ADVANCED ACCOUNTS

VOLUME II

ABOUT THE BOOK

This book covers a very wide range of topics of accounting. It can be used with great advantage while preparing for any B.Com.(Hons.) examination and CA (Foundation), CPT, PCC, ICWA, CS, CA (Inter.), CA (Final), CS (Foundation), and other similar examinations. Thus, it is a multi-pupose book. The book is already prescribed by The Institute of Chartered Accountants of India and the Institute of Company Secretaries of India for the paper in Accounting of their different examinations.

ADVANCED ACCOUNTS

VOLUME II

M.C. SHUKLA
T.S. GREWAL

S.C. GUPTA
Former Reader in Commerce
Hans Raj College
University of Delhi
Delhi

S. CHAND & COMPANY LTD.
(AN ISO 9001: 2000 COMPANY)
RAM NAGAR, NEW DELHI-110 055

S. CHAND & COMPANY LTD.

(An ISO 9001 : 2000 Company)

Head Office: 7361, RAM NAGAR, NEW DELHI - 110 055

Phone: 23672080-81-82, 9899107446, 9911310888

Fax: 91-11-23677446

Shop at: **schandgroup.com**; e-mail: **info@schandgroup.com**

Branches :

AHMEDABAD : 1st Floor, Heritage, Near Gujarat Vidhyapeeth, Ashram Road, **Ahmedabad** - 380 014, Ph: 27541965, 27542369, ahmedabad@schandgroup.com

BENGALURU : No. 6, Ahuja Chambers, 1st Cross, Kumara Krupa Road, **Bengaluru** - 560 001, Ph: 22268048, 22354008, bangalore@schandgroup.com

BHOPAL : Bajaj Tower, Plot No. 243, Lala Lajpat Rai Colony, Raisen Road, **Bhopal** - 462 011, Ph: 4274723. bhopal@schandgroup.com

CHANDIGARH : S.C.O. 2419-20, First Floor, Sector - 22-C (Near Aroma Hotel), **Chandigarh** -160 022, Ph: 2725443, 2725446, chandigarh@schandgroup.com

CHENNAI : 152, Anna Salai, **Chennai** - 600 002, Ph: 28460026, 28460027, chennai@schandgroup.com

COIMBATORE : Plot No. 5, Rajalakshmi Nagar, Peelamedu, **Coimbatore** -641 004, (M) 09444228242, coimbatore@schandgroup.com **(Marketing Office)**

CUTTACK : 1st Floor, Bhartia Tower, Badambadi, **Cuttack** - 753 009, Ph: 2332580; 2332581, cuttack@schandgroup.com

DEHRADUN : 1st Floor, 20, New Road, Near Dwarka Store, **Dehradun** - 248 001, Ph: 2711101, 2710861, dehradun@schandgroup.com

GUWAHATI : Pan Bazar, **Guwahati** - 781 001, Ph: 2738811, 2735640 guwahati@schandgroup.com

HYDERABAD : Padma Plaza, H.No. 3-4-630, Opp. Ratna College, Narayanaguda, **Hyderabad** - 500 029, Ph: 24651135, 24744815, hyderabad@schandgroup.com

JAIPUR : A-14, Janta Store Shopping Complex, University Marg, Bapu Nagar, **Jaipur** - 302 015, Ph: 2719126, jaipur@schandgroup.com

JALANDHAR : Mai Hiran Gate, **Jalandhar** - 144 008, Ph: 2401630, 5000630, jalandhar@schandgroup.com

JAMMU : 67/B, B-Block, Gandhi Nagar, **Jammu** - 180 004, (M) 09878651464 **(Marketing Office)**

KOCHI : Kachapilly Square, Mullassery Canal Road, Ernakulam, **Kochi** - 682 011, Ph: 2378207, cochin@schandgroup.com

KOLKATA : 285/J, Bipin Bihari Ganguli Street, **Kolkata** - 700 012, Ph: 22367459, 22373914, kolkata@schandgroup.com

LUCKNOW : Mahabeer Market, 25 Gwynne Road, Aminabad, **Lucknow** - 226 018, Ph: 2626801, 2284815, lucknow@schandgroup.com

MUMBAI : Blackie House, 103/5, Walchand Hirachand Marg, Opp. G.P.O., **Mumbai** - 400 001, Ph: 22690881, 22610885, mumbai@schandgroup.com

NAGPUR : Karnal Bag, Model Mill Chowk, Umrer Road, **Nagpur** - 440 032, Ph: 2723901, 2777666 nagpur@schandgroup.com

PATNA : 104, Citicentre Ashok, Govind Mitra Road, **Patna** - 800 004, Ph: 2300489, 2302100, patna@schandgroup.com

PUNE : 291/1, Ganesh Gayatri Complex, 1st Floor, Somwarpeth, Near Jain Mandir, **Pune** - 411 011, Ph: 64017298, pune@schandgroup.com **(Marketing Office)**

RAIPUR : Kailash Residency, Plot No. 4B, Bottle House Road, Shankar Nagar, **Raipur** - 492 007, Ph: 09981200834, raipur@schandgroup.com **(Marketing Office)**

RANCHI : Flat No. 104, Sri Draupadi Smriti Apartments, East of Jaipal Singh Stadium, Neel Ratan Street, Upper Bazar, **Ranchi** - 834 001, Ph: 2208761, ranchi@schandgroup.com **(Marketing Office)**

SILIGURI : 122, Raja Ram Mohan Roy Road, East Vivekanandapally, P.O., Siliguri, Dist., Jalpaiguri, (W.B.) (M) 09051064326 **(Marketing Office)**

VISAKHAPATNAM: Plot No. 7, 1st Floor, Allipuram Extension, Opp. Radhakrishna Towers, Seethammadhara North Extn., **Visakhapatnam** - 530 013, (M) 09347580841, visakhapatnam@schandgroup.com **(Marketing Office)**

First Edition 1960, Subsequent Editions and Reprints 1963, 64, 65, 66, 67, 68, 69, 70, 72, 73, 74 (Twice), 76, 77, 78, 80, 81 (Twice), 82, 83 (Twice), 84, 85, 86, 87, 88, 90, 92, 93, 94, 95, 96, 97 (Twice), 2000, 2001, 2002, 2003 (Twice), 2004, 2005, 2006
Reprint 2009, Reprint 2009 (With addition of Multiple Choice Questions)
Revised Edition 2011

ISBN : 81-219-1100-1 **Code** : 07A 201

PRINTED IN INDIA

By Rajendra Ravindra Printers Pvt. Ltd., 7361, Ram Nagar, New Delhi -110 055 and published by S. Chand & Company Ltd., 7361, Ram Nagar, New Delhi -110 055.

PREFACE TO THE SEVENTEENTH EDITION

I am privileged to present to the learned teachers and students a revised and updated seventeenth edition of **volume II** of '**Advanced Accounts**'.

The following are the important features of the present edition of the volume:

In Chapter 18, more information on Employees Stock Option has been provided and three illustrations on the topic have been added.

This volume deals with company accounts. There have been changes in rules, regulations and law concerning different topics. For example, there has been the Companies (Amendment) Act, 2001. In the light of these changes, material has been added or replaced at all the necessary places in the book to provide updated knowledge. In particular, there are vast changes in chapter 26 on Banks.

Chapter 29 of the book has been totally changed replacing old material by matter which is relevant in modern times.

Also, in all practical questions and illustrations, dates have been changed to give the problems a contemporary look; wherever found desirable, the amounts have also been changed.

Thus, an attempt has been made to make the book more useful.

Errors which have come to my notice have also been rectified. Of course, there may still be many other errors which have escaped notice. I am greatly indebted to the teachers and students of the subject who have been kind enough to point out errors and send suggestions for improvement. I earnestly request them to continue to do so.

I hope this edition will be welcomed by the students and teachers of Accounting with as much warmth and generosity as was accorded to the previous editions.

My thanks are also due to all those who have helped me in different ways in bringing out this edition. My special thanks are due to Ms Sadhana Tiwari for the her editorial support and Ajendra Negi DTP Operator who have worked hard for speedy revision of the book.

S.C. GUPTA

PREFACE TO THE FIRST EDITION

The aim of this work is to present to the reader the whole range of Book Keeping and Accountancy in one volume with precision and system as well as adequate details necessary to make the book one of practical utility.

The book differs from many others already in existence in that it deals in a lucid manner with all modern methods of preparation and presentation of accounts, keeping in view the exacting requirements of several enactments, especially the Companies Act, 1956. The book is replete with illustrations which have been graded with a view to enabling the student to progress along from the easy to the more complex points. To facilitate recapitulation and a better grasp of the subject, a large number of test problems with answers have been given at the end of each chapter. Certain portions of more advanced and complex nature have been marked with asterisks and may be ignored by those who do not wish to go into complexities.

The book fully covers the syllabi of all the Indian Universities for the various Commerce Examinations, as also the syllabi of the Intermediate and Final Examinations conducted by the Institute of Chartered Accountants of India. Mistakes and deficiencies are likely to be noticed by the reader, and we shall be grateful if they are pointed out to us. Any other suggestions to further increase the utility of the book will be acknowledged and incorporated in the next edition.

We regret very much the sad and premature demise of our co-author, Shri V. Sahai, while the book was in the Press. He brought to bear upon the book his vast experience of practical accounts. His contributions had definitely enhanced the value of the work. We trust and believe that the blending of our academic and practical experience has made the book useful not only to the students, but also to the practising accountants.

We are thankful to Shri Ajit Singh Sabherwal, M.A., B. Com., who has helped us in many ways, especially in the preparation of the index.

M.C. SHUKLA
T.S. GREWAL

CONTENTS

Chapter		Pages
18.	**Introduction — Shares, Debentures, etc.**	**18.1-18.185**
	General introduction	18.2
	Joint stock company	18.2
	Kinds of companies	18.2
	Private company and public company	18.2
	Privileges of a private limited company	18.3
	Floatation of companies	18.3
	Certificate of incorporation	18.4
	Prospectus	18.4
	Minimum subscription	18.6
	Certificate of commencement of business	18.6
	Return as to allotment	18.7
	Effect of irregular allotment	18.7
	Classes of shares	18.7
	Preference shares	18.7
	Kinds of preference shares	18.8
	Equity shares	18.8
	Share capital	18.9
	Management of companies	18.9
	General	18.9
	Powers of shareholders	18.9
	The board of directors	18.10
	Managing director	18.11
	Manager	18.11
	Meetings of shareholders	18.11
	Statutory meeting	18.11
	Annual general meeting	18.12
	Extraordinary general meeting	18.12
	Quorum	18.13
	Voting	18.13
	Resolutions	18.13
	Copies to be filed with the registrar	18.13
	Minutes books	18.13
	Accounts	18.14
	Statutory books	18.14
	Books of account	18.14
	Statistical books	18.15
	Issue of shares	18.15
	Use of application moneys	18.16
	Allotment of shares	18.17
	Calls	18.18
	Pro-rata allotment	18.23
	Calls in advance	18.27
	Calls in arrear	18.27
	Issue of shares at a premium	18.32
	Issue of shares at a discount	18.37
	Sweat equity shares	18.40
	Employees' stock option	18.40

Forfeiture and reissue of shares 18.45
Surrender of shares 18.46
Issue of shares for consideration other than cash 18.62
Issue of bonous shares 18.66
SEBI guidelines regarding bonus shares 18.66
Rights issue 18.68
Debentures 18.69
Distinction between debentures and shares 18.69
Classes of debentures 18.69
Issue of debentures 18.70
Debenture redemption reserve 18.75
Issue of debentures as a collateral security 18.78
Writing off discount, etc. on issue of debentures 18.80
Underwriting 18.81
Sub-underwriters 18.82
Brokerage 18.82
Marked applications 18.83
Underwriting commision 18.83
Calculation of liability of underwriters 18.83
Firm underwriting 18.86
Preparation of statutory report 18.88
Buy-back of shares 18.92
Redemption of preference shares 18.95
Redemption of debentures 18.116
Convertible debentures 18.132
Sinking fund for redemption of debentures 18.136
Purchase of business 18.161

19. Final Accounts 19.1–19.124

General 19.1
Requirements of law regarding the preparation of profit and loss account 19.2
General principles–same as for other concerns 19.7
Materiality 19.8
Prior period items 19.8
Extraordinary items 19.9
Changes in accounting policies 19.9
AS-5 (Prevised): Net profit or loss for the period, prior period items
And changes in accounting policies 19.10
AS-4 (revised) contingencies and events occurring after the balance sheet date 19.14
Debentures 19.18
Ascertaining profit for managerial remuneration 19.19
Remuneration to directors 19.21
Remuneration to the manager 19.22
Overall managerial remuneration 19.22
Schedule xiii-Appointment 19.22
Schedule xiii-Remuneration 19.23
Schedule xiv-Rates of depreciation 19.25
Calculation of commission 19.31
Appropriation items 19.35
Profits prior to incorporation 19.50
Divisible profits 19.56
Transfer to reserve 19.58
Depreciation 19.61

Unpaid dividend account ... 19.62
Capital profits ... 19.63
Dividends ... 19.63
Corporate divided tax ... 19.65
Appropriation of profits ... 19.65
Interest out of capital ... 19.70
Bonus shares ... 19.71
Form of balance sheet ... 19.74
Vertical form of balance sheet ... 19.82
Directors' report ... 19.98
Auditors' report ... 19.99
Filing of the profit & loss account and balance sheet ... 19.100

20. Valuation of Intangible Assets, Goodwill and Shares; Reorganisation and Reconstruction of Share Capital ... 20.1–20.112

Valuation of intangible assets ... 20.1
Meaning of intangible asset ... 20.1
Valuation of intangible assets ... 20.2
Recognition and initial measurement ... 20.3
Separate acquisition of intangible assets ... 20.3
Acquisition of intangible assets as part of an amalgamation ... 20.3
Acquisition of intangible assets by way of a Government grant ... 20.4
Internally generated intangible asset ... 20.4
Research phase ... 20.4
Development phase ... 20.4
Cost of an internally generated intangible asset ... 20.5
Recognition of an expense on intangible asset ... 20.5
Subsequent expenditure on intangible asset ... 20.6
Amortisation ... 20.6
Amortisation period ... 20.6
Amortisation method ... 20.6
Residual value ... 20.6
Review of amortisation period and amortisation method ... 20.6
Impairement losses ... 20.7
Retirements and disposals ... 20.7
Valuation of goodwill ... 20.7
Need ... 20.8
Components of goodwill ... 20.8
General factors affecting value of goodwill ... 20.9
Profitability ... 20.9
Yield expected by investors ... 20.14
Capital employed ... 20.15
Methods for evaluating goodwill ... 20.16
Super profits method ... 20.17
Annuity method ... 20.22
Capitalisation method ... 20.25
Valuation of shares ... 20.27
Need ... 20.27
Methods ... 20.28
Net assets method or intrinsic value ... 20.28
Yield basis or market value ... 20.29
Value based on earnings of company ... 20.33
Alteration of share capital ... 20.51
Conversion into stock ... 20.51

Increase or decrease of capital 20.52
Reserve liability 20.52
Reduction of capital 20.53
Surrender of shares 20.81
Variation of shareholders' rights 20.54
Schemes of reconstruction 20.88
Internal vs. external reconstruction 20.90
Legal position as regards external reconstruction 20.91

21. Amalgamation and External Reconstruction 21.1–21.146

Meaning of amalgamation 21.1
Types of amalgamation 21.1
Distinction between merger and purchase 21.2
Methods of accounting for amalgamation 21.2
Disclosures 21.4
Consideration 21.7
Accounting entries 21.10
External reconstruction 21.56
Distribution between external reconstruction and amalgamation 21.56
Dissenting shareholders 21.65
Inter-company owings 21.74
Unrealised profit on stock 21.83
Inter-company holdings 21.96
Amalgamation scheme 21.113
Accounting standard (AS)-14: Accounting for amalgamations 21.119

22. Holding Companies 22.1–22.120

General 22.1
Definitions 22.1
Advantages of holding companies 22.2
Disadvantages of holding companies 22.2
Legal definition and requirements 22.2
Accounts 22.4
AS-21: Consolidated financial statements 22.7
Consolidation of balance sheets and profit and loss accounts 22.12
Treatment of dividend 22.12
Debiting the subsidiary with profits etc. 22.14
Preparation of consolidated balance sheet 22.15
Cost of control and capital reserve 22.15
Minority interest 22.17
Capital profits and revenue profits 22.22
Controlling interest acquired during the course of the year 22.26
treatment relating to preference shares of the subsidiary 22.29
Unrealised profits 22.31
Mutual owings 22.33
Dividend out of preacquisition profits 22.36
Dividend out of post acquisition profits 22.37
Error relating to dividend from subsidiary company 22.37
Interim dividend 22.39
Proposed dividend 22.41
Change in value of fixed assets 22.47
Successive purchases of shares 22.66
Bonus shares 22.54
Consolidation of profit and loss accounts 22.73

Inter-company holdings 22.93
Foreign subsidiaries 22.95
Associated companies 22.99

23. Cash and Funds Flow Statements, Cash Budget and Working Capital 23.1–23.88

Cash flow statement 23.1
Introduction 23.1
Definition 23.2
Classification of activities 23.2
Non-cash transactions 23.5
The direct method 23.9
The indirect method 23.13
Advantages 23.30
Limitations 23.30
Distinction between cash flow statement and income statement 23.30
AS-3 (revised): Cash flow statements 23.31
Funds flow statement 23.43
Rules for drawing funds flow statement 23.44
Advantages 23.46
Limitations 23.46
Distinction between funds flow statement and cash flow statement 23.46
Distinction between funds flow statement and income statement 23.46
Distinction between statement showing changes in working capital and funds flow statement 23.47
Cash budget 23.66
Working capital 23.68
Concept of working capital 23.68
Factors determining working capital requirements 23.70
Estimating working capital requirements 23.72

24. Accounting Ratios 24.1–24.78

Importance of accounting ratios 24.1
Limitations 24.2
Various accounting ratios 24.3
Profitability ratios 24.5
AS-20: Earnings per share 24.9
Turnover, performance or activity ratios 24.23
Ratios to judge financial position and policies 24.26
Predictability of insolvency on the basis of ratios 24.65

25. Insurance Companies 25.1–25.48

General 25.1
Various types of insurance 25.1
Various terms 25.2
Regulation of Insurance Business 25.3
Final Accounts 25.3
A. Life Insurance Business 25.3
B. General Insurance Business 25.25
Reserve for Unexpired Risks 25.25

26. Bank 26.1–26.86

Legal provisions 26.1
Forms of business 26.1
Non-banking assets 26.2

Management 26.3
Minimum capital and reserves 26.3
Floating charge 26.4
Restrictions on dividends 26.4
Statutory reserve 26.4
Cash reserves and statutory liquidity reserve 26.4
Restrictions on loans and advances 26.5
Subsidiary companies 26.5
Control 26.5
Accounts and books 26 5
Demand drafts and telegraphic transfers 26.6
Travellers cheques and letters of credit 26.6
Acceptances, endorsements and other obligations 26.6
Bills for collection 26.7
Bills purchased and discounted 26.7
Rebate on bills discounted 26.7
Books required 26.10
Accounting year 26.11
Final accounts 25.11
Form of balance sheet 26.13
Form of profit and loss account 26.17
Guidelines of RBI 26.19
Notes on accounts and disclosure of accounting policies 26.28
Capital adequacy norms 26.30
Income from non-performing assets 26.35
Classification of bank advances 26.37
Principal accounting policies 26.46

27. Accounts of Electricity Companies .... 27.1 – 27.42

Legal provisions 27.1
Depreciation 27.1
Reasonable return 27.2
Clear profit 27.2
Disposal of surplus 27.3
Tariffs and dividends control reserve 27.6
Contingencies reserve 27.6
Development reserve 27.6
General reserve 27.6
Final accounts 27.7
Double account system 27.32
Replacement of an asset 27.36

28. Liquidation .... 28.1 – 28.71

Meaning of liquidation or winding up 28.1
Winding up by Court 28.1
Voluntary winding up 28.2
Members' voluntary winding up 28.2
Creditors' voluntary winding up 28.2
Consequences of winding up, generally 28.3
Preferential payments 28.3
Overriding preferential payments 28.4
Liquidator 28.5
Power and duties of liquidator 28.5

Preparation of statement of affairs 28.6
Deficiency/surplus account 28.9
Liquidator's final statement of account 28.13
Receiver for debentureholders 28.22
"B" list of contributories 28.28

29. Computerised Accounting System .... 29.1 – 29.5

Meaning 29.1
Features 29.1
Codification and grouping of accounts 29.1
Spread-sheet software 29.2
Customised accounting software 29.3
Enterprise resource planning (ERP) software 29.4
Outsourcing of accounting punction 29.4
Function 29.4
Choice of an alternative 29.5

30. Criticism of Financial Statements .... 30.1 – 30.18

Criticism 30.1
Forms in which accounts are drawn up 30.1
Reliability of information 30.5
Critical appreciation 30.7
Presentation 30.7
Single column or vertical statements 30.7
Method of preparing such statements 30.7
Common measurement statements 30.16

31. Inflation Accounting .... 31.1 – 31.42

Need 31.1
Objections 31.3
Current Purchasing Power method 31.5
Current Cost Accounting 31.12
Evaluation of CCA 31.25
SSAP 16 .... 31.27

32. Accounting for Human Resources of An Organisation and Social Responsibility .... 32.1 – 32.16

Introduction 32.1
Cost and replacement cost methods 32.1
Value approaches 32.2
A suggested approach 32.4
The two sides of the account 32.5
Value added statement 32.8

Multiple Choice Questions (Chapterwise) .... 1 – 15

Attention: Students

We request you, for your frank assessment, regarding some of the aspects of the book, given as under:

07 201 **Advanced Accounts Volume II**
M.C. Shukla, T.S. Grewal, S.C. Gupta ***Revised Edition 2011***

Please fill up the given space in neat capital letters. Add additional sheet(s) if the space provided is not sufficient, and if so required.

(i) What topic(s) of your syllabus that are important from your examination point of view are not covered in the book ?

....

....

....

....

(ii) What are the chapters and/or topics, wherein the treatment of the subject-matter is not systematic or organised or updated?

....

....

....

....

....

(iii) Have you come across misprints/mistakes/factual inaccuracies in the book? Please specify the chapters, topics and the page numbers.

....

....

....

....

....

(iv) Name top three books on the same subject (in order of your preference - 1, 2, 3) that you have found/heard better than the present book? Please specify in terms of quality (in all aspects).

1 ....

....

2 ....

....

3 ....

....

(v) Further suggestions and comments for the improvement of the book:

....

....

....

....

....

Other Details:

(i) Who recommended you the book? (Please tick in the box near the option relevant to you.)

☐ Teacher ☐ Friends ☐ Bookseller

(ii) Name of the recommending teacher, his designation and address:

....

....

....

(iii) Name and address of the bookseller you purchased the book from:

....

....

....

(iv) Name and address of your institution (Please mention the University or Board, as the case may be)

....

....

....

(v) Your name and complete postal address:

....

....

....

(vi) Write your preferences of our publications (1, 2, 3) you would like to have

....

....

The best assessment will be awarded half-yearly. The award will be in the form of our publications, as decided by the Editorial Board, amounting to Rs. 300 (total).

Please mail the filled up coupon at your earliest to:

Editorial Department
S. CHAND & COMPANY LTD.,
Post Box No. 5733, Ram Nagar,
New Delhi 110 055

18
Introduction — Shares, Debentures, etc.

SYNOPSIS

1. General introduction .. 18.2
(*a*) Joint stock company .. 18.2
Kinds of companies .. 18.2
Private company and public company .. 18.2
Privileges of a private limited company .. 18.3
(*b*) Floatation of companies .. 18.3
Certificate of incorporation .. 18.4
Prospectus .. 18.4
Minimum subscription .. 18.6
Certificate of commencement of business .. 18.6
Return as to allotment .. 18.7
Effect of irregular allotment .. 18.7
(*c*) Classes of shares .. 18.7
Preference shares .. 18.7
Kinds of preference shares .. 18.8
Equity shares .. 18.8
Share capital .. 18.9
(*d*) Management of companies .. 18.9
General .. 18.9
Powers of shareholders .. 18.9
The board of directors .. 18.10
Managing director .. 18.11
Manager .. 18.11
(*e*) Meetings of shareholders .. 18.11
Statutory meeting .. 18.11
Annual general meeting .. 18.12
Extraordinary general meeting .. 18.12
Quorum .. 18.13
Voting .. 18.13
Resolutions .. 18.13
Copies to be filed with the registrar .. 18.13
Minutes books .. 18.13
2. Accounts .. 18.14
(*a*) Statutory books .. 18.14
Books of account .. 18.14
Statistical books .. 18.15
(*b*) Issue of shares .. 18.15
Stockinvests .. 18.16
Use of application moneys .. 18.16
Allotment of shares .. 18.17
Calls .. 18.18
Pro-rata allotment .. 18.23
Calls in advance .. 18.27
Calls in arrear .. 18.27
Issue of shares at a premium .. 18.32
Issue of shares at a discount .. 18.37
Sweat equity shares .. 18.40
Employees' stock option .. 18.40
Forfeiture and reissue of shares .. 18.41
Surrender of shares .. 18.41
Issue of shares for consideration other than cash .. 18.57
Issue of bonous shares .. 18.61
SEBI guidelines regarding bonus shares .. 18.61
Rights issue .. 18.63
(*c*) Debentures .. 18.64
Distinction between debentures and shares .. 18.64
Classes of debentures .. 18.64
Issue of debentures .. 18.65
Debenture redemption reserve .. 18.70
Issue of debentures as a collateral security .. 18.73
Writing off discount, etc. on issue of debentures .. 18.75
(*d*) Underwriting .. 18.76
Sub-underwriters .. 18.77
Brokerage .. 18.77
Marked applications .. 18.78
Underwriting commision .. 18.78
Calculation of liability of underwriters .. 18.78
Firm underwriting .. 18.81
(*e*) Preparation of statutory report .. 18.83
(*f*) Buy-back of shares .. 18.87
(*g*) Redemption of preference shares .. 18.90
(*h*) Redemption of debentures .. 18.111
Convertible debentures .. 18.127
Sinking fund for redemption of debentures.. .. 18.131
(*i*) Purchase of business .. 18.156

1. GENERAL INTRODUCTION*

Joint Stock Company

A joint stock company is a voluntary association of persons formed for the purpose of some business for profit with common capital, divisible into transferable shares and possessing a corporate legal entity and a common seal. It is created by a process of law and can be put to an end only by a process of law. It is a legal person and is something different from its members. It is, therefore, capable of acting in its own name. But as it has no physical existence, it must act through its agents and all the contracts entered into by its agents must be under the seal of the company. The members as such do not carry on the business of the company. A group of persons who are individually called the directors and collectively form the Board of Directors are appointed. The company acts through the Board of Directors or subordinates appointed by the Board for the purpose.

Share capital of a company is divided into parts and each part is called a share. Every person who takes up a share or shares of a company become its member and continues to be a member so long as he holds even a single share. He is called a shareholder and is a part-owner of the company. But a person can be both a shareholder and a creditor of the same company and at the same time.

KINDS OF COMPANIES

Depending on the way they are formed, companies in India can be classified under the following two heads:—

(*i*) *Statutory companies:* These are the companies which are created by special acts of the Legislature, e.g., the State Bank of India, Life Insurance Corporation and State Trading Corporation. They are very small in number.

(*ii*) *Registered companies:* These are the companies which are formed and registered under the Companies Act, 1956 or earlier companies acts. Most of the companies are of this category. They are formed by fulfilling the legal formalities laid down in the Companies Act for the purpose. Certain documents have to be prepared and sent to Registrar of the Companies of the State in which the registered office of the company is to be situate along with the necessary fees. When the Registrar is satisfied that everything is in order and all the legal formalities have been complied with, he issues a Certificate of Incorporation which is really the birth certificate of the company.

Classification of companies on the basis of liability of members: From the point of view of the liability of the members, companies can be divided into the following three categories:-

(*i*) *Companies limited by shares:* In these companies, the liability of the members, called the shareholders, does not exceed the unpaid amount, if any, on the shares held by them. Most of the companies fall under this category.

(*ii*) *Companies limited by gurantee:* In these companies, the liability of the members is limited to the amount which the members undertake to contribute in the event of the winding up of the company. Companies limited by gurantee are not formed for the purpose of profit but for the promotion of art, science, culture, charity or sports, etc. They may or may not have a share capital. If such a company has a share capital, it is governed (excepting certain provisions), by the same provisions as govern companies limited by shares.

(*iii*) *Unlimited companies :* In this case, the liability of the members is not restricted; the members have to contribute the necessary amount to pay off the creditors of the company fully.

Private company and public company: There are two types of registerd companies– private companies and public companies. A private company is a company which has a minimum paid-up capital of Rs. 1,00,000 or such higher paid-up capital as may be prescribed by the Central Government and which by its articles of association (by-laws of the company),

(*i*) restricts the right of its members to transfer shares;

(*ii*) limits the number of its members to fifty (excluding employees who are members and ex-employees who continue to be members);

(*iii*) prohibits any invitation to the public to subscribe for any shares in, or debentures of the company; and

---

*What follows is meant only by way of general information. The student is advised to consult a good book on Company Law.

(*iv*) prohibits any invitation or acceptance of deposits from persons other than its (*i*) members (*ii*) directors or their relatives.

With regard to the second condition mentioned above, it should be noted that joint holders of shares are treated as a single member.

A public company means a company which

(*i*) is not a private company; and

(*ii*) has a minimum paid-up capital of Rs. 5,00,000 or such higher paid-up capital as may be prescribed;

A private company which is a subsidiary of a company which is not a private company is also a public company.

Distinction between a private company and a public company: The following are the main points of distinction between a private company and a public company:-

(*i*) *Minimum number:* The minimum number of persons required to form a private company is two whereas in the case of a public company, it is seven.

(*ii*) *Maximum number:* The maximum number of shareholders in the case of a private company is 50. This number excludes the persent and past employees of the company who may be members also. In public company, there is no restriction on maximum number of members.

(*iii*) *Minimum paid-up capital :* The minimum paid up capital in the case of a private company is Rs. 1,00,000 while in the case of a public company, it is Rs. 5,00,000.

(*iv*) *Restriction on invitation to the general public to subscribe to shares and debentures:* A private company, by its Articles of Association, must prohibit any invitation to the general public to subscribe to any shares in, or debentures of the company. There is no such restriction in the case of a public company.

(*v*) *Transferability of shares:* A private company, by its Articles of Association, restricts its member's right to transfer shares. In the case of a public company, shares are freely transferable.

(*vi*) *Special privileges:* A private company enjoys certain special privileges which are not enjoyed by a public company. For example, there is a statutory maximum limit of managerial remuneration payable in the case of a public company whereas this rule of overall maximum managerial remuneration does not apply to a private company which is not a subsidiary of a public company. To give you another example, a private company need not hold a statutory meeting or file with the Registrar of companies, a statutory report.

Privileges of a private limited company. The privileges and exemptions of a private limited company are as follows:

(1) Only two signatories to the Memorandum are sufficient.

(2) It is not required to, nor can it, issue prospectus or file a statement in lieu of prospectus.

(3) It may commence business immediately after incorporation.

(4) It may allot shares as soon as it receives the Certificate of Incorporation as provisions with regard to "minimum subscription" do not apply to it.

(5) It is not required to file a statutory report or hold a statutory meeting.

(6) Subject to Articles, only two members make a quorum.

(7) It need have only two directors.

(8) Director's consent to act as director and his contract to take up qualification shares need not be filed.

(9) The Profit and Loss Account, though filed with the Registrar, cannot be inspected by the public.

(10) Directors of private companies need not retire by rotation.

(11) Directors can be appointed by a single resolution.

(12) New shares need not be issued to the existing shareholders of the company in the first instance.

(13) It can grant loans to its directors without the sanction of the Central Government.

(14) Provisions regarding remuneration to managerial personnel do not apply to a private company.

(15) A person can be a managing director or a manager of more than two private companies.

(16) Restrictions on investments or loans in the same group of companies do not apply.

(*b*) **Floatation of companies:**

It is usually a "promoter" who thinks of the idea of a business to be run by a company. The promoter then makes detailed investigations to find out whether the idea is really a proposition; and if he thinks that the proposed company can run successfully, he takes such steps as will ensure its smooth running. He then gets the following documents prepared and sends them to the Registrar of Companies together with the necessary fees:-

(*a*) The Memorandum of Association. It contains six clauses- (*i*) the name of the company with "Limited" as the last word if the liability of the members is limited ("Private Limited" has to be used by private limited companies); (*ii*) the State in which the registered office is to be situate; (*iii*) the objects of the company*; (*iv*) a statement that the liability of the members is limited; (*v*) the amount of authorised share capital and its divisions into shares; and (*vi*) the declaration of association. The memorandum must be printed, divided into paragraphs, numbered consecutively, and must be signed by *at least seven* persons who each agree to take one share at least.

(*b*) The Articles of Association. It contains the rules and regulations for the conduct of the company's business. A private company has to prepare its own Articles of Association. But a public company may not prepare it, in which case provisions of Table A of the Companies Act will be applicable. Table A containes model articles.

(*c*) The agreement, if any which the company proposes to enter into with any individual for appointment as its managing or whole-time director or manager.

(*d*) In the case of a public company limited by shares, a list of the directors who have agreed to become the first directors of the company and their written consent to act as directors and take-up qualification shares, if any. This requirement does not apply to a private company. Further, if a separate list of directors is not filed, the subscribers to the memorandum will be deemd to be the first directors of the company.

(*e*) A declaration that all the requirements of the Companies Act and other formalities relating to registration have been complied with. It has to be signed by any of the following persons:-

(*i*) an advocate of the Supreme Court or of a High Court:

(*ii*) an attorney or a pleader entitled to appear before a High Court;

(*iii*) a secretary or a chartered accountant in whole-time practice in India, who is engaged in the formation of the company and

(*iv*) a person named in the articles of the company as a director, manager or secretary of the company

(*f*) Notice of the address of the Registered Office of the company. However, this notice may be given later within 30 days after registration.

Certificae of Incorporation. The Registrar will issue the *Certificate of Incorporation,* if he is satisfied that the requirements of the Companies Act have been complied with. He will enter the company's name in the Register. The company comes into existence.

Prospectus. A private limited company can commence business immediately after incorporation, but a public limited company has to wait till the Registrar grants to it the Certificate of Commencement of Business. For this purpose, the company has to issue a Prospectus (or prepare a Statement in lieu of Prospectus) signed by every director before its publication and file a copy with the Registrar. Section 2 (36) defines a Prospectus as " any document described or issued as a prospectus and includes any notice, circular, advertisement or other document inviting offers from the public for the subscription or purchase of any shares in, or debentures of, a body corporate". The main purpose of

* The objects have to be classified as:

(*i*) The main objects to be pursued by the company on its incorporation and objects incidental or ancillary to the attainment of the main objects; and

(*ii*) Other objects

A company is not allowed to pursue objects mentioned in (*ii*) above, unless the shareholders have agreed by a special resolution.

the Prospectus is to invite the public to subscribe for the shares and debentures of the comopany so that the company collects the necessary funds. Whenever the company makes a public issue of its shares or debentures, it will be required to publish a prospectus. It must be dated and that date, *prima facie,* will be the date of its issue. The Prospectus must be issued within 90 days of its date by newspaper advertisement or otherwise. The prospectus is the basis of contract between the company and the person who 'buys' the shares on the strength of the Prospectus. Therefore, if the Prospectus contains any misleading statement or if there is a material non-disclosure, the shareholder is entitled to rescind the contract within a resonable time but before winding up of the company. In addition to the right of rescission, the allottee of shares is entitled to claim compensation from any director, promoter or any other person who authorised the issue of the Prospectus.

If the Prospectus contains a statement made by an expert, he must not be a person who is or has been engaged or interested in the formation or promotion of or in the management of the company. Further, the expert's written consent to the inclusion of the statement (in the form and context in which it is included) must be obtained.

The Central Government vide Notification No, S.O. 666 (E) dated October 3, 1991 has revised the format of the prospectus as given in Schedule II of the Companies Act to ensure greater information regarding the company, its management, the project for which the money is proposed to be raised by the issue, financial preformance of the company during the five financial years immediately preceding the issue of prospectus and the management perception of the risk factors in the investment. The company has also to furnish particulars as to other listed companies under the same management within the meaning of the Section 370 (1B), which have made any capital issue during the last three years. It will also have to state whether it has obtained credit rating in case the prospectus is in connection with the issue of debentures or preference shares. The objective is to make the investor better placed to make an informed decision whether to invest or not to invest in shares or debentures offered by the company through a public issue. The draft prospectus is vetted by SEBI to ensure adequacy of disclosures.

Section 68A requires every prospectus to prominently reproduce the following:

"Any person who —

(a) makes in a fictitious name an application to a company for acquiring, or subscribing for, any shares therein, or

(b) otherwise induces a company to allot, or resister any transfer of, shares therein to him, or any other person in a fictitious name,

shall be punishable with imprisonment for a term which may extend to five years."

The Registrar may refuse to register a Prospectus, if-

(a) it does not show its date;

(b) it does not comply with requirements of Section 56 as to matters and reports to be set out;

(c) it contains statements of experts engaged or interested in the formation or management of the company;

(d) it does not contain the expert' s consent, when his opinion is permissible and is inserted.

(e) it does not contain the consent in writing of directors, and copy of the documents mentioned in section 60(1) or does not comply with the provisions of sections 60(2) with regard to statements that a copy of it has been filed with the Registrar; and

(f) it is not accompanied by the consent in writing of the auditor, legal adviser, etc., if named in the prospectus to act in that capacity.

A copy of every contract, or a memorandum giving full particulars of a contract not reduced to writing, and if any adjustment of figures has been made in any auditor's and accountant's report, then a written statement signed by the person making the report has to accompany the Prospectus.

Deposits: Section 58A provides that the Central Government, in consultation with the Reserve Bank of India, may make rules which must be followed by companies seeking to raise deposits from the public. The rules may provide the minimum limits for such *deposits* and also the form and the manner of the advertisement showing the financial position of the company. Acceptance of new deposits and renewal of old deposits are governed by the rules. As far as may be, the provisions of the Companies Act in respect of prospectus also apply to the advertisement for deposits. Every deposit accepted by a company after the commencement of the Companies (Amendenment) Act, 1988, shall be repaid in accordance with the terms and conditions of such deposits.

Minimum Subscription: For a new company issuing shares for the first time, minimum subscription means the amount which, in the opnion of the Board of Directors, is the minimum to be raised by the issue of shares so as to provide for the following:

(*i*) the price of any property purchased or agreed to be purchased;
(*ii*) all preliminary expenses, including underwriting commission and broberage;
(*iii*) repayment of money borrowed by the company for the above purposes;
(*iv*) working capital; and
(*v*) any other expenditure

The significance of the minimum subscription mentioned above is that if the newly incorporated public company fails to raise the minimum subscription, it will not be able to get certificate of commencement of business. Obviously, the purpose of this provision is to ensure that only companies with sufficient capital are allowed to commence business. If the company fails to raise minimum subscription within 120 days from the date of the first issue of prospectus, it is required to return whatever amount it has received from the applicants within the next ten days *i.e.,* within 130 days from the date of the issue of the prospectus.

There is another minimum subscription laid down by the SEBI for all the public and rights issues of shares. According to it, where a company does not receive 90% of the issued amount from public subscription plus accepted devolvepment from underwriters or from other sources in case of under-subscribed issues, within 60 days from the date of closure of the issue, the company will refund the subscription amount in full. It applies to all cases of public and rights issue but is not mandatory in case of resale of securities.

Prospectus states the minimum period for which the company will continue to receive applications for shares. It is called keeping the subscription list open. Subscription list must be kept open for at least three days. It shall not open before the beginning of the fifth day from the date of issue of prospectus.

The moneys received from applicants of shares have to be kept deposited in a scheduled bank until the certificate of commencement of business is obtained. In case a company has already received the certificate of commencement of business, application money has to be kept deposited in a scheduled bank until the entire amount payable on applications in respect of the minimum subscription has been received by the company.

Certificate of commencement of business. A private company, as already pointed out, can commence business on incorporation but other companies having share capital cannot do so unless they also obtain a certificate of commencement of business. This certificate will be granted if the following conditions have been fulfilled:

(1) The company has issued a Prospectus and has filed a copy with the Registrar or; if it has not issued a Prospectus, a Statement in lieu of Prospectus has been prepared and filed with the Registrar.
(2) The minimum number of shares which have to be paid for in cash has been subscribed and allotted.
(3) Every director has paid, in respect of shares for which he is bound to pay, an amount equal to what is payable on shares offered to the public on application and allotment.
(4) No money is, or may become, liable to be repaid to applicants for any shares or debentures offered for public subscription by reason of any failure to apply for, or to obtain, permission for the shares or debentures to be dealt with on any recognised stock exchange.
(5) A statutory declaration by the secretary or one of the directors that the aforesaid requirements

have been complied with is filed with the Registrar.

Note: Suitable provisions from amongst the above will also apply to companies limited by guarantee but not having a share capital.

Returns as to allotment. Within 30 days of making any allotment, the company must—

(a) file with the Registrar a return of the allotment stating the number and nominal amount of the shares comprised in the allotment, the names, addresses and occupations of the allottees, and the amount, if any, paid or due to be paid on each share;

(b) in the case of shares (not being bonus shares) allotted as fully or partly paid-up otherwise than in cash, produce for the inspection and examination of the Registrar the contract in writing constituting the title of the allottees to the allotment together with any contract of sale, or a contract for services or the other consideration in respect of which that allotment was made, such contract being duly stamped, and file with the Registrar verified copies of all such contracts and a return stating the number and nominal amount of shares so allotted, the extent to which they are to be treated as paid up, and the consideration for which they have been allotted; and

(c) in the case of bonus shares, file with the Registrar a return stating the number and nominal amount of the bonus shares so allotted with the names, addresses, and occupations of the allottees together with a copy of the resolution authorising the issue of such shares.

If shares have been issued at a discount the company must attach with the return the following:

(i) a copy of the relevant resolution of the company;

(ii) a copy of the order of the Central Government; and

(iii) a copy of the order of the Board if the discount offered exceeds 10%.

Notes: - (1) The return must not describe shares as having been allotted for cash unless cash has been actually received.

(2) The provisions as regards return as to allotment do not apply to reissue of forfeited shares.

Effect of irregular allotment. If a company, without complying with any of the conditions contained in sections 69 and 71 of the Companies Act (these relate to minimum subscription, etc.), makes an allotment, the applicant of the shares may avoid the allotment within 2 months after the statutory meeting, but not later than that. If the company is not required to hold a statutory meeting or if the allotment is made after such a meeting, the allotment can be avoided within 2 months of the allotment. The directors are liable to compensate the company or the allottee for any loss, damage, or costs suffered through irregular allotment.

(c) Classes of Shares

Share capital of a company is divided into certain indivisible units of a fixed amount. These units are called shares. 'Share' means share in the capital of a company. The person owning a share or shares of a company is called a shareholder. He is a part owner and risk bearer of the company. He gets income on his investment in shares in the form of dividends from the company. Dividend is that part of the profits of the company which is distributed among the shareholders for the shares held by them.

A public joint stock company can issue two classes of shares, *viz.*, preference shares and equity shares.

Preference Shares : Preference shares are those which carry

(i) a preferential right as to the payment of dividend during the lifetime of the company, and

(ii) a preferential right as to the return of capital when the company is wound up.

These shares carry a right of dividend at a fixed rate before any dividend can be paid on equity shares. The fixed rate of dividend payable is declared at the time of the issue of such shares. Whenever a reference is made to any preference shares issued, the fixed rate of dividend payable is also mentioned. For example, 12% preference shares mean that dividend at the rate of 12% per annum is payable on these preference shares. Of course, dividend is payable only if there are profits earned by the company and the Board of Directors decides to distribute them wholly or partly by way of dividends.

Kinds of Preference Shares. A preference share is (i) either cumulative or non-cumulative, *(ii)* redeemable or irredeemable, *(iii)* participating or non-participating and *(iv)* convertible or non-convertible.

(i) *Cumulative vs. Non-cumulative:* — The holders of cumulative preference shares are entitled to recover the arrears of preference dividend before any dividend is paid on equity shares. For example, if dividend has not been paid for the accounting years 2007-2008 and 2008-2009 on 10% cumulative preference shares and the company wants to distribute dividend on equity shares for the year 2009-2010, then dividend on preference shares for three years viz., 2007-2008, 2008-2009 and 2009-2010 10% per annum i.e., 30% dividend in all will have to be first paid on preference shares before any dividend can be paid on equity shares for 2009-2010. On the other hand, in case of non-cumulative preference shares, arrears of dividend do not accumulate and hence if dividend is to be paid to equity shareholders in any year, dividend at the fixed rate for only one year will have to be paid to preference shareholders before equity dividend is paid, even if preference shareholders have not received any dividend for a number of earlier years. In the abovementioned illustration, if the preference shares are non-cumulative, the company will have to pay 10% preference dividend only for 2009-2010 before paying equity dividend; the preference shareholders will lose dividend for 2007-2008 and 2008-2009. Unless specifically mentioned otherwise, preference ishares should be considered to be cumulative. In practice, they are always cumulative.

(ii) *Redeemable vs. Irredeemable:*— Redeemable preference shares are those preference shares whose amount can be returned by the company to their holders within the life time of the company subject to the terms of the issue and the fulfilment of certain legal conditions laid down in Sec. 80 of the Companies Act. The amount of irredeemable preference shares can be returned only when the company is wound up. After the commencement of the Companies (Amendment) Act, 1996, no company limited by shares shall issue any preference share which is irredeemable or is redeemable after the expiry of a period of 20 years from the date of issue.

(iii) *Participating vs. Non-participating:-* Participating preference shares are entitled not only to a fixed rate of dividend but also to a share in the surplus profits which remain after dividend has been paid at a certain rate to equity shareholders; the surplus profits are distributed in a certain agreed ratio between the participating preference shareholders and equity shareholders. Preference shareholders may also be given the right to participate in the surplus remaining after the equity share capital has been repaid in case of winding up of the company. Non-participating preference shares are entitled to only the fixed rate of dividend.

(iv) *Convertible vs. Non-convertible:*— The holders of convertible preference shares enjoy the right to get the preference shares converted into equity shares according to the terms of issue. The holders of non-convertible preference shares do not enjoy this right.

Equity Shares. Shares which are not preference shares are equity shares. The balance of profits remaining after appropriating preference dividend can be distributed among the equity shareholders as dividend. In case of winding up of the company, the payment is first made to creditors of the company. Then, the preference share capital is returned. Whatever remains belongs to equity shareholders.

Shares with differential rights

According to section 2 (46 A) as inserted by the Companies (Amendment) Act, 2000 a company can issue in accodance with the provisions of section 86, shares with differential rights as to dividend, voting or otherwise in accordance with such rules and subject to such conditions as may be prescribed.

Share Capital. Share capital means the capital raised by a company by the issue of shares. In this connection, the meaning of the following terms should be understood:—

(i) *Nominal or authorised capital:* This is the nominal or face value of the shares which the company is authorised to issue by its Memorandum of Association. This is the maximum capital which a company can have without altering the capital clause of the Memorandum of Association for an increase in its Authorised Capital.

(ii) *Issued capital :* It is the nominal value of the shares which are offered to the public for subscription. It cannot be more than the authorised capital.

(iii) *Subscribed capital :* It is the nominal value of the shares taken up by the public. If all the shares offered to the public are taken up by the public, subscribed capital will be equal to issued capital. But sometimes, all the shares which are offered to the public for subscription are not taken up by public. In such a case, only that part of the issued capital which is taken up by the public will be called subscribed capital.

(iv) *Called-up capital* : This is that part of the subscribed capital which has been called up. If the Board of Directors has called up the total amount payable on the shares, the called up capital will be equal to subscribed capital.

(v) *Paid-up capital :* This is that part of the called-up capital which has been paid-up by the shareholders or which is credited by the company as paid-up on the shares. If all the called-up capital has been received, paid-up capital will be equal to called-up capital. That part of the called-up capital which has not yet been received is called 'Calls in Arrear'. Thus, Called-up Capital - Calls in Arrear = Paid-up Capital.

(d) **Management of Companies**

General. The internal management of companies is carried on according to the articles of association. The articles define the relationship between members and between members and the company. On this basis, members are bound to each other but neither the company nor the members are bound to outsiders. Articles may supplement the terms of a special contract between the company and an outsider, but the outsider will not be able to take advantage of the Articles unless he is informed by the company that the company will observe the terms of the Articles.

The memorandum and articles of association constitute a notice to persons dealing with the company, and persons contracting with the company are presumed to know their contents. If a contract is entered into by the company contrary to the terms of the Memorandum or the Articles, the company is not bound by it. But outsiders are entitled to assume that the provisions of the Articles have been observed. This is known as the doctrine of "indoor management" or the rule in *Royal British Bank v. Tarquand.* For example, outsiders need not enquire into the validity of the election of directors.

Subject to the provisions of the law and the Memorandum, Articles define the powers of the shareholders, directors, managing director, etc. If directors exceed their powers as laid down in the Articles, the shareholders can ratify the act provided they are entitled to exercise the power themselves. A public limited company limited by shares need not prepare special articles of association. If it does not, Table A of the First Schedule to the Companies Act will apply. Also, if the special articles are silent on any point, the relevant provisions of Table A will apply.

Powers of Shareholders. Annually, in general meeting, the shareholders consider the annual accounts and the balance sheet and the directors' report and adopt them if they think fit. They also declare a dividend (not more than that recommended by the Board of Directors), elect directors in place of those who are due to retire and appoint auditors. In case of a public company and its subsidiary, the consent of the company in general meeting is necessary to-

(a) undertake lines of business other than those mentioned in the Memorandum as the main objects including those auxiliary to these;

(b) sell, lease or otherwise dispose of company's undertaking or substantial part of the undertaking;

(*c*) remit or give time for payment of any debt due by a director;

(*d*) invest, otherwise than in trust securities, the amount of compensation received by the company in respect of the compulsory acquisition after the commencement of the Act or of any-premises or property used for any such undertaking;

(*e*) borrow in excess of the aggregate paid-up capital plus reserves (temporary loans from company's bankers in the ordinary course: of thc business of the company being left out of account for this purpose); and

(*f*) contribute to charitable and other funds not relating to the company's business amounts exceeding Rs. 50,000 or 5% of its average net profits during the three preceding financial years, whichever is greater, in the course of any financial year.

'In respect of *(e)* and (*f*) above, the necessary resolution passed by the company in general meeting must specify the total amounts concerned. Temporary loans are defined as loans repayable on demand or within six months from the date of the loan, but not loans raised for the purpose of financing capital expenditure.

If the Board of Directors acts in the above-mentioned matters without the consent of the company, the third parties will be protected.

Further, the following should be kept in mind:

(*a*) The appointment of the sole selling agents by the Board must be approved by the company in general meeting within 6 months of the appointment; otherwise it will cease to be valid.

(*b*) Issues of bonus shares or debentures can be made only with the consent of the company in general meeting.

(c) Reorganisation of capital and amendment of the articles or memorandum of association also require the consent of the shareholders.

(*d*) Winding up, unless ordered by the Court, can be commenced only with the approval of the company in general meeting.

The Board of Directors. The management of a company is delegated to the Board of Directors. Directors are elected by the shareholders though some may be nominated by special interests like debentureholders, etc. The Companies Act contains a number of provisions in respect of directors.

Directors must act as a Board, i.e., decisions arrived at only at meetings of the directors will be binding except that, depending upon Articles, and subject to Section 289 of the Act, resolutions may also be adopted by circulation. Individual directors have no powers unless specific powers are delegated at a properly held meeting of the Board of Directors. The Board also has the power to appoint sub-committees to deal with specific matters. A meeting of the Board of Directors must be held once in every three calendar months. The Central Government has the power to exempt any class of companies from this provision. The quorum is two directors or one-third of the total number whichever is higher (not counting interested directors).

The directors are trustees for the company's property and it is their duty to apply the property for company's benefit alone. Any director using it for his personal benefit is guilty of breach of trust. The Board is also in the position of an agent and hence contracts signed by the directors on behalf of the company are binding on the company as far as third parties are concered, unless the contracts are beyond the powers of the company itself. The directors are not responsible for any loss suffered by the company, if they exercise reasonable care and skill in the exercise of their powers and discharge of their duties. But if the directors are guilty of gross negligence or of breach of trust, they must compensate the company for damage suffered by it and any provision in the articles absolving the directors from such liability is invalid. But if (according to section 633) the Court is satisfied that the director concerned acted honestly and reasonably and that, having regard to all the circumstances of the case, he ought fairly to be excused, the Court may relieve him, either wholly or partly, from his liability on such terms as it thinks fit.

The directors have the duty of general supervision of the affairs of the company even if there is a managing director. The following powers must be exercised only by the Board at its meetings (section 292):—

(i) the power to make calls;

(ii) the power to issue debentures;

(iii) the power to borrow moneys otherwise than on debentures;

(iv) the power to invest company's funds; and

(v) the power to make loans.

The powers specified in *(iii)*, *(iv)*, and *(v)* may be delegated by resolution at a Board meeting up to specified limits.

Section 292 does not cover the ordinary transactions with a bank.

Managing Director. The directors may appoint one of themselves as managing director. A managing director is "a director who, by virtue of an agreement with the company or of a resolution passed by the company in general meeting or by its Board, or, by virtue of its memorandum or articles of association is entrusted with substantial powers of management which would not otherwise be exercisable by him, and includes a director occupying the position of a managing director, by whatever name called." In the case of a public company and its subsidiary, amendment of any provision relating to the appointment or re-appointment of a managing director, whole-time director, or a director not liable to retirement by rotation will not be effective unless approved by the Central Government. A new managing director must be appointed only with the approval of the Central Government. Re-appointment also requires the sanction of the Central government (except appointment under schedule XIII of Companies Act). A managing director cannot act as such for more than two companies and in the case of the second company, unanimous approval of the Board of Directors is necessary. An undischarged insolvent, one who has at any time been adjudged an insolvent, one who suspends or has suspended payment to his creditors, one who makes or has at any time made a composition with the creditors or one who has been, at any time, convicted of an offence involving moral turpitude, cannot be appointed as managing director of any company.

Manager. A manager means "an individual who, subject to the superintendence, control and direction of the Board of Directors, has the management of the whole, or substantially the whole of the affairs of a company, and includes a director or any other person occupying the position of a manager, by whatever name called, and whether under a contract of service or not." A manager must be an individual. He is usually appointed by the Board of Directors. He cannot be appointed for more than five years at a time. The disqualifications and restrictions attaching to the managing director also attach to the manager.

Note: A company may have only one — either manager or managing director — but it may be permitted to have, say, two managing directors by the Central Government.

(e) Meetings of Shareholders

There are three kinds of general meetings of the company, namely, Statutory, Annual and Extraordinary. Every general meeting requires 21 days' notice in writing. A private company is not required to hold a statutory meeting.

Statutory Meeting. Every public company limited by shares, and limited by guarantee and having a share capital, must hold a general meeting of its members within a period of not less than one month nor more than six months from the date at which the company is entitled to commence business. The Board must, at least twenty-one days before the day of the meeting, forward to every member a report called the Statutory Report along with the notice of the meeting. The meeting is known as Statutory Meeting.

The *Statutory Report* must state the following:—

(a) the number of shares allotted distinguishing those allotted as fully or partly paid up otherwise than in cash, the extent to which they are partly paid up, the consideration for which the shares are allotted and the total amount received in cash;

(*b*) an abstract of the receipts and payments made up to a date within seven days of the report giving receipts and payments under distinctive heads and particulars of balance in hand;

(*c*) an account or estimate of the preliminary expenses including commission and discount paid or payable on the issue or sale of shares and debentures;

(*d*) names, addresses and occupations of its directors and auditors, and also of its manager, and secretary, if any, and any change that may have occurred since the date of incorporation;

(*e*) if any contract is to be modified, the particulars of such contracts with those of the proposed modification or the actual modification which is to be submitted for approval at the meeting;

(*f*) the extent to which underwriting contracts, if any, have not been carried out and the reason therefore;

(g) the arrears, if any, due on calls from directors, and manager; and

(*h*) the particulars of any commission or brokerage paid or to be paid in connection with the issue or sale of shares to any director.

At least two directors (one of them being the managing director, if there is one) must certify the report. The auditors of the company must also certify the report so far as it relates to the shares allotted by the company, cash received in respect thereof and the receipts and payments account. A copy of the report, duly certified, must be filed with the Registrar. It should be noted that a company cannot alter the terms of any contract referred to in the prospectus before the statutory meeting.

Procedure at the meeting. At the meeting, a list of members and of the number of shares held by them respectively must be produced and kept open and accessible to the members of the company during the continuance of the meeting. Any matter relating to the formation of the company or arising out of the Statutory Report can be raised without notice for discussion but, unless a notice has been given, a resolution cannot be passed. The meeting may be adjourned from time to time and a resolution may be passed at the adjourned meeting if due notice has been given in the meantime.

Annual General Meeting. Under section 166, every company without exception must hold, in addition to any other meeting, a general meeting specifying it as Annual General Meeting in the notice calling it. The first annual general meeting must be held within 18 months of the incorporation. It is not then necessary to hold any annual general meeting in the year of its incorporation or in the following year. Thereafter, an annual general meeting must be held every year but the interval between two annual general meetings must not be more than 15 months. The Registrar is allowed to extend the time by 3 months. The meeting can be held only in the city, town or village where the registered office is situate. It must be held during business hours and must not be held on a public holiday. If default is made in holding the meeting, the Central Government may, on the application of any member of the company, call or direct the calling of the general meeting. A notice of 21 days is necessary.

The usual business at the meeting is:

(a) Consideration of the annual accounts and the balance sheet and the report of the directors.

(*b*) Election of directors in place of those who retire.

(*c*) Appointment of auditors,

(*d*) Declaratioin of dividend.

All these matters are disposed of by simple majority.

It should be noticed that an annual general meeting can also transact business other than the four items enumerated above. But all such other business will be treated as special and proper notice must be given.

Extraordinary General Meeting. Every general meeting of the company, other than the statutory meeting and the annual general meeting, is an extraordinary general meeting. It is usually called by the directors for transacting some special or urgent business which has to be done before the next annual general meeting, Only the special business for which it is convened can be transacted at this meeting. Section 169 provides that an extraordinary general meeting must be called by the Board on the requisition of members holding 10% of the paid up capital carrying voting rights in respect of the matter to be discussed, and where a company has no share capital, on the requisition of members holding 10% of the total voting power in regard to the matter to be discussed. The meeting must be called within 21 days of the deposit of the requisition to be held on a day not later than 45 days from such date. The notice must state the matters for consideration at the meeting. If the Board does not hold the meeting within 45 days of the requisition, the requisitionists may hold the meeting within 3 months of the requisition. Notice of such meetings should be given in the same manner as for regular meetings. The requisitionists can recover from the company their reasonable expenses and the company can make good from the directors at fault.

Under section 186, the National Company Law Tribunal* may order a meeting of the company to be held either of its own accord or on the application of a director or a member entitled to vote.

Quorum. The quorum for the general meetings of the company is five persons personally present for public companies and two for private companies. But the Articles can fix a higher number.

Voting. At first, voting is by show of hands. In this case, every member present has one vote. But the Chairman or five members present in person or by proxy or members representing 10% of the paid-up capital or member(s) holding shares of not less than Rs. 50,000 may demand a poll in the case of a public company. In a private company, poll may be demanded by one member present in person or by proxy if not more than seven such members are personally present, and by two such members present in person or proxy, if more than seven such members are personally present. The voting shall be in accordance with the voting rights attached to each share. Only at a poll, proxies will be used.

Resolutions. The Companies Act recognises three types of resolutions: ordinary, special and a resolution requiring special notice. An *ordinary* resolution is one which is passed by a simple majority of votes cast on a show of hands or on a poll in favour of the resolution at a general meeting. A *special* resolution is one (1) in regard to which the intention to propose the resolution as a special resolution is specifically mentioned in the notice of the meeting, and (2) which is passed if the votes cast for it are not less than three times the votes cast against it.

A *resolution requiring special notice* is an ordinary resolution which may be passed by the members at a general meeting by a simple majority according to the provisions of the but a notice of the intention to move the resolution (which requires special notice) has be given to the company not less than 14 days before the meeting at which it is to be moved (excluding the day on which the notice is served and the day of the meeting) and the company must (upon receipt of such a notice) immediately give notice to the members of the intention to move such a resolution. Sections 225 and 284 of the companies Act mention four matters which require passing of a resolution wirte special notice. The Articles of the company may provide for additional makes in respect of which special notice is required.

Copies to be filed with the Registrar. Printed or type-written copies of the following resolutions and agreements must be filed with the Registrar within 30 days of the passing of the resolution:—

(1) special resolutions;

(2) resolutions agreed to by all members or classes of members;

(3) a resolution of the Board or an agreement appointing or re-appointing a managing director;

(4) resolutions or agreements agreed to by all the members of any class of shareholders but which would not have been effective but for such agreement and all resolutions or agreements which effectively bind all the members of any class of shareholders though not agreed to by all of them; and

---

* The National Company Law Tribunal has not become functional as yet. Hence, the authority is continued to be exercised by the Company Law Board.

(5) resolutions authorising directors to act under clauses *(a)*, *(d)* and (e) of sub-section (1) of Section 293;

(6) resolutions approving the appointment of sole selling agents; and

(7) resolution for voluntary winding up of the company.

Minutes Books. Every company must keep minutes containing a fair and correct summary of all proceedings of general meetings and Board meetings in books kept for that purpose. All appointments of officers made at any meetings must be included in the minutes.

In the case of Board meetings, the minutes must state the names of directors present and of those who may have dissented from any resolution passed at a meeting. The minutes of the general meeting are to be kept open for inspection by members.

2. ACCOUNTS

(*a*) Statutory Books:

Apart from the books required to record the company's transactions, the Companies Act requires some other books to be maintained mainly with a view to safeguarding the interests of the shareholders. Such books are known as **Statutory Books.** The following is the list of such books to be maintained by a company:-

1. Register of investments not held in company's name (open to members and debenture-holders). [Under sec. 49 (7)]
2. Register of fixed deposits.
3. Register of charges. [Under sec. 143 (1)]
4. Register of members. [Under sec. 150 (1)]
5. Index of members where the number is more than fifty, unless the register of members itself affords an index. [Under sec. 151 (1)]
6. Register of debentureholders. [Under sec. 152 (1)]
7. Index of debentureholders where the number is more than fifty; unless the register of debentureholders itself affords an index. [Under sec. 152 (2)]
8. Foreign register (and a duplicate) of members and debentureholders, if any. [Sections 157 and 158]
9. Minutes Books — books containing minutes of the general meetings of shareholders and the meetings of the Board of Directors. [Under sec. 193 (1)]
10. Register of contracts, companies and firms in which directors are interested directly or indirectly (open to members). [Under sec. 301 (1)]
11. Register of directors, managing director, manager and secretary. [Under sec. 303 (1)]
12. Register of directors' shareholdings (open to members and debentureholders during 14 days before and 3 days after the annual general meeting and to the Registrar and the Central Government). [Under sec. 307 (1)]
13. Register of loans made, gurantees given or securities provided to companies under the same management. [Under sec. 370 (1-C)]
14. Register of investment in shares and debentures of other companies.
15. Register of renewed and duplicate certificates.
16. Register of securities bought back [Section 77A]

Books of Account. Section 209 requires a company to maintain such books as will give a true and fair view in respect of:

(*a*) all sums of money received and expended by the company and the matters in respect of which the receipts and expenditure take place;

(*b*) all sales and purchases of goods by the company;

(*c*) all assets and liabilities of the company;

(*d*) and such particulars regarding utilisation of material or labour or other items of cost as may be prescribed by the Central Government in case the company belongs to a class of companies engaged in manufacturing, processing and mining activities.
Sub-section (3) makes it clear that the books to be maintained should be such as are necessary to give a true and fair view of the state of affairs of the company or branch office, as the case may be, and to explain its transactions. Such books must be kept on accural basis and according to the double entry system of accounting. They must be preserved for a minimum period of eight years immdiately preceding the current year.

These books are open to inspection of directors, the Registrar and officers authorised by the Central Government, and the officers authorised by the Securities and Exchange Board of India. Books of account have to be maintained at the registered office of the company. The Board of Directors may decide to keep all or any of the books of account at a place other than the registered office (but in India); within seven days of the decision, the Registrar must be notified of the full address of the place where the books are kept. Books relating to transactions at a branch (whether in or outside India) may be kept there but in that case proper summarised returns must be sent by the branch office to the registered office (or where the company is keeping books of account) at least quarterly.

Under section 209 (6) of the Companies Act, the following persons have been made responsible for keeping the books of account and securing compliance by the company with the requirements of section 209 of the Act:—

(*i*) where the company has a managing director or manager, such managing director or manager and all the officers and other employees of the company; and

(*ii*) where the company has neither a managing director nor manager, every director of the company.

If any person refered to above fails to take all resonable steps to secure compliance by the company with the requirements for keeping books of account or by his own wilful act causes any default by one company in this respect, he is punishable with imprisonment upto six months or with fine which may extend to Rs. 10,000 or with both.

Statistical Books. In addition to the statutory books mentioned earlier and the books of account, a company may choose to maintain a number of statistical books in order to keep a complete record of numerous details of certain transactions and activities of the company. The following statistical books are usually maintained by joint stock companies:—

(*i*) Share Application and Allotment Book

(*ii*) Share Calls Book

(*iii*) Share Certificate Book

(*iv*) Debentures Application and Allotment Book

(*v*) Debentures Calls Book

(*vi*) Register of Share Transfers

(*vii*) Dividend Book

(*viii*) Debenture Interest Book

(*ix*) Register of Documents Sealed

(*x*) Register of Share Warrants

(*xi*) Dividend Mandates Register

(*xii*) Register of Probates

(*xiii*) Register of Powers of Attorney

(*xiv*) Agenda Book

(*xv*) Register of Lost Share Certificates

(*xvi*) Register of directors' attendance.

(b) Issue of Shares. To collect capital from the public, a public company issues a document called the Prospectus inviting the public to submit applications to take up shares of the company. Subscription list for a public issue has to be kept open for at least 3 working days. The prospectus mentions the number and class of shares offered and the manner in which the amount of shares is payable by the public. Usually, the total amount of a share is payable in a number of instalments. A certain sum called the application money has to be paid along with the application which has to be made in a prescribed form.

Actually while framing the terms of the issue SEBI guidelines in this regard have to be followed. The following are a few examples of SEBI guideines:—

(*i*) In case of public issue at par, minimum number of shares for which application is to be made should be fixed at 200 shares of the face value of Rs. 10 each.

(*ii*) Where the issue is at a premium or comprises of debentures whether convertible or non-convertible, the amount payable in all in aspect of each instrument (i.e., on application, allotment and calls) by each applicant shall not be less than Rs. 2,000 irrespective of the size of the premium.

(*iii*) The minimum application money shall not be less than 25% of the issue price.

(*iv*) Where on application and on allotment, an amount exceeding Rs. 250 crores is raised, the amount to be called up on application/allotment and on various calls shall not exceed 25% of the total quantum of issue.

(*v*) The capital issued should be made fully paid up within 12 months from the date of the issue. Here, the term issue means 'allotment'. This guideline does not apply to issues of Rs. 500 crore or above.

When the application has been accepted and the shares have been alloted, the second instalment called the allotment becomes payable. Subsequent instalments will be payable as per terms of the issue and they are termed as calls and are serially numbered. Thus, the third instalment will be called the first call while the fourth instalment will be called the second call. The amount of a ten rupee share may be payable as to Rs. 2.50 p. with application, Rs. 3.50 p. on allotment, Rs. 2 on first call and Rs. 2 on second and first call.

Application money received will be debited to Bank and credited to Share Applications Account. If equity shares have been issued, the credit will be to Equity Share Applications Account and if preference shares have been issued, the credit will be to Preference Share Applications Account. Thus, for receipt of application money in respect of equity shares, the entry will be:

Bank Dr.
To Equity Share Applications Account
(Receipt of aplication money in respect of
...... equity shares @ Rs. ...... per share)

Use of application moneys: The application money has to be kept in a separate bank account maintained with a scheduled bank. The issuer company, till the date of allotment of shares, can use the application money only for the following:

(*i*) Adjustment of excess moneys against allotment of shares permitted to be dealt with in a Stock Exchange; or

(*ii*) Repayment of moneys for failure to get permission from the Stock Exchange.

On and from the date the allotment is made, the application moneys can be utilised by the company for the purposes for which the issue was made.

Allotment of shares. If the applications received are adequate to fulfil the condition of minimum subscription, the Board of Directors can proced to allot shares on applications received as per SEBI guidelines. All applications for identical number of shares have to be dealt with in an identical manner. In case of over subscription, allotment on a *pro-rata* basis has to be made subject to the condition that the number of shares alloted to every allotee is in marketable lot or a multiple thereof. Interested student is advised to go through the relevant detailed guidelines is this regard by SEBI. SEBI guidelines have been changed a few times and student should remember that SEBI may change them again. Letters of Regret along with refund of the application money are sent to applicants whose applications are rejected. Letters of Allotment are sent to other applicants in which the shareholders are requested to remit money due, if any, on allotment; the amount being called allotment money. The Board of Directors cannot allot more than the number of shares offered to the public in the prospectus even if it has received applications for a larger number.

If the company does not receive applications for at least 90% of the issued amount from the public subscription plus accepted development (*i.e.*, the amount not subscribed for by the public) from underwriters within 120 days from the date of the opening of the issue, the company has to refund the amopunt of subscription. In case of the disputed devolvepment also, the compny has to refund the subscription if the above conditions are not met. Section 73 of the Companies Act provides for payment of interest on excess application money from the expiry of the 78th day from the closing of the subscription list. Hence, the refund of application money within 120 days from the opening of subscription list is without prejudice to the company's liability for payment of interest on delayed refunds persuant to Section 73 of the Companies Act.

When allotment is made, two things are to be done simultaneously. Application money received in respetct of shares alloted is to be made part of share capital and allotment money in respect of the same shares is to be made due. Entries for the two are similar. Assuming that equity shares have been allotted, the journal entry will be as follows:

Equity Share Applications Account Dr.
Equity Share Allotment Account Dr.
To Equity Share Capital Account
(Capitalisation of application money in respect of equity shares @ Rs. ...... per share and allotment money due on the same number of equity shares @ Rs. ...... per share alloted by the Board of Directors)

Application money received with applications which have been rejected will be returned; the journal entry being as follows :—

Equity Share Applications Account Dr.
To Bank
(Refund of application money in respect of applications rejected by the Board of Directors)

As pointed out earlier, some applications may be accepted partially. The surplus application money on such an application will be transferred from Share Applications Account to Share Allotment Account to the extent of allotment money on shares allotted; the balance of surplus application money will be refunded unless the applicant has agreed to get it treated Calls in Advance in which case it will be transferred from Share Applications Account to Calls in Advance Account. If application money received with an application exceeds the total amount payable on shares allotted, such an excess will have to be refunded even in the case where the applicant has agreed to get the excess application money treated as Calls in Advance. Let us assume, a company issues equity shares of Rs. 10 each payable as follows :—

Rs. 2.50 with application,
Rs. 3.50 on allotment, and
Rs. 4 on first and final call.

Further assume that an applicant applies for 500 shares but his application is accepted partially and only 100 shares are allotted to him. The applicant must have paid Rs. 1,250 by way of application money. Application money on 100 shares is Rs. 250. Out of the surplus of Rs. 1,000, Rs. 350 will be appropriated towards allotment money, Rs. 400 will be treated as Calls in Advance and the balance, Rs. 250 will be refunded. The combined journal entry for disposal of remaining application money, after capitalisation of application money on 100 shares will be as follows : –

		Rs.	*Rs.*
	Equity Share Applications Account ... Dr.	1000	
	To Equity Share Allotment Account		350
	To Calls in Advance Account		400
	To Bank		250

One may not open separate applications and allotment accounts, but make entries regarding both applications and allotment in one account called 'Applications and Allotment Account'. If it is done, there will be no entry for transferring surplus application money on partially accepted applications to the extent it can be appropriated towards allotment money.

Calls. The balance due on shares after taking into account application money and allotment money may be asked for by the Board of Directors in a number of instalments depending upon the terms of the issue. Each such instalment is called a 'Call'. Wherever a call is made, the relevant share capital account is credited and a separate share call account is debited with the amount due. On receipt of the call, Bank is debited and the relevant Share Call Account is credited with the amount received. Suppose, in respect of some equity shares, there are in all two calls, the journal entries will be as follows :—

Equity Share First Call Account • Dr.
To Equity Share Capital Account
First call due in respect of ________equity shares
@ Rs. _______ per share.

Bank Dr.
To Equity Share First Call Account
Receipt of first call on __________equity shares
@ Rs. _______ per share.

Equity Share Second and Final Call Account Dr.
To Equity Share Capital Account
Second and final call due on ______equity shares
@ Rs. _________ per share.

Bank Dr.
To Equity Share Second and Final Call Account
Receipt of second and final call on _________equity shares
@ Rs.________per share.

According to Table A, no call can exceed one fourth of the nominal value of the shares or be payable at less than one month from the date fixed for the payment of the last preceding call and at least 14 days' notice must be given to the members for payment of a call.

It may also be noted here that shares may be issued at par, at a premium or at a discount. Issue of a share at par means that the total amount payable by the shareholder in respect of that share is equal to face value (or nominal value or par value) of the share. Suppose, a company issues shares of the face value of Rs. 10 each on which the shareholders are required to pay Rs. 4 per share with applications and Rs. 6 per share on allotment, there being no calls, we shall say that the company has issued shares at par because the total amount payable by the shareholder per share is Rs. 4 + Rs. 6 = Rs. 10 which is equal to the face value of one share.

If by the terms of the issue, the shareholders are required to pay more than the face value of the shares allotted to them, it is called an issue at a premium. On the other hand if the shareholders are required to pay less than the face value of the shares allotted to them, it is called issue of shares at a discount. First study a few illustrations relating to issue of shares at par.

Illustration 1. P Ltd. issued a prospectus inviting applications for 1,00,000 equity shares of Rs. 10 each, payable as to Rs. 2.50 p. with application, Rs. 3.50 p. on allotment and the balance on first and the final call. Applications were received for 99,000 shares only. All the applications were accepted in full. The call was also made in due course of time. All moneys were duly received. Journalise all the abovementioned transactions including cash transactions.

Solution:

Journal

	Particulars		L.F.	Dr.	Cr.
				Rs.	*Rs.*
	Bank	Dr.		2,47,500	
	To Equity Share Applications Account				2,47,500
	Receipt of application money on 99,000 equity shares @ Rs. 2.50 p. per share.				
	Equity Share Applications Account	Dr.		2,47,500	
	Equity Share Allotment Account	Dr.		3,46,500	
	To Equity Share Capital Account				5,94,000
	Capitatisation of application money @ Rs. 2.50 p. per share and allotment money due @ Rs. 3.50 per share on 99,000 equity shares allotted by the Borad of Directors.				
	Bank	Dr.		3,46,500	
	To Equity Share Allotment Account				3,46,500
	Receipt of allotment money on 99,000 equity shares @ Rs. 3.50 p. per share.				
	Equity Share First and Final Call Account	Dr.		3,96,000	
	To Equity Share Capital Account				3,96,000
	First and final call due on 99,000 equity shares @ Rs. 4 per share.				
	Bank	Dr.		3,96,000	
	To Equity Share First and Final Call Account				3,96,000
	Receipt of first and final call on 99,000 equity shares @ Rs. 4 per share.				

In practice, cash transactions are recorded in Cash Book. In a practical problem, if Cash Book has also been asked for, cash transactions should not be journalised.

Illustration 2. Jupiter Co. Ltd. issued 5,00,000 equity shares of Rs. 10 each payable as follows:—

Rs. 2.50 with application,

Rs. 3.50 on allotment ,

Rs. 2 on first call and,

Rs. 2 on second and final call.

Applications totalled 10,00,500 shares. One application for 500 shares was rejected on techincal grounds. All other applications were accepted allotting one share for every two shares applied for. The two calls were also made on due dates.

Assuming that all moneys were duly received, prepare cash book, journal and ledger accounts.

Solution:

Dr. **Cash Book (Bank Columns Only)** *Cr.*

		Rs.			*Rs.*
	To Equity Share Applications Account (Receipt of application money on 10,00,500 equity shares @ Rs. 2.50 per share)	25,01,250		By Equity Share Applications Account (Return of application money on 500 equity shares)	1,250
				By Balance c/d.	50,00,000
	To Equity Share Allotment Account (Receipt of balance of allotment money after adjusting excess application money)	5,00,000			
	To Equity Share First Call Account (Receipt of first call on 5,00,000 equity shares @ Rs. 2 per share)	10,00,000			
	To Equity Share Second and Final Call Account (Receipt of second and final call on 5,00,000 equity shares @ Rs. 2 per share)	10,00,000			
		50,01,250			50,01,250
	To Balance b/d	50,00,000			

Journal

			Dr.	*Cr.*
			Rs.	*Rs.*
	Equity Share Applications Account Dr.		12,50,000	
	Equity Share Allotment Account Dr.		17,50,000	
	To Equity Share Capital Account			30,00,000
	Application money @ Rs. 2.50 per share and allotment money @ Rs. 3.50 per share on 5,00,000 equity shares credited to Equity Share Capital Account on allotment.			
	Equity Share Applications Account Dr.		12,50,000	
	To Equity Share Allotment Accounts			12,50,000
	Transfer of surplus application money from Equity Share Applications Account to Equity Share Allotment Account.			

			Rs.	Rs.
Equity Share First Call Account	Dr.		10,00,000	
To Equity Share Capital Account				10,00,000
Amount due from equity shareholders in respect of first call on 5,00,000 equity shares @ Rs. 2 per share.				
Equity Share Second and Final Call Account	Dr.		10,00,000	
To Equity Share Capital Account				10,00,000
Second and final call due on 5,00,000 equity share @ Rs. 2 per share.				

Ledger

Equity Share Applications Account

Dr.	Rs.		Cr.	Rs.
To Equity Share Capital Account	12,50,000		By Bank	25,01,250
To Equity Share Allotment Account	12,50,000			
To Bank	1,250			
	25,01,250			25,01,250

Equity Share Allotment Account

Dr.	Rs.		Cr.	Rs.
To Equity Share Capital Account	17,50,000		By Equity Share Applications Account	12,50,000
			By Bank	5,00,000
	17,50,000			17,50,000

Equity Share First Call Account

Dr.	Rs.		Cr.	Rs.
To Equity Share Capital Account	10,00,000		By Bank	10,00,000

Equity Share Second and Final Call Account

Dr.	Rs.		Cr.	Rs.
To Equity Share Capital Account	10,00,000		By Bank	10,00,000

Equity Share Capital Account

Dr.	Rs.		Cr.	Rs.
To Balance c/d	50,00,000		By Equity Share Applications Account	12,50,000
			By Equity Share Allotment Account	17,50,000
			By Equity Share First Call Account	10,00,000
			By Equity Share Second and Final Call Account	10,00,000
	50,00,000			50,00,000
			By Balance b/d	50,00,000

Instead of opening two accounts namely Share Applications Account and Share Allotment Account, only one account called Share Applications and Allotment Account may be opened to serve the purpose of both the accounts.

In the following illustration, the treatment of Share Applications and Allotment Account should be noted.

Illustration 3. On 1st April, 2009, A Ltd. issued 4,00,000 equity shares of Rs. 10 each payable as follows :

Rs. 2.50 on application;
Rs. 3.50 on allotment;
Rs. 2 on 1st October, 2009; and
Rs. 2 on 1st February, 2010.

By 20th May, the issue was fully subscribed. Allotment was made on 1st June. All sums due on allotment were received by 1st July; those on 1st call were received by 20th October. When accounts were closed on 31st March, 2001, the second and final call on 1,000 shares had not been received.

Journalise the transactions.

Solution:

Journal

Date		Particulars		L.F.	Dr. Rs.	Cr. Rs.
2009 May	20	Bank To Equity Share Applications & Allotment Account Application money on 4,00,000 equity shares at Rs. 2.50 p. per share.	Dr.		10,00,000	10,00,000
June	1	Equity Share Applications & Allotment Account To Equity Share Capital Account Capitalisation of application money @ Rs. 2.50 per share and allotment money due @ Rs. 3.50 per share on 4,00,000 equity shares allotted by the Board of Directors vide resolution no........ dated 1st June, 2009.	Dr.		24,00,000	24,00,000
July	1	Bank To Equity Share Applications & Allotment Account Receipts of allotment money on 4,00,000 equity shares @ Rs. 3.50 per share.	Dr.		14,00,000	14,00,000
Oct.	1	Equity Share First Call Account To Equity Share Capital Account Amount due from members in respect of first call on 4,00,000 equity shares at Rs. 2 per share as per the Board of Directors' resolution no. ..... dated..... 1st October, 2009.	Dr.		8,00,000	8,00,000
Oct.	20	Bank To Equity Share First Call Account Receipt of the amounts due on first call @ Rs. 2 per share on 4,00,000 eqity shares.	Dr.		8,00,000	8,00,000
2010 Feb.	1	Equity Share Second & Final Call Account To Share Capital Account Amount due on 4,00,000 equity shares at Rs. 2 per share on second and final call, as per Directors' resolution no ...... dated .... 1st February, 2010.	Dr.		8,00,000	8,00,000

Mar.	31	Bank Dr. To Equity Share Second & Final Call Account Amount received against the final call on 3,99,000 shares at Rs. 2 per share.		7,98,000	7,98,000

Pro rata allotment. Pro rata means proportionately. Alloment on pro rata basis means that allotment on every application is made in the ratio which the total number of shares to be allotted on this basis bears to the total number of shares applied for in all such applications. If, 20,000 shares are allotted on pro rata basis on applications for 25,000 shares, it means that four shares are allotted for every five shares applied for. Usually applications are invited in multiples of a certain number of shares and it becomes possible to allot shares on pro rata basis without involving fractions of shares to be allotted. Shares are mostly alloted to the nearest multiple of marketable lot, mostly 100 shares.

Illustration 4. On 1st March, 2009 Alpha Co. Ltd. issued 12,500 10% preference shares of Rs. 25 each payable as to Rs. 8 with application, Rs. 12 on allotment and the balance in two equal calls of Rs. 2.50 per each. Subscription list (which was opened on 6th March, 2009) totalled 25,500 shares. The Board of Directors rejected one application for 500 shares and allotted shares on the remaining applications on pro rata basis on 1st April, 2009. First call was made three months after allotment whereas the second call was made four months after the first call. All moneys were duly received. In each case, a 14 days notice was served.

Pass journal entries, prepare cash book and show ledger accounts.

Solution:

Dr. **Cash Book (Bank Columns only)** *Cr.*

2009		*Rs.*	2009		*Rs.*
Mar. 6	To 10% Preference Share Applications & Allotment Account (Application money on 25,500 10% preference shares @ Rs. 8 per share)	2,04,000		By 10% Preference Share Applications & Allotment Account (Refund of application money on 500 10% preference shares @ Rs. 8 per share)	4,000
				By Balance c/d	3,12,500
April 1-14	To 10% Preference Share Applications & Allotment Account (Balance of allotment money in respect of 12,500 10% preference shares)	50,000			
July 1-14	To 10% Preference Share First Call Account (First call on 12,500 10% preference shares @ Rs.2.50 per share)	31,250			
Nov. 1-14	To 10% Preference Share Second & Final Call Account (Second & final call on 12,500 10% preference shares @ Rs. 2.50 per share)	31,250			
		3,16,500			3,16,500
	To Balance b/d	3,12,500			

Journal

Date		Particulars		L.F.	Dr. Rs.	Cr. Rs.
2009 April	1	10% Preference Share Applications & Allotment Account	Dr.		2,50,000	
		To 10% Preference Share Capital Account				2,50,000
		Application money @ Rs. 8 per share and allotment money @ Rs. 12 per share credited to 10% Preference Share Capital Account on allotment of 12,500 10% preference shares as per Board of Directors' resolution no. _____dated 1st April, 2009.				
July	1	10% Preference Share First Call Account	Dr.		31,250	
		To 10% Preference Share Capital Account				31,250
		First call money due on 12,500 10% preference shares @ Rs. 2.50 per share, as per Board of Directors' resolution no._______ dated 1st July, 2009.				
Nov.	1	10% Preference Share Second & Final Call Account	Dr.		31,250	
		To 10% Preference Share Capital Account				31,250
		Second and final call money due on 12,500 10% preference shares @ Rs. 2.50 per share as per Board of Directors' resolution no. _____ dated 1st November, 2009.				

Working Notes:

Shares Applied for	Shares Allotted	Application Money Received	Application Money	Appropriation towards Allotment Money	Refund
		Rs.	*Rs.*	*Rs.*	*Rs.*
500	—	4,000	—	—	4,000
25,000	12,500	2,00,000	1,00,000	1,00,000	—
25,500	12,500	2,04,000	1,00,000	1,00,000	4,000

	Rs.
Total allotment money on 12,500 10% preference shares @ Rs. 12 per share	1,50,000
Less : Amount of application money appropriated towards allotment money	1,00,000
Balance received after allotment	50,000

Ledger

10% Preference Share Applications & Allotment Account

Dr. / *Cr.*

Date	Particulars	Rs.	Date	Particulars	Rs.
2009 April 1	To 10% Preference Share Capital Account	2,50,000	2009 March 6	By Bank	2,04,000
	To Bank	4,000	April 1-14	By Bank	50,000
		2,54,000			2,54,000

10% Preference Share First Call Account

Dr.					Cr.
2009		Rs.	2009		Rs.
July 1	To 10% Preference Share Capital Account	1,87,500	July 1-14	By Bank	1,87,500

10% Preference Share Second and Final Call Account

Dr.					Cr.
2009		Rs.	2009		Rs.
Nov. 1	To 10% Preference Share Capital Account	1,87,500	Nov. 1-14	By Bank	1,87,500

10% Preference Share Capital Account

Dr.					Cr.
		Rs.	2009		Rs.
	To Balance c/d	3,12,500	April 1	By 10% Preference Share Applications & Allotment Account	2,50,000
			July 1	By 10% Preference Share First Call Account	31,250
			Nov. 1	By 10% Preference Share Second & Final Call Account	31,250
		3,12,500			3,12,500
				By Balance b/d	3,12,500

Where both the equity and preference shares are issued, the company will maintain separate application, allotment, call and capital accounts in respect of the two classes of shares. In a question on the issue of both classes of shares unless different dates have been mentioned in the question, it may be assumed that both classes of shares have been allotted on the same date and the dates for the making and receiving the different calls on the two classes of shares also concur.

Illustration 5. Keswani Co. Ltd. issued 7,50,000 equity shares of 10 each and 50,000 12% preference shares of Rs. 100 each, payable as under :—

	On Equity Shares	On Preference Shares
	Rs.	Rs.
With application	2.50	25
On allotment	3	30
On first call	2.25	45
On second call	2.25	--

The company received applications for 15,01,000 equity shares and 49,000 preference shares. Applications totalling 1,000 equity shares had to be rejected. Allotment on other applications for equity shares was made on a *pro rata* basis. All applications for preference shares were accepted in full. Calls were made on due dates. All moneys were duly received.

Show journal entries for the abovementioned transactions.

Solution:

Journal

			Dr.	Cr.
			Rs.	Rs.
	Bank Dr.		49,77,500	
	To Equity Share Applications & Allotment Account			37,52,500
	To 12% Preference Share Applications & Allotment Account			12,25,000
	Application money received on 15,01,000 equity shares @ Rs. 2.50 per share and 49,000 12% perference shares @ Rs. 25 per share.			

Particulars			Rs.	Rs.
Equity Share Applications & Allotment Account	Dr.		41,25,000	
12% Preference Share Applications & Allotment Account	Dr.		26,95,000	
To Equity Share Capital Account				41,25,000
To 12% Preference Share Capital Account				26,95,000
Capitalisation of application money @ Rs. 2.50 per share and allotment money due @ Rs. 3 per share on 7,50,000 equity shares and that of application money @ Rs. 25 per share and allotment money due @ Rs. 30 per share on 49,000 12% preference shares allotted as per resolution no_______ of the Board of Directors.				
Equity Share Applications & Allotment Account	Dr.		2,500	
To Bank				2,500
Return of application money on 1,000 equity shares @ Rs. 2.50 p. per share.				
Bank	Dr.		22,20,000	
To Equity Share Application & Allotment Account				7,50,000
To 12% Preference Share Applications & Allotment Account				14,70,000
Receipt of balance of allotment money on equity shares after appropriation of surplus application money and full preference share allotment money.				
Equity Share First Call Account	Dr.		16,87,500	
12% Preference Share First & Final Call Account	Dr.		22,05,000	
To Equity Share Capital Account				16,87,500
To 12% Preference Share Capital Account				22,05,000
First call due on 7,50,000 equity shares @ Rs. 2.25 per share and first & final call due on 49,000 12% preference shares @ Rs. 45 per share as per resolution no.________of the Board of Directors.				
Bank	Dr.		38,92,500	
To Equity Share First Call Account				16,87,500
To 12% Preference Share First & Final Call Account				22,05,000
First call received on 7,50,000 equity shares @ Rs. 2.25 per share and on 49,000 12% preference shares @ Rs. 45 per share.				
Equity Share Second Final Call Account	Dr.		16,87,500	
To Equity Share Capital Account				16,87,500
Second and final call due on 7,50,000 equity shares @ Rs. 2.25 per share as per resolution no. ______ of the Board of Directors.				
Bank	Dr.		16,87,500	
To Equity Share Second and Final Call Account				16,87,500
Second and final call received on 7,50,000 equity shares @ Rs. 2.25 p. per share.				

Working Notes:

Equity Shares Applied for	Equity Shares Allotted	Application Money Received	Application Money on Shares Allotted	Appropriation towards Allotment Money	Refund
		Rs.	*Rs.*	*Rs.*	*Rs.*
1,000	—	2,500	—	—	2,500
15,00,000	7,50,000	37,50,000	18,75,000	18,75,000	—
15,01,000	7,50,000	37,52,500	18,75,000	18,75,000	2,500

	Rs.
Total allotment money on equity shares Rs. 3 × 7,50,000	22,50,000
Less : Application money appropriated towards allotment money	18,00,000
Balance received after allotment of shares	7,50,000

Calls in Advance. A company, if its Articles of Association permit, may receive from shareholders the amount remaining unpaid on shares held by them even though the amount has not been called up. The amount so received is credited to Calls in Advance Account. When a call is made, the appropriate amount is transferred from Calls in Advance Account to the relevant call account.

Interest on calls in advance may be paid from the date of receipt of the advance to the date of appropriation (i.e. to the date of making the call). Entry for payment of such interest will be to debit Interest on Calls in Advance Account and to credit Bank. If surplus application money is treated as calls in advance, interest will be paid with effect from the date of allotment and not from the actual receipt of the application money. Interest on Calls in Advance is a nominal account and hence while preparing the final accounts of the company, it is transferred to Profit & Loss Account.

Calls in Arrear. Some shareholders may not pay allotment money or call in time. Share Allotment Account or Share Call Account is a personal account showing the amount due from the shareholders. If all moneys are duly received, these accounts will close. But if even after the expiry of the last date fixed for payment, some shareholders fail to pay, these accounts will show balances. The company may accept late payment of allotment money or call with or without interest for late payment. If interest is received, it will be debited to Bank and credited to Interest on Calls in Arrear Account, the latter account being transferred to Profit & Loss Account at the end of the accounting year.

A company may maintain a Calls in Arrear Account. In such a case, after the expiry of the last date for payment of allotment money or a call, the amounts not received by the company are transferred from Share Allotment Account or the relevant Share Call Account to Calls in Arrear Account. For receipt of calls in arrear, Bank will be debited and Calls in Arrear Account will be credited. Here also, for interest on calls in arrear for the period between the last date fixed for payment and the actual date of payment, Bank will be debited and Interest on Calls in Arrear Account will be credited. If nothing is given in the question, it may be assumed that 14 days notice was given for payment of a call. In the examination if notice period is not metioed, interest may be calculated from the date of making of the call with a note.

Sometimes in a practical problem on issue of shares, it is stated that the company has adopted Table A as its Articles of Association. While attempting such a problem, it is necessary to remember the following provisions of Table A :—

1. No call shall exceed one-fourth of the nominal value of the share or be payable at less than one month from the date fixed for the payment of the last preceding call. At least 14 days' notice must be given to the members for payment of the call.

2. If a sum called in respect of a share is not paid on or before the due date, the person concerned shall pay interest thereon from the due date to the time of actual payment at 5 per cent per annum. The Board shall be at liberty to waive interest or charge it at a lower rate.

3. The Board :

(*a*) may, if it thinks fit, receive from any member willing to advance the same, all or any part of the moneys uncalled and unpaid upon any shares held by him; and

(*b*) upon all or any of the moneys so advanced, may (until the same would, but for such advance, become presently payable) pay interest at such rate not exceeding, unless the company in general meeting shall otherwise direct, six per cent per annum as may be agreed upon between the Board and the member paying the sum in advance.

Briefly speaking, while attempting such a problem :

(*i*) interest on calls in advance should be paid @ 6% per annum.

(*ii*) interest on calls in arrear should be charged @ 5% per annum.

(*iii*) it should be assumed that 14 days' notices were given to pay calls.

Even if a company has framed its own Articles of Association but the document does not contain any provisions to the contrary, the relevant provisions of Table A of the Companies Act will be applicable.

Illustration 6. Goodluck Ltd. issued on 1st April, 2009 a prospectus inviting applications for 10,00,000 equity shares of Rs. 10 each, payable as stated below :–

With application	Rs. 2.50
On allotment	Rs. 2.50
On first call (three months after allotment)	Rs. 2.50
On second call (four months after first call)	Rs. 2.50

Every application had to be for a minimum of 500 shares. Prospectus also stated that the surplus application money, if any, remaining after appropriation towards allotment money, would be treated as calls in advance.

Subscriptions totalled 25,00,500 shares. On 1st May, 2009 the Board of Directors rejected one application for 500 shares on technical grounds and accepted all other applications, allotment being made on a *pro rata* basis.

One shareholder who had applied for 1,000 shares and to whom 400 shares had been allotted paid the final call two months late along with interest for late payment. All other moneys were received in time. The company has adopted Table A as its Articles of Assoication. It closes its books of account every year on 31st March.

Pass journal entries for all the abovementioned transactions during the year ended 31st March, 2010.

Solution:

Journal

				Dr.	Cr.
2009				Rs.	Rs.
Apr.	1	Bank	Dr.	62,51,250	
		To Equity Share Applications & Allotment Account			62,51,250
		Application money received in respect of 25,00,500 equity shares @ Rs. 2.50 per share.			
May.	1	Equity Share Applications & Allotment Account	Dr.	50,00,000	
		To Equity Share Capital Account			50,00.000
		Application money @ Rs. 2.50 per share and allotment money due @ Rs. 2.50 per share credited to Equity Share Capital Account in respect of 10,00,000 equity shares allotted by the Board of Directors vide resolution no.______dated 1st May, 2009.			

				Rs.	Rs.
May	1	Equity Share Applications & Allotment Account To Calls in Advance Account Surplus application money treated as calls in advance being transferred from Equity Share Applications and Allotment Account to Calls in Advance Account.	Dr.	12,50,000	12,50,000
"	3	Equity Share Applications & Allotment Account To Bank Refund of application money to the applicant whose application for 500 shares had to be rejected on technical grounds.	Dr.	1,250	1,250
Aug	1	Equity Share First Call Account To Equity Share Capital Account First call due on 10,00,000 equity shares @ Rs. 2.50 per share as per resolution no._______passed by Board of Directors on 1st August, 2009.	Dr.	25,00,000	25,00,000
"	"	Calls in Advance Account To Equity Share First Call Account Appropriation of calls in advance towards first call in respect of 10,00,000 equity shares @ Rs. 1.25 per share.	Dr.	12,50,000	12,50,000
"	"	Interest on Calls in Advance Account To Bank Interest paid on Rs. 12,50,000 for 3 months @ 6% per annum.	Dr.	18,750	18,750
"	14	Bank To Equity Share First Call Account Receipt of balance of first call on 10,00,000 equity shares @ Rs. 1.25 per share.	Dr.	12,50,000	12,50,000
Dec.	1	Equity Share Second & Final Call Account To Equity Share Capital Account Second & final call due on 10,00,000 equity shares @ Rs. 2.50 per share as per Board of Directors' resolution no._________dated 1st Dec., 2009.	Dr.	25,00,000	25,00,000
Dec.	14	Bank Calls in Arrear Account To Equity Share Second & Final Call Account Receipt of share and final call on 9,99,600 equity shares @ Rs. 2.50 per share; call in respect of 400 shares being in arrear.	Dr. Dr.	24,99,000 1,000	 25,00,000
2010 Feb.	14	Bank To Calls in Arrear Account To Interest on Calls in Arrear Account Receipt of calls in arrear along with interest for 2 months @ 5% per annum.	Dr.	1,008	 1,000 8
Mar.	31	Profit & Loss Account To Interest on Calls in Advance Account Transfer of Interest on Calls in Advance Account to Profit & Loss Account.	Dr.	18,750	18,750
"	"	Interest on Calls in Arrear Account To Profit & Loss Account Transfer of Interest on Calls in Arrear Account to Profit & Loss Account.	Dr.	8	8

Balance Sheet. Balance Sheet of a joint stock company has to be prepared in the prescribed form shown in Schedule VI Part I of the Companies Act. All items have to be shown under the prescribed heads and in the prescribed order. It will be discussed in detail in the chapter on final accounts of joint stock companies. For the time being in this chapter in every illustration where balance sheet has been shown, note carefully the order of items and the headings under which different items appear.

Illustration 7. Wye Ltd. was registered with an authorised capital of Rs. 2 crore divided into shares of Rs. 10 each. It issued at par 10,00,000 equity shares, the payment per share was to be made as follows :-

with application	Rs. 2.50,
on allotment	Rs. 3.50, and
on first and final call	Rs. 4

Applications were received for 9,90,000 shares. The Board of Directors accepted all the applications in full. All the allottees paid the allotment money in time. The call was also made. Call on 500 shares was received 5 months late along with iterest @ 12% per annum whereas call on 1,000 shares was still in arrear when the final accounts for the first year were prepared.

Record the abovementioned transactions in the books of the company and prepare the balance sheet as at the end of the year.

Solution:

Journal

			Dr.	Cr.
			Rs.	Rs.
	Equity Share Applications Account Dr. Equity Share Allotment Account Dr. To Equity Share Capital Account Application money @ Rs. 2.50 per share and allotment money @ Rs. 3.50 per share credited to Equity Share Capital Account on allotment of 9,90,000 equity shares as per resolution no_______ passed by the Board of Directors in its meeting dated________.		24,75,000 34,65,000	 59,40,000
	Equity Share First and Final Call Account Dr. To Equity Share Capital Account First and final call due on 9,90,000 equity shares @ Rs. 4 per share as per resolution no. ________ passed by the Board of Directors in its meeting dated______.		39,60,000	 39,60,000
	Calls in Arrear Account Dr. To Equity Share First and Final Call Account Transfer of call money not received till the last date fixed for payment to Calls in Arrear Account.		6,000	 6,000
	Interest on Calls in Arrear Account Dr. To Profit & Loss Account Transfer of Interest on Calls in Arrear Account to Profit & Loss Account at the end of the accounting year.		42	 42

Cash Book (Bank Columns Only)

Dr.		Rs.			Rs. Cr.
	To Equity Share Applications Account	24,75,000		By Balance c/d	98,96,042
	To Equity Share Allotment Account	34,65,000			
	To Equity Share First call Account	39,54,000			
	To Calls in Arrear Account	2,000			
	To Interest on Calls in Arrear Account	42			
		98,96,042			98,96,042
	To Balance b/d	98,96,042			

Ledger

Equity Share Applications Account

Dr.		Rs.			Rs. Cr.
	To Equity Share Capital	24,75,000		By Bank	24,75,000

Equity Share Allotment Account

Dr.		Rs.			Rs. Cr.
	To Equity Share Capital Account	34,65,000		By Bank	34,65,000

Equity Share First Call Account

Dr.		Rs.			Rs. Cr.
	To Equity Share Capital Account	39,60,000		By Bank	39,54,000
				By Calls in Arrear Account	6,000
		39,60,000			39,60,000

Calls in Arrear Account

Dr.		Rs.			Rs. Cr.
	To Equity Share First and Final Call Account	6,000		By Bank	2,000
				By Balance c/d	4,000
		6,000			6,000
	To Balance b/d	4,000			

Equity Share Capital Account

Dr.		Rs.			Rs. Cr.
	To Balance c/d	99,00,000		By Equity Share Applications Account	24,75,000
				By Equity Share Allotment Account	34,65,000
				By Equity Share First Call Account	39,60,000
		99,00,000			99,00,000
				By Balance b/d	99,00,000

Dr. **Interest on Calls in Arrear Account** Cr.

	Rs.		Rs.
To Profit & Loss Account	42	By Bank	42

Dr. **Profit & Loss Account** Cr.

	Rs.		Rs.
		By Interest on Calls in Arrear Account	40

Balance Sheet of Wye Ltd. as at the end of the year

Liabilities	*Rs.*	*Rs.*	*Assets*	*Rs.*
Share Capital			**Current Assets, Loans and Advances**	
Authorised:			(A) Current Assets	
20,00,000 Shares of Rs. 10 each		2,00,00,000	Cash at Bank	98,96,042
Issued:			(B) Loans and Advances	nil
10,00,000 Equity Shares of Rs. 10 each		1,00,00,000		
Subscribed:				
9,90,000 Equity Shares of Rs. 10 each, fully called up	99,00,000			
Less: Calls Unpaid	4,000	98,96,000		
Reserves and Surplus				
Profit & Loss Account		42		
		98,96,042		98,96,042

Issue of Shares at a Premium. When shares are issued at a price higher than the face value (also called par value or nominal value), it is called an issue of shares at a premium. Excess of issue price over face value is the amount of premium; it is a capital profit for the company and the amount so earned has to be credited to a separate account called Securities Premium Account.

There are no restrictions on issue of shares at a premium and the power to issue shares at a premium need not be taken in the Articles of Association. But there are restrictions on the ways securities premium can be used. According to Section 78 of the Companies Act, securities premium may be applied by the company for

(*i*) issuing to members of the company fully paid bonus shares; or
(*ii*) writing off the preliminary expenses of the company; or
(*iii*) writing off the expenses of, or the commission paid or discount allowed on issue of shares or debentures of the company; or
(*iv*) providing for the premium payable on the redemption of any redeemable preference shares or debentures.

According to the companies (Amendment) Act, 1999 a company may, object to fulfilment of certain conditions, use the amount of its securities Premium Account to buy back its own shares.

Any other application of securities premium will amount to a reduction of share capital. It is so because the provisions of the Companies Act relating to the reduction of share capital of a company apply to securities premium as if it were the paid-up share capital of the company. Reduction of share capital can be carried out by a company if the company is authorised by its Articles of Association to do so after passing a special resolution and getting sanction of the court.

The company may collect the amount of securities premium in a lump sum or in instalments. The amount of securities premium may be included in either application money or allotment money or a call. If nothing is mentioned to the contrary in a problem, it should be assumed that the entire amount of the securities premium is to be included in the allotment money.

If the amount of securities premium is included in the application money, the company will debit Bank and credit Share Applications Account with the amount received from applicants. On allotment of shares, the amount of securities premium in respect of shares allotted will be debited to Share Applications Account and credited to Securities Premium Account.

If securities premium is to be collected on allotment or a call, the company may adopt either of the following two courses:—

(*i*) When the allotment money (or the call) becomes due, Share Capital Account will be credited with the total amount becoming due on account of share capital and Securities Premium Account will be credited with the total amount of securities premium becoming due and with the total of the two, Share Allotment Account (or the relevant Share Call Account) will be debited. On receipt of the money, Bank will be debited and Share Allotment Account (or the relevant call account) will be credited with the total amount received.

(*ii*) In the second method, the amount of securities premium will be ignored when the entry for making the allotment money (or the call) due is passed; thus Share Allotment Account (or the relevant Share Call Account) will be debited and Share Capital Account will be credited with the total amount becoming due on account of share capital and no entry will be passed for securities premium becoming due. When the allotment money (or the relevant call) is actually received, Bank will be debited with the total amount received, Share Allotment Account (or the relevant Share Call Account) will be credited with the amount received on account of share capital and Securities Premium Account will be credited with the amount of premium received.

Considering that the Companies Act has placed restrictions on the applications of Securities Premium Account, the second method is considered better in which Securities Premium Account will be credited only when the amount of securities premium has actually been received in cash.

Illustration 8. Good Prospects Ltd. issued 5,00,000 equity shares of Rs. 10 each at a premium of Rs. 2 per share, the terms of payment per share were as follows :-

Rs. 3 with application

Rs. 4 on allotment

Rs. 5 on first and final call.

The issue was fully subscribed. The call was also duly made. All moneys were received in time.

Pass journal entries for all the transactions in each one of the following cases:—

Case I: Securities premium is included in the application money.

Case II: Securities premium is included in the allotment money.

Case III: Securities premium is included in the call.

Solution: ***Case I***

Journal

			Dr.	*Cr.*
			Rs.	*Rs.*
Bank	Dr.		15,00,000	
To Equity Share Applications Account				15,00,000
Application money received on 5,00,000 equity shares @ Rs. 3 per share including Rs. 2 per share as securities premium.				
Equity Share Applications Account	Dr.		15,00,000	
Equity Share Allotment Account	Dr.		20,00,000	
To Equity Share Capital Account				25,00,000
To Securities Premium Account				10,00,000
Transfer in respect of 5,00,000 equity shares from Equity Share Applications Account to Equity Share Capital Account a sum @ Re. 1 per share and to Securities Premium Account a sum @ Rs. 2 per share and the allotment money due on the same shares @ Rs. 4 per share.				

Particulars			Rs.	Rs.
Bank To Equity Share Allotment Account Receipt of allotment money on 5,00,000 equity shares @ Rs. 4 per share.	Dr.		20,00,000	20,00,000
Equity Share First & Final Call Account To Equity Share Capital Account First and final call due on 5,00,000 equity shares @ Rs. 5 per share.	Dr.		25,00,000	25,00,000
Bank To Equity Share First & Final Call Account Receipt of first and final call on 5,00,000 equity shares @ Rs. 5 per share.	Dr.		25,00,000	25,00,000

Case II

Journal

Particulars			Dr. Rs.	Cr. Rs.
Bank To Equity Share Applications Account Receipt of application money on 5,00,000 equity shares @ Rs. 3 per share.	Dr.		15,00,000	15,00,000
Either (*i*) Equity Share Applications Account Equity Share Allotment Account To Equity Share Capital Account To Securities Premium Account Capitalisation of application money @ Rs. 3 per share and allotment money due @ Rs. 4 per share including premium @ Rs. 2 per share on 5,00,000 equity shares alloted by the Board of Directors.	 Dr. Dr.		 15,00,000 20,00,000	 25,00,000 10,00,000
(*ii*) Bank To Equity Share Allotment Account Receipt of allotment money on 5,00,000 equity shares @ Rs. 4 per share including premium @ Rs. 2 per share.	Dr.		20,00,000	20,00,000
Or (*i*) Equity Share Applications Account Equity Share Allotment Account To Equity Share Capital Account Capitalisation of application money @ Rs. 3 per share and allotment money due @ Rs. 2 per share excluding premium @ Rs. 2 per share on 5,00,000 equity shares allotted by the Board of Directors.	 Dr. Dr.		 15,00,000 10,00,000	 25,00,000
(*ii*) Bank To Equity Share Allotment Account To Securities Premium Account Receipt of allotment money—amount received on account of share capital being credited to Equity Share Allotment Account and the amount of premium received being credited to Securities Premium Account.	Dr.		20,00,000	 10,00,000 10,00,000

Particulars		Dr. Rs.	Cr. Rs.
Equity Share First & Final Call Account	Dr.	25,00,000	
To Equity Share Capital Account			25,00,000
First and final call due on 5,00,000 equity shares @ Rs. 5 per share.			
Bank	Dr.	25,00,000	
To Equity Share First & Final Call Account			25,00,000
Receipt of first and final call on 5,00,000 equity shares @ Rs. 5 per share.			

Case III

Journal

Particulars		Dr. Rs.	Cr. Rs.
Bank	Dr.	15,00,000	
To Equity Share Applications Account			15,00,000
Receipt of application money on 5,00,000 equity shares @ Rs. 3 per share.			
Equity Share Applications Account	Dr.	15,00,000	
Equity Share Allotment Account	Dr.	20,00,000	
To Equity Share Capital Account			35,00,000
Application money @ Rs. 3 per share and allotment money @ Rs. 4 per share credited to Equity Share Capital Account on allotment of 5,00,000 equity shares.			
Bank	Dr.	20,00,000	
To Equity Share Allotment Account			20,00,000
Receipt of allotment money on 5,00,000 equity shares @ Rs. 4 per share.			
For first and final call,			
Either:			
(i) Equity Share First & Final Call Account	Dr.	25,00,000	
To Equity Share Capital Account			15,00,000
To Securities Premium Account			10,00,000
First and final call money due on 5,00,000 equity shares—amount @ Rs. 3 per share being credited to Equity Share Capital Account and premium @ Rs. 2 per share being credited to Securities Premium Account.			
(*ii*) Bank	Dr.	25,00,000	
To Equity Share First & Final Call Account			25,00,000
Receipt of first and final call on 5,00,000 equity shares @ Rs. 5 per share including premium @ Rs. 2 per share.			
Or			
(i) Equity Share First & Final Call Account	Dr.	15,00,000	
To Equity Share Capital Account			15,00,000
Amount becoming due on account of share capital on first and final call on 5,00,000 equity shares—the amount of securities premium being ignored for the time being.			

		Rs.	Rs.
(*ii*) Bank	Dr.	25,00,000	
To Equity Share First & Final Call Account			15,00,000
To Securities Premium Account			10,00,000
Receipt of first and final call on 5,00,000 equity shares—amount being received on account of share capital @ Rs. 3 per share being credited to Equity Share First & Final Call Account and the amount of securities premium @ Rs. 2 per share being credited to Securities Premium Account.			

If securities premium is included in the allotment money and surplus applications money is appropriated towards part payment of allotment money, first the appropriation will be made towards that part of the allotment money which is payable on account of share capital and the balance, if any, will be appropriated towards securities premium payable.

Illustration 9. Ideal Enterprises Ltd. was registered with an authorised share capital of Rs. 75,00,000. It issued 6,00,000 equity shares of Rs. 10 each at a premium of Rs. 2 per share, payable as to Rs. 3 with application, Rs. 4 (including premium) on allotment and the balance on first and final call.

Applications were received for 12,00,000 shares. The Board of Directors accepted all the applications, allotment being made on *pro rata* basis. All the shareholders paid the balance of allotment money and the call in time.

Pass journal entries for all the abovementioned transactions and prepare balance sheet of the company as it would appear immediately after the receipt of all the money due on call.

Solution:

Journal

		Dr. Rs.	Cr. Rs.
Bank	Dr.	36,00,000	
To Equity Share Applications Account			36,00,000
Receipt of application money on 12,00,000 equity shares @ Rs. 3 per share.			
Either			
(*i*) Equity Share Applications Account	Dr.	18,00,000	
Equity Share Allotment Account	Dr.	12,00,000	
To Equity Share Capital Account			30,00,000
Credit to Equity Share Capital Account for application money @ Rs. 3 per share and allotment money @ Rs. 2 per share on 6,00,000 equity shares — the amount of securities premium being ignored for the time being.			
(*ii*) Equity Share Applications Account	Dr.	18,00,000	
To Equity Share Allotment Account			12,00,000
To Securities Premium Account			6,00,000
Appropriation of surplus application money towards allotment money — first towards amount payable for share capital and the balance towards securities premium.			
(*iii*) Bank	Dr.	6,00,000	
To Securities Premium Account			6,00,000
Balance of allotment money received—the entire amount being securities premium.			

		Rs.	Rs.
Or			
(*i*) Equity Share Applications Account	Dr.	18,00,000	
Equity Share Allotment Account	Dr.	24,00,000	
To Equity Share Capital Account			30,00,000
To Securities Premium Account			12,00,000
Capitalisation of application money @ Rs. 3 per share and allotment money due @ Rs. 4 per share (including premium @ Rs. 2 per share) on 6,00,000 equity shares allotted by the Board of Directors as per resolution no. .... passed on			
(*ii*) Equity Share Applications Account	Dr.	18,00,000	
To Equity Share Allotment Account			18,00,000
Transfer of surplus applications money from Equity Share Application Account to Equity Share Allotment Account.			
(*iii*) Bank	Dr.	6,00,000	
To Equity Share Allotment Account			6,00,000
Receipt of balance of allotment money.			
Equity Share First & Final Call Account	Dr.	30,00,000	
To Equity Share Capital Account			30,00,000
First and final call due on 6,00,000 equity shares @ Rs. 5 per share as per resolution no. .... of the Board of Directors.			
Bank	Dr.	30,00,000	
To Equity Share First & Final Call Account			30,00,000
Receipt of first and final call on 6,00,000 equity shares @ Rs. 5 per share.			

Balance Sheet of Ideal Enterprise Ltd. as on . . .

Liabilities	*Rs.*	*Assets*	*Rs.*
Share Capital:		**Current Assets, Loans and Advances:**	
Authorised:	75,00,000	(A) Current Assets	
Issued & Subscribed:		Cash at Bank	72,00,000
6,00,000 Equity Shares of Rs. 10 each, fully paid up	60,00,000	(B) Loans and Advances	Nil
Reserves and Surplus:			
Securities Premium	12,00,000		
	72,00,000		72,00,000

Issue of Shares at a Discount. When a company issues shares at a price less than their face value, it is said to have issued them at a discount. For example, if a company issues shares of the face value of Rs. 100 each at Rs. 95 each, it will be said to have issued them at a discount of 5%. In order to issue shares at a discount, a company has to fulfil all the conditions laid down in Section 79 of the Companies Act. These conditions are as follows:—

(*i*) The shares to be issued at a discount must be of a class already issued;

(*ii*) The issue of the shares at a discount must be authorised by a resolution passed by the company in general meeting and sanctioned by the Central Government;

(*iii*) The resolution must specify the maximum rate of discount at which the shares are to be issued. If the maximum rate of discount specified in the resolution exceeds 10%, the issue shall not be sanctioned by the Central Government unless the Government is of the opinion that a higher percentage of discount may be allowed in the special circumstances of the case;

(*iv*) Not less than one year has, at the time of the issue, elapsed since the date on which the company was entitled to commence business;

(*v*) The shares to be issued at a discount must be issued within two months after the date on which the issue is sanctioned by the Central Government or within such extended time as the Central Government may allow.

In case of revival and rehabilitation of sick industrial companies, the provisions of section 79 shall have effect as if for the words "Central Government", "the word Tribunal" had been substituted.

After a company has issued shares at a discount, every subsequent prospectus for further issue of shares must contain particulars of the discount allowed on the issue of the shares or of so much of that discount as has not been written off by the date of the issue of the prospectus.

Discount allowed by the company on issue of shares is a capital loss. The amount is debited to 'Discount on Issue of Shares Account'. Mostly, the discount is adjusted in the allotment money. In this case, when the entry is passed for recording the allotment money due, the amount of discount is debited to Discount on Issue of Shares Account, the amount due after taking into consideration the discount is debited to Share Allotment Account and the total of the two is credited to Share Capital Account. On receipt of allotment money, Bank is debited and Share Allotment Account is credited with the amount actually received.

In the balance sheet, 'Discount on Issue of Shares Account' appears on the "Assets" side under the heading 'Miscellaneous Expenditure'. The account represents a fictitious asset and should be gradually written off by transfer to Profit and Loss Account although there is no legal compulsion to do so. It is also possible to apply Securities Premium Account to write off this account. To do so, Securities Premium Account will be debited and Discount on Issue of Shares Account will be credited.

Illustration 10. Following are the excerpts from the Balance Sheet of ABC Ltd. as on 31st March, 2009:

Liabilities	Rs.
Share Capital	
Authorised	5,00,00,000
Issued and Subscribed:	
25,00,000 Equity Shares of Rs. 10 each, fully paid up	2,50,00,000
1,00,000 14% Preference Shares of Rs. 100 each, fully paid up	1,00,00,000

In January, 2010 the company issued to public 50,000 14% preference shares of Rs. 100 each at a discount of 5%, the amount per share being payable as follows :—

With application	Rs. 25
On allotment	Rs. 45
On first and final call	Rs. 25

The issue was fully subscribed. The Board of Directors alloted the shares on 3rd February, 2010. The call was made on 3rd March, 2010. All the moneys were received.

Record the transactions relating to the issue in the books of the company and draw the balance sheet as it would appear after the collection of the amount of the call.

Solution:

Journal

Date		Particulars		Dr. Rs.	Cr. Rs.
2010 Feb.	3	14% Preference Share Applications Account	Dr.	12,50,000	
		14% Preference Share Allotment Account	Dr.	22,50,000	
		Discount on Issue of Shares Account	Dr.	2,50,000	
		To 14% Preference Share Capital Account			37,50,000
		Capitalisation of application money @ Rs. 25 per share, allotment money @ Rs. 45 per share becoming due and record of discount allowed @ Rs. 5 per share on allotment of 50,000 14% preference shares as per resolution no........passed by the Board of Directors			

				Rs.	Rs.
Mar.	3	14% Preference Share First & Final Call Amount Dr. To 14% Preference Share Capital Account First and final call due on 50,000 14% preference shares @ Rs. 25 per share as per resolution no......of the Board of Directors.		12,50,000	12,50,000

Dr. **Cash Book (Bank Columns Only)** Cr.

		Rs.			Rs.
	To 14% Preference Share Applications Account	12,50,000		By Balance c/d	47,50,000
	To 14% Preference Share Allotment Account	22,50,000			
	To 14% Preference Share First & Final Call Account	12,50,000			
		47,50,000			47,50,000
	To Balance b/d	47,50,000			

Ledger

Dr. **14% Preference Share Capital Account** Cr.

2010		Rs.	2010		Rs.
Mar. 31	To Balance c/d	1,50,00,000	Jan. 1	By Balance b/fd	1,00,00,000
			Feb. 3	By 14% Preference Share Applications Account	12,50,000
				By 14% Preference Share Allotment Account	22,50,000
				By Discount on Issue of Shares Account	2,50,000
			Mar. 3	By 14% Preference Share First & Final Call Amount	12,50,000
		1,50,00,000			1,50,00,000
				By Balance b/d	1,50,00,000

Dr. **14 % Preference Share Applications Account** Cr.

2010		Rs.	2010		Rs.
Feb. 3	To 14 % Preference Share Capital Account	12,50,000	?	By Bank	12,50,000

Dr. **14 % Preference Share Allotment Account** Cr.

2010		Rs.	2010		Rs.
Feb. 3	To 14 % Preference Share Capital Account	22,50,000	?	By Bank	22,50,000

Dr. **14 % Preference Share First & Final Call Account** Cr.

2010		Rs.	2010		Rs.
Mar. 3	To 14 % Preference Share Capital Account	12,50,000	?	By Bank	12,50,000

Dr. **Discount on Issue of Shares Account** Cr.

		Rs.			Rs.
2010 Feb. 3	To 14 % Preference Share Capital A/c	2,50,000	2010 Mar.31	By Balance c/d	2,50,000
	To Balance b/d	2,50,000			2,50,000

Balance Sheet of ABC Ltd. as on____

Liabilities	*Rs.*	Amount *Rs.*	*Assets*	Amount *Rs.*
Share Capital			**Net Sundry Assets**	3,50,00,000
Authorised:		5,00,00,000	**Current Assets, Loans and Advances**	
Issued:			(A) Current Assets	
25,00,000 Equity Shares of Rs. 10 each	2,50,00,000		Cash at Bank	47,50,000
1,50,000 14% Preference Shares of Rs. 100 each	1,50,00,000	4,00,00,000	(B) Loans and Advances	Nil
Subscribed:			**Miscellaneous Expenditure**	
25,00,000 Equity Shares of Rs. 10 each, fully paid up		2,50,00,000	Discount on Issue of Shares	2,50,000
1,50,000 14% Preference Shares of Rs. 100 each, fully paid up		1,50,00,000		
		4,00,00,000		4,00,00,000

Sweat Equity Shares

The Companies (Amendment) Act, 1999 introduced through section 79-A a new type of equity shares called 'Sweat Equity Shares'. The expresion 'sweat equity shares' means equity shares issued at a discount or for consideration other than cash for providing know-how or making available rights in the nature of intellectual property rights or value additions by whatever name called.

Not withstanding anything contained in section 79, which deals with the power of a company to issue shares at a discount, a company may issue sweat equity shares of a class of shares already issued, if the following conditions are fulfilled, namely:—

(*i*) the issue of sweat equity shares is authorised by a special resolution passed by the company in the general meeting;

(*ii*) the resolution specifies the number of shares, current market price, the consideration, if any, and the class or classes of directors or employees to whom such equity shares are to be issued;

(*iii*) not less than one year has, at the time of the issue, elapsed since the date on which the company was entitled to commence business;

(*iv*) the sweat equity shares of company, whose equity shares are listed on a stock exchange, are issued in accordance with the regulations made by the Securities and Exchange Board of India in this behalf. But in the case of company whose equity shares are not listed on any stock exchange, the sweat equity shares are issued in accordance with the guidelines as may be prescribed.

All the limitations, restrictions and provisions relating to equity shares are applicable to sweat equity shares also.

The entries for issue of these shares are the same as for issue of any other equity shares.

Employees' Stock Option

The scheme of employees' stock option was introduced by the Companies (Amendment) Act, 2000 through section 2 (15A). Employees' Stock Option means the option given to the whole-time directors, officers or employees of a company, which gives such directors, officers or employees the benefit or right to purchase or subscribe at a future date, tne securities offered by the company at a predetermined price.

This is a voluntary scheme on the part of a company to encourage its employees to have a higher participation in the company. The company may reserve a suitable percentage of shares of an issue of shares for the employees. The shares issued to employees under this scheme may be non-transferable for a few years.

Accounting Treatment. In order to understand the accounting treatment of employees stock option plan. It is necessary to know the meaning of various connected terms, which is briefly given below;–

Grant of option means giving an option to employees of the concern to subscribe to the shares of the concern.

Vesting is the process by which the employees are given the right to apply for the shares of the company in exercise of the options granted to them in pursuance of an employees stock option plan.

Vesting period is the time period during which the vesting of the options granted to the employees in pursuance of employees stock option scheme takes place.

Option discount means the excess of the market price of the share at the date of grant of option under ESOS over the exercise price of the option.

It should be remembered that option means a right to the employee but not an obligation on his part to take up the shares.

The accounting value of the options granted under ESOS is treated as another form of employee-compensation in the financial statements of the company; the amount is amortized on a straight line basis over the vesting period. For the record of this transaction, Employee Compensation Expense Account is debited and Employee Stock Options Outstanding Account is credited.

If a vested option lapses on the expiry of the exercise period, after the fair value of the option has been accounted for as employee compensation, Employee Stock Options Outstanding Account is debited and General Reserve is credited with an appropriate amount.

Illustration 11

The share capital of Carewell Ltd. is divided into equity shares of Rs. 10 each. On 1st April 2009, it granted 4,000 employees stock options at Rs. 25 per share when the market price of the share was Rs. 125. The options were to be exercised between 1st December, 2009 and 28th February, 2010. The employees exercised their options for 3,900 shares only; the remaining options lapsed. Carewell Ltd. closes its books of account on 31st March, every year.

Pass journal entries for the above mentioned transactions related to the financial year ended 31st March, 2010.

Solution:

Carewell Ltd.
Journal

				Rs.	*Rs.*
2009 April 1	Employee Compensation Expense A/c	Dr.		4,00,000	
	To Employee Stock Options Outstanding A/c				4,00,000
	Grant of 4,000 stock options to employees at Rs 25 when the market price is Rs. 125 per share				
1st Dec; 2009 to 28th Feb; 2010	Bank	Dr.		97,500	
	Employee Stock Options Outstanding A/c	Dr.		3,90,000	
	To Equity Share Capital A/c				39,000
	To Securities Premium A/c				4,48,500
	Allotment of 3,900 equity shares of Rs. 10 each at a premium of Rs. 115 each at Rs. 25 per share in exercise of options by employees under ESOS.				

			Rs.	Rs.
Mar. 1 2010	Employee Stock Options Outstanding A/c Dr. To Employee Compensation Expense A/c Entry for lapse of 100 stock options.		10,000	10,000
Mar. 31	Profit and Loss A/c Dr. To Employee Compensation Expense A/c Transfer of Employee Compensation Expense A/c to Profit & Loss A/c		3,90,000	3,90,000

If the vesting period covers more than one accounting year, the amount of employee compensation expense will be amortized on a straight line basis over the entire vesting period.

Illustration 12

On 1st April, 2006 MN Ltd. granted 10,000 employee stock options at Rs. 30 per share when the market price of a share was Rs. 140. The vesting period was 2½ years and the maximum exercise period was 6 months. 3,000 unvested options lapsed on 1st July, 2008. 6,500 options were exercised during the six months of exercise period; the remaining options lapsed. The company closed its books of account on 31st March every year.

Pass journal entries for all the transactions.

Solution:

MN Ltd.
Journal

			Rs.	Rs.
2007 Mar. 31	Employee Compensation Expense A/c Dr. To Employee Stock Options Outstanding A/c Employee Compensation Expense recognised for the year in respect of employee stock options; total discount of Rs. 110 per option being amortized on straight line basis over 2½ years		4,00,000	4,00,000
Mar. 31	Profit & Loss A/c Dr. To Employee Compensation Expense A/c Transfer of Employee Compensation Expense A/c to Profit & Loss A/c		4,40,000	4,40,000
2008 Mar. 31	Employee Compensation Expense A/c Dr. To Employee Stock Options Outstanding A/c Recognition of Employee Compensation Expense for the year in respect of ESOS		4,40,000	4,40,000
" "	Profit & Loss A/c Dr. To Employee Compensation Expense A/c Transfer of Employee Compensation Expense A/c to Profit & Loss A/c		4,40,000	4,40,000
2009 Mar. 31	Employee Stock Options Outstanding A/c Dr. To General Reserve A/c Excess of amount credited as outstanding over amount actually accepted by employees transferred to General Geserve		1,10,000	1,10,000

				Rs.	Rs.
Oct. 1 2008 to Mar. 31, 2009	Bank	Dr.		1,95,000	
	Employee Stock Options Outstanding A/c	Dr.		7,15,000	
	To Equity Share Capital A/c				65,000
	To Securities Premium A/c				8,45,000
	Allotment at 6,500 equity shares of Rs. 10 each of a premium of Rs. 130 per share @ Rs. 30 per share to employees who exercised their ESO.				
2009 Mar. 31	Employee Stock Option Outstanding A/c	Dr.		55,000	
	To General Reserve A/c				55,000
	Transfer of Employee Stock Option Outstanding A/c to General Reserve on lapse of 500 options at the end of exercise period.				

Working Note:

	Rs.
Total employee compensation expense recognised in 2006-07 and 2007-08; Rs. 4,40,000 plus Rs. 4,40,000	8,80,000
Less: Actual employee compensation expense on 7,000 options; Rs. 110 × 7,000	7,70,000
Excess transferred to General Reserve	1,10,000

Vesting of employee stock options may be conditional. Employee compensation expense will be recognised keeping in view the conditions imposed.

Illustration 13

On 1st April, 2006 Sunshine Ltd. granted 100 stock options to each one of its 500 employees @ Rs. 20 per share, the options to be available to those still in employment of the company at the time of vesting of options. The market value of fully paid equity share of Rs. 10 of the company was Rs. 80 on 1st April, 2006. The terms of the offer were that the options would vest at the end of year 1 if the earnings of the company increased by 9% or they would vest at the end of year 2 if the average increase in earnings of two years was 8% or lastly they would vest at the end of the year 3 if the average increase in earnings for three years was at least 6%. The options were to be exercised by the employees within 6 months of the vesting. The conditions for year 1 and year 2 were not met but the condition was satisfied in year 3.

2,500 unvested options lapsed on 31st March, 2007; 2,000 unvested options lapsed on 31st March, 2008 while 1,500 unvested options lapsed on 31st March, 2009. During the exercise-period 425 employees exercised the option; other options lapsed.

The company closed its books of account on 31st March every year.

You are required to pass journal entries and prepare Employee Stock Options Outstanding Account. Working notes be shown distinctly.

Solution:

Sunshine Ltd.
Journal

				Rs.	Rs.
2007 Mar. 31	Employee Compensation Expense Account	Dr.		14,25,000	
	To Employee Stock Options Outstanding Account				14,25,000
	Employee compensation expense recognised for the year				

Date	Particulars		L.F.	Rs.	Rs.
2007 Mar. 31	Profit and Loss Account To Employee Compensation Expense Account Transfer	Dr		14,25,000	14,25,000
2008 Mar. 31	Employee Compensation Expense Account To Employee Stock Options Outstanding Account Employee compensation expense recognised for the year	Dr.		3,95,000	3,95,000
" "	Profit and Loss Account To Employee Compensation Expense Account Transfer	Dr.		3,95,000	3,95,000
2009 Mar. 31	Employee Compensation Expense Account To Employee Stock Options Outstanding Account Employee compensation expense recognised for the year	Dr.		8,20,000	8,20,000
" "	Profit and Loss Account To Employee Compensation Expense Account Transfer	Dr.		8,20,000	8,20,000
Apr. 1 2009 to Sept. 30 2009	Bank Employee Stock Options Outstanding Account To Equity Share Capital Account To Securities Premium Account Allotment of 42,500 equity shares of Rs. 10 each at a premium of Rs. 70 each to employees @ Rs. 20 per share in pursuance of employee stock option scheme	Dr. Dr.		8,50,000 25,50,000	 4,25,000 29,75,000
2009 Sept. 30	Employee Stock Options Outstanding Account To General Reserve Account Transfer of balance of Employee Stock Options Outstanding Account to General Reserve on lapse of 1500 stock options	Dr.		90,000	90,000

Ledger

Employee Stock Options Outstanding Account

Date	Particulars	Rs.	Date	Particulars	Rs.
2007 Mar. 31	To Balance c/d	14,25,000	2007 Mar. 31	By Employee Compensation Expense Account	14,25,000
2008 Mar. 31	To Balance c/d	18,20,000	2007 Apr.1	By Balance b/d	14,25,000
			2008 Mar. 31	By Employee Compensation Expense Account	3,95,000
		18,20,000			18,20,000
2009 Mar. 31	To Balance c/d	26,40,000	2008 Apr. 1	To Balance b/d	18,20,000
			2009 Mar. 31	By Employee Compensation Expense Account	8,20,000
		26,40,000			26,40,000

2009			2009		
Apr. 1 to			Apr. 1	By Balance b/d	26,40,000
Sept 30	To Securities Premium Account	25,50,000			
Sept. 30	To General Reserve — transfer	90,000			
		26,40,000			26,40,000

Working Notes:

Recognition of Employee Compensation Expense

Particulars	Year ended 31.3.2007	Year ended 31.2.2008	Year ended 31.3.2009
Expected vesting period	2nd year	3rd year	3rd year
No. of options expected to vest	47,500	45,500	44,000
Total employee compensation expense @ (Rs 80 – Rs. 20) i.e. Rs. 60 per share	Rs. 28,50,000	Rs. 27,30,000	Rs. 26,40,000
Expense for the year	Rs. $\frac{28,50,000}{2}$ = Rs. 14,25,000	Rs. 27,30,000 × $\frac{2}{3}$ = Rs. 18,20,000	Rs. 26,40,000
Expense already recognised	Nil	Rs. 14,25,000	Rs. 14,25,000 + Rs. 3,95,000 = Rs. 18,20,000
Employee compensation expense recognised during the current year	Rs. 14,25,000	Rs. 3,95,000	Rs. 8,20,000

Forfeiture and Reissue of Shares. If a shareholder fails to pay allotment money or a call or a part thereof by the last date fixed for payment, the Board of Directors, if Articles of Association of the company empower it to do so, proceed to forfeit the shares on which allotment money or call has become in arrear. The Articles of Association lay down the procedure. A notice has to be served on the defaulter requiring him to pay the unpaid amount together with interest accrued by a certain date. The notice also must state that in the event of non-payment on or before the date so named, the shares in respect of which the notice has been served will be liable to be forfeited. When shares are forfeited, the shareholder's name is removed from the register of members and the amount already paid by him on shares is forfeited to the company. It is a capital gain and is credited to Forfeited Shares Account. A forfeited share may be reissued even at a loss. But the loss on reissue cannot exceed the gain on forfeiture of the share reissued.

As in the absence of any provisions to the contrary, provisions of Table A apply, it is necessary to note the following provisions of Table A relating to forfeiture and reissue of shares:-

1. If a member fails to pay any call or instalment of a call on or before the day appointed for payment thereof, the Board may, at any time thereafter during such time as any part of the call or instalment remains unpaid, serve a notice on him requiring payment of so much of call or instalment as is unpaid, together with any interest which may have accrued.
2. The notice aforesaid shall:
   (a) name a further day (not being earlier than the expiry of fourteen days from the date of the service of the notice) on or before which the payment required by the notice is to be made; and
   (b) state that, in the event of non-payment on or before the day so named, the shares in respect of which the call was made will be liable to be forfeited.

3. If the requirements of any such notice as aforesaid are not complied with, any shares in respect of which the notice has been given may, at any time, thereafter, before the payment required by the notice has been made, be forfeited by a resolution of the Board to that effect.

4. (a) A forefeited share may be sold or otherwise disposed of on such terms and in such manner as the Board thinks fit.

(b) At any time before a sale or disposal as aforesaid, the Board may cancel the forfeiture on such terms as it thinks fit.

Surrender of Shares: Sometimes, when a shareholder finds that he is unable to pay the calls made on him, he may voluntarily surrender shares to the company. The effect of surrender of shares is the same as that of forfeiture. The difference is that in case of surrender, the shareholder himself takes the initiative and the company is saved from the formalities of serving a notice and waiting till the period of the notice is over.

Entries on Forfeiture (or Surrender) and Reissue

(*i*) *When shares have been issued at par.* When shares which have been issued at par are forfeited, first find out the amount with which Share Capital Account has been credited in respect of forfeited shares; debit Share Capital Account with this amount. Now, this amount can be split in two parts; the amount which has been received and the amount which has not been received and because of which the shares have been forfeited. The amount which has been received is a capital gain to the company and is credited to Forfeited Shares Account (or Share Forfeiture Account or Shares Forfeited Account). The amount which has not been received may be lying in Calls in Arrear Account or if the company has not opened Calls in Arrear Account, in Share Allotment Account or different call accounts. Credit Calls in Arrear Account or Share Allotment Account and various call accounts as may be appropriate in the particular case with the amount not received. Suppose, a company issues equity shares of Rs. 10 each at par. Further assume that the application and allotment moneys @ Rs. 2.50 and @ Rs. 2.50 per share respectively are received in respect of all the shares, but the first call and the second call @ Rs. 3 and @ Rs. 2 per share respectively are not received in respect of 500 shares which are therefore forfeited. The following will be the entry on forfeiture of these shares if Calls in Arrear Account has not been opened :—

		Rs.	Rs.
Equity Share Capital Account	Dr.	5,000	
To Equity Share First Call Account			1,500
To Equity Share Second Call Account			1,000
To Forfeited Shares Account			2,500
Forfeiture of 500 equity shares, on which amount @ Rs. 5 per share has been received as application and allotment moneys for non-payment of the first call @ Rs. 3 per share and the second and final call @ Rs. 2 per share.			

If the amounts not received on the two calls have been transferred to Calls in Arrear Account, Equity Share First Call Account and Equity Share Second Call Account will stand closed and will be represented by Calls in Arrear Account. In this case, the entry on forfeiture of shares will be as follows:-

		Rs.	Rs.
Equity Share Capital Account	Dr.	5,000	
To Calls in Arrear Account			2,500
To Forfeited Shares Account			2,500

Narration of the entry will be the same as stated in the earlier case.

Alternatively, the total called up amount in respect of forfeited shares is debited to Share Capital Account and credited to Forfeited Shares Account. Then, Forfeited Shares Account is debited and

Share Allotment Account and various call accounts (or Calls in Arrear Account) are credited with the amount not received in respect of forfeited shares; it leaves a balance in Forfeited Shares Account which is equal to amount received in respect of forfeited shares. Thus, in this second method of passing entries on forfeiture of shares, the final effect is the same as in the first method. Entries for the abovementioned illustration under this method will be as follows:-

		Rs.	*Rs.*
1. Equity Share Capital Account	Dr.	5,000	
To Forfeited Shares Account			5,000
Transfer of called up amount in respect of 500 forfeited equity shares from Equity Share Capital Account to Forfeited Shares Account.			
2. *Either*			
Forfeited Shares Account	Dr.	2,500	
To Equity Share First Call Account			1,500
To Equity Share Second Call Account			1,000
or			
Forfeited Shares Account	Dr.	2,500	
To Calls in Arrear Account			2,500
Transfer of amount not received in respect of forfeited shares to Forfeited Shares Account.			

Forfeited shares can be reissued. They can be reissued even at a price lower than the paid up value of the reissued shares at the time of reissue. But the loss on reissue of a share cannot be more than the gain on forfeiture of that share credited to Forfeited Shares Account at the time of forfeiture. If a share is reissued at a loss, on reissue Bank is debited with cash received, Forfeited Shares Account is debited with loss suffered (or discount allowed) and Share Capital Account is credited will the total of the two amounts which is the paid up value of reissued shares. If the loss on reissue is less than the gain on forfeiture of a share, there is a net capital gain to the company which is transferred from Forfeited Shares Account to Capital Reserve; as such, Forfeited Shares Account is debited and Capital Reserve is credited.

If forfeited shares are reissued at a premium, the amount of such a premium will be credited to Securities Premium Account. If shares are reissued at par or at a premium, the amount of gain credited to Forfeited Shares Account at the time of forfeiture of these reissued shares will be transferred from Forfeited Shares Account to Capital Reserve.

If all the forfeited shares have not been reissued, Forfeited Shares Account will show a credit balance equal to gain on forfeiture of the shares not yet reissued.

Illustration 14. Amber Ltd. with an authorised capital of Rs. 1,00,00,000 offered to public 5,00,000 equity shares of Rs. 10 each payable as to Rs. 3 with application, Rs. 3 on allotment and the balance in two equal calls of Rs. 2 each. The company got the applications for all the shares offered. All the applications were accepted. One shareholder holding 800 shares did not pay the first call. After completing the legal formalities, the Board of Directors forfeited these shares. Consequently the second call was made on 4,99,200 shares only which was duly received in full. Then, the Board of Directors reissued three-fourths of the forfeited shares as fully paid up @ Rs. 9 per share.

Record the abovementioned transactions in the Cash Book, the Journal and the Ledger. Also, prepare the Balance Sheet as it would appear after all the abovementioned transactions have been recorded.

Solution:

Dr. **Cash Book (Bank Columns Only)** *Cr.*

	Rs.		Rs.
To Equity Share Applications Account (Application money received on 5,00,000 equity shares @ Rs. 3 per share)	15,00,000	By Balance c/d	50,02,200
To Equity Share Allotment Account (Allotment money received on 5,00,000 equity shares @ Rs. 2 per share)	15,00,000		
To Equity Share First Call Account (First call received on 4,99,200 equity share @ Rs. 2 per share,	9,98,400		
To Equity Share Second and Final call Account (Second and final call on 4,99,200 equity shares @ Rs. 2 per share)	9,98,400		
To Equity Share Capital Account (Reissue of 600 equity shares as fully paid up @ Rs. 9 per share)	5,400		
	50,02,200		50,02,200
To Balance b/d	50,02,200		

Journal

			Dr. Rs.	Cr. Rs.
	Equity Share Applications Account	Dr.	15,00,000	
	Equity Share Allotment Account	Dr.	15,00,000	
	To Equity Share Capital Account			30,00,000
	Capitalisation of application money @ Rs. 3 per share and allotment money becoming due at the same rate on allotment of 5,00,000 equity shares as per resolution no.______of the Board of Directors.			
	Equity Share First Call Account	Dr.	10,00,000	
	To Equity Share Capital Account			10,00,000
	First call due on 5,00,000 equity shares @ Rs. 2 per share as per resolution no.______of the Board of Directors.			
	Equity Share Capital Account	Dr.	6,400	
	To Equity Share First Call Account			1,600
	To Forfeited Shares Account			4,800
	Forfeiture of 800 equity shares for non-payment of first call.			
	Equity Share Second and Final Call Account	Dr.	9,98,400	
	To Equity Share Capital Account			9,98,400
	Second and final call due one 4,99,200 equity shares @ Rs. 2 per share as per resolution no.______of the Board of Directors.			

			Dr.	Cr.
	Forfeited Shares Account Dr. To Equity Share Capital Account The amount of discount allowed on reissue of 600 shares being debited to Forfeited Shares Account and credited to Equity Share Capital Account.		600	600
	Forfeited Shares Account Dr. To Capital Reserve Transfer of capital profit on reissue of 600 equity shares to capital reserve calculated as follows: Gain on forfeiture = Rs. 600 × (3+3) = Rs. 3,600; Loss on reissue = Rs. 600 × (10 – 9) = Rs.600; Net gain = Rs. 3,600 – Rs. 600 = Rs. 3,000.		3,000	3,000

Ledger

Dr. **Equity Share Applications Account** *Cr.*

		Rs.			Rs.
	To Equity Share Capital Account	15,00,000		By Bank	15,00,000

Dr. **Equity Share Allotment Account** *Cr.*

		Rs.			Rs.
	To Equity Share Capital Account	15,00,000		By Bank	15,00,000

Dr. **Equity Share First Call Account** *Cr.*

		Rs.			Rs.
	To Equity Share Capital Account	10,00,000		By Bank	9,98,400
				By Equity Share Capital Account	1,600
		10,00,000			10,00,000

Dr. **Equity Share Second and Final Call Account** *Cr.*

		Rs.			Rs.
	To Equity Share Capital Account	9,98,400		By Bank	9,98,400

Dr. **Equity Share Capital Account** *Cr.*

		Rs.			Rs.
	To Equity Share First Call Account	1,600		By Equity Share Applications Account	15,00,000
	To Forfeited Shares Account	4,800		By Equity Share Allotment Account	15,00,000
	To Balance c/d	49,98,000		By Equity Share First Call Account	10,00,000
				By Equity Share Second and Final Call Account	9,98,400
				By Bank	5,400
				By Forfeited Shares Account	600
		50,04,400			50,04,400
				By Balance b/d	49,98,000

Forfeited Shares Account

Dr.		Rs.			Rs. Cr.
	To Equity Share Capital Account	600		By Equity Share Capital Account	4,800
	To Capital Reserve	3,000			
	To Balance c/d	1,200			
		4,800			4,800
				By Balance b/d	1,200

Capital Reserve

Dr.		Rs.			Rs. Cr.
	To Balance c/d	3,000		By Forfeited Shares Account	3,000
				By Balance b/d	3,000

Balance Sheet of Amber Ltd. as on .....

Liabilities	*Rs.*	*Assets*	*Rs.*
Share Capital		**Current Assets, Loans and Advances**	
Authorised	1,00,00,000	(A) Current Assets	
Issued:		Cash at Bank	50,02,200
5,00,000 equity shares of Rs. 10 each	50,00,000	(B) Loans and Advances	Nil
Subscribed :			
4,99,800 equity shares of Rs. 10 each, fully paid up	49,98,000		
Forfeited Shares Account	1,200		
Reserves and Surplus			
Capital Reserve	3,000		
	50,02,200		50,02,200

Illustration 15. (*a*) X Ltd. forfeits 100 12% preference shares of Rs. 25 each, fully called up on which Rs. 1,500 have been received and reissues them as fully paid up to one of the directors upon payment of Rs. 2,300. Give the necessary journal entries.

(*b*) Y Ltd. forfeits 200 equity shares of Rs. 10 each issued at par for non-payment of the first call @ Rs. 2 per share and the second and final call @ Rs. 3 per share. The shares are reissued as fully paid up to one of the directors @ Rs. 9 per share. No entries are made on forfeiture but when the shares are reissued, the cash received is credited to Equity Share Capital Account. Give the rectifying entry.

Solution: (*a*) *In X Ltd'.s books:*

Journal

			Dr. Rs.	Cr. Rs.
	12% Preference Share Capital Account	Dr.	2,500	
	To Forfeited Shares Account			1,500
	To Calls in Arrear Account			1,000
	Forfeiture of 100 12% preference shares of 25 each, fully called up on which Rs. 1,500 have been received for non-payment of calls totalling Rs. 1,000.			
	Bank	Dr.	2,300	
	Forfeited Shares Account	Dr.	200	
	To 12% Preference Share Capital Account			2,500
	Reissue of 100 12% preference shares of Rs. 25 each as fully paid up to one of the directors upon payment of Rs. 2,300.			

	Forfeited Shares Account Dr.		1,300	
	To Capital Reserve			1,300
	Transfer of net capital profit from Forfeited Shares Account to Capital Reserve on reissue of 100 12% preference shares of Rs. 25 each as fully paid up for Rs. 2,300 which were earlier forfeited when Rs. 1,500 had been received on them.			

(b) Working Notes:

The following entries should have been passed on forfeiture and reissue of shares:-

Journal

			Dr.	Cr.
			Rs.	Rs.
	Equity Share Capital Account Dr.		2,000	
	To Equity Share First Call Account			400
	To Equity Share Second and Final Call Account			600
	To Forfeited Shares Account			1,000
	Forfeiture of 200 equity shares.			
	Bank Dr.		1,800	
	Forfeited Shares Account Dr.		200	
	To Equity Share Capital Account			2,000
	Reissue of 200 equity shares.			
	Forfeited Shares Account Dr.		800	
	To Capital Reserve			800
	Transfer of capital profit on reissue of forfeited shares to capital reserve.			

The net effect of all the abovementioned entries can be expressed as follows :-

			Rs.	Rs.
	Bank Dr.		1,800	
	To Equity Share First Call Account			400
	To Equity Share Second & Final Call Account			600
	To Capital Reserve			800

But only the following entry has been passed in the books :—

Journal

			Dr.	Cr.
			Rs.	Rs.
	Bank Dr.		1,800	
	To Equity Share Capital Account			1,800
	Cash received on reissue of forfeited shares debited to Bank and credited to Equity Share Capital Account.			

Thus, Bank has been correctly debited. Equity Share Capital Account has received an unwanted credit while Equity Share First Call Account, Equity Share Second & Final Call Account and Capital Reserve have not received the due credit. Hence, the following rectifying entry will be passed:—

Journal

			Dr.	Cr.
			Rs.	Rs.
	Equity Share Capital Account Dr.		1,800	
	To Equity Share First Call Account			400
	To Equity Share Second & Final Call Account			600
	To Capital Reserve			800
	Rectification of an error.			

(*ii*) **Forfeiture (or surrender) and reissue**—*When shares have been issued at a premium.*

If shares issued at a premium are forfeited, find out whether the premium on forfeited shares has been realised or not. If premium on forfeited shares has been received, Securities Premium Account must not be debited on forfeiture of shares. It is obligatory because of legal restrictions placed by section 78 of the Companies Act on the uses of securities premium received. It means that securities premium once received is not to be written back even if shares arè forfeited subsequently. Entry on forfeiture will therefore be passed as if the shares had been issued at par and no premium had been received. However, if the premium on forfeited shares has not been received but it has been credited to Securities Premium Account and debited to Share Allotment Account (or a Call Account) at the time of the premium becoming due; on forfeiture, Securities Premium Account will be debited and Share Allotment Account (or Call Account) will be credited with the premium not received. If the company credits Securities Premium Account only when the premium has been received, then the question of debiting Securities Premium Account on forfeiture will not arise.

On reissue, Securities Premium Account will not be credited if the premium had been received in respect of the shares before forfeiture. Of course if the reissue price exceeds the paid up value of reissued shares, Securities Premium Account will have to be credited with such an excess.

If shares on which securities premium had not been received till forfeiture are reissued, Securities Premium Account will be credited with the amount of securities premium in respect of reissued shares and the amount to be debited to Forfeited Shares Account will be calculated after taking this credit into consideration.

Illustration 16. Poonam Co. Ltd. offered to public for subscription 1,00,000 14% preference shares of Rs. 100 each at a premium of Rs. 10 per share. Payment was to be made as follows.

On application	Rs. 30
On allotment	Rs. 40 (including premium)
On first and final call	Rs. 40

Applications were received for all the shares offered and allotment was duly made. All moneys were duly received except the money on call on 100 shares which were forfeited after the requisite notices had been served. Later, all the forfeited shares were reissued as fully paid up @ Rs. 95 per share.

Journalise all the abovementioned transactions including cash transactions.

Solution:

Journal

	Particulars		L.F.	Dr. Rs.	Cr. Rs.
	Bank To 14% Preference Share Applications Account Receipt of application money @ Rs. 30 per share on 1,00,000 14% preference shares.	Dr.		30,00,000	 30,00,000
	14% Preference Share Applications Account 14% Preference Shares Allotment Account To 14% Preference Share Capital Account To Securities Premium Account Capitalisation of application money @ Rs. 30 per share and allotment money due @ Rs. 40 per share, including premium @ Rs. 10 per share, on allotment of 1,00,000 14% preference shares.	Dr. Dr.		30,00,000 40,00,000	 60,00,000 10,00,000
	Bank To 14% Preference Share Allotment Account Receipt of allotment money on 1,00,000 14% preference shares @ Rs. 40 per share including security premium @ Rs. 10 per share.	Dr.		40,00,000	 40,00,000
	14% Preference Share First and Final Call Account To 14% Preference Share Capital Account First and final call due on 1,00,000 14% preference shares @ Rs. 40 per share.	Dr.		40,00,000	 40,00,000
	Bank To 14% Preference Share First and Final Call Account Receipt of first and final call on 99,900 14% preference shares @ Rs. 40 per share.	Dr.		39,96,000	 39,96,000
	Calls in Arrear Account To 14% Preference Share First and Final Call Account Transfer to Calls in Arrear Account the amount of first and final call not received on 100 14% preference shares @ Rs. 40 per share.	Dr.		4,000	 4,000
	14% Preference Share Capital Account To Calls in Arrear Account To Forfeited Shares Account Forfeiture of 100 14% Preference shares for non-payment of first and final call of Rs. 40 per share.	Dr.		10,000	 4,000 6,000
	Bank Forfeited Shares Account To 14% Preference Share Capital Account Reissue of 100 14% preference shares of Rs. 100 each as fully paid up @ Rs. 95 per share.	Dr. Dr.		9,500 500	 10,000
	Forfeited Shares Account To Capital Reserve Transfer of balance of Forfeited Shares Account to Capital Reserve on reissue of all the forfeited shares.	Dr.		5,500	 5,500

Illustration 17. Neelam Co. Ltd. issues 5,00,000 equity shares of Rs. 10 each at a premium of 25%, Rs. 4 per share being payable along with application and the balance including premium being payable on allotment. Applications total 4,80,000 shares. All the applications are fully accepted. Allotment money on 200 shares is not received. After due notices have been served, these shares are forfeited. Later, all these shares are reissued as fully paid up @ Rs. 9 per share.

Pass journal entries for the above mentioned transactions crediting Securities Premium Account

(*a*) only when the amount of the premium has been received,

(*b*) as soon as the amount of the premium becomes due.

Solution:

Case (a)

Journal

Particulars			Dr. Rs.	Cr. Rs.
Bank	Dr.		19,20,000	
To Equity Share Applications Account				19,20,000
Application money received on 4,80,000 equity shares @ Rs. 4 per share.				
Equity Share Applications Account	Dr.		19,20,000	
Equity Share Allotment Account	Dr.		28,80,000	
To Equity Share Capital Account				48,00,000
Credit to Equity Share Capital Account for application money @ Rs. 4 per share and that part of the allotment money which is payable towards share capital namely @ Rs. 6 per share on allotment of 4,80,000 equity shares of Rs. 10 each at a premium of 25%.				
Bank	Dr.		40,78,300	
To Equity Share Allotment Account				28,78,800
To Securities Premium Account				11,99,500
Receipt of allotment money on 4,79,800 equity shares @ Rs. 8.50 per share; Rs. 6 per share towards share capital and Rs. 2.50 per share as premium.				
Equity Share Capital Account	Dr.		2,000	
To Equity Share Allotment Account				1,200
To Forfeited Shares Account				800
Forfeiture of 200 equity shares on which application money @ Rs. 4 per share has been received for non-payment of allotment money.				
Bank	Dr.		1,800	
Forfeited Shares Account	Dr.		700	
To Equity Share Capital Account				2,000
To Securities Premium Account				500
Reissue of 200 equity shares as fully paid up @ Rs. 9 per share.				
Forfeited Shares Account	Dr.		100	
To Capital Reserve				100
Transfer of balance of Forfeited Shares Account to Capital Reserve on reissue of all the forfeited shares.				

Case (b)

Journal

Particulars		L.F.	Dr. Rs.	Cr. Rs.
Bank	Dr.		19,20,000	
To Equity Share Applications Account				19,20,000
Application money received on 4,80,000 equity shares @ Rs. 4 per share.				
Equity Share Applications Account	Dr.		19,20,000	
Equity Share Allotment Account	Dr.		40,80,000	
To Equity Share Capital Account				48,00,000
To Securities Premium Account				12,00,000
Capitalisation of application money @ Rs. 4 per share and allotment money due @ Rs. 8.50 per share including securities premium @ Rs. 2.50 per share on allotment of 4,80,000 equity shares of Rs. 10 each at a premium of 25%.				
Bank	Dr.		40,78,300	
To Equity Share Allotment Account				40,78,300
Receipt of allotment money on 4,79,800 equity shares @ Rs. 8.50 per share including premium @ Rs. 2.50 per share.				
Equity Share Capital Account	Dr.		2,000	
Securities Premium Account	Dr.		500	
To Equity Share Allotment Account				1,700
To Forfeited Shares Account				800
Forfeiture of 200 equity shares on which application money @ Rs. 4 per share has been received for non-payment of allotment money @ Rs. 8.50 per share including securities premium @ Rs. 2.50 per share.				
Bank	Dr.		1,800	
Forfeited Shares Account	Dr.		700	
To Equity Share Capital Account				2,000
To Securities Premium Account				500
Reissue of 200 equity shares as fully paid up @ Rs. 9 per share.				
Forfeited Shares Account	Dr.		100	
To Capital Reserve				100
Transfer of balance of Forfeited Shares Account to Capital Reserve on reissue of all the forfeited shares.				

Illustration 18. Kay Ltd. with an authorised capital of Rs. 30,00,000 offered to public 2,00,000 equity shares of Rs. 10 each at a premium of Re. 1 each. The payment was to be made as follows:—

With application	Rs. 3
On allotment	Rs. 5 (including premium)
On first and final call	Rs. 3

Applications totalled 4,00,000 shares; Shares were allotted on a *pro rata* basis. Arun who had applied for 400 shares and to whom 200 shares had been allotted failed to pay the balance of allotment money due from him. His shares were forfeited and then reissued to Tarun as Rs. 8 (including premium of Re. 1) per share paid up @ Rs. 6 per share. Ramesh, another shareholder, failed to pay the call money on 100 shares held by him. His shares were also forfeited. Later, these shares were reissued as fully paid up to Suresh @ Rs. 12 per share.

Expenses of the issue came to Rs. 12,000 .

Prepare the Journal, the Cash Book, the Ledger and the Balance Sheet on the basis of the information given above.

Solution:

Journal

	Particulars		Dr. Rs.	Cr. Rs.
	Equity Share Applications Account	Dr.	6,00,000	
	Equity Share Allotment Account	Dr.	10,00,000	
	To Equity Share Capital Account			14,00,000
	To Securities Premium Account			2,00,000
	Capitalisation of application money @ Rs. 3 per share and allotment money becoming due @ Rs. 5 per share including premium @ Re. 1 per share on allotment of 2,00,000 equity shares alloted by the Board of Directors.			
	Equity Share Applications Account	Dr.	6,00,000	
	To Equity Share Allotment Account			6,00,000
	Transfer of surplus application money from Equity Share Applications Account to Equity Share Allotment Account.			
	Equity Share Capital Account	Dr.	1,400	
	Securities Premium Account	Dr.	200	
	To Equity Share Allotment Account			400
	To Forfeited Shares Account			1,200
	Forfeiture of 200 shares allotted to Arun on his application for 400 shares for non-payment of Rs. 400, balance of allotment money due from him after adjustment of surplus application money of Rs. 600 towards allotment money.			
	Forfeited Shares Account	Dr.	400	
	To Equity Share Capital Account			200
	To Securities Premium Account			200
	Concession given to Tarun on reissue of 200 shares to him.			
	Forfeited Shares Account	Dr.	8,00	
	To Capital Reserve			8,00
	Transfer of capital profit remaining after reissue of 200 shares from Forfeited Shares Account to Capital Reserve.			
	Equity Share First & Final Call Account	Dr.	6,00,000	
	To Equity Share Capital Account			6,00,000
	First and final call due on 2,00,000 equity shares @ Rs. 3 per share.			
	Equity Share Capital Account	Dr.	1,000	
	To Equity Share First & Final Call Account			300
	To Forfeited Shares Account			700
	Forfeiture of 100 equity shares for non-payment of call @ Rs. 3 per share.			
	Forfeited Shares Account	Dr.	700	
	To Capital Reserve			700
	Transfer of Forfeited Shares Account to Capital Reserve on reissue of 100 shares to Suresh.			

Cash Book (Bank Columns Only)

Dr.		Rs.			Rs. Cr.
	To Equity Share Applications Account	12,00,000		By Expenses on Issue of Shares Account	12,000
	To Equity Share Allotment Account	3,99,600		By Balance c/d	21,89,700
	To Equity Share Capital Account	1,200			
	To Equity Share First and Final Call Account	5,99,700			
	To Equity Share Capital Account	1,000			
	To Securities Premium Account	200			
		22,01,700			22,01,700
	To Balance b/d	21,89,700			

(*i*) *Calculation of amount due on allotment from Arun.* *Rs.*

Application money received = Rs. 3 × 400 = 1,200

Application money on 200 shares allotted = Rs. 3 × 200 = 600

Surplus application money = Rs. 1200 – Rs. 600 = 600

Total allotment money on 200 shares = Rs. 4 × 200 = 1,000

Amount due after appropriation of surplus application money = Rs. 1,000 – Rs. 600 = Rs. 400.

(*ii*) *Calculation of allotment money received:*

	Rs.
Total allotment money, Rs. 5 × 2,00,000	10,00,000
Less: Application money appropriated	6,00,000
	4,00,000
Less: Amount not paid by Arun on 200 shares, Rs. (5 × 200) – Rs. 600	400
	3,99,600

(*iii*) *Calculation of the amount of call received:*

		Rs.
Amount due on 2,00,000 shares = Rs. 3 × 2,00,000	=	6,00,000
Less: Amount not paid by Ramesh on 100 shares = Rs. 3 × 100	=	300
Amount received		5,99,700

Ledger

Equity Share Applications Account

Dr.		Rs.			Rs. Cr.
	To Equity Share Capital Account	6,00,000		By Bank	12,00,000
	To Equity Share Allotment Account	6,00,000			
		12,00,000			12,00,000

Equity Share Allotment Account

Dr.		Rs.			Rs. Cr.
	To Equity Share Capital Account	8,00,000		By Equity Share Applications Account	6,00,000
	To Securities Premium Account	2,00,000		By Bank	3,99,600
				By Equity Share Capital Account	200
				By Securities Premium Account	200
		10,00,000			10,00,000

Equity Share First & Final Call Account

Dr.	Rs.	Cr.	Rs.
To Equity Share Capital Account	6,00,000	By Bank	5,99,700
		By Equity Share Capital Account	300
	6,00,000		6,00,000

Equity Share Capital Account

Dr.	Rs.	Cr.	Rs.
To Equity Share Allotment Account	200	By Equity Share Applications Account	6,00,000
To Forfeited Shares Account	1,200	By Equity Share Allotment Account	8,00,000
To Equity Share First and Final Call Account	300	By Bank	1,200
To Forfeited Shares Account	700	By Forfeited Shares Account	200
To Balance c/d	20,00,000	By Equity Share First and Final Call Account	6,00,000
		By Bank	1,000
	20,02,400		20,02,400
		By Balance b/d	20,02,400

Forfeited Shares Account

Dr.	Rs.	Cr.	Rs.
To Equity Share Capital Account	200	By Equity Share Capital Account	1,200
To Securities Premium Account	200		
To Capital Reserve	800		
	1,200		1,200
To Capital Reserve Account	700	By Equity Share Capital Account	700

Expenses on Issue of Shares Account

Dr.	Rs.	Cr.	Rs.
To Bank	12,000	By Balance c/d	12,000
To Balance b/d	12,000		

Securities Premium Account

Dr.	Rs.	Cr.	Rs.
To Equity Share Allotment Account	200	By Equity Share Allotment Account	2,00,000
To Balance c/d	2,00,200	By Forfeited Shares Account	200
		By Bank	200
	2,00,400		2,00,400
		By Balance b/d	2,00,200

Capital Reserve Account

Dr.	Rs.	Cr.	Rs.
To Balance c/d	1,500	By Forfeited Shares Account	800
		By Forfeited Shares Account	700
	1,500		1,500
		By Balance b/d	1,500

Balance Sheet of Kay Ltd. as on .....

Liabilities	*Rs.*	*Assets*	*Rs.*
Share Capital :		**Current Assets, Loans and Advances:**	
Authorised	30,00,000	(A) Current Assets	
Issued & Subscribed :		Cash at Bank	21,89,700
2,00,000 Equity Shares of		(B) Loans and Advances	Nil
Rs. 10 each, fully paid up	20,00,000	**Miscellaneous Expenditure:**	
Reserves and Surplus:		Expenses on Issue of Shares Account	12,000
Capital Reserve	1,500		
Securities Premium	2,00,200		
	22,01,700		22,01,700

(iii) Forfeiture (or Surrender) and Reissue - *When shares have been issued at a discount:* If shares which have been issued at a discount are forfeited shares and the discount in respect of forfeited shares has been debited to Discount on Issue of Shares Account, on forfeiture while passing the entry for forfeiture, the amount of such discount is credited to Discount on Issue of Shares Account. On reissue of these shares, Discount on Issue of Shares Account is once again debited with the amount of the discount originally allowed on the shares reissued provided the amount received on reissue of these shares is less than the paid up value of these shares by at least the amount of such discount.

Illustration 19. *A* Ltd. invited applications for 1,00,000 shares of Rs. 100 each at a discount of 6% payable as follows:

	Rs.
On Application	25
On Allotment	34
On First and Final Call	35

The applications received were for 99,000 shares and all of these were accepted. All moneys due were received except the first and final call on 100 shares which were forfeited. 50 shares were re-issued @ Rs. 90 as fully paid. Assuming that all requirements of the law were complied with, pass entries in the Cash Book and Journal of the company. Also show how these transactions will be reflected in the company's balance sheet. *[C.S. (Inter) June, 1998 Modified]*

Solution:

Journal of *A* Ltd.

				Dr.	*Cr.*
				Rs.	*Rs.*
	Share Applications & Allotment Account	Dr.		58,41,000	
	Discount on Equity Shares Account	Dr.		5,94,000	
	To Equity Share Capital Account				64,35,000
	Allotment of 99,000 shares issued at a discount of 6%; Rs. 6 per share debited to Discount on Issue of Equity Shares Account, Rs. 59 per share (Rs. 25 on application and Rs. 34 on allotment), debited to Applications & Allotment Account. Allotment of shares has been made vide Board of Director's resolution no ...... dated				
	Equity Share First & Final Call Account	Dr.		34,65,000	
	To Equity Share Capital Account				34,65,000
	Amount due on 99,000 shares @ Rs. 35 per share on final call as per Board of Directors' resolution no ... dated.				

			Rs.	Rs.
	Equity Share Capital Account	Dr.	10,000	
	To Equity Share First & Final Call Account			3,500
	To Discount on Equity Shares Account			600
	To Equity Shares Forfeited Account			5,900
	Forfeiture of 100 equity shares for non-payment of the first and final call of Rs. 35 per share; the discount of Rs. 6 per share being written back and the amount of Rs. 59 - actually paid - being credited to Shares Forfeited Account, Directors' resolution no........dated.........			
	Discount on Issue of Shares Account	Dr.	300	
	Shares Forfeited Account	Dr.	200	
	To Equity Share Capital Account			500
	Discount allowed on 50 equity shares re-issued @ Rs. 90 as fully paid — the "Discount on Issue of Shares" being Rs. 6 per share, the balance of Rs. 4 per share debited to Shares Forfeited Account— Board of Directors' resolution no.......dated......			
	Shares Forfeited Account	Dr.	2,750	
	To Capital Reserve Account			2,750
	Profit remaining after re-issue of 50 shares transferred to Capital Reserve Account leaving the amount of gain on forfeiture on 50 shares, not yet reissued, in the Shares Forfeited Account.			

Dr. **Cash Book (Bank Columns Only)** **Cr.**

		Rs.			Rs.
	To Equity Share Applications & Allotment Account Application money received on 99,000 equity shares @ Rs. 25	24,75,000		By Balance c/d	93,07,000
	To Equity Share Applications & Allotment Account Allotment money received on 99,000 equity shares @ Rs. 34	33,66,000			
	To Equity Share First & Final Call Account First and final call received on 98,900 equity shares @ Rs. 35 per share	34,61,500			
	To Equity Share Capital Account Reissue of 50 equity shares as fully paid-up @ Rs. 90 per share	4,500			
		93,07,000			93,07,000
	To Balance b/d	93,07,000			

Balance Sheet of A Ltd. as on..........

Liabilities	*Rs.*	*Assets*	*Rs.*
Equity Share Capital (excluding the shares previously issued); 98,950 shares of Rs. 100 each, fully paid-up	98,95,000	Cash at Bank	93,07,000
Shares Forfeited Account	2,950	Discount on Issue of Shares Account - @ Rs. 6 on 98,950 shares	5,93,700
Capital Reserve Account	2,750		
	99,00,700		99,00,700

Illustration 20. Zed Ltd. issued 5,00,000 equity shares of Rs. 10 each at a discount of 10% payable as to Rs. 2.50 per share along with application, Rs. 2.50 per share on allotment and the balance on the first and the final call to be made six months after allotment. The issue was fully subscribed for.

Call on 300 shares was not received. These shares were forfeited. Half of these shares were reissued as fully paid up @ Rs. 8 per share. Two months later, the remaining forfeited shares were reissued as fully paid up @ Rs. 11 per share.

Pass journal entries for the above mentioned transactions.

Solution:

Journal

	Particulars		Dr. Rs.	Cr. Rs.
	Bank	Dr.	12,50,000	
	To Equity Share Applications and Allotment Account			12,50,000
	Receipt of application money on 5,00,000 equity shares @ Rs. 2.50 per share.			
	Equity Share Applications and Allotment Account	Dr.	25,00,000	
	Discount on Issue of Shares Account	Dr.	5,00,000	
	To Equity Share Capital Account			30,00,000
	Capitalisation of application money @ Rs. 2.50 per share and allotment money @ Rs. 2.50 per share (after adjusting discount @ 10%) becoming due on allotment of 5,00,000 equity shares.			
	Bank	Dr.	12,50,000	
	To Equity Share Applications and Allotment Account			12,50,000
	Receipt of allotment money on 5,00,000 equity shares @ Rs. 2.50 per share.			
	Equity Share First and Final Call Account	Dr.	20,00,000	
	To Equity Share Capital Account			20,00,000
	First and final call due on 5,00,000 equity shares @ Rs. 4 per share.			
	Bank	Dr.	19,98,800	
	To Equity Share First & Final Call Account			19,98,800
	Receipt of call on 4,99,700 equity shares @ Rs. 4 per share.			
	Calls in Arrear Account	Dr.	1,200	
	To Equity Share First & Final Call Account			1,200
	Transfer from Equity Share First & Final Call Account to Calls in Arrear Account, call not received on 300 shares @ Rs. 4 per share.			

		Rs.	Rs.
Equity Share Capital Account	Dr.	3,000	
To Discount on Issue of Shares Account			300
To Forfeited Shares Account			1,500
To Calls in Arrear Account			1,200
Forfeiture of 300 shares for non-payment of call.			
Bank	Dr.	1,200	
Discount on Issue of Shares Account	Dr.	150	
Forfeited Shares Account	Dr.	150	
To Equity Share Capital Account			1,500
Reissue of 150 equity shares of Rs. 10 each as fully paid up shares @ Rs. 8 per share.			
Forfeited Shares Account	Dr.	600	
To Capital Reserve			600
Transfer from Forfeited Shares Account to Capital Reserve, capital profit remaining on reissue of 150 shares forfeited shares.			
Bank	Dr.	1,650	
To Equity Share Capital Account			1,500
To Securities Premium			150
Reissue of remaining forfeited equity shares of Rs. 10 each as fully paid shares @ Rs. 11 each.			
Forfeited Shares Account	Dr.	750	
To Capital Reserve			750
Transfer of balance in Forfeited Shares Account to Capital Reserve on reissue of all the remaining shares forfeited shares.			

Issue of Shares for Consideration other than Cash: A company may issue shares for consideration other than cash. It may, for example, purchase some fixed assets for which it may make payment in the form of shares. Or it may take over a running business and the consideration for the business may be discharged by the company fully or partly in the form of its own shares. Entries will be as follows:—

Assets	Dr.
To Liabilities	
To Vendors	
Record of assets and liabilities taken over at agreed values and the consideration payable to vendors.	
Vendors	Dr.
To Share Capital Account	
To Securities Premium Account	
Discharge of consideration payable to vendors; share capital account being credited with the paid up value of shares issued to discharge the consideration and securities premium account being credited for the excess, if any, of agreed value over the paid up value of shares allotted.	

Shares may be allotted to promoters of the company as remuneration for the services rendered by them. The entry will be:

Goodwill Account	Dr.
or	
Incorporation Costs Account	Dr.
To Share Capital Account	

Similarly, a company may allot shares to brokers and underwriters to pay their commission. Brokerage is the act of procuring subscriptions for shares or debentures of the company. A broker receives commission on the shares and debentures subscribed through him. Underwriting is an arrangement by which a company, for commission called underwriting commission, secures a guarantee that the shares and debentures offered to the public will be taken up by the public and the shares and debentures not taken up by public will be taken up by the guarantor called the underwriter. When shares are allotted to discharge brokerage and underwriting commission, the following entries will be passed:—

Brokerage on Issue of Shares (or Debentures)	Dr.
To Broker	
Underwriting Commission	Dr.
To Underwriter	
Broker	Dr.
Underwriter	Dr.
To Share Capital Account	

Schedule VI part I of the Companies Act requires that in the balance sheet of the company, the following note be given for shares allotted for consideration other than cash :—

(Of the above shares , ... shares are allotted as fully paid up pursuant to a contract without payments being received in cash.)

Illustration 21. New Star Ltd. was registered with an authorised share capital of Rs. 25,00,000 divided into shares of Rs. 10 each. It acquired the business of M/s Karim & Sons, taking over the following assets at the values stated against each one of them:-

	Rs.
Freehold Premises	5,00,000
Machinery	3,00,000
Furniture	50,000
Stock	2,10,000
Sundry Debtors	40,000

The consideration was discharged by issue of 1,00,000 equity shares at a premium of 10%. The company allotted 1,000 shares at par to promoters as remuneration for their services.

The company offered to public 50,000 equity shares at a premium of 10% and 25,000 14% preference shares at par, the entire amount being payable on application. The entire issue was underwritten by M/s Sure & Fast for a commission of – 1.5% of the issue price payable in the form of equity shares of New Star Ltd. at par. The issue was fully subscribed to by the public.

Prepare the cash book, the journal, important ledger accounts and the balance sheet of the company.

Solution:

Dr. **Cash Book (Bank columns only)** *Cr.*

		Rs.			*Rs.*
	To Equity Share Applications and Allotment Account	5,50,000		By Balance c/d	8,00,000
	To 14% Preference Share Applications and Allotment Account	2,50,000			
		8,00,000			8,00,000
	To Balance b/d	8,00,000			

Journal

				Dr. Rs.	Cr. Rs.
		Freehold Premises	Dr.	5,00,000	
		Machinery	Dr.	3,00,000	
		Furniture	Dr.	50,000	
		Stock	Dr.	2,10,000	
		Sundry Debtors	Dr.	40,000	
		To M/s Karim & Sons			11,00,000
		Assets taken over from M/s Karim & Sons.			
		M/s Karim & Sons	Dr.	11,00,000	
		To Equity Share Capital Account			10,00,000
		To Securities Premium Account			1,00,000
		Allotment of 1,00,000 equity shares at a premium of 10% to M/s Karim & Sons to discharge consideration for the assets taken over from them.			
		Goodwill Account	Dr.	10,000	
		To Equity Share Capital Account			10,000
		Allotment of 1,000 equity shares of Rs. 10 each at par to promoters by way of remuneration for services rendered by them.			
		Equity Share Applications and Allotment Account	Dr.	5,50,000	
		14% Preference share Applications & Allotment Account	Dr.	2,50,000	
		To Equity Share Capital Account			5,00,000
		To Securities Premium Account			50,000
		To 14% Preference Share Capital Account			2,50.000
		Allotment of 50,000 equity shares of Rs. 10 each at a premium of 10% and 25,000 14% preference shares of Rs. 10 each at par.			
		Underwriting Commission	Dr.	12,000	
		To M/s Sure & Fast			12,000
		Underwriting commission due to M/s Sure & Fast @ 1.5% on Rs. 8,00,000, the issue price of shares offered to public.			
		M/s Sure & Fast	Dr.	12,000	
		To Equity Share Capital Account			12,000
		Allotment of 1,200 equity shares of Rs. 10 each at par to M/s Sure & Fast in payment of underwriting commission due to them.			

LEDGER ACCOUNTS

Dr. **Equity Share Capital Account** Cr.

		Rs.			Rs.
	To Balance c/d	15,22,000		By M/s Karim & Sons	10,00,000
				By Goodwill	10,000
				By Equity Share Applications and Allotment Account	5,00,000
				By M/s Sure & Fast	12,000
		15,22,000			15,22,000
				By Balance b/d	15,22,000

Securities Premium Account

Dr.		Rs.			Rs. Cr.
	To Balance c/d	1,50,000		By M/s Karim & Sons	1,00,000
				By Equity Share Applications and Allotment Account	50,000
		1,50,000			1,50,000
				By Balance b/d	1,50,000

14% Preference Share Capital Account

Dr.		Rs.			Rs. Cr.
	To Balance c/d	2,50,000		By 14% Preference Share Applications and Allotment Account	2,50,000
		2,50,000			2,50,000
				By Balance b/d	2,50,000

M/s Karim & Sons

Dr.		Rs.			Rs. Cr.
	To Equity Share Capital Account	10,00,000		By Freehold Premises	5,00,000
	To Securities Premium Account	1,00,000		By Machinery	3,00,000
				By Furniture	50,000
				By Stock	2,10,000
				By Sundry Debtors	40,000
		11,00,000			11,00,000

Equity Share Applications and Allotment Account

Dr.		Rs.			Rs. Cr.
	To Equity Share Capital Account	5,00,000		By Bank	5,50,000
	To Securities Premium Account	50,000			
		5,50,000			5,50,000

14% Preference Share Applications and Allotment Account

Dr.		Rs.			Rs. Cr.
	To 14% Preference Share Capital Account	2,50,000		By Bank	2,50,000

Underwriting Commission Account

Dr.		Rs.			Rs. Cr.
	To M/s Sure & Fast	12,000		By Balance c/d	12,000
	To Balance b/d	12,000			

M/s Sure & Fast

Dr.		Rs.			Rs. Cr.
	To Equity Share Capital Account	12,000		By Underwriting Commission	12,000

Note: Underwriting Commission Account may be written off by transfer to Securities Premium Account.

Balance Sheet of New Star Ltd. as at . . . . .

Liabilities	*Rs.*	*Assets*	*Rs.*
Share Capital:		**Fixed Assets:**	
Authorised :		Goodwill	10,000
2,50,000 Shares of Rs. 10 each	25,00,000	Freehold Premises	5,00,000
Issued and Subscribed :		Machinery	3,00,000
25,000 14% Preference Shares of		Furniture	50,000
Rs. 10 each fully paid up	2,50,000	**Current Assets, Loans and Advances:**	
1,52,200 Equity Shares of		(A) Current Assets	
Rs. 10 each fully paid up	15,22,000	Stock	2,10,000
(Of the above shares, 1,02,200		Sundry Debtors	40,000
equity shares are allotted as fully		Cash at Bank	8,00,000
paid up pursuant to contracts without		(B) Loans and Advances	nil
payments being received in cash)		**Miscellaneous Expenditure:**	
Reserves and Surplus:		Underwriting Commission	12,000
Securities Premium	1,50,000		
	19,22,000		19,22,000

Issue of Bonus Shares. Bonus shares are the shares allotted to existing equity shareholders without any consideration being received from them, in cash or in kind. They are issued to capitalise profits of the company. Bonus shares can be issued only if Articles of Association permit such an issue.

SEBI guidelines regarding issue of bonus shares :

SEBI has issued certain guidelines regarding issue of bonus shares. The following is the effect of these guidelines on a listed company :

(*i*) The bonus issue can be made only out of free reserves built out of the genuine profits or securities premium collected in cash.

(*ii*) Reserves created by revaluation of fixed assets are not available for issue of bonus shares.

(*iii*) The bonus issue cannot be made unless the partly-paid shares, if any, existing, are made fully paid-up.

(*iv*) The declaration of bonus issue, in lieu of dividend, cannot be made.

(*v*) Once the company announces bonus issue after the approval of the Board of Directors, it must implement the proposal within a period of six months from the date of such approval and it does not have the option of changing the decision.

(*vi*) If the Articles of Association of the company does not already contain a provision for capiitalisation of reserves etc; for issue of bonus shares, the company must pass a resolution at its general body meeting making provisions in the Articles of Association for capitalisation.

(*vii*) If consequent to the issue of bonus shares, the subscribed and paid-up capital exceeds the authorised share capital, the company has to pass a Resolution at its general body meeting for increasing the authorised capital.

(*viii*) No company can pending conversion of FCDs/PCDs, issue bonus shares unless similar benefit is extended to the holders of such FCDs/PCDs through reservation of shares in proportion to such convertible part of FCDs and PCDs. The shares so reserved may be issued at the time of conversion of such debentures on the same terms on which the bonus issue was made.

(*ix*) The company issuing bonus shares must not have defaulted in payment of interest or principal in respect of fixed deposits and interest on existing debentures or principle on redemption thereof. It also must have sufficient reason to believe that it has not defaulted in respect of the payment of statutory dues of the employees such as contribution to provident find, gratuity, bonus etc.

On issue of bonus shares, reserves used for such an issue are debited and Bonus to Equity Shareholders Account is credited with the amount for which bonus shares are issued. Then, Bonus to Equity Shareholders Account is debited and Equity Share Capital Account is credited with the amount of the issue.

After the issue of bonus shares, according to the schedule VI part I of the Companies Act, for bonus shares, the following note has to be given in the balance sheet of the company

(Of the above shares, ____shares are allotted as fully paid up by way of bonus shares).

After this note, the source from which bonus shares are issued, e.g., capitalisation of profits or reserves or from securities premium account has also to be mentioned.

Illustration 22. Ambitions Ltd. presents the following balance sheet to you:—

Balance Sheet

Liabilities	*Rs.*	*Assets*	*Rs.*
Share Capital:		Fixed Assets	
Authorised	20,00,000	Plant and Machinery	8,60,000
Issued and subscribed:		Furniture, Fittings & Fixtures	1,00,000
3,000 12% Preference Shares		Patents and Trade Mark	20,000
Rs. 100 each, fully paid up	3,00,000	Current Assets, Loans and Advances	
60,000 Equity Shares of Rs. 10		(A) Current Assets	
each, fully paid up	6,00,000	Stock	7,85,000
Reserves and Surplus		Debtors	1,07,000
Capital Reserve	1,30,000	Cash in Hand	4,500
Securities Premium	90,000	Cash at Bank	1,95,500
General Reserve	5,80,000	(B) Loans and Advances	
Profit & Loss Account	1,05,000	Bills of Exchange	40,000
Current Liabilities and Provisions:			
(A) Current Liabilities			
Sundry Creditors	1,25,000		
(B) Provisions			
Provision for Taxation	1,82,000		
	21,12,000		21,12,000

The company purchases fresh machinery for Rs. 1,25,000 for which it pays Rs. 25,000 in cash and allots 1,000 14% Preference Shares of Rs. 100 each as fully paid up to vendors. The company then issues one fully paid bonus equity share of Rs. 10 each for every three equity shares held to its equity shareholders. For this purpose, the balances in Profit & Loss Account and General Reserve are used to the necessary extent.

You are required to pass journal entries for the above mentioned transactions and redraft the company's balance sheet.

Solution:

Journal

				Dr.	*Cr.*
				Rs.	*Rs.*
	Machinery	Dr.		1,25,000	
	To Vendor				1,25,000
	Purchase of new machinery.				
	Vendor	Dr.		1,25,000	
	To Bank				25,000
	To 14% Preference Share Capital Account				1,00,000
	Payment of Rs. 25,000 in cash and allotment of 1,000 14% preference shares of Rs. 100 each to vendor to pay for the machinery.				

		Rs.	Rs.
Profit & Loss Account	Dr.	1,05,000	
General Reserve	Dr.	95,000	
To Bonus to Equity Shareholders Account			2,00,000
Use of Profit & Loss Account and General Reserve for issue of bonus shares of Rs. 2,00,000 to holders of equity shares of Rs. 6,00,000.			
Bonus to Equity Shareholders Account	Dr.	2,00,000	
To Equity Share Capital Account			2,00,000
Distribution of bonus shares.			

New Balance Sheet of Ambitions Ltd.

Liabilities	*Rs.*	*Assets*	*Rs.*
Share Capital:		Fixed Assets:	
Authorised	20,00,000	Plant and Machinery	9,85,000
Issued and Subscribed:		Furniture, Fittings & Fixtures	1,00,000
3,000 12% Preference Shares of Rs. 100 each, fully paid up	3,00,000	Patents and Trade Marks	20,000
1,000 14% Preference Shares of Rs. 100 each, fully paid up	1,00,000	**Current Assets, Loans and Advances:**	
80,000 Equity Shares of Rs. 10 each fully paid up	8,00,000	(A) Current Assets	
(Of the above shares, 1,000 14% Preference Shares are allotted as fully paid up pursuant to a contract without payments being received in cash)		Stock	7,85,000
(Of the above shares, 20,000 Equity Shares of Rs. 10 each are allotted as fully paid up by way of bonus shares, using credit balances in Profit & Loss Account and General Reserve)		Debtors	1,07,000
Reserves and Surplus:		Cash in hand	4,500
Capital Reserve	1,30,000	Cash at Bank	1,70,500
Securities Premium	90,000	(B) Loans and Advances	
General Reserve	4,85,000	Bills of Exchange	40,000
Current Liabilities and Provisions:			
(A) Current Liabilities			
Sundry Creditors	1,25,000		
(B) Provisions			
Provision for Taxation	1,82,000		
	22,12,000		22,12,000

Rights Issue. When a company which has already issued shares wants to make a further issue of shares, it is under a legal obligation to first offer the fresh issue to the existing shareholders unless the company has resolved otherwise by a special resolution. The right of the existing shareholder to buy shares from the company in this manner is transferable. If the market price of the shares is higher than the amount at which the company has offered new shares, the right to buy shares from the company will carry a price. Suppose, a company offers to its equity shareholders the right to buy one equity share of Rs. 100 each at Rs. 120 for every four equity shares of Rs. 100 each held. Suppose, the market value of one equity share is Rs. 180. Then, the value of the right will be calculated as follows:-

		Rs.
Market value of 4 equity shares Rs. 180 × 4	=	720
Add: Issue Price of 1 new equity share	=	120
Total price of 5 shares		840
Value of one share = Rs. 840/5	=	168
The value of right = Rs. 180 - Rs. 168	=	12

The whole process can be expressed in the form of the following formula also

$$\text{Value of rights} = \frac{\text{New Shares}}{\text{Total Shares}} \times (\text{Cum right price} - \text{New issue price})$$

Thus if we apply the formula in the abovementioned example, we will get, value of right
= Rs. 1/5 × (180 – 120)
= Rs. 1/5 × 60
= Rs. 12.

It gives us the value of right attached to each share held. But in order to buy the share from the company, a person will have to buy 4 such rights because the company will issue one share against four shares held.

Debentures. A debenture may be defined as an acknowledgment (mostly under seal of the company) of a debt or loan raised by a company. Just as share capital of a company is divided in a large number of parts, each part being called a share, a loan raised by a company may be divided in a large number of parts, each part being called a debenture. Debentures are serially numbered. They enable the company to raise a loan easily by enabling investors to buy as many debentures as they want.

Debenture is a creditorship security; company has to pay interest to debentureholders at the agreed rate. It is usual to prefix 'Debentures' with the annual rate of interest. Thus, if interest @ 10% per annum has to be paid on certain debentures, these debentures will be called 10% Debentures.

Distinction between Debentures and Shares. The following are the points of distinction between debentures and shares :-

(*i*) *Creditorship Security v. Ownership Security:* Whereas a debenture is a creditorship security, a share is an ownership security. It means that a debentureholder is a creditor of the company, while a shareholder is a part-owner of the company. It is the fundamental distinction between a debenture and a share.

(*ii*) *Certainty of return:* A debentureholder is certain of return on his investment. The company has to pay interest on debentures at the fixed rate agreed upon at the time of issue even if it suffers heavy losses. A shareholder cannot get dividends if the company does not earn profits. As a matter of fact, even when a company earns a profit, its Directors may decide to plough back the profits and not declare a dividend. Thus, there is no certainty of return on investment in shares.

(*iii*) *Order of repayment on winding up:* In case of winding up of a company, the amount of debentures will be repaid before any amount is paid to shareholders to return share capital.

(*iv*) *Restrictions on issue at a discount:* There are no restrictions on issue of debentures at a discount, but there are legal conditions which have to be fulfilled to issue shares at a discount.

(*v*) *Mortgage:* There can be mortgage debentures. It means that assets of the company can be mortgaged in favour of debentureholders by way of security. But there can be no mortgage shares.

(*vi*) *Convertibility:* Debentures which can be converted into shares at the option of debenture-holders can be issued. But shares convertible into debentures cannot be issued.

Classes of Debentures. Debentures may be classified into different categories from different points of view:

(*a*) *Redemption:* From the point of view of redemption, debentures can be classified as (i) redeemable and (ii) irredeemable. Redeemable debentures are those that will be repaid by the company within or at the end of the specified period. Irredeemable debentures are those that are repayable only at the time of winding up of the company. Debentures are invariably, redeemable.

(*b*) *Security:* From the point of view of security, debentures can be classified into (i) mortgage debentures and (ii) naked or simple debentures. Mortgage debentures are those that are secured. A mortgage deed is signed by the company and the representatives or trustees of the debentureholders whereby a charge is created on the assets of the company in favour of debentureholders. The charge may be on particular assets in which case it will be called a fixed charge or it may be a charge on all the free assets of the company in which case it will be called a general charge. Simple or naked debentures are those that carry no security in which case, debentureholders have the position of unsecured creditors of the company.

(*c*) *Record:* From the point of view of record; debentures may be classified as (i) registered debentures and (ii) bearer debentures. In the case of registered debentures, the company maintains a register of debentureholders in which a record of the names, addresses and holdings of all the debentureholders is maintained. Transfer of registered debentures requires a transfer deed which has to be lodged with the company for the necessary changes to the recorded in the register of debentureholders. On the other hand, bearer debentures are transferable by mere delivery because the company keeps no record of their holders. Payment of interest is made on the production of coupons attached to the debentures.

(*d*) *Priority:* From the point of view of priority in the payment of interest and repayment of the principal amount, there may be different series of debentures which may be termed as (i) first debentures and (ii) second debentures etc. The debentures which have to be repaid and on which interest has to be paid in preference to other debentures are known as first debentures. The debentures which will be paid and on which interest will be paid after the first debentures have been dealt with are known as Second Debentures.

(*e*) *Convertibility:* Debentures may be (i) convertible or (ii) non-convertible. Convertible debentures are those debentures which are convertible into shares at the option of the debentureholders according to the terms of the issue. Non-convertible debentures do not confer any such right on the debentureholders and hence cannot be converted into shares.

Issue of Debentures. Debentures are issued in the same manner in which shares are issued. The company issues a prospectus inviting applications along with a sum of money called application money. After scrutiny, the Board of Directors makes allotment of debentures. If the entire sum of money has not been asked for along with applications another sum of money called, allotment money may be asked for. Subsequently there may be a few calls even. But mostly, the entire amount is received on application or on application and allotment.

Entries for issue of debentures are similar to those passed for issue of shares, only the names of the accounts are changed. There are Debenture Applications Account, Debenture Allotment Account (or Debenture Applications and Allotment Account), Debenture First Call Account, Debenture Second Call Account, Debenture Third and Final Call Account etc. Instead of crediting Share Capital Account, Debentures Account is credited.

When applications are received, the entry is:

Bank	Dr.	with the actual amount received.
To Debentures Applications Account		

On allotment, the application money on debentures allotted is transferred to Debentures Account. Thus —

Debentures Applications Account	Dr.	application money on debentures allotted.
To Debentures Account		

The amount on applications which are rejected will be refunded. The entry, therefore, is:

Debentures Applications Account	Dr.	application money on rejected
To Bank		applications.

Like shares, surplus application money on partially accepted applications will be transferred to Debentures Allotment Account. Thus -

Debentures Applications Account	Dr.	surplus application money on
To Debentures Allotment Account		partially accepted applications.

The amount due on allotment of debentures is journalised as:

Debentures Allotment Account	Dr.	gross amount due on allotment.
To Debentures		

On receipt of the allotment money, bank will be debited and the Debentures Allotment Account credited.

It is usual to prefix "Debentures," with the rate of interest. Thus, if the rate of interest is 14 per cent, the name given will be "14% Debentures".

Premium on Issue of Debentures Account and Discount on Issue of Debentures Account take place of Securities Premium Account and Discount on Issue of Shares Account respectively.

Like shares, debentures may be issued at par, at a premium or at a discount. But the law does not lay down any maximum limit for discount on issue of debentures. The sanction of the Company Law Board is also not needed.

Debentures are invariably redeemable. They may be redeemable at par or at a premium. Redemption of debentures at a premium means that the company pays to the debenture holders, at the time of redemption, a sum higher than the face value of debentures held by them.

If a company issues debentures on the condition that it would redeem them at a premium, this additional liability should be recorded in a separate account called 'Premium on Redemption of Debentures Account' and shown along with the liability 'Debentures' on the liabilities side of the balance sheet.

As debentures can be issued at par, at a premium or at a discount and can be redeemable at par or at a premium, there are a number of possible cases of entries to be passed at the time of issue of debentures. Summarised entries for typical cases are given below :—

(*i*) When debentures are issued at par and are also redeemable at par:

Bank	Dr	(with amount received)
To Debentures		(with face value)

(*ii*) When debentures are issued at a discount but are redeemable at par:

Bank	Dr	(with amount received)
Discount on Issue of Debentures Account	Dr	(with discount allowed)
To Debentures		(with face value)

(*iii*) When debentures are issued at a premium but are redeemable at par:

Bank	Dr	(with amount received)
To Debentures		(with face value)
To Premium on Issue of Debentures Account		(with premium charged)

The name of Share Premium has been changed to Securities Premium. Debentures are also securities. Hence, premium on issue of debentures can logically be credited to Securities Premium Account. Then, restrictions on the use of premium on issue of shares will be applicable to the use of premium on issue of debentures also.

(*iv*) When debentures are issued at par but are redeemable at a premium:

Bank	Dr	(with amount received)
Loss on Issue of Debentures Account	Dr	(with premium payable on redemption)
To Debentures		(with face value)
To Premium on Redemption of Debentures Account		(with premium payable on redemption)

Premium on Redemption of Debentures must be distinguished from Premium on Issue of Shares; the former is a liability to be shown along with Debentures under the heading Secured Loans while the latter is a capital profit to be shown under Reserves and Surplus.

(*v*) When debentures are issued at a discount but are redeemable at a premium:

Bank	Dr	(with amount received)
Discount on Issue of Debentures Account	Dr	(with discount allowed)
Loss on Issue of Debentures Account	Dr	(with premium payable on redemption)
To Debentures		(with face value)
To Premium on Redemption of Debentures Account		(with premium payable on redemption)

Alternatively, discount allowed on issue of debentures as well as the amount of premium payable on redemption may be debited to Loss on Issue of Debentures Account, in which case the journal entry will be as follows:—

Bank	Dr	(with amount received)
Loss on Issue of Debentures Account	Dr	(with excess of amount payable on redemption over issue - price)
To Debentures		(with face value)
To Premium on Redemption of Debentures Account		(with premium payable on redemption)

If there are certain expenses on issue of debentures, the following entry will also be passed:

Expenses on Issue of Debentures Account	Dr	(with the amount of expenses)
To Bank		

Expenses on Issue of Debentures Account. Discount on Issue of Debentures Account and Loss on Issue of Debentures Account may be transferred to Cost of Issue of Debentures Account by means of the following journal entry:

Cost of Issue of Debentures Account	Dr
To Expenses on Issue of Debentures Account	
To Discount on Issue of Debentures Account	
To Loss on Issue of Debentures Account	

Cost of Issue of Debentures Account, Expenses on Issue of Debentures Account, Discount on Issue of Debentures Account and Loss on Issue of Debentures Account represent capital losses and their balances are shown in the balance sheet of the company on the Assets side under the broad heading, Miscellaneous Expenditure. According to the provisions of the Companies Act, the amount of such a loss need not be written off. But sound principles of accountancy demand that the loss should be gradually and suitably written off over the life span of debentures in respect of which the loss has been incurred. Alternatively, the loss may be wholly or partly be transferred to Securities Premium Account.

Premium on Issue of Debentures Account represents a capital profit and should be transferred to Capital Reserve. Premium on Redemption of Debentures Account is a personal account. At the time of redemption of debentures, Premium on Redemption of Debentures Account is transferred to Sundry Debentureholders Account.

Illustration 23. White Ltd. issues 10,000 12% Secured Debentures of Rs. 100 each. Give journal entries if the Debentures are redeemable at par and are issued (*i*) at par, (*ii*) at a discount of 2 per cent and (*iii*) at a premium of 3 per cent.

Also show the entries which will be made if the Debentures are redeemable at a premium of 5 per cent and are issued (*i*) at par and (*ii*) at a discount of 2 per cent.

Also show in each case, how the figures will appear in the balance sheet.

Solution:

Journal

		Dr. Rs.	Cr. Rs.
Debentures redeemable at par			
(*i*) Issued at par:–			
Bank	Dr	10,00,000	
To 12% Debentures			10,00,000
Issue of 10,000 12% Debentures of Rs. 100 each at par.			
(*ii*) Issued at a discount:–			
Bank	Dr	9,80,000	
Discount on Issue of Debentures Account	Dr	20,000	
To 12% Debentures			10,00,000
Issue of 10,000 12% Debentures of Rs. 100 each at a discount of 2%.			
(*iii*) Issued at a premium:–			
Bank	Dr	10,30,000	
To 12% Debentures			10,00,000
To Premium on Issue of Debentures Account/ Securities Premium Account			30,000
Issue of 10,000 12% Debentures of Rs. 100 each at a premium of 3%.			
(*i*) Debentures issued at par but redeemable at a premium of 50%			
Bank	Dr	10,00,000	
Loss on Issue of Debentures Account	Dr	50,000	
To 12% Debentures			10,00,000
To Premium on Redemption of Debentures Account			50,000
Issue of 10,000 12% Debentures of Rs. 100 each issued at par but redeemable at a premium of 5%.			
(*ii*) Debentures issued at a discount of 2% but redeemable at a premium of 5%:–			
Bank	Dr	9,80,000	
Loss on Issue of Debentures Account	Dr	70,000	
To 12% Debentures			10,00,000
To Premium on Redemption of Debentures Account			50,000
Issue of 10,000 12% Debentures issued at a discount of 2% but redeemable at a premium of 5%.			

Balance Sheet

Liabilities	*Rs.*	*Assets*	*Rs.*
Debentures redeemable at par		**Current Assets, Loans and Advances:**	
(i) Issued at par		(A) Current Assets	
Secured Loans:		Cash at Bank	10,00,000
12% Debentures	10,00,000	(B) Loans and Advances	nil
	10,00,000		10,00,000
(ii) Issued at a discount			
Secured Loans:		**Current Assets, Loans and Advances:**	
as show above		10,00,000 (A) Current Assets	
12% Debentures		Cash at Bank	9,80,000
		(B) Loans and Advances	nil
		Miscellaneous Expenditure:	
		Discount on Issue of Debentures Account	20,000
	10,00,000		10,00,000

	Rs.		Rs.
(iii) Issued at a premium			
Reserves and Surplus:		**Current Assets, Loans and Advances:**	
Premium on Issue of Debentures		(A) Current Assets	
Account/Securities Premium	30,000	Cash at Bank	10,30,000
Secured Loans:		(B) Loans and Advances	nil
12% Debentures	10,00,000		
	10,30,000		10,30,000
Debentures redeemable at a premium of 5%		**Current Assets, Loans and Advances:**	
		(A) Current Assets	
(i) Issued at par		Cash at Bank	10,00,000
Secured Loans:		(B) Loans and Advances	nil
12% Debentures	10,00,000	**Miscellaneous Expenditure:**	
Premium on Redemption		Loss on Issue of Debentures Account	50,000
of Debentures	50,000		
	10,50,000		10,50,000
(ii) Issued at a discount			
Secured Loans:		**Current Assets, Loans and Advances:**	
12% Debentures	10,00,000	(A) Current Assets	
Premium on Redemption of	50,000	Cash at Bank	9,80,000
Debentures		(B) Loans and Advances	nil
		Miscellaneous Expenditure	
		Loss on Issue of Debentures Account	70,000
	10,50,000		10,50,000

Debentures may be issued for consideration other than cash. Such an issue may be made at par, at a premium or at a discount. When a company takes over a running business, very frequently it discharges a part of the consideration in the form of its debentures.

Illustration 24. Pee Co. Limited took over certain fixed assets for Rs. 3,15,000 from the liquidator of Tee Limited which was being wound up and allotted 3,000 13% Debentures at a premium of 5% to the liquidator to satisfy the consideration.

The company then issued a prospectus inviting the public to subscribe 10,000 12% Debentures of Rs. 100 each at a discount of 2%, payable as follows:-

	Rs.
With application	35
On allotment	23
On first and final call	40

Applications were received for 9,000 debentures only. All the applications were accepted. In course of time the call was also made. All the moneys were duly received.

Prepare the Cash Book and the Journal.

Solution:

Dr. **Cash Book (Bank Columns Only)** *Cr.*

		Rs.			*Rs.*
	To 12% Debentures Applications and Allotment Account (Application money on 9,000 12 % Debentures @ Rs. 35 each)	3,15,000		By Balance c/d	8,82,000
	To 12% Debentures Applications and Allotment Account (Allotment money on 9,000 12% Debentures @ Rs. 23 each)	2,07,000			
	To 12% Debentures First and Final Call Account				

	(First and final call on 9,000 12% Debentures @ Rs. 40 each)	3,60,000		
		8,82,000		8,82,000
	To Balance b/d	8,82,000		

Journal

			Dr. Rs.	Cr. Rs.
Fixed Assets	Dr		3,15,000	
To Liquidator of Tee Ltd.				3,15,000
Purchase of fixed assets for an agreed value of Rs. 3,15,000.				
Liquidator of Tee Ltd.	Dr		3,15,000	
To 13% Debentures				3,00,000
To Premium on Issue of Debentures/Securities Premium				15,000
Issue of 3,000 13% Debentures of Rs. 100 each at a premium of 5% in discharge of consideration.				
12% Debenture Applications and Allotment Account	Dr		5,22,000	
Discount on Issue of Debentures Account	Dr		18,000	
To 12% Debentures				5,40,000
Application money @ Rs. 35 per debenture and allotment money @ Rs. 23 per debenture (after adjustment of discount of Rs. 2 per debenture) on 9,000 12% Debentures debited to 12% Debenture Applications and Allotment Account, the discount allowed debited to Discount on Issue of Debentures Account and the total of the two amounts credited to 12% Debentures Account on allotment of debentures.				
12% Debenture First and Final Call Account	Dr		3,60,000	
To 12% Debentures				3,60,000
First and final call due on 9,000 12% Debentures @ Rs. 40 per debenture.				

Debenture Redemption Reserve : As per SEBI guidelines, in case of issue of debentures with maturity of more than 18 months, debenture redemption reserve has to be created. The following points are also noteworthy :—

(*i*) A moratorium upto the date of commercial production can be provided for creation of the debenture redemption reserve in respect of debentures raised for project finance.

(*ii*) The debenture redemption reserve may be created either in equal instalments for the remaining period or with higher amounts if profits permit.

(*iii*) In the case of partly convertible debentures, debenture redemption reserve should be created in respect of non-convertible portion of debenture issue on the same lines as applicable for fully non-convertible debenture issue. In respect of non-convertible issues by new companies, the creation of debenture redemption reserve should commence from the year the company earns profits for the remaining life of debentures.

(*iv*) Company should create DRR equivalent to 50% of the amount of debenture issue before debenture redemption commences. Withdrawal from DRR is permissible only after 10% of the debenture liability has been actually redeemed by the company.

(*v*) Debenture redemption reserve will be treated as a part of General Reserve for consideration of bonus issue proposals.

The entry for creation of debenture redemption reserve will be as follows :—

Profit and Loss Appropriation Account Dr. with the amount of the instalment
To Debenture Redemption Reserve

Illustration 25. On 1st April 2006, a company issued 1,000 14% debentures of Rs. 1,000 each at Rs. 950. Terms of issue provided that beginning with April 2008, Rs. 50,000 of debentures should be redeemed, either by drawings at par or by purchase in the market every year. The expenses of the issue amounted to Rs. 8,000 which were written off in 2006-07. The company wrote off Rs. 10,000 from the Discount on issue of Debentures every year. In 2008-09, the debentures to be redeemed were repaid at the end of the year by draw of lots. In 2009-2010, the company purchased for cancellation 50 debentures at the ruling price of Rs. 980 on 31st March, 2010, the expenses being Rs. 500. Interest is payable yearly. Every year, an appropriate amount was also credited to Debenture Redemption Reserve. Ignore income tax.

Give journal entries and the balance sheet (as far as it relates to debentures) on 31st March, 2010.

Solution:

Journal

Date		Particulars		Dr. Rs.	Cr. Rs.
2006 April	1	Bank	Dr.	9,50,000	
		Discount on Issue of Debentures Account	Dr.	50,000	
		To 14% Debentures			10,00,000
		The issue of 1,000 14% debentures of Rs. 1,000 each at Rs. 950.			
"	"	Debentures Issue Expenses Account	Dr.	8,000	
		To Bank			8,000
		The expenses of Rs. 8,000 incurred on issue of the debentures.			
2007 Mar.	31	Interest on Debentures Account	..Dr.	1,40,000	
		To Bank			1,40,000
		Payment of interest for the year on debentures.			
"	"	Profit and Loss Account		1,58,000	
		To Interest on Debentures Account			1,40,000
		To Debentures Issue Expenses Account			8,000
		To Discount on Issue of Debentures Account			10,000
		Transfer of Interests on Debentures Account and Debentures Issue Expenses Account to Profit and Loss Account and writing off Rs. 10,000 of Discount on Issue of Debendures.			
"	"	Profit and Loss Appropriation Account	..Dr.	2,50,000	
		To Debenture Redemption Reserve			2,50,000
		Creation of Debenture Redemption Reserve for redemption of debentures.			
2008 Mar.	31	Interest on Debentures Account	..Dr.	1,40,000	
		To Bank			1,40,000
		Payment of interest for the year on debentures.			
"	"	Profit and Loss Account	..Dr.	1,50,000	
		To Interest on Debentures Account			3,40,000
		To Discount on Issue of Debentures Account			10,000
		Transfer of Interest on Debentures Account to Profit and Loss Account and writing off Rs. 10,000 of Discount of Issue of Debentures.			

Date		Particulars		Rs.	Rs.
2008 Mar.	31	Profit and Loss Appropriation Account	..Dr.	2,50,000	
		To Debenture Redemption Reserve			2,50,000
		Bringing up Debentures Redemption Reserve equal to 50% of the amount of Debentures to facilitate part redemption of debentures.			
2009 Mar.	31	Interest on debentures Account	..Dr.	1,40,000	
		14% Debentures	..Dr.	50,000	
		To Bank			1,90,000
		Payment of yearly interest on debentures and redemption of debentures of the paid up value of Rs. 50,000 at par by draw of lots.			
”	”	Profit and Loss Account	..Dr.	1,50,000	
		To Interest on Debentures Account			1,40,000
		To Disccount on Issue of Debentures Account			10,000
		Transfer of Interest on Debentures Account to Profit and Loss Account and writing off Rs. 10,000 of Discount on Issue of Debentures.			
”	”	Profit and Loss Application Account	..Dr.	2,50,000	
		To Debenture Redemption Reserve			2,50,000
		Increase made in Debenture Redemption Reserve			
”	”	Debenture Redemption Reserve	..Dr.	50,000	
		To General Reserve			50,000
		Trasnfer of the par value of debentures redeemed this year from Debenture Redemption Reserve to General Reserve			
2010 Mar.	31	Interest on Debentures Account	..Dr.	1,33,000	
		To Bank			1,33,000
		Payment of yearly interest on debentures for Rs. 9,50,000			
“	”	14% Debentures	..Dr.	50,000	
		To Bank			49,500
		To Profit on Redemption of Debentures			500
		Purchase of 50 Debentures in the market for cancellation @ Rs. 980 plus expenses Rs. 500.			
“	”	Profit on Redemption of Debentures	..Dr.	500	
		To Disccount on Issue of Debentures Account			500
		Use of profit on redemption of debentures to partly write off discount on issue of debentures.			
”	”	Profit and Loss Account	..Dr.	1,42,500	
		To Interest on Debentures Account			1,33,000
		To Discount on Issue of Debentures Account			9,500
		Transfer of Interest on Debentures Account to Profit and Loss Account and writing off Rs. 9,500 of discount on Issue of Debentures, making total write off for the year equal to Rs. 10,000			
”	”	Profit and Loss Appropriation Account	... Dr.	2,50,000	
		To Debenture Redemption Reserve			2,50,000
		Further credit to Debenture Redemption reserve, making the total credit equal to the face value of debentures issued.			

"	"	Debenture Redemption Reserve ..Dr. To General Reserve Transfer from Debenture Redemption Reserve to General Reserve, the face value of debentures redeemed during the year.	50,000	50,000

Balance Sheet as on March 31, 2000

Liabilities	*Rs.*	*Assets*	*Rs.*
Reserves and Surplus:		**Miscellaneous Expenditure:**	
General Reserve	1,00,000	Discount on Issue of Debenture	10,000
Debenture Redemption Reserve	9,00,000		
Secured Loan:			
900 14% Debentures of Rs. 1,000 each	9,00,000		

Issue of Debentures as a Collateral Security. A company may issue debentures in favour of a lender of money as a collateral (subsidiary or secondary) security for a loan raised by it. The debentures remain dormant with the lender unless and until the company makes a default in the repayment of the loan for whose security the debentures have been issued. No entry need be passed for issue of such debentures. However, if an entry is desired, the following entry may be passed:-

Debentures Suspense Account Dr
To Debentures Account
Face value of debentures issued by way of collateral security.

In the balance sheet, both Debentures Account and Debentures Suspense Account will appear on the Liabilities side, Debentures Suspense Account being deducted from Debentures Account. It may be shown as follows :

Balance Sheet

Debentures
Less: Debentures Suspense Account

When the loan is repaid, the above entry is reversed as follows :

Debentures Suspense Account Dr
To Debentures Account

Illustration 26. Kalpana Ltd. raised a bank loan of Rs. 2,50,000 and issued by way of a collateral security, 250 14% Debentures of Rs. 1,000 each. The company further issued to public 8,000 12% Debentures of Rs. 100 each at a discount of 2% payable as to Rs. 50 on application and the balance on allotment. The issue was underwritten by M/s Ajanta Underwriters for a commission of 1% of nominal value of debentures underwritten. The whole of the issue was subscribed to by the members of the public. The company paid the underwriting commission in the form of its 12% Debentures of Rs. 100 each issued at par. Pass journal entries for the above mentioned transactions and draw the balance sheet of the Kalpana Ltd.

Solution:

Journal

			Dr. *Rs.*	Cr. *Rs.*
	Bank To Bank Loan Amount of bank loan raised.	Dr	2,50,000	2,50,000
	14% Debentures Suspense Account To 14% Debentures Account Issue of 14% Debentures in favour of bank by way of a collateral security.	Dr	2,50,000	2,50,000

Particulars		Dr (Rs.)	Cr (Rs.)
Bank	Dr	4,00,000	
To 12% Debenture Applications Account			4,00,000
Receipt of application money on 8,000 12% Debentures @ Rs. 50 per debenture.			
12% Debenture Applications Account	Dr	4,00,000	
12% Debenture Allotment Account	Dr	3,84,000	
Discount on Issue of Debentures Account	Dr	16,000	
To 12% Debentures Account			8,00,000
Allotment of 8,000 12% Debentures of Rs. 100 each at a discount of Rs. 2 per debenture.			
Underwriting Commission on Issue of Debentures Account	Dr	8,000	
To M/s Ajanta Underwriters			8,000
Underwriting commission payable to M/s Ajanta Underwriters @ 1% on Rs. 8,00,000, the nominal value of debentures underwritten.			
M/s Ajanta Underwriters	Dr	8,000	
To 12% Debentures Account			8,000
Allotment of 80 12% Debentures of Rs. 100 each at par to M/s Ajanta Underwriters by way of payment of underwriting commission due to them.			
Bank	Dr	3,84,000	
To 12% Debenture Allotment Account			3,84,000
Receipt of allotment money on 8,000 12% Debentures @ Rs. 48 per debenture.			

Balance Sheet of Kalpana Ltd. as on . . . .

Liabilities		*Rs.*	*Assets*	*Rs.*
Secured Loans:			**Current Assets, Loans and Advances:**	
14% Debentures	2,50,000		(A) Current Assets	
Less: 14% Debentures			Cash at Bank	10,34,000
Suspense Account	2,50,000	nil	(B) Loans and Advances	nil
12% Debentures		8,08,000	**Miscellaneous Expenditure:**	
Bank Loan		2,50,000	Underwriting Commission on Issue of Debentures Account	16,000
			Discount on Issue of Debentures Account	8,000
		10,58,000		10,58,000

Working Notes :-

Dr. **Cash Book (Bank Columns Only)** *Cr.*

		Rs.			*Rs.*
	To Bank Loan	2,50,000		By Balance c/d	10,34,000
	To 12% Debentures Applications Account	4,00,000			
	To 12% Debenture Allotment Account	3,84,000			
		10,34,000			10,34,000
	To Balance b/d	10,34,000			

Dr. **12% Debentures Account** Cr.

		Rs.			Rs.
	To Balance c/d	8,08,000		By 12% Debenture Applications Account	4,00,000
				By 12% Debenture Allotment Account	3,84,000
				By Discount on issue of Debentures Account	16,000
				By M/s Ajanta Underwriters	8,000
		8,08,000			8,08,000
				By Balance b/d	8,08,000

Writing off discount etc. on issue of debentures. A company is not legally bound to write off discount or loss or expenses on issue of debentures (cost of issue of debentures). But prudence demands that such amounts should be gradually written off by transfer to Profit & Loss Account on some reasonable basis.

If the debentures are redeemable at the end of a certain period say ten years, it will be reasonable to write off one-tenth of the cost of issue of debentures every year. If the debentures are to be repaid by instalments, the amount to be written off each year should be in proportion to the amount outstanding against debentures because that represents the benefit which the company reaps from the issue of debentures. Suppose, a company issues debentures for Rs. 10,00,000 and redeems at the end of each year debentures of Rs. 1,00,000. Then, the total cost of issue of debentures should be written off in ten years in the ratio of 10:9:8:7:6:5:4:3:2:1. If debentures remain outstanding only for a part of a year, the amount to be written off at the end of that year should be proportionately reduced.

Illustration 27. Vaishali Co. Limited closes its books of accounts every year on 31st March. On 1st May, 1999 it issues 8% Debentures of the face value of Rs. 5,00,000 at a discount of 3%. Expenses of issue amount to Rs. 3,000. Calculate the amounts of the cost of Issue of Debentures to be written off in different accounting years in each one of the following cases:-

(*a*) All the debentures will be redeemed after 10 years on 1st May, 2009:

(*b*) Every year debentures of the face value of Rs. 1.00,000 will be redeemed; the first redemption taking place on 1st May, 2000.

(*c*) Debentures will be redeemed in five equal yearly instalments of Rs. 1,00,000 each, the first instalment being payable on 1st May, 2003.

Solution:

Discount allowed on issue of debentures = 3/100 × Rs. 5,00,000 = Rs. 15,000

Expenses on issue of debentures = Rs. 3,000

Total cost of issue of debentures to be written off = Rs. 15,000 + Rs. 3,000 = Rs. 18,000

(*a*) As debentures will be redeemed after 10 years, one-tenth of the total cost of issue of debentures should be written off for every completed year.

But in the accounting year 1999-2000, debentures remain outstanding for 11 months only (i.e., from 1st May, 1999 to 31st March, 2000). Hence, amount to be written off in accounting year 1999-2000 = Rs. 18,000 × 1/10 × 11/12 = Rs. 1,650 The amount to be written off in each one of the next nine accounting years = Rs. 18,000 × 1/10 = Rs. 1,800

In the accounting year 2009-10, debentures remain outstanding for only 1 month (i.e. from 1st April, 2009 to 1st May, 2009). Hence, amount to be written off in accounting year 2009-10 = Rs. 18,000 × 1/10 × 1/12 = Rs. 150.

(*b*) Debentures of Rs. 1,00,000 are redeemed after each completed year. Hence, during the years 1999-2000, 2000-01, 2001-02, 2002-03 and 2003-04 debentures of the face value of Rs. 5 lakh Rs. 4 lakh, Rs. 3 lakh, Rs. 2 lakh and Re. 1 lakh respectively remain outstanding. Cost of issue of debentures should be written off in the ratio of 5 : 4 : 3 : 2 : 1. Total of the ratios = 5 + 4 + 3 + 2 + 1 = 15. Cost of issue of debentures to be written off for the period between 1st May, 1999 and 1st May, 2000 = Rs. 18,000 × 5/15 = Rs. 6,000. But in accounting year 1999-2000, debentures of Rs. 5 lakhs remain outstanding only for 11 months (i.e. from 1st May, 1999 to 31st March, 2000). Hence, amount to be written off in 1989 = Rs. 18,000 × 5/15 × 11/12 = Rs. 5,500.

In the accounting year 2000-01, debentures of Rs. 5,00,000 remain outstanding for 1 month and those of Rs. 4,00,000 remain outstanding for 11 months.

Hence, amount to be written off in the accounting year 2000-01 = Rs. (18,000 × 5/15 × 1/12) + Rs. (18,000 × 4/15 × 11/12) = Rs. 500 + Rs. 4,400 = Rs. 4,900

Applying similar reasoning, we can calculate the amounts to be written off in other years as follows:-

Amount to be written off in 2001-02
= Rs. (18,000 × 4/15 × 1/12) + Rs. (18,000 × 3/15 × 11/12)
= Rs. 400 + 3,300 = Rs. 3,700

Amount to be written off in 2002-03
= Rs. (18,000 × 3/15 × 1/12) + Rs. (18,000 × 2/15 × 11/12)
= Rs. 300 + Rs. 2,200 = Rs. 2,500

Amount to be written off in 2003-04
= Rs. (18,000 × 2/15 × 1/12) + Rs. (18,000 × 1/15 × 11/12)
= Rs. 200 + Rs. 1,100 = Rs. 1,300

Amount to be written off in 2004-05
= Rs. 18,000 × 1/15 × 1/12 = Rs. 100.

(*c*) During the first four complete years, debentures of Rs. 5 lakh remain outstanding and during the next four complete years debentures of Rs. 4 lakh, Rs. 3 lakh, Rs. 2 lakh and Rs. 1 lakh respectively remain outstanding. Hence, ratio in which the cost of issue of debentures should be written off for eight complete years = 5 : 5 : 5 : 5 : 4 : 3 : 2 : 1. Total of ratios = 5 + 5 + 5 + 5 + 4 + 3 + 2 + 1 = 30.

Amount to be written off in accounting year 1999-2000 (for 11 months from 1st May, 1999 to 31st March, 2000)
= Rs. 18,000 × 5/30 × 11/12 = Rs. 2,750.

In each of the accounting years of 2000-01, 2001-02 and 2002-03 the amount to be written off
= Rs. 18,000 × 5/30 = Rs. 3,000.

Amount to be written off in 2003-04
= Rs. (18,000 × 5/30 × 1/12) + Rs. (18,000 × 4/30 × 11/12)
= Rs. 250 + Rs. 2,200 = Rs. 2,450

Amount to be written off in 2004-05
= Rs. (18,000 × 4/30 × 1/12) + Rs. (18,000 × 3/30 × 11/12)
= Rs. 200 + Rs. 1,650 = Rs. 1,850.

Amount to be written off in 2005-06
= Rs. (18,000 × 3/30 × 1/12) + Rs. (18,000 × 2/30 × 11/12)
= Rs. 150 + Rs. 1,100 = Rs. 1,250.

Amount to be written off in 2006-07
= Rs. (18,000 × 2/30 × 1/12) + Rs. (18,000 × 1/30 × 11/12)
= Rs. 100 + Rs. 550 = Rs. 650.

Amount to be written off in 2007-08
= Rs. 18,000 × 1/30 × 1/12
= Rs. 50.

(*d*) Underwriting:

Underwriting in the context of a company means undertaking a responsibility or giving a guarantee that the shares or debentures offered to the public will be subscribed for. There are firms which undertake this sort of work and are very useful to companies which want to raise funds by the issue of shares or debentures. If the shares or debentures are not taken up by the public wholly, the underwriters will have to take them up and pay for them. For this service, they charge a commission which is generally calculated at a specified rate on the issue price of the whole of the shares or debentures underwritten. Even if the public takes up all the shares or debentures offered and the underwriters are not called upon to take up any share, commission will be payable on the whole of the shares or debentures underwritten. A company cannot pay any commission on issue of shares unless it is permitted by its Articles.

Commission cannot be paid to any person on shares or debentures which are not offered to the public for subscription [section 76 (4A)]. The amount or rate per cent of the commission paid or payable as also the number of shares (or debentures) which a person has agreed to subscribe for commission has to be disclosed in the prospectus or the statement in lieu of prospectus, as the case may be. The directors must also state in the prospectus that, in their view, the underwriters are capable of meeting their obligations under the underwriting contract.

The law limits the commission in case of issue of shares to 5% (or a lower rate if the Articles so state) of the issue price of shares and in case of issue of debentures to 2 1/2% or such lower rate as is provided in the Articles. However, pursuant to Guidelines issued by the Stock Exchange division of the Department of Economic Affairs, Ministry of Finance vide their reference No. F14/1/SE/85, dated 7th May, 1985, the following rates for payment of underwriting commission are in force–

	On amount devolving on the underwriters (per cent)	*On amounts by the Public (per cent)*	
(A) Equity shares	2.5	2.5	
(B) Preference shares/convertible and non-convertible debentures			
(a) For amounts upto Rs. 5 lakh	2.5	1.5	
(b) For amounts in excess of Rs. 5 lakh		2	1

(i) The rates of underwriting commission mentioned above are maximum ceiling rates, within which any company will be free to negotiate the same with the underwriters.

(ii) Underwriting commission will not be payable on amounts taken up by the promoters group, employees, directors, their friends and business associates.

Sub-underwriters. In addition to the underwriter, there may be several underwriters working under him. These will be called sub-underwriters. They are responsible only to the underwriter and generally have no privity of contract with the company. For subscriptions procured by the sub-underwriters, the underwriter receives a small commission payable, called *overall commission*. The limits for commission cover commission to the sub-underwriters and the overall commission.

Brokerage. Brokerage, as against underwriting, is merely the act of procuring subscriptions for shares or debentures without any responsibility. A broker receives commission on the shares subscribed through him but is under no obligation to take up any shares that may remain unsold. Brokerage can be paid in addition to the underwriting commission, if any.

The Ministry of Finance (Department of Economic Affairs) vide its letter dated 7th May, 1987 has laid down the following rules regarding brokerage :

(i) Brokerage applicable to all types of public issues of industrial securities is fixed at 1.5 per cent whether the issue is underwritten or not.

(ii) The mailing cost and other out-of-pocket expenses for canvassing of public issues, etc. will be borne by the stock brokers and no payment on that account will be made by the companies. A clause to this effect must be included in the agreement to be entered into between the broker and the company.

(iii) The listed companies are allowed to pay brokerage on private placement of capital at the maximum rate of 0.5 per cent.

(iv) Brokerage will not be allowed in respect of promoters quota, including the amounts taken up by the directors, their friends and the employees; and in respect of the right issues taken up or renounced by the existing shareholders.

(v) Brokerage will not be paid when the applications are made by the institutions/banks against their underwriting commitments or on the amounts devolving on them as underwriters consequent to under-subscription of the issues.

Marked applications. Underwriters or brokers issue application forms for shares or debentures to members of the public. Such application forms are stamped with the name of the underwriters or brokers. The company can then find out how many shares have been applied for through a particular broker or underwriter. Such applications are known as Marked Applications. Those applications which do not bear the stamp of the underwriter or the broker are known as Unmarked Applications. If there is a sole underwriter who has underwritten the whole of issue, it does not matter whether applications are marked or not as he will be given credit for all applications whether sent through him or directly. But as will be seen later, it does matter if there are two or more underwriters or if the issue has been only partially underwritten.

Underwriting commission. The entry for underwriting commission or brokerage is :

Underwriting Commission (or Brokerage) on Issue of Shares (or Debentures) .. Dr.
  To Underwriter (or Broker).

Calculation of liability of Underwriter—Partial Underwriting. As explained above, if an underwriter underwrites the whole of the issue, the shares or debentures left unsubscribed by the public will have to be taken up by the underwriter. But if the underwriter undertakes responsibility for only part of the issue, the company will have to set against the underwriter's undertaking, applications received through him (marked applications). Suppose, out of an issue of 10,000 shares, only 6,000 shares are underwritten. Then, if the marked applications amount to 5,400 shares, the underwriter's liability will be 600 shares (6,000 – 5,400). But, if all the shares are subscribed (even though the marked applications are less than the number underwritten) the underwriter has no liability.

Suppose, A and B, two underwriters, underwrite 4,000 and 6,000 shares. Total applications are for 8,000 shares out of which marked applications are for A 3,500 and for B 4,000. Then the liabilities of A and B for the 2,000 unsubscribed shares (10,000—8,000) will be determined as follows:

	A	B
Gross Liability	4,000	6,000
Less: unmarked applications* in the ratio of 4:6	– 200	– 300
	3,800	5,700
Less: marked applications	– 3,500	– 4,000
	300	1,700

If the marked applications for one underwriter exceed his liability, the surplus should be distributed among other underwriters in the ratio of their gross liability or in the ratio of the number of shares underwritten.

Another way of fixing the liabilities of the underwriters is to deduct the marked applications from the gross liability and to distribute the liability for unapplied for shares in the ratio of the remaining liability. In the above example, the liabilities of A and B will be fixed as under:

	A	B
Gross Liability	4,000	6,000
Less: Marked applications	– 3,500	– 4,000
Remaining Liability	500	2,000
Liability for unapplied for shares, (2,000) in the ratio of 5:20	400	1,600

*Out of total application for 8,000 shares marked applications are 3,500 for *A* and 4,000 for *B* (total 7,500 shares). Hence the remaining are unmarked. Unmarked applications should be "credited" to the underwriters in the ratio of their gross liability.

If details of marked applications are not available, all the applications received should be "credited" to various underwriters in the ratio of their gross liability; only the balance will have to be subscribed by them. It should be noted that if there is only one underwriter who underwrites only part of the issue, the company itself should be treated as an underwriter for the remaining part.

Illustration 28:.A joint stock company issues 20,000 shares. The issue is underwritten by X, Y, Z in the ratio of 5:3:2 respectively. Unmarked applications total 1,000 whereas marked applications are as follows :

X 8,000
Y 2,850
Z 4,150

Calculate the net liability of each one of the underwriters.

Solution:

Statement of Liability of Underwriters

	X	*Y*	*Z*	Total
Gross Liability	10,000	6,000	4,000	20,000
Less: Unmarked applications 1,000 in the ratio of 10:6:4	– 500	– 300	– 200	– 1,000
	9,500	5,700	3,800	19,000
Less: Marked applications	8,000	2,850	4,150	15,000
	1,500	2,850	– 350	4,000
Credit for Z's oversubscription to X and Y in the ratio of 10:6	– 219	– 131	+ 350	—
	1,281	2,719	—	4,000

Illustration 29. A company issues 10,000 equity shares of Rs. 100 each at par and 500 debentures of Rs. 1,000 each @ Rs. 950. The whole of the issue has been underwritten by M/s. P. Bhalla & Co. for a commission of 2 per cent on shares and 1 per cent on debentures (nominal value). The whole of the shares were applied for but only 400 debentures were applied for. All applications were accepted. Give journal entries and show the entries in the balance sheet assuming all amounts have been received.

Solution:

Journal

			Dr.	*Cr.*
			Rs.	*Rs.*
	Bank ...Dr. To Equity Share Capital Account Payment received for 10,000 equity shares of Rs. 100 each, issued at par.		10,00,000	10,00,000
	Bank ...Dr. Discount on Issue of Debentures Account ...Dr. To Debentures Payment received for 400 debentures of Rs. 1,000 each issued @ Rs. 950 per debenture.		3,80,000 20,000	4,00,000
	M/s. P. Bhalla & Co. ...Dr. Discount on Issue of Debentures Account ...Dr. To Debentures Allotment of 100 debentures to the underwriters, being the debentures not taken up by the public, as per agreement dated....		95,000 5,000	1,00,000
	Underwriting Commission on Issue of Debentures A/c ...Dr. Underwriting Commission on Issue of Shares A/c ...Dr. To M/s. P. Bhalla & Co. Underwriting commission due to the underwriters @ 1% on Rs. 5,00,000 the nominal value of debentures and @ 2% on Rs. 10,00,000 the nominal value of shares.		5,000 20,000	25,000
	Bank ...Dr. To M/s. P.Bhalla & Co. Receipt of amount due from the underwriters.		70,000	70,000

Balance Sheet

Liabilities	*Rs.*	*Assets*	*Rs.*
Share Capital		**Current Assets, Loans and Advances**	
Issued and subscribed:		**(A) Current Assets**	
10,000 Equity Shares of		Bank	14,50,000
Rs. 100 each fully paid	10,00,000	**(B) Loans and Advances**	
		Miscellaneous Expenditure	
Secured Loans		Underwriting Commission on Issue of	
500 Debentures of Rs. 1,000 each	5,00,000	Shares	20,000
		Underwriting Commission on Issue of	
		Debentures	5,000
		Discount on Issue of Debentures	25,000
	15,00,000		15,00,000

When there is discount on issue of debentures as well as commission or expenses on issue of debentures, it is usual to transfer both to one account named "Cost of Issue of Debentures Account". In the above illustration, the entry will be as follows :—

		Rs.	*Rs.*
Cost of Issue of Debentures Account	Dr.	30,000	
To Underwriting Commission of Issue of Debentures A/c			5,000
To Discount on Issue of Debentures A/c			25,000

Illustration 30. A company issues 1,000 14% Debentures of Rs. 1,000 each at a premium of 20%. Sixty per cent of the issue was underwritten by M/s. Bulls & Bears for a commission @ 1.5% of the issue price of debentures underwritten. Applications were received for 800 debentures which were accepted and payment of these was received in full. Give journal entries.

Solution:

Since M/s. Bulls & Bears underwrite 60% of the issue, the company must itself be treated as an underwriter of the remaining 40%. In the absence of any information, the applications for 800 debentures must be deemed to have been marked 60% in favour of the underwriters, viz., 480 debentures. The underwriters are, therefore, liable to take up 120 debentures (600 - 480). The journal entries are as follows:-

Journal

				Dr. *Rs.*	Cr. *Rs.*
		Bank Dr.		9,60,000	
		To 14% Debentures Account			8,00,000
		To Premium on Issue of Debentures/ Securities Premium			1,60,000
		Allotment of 800 debentures applied for, payment being @ Rs. 1,200 per debenture, as per Directors' resolution ...			
		M/s. Bulls & Bears ...Dr.		1,44,000	
		To 14% Debentures Account			1,20,000
		To Premium on Issue of Debentures/Securities Premium			24,000
		Allotment of 120 debentures to the underwriters in pursuance of their agreement, dated......			
		Underwriting Commission on Issue of Debentures Account ...Dr.		10,800	
		To M/s. Bulls & Bears			10,800
		The commission @ 1 1/2% on 600 debentures calculated at the issue price of Rs. 1,200 per debenture.			
		Bank ...Dr.		1,33,200	
		To M/s. Bulls & Bears			1,33,200
		The amount received from the underwriters in settlement.			

Firm underwriting. When an underwriter agrees to buy or subscribe a certain number of shares or debentures irrespective of the result of the issue of the prospectus, it is a case of firm underwriting. Strictly speaking, an underwriter is not allowed to set off his firm underwriting against his liability otherwise determined. This means that he will have to subscribe both for shares underwritten firm and for shares which, ignoring firm underwriting, he has to take under the underwriting contract. Suppose, A underwrites 6,000 shares and also 500 shares firm, the total issue being 10,000 shares. The marked applications are 5,400. He will have to take 1,100 shares in all-500 underwritten firm and 600 under the underwriting agreement. This, of course, is subject to the terms of the contract. If the contract so provides, the net liability of the underwriter will be calculated after taking the firm underwriting into account.

Illustration 31. The following underwriting takes place:

A 6,000 shares; *B* 2,500 shares and *C* 1,500 shares.

In addition there is firm underwriting :

A, 800 shares; *B*, 300 shares and *C*, 1,000 shares.

The share issue is 10,000. Total subscription including firm underwriting was 7,100 shares and the forms included the following marked forms:

A, 1,000 shares; *B*, 2,000 shares; and *C*, 500 shares.

Show the allocation of liability of the underwriters. (*C.A. Final*)

Solution:

Statement of Liability of Underwriters

If shares underwritten firm are treated as unmarked applications

	A	*B*	*C*	*Total*
Gross Liability	6,000	2,500	1,500	10,000
Less: allocation of unmarked applications (7,100, total applications, minus 3,500 marked forms)	– 2,160	– 900	– 540	– 3,600
Balance	3,840	1,600	960	6,400
Less: Marked forms	– 1,000	– 2,000	– 500	– 3,500
Balance	2,840	– 400	460	2,900
Credit for *B*'s over-subscription to *A* and *C* in the ratio of 60 : 15 (gross liability)	– 320	+ 400	– 80	—
Net liability for shares left unsubscribed	2,520	—	380	2,900
Add: Firm underwriting	+ 800	+ 300	+ 1,000	+ 2,100
Total shares to be acquired	3,320	300	1,380	5,000

If shares underwritten firm are treated as marked applications:

Total subscription is 7,100 shares. The performances of the underwriters are as follows:

	Marked		Firm underwriting		
A	1,000	marked plus	800	shares under firm underwriting or total	1,800
B	2,000	" "	300	" " " " "	2,300
C	500	" "	1,000	" " " " "	1,500
Total	3,500		2,100		5,600

Unmarked applications are, therefore 7,100 minus 5,600 or 1,500 shares. Liability of the underwriters is as under:—

	A	*B*	*C*	*Total*
Gross Liability	6,000	2,500	1,500	10,000
Allocations of unmarked applications in the ratio of 60:25:15	– 900	– 375	– 225	– 1,500
Balance	5,100	2,125	1,275	8,500
Marked forms plus firm underwriting	– 1,800	– 2,300	– 1,500	– 5,600
Net Liability	3,300	+ 175	+ 225	2,900
Credit for B's and C's over-subscription	– 175 – 225	—	—	—
Shares to be acquired under the agreement	2,900	—	—	2,900
Add: Firm underwriting	+ 800	+ 300	+ 1,000	+ 2,100
Total shares to be acquired	3,700	300	1,000	5,000

Illustration 32. Sam Ltd. invited applications from public for 1,00,000 equity shares of Rs. 10 each at a premium of Rs. 5 per share. The entire issue was underwritten by the underwritters A, B, C and D to the extent of 30%, 30%, 20% and 20% respectively with the provision of firm underwriting of 3,000, 2,000, 1,000 and 1,000 shares respectively. The underwriters were entitled to the maximum commission permitted by law.

The company received applications for 70,000 shares from public out of which applications for 19,000, 10,000, 21,000 and 8,000 shares were marked in favour of A, B, C and D respectively.

Calculate the liability of each one of the underwriters. Also ascertain the underwriting commission payable to the different underwriters. *[C.S. (Inter) June, 1997]*

Solution:

In case the shares underwritten firm are treated as marked applications:

Calculation of Liability of Underwriters

(Number of shares)

	A	*B*	*C*	*D*	*Total*
Gross Liability	30,000	30,000	20,000	20,000	1,00,000
Less: Unmarked application	3,600	3,600	2,400	2,400	12,000
Balance	26,400	26,400	17,600	17,600	88,000
Less: Marked application plus shares underwritten firm	22,000	12,000	22,000	9,000	65,000
Balance	4,400	14,400	– 4,400	8,600	23,000
C's over-subscription credited to A, B and D in one ratio of 3 : 3 : 2	– 1,650	– 1,650	+ 4,400	– 1,100	—
Net Liability	2,750	12,750	Nil	7,500	23,000
Add: Firm underwriting	3,000	2,000	1,000	1,000	7,000
Total Liability	5,750	14,750	1,000	8,500	30,000

In case the shares underwritten firm are treated as unmarked application:

Calculation of Liability of Underwriters

(Number of shares)

	A	*B*	*C*	*D*	*Total*
Gross Liability	30,000	30,000	20,000	20,000	1,00,000
Less: Unmarked applications	5,700	5,700	3,800	3,800	19,000
Balance	24,300	24,300	16,200	16,200	81,600
Less: Marked application	19,000	10,000	21,000	8,000	58,000
Balance	5,300	14,300	– 4,800	8,200	23,000
C's over subscription credited to A, B and C	– 1,800	– 1,800	+ 4,800	– 1,200	—

Net Liability	3,500	12,500	Nil	7,000	23,000
Add: Firm underwriting	3,000	2,000	1,000	1,000	7,000
Total Liability	6,500	14,500	1,000	8,000	30,000

Working Note:

Application received from public	70,000
Add: Shares underwritten firm	7,000
Total applications	77,000
Less: Marked applications	58,000
Unmarked application	19,000

Calculation of underwriting commission:

As per law in force, underwriting commission is payable @ $2\frac{1}{2}$% of the issue price of shares.

Underwriting commission payable to A = $2\frac{1}{2}$% of (Rs. $15 \times 30{,}000$)

" " " " = Rs. 11,250

" " " " B = Rs. 11,250

" " " " C = $2\frac{1}{2}$% of (Rs. $15 \times 20{,}000$)

= Rs. 7,500

" " " " D = Rs. 7,500

(e) Preparation of Statutory Report:

A new public company has to hold a statutory meeting soon after it receives its certificate for commencement of business and it has to send to its members a report called the statutory report. From the accounts point of view, the report has to contain the following information:-

(*a*) regarding shares issued together with their classes and consideration, and

(*b*) regarding the amounts received and disbursed by the company, grouped under prominent headings.

It has been seen how a new company receives cash by the issue of shares and debentures. These will be the two prominent sources from which cash is received. Payments by a new company are made for preliminary expenses (which may be treated as expenses for the formation of the company, e.g., preparation and printing of the Memorandum and the Articles, expenses for obtaining the certificate of commencement of business, etc.), underwriting commission, brokerage, acquisition of assets and for meeting day-to-day expenses.

The form of the Statutory Report is given below:-

Form No. 22

No. of Company ....

Nominal Capital Rs. ....

THE COMPANIES ACT, 1956
Statutory Report*
(Pursuant to section 165)

Name of Company ....

Statutory Report of the .... Limited.

Certified and filed pursuant to section 165 (5).

Date of notice of holding statutory meeting ....

Date of meeting ....

***Adapted in view of abolition of the system of managing agents and secretaries and treasurers.**

Place where the meeting is to be held ....

Presented by ....

....

....

The Board of Directors submits this statutory report to the members in pursuance of section 165.

2. Shares allotted and cash received up to ....

	No. of shares.	Nominal value of each share	Cash received up to ....
(a) Allotted subject to payment thereof in cash.			
(*i*) Equity			
(*ii*) Redeemable Preference Shares			
(*iii*) Preference Shares other than Redeemable Preference Shares			
(*b*) Allotted as fully paid up otherwise than in cash and the consideration for which they have been allotted.			
(*i*) Equity			
(*ii*) Redeemable Preference Shares			
(*iii*) Preference Shares other than Redeemable Preference Shares			
(*c*) Allotted as partly paid up to the extent of Rs. ..... per share, and the consideration for which they have been so allotted.			
(*i*) Equity			
(*ii*) Redeemable Preference Shares			
(*iii*) Preference Shares other than Redeemable Preference Shares.			

2. Abstract of receipts and payments up to .....

Receipts	*Rs.*	*Payments*	*Rs.*
Shares			
Equity		Preliminary expenses	
		Commission on issue or sale of shares.	
Redeemable Preference Shares		....	
		Discount on issue or sale of shares.	
Preference shares other than Redeemable Preference Shares			
		Capital Expenditure	
Advance payment for shares		Land	
Debentures		Buildings	
		Plant	
Loans		Machinery	
Deposits		*Other Items to be specified*	
Other sources (to be specified)........................			
		Balances :	
		In hand	
		At Banks	
		At Post Office Savings Bank	

Total Total

3. Preliminary expenses as estimated in the Prospectus or Statement in lieu of Prospectus

	Preliminary expenses actually incurred up to aforesaid date *Rs.*	Preliminary expenses estimated to be incurred after the aforesaid date *Rs.*
Law Charges		
Other charges in connection with the preparation of the Memorandum and Articles of Association		
Printing expenses		
Registration charges		
Advertisement charges		
Commission on issue or sale of shares		
Discount on issue or sale of shares		
Other initial expenses (to be specified as far as possible)		
Total Rs.		

4. Names, addresses and occupations of the Company's Directors, Auditors, Manager and Secretary.

	Name(s)	Address(es)	Occupation(s)	Particulars of change(s), date of change, if any, in entries in columns (1), (2) and (3) since the date of incorporation
	1	2	3	4
A.	Directors			
B.	Auditors			
C.	Manager			
D.	Secretary			

These particulars must include dates of changes.

5. Particulars of any contract which is to be submitted to the statutory meeting for approval.

(If any modification or proposed modification of a contract is to be submitted for such approval, brief particulars of contract and particulars of modification or proposed modification should be given).

6. Underwriting contracts

Brief description of each contract.

If contract not carried out fully, extent to which it has not been carried out and reasons therefor.

7. The arrears, if any, due on calls from Directors and Manager.

NAMES

DIRECTORS : Amount due

8. Particulars of any commission or brokerage paid or to be paid in connection with the issue or sale of shares to any director or manager.

Name	Commission or Brokerage paid or to be paid
Directors	
________________	on Shares
________________	on Debentures
________________	

Dated this..................day of......................20...............

We hereby certify that the above report is correct.

Signatures of two or more Directors.*

We hereby certify as correct so much of the report as relates to the shares allotted by the company and to the cash received in respect of such shares and to the receipts and payments.

Date this. . . . . day of . . . . .20. . . . . Auditors.

Illustration 33. A company incorporated on 1st May, 2009 issued a prospectus inviting applications for (1) 1,000 14% Redeemable Preference Shares of Rs. 100 each; (2) 5,000 Equity Shares of Rs. 100 each and (3) 2,000 14% Debentures of Rs. 100 each. The whole of the issue was underwritten for a maximum commission allowed as per law. All the shares and debentures were subscribed and the whole of the sums due (except final call of Rs. 40 on equity shares) was received by the 15th June, 2009. Preliminary Expenses of the company amounted to Rs. 6,500 which were paid on 6th June. The company acquired plant and machinery for Rs. 1,50,000 out of which Rs. 1,25,000 was paid on 30th June, the balance being still outstanding. Lands were acquired for cash payment of Rs. 1,00,000 on 30th June, 2009 and contract for erection of buildings was placed against which a sum of Rs. 25,000 was paid on 30th June, 2009. Underwriting Commission was paid.

The company acquired certain patents and trade marks for Rs. 50,000, the payment for which was made in the form of fully paid equity shares, allotted on 1st June, 2009. The company received its Certificate of Commencement of Business on 10th June, 2009. It held its statutory meeting on 25th July, 2009 and the Statutory Report was sent on 3rd July with information up to 30th June, 2009. Show the particulars relating to shares allotted and receipts and payments of the company, assuming salaries up to 30th June amount to Rs. 4,800 and other expenses to Rs. 3,800. All cash except Rs. 500 (kept in hand) is at a bank. Show these particulars in the Statutory Report. Also prepare balance sheet as on 30th June, 2009.

Solution:

Extracts from the Statutory Report of . . . . . .Ltd.

(Pursuant to Section 165)

1. Shares allotted and cash received up to 30th June, 2009 :—

No. of Shares	*Nominal value of each share*	*Cash received up to 30th June, 2009*
	Rs.	*Rs.*
1,000 14% Redeemable Preference Shares	100	1,00,000
5,000 Equity Shares (Rs. 60 paid)	100	3,00,000
500 Equity Shares	100	nil (issued for patents and trade marks).

2. Abstract of Receipts and Payments up to June 30th, 2009 :
(Made up-to-date within seven days of the Report)

Receipts	*Rs.*	*Payments*	*Rs.*
Shares :		Preliminary Expenses	6,500
Equity	3,00,000	Commission on issue of shares	14,000
Redeemable Preference Shares	1,00,000	Discount on issue of shares	nil
Debentures	2,00,000	Commission on issue of debentures	3,000
Loans	nil	Capital Expenditure :	
Deposits	nil	Lands	1,00,000
Other Sources	nil	Building (advance)	25,000
		Plant and Machinery	1,25,000
		Other items :	
		Salaries	4,800
		General Expenses	3,800
		Balances :	
		In hand	500
		At Bank	3,17,400
		At Post Office Savings Banks	nil
	6,00,000		6,00,000

*Where there is a managing director, he shall be one of the signatories.

The Balance Sheet of the company as on 30th June, 2009 would be as follows :

Liabilities	Rs.	Assets	Rs.
Share Capital :		Land	1,00,000
1,000 Redeemable 14%		Plant and Machinery	1,50,000
Preference Shares of Rs. 100		Advance Payment for Buildings	25,000
each, fully paid	1,00,000	Patents and Trade Marks	50,000
5,000 Equity shares of Rs. 100		Cash in hand	500
each, Rs. 60 paid	3,00,000	Cash at Bank	3,17,400
500 Equity shares of Rs. 100		Miscellaneous Expenses:-	
fully paid, issued to vendors	50,000	Preliminary Expenses	6,500
14% Debentures	2,00,000	Underwriting Commission on issue	
Creditors for Machinery	25,000	of shares	14,000
		Underwriting Commission on	
		issue of Debentures	3,000
		Salaries and General Expenses paid	8,600
	6,75,000		6,75,000

(f) Buy-back of Shares

According to section 77 of the Companies Act, a company limited by shares and a company limited by guarantee and having a share capital cannot buy its own shares unless the consequent reduction of capital is effected and sanctioned in accordance with the provisions of the Act. But the Companies (Amendment) Act, 1999 introduced sections 77A, 77AA and 77B according to which it has now become possible for a company to buy-back its own shares subject to fulfilment of certain conditions.

Conditions: For a buy-back of shares, the following conditions have to be satisfied:—

(*a*) The buy-back is authorised by the Articles of Association of the company.

(*b*) A special resolution has been passed in general meeting of the company authorising the buy-back.

However as per the companies (Amendment) Act, 2001 the Board of Directors is now empowered to buy back upto 10 per cent of the total paid-up capital and free reserves of the company without approval of shareholders in the general meeting.

(*c*) The buy-back does not exceed 25 per cent of the total paid-up capital and free reserves of the company. Further, the buy-back of equity shares in any financial year cannot exceed 25 per cent of its total paid-up equity capital in that financial year.

(*d*) The ratio of the debt owed by the company is not more than twice the capital and its free reserves after such buy-back. However, the Central Government may prescribe a higher ratio of the debt than that specified in this clause for a class or classes of companies.

(*e*) All the shares are fully paid-up.

(*f*) The buy-back of the shares listed on any stock exchange is in accordance with the regulations made by the Securities and Exchange Board of India (SEBI) in this behalf. The buy-back of shares which are not listed on any stock exchange has to be in accordance with the guidelines as may be specified.

Resrictions on Buy-back :

A buy-back cannot be made:

(*i*) through any subsidiary company including its own subsidiary company; or

(*ii*) through any investment company or group of investment companies; or

(*iii*) if a default by the company is subsisting in repayment of deposit or interest payable thereon, redemption of debentures or preference shares or payment of dividend to any shareholders or repayment of any term loan or interest payable thereon to any financial institution or bank.

Contents of notice of meeting :

The notice of the meeting at which special resolution is proposed to be passed for buy-back has to be accompanied by an explanatory statement stating—

(*i*) a full and complete disclosure of all material facts;
(*ii*) the necessity for the buy-back;
(*iii*) the class of shares intended to be purchased under the buy-back;
(*iv*) the amount to be invested under the buy-back; and
(*v*) the time limit for completion of buy-back.

Time-limit for buy-back: In any case, the buy-back has to be completed within twelve months from the date of passing the special resolution.

Sources for buy-back: The company may purchase its own shares from out of:

(*i*) its free reserves, or
(*ii*) the securities premium account; or
(*iii*) the proceeds of any shares or other specified securities like employees' stock option.

No buy-back of shares can be made out of the proceeds of an earlier issue of the same kind of shares.

Picking shares for buy-back: The buy-back may be—

(*a*) from the existing shareholders on a proportionate basis; or
(*b*) from the open market; or
(*c*) from odd lots, that is to say, where the lot of shares of a public company whose shares are listed on a recognised stock exchange is smaller than such marketable lot as may be specified by the stock exchange; or
(*d*) by purchasing the shares issued to employees of the company pursuant to a scheme of stock option or sweat equity.

Declaration of solvency: Before a buy-back, a listed company has to file with the Registrar of companies and the SEBI, a declaration of solvency stating that the Board of Directors has made a full inquiry into the affairs of the company as a result of which they have formed an opinion that the Company is capable of meeting its liabilities and will not be rendered insolvent within a period of one year of the date of declaration adopted by the Board. The declaration has to be signed by at least two directors of the company, one of them being managing director, if any.

Method of fixation of price for buy-back: The price at which the shares are bought-back may be decided by either of the following methods:

The company may fix a price for buy-back of shares and invite its shareholders to offer within a specified period of time shares at the fixed price for buy-back. In case of oversubscription, all applications are accepted on a *pro-rata* basis.

Alternatively, the company may announce a range of price called a band and invite its shareholders to submit tenders within the specified period of time offering shares at prices within the announced band. The company will choose the lowest offered price at which it is able to repurchase the requisite number of shares. Different shareholders may have quoted different prices but all the shareholders whose shares are bought-back get the same price.

Deposit in an escrow account: The SEBI requires the company going in for a buy-back of shares to deposit in an escrow account a specified percentage of total consideration payable for the buy-back. Escrow account means an account in which money is held until a specified duty has been performed; in the present case it means till the consideration for buy-back of shares has been paid to the shareholders. The escrow account, in case of buy-back, may consist of (*i*) cash deposited with a scheduled commercial bank, (*ii*) bank guarantee in favour of merchant banker handling the buy-back and (*iii*) deposit of acceptable securities with appropriate margin, with the banker.

Important things after buy-back: After the buy-back, the company is required to extinguish and physically destroy the shares so bought-back within 7 days of the last date of completion of buy-back. The company is not allowed to make further issue of the same kind of shares as bought-back within a period of 24 months of the buy-back. The companies (Amendment) Act, 2001 has reduced this period of 24 months to 6 months. But the company may issue bonus shares. It may also discharge its subsisting obligations such as conversion of preference shares or debentures into equity shares.

Advantages of buy-back: The main advantage of buy-back of shares is that it facilitates capital restructuring of the company. By getting rid of the capital not required by it, the company is able to step-up its earning per share. The buy-back can also be used by the company to thwart or frustrate the hostile tabe-over of the company by undesirable persons.

Entries:

(*i*) If buy-back is made out of the proceeds of a fresh issue, first of all entries for the issue of new shares should be made.

(*ii*) If the shares are bought-back at their face value, Share Capital Account will be debited and Bank, credited.

(*iii*) If the shares are bought-back at a price higher than their face value, the amount paid over and above the face value will be debited to General Reserve or Securities Premium Account.

(*iv*) If shares are bought back at a discount, the amount of the discount will be credited to Capital Reserve.

(*v*) If the buy-back is made out of free reserves, the nominal value of the shares purchased shall be transferred to Capital Redemption Reserve Account. Free reserves mean those reserves which as per the latest audited balance sheet of the company, are free for distribution as dividend and will include Securities Premium Account.

Illustration 34:

Zaveri Ltd. resolved to buy back 3,00,000 of its fully paid equity shares of Rs. 10 each at Rs. 12 per share. For the purpose, it issued 10,000 13% preference shares of Rs. 100 each at par, the total sum being payable with applications. The company uses Rs. 8,50,000 of its balance in Securities Premium Account apart from its adequate balance in General Reserve Account to fulfil the legal requirements regarding buy-back.

Pass journal entries for all the transactions involved in the buy-back.

Solution:

Journal

	Particulars		Rs.	Rs.
	Bank ...Dr.		10,00,000	
	To 13% Preference Share Application & Allotment Account			10,00,000
	Receipt of application money on 10,000 13% preference shares @ Rs. 100 per share.			
	13% Preference Share Application & Allotment Account ...Dr.		10,00,000	
	To 13% Preference Share Capital Account			10,00,000
	Capitalisation of application money @ Rs. 100 per share on 10,000 13% preference shares allotted by the Board of Directors			
	Securities Premium Account ...Dr.		8,50,000	
	General Reserve Account ...Dr.		11,50,000	
	To Capital Redemption Reserve Account			20,00,000
	Creation of Capital Redemption Reserve for buy-back of equity shares to the extent not covered by fresh issue of preference shares.			
	Equity Share Capital Account ...Dr.		30,00,000	
	General Reserve Account ...Dr.		6,00,000	
	To Sundry Equity Shareholders			36,00,000
	Amount payable to sundry equity shareholders on buy-back of 3,00,000 equity shares of Rs. 10 each at Rs. 12 per share.			
	Sundry Equity Shareholders ...Dr.		36,00,000	
	To Bank			36,00,000
	Payment made to sundry equity shareholders for buy-back of shares.			

(g) Redemption of Preference Shares

Section 80 of the Companies Act allows a company, if authorised by its Articles of Association, to issue preference shares which can be redeemed by the company according to the terms of the issue; but the following legal restrictions apply to such redemption:—

1. No shares can be redeemed unless they are fully paid, i.e. partly paid shares must become fully paid before they can be redeemed.
2. Shares can be redeemed only out of profits of the company which would otherwise be available for dividend or out of the proceeds of a fresh issue of shares made for the purpose of the redemption. Both sources can be used simultaneously, i.e. a part of the amount needed for redemption may be collected by issue of new shares and the balance by using the profits that would otherwise be available for distribution of dividends.
3. To the extent that the shares are redeemed out of profits, Capital Redemption Reserve Account must be credited, debiting the Profit & Loss Account, General Reserve or other accounts showing profits otherwise available for distribution of dividends. Capital Redemption Reserve Account can be utilised for the issue of fully paid bonus shares to the members of the company; otherwise it must be maintained intact unless sanctioned by the Court. The provisions of the Companies Act relating to the reduction of share capital of a company apply to Capital Redemption Reserve Account as if it were paid up share capital of the company.
4. Before the shares are redeemed, the premium, if any, payable on redemption must be provided for out of the profits of the company or out of Securities Premium Account.

Purpose of legal restrictions on redemption of Preference Shares: The purpose of all the legal restrictions on redemption of preference shares is not to allow redemption of preference shares affect adversely the security available to the creditors of the company. Consider the following balance sheet of a joint stock company:-

Balance Sheet

Liabilities	*Rs.*	*Assets*	*Rs.*
50,000 Equity Shares of Rs. 10 each, fully paid	5,00,000	Sundry Assets	14,50,000
1,500 10% Preference Shares of Rs. 100 each, Rs. 80 called and paid up	1,20,000		
General Reserve	2,80,000		
Profit & Loss Account	1,00,000		
Sundry Creditors	4,50,000		
	14,50,000		14,50,000

Security available to Sundry Creditors is Rs. 6,50,000 calculated as follows:—

	Rs.
Fully paid equity shares	5,00,000
Partly paid preference shares	1,20,000
Amount which can be called on preference shares Rs. 20 × 1500	30,000
	6,50,000

The amounts in General Reserve and Profit & Loss Account cannot be depended upon because they can disappear at any time by distribution of dividends. On the other hand, uncalled amount on preference share has been included in the amount of security available to creditors because in case of winding up, if the amount otherwise available is insufficient to make full payment to the creditors, the liquidator will call upon the preference shareholders to pay the uncalled amount and he will use this amount also to meet the creditors' claim. The purpose of imposing the restriction that the preference shares must be fully paid before they can be redeemed is to ensure that the uncalled amount on preference shares is not lost to creditors by way of security due to redemption.

The fact that the security available to creditors remains intact when preference shares are redeemed out of proceeds of a fresh issue of shares made for the purpose is obvious. But it should be understood that even when the company redeems preference shares out of profits otherwise available for dividends, the effect is indirectly the same. In this case, the amount of preference shares to be redeemed is transferred from accounts showing divisible profits to Capital Redemption Reserve Account which can be used only for one purpose, namely issue of fully paid bonus shares. Section 80(d) of the Companies Act makes it clear that the provisions of the Act relating to the reduction of the share capital of a company shall apply to the Capital Redemption Reserve Account as if it were paid up share capital of the company. If in the example given earlier, the company makes a final call of Rs. 20 each on preference shares bringing up the paid up preference share capital to Rs. 1,50,000 and then redeems all the preference shares at par, transferring Rs. 1,50,000 from General Reserve to Capital Redemption Reserve Account, the balance sheet of the company will be as follows:—

Balance Sheet

Liabilities	*Rs.*	*Assets*	*Rs.*
50,000 Equity Shares of Rs. 10 each, fully paid	5,00,000	Sundry Assets	13,30,000*
Capital Redemption Reserve Account	1,50,000		
General Reserve	1,30,000		
Profit & Loss Account	1,00,000		
Sundry Creditors	4,50,000		
	13,30,000		13,30,000

*The balance of Sundry Assets can be calculated as follows :—

	Rs.
Opening Balance	14,50,000
Add: Cash received on final call on preference shares	30,000
	14,80,000
Less: Cash paid to redeem preference shares of Rs. 1,50,000	1,50,000
Closing balance of Sundry Assets	13,30,000

The amount of security available to creditors is still Rs. 6,50,000 which is total of Rs. 5,00,000 of Equity Share Capital and Rs. 1,50,000 of Capital Redemption Reserve Account.

If Capital Redemption Reserve Account is utilised for issue of fully paid bonus shares, the balance sheet will be as follows:-

Balance Sheet

Liabilities	*Rs,*	*Assets*	*Rs.*
65,000 Equity Shares of Rs. 10 each, fully paid (Of the above shares, 15,000 Equity Shares have been allotted as fully paid up by way of bonus shares)	6,50,000	Sundry Assets	13,30,000
General Reserve	1,30,000		
Profit and Loss Account	1,00,000		
Sundry Creditors	4,50,000		
	13,30,000		13,30,000

It is obvious that the security available to the creditors is still Rs. 6,50,000.

Interpretation of 'Proceeds of a fresh issue'. In the light of the purpose of law in imposing restrictions on redemption of preference shares explained earlier, the correct interpretation of the phrase 'proceeds of a fresh issue of shares' used in section 80 of the Companies Act can be made. The word 'proceeds' does not include the amount of the premium if shares are issued at a premium but stands for the actual amount received if shares are issued at par or at a discount. When the shares are issued at a premium, the amount of securities premium received cannot be depended upon as security to creditors because the amount can be used by the company in writing off certain expenses specified in section 78 of the Companies Act which does not mention redemption of preference shares as one of the purposes for which securities premium can be used. Of course, securities premium can be used for buy-back of shares but for that, certain conditions have to be fulfilled and hence, that is a special case.

Capital Redemption Reserve Account. As only those profits which are otherwise available for dividends can be used for redemption of preference shares, transfer to Capital Redemption Reserve Account should be made only from such accounts as represent divisible profits. Amounts in Securities Premium Account, Forfeited Shares Account, Profit Prior to Incorporation Account and Capital Reserve Account must not be transferred to Capital Redemption Reserve Account. The credit balances in Profit & Loss Account, General Reserve, Dividend Equalisation Reserve are the examples of the balances available for distribution of dividend and hence for transfer to Capital Redemption Reserve Account.

Illustration 35:

A company has 40,000 12% redeemable preference shares of Rs. 100 each, fully paid. The company decides to redeem the shares on December 31, 2009 at a premium of 5 per cent. The company makes the following issues:—

(a) 1,00,000 equity shares of Rs. 10 each at a premium of 10 per cent.

(b) 10,000 14% debentures of Rs. 100 each.

The issue was fully subscribed and all the amounts were received. The redemption was duly carried out. The company has sufficient profits. Give journal entries.

Solution:

Journal

					Dr. Rs.	Cr. Rs.
2009 Dec.	31	Bank	Dr.		11,00,000	
		To Equity Share Capital Account				10,00,000
		To Securities Premium Account				1,00,000
		Allotment of 1,00,000 equity shares of Rs. 10 each at a premium of Re. 1 per share.				
"	"	Bank	Dr.		10,,00,000	
		To 14% Debentures				10,,00,000
		Allotment of 10,000 14% debentures of Rs. 100 each.				
"	"	Profit and Loss Account	Dr.		1,00,000	
		Securities Premium	Dr.		1,00,000	
		To Premium on Redemption of Preference Shares Account				2,00,000
		The provision of premium of 5% payable on redemption of 40,000 redeemable preference shares of Rs. 100 each.				
"	"	Profit and Loss Account	Dr.		30,00,000	
		To Capital Redemption Reserve Account				30,00,000
		The amount transferred to Capital Redemption Reserve Account—the amount uncovered by the face value of the shares issued.				
"	"	12% Redeemable Preference Share Capital Account	Dr.		40,00,000	
		Premium on Redemption of Preference Shares Account	Dr.		2,00,000	
		To Bank				42,00,000
		The repayment of the 40,000 redeemable preference shares of Rs. 100 each at a premium of Rs. 5 per share.				

Illustration 36:

The following extract of Ronnie Limited's Balance Sheet is given to you:—

Liabilities	*Rs.*
Share Capital:	
Authorised	35,00,000
Issued and subscribed:	
1,50,000 Equity Shares of Rs. 10 each, fully paid up	15,00,000
5,000 11% Redeemable Preference Shares of Rs. 100 each, Rs. 90 called and paid up	4,50,000
Reserves and Surplus:	
Capital Reserve	75,000
Securities Premium	15,000
General Reserve	1,60,000
Profit and Loss Account	1,85,000

The company decides to redeem all the preference shares at a premium of 1%. For the specific purpose of such redemption, it issues 2,000 14% redeemable preference shares of Rs. 100 each at a premium of 5%, the entire amount being payable along with application. The whole issue is taken up by the public. The redemption of 11% redeemable preference shares is duly completed.

Journalise the abovementioned transactions.

Solution:

Journal

		Dr. Rs.	Cr. Rs.
11% Redeemable Preference Share Final Call Account	Dr.	50,000	
To 11% Redeemable Preference Share Capital Account			50,000
Final call of Rs. 10 each made on 5,000 11% redeemable preference shares.			
Bank	Dr.	50,000	
To 11% Redeemable Preference Share Final Call Account			50,000
Receipt of final call on 5,000 11% redeemable preference shares @ Rs. 10 per share.			
Bank	Dr.	2,10,000	
To 14% Redeemable Preference Share Applications & Allotment Account			2,10,000
Receipt of application money on 2,000 14% redeemable preference shares.			
14% Redeemable Preference Share Applications and Allotment Account	Dr.	2,10,000	
To 14% Redeemable Preference Share Capital Account			2,00,000
To Securities Premium Account			10,000
Allotment of 2,000 14% redeemable preference shares of Rs. 100 each issued at a premium of 5%.			
General Reserve	Dr.	1,60,000	
Profit & Loss Account	Dr.	1,40,000	
To Capital Redemption Reserve Account			3,00,000
Creation of Capital Redemption Reserve Account out of divisible profits for the amount of preference shares being redeemed not covered by the face value of fresh issue of preference shares.			
Securities Premium Account	Dr.	5,000	
To Premium on Redemption of Preference Shares Account			5,000
Provision made out of Securities Premium Account for the premium on redemption of preference shares.			

	Dr. Rs.	Cr. Rs.
11% Redeemable Preference Share Capital Account Dr.	5,00,000	
Premium on Redemption of Preference Shares Account Dr.	5,000	
To Sundry Preference Shareholders Account		5,05,000
Amount due to sundry preference shareholders on redemption of preference shares.		
Sundry Preference Shareholders Account Dr.	5,05,000	
To Bank		5,05,000
Payment made to sundry preference shareholders to redeem 5,000 11% redeemable preference shares of Rs. 100 each at a premium of 1%.		

Illustration 37:

On 31st March, 2010 the balance sheet of Utopia Limited stood as follows:—

Liabilities	*Rs.*	*Assets*	*Rs.*
Share Capital :		**Fixed Assets :**	
Authorised	20,00,000	Land and Buildings	5,00,000
Issued and Subscribed :		Plant and Machinery	10,00,000
1,00,000 Equity Shares of Rs. 10 each, fully paid	10,00,000	Furniture, Fittings and Fixtures	3,90,000
		Investments:	
4,500 12% Redeemable Preference Shares of Rs. 100 each, fully paid	4,50,000	Units of the Unit Trust of India	1,45,000
Reserves and Surplus :		**Current Assets, Loans and Advances:**	
		(A) Current Assets	
Capital Reserve	12,500	Stock	9,10,200
Securities Premium	20,000	Debtors	1,42,800
General Reserve	8,30,500	Cash in hand	8,500
Profit and Loss Account	3,87,000	Cash at Bank	1,02,500
Current Liabilities and Provisions :		(B) Loans and Advances	
(A) Current Liabilities		Unexpired Insurance	1,000
Sundry Creditors	2,50,000		
(B) Provisions			
Provision for Taxation	2,50,000		
	32,00,000		32,00,000

On 1st April, 2010 in order to redeem all of its preference shares at a premium of 5%, the company issued 20,000 equity shares of Rs. 10 each at a premium of 10% and sold all of its investments in the Units for Rs. 1,58,000.

After the redemption of the preference shares, the company issued one fully paid equity share of Rs. 10 as bonus for every four shares held by its members.

Show journal entries for all the abovementioned transactions and prepare the balance sheet of the company immediately after the issue of bonus shares.

Solution:

Journal

	Dr. Rs.	Cr. Rs.
Bank Dr.	2,20,000	
To Equity Share Applications & Allotment Account		2,20,000
Receipt of application money on 20,000 equity shares @ Rs. 11 per share.		

Particulars		Dr. Rs.	Cr. Rs.
Equity Securities Applications & Allotment Account	Dr.	2,20,000	
To Equity Share Capital Account			2,00,000
To Securities Premium Account			20,000
Allotment of 20,000 equity shares of Rs. 10 each at a premium of 10%.			
Bank	Dr.	1,58,000	
To Units of the Unit Trust of India			1,58,000
Sale proceeds of the units of the Unit Trust of India.			
Units of the Unit Trust of India	Dr.	13,000	
To Profit and Loss Account			13,000
Transfer of profit on sale of investments to Profit and Loss Account.			
Securities Premium Account	Dr.	22,500	
To Premium on Redemption of Preference Shares Account			22,500
Utilisation of Securities Premium Account for making provision for premium payable on redemption of preference shares.			
General Reserve	Dr.	2,50,000	
To Capital Redemption Reserve Account			2,50,000
Creation of Capital Redemption Reserve Account for the amount not covered by fresh issue of shares to redeem preference shares.			
12% Redeemable Preference Share Capital Account	Dr.	4,50,000	
Premium on Redemption of Preference Shares Account	Dr.	22,500	
To Sundry Preference Shareholders Account			4,72,500
Amount payable to Sundry Preference Shareholders on redemption of preference shares at a premium of 5%.			
Sundry Preference Shareholders Account	Dr.	4,72,500	
To Bank			4,72,500
Payment made to sundry preference shareholders.			
Capital Redemption Reserve Account	Dr.	2,50,000	
Capital Reserve	Dr.	12,500	
Securities Premium Account	Dr.	17,500	
General Reserve	Dr.	20,000	
To Bonus to Equity Shareholders Account			3,00,000
Use of Capital Redemption Reserve Account, Capital Reserve, Securities Premium and General Reserve to provide for bonus shares to be issued to equity shareholders of Rs. 12,00,000.			
Bonus to Equity Shareholders Account	Dr.	3,00,000	
To Equity Share Capital Account			3,00,000
Issue of fully paid bonus shares to equity shareholders @ one equity share for every four shares held.			

Working Notes:

Cash Book (Bank Columns only)

Dr.	Rs.	Cr.	Rs.
To Balance b/fd	1,02,500	By Sundry Preference Shareholders	4,72,500
To Equity Share Applications & Allotment Account	2,20,000	By Balance c/d	8,000
To Units of the Unit Trust of India	1,58,000		
	4,80,500		4,80,500
To Balance b/d	8,000		

Equity Share Capital Account

Dr.		Rs.			Rs. Cr.
	To Balance c/d	15,00,000		By Balance b/fd	10,00,000
				By Equity Share Applications & Allotment Account	2,00,000
				By Bonus to Equity Shareholders	3,00,000
		15,00,000			15,00,000
				By Balance b/d	15,00,000

Securities Premium Account

Dr.		Rs.			Rs. Cr.
	To Premium on Redemption of Preference Shares	22,500		By Balance b/fd	20,000
	To Bonus to Equity Shareholders	17,500		By Equity Share Applications & Allotment Account	20,000
		40,000			40,000

General Reserve

Dr.		Rs.			Rs. Cr.
	To Capital Redemption Reserve	2,50,000		By Balance b/fd	8,30,500
	To Bonus to Equity Shareholders	20,000			
	To Balance c/d	5,60,500			
		8,30,500			8,30,500
				By Balance b/d	5,60,500

Balance Sheet of Utopia Limited
as on ....

Liabilities		*Rs.*	*Assets*	*Rs.*
Share Capital:			**Fixed Assets:**	
Authorised		20,00,000	Land and Buildings	5,00,000
Issued and subscribed : 1,50,000 Equity Shares of Rs. 10 each, fully paid		15,00,000	Plant and Machinery	10,00,000
(Of the above shares, 30,000 equity shares are allotted as fully paid up by way of bonus shares)			Furniture, Fittings and Fixtures	3,90,000
			Current Assets, Loans and Advances:	
			(A) Current Assets	
Sources:			Stock	9,10,200
Capital redemption reserve	2,50,000		Debtors	1,42,800
Capital reserve	12,500		Cash in hand	8,500
Securities premium	17,500		Cash at Bank	8,000
General Reserve	20,000		(B) Loans and Advances	
Reserves and Surplus:			Unexpired Insurance	1,000
General Reserve		5,60,500		
Profit and Loss Account		4,00,000		
Current Liabilities and Provisions				
(A) Current Liabilities :				
Sundry Creditors		2,50,000		
(B) Provisions				
Provision for Taxation		2,50,000		
		29,60,500		29,60,500

Illustration 38:

Following is the Balance Sheet of R. Ltd. as on March 31, 2010 :

Liabilities		*Rs.*	*Assets*	*Rs.*
5,000 Equity Shares of Rs. 100 each, fully paid		5,00,000	Cash at Bank	4,40,000
2,000 12% Redeemable Preference Shares of Rs. 100 each, fully called	2,00,000		Other Assets	6,10,000
Less: Calls in arrear (Rs. 20 per share)	2,000	1,98,000		
1,000 14% Redeemable Preference Shares of Rs. 100 each, Rs. 60 paid		60,000		
Profit and Loss Account		2,40,000		
Creditors		52,000		
		10,50,000		10,50,000

On the above date the preference shares are redeemed to the extent possible, at a premium of 5 per cent. Journalise and give the amended balance sheet.

Solution:

Journal

				Dr. *Rs.*	*Cr.* *Rs.*
2010 Mar.	31	Profit and Loss Account	Dr.	2,10,000	
		To Premium on Redemption of Preference Shares Account			10,000
		To Capital Redemption Reserve Account			2,00,000
		The transfer of the requisite sums from the Profit & Loss Account to provide premium of 5% and the capital sum of redemption of 2,000 shares of Rs. 100 each.			
"	"	12% Redeemable Preference Share Capital Account	Dr.	1,90,000	
		Premium on Redemption of Preference Shares Account	Dr.	9,500	
		To 12% Redeemable Preference Shareholders			1,99,500
		The sum payable to those redeemable preference shareholders who have got fully paid shares.			
"	"	12% Redeemable Preference Shareholders	Dr.	1,99,500	
		To Bank			1,99,500
		The payment of the amount due to the redeemable preference shareholders.			

Notes : (*i*) Partly paid shares cannot be redeemed.

(*ii*) In respect of shares on which the call is due, it would be proper to create the full capital redemption reserve but to redeem them only when the call has been collected.

Balance Sheet of R. Ltd. as on March 31, 2010

Liabilities	*Rs.*	*Rs.*	*Assets*	*Rs.*
5,000 Equity Shares of Rs. 100 each, fully paid		5,00,000	Cash at Bank	2,40,500
100 12% Redeemable Preference Shares of Rs. 100 each	10,000		Other Assets	6,10,000
Less: calls in arrear	2,000	8,000		
1,000 14% Redeemable Preference Shares of Rs. 100 each, Rs. 60 paid		60,000		

	Rs.		Rs.
Premium Payable on Redemption of Preference Shares	500		
Capital Redemption Reserve Account	2,00,000		
Profit and Loss Account	30,000		
Creditors	52,000		
	8,50,500		8,50,500

Illustration 39:

On 1st April, 2010 the following balances were extracted from the ledger of Enkay Limited:

		Rs.
(1)	10% Redeemable Preference Share Capital Account : 5,000 Shares of Rs. 100 each, fully called-up	5,00,000
(2)	Calls Unpaid Account : Final call on 100 10% Redeemable Preference Shares @ Rs. 20 each	2,000
(3)	Securities Premium Account	14,000
(4)	General Reserve	1,60,000
(5)	Profit and Loss Account	1,18,546
(6)	Declared Preference Dividend, not yet paid	49,800

The company redeemed all the preference shares at a premium of 5% and for the purpose, it issued equity shares of Rs. 10 each at a premium of Re. 1 each for such an amount as was necessary for the purpose after utilising the available profits to the maximum possible extent. It also paid the declared preference dividend.

Show journal entries for all the abovementioned transactions.

Solution:

Working Notes :

Divisible profits available = Rs. 1,60,000 + Rs. 1,18,546 = Rs. 2,78,546

Face value of shares to be redeemed = Rs. 5,00,000

Minimum amount of new issue = Rs. 5,00,000 – Rs. 2,78,546 = Rs. 2,21,454.

But as no fraction of a share can be allotted, and new shares are of Rs. 10 each, the minimum amount of new issue = Rs. 2,21,460

Securities premium to be received = 10% of Rs. 2,21,460 = Rs. 22,146.

Total securities premium = Rs. 14,000 + Rs. 22,146 = Rs. 36,146

Premium payable on redemption of preference shares = Rs. 5/100 x 5,00,000 = Rs. 25,000

As the total share premium after the new issue would be sufficient to take care of the premium payable on redemption of preference shares, the company can proceed to redeem the preference shares by issuing 22,146 new equity shares of Rs. 10 each.

Solution:

Journal

			Dr. Rs.	Cr. Rs.
	Bank Dr.		2,43,606	
	To Equity Share Capital Account			2,21,460
	To Securities Premium Account			22,146
	Allotment of 22,146 equity shares of Rs. 10 each at a premium of Re. 1 per share.			

Particulars		Rs.	Rs.
Securities Premium Account	Dr.	25,000	
To Premium on Redemption of Preference Shares Account			25,000
Utilisation of Securities Premium Account for meeting the premium payable on redemption of preference shares.			
General Reserve	Dr.	1,60,000	
Profit and Loss Account	Dr.	1,18,540	
To Capital Redemption Reserve Account			2,78,540
Creation of Capital Redemption Reserve Account out of divisible profits for redemption of preference shares.			
Declared Preference Dividend Account	Dr.	49,800	
To Bank			49.800
Payment of declared preference dividend.			
Bank	Dr.	2,000	
To Calls in Arrear Account			2,000
Receipt of calls in arrear in respect of preference shares.			
10% Redeemable Preference Share Capital Account	Dr.	5,00,000	
Premium on Redemption of Preference Shares Account	Dr.	25,000	
To Preference Shareholders Account			5,25,000
Amount payable to preference shareholders on redemption of preference shares at a premium of 5%.			
Preference shareholders Account	Dr.	5,25,000	
To Bank			5,25,000
Payment made to preference shareholders to redeem all the preference shares at a premium of 5%.			

Illustration 40:

From the following particulars, determine the minimum amount of fresh issue of shares of Rs. 10 each to be made at a discount of Re. 1 per share for redemption of preference shares at a premium of 5%.

	Rs. in lakhs
(i) Fully paid redeemable preference shares	800
(ii) Revaluation reserve	100
(iii) Capital reserve	20
(iv) General reserve	270
(v) Credit balance of profit and loss account	80
(vi) Securities premium account	30

Solution:

	Rs. in lakhs
Paid up value of redemable preference shares	800
Add: Premium @ 5% to be paid on redemption of preference shares	40
Total amount required	840
Provision for premium on redemption of preference shares out of:	
Securities premium account	30
Credit balance of profit and loss account	10
	40
Amount available for capital redemption reserve:	
General reserve	270
Credit balance of profit and loss account (Rs. 80 lakh – Rs. 10 lakh)	70
	340

Rs. in lakh

Fresh shares have to be issued to collect
(Rs. 800 – 340 lakh) = Rs. 460 lakh
Number of shares of Rs. 10 each to be issued at

a discount of Re. 1 per share = $\frac{460\,\text{lakh}}{10} \times \frac{10}{9}$ = 51,111.1 shares

As fraction of a share cannot be issued 51,11,112 shares of Rs. 10 each amounting to Rs. 5,11,11,120 will have to be issued.

Illustration 41:

The following is an extract from the balance sheet of Abhinav Limited as on 31st March, 2009:

	Rs.	*Rs.*
Share Capital		
20,000 12% Preference Shares of Rs. 50 each, fully paid		10,00,000
1,00,000 Equity Shares of Rs. 10 each, Rs. 7.50 per share called up	7,50,000	
Less: Calls unpaid	7,500	7,42,500
Securities Premium Account		50,000
General Reserve		6,00,000
Calls in Advance (final call on equity shares)		2,500

On 1st April, 2009 the Board of Directors decide the following :

(*i*) The fully paid preference shares are to be redeemed at a premium of 5% in May, 2009 and, for that purpose, 50,000 equity shares of Rs. 10 each are to be issued at par to be paid for in full on application in April, 2009.

The final call of Rs. 2.50 per share is to be made in July, 2009.

The 1,000 equity shares owned by A, an existing shareholder, who failed to pay the allotment money of Rs. 2.50 per share and the first call of Rs. 2.50 per share, were forfeited in the month of June, 2009.

The above decisions were duly complied with according to the time schedule laid down.

The amount due on the issue of fresh equity shares and on final call were duly received except from B, who has failed to pay the first call money on his 1,000 shares has failed to pay the final call money also. These shares of B were forfeited in the month of August, 2009.

Of the total shares forfeited, 1,500 were issued to X in September, 2009, credited as fully paid at Rs. 9 per share, the whole of A's shares being included.

Pass journal entries in the books of the Company to record these transactions and show the relevant items on the liabilities side of the balance sheet (necessary extracts) according to the form prescribed by the Companies Act, 1956. Assume that the resources required for payment are available.

[*Adapted, B.Com., (Hons.) Delhi, 1988*]

Solution:

Journal

			Dr.	*Cr.*
2009			*Rs.*	*Rs.*
April	Bank	Dr.	5,00,000	
	To Equity Share Applications & Allotment Account			5,00,000
	Receipt of application money @ Rs. 10 per share in respect of 50,000 equity shares.			
	Equity Share Applications & Allotment Account	Dr.	5,00,000	
	To Equity Share Capital Account			5,00,000
	Allotment of 50,000 equity shares of Rs. 10 each at par			

Date	Particulars		Rs.	Rs.
2009				
May	General Reserve	Dr.	5,00,000	
	To Capital Redemption Reserve			5,00,000
	Creation of Capital Redemption Reserve out of General Reserve for redemption of preference shares for the amount not covered by fresh issue of shares.			
	Securities Premium Account	Dr.	50,000	
	To Premium on Redemption of Preference Shares Account			50,000
	Use of Securities Premium to provide premium payable on redemption of preference shares.			
	12% Preference Share Capital Account	Dr	10,00,000	
	Premium on Redemption of Preference Shares Account	Dr.	50,000	
	To Sundry Preference Shareholders			10,50,000
	Amount payable to sundry preference shareholders on redemption.			
	Sundry Preference Shareholders Account	Dr.	10,50,000	
	To Bank			10,50,000
	Payment made to sundry preference shareholders.			
June	Equity Share Capital Account	Dr.	7,500	
	To Calls in Arrear Account			5,000
	To Forfeited Shares Account			2,500
	Forfeiture of 1,000 equity shares held by A for non-payment of allotment money @ Rs. 2.50 per share and first call money @ Rs. 2.50 per share.			
July	Equity Share Second & Final Call Account	Dr.	2,47,500	
	To Equity Share Capital Account			2,47,500
	Second and final call due in respect of 99,000 equity shares @ Rs. 2.50 per share.			
	Calls in Advance	Dr.	2,500	
	To Equity Share Second & Final Call Account			2,500
	Transfer of Calls in Advance to Equity Share Second & Final Call Account.			
	Bank	Dr.	2,42,500	
	To Equity Share Second & Final Call Account			2,42,500
	Receipt of second and final call in respect of 97,000 equity shares @ Rs. 2.50 per share.			
	Calls in Arrear Account	Dr.	2,500	
	To Equity Share Second & Final Call Account			2,500
	Amount not received in respect of shares held by B transferred to Calls in Arrear A/c.			
Aug.	Equity Share Capital Account	Dr.	10,000	
	To Calls in Arrear Account			5,000
	To Forfeited Shares Account			5,000
	Forfeiture of 1,000 equity shares held by B for non-payment of first as well as second calls.			
Sept.	Bank	Dr.	13,500	
	Forfeited Shares Account	Dr.	1,500	
	To Equity Share Capital Account			15,000
	Reissue of 1,500 equity shares as fully paid at Rs. 9 per share.			
	Forfeited Shares Account	Dr.	3,500	
	To Capital Reserve			3,500
	Transfer from Forfeited Shares Account to Capital Reserve net gain on reissue of 1,500 forfeited shares.			

Balance Sheet
(*Releant extracts on liabilities side*)

Liabilities		*Rs.*
Share Capital		
Authorised:		?
Issued		
1,50,000 Equity Shares of Rs. 10 each		15,00,000
Subscribed:		
1,49,500 Equity Shares of Rs. 10 each, fully paid		14,95,000
Forfeited Shares Account		2,500
Reserves and Surplus:		
Capital Redemption Reserve:		
Balance as on 31st March, 2009	Nil	
Add: Additions thereafter	5,00,000	5,00,000
Capital Reserve:		
Balance as on 31st March, 2009	Nil	
Add: Additions thereafter	3,500	3,500
General Reserve:		
Balance as on 31st March, 2009	6,00,000	
Less: Transfer to Capital Redemption Reserve	5,00,000	1,00,000

Illustration 42:

The following the Balance Sheet of Trinity Ltd. as at 31.3.2008:

Trinity Ltd.
Balance Sheet as at 31st March, 2008

Liabilities	*Rs.*	*Assets*	*Rs.*	*Rs.*
Share Capital		**Fixed Assets**		
Authorised		Gross Block		4,00,000
10,000 10% Redeemable		*Less*: Depreciation		1,00,000
Preference				3,00,000
Shares of Rs. 10 each	1,00,000	**Investments**		1,00,000
90,000 Equity Shares of Rs. 10 each	9,00,000			
	10,00,000			
Issued, Subscribed and Paid-up Capital		**Current Assets and Loans and Advances**		
10,000 10% Redeembable				
Preference Shares of Rs. 10 each	1,00,000	Inventory	1,25,000	
50,000 Equity Shares of Rs. 10 each	5,00,000	Debtors	1,25,000	
		Cash and Bank balances	1,50,000	4,00,000
(A)	6,00,000	**Miscellaneous Expenditure**		
Reserves and Surplus		(to the extent not		
Securities Premium	70,000			
General Reserve	1,20,000	written off)		20,000
Profit and Loss account	18,500			
(B)	2,08,500			
Current Liabilities and Provisions (C)	11,500			
Total (A + B + C)	8,20,000	Total		8,20,000

For the year ended 31.3.2009 the company made a net profit of Rs. 15,000 after providing Rs. 20,000 depreciation and writing off the miscellaneous expenditure amounting to Rs. 20,000.

The following additional information is available with regard to company's operation:

(*i*) The preference dividend for the year ended 31.3.2009 was paid before 31.3.2009.

(*ii*) Except cash and bank balances other current assets and current liabilities as on 31.3.2009, was the same as on 31.3.2008.

(*iii*) The company redeemed the preference shares at a premium of 10%.

(*iv*) The company issued bonus shares in the ratio of one share for every five equity shares held as on 31.3.2009.

(*v*) To meet the cash requirements of redemption, the company sold a portion of the investments, so as to leave a minimum balance of Rs. 30,000 after such redemption.

(*vi*) Investments were sold at 90% of cost on 31.3.2009.

You are required:

(*a*) Prepare necessary journal entries to record redemption and issue of bonus shares.

(*b*) Prepare the cash and bank account.

(*c*) Prepare the Balance Sheet as at 31st March, 2009 incorporating the above transactions.

[*C.A. (Inter.) Nov., 1996 Modified*]

Solution:

Books of Trinity Ltd.

Journal

(*a*)

			Rs.	Rs.
	Bank Dr.		45,000	
	Profit and Loss Account Dr.		5,000	
	To Investments			50,000
	Sale of investments; loss on sale being transferred to profit and loss account			
	General Reserve Dr.		1,00,000	
	To Capital Redemption Reserve			1,00,000
	Creation of capital redemption reserve to redeem preference shares			
	Securities Premium Dr.		10,000	
	To Premium on Redemption of Preference Share Account			10,000
	Premium on redemption of preference shares provided out of securities premium.			
	10% Redeemable Preference Share Capital Account Dr.		1,00,000	
	Premium on Redemption of Preference Shares Account Dr.		10,000	
	To Sundry Preference Shareholder			1,10,000
	Amount payable to sundry preference shareholders on redemption of preference shares at a premium			
	Sundry Preference Shareholders Dr.		1,10,000	
	To Bank			1,10,000
	Payment made to sundry preference shareholders			
	Capital Redemption Reserve Dr.		1,00,000	
	To Bonus to Equity Shareholders Account			1,00,000
	Use of capital redemption reserve to issus bonus shares in the ratio of 1 : 5			
	Bonus to Equity Shareholders Account Dr.		1,00,000	
	To Equity Share Capital Account			1,00,000
	Issue of bonus shares			

(*b*) *Dr.* **Cash and Bank Account** *Cr.*

	Rs.	*Rs.*		*Rs.*
To Balance b/f		50,000	By Preference dividend	10,000
To Cash from operations:			By Preference shareholders	1,10,000
Profit	15,000		By Balance c/f	30,000
Add: Depreciation	20,000			
Add: Miscellanous expenditure written off	20,000			
		55,000		
To Investments		45,000		
		1,50,000		1,50,000

(*c*)

Balance Sheet of Trinity Limited
As at 31st March, 2009 (after redemption)

	Rs.	*Rs.*		*Rs.*	*Rs.*	*Rs.*
Liabilities			**Assets**			
Share Capital			**Fixed Assets**			
Authorised		10,00,000	Gross Block		4,00,000	
Issued, Subscribed and Paid up:			*Less*: Depreciation			
60,000 Eqauity Shares of Rs. 10 each,			upto 31.3.98	1,00,000		
fully paid-up		6,00,000	For the year	20,000		
(10,000 shares have been					1,20,000	
allotted as bonus shares)						2,80,000
Source: Capital Redemption Reserve			**Investments**			
Reserves and Surplus			(Market value, Rs. 45,000)			50,000
Securities Premium	60,000		**Current Assets, Loans and Avances**			
General Reserve	20,000		(A) Current Assets:			
Profit and Loss Account	18,500		Inventory		1,25,000	
		98,500	Debtors		1,25,000	
Current Liabilities and Provisions			Cash and Bank Balances		1,30,000	
(A) Current Laibilities:						3,80,000
Sundry Creditors		11,500	(B) Loans and Advances			Nil
(B) Provisions		Nil				
		7,10,000				7,10,000

Working Notes:

	Rs.	*Rs.*
(*i*) Profit and Loss Account for the year ending 31st March, 2009 :		
Balance as on 1.4.2008		18,500
Add: Profit for the year		15,000
		33,500
Less: Preference dividend	10,000	
Loss on sale of investments	5,000	15,000
Balance as on 31.3.2009		18,500
(*ii*) General Reserve		1,20,000
Less: Transfer to Capital Redemption Reserve		1,00,000
Balance as on 31.3.2009		20,000

	Rs.
(iii) Securities Premium	70,000
Less: Premium on Redemption of Preference shares	10,000
Balance as on 31.3.2009	60,000
(iv) Capital Redemption Reserve	1,00,000
Less: Transfer for Bonus Shares	1,00,000
Balance as on 31.3.2009	NIL
(v) Sale of Investments:	
Cost of Investments	50,000
Cash received	45,000
Loss on Sale of Investments	5,000
Total Investments	1,00,000
Less: Cost of Investments sold	50,000
Cost of Investments on hand	50,000
Market value, (90% of 50,000)	45,000

Illustration 43:

On 31st March, 2010 the summarised balance sheet of Madhu Limited stood as follows:—

Liabilities	*Rs.*	*Assets*	*Rs.*
Share Capital:		Fixed Assets	6,00,000
Authorised	10,00,000	Cash at Bank	2,00,000
Issued and subscribed:		Other Current Assets	3,00,000
5,000 Equity Shares of Rs. 100 each, fully paid up	5,00,000		
2,500 13% Redeemable Preference Shares of Rs. 100 each, fully paid up	2,50,000		
Reserves and Surplus:			
Securities Premium	10,000		
Dividend Equalisation Reserve	1,02,000		
Profit and Loss Account	38,000		
Current Liabilities	2,00,000		
	11,00,000		11,00,000

The company redeemed all its preference shares at a premium of 10% issuing fresh equity shares of Rs. 100 each at a premium of 5% for minimum amount necessary after using all of its divisible profits for purpose of redemption.

After ascertaining the amount for which first equity shares were issued, show journal entries for all the transactions concerning the redemption of preference shares and prepare the balance sheet as it would appear immediately after the redemption.

Solution:

Divisible profits = Rs. 1,02,000 + Rs. 38,000 = Rs. 1,40,000

Minimum issue of equity shares = Rs. 2,50,000 – Rs. 1,40,000 = Rs. 1,10,000

Premium on Rs. 1,10,000 @ 5% = Rs. 5,500.

Total balance in Securities Premium Account will be = Rs. 10,000 + Rs. 5,500 = Rs. 15,500.

Premium payable on redemption of preference shares = Rs. 10/100 x 2,50,000 = Rs. 25,000.

As total balance in Securities Premium Account falls short of the amount of premium required to be paid on redemption of preference shares, the amount of fresh issue will have to be calculated with the help of an equation.

Let us assume amount of fresh issue is x.

Redeemable preference shares + Premium payable on redemption = Balance of Securities Premium Account + Divisible Profits + x + (x x rate of premium on fresh issue/100)

Therefore, Rs. 2,50,000 + Rs. 25,000 = Rs. 10,000 + Rs. 1,40,000 + x + (x x 5/100)
or Rs. 2,75,000 = Rs. 1,50,000 + x + 5x/100
or Rs. 2,75,000 – Rs. 1,50,000 = x + 5x /100
or Rs. 1,25,000 = x + 5x /100
or Rs. 1,25,00,000 = 100x + 5x
or Rs. 1,25,00,000 = 105x
or x = Rs. 1,25,00,000/105
Therefore, x = Rs. 1,19,048

As shares issued are of Rs. 100 each, the company must have issued equity shares of Rs. 1,19,100.

Journal

	Particulars			Dr. Rs.	Cr. Rs.
	Bank	Dr.		1,20,055	
	To Equity Share Capital Account				1,19,100
	To Securities Premium Account				5,955
	Allotment of 1,191 equity shares of Rs. 100 each at a premium of 5%.				
	Securities Premium Account	Dr.		15,955	
	Profit & Loss Account	Dr.		9,045	
	To Premium on Redemption of Preference Shares Account				25,000
	Premium payable on redemption of preference shares being set off against Securities Premium Account and Profit & Loss Account.				
	13% Redeemable Preference Share Capital Account	Dr.		2,50,000	
	Premium on Redemption of Preference Shares Account	Dr.		25,000	
	To Sundry Preference Shareholders				2,75,000
	Amount payable to preference shareholders on redemption.				
	Dividend Equalisation Reserve	Dr.		1,02,000	
	Profit & Loss Account	Dr.		28,900	
	To Capital Redemption Reserve Account				1,30,900
	Credit to Capital Redemption Reserve Account for the amount of redeemable preference shares not covered by face value of fresh issue of shares.				
	Sundry Preference Shareholders Account	Dr.		2,75,000	
	To Bank				2,75,000
	Payment to preference shareholders.				

Balance Sheet of Madan Limited (after redemption of preference shares)

Liabilities	*Rs.*	*Assets*	*Rs.*
Share Capital:		**Fixed Assets**	6,00,000
Authorised	10,00,000	Cash at Bank	50,055
Issued and Subscribed:		**Current Assets**	3,00,000
6,191 Equity Shares of Rs. 100 each, fully paid up	6,19,100	Other Current Assets	
Reserves and Surplus:			
Capital Redemption Reserve	1,30,900		
Profit and Loss Account	55		
Current Liabilities	2,00,000		
	9,50,055		9,50,055

Working Notes:

Cash Book (Bank Columns Only)

Dr.	Rs.		Cr. Rs.
To Balance b/fd	2,00,000	By Sundry Preference Shareholders	2,75,000
To Equity Share Capital	1,19,100	By Balance c/d	50,055
To Securities Premium	5,955		
	3,25,055		3,25,055
To Balance b/d	50,055		

Profit and Loss Account

	Rs.		Rs.
To Premium on Redemption of Preference shares	9,045	By Balance b/fd	38,000
To Capital Redemption Reserve	28,900		
To Balance c/d	55		
	38,000		38,000
		By Balance b/d	55

Illustration 44:

The relevant section of the Balance Sheet of Tee Limited as on 31st March, 2010 is given below:—

Liabilities	Rs.
Share Capital:	
Authorised:	8,00,000
Issued and Subscribed :	
40,000 Equity Shares of Rs. 10 each, fully paid up	4,00,000
1,500 10% Redeemable Preference Shares of Rs. 100 each, fully paid up	1,50,000
Reserves and Surplus:	
Profit Prior to Incorporation	20,000
Capital Reserve	7,500
Securities Premium	5,000
General Reserve	40,000
Profit and Loss Account	30,000

The preference shares were due to be redeemed at a premium of 5%. As the divisible profits were inadequate, the company after completing the legal formalities issued the minimum amount of equity shares of Rs. 10 each at a discount of 10%. All the preference shares were then redeemed.

You are required to pass journal entries for all the abovementioned transactions.

Solution:

Calculation of the amount of fresh issue of shares:

Amount of premium payable on redemption of preference shares = Rs. 5/100 x 1,50,000 = Rs. 7,500.

Balance of Securities Premium Account = Rs. 5,000

Additional amount to be met out of divisible profits or proceeds of fresh issue = Rs. 7,500 - Rs. 5,000 = Rs. 2,500

Issue price of fresh issue = Rs. 1,50,000 + Rs. 2,500 - Rs. 40,000 - Rs. 30,000 = Rs. 82,500

Nominal value of the issue = Rs. 82,500 x 100/90 = Rs. 91,667

As shares are of Rs. 10 each, the face value of new issue must be Rs. 91,670.

Journal

	Dr.	Cr.
	Rs.	*Rs.*
Bank Dr. Discount on Issue of Shares Account Dr. To Equity Share Capital Account Allotment of 9,167 equity shares of Rs. 10 each at a discount of 10%.	82,503 9,167	 91,670
Securities Premium Dr. General Reserve Dr. To Premium on Redemption of Preference Shares Account Use of Securities Premium and General Reserve to provide premium on redemption of preference shares.	5,000 2,500	 7,500
10% Redeemable Preference Share Capital Account Dr. Premium on Redemption of Preference Shares Account Dr. To Sundry Preference Shareholders Account Amount payable to Sundry Preference Shareholders to redeem preference shares at a premium of 5%.	1,50,000 7,500	 1,57,500
General Reserve Dr. Profit & Loss Account Dr. To Capital Redemption Reserve Account Credit to Capital Redemption Reserve Account for the amount not covered by fresh issue of shares.	37,500 29,997	 67,497
Sundry Preference Shareholders Account Dr. To Bank Payment to preference shareholders to redeem preference shares.	1,57,500	 1.57,500

Illustration 45:

Brisk Trading Corporation Ltd. has an authorised capital of Rs. 75,00,000 divided into shares of Rs. 100 each. On 31st March, 2009 its Balance Sheet appeared as follows:—

Liabilities	*Rs.*	*Assets*	*Rs.*
Subscribed Share Capital:		Furniture, Fixtures & Fittings	4,15,000
30,000 Equity Shares of Rs. 100 each, fully paid	30,00,000	Stock	40,65,000
20,000 14% Redeemable Preference Shares of Rs. 100 each, fully paid	20,00,000	Debtors	12,30,000
Capital Reserve	25,000	Cash at Bank	33,90,000
Securities Premium	10,000		
General Reserve	10,00,000		
Profit & Loss Account	20,000		
Sundry Creditors	18,05,000		
Preference Dividend Payable	1,40,000		
Equity Dividend Payable	3,00,000		
Provision for Taxation	7,26,000		
Corporate Dividend Tax Payable	74,000		
	91,00,000		91,00,000

After payment of corporate dividend tax and dividend to all its shareholders, the company decided to redeem all the preference shareholders at a premium of 10%. For the purpose, it issued new equity shares of Rs. 100 each at a premium of 5% to the minimum possible extent, utilizing the accumulated profits to the maximum possible extent.

(*a*) Pass journal entries and redraft the balance sheet immediately after the redemption of preference shares. Show calculations clearly.

(*b*) Calculate the amount of face value of equity shares that the company would be required to issue if the new issue were made at a discount of 5%.

Solution:

(*a*) Working Notes:

		Rs.
Amount of preference shares to be redeemed	=	20,00,000
Add: Premium to be paid on redemption = Rs. 20,00,000 × 10/100	=	2,00,000
Total amount to be paid	=	22,00,000
Accumulated revenue profits:		
General Reserve	=	10,00,000
Add: Profit & Loss Account	=	20,000
		10,20,000
Balance of Securities Premium Account	=	10,000

The balance is to be raised by issue of equity shares of Rs. 100 each at a premium of 5%.

Let us assume face value of the fresh issue = x

Then, premium to be received = $5x/100$

Total amount raised = $x + 5x/100$

Then, $x + 5x/100 = 22{,}00{,}000 - 10{,}20{,}000 - 10{,}000$

or $x + 5x/100 = 11{,}70{,}000$

Multiplying both the sides by 100, we get,

$100x + 5x = 1{,}70{,}00{,}000$

or $105x = 11{,}70{,}00{,}000$

or $x = 11{,}70{,}00{,}000/105$

Therefore x = 11,14,286 (to the nearest rupee)

As the equity shares to be issued are of Rs. 100 each, the face value of the fresh issue will have to be Rs. 11,14,300.

Journal

		Dr. Rs.	Cr. Rs.
Corporate Dividend Tax Payable	Dr.	73,000	
Preference Dividend Payable	Dr.	1,40,000	
Equity Dividend Payable	Dr.	3,00,000	
To Bank			5,13,000
Payment of corporate dividend tax and dividend.			
Bank	Dr.	11,70,015	
To Equity Share Capital Account			11,14,300
To Securities Premium Account			55,715
Allotment of 11,143 equity shares of Rs. 100 each at a premium of 5%.			
Securities Premium Account	Dr.	65,715	
General Reserve	Dr.	1,34,285	
To Premium on Redemption of Preference Shares Account			2,00,000
Use of Securities Premium to the fullest extent and then of General Reserve to provide premium payable on redemption of preference shares			
General Reserve	Dr.	8,65,715	
Profit & Loss Account	Dr.	20,000	
To Capital Redemption Reserve Account			8,85,715
Creation of Capital Redemption Reserve for the amount not covered by fresh issue of shares for redemption of preference shares.			

			Rs.	Rs.
	14% Redeemable Preference Share Capital Account	Dr.	20,00,000	
	Premium on Redemption of Preference Shares Account	Dr.	2,00,000	
	To Sundry Preference Shareholders Account			22,00,000
	Amount payable to sundry preference shareholders on redemption of preference shares.			
	Sundry Preference Shareholders Account	Dr.	22,00,000	
	To Bank			22,00,000
	Payment to sundry preference shareholders to redeem preference shares.			

Working Notes:

Cash Book (Bank Columns only)

Dr.	Rs.		*Cr.* Rs.
To Balance b/fd	33,90,000	By Corporate Dividend Tax Payable	74,000
To Equity Share Capital Account	11,14,300	By Preference Dividend Payable A/c	1,40,000
To Securities Premium Account	55,715	By Equity Dividend Payable A/c	3,00,000
		By Sundry Preference Shareholders Account	22,00,000
		By Balance c/d	18,66,015
	45,60,015		45,30,015
To Balance b/d	18,46,015		

Balance Sheet
as at 31st March, 2009

Liabilities	Rs.	*Assets*	Rs.
Share Capital:		**Fixed Assets:**	
Authorised:		Furniture, Fixtures & Fittings	4,15,000
75,000 Shares of Rs. 100 each	75,00,000	**Current Assets, Loans and Advances:**	
Issued & Subscribed:		(A) Current Assets	
41,143 Equity Shares of Rs.100		Stock	40,65,000
each, fully paid up	41,14,300	Debtors	12,30,000
Reserves and Surplus:		Cash at Bank	18,46,015
Capital Reserve	25,000	(B) Loans and Advances	nil
Capital Redemption Reserve	8,85,715		
Current Liabilities and Provisions:			
(A) Current Liabilities			
Sundry Creditors	18,05,000		
(B) Provisions			
Provisions for Taxation	7,26,000		
	75,56,015		75,56,015

(*b*) Let us assume the face value of the fresh issue = x

Then discount allowed = $5x/100$

Then,

$$x - 5x/100 = 22,00,000 - 10,20,000 - 10,000$$

or $$x - 5x/100 = 11,70,000$$

Multiplying both the sides by 100, we get

$$100x - 5x = 11,70,00,000$$

or $$95x = 11,70,00,000$$

or $$x = 11,70,00,000/95$$

Therefore, $$x = 12,31,579 \text{ (to the nearest rupee)}$$

As the shares to be issued are of Rs. 100 each the face value of the fresh issue will be Rs. 12,31,600.

(h) Redemption of Debentures

Debentures are invariably redeemable. The Companies Act has not laid down any conditions for the redemption of debentures. Of course, the terms laid down for the redemption of the debentures in the prospectus at the time of issue of the debentures will have to be complied with by the company. Debentures may be redeemed in one of the following three ways:—

(*i*) *In one lot:* All the debentures may be redeemed in one lot at the end of a specified period of time or even before the expiry of the specified period of time by serving a notice to debentureholders.

(*ii*) *In instalments by draw of lots:* The debentures may be redeemed in instalments. For example one-tenth of the total debentures may be redeemed every year for ten years by draw of lots. Lot will have to be drawn every year to determine which particular debentures have to be redeemed in that particular year.

(*iii*) *By purchase of debentures in the open market:* A company may reserve the right to buy its debentures in the open market. If the company cancels the debentures so purchased, it will amount to redemption of these debentures.

Cancellation of debentures may take place in one of the two ways:—

(*a*) *Immediate Cancellation:* The company may cancel the debentures immediately after their purchase in the open market.

(*b*) *Cancellation after holding them for some time as 'Own Debentures'.* The company may hold the debentures purchased in the open market for some time as investments in 'Own Debentures'. It is done when the company wants to keep open its option of reselling the debentures. But after some time, it may decide to cancel the debentures held. After cancellation, the debentures stand redeemed and cannot be resold.

The company may redeem only a part of the debentures by purchase in the open market. The remaining debentures may be redeemed at the expiry of the stipulated period of time.

When a company redeems its debentures in one lot at the expiry of a specified period of time or in instalments by draw of lots, the debentures may be redeemed either at par or at a premium according to the terms of issue. But if the company redeems debentures by purchase in the open market the debenture may be redeemed at a premium, at par or even at a discount. Debentures will be redeemed at a discount when the company is able to buy the debentures in the open market at a price lower than the face value of the debentures.

Before redemption starts, there must be a balance of at least 50% of the amount of debentures issued in the Debenture Redemption Reserve.

Entries: When debentures are redeemed other than by purchase in the open market, the following entries will be passed:

(1) When debentures are redeemed at par:

(i)	Debentures Account To Sundry Debentureholders	Dr.	(with face value of debentures being redeemed)
(*ii*)	Sundry Debentureholders To Bank	Dr.	(with face value of debentures being redeemed)

(2) When debentures are redeemed at a premium:-

(*i*)	Debentures	Dr.	(with face value of debentures to be redeemed)
	Premium on Redemption of Debentures Account	Dr.	(with premium being paid on redemption)
	To Sundry Debentureholders		(with total amount payable)
(*ii*)	Sundry Debentureholders To Bank		(with total amount payable)

When debentures are redeemed by cancelling then immediately after their purchase in the open market, redemption will be recorded as follows:—

(1) When purchase price is equal to the face value of debentures:

Debentures	Dr.	(With face value of debentures)
To Bank		

(2) When purchase price is higher than the face value of debentures:

(*i*) Debentures	Dr.	(with face value)
Loss on Redemption of Debentures Account	Dr.	(with extra amount paid)
To Bank		(with actual amount paid)
(*ii*) Securities Premium Account		
or		*or*
Profit & Loss Account	Dr.	(with extra amount paid.)
To Loss on Redemption of Debentures A/c		

(3) When purchase price is lower than the face value of debentures :

(*i*) Debentures	Dr.	(with face value)
To Bank		(with the amount paid)
To Profit on Redemption of Debentures Account		(with excess of face value over the amount paid)
(ii) Profit on Redemption of Debentures Account	Dr.	(with excess of face value over the amount paid)
To Capital Reserve		

A company may buy its own debentures, hold them as investments for some time and then redeem them by cancellation. Entries in this case will be as follows:

When debentures are purchased as investments:

Own Debentures Account	Dr.	(with amount for which debentures purchased)
To Bank		

When 'own debentures' held as investments are cancelled:

(1) In case purchase price of own debentures is equal to the face value of debentures:

Debentures	Dr.	(with face value)
To Own Debentures		(with purchase price of own debentures cancelled)

(2) In case purchase price of own debentures is higher than the face value of debentures:

(*i*) Debentures	Dr.	(with face value)
Loss on Cancellation of Own Debentures	Dr.	(with extra amount paid)
To Own Debentures		(with purchase price of own debentures cancelled)
(*ii*) Securities Premium Account		
or		
Profit & Loss Account	Dr.	(with excess of purchase price of own debentures cancelled over their face value)
To Loss on Cancellation of Own Debentures A/c		

(3) If purchase price is lower than the face value of debentures:

(*i*) Debentures	Dr.	(with face value)
To Own Debentures Account		(with the amount paid)
To Profit on Cancellation of Own Debentures Account		(with excess of face value over purchase price of own debentures cancelled).
(*ii*) Profit an Cancellation of Own Debentures Account	Dr.	(with excess of face value over purchase price of own debentures cancelled)
To Capital Reserve		

By the terms of issue, the debentures may be redeemable at a premium and the company may, at the time of allotment of debentures, credit Premium on Redemption of Debentures Account with the amount of the premium payable at the time of debentures. The company may reserve the right of redeeming any of these debentures by purchase in the open market. If the company redeems any of such debentures by purchasing them in the open market and then cancelling them, while passing entries on cancellation, Debentures Account will be debited with face value of debentures cancelled and Premium on Redemption of Debentures Account will be debited with premium agreed to be paid on redemption according to the terms of the issue. Profit or loss on cancellation will be calculated by comparing the purchase price of debentures cancelled with this face value plus the premium payable on redemption according to the terms of the issue. Suppose, a company issues debentures of Rs. 100 each redeemable at a premium of 5%. If it buys one debenture for Rs. 97 and cancels it, the capital profit on cancellation is Rs. 8.

Illustration 46:

On 1st January, 2000 New Castle Limited allotted 10,000 9% Debentures of Rs. 100 each at par, the total amount having been received along with applications.

(*i*) On 1st January, 2002 the company purchased in the open market 1,000 of its own debentures @ Rs. 101 each and cancelled them immediately.

(*ii*) On 1st January, 2005 the company redeemed at par debentures for Rs. 3,00,000 by draw of a lot.

(*iii*) On 1st January, 2006, the company purchased debentures of the face value of Rs. 2,00,000 for Rs. 1,97,800 in the open market, held them as investments for one year and then cancelled them.

(*iv*) Finally, as per resolution of the board of directors, the remaining debentures were redeemed at a premium of 2% on 1st January, 2010 when Securities Premium Account in the company's ledger showed a balance of Rs. 30,000.

Pass journal entries for the abovementioned transactions ignoring debenture redemption reserve, debenture - interest and interest on own debentures.

Solution:

Journal

Date		Particulars		Dr. Rs.	Cr. Rs.
2000 Jan.	1	Bank	Dr.	10,00,000	
		To 9% Debenture Applications & Allotment Account			10,00,000
		Application money on 10,000 debentures @ Rs. 100 per debenture.			
		9% Debentures Applications & Allotment Account	Dr.	10,00,000	
		To 9% Debentures Account			10,00,000
		Allotment of 10,000 9% Debentures of Rs. 100 each at par.			
(*i*) 2002 Jan.	1	9% Debentures Account	Dr.	1,00,000	
		Loss on Redemption of Debentures Account	Dr.	1,000	
		To Bank			1,01,000
		Redemption of 1,000 9% Debentures of Rs. 100 each by purchase in the open market @ Rs. 101 each.			
"	"	Profit & Loss Account/Securities Premium Account	Dr.	1,000	
		To Loss on Redemption of Debentures Account			1,000
		Loss on redemption of debentures being written off by transfer to Profit & Loss Account or Securities Premium Account.			
(*ii*) 2005 Jan.	1	9% Debentures Account	Dr.	3,00,000	
		To Sundry Debentureholders			3,00,000
		Amount payable to Sundry debentureholders on redemption of debentures for Rs. 3,00,000 at par by draw of a lot.			
"	"	Sundry Debentureholders	Dr.	3,00,000	
		To Bank			3,00,000
		Payment made to Sundry debentureholders for redeeming debentures of Rs. 3,00,000 at par.			

				Rs.	Rs.
(iii) 2006 Jan.	1	Own Debentures	Dr.	1,97,800	
		To Bank			1,97,800
		Purchase of own debentures of the face value of Rs. 2,00,000 for Rs. 1,97,800.			
2007 Jan.	1	9% Debentures	Dr.	2,00,000	
		To Own Debentures			1,97,800
		To Profit on Cancellation of Own Debentures Account			2,200
		Cancellation of own debentures of the face value of Rs. 2,00,000 purchased last year for Rs. 1,97,800.			
"	"	Profit on Cancellation of Own Debentures Account	Dr.	2,200	
		To Capital Reserve Account			2,200
		Transfer of profit on cancellation of own debentures to capital reserve.			
(iv) 2010 Jan.	1	9% Debentures Account	Dr.	4,00,000	
		Premium on Redemption of Debentures Account	Dr.	8,000	
		To Sundry Debentureholders			4,08,000
		Amount payable to holders of debentures of the face value of Rs. 4,00,000 on redemption at a premium of 2% as per resolution no..............of the board of directors.			
"		Sundry Debentureholders	Dr.	4,08,000	
		To Bank			4,08,000
		Payment to sundry debentureholders.			
"	"	Securities Premium Account	Dr.	8,000	
		To Premium on Redemption of Debentures Account			8,000
		Utilisation of a part of the balance in Securities Premium Account to write off premium paid on redemption of debentures.			

Ex-interest price and cum-interest price. When debentures are purchased in the open market, a distinction has to be made between the capital portion and the revenue portion of the total amount paid for acquiring the debentures. The phrase 'cum interest price' is used to denote the total amount paid to the seller to acquire the debentures. If the interest accrued on purchased debentures from the previous date of payment of debenture - interest to the date of the transaction is deducted from the cum-interest price, we will get ex-interest price which is the capital portion of the total amount paid, the accrued interest being the revenue portion.

Suppose on 1st April, 2009 a joint stock company allots 10,000 12% Debentures of Rs. 100 each at par. Interest on debentures is payable half yearly on 30th September and 31st March. On 31st May, 2010 the company buys in the open market 100 of its 12% Debentures paying a total sum of Rs. 9,900 to the seller. Here, the total price paid per debenture is Rs. 99; it is the cum-interest quotation of the debentures purchased. The previous date of payment of debenture - interest was 31st March 2010. Interest accrued on one debenture of Rs. 100 from 31st March, 2010 to 31st May, 2010 the date of the transaction @ 12% per annum is Rs. 2. Hence, the ex-interest quotation of the debentures purchased is Rs. 99 - Rs. 2 = Rs. 97. For 100 debentures, the ex-interest price is Rs. 9,700.

Whatever may be the purpose of purchase of debentures in the open market, the accrued interest should be debited to Debentures, Interest Account. If debentures have been purchased for immediate cancellation, the ex-interest price should be compared with the face value of debentures purchased to ascertain the profit or loss on cancellation. If debentures have been purchased to be held as investments, the ex-interest price is debited to Investments in Own Debentures Account or simply

Own Debentures Account. On resale of own debentures also, a distinction between ex-interest price and cum-interest price has to be made. Cum interest price is the total amount realised. Interest accrued is credited to Interest on Own Debentures Account and the balance which is the ex-interest price is credited to Own Debentures Account. Ex-interest sale price is compared with the ex-interest purchase price to ascertain the profit or loss on resale of own debentures. On cancellation of own debentures ex-interest purchase price is compared with the face value of own debentures cancelled to ascertain the profit or loss on cancellation.

Entries concerning Own Debentures:

(1) When own debentures are purchased:

Own Debentures Account	Dr.	ex-interest price
Debentures Interest Account	Dr.	interest accrued
To Bank		cum interest price

(2) Every time interest on own debentures becomes due:

Debentures Interest Account	Dr.	with interest saved.
To Interest on Own Debentures Account		

At the end of every accounting year, Debentures Interest Account and Interest on Own Debentures Account will be transferred to Profit and Loss Account.

(3) When own debentures are resold:

(*i*)

Bank	Dr.	cum interest price
To Own Debentures Account		ex-interest price
To Interest on Own Debentures Account		interest accrued

(*ii*) Either

Own Debentures Account	Dr.	excess of ex-interest resale price over ex-interest purchase price
To Profit on Resale of Own Debentures Account		

Or

Loss on Resale of Own Debentures Account	Dr.	excess of ex-interest purchase price over ex-interest resale purchase price
To Own Debentures Account		

Profit on Resale of Own Debentures Account and Loss on Resale of Own Debentures Account represent revenue profit and revenue loss respectively and hence are closed by transfer to Profit and Loss Account.

(4) When own debentures are cancelled:

(*i*) If ex-interest purchase price of own debentures cancelled is less than their face value:

Debentures Account	Dr.	face value
To Own Debentures Account		ex-interest purchase price
To Profit on Cancellation of Own Debentures Account		excess of face value over ex-interest purchase price

Profit on Cancellation of Own Debentures Account represents a capital profit and should be transferred to Capital Reserve by means of the following entry:

Profit on Cancellation of Own Debentures Account	Dr.	
To Capital Reserve		

(*ii*) If ex-interest purchase price of own debentures cancelled is more than their face value:

Debentures Account	Dr.	face value
Loss on cancellation of Own Debentures Account	Dr.	excess of *ex*-interest purchase price over face value
To Own Debentures Account		ex-interest purchase price.

Loss on Cancellation of Own Debentures Account represents a capital loss and may be closed by transfer to Securities Premium Account or Profit & Loss Account by means of the following entry:

Securities Premium Account Dr.
Profit and Loss Account Dr.
To Loss on Cancellation of Own Debentures Account

On cancellation of own debentures, the following entry should also be passed with the interest accrued from the previous date of payment of debenture - interest to the date on which own debentures are cancelled :—

Debentures Interest Account Dr.
To Interest on Own Debentures Account

Illustration 47:

B Ltd. purchases for immediate cancellation 2,000 of its own 12% Debentures of Rs. 100 each on 1st December, 2009, the dates of interest being 31st March and 30th September.

Pass the necessary journal entries relating to the cancellation if

(*i*) debentures are purchased at Rs. 92 ex-interest.

(*ii*) debentures are purchased at Rs. 92 cum-interest.

Solution

Journal

Date		Particulars		L.F.	Dr. Rs.	Cr. Rs.
2009						
Dec.	1	12% Debentures Account	Dr.		2,00,000	
		Debentures Interest Account	Dr.		4,000	
		To Bank				1,88,000
		To Profit on Cancellation of Debentures Account				16,000
		Immediate cancellation of 2,000 12% Debentures purchased at Rs. 92 ex-interest, amount paid calculated as follows:- Ex-interest price = Rs. 92 × 2,000 = Rs. 1,84,000, Interest paid Rs. 4,000.				
"	"	Profit on Cancellation of Debentures Account	Dr.		16,000	
		To Capital Reserve Account				16,000
		Transfer of Profit on Cancellation of Debentures Account to Capital Reserve Account.				
(*ii*)						
2009						
Dec.	1	12% Debentures Account	Dr.		2,00,000	
		Debentures Interest Account	Dr.		4,000	
		To Bank				1,84,000
		To Profit on Cancellation of Debentures A/c				20,000
		Immediate cancellation of 2,000 12% Debentures purchased at Rs. 92 cum-interest.				
"	"	Profit on Cancellation of Debentures Account	Dr.		20,000	
		To Capital Reserve Account				20,000
		Transfer of Profit on Cancellation of Debentures Account to Capital Reserve Account.				

Illustration 48:

On 31st March, 2009 A Ltd.'s Balance Sheet showed 10,000 12% Debentures of Rs. 100 each outstanding. Interest on debentures is payable on 30th September and 31st March every year. On

1st August, 2009, the company purchased 500 of its own debentures as investment at Rs. 97 ex-interest.

Pass journal entries supposing:

(*a*) the company cancels all its own debentures on 1st March, 2010

(*b*) the company resells all its own debentures at Rs. 105 cum-interest on 1st March, 2010.

Solution:

Journal

Date		Particulars		Dr. Rs.	Cr. Rs.
2009 (*a*) Aug.	1	Own Debentures Account	Dr.	48,500	
		Debentures Interest Account	Dr.	2,000	
		To Bank			50,500
		Purchase of 500 of Own Debentures of Rs. 100 each at Rs. 97 ex-interest. Amount of interest paid being: Rs. 12/100 × 4/12 × 50,000 = Rs. 2,000.			
Sep.	30	Debentures Interest Account	Dr.	58,000	
		To Bank			57,000
		To Interest on Own Debentures Account			1,000
		Payment of half year's interest on 9,500 debentures and credit of 2 months' interest on 500 debentures to Interest on Own Debentures Account.			
2010 Mar.	1	12% Debentures Account	Dr.	50,000	
		To Own Debentures Account			48,500
		To Profit on Cancellation of Own Debentures Account			1,500
		Cancellation of 500 own debentures purchased earlier at Rs. 97 ex-interest.			
2010 Mar.	1	Profit on Cancellation of Own Debentures Account	Dr.	1,500	
		To Capital Reserve Account			1,500
		Transfer of Profit on Cancellation of Own Debentures Account to Capital Reserve Account.			
"	"	Debentures Interest Account	Dr.	2,500	
		To Interest on Own Debentures Account			2,500
		Interest accrued on 500 Own Debentures from the last date of payment of interest (30th September, 1999) to the date of cancellation of debentures (1st March, 2000).			
Mar.	31	Debentures Interest Account	Dr.	57,000	
		To Bank			57,000
		Payment of half yearly interest on 9,500 debentures in cash.			
"	"	Profit and Loss Account	Dr.	1,19,500	
		To Debentures Interest Account			1,19,500
		Transfer of Debentures Interest Account to Profit and Loss Account.			
"	"	Interest on Own Debentures Account	Dr.	3,500	
		To Profit and Loss Account			3,500
		Transfer of Interest on Own Debentures Account to Profit and Loss Account.			

(*ii*)				Rs.	Rs.
2010					
Mar.	1	Bank	Dr.	52,500	
		To Own Debentures Account			50,000
		To Interest on Own Debentures Account			2,500
		Resale of 500 Own Debentures at Rs. 105 cum-interest, ex-interest price being credited to Own Debentures Account and 5 months' interest to Interest on Own Debentures Account.			
"	"	Own Debentures Account	Dr.	1,500	
		To Profit on Resale of Own Debentures Account			1,500
		Profit on resale of Own Debentures being excess of ex-interest sale price over ex-interest purchase price transferred from Own Debentures Account to Profit on Resale of Own Debentures Account.			
"	"	Interest on Own Debentures Account	Dr.	2,500	
		Profit on Resale of Own Debentures Account	Dr.	1,500	
		To Profit and Loss Account			4,000
		Transfer of Interest on Own Debentures and Profit on Resale of Own Debentures Account to Profit and Loss Account.			

Illustration 49:

On 1st April, 2008 Sumitra Limited issued 25,000 12% Debentures of Rs. 100 each at par. According to the terms of the issue, interest was payable half yearly on 30th September and 31st March and the company reserved the right to buy any number of debentures in the open market to be held as investments or to be cancelled at any time.

During the accounting year ended 31st March, 2009 the company purchased 200 of its debentures at Rs. 102 cum- interest on 31 July, 2008 and 800 of its debentures at Rs. 99 ex-interest on 28th February, 2009.

On 30th June, 2009 the company sold one half of the debentures purchased on 28th February, 2009 at Rs. 104 cum-interest. On 30th November, 2009 the company purchased 1,500 debentures at Rs. 97.50 and on 31st December, 2009 it cancelled 600 debentures purchased in 2008-09 and still lying with it.

Pass journal entries for all the transactions relating to debentures for the accounting years 2008-09 and 2009-2010. Also prepare important ledger accounts. Ignore creation of debenture redemption reserve.

Solution:

Journal

				Dr.	Cr.
2008				Rs.	Rs
April	1	Bank	Dr.	25,00,000	
		To 12% Debentures Account			25,00,000
		Issue of 25,000 12% Debentures of Rs. 100 each at par.			
July	31	Own Debentures Account	Dr.	19,600	
		Debentures Interest Account	Dr.	800	
		To Bank			20,400
		Purchase of 200 of Own Debentures at Rs. 102 cum-interest.			
Sept.	30	Debentures Interest Account	Dr.	1,49,200	
		To Bank			1,48,800
		To Interest on Own Debentures Account			400
		Payment of half year's interest on 24,800 debentures and credit of 2 months' interest on 200 debentures to Interest on Own Debentures Account.			

Date		Particulars		Rs.	Rs.
2009					
Feb.	28	Own Debentures Account	Dr.	79,200	
		Interest Debentures Account	Dr.	4,000	
		To Bank			83,200
		Purchase of 800 debentures at Rs. 99 ex-interest.			
Mar.	31	Debentures Interest Account	Dr.	1,46,000	
		To Bank			1,44,000
		To Interest on Own Debentures Account			2,000
		Payment of half year's interest on 24,000 debentures in cash and credit of half year's interest on 200 debentures and one month's interest on 800 debentures to interest on Own Debentures Account.			
"	"	Profit and Loss Account	Dr.	3,00,000	
		To Debentures Interest Account			3,00,000
		Transfer of Debentures Interest Account to Profit and Loss Account.			
"	"	Interest on Own Debentures Account	Dr.	2,400	
		To Profit & Loss Account			2,400
		Transfer of Interest on Own Debentures Account to Profit and Loss Account.			
2009					
June	31	Bank	Dr.	41,600	
		To Own Debentures Account			40,400
		To Interest on Own Debentures Account			1,200
		Sale of 400 own debentures at Rs. 104 cum-interest.			
"	"	Own Debentures Account	Dr.	800	
		To Profit on Sale of Own Debentures Account			800
		Profit on sale of 400 own debentures.			
Sept.	31	Debentures Interest Account	Dr.	1,50,000	
		To Bank			1,46,400
		To Interest on Own Debentures Account			3,600
		Payment in cash six months' interest on 24,400 debentures and credit of 6 months' interest on 600 debentures to Interest on Own Debentures Account.			
Nov.	30	Own Debentures Account	Dr.	1,46,250	
		Debentures Interest Account	Dr.	3,000	
		To Bank			1,49,250
		Purchase of 1,500 debentures at Rs. 97.50 p. ex-interest.			
Dec.	31	12% Debentures Account	Dr.	60,000	
		To Own Debentures Account			59,200
		To Profit on Cancellation of Own Debentures			800
		Cancellation of 200 own debentures purchased at Rs. 98 ex-interest and 400 own debentures purchased at Rs. 99 ex-interest.			
"	"	Profit on Cancellation of Own Debentures Account	Dr.	800	
		To Capital Reserve Account			800
		Transfer of Profit on Cancellation of Own Debentures Account to Capital Reserve Account.			
"	"	Debentures Interest Account	Dr.	1,800	
		To Interest on Own Debentures Account			1,800
		Interest accured for 3 months on 600 own debentures cancelled.			

				Rs.	Rs.
2010 Mar.	31	Debentures Interest Account	Dr.	1,43,400	
		To Bank			1,37,400
		To Interest on Own Debentures Account			6,000
		Payment of 6 months' interest on 22,900 debentures in cash and credit of 4 months' interest on 1,500 debentures to Interest on Own Debentures Account.			
"	"	Profit and Loss Account	Dr.	2,98,200	
		To Debentures Interest Account			2,98,200
		Transfer of Debentures Interest Account and Profit & Loss Account.			
	"	Profit on Sale of Own Debentures Account	Dr.	1,200	
		Interest on Own Debentures Account	Dr.	12,600	
		To Profit & Loss Account			13,800
		Transfer of Profit on Sale of Own Debentures Account and Interest on Own Debentures Account to Profit and Loss Account.			

Ledger

Own Debentures Account

Dr.					Cr.
2008		Rs.	2009		Rs.
July 31	To Bank	19,600	Mar. 31	By Balance c/d	98,800
2009 Feb. 28	To Bank	79,200			
		98,800			98,800
2009			2009		
Apr. 1	To Balance b/d	98,800	June 30	By Bank	40,400
June 30	To Profit on Sale of Own Debentures Account	800	Dec. 31	By 12% Debentures Account	59,200
Nov. 30	To Bank	1,46,250	2010 Mar. 31	By Balance c/d	1,46,250
		2,45,850			2,45,850
2010 Apr. 1	To Balance b/d	1,46,250			

Interest on Own Debentures Account

		Rs.			Rs.
2009			2008		
Mar. 31	To Profit & Loss Account —transfer	2,400	Sept. 30	By Debentures Interest Account	400
			2009 Mar. 31	By Debentures Interest Account	2,000
		2,400			2,400
2010			2009		
Mar. 31	To Profit & Loss Account—transfer	12,600	June 30	By Bank	1,200
			Sept. 30	By Debentures Interest Account	3,600
			Dec. 31	By Debentures Interest Account	1,800
			2010 Mar. 31	By Debentures Interest Account	6,000
		12,600			12,600

Debentures Interest Account

Dr.					Cr.
2008		Rs.	2009		Rs.
July 31	To Bank	800	Mar. 31	By Profit & Loss Account—transfer	3,00,000
Sept. 30	To Bank	1,48,800			
" "	To Interest on Own Debentures Account	400			

Date	Particulars	Rs.	Date	Particulars	Rs.
2009					
Feb. 28	To Bank	4,000			
Mar.	To Bank	1,44,000			
" "	To Interest on Own Debentures Account	2,000			
		3,00,000			3,00,000
2009			2010		
Sept 30	To Bank	1,46,400	Mar. 31	By Profit & Loss Account—transfer	2,98,200
" "	To Interest on Own Debentures Account	3,600			
Nov. 30	To Bank	3,000			
Dec. 31	To Interest on Own Debentures Account	1,800			
2010					
Mar. 31	To Bank	1,37,400			
" "	To Interest on Own Debentures Account	6,000			
		2,98,200			2,98,200

12% Debentures Account

Date	Particulars	Rs.	Date	Particulars	Rs.
2009			2008		
Mar. 31	To Balance c/d	25,00,000	Apr. 1	By Bank	25,00,000
2009			2009		
Dec. 31	To Own Debentures	59,200	Apr. 1	By Balance b/d	25,00,000
" "	To Profit on cancellation of Own Debentures Account	800			
2010					
Mar. 31	To Balance c\d	24,40,000			
		25,00,000			25,00,000
			Apr. 1	By Balance b/d	24,40,000

Illustration 50:

The summarised balance sheet of Convertible Limited, as on 31st March, 2010 stood as follow:—

Liabilities:	Rs.
Share Capital: 5,00,000 equity shares of Rs. 10 each, fully paid	50,00,000
General Reserve	75,00,000
Debentures Redemption Fund	50,00,000
12.5% Convertible Debentures 1,00,000 Debentures of Rs. 100 each	1,00,00,000
Other Loans	50,00,000
Current Liabilities and Provisions	1,25,00,000
	4,50,00,000
Assets:	
Fixed Assets (at cost less depreciation)	1,60,00,000
Debenture Redemption Fund Investments	40,00,000
Cash and Bank Balances	50,00,000
Other Current Assets	2,00,00,000
	4,50,00,000

The debentures are due for redemption on 1st April, 2010. The terms of issue of debentures provided they were redeemable at a premium of 5% and also conferred option to the debenture-holders to convert 20% of their holding into equity shares at a predetermined price of Rs. 15.75 per share and receive the payment in cash for the remaining debentures.

Assuming that :-

(*i*) except for 100 debentureholders holding 25,000 debentures in all, the rest of them exercised the option for maximum conversion;

(*ii*) the investments realise Rs. 44 lakh on sale; and

(*iii*) all the transactions are put through, without any lag, on 1st April, 2010.

Redraft the balance sheet of the company as on 1st April, 2010 after giving effect to the redemption. Show your calculations in respect of the number of equity shares to be allotted and the cash payment necessary.

[*Adapted C.A.* (*Inter.*) *Nov. 1985*]

Solution:

Convertible Limited
Balance Sheet as on April 1, 2010

Liabilities	*Rs.*	*Assets*	*Rs.*
Share Capital:		*Fixed Assets:*	
6,00,000 Equity Shares of Rs. 10 each	60,00,000	Fixed Assets (at cost less depreciation)	1,60,00,000
Reserves & Surplus:		*Current Assets, Loans and Advances:*	
Securities Premium	75,000	(A) Current Assets	
General Reserve	1,29,00,000	Cash and Bank Balance	4,75,000
Unsecured loans		Other Current Assets	2,00,00,000
Sundary Loans	50,00,000	(B) Loans and Advances	Nil
Current Liabilities & Provisions	1,25,00,000		
	3,64,75,000		3,64,75,000

Working Notes:

(*i*) *Calculation of number of shares to be allotted:* Number of debentures opting for conversion = 1,00,000 – 25,000 = 75,000

As they are entitled to convert a maximum of 20% of the holding, the number of debentures to be converted into equity shares = 75,000 × 20/100 = 15,000

Amount for which equity shares are to be allotted to convert 15,000 debentures = Rs. 105 × 15,000 = Rs. 15,75,000. The predetermined price of one equity share being Rs. 15,75, the number of equity shares of Rs. 10 each to be allotted 15,75,000/15.75 = 1,00,000

(*ii*) *Cash to be paid:* Number of debentures left after conversion into equity shares 1,00,000 – 15,000 = 85,000

Amount to be paid to redeem them at a premium of 5% = Rs. 105 × 85,000 = 89,25,000

(*iii*)

Dr. **Cash Book (Bank Columns only)** *Cr.*

	Rs.		*Rs.*
To Balance b/fd	50,00,000	By Debentureholders Account	89,25,000
To Debenture Redemption Fund Investment	44,00,000	By Balance c/d	4,75,000
	94,00,000		94,00,000
To Balance b/d	4,75,000		

Dr. **General Reserve** *Cr.*

	Rs.		*Rs,*
To Balance c/d	1,29,00,000	By Balance b/fd	75,00,000
		By Debentures Redemption Fund	54,00,000
	1,29,00,000		1,29,00,000
		By Balance b/d	1,29,00,000

Securities Premium Account

Dr.	Rs.		Cr. Rs.
To Premium on Redemption of Debentures Account	5,00,000	By Bank	5,75,000
To Balance c/d	75,000		
	5,75,000		5,75,000
		By Balance b/d	75,000

Illustration 51:

(*i*) Swati Associates Ltd. has issued 10,000 12% Debentures of Rs. 100 each on 1.4.2007. These debentures are redeemable at par after 3 years. Interest is payable annually.

(*ii*) On January 1, 2009, it buys 1,500 debentures from the market at Rs. 98 per debenture. These are sold away on September 30, 2009 at Rs. 105 per debenture.

(*iii*) On April 1, 2009, it buys 1,000 debentures at Rs. 104. These are cancelled on July 1, 2009.

(*iv*) On January 1, 2010, it buys 2,000 debentures at Rs. 106. These debentures alongwith other debentures are redeemed on 31st March, 2010.

Pass Journal entries and prepare the relevant ledger accounts showing the above transactions. Ignore creation of debenture redemption reserve.

[*C.A. (Inter.) Nov. 1988, Modified*]

Solution:

Journal

Date		Particulars		Dr. Rs.	Cr. Rs.
2007 April	1	Bank	Dr.	10,00,000	
		To 12% Debentures Account			10,00,000
		Allotment of 10,000 12% Debentures of Rs. 100 each at par for cash.			
2008 March	31	Debenture Interest Account	Dr.	1,20,000	
		To Bank			1,20,000
		Payment of debenture interest @ 12% on 10,000 Debentures of Rs. 100 each.			
” ”	”	Profit & Loss Account	Dr.	1,20,000	
		To Debentures Interest Account			1,20,000
		Transfer of Debenture Interest Account to Profit & Loss Account.			
2009 Jan.	1	Own Debentures Account	Dr.	1,47,000	
		Debenture Interest Account	Dr.	13,500	
		To Bank			1,60,500
		Purchase of 1,500 own debentures from the open market, amount paid being calculated as follows:- Ex-interest price = Rs. 98 x 1,500 = Rs. 1,47,000; Interest paid = Rs. 1,50,000 $\times \frac{9}{12} \times \frac{12}{100}$ Rs. 13,500; Total = Rs. 1,60,500			
Mar.	31	Debenture Interest Account	Dr.	1,06,500	
		To Bank			1,02,000
		To Interest on Own Debentures Account			4,500
		Payment of yearly interest in cash on 8,500 debentures and credit given to Interest on Own Debentures Account for interest for 3 months (Jan. to March) in respect of 1,500 shares held by the company itself.			

Date		Particulars		Rs.	Rs.
Mar.	31	Profit and Loss Account	Dr.	1,20,000	
		To Debenture Interest Account			1,20,000
		Transfer of Debenture Interest Account to Profit and Loss Account.			
"	"	Interest on Own Debentures Account	Dr.	4,500	
		To Profit and Loss Account			4,500
		Transfer of Interest on Own Debentures Account to Profit and Loss Account.			
2009 April	1	Own Debentures Account	Dr.	1,04,000	
		To Bank			1,04,000
		Purchase of 1,000 debentures @ Rs. 104.			
July	1	12% Debentures Account	Dr.	1,00,000	
		Loss on Cancellation of Own Debentures Account	Dr.	4,000	
		To Own Debentures Account			1,04,000
		Cancellation of 1,000 own debentures of Rs. 100 each, purchased earlier @ Rs. 104.			
July	1	Debenture Interest Account	Dr.	3,000	
		To Interest on Own Debentures Account			3,000
		Interest accrued on 1,000 own debentures till the date of cancellation, Rs. 1,00,000 × 3 × 12/100 × 12 = Rs. 3,000.			
Sept.	30	Bank	Dr.	1,66,500	
		To Own Debentures Account			1,57,500
		To Interest on Own Debentures Account			9,000
		Resale of 1,500 own debentures, cash received being calculated as follows: Ex-interest price = Rs. 105 × 1,500 = Rs. 1,57,500 Interest received = Rs. $1,50,000 \times \frac{6}{12} \times \frac{12}{100}$ = Rs. 9,000 Total = Rs. 1,66,500			
2009 Sep.	30	Own Debentures Account	Dr.	10,500	
		To Profit on Resale of Own Debentures Account			10,500
		Excess of ex-interest sale price over ex-interest purchase price credited to Profit on Resale of Own Debentures Account; calculation being made as follows:- Sale Price = Rs. 105 × 1,500 = Rs. 1,57,500 Purchase Price = Rs. 98 × 1,500 = Rs. 1,47,000			
2010 Jan.	1	Own Debentures Account	Dr.	2,12,000	
		Debenture Interest Account	Dr.	18,000	
		To Bank			2,30,000
		Purchase of 2,000 debentures at Rs. 106 per debenture from the open market, interest paid for 9 months calculated as follows : Rs. 2,00,000 × 9 × 12/100 × 12 = Rs. 18,000			
Mar.	31	12% Debentures Account	Dr.	2,00,000	
		Loss on Cancellation of Own Debentures Account	Dr.	12,000	
		To Own Debentures Account			2,12,000
		Cancellation of 2,000 own debentures of Rs. 100 each, earlier purchased at Rs. 106 each.			
"	"	Debenture Interest Account	Dr.	6,000	
		To Interest on Own Debentures Account			6,000
		Interest accrued on 2,000 debentures since the date of purchase to the date of cancellation i.e., for 3 months Rs. 2,00,000 × 3 × 12/100 × 12 = Rs. 6,000			

Date		Particulars		Rs.	Rs.
2010					
Mar.	31	Debenture Interest Account	Dr.	84,000	
		To Bank			84,000
		Interest paid in cash for one year in respect of 7,000 debentures of Rs. 100 each @ 12%.			
"	"	12% Debentures Account	Dr.	5,50,000	
		To Bank			5,50,000
		Redemption of 5,500 debentures of Rs. 100 each at par.			
"	"	Profit and Loss Account	Dr.	1,27,000	
		To Debenture Interest Account			1,11,000
		To Loss on Cancellation of Own Debentures Account			16,000
		Transfers.			
"	"	Profit on Resale of Own Debentures Account	Dr.	10,500	
		Interest on Own Debentures Account	Dr.	18,000	
		To Profit & Loss Account			28,500
		Transfers.			

12% Debentures Account

Dr. *Cr.*

Date	Particulars	Rs.	Date	Particulars	Rs.
2008 Mar. 31	To Balance c/d	10,00,000	2007 April 1	By Bank	10,00,000
2009 Mar. 31	To Balance c/d	10,00,000	2008 April 1	By Balance b/d	10,00,000
2009 July 1	To Own Debentures	1,00,000	2009 April 1	By Balance b/d	10,00,000
2010 Mar. 31	To Own debentures	2,00,000			
" "	To Bank	7,00,000			
		10,00,000			10,00,000

Debenture Interest Account

Dr. *Cr.*

Date	Particulars	Rs.	Date	Particulars	Rs.
2008 Mar. 31	To Bank	1,20,000	2008 Mar. 31	By Profit & Loss Account (transfer)	1,20,000
2009 Jan. 1	To Bank	13,500	2009 Mar. 31	By Profit & Loss Account (transfer)	1,20,000
Mar. 31	To Bank	1,02,000			
" "	To Interest on Own Debentures Account	4,500			
		1,20,000			1,20,000
2009 July 1.	To Interest on Own Debentures Account	3,000	2010 Mar 31	By Profit & Loss Account (transfer)	1,11,000
2010 Jan. 1	To Bank	18,000			
Mar. 31	To Interest on Own Debentures Account	6,000			
" "	To Bank	84,000			
		1,11,000			1,11,000

Profit & Loss Account (Extracts)

Dr.					Cr.
2008		Rs.			Rs.
Mar. 31	To Debenture Interest Account	1,20,000			
2009			2009		
Mar. 31	To Debenture Interest Account	1,20,000	Mar. 31	By Interest on Own Debentures Account	4,500
2010			2010		
Mar. 31	To Debenture Interest Account	1,11,000	Mar. 31	By Profit on Resale of Own Debentures Account	10,500
" "	To Loss on Cancellation of of Own Debentures Account	16,000	" "	By Interest on Own Debentures Account	18,000

Own Debentures Account

Dr.					Cr.
2009		Rs.	2009		Rs.
Jan. 1	To Bank	1,47,000	Mar. 31	By Balance c/d	1,47,000
April 1	To Balance b/d	1,47,000	July 1	By 12% Debentures Account	1,00,000
" "	To Bank	1,04,000			
Sept. 30	To Profit on Resale of Own Debentures Account	10,500	" "	By Loss on Cancellation of Own Debentures Account	4,000
2010					
Jan. 1	To Bank	2,12,000	Sept. 30	By Bank	1,57,500
			2010		
			Mar. 31	By 12% Debentures Account	2,00,000
			" "	By Loss on Cancellation of Own Debentures Account	12,000
		4,73,500			4,73,500

Interest on Own Debentures Account

Dr.					Cr.
2009		Rs.	2009		Rs.
Mar. 31	To Profit & Loss Account-transfer	4,500	Mar. 31	By Debenture Interest Account	4,500
2010			2009		
Mar. 31	To Profit & Loss Account-transfer	18,000	July 1	By Debenture Interest Account	3,000
			Sept. 30	By Bank	9,000
			2010		
			Mar. 31	By Debenture Interest Account	6,000
		18,000			18,000

Loss on Cancellation of Own Debentures Account

Dr.					Cr.
2009		Rs.	2010		Rs.
July 1	To Own Debentures Account	4,000	Mar 31	By Profit & Loss Account-transfer	16,000
2010					
Mar. 31	To Own Debentures	12,000			
		16,000			16,000

Profit on Resale of Own Debentures Account

Dr.					Cr.
2010		Rs.	2009		Rs.
Mar. 31	To Profit & Loss Account-transfer	10,500	Sept. 30	By Own Debentures Account	10,500

Convertible Debentures. Holders of convertible debentures enjoy the option of getting the debentures held by them converted into shares according to the term of the issue. To issue convertible debentures, a company requires the consent of its shareholders by special resolution and that of the Central Government so that at the time of conversion of debentures into shares, the provisions of section 81 of the Companies Act are not attracted which require that a fresh issue of shares must first be offered to the existing equity shareholders.

Debentures issued at a discount cannot be converted into fully paid shares of the same face value without undergoing the procedure for issue of shares at a discount prescribed by section 79 of the Companies Act. But it would be legal to issue shares in lieu of debentures with a paid up value equal to the amount actually received on debentures. For example a debenture of Rs. 100 issued at a discount of 10% can be converted into a share of Rs. 100, Rs. 90 paid up or into 9 fully paid up shares of Rs. 10 each. It does not involve issue of shares at a discount because in both cases the paid up value of share or shares issued in lieu of a debenture is the same as the amount actually received on a debenture.

Illustration 52:

On 1st July, 2007, Ispat Limited issued 10,000 9% Mortgage Debentures of Rs. 150 each at par, the interest being payable half yearly on 1st January and 1st July. According to the terms of the issue, the debentureholders had the option of getting the debentures converted into equity shares of Rs. 100 each at a premium of Rs. 50 each on 1st January, 2010. The company had the right to buy at any time its debentures in the open market for cancellation.

On 1st May, 2008 the company purchased 1,000 debentures at Rs. 148 cum-interest and on 1st November, 2009 it purchased 1,500 debentures at Rs. 146 ex-interest; the debentures being cancelled immediately in both the cases. On 1st January, 2010 holders of 4,100 debentures exercised their option, getting their debentures converted into equity shares.

The company closed its books of account every year on 31st March. You are required to show journal entries for all the transactions relating to debentures during 2007-08, 2008-09 and 2009-2010. Also show the relevant portions of the 'Liabilities' side of the balance sheet of the company as on 31st March, 2010.

Solution:

Journal

Date		Particulars		Dr. Rs.	Cr. Rs.
2007 July	1	Bank	Dr.	15,00,000	
		To 9% Mortgage Debentures			15,00,000
		Allotment of 10,000 9% Debentures of Rs. 150 each at par.			
2008 Jan	1	Debentures Interest Account	Dr.	67,500	
		To Bank			67,500
		Payment on interest for 6 months on Rs. 15,00,000 @ 9% per annum.			
Mar.	31	Debentures Interest Account	Dr.	33,750	
		To Accrued Debentures Interest Account			33,750
		Accrued interest on Debentures for 3 months.			
Mar.	31	Profit & Loss Account	Dr.	1,01,250	
		To Debentures Interest Account			1,01,250
		Transfer of Interest on Debentures Account to Profit and Loss Account at the end of the accounting year.			

Date		Particulars		Rs.	Rs.
2008 May	1	9% Mortgage Debentures Account	Dr.	1,50,000	
		Accrued Debentures Interest Account	Dr.	3,375	
		Debentures Interest Account	Dr.	1,125	
		To Bank			1,48,000
		To Capital Reserve			6,500
		Cancellation of debentures of the face value of Rs. 1,50,000 by purchase in the open market for a total cum-interest price of Rs. 1,48,000 which included accrued interest for 3 months Rs. 3,375 for 2007-08 and accrued interest for 1 month Rs. 1,125 for April, 2008; the profit on cancellation being credited to Capital Reserve.			
July	1	Accrued Debentures Interest Account	Dr.	30,375	
		Debentures Interest Account	Dr.	30,375	
		To Bank			60,750
		Payment of interest on debentures of Rs. 13,50,000 for 6 months-3 months of 2007-08 and 3 months of 2008-09.			
2009 Jan	1	Debentures Interest Account	Dr.	60,750	
		To Bank			60,750
		Payment of interest.			
Mar.	31	Debentures Interest Account	Dr.	30,375	
		To Accrued Debentures Interest Account			30,375
		Accrued interest.			
Mar.	31	Profit & Loss Account	Dr.	1,22,625	
		To Debentures Interest Account			1,22,625
		Transfer.			
July	1	Accrued Debentures Interest Account	Dr.	30,375	
		Debentures Interest Account	Dr.	30,375	
		To Bank			60,750
		Payment of interest for 3 months of 2008-09 and 3 months of 2009-2010.			
Nov.	1	9% Mortgage Debentures Account	Dr.	2,25,000	
		Debentures Interest Account	Dr.	6,750	
		To Bank			2,25,750
		To Capital Reserve			6,000
		Cancellation of debentures of the face value of Rs. 2,25,000 by purchase for an ex-interest price of Rs. 2,19,000 and Rs. 6,750 for interest for 4 months - profit on cancellation being credited to Capital Reserve.			
2010 Jan	1	Debentures Interest Account	Dr.	50,625	
		To Bank			50,625
		Payment of interest for 6 months on Rs. 11,25,000.			
"	"	9% Mortgage Debentures Account	Dr.	6,15,000	
		To Equity Share Capital Account			4,10,000
		To Securities Premium Account			2,05,000
		Conversion of Rs. 4,100 debentures of Rs. 150 each into 4,100 equity shares of Rs. 100 each issued at a premium of 50%.			
Mar.	31	Debentures Interest Account	Dr.	11,475	
		To Accrued Debentures Interest Account			11,475
		Accrued interest on debentures of Rs. 5,10,000 for 3 months @ 9% per annum.			
"	"	Profit & Loss Account	Dr.	99,225	
		To Debentures Interest Account			99,225
		Transfer of Interest on Debentures Account to Profit and Loss Account at the end of the accounting year.			

Balance Sheet (Liabilities Side) of Ispat Limited as on 31st March, 2010

	Rs.
Share Capital:	
4,100 Equity Shares of Rs. 100 each	4,10,000
Reserves and Surplus:	
Capital Reserve	12,500
Securities Premium	2,05,000
Secured Loans:	
9% Mortgage Debentures	5,10,000
Current Liabilities:	
Accrued Debentures Interest	11,475

Working Notes:

Dr. **Debentures Interest Account** *Cr.*

Date	Particulars	Rs.	Date	Particulars	Rs.
2008			2008		
Jan 1	To Bank	67,500	Mar. 31	By Profit & Loss Account-transfer	1,01,250
Mar. 31	To Accrued Debentures Interest	33,750			
		1,01,250			1,01,250
2008			2009		
May. 1	To Bank	1,125	Mar. 31	By Profit & Loss Account-transfer	1,22,625
July 1	To Bank	30,375			
2009					
Jan. 1	To Bank	60,750			
Mar. 31	To Accrued Debentures Interest	30,375			
		1,22,625			1,22,625
2009			2010		
July 1	To Bank	30,375	Mar. 31	By Profit & Loss Account-transfer	99,225
Nov. 1	To Bank	6,750			
2010					
Jan. 1	To Bank	50,625			
Mar. 31	To Accrued Debentures Interest	11,475			
		99,225			99,225

9% Mortgage Debentures Account

Date	Particulars	Rs.	Date	Particulars	Rs.
2008			2007		
Mar. 31	To Balance c/d	15,00,000	April 1	By Bank	15,00,000
			2008		
May 1	To Bank	1,43,500	Apr. 1	By Balance b/d	15,00,000
" "	To Capital Reserve	6,500			
2009					
Mar. 31	To Balance c/d	13,50,000			
		15,00,000			15,00,000
2009			2009		
Oct 1	To Bank	2,19,000	Apr. 1	By Balance b/d	13,50,000
" "	To Capital Reserve	6,000			
2010					
Jan. 1	To Equity Share Capital Account	4,10,000			
	To Securities Premium Account	2,05,000			
" "	To Balance c/d	5,10,000			
Mar. 31		13,50,000			13,50,000
			2010		
			Apr. 1	By Balance b/d	5,10,000

Interest accrued on 31st March, 2008 = $\frac{\text{Rs. } 15{,}00{,}000 \times 3 \times 9}{100 \times 12}$ = Rs. 33,750

Interest accrued on 31st March, 2009 = $\frac{\text{Rs. } 13{,}50{,}000 \times 3 \times 9}{100 \times 12}$ = Rs. 30,375

Interest accrued on 31st March, 2010 = $\frac{\text{Rs. } 5{,}10{,}000 \times 3 \times 9}{100 \times 12}$ = Rs. 11,475

Accrued interest on Rs. 1,50,000 for 3 months = $\frac{\text{Rs. } 1{,}50{,}000 \times 3 \times 9}{100 \times 12}$ = Rs. 3,375

Accrued interest on Rs. 1,50,000 for 1 month = $\frac{\text{Rs. } 3375}{3}$ = Rs. 1,125

Cum-interest price of 1,000 debentures = Rs. 148 × 1000 = Rs. 1,48,000
Ex-interest price of 1,000 debentures = Rs. 1,48,000 – Rs. 3,375 – Rs. 1,125 = Rs. 1,43,500
Capital profit on cancellation of 1,000 debentures = Rs. 1,50,000 – Rs. 1,43,500 = Rs. 6,500
Ex-interest price of 1,500 debentures = Rs. 146 × 1500 = Rs. 2,19,000
Capital profit on cancellation of 1,500 debentures = Rs. 2,25,000 – Rs. 2,19,000 = Rs. 6,000

Illustration 53.

Libra Limited made a public issue in respect of which the following information is available:

(*a*) Number of partly convertible debentures issued 2,00,000; face value and issue price Rs. 100 per debenture.

(*b*) Convertible porition per debenture 60%, date of conversion on expiry of 6 months from the date of allotment.

(*c*) Date of closure of subscription lists 1.5.2009, date of allotment 1.6.2009, rate of interest on debentures 12% payable from the date of allotment, value of equity share for the purpose of conversion Rs. 60 (Face value, Rs. 10).

(*d*) Underwriting commission @ 2% on the amount devolving on the underwriters and @ 1% on the amount subscribed for by the public.

(*e*) Number of debnetures applied for 1,50,000.

(*f*) Interest payable on debentures half-yearly on 30th September and 31st March.

Write relevant journal entries for all transactions arising out of the above during the year ended 31st March, 2010 (including cash and bank entries). [*C.A.* (*Inter.*) *May, 1995 Modified*]

Solution:

Journal

			Dr.	*Cr.*
2009			*Rs. '000*	*Rs. '000*
May	1	Bank Dr.	15,000	
		To 15% Debenture Application & Allotment Account		
		Application money received on 1,50,000 15% debentures @ Rs. 100 per debenture.		
June	1	15% Debenture Applications & Allotment Account Dr.	15,000	
		Underwriters Dr.	50,000	
		To 15% Debentures Account		20,000
		Allotment of 1,50,000 15% debentures to applicants and 50,000 15% debentures to underwriters.		
"	"	Underwriting Commission Account Dr.	2,50	
		To Underwriters		2,50
		Commission @2% on Rs. 50,00,000 the amount devolving on the underwriters and @1% on Rs. 1,50,00,000, the amount subscribed for by the public.		

				Rs.	Rs.
June	1	Bank Dr.		47,50	
		To Underwriters			47,50
		Amount received from underwriters in settlement of account			
Sept.	30	Interest on Debentures Account Dr.		8,00	
		To Bank			8,00
		Interest paid on debentures for 4 months @ 12% per annum on Rs. 2 crore			
Dec.	1	15% Debentures Account Dr.		1,20,00	
		To Equity Shares Capital Account			20,00
		To Securities Premium Account			1,00,00
		Conversion of 60% of the amount of debentures into shares of 60 each with a face value of Rs. 10 each.			
2010					
Mar.	31	Interest on Debentures Account Dr.		7,20	
		To Bank			7,20
		Interest paid on debentures for half year, calculated as follows: On Rs. 80 lakh for 6 months = Rs. 4,80,000 On Rs. 120 lakh for 2 months = Rs. 2,40,000 Rs. 7,20,000			

Sinking Fund for Redemption of Debentures. A sinking fund may be created to collect funds for redemption of debentures after their specified life. It enables the company to redeem the debentures without upsetting its working capital. With the help of Sinking Fund Tables, an amount to be set aside every year out of the profits of the company is ascertained. The annual instalment is invested in some safe securities. The interest received on investments is also invested. When debentures are to be redeemed, the investments are sold out to provide cash for redemption.

Entries in the case of a sinking fund for redemption of debentures are as follows:-

At the end of the first year :

(*i*) Profit and Loss Appropriation Account Dr. — with annual instalment ascertained with the help of Sinking Fund Tables
To Debenture Redemption Fund

(*ii*) Debenture Redemption Fund Investments Account Dr. — with the amount of investments made
To Bank

In each one of the subsequent years (except the last year);

(*i*) Bank Dr. — with the amount of interest received on investments
To Interest on Debenture Redemption Fund Investments Account

(*ii*) Interest on Debenture Redemption Fund Investments Account Dr. — Transfer of interest received to Sinking Fund
To Debenture Redemption Fund Account

(*iii*) Profit & Loss Appropriation Account Dr. — with annual instalment
To Debenture Redemption Fund

(*iv*) Debenture Redemption Fund Investments Account Dr. — with the amount invested
To Bank

In the last year:

(*i*) Bank Dr. — with interest received
To Interest on Debenture Redemption Fund

Investments Account

(*ii*)	Interest on Debenture Redemption Fund Investments Account To Debenture Redemption Fund Account	Dr.	Transfer of interest received
(*iii*)	Profit & Loss Appropriation Account To Debenture Redemption Fund Account	Dr.	with annual instalment
(*iv*)	Bank To Debenture Redemption Fund Investments Account	Dr.	with sale process of all the investments
(*v*)	*Either* Debenture Redemption Fund Investments Account To Debenture Redemption Fund Account	Dr.	Transfer of profit on sale of investments
	Or Debenture Redemption Fund To Debenture Redemption Fund Investments Account	Dr.	Transfer of loss on sale of investments
(*vi*)	Debenture Redemption Fund Account To General Reserve	Dr.	Transfer of balance in Debenture Redemption Fund Account to General Reserve after redemption of debentures.

In the abovementioned scheme of entries, Debenture Redemption Fund Account, Debenture Redemption Fund Investments Account and Interest on Debenture Redemption Fund Investments Account may be named Sinking Fund Account, Sinking Fund Investments Account and Interest on Sinking Fund Investments Account respectively. Then, the scheme may be used to collect funds to repay any liability. The scheme is similar to the Depreciation Fund (discussed in the chapter on Depreciation) which is a sinking fund to replace a wasting asset.

Distinction between Sinking Fund to replace a wasting asset and one to repay a liability.

A sinking fund can be raised to collect funds either to replace a wasting asset or to repay a liability. But there are the following points of distinction between the two :—

(*i*) *Revenue Expense v. Appropriation of Profits :* In the case of sinking fund to replace a wasting asset, the annual instalment is really depreciation on the wasting asset and hence is a charge against profits. Consequently, the annual instalment is debited to Profit and Loss Account. On the other hand, in the case of a sinking fund to repay a liability, the annual instalment is an appropriation of profits and hence is debited to Profit and Loss Appropriation Account. It is setting aside a part of profits to be used for repayment of a liability. Thus, while Depreciation Fund represents accumulated depreciation on a wasting asset, Fund created for the repayment of a liability like Debenture Redemption Fund represents profits set aside gradually to repay a liability.

(*ii*) *Use of sale proceeds of investments :* In the case of the sinking fund for the replacement of a wasting asset, the sale proceeds of sinking fund investments are used to buy a new asset to replace the wasting asset while in the case of the sinking fund for the repayment of a liability, the sale proceeds of sinking fund investments are used to pay off the liability.

(*iii*) *Disposal of the balance of Sinking Fund :* In the case of the sinking fund for the replacement of a wasting asset, Depreciation Fund's credit balance is used to write off the debit balance of the asset which is to be replaced. In the case of a sinking fund for the repayment of a liability, after the liability has been paid off, the sinking fund's balance is transferred to general reserve which can be used to meet any losses or even to pay dividends.

Special points regarding sinking fund for redemption of debentures : The following points should be kept in mind while operating a sinking fund for redemption of debentures :

(*i*) If the terms of the issue of debentures lay down that the debentures will be redeemed at a premium, the amount to be collected by means of sinking fund must include the amount of the premium payable on redemption.

(*ii*) If investments are made in bonds, debentures or other securities available at a certain price, it may not be possible to invest exactly the same amount as is the balance of Sinking Fund because securities can be purchased only in whole numbers. In such a case, there may be over-investment or under-investment. But such a number of securities must be purchased as to keep the balance of Sinking Fund Investments Account as near as possible to the balance of Sinking Fund.

(*iii*) The face value and market price of securities may differ. In such a case, it must be remembered that interest on securities will be received on the face value and not on the market value.

(*iv*) If debentures are redeemed in instalments, as and when debentures are redeemed, the face value of debentures redeemed (plus premium payable, if any, on redemption according to the terms of the issue) should be transferred from Sinking Fund to General Reserve. When all the debentures have been redeemed, the balance of Sinking Fund should be transferred to General Reserve.

Illustration 54:

On 1st April, 2006, Old Guards Limited issued 12% Debentures for Rs. 5,00,000 at par redeemable at a premium of 2% after four years on 31st March, 2010. To collect funds for redemption, the company decided to establish a Sinking Fund; investments which were to be made to the nearest rupee were to earn interest @ 10% per annum. Sinking Fund Tables show that Re. 0.2155 invested every year for four years @ 10% per annum will accumulate Re. 1.

On 31st March, 2010 the investments were sold at a loss of 1% and the debentures were duly redeemed.

Give journal entries and ledger accounts for the four accounting years ended 31st March, 2010. Entries relating to interest on debentures and for writing off Loss on Issue of Debentures Account need not be presented. All calculations may be made to the nearest rupee.

Solution:

Amount to be collected for redemption:	
Par value of debentures	Rs. 5,00,000
Add: Premium @ 2% payable on redemption	Rs. 10,000
Total	Rs. 5,10,000

Annual instalment = Rs. 5,10,000 x 0.2155 = Rs. 1,09,905

Journal

				Dr.	Cr.
2006				Rs.	Rs.
April	1	Bank	Dr.	5,00,000	
		Loss on Issue of Debentures Account	Dr.	10,000	
		To 12% Debentures Account			5,00,000
		To Premium on Redemption of Debentures Account			10,000
		Issue of 12% Debentures of the face value of Rs. 5,00,000 at par redeemable at a premium of 2%.			
2007					
March	31	Profit & Loss Appropriation Account	Dr.	1,09,905	
		To Debenture Redemption Fund			1,09,905
		Annual instalment needed to build up a sinking fund of Rs. 5,10,000 in four years.			
"	"	Debenture Redemption Fund Investments Account	Dr.	1,09,905	
		To Bank			1,09,905
		Investment of the Debenture Redemption Fund.			

Date		Particulars		Rs.	Rs.
2008 March	31	Bank	Dr.	10,991	
		To Interest on Debenture Redemption Fund Investment Account			10,991
		Receipt of interest @ 10% per annum on Rs. 1,09,905.			
"	"	Interest on Debenture Redemption Fund Investments Account	Dr.	10,991	
		To Debenture Redemption Fund			10,991
		Transfer of interest received to Debenture Redemption Fund.			
"	"	Profit & Loss Appropriation Account	Dr.	1,09,905	
		To Debenture Redemption Fund			1,09,905
		Annual instalment credited to Debenture Redemption Fund.			
"	"	Debenture Redemption Fund Investments Account	Dr.	1,20,896	
		To Bank			1,20,896
		Investment of the annual instalment and the interest received during the year.			
2009 March	31	Bank	Dr.	23,080	
		To Interest on Debenture Redemption Fund Investments Account			23,080
		Interest received on total investment of Rs. 2,30,801.			
"	"	Interest on Debenture Redemption Fund Investments Account	Dr.	23,080	
		To Debenture Redemption Fund			23,080
		Transfer of interest to Debenture Redemption Fund.			
"	"	Profit and Loss Appropriation Account	Dr.	1,09,905	
		To Debenture Redemption Fund			1,09,905
		Annual instalment credited to Debenture Redemption Fund.			
"	"	Debenture Redemption Fund Investments Account	Dr.	1,32,985	
		To Bank			1,32,985
		Investment of the annual instalment and the interest received during the year.			
2010 March	31	Bank	Dr.	36,379	
		To Interest on Debenture Redemption Fund Investments Account			36,379
		Receipt of interest on total investments of Rs. 3,63,786 @ 10%.			
"	"	Interest on Debenture Redemption Fund Investments Account	Dr.	36,379	
		To Debenture Redemption Fund			36,379
		Interest received transferred to Debenture Redemption Fund.			
"	"	Profit and Loss Appropriation Account	Dr.	1,09,905	
		To Debenture Redemption Fund			1,09,905
		Annual instalment credited to Debenture Redemption Fund.			
2010 March	31	Bank	Dr.	3,60,148	
		To Debenture Redemption Fund Investments Account			3,60,148
		Sale proceeds of investment.			
"	"	Debenture Redemption Fund	Dr.	3,638	
		To Debenture Redemption Fund Investments Account			3,638
		Transfer of loss on sale of investments to Debenture Redemption Fund.			
"	"	12% Debentures Account	Dr.	5,00,000	
		Premium on Redemption of Debentures Account	Dr.	10,000	
		To Sundry Debentureholders			5,10,000
		Payment to be made to Sundry Debenture holders to redeem 12% Debentures of the face value of Rs. 5,00,000 at a premium of 2%.			

Date		Particulars		L.F.	Rs.	Rs.
2010						
March	31					
"	"	Sundry Debenture-holders	Dr.		5,10,000	
		To Bank				5,10,000
		Payment made to sundry debenture-holders.				
"	"	Debenture Redemption Fund	Dr.		5,06,432	
		To General Reserve				5,06,432
		Transfer of balance of Debenture Redemption Fund to General Reserve after redemption of debentures.				

Ledger

Dr. 12% Debentures Account Cr.

Date	Particulars	Rs.	Date	Particulars	Rs.
2007			2006		
March 31	To Balance c/d	5,00,000	April 1	By Bank	5,00,000
2008			2007		
March 31	To Balance c/d	5,00,000	April 1	By Balance b/d	5,00,000
2009			2008		
March 31	To Balance c/d	5,00,000	April 1	By Balance b/d	5,00,000
2010			2009		
March 31	To Sundry Debentureholders	5,00,000	April 1	By Balance b/d	5,00,000

Dr. Premium on Redemption of Debentures Account Cr.

Date	Particulars	Rs.	Date	Particulars	Rs.
2007			2006		
March 31	To Balance c/d	10,000	April 1	By Loss on Issue of Debentures Account	10,000
2008			2007		
March 31	To Balance c/d	10,000	April 1	By Balance b/d	10,000
2009			2008		
March 31	To Balance c/d	10,000	April 1	By Balance b/d	10,000
2010			2009		
March 31	To Sundry Debentureholders	10,000	April 1	By Balance b/d	10,000

Dr. Debenture Redemption Fund Cr.

Date	Particulars	Rs.	Date	Particulars	Rs.
2007			2007		
March 31	To Balance c/d	1,09,905	Mar. 31	By Profit and Loss Appropriation Account	1,09,905
2008			2007		
March 31	To Balance c/d	2,30,801	April 1	By Balance b/d	1,09,905
			2008		
			Mar. 31	By Interest on D.R.F. Investments	10,991
			Mar. 31	By Profit and Loss Appropriation Account	1,09,905
		2,30,801			2,30,801
2009			2008		
March 31	To Balance c/d	3,63,786	April 1	By Balance b/d	2,30,801
			2009		
			Mar. 31	By Interest on D.R.F. Investments Account	23,080
			" "	By Profit and Loss Appropriation Account	1,09,905
		3,63,786			3,63,786

		Rs.			Rs.
2010			2009		
March 31	To D.R.F. Investments Account	3,638	April 1	By Balance b/d	3,63,786
	To General Reserve – Transfer	5,06,432	2010	By Interest on D.R.F.	
			Mar. 31	Investments Account	36,379
			" "	By Profit and Loss Appropriation Account	1,09,905
		5,10,070			5,10,070

Debenture Redemption Fund Investment Account

		Rs.			Rs.
2007			2007		
Mar. 1	To Bank	1,09,905	Mar. 31	By Balance c/d	1,09,905
2007			2008		
April 1	To Balance b/d	1,09,905	Mar. 31	By Balance c/d	2,30,801
2008					
March 31	To Bank	1,20,896			
		2,30,801			2,30,801
2008			2009		
April 1	To Balance b/d	2,30,801	Mar. 31	By Balance c/d	3,63,786
2009					
March 31	To Bank	1,32,985			
		3,63,786			3,63,786
2009			2010		
April 1	To Balance b/d	3,63,786	Mar. 31	By Bank	3,60,148
				By Debentures Redemption Fund-transfer of loss	3,638
		3,63,786			3,63,786

Interest on Debenture Redemption Fund Investment Account

		Rs.			Rs.
2008			2008		
March 31	To Debenture Redemption Fund— transfer	10,991	Mar. 31	By Bank	10,991
2009			2009		
March 31	To Debenture Redemption Fund— Transfer	23,080	Mar. 31	By Bank	23,080
2010			2010		
March 31	To Debenture Redemption Fund— Transfer	36,379	Mar. 31	By Bank	36,379

Sundry Debentureholders Account

		Rs.			Rs.
2010			2010		
March 31	To Bank	5,10,000	Mar. 31	By Debentures	5,00,000
			" "	By Premium on Redemption of Debentures Account	10,000
		5,10,000			5,10,000

Illustration 55:

The following was the balance sheet of Brite Ltd. as on 31st March, 2010 :

Liabilities	Rs.	Assets	Rs.
7,500 Equity Shares of Rs. 100 each, fully paid	7,50,000	Fixed Assets	7,80,000
2,000 15% Preference Shares of Rs. 100 each, fully paid	2,00,000	Debenture Redemption Fund Investments	88,500
General Reserve	6,30,000	Stock	6,00,800
Profit and Loss Account	50,000	Debtors	2,60,700
Debenture Redemption Fund	88,480	Cash at Bank	3,00,000
12% Debentures	1,00,000		
Sundry Creditors	2,11,520		
	20,30,000		20,30,000

On this date, the company redeemed at a premium of 5% all its preference shares and debentures. For the purpose, it sold all the investments at Rs. 90,000 and allotted to its existing equity shareholders 1,500 equity shares of Rs. 100 each at par, the entire amount being received forthwith.

After the redemption of preference shares and debentures, the company issued one fully paid bonus share of Rs. 100 for every three shares held. Show journal entries for all the above-mentioned transactions including cash transactions and prepare the balance sheet thereafter.

[*Adapted, B.Com. (Hons.) Delhi, 1989*]

Solution:

Journal

Date		Particulars		Dr. Rs.	Cr. Rs.
2010 March	31	Bank	Dr.	90,000	
		To Debenture Redemption Fund Investments Account			90,000
		Sale proceeds of D.R.F. Investments.			
"	"	Debenture Redemption Fund Investments Account	Dr.	1,500	
		To Debenture Redemption Fund Account			1,500
		Transfer of profit on sale of investments from Debenture Redemption Fund Investments Account to Debenture Redemption Fund Account.			
"	"	Bank	Dr.	1,50,000	
		To Equity Share Applications & Allotment Account			1,50,000
		Receipt from existing shareholders total amount for 1,500 equity shares @ Rs. 100 each.			
"	"	Equity Share Applications and Allotment Account	Dr.	1,50,000	
		To Equity Share Capital Account			1,50,000
		Allotment of 1,500 equity shares of Rs. 100 each at par to existing shareholders.			
"	"	General Reserve	Dr.	50,000	
		To Capital Redemption Reserve			50,000
		Creation of Capital Redemption Reserve for redemption of preference shares for the amount not covered by fresh issue of equity shares.			
"	"	Debenture Redemption Fund	Dr.	5,000	
		To Premium on Redemption of 12% Debentures Account			5,000
		Use of Debenture Redemption Fund to provide premium on redemption of 12% debentures.			

2010				Rs.	Rs.
March	31	General Reserve	Dr.	10,000	
		To Premium on Redemption of 15% Preference Shares Account			10,000
		Provision for premium payable on redemption of 15% preference shares.			
		15% Preference Share Capital Account	Dr.	2,00,000	
		Premium on Redemption of 15% Preference Shares Account	Dr.	10,000	
		To Sundry Preference Shareholders Account			2,10,000
		Total amount payable to sundry preference shareholders on redemption of 15% preference shares at a premium of 5%.			
		12% Debentures Account	Dr.	1,00,000	
		Premium on Redemption of 12% Debentures Account	Dr.	5,000	
		To Sundry Debentureholders Account			1,05,000
		Amount payable to sundry debentureholders on redemption of 12% debentures at a premium of 5%.			
		Sundry Preference Shareholders Account	Dr.	2,10,000	
		Sundry Debentureholders	Dr.	1,05,000	
		To Bank			3,15,000
		Payment made to sundry preference shareholders and debentureholders to redeem the securities at a premium of 5%.			
		Debenture Redemption Fund	Dr.	84,980	
		To General Reserve			84,980
		Transfer of balance of Debenture Redemption Fund to General Reserve on redemption of all the debentures.			
		Capital Redemption Reserve	Dr.	50,000	
		General Reserve	Dr.	2,50,000	
		To Bonus to Equity Shareholders Account			3,00,000
		Use of Capital Redemption Reserve and General Reserve to provide for bonus shares to be issued in the ratio of 1:3 to the existing shareholders.			
		Bonus to Equity Shareholders Account	Dr.	3,00,000	
		To Equity Share Capital Account			3,00,000
		Allotment of 3,000 equity shares of Rs. 100 each at par to existing shareholders by way of bonus in the ratio of 1:3.			

Working Notes:

(*i*)

Dr. **Debenture Redemption Fund Account** *Cr.*

		Rs.			Rs.
	To Premium on Redemption of 12% Debentures Account	5,000		By Balance b/fd	88,480
	To General Reserve–transfer of balance	84,980		By Debenture Redemption Fund Investments Account — profit on sale	1,500
		89,980			89,980

(ii)

General Reserve

Dr.	Rs.		Cr. Rs.
To Capital Redemption Reserve	50,000	By Balance b/fd	6,30,000
To Premium on Redemption of 15% Preference Shares Account	10,000	By Debenture Redemption Fund Account	84,980
To Bonus to Equity Shareholders Account	2,50,000		
To Balance c/d	4,04,980		
	7,14,980		7,14,980
		By Balance b/d	4,04,980

(iii)

Cash Book (Bank Columns Only)

	Rs.		Rs.
To Balance b/fd	3,00,000	By Sundry Preference Shareholders Account	2,10,000
To Debenture Redemption Fund Investments Account	90,000	By Sundry Debentureholders Account	1,05,000
To Equity Share Applications & Allotment Account	1,50,000	By Balance c/d	2,25,000
	5,40,000		5,40,000
To Balance b/d	2,25,000		

Brite Ltd.
Balance Sheet
as at 31st March, 2010

	Rs.		Rs.
Share Capital		**Fixed Assets**	7,80,000
Subscribed :		**Current Assets, Loans and Advances**	
12,000 Equity Shares of Rs. 100 each, fully paid	12,00,000	(A) Current Assets	
(Of the above shares, 3,000 equity shares are allotted as fully paid up by way of bonus shares)		Stock	6,00,800
Sources: Rs.		Debtors	2,60.700
Capital Redemption Reserve 50,000		Cash at Bank	2,25,000
General Reserve 2,50,000		(B) Loans and Advances	Nil
Reserves and Surplus			
General Reserve	4,04,980		
Profit & Loss Account	50,000		
Current Liabilities and Provisions			
(A) Current Liabilities : Creditors	2,11,520		
(B) Provisions	Nil		
	18,66,500		18,66,500

Illustration 56:

L.B. Ltd. had 12% Debentures of Rs. 2,00,000 outstanding in its books as on 1.4.2009. It also had a balance of Rs. 80.000 in Sinking Fund Account represented by 10% investments (Face value, Rs. 1,00,000)

On 31.12.2009 it sold investments of the face value of Rs. 20,000 @ Rs. 90 cum-interest and with the proceeds purchased own debentures of the face value of Rs. 20,000 for immediate cancellation.

The interest dates for both debentures and investments were 30th September and 31st March. Annual appropriations to Sinking Fund came to Rs. 21,000.

Pass journal entries and prepare the necessary ledger accounts for the year ended 31st March, 2010. [*Adapted C.W.A. (Final) June 1985*].

L.B. Ltd.
Journal

Date		Particulars		Dr. Rs.	Cr. Rs.
2009 Sept.	30	Bank Dr. To Interest on Sinking Fund Investments Account Receipt of half yearly interest on Sinking Fund Investments of the nominal value of Rs. 1,00,000.		5,000	5,000
"	"	Debentures Interest Account Dr. To Bank Payment of interest on Debentures of Rs. 2,00,000 @ 12% per annum for six months.		12,000	12,000
Dec.	31	Bank Dr. To Sinking Fund Investments Account To Interest on Sinking Fund Investments Account Sale proceeds of sinking fund investments of the face value of Rs. 20,000 @ Rs. 90 cum interest; interest $= \frac{\text{Rs. } 20,000 \times 3 \times 100}{100 \times 12} = \text{Rs. } 500$		18,000	17,500 500
"	"	Sinking Fund Investments Account Dr. To Sinking Fund Account Profit on sale of sinking fund investments costing Rs. 16,000 transferred from Sinking Fund Investments Account to Sinking Fund Account.		1,500	1,500
Dec.	31	12% Debentures Account Dr. Debentures Interest Account Dr. To Bank To Sinking Fund Account Purchase of 12% Debentures of the face value of Rs. 20,000 for Rs. 18,000 cum interest for immediate cancellation, profit on cancellation being credited to Sinking Fund Account.		20,000 600	18,000 2,600
"	"	Sinking Fund Account Dr. To Capital Reserve Transfer of capital profit of Rs. 2,600 on cancellation of 12% Debentures from Sinking Fund Account to Capital Reserve.		2,600	2,600
"	"	Sinking Fund Dr. To General Reserve Transfer from Sinking Fund to General Reserve face value of debentures cancelled.		20,000	20,000
2010 Mar.	31	Bank Dr. To Interest on Sinking Fund Investments Account Receipt of half yearly interest on Sinking Fund Investments of the nominal value of Rs. 80,000.		4,000	4,000
"	"	Debentures Interest Account Dr. To Bank Payment of interest on Debentures of Rs. 1,80,000 @ 12% per annum for six months.		10,800	10,800

Date		Particulars		Rs.	Rs.
2010 March	31	Interest on Sinking Fund Investments Account	Dr.	9,500	
		To Sinking Fund			9,500
		Transfer of total interest earned during the year in respect of sinking fund investments from Interest on Sinking Fund Investments Account to Sinking Fund.			
"	"	Profits & Loss Appropriation Account	Dr.	21,000	
		To Sinking Fund			21,000
		Annual appropriation.			
"	"	Sinking Fund Investments Account	Dr.	30,500	
		To Bank			30,500
		Fresh investments equal to annual appropriation to Sinking Fund plus interest received on Sinking Fund Investments during the year.			
"	"	Profit & Loss Account	Dr.	23,400	
		To Debentures Interest Account			23,400
		Transfer of Debentures Interest Account to Profit & Loss Account.			

Ledger

12% Debentures

Dr. Cr.

Date	Particulars	Rs.	Date	Particulars	Rs.
2009 Dec. 31	To Bank	17,400	2009 April 1	By Balance b/fd	2,00,000
" "	To Sinking Fund Account (profit on cancellation)	2,600			
2010 Mar. 31	To Balance c/d	1,80,000			
		2,00,000			2,00,000
			2010 April 1	By Balance b/d	1,80,000

Sinking Fund

Dr. Cr.

Date	Particulars	Rs.	Date	Particulars	Rs.
2009 Dec. 31	To Capital Reserve (transfer of profit on cancellation)	2,600	2009 April 1	By Balance b/fd	80,000
" "	To General Reserve	20,000	Dec. 31	By Sinking Fund Investments Account (profit on sale of investments)	1,500
2010 Mar. 31	To Balance c/d	92,000		By 12% Debentures (profit on cancellation)	2,600
			2010 Mar 31	By Interest on Sinking Fund Investments Account	9,500
			" "	By Profit & Loss Appropriation Account (Annual appropriation)	21,000
		1,14,600			1,14,600
			2010 April 1	By Balance b/d	92,000

Dr. **Sinking Fund Investments Account** Cr.

		Rs.			Rs.
2009			2009		
April 1	To Balance b/fd (face value Rs. 1,00,000)	80,000	Dec. 31	By Bank (sale – face value Rs. 20,000)	17,500
Dec. 31	To Sinking Fund (profit on sale) (Rs. 17,500 - Rs. 16,000)	1,500	2010 Mar. 31	By Balance c/d	94,500
2010 Mar. 31	To Bank (fresh investments)	30,500			
		1,12,000			1,12,000
2010 April 1	To Balance b/d	94,500			

Dr. **Interest on Sinking Fund Investments Account** Cr.

		Rs.			Rs.
2010			2009		
Mar. 31	To Sinking Fund – transfer	9,500	Sept. 30	By Bank (on Rs. 1,00,000 for 6 months)	5,000
			Dec. 31	By Bank (Rs. 20,000 × 3/12 × 10/100 × 12)	500
			2010 Mar. 31	By Bank (on Rs. 80,000 for 6 months)	4,000
		9,500			9,500

Debentures Interest Account

		Rs.			Rs.
2009			2010		
Sept. 30	To Bank	12,000	Mar. 31	By Profit & Loss Account - transfer	23,400
Dec. 31	To Bank	600			
2010 Mar. 31	To Bank	10,800			
		23,400			23,400

Illustration 57:

On 1st April, 2009, the books of Atul Limited showed that 9,000 12% Debentures of Rs. 100 each were outstanding. On this date, the Debenture Redemption Fund showed a balance of Rs. 5,70,000 represented by 8% Port Trust Bonds of the face value of Rs. 6,00,000. The date of interest both for debentures and bonds was 31st March.

On 30th March, 2009, 500 Debentures were purchased in the market @ Rs. 96 and cancelled immediately, the amount required being raised by selling Port Trust Bonds of the nominal value of Rs. 50,000.

On 31st March, 1998, the annual instalment of Rs. 60,000 plus the interest received during the year on Debenture Redemption Fund Investments were invested in 8% Port Trust Bonds of Rs. 100 each available at Rs. 95 each to the maximum possible extent.

Give journal entries for all the abovementioned transactions. Also show important ledger accounts for the year ended 31st March, 2010.

Solution:

Working Notes:

Amount required to purchase 500 debentures on 30th June, 2009:

Ex-interest price = Rs. 96 × 500 = Rs. 48,000

Interest on Rs. 50,000 for 3 months @ 12% p.a. = $\frac{\text{Rs. } 50{,}000 \times 3 \times 12}{100 \times 12}$ = Rs. 1,500

Cum - interest price = Rs. 48,000 + Rs. 1,500 = Rs. 49,500

Interest on bonds of Rs. 50,000 for 3 months @ 8% p.a. = $\frac{\text{Rs. } 50{,}000 \times 3 \times 8}{100 \times 12}$ = Rs. 1,000

Ex-interest price received for bonds of Rs. 50,000 = Rs. 49,500 – Rs. 1,000 = Rs. 48,500
Ex-interest purchase price of bonds of face value of Rs. 6,00,000 = Rs. 5,70,000
Hence, ex-interest purchase price of bonds of face value of Rs. 50,000 = Rs. 5,70,000/6,00,000 × 50,000 = Rs. 47,500
Profit = Rs. 48,500 – Rs. 47,500 = Rs. 1,000
Interest received on bonds of Rs. 5,50,000 on 31st March, 2010
= Rs. 5,50,000 × 8/100 = Rs. 44,000.

Journal

				Dr.	Cr.
2009				*Rs.*	*Rs.*
June	30	Bank	Dr.	49,500	
		To Debenture Redemption Fund Investments Account			48,500
		To Interest on Debenture Redemption Fund Investments Account			1,000
		Sale proceeds of port trust bonds of the nominal value of Rs. 50,000.			
"	"	Debenture Redemption Fund Investments Account	Dr.	1,000	
		To Debenture Redemption Fund			1,000
		Transfer of profit on sale of bonds to Debenture Redemption Fund.			
"	"	Own Debentures Account	Dr.	48,000	
		Debentures Interest Account	Dr.	1,500	
		To Bank			49,500
		Purchase of 500 own debentures @ Rs. 96 ex-interest.			
"	"	12% Debentures Account	Dr.	50,000	
		To Own Debentures Account			48,000
		To Capital Reserve			2,000
		Cancellation of 500 own debentures, profit being credited to Capital Reserve.			
"	"	Debenture Redemption Fund	Dr.	50,000	
		To General Reserve			50,000
		Transfer from Debenture Redemption Fund to General Reserve a sum equal to the face value of own debentures cancelled.			
2010					
Mar.	31	Bank	Dr.	44,000	
		To Interest on Debenture Redemption Fund Investments Account			44,000
		Interest received on Port Trust Bonds of the face value of Rs. 5,50,000.			
"	"	Interest on Debentures Account	Dr.	1,02,000	
		To Bank			1,02,000
		Interest paid on debentures for Rs. 8,50,000 @ 12% p.a. for 1 year.			
"	"	Interest on Debenture Redemption Fund Investments Account	Dr.	45,000	
		To Debenture Redemption Fund			45,000
		Transfer of interest received during the year on port trust bonds to Debenture Redemption Fund.			
"	"	Profit & Loss Appropriation Account	Dr.	60,000	
		To Debenture Redemption Fund			60,000
		Annual instalment credited to Debenture Redemption Fund.			

				Rs.	Rs.
2010					
Mar.	31	Debenture Redemption Fund Investments Account	Dr.	1,04,975	
		To Bank			1,04,975
		Purchase of 1,105 port trust bonds of Rs. 100 each at Rs. 95 each, the maximum that can be purchased for Rs. 1,05,000.			
"	"	Profit and Loss Account	Dr.	1,03,500	
		To Debenture Interest Account			1,03,500
		Transfer of interest on debentures for the year to Profit & Loss Account.			

Dr. 12% Debentures Account Cr.

		Rs.			Rs.
2009			2009		
June 30	To Own Debentures A/c	48,000	Apr. 1	By Balance b/fd	9,00,000
" "	To Capital Reserve	2,000			
2010					
Mar. 31	To Balance c/d	8,50,000			
		9,00,000			9,00,000
			2010		
			Apr. 1	By Balance b/d	8,50,000

Dr. Debenture Redemption Fund Cr.

		Rs.			Rs.
2009			2009		
June 30	To General Reserve	50,000	Apr. 1	By Balance b/fd.	5,70,000
2010			June 30	By Debenture Redemption Fund Investments Account	1,000
Mar. "	To Balance c/d	6,26,000	2010		
			Mar. 31	By Interest on Debenture Redemption Fund Investments Account	45,000
			" "	By Profit & Loss Appropriation Account	60,000
		6,76,000			6,76,000
			2010		
			Apr. 1	By Balance b/d	6,26,000

Dr. Debenture Redemption Fund Investments Account Cr.

		Face value Rs.	Rs.			Face value Rs.	Rs.
2009				2009			
Apr. 1	To Balance b/fd	6,00,000	5,70,000	June 31	By Bank	50,000	48,500
June 30	To Debenture Redemption Fund	—	1,000	2010			
				Mar. 31	By Balance c/d	6,60,500	6,27,475
2010							
Mar. 31	To Bank	1,10,500	1,04,975				
		7,10,500	6,75,975			7,10,500	6,75,975
2010							
Apr. 1	To Balance b/d	6,60,500	6,27,475				

Interest on Debenture Redemption Fund Investments Account

		Rs.			Rs.
2010			2009		
Mar. 31	To Debenture Redemption Fund—transfer	45,000	June 30	By Bank	1,000
			2010		
			Mar. 31	By Bank	44,000
		45,000			45,000

Debentures Interest Account

2009		Rs.	2010		Rs.
June 30	To Bank	1,500	Mar. 31	By Profit & Loss Account-transfer	1,03,500
2010					
Mar. 31	To Bank	1,02,000			
		1,03,500			1,03,500

Illustration 58:

X Ltd. had Rs. 10,00,000 11% debentures outstanding on 1st April, 1997. On that date, Debenture Redemption Fund was Rs. 8,70,000 represented by Rs. 4,00,000 Own Debentures purchased at 96% on the average and Rs. 5,40,000 8% Government Loan. The annual instalment for Debenture Redemption Fund was Rs. 50,000.

On 31st March, 2010 the investments in Government Loan were sold at 95% and all debentures were redeemed or cancelled as necessary at a premium of 5%. The dates of interest for debentures as well as Government Loan were 30th September and 31st March.

Prepare ledger accounts relating to the abovementioned matters for the year ended 31st March, 2010.

Solution:

Working Notes:

	Rs.
Total of Debenture Redemption Fund Investments	8,70,000
Less: Purchase price of Own Debentures of face value of Rs. 4,00,000 at 96%	3,84,000
Purchase price of 8% Government Loan of the face value of Rs. 5,40,000	4,86,000

Ledger

11% Debentures Account

Dr. *Cr.*

2010		Rs.	2009		Rs.
Mar. 31	To D.R.F. Investments (Own Debentures) A/c	4,00,000	Apr. 1	By Balance b/fd	10,00,000
" "	To Sundry Debentureholders Account	6,00,000			
		10,00,000			10,00,000

Debentures Interest Account

Dr. *Cr.*

2009		Rs.	2010		Rs.
Sep. 30	To Bank (On Rs. 6,00,000)	33,000	Mar. 31	By Profit & Loss Account—transfer	1,10,000
" "	To Interest on D.R.F. Investments Account (On Rs. 4,00,000)	22,000			
2010					
Mar. 31	To Bank	33,000			
" "	To Interest on D.R.F. Investments Account	22,000			
		1,10,000			1,10,000

Dr. Interest on Debenture Redemption Fund Investments Account Cr.

		Rs.			Rs.
2010			2009		
Mar. 31	To Debenture Redemption Fund—transfer	87,200	Sept. 30	By Bank (on Rs. 5,40,000 of Govt. Loan)	21,600
			" "	By Debentures Interest Account (on Rs. 4,00,000)	22,000
			2010		
			Mar. 31	By Bank	21,600
			" "	By Debentures Interest Account	22,000
		87,200			87,200

Dr. Debenture Redemption Fund Investments (Own Debentures) Account Cr.

		Nominal Value Rs.	Rs.			Nominal Value Rs.	Rs.
2009				2010			
Apr. 1	To Balance b/fd	4,00,000	3,84,000	Mar. 31	By 11% Debentures Account	4,00,000	4,00,000
2010							
Mar. 31	To Capital Reserve (profit on cancellation)		16,000				
		4,00,000	4,00,000			4,00,000	4,00,000

Dr. Debenture Redemption Fund Investments (Govt. Loan) Account Cr.

		Nominal Value Rs.	Rs.			Nominal Value Rs.	Rs.
2009				2010			
Apr. 1	To Balance b/fd	5,40,000	4,86,000	Mar. 31	By Bank	5,40,000	5,13,000
2010							
Mar. 31	To Debenture Redemption Fund Account (profit on sale)		27,000				
		5,40,000	5,13,000			5,40,000	5,13,000

Dr. Debenture Redemption Fund Cr.

		Rs.			Rs.
2010			2009		
Mar. 31	To Premium on Redemption of Debentures Account	30,000	Apr. 1	By Balance b/fd	8,70,000
" "	To General Reserve — transfer	10,04,200	1998		
			Mar. 31	By Interest on D.R.F. Investments	87,200
			" "	By D.R.F. Investments (Govt. Loan) Account	27,000
			" "	By Profit & Loss Appropriation A/c	50,000
		10,34,200			10,34,200

Dr. Sundry Debentureholders Account Cr.

		Rs.			Rs.
2010			2010		
Mar. 31	To Bank	6,30,000	Mar. 31	By 11% Debentures Account	6,00,000
			" "	By Premium on Redemption of Debentures Account	30,000
		6,30,000			6,30,000

Dr. **Premium on Redemption of Debentures Account** Cr.

2010		Rs.	2010		Rs.
Mar. 31	To Sundry Debentureholders	30,000	Mar. 31	By Debenture Redemption Fund	30,000

Illustration 59:

On 31st March, 2009, the following balances were extracted from the books of X Ltd.:—

		Rs.	Rs.	Rs.
12% Mortgage Debentures				15,00,000
Debenture Redemption Fund				9,13,000
Debenture Redemption Fund Investments :				
9% Port Trust Bonds	(Rs. 5,00,000)		4,50,000	
Own Debentures	(Rs. 3,00,000)		2,85,000	7,35,000

Face value of each bond and debenture was Rs. 100. Interest dates in both cases are 30th September and 31st March.

The investments were as on 1st April, 2008; the investments in respect of 2008-09 were made on 1st April, 2009 in the form of Port Trust Bonds purchased at Rs. 89.

On 31st July, 2009, the company purchased Own Debentures of the face value of Rs. 2,00,000 @ 94, the required amount being realised by sale of Port Trust Bonds at Rs. 91. The company resold Own Debentures of the face value of Rs. 1,00,000 @ Rs. 99 cum-interest on 31st December, 2009 and cancelled the remaining debentures held by it on 28th February, 2010.

Prepare ledger accounts for the year ended 31st March, 2000.

Solution:

Working Notes:

1. Amount to be invested for 2008-09 = Rs. 9,13,000 – Rs. 7,35,000 = Rs. 1,78,000.
2. Face value of Bonds purchased on 1st April, 2009

$$= \text{Rs. } 1{,}78{,}000 \times \frac{100}{89} = \text{Rs. } 2{,}00{,}000$$

3. Amount required to purchase own debentures of Rs. 2,00,000 on 31st July, 2009:

$$\text{Principal amount} = \frac{\text{Rs. } 2{,}00{,}000 \times 94}{100} = \text{Rs. } 1{,}88{,}000$$

$$\text{Interest for 4 months} = \frac{\text{Rs. } 2{,}00{,}000 \times 4 \times 12}{100} = \text{Rs. } 8{,}000$$

$$\text{Total} = \text{Rs. } 1{,}96{,}000$$

$$\text{Interest for 4 months on 1 bond} = \frac{\text{Rs. } 2{,}00{,}000 \times 4 \times 12}{100 \times 12} = \text{Rs. } 3$$

Cum-interest selling price of 1 bond = Rs. 91 + Rs. 3 = Rs. 94.
No. of bonds sold to get Rs. 1,96,000 = 1,96,000/94 = 2,086
Interest received = Rs. 3 × 2,086 = Rs. 6,258
Ex-interest purchase price of each bond purchased earlier than 2009-2010
= Rs. 4,50,000/5,00,000 × 100 = Rs. 90
Profit on sale of 2,086 bonds (on FIFO basis) = Rs. (91 – 90) × 2,086 = Rs. 2,086.

4. Interest on 1 debenture for 3 months = Rs. 3
Ex-interest selling price of 1 debenture = Rs. 99 – Rs. 3 = Rs. 96.
Ex-interest purchase price of each debenture purchased earlier than 2009-2010
= Rs. 2,85,000/3,00,000 x 100 = Rs. 95
Profit on sale of 1,000 own debenture on FIFO basis = Rs. (96 – 95) × 1,000 = Rs. 1,000.

5. Interest on Debenture Redemption Fund Investments for 2008-09:
   Interest on Port Trust Bonds : 9% on Rs. 5,00,000 = Rs. 45,000
   Interest on Own Debentures : 12% on Rs. 3,00,000 = Rs. 36,000
   Total = Rs. 81,000
   Amount to be invested for 2008-09 = Rs. 1,78,000
   Hence, annual instalment = Rs. 1,78,000 – Rs. 81,000 = Rs. 97,000

Ledger

12% Mortgage Debentures Account

Dr.					*Cr.*
2010		*Rs.*	2009		*Rs.*
Feb. 28	To Debenture Redemption Fund Investments (Own Debentures) Account	4,00,000	Apr. 1	By Balance b/fd	15,00,000
Mar. 31	To Balance c/d	11,00,000			
		15,00,000			15,00,000
			2010 Apr. 1	By Balance b/d	11,00,000

Debenture Interest Account

Dr.					*Cr.*
2009		*Rs.*	2010		*Rs.*
July 31	To Bank	8,000	Mar. 31	By Profit & Loss Account-transfer	1,76,000
Sept. 30	To Bank	60,000			
" "	To Interest on D.R.F. Investments Account	22,000			
2010					
Feb. 28	To Interest on D.R.F. Investments Account	20,000			
Mar. 31	To Bank	66,000			
		1,76,000			1,76,000

Interest on Debenture Redemption Fund Investments Account

Dr.					*Cr.*
2010		*Rs.*	2009		*Rs.*
Mar. 31	To Debenture Redemption Fund –transfer	95,484	July 30	By Bank	6,258
			Sept. 30	By Debenture Interest	22,000
			" "	By Bank	22,113
			Nov. 30	By Bank	3,000
			Dec. 31	By Debenture Interest	20,000
			2010 Mar. 31	By Bank	22,113
		95,484			95,484

Debenture Redemption Fund Investments (Port Trust Bonds) Account

Dr.							*Cr.*
2009		*Face Value Rs.*	Rs.	2009		*Face Value Rs.*	*Rs.*
Apr. 1	To Balance b/fd	5,00,000	4,50,000	July 30	By Bank	2,08,600	1,89,826
" "	To Bank	2,00,000	1,78,000	2010 Mar. 31	By Balance c/d	4,91,400	4,40,260
July 31	To Debenture Redemption Fund (Profit)		2,086				
		7,00,000	6,30,086			7,00,000	6,30,086
2010 Apr. 1	To Balance b/d	4,91,400	4,40,260				

Dr. **Debenture Redemption Fund Investments (Own Debentures) Account.** *Cr.*

		Face Value Rs.	Rs.			Face Value Rs.	Rs.
2009				2009			
Apr. 1	To Balance b/fd	3,00,000	2,85,000	Dec. 31	By Bank	1,00,000	96,000
July 31	To Bank	2,00,000	1,88,000	2010			
Dec. 30	To Debenture Redemption Fund (Profit)		1,000	Feb. 28	By 12% Debentures Account	4,00,000	4,00,000
2010							
Feb. 28	To Capital Reserver (Profit on cancellation)		22,000				
		5,00,000	4,96,000			5,00,000	4,96,000

Dr. **Debenture Redemption Fund** *Cr.*

		Rs.			Rs.
2010			2009		
Feb. 28	To General Reserve	4,00,000	Apr. 1	By Balance b/fd	9,13,000
Mar. 31	To Balance c/d	7,08,570	July 31	By D.R.F.I (Port Trust Bonds) Account	2,086
			Dec. 31	By D.R.F.I (Own Debentures) Account	1,000
			2010		
			Mar. 31	By Interest on D.R.F. Investments Account	95,484
			" "	By Profit & Loss Appropriation Account	97,000
		11,08,570			11,08,570
			2010		
			Apr. 1	By Balance b/d	7,08,570

Debenture Redemption Fund Insurance Policy. To get money for the redemption of debentures after a specified period of time, a company may take an insurance policy. It is called Debenture Redemption Fund Insurance Policy. Entries will be passed as follows :—

(*i*) Every year, when the insurance premium is paid:
Debenture Redemption Fund Insurance Policy Account ... Dr. With premium paid
To Bank

(*ii*) At the end of each accounting year :—
Profit & Loss Appropriation Account ... Dr. With premium paid
To Debenture Redemption Fund

(*iii*) On the maturity of the insurance policy :—
(*a*) Bank ... Dr. With amount of the policy received
To Debenture Redemption Fund Insurance Policy Account.
(*b*) Debenture Redemption Fund Insurance Policy Account ... Dr. With excess of amount of policy over total premium paid
To Debenture Redemption Fund

(*iv*) After the redemption of debentures :
Debenture Redemption Fund ... Dr. With balance in Debenture Redemption Fund
To General Reserve

Illustration 60

On 1st April, 2008 the following balances appeared in the books of Fairdeal Co. Ltd. :—

	Rs.
10% Mortgage Debentures	10,00,000
Debenture Redemption Fund	7,16,400
Debenture Redemption Fund Insurance Policy	7,16,400

On 1st April, 2008 the company paid the annual premium of Rs. 79,600. On 31st March, 2009 the policy amount of Rs. 10,00,000 was received and all the debentures were redeemed at par.

Show the abovementioned three ledger accounts for the year ended 31st March, 2009.

Solution:

Dr. **10% Mortgage Debentures Account** *Cr.*

		Rs.			Rs.
2009			2008		
Mar. 31	To Bank	10,00,000	April 1	By Balance b/fd	10,00,000

Dr. **Debenture Redemption Fund Insurance Policy Account** *Cr.*

		Rs.			Rs.
2008			2009		
April 1	To Balance b/fd	7,16,400	Mar. 31	By Bank	10,00,000
" "	To Bank	79,600			
2009					
Mar. 31	To Debenture Redemption Fund (Profit)	2,04,000			
		10,00,000			10,00,000

Dr. **Debenture Redemption Fund** *Cr.*

		Rs.			Rs.
2009			2008		
Mar. 31	To General Reserve—transfer	10,00,000	April 1	By Balance b/fd	7,16,400
			2009		
			Mar. 31	By Debenture Redemption Fund Insurance Policy Account	2,04,000
			" "	By Profit & Loss Appropriation Account	79,600
		10,00,000			10,00,000

Illustration 61

The following was the balance sheet of Adarsh Trading Co. Ltd. as on 31st March, 2009 :—

Liabilities	*Rs.*	*Assets*	*Rs.*
Share Capital		Fixed Assets	
Authorised	25,00,000	Land and Buildings	11,50,000
Issued and subscribed:		Furniture, Fixtures and Fittings	3,75,000
1,00,000 Equity Shares of		Investments	
Rs. 10 each, fully paid up	10,00,000	Debenture Redemption Fund Investments	2,81,000
3,000 13% Redeemable Preference		Current Assets, Loans and Advances	
Shares of Rs. 100 each, fully paid up	3,00,000	(A) Current Assets	
Reserves and Surplus		Stock	7,60,000
Capital Reserve	30,000	Debtors	6,65,000
General Reserve	8,00,000	Cash at Bank	2,75,000
Profit and Loss (Appro.) Account	2,00,000	(B) Loans and Advances	Nil
Debenture Redemption Fund	3,35,000	Miscellaneous Expenditure	
Secured Loans		Discount on Issue of Debentures	9,000
9% Debentures	4,50,000		

	Rs.		Rs.
Current Liabilities and Provisions			
(A) Current Liabilities			
Sundry Creditors	1,50,000		
(B) Provisions			
Provision for Taxation	2,50,000		
	35,15,000		35,15,000

On 1st April, 2009 the company offered to its preference shareholders and debentureholders the option to get their holdings converted into equity shares of Rs. 10 each to be considered as worth Rs. 20 each. One-half of the preference shareholders and one-third of the debentureholders in value exercised their option in favour of conversion.

The company sold all the investments for Rs. 2,76,000, allotted 20,000 equity shares of Rs. 10 each at a premium of 100% to the public for cash and redeemed at par all remaining debentures and preference shares. It then issued to its equity shareholders one fully paid equity share of Rs. 10 by way of bonus for every two shares held using revenue reserves to the minimum possible extent.

Pass journal entries for all the abovementioned transactions and prepare the balance sheet as it would appear after the completion of these transactions.

Solution:

Journal

		Dr.	Cr.
		Rs.	Rs.
13% Preference Share Capital Account	Dr.	1,50,000	
To Equity Share Capital Account			75,000
To Securities Premium Account			75,000
Conversion of 1,500 13% Redeemable Preference Shares of Rs. 100 each into 7,500 Equity Securities of Rs. 10 each issued at a premium of 100%.			
9% Debentures Account	Dr.	1,50,000	
To Equity Share Capital Account			75,000
To Securities Premium Account			75,000
Conversion of 9% Debentures of Rs. 1,50,000 into 7,500 Equity Shares of Rs. 10 each issued at a premium of 100%.			
Bank	Dr.	2,76,000	
To Debenture Redemption Fund Investments Account			2,76,000
Sale proceeds of investments.			
Debenture Redemption Fund	Dr.	5,000	
To Debenture Redemption Fund Investments Account			5,000
Loss on sale of investments being transferred to Debenture Redemption Fund.			
Bank	Dr.	4,00,000	
To Equity Securities Capital Account			2,00,000
To Securities Premium Account			2,00,000
Allotment for cash 20,000 equity shares of Rs. 10 each at a premium of Rs. 10 each.			
13% Preference Share Capital Account	Dr.	1,50,000	
9% Debentures Account	Dr.	3,00,000	
To Bank			4,50,000
Redemption of remaining preference shares and debentures at par.			

		Rs.	Rs.
Debenture Redemption Fund	Dr.	3,30,000	
To General Reserve			3,30,000
Transfer of Debenture Redemption Fund to General Reserve.			
Securities Premium Account	Dr.	9,000	
To Discount on Issue of Debentures Account			9,000
Transfer of Discount on Issue of Debentures Account to Securities Premium Account.			
Capital Reserve	Dr.	30,000	
Securities Premium Account	Dr.	3,41,000	
General Reserve	Dr.	3,04,000	
To Bonus to Equity Shareholders Account			6,75,000
Use of reserves to issue bonus shares.			
Bonus to Equity Shareholders Account	Dr.	6,75,000	
To Equity Share Capital Account			6,75,000
Issue of bonus shares.			

Balance Sheet of Adarsh Trading Co. Ltd. :
as on ____________

Liabilities	*Rs.*	*Assets*		*Rs.*
Share Capital:		**Fixed Assets:**		
Authorised:	25,00,000	Land and Buildings		11,50,000
Issued and subscribed:		Furniture, Fixtures and Fittings		3,75,000
2,02,500 Equity Shares of		**Current Assets, Loans and Advance:s**		
Rs. 10 each, fully paid up	20,25,000	(A) Current Assets		
(Of the above shares, 67,500 equity		Stock		7,60,000
shares have been allotted as fully		Debtors		6,65,000
paid up by way of bonus shares)		Cash at Bank	5,01,000	
Sources : Capital Reserve Rs. 30,000;				
Securities Premium Rs. 3,41,000;		(B) Loans and Advances		nil
and General Reserve Rs. 3,04,000				
Reserves and Surplus:				
General Reserve	8,26,000			
Profit and Loss Account	2,00,000			
Current Liabilities and Provisions:				
(A) Current Liabilities				
Sundry Creditors	1,50,000			
(B) Provisions				
Provision for Taxation	2,50,000			
	34,51,000			34,51,000

Working Notes:

(*i*) Calculation of closing balance of Cash at Bank :

		Rs.
Opening balance		2,75,000
Add: Sale proceeds of investments		2,76,000
Issue of equity shares		4,00,000
		9,51,000
Less: Payment to debentureholders	3,00,000	
Payment to preference shareholders	1,50,000	4,50,000
Closing balance		5,01,000

(*ii*) Opening balance of Equity Share Capital Account	10,00,000
Add: Issue to preference shareholders	75,000
Issue to debentureholders	75,000

	Rs.
Issue for cash	2,00,000
	13,50,000
Add: Bonus Issue	6,75,000
Closing balance	20,25,000
(*iii*) Opening balance of General Reserve	8,00,000
Add: Debenture Redemption Fund (Rs. 3,35,000 - Rs. 5,000)	3,30,000
	11,30,000
Less: Use for bonus Issue	3,04,000
Balance	8,26,000
(*iv*) Balance of Securities Premium Account used for bonus Issue :	
Securities Premium on conversion of preference shares	75,000
Securities Premium on conversion of debentures	75,000
Securities Premium received on issue of shares for cash	2,00,000
	3,50,000
Less: Amount used to write off Discount on Issue of Debentures	9,000
Balance used for bonus issue	3,41,000

Illustration 62

The terms of an issue of Rs. 10,00,000 14% Debentures of Rs.10 each included the following:

(*a*) Interest payable half-yearly on 31st March and 30th September.

(*b*) Twenty five per cent of the profits of any year to be applied in redeeming debentures and, upon being redeemed, they are to be cancelled.

(*c*) The company may purchase its debentures in the open market without limitation to the amount redeemable as above; those to be redeemed, if not obtained by purchase, being drawn by lot and surrendered at Rs. 10.50.

(*d*) Any debentures purchased in excess of the obligatory amount may, entirely at the option of the company, be cancelled or kept alive for reissue.

(*e*) Upon giving three months' notice, the company can redeem the debentures outstanding at Rs. 11.

On 1st October, 2009 —

(*i*) Rs. 4,82,000 debentures had been redeemed and cancelled.

(*ii*) The profits for the year to date were Rs. 4,20,000.

(*iii*) The company held Rs. 2,82,000 of its live debentures (cost Rs. 2,53,800).

On the above date the debentures to be redeemed and cancelled were appropriated out of the company's holding, and three months' notice to redeem the outside debentures was given.

The redemption was duly completed on 1st January, 2010 and the interest for three months duly paid.

On 31st March, 2010 it was resolved that the remaining debentures should be cancelled.

Show journal entries and ledger accounts ignoring income tax and SEBI guidelines on creation of capital Redemption Revenue. *(Adapted from C.A. Final)*

Solution:

It should be noted that out of Rs. 10,00,000 debentures, Rs. 4,82,000 debentures have already been cancelled. Hence, the amount outstanding on 1st October, 2009 is Rs. 5,18,000. Out of this latter sum, debentures worth Rs. 2,82,000 (cost Rs. 2,53,800) are held by the company alive. Outside debentures are, therefore, Rs. 2,36,000, i.e., Rs. 5,18,000 – Rs. 2,82,000.

Journal

			Dr.	Cr.
2009			*Rs.*	*Rs.*
Oct.	1	Profit and Loss Appropriation Account Dr. To Debenture Redemption Fund Account The sum (25% of profits) to be used for redemption of debentures, as per terms of issue of debentures.	1,05,000	1,05,000
"	"	14% Debentures Dr. To Own Debentures Account To Profit on Redemption of Debentures Account The cancellation of debentures of the face value of Rs. 1,05,000 out of own holding - the cost of such debentures being Rs. 94,500, i.e., 2,53,800/2,82,000 x 1,05,000, the balance transferred to Profit on Redemption of Debentures Account.	1,05,000	94,500 10,500
2010				
Jan.	1	14% Debentures Dr. Premium on Redemption of Debentures Account Dr. To Debentureholders The redemption of outside debentures (5,18,000 - 2,82,000) at Rs. 11 per debenture in accordance with terms of the issue; three months' notice having been given on 1st October, 2009.	2,36,000 23,600	2,59,600
"	"	Debentures Interest Account Dr. To Debentureholders Interest for 3 months on Rs. 2,36,000 @ 14% payable to the debentureholders.	8,260	8,260
"	"	Debentureholders Dr. To Bank The amount due to debentureholders paid.	2,67,860	2,67,860
Mar.	31	14% Debentures Dr. To Own Debentures Account To Profit on Redemption of Debentures Account Cancellation of the remaining debentures on hand. Cost: 2,53,800/2,82,000 × 1,77,000 or Rs. 1,59,300 and profit: Rs. 1,77,000 – 1,59,300 or Rs. 17,700	1,77,000	1,59,300 17,700
		Debentures Interest Account Dr. To Debentures Redemption Fund Account Saving of interest on Rs. 1,77,000 (held by the company) for 6 months credited to Debenture Redemption Fund.	12,390	12,390
"	"	Profit on Redemption of Debentures Account Dr. To Debenture Redemption Fund Account Transfer of the profit on redemption to D.R. Fund.	28,200	28,200
"	"	Debenture Redemption Fund Account Dr. To Premium on Redemption of Debentures Account Transfer of the Premium on Redemption of Debentures to Debenture Redemption Fund Account.	23,600	23,600
"	"	Debentures Redemption Fund Account Dr. To Capital Reserve Transfer of unused amount of profit on redemption of debentures lying in Debentures Redemption Fund to Capital Reserve.	4,600	4,600
"	"	Debentures Redemption Fund Account Dr. To General Reserve Redemption having been completed, the balance in Debebtures Redemption Fund transferred to General Reserve.	1,17,390	1,17,390

Ledger Accounts:

14% Debentures

Dr. / Cr.

Date	Particulars	Rs.	Rs.	Date	Particulars	Rs.
2009				2009		
Oct. 1	To Sundries -			Oct. 1	By Balance b/d	5,18,000
	Own Debentures		94,500			
	Profit on Redemption of Debentures		10,500			
2010						
Jan. 1	To Debentureholders		2,36,000			
Mar. 31	To own Debentures		1,59,300			
	To profit on Red. of Debentures			17,700		
			5,18,000			5,18,000

Own Debentures Account

Dr. / Cr.

Date	Particulars	Rs.	Date	Particulars	Rs.
2009			2009		
Oct. 1	To Balance b/d (nominal value Rs. 2,82,000)	2,53,800	Oct. 1	By 14% Debentures — cancellation	94,500
			2010		
			Mar. 31	By 14% Debentures — cancellation	1,59,300
		2,53,800			2,53,800

Debentures Redemption Fund Account

Dr. / Cr.

Date	Particulars	Rs.	Date	Particulars	Rs.
2010			2009		
Mar. 31	To Premium on Redemption of Debentures Account	23,600	Oct. 1	By Profit and Loss (App.) A/c	1,05,000
" "	To Capital Reserve	4,600	2010		
" "	To General Reserve	1,17,390	Mar. 31	By Profit on Redemption of Debentures Account	28,200
			" "	By Debentures Interest Account	12,390
		1,45,590			1,45,590

Profit on Redemption of Debentures Account

Dr. / Cr.

Date	Particulars	Rs.	Date	Particulars	Rs.
2010			2009		
Mar. 31	To Debenture Redemption Fund Account	28,200	Oct. 1	By 14% Debentures	10,500
			2010		
			Mar. 31	By 14% Debentures	17,700
		28,200			28,200

Premium on Redemption of Debentures Account

Dr. / Cr.

Date	Particulars	Rs.	Date	Particulars	Rs.
2010			2010		
Jan. 1	To Debentureholders	23,600	Mar. 31	By Debenture Redemption Fund Account	23,600

Debentureholders

Dr. / Cr.

Date	Particulars	Rs.	Date	Particulars	Rs.
2010			2010		
Jan. 1	To Bank Account	2,67,860	Jan. 1	By 5% Debentures	2,36,000
			" "	By Premium on Redemption of Debentures Account	23,600
			" "	By Debentures Interest Account	8,260
		2,67,860			2,67,860

Debentures Interest Account

Dr.					Cr.
2010		*Rs.*	2010		*Rs.*
Jan. 1	To Debentureholders	8,260	Mar. 31	By Profit and Loss Account	21,650
Mar. 31	To Debenture Redemption Fund Account	12,390			
		21,650			21,650

General Reserve

Dr.					Cr.
			2010		*Rs.*
			Mar. 31	By Debenture Redemption Fund Account	1,17,390

(i) Purchase of Business:

A company may start an entirely new business or it may start with buying an existing business, either that of a partnership or of a limited company. Frequently, later in its life, a company buys businesses. The purchase price or purchase consideration may be discharged in the form of shares, debentures or cash. The price paid for the business will naturally depend on the valuation of its assets including goodwill.

In case the business is purchased for a lump sum, goodwill will be the difference between the price paid and the value of net tangible assets. A company pays Rs. 10 lakh for a business which has tangible assets amounting to Rs. 1 lakh and which owes Rs. 2 lakh to sundry creditors. The net tangible assets are Rs. 9 lakh and goodwill will be Rs. 1 lakh i.e., Rs. 10 lakh less 1 lakh. It may happen that a company pays less than the value of net assets. The company then makes a profit. Such a profit is treated as capital profit and is to be credited to Capital Reserve. In other words, if net tangible assets exceed the 'purchase consideration', the difference will be treated as Capital Reserve.

Following is the balance sheet of A and B on the basis of which their business will be taken over by AB Ltd.:—

Balance Sheet of M/s A and B

	Rs.		*Rs.*
Sundry Creditors	1,50,000	Goodwill	75,000
Mrs. *A*'s Loan	1,00,000	Land and Buildings	1,50,000
A's Capital	1,80,000	Plant and Machinery	2,00,000
B's Capital	1,50,000	Patents and Trade Marks	40,000
		Stock	55,000
		Sundry Debtors	45,000
		Cash at Bank	15,000
	5,80,000		5,80,000

The company pays Rs. 3,00,000 for the business but does not take over Mrs. A's Loan. The net assets (excluding goodwill) of the company will be :

	Rs.
Land and Buildings	1,50,000
Plant and Machinery	2,00,000
Patents and Trade Marks	40,000
Stock	55,000
Sundry Debtors	45,000
Cash at Bank	15,000
	5,05,000
Less: Sundry Creditors	1,50,000
Net Tangible Assets	3,55,000

Since the company pays only Rs. 3,00,000 for net tangible assets worth Rs. 3,55,000, the Capital Reserve is Rs. 55,000.

In case a lump sum amount is not settled as purchase consideration, it will be equal to the net assets, including goodwill, acquired. In the example given above, if the company takes over all the assets and no liabilities, the company will pay Rs. 5,80,000. If the company also agrees to pay the trade creditors, it will deduct Rs. 1,50,000 and pay only Rs. 4,30,000. If the company takes over Mrs. *A*'s Loan also, it will further deduct Rs. 1,00,000 and pay only Rs. 3,30,000.

Entries in the books of the purchasing company. The following entries are necessary to record the purchase of business :—

1. Debit Business Purchase Account } with the purchase price agreed upon.
   Credit Vendor }
2. Debit various assets taken over at the value at which the company wants to record them in its books.
   Credit various liabilities taken over at the values agreed upon.
   Credit Business Purchase Account with the purchase consideration.
   If the credits exceed the debits, the difference is Goodwill and should be debited as such.
   If the debits exceed the credits, the difference is capital profit and should be credited to Capital Reserve.

(*Note.* The student should remember to calculate goodwill or capital reserve not by taking the balance sheet figures of the vendor *but the figures* at which the company wants to record, in its books, the assets and liabilities taken over.)

3. On payment to the Vendor :
   Debit the Vendor
   Credit : Bank (if cash is paid)
   Securities Capital (if shares are issued, paid up value)
   Securities Premium (if any)
   Debentures (nominal value of debentures that may be issued)
   Premium on Issue of Debentures Account (if any)

   Entries in the books of the vendor will be such as to close the books. In the case of partnership, such entries have already been noted. In the case of companies, the entries are similar but will be discussed in a subsequent chapter.

Illustration 63

A company was formed with an authorised capital of Rs. 5 crore divided into 25 lakh equity shares of Rs. 10 each and 25 lakh preference shares of Rs. 10 each to acquire the going concern of M/s. Karamchand & Co. whose balance sheet stood as follows :—

Liabilities	*Rs.'000*	*Assets*	*Rs.'000*
Bills Payable	350	Cash at Bank	450
Sundry Creditors	640	Book Debts	750
Capital	13,210	Insurance Policy	400
		Stock in Trade	3,100
		Plant and Machinery	5,000
		Freehold Premises	4,500
	14,200		14,200

The purchase price was agreed upon at Rs. 1 crore, 75 lakh to be paid, Rs. 50 lakh in fully paid equity shares, Rs. 50 lakh in fully paid preference shares, Rs. 30 lakh in redeemable debentures and the balance in cash. The company does not take over the insurance policy, values the stock and plant and machinery at 10 per cent less than the book value and the freehold premises at 20% more than the book value. The liabilities will be discharged by the company.

The balance of both kinds of shares was issued to and paid up by the public with the exception of 60,000 equity shares held by Jamnadas on which he did not pay the last call of Rs. 3 per share, and which were subsequently forfeited and reissued at a discount of 20 per cent.

Give journal entries to record the above and prepare the balance sheet of the company.

(Adapted from R.A. First)

Solution:

Journal of .....Ltd.

			Dr.	Cr.
			Rs.'000	Rs.'000
	Business Purchase Account	Dr.	17,500	
	To M/s. Karamchand & Co.			17,500
	The purchase of business of M/s.......... Karamchand & Co. for Rs. 1,75,000 as per agreement dated			
	Cash at Bank	Dr.	450	
	Sundry Debtors	Dr.	750	
	Stock in Trade	Dr.	2,790	
	Plant and Machinery	Dr.	4,500	
	Freehold Premises	Dr.	5,400	
	Goodwill	Dr.	4,600	
	To Bills Payable			350
	To Sundry Creditors			640
	To Business Purchase Account			17,500
	Various assets and liabilities taken over (recorded at adjusted figures) ; Goodwill calculated by deducting the value of other assets from the total of Bills Payable, Sundry Creditors and Business Purchase Account.			
	Equity Shares Applications, Allotment, First Call, etc.	Dr.	14,000	
	To Equity Share Capital Account			14,000
	The credit of Rs. 7 per share to Equity Share Capital on 20 lakh shares left for issue to the public.			
	Bank	Dr.	14,000	
	To Equity Shares Applications, Allotment, First Call etc.			14,000
	The receipt of Rs. 7 per share on all the 20 lakh shares.			
	Bank	Dr.	20,000	
	To Preference Share Capital Account			20,000
	The issue and allotment of 20 lakh preference shares to the public, the whole of the amount being received in cash.			
	Equity Shares Final Call Account	Dr.	6,000	
	To Equity Share Capital Account			6,000
	The amount due on 20 lakh shares @ Rs. 3 per share as final call.			
	Bank Account	Dr.	5,800	
	To Equity Shares Final Call Account			5,800
	The amount received as final call on the equity shares except on 60,000 shares.			
	M/s. Karamchand & Co.	Dr.	17,500	
	To Equity Share Capital Account			5,000
	To Preference Shares Capital Account			5,000
	To Redeemable Debentures			5,000
	To Bank			4,500
	The discharge of the purchase consideration as per agreement.			
	Equity Share Capital Account	Dr.	600	
	To (Equity Shares) Final Call Account			180
	To Shares Forfeited Account			480
	The forfeiture of 60,000 equity shares of Rs. 10 each for non-payment of the final call of Rs. 3.			

			Rs.'000	Rs.'000
	Bank	Dr.	480	
	Shares Forfeited Account	Dr.	120	
	To Equity Shares Capital Account			600
	Issue of 60,000 forfeited shares at a discount of 20%.			
	Shares Forfeited Account	Dr.	300	
	To Capital Reserve Account			300
	Balance in the Shares Forfeited Account transferred to Capital Reserve as required by law.			

Balance Sheet of ....Ltd. as on....

Liabilities	*Rs.'000*	*Assets*	*Rs.'000*
Share Capital:		**Fixed Assets:**	
Authorised:	50,000	Goodwill	4,600
Issued and Subscribed:		Freehold Premises	5,400
25 lakh Preference Shares of		Plant and Machinery	4,500
Rs. 10 each fully paid	25,000	**Current Assets, Loans and Advances:**	
25 lakh Equity Shares of		(A) Current Assets	
Rs. 10 each fully paid in cash	25,000	Stock in Trade	2,790
(All the above shares have been		Sundry Debtors	750
allotted as fully paid up pursuant		Cash at Bank	36,250
to a contract without payments		(B) Loans and Advances	Nil
being received in cash)			
Reserves and Surplus:			
Capital Reserve	300		
Secured loans:			
Debentures	3,000		
Current Liabilities and Provisions:			
(A) Current Liabilities			
Sundry Creditors	640		
Bills Payable	350		
(B) Provisions	Nil		
	54,290		54,290

Interest to Vendors. If there is a delay in the settlement and discharge of the purchase consideration, the vendors are generally entitled to interest at an agreed rate from the date of purchase to the date of settlement. Suppose, in the above illustration, the business is purchased as from 1st April, 2009 and that the settlement is made on 31st August 2009. In that case. M/s. Karamchand & Co. will be entitled to interest on Rs. 1 crore 75 lakh at 12% (say) for five months. This amounts to Rs. 8,75,000 and should be debited, on payment, to Interest to Vendors Account. This is charged to the Profit and Loss Account.

Debtors and creditors taken over on behalf of the debtors. Often, a company does not take over the debtors and creditors belonging to the vendor but merely agrees to collect the debts and pay the creditors on behalf of the vendor. This means that any profit or loss made in the process will belong to the vendor. The entries to be made in such a case will be as follows :—

1. At the time of the acquisition of the business :

   Debit Vendors' Debtors at the book value.

   Credit Vendors' Creditors at the book value.

   Credit Vendors' Suspense Account with the difference.

Note. The Debtors and Creditors, in this case, will not be included when the main entries for purchase of business are passed.

2. When debtors are realised :

Debit Bank } with the amount
Credit Vendors' Debtors } realised.

3. When creditors are paid :

Debit Vendors' Creditors } with the amount
Credit Bank } paid.

4. Any loss suffered on realisation of debts will be transferred to Vendors' Suspense Account, thus :

Debit Vendors' Suspense Account.
Credit Vendors' Debtors.

The entry will be reversed if there is a profit.

5. Any gain on payment to creditors will be credited to Vendor's Suspense Account, thus:-

Debit Vendors' Creditors
Credit Vendors' Suspense Account

The entry will be reversed if there is a loss on payment to creditors.

6. If the company is entitled to any commission for the work done:

Debit Vendors' Suspense Account
Credit Commission Account

7. On payment to the Vendor of the amount due in respect of debtors and creditors :

Debit Vendors' Suspense Account
Credit Bank or
Debentures or
Share Capital (as the case may be).

Illustration 64. On 1st March, 2009 a company bought certain assets from R. Hardas. The company also undertook to collect his debts amounting to Rs. 1,30,000 and to pay his creditors for Rs. 30,000 for a commission of 3 per cent on amounts collected and one per cent on amounts paid. The debtors realised Rs. 1,20,000 only out of which Rs. 28,500 was paid to creditors in full settlement. R. Hardas received 14% debentures of the face value of Rs. 50,000 at 95% and the balance in cash. Journalise

Solution:

Journal

Date		Particulars		L.F.	Dr.	Cr.
2009					Rs.	Rs.
March	1	Vendor's Debtors	Dr.		1,30,000	
		To Vendor's Creditors				30,000
		To Vendor's Suspense Account				1,00,000
		The Vendor's debtors and creditors taken over for collection and payment on behalf of the vendor, as per agreement dated....				
		Bank	Dr		1,20,000	
		Vendor's Suspense Account	Dr.		10,000	
		To Vendor's Debtors				1,30,000
		The sum realised from debtors, the loss of Rs. 10,000 i.e. Rs. (1,30,000 – 1,20,000) debited to Vendor's Suspense A/c.				
		Vendor's Creditors Account	Dr.		30,000	
		To Bank				28,500
		To Vendor's Suspense Account				1,500
		The payment in full settlement of Rs. 28,500 to creditors, the profit of Rs. 1,500 credited to Vendor's Suspense A/c.				

		Rs.	Rs.
Vendor's Suspense Account	Dr.	3,885	
To Commission Account			3,885
The commission earned for collection of debts and payment of creditors- 3% on Rs. 1,20,000 Rs. 3,600 1% on Rs. 28,500 Rs. 285 3,885			
Vendor's Suspense Account	Dr.	87,615	
Discount on Issue of Debentures Account	Dr.	2,500	
To 14% Debentures			50,000
To Bank			40,115
The settlements of the vendor's account in respect of debtors and creditors by the issue of Rs. 50,000 debentures at a discount of 5% and the balance in cash.			

An alternative method. Vendor's debtors and creditors not taken over may also be dealt with in the following manner:

(*i*) Debit Vendor's Debtors Account
Credit Debtors' Suspense Account
(*ii*) Debit Creditors' Suspense Account
Credit Vendor's Creditors Account
} with the respective amounts.

(*iii*) On collection of amounts from vendors' debtors —
(a) Debit Bank
Credit Vendor's Debtors Account
(b) Debit Debtors' Suspense Account
Credit Vendors
} with the cash collected.

(*iv*) On discounts allowed to Vendor's debtors, bad debts written off, etc.
Debit Debtors' Suspense Account
Credit Vendor's Debtors Account.

(*v*) On payment being made to Vendor's creditors —
(a) Debit Vendor's Creditors Account
Credit Bank.
(b) Debit Vendor.
Credit Creditors' Suspense Account

(*vi*) On discounts being allowed by the creditors —
Debit Vendor's Creditors Account
Credit Creditors' Suspense Account.

(*vii*) On commission being chargeable to the Vendor for the work —
Debit Vendor
Credit Commission Account.

The above-mentioned entries will ensure that the balance in the Vendor's Debtors Account will equal that in the Debtors' Suspense Account; so also in the case of vendor's creditors. The vendor is credited with actual cash collected from the vendor's debtors and debited with actual payment made to the vendor's creditors and also with the commission that may be chargeable to them.

The illustration given above will be worked out as follows under this method.

Journal

				Dr.	Cr.
2009				Rs.	Rs.
March	1	Vendor's Debtors Account	Dr.	1,30,000	
		To Debtors' Suspense Account			1,30,000
		Vendor's debtors to be collected on behalf of the vendor.			
		Creditors' Suspense Account	Dr.	30,000	
		To Vendor's Creditors Account			30,000
		Creditors to be paid on behalf of the vendor.			
		Bank	Dr.	1,20,000	
		To Vendor's Debtors Account			1,20,000
		Cash collected from Vendor's Debtors.			
		Debtors' Suspense Account	Dr.	1,20,000	
		To Vendor			1,20,000
		Amount due to vendor in respect of cash collected from his debtors.			
		Debtors' Suspense Account	Dr.	10,000	
		To Vendor's Debtors Account			10,000
		"Loss" on vendor's debtors.			
		Vendor's Creditors Account	Dr.	28,500	
		To Bank			28,500
		Amount paid to vendor's creditors.			
		Vendor	Dr.	28,500	
		To Creditors' Suspense Account			28,500
		Amount recoverable from vendor in respect of payment to his creditors.			
		Vendor's Creditors Account	Dr.	1,500	
		To Creditors' Suspense Account			1,500
		"Gain" on vendors' creditors.			
		Vendor	Dr.	3,885	
		To Commission Account			3,885
		Commission chargeable to the vendor.			
		Vendor	Dr.	87,615	
		Discount on Issue of Debentures Account	Dr.	2,500	
		To 14% Debentures			50,000
		To Bank			40,115
		Settlement of vendor's claim in respect of collections and payments on his behalf.			

Illustration 65. The Balance Sheet of Gobind Sewa Ram was as follows :—

Balance Sheet on 31st March, 2009

	Rs.	Rs.		Rs.	Rs.
Creditors	31,000		Sundry Assets		1,05,000
Less: Reserve	1,000	30,000	Debtors	67,200	
Loans		20,000	*Less:* Provision	2,200	65,000
Govind Sewa Ram		1,20,000			
		1,70,000			1,70,000

On 15th July, 2009, G.S. Ltd. was incorporated, taking over all the assets (except Debtors) and the liability for loans; interest at 12 per cent per annum on the purchase price to be allowed to the vendors from 1st April, 2009 to the date of completion. The credit balance of Gobind Sewa Ram's capital to be satisfied by the issue of equity shares in G.S. Ltd.

The loan-holders accept 14% per cent preference shares in discharge of their debts. The company, as agent for the vendor, agrees to collect the debts, which realise ultimately Rs. 63,000 out of which it pays, as agent for the vendor, the creditors at the net figure shown in the balance sheet. Of the balance, it pays on account to Gobind Sewa Ram the sum of Rs. 10,000; the amount remaining undrawn by Govind Sewa Ram, including interest, to be discharged in the form of Rs. 25,000 debentures at 96 and balance in cash. The new company is entitled to all intervening profit (i.e., between 1st April, 2009 and 15th July, 2009)

Show the opening entries of G.S. Ltd. and the closing entries of Govind Sewa Ram in respect of the above, assuming that the date of completion is 31st August, 2009. Ignore income tax.

(*B.Com., Agra and C.A. Final*)

Solution:

Journal of G.S. Ltd.

Date		Particulars		Dr. Rs.	Cr. Rs.
2000 July	15	Sundry Assets	Dr.	1,05,000	
		To Loans			20,000
		To Govind Sewa Ram			85,000
		Assets of Govind Sewa Ram and his loans taken over as per agreement dated			
	15	Vendor's Debtors	Dr.	67,200	
		To Vendor's Creditors			31,000
		To Govind Sewa Ram Suspense Account			36,200
		Debtors and creditors of the vendor to be collected and paid on his behalf as per agreement dated........			
		Bank	Dr.	63,000	
		Govind Sewa Ram Suspense Account	Dr.	4,200	
		To Vendor's Debtors			67,200
		Amount collected from vendor's debtors and the loss transferred to Vendor's Suspense Account.			
		Vendor's Creditors	Dr.	31,000	
		To Bank			30,000
		To Govind Sewa Ram Suspense Account			1,000
		Payment to vendor's creditors at the net amount (i.e., less discount); the profit transferred to Vendor's Suspense Account.			
		Govind Sewa Ram Suspense Account	Dr.	10,000	
		To Bank			10,000
		Payment of Rs. 10,000 on account, to the vendor in respect of amount collected from debtors.			
Aug.	31	Govind Sewa Ram Suspense Account	Dr.	23,000	
		To Govind Sewa Ram			23,000
		Balance in the Vendor's Suspense Account transferred to his account.			

				Rs.	Rs.
Aug.	31	Interest to Vendor's Account	Dr.	4,250	
		To Govind Sewa Ram			4,250
		Interest at 12% on Rs. 85,000 for five months (1st Apr. to 31st Aug.) credited to the vendor.			
"	"	Govind Sewa Ram	Dr.	1,10,125	
		Discount on Issue of Debentures Account	Dr.	1,000	
		To Equity Share Capital Account			85,000
		To Debentures			25,000
		To Bank			1,125
		Discharge of the amount due to the vendor as under: equity shares Rs. 85,000; debentures of Rs. 25,000 at Rs. 96 and the balance in cash.			
"	"	Loan	Dr.	20,000	
		To 14% Preference Share Capital Account			20,000
		Loan of Rs. 20,000 discharged by allotment of 14% preference shares.			

BOOKS OF GOVIND SEWA RAM
Journal

				Dr.	Cr.
2009				Rs.	Rs.
April	1	Realisation Account	Dr.	1,73,200	
		To Sundry Assets			1,05,000
		To Sundry Debtors			67,200
		To Reserve on Creditors			1,000
		Transfer of the various assets and the reserve on creditors to Realisation Account.			
"	"	Sundry Creditors	Dr.	31,000	
		Loans	Dr.	20,000	
		Provision on Debtors Account	Dr.	2,200	
		To Realisation Account			53,200
		Transfer of various liabilities and the provision on debtors to Realisation Account.			
July	15	G.S. Ltd.	Dr.	85,000	
		To Realisation Account			85,000
		Amount payable by G.S. Ltd. on acquisition of the business by the company.			
		G.S. Ltd.	Dr.	63,000	
		To Realisation Account			63,000
		The amount realised by G.S. Ltd. from debtors.			
		Realisation Account	Dr.	30,000	
		To G.S. Ltd.			30,000
		Amount paid to creditors by G.S. Ltd.			
		Bank	Dr.	10,000	
		To G.S. Ltd.			10,000
		Receipt of Rs. 10,000 from G.S. Ltd. on account.			

				Rs.	Rs.
Aug.	31	G.S. Ltd.	Dr	4,250	
		To Realisation Account			4,250
		Interest payable by G.S. Ltd. on Rs. 85,000 for five months at 12%.			
"	"	Shares in G.S. Ltd.	Dr.	85,000	
		Debentures in G.S. Ltd.	Dr.	24,000	
		Bank	Dr.	1,125	
		To G.S. Ltd.			1,10,125
		Receipt of shares, debentures and cash from G.S. Ltd. in settlement.			
"	"	Realisation Account	Dr.	125	
		To Govind Sewa Ram Capital Account.			125
		Profit on realisation transferred to Capital Account.			
"	"	Govind Sewa Ram Capital Account	Dr.	1,20,125	
		To Bank			11,125
		To Debentures in G.S. Ltd.			24,000
		To Shares in G.S. Ltd.			85,000
		Shares, debentures and cash handed over to the proprietor.			

***Entries, when the same account books are continued.** The treatment detailed above applies when the purchasing company starts new books of account. However, often a company decides to continue the same books of account as were being maintained by the seller. In such a case, the following steps will be necessary:

1. If assets and liabilities, which are to be taken over by the purchasing company; are to be revalued, a profit and loss adjustment account should be prepared and the balance transferred to the capital accounts of partners (or shareholders' account if the vendor is a company).
2. If certain assets or liabilities are not taken over by the purchasing company, these should be transferred to the capital accounts of the partners in the ratio of their capitals. If the asset is worthless, it should be transferred in the profit-sharing ratio. In case the vendor is a company, the assets not taken over by the purchasing company will be realised and the liabilities that are not taken over by the purchasing company will be paid. Usually, a separate Bank account is opened for this purpose.
3. The capital accounts of partners (or Shareholders' Account) will be debited and Share Capital Account (for shares issued) or Debentures Account (for debentures issued) and Bank (for cash paid) should be credited.

It will be noted no entries will be required to close the books of the vendor and no special entries will be required to open the books of the purchasing company.

An alternative to the steps Nos. 2 and 3 is to : (1) debit Purchase of Business Account with the amount agreed as purchase price and credit Share Capital (for shares issued), Debentures (for debentures issued) and Bank (for cash paid); and (2) transfer to Purchase of Business Account, the Capital Accounts of partners (or Shareholders' Account) and the assets and liabilities not taken over by the purchasing company.

You will find in the chapter on Amalgamation that the vendor company is known as transferor company and the purchasing company is referred to as the transferee company.

Illustration 66. The following is the Balance Sheet of M/s. A and B as on March 31, 2009:-

Liabilities	*Rs.*	*Assets*	*Rs.*
Sundry Creditors	20,000	Land and Buildings	1,00,000
Mrs. A's Loan	90,000	Plant and Machinery	80,000
Capitals - A	1,20,000	Stock in Trade	30,000
B	80,000	Sundry Debtors	50,000
		Investments	40,000
		Cash at Bank	10,000
	3,10,000		3,10,000

Profits were shared as 2/3 to A and 1/3 to B. On 1st April, 2009 A B Ltd. purchased the business of M/s. A and B for a payment of Rs. 3,00,000 to be made in the form of equity shares of Rs. 100 each credited as Rs. 80 paid. The company does not take over the investments and Mrs. A's Loan. The company also decides to revalue land and buildings at Rs. 1,35,000, plant and machinery at Rs. 70,000 and to create a provision for doubtful debts on debtors @ 5%. There was a claim by a worker for Rs. 3,000 for injuries in an accident. The company decided to admit the claim. Out of the investments, Rs. 6,000 worth are worthless. Mrs. A agrees to receive the remaining investments and 700 shares of A B Ltd. in settlement of her loan.

The company decides to retain the books of account of the firm. Journalise.

Solution:

Journal

Date		Particulars		L.F.	Dr. Rs.	Cr. Rs.
2009 April	1	Land and Buildings	Dr.		35,000	
		To Revaluation Account				35,000
		Increase in the value of land and buildings, for sale of business to A B Ltd.				
"	"	Revaluation Account	Dr.		15,500	
		To Plant and Machinery				10,000
		To Provision for Doubtful Debts				2,500
		To Liability for Accident				3,000
		Decrease in the value of the plant and machinery, creation of provision for doubtful debts and creation of liability for compensation, to be brought into account for sale of business to A B Ltd.				
"	"	Revaluation Account	Dr.		19,500	
		To A's Capital Account				13,000
		To B's Capital Account				6,500
		Transfer of profit on revaluation to partners' capital accounts.				
"	"	Goodwill Account	Dr.		30,500	
		To A's Capital Account				20,333
		To B's Capital Account				10,167
		Raising of goodwill account, the amount calculated as under—				

	Rs.	Rs.
Land and Building		1,35,000
Plant and Machinery		70,000
Stock		30,000
Sundry Debtors (net)		47,500
Cash at Bank		10,000
		2,92,500
Less: Sundry Creditors	20,000	
Liability for accident	3,000	23,000
Net assets		2,69,500
Amount to be paid		3,00,000
Goodwill, Rs. (3,00,000 – 2,69,500)		30,500

Date		Particulars		L.F.	Dr. Rs.	Cr. Rs.
"	"	A's Capital Account	Dr.		4,000	
		B's Capital Account	Dr.		2,000	
		To Investments				6,000
		Transfer of investments worth Rs. 6,000 to capital accounts of A and B in the profit-sharing ratio because they are worthless.				

Date		Particulars		Rs.	Rs.
2009					
April	1	Mrs. A's Loan	Dr.	90,000	
		To Investments			34,000
		To Equity Share Capital Account			56,000
		Settlement of Mrs. A's loan by the remaining investments and by allotment to her of 700 equity shares of Rs. 100 each credited as Rs. 80 paid up.			
"	"	A's Capital Account	Dr.	1,49,280	
		B's Capital Account	Dr.	94,640	
		To Equity Share Capital Account			2,43,920
		Allotment of 1,866 equity shares of Rs. 100 each Rs. 80 paid to A and of 1,183 similar shares to B.			
"	"	A's Capital Account	Dr.	53	
		B's Capital Account	Dr.	27	
		To Bank			80
		Remaining balance paid to them in cash (for fractions of shares).			

Alternatively —

Entries for revaluation of assets and goodwill will be similar to the ones already passed. The other entries will be:

Date		Particulars		Rs.	Rs.
2009					
April	1	Purchase of Business Account	Dr.	3,00,000	
		To Equity Share Capital Account			2,99,920
		To Bank			80
		Allotment of 3,749 equity shares (700 to Mrs. A, 1,866 to A and 1,183 to B) and payment of Rs. 80 in cash to avoid fractions of shares, on transfer of business to A B Ltd.			
"	"	Purchase of Business Account	Dr.	40,000	
		To Investments			40,000
		Investments not taken over by the company.			
"	"	Mrs. A's Loan	Dr.	90,000	
		A's Capital Account	Dr.	1,53,333	
		B's Capital Account	Dr.	96,667	
		To Purchase of Business Account			3,40,000
		Transfer of Mrs. A's Loan and the capital accounts (adjusted) to the Purchase of Business Account.			

EXERCISE XVIII

Practical

1. Smriti Ltd. invited applications for 5,00,000 equity shares of Rs. 10 each payable as follows :—

With application	Rs. 2.50
On allotment	Rs. 3.50
On first call	Rs. 2
On second & final call	Rs. 2

Applications totalled 4,70,000 shares. The Board of Directors accepted all the applications. Both the calls were made. All the moneys were duly received. You are required to :-

(i) pass journal entries for all the transactions including cash transactions,

(ii) prepare cash book,

(iii) show ledger accounts, and

(iv) draw balance sheet after the receipt of final call money.

(Total of Balance Sheet Rs. 47,00,000)

2. Vishwash Ltd. with an authorised share capital of Rs. 90,00,000 divided into shares of Rs. 10 each issued a prospectus inviting application for 6,00,000 equity shares of Rs. 10 each issued at a premium of Rs. 2 per share payable as to Rs. 3 with application, Rs. 5 on allotment and the balance on first and final call to be made three months after the date of allotment.

Applications were received for 12,00,500 shares. An application for 500 shares was rejected on technical grounds while *pro rata* allotment was made on the remaining applications on 27th November, 2009.

All the allottees paid the allotment money due.

The call was made on 27th February, 2010 as scheduled. By 31st March, 2010 all the shareholders barring one shareholder holding 200 shares had paid the call.

Prepare Journal, Cash Book and Ledger. Also draw Balance Sheet as at 31st March, 2010.

[*Total of Balance Sheet Rs. 71,99,200*]

3. Bee Ltd. having a nominal capital of Rs. 20,00,000 in shares of Rs. 10 each, invited applications for 1,00,000 equity shares, payable as follows :—

On application	Rs. 3
On allotment	Rs. 3
On first call	Rs. 2
On second & final call	Rs. 2

The company received applications for 99,000 shares. All the applications were accepted. All moneys due as stated above were received with the exception of the second and final call on 200 shares; these shares were forfeited and reissued as fully paid @ Rs. 9 per share. Expenses of the issue came to Rs. 10,000.

Record the entries relating to above-mentioned matters in the journal of the company and show the balance sheet of the company as finally emerging.

(*Balance Sheet Total Rs. 9,91,400*)

4. On February 1, 2009 the Directors of Alpha Ltd., issued 50,000 equity shares of Rs. 10 each at Rs. 12 per share, payable as to Rs. 5 on application (including premium), Rs. 4 on allotment and the balance on May 1, 2009.

The lists closed on February 10, 2009 by which date applications for 75,000 shares had been received. Allotment was made to all the applicants on a *pro rata* basis. All moneys were duly received except that one shareholder who had applied for 750 shares did not pay the call. After the necessary legal formalities, the shares of the defaulting shareholder were forfeited on September, 2009. These shares were later reissued as fully paid up at Rs. 8 per share on November 1, 2000.

Journalise the transactions. (*Capital Reserve Rs. 2,500*)

5. *B* Limited purchased certain patents under an agreement, dated 15th July, at a cost of Rs. 1,10,000, Rs. 10,000 of which was to be paid to the vendor in cash and Rs. 1,00,000 in fully paid Rs. 10 equity shares. Further capital was issued to the public to the extent of Rs. 2,00,000 as follows:

(*i*) Rs. 1,50,000 in Rs. 10 Equity Shares payable as to Re. 2.50 on application, Rs. 2.50 on allotment and Rs. 5 at the end of three months.

(*ii*) Rs. 50,000 in 14% Preference Shares of Rs. 100 each payable as to Rs. 40 on application, Rs. 40 on allotment and Rs. 20 at the end of three months.

The patents passed to the company in accordance with the agreement on 31st July, which was also the date of allotment. The shares were fully subscribed and duly paid for with the exception of 200 equity shares which were forfeited for non-payment of the final call.

Make entries in the cash book, journal and ledger of the company and prove by a balance sheet the correctness of your entries.

(*Cash Book Balance, Rs. 1,89,000; Total of Balance Sheet, Rs. 2,99,000*)

6. On 1st April, 2009, Brite Ltd. was registered with nominal capital of 6,00,000 Equity Shares of Rs. 10 each. On 5th April, 1,00,000 shares were allotted at par, cash being received in full forthwith. On February 4, 2010 the balance of shares were offered to the public at a premium of Rs. 2.50 per share, the whole issue having been underwritten for a commission of 2 per cent of the issue price. Only 2,80,000 shares were subscribed by and allotted to the public. Rs. 3.50 per share was payable on application, Rs. 4 on allotment and a first call of Rs. 3 per share was payable on 15th March, 2010. The whole of the money due from the public was paid; the underwriters had paid the application and allotment money, but had not paid the first call before the end of the accounting year ended 31st March, 2010.

Give the necessary journal entries for these transactions and show how they would appear in the company's Balance Sheet at 31st March, 2010, assuming that the underwriting commission had not been paid yet.

(*Total of Balance Sheet, Rs. 57,15,000*)

7. The issued share capital of Alfa Limited consists 1,00,000 equity shares of Rs. 10 each fully paid up. The company offers to its shareholders shares on rights basis in the ratio of 1 : 1; the shares of Rs. 10 each being offered at a premium of Rs. 10 per share. Half of the price was payable with the application and the balance was payable on allotment, distribution being as follows:

	With application	*On allotment*
	Rs.	*Rs.*
Share capital	5	5
Securities premium	5	5
	10	10

All the shareholders accepted the offer. One shareholder holding 300 shares paid the full offer price with his application. Another shareholder holding 200 shares failed to pay the allotment money and his shares were subsequently forfeited. Later the shares were reissued as fully paid up for Rs. 4,000 cash.

Journalise the abovementioned transactions. *[C.S. (Inter) June, 1997 Modified]*

(Transfer to capital reserve, Rs. 1,000)

8. (*a*) The directors of a company forfeited 100 equity shares of Rs. 10 each on which Rs. 400 had been paid. The shares were reissued to one of the directors upon payment of Rs. 750. Give the necessary journal entries.

(*b*) The directors of a company forfeited 100 equity shares of Rs. 10 each for non-payment of the first call of Rs. 2 and the final call of Rs. 2. The shares were reissued to one of the directors upon payment of Rs. 8 per share. No entries were made on forfeiture but when the shares were reissued, the cash received was credited to the Share Capital Account. Give the necessary rectifying journal entry.

[Capital Reserve (a) Rs. 150; (b) Rs. 400]

9. B Ltd. registered with Table A as its articles was formed with an authorised capital of 2,00,000 equity shares of Rs. 10 each. On 1st October, 2008 1,00,000 shares were issued, fully paid, to the vendors and 80,000 were subscribed for by the public. On the latter, Rs. 2.50 a share was payable on application, Rs. 2.50 on allotment, Rs. 2.50 on first call due on 1st December, and Rs. 2.50 on the second call due on 1st March, 2009.

On the shares subscribed for by the public there had been paid on 30th September, 2009 the following:

On 60,000 shares	the full amount called
On 18,000 shares	Rs. 7.50 per share
On 500 shares	Rs. 5.00 per share
On 1,500 shares	Rs. 2.50 per share.

On 30th September, 2009 the directors forfeited the shares on which less than Rs. 7.50 had been paid. The calls in arrear on the 18,000 shares were collected on 31st October, 2009 together with the necessary interest. The forfeited shares were reissued on the same date to M at Rs. 8 per share.

Submit journal entries for the transactions and set out the capital items as they should appear in the company's balance sheet as at 31st March, 2009 and 31st March, 2010.

[Balance Sheet Totals as at 31st March, 2009, Rs. 17,41,250 and as at 31st March 2010, Rs. 18,03,750; Transfer to Capital Reserve Rs. 2,250]

10. A prospectus issued by a company invited applications for 2,00,000 equity shares of Rs. 10 each, payable Rs. 2 on application, Rs. 2 on allotment and the balance in two equal instalments at intervals of three months each after allotment which was made on June 15, 2009.

The vendor was to receive 20,000 fully paid equity shares as part payment of the purchase consideration of Rs. 16,00,000 made up as follows : Land and Building Rs. 6,00,000, Plant Rs. 3,50,000, Stock in Trade Rs. 4,50,000 and the balance as Goodwill.

The offer was over-subscribed by 20,000 shares and the amount due on allotment was received in full. Rs. 5,25,000 and Rs. 5,20,000 were received on first and second calls respectively. Show the accounts concerned after opening the books, recording the above receipts on account of capital, and paying the balance of the purchase consideration to the vendor.

Journal entries are not required. *(Cash Book Balance Rs. 4,45,000)*

11. In May, 2009, the Universal Store Ltd. offered for subscription 10,000 14% Debentures of Rs. 100 each at the issue price of 94% payable Rs. 25 per debenture on application, Rs. 50 on allotment and the balance on 1st August, 2009. Interest was to be payable half yearly, on 30th September and 31st March; the first coupon, payable on 30th September, 2009 being 3 per cent. The issue was fully taken up.

Simultaneously, the company issued 10,000 equity shares of Rs. 100 each at a discount of 5%, terms of payment being similar to that of debentures. Assume that the legal formalities have been observed.

Journalise the transactions and show how they would appear in the company's balance sheet as at 31st March, 2010.

[P. & L A/c, Rs. 1,00,000 (Interest) to be shown on the assets side; Bank balance Rs. 17,90,000; Balance Sheet Total Rs. 20,00,000]

12. Ratan & Co. Ltd. issued 10,000 shares of Rs. 100 each at a premium of Rs. 20 per share. The entire issue was underwritten as follows:

A 5,000 shares (firm underwriting 1,000 shares),
B 3,000 shares (firm underwriting 500 shares), and
C 2,000 shares (firm underwriting 500 shares).

Shares applied for were 9,000 shares, the following being the marked forms:

A 3,500 shares
B 1,400 shares and } including firm underwriting.
C 1,600 shares

What is the liability of each underwriter and how much commission will each get, assuming it is the maximum allowed by law?

(Total Liability : A 1,187 shares; B 1,313 shares; C 500 shares)

13. Emess Ltd. issued 40,000 shares which were underwritten as—

P: 24,000 share; Q: 10,000 shares; and R: 6,000 shares. The underwriters made applications for firm underwriting as under:

P: 3,200 shares; Q: 1,200 shares; and R: 4,000 shares. the total subscription excluding firm underwriting (including marked applications) were 20,000 shares, the marked applications were — P: 4,000 shares: Q: 8,000 shares: and R: 2,000 shares.

Prepare a statement showing the net liability of underwriters. *[C.S. Inder, June 1998]*

(Total liability: P 13,280 shares; Q 1,200 shares and R 5,520 shares)

14. Kusum Ltd. has authorised capital of Rs. 25,00,000 divided into 1,00,000 equity shares of Rs. 25 each. The company issued for subscription 25,000 shares at a premium of Rs. 10 each. The entire issue was underwritten as follows:

A — 15,000 shares (firm underwriting – 2,500 shares),
B — 7,500 shares (firm underwriting – 1,000 shares), and
C — 2,500 shares (firm underwriting – 500 shares).

Out of total issue, 22,500 shares including firm underwriting were subscribed.

The following were the marked forms:

A — 8,000 shares
B — 5,000 shares
C — 2,000 shares

Calculate the liability of each underwriter. *[C.S. (Inter) June, 1995]*

(Total liability; A 4,833 shares; B 1,167 shares; C 500 shares Alternatively, A 4,667 shares; B 1,333 shares; C 500 shares)

15. Nirman Ltd. issued 80,000 equity shares which were underwriten as follows:–

Underwriter	*Shares underwriter*
A Ltd.	48,000
B Ltd.	20,000
C Ltd.	12,000

The avobementioned underwriters made application for firm underwriting as follows:–

A Ltd.	6,400 shares
B Ltd.	8,000 shares
C Ltd.	2,400 shares

The total applications excluding firm underwriting but including marked applications were for 40,000 shares. The marked applications were as under:–

A Ltd.	8,000 shares
B Ltd.	10,000 shares
C Ltd.	4,000 shares

The underwriting contracts provide that underwriters be given credit for firm applications and that credit for unmarked application be given in proportion to the shares underwritten.

You are required to show the allocation of liability. *[C.A. (Inter) Nov; 1997 Modified]*

(Total liability: A Ltd. 27,200 shares; B Ltd. 8,000 shares and C Ltd. 4,800 shares)

16. X Ltd. issued 10,000 14% Debentures of Rs. 100 each at a discount of 6%. Eighty per cent of the issue was underwritten by M/s. A.B. Co., for a commission of 1 per cent on the nominal value of the debentures.

Applications were received for 7,500 Debentures. Journalise the transactions, assuming all moneys due have been received. Also show the entries in the balance sheet of the company.

(Balance Sheet, Rs. 9,50,000)

17. *C* Ltd. made an issue, which was fully subscribed, of Rs. 2,00,000 14% First Mortgage Debentures (Rs. 100 each) at 98%. The lists opened and closed and the stock was allotted on 31st October, subscriptions being payable 10% on application, 40% on allotment, 25% on 31st December and 23% on 31st March. Under the terms of the issue, payment could be made in full on allotment, interest on any amounts prepaid being allowable at the rate of 12% per annum; such interest was payable by the company on 31st March. The allottees of one-half of the Debentures took advantage of the pre-payment terms. The others paid on the due dates. Journalise.

(Interest on calls in advance Rs. 1,650)

18. *B* Ltd. made an issue of 10,000 14% Mortgage Debentures of Rs. 100 each at 96. The whole of the issue was underwritten by M/s S.C. & Co. 8,500 debentures were applied for and allotted to the public. The underwriters discharged their liability and were paid their commission which was at the rate of 1% on the nominal value of the debentures. Give journal entries, ledger accounts and show the balance sheet of the company.

(Balance Sheet, Rs. 10,00,000)

19. *A* Ltd. offered to the public 5,000 14% Mortgage Debentures of Rs. 100 each at Rs. 105. 80% of the issue was underwritten by M/s. Stocks & Shares for a commission @ 1.5% of the issue price of debentures underwritten. Applications were received from the public for 4,000 debentures which were allotted. Show the balance sheet of the company. *(Balance Sheet Total Rs. 5,04,000)*

20. Active Limited made the following issues of Debentures :

(*i*) For cash @ 90% 6,000 Debentures of Rs. 100 each.

(*ii*) To a creditor who supplied machinery costing Rs. 1,00,000, 1,100 Debentures of Rs. 100 each.

(*iii*) To Bank for a loan of Rs. 7,00,000 as collateral security, 10,000 Debentures of Rs. 100 each.

Jouranlise the transactions.

21. Give journal entries for the following:

(*i*) The Board of Directors forfeit 2,000 equity shares (issued at par) on account of non-payment of final call of Rs. 2 per share. Later, these shares of Rs. 10 each are re-issued as fully paid up at a premium of Re.1 per share.

(*ii*) The company allots 60,000 equity shares of Rs. 10 each as fully paid to the Liquidator of V Co. Ltd. in full satisfaction of consideration of Rs. 6,60,000 for the business purchased from V Co.

(*iii*) The company allots 1,000 12% debentures of Rs. 100 each at an issue price of Rs. 96 per debenture redeemable at a premium of Rs. 8 per debenture. (The liability of premium is also to be recorded at the time of issue of debentures).

(*iv*) 3,000 fully convertible debentures of Rs. 100 each are converted into 20,000 equity shares of Rs. 10 each at a premium of Rs. 5 per share. *[B. Com. (Hons.) Delhi 1991]*

22. M. Ltd. issued 4,000 12% Debentures of Rs. 100 each at 105. The debentureholders had the option of converting, within one year, debentures into 14% Redeemable Preference Shares of Rs. 100 at Rs. 125.

At the end of the first year, the interest on debentures was outstanding. Holders of 200 debentures decided to take advantage of the option. Give journal entries and show the balance sheet of the company.

(Balance Sheet Total Rs. 4,68,000)

23. D. Ltd. issued 10,000 Debentures of Rs. 100 each at a discount of 6%. The Debentures are to be redeemed at the rate of Rs. 1,00,000 each year commencing with the end of the fifth year. How much Discount on Issue of Debentures should be written off each year ?

(Total of ratios 95; each of the first five years Rs. 6,315.79)

24. The following is the Balance Sheet at Abhipraya Limited as on 31st March, 2009:

	Rs.		*Rs.*
Share Capital :		Fixed Assets	24,00,000
5,000, 12% Redeemable Pref.		Stock	5,00,000
Shares of Rs. 100 each	5,00,000	Debtors	50,000
10,000 Equity Shares of		Cash	50,000
Rs. 100 each	10,00,000		

Capital Reserve	1,00,000	
Securities Premium Account	1,00,000	
General Reserve	2,00,000	
Profit and Loss Account	1,00,000	
Current Liabilities	10,00,000	
	30,00,000	30,00,000

The Preference Shares are to be redeemed on 1st April, 2010 at 10 per cent premium.

On 1st April, 2010, a fresh issue of equity shares was made to the extent it is required under the Companies Act for the purpose of the redemption of preference shares.

The shortfall in cash resources for the purpose of redemption after utilizing the proceeds of fresh issue was met by raising a bank loan, the cash balance of Rs. 50,000 being the minimum the company requires for its trading operations.

Draft journal entries in the books of the company to record these share capital transactions and prepare the balance sheet, in the form prescribed by the Companies Act 1956, immediately after redemption.

[Adapted B.Com. (Hons.) Delhi, 1987]

(Capital Redemption Reserve Rs. 3,00,000; Balance Sheet Total Rs. 30,00,000)

25. Ajanta Trading Co. Ltd. has an authorised capital of Rs. 60,00,000 divided into 10,000 14% redeemable preference shares of Rs. 100 each and 5,00,000 equity shares of Rs. 10 each. On 31st March, 2009 all the abovementioned shares were fully paid; Securities Premium showed a balance of Rs. 7,50,000 whereas General Reserve and Profit & Loss Account stood at Rs. 24,50,000 and Rs. 3,75,000 respectively.

The company decided to redeem all the preference shares at a premium of Rs. 2 per share and for this specific purpose, the company issued for cash 50,000 equity shares of Rs. 10 each at a premium of Rs. 4 per share, payable in full with application. The issue was fully subscribed; the expenses of the issue amounting to Rs. 75,000. It is the intention of the directors that the minimum reduction should be made in revenue reserves. Jouranalise all the abovementioned transactions.

26. Spolight Limited has issued Share Capital of 60,000, 14% Redeemable Preference Shares of Rs. 20 each and 4,00,000 Equity Shares of Rs. 10 each. The Preference Shares are redeemable at a premium of 5 per cent on 1st April, 2009.

As at 31 March, 2009 the company's Balance Sheet showed the following position:

Liabilities	*Rs.*	*Assets*	*Rs.*
Issued Share Capital :		Plant and Machinery	25,00,000
60,000, 14% Redeemable Preference		Furniture and Fixtures	9,00,000
Shares of Rs. 20 each fully paid	12,00,000	Investments	3,50,000
4,00,000 Equity Shares of Rs 10 each		Stock	15,00,000
fully paid	40,00,000	Debtors	14,00,000
Profit and Loss A/c	7,00,000	Balance at Bank	3,50,000
Sundry Creditors	11,00,000		
	70,00,000		70,00,000

In order to facilitate the redemption of preference shares, it was decided:

(*a*) to sell all the investments for Rs. 3,00,000.

(*b*) to finance part of the redemption from company funds subject to leaving of balance in Profit and Loss Account of Rs 2,00,000.

(*c*) to issue sufficient equity shares of Rs. 10 each at a premium of Rs. 2 per share to raise the balance of funds required.

All the abovementioned decisions were fully carried out and the preference shares were duly redeemed.

You are required to prepare

(*i*) Journal entries to record the above transactions, and

(*ii*) A memorandum balance sheet as on completion of redemption.

(Adapted I.C.W.A. Inter June, 1981)

(Fresh Issue of 75,000 shares, Balance Sheet Total Rs 65,90,000)

27. The following balances are appearing in the books of Well-done Limited:

	Rs.
Redeemable Preference Share Capital	5,00,000

Calls-in-arrear (Redeemable Preference Shares)	10,000
General Reserve	3,00,000
Securities Premium	40,000
Development Rebate Reserve	2,00,000

It is ascertained that:

Preference shares are of Rs. 100 each fully called, due for immediate redemption at a premium of 10%.

Calls in arrear are on account of final call on 500 shares held by four members whose whereabouts are not known.

Balance of general reserve and securities premium is to be fully utilised for the purposes of redemption and the shortfall is to be made good by issue of equity shares of Rs. 10 each at par.

The redemption of preference shares was duly carried out.

You are required to give the journal entries and the relevant extracts from the liabilities side of the balance sheet as they would appear after the redemption is carried out.

(Adapted C.A. Inter)

(Amount transferred to Capital Redemption Reserve Rs. 2,90,000; Preference Shares Redemption Suspense Account Rs. 55,000)

28. The following is the Balance Sheet of Oskar India Ltd. at 31st March, 2009:

Liabilities	*Rs.*	*Assets*	*Rs.*
Preference Share Capital:		Fixed assets	6,00,000
2,500 shares of Rs. 100 each,		Investments	50,000
fully called-up	2,50,000	Bank	90,000
Less: Final call of Rs. 20 per			
share unpaid	2,000		
	2,48,000		
Equity Share Capital:			
30,000 shares of Rs. 10 each,			
fully paid-up	3,00,000		
Securities Premium	15,000		
Profit & Loss Account	1,50,000		
Creditors	27,000		
	7,40,000		7,40,000

On 30th September, 2009s, the Board of Directors decided to redeem the preference shares at a premium of 10% and to sell the investments at its market price of Rs. 40,000. They also decided to issue sufficient number of equity shares of Rs. 10 each at a premium of Re. 1 per share, required after utilising the Profit and Loss Account leaving a balance of Rs. 50,000. Premium on redemption is required to be set off against Securities Premium Account.

Repayments on redemption were made in full except to one shareholder holding 50 shares due to his leaving India for good. Assume that calls in arrears were received in full.

You are required to show the journal entries and the balance sheet of the company after redemption. Assumptions made should be shown in the working.

[Adapted Co. Sec. (Inter) Dec. 1987] *(No. of new shares 16,000; Total of Balance Sheet Rs. 6,38,500)*

29. X Ltd. has the following balance sheet as on 31 March, 2010.

	Rs.		*Rs.*
Share Capital:		Fixed Assets	22,00,000
Issued, subscribed and fully paid up		Current Assets	8,00,000
10,000 Equity Shares of Rs. 100 each	10,00,000		
5,000 Preference Shares of Rs. 100 each	5,00,000		
Capital Reserve	1,00,000		
Securities Premium Account	1,00,000		
General Reserve	2,00,000		
Profit and Loss Account	1,00,000		
Current Liabilities	10,00,000		
	30,00,000		30,00,000

The preference shares are to be redeemed at 10 per cent premium. Fresh issue of equity shares is to be made to the extent it is required under the Companies Act for the purpose of this redemption. The shortfall in funds for the purpose of the redemption after utilising the proceeds of the fresh issue are to be met by taking a bank loan. Show journal entries.

(Adapted C.A. Inter)

(Amount transferred to Capital Redemption Reserve Rs. 3,00,000)

30. The following balances were extracted from the books of Redemption Limited as on 31st March, 2010:

	Rs.
2,000 14% redeemable preference shares of Rs. 100 each, fully called up	2,00,000
Less: Calls in arrear at Rs. 20 per share on 300 shares	6,0000
	1,94,000
Capital reserve	10,000
General reserve	50,000

The preference shares were redeemed on 1st April, 2010 at a premium of Rs. 5 per share. The company issued 13,000 equity shares of Rs. 10 each, at par, for the purpose of redeeming the preference shares, which were fully subscribed and duly allotted.

You are required to show the journal entries showing the transactions relating to the redemption of shares and the relevant extracts on the liabilities side of the balance sheet after such redemption.

(Adapted C.A. Inter)

(Capital Redemption Reserve Account Rs. 40,000)

Notes (1) Premium on redemption should not be met out of capital reserve because it may be out of appreciation of assets, and (2) Redeemable preference shares having calls in arrear will be redeemed later when they become fully paid up.

31. Following are the extracts of Bharat Co. Ltd.'s balance sheet as at 31st March, 2010:

Liabilities	*Rs.*
15,000 14% Redeemable Preference Shares of Rs. 100 each, fully paid	15,00,000
Capital Reserve	20,000
Securities Premium	5,000
General Reserve	6,70,000
Profit & Loss Account	40,000

The company redeems all its preference shares at a premium of 10%. For the purpose it issues equity shares of Rs. 100 each at a premium of 10% to the minimum possible extent.

Pass journal entries. *[Fresh issue Rs. 8,500 shares]*

32. X Ltd. whose issued share capital on 31st March, 2010 consisted of 2,40,000 10% preference shares of Rs. 10 each fully paid-up and 6,00,000 equity shares of Rs. 10 each fully-paid up, decided to redeem its preference shares at a premium of Re. 1 per share. The company's balance sheet as at 31st March, 2010 showed a balance of Rs. 28,00,000 in its general reserve. The redemption was carried out partly out of profits and partly out of the proceeds of a fresh issue of 1,20,000 equity shares of Rs.10 each at a premium of Rs. 3.50 p. share. The premium payable on redemption of preference shares was met out of the premium received on the new issue of equity shares.

Three months after the redemption of preference shares, the company issued one fully paid-up equity share by way of bonus for every five shares held by the equity shareholders. For the purpose, capital reserves were used to the maximum possible extent.

You are required to pass the necessary journal entries for all the abovementioned transactions.

(**Hint:** Amount of securities premium available for issue of bonus shares = Rs. 4,20,000 – Rs. 2,40,000 = 1,80,000. Amount of bonus shares = Rs. $\frac{1}{5}$ (60,00,000 + 12,00,000 = Rs. 14,40,000)

33. The following is the summarised balance sheet of X Ltd. as on 31st March, 2010:–

Liabilities	*Rs.*
1,00,000 Equity Shares of Rs. 10 each, fully paid up	10,00,000
60,000 10% Preference Shares of Rs. 10 each Rs. 8 called and paid up	4,80,000
Capital Reserve	2,00,000
Securities Premium Account	1,20,000
General Reserve	2,50,000
Profit and Loss Account	4,00,000

	Rs.
Sundry Creditors	2,00,000
	26,50,000
Assets	***Rs.***
Net Block	10,00,000
Investments	4,00,000
Inventories	4,50,000
Accounts Receivable	7,80,000
Cash at Bank	20,000
	26,50,000

On 1st April, 2010, the company made a final call on its preference shares. The call was paid by all the shareholders. Thereafter, the company redeemed the fully paid preference shares at a premium of 10%. For this purpose, the company sold its investments for Rs. 4,40,000 and issued 2,000 11% preference shares of Rs. 100 each, the full amount being received with applications.

After the redemption of preference shares, the company issued fully paid bonus shares in the ratio of one equity shares for every two equity shares held.

Pass journal entries for all the abovementioned transactions and prepare the balance sheet of the company immediately after the completion of these transactions. Make the necessary assumptions.

[Adapted B.Com. (Hons.), Delhi 1999]

(Balance sheet total Rs. 23,50,000 and Cash balance Rs. 1,20,000)

34. A limited company has an authorised capital of Rs. 10 crore in shares of Rs. 10 each of which 60 lakh shares have been issued and are fully paid. A summary of its balance sheet on 31st March, 2010 is as follows:

Liabilities	*Rs. in lakhs*	*Assets*	*Rs. in lakhs*
Share Capital:	600	Fixed Assets (net)	1,100
Debenture redemption fund	480	Debenture redemption fund investments	
Profit and loss account	190	(cost) market value Rs. 408 lakh)	480
12% Debentures redeemable at 102%	500	Current assets	300
Current liabilities	110		
	1,880		1,880

Interest on the debentures had been paid upto 31st March, 2010. On 1st April, 2010, the directors gave notice to redeem the 12% debentures on 1st July, 2010 giving the holders the option to be repaid either wholly in cash or by issue of four shares of Rs. 10 each (fully paid) for every Rs. 100 debentures.

Sixty per cent of the holders exercised the option to take shares, and the cash for the remainder was obtained by realising a sufficient amount of the investment at their market value on 31st March, 2010.

Draft journal entries to record these transactions and any consequential transfers which you consider necessary. *[C.S. (Inter) Dec. 1994 Modified]*

(Balance of Debentures Redemption Fund Rs. 480 lakh)

(**Hint:** Total amount required for redemption = Rs. 200 lakh + Rs. 4 lakh = Rs. 204 lakh, cost of investment sold to collect Rs. 204 lakh = Rs. 240 lakh. Loss on sale = Rs. 240 lakh – 204 lakh = Rs. 36 lakh).

35. S Ltd. made an issue of 1,000 14% Debentures of Rs. 500 each on 1st April, 2007 at the issue price of Rs. 480. The terms of issue provided that beginning with 2009-2010 Rs. 20,000 Debentures should be redeemed either by purchase in the market or by drawings by lot at par. The expenses of issue amounted to Rs. 4,000 which were written off in 2007-08. In 2008-09 and 2009-2010, Rs. 5,000 were written off the Discount on Issue of Debentures.

In 2009-2010 the company purchased Rs. 6,000 Debentures @ Rs. 470 on 31st December cum-interest and Rs. 10,000 Debentures @ Rs. 475 ex-interest on 28th February, the expenses being Rs. 400. On 31st March, the debentures necessarily to be redeemed were paid off at par by drawings by lot. Assuming the interest is payable on 30th September and 31st March, pass journal entries to record the above transactions including interest on debentures. *(Profit on redemption, Rs. 570 and Rs. 500)*

36. Gamma Ltd. has an authorised capital of Rs. 15,00,000 in shares of Rs. 10 each of which 80,000 shares have been issued and are fully paid. The following is the summary of the Balance Sheet as on March 31, 2009:

	Rs.		Rs.
Share Capital	8,00,000	Fixed Assets (net)	12,50,000
Debentures Redemption Reserve	3,00,000	Investments at cost	1,85,000
General Reserve	2,00,000	Stock-in-Trade	1,80,000
14% Debentures	4,00,000	Sundry Debtors	1,07,000
Current Liabilities	1,70,000	Balance at Bank	1,48,000
	18,70,000		18,70,000

The following transactions took place:

(1) On August 1, 2009, new shares were offered to the existing shareholders, in the ratio of one for every five shares held, new shares at a price of Rs. 12.50 per share payable as to Rs. 5 on application, and the balance on allotment. The shareholders took up all the shares to which they were entitled and the amounts due on allotment, which took place on August 17, 2009, were all received by August 22, 2009.

(2) On September 1, 2009, all the investments were realised, the net proceeds, amounting to Rs. 1,66,000 being received on September 12.

(3) On September 30th, 1999, all outstanding Debentures were redeemed at a premium of 5 per cent and half year's interest due on that date was paid.

(4) Expenses of the share issue amounted to Rs. 5,000 and were paid on September 20.

Journalise the entries to record the above transactions, utilising the Securities Premium Account to the full extent permitted by law

[Adapted from C.A. (Eng.) Inter]

37. A company issued 5,000 14% Debentures of Rs. 100 each at par on 1st April, 2005 redeemable at par on 31st March, 2010. A Sinking Fund was established for the purpose. It was expected that investment would earn 10 per cent net. Sinking Fund tables show that Re. 0.1638 amounts to Re. 1 at the end of five years @ 10%. On 31st March, 2010 the investment realised Rs. 3,90,000. On that day the company's bank balance stood at Rs. 1,45,600. The Debentures were duly redeemed. Give the necessary ledger accounts.

(Profit on sale of investment Rs. 9,902 ; Transfer to General Reserve Rs. 5,09,910)

38. X Ltd. issued 2000 12% Debentures of Rs. 100 each at par on 1st April, 2007. These debentures are redeemable at the end of the fifth year at 5% premium. It was resolved that Sinking Fund should be formed and invested in 10% Development Bonds of Rs. 100 each. Interest of Bonds is payable on 31st March every year.

Reference to Sinking Fund Table shows that Re. 0.1638 invested at the end of every year at 10% compound interest will produce Re. 1 at the end of the fifth year.

10% Development Bonds of the required amount were purchased on different dates at the following prices:

On March 31, 2008	Rs. 94
On March 31, 2009	Rs. 96
On March 31, 2010	Rs. 98

You are required to show Debenture Redemption Fund, Debenture Redemption Fund Investments Account and Interest on Debenture Redemption Find Investments Accounts for the first three years in the books of X Ltd. Accounting year of the company ends on 31st March.

[Adapted B.Com. (Hons.) Delhi, 1997]

(Balances: Debenture Redemption Fund Rs. 1,14,474; Debenture Redemption Fund Investments Accounts Rs. 1,14,462; Interest Rs. 3,660 and Rs. 7,620; Bonds purchased 366, 396 and 429)

39. On 1st October 2007, a company issued 10,000 12% Debentures of Rs. 100 each (interest payable on 30th September and 31st March). The company is allowed to purchase own debentures which may be cancelled or kept or reissued at the company's option. The company made the following purchases in the open market:

On 31st August, 2008, 1,000 Debentures @ Rs. 98 ex-interest

On 31st December, 2009, 500 Debentures @ Rs. 97 cum interest.

The debentures purchased on 31st August 2008 were cancelled on 31st March, 2010. Give entries to record the transactions and show the balance sheet on 31st March, 2010.

(Profit on redemption Rs. 2,000)

40. Moon Ltd. issued on 1st April, 2006 20,000, 12% debentures of Rs. 100 each, redeemable at the option of the company after the second year at Rs. 104 upon two months' notice. the following debentures were purchased in the open market:

(*i*) on 12th June, 2008, Rs. 4,000 nominal at cum-interest cost of Rs. 4,025; and

(*ii*) on 24th August 2008, Rs. 7,000 nominal at ex-interest cost of Rs. 6,915.

These debentures were retained as investments till 30th September, 2009 when the debentures were cancelled. Due dates for interests on debentures are 30th September and 31st March. The books of accounts are closed every year on 31st March.

Show the following ledger accounts for the year 2008-2009 and 2009-2010:

(*i*) 12% debentures account.

(*ii*) Own debentures account.

(*iii*) Interest on own debentures account.

(*iv*) Interest on debentures account.

[*C.S. (Inter), June 1999, Adapted C.A. (Inter)*] (*Profit on redemption Rs. 156 or Rs. 596*)

41. A company had Rs. 4,50,000 14% Debentures outstanding on 1st April, 2009 (redeemable on 31st March, 2010). On that date the Sinking Fund stood at Rs. 3,74,500 represented by Rs. 50,000 own debentures purchased at an average price of Rs. 99 per debenture and Rs. 3,30,000 10 per cent stock. The annual instalment was Rs. 35,500.

On 31st March, 2010 investments were realised at 98% and the Debentures were redeemed. Pass journal entries and write up the accounts for the year ended 31st March, 2010.

(*Capital profit on cancellation of own debentures Rs. 500; loss on sale of 10 per cent stock Rs. 1,600*)

42. A company had issued, some time ago, 10,000 12% Debentures of Rs. 100 each at Rs. 97.50 redeemable at the end of 10 years at par, or previously by six months' notice at Rs. 102 at the company's option.

On March 31st, 2009 the accounts showed balances in Debentures Redemption Fund of Rs. 53,500 represented by 10% Rs. 42,800 nominal value Government Loan Bonds, purchased at an average price of Rs. 101, and Rs. 10,272 uninvested in cash.

On 1st April, 2009 the company decided to purchase Rs. 11,000 of its own Debentures at an inclusive cost of Rs. 10,272 instead of further Government Loan Bonds and this was carried out forthwith. On 30th September, 1999, the company gave six months' notice to holders of Rs. 40,000 worth of Debentures and on 31st March, 2010 carried out the redemption by sale of Rs. 40,800 of Government Loan Bonds at par and cancelled the same together with their own holding.

Journalise the foregoing transactions as well as those for interest on Government Loan Bonds and on the company's own debentures throughout the year ended 31st March, 2010 the interest on the Bonds being payable on 31st March, and on the Debentures on 30th September and 31st March.

(*Adapted C. A. Inter*)

(*Capital profit on cancellation of own debentures Rs. 728; loss on sale of investment Rs. 408*)

43. The Balance Sheet of Industrial Enterprises Ltd. as at 31st March, 2008 disclosed the following information:

	Rs.	
1. 14% 2000 Debentures	17,00,000	
2. Debentures Redemption Fund	11,63,600	
3., Turbine Replacement Fund	7,75,700	
4. Investments:		
10% Government Securities (purchased at par) being investments of		
	Rs.	Rs.
Debenture Redemption Fund	11,63,600	
Turbine Replacement Fund	7,75,700	19,39,300
Turbine at cost		11,21,700

The contribution to the Debenture Redemption Fund and Turbine Replacement Fund was Rs. 1,39,070 and Rs. 87,190 respectively per year both for 2008-09 and 2009-2010. Debentures fell due for payment on 31st March, 2010. Prepare the above accounts in the books of the company for 2008-09 and 2009-2010, assuming that securities were realised on 31st March, 2010 at cost and interest on securities on 31st March was immediately invested. A new turbine was purchased for Rs. 13,00,000 and the old turbine was sold for Rs. 3,00,000 in 2009-2010. How would you show the above accounts in the Balance Sheet on 31st March, 2010.

44. A company had Rs. 8,60,000 14% Debentures outstanding on April 1, 2009. On that date the Sinking Fund was Rs. 7,49,000 represented by Rs. 1,50,000 own debentures purchased at Rs. 90 on an average and Rs. 7,00,000 10% Government Loan. The annual contribution to the Sinking Fund was Rs. 20,000. On 31st March, 2010, the investments were realised at 90% and all debentures were redeemed (or cancelled as the case may be) at a premium of 4%.

Pass journal entries and prepare accounts relating to the matters stated above.

[*Adapted from C.A. (Inter)*]

(*Capital profit on cancellation of own debentures Rs. 15,000; Profit on sale of investment Rs. 16,000*)

45. Wye Ltd. issued 5,000 14% Debentures of Rs. 100 each. On 1st April, 2009 the Sinking Fund showed a balance of Rs. 2,70,000 represented by 10% Government Loan of the face value of Rs. 3,00,000. Interest dates in both cases were 30th September and 31st March. On 30th June, 1999, 300 Debentures were purchased in the market @ Rs. 92 and cancelled; the amount required being raised by selling Government loan of the face value of Rs. 30,000. The annual appropriation to Sinking Fund is Rs. 81,900. Give journal entries recording these transactions. Also show important ledger accounts for the year ended 31st March, 2010.

46. MM Ltd. had the following among their ledger opening balances as on April 1, 2009:

	Rs.
11% Debentures A/c (1999 issue)	50,00,000
Debenture Redemption Fund A/c	45,00,000
13.5% Debentures in XX Ltd. A/c (Face value Rs. 20,00,000)	19,50,000
Own Debentures A/c (Face value Rs. 20,00,000)	18,50,000

As 31st March, 2010 was the date for redemption of the 1999 Debentures, the company started buying own debentures and made the following purchases in the open market:

1-5-2009 2,000 debentures at Rs. 98 cum-interest.

1-9-2009 2,000 debentures at Rs. 99 ex-interest. Half-yearly interest is due on the debentures on the 30th September and 31st March in the case of both the companies.

On 31st March, 2010, the debentures in XX Ltd. were sold for Rs. 95 each ex-interest. On that date, the outstanding debentures of MM Ltd. were redeemed by payment and by cancellation.

Show the entries in the following ledger accounts of MM Ltd. during 2009-2010—

(a) Debenture Redemption Fund A/c

(b) Own Debentures A/c.

The face value of a debenture was Rs. 100.

(Round off calculations to the nearest rupee) [*Adapted C.A. (Inter) Nov. 1984*]

[*Hints : Profit on cancellation, Rs. 1,57,833 will be transferred to capital reserve. Interest on own debentures Rs. 2,53,000. Transfer from Debenture Redemption Fund to General Reserve, Rs. 49,73,000*]

47. The following balances appeared in the books of Lee Ltd. on 31st March, 2009:

		Rs.	*Rs.*
14% Mortgage Debentures			10,00,000
Sinking Fund			5,41,400
Sinking Fund Investments:		*Rs.*	
10% Port Trust Bonds	(Rs. 4,00,000)	3,60,000	
Own Debenture	(Rs. 1,00,000)	90,000	4,50,000

Interest dates in both cases are 30th September and 31st March.

The investments were as on 1st April, 2008; the investments in respect of 2008-09 were made on 1st April, 2009 in the form of Port Trust Bonds purchased at 92%.

On June 30, 2009, the company purchased own debenture of the face value of Rs. 1,00,000 @ 93, the required amount being realised by sale of Port Trust Bonds (to the nearest Rs. 100) at Rs. 92.75. The company resold own debentures of the face value of Rs. 50,000 @ 97 cum-interest on 28th February, 2010, and cancelled the remaining debentures held by it on 31st March.

Prepare ledger accounts arising out of above for 2009-2010.

(*Annual appropriation Rs. 37,400*)

48. Tee Ltd. issued on 1st April, 2006 3,000 14% Redeemable Preference Shares of Rs. 100 each, payment having been received in cash on that date. These shares were redeemable on 31st March, 2010 at a premium of 10%. The company decided to establish a sinking fund for the purpose and make suitable investments which were expected to earn a net yield of 12% p.a. Tables show that to produce Re. 1 in four years at 12% p.a., an annual investment of Re. 0.2092 is required.

Prepare ledger accounts for the four years, assuming the investments to have been sold at par and the redemption to have been carried out as planned.

(*Annual appropriation Rs. 69,047*)

49. The summarised Balance Sheet of Notsogay Ltd. on March 31, 2010 was as follows:

	Rs.		*Rs.*
Share Capital:		Goodwill	2,00,000
12% Redeemable Preference Shares		Other Fixed Assets at Cost	6,12,000
of Rs. 10 each fully paid *less* calls		Stock	4,50,000

	Rs.		Rs.
in arrear, Rs. 10,000 @ Rs. 2 per share	1,90,000	Debtors	2,15,000
		Discount on Issue of Debentures	12,000
14% Redeemable Preference Shares of Rs. 10 each, Rs. 8 called up	2,00,000		
Equity Shares of Rs. 10 each	4,00,000		
Profit and Loss Account	2,60,000		
14% Debentures	3,00,000		
Bank Loan	50,000		
Creditors	89,000		
	14,89,000		14,89,000

Wanting to redeem the preference shares and the debentures, the company offered to the redeemable preference shareholders and debenture-holders the option to convert their holdings into equity shares which are to be treated as worth Rs. 12.50. One-half of the preference shareholders and one-third of the debentureholders agreed to do this.

The company issued 30,000 equity shares @ Rs. 12.50 to the public for cash and with the funds available paid off the bank loan and redeemed the remaining preference shares and debentures. Journalise the transactions and show how the balance sheet will appear after the transactions have been completed.

(Total of Balance Sheet Rs. 15,52,000 after writing off Discount of Debentures)

50. Brown and Black are proprietors of competing businesses. They decide for their own protection to amalgamate and for this purpose float a company called Brown and Black Ltd., with an authorised capital of Rs. 10,00,000 divided into 60,000 equity shares of Rs. 10 each and 4,000 14% preference shares of Rs. 100 each.

On the date of the transfer, Brown's assets amount to Rs. 2,65,350 excluding goodwill. His liabilities at the same time amount to Rs. 32,600. On the same date, Black's assets amount to Rs. 1,95,000 excluding goodwill and his liabilities Rs. 15,000. It is agreed that the company will take over the assets and liabilities of both Brown and Black and will issue to each 15,000 equity shares fully paid up and pay the balance in cash. It is also agreed that fully paid up preference shares will be issued to them on account of goodwill which is to be valued on the basis of two years' purchases of the average of the last three years' profits which are as follows:

	Brown	*Black*
	Rs.	*Rs.*
1st year	16,000	8,000
2nd year	12,000	11,000
3rd year	11,000	14,000

In addition to the above, the public subscribe and pay in full for 20,000 equity shares and the remaining preference shares. The company also pays Rs. 15,000 as preliminary expenses.

You are required to show the vendors' accounts in the company's ledger and prepare the balance sheet of the company after these transactions are completed.

(Adapted R.A. First) (Total of Balance Sheet, Rs. 9,47,600)

51. The Balance Sheet of P, Q & R, stood as under when they sold off the concern to a newly started joint stock company:

	Rs.		*Rs.*
P Capital	90,000	Land and Buildings	56,000
Q's Capital	60,000	Machinery	28,000
R's Capital	30,000	Stock	52,000
Creditors	16,000	Debtors	36,000
		Bills Receivable	24,000
	1,96,000		1,96,000

The joint stock company is started with a capital of Rs. 4,00,000 divided into 40,000 shares of Rs. 10 each. It also issues debentures for Rs. 2,00,000 at a discount of 5%. The entire concern of P, Q and R is taken up by the company on agreeing to pay them Rs. 96,000 by the allotment of 9,600 shares fully paid and Rs. 96,000 in cash.

All the debentures and the remaining shares are issued to the public which are all taken up and paid for with the exception of 4,000 shares, held by A on which he has not paid the final call of Rs. 4 per share which were forfeited and reissued as fully paid at a discount of Rs. 2 per share. The company paid Rs. 2,000 for preliminary expenses.

Pass the necessary journal entries in the books of the company and prepare also the balance sheet.

(Adapted from R.A. First) (Total of Balance Sheet Rs. 6,32,000)

52. A company which purchased the business of M/s. X and Y agreed to collect their debts and pay off their creditors for a commission of 3% on amounts collected and 2 per cent on amounts paid, any loss or profit in the process being that of the vendors. The debtors on the date of acquisition were Rs. 40,000 and creditors were Rs. 6,000.

Three months later the company reported that out of the debtors, Rs. 24,000 had been collected including Rs. 1,500 previously written off as a bad debt. Discounts allowed were Rs. 600. Creditors were paid off in full, the discount earned being Rs. 200. But a claim of Rs. 500 for damages had to be admitted and paid in respect of a late supply of goods to one of their customers by the firm.

Journalise the transactions in the books of the company.

(*Commission Rs. 846; Net payment Rs. 16,854*)

53. Zee Co. Ltd. agreed to collect the debts and pay the creditors on behalf of Zed Co. from whom the company had acquired a running business. The firm's debtors and creditors totalled Rs. 50,000 and Rs. 20,000 respectively. In due course, the company paid the creditors Rs. 15,600, the creditors allowing discount @ 2 1/2%. This was the amount collected from debtors, including a debt of Rs. 250 previously written off as bad. Discounts allowed and bad debts written off respectively were Rs. 500 and Rs. 300.

The company is entitled to a commission of 5% on amounts collected and 1% on amounts paid. Prepare ledger accounts in the books of the company.

(*Commission Rs. 936*)

Essay Type

1. What do you mean by a joint stock company ? Briefly describe its main characteristics.
2. What are the different types of joint stock companies ?
3. Define a private company. How will you distinguish between a private company and a public company ?
4. Describe the privileges and exemptions enjoyed by a private limited company.
5. Explain the following documents :-
   (i) Memorandum of Association, (ii) Articles of Association, (iii) Table A, (iv) Prospectus, (v) Statement in lieu of Prospectus.
6. What is minimum subscription ? What is its significance ?
7. Enumerate the conditions which must be fulfilled by a public joint stock company to obtain a certificate of commencement of business.
8. Define 'preference shares'. What are the different kinds of preference shares ?
9. Describe the guidelines for the issue of cummulative convertible preference shares.
10. Explain in the context of share capital the meaning of the terms (i) authorised, (ii) issued, (iii) subcribed, (iv) called-up and (v) paid-up.
11. What is a Statutory Report ?
12. What do you understand by Annual General Meeting of shareholders ? What is the business conducted at such a meeting ?
13. Explain the different types of resolutions which may be passed at meetings of shareholders of a public limited company.
14. What do you understand by 'pro-rata' allotment ?
15. Explain (i) Calls in Advance and (ii) Calls in Arrear. What are the provisions of Table A regarding them?
16. What is the effect of forfeiture of shares ? How does forfeiture of shares differ from surrender of shares?
17. What are the purposes for which the balance of Securities Premium Account may be applied?
18. What are the conditions which must be fulfilled for the issue of shares at a discount ?
19. What is the purpose of issue of bonus shares ? What are the conditions which have to be fulfilled while making such an issue ?
20. What do you understand by a Rights Issue of shares ?
21. Define a debenture. Also enumerate the points of distinction between a debenture and a share.
22. Describe the different classes of debentures.
23. What do you understand by the term underwriting ? What is the maximum understanding commission that can be paid in respect of underwriting of (i) shares and (ii) debentures ?
24. Explain the term Firm Underwriting.
25. What are the conditions which must be fulfilled for redemption of preference shares ? What is the purpose of these legal restrictions ?
26. What are the different ways in which debentures may be redeemed ?
27. Clearly distinguish between ex-interest price and cum-interest price.
28. What do you understand by 'Convertible Debentures'?
29. What are the points of distinction between a sinking fund to replace a wasting asset and the one to repay a liability ?
30. Explain Sinking Fund for Redemption of Debentures.

19

FINAL ACCOUNTS

SYNOPSIS

1. General .. 19.1
   Requirements of law regarding the preparation of Profit and Loss Account .. 19.2
   General Principles–same as for other concerns .. 19.7
   Materiality .. 19.8
   Prior Period Items .. 19.8
   Extraordinary Items .. 19.9
   Changes in Accounting Policies .. 19.9
   AS-5 (Revised): Net Profit or Loss for the Period, Prior Period Items and Changes in Accounting Policies .. 19.10
   AS-4 (Revised) Contingencis and Events Occurring After the Balance Sheet Date .. 19.14
   Debentures .. 19.18
   Ascertaining profit for managerial remuneration .. 19.19
   Remuneration to Directors .. 19.21
   Remuneration to the manager .. 19.22
   Overall managerial remuneration .. 19.22
   Schedule XIII-Appointment .. 19.22
   Schedule XIII-Remuneration .. 19.23
   Schedule XIV-Rates of depreciation ... 19.25
   Calculation of commission .. 19.31
   Appropriation Items .. 19.35
   Profits Prior to Incorporation .. 19.50
2. Divisible Profits .. 19.56
   Transfer to Reserve .. 19.58
   Depreciation .. 19.61
   Unpaid Dividend Account .. 19.62
   Capital Profits .. 19.63
   Dividends .. 19.63
   Corporate Divided tax .. 19.65
   Appropriation of Profits .. 19.65
   Interest out of Capital .. 19.70
   Bonus Shares .. 19.71
3. Form of Balance Sheet .. 19.74
   Vertical form of Balance Sheet .. 19.82
4. Directors' Report .. 19.98
   Auditors' Report .. 19.99
   Filing of the Profit & Loss Account and Balance Sheet .. 19.100

1. GENERAL

A limited company must prepare every year the Profit and Loss Account and the Balance Sheet. Section 209 makes it compulsory for a company to keep certain books of account. Section 210 governs the preparation of the final accounts. The important portions of this section read as follows:

"(1) At every annual general meeting of company held in pursuance of section 166, the Board of Directors of the company shall lay before the company —

(*a*) the balance sheet as at the end of the period specified in sub-section (3); and

(*b*) a profit and loss account for that period.

(2) In case of a company not carrying on business for profit, an income and expenditure account shall be laid before the company at its annual general meeting instead of profit and loss account, and all references to 'profit and loss account', 'profit' and 'loss' in this section and elsewhere in this Act, shall be construed, in relation to such a company, as references respectively to the 'income and expenditure account', 'the excess of income over expenditure' and 'the excess of expenditure over income'.

(3) The profit and loss account shall relate —

(*a*) in the case of the first annual general meeting of the company, to the period beginning with the incorporation of the company and ending with a day which shall not precede the day of the meeting by more than nine months; and

(*b*) in the case of any subsequent annual general meeting of the company, to the period beginning with the day immediately after the period for which the account was last submitted and ending with a day which shall not precede the day of the meeting by more than six months, or in cases where an extension of time has been granted for holding the meeting under the second proviso to sub-section (1) of section 166, by more than six months and the extension so granted.

(4) The period to which the account aforesaid relates is referred to in this Act as a 'financial year', and it may be less or more than a calendar year, but it shall not exceed fifteen months.

Provided that it may extend to eighteen months, where special permission has been granted in that behalf by the Registrar".

It would appear from reading sub-section (3) and (4) that the period for which the profit and loss account has to be prepared may be less or more than a year. In actual practice, however, it would be rare to find a company which does not prepare its accounts for a full year, except in the first instance where a company may prepare its accounts for a period beginning with the date of its incorporation and ending on 31st March.

In view of the amendment in the Income-tax Act, 1961, the financial year must begin on 1st April and end on 31st March in the subsequent calendar year.

The information to be given in the Profit and Loss Account is set out in Part II of Schedule VI of the Companies Act. To give this information, so far as it is applicable, is obligatory under Section 211(2). But this is subject to the provision of the same section: "Every profit and loss account of a company shall give a true and fair view of the profit or loss of the company for the financial year".

This means that a person perusing the Profit and Loss Account should be able to form a fair view (*i.e.*, not a misleading one) of the profit earned or loss suffered by the company during the year as well as the significant factors leading to the result. Generally, information required under Part II of Schedule VI to the Act has to be disclosed. All material facts having an influence on the figure of profit or loss disclosed by the profit and loss account must be disclosed. In particular, the effect of a change in the basis of accounting such as change in the method of valuation of stock or of providing depreciation has to be clearly stated.

The Central Government may by notification exempt any class of companies from compliance with any of the requirements in Schedule VI if, in its opinion, it is necessary to do so in the public interest. Insurance, banking, electricity companies or any other class of companies for which a form of profit and loss has been specified by an Act governing such companies are exempt from the requirements of sub-section (2) of Section 211, *i.e.*, compliance with Schedule VI. Further, such companies need not disclose any pieces of information which they are not required to do under the respective Acts governing them.

Part II of Schedule VI is reproduced below (with adaptation necessitated by the abolition of managing agents and secretaries and treasurers).

SCHEDULE VI, Part II

Requirements as to Profit and Loss Account:

1. The provisions of this Part shall apply to the income and expenditure account referred to in sub-section (2) of section 210 of the Act, in like manner as they apply to a profit and loss account, but subject to the modification of reference as specified in that sub-section.

2. The profit and loss account (*a*) shall be so made out as clearly to disclose the result of the working of the company during the period covered by the account, and (*b*) shall disclose every material feature, including credits or receipts and debits or expenses in respect of non-recurring transactions or transactions of an exceptional nature.

3. The profit and loss account shall set out the various items relating to the income and expenditure of the company arranged under the most convenient heads; and, in particular, shall disclose the following information in respect of the period covered by the account:—

(*i*) (*a*) The turnover, that is, the aggregate amount for which sales are effected by the company, giving the amount of sales in respect of each class of goods dealt with by the company, and indicating the quantities of such sales for each class separately.

(*b*) Commission paid to sole selling agents within the meaning of section 294 of the Act.

(*c*) Commission paid to other selling agents.

(*d*) Brokerage and discount on sales, other than the usual trade discount.

(*ii*) (*a*) In the case of manufacturing companies:—

(1) The value of the raw material consumed, giving item-wise break-up and indicating the quantities thereof. In this break-up, as far as possible, all important basic raw materials shall be shown as separate items. The intermediates or components procured from other manufacturers may, if their list is too large to be included in the break-up, be grouped under suitable headings without mentioning the quantities, provided all those items, which in value individually account for 10% or more of the total value of the raw material consumed, shall be shown as separate and distinct items with quantities thereof in the break-up.

(2) The opening and closing stocks of goods produced, giving break-up in respect of each class of goods and indicating the quantities thereof.

(*b*) In the case of trading companies, the purchases made and the opening and closing stocks, giving break-up in respect of each class of goods traded in by the company and indicating the quantities thereof.

(*c*) In the case of companies rendering or supplying services, the gross income, derived from services rendered or supplied.

(*d*) In the case of a company, which falls under more than one of the categories mentioned in (*a*), (*b*) and (*c*) above, it shall be sufficient compliance with the requirements therein if the total amounts are shown in respect of the opening and closing stocks, purchases, sales and consumption of raw material with value and quantitative break-up and the gross income from services rendered is shown.

(*e*) In the case of other companies, the gross income derived under different heads.

Note 1:—The quantities of raw materials, purchases, stocks and the turnover, shall be expressed in quantitative denominations in which these are normally purchased or sold in the market.

Note 2:—For the purpose of items (*ii*) (*a*), (*ii*) (*b*) and (*ii*) (*d*) the items for which the company is holding separate industrial licences, shall be treated as separate classes of goods, but where a company has more than one industrial licence for production of the same item at different places or for expansion of the licensed capacity, the item covered by all such licences shall be treated as one class. In the case of trading companies, the imported items shall be classified in accordance with the classification adopted by the Chief Controller of Imports and Exports in granting the import licences.

Note 3:—In giving the break-up of purchases, stocks and turnover, items like spare parts and accessories, the list of which is too large to be included in the break-up, may be grouped under suitable headings without quantities, provided all those items, which in value individually account for 10% or more of the total value of the purchases, or turnover, as the case may be, are shown as separate and distinct items with quantities thereof in the break-up.

(*iii*) In the case of all concerns having work-in-progress the amounts for which such works have been completed at the commencement and at the end of the accounting period.

(*iv*) The amount provided for depreciation, renewals or diminution in the value of fixed assets.

If such provision is not made by means of a depreciation charge, the method adopted in making such provision.

If no provision is made for depreciation, the fact that no provision has been made shall be stated and the quantum of arrears of depreciation computed in accordance with Section 205(2) of the Act shall be disclosed by way of a note.

(*v*) The amount of interest on the company's debentures and other fixed loans, that is to say, loans for fixed periods, stating separately the amount of interest, if any, paid or payable to the managing director and the manager, if any.

(*vi*) The amount of charge for Indian Income Tax and other Indian taxation on profits, including, where practicable, with Indian income-tax, any taxation imposed elsewhere to the extent of the relief, if any, from Indian income-tax and distinguishing, where practicable, between income tax and other taxation.

*(*vii*) The amounts reserved for:—
- (*a*) repayment of share capital, and
- (*b*) repayment of loans.

*(*viii*) (*a*) The aggregate, if material, of any amounts set aside or proposed to be set aside, to reserves but not including provisions made to meet any specific liability, contingency, or commitment known to exist at the date as at which the balance sheet is made up.
- (*b*) The aggregate, if material, of any amounts withdrawn from such reserves.

(*ix*) (*a*) The aggregate, if material, of the amounts set aside to provisions made for meeting specific liabilities, contingencies, or commitments.
- (*b*) The aggregate, if material, of the amounts withdrawn from such provisions, as no longer required.

(*x*) Expenditure incurred on each of the following items, separately for each item:—
- (*a*) Consumption of stores and spare parts.
- (*b*) Power and fuel.
- (*c*) Rent.
- (*d*) Repairs to buildings.
- (*d*) Repairs to machinery.
- (*f*) (1) Salaries, wages and bonus.
  - (2) Contribution to provident and other funds.
  - (3) Workmen and staff welfare expenses to the extent not adjusted from any previous provision or reserve.

Note : — Information in respect of this should also be given in the balance sheet under the relevant provision or reserve account.

- (*g*) Insurance.
- (*h*) Rates and taxes, excluding taxes on income.
- (*i*) Miscellaneous expenses, provided that any item under which the expenses exceed 1 per cent of the total revenue of the company or Rs. 5,000, whichever is higher, shall be shown as a separate and distinct item against an appropriate account head in the Profit and Loss Account and shall not be combined with any other item to be shown under 'Miscellaneous Expenses'.

(*xi*) (*a*) The amount of income from investments distinguishing between trade investments and other investments.
- (*b*) Other income by way of interest, specifying the nature of the income.
- (*c*) The amount of income-tax deducted if the gross income is stated under sub-paragraphs (*a*) and (*b*) above.

(*xii*) (*a*) Profits or losses on investments showing distinctly the extent of the profits or losses earned or incurred on account of membership of a partnership firm, to the extent not adjusted from any previous provision or reserve.

Note :— Information in respect of this item should also be given in the balance sheet under the relevant provision or reserve account.

(*b*) Profits or losses in respect of transactions of a kind not usually undertaken by the company or undertaken in circumstances of an exceptional or non-recurring nature, if material in amount.

(*c*) Miscellaneous income.

(*xiii*) (*a*) Dividends from subsidiary companies.

(*b*) Provision for losses of subsidiary companies.

*(*xiv*) The aggregate amount of the dividends paid and proposed, and stating whether such amounts are subject to deduction of income-tax or not. (Actually now no tax is to be deducted from dividend; rather corporate dividend tax has to be paid on dividends.)

(*xv*) Amount, if material, by which any items shown in the profit and loss account are affected by any change in the basis of accounting.

4. The profit and loss account shall also contain or give by way of a note detailed information, showing separately the following payments provided or made during the financial year to the directors (including managing directors) or manager, if any, by the company, the subsidiaries of the company and any other person:—

(*i*) managerial remuneration under section 198 of the Act paid or payable during the financial year to the directors (including managing directors) or manager, if any;

(*ii*) other allowances and commission including guarantee commission (details to be given);

(*iii*) any other perquisites or benefits in cash or in kind (stating approximately money value where practicable);

(*iv*) Pensions, etc., —

(*a*) pensions,

(*b*) gratuities,

(*c*) payments from provident funds, in excess of own subscriptions and interest thereon,

(*d*) compension for loss of office,

(*e*) consideration in connection with retirement from office.

4A. The profit and loss account shall contain or give by way of a note a statement showing the computation of net profits in accordance with section 349 of the Act with the relevant details of the calculation of the commissions payable by way of percentage of such profits to the directors (including managing directors) or manager, if any.

4B. The profit and loss account shall further contain or give by way of a note detailed information in regard to amounts paid to the auditor, whether as fees, expenses or otherwise for services rendered:—

(*a*) as auditor; and,

(*b*) as adviser in any other capacity in respect of

(*i*) taxation matters,

(*ii*) company law matters,

(*iii*) management services; and

(*c*) in any other manner.

[The Institute of Chartered Accountants of India has stated, in its Statement styled "Payment to Auditors for Other Services", that the remuneration to the auditor for other services should be classified as follows:

(1) for tax representation;

(2) for company law matters;

(3) for management services;

(4) for internal auditing; and

(5) for other services.]

4C. In the case of manufacturing companies, the profit and loss account shall also contain by way of a note, in respect of each class of goods manufactured, detailed quantitative information in regard to the following, namely;

(*a*) the licensed capacity (where licence is in force);
(*b*) the installed capacity; and
(*c*) the actual production

Note 1 : — The licensed capacity and installed capacity of the company as on the last date of the year to which the profit and loss account relates shall be mentioned against items (*a*) and (*b*) above respectively.

Note 2 : — Against item (*c*), the actual production in respect of the finished products meant for sale shall be mentioned. In cases where semi-processed products are also sold by the company, separate details thereof shall be given.

Note 3 : — For the purposes of this paragraph, the items for which the company is holding separate industrial licences shall be treated at separate classes of goods but where a company has more than one industrial licence for production of the same item at different places, or for expansion of the licensed capacity, the items covered by all such licences shall be treated as one class.

4D. The profit and loss account shall also contain by way of a note the following information, namely:—

(*a*) value of imports calculated on C.I.F. basis by the company during the financial year in respect of:—
   (*i*) raw materials;
   (*ii*) components and spare parts;
   (*iii*) capital goods;

(*b*) expenditure in foreign currency during the financial year on account of royalty, knowhow, professional consultation fees, interest, and other matters;

(*c*) value of all imported raw materials, spare parts and components consumed during the financial year and the value of all indigenous raw materials, spare parts and components similarly consumed and the percentage of each of the total consumption;

(*d*) the amount remitted during the year in foreign currencies on account of dividends, with a specific mention of the number of non-resident shareholders, the number of shares held by them on which the dividends were due and the year to which the dividends related;

(*e*) earnings in foreign exchange classified under the following heads, namely:
   (*i*) export of goods calculated on F.O.B. basis;
   (*ii*) royalty, know-how, professional and consultation fees;
   (*iii*) interest and dividend;
   (*iv*) other income, indicating the nature thereof

5. The Central Government may direct that a company shall not be obliged to show the amount set aside to provisions other than those relating to depreciation, renewal or diminution in value of assets, if the Central Government is satisfied that the information should not be disclosed in the public interest and would prejudice the company, but subject to the condition that in any heading stating an amount arrived at after taking into account the amount set aside as such, the provision shall be so framed or marked as to indicate that fact.

6. (1) Except in the case of the first profit and loss account laid before the company after the commencement of the Act, the corresponding amount for the immediately preceding financial year for all items shown in the profit and loss account shall also be given in the profit and loss account.

(2) The requirement in sub-clause (1) shall, in the case of companies preparing quarterly or half-yearly accounts, relate to the profit and loss account for the period ended on the corresponding date of the previous year.

Note : Items which have been marked with an asterisk are really appropriation of profits. The asterisks have been placed by the author.

Main Points. The main features of the requirements of the law with regard to the Profit and Loss Account are the following:—

(1) There is no need to split the account into the three sections into which it used to be divided (viz., Trading Account, Profit and Loss Account and Appropriation Account, the last to depict how the profits earned were distributed). Only one account (called Profit and Loss Account) may do. However, the splitting of the account into the three sections is not forbidden, and is recommended due to the reason, that, in that manner, the gross profit and the true net profit (or loss) can be readily known. It is particularly recommended that appropriations of profit should be shown in a separate section called the Profit and Loss Appropriation Account, popularly known as "below the line". Items which have to be taken into consideration for determining the profits earned or loss suffered are shown "above the line".

(2) On the left hand side of each of the two sides (Dr. and Cr.) figures relating to the previous year should be given.

(3) The information given should be as complete as possible. If there is any departure from usual accountancy practice (for example, not providing for depreciation), the fact should be indicated by a note.

(4) Remuneration received by managing directors or manager either from the company or its subsidiaries should be indicated separately.

(5) Above all, the Profit and Loss Account must be made out in such a manner that it discloses a "true and fair view" of the profit or loss of the company for the financial year. This would mean that items of extra-ordinary nature or those unrelated to the company's business or items relating to previous years, and material in amount, or drawings out of reserves or profits resulting from revaluation of assets or out of a changed basis of accounting, such as a different method of valuing stock or providing depreciation, should be separately stated. "Window Dressing", that is, showing a position much better than it actually is or the other way-creating secret reserves-would be contrary to the spirit of law.

(6) Part II of Schedule VI uses two terms "if material" and "if material in amount" in respect of information to be disclosed in the Profit and Loss Account. The term "if material" would require disclosure of any figure, even if small in amount, which would point to a change in methods of accounting or to future commitments (like a long-term lease). Figures which affect the profit or loss substantially should be shown separately. Figures, which are not material may be grouped together.

(7) The Profit and Loss Account has to give information about both quantities and values of various types of raw material purchased and about quantities and values of various products comprised in the turnover. This should enable a comparative study of the company's performance in terms of input-output relationships.

General Principles:

The student will note that there is no fundamental difference between the preparation of the Trading and Profit and Loss Account for a sole proprietor or a partnership or for a company. The same principles hold good. To repeat, the following points have to be kept in mind in general:—

(*a*) A point of importance is that of matching revenue and expenditure. All expenses incurred for the purpose of earning an income shown in the Profit and Loss Account should be debited to the account. Expenses incurred against which revenue has still to be earned should be carried forward to the period in which revenue will be credited to the Profit and Loss Account. Revenue expenditure may be treated as deferred on this basis, to take an example.

(*b*) Expenditure of revenue nature alone, and that relating to only the period concerned, should be debited. Capital expenditure or expenditure relating to the past period or the future should be excluded.

(*c*) Even if some expenditure relating to the period for which accounts are being prepared has not been actually paid for, it should be brought into books, and if it is of revenue nature should be debited to the Profit and Loss Account.

(*d*) The above three points, (*a*) , (*b*) and (*c*), hold equally good for incomes of the company. This is to say, only the revenue income relating to the period concerned but all the incomes relating to the period, even if they have not been actually received in cash, should be credited to the Profit and Loss Account.

(*e*) Losses suffered by accident or otherwise should be debited to the Profit and Loss Account. Diminution in the value of assets due to wear and tear and passage of time should be brought into account. But it is not advisable to bring into account appreciation in the value of assets.

(*f*) Adjustments for prior years should be shown separately, unless they are immaterial.

The above principles hold good for a company also. But there are some differences in the accounts relating to, say a partnership and those relating to a company. The important differences are:

(*a*) The heading in case of a partnership is usually Trading and Profit and Loss Account; in case of a company the heading is only Profit and Loss Account.

(*b*) There are certain items like Interest on Debentures, Directors' Fees, etc., which appear in a company's Profit and Loss Account but not in accounts of a partnership. Income-tax on profits is treated as an expenditure in the case of companies.

(*c*) The profit or loss disclosed by accounts of partnership is transferred to the capital accounts (or current accounts) of partners, but the profit or loss disclosed by the profit and loss account of a company is not transferred to the Share Capital Account; it is transferred to a separate account called Profit and Loss Appropriation Account whose balance, after appropriations, if any, is shown separately.

(*d*) There are special features relating to the division (or appropriation) of profits of a company.

Materiality. The concept of materiality is vital to the preparation of final statements of account on a true and fair basis which means that those who study the profit and loss account and the balance sheet should be able to form a good idea of profit earned (or loss suffered) by the company during the year and of its financial position at the end of the year. Materiality is a relative term - what is material for one company may not be material for another. An error of Rs. 5,000 in stock-taking, in the case of a company where the value of stock runs into crores of rupees is surely too small to deserve special treatment but not so if the value of the stock is, say, only Rs. 50,000. The undermentioned general rules may help in this regard:—

(*i*) As far as possible, figures relating to previous years, representing adjustments, should be reported separately, preferably below the line (*i.e.,* in the appropriation section). Suppose, a fairly big debt written off in the past is recovered. The amount should be credited in the profit and loss account as a separate item and not credited to Bad Debts Account so as to reduce the figure of bad debts to be written off in the current year. If, on settlement of tax liability relating to past years, the actual amount differs from the provision already made, the difference should be separately debited or credited, as the case may be, in the profit and loss appropriation account.

(*ii*) Whether an amount is material or not should be judged having regard to the size of the net profit as well as the size of the sub-group to which the item belongs. For example, an adjustment of purchase price results in an extra amount to be paid in respect of purchases made in the previous year. This should be stated separately in the profit and loss account if the amount appears to be large having regard to current year's purchases and also to the net profit. In case of a balance sheet, this rule will apply with reference to the total of assets and liabilities as well as the particular sub-group involved. A contingent liability, for instance, should be reported separately if the amount is large enough in view of the total amount of contingent liabilities and total liabilities.

2. Prior Period Items. Since the purpose of the profit and loss account is to reveal the profit or loss for the period under report, it is clearly necessary to distinguish amounts that pertain to the previous periods from those concerning the current period, *if the former are material.* Adjustments for previous periods become necessary since it is not possible to reopen the accounts for a period once these have been adopted by the shareholders in the annual general meeting. These adjustments are made preferably below the line, that is, in the appropriation section of the Profit and Loss Account. But it is legally sufficient if these are separately stated or even if the concerned accounts are disclosed in a bracket, the Profit and Loss Account stating the total amount. Suppose purchases for 2009-2010 total Rs. 5,40,000 but a purchase of Rs. 50,000 in 2008-09 was omitted to be recorded then but has to be recorded in 2009-2010. The amount of purchase in the 2009-2010 Profit and Loss Account may be stated as follows:

Purchases Rs. 5,90,000
(Including purchases relating to 2008-2009, Rs. 50,000)

But as stated already, it would be better to state the purchases in the Profit and Loss Account at Rs. 5,40,000 and show the amount of Rs. 50,000 in the Profit and Loss Appropriation Account.

The Institute of Chartered Accountants of India defines Prior Period Items as "income or expenses which asrise in the current period as a result of errors or omissions in the preparation of the financial statements of one or more prior periods." Prior Period Items should not be confused with correction of estimates as a result of availability of additional information in subsequent periods. Such correction, if material, should still be disclosed separately. Suppose; the provision for taxation on 1st April, 2009 stands at Rs. 6,00,000; the tax liability till that date is settled for Rs. 5,40,000 and the liability for 2009-2010 is estimated at Rs. 3,40,000. The correct treatment is to show the saving of Rs. 60,000 in the P & L Appropriation Account and show the full debit of Rs. 3,40,000 as Provision for Taxation above the line. To show a debit of only Rs. 2,80,000 will be wrong. Revised AS 5, the Accounting Standard issued by the Institute of Chartered Accountants of India, is reproduced a little later; it should be gone through carefully.

3. Extraordinary Items. These are defined by the Institute as "income or expenses that arise from events or transactions that are clearly distinct from the ordinary activities of the enterprise and, therefore, are not expected to recur frequently or regularly." These losses which arise from events or transactions that are distinct from the ordinary activities of the business and which are both material and expected not to recur frequently or regularly. These would include material adjustments necessitated by circumstances which though related to previous periods are determined in the current period." The following are a few examples of extraordinary items:—

1. Profit or loss on sale of raw materials, when this has not been the practice.
2. Profit or loss on speculation, where this has not been resorted to regularly.
3. Loss due to earthquake.
4. Wages to be paid for the previous years where the higher wages are to take effect with retrospective effect.

The nature and amount of extraordinary or exceptional items should be separately disclosed so that the effect on current income is clearly discernible. It would be better to disclose such an amount below the line. It should be noted that incomes or expenses arising from the ordinary activities of the enterprise, though abnormal in amount are not extraordinary items, for example a very large debt from a regular trade customer written off.

As a result of uncertainties inherent in business activities, many financial statement items cannot be measured with precision but can only be estimated. Estimates may be required, for example, of bad debts, inventory obsolescence, or the useful lives of depreciable assets. An estimate may have to be revised if changes occur regarding the circumstances on which the estimate was based, or as a result of new information, more experience, or subsequent developments. The revision of the estimate, by its nature, does not bring the adjustment within the definitions of an extraordinary item or prior period item.

4. Changes in Accounting Policies. It is well known that any change in accounting policies (such as in the method of valuation of inventories or provision for depreciation) has to be disclosed along with the amount by which the profit or loss of the year under report is affected, if the amount is material. Such a change may cloud the profit or loss disclosed. Therefore, the Institute of Chartered Accountants of India recommends, through its Accounting Standard 5 (Revised), that a change in an accounting policy should be made only if the adoption of a different accounting policy is required by statute or for compliance with an accounting standard or if it is considered that the change would result in a more appropriate presentation of the financial statements of the enterprise.

Now study carefully the revised AS-5 given below. In this Accounting Standard, the standard portions have been set in bold type. These should be read in the context of the background material which has been set in normal type and in the context of the Preface to the Statements of Accounting Standards.

AS-5 (REVISED): NET PROFIT OR LOSS FOR THE PERIOD, PRIOR PERIOD ITEMS AND CHANGES IN ACCOUNTING POLICIES

The following is the text of the revised Accounting Standard (AS) 5, Net Profit or Loss for the Period, Prior Period Items and Changes In Accounting Policies, issued by the Council of the Institute of Chartered Accountants of India.

This revised standard comes into effect in respect of accounting periods commencing on or after 1.4.1996, and is mandatory in nature. It is clarified that in respect of accounting periods commencing on a date prior to 1.4.1996. Accounting Standard (AS) 5 as originally issued in November, 1982 (and subsequently made mandatory), will apply.

OBJECTIVE

The objective of this Statement is to prescribe the classification and disclosure of certain items in the statement of profit and loss so that all enterprises prepare and present such a statement on a uniform basis. This enhances the comparability of the financial statements of an enterprise over time and with the financial statements of other enterprises. Accordingly, this Statement requires the classification and disclosure of extraordinary and prior period items, and the disclosure of certain items, within profit or loss from ordinary activities. It also specifies the accounting treatment for changes in accounting estimates and the disclosures to the made in the financial statements regarding changes in accounting policies.

SCOPE

1. This Statement should be applied by an enterprise in presenting profit or loss from ordinary activities, extraordinary items and prior period items in the statement of profit and loss, in accounting for changes in accounting estimates, and in disclosure of changes in accounting policies.

2. This Statement deals with, among other matters, the disclosure of certain items of net profit or loss for the period. These disclosures are made in addition to any other disclosures required by other Accounting Standards.

3. This Statement does not deal with the tax implications of extraordinary items, prior period items, changes in accounting estimates, and changes in accounting policies for which appropriate adjustments will have to be made depending on the circumstances.

DEFINITIONS

4. The following terms are used in this Statement with the meanings specified:

Ordinary activities **are any activities which are undertaken by an enterprise as part of its business and such related activities in which the enterprise engages in furtherance of, incidental to, or arising from, these activities.**

Extraordinary items **are income or expenses that arise from events or transactions that are**

clearly distinct from the ordinary activities of the enterprise and, therefore, are not expected to recur frequently or regularly.

Prior period items **are income or expenses which arise in the current period as a result of errors or omissions in the preparation of the financial statements of one or more prior periods.**

Accounting policies **are the specific accounting principles and the methods of applying those principles adopted by an enterprise in the preparation and presentation of financial statements.**

NET PROFIT OR LOSS FOR THE PERIOD

5. All items of income and expenses which are recognised in a period should be included in the determination of net profit or loss for the period unless an Accounting Standard requires or permits otherwise.

6. Normally, all items of income and expense which are recognised in a period are included in the determination of the net profit or loss for the period. This includes extraordinary items and the effects of changes in accounting estimates.

7. The net profit or loss for the period comprises the following components, each of which should be disclosed on the face of the statement of profit and loss:

(a) Profit or loss from ordinary activities and

(b) Extraordinary items.

EXTRAORDINARY ITEMS

8. Extraordinary items should be disclosed in the statement of profit and loss as a part of net profit or loss for the period. The nature and the amount of each extraordinary item should be separately disclosed in the statement of profit and loss in a manner that its impact on current profit or loss can be perceived.

9. Virtually all items of income and expense included in the determination of net profit or loss for the period arise in the course of the ordinary activities of the enterprise. Therefore, only on rare occasions does an event or transaction give rise to an extraordinary item.

10. Whether an event or transaction is clearly distinct from the ordinary activities of the enterprise is determined by the nature of the event or transaction in relation to the business ordinarily carried on by the enterprise rather than by the frequency with which such events are expected to occur. Therefore, an event or transaction may be extraordinary for one enterprise but not for another enterprise because of the differences between their respective ordinary activities. For example, losses sustained as a result of an earthquake may qualify as an extraordinary item for many enterprises. However, claims from policyholders arising from an earthquake do not qualify as an extraordinary item for an insurance enterprise that insures against such risks.

11. Examples of events or transactions that generally give rise to extraordinary items for most enterprises are:—

Attachment of property of the enterprise; or

an earthquake.

PROFIT OR LOSS FROM ORDINARY ACTIVITIES

12. When items of income and expense within profit or loss from ordinary activities are of such size, nature or incidence that their disclosure is relevant to explain the performance of the enterprise for the period, the nature and amount of such items should be disclosed separately.

13. Although the items of income and expense described in paragraph 12 are not extraordinary items, the nature and amount of such items may be relevant to users of financial statements in understanding the financial position and performance of an enterprise and in making projections about financial position and performance. Disclosure of such information is sometimes made in the notes to the financial statements.

14. Circumstances which may give rise to the separate disclosure of items of income and expense in accordance with paragraph 12 include:

(*a*) the write-down of inventories to net realisable value as well as the reversal of such write-downs;
(*b*) a restructuring of the activities of an enterprise and the reversal of any provisions for the costs of restructuring;
(*c*) disposals of items of fixed assets;
(*d*) disposals of long-term investments;
(*e*) legislative changes having retrospective application;
(*f*) litigation settlements; and
(*g*) other reversals of provisions.

PRIOR PERIOD ITEMS

15. The nature and amount of prior period items should be separately disclosed in the statement of profit and loss in a manner that their impact on the current profit or loss can be perceived.

16. The term 'prior period items', as defined in this Statement, refers only to income or expenses which arise in the current period as a result of errors or omissions in the preparation of the financial statements of one or more prior periods. The term does not include other adjustments necessitated by circumstances, which though related to prior periods, are determined in the current period *e.g.*, arrears payable to workers as a result of revision of wages with retrospective effect during the current period.

17. Errors in the preparation of the financial statements of one or more prior periods may be discovered in the current period. Errors may occur as a result of mathematical mistakes, mistakes in applying accounting policies, misinterpretation of facts, or oversight.

18. Prior period items are generally infrequent in nature and can be distinguished from changes in accounting estimates. Accounting estimates by their nature are approximations that may need revision as additional information becomes known. For example, income or expense recognised on the outcome of a contingency which previously could not be estimated reliably does not constitute a prior period item.

19. Prior period items are normally included in the determination of net profit or loss for the current period. An alternative approach is to show such items in the statement of profit and loss after determination of current net profit or loss. In either case, the objective is to indicate the effect of such items on the current profit or loss.

CHANGES IN ACCOUNTING ESTIMATES

20. As a result of the uncertainties inherent in business activities, many financial statement items cannot be measured with precision but can only be estimated. The estimation process involves judgements based on the latest information available. Estimates may be required, for example, of bad debts, inventory obsolescence, or the useful lives of depreciable assets. The use of reasonable estimates is an essential part of the preparation of financial statements and does not undermine their reliability.

21. An estimate may have to be revised if changes occur regarding the circumstances on which the estimate was based, or as a result of new information, more experience or subsequent developments. The revision of the estimate, by its nature, does not bring the adjustment within the definitions of an extraordinary item or a prior period item.

22. Sometimes, it is difficult to distinguish between a change in an accounting policy and a change in an accounting estimate. In such cases, the change is treated as a change in an accounting estimate, with appropriate disclosure.

23. The effect of a change in an accounting estimate should be included in the determination of net profit or loss in:

(a) the period of the change, if the change affects the period only; or
(b) the period of the change and future periods, if the change affects both.

24. A change in an accounting estimate may affect the current period only or both the current period and future periods. For example, a change in the estimate of the amount of bad debts is recognised immediately and, therefore, affects only the current period. However, a change in estimated useful life of a depreciable asset affects the depreciation in the current period and in each period during the remaining useful life of the asset. In both cases, the effect of the change relating to the current period is recognised as income or expense in the current period. The effect, if any, on future periods, is recognised in future periods.

25. The effect of a change in an accounting estimate should be classified using the same classification in the statement of profit and loss as was used previously for the estimate.

26. To ensure the comparability of financial statements of different periods, the effect of a change in an accounting estimate which was previously included in the profit or loss from ordinary activities is included in that component of net profit or loss. The effect of a change in an accounting estimate that was previously included as an extraordinary item is reported as an extraordinary item.

27. The nature and amount of a change in an accounting estimate which has a material effect in the current period, or which is expected to have a material effect in subsequent periods, should be disclosed. If it is impracticable to quantify the amount, this fact should be disclosed.

CHANGES IN ACCOUNTING POLICIES

28. Users need to be able to compare the financial statements of an enterprise over a period of time in order to identify trends in its financial position, performance and cash flows. Therefore, the same accounting policies are normally adopted for similar events or transactions in each period.

29. A change in an accounting policy should be made only if the adoption of a different accounting policy is required by statute or for compliance with an accounting standard or if it is considered that the change would result in a more appropriate presentation of the financial statements of the enterprise.

30. A more appropriate presentation of events or transactions in the financial statements occurs when the new accounting policy results in more relevant or reliable information about the financial position, performance or cash flows of the enterprise.

31. The following are not changes in accounting policies:

(*a*) the adoption of an accounting policy for events or transactions that differ in substance from previously occurring events or transactions *e.g.*, introduction of a formal retirement gratuity scheme by an employer in place of ad hoc ex-gratia payments to employees on retirement; and

(*b*) the adoption of a new accounting policy for events or transactions which did not occur previously or that were immaterial.

32. Any change in an accounting policy which has a material effect should be disclosed. The impact of, and the adjustments resulting from, such change, if material, should be shown in the financial statements of the period in which such a change is made, to reflect the effect of such change. Where the effect of such change is not ascertainable, wholly or in part, the fact should be indicated. If a change is made in the accounting policies which has no material effect on the financial statements for the current period but which is reasonably expected to have a material effect in later periods, the fact of such change should be appropriately disclosed in the period in which the change is adopted.

33. *A change in accounting policy consequent upon the adoption of an Accounting Standard should be accounted for in accordance with the specific transitional provisions, if any, contained in that Accounting Standard. However, disclosures required by paragraph 32 of this Standard should be made unless the transitional provisions of any other Accounting Standard require alternative disclosures in this regard.

5. Contingencies and Events Occurring after the Balance Sheet Date.

In its Accounting Standard 4 (Revised), the Institute of Chartered Accountants of India deals with these two classes of events . Results of contingencies, as the term implies, lie in the future though the seed is already sown, *i.e.*, the ultimate outcome, gain or loss, will be known or determined only on the occurrence, or non-occurrence, of one or more uncertain future events. Contingencies are disclosed by way of notes at the foot of the balance sheet. But if there is a probability of a loss arising, it would be better to make a provision in this regard; judgment of management is naturally to be relied upon.

* This paragraph has been added in this Standard pursuant to a limited revision made in 2001. This revision comes into effect in respect of accounting periods commencing on or after 1.4.2001.

"Events occurring after the balance sheet date are those significant events, both favourable and unfavourable, that occur between the balance sheet date and the date on which the financial statements are approved by the Board of Directors...". Such events are of two types:

(*i*) those that provide further evidence of conditions that existed at the balance sheet date, and

(*ii*) those that are indicative of conditions that arose subsequent to the balance sheet date.

The former type of events are considered for preparing estimates etc. relating to the year under report; for example, insolvency of a debtor after the balance sheet date is considered for estimating the doubtful debts so that a proper provision is made. Proper provision for taxation cannot be made till the profit before tax is known. Events of the second type generally are not considered, though the Directors in their report to the shareholders should touch upon the important events. "Proposed dividend" is an event after the balance sheet date but it is required to be statutorily disclosed. Also, **if the event concerned is so serious as to affect the existence or substratum of the enterprise** (*e.g.*, destruction of a major factory by fire), disclosure is usually made.

Now study the revised Accounting Standard-4.

AS-4 (REVISED)*: CONTINGENCIES AND EVENTS OCCURRING AFTER THE BALANCE SHEET DATE

The following is the text of the revised Accounting Standard (AS) 4, 'Contingencies and Events Occurring after the Balance Sheet Date' issued by the Council of the Institute of Chartered Accountant of India.

This revised standard comes into effect in respect of accounting periods commencing on or after 1.4.1995 and is mandatory in nature. It is clarified that in respect of accounting periods commencing on a date prior to 1.4.1995, Accounting Standard 4 as originally issued in November, 1982 (and subsequently made mandatory) applies.

Introduction

1. This Statement deals with the treatment in financial statements of:

(*a*) contingencies, and

(*b*) events occurring after the balance sheet date.

2. The following subjects, which may result in contingencies, are excluded from the scope of this Statement in view of special considerations applicable to them;

(*a*) liability of life assurance and general insurance enterprises arising from policies issued;

(*b*) obligations under retirement benefit plans; and

(*c*) commitments arising from long-term lease contracts.**

Definitions

3. The following terms are used in this Statement with the meanings specified:

3.1 A *contingency* is a condition or situation, the ultimate outcome of which, gain or loss, will be known or determined only on the occurrence, or non-occurrence, of one or more uncertain future events.

3.2 *Events occurring after the balance sheet date* are those significant events, both favourable and unfavourable, that occur between the balance sheet date and the date on which the financial statements are approved by the Board of Directors in the case of a company, and by the corresponding approving authority in the case of any other entity.

Two types of events can be identified:

(*a*) those which provide further evidence of conditions that existed at the balance sheet date; and

(*b*) those which are indicative of conditions that arose subsequent to the balance sheet date.

---

*Revised in January 1995,

** Further, pursuant to AS 29, 'Provisions, Contingent Liabilities and Contingent Assets' becoming mandatory in respect of accounting periods commencing on or after 1-4-2004, all paragraphs of this Standard that deal with contingencies (viz. paragraphs 1(a), 2, 3.1, 4 (4.1 to 4.4), 5 (5.1 to 5.6), 6, 7 (7.1 to 7.3), 9.1 (relevant portion), 9.2, 10, 11, 12 and 16 stand withdrawn except to the extent they deal with impairment of assets not covered by other Indian Accounting Standards. For example, impairment of receivables (commonly referred to as the provision for bad and doubtful debts) would continue to be covered by AS-4.

Explanation

4. Contingencies.

4.1 The term "contingencies" used in this Statement is restricted to conditions or situations at the balance sheet date, the financial effect of which is to be determined by future events which may or may not occur.

4.2. Estimates are required for determining the amounts to be stated in the financial statements for many ongoing and recurring activities of an enterprise. One must, however, distinguish between an event which is certain and one which is uncertain. The fact that an estimate is involved does not, of itself, create the type of uncertainty which characterises a contingency. For example, the fact that estimates of useful life are used to determine depreciation, does not make depreciation a contingency; the eventual expiry of the useful life of the asset is not uncertain. Also, amounts owed for services received are not contingencies as defined in paragraph 3.1, even though the amounts may have been estimated, as there is nothing uncertain about the fact that these obligations have been incurred.

4.3 The uncertainty relating to future events can be expressed by a range of outcomes. This range may be presented as quantified probabilities, but in most circumstances, this suggests a level of precision that is not supported by the available information. The possible outcomes can, therefore, usually be generally described except where reasonable quantification is practicable.

4.4 The estimate of the outcome and of the financial effect of contingencies are determined by the judgement of the management of the enterprise. This judgement is based on consideration of information available up to the date on which the financial statements are approved and will include a review of events occurring after the balance sheet date, supplemented by experience of similar transactions and, in some cases, reports from independent experts.

5. ***Accounting Treatment of Contingent Losses***

5.1 The accounting treatment of a contingent loss is determined by the expected outcome of the contingency. If it is likely that a contingency will result in a loss to the enterprise, then it is prudent to provide for that loss in the financial statements.

5.2 The estimation of the amount of a contingent loss to be provided for in the financial statements may be based on information referred to in paragraph 4.4.

5.3 If there is conflicting or insufficient evidence for estimating the amount of a contingent loss, then disclosure is made of the existence and nature of the contingency.

5.4 A potential loss to an enterprise may be reduced or avoided because a contingent liability is matched by a related counter-claim or claim against a third party. In such cases, the amount of the provision is determined after taking into account the probable recovery under the claim if no significant uncertainty as to its measurability or collectability exists. Suitable disclosure regarding the nature and gross amount of the contingent liability is also made.

5.5 The existence and amount of guarantees, obligations arising from discounted bills of exchange and similar obligations undertaken by an enterprise are generally disclosed in financial statements by way of note, even though the possibility that a loss to the enterprise will occur, is remote.

5.6 Provisions for contingencies are not made in respect of general or unspecified business risks since they do not relate to conditions or situations existing at the balance sheet date.

Accounting Treatment of Contingent Gains

6. Contingent gains are not recognised in financial statements since their recognition may result in the recognition of revenue which may never be realised. However, when the realisation of a gain is virtually certain, then such gain is not a contingency and accounting for the gain is appropriate.

7. *Determination of the amounts at which Contingencies are included in Financial Statements*

7.1 The amount at which a contingency is stated in the financial statements is based on the information which is available at the date on which the financial statements are approved. Events occurring after the balance sheet date that indicate that an asset may have been impaired, or that a liability may have existed, at the balance sheet date are, therefore, taken into account in identifying contingencies and in determining the amounts at which such contingencies are included in financial statements.

7.2 In some cases, each contingency can be separately identified, and the special circumstances of each situation considered in the determination of the amount of contingency. A substantial legal claim against the enterprise may represent such a contingency. Among the factors taken into account by management in evaluating such a contingency are the progress of the claim at the date on which the financial statements are approved, the opinions, wherever necessary, of legal experts or other advisers, the experience of the enterprise in similar cases and the experience of other enterprises in similar situations.

7.3 If the uncertainties which created a contingency in respect of an individual transaction are common to a large number of similar transactions, then the amount of the contingency need not be individually determined, but may be based on the group of similar transactions. An example of such contingencies may be the estimated uncollectable portion of accounts receivable. Another example of such contingencies may be the warranties for products sold. These costs are usually incurred frequently and experience provides a means by which the amount of the liability or loss can be estimated with reasonable precision although the particular transactions that may result in a liability or a loss are not identified. Provision for these costs results in their recognition in the same accounting period in which the related transactions took place.

8. *Events Occurring after the Balance Sheet Date*

8.1 Events which occur between the balance sheet date and the date on which the financial statements are approved, may indicate the need for adjustments to assets and liabilities as at the balance sheet date or may require disclosure.

8.2 Adjustments to assets and liabilities are required for events occurring after the balance sheet date that provide additional information materially affecting the determination of the amounts relating to conditions existing at the balance sheet date. For example, an adjustment may be made for a loss on a trade receivable account which is confirmed by the insolvency of a customer which occurs after the balance sheet date.

8.3 Adjustments to assets and liabilities are not appropriate for events occurring after the balance sheet date, if such events do not relate to conditions existing at the balance sheet date. An example is the decline in market value of investments between the balance sheet date and the date on which the financial statements are approved. Ordinary fluctuations in market values do not normally relate to the condition of the investments at the balance sheet date, but reflect circumstances which have occurred in the following period.

8.4 Events occurring after the balance sheet date which do not affect the figures stated in the financial statements would not normally require disclosure in the financial statements although they may be of such significance that they may require a disclosure in the report of the approving authority to enable users of financial statements to make proper evaluations and decisions.

8.5 There are events which, although they take place after the balance sheet date, are sometimes reflected in the financial statements because of statutory requirements or because of their special nature. Such items include the amount of dividend proposed or declared by the enterprise after the balance sheet date in respect of the period convered by the financial statements.

8.6 Events occurring after the balance sheet date may indicate that the enterprise ceases to be a going concern. A deterioration in operating results and financial position, or unusual changes affecting the existence or substratum of the enterprise after the balance sheet date (e.g., destruction of a major production plant by a fire after the balance sheet date) may indicate a need to consider whether it is proper to use the fundamental accounting assumption of going concern in the preparation of the financial statements.

9. *Disclosure*

9.1 The disclosure requirements herein referred to apply only in respect of those contingencies or events which affect the financial position to a material extent.

9.2 If a contingent loss is not provided for, its nature and an estimate of its financial effect are generally disclosed by way of note unless the possibility of a loss is remote (other than the circumstances mentioned in paragraph 5.5). If a reliable estimate of the financial effect cannot be made, this fact is disclosed.

9.3 When the events occurring after the balance sheet date are disclosed in the report of the approving authority, the information given comprises the nature of the events and an estimate of their financial effects or a statement that such an estimate cannot be made.

Accounting Standard

Contingencies

10. The amount of a contingent loss should be provided for by a charge in the statement of profit and loss if:

(*a*) it is probable that future events will confirm that, after taking into account any related probable recovery, an asset has been impaired or a liability has been incurred as at the balance sheet date, and

(*b*) a reasonable estimate of the amount of the resulting loss can be made.

11. The existence of a contingent loss should be disclosed in the financial statements if either of the conditions in paragraph 10 is not met, unless the possibility of a loss is remote.

12. Contingent gains should not be recognised in the financial statements.

Events Occurring after the Balance Sheet Date

13. Assets and liabilities should be adjusted for events occurring after the balance sheet date that provide additional evidence to assist the estimation of amounts relating to conditions existing at the balance sheet date or that indicate that the fundamental accounting assumption of going concern (i.e., the continuance of existence or substratum of the enterprise) is not appropriate.

14. Dividends stated to be in respect of the period covered by the financial statements, which are proposed or declared by the enterprise after the balance sheet date but before approval of the financial statements, should be adjusted.

15. Disclosure should be made in the report of the approving authority of those events occurring after the balance sheet date that represent material changes and commitments affecting the financial position of the enterprise.

Disclosure

16. If disclosure of contingencies is required by paragraph 11 of this Statement, the following information should be provided:

(*a*) the nature of the contingency;

(*b*) the uncertainties which may affect the future outcome.

(*c*) an estimate of the financial effect, or a statement that such an estimate cannot be made.

17. If disclosure of events occurring after the balance sheet date in the report of the approving authority is required by paragraph 15 of this Statement, the following information should be provided:

(*a*) the nature of the event;

(*b*) an estimate of the financial effect, or a statement that such an estimate cannot be made.

Illustration 1:

The draft accounts of P Ltd. showed a profit for the year ended 31st March, 2010 of Rs 7,00,000 after tax but before taking into accounting the following items. It had retained earnings at the beginning of the year of Rs. 5,00,000.

1. Cost of closing a plant during the year Rs. 1,00,000. Another plant was closed five years ago.

2. The sale for Rs. 1,50,000 of an investment acquired 5 years ago at a cost of Rs. 20,000.

3. The directors have decided to write off goodwill appearing at Rs. 2 lakh in the beginning of the year.

4. A debt of Rs. 2,40,00 from a customer company (now in liquidation) has remained outstanding since 31st March, 2009, when no provision was made; the expected dividend is 10 p. in the rupee.

5. The taxation liability for prior year was agreed and showed that Rs. 10,000 had been underprovided; the provision for tax for the year was Rs. 6,50,000.

6. It was announced on 10th April, 2010 by a foreign government that one of the overseas plants would be nationalised, but compensation has been promised based on four times the expected annual profit. This has averaged Rs. 50,000 for the last five years. The net assets attributable to the plant and included in the balance sheet 31st March, 2010 are Rs. 3,00,000.

7. A professional valuation of buildings owned by the company has shown a surplus over book values of Rs. 4,00,000.

8. Research and development expenditure carried forward at the beginning of the year amounted to Rs. 2,50,000. The previous policy has not changed and on the new basis only Rs. 1,00,000 would have been carried forward.

You are required to state how these items will be dealt with in the final statements of account.

(*Adapted C.A. Eng. P.E.I.*)

Answer: The following is the suggested treatment of each of the items alongwith reasons (state briefly):—

	Item	*Treatment*	*Reasons*
1.	Closure costs, Rs. 1,00,000	Extraordinary item, should be shown separately in the P & L A/c.	(*i*) Material (*ii*) Derives from events outside the ordinary activities of the business. (*iii*) Abnormal and not expected to recur pequently or regularly
2.	Sale of an investment	Profit on sale, Rs. 1,30,000, is extraordinary item and should be shown as a separate item in the P & L A/c.	(*i*) Material (*ii*) Derives from an event not connected with the ordinary activities of the business. (*iii*) Abnormal income and not expected to recur frequently or regularly.
3.	Writing off of goodwill	The write-off is an extraordinary item and should be distinctively disclosed in the P & L A/c.	(*i*) Material (*ii*) Not connected with the ordinary activities of the business.
4.	Bad debt Rs. 2,16,000	Exceptional item to be disclosed separately	(*i*) Material (*ii*) Not concerned with the ordinary activities of the business for the (*iii*) Abnormal in size and incidence.
5.	Under-provision of tax in prior years	Rs. 10,000 may be included with total tax charge; need not be separately disclosed.	Not material.
6.	Nationalisation of overseas palnt	Loss of Rs. 1,00,000 does not concern the year's account but it is a significant item to be included in the Directors' Report.	It is an event after the balance sheet date but does not affect the substratum of the company.
7.	Surplus on revaluation of buildings	Rs. 4,00,000 should be credited direct to capital reserves.	It is an uncrealised capital gain, not available for paying dividend.
8.	Change in accounting policy concerning R & D expenditure	Reduce opening reserves by Rs. 1,50,000 or show as prior year adjustment in the P & L A/c (below the line). Disclose change in the accounting policy.	Prior year adjustment arising from change in accounting policy should not affect current year's results.

Special points:

Debentures. (*a*) *Interest on debentures.* Interest for the full period for which the accounts are being prepared or for which the debentures have been outstanding during such a period should be provided. Suppose, the following two items appear in a company's trial balance at the end of a year:—

	Dr. *Rs.*	*Cr.* *Rs.*
14% Debentures (issued 4 years ago)		4,00,000
Interest on Debentures	14,000	

Interest for the full year on Rs. 4,00,000 @ is Rs. 56,000. Because the amount paid is only Rs. 14,000, another Rs. 42,000 is still due. Since usually debenture interest is paid half yearly, it would appear that Rs. 28,000 is already due for payment but that Rs. 14,000 is not yet payable. The term used for the former is "Accrued and Due" or "Outstanding"; the term for the latter is "Accrued" or "Accrued but not due"; Interest Outstanding will be shown in the Balance Sheet along with Debentures and Interest Accrued will be shown as a current liability. However, both items are short-term liabilities.

The Profit and Loss Account will be debited by Rs. 56,000. But one should remember that *interest paid on moneys borrowed for construction of an asset should be added to the cost of the asset concerned for the period of construction.* Once the asset comes into use, the interest paid will be a charge against revenue and debited to the Profit and Loss Account. This is according to legal decisions in income-tax cases and has the approval of the Institute of Chartered Accountants of India.

(*b*) *Income tax on interest on debentures.* Under the Income-tax Act, it is the duty of those who pay interest on securities to deduct tax from the interest payable at the prescribed rate and deposit it with the Government. (In case the securities are declared tax-free by the Government, the deduction will not be made. Also no deduction will be made or deduction will be made at a lower rate if the income-tax officer gives a certificate to this effect to the person whom the interest is payable). The rate for deduction of income-tax at source is now-a-days 10%; rates change usually with every Finance Act which is passed every year by the Parliament.

The practical effect is that if a person holds, say, Rs. 10,000 14% Debentures of a company, the interest payable to him by the company is Rs. 1,400. But the company will have to deduct Rs. 140 (10% of Rs. 1,400) as tax, deposit it with the Government, and pay to the debentureholder only Rs. 1,260, the balance. The entries for interest on debentures, as a whole, therefore, are as follows:—

Interest on Debentures	Dr.	gross amount due.
To Sundry Debentureholders		gross amount *less* tax deducted.
To Income-tax Payable		tax deducted from the interest.

Income-tax payable is a liability and will appear in the Balance Sheet until paid off.

(*c*) *Discount or Cost of Issue of Debentures.* Discount or commission or cost of issue of debentures appears in the balance sheet but these should be written off as early as possible and in any case not later than the date of redemption of the debentures. Suppose, the following two entries appear in a company's trial balance on 31st March, 2010:—

	Rs.	*Rs.*
14% Debentures (to be redeemed on 31st March, 2014)		3,00,000
Discount on Issue of Debentures	15,000	

In this case, it would be advisable to write off one-fifth of Rs. 15,000, viz., Rs. 3,000 because the Debentures have to be redeemed in five years' time (counting from 1st April, 2009).

Ascertaining profit for managerial remuneration. Section 349 lays down how the net profits of the company will be ascertained for the purpose of the calculation of remuneration to directors, manager or managing director. It corresponds more or less to the accepted ideas of calculating net profits of a concern. The following credits or incomes in addition to the gross profit should be taken into account:

Bounties and subsidies received from any Government, or any public authority constituted or authorised in this behalf, by any Government, unless and except in so far as the Centreal Government otherwise directs.

The following "incomes" or credits should not be taken into account:

(*a*) premium on shares or debentures issued or sold by the company;

(*b*) profits on sales by the company of forfeited shares;

(*c*) profits of a capital nature including profits from the sale of the undertaking or any of the undertaking of the company, or any part thereof; and

(*d*) profits from the sale of any immovable property or fixed assets of a capital nature comprised in the undertaking or any of the underkings of the company, unless the business of the company consists, whether wholly or partly, of buying and selling such property or assets.

But where the amount for which any fixed asset is sold exceeds its written down value (calculated according to section 350), credit should be given for so much of the excess as is not higher than the difference between the original cost of that fixed asset and its written down value. Suppose, a machine purchased for Rs. 30,000, written down to Rs. 18,000 by writing off depreciation, is sold for Rs. 35,000. The managerial personnel are entitled to commission on Rs. 12,000, *i.e.*, excluding the profit over and above the original cost.

From the incomes of the company, the following have to be deducted:—

(*a*) all the usual working charges;

(*b*) directors' remuneration;

(*c*) bonus or commission paid or payable, to any member of the company's staff, or to any engineer, technician or person employed or engaged by the company, whether on a whole-time or on a part-time basis;

(*d*) any tax notified by the Central Government as being in the nature of a tax on excess or abnornal profits;

(*e*) any tax on business profits imposed for special reasons or in special circumstances and notified by the Central Government in this behalf:

(*f*) interest on debentures issued by the company;

(*g*) interest on mortgages executed by the company and on loans and advances secured by a charge on its fixed or floating assets;

(*h*) interest on unsecured loans and advances;

(*i*) expenses on repairs, whether to immovable property or to movable property, provided the repairs are not of a capital nature;

(*j*) contributions to charitable and other funds not directly relating to the business of the company not exceeding Rs. 50,000 or 5 per cent of its average net profits during the three financial years immediately preceding, whichever is greater. These limits can be exceeded with the consent of the company in general meeting.

(*k*) depreciation calculated according to section 350. Under section 350 the depreciation (for the purpose of calculating commission to managerial personnel) is to be calculated according to the rates given in Schedule XIV of the Companies Act, 1956. Depreciation includes only normal depreciation including extra and multiple shift allowances, excluding any special, initial or other depreciation or any development rebate. (Deduction on account of special, initial or other depreciation or any development rebate has since been withdrawn under the Income-tax Act.)

If an asset is sold, discarded, demolished or destroyed before it is completely written off, the excess of the written down value over its sale proceeds (or its scrap value) has to be written off in the financial year in which the asset is sold, discarded, demolished or destroyed;

(*l*) the excess of expenditure over income which arises in computing the net profit in accordance with section 349 in any year (after the commencement of the Act) in so far as this excess has not been deducted in any subsequent year preceding the year in respect of which the net profits have to be ascertained;

(*m*) any compensation or damages to be paid in virtue of any legal liability including a liability arising from a breach of contract;

(*n*) any sum paid by way of insurance against the risk of meeting any liability such as is referred to in (*m*); and

(*o*) debts considered bad and written off or adjusted during the year of account.

Profits on which remuneration has to be allowed should be ascertained without deducting the following:—

(*a*) income tax and super tax payable by the company under the Income-tax Act or any other tax on the incomes of the company not covered by (*d*) and (*e*) above.

(*b*) any compensation, damages or payments made voluntarily, that is to say, otherwise than in virtue of a liability such as is referred to in (*m*) above; and

(*c*) loss of a capital nature including loss on sale of the undertaking or any of the undertakings of the company or of any part thereof not including any excess of written down value over its sales proceeds or scrap value of any asset sold, discarded, demolished or destroyed. (This excess has to be written off to the P. & L. A/c).

It should be noted that the Profit and Loss Account should have a statement attached showing how the profit has been ascertained for the purpose of commission due to directors, managing director or manager.

Remuneration to Directors. Subject to section 198 which relates to the overall managerial remuneration (discussed later), the remuneration to directors is governed by section 309 of the Companies Act. It is to be determined either by the articles of the company or by a resolution or, if the articles so required, by a special resolution, passed by the company in general meeting subject to the following:—

(*a*) A whole-time director or a managing director may be paid remuneration either by way of a monthly payment or at a specified percentage of the net profits of the company or partly by one way and partly by the other. But except with the approval of the Central Government:—

  (*i*) if there is only one whole-time or managing director the percentage cannot exceed five; and

  (*ii*) if there are more than one whole-time director, the percentage cannot exceed ten for all of them together.

(*b*) Part-time directors (*i.e.*, those who are neither whole-time nor managing directors) may receive monthly, quarterly or annual payment with the approval of the Central Government or by way of commission if the company by special resolution authorises such payment. The total remuneration cannot exceed (1) one per cent of the net profits of the company if the company has a managing or whole-time director, or manager; or (2) three per cent of the net profits if the company has no manager, managing or whole-time director. The rates of one and three per cent respectively can be increased by the company in general meeting with the approval of the Central Government.

(*c*) A director who is in receipt of any commission from the company and who is either a whole-time or managing director cannot receive any commission or other remuneration from any subsidiary of such company.

It should be noted that remuneration to a director will include any remuneration paid to him for services rendered by him in any capacity except when (*a*) the services rendered are of a professional nature, and (*b*) in the opinion of the Central Government, the director possesses the requisite qualification for the practice of the profession.

In addition, a director may receive remuneration by way of a fee for each meeting of the Board, or a committee thereof attended by him according to the Companies Act, but the Government has decided that in case of whole-time or managing directors, no sitting fees will be payable.

Section 309 does not apply to a private company unless it is a subsidiary of a public company.

According to section 310, in the case of a public company, or a private company, which is a subsidiary of a public company, any increase in the remuneration payable to the directors requires the approval of the Central Government except in the following cases:—

(*a*) in cases where Schedule XIII is applicable (discussed later) and the increase is in accordance with the conditions specified in that Schedule; and

(*b*) where the increase is made in the fee payable for attending each meeting of the Board or a committee thereof and the increased rate does not exceed such sum as may be prescribed. (The prescribed sum is Rs. 2,000 vide rule 10B of General Rules and Forms).

Similarly, according to section 311, for a public company, and a private company, which is a subsidiary of a public company, any increase in the remuneration of the managing or whole-time director on reappointment or appointment after the commencement of the Companies Act, 1956 requires approval of the Central Government except in cases where Schedule XIII is applicable and the increase is in accordance with the conditions specified in that Schedule.

Remuneration to the manager. Section 387 governs the remuneration to manager. A manager may receive remuneration by way of a monthly payment or by way of a specific percentage of the net profits of the company (calculated according to sections 349, 350 and 351) or partly by way of a monthly payment and partly by way of percentage of profits. The total remuneration cannot exceed five per cent of the net profits except with the approval of the Central Government.

Overall managerial remuneration. Section 198 puts a maximum limit (exclusive of any fees payable to directors, for attending meetings of the Board or any committee of the Board) of eleven per cent of the net profits on total remuneration payable by the company to its directors, including managing directors and its manager (if any).

Managerial remuneration includes any expenditure incurred by the company:

(*a*) in providing any rent-free accommodation, or any other benefit or amenity in respect of accommodation free of charge;

(*b*) in providing any other benefit or amenity free of charge or at a concessional rate;

(*c*) in respect of any obligation or service which, but for such expenditure by the company, would have been incurred by the person concerned; and

(*d*) to effect any insurance on the life of, or to provide any pension, annuity or gratuity for, the person concerned or his spouse or child.

However, if in any financial year a company has no profits or its profits are inadequate, the company may pay to its managing or whole-time director or manager remuneration according to schedule XIII, part II, section II.

Prohibition of tax-free payments

Section 200 prohibits the payment to any officer or employee remuneration free of tax or remuneration calculated by reference to or varying with the tax payable by him.

SCHEDULE XIII

[See sections 198, 269, 310 and 311]

CONDITIONS TO BE FULFILLED FOR THE APPOINTMENT OF A MANAGING OR WHOLE-TIME DIRECTOR OR A MANAGER WITHOUT THE APPROVAL OF THE CENTRAL GOVERNMENT

PART I
APPOINTMENTS

1. No person shall be eligible for appointment as a managing or whole-time director or a manager of a company unless he satisfies the following conditions, namely:—

(*a*) he had not been sentenced to imprisonment for any period, or to a fine exceeding one thousand rupees, for the conviction of an offence under any of the following Acts, namely:—

(*i*) the Indian Stamp Act, 1899 (2 of 1899),

(*ii*) the Central Excises and Salt Act, 1944 (1 of 1944),
(*iii*) the Industries (Development and Regulation) Act, 1951 (65 of 1951),
(*iv*) the Prevention of Food Adulteration Act, 1954 (37 of 1954),
(*v*) the Essential Commodities Act, 1955 (10 of 1955),
(*vi*) the Companies Act, 1956 (1 of 1956),
(*vii*) the Securities Contracts (Regulations) Act, 1956 (42 of 1956),
(*viii*) the Wealth-tax Act, 1957 (27 of 1957),
(*ix*) the Income-tax Act, 1961 (43 of 1961),
(*x*) the Customs Act, 1962 (52 of 1962),
(*xi*) the Monopolies and Restrictive Trade Practices Act, 1969 (54 of 1969),
(*xii*) the Foreign Exchange Regulation Act, 1973 (46 of 1973),
(*xiii*) the Sick Industrial Companies (Special Provisions) Act, 1985 (1 of 1986),
(*xiv*) the Securities and Exchange Board of India Act, 1992 (15 of 1992),
(*xv*) the Foreign Trade (Development and Regulation) Act, 1992 (22 of 1992).

(*b*) he had not been detained for any period under the Conservation of Foreign Exchange and Prevention of Smuggling Activities Act, 1974 (52 of 1974);

Provided that where the Central Government has given its approval to the appointment of a person convicted or detained under sub-paragraph (*a*) or sub-paragraph (*b*), as the case may be, no further approval of the Central Government shall be necessary for the subsequent appointment of that person if he had not been so convicted or detained subsequent to such approval;

(*c*) he has completed the age of twenty-five years and has not attained the age of seventy years or the age of retirement, if any, specified by the company, whichever is earlier

if the appointment is made at the age of 69 years; and thereafter the appointed crosses the age of 70 years during the tenure of his appointment, no approval of the Central Government is required for the latter part of his appointment which may fall outside the upper age limit.

(*d*) where he is managerial person in more than one company, he opts to draw remuneration from only one company;

(*e*) he is resident in India.

Explanation: For the purpose of this schedule, resident in India includes a person who has been staying in India for a continuous period of not less than twelve months immediately preceding the date of his appointment as a managerial person and who has come to stay in India,—

(*i*) for taking up employment in India, or
(*ii*) for carrying on a business or vocation in India.

PART II
REMUNERATION

Section I. — Remuneration payable by companies having profits;

Subject to the provisions of sections 198 and 309, a company having profits in a financial year may pay any remuneration, by way of salary, dearness allowance, perquisites, commission and other allowances, which shall not exceed five per cent of its net profits for one such managerial person, and if there is more than one such managerial person, ten per cent for all of them together.

Section II.— Remuneration payable by companies having no profits or inadequate profits:

1. Notwithstanding anything contained in this part, where in any financial year during the currency of tenure of the managerial person, a company has no profits or its profits are inadequate, it may pay remuneration to a managerial person, by way of salary, dearness allowance, perquisites and any other allowances, not exceeding ceiling limits of Rs. 24,00,000 per annum or Rs. 2,00,000 per month calculated on the following scale:—

	where the effective capital of the company is—	*monthly salary, payable shall not exceed—*
(*i*)	less than Rs. 1 crore	Rs. 75,000
(*ii*)	Rs. 1 crore or more but less than Rs. 5 crore	Rs. 1,00,000
(*iii*)	Rs. 5 crores or more but less than Rs. 25 crore	Rs. 1,25,000
(*iv*)	Rs. 25 crore or more but less than 100 crore	Rs. 1,50,000
(*v*)	Rs. 100 crore or more	Rs. 2,00,000

[Press Note No. 3/2000 dated 6.3.2000 issued by Ministry of Law, Justice and Company Affairs (Deptt. of Company Affairs)]

Explanation I: For the purposes of Section II of this Part, "effective capital" means the aggregate of the paid-up share capital (excluding share application money or advances against shares); amount; if any, for the time being standing to the credit of securities premium account; reserves and surplus (excluding revaluation reserve; long-term loans and deposits repayable after one year (excluding working capital loans, overdrafts, interest due on loans unless funded, bank guarantee etc., and other short-term arrangements) as reduced by the aggregate of any investments (except in the case of investments by an investment company whose principal business is acquisition of shares, stock, debentures or other securities), accumulated losses and preliminary expenses not written off.

Explanation II: (*a*) Where the appointment of the managerial person is made in the year in which company has been incorporated, the effective capital shall be calculated as on the date of such appointment;

(*b*) in any other case, the effective capital shall be calculated as on the last date of the financial year preceding the financial year in which the appointment of the managerial person is made.

Perquisites:

2. A managerial person shall also be a eligible to the following perquisites which shall not be included in the computation of the ceiling on remuneration specified in paragraph 1 of this Section:

(*a*) contribution to provident fund, superannuation fund or annuity fund to the extent these **either singly or put together are not taxable under the Income-tax Act, 1961,**

(*b*) gratuity payable at a rate not exceeding half a month's salary for each completed year of service, and

(*c*) encashment of leaves at the end of the tenure.

Perquisites for expatriates:

3. In addition to the perquisities specified in paragraph 2 of this section, an expatriate managerial person (including a non-resident Indian) shall be eligible to the following perquisites which shall not be included in the computation of the ceiling on remuneration specified in paragraph 1 of this section:

(*a*) *Children's education allowance*: In case of children studying in or outside India, an allowance limited to a maximum of Rs. 5,000 per month per child or actual expenses incurred, whichever is less. Such allowance is admissible upto a maximum of two children.

(*b*) *Holiday passage for children studying outside India/family staying abroad*: Return holiday passage once in a year be economy class or once in two years by first class to children and to the members of the family from the place of their study or stay abroad to India if they are not residing in India which the managerial person.

(*c*) *Leave travel concession*: Return passage for self and family in accordance with the rules specified by the company where it is proposed that the leave be spent in home country instead of anywhere in India.

Explanation: For the purposes of this Part, family means the spouse, dependent children and dependent parents of the managerial person.

Section III—Remuneration payable to a managerial person in two companies:

Subject to the provisions of section I and II, a managerial person shall draw remuneration from one or both companies, provided that the total remuneration drawn from the companies does not exceed the higher maximum limit admissible from any one of the companies of which he is a managerial person.

PART III

PROVISIONS APPLICATION TO PARTS I AND II OF THIS SCHEDULE

1. The appointment and remuneration referred to in Parts I and II of this Schedule shall be subject to approval by a resolution of the shareholders in general meeting.

2. The auditor or the secretary of the company or where the company has not appointed a secretary, a secretary in whole-time practice shall certify that the requirements of this Schedule have been complied with and such certificate shall be incorporated in the return filed with the Registrar under sub-section (2) of section 269.

SCHEDULE XIV

[*See sections 205 and 350*]

RATES OF DEPRECIATION

Name of assets	Single shift		Double shift		Triple shift	
	W.D.V.	S.L.M.	W.D.V.	S.L.M.	W.D.V.	S.L.M.
1	2	3	4	5	6	7
I. (*a*) **Buildings** (other than factory buildings) [NESD]	5%	1.63%	—	—	—	—
(*b*) Factory Buildings	10%	3.34%	—	—	—	—
(*c*) Purely temporary erections such as wooden structures	100%	100%	—	—	—	—
II. Plant and Machinery						
(*i*) General rate applicable to—						
(*a*) plant and machinery (not being a ship) other than continuous process plant for which no special rate has been prescribed under (*ii*) below	13.91%	4.75%	20.87%	7.42%	27.82%	10.34%
(*b*) continuous process plant, other than those for which no special rate has been prescribed under (*ii*) below (NESD)	15.33%	5.28%	—	—	—	—
(*ii*) Special rates						
A.1. Cinematograph films-Machinery used in the production and exhibition of cinematograph films [NESD]						
(a) Recording equipment, reproducing equipment, developing machines, printing machines, editing machines, synchronisers and studio lights except bulbs	20%	7.07%	—	—	—	—
(*b*) Projecting equipment of film exhibiting concerns						

1	2	3	4	5	6	7
2. Cycle [NESD]	20%	7.07%	—	—	—	—
3. Electrical machinery, X-Ray and electrotherapeutic apparatus and accessories thereto, medical, diagnostic equipments, namely, Catscan, Ultrasound Machines, ECG Monitors, etc, (NESD)	20%	7.07%	—	—	—	—
4. Juice boiling pans (karhais) (NESD)	20%	7.07%	—	—	—	—
5. Motor-cars, motor cycles, scooters and other mopeds (NESD)	25.89%	9.5%	—	—	—	—
6. Electrically operated vehicles including battery powered or fuel cell powered vehicles (NESD)	20%	7.07%	—	—	—	—
7. Sugarcane crushers (indigenous kolhus and belances) (NESD)	20%	7.07%	—	-	—	—
8. Glass manufacturing concerns except direct fire glass melting furnaces-Recuperative and regenerative glass melting furnaces	20%	7.07%	30%	11.31%	40%	16.21%
9. Machinery used in the manufacture of electronic goods or components	15.62%	5.38%	23.42%	8.46%	31.23%	11.87%
B. 1. Aeroplanes, Aeroengines, Simulators, Visual Systems and Quick Engine Change Equipment (NESD)	16.2%	5.6%	—	—	—	—
2. Concrete pipes manufacture-Moulds [NESD]						
3. Drum container manufacture-Dies [NESD]						
4. Earth-moving machinery employed in heavy construction works, such as dams, tunnels, canals, etc. [NESD]						
5. Glass manufacturing concerns except direct fire glass melting furnaces-Moulds [NESD]	30%	11.31%				
6. Moulds in iron foundaries [NESD]						
7. Mineral oil concerns-Field operations (above ground) Portable boilers, drilling tools, well-head tansk, rigs, etc. [NESD]						
8. Mines and quarries-Portable underground machinery and earth-moving machinery used in open cast mining [NESD]						

1	2	3	4	5	6	7
9. Motor buses and motor lorries other than those used in a business of running them on hire [NESD]						
9A. Motor tractors, harvesting combines [NESD]	30%	11.31%				
10. Patterns, dies and templates [NESD]						
11. Ropeway structures-Ropeways, ropes and trestle sheaves and connected parts [NESD]						
12. Shore and other leather goods factories-Wooden lasts used in the manufacture of shoes.	30%	11.31%	45%	18.96%	60%	29.05%
C. 1. Motor buses, motor lorries and motor taxies used in a business of running them on hire [NESD]						
2. Rubber and plastic goods factories-Moulds [NESD]	40%	16.21%				
3. Data processing machines including computers [NESD]						
4. Gas cylinders including valves and regulators [NESD]						
D. 1. Artificial silk manufacturing machinery wooden parts						
2. Cinematograph films-Bulbs of studio lights						
3. Flour mills-Rollers						
4. Glass manufacturing concerns-Direct fire glass melting furnaces						
5. Iron and Steel industries-Rolling mill rolls						
6. Match factories-Wooden match frames						
7. Mineral oil concerns(*a*) Plant used in field operations (below ground)-Distribution-returnable packages; (*b*) Plant used in field operations (below ground) but not including assets used in field operations (distribution)-Kerbside pumps including underground tanks and fittings	100%	100%	—	—	—	—
8. Mines and quarries- (*a*) Tubs, winding ropes, haulage ropes and sand stowing pipes (*b*) Safety lamps						
9. Salt works-Salt pans, reservoirs and condensers, etc., made of earthy, sandy or clay material or any other similar material						
10. Sugar works-rollers	100%	100%				

1	2	3	4	5	6	7
III. Furniture and Fittings						
1. General Rates [NESD]	18.1%	6.33%	—	—	—	—
2. Rate for furniture and fittings used in hotels, restaurants and boarding houses, schools, colleges and other educational institutions, libraries, welfare centres, meeting halls, cinema houses, theatres and circuses, and for furniture and fittings let out on hire for use on the occasion of marriages and similar functions [NESD]	25.88%	9.5%	—	—	—	—
IV. Ships						
1. Ocean-going ships-						
(*i*) Fishing vessels with wooden hull [N.E.S.D.]	27.05%	10%	—	—	—	—
(*ii*) Dredgers, tugs, barges, survey launches and other similar ships used mainly for dredging purposes [N.E.S.D.]	19.8%	7%	—	—	—	—
(*iii*) Other ships [N.E.S.D.]	14.6%	5%	—	—	—	—
2. Vessels ordinarily operating on inland waters-						
(*i*) Speed boats [N.E.S.D.]	20%	7.07%	—	—	—	—
(*ii*) Other vessels [N.E.S.D.]	10%	3.34%	—	—	—	—
W.D.V. means written down value.						
S.L.M. means straight line method.						

NOTES

1. "Buildings" include roads, bridges, culverts, wells and tube-wells.
2. "Factory buildings" does not include offices, godowns, officers' and employees' quarters, roads, bridges, culverts, wells and tube-wells.
3. "Speed boat" means a motor boat driven by a high speed internal combustion engine capable of propelling the boat at a speed exceeding 24 kilometres per hour in still water and so designed that when running at a speed it will plane, *i.e.,* its bow will rise from the water.
4. Where, during any financial year, any addition has been made to any asset, or where any asset has been sold, discarded, demolished or destroyed, the depreciation on such assets shall be calculated on a *prorata* basis from the date of such addition or, as the case may be, up to the date on which such asset has been sold, discarded, demolished or destroyed.
5. The following information should also be disclosed in the accounts:
   (*i*) depreciation methods used; and
   (*ii*) depreciation rates or the useful lives of the assets, if they are different from the principal rates specified in the Schedule.
6. The calculations of the extra depreciation for double shift working and for triple shift working shall be made separately in the proportion which the number of days for which the concern worked double shift or triple shift, as the case may be, bears to the normal number of working days during the year. For this purpose, the normal number of working days during the year shall be deemed to be —
   (*a*) in the case of a seasonal factory or concern, the number of days on which the factory or concern actually worked during the year or 180 days, whichever is greater;

(*b*) in any other case, the number of days on which the factory or concern actually worked during the year or 240 days, whichever is greater.

The extra shift depreciation shall not be charged in respect of any item of machinery or plant which has been specifically, excepted by inscription of the letters "NESD" (meaning "no extra shift depreciation") against it in sub-items above and also in respect of the following items of machinery and plant to which the general rate of depreciation of 13.91% per cent applies:

(1) Accounting machines.
(2) Air-conditioning machinery including room air-conditioners.
(3) Building contractor's machinery.
(4) Calculating machines.
(5) Electrical machinery—switchgear and instruments, transformers and other stationary plant and wiring and fitting of electric light and fan installations.
(6) Hydraulic works, pipelines and sluices.
(7) Locomotives, rolling stocks, tramways and railways used by concerns, excluding railway concerns.
(8) Mineral oil concerns—field operations:
   (*a*) Prime movers
   (*b*) Storage tanks (above ground)
   (*c*) Pipelines (above ground)
   (*d*) Jetties and dry docks
(9) Mineral oil concerns—field operations (distribution)—Kerbside pumps, including underground tanks and fittings.
(10) Mineral oil concerns—refineries:
   (*a*) Prime movers
   (*b*) L.P.G. Plant
(11) Mines and quarries:
   (*a*) Surface and underground machinery (other than electrical machinery and portable underground machinery)
   (*b*) Head-gears
   (*c*) Rails
   (*d*) Shafts and inclines
   (*e*) Tramways on the surface.
(12) Neo-post franking machines.
(13) Office machinery
(14) Overhead cables and wires.
(15) Railway sidings.
(16) Refrigeration plant container, etc. (other than racks).
(17) Ropeway structures:
   (*i*) Trestle and station steel work,
   (*ii*) Driving and tension gearing.
(18) Salt works—Reservoirs, condensers, salt pans, delivery channels and piers if constructed of masonry, concrete, cement, asphalt or similar materials, barges and floating plant; piers, quays and jetties; and pipelines for conveying brine if constructed of masonry, concrete, cement, asphalt or similar materials.
(19) Surgical instruments.
(20) Tramways electric and tramways run by internal combustion engines—permanent way; cars—car trucks, car bodies, electrical equipment and motors; tram cars including engines and gears.

(21) Typewriters.
(22) Weighing machines.
(23) Wireless apparatus and gear, wireless appliances and accessories.

7. 'Continuous process palnt' means a plant which is required and designed to operate 24 hours a day.
8. Notwithstanding any thing mentioned in this schedule, depreciation on assets, whose actual cost does not exceed five thousand rupees, shall be provided at the rate of hundred per cent. Provided that where the aggregate actual cost of individual items of plant and machinery costing Rs. 5,000 or less constitute more than 10 per cent of the total actual cost of plant and machinery, rates of depreciation applicable to such items shall be the rates as specified in item II of the schedule. (The second sentence of this note no. 8 has been added on 1st March 1995).

The abovementioned schedule XIV is the one amended vide Notification No. GSR 788 (E), dated 4-11-1994 issued by the Ministry of Law, Justice and Company Affairs, Department of Company Affairs. The changes made in Schedule XIV as per the abovementioned Notification shall apply in respect of the accounts of the companies closed on or after the date of issue of the Notification. The revised rates of depreciation shall apply to assets acquired by the companies on or after that date. As regards applicability of these changes to existing assets, the companies have been advised by the Ministry of Law, Justice & Company Affairs, Department of Company Affairs to follow the recommendation of Institute of Chartered Accountants of India contained in its Guidance Notes on the "Accounting for Depreciation in Companies". These recommendations are given below:

(*a*) A company following the written down value (W.D.V.) method of depreciation in respect of its assets should apply the relevant W.D.V. rates prescribed in Schedule XIV to the written down value as at the end of the previous financial year as per the books of the company.

(*b*) A company following the straight line method of depreciation in respect of its assets existing on the date of Schedule XIV into force may adopt any of the following alternative bases of computing the depreciation charge:

(*i*) The specified period may be recomputed by applying to the original cost, the revised rate as prescribed in Schedule XIV and depreciation charge calculated by allocating the unamortized value as per the books of account over the remaining part of the recomputed specified period.

(*ii*) The company can continue to charge depreciation on straight line basis at old rates in respect of assets existing on the date on which the new provision relating to depreciation came into force.

(*iii*) SLM rates prescribed Schedule XIV can be straightaway applied to the original cost of all the assets including the existing assets from the year of change of the rate.

Illustration 2:

The following Profit and Loss Account is presented by A Ltd. for the year ended March 31, 2010:—

Profit and Loss Account

	(*Rs. in '000*)		(*Rs. in '000*)
To Salaries and Wages	1,28,00	By Gross Profit b/fd	6,08,00
To Directors' Fees	1,00	By Profit on sale of company's land	25,00
To Repairs	27,00		
To Depreciation	90,00	By Subsidy received from State Government	50,000
To Scientific Research (New Laboratory set up)	20,00		
To General Charges	18,00		
To Interest on Debentures	24,00		
To Income Tax	1,16,00		

	(*Rs. in '000*)	(*Rs. in '000*)
To Proposed Dividend	1,00,00	
To Provision for Corporate Dividend tax	11,00	
To Balance c/fd	1,48,00	
	6,83,00	6,83,00

The amount of depreciation as per Schedule XIV comes to Rs. 82,00,000. The effective capital of the company is Rs. 4 crore. Calculate the remuneration payable to the managing director of the company.

Solution:

		(*Rs in '000*)
Gross Profit as disclosed by the Profit and Loss Account		6,08,00
Add: Subsidy received		50,00
		6,58,00
Less: Deductions to be made:	(*Rs in '000*)	
Salaries and Wages	1,28,00	
Directors' Fees	1,00	
Repairs	27,00	
Depreciation	82,00	
General Charges	18,00	
Interest on Debenture	24,00	2,80,00
Profit according to Section 349		3,78,00

Remuneration payable to the managing director @ 5% = Rs. 18,90,000.

In the above case, we may also proceed by taking the balance of profit as reported and then making adjustments for items to be excluded. Thus:—

	(*Rs in '000*)
Balance of profit as per Profit and Loss Account	1,48,00
Add: Proposed Dividend, being appropriation	1,00,00
Provision for Corporate Dividend tax	11,00
Income-Tax (managing director's remuneration is calculated on profit before tax)	1,16,00
Scientific Research, being capital expenditure	20,00
Excess Depreciation (Rs. 90,00,000 – Rs. 82,00,000)	8,00
	4,03,00
Less: Capital profit on sale of land	25,00
Profit according to Section 349	3,78,00

Remuneration payable to the managing director on Rs. 3,78,00,000 @ 5% = Rs. 18,90,000.

Calculation of Commission. The law permits payment of commission to managerial personnel on net profit calculated before taking into account the commission. If the profits are, for example, Rs. 7,20,00,000, a managing director (if there is only one) can receive up to 5% of Rs. 7,20,00,000 or Rs. 36,00,000 as his remuneration (the exact amount depends upon the Articles or the appropriate resolution of the company). If there are two or more than two whole-time directors, the total remuneration to all of them cannot exceed Rs. 72,00,000, i.e., 10% of Rs. 7,20,00,000. But the company may, if it so desire, calculate the commission on profits remaining after charging such commission. In such a case, the commission to a managing director (if there is no other whole-time director) will be Rs. 7,20,00,000 × 5/105 or Rs. 34,28,571 in the example given above.

If there is no whole-time director or manager, part-time directors put together can receive, apart from the fees for attending meetings, a commission of 3 per cent (maximum) of the net profits. Otherwise, the part-time directors may receive up to one per cent of the net profits. If there whole-time directors and others are part-time directors, the whole-time directors together can be paid upto 10 per cent of the net profits and part-time directors can be paid upto 1 per cent of the profits. Moreover, the remuneration paid to one need not be deducted from the profits for the purpose of calculating commission to the other. Suppose, the total profits are Rs. 6,00,00,000. The two whole-time directors can get upto Rs. 60,00,000 in all (10% of the profits) and the part-time directors can get upto Rs. 6,00,000, *i.e.*, 1% of Rs. 6,00,00,000.

But a different arrangement is permissible—that the remuneration payable to the whole-time directors should be calculated on profits remaining after payment of commission to part-time directors and that the commission to part-time directors should be calculated after the remuneration to the whole-time directors has been deducted. Taking the example given above, the calculation will be as follows:—

Suppose, the remuneration payable to the whole-time directors is x :

Then, the profits remaining after charging x are Rs. 6,00,00,000 – x ;

and the commission payable to part-time directors is 1/100 (6,00,00,000 – x);

The profits remaining after charging the commission to part-time directors will be Rs. 6,00,00,000 – 1/100 (6,00,00,000 – x).

Then, $x = 1/10[6{,}00{,}00{,}000 - 1/100\,(6{,}00{,}00{,}000 - x)]$

Solving the equation, one gets

$$10x = 6{,}00{,}00{,}000 - 1/100\,(6{,}00{,}00{,}000 - x)$$

or $$1{,}000x = 6{,}00{,}00{,}00{,}000 - 6{,}00{,}00{,}000 + x)$$

or $$1{,}000\,x - x = 6{,}00{,}00{,}00{,}000 - 6{,}00{,}00{,}000$$

or $$999x = 5{,}94{,}00{,}00{,}000$$

Hence $$x = 59{,}45{,}946$$

The commission to whole-time directors is Rs. 59,45,946. The remaining profits are Rs. 5,40,541. Hence, the commission to part-time directors @ 1% of Rs. 5,40,54,054 i.e. Rs. 5,40,541

The agreement with the managerial personnel could of course introduce greater complication of calculating the remuneration. For instance, the commission or remuneration payable could be calculated after deducting such commission or remuneration. If this were the case, the example given above, the calculations would be as under:—

Suppose, the remuneration to the whole time directors is x.

Then, the commission to the part-time directors would be 1/101 (6,00,00,000 – x).

or $$x = 10/110\,[6{,}00{,}00{,}000 - 1/101\,(6{,}00{,}00{,}000 - x)]$$

or $$x = 1/11[6{,}00{,}00{,}000 - 1/101\,(6{,}00{,}00{,}000 - x)]$$

or $$11x = 6{,}00{,}00{,}000 - 1/101\,(6{,}00{,}00{,}000 - x)]$$

Multiplying both the sides by 101, we get

or $$1{,}111x = 6{,}06{,}00{,}00{,}000 - 6{,}00{,}00{,}000 + x$$

or $$1{,}111\,x - x = 6{,}06{,}00{,}00{,}000 - 6{,}00{,}00{,}000$$

or $$1{,}110x = 6{,}00{,}00{,}00{,}000$$

Hence $$x = 54{,}05{,}406$$

The remaining profit are Rs. 5,45,94,594. The part-time director's commission is 1/101 of Rs. 5,45,94,594 or Rs. 5,40,541.

Illustration 3:

Determine the maximum remuneration payable to the part-time directors and manager of B Ltd. (a manufacturing company) under section 309 and 387 of the Companies Act, 1956 from the following particulars:

Before charging any such remuneration, the profit and loss account showed a credit balance of Rs. 2,31,00,000 for the year ended 31st March, 2010 after taking into account the following matters:

	Rs.
(*i*) Capital expenditure	52,50,000

		Rs.
(*ii*)	Subsidy received from government	42,00,000
(*iii*)	Depreciation	10,50,000
(*iv*)	Bonus to foreign technicians	31,50,000
(*v*)	Provision for taxation	2,87,00,000
(*vi*)	Compensation paid to injured workman	10,50,000
(*vii*)	Loss on sale of fixed assets	7,00,000
(*viii*)	Profit on sale of investment	21,00,000

Company is providing depreciation as per section 350 of the Companies Act, 1956.

[*Adapted Co. Sec.* (*inter*)]

Solution:

Calculation of profit for the purpose of determination of Managerial Remuneration:

Net profit as per Profit and Loss Account	2,31,00,000
Add: Capital Expenditure	52,50,000
Provision for Taxation	2,87,00,000
	5,70,50,000
Less: Profit on sale of investment	21,00,000
	5,49,50,000
Less: Part-time directors' commission @ 1%	5,49,500
Net Profit for sec. 387	5,44,00,500

Manager's Remuneration @ 5% of Rs. 5,44,00,500 = Rs. 27,20,025

Total Managerial Remuneration Payable = Rs. 27,20,025 + Rs. 5,49,500 = Rs. 32,69,525.

Illustration 4:

C Ltd. employs a manager who is entitled to a salary of Rs. 1,20,000 per month, and in addition, to a commission of 2 per cent of the net profit of the company before such salary or commission. The Profit and Loss Account for the company's financial year ending 31st March, 2010 is as follows:

	(*Rs. in '000*)		(*Rs. in '000*)
To General Expenses	12,60	By Gross Profit b/fd	1,32,00
To Staff Salaries and Bonus	27,40	By Subsidy from the State Government	5,00
To Ex-gration Payment to two Employees	80	By Profit on sale of Machinery and Plant	
To Charitable Donations	2,00	(Difference between price realised and	
To Depreciation	11,00	written-down value)	8,00
To Manager's Salary	14,40		
To Commission to Manager			
(on account)	1,40		
To Income-tax	27,00		
To Balance c/fd	48,40		
	1,45,00		1,45,00

The amount realised on sale of the Machinery and Plant was Rs. 32 lakh while the cost was Rs. 30 lakh. The company has provided depreciation as per Schedule XIV. The effective capital of the company is Rs. 25 crore.

Calculate the commission payable to manager.

Solution:

	(*Rs. in '000*)
Profit as per Profit and Loss Account	48,40
Add: Items not to be deducted for computing profit for the purpose of calculating commission:	
Ex-gratia Payment to two Employees	80
Manager's Salary	14,40

	(*Rs. in '000*)
Commission to the Manager (on account)	1,40
Income-tax	27,00
	92,00
Less: Capital profit on sale of Machinery and Plant: (Rs. 32,00 thousand – Rs. 30,00 thousand)	2,00
Profit on which commission is to be calculated	90,00
Commission @ 2% on Rs. 90,00 thousand;	1,80
Amount still to be paid (Rs. 1,80 thousand – 1,40 hundred)	40

Commission payable on profits available for dividend. "Profits available for dividend" would mean profits remaining after taxation and appropriations which have to be made compulsorily. But in the absence of any agreement to the contrary, appropriation of profits, such as transfer to the reserve funds, which are at the discretion of the directions should not be deducted. Taxes must be computed after charging all remuneration, including the commission to the staff. Thus, commission to staff and taxes would be inter-related. If profits are x, T is tax and c is commission, then c would be based on $x - t$ and t would be based on $x - c$. In other words, one has to be deducted from the profits before the other can be calculated.

Taking the above illustration again, suppose the manager is entitled to a commission on profits remaining after taxation and that the rate of income-tax is 50% on ordinary profits and again 50% on capital profits. The calculation would be as under:

Assume commission is c and taxation is t.

Profit for computation of taxation

	(*Rs. in lakhs*)	(*Rs. in lakhs*)
Profit as per profit and Loss A/c	381	384
Add: Items not to be deducted:—		
Ex-gratia payment to two employees	8	8
Manager's Saraly	48	
Commission to the Manager (on account)	10	10
Income-tax	370	370
	820	772
Less: Profit on sale of Machinery	20	20
	800	752
Less: t and c	t	c
	?	??

$$t = (752 - c) \times 50/100 + 50/100 \times 20$$
$$= (752 - c) \times 1/2 + 10$$

Substituted the value of t, we get

$$c = 2/100\ [800 - 1/2\ (752 - c) - 10]$$

or $$c = 2/100\ (790 - 1/2)\ (75 - c)$$

or $$c = 1/100\ (1580 - 752 + c)$$

or $$100\ c = 1580 - 752 + c$$

or $$99c = 828$$

Hence $$c = 8.36$$

$$t = 50/100\ (752 - 8.36) + 50/100 \times 20$$
$$t = 752/2 - 8.36/2 + 10$$

Hence, $$t = 3.82$$

Taxation. It has been accepted by the various accountancy bodies that income-tax or tax on profits is a charge against revenue even though the amount payable clearly depends on uncertain factors like the views of the Finance Minister and though there will be no liability if there is no profit. Since the actual amount payable will be known long after the preparation of the Profit and Loss Account, the liability for taxes has to be estimated and provided for on that basis. The amount has to be debited to the Profit and Loss Account (above the line) and credited to the Provision for Taxation Account. Sales Tax should normally be deducted from Sales Account if not already recorded separately; but if an extraordinary amount, not recovered from customers, is payable, it should be debited to the Profit and Loss Account.

In the balance sheet, the provision for taxation should contain only those accounts in respect of which assessment has not been made. If the tax payable for a period has been determined, the amount, if unpaid, should be shown as a liability under current liabilities. The amount of the tax paid in advance may be either shown as advance on the assets side or deducted from the provision for taxation on the liabilities side.

Any adjustment on account of previous years should be debited or credited below the line – in the appropriation section of the Profit and Loss Account — as otherwise the Profit and Loss Account will not disclose a figure of profit or loss fully relevant to the current year. Suppose, in 2009-2010 the Provision for Taxation stood at Rs. 1,65,000 and the liability for 2009-2010 comes to only Rs. 1,29,00,000. Then, Rs. 36,00,000 should be credited to the Profit and Loss Appropriation Account by debit to the Provision for Taxation Account or to General Reserve.

Dividends. Dividends to shareholders will be considered in detail a little later. Here it will be sufficient to say that dividends represent appropriation of profits and should be shown in the "appropriation" section of the Profit and Loss Account. If, however, one consolidated account is shown, dividends paid (and proposed) should be debited therein. Provision for Corporate Dividend Tax has also to be made on dividends proposed or declared.

Other appropriation items like transfer to General Reserve, or to Sinking Fund for Redemption of Debentures (or other liability) or anything that represents division of profits should also be shown in the Profit and Loss Account (in the appropriation section if that is to be shown separately). Any withdrawal of material amounts from provisions or reserves created in previous years should be separately shown, preferably in the appropriation section.

Illustration 5:

From the following figures taken from the books of U Ltd., prepare the Profit and Loss Account for the year ended on 31st March, 2010 and the Balance Sheet as on that date. The form prescribed by the law for the Balance may be ignored.

	Rs. in lakhs		*Rs. in lakhs*
Cash in hand	5	Repairs	39
Machinery	89,27	Postage and Stationery	21
Unclaimed Dividends	17	Rent, Rates and Taxes	62
Freehold Land	15,04	Carriage	20
Preliminary Expenses	83	Travelling Expenses	10
Sinking Fund for Redemption of Debentures	25,00	Subscribed and fully called Share Capital	1,25,00
		Discount on Issue of Debentures Account	50
Sundry Debtors	25,00	Interest on Sinking Fund Investments	1,44
Depreciation on Machinery	5,50	Sinking Fund Investments	25,00
Wages	7,50	Sundry Creditors	20,36
Salaries	2,09	Goodwill	5,00
Purchases	64,70	Miscellaneous Receipts	4
Bad Debts	34	Loose Tools	42
Directors' Remuneration	74	14% Debentures to be redeemed on March 31, 2015	20,00
Auditors' Fees	25		
Interest on Debentures less tax @ 10%	1,26	Provision for Bad Debts	1,00
Insurance	1,30	Interest Receivable on Government Loan	50
Depreciation on Buildings	1,50	Sales	98,35

	Rs. in lakhs		Rs. in lakhs
Cash at Bank	1,40	P. & L. A/c balance (Cr.)	96
General Reserve	4,76	Returns from Customers	47
Returns from Purchases	35	Depreciation Provision	20,24
10% Free of tax Government Loan	10,00	Bank Charges	1
Motive Power	1,90	Discount on Sales	13
Bills Payable	75	Stock (1st April, 2009)	13,00
Buildings	45,06	General Expenses	14

1. Provision for bad debts is to be maintained at 5% on sundry debtors.
2. Write off the whole of the preliminary expenses and one-fifth of the balance of Discount on issue of Debentures Account.
3. Rs. 200 lakh is the annual instalment for the Sinking Fund for Redemption of Debentures.
4. The closing stock is Rs. 1,370 lakh including goods worth Rs. 30 lakh received on the last day and for which entries have not yet been passed.
5. The authorised capital of the company is Rs. 150 crore divided into 15 crore shares of Rs. 10 each.
6. Make a provision for income tax @ 35% of net profits.
7. Transfer Rs. 1,00 lakh to General Reserve.

Solution:

Profit and loss Account of U Ltd. for the year ended 31st March, 2010

Dr. *Cr.*

Figures for 2008-2009 (Rs. in lakhs)	*Particulars*		*Amount (Rs. in lakhs)*	*Figures for 2008-2009 (Rs. in lakhs)*	*Particulars*		*Amount (Rs. in lakhs)*
	To Opening Stock : (2)			96,64	By Sales		97,88
7,00	Finished Goods	8,00			By Closing Stock : (2)		
5,50	Raw Materials	5,00	13,00	8,00	Finished Goods	9,60	
				5,00	Raw Materials	4,10	13,70
64,20	To Purchase of Materials		64,65				
7,30	To Wages		7,50				
1,70	To Motive Power		1,90				
18	To Carriage		20				
23,76	To Gross Profit c/d		24,33				
1,11,58			1,11,58	1,11,58			1,11,58
1,98	To Salaries		2,09	23,76	By Gross Profit b/d		24,33
5,50	To Depreciation on Machinery		5,50	1,00	By Intt. on Invest. Recd.	50	
1,50	To Depreciation on buildings		1,50		*Add*: Outstanding	50	1,00
13	To Repairs		39	1,44	By Interest on Sinking		
29	To Insurance		30		Fund Investment (3)		1,44
2,80	To Interest on Debentures (4)			2	By Miscellaneous Receipts		4
	(paid 12,600 × 100/90	1,40					
	Add: Outstanding	1,40	2,80				
1,00	To Provision for Bad						
	Debts required	1,25					
	Add: Bad Debts	34					
		159					
	Less: Existing						
	Provision	1,00	59				
13	To General Expenses		14				
18	To Postage and Stationery		21				

(Rs. in lakhs)		(Rs. in lakhs)	(Rs. in lakhs)		(Rs. in lakhs)
60	To Rent, Rates and Taxes	62			
9	To Travelling Expenses	10			
	To Opening Stock : (2)		96,64	By Sales	97,88
83	To Preliminary Expenses written off	83			
10	To Discount on Issue of Debentures : 1/5 written off	10			
1	To Bank Charges	1			
12	To Discount on Sales	13			
25	To Auditors' Fees	25			
69	To Directors' Remuneration	74			
3,51	To Provision for Taxation	3,68			
6,51	To Net Profit	6,83			
26,22		26,81	26,22		26,81

Profit and Loss Appropriation Account

Figures for 2008-2009 (Rs. in lakhs)	*Particulars*	*Amount (Rs. in lakhs)*	*Figures for 2008-2009 (Rs. in lakhs)*	*Particulars*	*Amount (Rs. in lakhs)*
3,44	To Transfer to Sinking Fund for Redemption of Debentures (Rs. 2,00,00 + Rs. 1,44,000 Interest)	3,44	39	By Balance b/fd	96
			6,51	By Net Profit for the year b/d	6,83
1,00	To General Reserve	1,00			
2,46	To Balance carried to Balance Sheet	3,35			
6,90		7,79	6,90		7,79

Notes:

(1) Figures for the year ending 31st March, 2009 have been assumed.

(2) The law requires the opening and closing stocks of finished products to be separately stated. Hence, the figures given in the question have been split into stocks of finished goods and raw materials on an assumed basis.

(3) Interest on Sinking Fund Investments has been shown in the Profit and Loss Account because the law requires all interest to be shown there. This is opposed to the general accountancy practice. However, the effect of this departure from accountancy practice is nullified by transferring Rs. 3,44,000 (Rs. 2,00,000, the annual instalment plus Rs. 1,44,000, the Interest on Sinking Fund Investments) to the Sinking Fund.

(4) The amount of interest shown in the trial balance is the net amount after deducting tax which is @ 10% of gross amount. If interest is Rs. 100, Rs. 10 would be the tax and Rs. 90 would be the net amount paid. The gross interest, therefore, is found by multiplying Rs. 1,26,000 by 100/90. This is Rs. 1,40,000. The year's interest on Rs. 20,00,000 @ 14% comes to Rs. 2,80,000. Hence, Rs. 1,40,000 is to be provided. Income tax deducted (or deductible) at source on Rs. 2,80,000 @ 10% or Rs. 28,000 has been added to the liability for income tax deducted at source.

(5) It is not necessary or usual to give details of prepaid or outstanding item in the Profit and Loss Account itself.

Balance Sheet of U Ltd. as on 31st March, 2010
(not in prescribed form)

Liabilities	*Rs. in Lakhs*	*Rs. in lakhs*	*Assets*	*Rs. in Lakhs*	*Rs. in lakhs*
Share Capital			Fixed Assets:		
Authorised:			Goodwill		5,00
15 crore shares of Rs. 10 each		1,50,00	*Machinery at cost	89,27	
Subscribed:			*Less*: Depreciation written off		
12 crore 50 lakh Equity Shares			to date	15,50	73,77
of Rs. 10 each			Freehold Land		15,04
fully called and paid-up		1,25,00	*Buildings at cost	45,06	
General Reserve		5,76	*Less*: Depreciation written		
Sinking Fund for Redemption			off upto date	4,74	40,32
of Debenture		28,44	Loose Tools		42
Profit and Loss Appropriation Account		3,35	Current Assets:		
14% Debentures (2,015)		20,00	Stock: Finished Goods	9,60	
Interest outstanding	1,40		Raw Materials	4,10	13,70
Less: Tax @ 10%	14	1,26	Sundry Debtors	25,00	
Current Liabilities:			*Less*: Provision for Bad Debts	1,25	23,75
Sundary Creditors	20,36		Cash at Bank		1,40
Add: Unrecorded purchase	30	20,66	Cash in Hand		5
Bills Payable		75	Investments:		
Unclaimed Dividend		17	10% free of tax Government Loan		10,00
Provision for Taxation		3,68	Interest outstanding thereon		50
Income-tax Deducted at Sources		28	Sinking Fund Investment		25,00
			Discount on Issue of Debentures		
			(balance not yet written off)		40
		2,09,35			2,09,35

Alternatively, the profit and loss account can be presented as follows:—

Profit and Loss Account of U Ltd. for the year ended March 31, 2010

Figures for 2008-2009 (Rs. in lakhs)	*Particulars*	*Rs. in Lakhs*	*Amount (Rs. in lakhs)*	*Figures for 2008-2009 (Rs. in lakhs)*	*Particulars*	*Rs. in Lakhs*	*Amount (Rs. in lakhs)*
	To Opening Stock:			96,64	By Sales		97,88
7,00	Finished Goods	8,00			By Closing Stock:		
5,50	Raw Materials	5,00	13,00	8,00	Finished Goods	9,60	
64,20	To Purchase of Materials		64,65	5,00	Raw Materials	4,10	13,70
7,30	To Wages		7,50	1,00	By Interest on Investments		
1,70	To Motive Power		1,90		(received and outstanding)		1,00
18	To Carriage		20	1,44	By Interest on Sinking		
1,98	To Salaries		2,09		Fund Investments		1,44
5,50	To Depreciation on			2	By Miscellaneous		
	Machinery		5,50		Receipts		4
1,50	To Depreciation on						
	Buildings		1,50				

* It is better, and as will be seen later required by law, that the value of fixed assets be shown at cost less depreciation written off to date. Since, the books maintain "Depreciation Provision", the value of Machinery and Buildings shown in the books is the cost. It has been assumed that Depreciation Provision consists of Rs. 15,50,000 as depreciation on Machinery and Rs. 4,74,000 as depreciation on Buildings. The current year's depreciation of Rs. 5,50,000 on Machinery and Rs. 1,50,000 on Buildings stands included in the Depreciation Provision figure of 20,24,000 since the figures of depreciation appear in the trial balance.

(Rs. in lakhs)			(Rs. in lakhs)	(Rs. in lakhs)		(Rs. in lakhs)
13	To Repairs to Machinery		39			
29	To Insurance		30			
2,80	To Interest on Debentures (paid and outstanding)		2,80			
1,00	To Bad Debts	34				
	Add: Additional Provision required	25	59			
13	To General Expenses		14			
18	To Postage and Stationery		21			
60	To Rent, Rates & Taxes		62			
9	To Travelling Expenses		10			
83	To Preliminary expenses written off		83			
10	To Discount on Issue of Debentures; 1/5 written off		10			
1	To Bank Charges		1			
12	To Discount on Sales		13			
25	To Auditor's Fees		25			
69	To Directors' Remuneration		74			
3,51	To Provision for Income tax		3,68			
3,44	To Transfer to Sinking Fund for Redemption of Debentures		3,44			
1,00	To General Reserve		1,00			
2,07	To Balance of Profit		2,39			
11,210			11,406	11,210		11,406

Illustration 6:

The following is the trial balance of Bee Ltd. as on 31st March, 2010:

	(Rs. in '000)		(Rs. in '000)
Stock as on 1.4.2009	75,00	Purchase returns	10,00
Purchases	2,45,00	Sales	3,40,00
Wages	30,00	Discount	3,00
Carriage inwards	95	Profit and loss account	16,35
Furniture	17,00	Share capital	1,00,00
Salaries	7,50	Creditors	17,50
Rent	4,00	General reserve	15,50
Sundry trade expenses	6,05	Bills payable	7,00
Dividend paid for 2008-2009	9,00		
Corporate dividend tax paid	1,35		
Debtors	28,50		
Plant and machinery	29,00		
Cash at bank	46,20		
Patents	4,80		
Bills receivable	5,00		
	5,09,35		5,09,35

Prepare the profit and loss account for the year ended 31st March, 2010 and a balance sheet as on that date after considering the following adjustments:

(*i*) Stock as on 31st march, 2010 was valued at Rs. 88,10,000.

(*ii*) Make a provision for income-tax at 35%.

(*iii*) Depreciate plant and machinery at 15%; furniture at 10%; and patents at 5%.

(*iv*) On 31st March, 2010 outstanding rent amount to Rs. 80,000.

(v) The Board recommends payment of a dividend @ 15% per annum. Transfer the minimum required amount to general reserve. Also make a provision for corporate dividend tax @ 15% of the amount proposed to be distributed.
(vi) Provide Rs. 31,000 for doubtful debts.
(vii) Provide Rs. 5,20,000 for managerial remuneration. (*C.S.* (*Inter*) *June, 1998 modified*)

Solution.

Dr. **Profit and Loss Account for the year ended 31st March, 2010** *Cr.*

	(*Rs. '000*)	(*Rs. '000*)		(*Rs. '000*)
To Opening stock		75,00	By Sales	3,40,00
To Purchases	2,45,00		By Closing stock	88,10
Less: Purchases returns	10,00	2,35,00		
To Wages		30,00		
To Carriage inwards		95		
To Gross profit c/d		87,15		
		4,28,10		4,28,10
To Salaries		7,50	By Gross profit b/d	87,15
To Rent	4,00		By Discount	3,00
Add: Outstanding rent	80	4,80		
To Sundry trade expenses		6,05		
To Depreciation on:				
Plant and machinery	4,35			
Furniture	1,70			
Patents	24	6,29		
To Provision for bad debts		31		
To Outstanding managerial remuneration		5,20		
To Provision for income tax @ 35%		21,00		
To Net profit c/d		39,00		
		90,15		90,15
To Dividend paid for 2008-2009		9,00	By Balance b/fd	1635
To Corporate dividend tax paid		1,35	By Net profit for the year b/d	39,00
To General reserve, 5% of Rs. 39 lakh		1,95		
To Proposed dividend @15%		15,00		
To Provision for corporate dividend tax @ 15% on proposed dividend		2,25		
To Balance carried to balance sheet		25,80		
		55,35		55,35

Balance Sheet as at 31st March, 2010

Liabilities	(*Rs. '000*)	(*Rs. '000*)	*Assets*	(*Rs. '000*)	(*Rs. '000*)
Share Capital			**Fixed Assets**		
Authorised		?	Palnt and machinery	29,00	
Issued and Subscribed		1,00,00	*Less*: Depreciation	4,35	24,65
Reserves and Surplus			Furniture	17,00	
General Reserve	15,50		*Less*: Depreciation	1,70	15,30
Add: Addition made			Patents	4,80	
during the year	1,95	17,45	*Less*: Depreciation	24	4,56
Surplus i.e. credit balance			**Current Assets, Loans and**		
of profit and loss			**Advances**		
(appropriation) account		25,80	(A) Current Assets		
			Stock		88,10

	(Rs. '000)	*(Rs. '000)*		*(Rs. '000)*	*(Rs. '000)*
Current Liabilities and Provisions			Debtors	28,50	
(A) Current liabilities			*Less*: Provision for bad		
Bill payable		7,00	debts	31	28,19
Creditors		17.50	Cash at bank		46,20
Rent Outstanding		80	(B) Loans and Advances		
Managerial remuneration outstanding		5,20	Bills receivable		5,00
(B) Provisions					
Provision for taxation		21,00			
Provision for corporate dividend tax on proposed dividiend		2,25			
Proposed dividend @ 15%		15,00			
		2,12,00			2,12,00

Illustration 7:

The following is the trial balance of Nakul Ltd. as on 31st March, 2010:

	(Rs. '000)		*(Rs. '000)*
Stock, 1st April, 2009	75,00		
Purchases Returns			10,00
Purchases and Sales	2,45,00		3,40,00
Wages		30,00	
Discount			3,00
Carriage Inwards	95		
Furniture and Fittings	17,00		
Salaries	7,50		
Rent	4,00		
Sundry Expenses	7,05		
Profit and Loss Appropriation Account, 31st March, 2009			16,35
Dividend paid for 2008-2009	9,00		
Corporate Dividend Tax	1,35		
Equity Share Capital			1,00,00
Debtors and Creditors	27,50		17,50
Plant and Machinery	29,00		
Cash at Bank	46,20		
General Reserve			15,50
Patents and Trade Marks	4,80		
Bills Receivable and Bills Payable	5,00		7,00
	5,09.35		5,09,35

Prepare Trading Account, Profit and Loss Account, and Profit and Loss Appropriation Account for the year ended 31st March, 2010 and Balance Sheet at that date. Take into consideration the following adjustments:

(*i*) Stock on 31st March, 2010 was valued at Rs. 79,24,000.

(*ii*) Make a provision for income tax @ 35%.

(*iii*) Depreciate plant and machinery @ 15%, furniture and fittings @ 10% and patents and trade marks @ 5%.

(*iv*) On 31st March, 2001 outstanding rent amounted to Rs. 80,000 while outstanding salaries totalled Rs. 65,000.

(*v*) Provide for managerial remuneration @10% of the net profits before tax but after such managerial remuneration.

(*vi*) The Directors propose a dividend @15% per annum for the year ended 31st March, 2010 after the minimum transfer to general reserve as required by law.

Make a provision for corporate dividend tax @ 15%. (*B.Com. (Hons.) Delhi, 1990 Modified*]

Solution:

Dr. **Trading and Profit & Loss Account for the year ended 31st March, 2010** Cr.

	(Rs. '000)	(Rs. '000)		(Rs. '000)
To Stock on 1st April, 2009		75,00	By Sales	3,40,00
To Purchases	2,45,00		By Stock on 31st March, 2010	79,24
Add: Purchases Returns	10,00	2,35,00		
To Wages		30,00		
To Carriage Inwards		95		
To Gross Profit c/d		78,29		
		4,19,24		4,19,24
To Salaries	7,50		By Gross Profit b/d	78,29
Add: Outstanding salaries	65	8,15	By Discount Received	3,00
To Rent	4,00			
Add: Outstanding Rent	80	4,80		
To Sundry Expenses		7,05		
To Depreciation on:				
Plant and Machinery @15%	4,35			
Furniture and Fittings @ 10%	1,70			
Patents and Trade Marks @5%	24	6,29		
To Managerical Remuneration @10%		5,00		
To Provision for Income Tax @ 35%		17,50		
To Net Profit carried to Profit and Loss Application Account		32,50		
		81,29		81,29

Profit and Loss Appropriation Account for the year ended 31st March, 2010

	Rs.		Rs.
To Dividend Paid for 2008-2009	9,00	By Balance c/fd	16,35
To Corporate Dividend Tax	90	By Net Profits for the year b/d	32,50
To General Reserve, 5% of Rs. 32,50,000	1,35		
To Proposed Dividend @ 15%	15,00		
To Provision for Corporate Dividend Tax @ 15%	2,25		
To Balance carried to Balance Sheet	19,62		
	48,85		48,85

Balance Sheet as at 31st March, 2010

Liabilities	(Rs. '000)	(Rs. '000)	*Assets*	(Rs. '000)	(Rs. '000)
Share Capital			**Fixed Assets**		
Authorised		?	Palnt and Machinery	29,00	
Issued and Subscribed:			*Less*: Depreciation for the year	4,35	24,65
Equity Share Capital		1,00,00	Furniture and Fittings	17,00	
Reserves and Surplus			*Less*: Depreciation for the year	1,70	15,30
General Reserve	15,50		Patents and Trade Marks	4,80	
Add: Addition during the year	1,63	17,13	*Less*: Depreciation for the year	24	4,56
Surplus i.e. credit balance of profit and loss (appropriation) account		10,62	**Current Assets, Loans and Advances**		
			(A) Current Assets		
Current Liabilities and Provisions			Stock		79,24
(A) Current Liabilities			Debtors		27,50
Bill payable		7,00	Cash at Bank		46,20

	(Rs. '000)	(Rs. '000)		(Rs. '000)	(Rs. '000)
Creditors		17,50	(B) Loans and Advances		
Outstanding Expenses:			Bills Receivable		5,00
Rent	80				
Salaries	65				
Managerial Remuneration	5,00	6,45			
(B) Provisions					
Provision for Income tax		17,50			
Provision for Corporate Dividend Tax		2,25			
Proposed Dividend		15,00			
		2,02,45			2,02,45

Note: Due to absence of information, figures for the previous year have not been given.

Illustration 8:

The following is the trial balance of Subhash Ltd. as on 31st March, 2010:

(*Figures in Rs. '000*)

Debit Balances	*Rs.*	*Credit Balances*	*Rs.*
Land, at cost	110	Equity Capital (Shares of Rs. 10 each)	150
Plant & Machinery, at cost	385	10% Debentures	100
Debtors	48	General Reserve	65
Stock (31.3.2010)	43	Profit & Loss Account	36
Adjusted Purchases	10	Securities Premium	20
Factory Expenses	160	Sales	350
Administration Expenses	30	Creditors	26
Selling Expenses	15	Provision for Depreciation	86
Debenture Interest	10	Suspense Account	2
Interim Dividend Paid	9		
	835		835

Additional Information:

(*a*) On 31.3.2010, the company issued bonus shares to the shareholders on 1:3 basis. No entry relating to this has yet been made.

(*b*) The authorised share capital of the company is 25,000 shares of Rs. 10 each.

(*c*) The company on the advice of independent valuer wishes to revalue the land at Rs. 1,80,000.

(*d*) Proposed final dividend 10%. Ignore Corporate Dividend Tax.

(*e*) Suspense account of Rs. 2,000 represents cash received for the sale of some of the machinery on 1.4.2000. The cost of the machinery was Rs. 5,000 and the accumulated depreciation thereon was Rs. 4,000.

(*f*) Depreciation is to be provided on plant and machinery at 10% on cost.

You are required to prepare Subhash Limited's profit & loss account for the year ended 31.3.2010 and a balance sheet on that date in vertical form as per the provisions of Schedule VI of the Companies Act, 1956.

Your answer to include detailed schedules only for the following:

(1) Share Capital,

(2) Reserve & Surplus, and

(3) Fixed Assets,

Ignore previous years' figures and taxation. [*C.A.* (*Inter.*) *May, 1997 Modified*]

Solution:

Subhash Limited
Balance Sheet as at 31.3.2010

	Schedule No.			(Rs. '000)
I. Sources of Funds				
(1) Shareholders Funds				
(*a*) Capital	1	200		
(*b*) Reserves & Surplus	2	200		400
(2) Loan Funds				
10% Debentures				100
	Total			500
II. Application of Funds				
(1) Fixed Assets	3			
Land			180	
Gross Block, Rs. (385 – 5) thousand		380		
Less: Depreciation Rs. (86 + 38 – 4) thousand		120	260	440
(2) Current Assets				
Stock		43		
Debtors		48		
Cash		10	101	
Less: Current Liabilities				
Creditors		26		
Proposed Dividend		15	41	60
	Total			500

Profit and Loss Account for the year ended 31.3.2010

	(Rs. '000)	(Rs. '000)	(Rs. '000)
Sales			350
Other Income (profit on sale of machine)			1
Total Income			351
Less: Expenses:			
Purchases		160	
Factory Expenses		30	
Administration Expenses		15	
Selling Expenses		15	
Depreciation		38	
Interest on Debentures		10	268
Net Profit before Dividend			83
Dividend: Interim	9		
Final	15		24
Balance Carried to Balance Sheet			59

SCHEDULES

SCHEDULE 1
Share Capital

	(Rs. '000)
Authorised	
25,000 Shares of Rs. 10 each	2,50
Issued, subscribed and fully paid-up:	

	(Rs. '000)
20,000 shares of Rs. 10 each (Of the above, 5,000 shares are alloted as fully paid by way of bonus shares.)	2,00

Bonus shares were issued by utilising the general reserve.

SCHEDULE 2

Reserves and Surplus

	Rs. '000
Premium Account Securities	20
Revaluation Reserve	70
General Reserve	15
Balance in Profit & Loss Account	95
	2,00

SCHEDULE 3

Fixed Assets	As on 1/4/2009 Rs. '000	Additions Rs. '000	Deletions Rs. '000	Depreciation Rs. '000	Net Block Rs. '000
Land	1,10	70	—	—	1,80
Plant & Machinery	3,85	—	5	1,20	2,60
Total	4,95	70	5	1,20	4,40

Land was revalued upward by Rs. 70 thousand during the year.

Working Notes:

(*i*) Bonus shares have been issued on 1:3 basis.

Hence, bonus shares have been issued for $\frac{150 \text{ thousand}}{3}$ = 50 thousand.

Equity Share Capital = Rs. (150 + 50) thousand = Rs. 200 thousand.

General Reserve = Rs. (65 – 50) thousand = Rs. 15 thousand.

(*ii*) Due to revaluation of land, there is Revaluation Reserve for 70 thousand.

Illustration 9:

E Ltd. manufactures and sells food products. The following draft financial statements were prepared by the chief accountant for the year ended 31.3.2010 and placed before you for advice:

Profit and Loss Statement for the year ended 31.3.2010

	(Figures in Rs. lakhs)
Sales and other income	3,500
Cost of goods sold including operating expenses and depreciation	2,740
Operating profit	760
Profit on sale of property	200
Interest charges	300
Profit before tax	660
Tax provision	330
Profit after tax	330
Proposed dividend	300
Provision for corporate dividend tax	33
Profit retained	30
Add: Opening balance of profit	360
Profit carried to balance sheet	357

Balance Sheet as on 31.3.2010

(Figures in Rs. lakhs)

Liabilities		*(Rs. '000)*	*Assets*		*(Rs. '000)*
Share capital		3,000	Fixed assets	5,000	
General reserve		540	*Less*: Depreciation	1,000	4,000
Profit and Loss account balance		357	Current assets		
Secured loans		2,000	Stock	800	
Current liabilities and provisions			Debtors	1,000	
Creditors	240		Royalty receivable	100	
Provision for tax	330		Advance tax	200	
Proposed dividend	300		Cash balance	550	2,650
Provision for Corporate			Miscellaneous expenditure		
Dividend tax	33	903	to the extent not written off		150
		6,800			6,800

You are provided with further information as follows:

(*a*) On 1.4.2009 E Ltd. had sold some of its fixed assets for Rs. 100 lakh [written down value Rs. 250 lakh]. These assets were revalued earlier. As on 1.4.2009 the revaluation reserve corresponding to these assets stood at Rs. 200 lakh. The profit on sale of property as shown in the profit and loss statement represented the transfer of this amount. Loss on sale of the asset was included in the cost of goods sold etc.

(*b*) During the year E Ltd. undertook restructuring exercise of its operations at a cost of Rs. 150 lakh. This amount stood included in "miscellaneous expenditure to the extent not written off".

(*c*) Included in sales and other income is a sum of Rs. 100 lakh representing royalty receivable for supply of know-how to a company in South-East Asia. As per agreement the amount is to be received in US Dollars. However, exchange permission was denied to the company in South-East Asia for remitting the same.

(*d*) E Ltd. purchased fixed assets costing Rs. 1,825 lakh on 1.4.2009 and the same was fully financed by foreign currency loan [i.e. US Dollars] repayable in five equal instalments annually. [Exchange rate at the time of purchase was 1 US Dollar = Rs. 36.50]. As on 31.3.2010 the first instalment was paid when 1 US Dollar fetched Rs. 41.50. The entire loss on exchange was included in cost of goods sold etc. E Ltd. normally provides depreciation on fixed assets at 20% on WDV basis.

(*e*) Dividend at 10% on paid up equity capital is to be maintained as in prior years.

You are required to redraft the financial statements of E Ltd. for the year ended 31.3.2010 in accordance with relevant provisions of accounting standards. Journal entries (wherever applicable) in respect of the information given are to be shown. Schedule, previous year's figures and cash flow statement are not required. *[Adapted C.A. (Final), Nov., 1998]*

Solution:

(*a*) According to paras 14.4 and 32 of Accounting Standard 10 on Accounting for Fixed Assets, on disposal of a previously revalued item of fixed asset, the difference between net disposal proceeds and the net book value should be charged or credited to the profit and loss statement except that, to the extent such a loss is related to an increase which was previously recorded as a credit to revaluation reserve and which has not been subsequently reversed or utilised, it is charged directly to that account. The amount standing in revaluation reserve following the retirement or disposal of an asset which relates to that asset may be transferred to general reserve.

Hence, adjustments are required as follows:—

Journal

(*Rs. in lakhs*)

	Dr.	Cr.
Either		
Profit on Sale of Property Account ....Dr.	200	
To Loss on Sale of Fixed Assets Account		150
To General Reserve		50
Use of Profit on Sale of Property Account to write off Loss on Sale of Fixed Assets Account, the remaining balance in the former account being credited to General Reserve.		
Or the following two entire		
Profit on Sale of Property Account ...Dr.	200	
To Revaluation Reserve		200
Transfer of Profit on Sale of Property Account to Revaluation Reserve.		
Revaluation Reserve ...Dr.	200	
To Loss on Sale of Fixed Assets Account		150
To General Reserve		50
Transfer of Loss on Sale of Fixed Assets Account to Revaluation Reserve; the balance remaining in Revaluation Reserve being transferred to General Reserve.		

(*b*) According to para 12 of Accounting Standard-5 (Revised) on Net Profit or Loss for the Period, Prior Period items and Changes in Accounting Policies, when items of income and expense within profit or loss from ordinary activities are of such size, nature or incidence that their disclosure is relevant to explain the performance of the enterprise for the period, the nature and amount of such items should be disclosed separately.

Hence, it is wrong to show the reconstructing cost of Rs. 150 lakh under 'miscellaneous expenditure'. The amount requires a separate disclosure in the Profit and Loss Account.

(*c*) According to para 9.2 of AS 9 on Revenue Recognition, where the ability to assess the ultimate collection with reasonable certainty is lacking at the time of raising any claim, *e.g.*, for escalation of price, export incentives, interest etc., revenue recognition is postponed to the extent of uncertainty involved. In such cases, it may be appropriate to recognise revenue only when it is reasonably certain that the ultimate collection will be made. The necessary adjustment journal entry is as follows:—

Journal

(*Rs. in lakhs*)

	Dr.	Cr.
Sales and Other Income ....Dr.	100	
To Royalty Receivable Account		100
Adjustment mode for Uncertain collection of royalty receivable.		

Alternatively, one may apply para 9.3 of AS 9, after making reasonable assumption as to the timing of the uncertainty. According to para 9.3, when the uncertainty relating to collectability arises subsequent to the time of sale or the rendering of the service, it is more appropriate to make a separate provision to reflect the uncertainty rather than to adjust the amount of revenue originally recorded.

(*d*) Exchange differences arising on repayment of liabilities incurred for the purpose of acquiring fixed assets, which are carried in terms of historical cost, should be adjusted in the carrying amount of the respective fixed assets. The carrying amount of such fixed assets should to the extent not already so adjusted or otherwise accounted for, also be adjusted to account for any increase or decrease in the liability of the enterprise, as expressed in the reporting currency by applying the closing rate, for making payment towards the whole or a part of the cost of the assets or for repayment of the whole or a part of the monies borrowed by the enterprise from any person, directly or indirectly, in foreign currency specifically for the purpose of acquiring those assets.

Thus, the entire loss on exchange should be added to the carrying amount of fixed assets and not to the cost of goods sold.

Further, depreciation on the revised unamorised depreciable amount should also be provided, in accordance with para 25 of AS 6 (Revised) on Depreciation Accounting.

$$\text{Now, foreign currency loan} = \frac{\text{Rs.1,825 lakh}}{\text{Rs.36.50}} = \text{50 lakh U.S. Dollars.}$$

Loss of Foreign exchange (including loss on payment of first instalment)
= 50 lakh U.S. Dollers × (41.50 – 36.50) = Rs. 250 lakh
Additional depreciation to be provided = 20% of Rs. 250 lakh = Rs. 50 lakh.

Journal

(*Rs. in lakhs*)

			Dr.	Cr.
	Fixed Assets ...Dr.		250	
	To Loss of Foreign Exchange/Cost of Goods Sold etc.			250
	Increase in the cost of fixed assets due to loss of foreign exchange.			
	Depreciation Account ...Dr.		50	
	To Provision for Depreciation Account			50
	Additional depreciation provided due to increase in the cost of fixed assets on account of loss of foreign exchange.			

E Ltd.
Balance Sheet as at 31.3.2010

(*Rs. in lakhs*)

I. SOURCES OF FUNDS			
(1) Shareholders' Funds			
(*a*) Capital		3,000	
(*b*) Reserves & Surplus			
General reserve	590		
Profit and loss account	307	897	3,887
(2) Loan funs:			
(*a*) Secured loans		2,000	
(*b*) Unsecured loans		—	2,000
Total			5,897
II. Application of Funds			
(1) Fixed assets:			
(*a*) Gross block	5,000		
Exchange difference capitalised	250	5,250	
(*b*) *Less*: Depreciation (1,000 + 50)		1,050	
(*c*) Net block		4,200	
(*d*) Capital work in progress		—	4,200
(2) Investments			
(3) Current assets, loans and advances:			
(*a*) Investories		800	
(*b*) Sundry debtors		1,000	
(*c*) Cash balance		550	

(*d*) Other current assets		—	
(*e*) Loans and advances (Advance tax)		200	
		2,550	
Less: Current liabilities and provisions:			
(*a*) Liabilities		240	
(*b*) Provisions			
Provision for taxation	280		
Provision Corporate Dividend tax	33		
Proposed dividend	300	613	
		853	
Net current assets			1,697
(4) Miscellaneous expenditure (to the extent not written off or adjusted)			
Total			5897

Profit and Loss Account
for the year ended 31st March, 2010

	(*Rs. in lakhs*)
Sales and other income	3,400 *
Cost of goods sold including operating expenses and depreciation	(2,390) **
Restructuring cost	(150)
Interest charges	(300)
Profit before taxation	560
Provision for tax (@ 50%)	(280)
Net profit	280
Balance brought forward from previous year	360
Profit available for appropriation	640
Proposed dividend	(300)
Provision for Corporate Dividend Tax	(33)
Balance carried forward	307

	(*Rs. in lakhs*)
*Sales and other income, as given	3,500
Less: Adjustment for royalty receivable	100
Amount appearing in income statement	3,400

		(*Rs. in lakhs*)
**Cost of goods sold etc., as given		2,740
Less: Loss on sale of fixed to Profit on sale of Property Account	150	
Loss of foreign exchange debited to fixed assets account	250	400
		2,340
Add: Additional depreciation on fixed assets		50
Amount appearing in income statement		2,390

Notes on Accounts: The royalty receivable in US Dollars for supply of know-how to a company in South-East Asia amounting to Rs. 100 lakh has not been recognised as exchange permission has been denied to the company in South-East Asia for remitting the same.

Notes:

(*i*) In the absence of any information regarding interest on foreign currency loan taken for financing purchase of fixed assets, no provision has been made for interest liability.

(*ii*) It has been assumed that restructuring costs are of revenue nature.

(*iii*) Current year profit after tax is only Rs. 280 lakh as against the proposed dividend of Rs. 300 lakh. Hence, in order to ensure sufficient compliance with section 205 of the Companies Act, 1956, past profits are utilised to make up the shortfall. It is also assumed that there are no arrears of depreciation.

Profits Prior to Incorporation:

It may happen in case of new companies that a running business is taken over from a certain date, whereas the company may be incorporated at a later date. The company would be entitled to all profits earned after the date of purchase of business unless the agreement with the vendors provides otherwise. But profits up to the date of incorporation of the company have to be treated as capital profits because these are the profits which have been earned even before the company came into existence. Such profits are known as profits prior to incorporation. It should be remembered that a public company cannot commence business till it receives the certificate of commencement of business. Therefore, it would be prudent to treat all profits earned before commencement of business as capital profits. However, strictly speaking, "Profit Prior to Incorporation" means only the profits earned up to the date of incorporation and not upto the date of the certificate of commencement of business.

For correct allocation of profits, a profit and loss account should be prepared on the date of incorporation; but this would mean taking stock which is inconvenient. The usual practice, therefore, is to prepare the profit and loss account only at the end of the year and then to allocate the profit between the two periods—up to incorporation and after. The allocation is done on the following basis:—

(*a*) Gross profit should be allocated according to the ratio of sales for the two periods.

(*b*) Expenses that are connected with sales, (such as discount allowed, bad debts, commission to salesmen, advertising, etc.) should be allocated in the ratio of sales.

(*c*) Expenses that are incurred on the basis of time (such as salaries, rent, interest, etc.,) should be allocated in the ratio of the time before incorporation and after.

(*d*) Expenses that are solely incurred for the company on and after its incorporation (for example, preliminary expenses or interest on debentures or directors' fees) should be charged wholly to the post-incorporation period.

Gross profit minus the total of expenses for the pre-incorporation period will give the profit prior to incorporation. The entry to be passed will be :

Profit and Loss Account ...Dr.
To Profit Prior to Incorporation

Profit Prior to Incorporation will appear in the balance sheet along with other capital profits. The remaining profits will be treated as revenue profits and available for dividends, etc.

Illustration 10:

G Ltd. was incorporated on the 1st August, 2009 and received its certificate for commencement of business on 1st September, 2009. The company bought the business of M/s Active and Slow with effect from 1st April, 2009. From the following figures relating to the year ending 31st March, 2010 find out the profits available for dividends:—

(*a*) Sales for the year were Rs. 60 crore out of which sales up to 1st August were Rs. 25 crore and upto 1st September Rs. 30 crore.

(*b*) Gross Profit for the year was Rs. 18 crore.

(*c*) The expenses debited to the Profit and Loss Account were:—

	Rs. '000
Rent	9,000
Salaries	15,000
Directors' Fees	4,800
Interest on Debentures	5,000
Audit Fees	1,500
Discount on Sales	3,600
Depreciation	24,000
General Expenses	4,800
Advertising	18,000

	Rs. '000
Stationery and Printing	3,600
Commission on Sales	6,000
Bad Debts	1,500
(Rs. 5,000, relate to debts created prior to incorporation)	
Interest to vendor on purchase consideration upto 1st October, 2000	3,000

Solution:

Profit-prior to and after Incorporation

	Basis of allocation	*Prior to Incorporation Rs. '000*	*After Incorporation Rs. '000*
Gross Profit	Sales	7,500	
Expenses:			
Rent	Time	3,000	6,000
Salaries	Time	5,000	10,000
Directors' Fees	—	—	4,800
Interest on Debentures	—	—	5,000
Audit Fees*	Time	500	1,000
Discount on Sales	Sales	1,500	2,100
Depreciation	Time	8,000	16,000
General Expenses	Time	1,600	3,200
Advertising	Sales	7,500	10,500
Stationery and Printing	Time	1,200	2,400
Commission on Sales	Sales	2,500	3,500
Bad Debts	—	500	1,000
Interest to Vendor	Time	2,000	1,000
Total		33,300	66,500
Profit (Gross Profit less Expenses)		41,700	38,500

The ratio of sales is 25 crore: 35 crore or 5 : 7. The ratio of time is four months (upto 1st August) to 8 months or 1 : 2, except in case of interest to vendor. In this case (the interest paid is for 6 months out of which interest for four months (upto 1st August) is charged to the period prior to incorporation. Bad debts have been allocated according to the indication given in the question.

Illustration 11:

New Ventures Ltd. was incorporated on 1st July, 2009 with an authorised capital consisting of 50,000 equity shares of Rs. 10 each to take over the running business of Random Brothers as from 1st April, 2009. The following is the summarised Profit & Loss Account for the year ended 31st March, 2010:—

	Rs. '000			Rs. '000
Cost of sales for the year	1,60,000	Sales:—		
Administrative Expenses	17,680	1st April, 2009 to 30th		
Selling Commission	8,750	June, 2009	60,000	
Goodwill written off	2,200	1st July, 2009 to 31st		
Interest paid to ventors		March, 2010	1,90,000	2,50,000
(loan repaid on 1st February)	3,730			
Distribution expenses (60% variable)	12,500			
Preliminary expenses written off	3,100			

*Audit fees have been allocated between the two periods because audit must have been conducted also for transactions taking place prior to incorporation. However, since audit fees arise only when the company is formed, it would be permissible to charge it wholly to the period after incorporation.

	Rs.		Rs.
Debenture interest	3,200		
Depreciation	4,440		
Directors' fees	1,200		
Net profit	33,200		
	2,50,000		2,50,000

The company deals in one type of product. The unit cost of sales was reduced by 10 per cent in the post-incorporation period as compared to the pre-incorporation period in the year. You are required to apportion the net profit amount between pre-incorporation and post-incorporation periods showing the basis of apportionment. How will pre-incorporation profit be dealt with in the books of account of the company? [*Adapted C.S. (Inter.) June, 1987*]

Solution:

Calculation of pre-incorporation and post-incorporation profits:—

Sales Ratio = 6 : 19

Time Ratio = 3 : 9 or 1 : 3

	Basis of Apportionment	*Pre-incorporation*	*Post-incorporation*
		Rs. '000	*Rs. '000*
Sales	Actual	60,000	1,90,000
Less: Cost of sales	Sales	38,400	1,21,600
Administrative expenses	Time	4,420	13,260
Selling commission	Sales	2,100	6,650
Goodwill	Post-incorporation	—	2,200
Interest to vendors (till 1st Feb.)	Time (3 : 7)	1,119	2,611
Distribution expenses :			
Variable (60%), Rs. 7,500	Sales	1,800	5,700
Fixed (40%), Rs. 5,000	Time	1,250	3,750
Preliminary expenses	Post-incorporation	—	3,100
Debenture interest	"	—	3,200
Depreciation	Time	1,110	3,330
Directors' fees	Post-incorporation	—	1,200
		50,199	1,66,601
Profit		9,801	23,399

Pre-incorporation profit amounting to Rs. 9,801 thousand is a capital profit; it will be credited to Capital Reserve Account.

Sometimes, the sales figure for the period prior to incorporation is not given directly but has to be calculated from the ratio of sales of various months. Suppose, (*a*) a company is incorporated on Ist August, 2009, having taken over a running business on Ist April, 2009; (*b*) sales for the year ending 31st March, 2010 are Rs. 95 lakh; and (*c*) sales for the each one of the first five months of the accounting year are half of what they are for each one of the seven subsequent months of the accounting year. Thus, if the sales figure for each one of the first five months is 1, the sales for each one of the subsequent seven months are 2; total for the first five months is 5 and that for the subsequent seven months 14. Now, sales for four months upto Ist August, 2009 would be 1 × 4 *i.e.*, 4 and sales for the following eight months would be 1 + 2 × 7 or 1 + 14 i.e. 15. The ratio between pre-incorporation sales and post-incorporation sales is 4 : 15. Hence, total sales during the pre-incorporation period are Rs. 95 lakh × 4/19 = Rs. 20 lakh and the total sales during the post-incorporation period are Rs. 75 lakh.

Examples:

(1) A company takes over a business w.e.f. Ist April, 2009 and is incorporated on Ist August,

2009, sales for the full year ending 31st March, 2010 are Rs. 12 crore; the sales for the months of April, June and December are one and a half times the average; sales for the month of May are half the average and for march are twice the average. The sales for the months of April to July will be calculated as under:—

		Rs. in Crores
Average sale per month = Rs. 12 crore ÷ 12 = Rs. 1 crore		
Sales for :	April (1½ times the average)	1.5
	May (½ the average)	0.5
	June (1½ the average)	1.5
	December (1½ times the average)	1.5
	March (twice the average)	2.0
Total for five months		7.0

Therefore, sales for the remaining seven months = Rs. 12 crore – Rs. 7 crore = 5 crore.

Average for each one of the seven months = Rs. 5 crore ÷ 7 = Rs. 71,42,857.

Hence, total sales for the four months, April, 2009 to July 2009 are Rs. (1,50,00,000 + 50,00,000 + 1,50,00,000 + 71,42,857) = Rs. 4,21,42,857.

(2) A company incorporated on August 1, 2009 took over the business of a firm w.e.f. April 1, 2009. For the year ended 31st March, 2010 the gross profit was Rs. 9,75,00,000; the sales for the first four months of the year ended 31st March, 2010 were one-fourth of the total sales for the year. As from August 1, 2009, the prices of the goods went up from the 5% and the selling price was raised by 8%; the mark-up in the pre-incorporation period was 25% on cost. What is the amount of gross profit earned by the company during the post-incorporation period of eight months?

	Margain		
	Prior to August 1	*After August 1*	
Cost of goods purchased	Rs. 100	Rs. 105	(i.e. 100 + 5%)
Selling Price	Rs. 125	Rs. 135	(i.e. 125 + 8%)
Margin on Selling Price	25/125	30/135	

If total sales is S, then sale before August 1 is $1/4S$ and that after August 1 is $3/4S$.

Therefore, $\frac{25}{125} \times \frac{1}{4} S + \frac{30}{135} \times \frac{3}{4} S = 9{,}75{,}50{,}000$

or $\frac{1}{20} S + \frac{1}{6} S \qquad = 9{,}75{,}50{,}000$

$3S + 10S = 58{,}50{,}00{,}000$

Hence, $\qquad S = 45{,}00{,}00{,}000$

Sale after August 1: 45,00,00,000 × 3/4 = Rs. 33,75,50,000.

Gross Profit on Rs. 33,75,50,000 = 33,75,50,000 × 30/135 = Rs, 7,50,00,000.

Illustration 12:

A company was incorporated on 1st August, 2009 to take over a business from the preceding 1st April. The accounts were made upto 31st March, 2010 as usual and the trading and profit and loss account gave the following result:

	(Rs. '000)		(Rs. '000)
To Opening stock	1,40,00	By Sales	12,00,00
To Purchases	9,10,00	By Closing stock	1,50,00
To Gross profit c/d	3,00,00		
	13,50,00		13,50,00
To Rent, rates and insurance	18,00	By Gross profit b/d	3,00,00
To Directors' fees	20,00		
To Salaries	51,00		

	(Rs. '000)		(Rs. '000)
To Office expenses	48,00		
To Travellers' commission	12,00		
To Discounts	15,00		
To Bad debts	3,00		
To Audit fee	7,50		
To Depreciation	6,00		
To Debenture interest	4,50		
To Net profit	1,15,00		
	3,00,00		3,00,00

It is ascertained that the sales for February, 2010 and March, 2010 are one and half times the average for the year. Apportion the year's profit between the pre-incorporation and the post-incorporation period. [*C.S. (Inter.) Dec. 1995 Modified*]

Solution:

Statement showing profit prior to and after incorporation

Items	*Basis of apportionment*	*Pre-incorporation period* Rs. '000	*Post-incorporation period* Rs. '000
Gross profit	Sales, 1: 3	75,00	2,25,00
Less expenses:			
Rent, rates and insurance	Time, 1 : 2	6,00	12,00
Directors' fees	Post-incorporation	—	20,00
Salaries	Time, 1 : 2	17,00	34,00
Office expenses	Time, 1 : 2	16,00	32,00
Travellers' commission	Sales, 1 : 3	3,00	9,00
Discounts	Sales, 1 : 3	3,75	11,25
Bad debts	Sales, 1 : 3	1,00	2,00
Audit fee*	Time, 1 : 2	2,50	5,00
Depreciation	Time, 1 : 2	2,00	4,00
Debenture interest	Post-incorporation	—	4,50
Total expenses		51,25	1,33,75
Profit (gross profit-expenses)		13,75	91,25
		75,00	2,25,00

*Alternatively, audit fee may be wholly charged to post-incorporation period.

Working Notes:

(*i*) Time ratio = 4 months : 8 months = 1 : 2

(*ii*) *Sales ratio*:

Sales for the year = Rs. 12 crore

Monthly average = Rs. 1 crore

Sales for February 2010/March 2010 = 1.5 × Rs. 1 crore = Rs. 1.5 crore.

Sales from 1st August, 2009 to 31st January, 2010

= 6 × Rs. 1 crore = Rs. 6 crore

Sales from 1st February, 2010 to 31st March, 2010 = 2 × Rs. 1.5 crore = Rs. 3 crore

Post-incorporation sales = Rs. 6 crore + Rs. 3 crore = Rs. 9 crore

Pre-incorporation sales = Rs. 12 crore – Rs. 9 crore = Rs. 3 crore

Hence, sales ratio between pre-incorporation period and post-incorporation period = Rs. 3 crore : Rs. 9 crore = 1 : 3.

Illustration 13

Green Company Ltd. was formed to take over a running business with effect from 1st April, 2009. The company was incorporated on 1st August, 2009, and the certificate of commencement of business was received on 1st October, 2009. The following profit and loss account has been prepared for the year ended 31st March, 2010.

Profit and Loss Account for the year ended 31st March, 2010

	Rs.		*Rs.*
To Salaries	2,40,000	By Gross profit b/f	16,00,000
To Printing and stationery	24,000		
To Travelling expenses	84,000		
To Advertisement	80,000		
To Miscellaneous trade expenses	1,89,000		
To Rent (office building)	1,32,000		
To Electricity charges	21,000		
To Directors' fees	56,000		
To Bad debts	16,000		
To Commission to selling agents	80,000		
To Audit fees	30,000		
To Debenture interest	15,000		
To Interest paid to vendors	21,000		
To Selling expenses	1,26,000		
To Depreciation on fixed assets	48,000		
To Net profit c/f	4,38,000		
	16,00,000		16,00,000

The following additional information is provided to you:

(*i*) Total sales for the year, which amounted to Rs. 96,00,000 arose evenly upto the date of the certificate of commencement of business, whereafter they spurted to record an increase of two-thirds during the rest of the year.

(*ii*) Rent of office building was paid @ Rs. 10,000 per month upto September, 2009, and thereafter it was increased by Rs. 2,000 per month.

(*iii*) Travelling expenses include Rs. 24,000 towards sales promotion.

(*iv*) Depreciation include Rs. 3,000 for assets acquired in the post-incorporation period.

(*v*) Consideration was discharged by the company on 30th September, 2009 by issuing equity shares of Rs. 10 each.

Prepare the profit and loss account in columnar form showing distinetly the allocation of profits between pre-incorporation and post-incorporation periods, indicating the basis of allocation regarding each item. [*C.S. (Inter.) Dec. 1997 Modified*]

[*C.A. (PCE) May. 2010 Modified*]

Solution:

Profit and Loss Account for the year ended 31st March, 2010

Items	*Basis of apportionment*	*Pre-incorporation period Rs.*	*Post-incorporation period Rs.*
Gross profit	Sales, 1: 3	4,00,000	12,00,000
Less expenses:			
Salaries	Time, 1 : 2	80,000	1,60,000
Printing and stationery	Time, 1 : 2	8,000	16,000
Travelling expenses (sales promotion)	Sales, 1 : 3	6,000	18,000
Travelling expenses (others)	Time, 1 : 2	20,000	40,000
Advertisement	Sales, 1 : 3	20,000	60,000

		Rs.	Rs.
Miscellaneous trade expenses	Time, 1 : 2	63,000	1,26,000
Rent (office building)	Actual	40,000	92,000
Electricity charges	Time, 1 : 2	7,000	14,000
Directors' fees	Post-incorporation	—	56,000
Bad debts	Sales, 1 : 3	4,000	12,000
Commission to selling agents	Sales, 1 : 3	20,000	60,000
Audit fees*	Time, 1 : 2	10,000	20,000
Debenture interest	Post-incorporation	—	15,000
Interest paid to vendors	Time, 2 : 1	14,000	7,000
Selling expenses	Sales, 1 : 3	31,500	94,500
Depreciation on fixed assets acquired in post-incorporation period	Post-incorporation	—	3,000
Depreciation on fixed assets acquired from vendors	Time, 1 : 2	15,000	30,000
Total expenses		3,38,500	8,23,500
Profit (gross profit less expenses)		61,500	3,76,500
		4,00,000	12,00,000

**Note*: Alternatively, audit fee may be charged wholly to the post-incorporation period.

Working Notes:

(*i*) Time ratio = 4 months : 8 months = 1 : 2

(*ii*) *Sales ratio*:

Suppose sales upto the date of the certificate of commencement of business = x.

Then, Sales during the rest of the year = $1\frac{2}{3}x = \frac{5}{3}x$

Hence, $x + \frac{5}{3}x$ = Rs. 96,00,000

Multiplying both the sides by 3, we get

$3x + 5x$ = Rs. 2,88,00,000

$\therefore$ x = Rs. 36,00,000

Sales upto 1st August i.e. for 4 months = Rs. 36,00,000 × $\frac{4}{6}$ = Rs. 24,00,000.

Post-incorporation sales = Rs. 96,00,000 – Rs. 24,00,000 = Rs. 72,00,000.

Ratio of sales between pre-incorporation period and post – incorporation sales = 24 : 72 = 1 : 3

(*iii*) Rent for the first four months = Rs. 10,000 × 4 = Rs. 40,000

Rent for post-incorporation period = Rs. 1,32,000 – Rs. 40,000 = Rs. 92,000.

2. DIVISIBLE PROFITS

Profits available for dividend to shareholders are known as divisible profits. From the strict accountancy points of view, it is essential that dividends should be declared, unless there are compelling reasons otherwise, only if profits remain after meeting all expenses, losses, depreciation on fixed as well as on fluctuating assets, taxation, writing off past losses and after transferring a reasonable amount to reserves. Profits of extraordinary nature, that is, non-recurring profits of profits arising from sale of fixed assets or redemption of fixed liabilities, should not be disturbed as dividend. Prudence demands that assets should not be revalued—at least not for the purpose of declaring a dividend. In respect of dividends, the Articles of the company concerned should be complied with unless these contravene the provisions of law.

Dividends cannot be declared except out of profits. If a company declares and pays a dividend in the absence of profits, the directors will have to make good the amount to the company from their own pockets. However, there is a certain amount of difference attached to the meaning of "divisible profits" under the law and under general accountancy practice. The legal position in India is now clearly stated in section 205 of the Companies Act. It is reproduced below:

"(1) No dividend shall be declared or paid by a company for any financial year except out of the profits of the company for that year arrived at after providing for depreciation in accordance with the provision of sub-section (2) or out of the profits of the company for any previous financial year or years arrived at after providing for depreciation in accordance with those provisions and remaining undistributed or out of both or out of moneys provided by the Central Government or a State Government for the payment of dividend in pursuance of a guarantee given by that Government:

Provided that—

(*a*) if the company has not provided for depreciation for any previous financial year or years which falls or fall after the commencement of the Companies (Amendment) Act, 1960, it shall, before declaring or paying dividend for any financial year provide for such depreciation out of the profits of that financial year or out of the profits of any other previous financial year or years;

(*b*) if the company has incurred any loss in any previous financial year or years, which falls or fall after the commencement of the Companies (Amendment) Act, 1960, then the amount of the loss or an amount which is equal to the amount provided for depreciation for that year or those years whichever is less, shall be set off against profits of the company for the year for which dividend is proposed to be declared or paid or against the profits of the company for any previous financial year or years, arrived at in both cases after providing for depreciation in accordance with the provisions of sub-section (2) or against both;

(*c*) the Central Government may, if it thinks necessary to do so in the public interest, allow any company to declare or pay dividend for any financial year out of the profits of the company for that year or any previous financial year or years without providing for depreciation:

Provided further that it shall not be necessary for a company to provide for depreciation as aforesaid where dividend for any financial year is declared or paid out of the profits of any previous financial year or years which falls or fall before the commencement of the Companies (Amendment) Act, 1960.

(2) For the purpose of sub-section (1), depreciation shall be provided either—

(*a*) to the extent specified in section 350; or

(*b*) in respect of each item of depreciable asset, for such an amount as is arrived at by dividing ninety-five per cent of the original cost thereof to the company by the specified period in respect of such assets; or

(*c*) on any other basis approved by the Central Government which has the effect of writing off by way of depreciation ninety-five per cent of the original cost to the company of each such depreciable asset on the expiry of the specific period; or

(*d*) as regards any other depreciable asset for which no rate of depreciation has been laid down by this Act or any rules made thereunder, on such basis as may be approved by the Central Government by any general order published in the Official Gazette or by any special order in any particular case:

Provided that where depreciation is provided for in the manner laid down in clause (*b*) or clause (*c*), then, in the event of the depreciable asset being sold, discarded, demolished or destroyed the written down value thereof at the end of the financial year in which the asset is sold, discarded, demolished or destroyed, shall be written off in accordance with the proviso to section 350.

(2A) Notwithstanding anything contained in sub-section (1), on and from the commencement of the Companies (Amendment) Act, 1974,* no dividend shall be declared or paid by a company for any financial year out of the profits of the company for that year arrived at after providing for depreciation in accordance with the provisions of sub-sections (2) except after the transfer to the reserves of the company of such percentage of its profits for that year, not exceeding ten per cent. as may be prescribed;

Provided that nothing in this sub-section shall be deemed to prohibit the voluntary transfer by a company of a higher percentage of its profits to the reserves in accordance with such rules as may be made by the Central Government in this behalf.

(2B) A company which fails to comply with the provisions of section 80A shall not, so long as such failure continues, declare any dividend on its equity shares.

(3) No dividend shall be payable except in cash:

Provided that nothing in this sub-section shall be deemed to prohibit the capitalization of profits or reserves of a company for the purpose of issuing fully paid-up bonus shares or paying up any amount, for the time being unpaid, on any shares held by the members of the company.

(4) Nothing in this section shall be deemed to affect in any manner the operation of section 208.

(5) For the purposes of this section—

(*a*) "specified period" in respect of any depreciable asset shall mean the number of years at the end of which at least ninety-five per cent of the original cost of that asset to the company will have been provided for by way of depreciation if depreciation were to be calculated in accordance with the provisions of section 350; and

(*b*) any dividend payable in cash may be paid by cheque or warrant sent through the post directed to the registered address of the shareholder entitled to the payment of the dividend or in the case of joint shareholders to the registered address of that one of the joining shareholders which is first named on the register of members, or to such person and to such address as the shareholder or the joint shareholders may in writing direct."

Transfer to Reserve : The Government compels companies to transfer to reserve a part of their profits (not exceeding 10%). The transfer to reserves is out of after-tax profits.

The Government have promulgated the following rules about transfer to reserves:—

(1) No dividend shall be declared or paid by a company for any financial year out of the profits of the company for that year arrived at after providing for depreciation in accordance with the provisions of sub-section (2) of section 205 of the Act, except after the transfer to the reserves of the company of a percentage of its profits for that year as specified below:—

(*i*) Where the dividend proposed exceeds 10 per cent but not 12.5 per cent of the paid up capital, the amount to be transferred to the reserves shall not be less than 2.5 per cent of the current profits;

(*ii*) Where the dividend proposed exceeds 12.5 per cent but does not exceed 15 per cent of the paid up capital, the amount to be transferred to the reserves shall not be less than 5 per cent of the current profits;

(*iii*) Where the dividend proposed exceeds 15 percent, but does not exceed 20 per cent of the paid up capital, the amount to be transferred to the reserves shall not be less than 7.5 per cent of the current profits; and

(*iv*) Where the dividend proposed exceeds 20 per cent of the paid up capital, the amount to be transferred to reserves shall not be less than 10 per cent of the current profits.

(2) Nothing in (1) above shall be deemed to prohibit the voluntary transfer by a company of a percentage higher than 10 per cent of its profits to its reserves for any financial year, so however, that:—

(*i*) Where a dividend is declared,

(*a*) a minimum distribution sufficient for the maintenance of dividends to shareholders at rate equal to the average of the rates at which dividends declared by it cover the three years immediately preceding the financial year; or

(*b*) in a case where bonus share have been issued in the financial year in which the dividend is declared or in the three years immediately preceding the financial year, a minimum distribution sufficient for the maintenance of dividends to shareholders at an amount equal to the average amount (quantum) of dividend declared over the three years immediately preceding the financial year, is ensured:

Provided that a case where the net profits after tax are lower by 20 per cent or more than the average net profits after tax of the two financial years immediately preceding, it shall not be necessary to ensure such minimum distribution.

(*ii*) Where no dividend is declared, the amount proposed to be transferred to its reserves from the current profits shall be lower than the average amount of the dividends to the shareholders declared by it over the three years immediately preceding the financial year.

Declaration of dividend out of reserve. The Government have promulgated the following rules regarding utilisation of reserves for payment of dividend.

In the event of inadequacy or absence of profits in any year, dividend may be declared by a company for that year out of the accumulated profits earned by it in previous years and transferred by it to the reserves, subject to the conditions that:—

(*i*) The rate of the dividend declared shall not exceed the average of the rates at which dividend was declared by it in the five years immediately preceding that year or ten per cent of its paid-up capital, whichever is less:

(*ii*) the total amount to be drawn from the accumulated profits earned in previous years and transferred to the reserves shall not exceed an amount equal to one-tenth of the sum of its paid up capital and free reserves and the amount so drawn shall first be utilised to set off the losses incurred in the financial year before any dividend in respect of preference or equity shares is declared; and

(*iii*) the balance of reserves after such drawal shall not fall below fifteen per cent of its paid up share capital.

Explanation. For the purpose of this rule, "profits earned by a company in previous years and transferred by it to the reserves" shall mean the total amount of net profits after tax, transferred to reserves as at the beginning of the year for which the dividend is to be declared; and in computing the said amount, all items of capital reserves including reserves created by revaluation of assets shall be excluded.

Illustration 14:

(*a*) Zed Ltd. closes its accounts on 31st March each year. Its paid up share capital consists of

(*i*) 50 lakh 11% Preference Shares of Rs. 10 each fully paid, Rs. 5 crore and

(*ii*) 2 crore Equity Shares of Rs. 10 each, fully paid, Rs. 20 crore.

The profit earned after tax and dividends paid by the company have been the following:—

	Profit *Rs. in lakhs*	*Total Dividend paid* *Rs. in lakhs*
2004-2005	520	255
2005-2006	480	255
2006-2007	530	295
2007-2008	560	315
2008-2009	600	335

During 2009-2010 the company earned a profit of Rs. 522 lakh. The company desires to transfer Rs. 250 lakh to Reserves because of a contemplated project. Comment on the proposal. Will your answer differ if the profit earned during 2009-2010 was only Rs. 450 lakh?

(*b*) Wye Ltd. has only one type of capital viz. 4 crore equity shares of Rs. 10 each. It also has got reserves totalling Rs. 20 crore. The company closes its books each year on 31st March. It has been paying dividends at the rate of 12½% upto 2006-07 and 15% thereafter. In 2009-2010 the company suffered a loss of Rs. 250 lakh therefore, it wishes to draw from reserves an amount to pay dividend at 12%. Advise the company.

Answer:

Under the Transfer to Reserve Rules, issued under the Companies Act, a company must have a minimum distribution to ensure dividend at a rate equal to the average for the three immediately preceding years (except where the profit earned is 20% less than the average for the two preceding years). Zed. Ltd has paid dividend for three years as shown below:—

	Total dividend	*Pref. dividend*	*Equity dividend*	*Rate of equity dividend*
	Rs. in lakhs	*Rs. in lakhs*	*Rs. in lakhs*	
2006-2007	295	55	240	12%
2007-2008	315	55	260	13%
2008-2009	335	55	280	14%

The average of equity dividend for the three years is 13%. The minimum distribution required, therefore, is Rs. 315 lakh i.e.

	Rs.
11% on Rs. 5 crore Preference Capital	55
13% on Rs. 20 crore Equity Capital	260
	315

The average of the profit for 2007-08 and 2008-09 comes to Rs. 580 lakh, profit for 2009-2010 Rs. 522 lakh, is less than the average by only 10%.

If the company transfers Rs. 250 lakh to reserves, it will be violating the Transfer to Reserves Rules. The company must pay Rs. 315 lakh as dividend and transfer only Rs. 207 lakh to Reserves.

If the profit earned is Rs. 450 lakh, the company need not ensure the minimum distribution as computed above since the profit is below the average profit for two years by more than 20%.

(*b*) The Rules governing utilisation of reserves for payment of dividend restrict the withdrawals to the lower of:

(*i*) an amount sufficient to ensure dividend at the average rate for the previous five years or 10% whichever is less; and

(*ii*) 1/10 of paid up capital and free reserves, subject to the remaining balance in reserves being at least 15% of the paid up capital.

The average dividend for five years is 13.5%, *i.e.*, (12½% × 3 + 15% × 2). Therefore, in the first instance only 10% dividend will be allowed. This will absorb Rs. 650 lakh, *i.e.*,

	Rs. in lakhs
Loss	250
Dividend @ 10%	400
	650

But, more than 1/10 of the paid-up capital and free reserves cannot be withdrawn from reserves. The paid-up capital being Rs. 40 crore and the reserves being Rs. 20 crore, the amount that can be drawn is Rs. 6 crore — the balance then left will be more than 15% of the paid-up capital. The withdrawal from reserves must first be used to set off the loss which is Rs. 2.5 crore. The balance of Rs. 3.5 crore may be paid as dividend. The rate will then be 8¼%. The company must be satisfied with paying this dividend.

Depreciation. Section 205 has now brought legal and accountancy positions quite close. Previously, it was possible to declare dividends without writing off depreciation on fixed assets (*Verner vs. General Commercial Trust*) and without providing for previous losses (*Ammonia Soda Co. vs. Chamberlain*) provided the Articles did not prohibit such a distribution.

Arrears of depreciation or accumulated losses in respect of financial years falling *before* the commencement of the Companies (Amendment) Act of 1960, *need not* be provided still. But for financial years falling after the commencement of the Companies (Amendment) Act of 1960, dividends cannot be declared unless—

(*a*) depreciation has been written off the fixed assets in respect of the financial year for which dividend is to be declared according to section 205 (2);

(*b*) arrears of depreciation on fixed assets in respect of any previous year [falling after the commencement of the Companies (Amendment) Act, 1960] have been deducted from the profits; and

(*c*) losses incurred by the company in the previous years falling after the commencement of the Companies (Amendment) Act of 1960 or the amounts of depreciation provided whichever are less have been deducted.

Distinction has to be made between depreciation provided for (that is recorded in books) and not provided for. In respect of financial years falling after 28th December, 1960 (the date of commencements of the Companies Amendment Act, 1960), depreciation not provided for (arrears) must first be deducted before paying dividend out of the profits of the year for which dividend is to be paid or out of profits of any of the previous years. But in case of depreciation provided for in a year in which there is a loss, it is sufficient if the amount of depreciation or the amount of the total loss is deducted out of subsequent profits before payment of dividend. Further, dividends may be declared out of past profits without providing for subsequent depreciation or losses.

However, the Central Government may, if it thinks necessary so to do in the public interest, allow any company to declare or pay dividend for any financial year out of the profits of the company for that year or any previous financial year or years without providing for depreciation.

For the sake of clarity, let us take an example. Suppose, the proper amount of depreciation to be written off for the year ended 31st March, 2009 comes out to be Rs. 95 lakh out of which the company provides for only Rs. 60 lakh, leaving depreciation amounting to Rs. 35 lakh unprovided for and the Profit and Loss Account shows a loss of Rs. 80 lakh. Further assume that for the year ended 31st March, 2010, the Profit and Loss Account of the company shows a profit of Rs. 1 crore 50 lakh after providing in full for the depreciation for the 2009-2010. Now, if the company wants to declare a dividend out of the profits for the year 2009-2010, the company must deduct from the profits for the year the following:—

(*i*) Rs. 35 lakh, the amount of depreciation not provided for in the year 2008-2009; and

(*ii*) either Rs. 80 lakh, the amount of loss for the year 2008-2009; or Rs. 60 lakh, the amount of depreciation actually provided for in the final accounts of the company for the year 2008-2009. Prudence demands that the loss of Rs. 80 lakhs be deducted leaving the profit for 2009-2010 at Rs. 35 lakh only. However, the law permits, in the abovementioned case, a deduction of Rs. 60 lakh only leaving the figure of profit for 2009-2010 at Rs. 55 lakh. If the later course is adopted, the remaining amount of loss, Rs. 20 lakh, should better be provided for as a matter of prudence, out of the profits for the year 2010-2011 or later years before a dividend for the year concerned is declared.

Section 205(2) lays down how depreciation is to be calculated. According to it, depreciation should be provided either:

(*a*) To the extent specified in section 350, i.e. the amount of depreciation on assets as shown by the books of the company at the end of the financial year expiring at the commencement of this Act or immediately thereafter and at the end of each subsequent financial year at the rate specified in Schedule XIV; or

(*b*) in respect of each item of depreciable assets for such an amount as is arrived at by dividing 95 per cent of the original cost thereof to the company be by specified period in respect of such assets; or

(*c*) on any other basis approved by the Central Government which has the effect of writing off by way of depreciation 95 per cent of the original cost to the company of each such depreciable assets on the expiry of the specified period; or

(*d*) as regards any other depreciable asset for which no rate of depreciation has been laid down by this Act or any rules made thereunder, on such basis as may be approved by the Central Government by any general order published in the Official Gazette or any special order in any particular case.

According to Section 350, if any asset is sold, discarded, demolished or destroyed for any reason before depreciation of such asset has been provided for in full, the excess, if any, of the written-down value of such asset over its sale proceeds or, as the case may be, its scrap value, shall be written off in the financial year in which the asset is sold, discarded, demolished or destroyed.

The amount of depreciation charged on the fixed assets every year is debited to the Profit and Loss Account and credited to the Provision for Depreciation Account which is allowed to accumulate from year to year. The amount of depreciation may be debited to Depreciation Account and credited to Provision for Depreciation Account. Depreciation Account is transferred to the Profit and Loss Account. In the Balance Sheet, the balance of Provision for Depreciation Account is shown by way of a deduction from the cost of the Fixed Asset.

If any asset is purchased during an accounting period, depreciation may be provided for the full year giving a note to this effect but according to sound principles of Accountancy, depreciation should be provided only for that part of the year for which the asset has been in use. If there is any change in an accounting year in the method of providing for depreciation, the fact must be disclosed along with the quantum of effect on the profit/loss of the company. If depreciation is provided for any previous year or years, it is to be treated as an appropriation of profits and not a charge against profits.

Part II of Schedule VI of the Companies Act requires that the Profit and Loss Account must disclose the amount provided for depreciation, renewals or diminution in value of fixed assets. If such provision is not made by means of a depreciation charge, the method adopted for making such provision shall be stated. If no provision is made for depreciation, the fact that no provision has been made shall be stated and the quantum of arrears of depreciation computed in accordance with section 205(2) of the Act shall be disclosed by way of a note.

The law does not make it compulsory for a company to provide for depreciation on fixed assets. All that it requires is that dividens must not be declared without providing for depreciation.

Payment of Dividend. Any dividend payable in cash may be made by cheque or warrant sent through the post directed to the registered address of the shareholder entitled to the payment of dividend.

Unpaid Dividend Account. Section 205A provides that where, after the commencement of the Companies (Amendment) Act, 1974, a dividend has been declared by a company but has not been paid or claimed, within thirty days from the date of the declaration to any shareholder entitled to the payment of the dividend, the company shall within seven days from the date of expiry of the said period of thirty days, transfer the total amount of such dividend to a special account called "Unpaid Dividend Account of ...... Company Limited" in a scheduled bank. In case of default, interest on the amount not transferred to the said account at the rate of twelve per cent per annum from the date of default will have to be paid by the company. After the transfer has been made, naturally the dividend concerned will be paid out of Unpaid Dividend Account. If any money transferred to this account remains unpaid or unclaimed for a period fo seven years from the date of the transfer, it will be transferred by the company to the Investor Education and Protection Fund established under sub-section (1) of section 205C. Such unpaid dividend cannot be later claimed by the shareholder concerned on or after the commencement of the Companies (Amendment) Act, 1999.

Goodwill previously written off may be written back, if the Articles permit, upto its reasonable value; the amount may be credited to the Profit and Loss Account unless it appears that the item has been irrevocably written off (*Stapley vs. Read Bros.*). Presumably, there being no legal decision on the point, fixed assets, previously written off, may also be written up to their reasonable value.

Preliminary expenses need not be written off (*Bale vs. Cleland*). But the same may also be charged to the Profit and Loss Account.

Capital profits, as opposed to current or revenue profits, arise in special circumstances and are connected with acquisition of business, fixed assets and long-term liabilities.

Capital profits can be used to write off fictitious assets like discount on issue of shares or debentures, underwriting commission, etc. Only in certain circumstances can they be used for declaring a dividend.

Capital profits can be distributed only if (1) they are realised in cash; (2) surplus remains after a revaluation of all assets, and (3) the Articles do not forbid such distribution. (*Foster vs. New Trinidad Lake Asphalte Co. and Lubbock vs. British Bank of South America.*) Capital profits available for dividends should not be included in Capital Reserve since by definition Capital Reserve means a reserve which cannot be used for paying a dividend.

The following are the examples of capital profits:

(*a*) Profit prior to incorporation.

(*b*) Premium on issue of shares. The amount is credited to Securities Premium Account and can be applied by the company only for those purposes which are laid down in Section 78 of the Companies Act.

(*c*) Profit remaining on reissue of forfeited shares. The amount is transferred to Capital Reserve and is not available for dividend.

(*d*) The credit to the Capital Redemption Reserve Account for redemption of redeemable preference shares. The amount is available only for issue of fully-paid bonus shares.

(*e*) Premium on issue of debentures. Not available for distribution of dividend.

(*f*) Profit on redemption of debentures. Not available for distribution of dividend.

(*g*) Profit on sale of fixed assets to the extent the sale proceeds exceeds the original cost of the fixed assets sold.

(*h*) Profit on acquisition of business - that is, excess of the value of tangible assets acquired over the liabilities taken over and the consideration.

Profit from subsidiary companies. Profit of subsidiary companies must not be included in divisible profits unless the subsidiary company has declared a dividend (and only the dividend may be treated as divisible profit). Losses of subsidiary companies need not be debited to the Profit and Loss Account of the holding company but it would be better if a provision is created to meet the holding company's share of the loss of the subsidiary company.

Dividends received out of profits existing on the date of acquisition of the controlling shares in the subsidiary company must be treated as a capital receipt.

Dividends:

It is the general meeting of shareholders that declares a dividend but the rate of dividend cannot exceed the one recommended by the board of directors. However, an interim dividend (that is, dividend pending finalisation of accounts) may be declared by the Board of Directors, if the Articles authorise them to do so. In the absence of any indication to the contrary (which indication will be found in the articles), the rate applies to the paid up capital. Thus, if a company has issued 50 lakh shares of Rs. 10 each on whcih Rs. 7.50 per share has been paid up and if the dividend declared is at the rate of 10%, total dividend payable will be 10% of Rs. 375 lakh (the paid up capital) or

Rs. 37,50,000. There is nothing to prevent a company from declaring dividend on the full nominal value of the share even if the paid up amount is less. Calls in advance cannot be treated as part of paid up capital for declaration of dividends. Dividends on shares upon which there are calls in arrear should be calculated on the amount actually paid. However, a company has the power to forbid, by suitable provisions in the Articles, the payment of dividend on shares on which there are calls in arrear. Further (according to Table A), unless otherwise provided in the terms of issue, the period also has to be taken into consideration. Suppose 1 crore equity shares of Rs. 10 each were Rs. 8 paid up on 1st April, 2009 and the call of Rs. 2 was made and paid on 1st October, 2009, a dividend of 10% for 2009-2010 will mean Rs. 90 lakh as shown below:

10% on Rs. 8 crore for full year	Rs. 80 lakh; and
10% on Rs. 2 crore for 6 months	Rs. 10 lakh

Table A also permits the Board of Directors to apply the dividend payable to a shareholder towards any amount due from him on account of calls or otherwise in relation to the shares of the company.

Under Section 206, a dividend can be paid only to the registered holder of shares or to his order or to his bankers. However, in case a share warrant has been issued in respect of fully paid up shares under section 114, the dividend may be paid to the bearer of the share current or to his bankers. Under section 114, a public company, if authorised by its articles, may with the previous approval of the Central Government issue in respect of fully paid shares, share warrants for payment of dividend on those fully paid shares.

The dividend or the warrant for it must be posted to the registered address of the shareholder within 30 days of the declaration of the dividend except in certain circumstances (Section 207). Every director of the company shall, if he is knowingly a party to the default, be punishable with simple imprisonment for a term which may extend to 3 years and shall also be liable to a fine of Rs. 1,000 for every day during which such default continues and the company shall be liable to pay simple interest @ 18% per annum during the period for which such default continues.

Interim dividend. Directors usually have the power (Table A contains such a power) to pay dividend for the current year before the year is closed. Such a dividend is known as interim dividend. Since the profits of the company cannot be known exactly till the accounts are closed, the directors have to be extremely careful. If an interim dividend is paid and it is found subsequently that the company's profits are inadequate to cover the dividend, it will amount to payment of dividend out of capital which is forbidden by law. The directors will then have to make good the amount.

Usually, therefore, the directors get the accounts prepared upto a certain date and then declare a dividend on a very conservative basis. The interim dividend is usually paid for a period of six months. Thus, if a company pays interim dividend of twenty per cent per annum on a capital of Rs. 5 crore, the total amount will be Rs. 50 lakh. But if the resolutiond declaring the dividend were to simply state the rate to be 20%, the total dividend would be Rs. 1 crore, i.e., 20% of Rs. 5 crore. The directors may recommend another dividend when the final figures for the profit are available. Such dividend will then be termed as Final Dividend.

When final dividend is declared, interim dividend is not adjusted unless the resolution specified otherwise. A company pays interim dividend at the rate of 10% on Rs. 10 crore, i.e., Rs. 1 crore. At the end of the year, it declares a final dividend of 25%; the amount comes to Rs. 2.5 crore, i.e., 25% on Rs. 10 crore. Total dividend during the year will be Rs. 3.5 crore.

Section 205(1A) provides that the Board of directors may declare interim dividend and the amount of dividend including interim dividend shall be deposited in a separate bank account.

Income-tax meaning of dividends. From the income-tax point of view any release of assets in favour of the shareholders to the extent the company has profit, will be treated as dividend. The most usual case is release of cash. But even if cash is paid, not as dividend but as return of capital, income-tax authorities will treat it as dividend to the extent it is covered by the accumulated profits. Consider the following balance sheet of a company.

	Rs. (in crores)		Rs. (in crores)
Share Capital		Sundry Assets	8
1 crore shares of Rs. 10 each fully paid	10	Cash at Bank	6
General Reserve	4		
	14		14

Suppose, the company decides to retun Rs. 3 to the shareholders as return of capital and obtains court sanction for it. The company will pay Rs. 3 crore to the shareholders. It will be treated as dividend. It makes no difference if instead of cash, other assets had been distributed. But distribution of bonus shares will not be treated as dividend because it involves no release of assets. Bonus debentures will, however, be treated as dividend.

Corporate Dividend Tax. The Finance Act, 1997 introduced additional income tax, called tax on distributed profits, on joint stock companies on the anounts of their profits distributed by them among the shareholders as dividends. This tax is popularly known as corporate dividend tax or simply dividend tax. Section 115-0(1) of the Income tax Act lays down that any amount declared, distributed or paid by a domestic company by way of dividends, whether interim or otherwise shall be subject to tax on distributed profits. Further, section 115-0(3) lays down that the tax has to be paid within 14 days from the date of (*i*) declaration of dividend, (*ii*) distribution of dividend or (*iii*) payment of dividend, whichever is earliest. Like rates of income tax, the rate of corporate dividend tax may vary from one financial year to the other financial year. The present rate is 15 per cent. The Finance Act fixes the rate; hence it is subject to change.

As corporate dividend tax is levied on the profits distributed, it should be shown below the line *i.e.* in Profit and Loss Appropriation Account. In the case of interim dividend, the tax will normally be paid in the same accounting year in which the dividend is declared and paid. In the case of proposed dividend, a provision for corporate dividend tax on the amount proposed to be distributed should be made and shown along with the Proposed Dividend in the Profit and Loss Appropriation Account. In the balance sheet, it should be shown along with Provision for Income Tax.

Corporate Dividend Tax was withdrawn by the Finance Act, 2002. It has been reintroduced by the Finance Act, 2003.

Dividends from the domestic companies in the hand of shareholders are now exempt from income tax and hence the question of deduction of income tax at source from dividends by the companies no longer arises.

Appropriation of Profits:

This applies only to divisible profits, that is, to profits remaining after all charges against the current income have been taken into account. Once a surplus that can be shared by various parties is established, the question of its disposal arises. The directors may decided to retain a certain amount to strengthen the company's finances and the shareholders will appreciate a share in the form of dividends. The amount retained may take the form of transfer to various reserves or just a balance left. The account showing the disposal of the profits is known as the Profit and Loss Appropriation Account. The amount brought forward from the previous year is put on the credit side together with current year's profits and any transfer from reserves. On the debit side, the following items are usually found:

(*i*) Transfer to General Reserve;

(*ii*) Transfer to Dividend Equalisation Reserve: Dividend Equalisation Fund means a fund accumulated out of profits otherwise available for dividends with the purpose of making the rate of dividend uniform from year to year. If dividends fluctuate, speculators are encouraged. When good profits are made, a part of them is put to the Dividend Equalisation Reserve which can be drawn upon to pay dividends when profits are small.

(*iii*) Transfer to Sinking Fund for Redemption of Debentures;

(*iv*) Dividends (paid and proposed); and

(*v*) Corporate Dividend Tax paid; and provision for the same on proposed dividend.

(*vi*) Balance.

Illustration 14:

On 1st April, 2009 the subscribed share capital of Surya Ltd. stood at Rs. 12.5 crore divided into 1 crore fully paid equity shares of Rs. 10 each and 2.5 lakh fully paid 12% preference shares of Rs. 100 each. On the same date, Profit and Loss Appropriation Account showed an opening balance of Rs. 1 crore 42 lakh.

During the year ended 31st March, 2010 the company paid an interim dividend @ 10% on its equity shares, paying preference dividend for the entire year 2009-2010. On 31st March, 2010 the company's Profit and Loss Account showed that the company had earned for the year Rs. 3 crore 70 lakh as profit after tax. The Board of Directors decided to transfer Rs. 60 lakh to Debenture Redemption Reserve and 10% of the net profit for the year to General Reserve. The Board also proposed a final dividend @ 11% on equity shares over and above the interim dividend already distributed. The company is required to pay corporate dividend tax @ 15%.

Prepare Profit and Loss Appropriation Account for the year needed 31st March, 2010.

Solution:

Profit and Loss Appropriation Account for the year ended 31st March, 2010

	(Rs. '000)		*(Rs. '000)*
To Interim Preference Dividend—		By Balance b/fd	14,200
@ 12% on Rs. 2.5 crore	3,000	By Net Profit for the year	37,000
To Interim Equity Dividend—			
@ 10% on Rs. 10 crore	10,000		
To Corporate Dividend Tax Paid—			
@ 15% on Rs. 1.3 crore	1,950		
To Debenture Redemption Reserve	6,000		
To General Reserve—			
10% of Rs. 3 crore 70 lakh	3,700		
To Proposed Final Equity Dividend—			
@ 11% on Rs. 10 crore	11,000		
To Provision for Corporate Dividend Tax—			
@ 15% on Rs. 1.1 crore	1,650		
To Balance carried to balance sheet	13,900		
	51,200		51,200

Illustration 15:

For the year ended 31st March, 2010 the profits of W Ltd. before charging depreciation on fixed assets and managing directors' commission amounted to Rs. 20 crore. Depreciation amounted to Rs. 8 crore and commission was payable to the managing director at 5% of the profits. The paid up capital of the company consisted of 30 lakh 10% preference shares of Rs. 100 each and 4 crore equity shares of Rs. 10 each. Interim dividends on preference and equity shares were paid during the year at Rs. 5 and Rs. 0.50 per share respectively. There was a credit balance of Rs. 4,90,00,000 brought forward from the previous year. The following appropriations were passed at the Annual General Meeting of the company:

(*a*) To pay the balance of the year's dividend on preference shares.

(*b*) To pay a final dividend on equity shares at Rs. 0.75 per share and corporate dividend tax @ 15%.

(*c*) To provide for taxation @ 35%.

(*d*) To transfer Rs. 50 lakh to General Reserve.

(*e*) To carry forward the balance.

Write up the Profit and Loss Appropriation Account.

Solution:

Dr.	**Profit and Loss Account**		*Cr.*
	(Rs. '000)		*(Rs. '000)*
To Depreciation	80,000	By Profit for the year	2,00,000
To Managing Director's Commission, 5% of Rs. 12 crore	6,000		
To Provision for Taxation @35%	39,900		
To Net Profit c/d	74,100		
	2,00,000		2,00,000
To Interim Preference Dividend	15,000	By Balance b/fd	49,000
To Interim Dividend on Equity Shares, Re. 0.50 on 4 crore shares	20,000	By Net Profit for the year b/d	74,100
To Corporate Dividend Tax @ 15%	5,250		
To General Reserve — transfer	5,000		
To Final Preference Dividend	15,000		
To Final dividend on Equity Shares, Re 0.75 on 4 crore shares	30,000		
To Provision for Corporate Dividend Tax	6,750		
To Balance c/d	26,100		
	1,23,100		1,23,000
		By Balance b/d	29,300

Illustration 15:

The Balance Sheet of Zee Ltd. as at 31-3-2010 is given below:

	Rs. in lakhs		*Rs. in lakhs*
Issued and Paid-up Share Capital :		Freehold Property	200
20 lakh Equity Shares of Rs. 10 each	200	Stock-in-trade	120
Profit and Loss Account	181	Sundry Debtors	100
12% Debenture	120	Cash and Bank balances	181
Sundry Creditors	100		
	601		601

It was resolved at the Annual General Meeting:—

(*i*) to pay a dividend of 10% and corporate dividend tax @ 15%.

(*ii*) to issue one bonus share for every four shares held.

(*iii*) to give existing shareholders the option to buy one Rs. 10 share @ Rs. 14 for every four shares held prior to bonus distribution.

(*iv*) to repay the debentures at a premium of 4%.

All the shareholders took up the option in (iii) above. Pass journal entries and draw up the Balance Sheet after the above transactions have been given effect to. (Ignore tax on income).

[*Adapted C.W.A. (Inter) Dec. 1985*]

Solution:

Journal

			Dr. Rs. in lakhs	Cr. Rs. in lakhs
(i)	Profit and Loss Appropriation Account	Dr.	23	
	To Dividend Payable Account			20
	To Corporate Dividend Tax Payable			3
	10% dividend on 20 lakh equity shares of Rs. 10 each @ 10% and corporate dividend tax payable thereon @15%.			
	Dividend Payable Account	Dr.	20	
	Corporate Dividend Tax	Dr.	3	
	To Bank			23
	Payment of dividend and corporate dividend tax thereon.			
(ii)	Profit and Loss Appropriation Account	Dr.	50	
	To Bonus to Equity Shareholders Account			50
	Bonus payable to equity shareholders.			
	Bonus to Equity Shareholders Account	Dr.	50	
	To Equity Share Capital Account			50
	Allotment of 5 lakh equity shares of Rs. 10 each as bonus shares to equity shareholders.			
(iii)	Bank	Dr.	70	
	To Equity Share Capital Account			50
	To Securities Premium Account			20
	Allotment of 5 lakh equity shares of Rs. 10 each at a premium of Rs. 4 per share on rights basis.			
(iv)	Securities Premium Account	Dr.	4.8	
	To Premium on Redemption of Debentures Account			4.8
	Premium on redemption of debentures charged to Securities Premium Account.			
	12% Debentures Account	Dr.	120	
	Premium on Redemption of Debentures Account	Dr.	4.8	
	To Debentureholders Account			124.8
	Amount payable on redemption of debentures alongwith premium.			
	Debentureholders Account	Dr.	124.8	
	To Bank			124.8
	Amount due to debentureholders paid off.			

Balance Sheet of Zee Ltd. as at 31-3-2010

Liabilities	*Rs. in lakhs*	*Assets*	*Rs. in lakhs*
Share Capital :		**Fixed Assets**	
Issued and Subscribed :		Freehold Poperty	200
30 lakh equity shares of Rs. 10 each,		**Current Assets, Loans and Advances**	
fully paid -up	300	(A) Current Assets	
(Of the above shares, 5 lakh		Stock-in-trade	120
shares have been allotted		Sundry Debtors	100
as fully paid up by way of bonus		Cash and Bank Balances	103.2
shares out of P. and L. A/c)		(B) Loans and Advances	nil

	Rs. in lakhs		Rs. in lakhs
Reserves & Surplus			
Securities Premium	15.2		
Profit and Loss A/c	108		
Current Liabilities			
(A) Current Liabilities			
Sundry Creditors	100		
(B) Provisions	nil		
	523.2		523.2

Illustration 16:

The articles of association of Diana Ltd. provide for the following :–

(1) That 10 per cent of the profits of each year shall be transferred to Reserve Fund;

(2) That an amount equal to 10 per cent of equity dividend shall be set aside for bonus to staff;

(3) That the balance available for distribution shall be applied;

(*a*) in paying 7 per cent on cumulative preference shares;

(*b*) in paying 10 per cent on equity shares;

(*c*) one-third of the balance available as additional dividend on preference shares and 2/3rds as additional equity dividend.

A further condition was also imposed by the Articles, viz., that the balance carried forward shall not be reduced by the provisions under (2), (3b) or (3c) below a sum equal to 6% of the preference share capital.

The company has issued 26,000 7% cumulative participating preference shares of Rs. 100 each fully paid up, and 2,60,000 equity shares of Rs. 10 each fully paid. The profit for the year 2009-2010 was Rs. 14,42,989 and the balance brought forward from the previous year was Rs. 1,57,170. Provide Rs. 6,27,300 for taxation before making other appropriations.

Prepare the Profit and Loss Appropriation Account. Ignore corporate dividend tax.

(*Adapted from C.A. Final*)

Solution:

Dr. **Profit and Loss Appropriation Account** *Cr.*

		Rs.		Rs.
To Provision for Taxation		6,27,300	By Balance b/d	1,57,170
To Transfer to Reserve Fund :			By Profits for the year	14,42,989
10% of profit at this stage		81,569		
To Provision for Staff Bonus :				
10% of Equity Dividend	Rs. 26,000			
10% of additional Equity Dividend	Rs. 16,500	42,500		
To Preference Shares Dividend :				
7% of Rs. 26,00,000		1,82,000		
Additional Dividend		82,500		
To Equity Dividend :				
10% of Rs. 26,00,000		2,60,000		
Additional Dividend		1,65,000		
To Balance c/fd		1,59,290		
		16,00,159		16,00,159

Notes:

(1) Without considering the additional dividends and the bonus payable to the staff on additional equity dividend, the balance left in the Profit and Loss Appropriation Account is Rs. 4,23,290. Out of this, a minimum sum of Rs. 1,56,000, i.e., 6% on Rs. 26,00,000 is to be carried forward. This amount has been increased to Rs. 1,59,290 to make the balance left a round figure.

(2) After carrying forward a balance of Rs. 1,59,290, a sum of Rs. 2,64,000 is left to be shared among the preference shareholders, equity shareholders and the staff (who will get 10% of whatever dividend is paid to the equity shareholders). According to the articles, preference shareholders get half of what equity shareholders get by way of additional dividend. Thus, if equity share holders get x, preference shareholders get 1/2x and the staff gets 1/10x. Therefore:

$$x+\frac{1}{2}x+\frac{1}{10}x = 2{,}64{,}000$$

$$10x + 5x + x = 26{,}40{,}000;$$

$16x = 26{,}40{,}000$; hence $x = 1{,}65{,}000$

Therefore: Equity Dividend (additional) is Rs. 1,65,000;
Preference dividend (additional) is Rs. 82,500; and
Additional Staff Bonus is Rs. 16,500.

Separate bank account for dividends. According to section 205(1A), within five days from the date of declaration of dividend, a company has to open a separate bank account for the payment of dividends. From the general bank account, the amount of dividends to be paid is transferred to a separate account called Dividend Bank Account. All dividend warrants will then be paid out of Dividend Bank Account. The balance of Dividend Bank Account will be equal to the dividends which have not yet been claimed.

Interest out of Capital:

As has been pointed out earlier, dividends cannot be paid except out of profits or in other words, dividends cannot be paid out of capital. In certain cases, however, the Central Government has the power to permit payment of interest to shareholders even when there is no profit. A company which has to wait rather a long period before it can commence production (because construction of works may take long) may find the shareholders restive if nothing is given to them by way of yield. Moreover, if construction is carried on with borrowed funds, interest will have to be paid; hence there is some theoretical justification for payment of interest to the shareholders. Section 208 governs payment of interest in such cases. The company is allowed to pay interest on such shares as are issued for the purpose of defraying the expenses of the construction of any works or building or of providing any plant which cannot be made profitable for a lengthy period, subject to the following conditions :—

(a) The payment is authorised by Articles or by a special resolution.

(*b*) Prior sanction of the Central Government is obtained.

(*c*) The payment of interest is made only for such period as may be determined by the Central Government.

But the period cannot extend beyond the close of the half year next after the half year in which the works, buildings, etc., have been actually completed. For example, if the construction is over on 10th January, 2009 interest cannot be paid after 30th September, 2009.

(*d*) The rate of interest does not exceed four per cent per annum or such other rate as the Central Government may, by notification in the Official Gazette, direct.

The Central Government can order an enquiry at the company's cost before according its sanction. The company can treat the interest so paid as part of the cost of construction.

Bonus Shares:

Sometimes the company may not be in a position to pay cash dividends in spite of adequate profits because of the adverse effect on the working capital of the company. Moreover, all prudent companies build up reserves for purposes of expansion and for building up financial strength. Later, however, to satisfy shareholders and to portray a realistic relationship between capital and profits earned, the company may issue shares, without payment being required, to the existing equity shareholders. Such shares are known as bonus shares. Bonus shares can be issued only if such an issue is permitted by the Articles of Association.

Guidelines for Issue of Bonus Shares

In keeping with the pace of liberalisation and reforms in the primary market, the Securities and Exchange Board of India (Primary Market Department) vide its press release dated 15.4.1994 modified the guidelines for bonus shares. The modified guidelines are as follows:-

(*i*) These guidelines are applicable to existing listed companies who shall forward a certificate duly signed by the issuer and duly countersigned by its statutory auditor or by a company secretary in practice to the effect that the terms and conditions for issue of bonus shares as laid down in these guidelines have been complied with.

(*ii*) Issue of bonus shares after any public/rights issue is subject to the condition that no bonus issue shall be made which will dilute the value or rights of the holders of debentures, convertible fully or partly.

In other words, no company shall, pending conversion of FCDs/PCDs, issue any shares by way of bonus unless similar benefit is extended to the holders of such FCDs/PCDs, through reservation of shares in proportion to such convertible part of FCDs or PCDs. The shares so reserved may be issued at the time of conversion(s) of such debentures on the same terms on which the bonus issues were made.

(*iii*) The bonus issue is made out of free reserves built out of the genuine profits or securities premium collected in cash only.

(*iv*) Reserves created by revaluation of fixed assets are not capitalised.

(*v*) The declaration of bonus issue, in lieu of dividend, is not made.

(*vi*) The bonus issue is not made unless the partly-paid shares, if any existing, are made fully paid-up.

(*vii*) The company —

1. has not defaulted in payment of interest or principal in respect of fixed deposits and interest on existing debentures or principal on redemption thereof, and
2. has sufficient reason to believe that it has not defaulted in respect of the payment of statutory dues of the employees such as contribution to provident fund, gratuity, bonus etc.

(*viii*) A company which announces a bonus issue after the approval of the Board of Directors must implement the proposal within a period of six months from the date of such approval and shall not have the option of changing the decision.

(*ix*) There should be a provision in the Articles of Association of the company for capitalisation of reserves, etc. and if not, the company shall pass a Resolution at its General Body Meeting making provision in the Articles of association for capitalisation of reserves etc.

(*x*) Consequent to the issue of bonus shares, if the subscribed and paid-up capital exceed the authorised share capital, a Resolution shall be passed by the company at its General Body Meeting for increasing the authorised capital.

The application has to be supported by a certificate from the auditor of the company in regard to the facts stated and the fact that the guidelines have been complied with. It has to be affirmed by the Principal Officer of the company.

Bonus shares are generally issued in the following circumstances:—

(*a*) When the company's cash resources are inadequate for a cash dividend.

(*b*) When the company wants to build up cash resources for expansion or other purposes like repayment of liability. Many of the present large companies have achieved their position by refusing to distribute all their profits as cash dividends. The accumulated profits are later converted into shares.

(*c*) When the company, having built up large reserve, wishes to show to the outsiders (and also the shareholders) the correct earning capacity. Suppose, a company has the following summarised balance sheet :

	Rs.		*Rs.*
Share Capital	50,00,000	Net Assets	1,50,00,000
General Reserve	1,00,00,000		
	1,50,00,000		1,50,00,000

Suppose further, that the company earns during a year Rs. 20,00,000. A superficial view will show that the company earns 40 per cent on its capital. This may give rise to accusations against the company of profiteering. Labour may also feel restive and may demand a much greater share in the company's revenues. The correct position is that the company earns Rs. 20 lakh on Rs. 150 lakh. The yield, therefore, works out to be 13.33% which appears to be much more reasonable than forty per cent. To present a correct picture, the company may decide to convert the reserves into shares and distribute the shares among the shareholders.

Bonus shares can be issued out of the following :—

(1) Balance in the Profit and Loss Account;

(2) General Reserves or other reserves accumulated out of profits;

(3) Balance in the Sinking Fund for Redemption of Debentures after the debentures have been redeemed;

(4) Realised capital profits and reserves;

(5) Capital Redemption Reserve Account (created out of profits for the redemption of redeemable preference shares);*

(6) Premium received on issue of shares.*

Bonus Shares can be issued in the form of fully paid shares at par, or at a premium. But the bonus can also be distributed, at least theoretically, by way of making partly paid shares fully paid, that is to say, the bonus can be applied towards the call that may be due on the shares. This last form of bonus means that the liability of the shareholders on partly paid shares is extinguished. But SEBI guidelines do not permit it.

From the point of view of the company, allotment of bonus shares has the advantage that it does not result in the release of resources of the company. Because of the bonus issue, the profits become part of the share capital which increases the creditworthiness of the company. It may be resorted to by the company in case of expansion of its business; it will, however, not increase the total resources at the disposal of the company. It can also the used by the company to reduce its abnormally high rate of dividend as it will increase the amount of share capital without increasing the profitability of the company.

It should be remembered that when bonus shares are distributed, the shareholders may not gain at all. This is because of the fact that the market value of the shares depends upon the dividend received. If the company issues bonus shares, the profits (which do not increase) will have to be distributed over a larger number of shares, thus reducing the dividend per share. This will result in a fall in the value of the shares in the market. Thus, the shareholder will have a larger number of

*Only fully paid bonus shares can be issued out of the Capital Redemption Reserve Account or Securities Premium Account.

shares but the total value of his holding will not increase because each share now is of a smaller value. Hence, the shareholder makes no entry in his books on receipt of bonus shares. However, the shareholder will benefit in the form of capital appreciation if there is a net increase in the amount of dividend received by him.

The company has to make the following entries in its books :—

1. Debit Profit and Loss Appropriation Account (or General Reserve or Securities Premium Account or Capital Redemption Reserve Account, depending from what source the bonus is being given).
   Credit Bonus to Equity Shareholders Account.
2. Debit Bonus to Equity Shareholders Account with the total amount.
   Credit Share Capital Account with the nominal value of shares issued.
   Credit Securities Premium Account with the premium, if any, on the bonus shares.

The fact of the issue of the bonus shares has to be disclosed in the balance sheet. Mention must be made of the number and the amount of shares issued as bonus shares and also source from which the bonus shares have been issued.

Illustration 17:

The balance sheet of A Ltd. on March 31, 2010 was as follows :—

	Rs. '000		*Rs. '000*
Share Capital :			
20 lakh Equity Shares of		Sundry Assets	47,500
Rs. 10 each	20,000		
Securities Premium	5,000		
General Reserve	10,000		
Profit and Loss Account	8,000		
Sundry Creditors	4,500		
	47,500		47,500

The company decided to issue bonus shares at the rate of three shares for every four shares held and decided, for this purpose, to utilise the securities premium, Rs. 60 lakh out of reserve and the balance out of the Profit and Loss. Account. Give journal entries to give effect to the above and give the amended balance sheet.

Solution:

Journal

			Dr.	*Cr.*
2010			*Rs. '000*	*Rs.'000*
Mar. 31	Securities Premium Account	...Dr.	5,000	
	General Reserve	...Dr.	6,000	
	Profit and Loss Account	...Dr.	4,000	
	To Bonus to Equity Shareholders Account			15,000
	The amount of bonus shares numbering 15 lakh i.e. 20 lakh × 3/4 to be distributed among the equity shareholders, as per resolution no......			
	Bonus to Equity Shareholders Account	...Dr.	15,000	
	To Share Capital Account			15,000
	The allotment of bonus shares, as per resolution no......			

Balance Sheet of A Ltd. as at 31st March, 2010

	Rs. '000		*Rs. '000*
Share Capital		Sundry Assets	47,500
35 lakh equity shares of Rs. 100 each, fully paid	35,000		
[Of the above, 15 lakh equity shares were issued as bonus shares out of Securities Premium Account (Rs. 50 lakh) General Reserve (Rs. 60 lakh) and Profit and Loss Account (Rs. 40 lakh)]			
General Reserve	4,000		
Profit and Loss Account	4,000		
Sundry Creditors	4,500		
	47,500		47,500

Public Deposits. The Companies (Amendment) Act, 1974 introduced sections 58A and 58B to regulate acceptance of deposits by non-banking companies. The Central Government in consultation with the Reserve Bank of India may prescribe the limits up to which, the manner in which and the conditions subject to which deposits may be invited or accepted by company either from the public or from its members.

Briefly, the company has put to an advertisement in at least one newspaper of English and a regional language and the advertisment must contain all the information about the company as prescribed. No company can accept or renew any deposit which is repayable on demand or on notice or after a period of less than six months or more than 36 months from the date of acceptance or renewal of such deposit. However, for the purpose of meeting any short-term requirements of funds, a company may accept or renew deposits for a period of less than 6 months provided that such deposits do not exceed ten per cent of the aggregate of the paid-up share capital and free reserves of the company and are repayable not earlier than three months from the date of such deposits or renewal thereof.

Generally, the amount of public deposits is not to exceed 35% of the paid-up share capital and free reserves—composed of 10% of the paid-up share capital and free reserves from shareholders, or against unsecured debentures or from others against guarantee provided by any directors, and the remaining from the general public. For the purpose of arriving at the aggregate of the paid-up share capital and free reserves, the amount of accumulated balance of loss, balance of deferred revenue expenditure and other intangible assets, if any, will be deducted.

In case to the interest payable to a depositor exceeds Rs. 2,500 in a year, the company will deduct income-tax at source at prescribed rate.

3. FORM OF BALANCE SHEET

Section 210 of the Companies Act requires preparation of a balance sheet at the end of each specified period. Section 211 requires the balance sheet to be set up in the prescribed form (but exempts banking, insurance and electricity companies and also other companies governed by any other special Act). The Central Government has the power to exempt any class of companies from compliance with the requirements of the prescribed form if it is in the public interest. The "form" is designed to elicit proper information but, nevertheless, a company has the obligation of preparing balance sheet in such a way, so as to give a true and fair view of the state of affairs of the company as at the end of the financial year.

The form of the Balance Sheet as given in Schedule VI of the Companies Act is given below. Notes and instruction regarding various items are given in brackets below each item. As a general rule, if the information required to be given under any of the items or sub-items in the prescribed form cannot be conveniently included in the Balance Sheet itself, it should be furnished in a separate schedule or schedules to be annexed to the Balance Sheet.

SCHEDULE VI–PART I
(See section 211)
Form of Balance Sheet

(The balance sheet of a company shall be either in horizontal form or vertical form)

A. Horizontal Form

Balance Sheet of . . . .(Here enter the name of the company) as at . . . .(Here enter the date at which the balance sheet is made out.)

Figures for the previous year Rs.	*LIABILITIES*	*Figures for the current year Rs.*	*Figures for the previous year Rs.*	*ASSETS*	*Figures for the current year Rs.*
	SHARE CAPITAL Authorised. . . . . . shares of Rs. . . . . . .each. Issued: (distinguishing between the various classes of capital and stating the particulars specified below, in respect of each class) .... shares of Rs. .... .each. Subscribed: (distinguishing between the various classes of capital and stating the particulars specified below, in respect of each class) ...... shares of Rs. ...... each Rs. ...... called up. (Of the above shares...... .shares are allotted as fully paid-up pursuant to a contract without payments being received in cash.) (Of the above shares . . . . . shares are allotted as fully paid-up by way of bonus shares.) *Specify the source from which bonus shares are issued, e.g., capitalisation of profits or Reserves or from Securities Premium Account.* *Less* : Calls unpaid: (*i*) By directors (*ii*) By others *Add* : Forfeited shares : (amount originally paid up)			FIXED ASSETS : Distinguishing as far as possible between expenditure upon (*a*) goodwill (*b*) land (*c*) buildings (*d*) leaseholds (*e*) railway sidings (*f*) plant and machinery (*g*) furniture and fittings (*h*) development of property (*i*) patents, trade marks and designs (*j*) livestock, and (*k*) vehicles, etc. *(Under each head the original cost and the additions thereto and deductions therefrom during the year, and the total depreciation written off or provided up to the end of the year is to be stated. Depreciation written off or provided shall be allotted under the different asset heads and deducted in arriving at the value of Fixed Assets. [Also see note (11)].* *In every case where the original cost cannot be ascertained, without unreasonable expense or delay, the valuation shown by the books is to be*	

Figures for the previous year Rs.	LIABILITIES	Figures for the current year Rs.	Figures for the previous year Rs.	ASSETS	Figures for the current year Rs.
	(Any capital profit on reissue of forfeited shares should be transferred to Capital Reserve). *Notes:* 1. *Terms of redemption or conversion (if any) of any redeemable preference capital are to be stated together with earliest date of redemption or conversion.* 2. *Particulars of any option on unissued Share Capital are to be specified.* 3. *Particulars of the different classes of preference shares are to be given.* *These particulars are to be given along with Share Capital.* In the case of subsidiary companies, the number of shares held by the holding company as well as by the ultimate holding company and its susidiaries shall be separately stated in respect of Subscribed Share Capital. The auditor is not required to certify the correctness of such share-holdings as certified by the management. **RESERVES AND SURPLUS :** (1) Capital Reserves (2) Capital Redemption Reserve (3) Securities Premium Account (showing details of its utilisation in the manner provided in Section 78 in the year of utilisation). (4) Other Reserves specifying the nature of each Reserve and the amount in respect thereof. *Less* : Debit balance in profit and loss account (if any). *(The debit balance in the Profit and Loss Account shall be shown as a deduction from the uncommitted reserves, if any).*			*given. For the purpose of this paragraph, such valuation shall be the net amount at which an asset stood in the company's books at the commencement of this Act after deduction of the amounts previously provided or written off for depreciation or diminution in value, and where any such asset is sold, the amount of sale proceeds shall be shown as deduction.* *Where sums have been written off on a reduction of capital or a revaluation of assets, every balance-sheet, (after the first balance-sheet) subsequent to the reduction or revaluation shall show the reduced figures with the date of the reduction in place of the original cost.* *Each balance sheet for the first five years subsequent to the date of the reduction, shall show also the amount of the reduction made.* *Similarly, where sums have been added by writing up the assets, every balance-sheet subsequent to such writing up shall show the increased figures with the date of the increase in place of the original cost. Each balance-sheet for the first five years subsequent to the date of the writing up shall also show the amount of increase made.* *Explanation : Nothing contained in the preceding two paragraphs shall apply to any adjustment made in accordance with the second paragraph.* **INVESTMENTS :** Showing nature of investments and mode of valuation, for example, cost or market value, and distinguishing between—	

(5) Surplus, i.e., balance in profits and loss account after providing for proposed allocations, namely: Dividend, bonus or reserves
(6) Proposed additions to reserves.
(7) Sinking Funds.

(Additions and deductions since last balance-sheet to be shown, under each of the specified heads. The word "fund" in relation to any "Reserve" should be used only where such Reserve is specifically represented by earmarked investments).

SECURED LOANS :

(1) Debentures.
(2) Loans and Advances from Banks.
(3) Loans and Advances from Subsidiaries.
(4) Other Loans and Advances.

(Loans from directors and/or manager should be shown separately.)

Interest accrued and due on Secured Loans should be included under the appropriate sub-heads under the head "Secured Loans".

The nature of security to be specified in each case.

Where loans have been guaranteed by manager and/or directors, a mention thereof shall also be made and also the aggregate amount of such loans under each head.

In case of Debentures, terms of redemption or conversion (if any) are to be stated together with earliest date of redemption or conversion.

UNSECURED LOANS :

(1) Fixed Deposits.
(2) Loans and Advances from Subsidiaries.
(3) Short Term Loans and Advances :
 (*a*) From Banks.
 (*b*) From Others.
 (Short term loans include those which are due for repayment not later than one year as at the date of the balance-sheet.)

(1) Investments in Government or Trust Securities.
(2) Investments in shares, debentures or bonds. *(Showing separately shares fully paid-up and partly paid-up and also distinguishing the different classes of shares and showing also in similar details investments in shares, debentures or bonds of subsidiary companies).*
(3) Immovable properties.
(4) Investments in the capital of partnership firms.
(5) Balance of unutilised monies raised by issue.

(Aggregate amount of company's quoted investments and also the market value thereof shall be shown).

(Aggregate amount of company's unquoted investments shall also be shown).

(All unutilised monies out of the issue must be separately disclosed in the balance sheet of the company indicating the form in which such unutilised funds have been invested).

CURRENT ASSETS, LOANS AND ADVANCES:

(A) CURRENT ASSETS :

(1) Interest accrued on Investments.
(2) Stores and spare parts.
(3) Loose Tools.
(4) Stock-in-trade.
(5) Work-in-progress.

[In respect of (2) and (4), mode of valuation of stock shall be stated and the amount in respect of raw materials shall also be stated separately where practicable. Mode of valuation of works-in-progress shall be stated].

(6) Sundry Debtors—
 (*a*) Debts outstanding for a period exceeding six months.

Figures for the previous year Rs.	LIABILITIES	Figures for the current year Rs.	Figures for the previous year Rs.	ASSETS	Figures for the current year Rs.
	(4) Other Loans and Advances : (*a*) From Banks. (*b*) From Others. *(Loans from directors and/or manager should be shown separately.)* Interest accrued and due on Unsecured Loans should be included under the appropriate sub-heads under the head "Unsecured Loans". *Where Loans have been guaranteed by manager, and/or directors, a mention thereof shall also be made together with the aggregate amount of such loans under each head.* **CURRENT LIABILITIES AND PROVISIONS :** A. CURRENT LIABILITIES (1) Acceptances. (2) Sundry Creditors. (*i*) Total outstanding dues to small scale industrial undertabling(s); and (*ii*) Total outstanding dues of creditors other than small scale industrial undertabling(s) The name (s) of the small scale industrial undertabling (s) to whom the company owes a sum exceeding Rs. 1 lakh which is outstanding for more than 30 days, are to be disclosed) [A small scale industrial undertabling has the same meaning as assigned to it under clause (j) of section 3 of the Industrial (Development and Regulation) Act, 1951.] (3) Subsidiary Companies. (4) Advance payments and unexpired discounts for the portion for which value has still to be given, e.g.,			(*b*) Other debts. *Less* : Provision *(The amounts to be shown under Sundry Debtors shall include the amounts due in respect of goods sold or services rendered or in respect of other contractual obligations but shall not include the amounts which are in the nature of loans or advances).* In regard to Sundry Debtors particulars to be given separately of— (*a*) *debts considered good and in respect of which the company is fully secured ;* (*b*) *debts considered good for which the company holds no security other than the debtor's personal security ; and* (*c*) *debts considered doubtful or bad.* *Debts due by directors or other officers of the company or any of them either severally or jointly with any other person or debts due by firms or private companies respectively in which any director is a partner or a director or a member to be separately stated.* *Debts due from other companies under the same management within the meaning of sub-section (IB) of Section 370 to be disclosed with the names of the companies. The maximum amount due by directors or other officers of the company at any time during the year to be shown by way of a note.* *The provision to be shown under this head should not exceed the amount of debts stated to be considered doubtful or bad and any surplus of such provision, if already created, should be shown at*	

in the case of the following classes of companies:—

Newspaper, Fire Insurance,
Theatres, Clubs, Banking,
Steamship Companies, etc.

(5) Unclaimed Dividends

(6) Other Liabilities (if any).

(7) Interest accrued but not due on loans.

B. PROVISIONS

(8) Provision for Taxation.

(9) Proposed Dividends.

(10) For Contingencies.

(11) For Provident Fund Scheme.

(12) For insurance, pension and similar staff benefit schemes.

(13) Other provisions.

A foot-note to the balance sheet may be added to show separately :—

(1) Claims against the company not acknowledged as debts.

(2) Uncalled liability on shares partly paid.

(3) Arrears of fixed cumulative dividends.

(*The period for which the dividends are in arrear or if there is more than one class of shares, the dividends on each such class that are in arrear, shall be stated*).

(4) Estimated amount of contracts remaining to be executed on capital account and not provided for.

(5) Other money for which the company is contingently liable.

(*The amount of any guarantees given by the company on behalf of directors or other officers of the company shall be stated and where practiable, the general nature and amount of each such contingent liability, if material, shall also be specified*).

every closing under "Reserves and Surplus" (in the Liabilities side) under a separate sub-head "Reserve for Doubtful or Bad Debts.")

(7A) Cash balance on hand.

(7B) Bank balances—

(*a*) with Scheduled Banks; and

(*b*) with others.

(In regard to bank balances, particulars to be given separately of—

(*a*) *the balances lying with Scheduled Banks on current accounts, call accounts and deposit accounts ;*

(*b*) *the names of the bankers other than Scheduled Banks and the balances lying with each such banker on current accounts, call accounts and deposit accounts and the maximum amount outstanding at any time during the year with each such banker ; and*

(*c*) *the nature of the interest, if any, of any director or his relative in each of the bankers [other than Scheduled Banks referred to in (b) above.*]

(B) LOANS AND ADVANCES :

(8) (*a*) Advances and loans to subsidiaries.

(*b*) Advances and loans to partnership firms in which the company or any of its subsidiaries is a partner.

(9) Bills of Exchange.

(10) Advances recoverable in cash or in kind or for value to be received, e.g., rates, taxes, insurance, etc.

(11) Balances with customs, port trust, etc. (where payable on demand).

[*The instructions regarding Sundry Debtors apply to "Loans and Advances" also. The amounts due from other companies under the same*

Figures for the previous year Rs.	LIABILITIES	Figures for the current year Rs.	Figures for the previous year Rs.	ASSETS	Figures for the current year Rs.
				management within the meaning of sub-section (IB) of Section 370 should also be given with the names of the companies; the maximum amount due from every one of these at any time during the year must be shown]. **MISCELLANEOUS EXPENDITURE** (to the extent not written off or adjusted). (1) Preliminary expenses. (2) Expenses including commission or brokerage on underwriting or subscription of shares or debentures. (3) Discount allowed on the issue of shares or debentures. (4) Interest paid out of capital during construction (also stating the rate of interest). (5) Development expenditure not adjusted. (6) Other items (specifying nature). **PROFIT AND LOSS ACCOUNT** (*Show here the debit balance of profit and loss account carried forward after deduction of the uncommitted reserves, if any*).	

Notes : (1) Paise can also be given in addition to Rupees, if desired.

(2) Dividends declared by subsidiary companies after the date of the balance-sheet should not be included unless they are in respect of a period which closed on or before the date of the balance-sheet.

(3) Any reference to benefits expected from contracts to the extent not excecuted shall not be made in the balance-sheet but shall be made in the Board's report.

(4) Particulars of any redeemed debentures which the company has power to issue should be given.

(5) Where any of the company's debentures are held by a nominee or a trustee for the company, the nominal amount of the debentures and the amount at which they are stated in the books of the company shall be stated.

(6) A statement of investments (whether shown under "Investments" or under "Current Assets" as Stock-in-Trade) separately classifying trade investments and other investments should be annexed to the balance sheet, showing the names of the bodies corporate (including separately the names of the bodies corporate under the same management) in whose shares or debentures, investments have been made (including all investments whether existing or not, made subsequent to the date as at which the previous balance sheet was made out) and the nature and extent of the investments so made in each such body corporate; provided that in the case of an investment company, that is to say, a company whose principal business is the acquisition of shares, stock, debentures or other securites, it shall be sufficient if the statement shows only the investments existing on the date as at which the balance sheet has been made out. In regard to the investments in the capital of partnership firms, the names of the firms (with the names of all their partners, total capital and the shares of each partner) shall be given in the statement.

(7) If, in the opinion of the Board, any of the current assets, loans and advances have not a value on realisation in the ordinary course of business at least equal to the amount at which they are stated, the fact that the Board is of that opinion shall be stated.

(8) Except in the case of the first balance-sheet laid before the company after the commencement of the Act, the corresponding amounts of the immediately preceding financial year for all items shown in the balance sheet shall be also given in the balance sheet. The requirements in this behalf shall, in case of companies preparing quarterly or half-yearly accounts, etc., relate to the balance sheet for the corresponding date in the previous year.

(9) Current accounts with Directors and Manager, whether they are in credit or debit, shall be shown separately.

(10) The information required to be given under any of the items or sub-items in the Form, if it cannot be conveniently included in the balance-sheet itself, shall be furnished in a separate Schedule or Schedules to be annexed to and form part of the balance-sheet. This is recommended when items are numerous.

(11) Where the original cost of fixed assests and additions and deductions thereto, relate to any fixed asset which has been acquired from a country outside India, and in consequence of a change in the rate of exchange at any time after the acquisition of such assets, there has been an increase or reduction in the liability of the company, as expressed in Indian currency, for making payment towards the whole or a part of the cost of the asset, or for repayment of the whole or a part of moneys borrowed by the company from any person, directly or indirectly, in any foreign currency specifically for the purpose of acquiring the asset (being in either case the liability existing immediately before the date on which the change in the rate of exchange takes effect), the amount by which the liability is so increased or reduced during the year, shall be added to, or as the case may be, deducted from the cost, and the amount arrived at after such addition or deduction shall be taken to be the cost of the fixed assets.

Explanation 1. This paragraph shall apply in relation to all balance-sheets that may be made out as at the 6th day of June, 1966, or any day thereafter and where, at the date of issue of the notification of the Government of India, in the Ministry of Industrial Development and Company Affairs (Department of Company Affairs), G.S.R. No. 129, dated the 3rd day of January, 1968, any balance sheet in relation to which the paragraph applies, has already been made out and laid before the company in annual general meeting, the adjustment referred to in this paragraph may be made in the first balance sheet made out after the issue of the said notification.

Explanation 2. In this paragraph, unless the context otherwise requires, the expressions "rate of exchange", "foreign currency" shall have the meanings respectively assigned to them under sub-section (1) of section 43A of the Income-tax Act, 1961 (43 of 1961), and Explanation 2 and Explanation 3 of the said sub-section shall, as far as may be, apply in relation to the said paragraph as they apply to the said sub-section(1).

B. Vertical Form of Balance Sheet

Name of the Company ....

Balance Sheet as at ....

	Schedule No.	Figures as at the end of the current year	Figures as at the end of the previous financial year
I. SOURCE OF FUNDS			
(1) Shareholders' Funds:			
(*a*) Capital	...	......	......
(*b*) Reserves and Surplus	...	......	......
(2) Loan Funds:			
(*a*) Secured Loans	...	......	......
(b) Unsecured Loans	...	....	......
Total			
II. APPLICATION OF FUNDS			
(1) Fixed Assets:			
(*a*) Gross Block	...	......	......
(*b*) *Less:* Depreciation	...	......	......
(*c*) Net Block	...	......	......
(*d*) Capital Work-in-progress	...	......	......
(2) Investments	...	......	......
(3) Current Assets, Loans and Advances			
(*a*) Inventories	...	......	......
(*b*) Sundry Debtors	...	......	......
(*c*) Cash and Bank Balances	...	......	......
(*d*) Other Current Assets	...	......	......
(e) Loans and Advances	...	......	......
Less : **Current Liabilities and Provisions**			
(*a*) Liabilities	...	......	......
(*b*) Provisions	...	......	......
Net Current Assets			
(4) (*a*) Miscellaneous expenditure to the extent not written off or adjusted	...	......	......
(*b*) Profit and Loss Account	...	......	......
Total			

Notes: 1. Details under each of the above items shall be given in separate Schedules. The Schedules shall incorporate all the information required to be given under Part IA of the Schedule VI read with Notes containing General Instruction for Preparation of Balance Sheet.

2. The Schedules, referred to above, accounting policies and explanatory notes that may be attached shall form an integral part of the balance sheet.

3. The figures in the balance sheet may be rounded to the nearest "000" or "00" as may be convenient or may be expressed in terms of decimals of thousands.

4. A footnote to the balance sheet may be added to show separately contingent liabilities.

By Notification No. GSR 388 (E), dated May 15, 1995, the Central Government has inserted Part IV in the Schedule VI to the Act. The summarised disclosure requirements of the said Part are as under:

(*i*) Registration details.

(*ii*) Capital raised during the year of account.

(*iii*) Position of mobilisation and deployment of funds.

(*iv*) Performance of the company.

(*v*) Three principal products/services of the company (as per monetary terms) together with ITC codes of such products.

This amendment will take effect in respect of account closed on or after 16.5.95.

PART IV

Balance Sheet Abstract and Company's General Business Profile

I. Registration Details

Registation No. [ ] State Code [ ] (Refer Code list I)

Balance Sheet Date [ ] Date [ ] Month [ ] Year

II. Capital Raised during the Year (Amount in Rs. Thousands)

Public Issue [ ] Rights Issue [ ]

Bonus Issue [ ] Private Placement [ ]

III. Position of Mobilisation and Deployment of Funds (Amount in Rs. Thousands)

Total Liabilities [ ] Total Assets [ ]

Paid-up Capital [ ] Reserve & Surplus [ ]

Secured Loans [ ] Unsecured Loans [ ]

Application of Funds

Net Fixed Assets [ ] Investments [ ]

Net Current Assets [ ] Miscellaneous Expenditure [ ]

Accumulated Losses [ ]

IV. Performance of Company (Amount in Rs. Thousands)

Turnover [ ] Total Expenditure [ ]

+ – Profit/Loss Before Tax [ ] + – Profit/Loss After Tax [ ]

(Please tick appropriate box, + for Profit, – for Loss)

Earning per Share in Rs. [ ] Dividend Rate % [ ]

V. Generic Names of Three Principal Products/Services of Company (as per monetary terms)

Item Code No. (ITC Code) [ ]

Product Description

Item Code No.
(ITC Code)

Product Description

Item Code No.
(ITC Code)

Product Description

Note: For ITC code of products please refer to the publication Indian Trade Classification based on harmonised commodity description and coding system by Ministry of Commerce, Directorate General of Commercial Intelligence and Statistics, Kolkata-700 001.

Annexure - I
Code List 1 : State Codes

State Code	State Name	State Code	State Name
01	Andhra Pradesh	02	Assam
03	Bihar	04	Gujarat
05	Haryana	06	Himachal Pradesh
07	Jammu & Kashmi	08	Karnataka
09	Kerala	10	Madhya Pradesh
11	Maharashtra	12	Manipur
13	Meghalaya	14	Nagaland
15	Orissa	16	Punjab
17	Rajasthan	18	Tamil Nadu
20	Uttar Pradesh	21	West Bengal
22	Sikkim	23	Arunachal Pradesh
24	Goa	52	Andaman Islands
53	Chandigarh	54	Dadra Island
55	Delhi	56	Daman & Diu
57	Lakshwadeep	58	Mizoram
59	Pondicherry		

Illustration 18:

From the following particulars furnished by Pioneer Ltd., prepare the Balance Sheet as at 31st **March, 2010, as required by Part I, Schedule VI of the Companies Act.**

	Rs.	Dr. Rs.	Cr. Rs.
Equity Share Capital (Rs. 10 each, fully paid up)			10,00,000
Calls in Arrears		1,000	
Land		2,00,000	
Buildings		3,50,000	
Plant and Machinery		5,25,000	
Furniture		50,000	
General Reserve			2,10,000
Loan From State Finane Corporation			1,50,000
Stock:			
Finished Goods	2,00,000		
Raw Materials	50,000	2,50,000	
Provision for Taxation			61,880
Sundry Debtors		2,00,000	
Advances		42,700	
Proposed Dividend			60,000
Provision for Corporate Dividend Tax			6,120
Profit and Loss Account			1,00,000
Cash Balance		30,000	
Cash at Bank		2,47,000	
Preliminary Expenses		13,300	
Loans (Unsecured)			1,21,000
Sundry Creditors (For Goods and Expenses)			2,00,000
		19,09,000	19,09,000

The following additional information is also provided:—

(*a*) Miscellaneous Expenses included Rs. 5,000 audit fees and Rs. 700 for out of pocket expenses paid to the auditors.

(*b*) 2,000 equity shares were issued for consideration other than cash.

(*c*) Debtors of Rs. 52,000 are due for more than six months.

(*d*) The cost of assets:

	Rs.
Buildings	4,00,000
Plant and Machinery	7,00,000
Furniture	62,500

(*e*) The balance of Rs. 1,50,000 in the Loan from State Finance Corporation Account is inclusive of Rs. 7,500 for interest accrued but not due. The loan is secured by hypothecation of the Plant and Machinery.

(*f*) Balance at Bank includes Rs. 2,000 with Perfect Bank Ltd., which is not a Scheduled Bank.

(*g*) Bills receivable for Rs. 2,75,000 maturing on 30th June, 2010, have been discounted.

(*h*) The company had contract for the erection of machinery at Rs. 1,50,000 which is still incomplete.

[*Adapted C.A. (Inter) May, 1989*]

Solution:

Balance Sheet of Pioneer Ltd.
as at 31st March, 2010

Liabilities	*Rs.*	*Rs.*	*Assets*	*Rs.*	*Rs.*
Share Capital			**Fixed Assets**		
Authorised		?	Land, at cost		2,00,000
Issued and Subscribed:			Buildings, at cost	4,00,000	
1,00,000 Equity Shares, Rs. 10 each		10,00,000	*Less*: Depreciation written		
(Of the above shares, 2,000 equity			off to date	50,000	3,50,000
shares are allotted as fully			Plant and Machinery,	7,00,000	
paid up pursuant to a contract			at Cost		
without payment being received			*Less*: Depreciation written		
in cash)			written off to date	1,75,000	5,25,000
Less: Calls-in-arrear		1,000	Furniture, at cost	62,500	
		9,99,000			
Reserves and Surplus			*Less*: Depreciation written		
General Reserve		2,10,000	off to date	12,500	50,000
Profit and Loss (Appropriation)			**Current Assets, Loans and**		
Account		1,00,000	**Advances**		
Secured Loans			(A) Current Assets Stock:		
Loan from State			Finished Goods	2,00,000	
Finane Corporation	1,42,500		Raw Materials	50,000	2,50,000
Add: Interest accured but			Sundry Debtors		
not due	7,500	1,50,000	(*a*) Debts outstanding		
(Secured by hypothecatiuon of			for more than six months	52,000	
Plant and Machinery)			(*b*) Other Debts	1,48,000	2,00,000
Unsecured Loans		1,21,000	Bank Balance		
Current Liabilities and Provisions			(*a*) with Scheduled		
(A) Current Liabilities			Banks	2,45,000	
Sundry Creditors for			(*b*) With Others	2,000	2,47,000
goods and expenses		2,00,000	(B) Loans and Advances		
(B) Provisions			Advances		42,700
Provision for Tax		61,880	Miscellaneous Expenditure		
Provision of Corporate			Preliminary Expenses		13,300
Dividend Tax		6,120			
Proposed Dividend		60,000			
Contingent Liabilities not Provided for:					
1. Bills receivable for Rs. 2,75,000 **maturing on 30th June, 2010** have been discounted.					
2. The company had contract for the ereaction of machinery at Rs. 1,50,000 which is still incomplete.					
		19,08,000			19,08,000

Illustration 19:

The following is the trial balance of Lakshmi Co. Ltd. as at 31st March, 2010:

	Rs. '000	*Rs. '000*
Stock, 1st April, 2009	75,000	
Purchases Returns		10,000
Purchases and Sales	2,45,000	3,40,000
Wages	30,000	
Discount		3,000
Carriage Inward	950	
Furniture and Fittings	17,000	

	Rs. '000	*Rs. '000*
Salaries	7,500	
Rent	4,000	
Sundry Expenses	7,050	
Profit and Loss Appropriation Account, 31st March, 2009		16,350
Dividends paid for 2008-2009	9,000	
Corporate Dividend Tax Paid @ 15%	1,350	
Share Capital		1,00,000
Debtors and Creditors	27,500	17,500
Plant and Machinery	29,000	
Cash at Bank	46,200	
General Reserve		15,500
Patents and Trade Mark	4,800	
Bills Receivable and Bills Payable	5,000	7,000
	5,09,350	5,09,350

Prepare Trading Account, Profit and Loss Account, and Profit and Loss Appropriation Account for the year ended 31st March, 2010 and Balance Sheet at that date. Take into consideration the following adjustments:

(*i*) Stock on 31st March, 2010 was valued at Rs. 8,80,00,000.

(*ii*) Make a provision for income tax @ 35%.

(*iii*) Depreciate Plant and Machinery @ 15%, Furniture and Fittings @ 10% and Patents and Trade Marks @ 5%.

(*iv*) On 31st March, 2010, outstanding rent amounted to Rs. 8,00,000 while outstanding salaries totalled Rs. 9,00,000.

(*v*) The Board of Directors propose a dividend @ 15% per annum for the year ended 31st March, 2010 after the minimum transfer to General Reserve as required by law. The rate of corporate dividend tax is 15%.

(*vi*) Make a provision for doubtful debts amounting to Rs. 5,10,000.

(*vii*) Provide for managerial remuneration @10% of the net profits before tax and before deducting managerial remuneration.

Solution:

Trading and Profit & Loss Account of Lakshmi Co. Ltd.
for the year ended 31st March, 2010

Dr. *Cr.*

Figures for previous year Rs. '000	*Particulars*	*Rs. '000*	*Figures the current year Rs. '000*	*Figures for previous year Rs. '000*	*Particulars*	*Figures the current year Rs. '000*
	To Stock, 1st April, 2009		75,000		By Sales	3,40,000
	To Purchases	2,45,000			By Stock, 31st March, 2010	88,000
	Less: Returns	10,000	2,35,000			
	To Wages		30,000			
	To Carriage Inward		950			
	To Gross Profit c/d		87,050			
			4,28,000			4,28,000
	To Salaries	7,500			By Gross Profit b/d	87,050
	Add: Outstanding Salaries	900	8,400		By Discount	3,000

Rs. '000		Rs. '000	Rs. '000	Rs. '000		Rs. '000
	To Rent	4,000				
	Add: Outstanding Rent	800	4,800			
	To Sundry Expenses		7,050			
	To Provision fror Doubtful Debts		510			
	To Depreciation on:					
	Plant & Machinery @ 15%		4,350			
	Furniture & Fittings @ 10%		1,700			
	Patents & Trade Marks @ 5%		240			
	To Outstanding Managerial Remuneration & 10% of Rs. 63,000		6,300			
	To Provision for Income Tax @ 35% on Rs. 56,700		19,845			
	To Net Profit c/d		36,855			
			90,050			90,050
	To Dividends paid for 2008-2009		9,000		By Balance b/fd	16,350
	To Corporate Dividend Tax Paid		1,350		By Net Profit for the year b/d	36,855
	To Transfer to General Reserve @ 5% of Net Profit		1,843			
	To Proposed Dividend @ 15%		15,000			
	To Provision for Corporate Dividend Tax @ 15%		2,250			
	To Balance carried to Balance Sheet		23,276			
			53,205			53,205

Balance Sheet of Lakshmi Co. Ltd.
as at 31st March, 2010

Figures for the previous year Rs. '000	*Liabilities*	*Rs. '000*	*Figures for the current year Rs. '000*	*Figures for the previous year Rs. '000*	*Assets*	*Rs. '000*	*Figures for the current year Rs. '000*
	Share Capital				**Fixed Assets**		
	Authorised		?		Plant and Machinery	29,000	
	Issued & Subscribed		1,00,000		*Less*: Dep. @ 15%	4,350	24,650
	Reserves and Surplus				Furniture and Fittings	17,000	
	General Reserve				*Less*: Depreciation @ 10%	1,700	15,300
	Balance as on 1st April, 2009	15,500			Patent and Trade Marks	4,800	
	Add: addition made during the year	1,843	17,343		*Less*: Dep. @ 5%	240	4,560
	Profit & Loss Account		23,752		**Current Assets, Land and Advances**		
	Current Liabilities and Provisions				(A) Current Assets		
	(A) Current Liabilities				Stock		88,000
	Acceptances		7,000		Debtors	27,500	
	Creditors		17,500		*Less*: Provision for Doubtful Debts	510	26,990
	Outstanding Expenses:				Cash at Bank		46,200
	Rent		800		(B) Loans and Advances		
					Bills of Exchange		5,000

Rs. '000		*Rs. '000*	*Rs. '000*		*Rs. '000*
	Salaries	900			
	Managerial Remuneration	6,300			
	(B) Provisions				
	Provisions for Taxation	19,845			
	Provision for Corporate Dividend Tax	2,250			
	Proposed Dividend	15,000			
		2,10,700			2,10,700

Illustration 20:

Auto Parts Manufacturing Co. Ltd. was registered with a nominal capital of Rs. 10 crore dividend into shares of Rs. 10 each, of which 40 lakh shares had been issued and fully called.

The following is the Trial Balance extracted on 31st March, 2010.

	Rs. '000	*Rs. '000*
Stock, (1st April, 2009)	18,642	
Manufacturing Wages	10,974	
Manufacturing Expenses	1,924	
Purchases and Sales	71,821	1,16,990
Machinery Repairs	861	
Carriage Inwards	491	
Carriage Outwards	926	
Advance payment of Income-tax	1,429	
Bank Loan (at 18%)		5,000
Interest on Loan	450	
Debtors and Creditors	16,440	9,222
Profit and Loss Account, 1st April, 2009		864
Bank Current Account	10,686	
Cash in hand	192	
Leasehold Factory	16,421	
Plant and Machinery	12,840	
Loose Tools	1,250	
Share Capital		40,000
Calls in Arrear	100	
Rates and Electricity (Factory Rs. 1,421 thousand, Office Rs. 340 thousand)	1,761	
Directors' Fees and Remuneration	1,200	
Office Salaries and Expenses	1,300	
Auditors' Fees	125	
Office Furnitures	500	
Commission	860	
Returns	1,264	981
Preliminary Expenses	600	
	1,73,057	1,73,057

You are required to prepare Trading and Profit and Loss Account for the year ending March 31, 2010 and Balance Sheet as at that date after taking into consideration the following adjustments:

1. Write off one-third of Preliminary Expenses.
2. Depreciation is to be provided on:
   Plant and Machinery @ 15%; and
   Office Furniture @ 10%.
3. Manufacturing Wages Rs. 189 thousand and Office Salaries Rs. 120 thousand had accrued due.

4. Provide for Interest on Bank Loan for 6 months.
5. The Stock was valued at Rs. 12,484 thousand and Loose Tools at Rs. 1,000 thousand.
6. Provide Rs. 850 thousand on Debtors for Doubtful Debts.
7. Provide further Rs. 312 thousand for Discount on Debtors.
8. Make a Provision for Income Tax @ 40%.
9. The Directors recommend dividend at 15% for the year ending 31st March, 2001 after transferring 5% of net profits to General Reserve. Make a provision for corporate dividend tax @ 15%. *[Adapted C.W.A. (Inter.) Dec. 1988]*

Solution:

Profit and Loss Account of Auto Parts Manufacturing Co.
for the year ended 31st March, 2010

Dr. *Cr.*

	Rs. '000	*Rs. '000*		*Rs. '000*	*Rs. '000*
To Opening Stock		18,642	By Sales	1,16,990	
To Purchases	71,821		*Less*: Sales Returns	1,264	
Less: Purchase Returns	981	70,840			1,15,726
To Manufacturing Wages	10,974		By Closing Stock		12,484
Add: Outstanding Wages	189	11,163			
To Manufacturing Expenses		1,924			
To Carriage Inwards		491			
To Rates and Electricity		1,421			
To Gross Profit c/d		23,729			
		1,28,210			1,28,210
			By Gross Profit b/d		23,729
To Office Salaries and Expenses	1,300				
Add: Outstanding Salaries	120	1,420			
To Carriage Outwards		926			
To Machinery Repairs		861			
To Interest on Bank Loan	450				
Add: Outstanding Interest	450	900			
To Rates and Electricity		340			
To Directors' Fees and Remuneration		1,200			
To Auditors' Fees		125			
To Commission		860			
To Provision for Doubtful Debts		850			
To Provision for Discount on Debtors		312			
To Depreciation on:					
Plant and Machinery @ 15%	1,926				
Office Furniture @ 10%	50	1,976			
To Loose Tools written off		250			
To Preliminary Expenses written off		200			
To Provision for Taxation		5,404			
To Net Profit c/d		8,105			
		23,729			23,729
To General Reserve @ 5%		406	By Balance b/fd		864
To Proposed Dividend @ 15%		5,985	By Net Profit b/d		8,105
To Provision for Corporate Dividend Tax		898			
To Balance c/d		1,680			
		8,969			8,969

Balance Sheet of Auto Parts Manufacturing Co.
as at 31st March, 2010

Liabilities	*Rs. '000*	*Rs. '000*	*Assets*	*Rs. '000*	*Rs. '000*
Share Capital			**Fixed Assets**		
Authorised		?	Leasehold Factory		16,421
Issued and Subscribed	40,000		Plant and Machinery	12,480	
Less: Calls-in-arrear	100	39,900	*Less*: Depreciation	1,926	10,914
Reserves and Surplus			Office Furniture	500	
General Reseve		406	*Less*: Depreciation	50	450
Profit and Loss Account		1,680	**Current Assets, Loans and Advances**		
Secured Loans:					
Bank Loan	5,000		(A) Current Assets		
Add: Outstanding			Loose Tools		1,000
Interest	450	5,450	Stock		12,484
Current Liabilities and Provisions			Sundry Debtors	16,440	
(A) Current Liabilities			*Less*: Provision for		
Creditors for goods		9,222	Doubtful Debts	850	
Creditors for expenses		309		15,590	
(B) Provisions			*Less*: Provision for		
Provision for Taxation		5,404	Discount on Debtors	312	15,278
Provision for Corporation			Cash in hand		192
Dividend		698	Bank Current Account		10,686
Proposed Dividend		5,985	(B) Loans and Advances		
			Advance Payment of		
			Income-Tax		1,429
			Miscellaneous Expenditure		
			(to the extent not written off		
			or adjusted)		
			Preliminary Expenses		400
		69,254			69,254

Illustration 21:

The following balances are extracted from the books of Raj Ltd., a real estate company, on 31st March, 2010:

	Dr. (*Rs. '000*)	*Cr.* (*Rs. '000*)
Sales		2760
Purchases of Materials	1218	
Equity Share Capital, fully paid shares of Rs. 10 each		100
Land purchased in the year as stock	73	
Leasehold Premises	42	
Creditors		463
Debtors	735	
Directors' Salaries	39	
Wages	111	
Work in Progress on 01-04-2009	210	
Sub-contractors' Cost	894	
Equipment, Fixtures and Fittings at cost on 01-04-2009	264	
Stock on 01.04.2009	59	
Profit and Loss Account, credit balance on 01.04.2009		128
Secured Loan		112
Bank Overdraft		105

	(Rs. '000)	(Rs. '000)
Interest on Loan and Overdraft	22	
Depreciation on Equipment on 01.04.2009		164
Administration Expenses	147	
Office Salaries	18	
	3,832	3,832

You also obtain the following information :

(*a*) On 31st March, 2010, stock on hand including the land acquired during the year, is valued at Rs. 1,42,000. Work in progress at that date is valued at Rs. 1,40,000.

(*b*) On 1st October, 2009 the company moved to new premises. The premises are on a 12 year lease and the lease premium paid amounted to Rs. 42,000. The company used sub-contract labour of Rs. 40,000 and materials at cost of Rs. 38,000 in the refurbishment of the premises. These are to be considered as part of the cost of leasehold premises.

(*c*) A review of the debtors reveals specific doubtful debts of Rs. 35,000 and the directors wish to provide for these together with a general provision based on 2% of the balance.

(*d*) Depreciation on equipment, fixtures and fittings is provided at 15% on the written down value.

(*e*) Raj Ltd. sued Bright Ltd. for supplying defective materials which have been written off as valueless. The directors are confident that Bright Ltd. will agree for a settlement at Rs. 50,000.

(*f*) The directors propose a dividend of 25%. A provision for corporate dividend tax is to be made @ 15%.,

(*g*) Rs. 20,000 is to be provided as audit fee.

(*h*) The company will provide 35% of the pre-tax profit as bonus to employees in the accounts before charging the bonus.

(*i*) Income tax to be provided at 35% of the profits. Assume that depreciation calculated according to Income Tax Act amounts to Rs. 25,000.

You are required :

(*a*) to prepare the company's financial statements for the year ended 31st March, 2010 as near as possible to proper form of company final accounts; and

(*b*) to prepare a set of Notes on Accounts including significant accounting policies.

Notes : Workings should form part of your answer.
Previous year figures can be ignored.
Figures are to the be rounded off to the nearest thousand.

(*C.A. Final, Nov; 1996 Modified*)

Solution :

Raj Ltd.
Balance Sheet as at 31st March, 2010

(Rs. in thousands)

1. SOURCES OF FUNDS		
(1) Shareholders' funds:		
(*a*) Capital	100	
(*b*) Reserves and surplus	224	
		324
(2) Loan funds:		
(*a*) Secured loans	112	
(*b*) Unsecured loans	—	
		112
TOTAL		436

(Rs. in thousands)

II. APPLICATION OF FUNDS		
(1) Fixed assets:		
(*a*) Gross block	384	
(*b*) *Less*: Depreciation	184	
(*c*) Net block	200	
(*d*) Capital work in progress	—	
		200
(2) Investments		
(3) Current assets, loans and advances:		
(*a*) Inventories	282	
(*b*) Sundry debtors	686	
(*c*) Cash and bank balances	—	
(*d*) Other current assets	—	
(*e*) Loans and advances	—	
	968	
Less: Current liabilities and provisions:		
(*a*) Current liabilities	588	
(*b*) Provisions	144	
	732	
Net current assets		236
(4) Miscellaneous expenditure (to the extent not written off or adjusted)		—
TOTAL		436
Contingent liabilities	Nil	

Profit and Loss Account for the year ended 31st March, 2010

(Rs. in thousands)

Income		
Sales		2,760
Expenditure		
Manufacturing expenses	2,205	
Other expenses	297	
Interest	22	
Depreciation on fixed assets	20	
		2,544
Profit before Taxation		216
Provision for income-tax		91
Net Profit		125
Balance brought forward from previous year		128
		253
Appropriations:		
Transfer to general reserve, 10% of net profit	13	
Proposed equity dividend @25%	25	
Provision for corporate dividend tax	4	42
Balance Carried to Balance Sheet		211

NOTES ON BALANCE SHEET AND PROFIT AND LOSS ACCOUNT

1. **Accounting Policies**: The accounts have been prepared primarily on historical cost concept. The significant accounting policies followed by the company are as follows:–
   (*a*) *Fixed Assets* : Fixed assets are shown at cost *less* depreciation. Cost comprises the purchase price and other attributable expenses.

The cost of leasehold premises includes the cost of refurbishment to the extent of Rs. 78,000.

(*b*) *Depreciation*: Depreciation on equipment, fixtures and fittings has been provided on written down value basis at 15% per annum. Leasehold premises and improvements are being amortised over the lease period.

(*c*) *Valuation of Inventories*: Inventories are valued at the lower of historical cost or net realisable value.

2. **Other Matters**: Bright Ltd. has been sued for supplying defective materials which have been written off as valueless. It is hoped that Bright Ltd. will agree for a settlement at Rs. 50,000; but being a contingent gain, it has not been recognised in the accounts.

Working Notes:

		Rs. in '000
(*i*) *Calculation of manufacturing expenses* :		
Opening stock	59	
Opening work-in-progress	210	
		269
Purchases of materials, Rs. (1,218-38) thousand		1,180
Purchase of land as stock		73
Wages		111
Sub-contractors' cost, Rs. (894–40) thousand		854
		2,487
Less : Closing stock	142	
Closing work-in-progress	140	282
		2,205
(*ii*) *Calculation of 'Other expenses'*		
Administration expenses		147
Office salaries		18
Directors' salaries		39
Provision for doubtful debts		
Specific doubtful debts	35	
Others : 2% of Rs. (735–35) thousand	14	49
Audit fee		20
Bonus as per working note (*iii*)		24
		297
(*iii*) *Calculation of bonus* :		
Sales		2,760
Less : Manufacturing expenses	2,205	
Other expenses, excluding bonus	273	
Depreciation	20	
Interest	22	2,520
Profit before tax		240
Bonus @ 10%		24
(*iv*) *Gross block* :		
Equipment, fixtures and fittings		264
Leasehold premises, Rs. (42 + 40 + 38) thousand		120
		384
(*v*) *Depreciation* :		
On equipment, fixtures and fittings :		
Accumulated depreciation as on 1.4.2000	164	
For current year, 15% of Rs. (264–164) thousand	15	179
Amount of leasehold premises, written off,		
1/12 × ½ × Rs. 120 thousand		5
		184

		Rs. in '000
(vi) *Current liabilities* :		
Sundry creditors		463
Bank overdraft		105
Outstanding audit fee		20
		588
(vii) *Calculation of provision for taxation* :		
Profit as per profit and loss account		216
Add back : Provision for doubtful debts	49	
Leasehold premises, written off	5	
Depreciation on equipment, fixtures and fittings	15	69
		285
Less : Depreciation under the Income-tax Act		25
		260
Provision for income-tax @ 35%		91
(viii) *Provisions* :		
Provision for income tax		91
Provision for corporate dividend tax		4
Proposed equity dividend		25
Provision for bonus		24
		144

Illustration 22:

The following information has been extracted from the books of account of Jay Ltd. as at 31st March, 2010:—

	Dr. (Rs. '000)	Cr. (Rs. '000)
Administration expenses	248	
Cash at bank and on hand	114	
Cash received on sale of fittings		5
Long-term loan		35
Interest on long-term loan	7	
Investments	100	
Income from investments		15
Depreciation on fixtures, fittings, tools and equipment as on 1st April, 2009		130
Distribution costs	51	
Factory closure costs	30	
Fixtures, fittings, tools and equipment, at cost	340	
Profit and loss account at 1st April, 2009		40
Purchase of equipment	60	
Purchases of goods for resale	855	
Sales (net of excise duty)		1,500
Share capital (50,000 shares of Rs. 10 each, fully paid)		500
Stock at 1st April, 2009	70	
Trade creditors		40
Trade debtors	390	
	2,265	2,265

The following additional information is provided to you :–

(*i*) The stocks at 31st March, 2010 (valued at the lower of cost or net realisable value) was estimated to be worth Rs. 1,00,000.

(*ii*) Fixtures, fittings, tools and equipment all related to administration. Depreciation is charged @ 20% per annum on cost. A full year's depreciation is charged in the year of acquisition, but no depreciation is charged in the year of disposal.

(*iii*) During the year to 31st March, 2010, the company purchased Rs. 60,000 of equipment. It also sold some fittings (which had originally cost Rs. 30.000) for Rs. 5,000 and for which depreciation of Rs. 15,000 had been set aside.

(*iv*) Make a provision for income - tax @ 40%. Factory closure cost is to be presured as an allowable expenditure for income tax purposes. Assume depreciation for the year under the Income-tax Act comes to Rs. 84,000.

(*v*) The company transfers Rs. 15,000 to general reserve and proposes to pay a dividend @ 20%. A provision for corporate dividend tax @ 15% is also mode.

Prepare Jay Ltd.'s profit and loss Account for the year ended 31st March, 2010 and a Balance Sheet as at that date in accordance with the Companies Act, 1956 in the vertical form along with the Notes on Accounts containing only the significant accounting policies. Details of the schedules are not required.

Solution :

Balance Sheet as at 31st March, 2010

	(Rs. in thousands)	*(Rs. in thousands)*
I. SOURCES OF FUNDS		
(1) Shareholders' funds:		
(*a*) Capital	500	
(*b*) Reserves and surplus	87	
TOTAL		587
(2) Loan funds:		
(*a*) Secured loans	35	
(*b*) Unsecured loans	—	35
TOTAL		622
II. APPLICATION OF FUNDS		
(1) Fixed assets:		
(*a*) Gross block	370	
(*b*) Less: Depreciation	189	
(*c*) Net block	181	
(*d*) Capital work in progress	—	181
(2) Investments		100
(3) Current assets, loans and advances:		
(*a*) Inventories	100	
(*b*) Sundry debtors	390	
(*c*) Cash and bank balances	114	
(*d*) Other current assets	—	
(*e*) Loans and advances	—	
	604	
Less: Current liabilities and provisions :		
(*a*) Current Liabilities	40	
(*b*) Provisions	223	
	263	
Net current assets		341
(4) Miscellaneous expenditure (to the extent not written off or adjusted)		—
TOTAL		622
Contingent liabilities		Nil

Profit and Loss Account
for the year ended 31st March, 2010

	(Rs. in thousand)	(Rs. in thousands)
INCOME		
Sales (net of excise duty)		1,500
Increase in stock		30
Income from investments		15
		1,545
EXPENDITURE		
Purchases of goods for resale	855	
Administration expenses	248	
Distribution costs	51	
Loss on sale of fittings	10	
Depreciation	74	
Interest on long term loan	7	1,245
Profit before Extraordinary Item		300
Factory closure costs		30
Profit before Taxation		270
Provision for income-tax @40%		108
Net Profit		162
Balance brought forward from previous year		40
Profit Available for Appropriations		202
Appropriations :		
Transfer to general reserve	15	
Proposed dividend @ 20%	100	
Provision for corporate dividend tax @ 15%	15	130
Balance Carried to Balance Sheet		72

NOTES ON ACCOUNTS

Significant Accounting Policies :

(*i*) *Basis of preparation of financial statements* : The financial statements have been prepared on the basis of historical cost concept in accordance with the generally accepted accounting principles and the provisions of the Companies Act, 1956.

(*ii*) *Valuation of Inventories* : Inventories are valued at the lower of historical cost or the net realisable value.

(*iii*) *Valuation of Investments* : Investments are valued at lower of cost or net realisable value.

(*iv*) *Depreciation* : Depreciation on fixed assets is provided using the straight-line method, based on the period of five years. Depreciation on additions is provided for the full year but no depreciation is provided on the assets sold in the year of their disposal.

Working Notes

	Rs. in thousands	Rs. in thousands
(*i*) Fixtures, fittings, tools and equipment :		
Gross block as on 1.4.2009	340	
Additions during the year	60	
	400	
Deductions during the year	30	
Gross block as on 31.3.2010		370
Depreciation provision as on 1.4.2009	130	
Depreciation for the year @ 20%	74	
	204	
Deductions during the year	15	
Depreciation provision as on 31.3.2010		189
Net block		181

		Rs. in thousands	Rs. in thousands
(ii)	Calculation of provision for income-tax		
	Profit as per profit and loss account		270
	Add back : Loss on sale of fittings	10	
	Depreciation	74	84
			354
	Less: Depreciation under the Income-tax Act		84
			270
	Provisions for income tax @ 40%		108
(iii)	Provisions :		
	Provision for income tax		108
	Provision for corporate dividend tax		15
	Proposed dividend		100
			223

4. DIRECTORS' REPORT, ETC.

Previously, it was the practice with most Indian companies to send to the shareholders a copy of the balance sheet and the profit and loss account accompanied by only the briefest possible report from the directors. Apart from matters dealing with the disposal of profits, i.e., recommendations regarding transfer to reserves and dividends, it was not unusual to come across a report which described the performance as "satisfactory considering the circumstances" and gave no other information. This is clearly unsatisfactory as the shareholders are entitled to get all information which can be safely given to them without prejudice to the company's future operations. It is the duty of the directors to describe the conditions prevailing in the industry generally from various points of view—financial, commercial, labour, and taxation—and then to point out the various difficulties which the company encountered during the year and the advantages which the company enjoyed. The Report should also deal with significant events that have occurred after the close of the financial year for which accounts have been presented, e.g., the effect of new taxes. Also, the Report is the place where likely future developments can be mentioned. The future benefits of a contract already entered into, for instance, cannot be entered in final statements of accounts—they can only be stated in the Directors' Report. Also events after the date of the balance sheet have to find a mention in the Directors' Report.

Suitable statistical information regarding sales, profits, wages and dividends accompanied by suitable graphs (which should be designed with care lest they should give a false impression) should be given. Section 217 of the Companies Act, 1956 makes it compulsory for the balance sheet laid before a company in general meeting to be accompanied by a report by the Board of Directors. The report must deal with the following :—

(*a*) The state of the company's affairs;

(*b*) The amounts, if any, which the Board proposes to carry to any reserves in such balance sheet;

(*c*) The amount, if any, which the Board recommends, should be paid by way of dividend;

(*d*) Material changes and commitments, if any, affecting the financial position of the company which have occurred between the end of the financial year of the company to which the balance sheet relates and the date of the report.

(*e*) the conservation of energy, technology absorption, foreign exchange earnings and outgo, in such manner as may be prescribed. Refer Companies (Disclosure of Particulars in the Report of Board of Directors) Rules, 1988.

Further, the Board's report should deal with the following for proper appreciation of the state of the company's affairs (unless the disclosures will, in the opinion of the Board, harm the company's business) :—

(*a*) Changes which have occurred during the financial year in the nature of the company's business;

(*b*) Similar changes in the company's subsidiaries or in the nature of the business carried on by them; and

(*c*) Changes in the classes of business in which the company has an interest.

(*d*) The name of every employee who (*i*) if employed throughout the year received a total remuneration of Rs. 12,00,000 (w.e.f. 25.10.2000) or more in the year; or (*ii*) if employed for part of the financial year and was in receipt of remuneration for any part of that year at a rate which in the aggregate was not less than Rs. 1,00,000 per month (w.e.f. 25.10.2000) or (*iii*) if employed throughout the financial year or part thereof received remuneration which, in the aggregate, or as the case may be, at a rate which, in the aggregate, exceeded that drawn by the managing director or whole-time director or manager and held by himself or along with his spouse and dependent children not less than 2% of the equity shares of the company. The term remuneration has the same meaning as in the *Explanation* to Sec. 198. It has to be disclosed whether any such employee is a relative of any director or manager of the company; the name of such director must also be stated. Companies normally disclose the job assigned to the employees concerned and also their qualification.

According to section 217(2AA), the Board's report is also to include a Directors' Responsibility Statement, indicating therein—

(*i*) that in the preparation of the annual accounts, the applicable accounting standards have been followed along with proper explanation relating to material departures;

(*ii*) that the directors have selected such accounting policies and applied them consistently and made judgements and estimates that are reasonable and pendent so as to give a true and fair view of the state of affairs of the company at the end of the financial year and of the profit or loss of the company for that period;

(*iii*) That the directors have taken proper and sufficient care for the maintenance of adequate accounting records in accordance with the provisions of the Companies Act for safeguarding the assets of the company and for preventing and detecting fraud and other irregulanties;

(*iv*) that the directors have prepared the annual accounts on a going concern basis.

According to section 217(2B), the Board's report will also specify the reasons for the failure, if any, to complete the buy-back within the specified in sub-section (4) of section 77A.

In addition to the above, sub-section (3) of section 217 declares :

"The Board shall also be bound to give the fullest information and explanations in its report aforesaid, or in cases falling under the proviso to section 222 in an addendum to that report, on every reservation, qualification or adverse remark contained in the auditors report".

The proviso to section 222 enables the Board to give information (as is allowed to be given in a statement) annexed to the accounts in the Board's report itself. To that extent, the report will be considered as annexed to the accounts and will have to be audited.

The report of the directors should be signed by the chairman if he is so authorised but, it he is not, the report has to be signed by the company's manager or secretary, if any, and by not less than two directors of the company, one of whom shall be the managing director where there is one.

Auditors' Report :

A company must get its accounts audited by qualified auditors. Sections 224 to 233 of the Companies Act deal with appointment, powers and duties of the auditors. The auditors have to report on the accounts, balance sheet and the profit and loss account examined by them. The report is addressed to the shareholders and it is the duty of the directors to attach the report to the balance sheet so that every shareholder gets a copy of the report.

The report is called clean or clear if it is unqualified. But if the report contains some adverse remarks or remarks to call the attention of the shareholders to certain facts, it is called a qualified report. As seen above, the directors must themselves comment on every reservation, qualification and adverse remarks contained in the report.

Below is given a specimen of an unqualified report :

"We have audited the attached Balance Sheet of *A, B, C,* Ltd. as on 31st March, 2010, and also the annexed Profit and Loss Account of the company for the year ended on that date and report that:

(1) We have obtained all the information and explanations which to the best of our knowledge and belief were necessary for the purpose of our audit;

(2) In our opinion, proper books of account as required by law have been kept by the company so far as it appears from our examination of the books (and according to the reports of the Branch Auditors* where such audit has not been done by us);

(3) The Balance Sheet and Profit and Loss Account dealt with by the report are in agreement with the books of account (and audited returns from branches*);

(4) The reports of the Branch Auditors have been forwarded to us and have been considered in preparing our report*;

(5) In our opinion and to the best of our information and according to the explanations given to us, the Accounts (together with notes thereon and documents annexed thereto) give the information required by the Companies Act, 1956 in the manner so required and give a true and fair view :

(*a*) in the case of the Balance Sheet, of the state of the affairs of the company as at 31st **March, 2010 and**

(*b*) in the case of the Profit and Loss Account, of the profit (or loss) for the year ended on that date. ....

Chartered Accountants."

In addition, now auditors have to give their remarks on a number of points contained in the Manufacturing and Other Companies (Auditor's Report) Order, 1975 issued under section 227 (4A) of the Companies Act. Students are advised to consult a book on Auditing if they are interested in details.

Filing, etc., of the Balance Sheet with the Registrar:

Every balance sheet and every profit and loss account of a non-banking company must be signed by its manager or secretary, if any, and by not less than two directors one of whom shall be a managing director, if there is one. If only one director is in India for the time being, his signatures alone together with a statement explaining why he alone is signing will be enough. Before the Balance Sheet and Profit and Loss Account are signed, they must be approved by the Board of Directors.

The annual accounts (meaning the balance sheet, the profit and loss account, the auditor's report and every other document annexed or attached to the Balance Sheet) have to be laid before the company in general meeting. The following classes of persons must be sent a copy of the annual accounts together with the auditor's report at least 21 days before the meeting.

(*a*) Members, unless they are not entitled to have a notice of the general meeting;

(*b*) Debentureholders, excluding holders of bearer debentures and excluding those who are not entitled to have a notice of the meeting;

(*c*) Trustees for debentureholders; and

(*d*) Persons who are entitled to have a notice of general meetings.

Members or debentureholders of the company can obtain, without charge, a copy of the annual accounts by making a demand for them. Those who have deposited moneys with the company may obtain a copy of the annual accounts on payment of one rupee.

It is an offence to issue, circulate or publish a copy of a balance sheet or profit or loss account which is not signed as required by the Act and which is not accompanied by documents that are required to be annexed or attached.

After the accounts have been laid before the company in general meeting and have been considered by it, copies of the accounts have to be filed with the Registrar. Sub-sections (1) and (2) of Section 220, dealing with the matter, read as follows :

"(1) After the balance sheet and the profit and loss account have been laid before a company at an annual general meeting as aforesaid, these shall be filed with the Registrar within thirty days from the date on which the balance sheet and the profit and loss account were so laid-

(a) three copies of the balance sheet and the profit and loss account, signed by the managing director, manager or secretary of the company, or if there be none of these, by a director of the company, together with three copies of all documents which are required by this Act, to be annexed or attached to such balance sheet or profit and loss account;

Provided that in the case of a private company copies of the balance sheet and copies of the profit and loss account shall be filed with the Registrar separately.

Provided further that—

(i) in the case of a private company which is not a subsidiary of a public company, or

(ii) in the case of a private company of which the entire paid-up share capital is held by one or more bodies incorporated outside India or

(iii) in the case of a company which becomes a public company by virtue of section 43A, if the Central Government directs that it is not in the public interest that any person other than a member of the company shall be entitled to inspect, or obtain copies of the profit and loss account of the company, no person other than a member of the company concerned shall be entitled to inspect or obtain copies of, the profit and loss account of that company under Section 610.

(2) If the annual general meeting of a company before which a balance sheet is laid as aforesaid does not adopt the balance sheet, a statement of that fact and of the reasons therefore shall be annexed to the balance sheet and to the copies thereof required to be filed with the Registrar".

Other Annual Returns. It should be remembered that in addition to copies of the balance sheet and the profit and loss account, a company having share capital has to submit (under Section 159), within 60 days of the annual general meeting, to the Registrar a return (in the form set out in Part II of Schedule V or as near thereto as circumstances permit) regarding :-

(*a*) its registered office,

(*b*) the register of its members,

(*c*) the register of its debentureholders,

(*d*) its shares and debentures,

(*e*) its indebtedness,

(*f*) its members and debentureholders, past and present, and

(*g*) directors, managing directors, managers and secretaries, past and present.

If any of the five immediately preceding returns has given as at the date of the annual general meeting with reference to which it was submitted, the full particulars required as to past and present members and the shares held and transferred by them, the return in question may contain only such of the particulars as relate to persons ceasing to be or becoming members since that date and to shares transferred since that date or to changes as compared with that date in the number of shares held by a member.

In case the company has converted its shares into stock and has given notice of conversion to the Registrar, the return should state the amount of stock held by each member instead of the number of shares.

If a company does not have share capital, the annual return should contain the following particulars:—

(*a*) the address of the registered office of the company;

(*aa*) the names of members and the respective dates on which they became members and the names of persons who ceased to be members since the date of the annual general meeting of the immediately preceding year, and the dates on which they so ceased; and

(*b*) all such particulars with respect to the persons, who, at the date of the return, were the directors of the company, its managing agents, its manager and its secretary as are set out in Section 303.

The return must have a statement annexed thereto containing particulars of the total amount of the indebtedness of the company in respect of all charges required to be registered with the Registrar.

The copy of the annual return filed with the Registrar has to be signed both by a director and by the manager or secretary of the company, or where there is none of these, by two directors of the company, one of them being the managing director where there is one. Along with the return, a certificate signed by both the signatories of the return has to be sent. The certificate has to state:

(*a*) that the return states the facts as they stood on the day of the annual general meeting correctly and completely, (*aa*) that since the date of the last annual return the transfer of all shares and debentures and the issue of all further certificates of shares and debentures have been appropriately recorded in the books maintained for the purpose; and (*b*) in the case of a private company also (i) that the company has not, since the date of the previous annual general meeting (or in the case of a first return since the date of the incorporation) issued any invitation to the public to subscribe for any shares or debentures of the company, (*ii*) that where the annual return discloses the fact that the number of members of the company exceeds fifty, the excess consists wholly of persons who are not to be included in reckoning the number of fifty [under sub-clause (*b*) of clause (*iii*) of sub-section (1) of Section 3.] The above are the provisions contained in Sections 159, 160 and 161 of the Companies Act, 1956.

The student is advised to carefully go through the published accounts of a company and note the information that is required to be given compulsorily under law and that given voluntarily by the management as well as the manner in which it is given in both cases, particularly the schedules that are prepared to give details whereof only a summarised figure is stated in the balance sheet or the profit and loss account.

EXERCISE XIX

Practical

1. The Alfa manufacturing company limited was registered with a nominal capital of Rs. 60,00,000 in Equity Shares of Rs. 10 each. The following is the list of balances extracted from its books on 31st March, 2010:

	Rs.
Calls-in-arrear	75,000
Premises	30,00,000
Plant and Machinery	33,00,000
Interim Dividend paid on 1st November, 2009	3,92,500
Corproate Dividend Tax	39,250
Stock, 1st April, 2009	7,50,000
Fixtures	72,000
Sundry Debtors	8,70,000
Goodwill	2,50,000
Cash in hand	7,500
Cash at Bank	3,99,000
Purchases	18,50,000
Preliminary Expenses	50,000
Wages	8,48,650
General Expenses	68,350
Freight and Carriage	1,31,150
Salaries	1,45,000
Directors' Fees	57,250
Bad debts	21,100
Debenture Interest paid	1,80,000
Share Capital	40,00,000
12% Debentures	30,00,000
Profit and Loss Account (Credit Balance)	3,01,750
Bills Payable	3,70,000
Sundry Creditors	4,00,000
Sales	41,50,000
General Reserve	2,50,000
Bad debts Provision 1st April, 2009	35,000

Prepare Trading and Profit and Loss Account and Balance Sheet in proper form after making the following adjustments:

(*i*) Depreciate Plant and Machinery by 15%.

(*ii*) Write off Rs. 5,000 from Preliminary Expenses.

(*iii*) Provide half year's debenture interest due.
(*iv*) Leave Bad and Doubtful Debts Provision at 5% on Sundry Debtors.
(*v*) Provide for Income Tax @ 35%.
(vi) Stock on 31st March, 2010 was Rs. 9,50,000.

(*Adapted B.Com., Delhi*)
(*Gross Profit Rs. 15,20,200; Net Profit Rs. 2,34,000; P. & L. App. A/c bal. Rs. 1,04,000; Balance Sheet Total Rs. 83,55,000*)

2. The following is the Trial Balance of L.N. Manufacturing Co. Ltd. as at 31st March, 2010:

	Dr.	*Cr.*
Stock 1st April, 2009	7,50,000	—
Sales	—	35,00,000
Purchases	24,50,000	—
Productive Wages	5,00,000	—
Discounts	70,000	50,000
Salaries	75,000	—
Rent	49,500	—
General Expenses including Insurance	1,70,500	—
Profit and Loss Account, 1st April, 2009	—	1,63,800
Dividends paid	90,000	—
Corporate Dividend Tax @ 15%	13,500	—
Capital-1,00,000 shares of Rs. 10 each	—	10,00,000
Sundry Debtors and Creditors	3,75,000	1,75,000
Plant and Machinery	2,90,000	—
Cash in hand and at Bank	1,62,000	—
General Reserve	—	1,55,000
Bad debts	48,300	—

You are required to prepare Trading Account, and Profit and Loss Account for the year ended 31st March, 2010 and the Balance Sheet at that date. You are also to make provision in respect of the following:

(*a*) Stock on 31st March, 2010 : Rs. 8,20,000.
(*b*) Depreciate Machinery @ 15% per annum.
(*c*) Provide 5% discount on debtors.
(*d*) Allow 2.5% discount on creditors.
(*e*) Provide Managing Director's Commission @ 5% on the net profits before deducting his commission.
(*f*) One month's rent @ Rs. 54,000 per annum was due on 31st March, 2010.
(*g*) Six months Insurance was unexpired at Rs. 7,500 per annum.
(*h*) Make a provision for Income Tax @ 35%.

(*Adapted from B.Com., Delhi*)
(*Gross Profit Rs. 6,20,000; Net Profit Rs. 1,22,311; Managing Director's remuneration Rs. 9,904; P. & L. App. A/c balance Rs. 1,82,611; Balance Sheet Total Rs. 15,88,500*)

3. The following is the Trial Balance of A.B.C. Company Ltd., as on 31st March, 2010. Prepare Trading and Profit and Loss Account in the form prescribed under the Companies Act, 1956. Give the Auditor's Certificate at the foot of the Balance Sheet.

	Dr. *Rs.*	*Cr.* *Rs.*
Authorised Capital—		
50,000 shares at Rs. 10 per share		5,00,000

Subscribed Capital— 10,000 shares at Rs. 10 per share		1,00,000
Calls in Arrear	6,400	
Land	10,000	
Buildings	25,000	
Plant & Machinery	15,000	
Furniture & Fixture	3,200	
Carriage Inwards	2,300	
Wages	21,400	
Salaries	4,600	
Bad Debts Provision, 1st April, 2009		1,400
Sales		80,000
Sales Returns	1,700	
Bank Charges	100	
Coal, Gas & Water	700	
Rates & Taxes	800	
Purchases	50,000	
Purchases Returns		3,400
Bills Receivable	1,200	
General Expenses	1,900	
Sundry Debtors	42,800	
Sundry Creditors		13,200
Stock, 1st April, 2009	25,000	
Fire Insurance	400	
Cash at Bank	13,000	
Cash in hand	2,500	
Securities Premium		6,000
General Reserve		24,000
	2,28,000	2,28,000

Charge depreciation on Buildings @ 5%; on Plant and Machinery @ 15% and Furniture and Fixture @ 10%. Make a provision of 5% on Sundry Debtors for Bad Debts. Carry forward the following unexpired amounts :

	Rs.
Fire Insurance	120
Provide for the following outstanding liabilities :	
Wages	3,200
Salaries	500
Rates & Taxes	200

The value of Stock as on 31st March, 2010, was Rs. 30,000.

(*Adapted B.Com., Delhi*)

(*Gross Profit Rs. 9,100; Net Loss, Rs. 3,840; Total of Balance Sheet, Rs. 1,36,860*)

4. The following balances appeared in the books of Bright Ltd. as on 31st March, 2010:

	Debit Rs.	*Credit Rs.*
Equity shares of Rs. 10 each, fully paid up		6,00,000
General reserve		2,30,000
Unclaimed dividend		526
Trade creditors		42,858
Buildings (*at cost*)	2,50,000	
Purchases	5,00,903	
Sales		10,83,947
Manufacturing expenses	3,50,000	
Establishment charges	26,814	

	Debit Rs.	Credit Rs.
General charges	31,078	
Machinery (*at cost*)	2,30,000	
Furniture (*at cost*)	35,000	
Opening stock	1,72,058	
Book debts	1,02,380	
Investments	2,88,950	
Provision for depreciation on fixed assets		91,000
Advance payment of income-tax	50,000	
Cash at bank	72,240	
Directors' fees	1,800	
Interest on investments		8,544
Profit and loss account (1.4.2009)		16,848
Staff provident fund		37,500
	21,11,223	21,11,223

From the abovementioned balances and the following information prepare the company's balance sheet as on 31st March, 2010 and its profit and loss account for the year ended on that date:

(*i*) The stock on 31st March, 2010 was valued at Rs. 1,48,680.

(*ii*) Provide Rs. 29,000 for depreciation of fixed assets and Rs. 8,000 for managing director's remuneration.

(*iii*) Interest accrued on investments amounted to Rs. 2,750.

(*iv*) Make a provision of Rs. 50,000 for income-tax.

(*v*) The directors propose a dividend @ 8% after transfer of Rs. 25,000 to general reserve. Also provide for dividend tax @ 15% of the proposed dividend.

[*C.S. (Inter.) Dec., 1998 Modified*]

[*Gross Profit Rs. 2,09,666; Net profit Rs. 74,268; Balance of profit and loss appropriation account Rs, 10,916; Total of balance sheet Rs. 10,60,000*]

5. The Auto Parts Manufacturing Co. Ltd. was registered will an authorised share capital of Rs. 10,00,000 divided into shares of Rs. 10 each, of which 40,000 equity shares had been issued and fully paid-up.

The following is the trial balance extracted on 31st March, 2010:—

	Debit Rs.	Credit Rs.
Stock (1st April, 2009)	1,86,420	
Purchase and Sales	7.18.210	11.69.900
Returns	12,680	9,850
Manufacturing Wages	1,09,740	—
Sundry Manufacturing Expenses	19,240	—
Carriage Inwards	4,910	—
18% Bank Loan (Secured)	—	50,000
Interest on Bank Loan	4,500	—
Office Salaries and Expenses	17,870	—
Audit Fees	8,600	—
Director's Remuneration	26,250	—
Preliminary Expenses	6,000	—
Freehold Premises	1,64,210	—
Plant and Machinery	1,28,400	—
Furniture	5,000	—
Loose Tools	12,500	—
Debtors and Creditors	1,05,400	62,220
Cash in hand	19,530	—
Cash at Bank	96,860	—

	Debit Rs.	Credit Rs.
Advance Payment of Tax	84,290	—
Profit and Loss Account on 1st April, 2009	—	38,640
Equity Share Capital	—	4,00,000
	17,30,610	17,30,610

You are required to prepare Profit & Loss Account for the year ended 31st March, 2010 and a Balance Sheet as at that date after taking into consideration the following adjustments:

(*i*) On 31st March, 2010, outstanding Manufacturing wages and outstanding office salaries stood at Rs. 1,890 and Rs. 1,200 respectively. On the same date, stock was valued at Rs. 1,60,520 and loose tools at Rs. 10,000.

(*ii*) Provide for interest on bank loan for 6 months.

(*iii*) Depreciation on plant and machinery is to be provided @ 15% while on office furniture it is to be @ 10%.

(*iv*) Write off one-third of balance of preliminary expenses.

(*v*) Make a provision for income tax @ 35% of book profits.

(*vi*) The directors recommended a maiden (first) dividend @ 15% for the year ending 31st March, 1999 after a transfer of 5% of net profits to general reserve. Also make a provision for tax on distributed profits @15% of the proposed dividend.

[*B.Com. (Hons.) Delhi, 1991 Modified*]

[*Gross profit Rs. 2,87,180; Net profit Rs. 1,30,000; Balance of profit and loss appropriation account Rs, 93,140; Total of balance sheet Rs. 7,58,450*]

6. The following balances have been extracted from the books of account of Johri Co. Ltd. as on 31st March, 2010:

Credit Balance	*Rs.*	*Debit Balance*	*Rs.*
Equity Share Capital	40,00,000	Premises	30,72,000
12% Debentures	30,00,000	Plant	33,00,000
Profit and Loss Account, (1st April, 2009)	3,05,677	Furniture	2,00,000
		Stock (1st April, 2009)	7,50,000
Bills Payable	3,70,000	Debtors	8,70,000
Creditors	4,00,000	Goodwill	50,000
Sales	41,50,000	Cash at Bank	14,06,500
General Reserve	12,50,000	Cash in Arrier	75,000
Provision for Bad Debts		Interim Dividend Paid	3,92,500
(1st April, 2009)	35,000	Tax on Distributed Profits Paid	43,175
		Purchases	18,50,000
		Preliminiary Expenses	50,000
		Wages	9,79,800
		Salaries	2,02,250
		Debenture Interest Paid	1,80,000
		Bad Debts	21,100
		General Expenses	68,350
	1,35,10,675		1,35,10,675

Additional information:

(*a*) Depreciate plant by 15% and furniture by 10%.

(*b*) Write off preliminary expenses to the extent of Rs. 5,000.

(*c*) Half year's interest on debentures in due.

(*d*) Create a provision for bad debts @ 5% on debtors.

(*e*) Provide for income tax @ 38.5% on book profits.

(*f*) Stock on 31st March, 2009 was valued at Rs. 10,10,000.

(*g*) A claim of Rs. 25,000 for workmen's compensation is being disputed by the company.

(*h*) Issued and subscribed share capital consists of 4,00,000 equity shares of Rs. 10 each, fully called up.

Prepare Profit and Loss Account for the year ended 31st March, 2010 and Balance Sheet as at that date.

[*B.Com. (Hons.) Delhi, 1993 Modified*]

[*Gross profit Rs. 15,80,200; Net profit Rs. 2,46,000; Balance of profit and loss appropriation account Rs, 1,16,000; Total of balance sheet Rs. 93,95,000*]

Hints: Book profit before income tax = Rs. (15,80,200 – 2,02,250 – 3,60,000 – 29,600 – 5,15,000 – 5,000) = Rs. 4,00,000.

Provision for income tax @ 38.5% = $\frac{38.5}{100}$ × Rs. 4,00,000 = Rs. 1,54,000.

7. The following is the trial balance of Ema Ltd. as on 31st March, 2010:

Debit	*Rs.*	*Credit*	*Rs.*
Advance tax for 2009-2010	2,15,000	Shares forfeiture a/c	6,000
Interim dividend	50,000	Preference share capital	2,00,000
Dividend tax paid	7,500	Equity share capital	5,00,000
Capital redemption a/c	2,20,000	General reserve	2,00,000
Discount on issue of debenture a/c	6,000	Securities premium a/c	20,000
Share reissue a/c	2,000	Profit & loss a/c	1,52,500
Fixed assets	10,00,000	Operating profit for 2009-2010 (before tax)	6,02,000
Investments	3,00,000	13% debentures	1,00,000
Current assets	1,90,000	Current liabilities	2,10,000
	19,90,500		19,90,500

The following additional information is provided to you.

(*i*) On 31st March, 2010 the issued share capital consists of 50,000 equity shares of Rs. 10 each fully paid up. Share reissue account represents discount allowed at the time of reissue of 1,000 forfeited equity shares which were earlier forfeited for the non-payment of the final call.

(*ii*) Subsequent to the reissue of equity shares as noted above, the preference share capital was redeemed out of profits otherwise available for dividend; the directors deciding to pay a premium of 10% to the preference shareholders. The company also issued bonus shares to equity shareholders in the ratio of 2 : 5 out of capital redemption reserve account. Both the redemption of preference shares and the issue of bonus shares have not been recorded in the books except that the amount paid to the preference shareholders has been debited to the capital redemption account.

(*iii*) Provision for tax is required at 35%.

(*iv*) The Board of Directors has proposed a final dividend of 20% on equity shares after appropriating profits as per law. Provision for corporate dividend tax @ 15% of the proposed dividend is also made.

(*v*) The board of Directors has decided to record the upward revaluation of fixed assets by 25%.

(*vi*) Rs. 2,000, out of discount on issue of debentures account, is yet to be written off against the profit for the current year.

You are required to prepare the profit and loss account of the company for the year ended 31st

March, 2010 and its balance sheet as on that date after passing journal entries for the necessary adjustments.

[C.S. (Inter.) June, 1997 Modified]

[Net Profit Rs. 3,90,000; Profit and Loss Appropriation Account balance Rs. 2,86,600; Total of Balance Sheet Rs. 19,59,000]

8. The undermentioned balances appeared in the books of the Pioneer Flour Mills Co. Ltd. as at 31st March, 2010:—

	Rs.		*Rs.*
Share Capital (Authorised and Issued), 6,00,000 shares of Rs. 10 each	60,00,000	Furniture	2,00,000
		Stocks	17,20,580
		Book Debts	17,83,800
General Reserve	25,00,000	Investments	28,89,500
Unclaimed Dividends	65,260	Cash at Bank	19,22,400
Trade Creditors	10,78,580	Directors' fees	18,000
Buildings	10,00,000	Interim Dividend	6,00,000
Purchases	50,09,030	Interest	85,440
Sales	1,18,39,470	Advance Payment of Income Tax	8,00,000
Manufacturing Expenses	35,90,000	Profit & Loss A/c 1st Apr., 2009 (Cr.)	2,58,480
Establishment	2,68,140	Staff Provident Fund	3,75,000
General Charges	3,10,780	Corporate Dividend Tax	60,000
Plant and Machinery	20,00,000		

From these balances and the following information prepare the company's Balance Sheet as at 31st March, 2010 and its Profit and Loss Account for the year ended on that date :-

(*a*) The stocks of wheat and flour on 31st March, 2010 were valued at Rs. 14,86,800.

(*b*) Depreciation is to be provided on the written down values of fixed assets at the following rates :

Buildings 5%;
Plant and Machinery 15%;
Furniture 10%.

(*c*) Interest accrued on investment amounted to Rs. 27,500.

(*d*) A claim of Rs. 25,000 for workmen's compensation is being disputed by the company.

(*e*) Provide Rs. 15,000 for the company's contribution to the Staff Provident Fund.

(*f*) Establishment includes Rs. 60,000 paid to the Manager who is entitled to remuneration @ 5% of profit before such remuneration.

(*g*) Make a Provision for Income Tax @ 35%.

(Gross Profit Rs. 30,06,660; Net Profit Rs. 13,57,067; Total of Balance Sheet Rs. 1,17,40,000)

Hints: Prepare trial balance first. Claim of Rs. 25,000 is a contingent liability.

9. The following balances appeared in the books of Ram Flour Mill Co. Ltd., as on 31st March, 2010:—

	Rs.	*Rs.*
Stock of Wheat	4,750	—
Stock of Flour	8,000	—
Wheat Purchases	2,02,500	—
Manufacturing Expenses	45,000	—
Flour Sales	—	2,79,500
Salaries and Wages	6,500	—
Establishment	2,850	—
Interest	—	250
Rent Received	—	400
Profit & Loss Account	—	7,950
Directors' Fees	100	—

	Rs.	Rs.
Dividend (for 1999-2000)	4,500	—
Corporate Dividend Tax	675	—
Land	6,000	—
Buildings	25,250	—
Plant & Machinery	25,250	—
Furniture	2,550	—
Motor Vehicles	2,550	—
Stores & Spare Parts	9,150	—
Advances	12,250	—
Book Debts	25,850	—
Investments	2,000	—
Share Capital	—	36,000
Pension Fund	—	11,500
Dividend Equalization Reserve	—	5,000
Taxation Provision	—	4,250
Unclaimed Dividends	—	450
Deposits	—	800
Trade Creditors	—	60,000
Cash in hand and at Bank	20,600	—
	4,06,375	4,06,375

From the above balances and following information, prepare the company's Balance Sheet as on 31st March, 2010 and the Profit and Loss Account for the year ended on that date.

(*a*) Stocks on 31st March, 2010 were :-
Wheat at cost Rs. 7,450; Flour at market rate Rs. 10,850.

(*b*) Outstanding Expenses : Manufacturing Expenses, Rs. 11,250, Salaries and Wages Rs. 600, Establishment Rs. 500.

(*c*) Provide Depreciation :-
Building @ 5% p.a.; Plant and Machinery @ 15% p.a.; Furniture @ 10% p.a.; Motor Vehicles 20 % p.a.

(*d*) Interest accrued on Government Securities Rs. 50.

(*e*) The Taxation Provision in the Trial Balance is after payment of taxes for assessment up to 31st March, 2009. The only liability for taxes is in respect of profits for 2009-2010 for which a provision of 35% of net profit is considered necessary.

(*f*) The directors propose a dividend of 20% after transfer of Rs. 5,000 to General Reserve. Provision for corporate dividend tax @ 15% is also to be made.

(*g*) The authorised capital consists of 6,000 equity shares of Rs. 10 each, of which 3,000 shares are issued and fully paid.

(Adapted from C.A. Final)

(Gross Profit Rs. 26,300; Net Profit, Rs. 6,912; P. & L. App. A/c balance Rs. 882; Total of Balance Sheet, Rs. 1,43,985.)

10. From the following particulars prepare (a) Spinning Account, (b) Weaving Account, (c) Trading Account of Shantipur Cotton Mills, Ltd., for the year ending 31st March, 2010 :—

	Spinning Dept. Rs.	*Weaving Dept.* Rs.
Cotton	8,26,160	..
Purchase of Yarns, etc.	..	41,060
Brokerage Charges, etc.	2,970	..
Freight & Carriage	11,870	7,630
Wages & Salaries	1,78,020	2,87,800
Coal	19,870	11,270

	Spinning Dept. Rs.	Weaving Dept. Rs.
Oil, Tallow, Waste, etc.	3,060	1,650
Gas, Electric Light & Water	2,650	1,280
Cords, Ropes, Roller Leather & Cloth	7,860	..
Skips, Bobbins & Skewers	2,080	1,140
Brushes, Starch & Binding	2,860	..
Strapping & Laces	1,210	960
Packing Paper & Twine	2,970	..
Rates, Taxes & Insurance	4,360	2,260
Mill Charges & Sundry Stores	2,060	1,970
Horse & Stable Expenses	1,870	1,120
Repairs to Buildings, Engines, Boilers, Gearing, etc.	12,870	4,780
Depreciation of Plant and Machinery	22,060	20,870
Sale of Yarns	68,160	..
Sales of Waste	26,320	1,360
Sale of Sundries	890	950
Shuttles, Pickers, Picking Bands, etc.	..	5,380
Reeds, Combs & Healds	..	3,090
Brushes & Sundries	..	1,050
Flour & Sizing Materials	..	15,940
Goods Purchased	..	86,750
Bleaching, Dyeing & Printing	..	2,84,870
Carriage	..	3,390
Packing	..	2,730
Sale of Bought Goods	..	94,270
Sales of Cloth :-		
Grey	..	6,17,280
White	..	16,09,160
Dyed	..	1,26,140
	1st April, 2009	31st March, 2010
Stocks of Cloth :-		
At Mills	4,07,850	4,07,530
At Warehouse	7,50,160	7,60,170
At Bleachers & Dyers	95,280	84,270

(Adapted C.A. Final)

(Cost of yarn, Rs. 10,09,430; Cost of Weaving, Rs. 14,16,370; Gross Profit, Rs. 6,51,320)

11. The following are the balances from the Ledger of Mount-View Hotel, Ltd., on 31st March, 2010:

	Rs.
Share Capital—Credit balance on 1st April, 2009	56,685
Preliminary Expenses	7,500
Freehold Premises	46,800
Furniture and Fittings	8,934
Glass and China	1,101
Linen	840
Cutlery and Plate	390
Rates, Taxes and Insurance	1,713
Salaries	2,400
Wages	4,305
Stocks on 1st April, 2009 :	
Wines, Rs. 1,239; Spirits, Rs. 378; Beer, Rs. 165	1,782
Minerals, Rs. 147; Cigars and Cigarettes, Rs. 114	261
Sundry Provisions and Stores, Rs. 183; Coal, Rs. 150	333

	Rs.
Purchases :	
Meat, Rs. 3,627; Fish and Poultry Rs. 3,960 ;	7,587
Sundry Provisions and Stores, Rs. 5,220	5,220
Wines, Rs. 1,881; Spirits, Rs. 2,190; Beer, Rs. 1,152	5,223
Minerals, Rs. 1,050; Cigars and Cigarettes, Rs. 240	1,290
Laundry	951
Coal and Gas	2,160
Electric Light	1,128
General Expenses	1,710
Sales :	
Wines, Rs. 5,870; Spirits, Rs. 6,335; Beer, Rs. 3,863	16,068
Minerals, Rs. 2,160; Cigars and Cigarettes, Rs. 390	2,550
Meals	23,829
Rooms	9,375
Fires in Bedrooms	582
Washing Charges	219
Repairs, Renewals, and Depreciation :—	
Premises, Rs. 348; Furniture and Fittings Rs. 660	1,008
Glass and China, Rs. 609; Linen, Rs. 390	999
Cutlery and Plate	207
Cash Book—Debit balances :	
In Bank	8,148
In Hand	219
Visitors Accounts unpaid	489
Sundry Creditors	3,390

Stocks on 31st March, 2010 were valued as follows :-
Wines, Rs. 1,197; Spirits, Rs. 333; Beer, 174;
Minerals, Rs. 357; Cigars and Cigarettes, Rs. 69;
Sundry Provisions and Stores, Rs. 141; Coal, Rs.99.

The manager is entitled to a commission of 5% of the net profits after charging his commission. The authorised share capital is 1,00,000 shares of Rs. 10 each of which 57,000 shares were issued, the whole of the amount being called up. The final call on 210 shares @ Rs. 1.50 per share was unpaid; the directors forfeited these shares at their meeting held on 15th March, 2010.

The tax liability is to be provided for @ 35% and the directors propose to declare a dividend at the rate of 10 per cent. Provision for corporate dividend tax @ 15% is also to be made. Prepare the Final Accounts for presentation to the shareholders.

(*Adapted from C.A. Final*)

(Commission Rs. 796; Net Profit after tax Rs. 10,348; Total of Balance Sheet, Rs. 76,791)

12. The Accountant of X Ltd. Merchants and Commission Agents, left on 31st March, 2010 leaving his books partially prepared. The balances still, to be dealt with, are as follows:

	Rs		Rs.
Furniture at cost, less depreciation	3,90,000	Sales ex-consignments not closed	3,25,000
Godowns (at cost)	13,00,000	General Reserve	2,60,000
Buildings (at cost)	11,05,000	Preference Shares of Rs. 100 each	13,00,000
Sundry Debtors	2,65,850	Equity Shares of Rs. 10 each,	
Debenture Interest	62,400	Rs. 7.50 called up	9,75,000
Income Tax assessed and		Sundry Consignors' balances	1,30,000
paid for 2008-2009	55,000	12% Debentures with a general charge	10,40,000
Bills Receivable	26,000	Provision for Income Tax for 2008-2009	54,000
Cash at Bank	4,00,000	Current Account balance of Subsidiaries	52,000
Cash in Hand	1,20,000	Trade Creditors	4,39,000
Discount on Issue of Debentures—		Commission on Sales ex-consignment	2,000

	Rs		Rs.
Balance on 1st April, 2009	13,000	Profit and Loss Appropriation Account, balance on 1st April, 2009	2,12,550
Preference Dividend for half year to 30th September, 2009	78,000	Trading Account for 2000-2001	6,36,150
Final Dividend for 2008-2009	97,500	Suspense Account	16,000
Corporate Dividend Tax Paid	17,550		
Bills paid against consignments not closed	3,90,000		
Charges paid against unsold consignments	10,400		
Stock—31st March, 2010	3,95,000		
Investment (at cost) in subsidiary companies	7,56,000		
Calls in Arrear @ Rs. 2,50 per share	10,000		
	54,91,700		54,91,700

You will have to provide : a Provision of Rs. 19,500 for Doubtful Debts, 10% Depreciation on Furniture and 5% on Godowns and Buildings; Rs. 6,500 to write off Discount on Issue of Debentures. Make a Provision for Income Tax @ 35%. You are further informed that :

(1) Bills Receivable for Rs. 9,750, maturing after 31st March, 2010 had been discounted.

(2) Stock includes a sum of Rs. 39,000 in respect of unsold goods in stores ex-sundry consignments, invoiced proforma at that figure.

(3) The directors recommend a dividend of 10% on equity shares. Assume the rate of corporate dividend tax to be 10%.

(4) Suspense Account represents the amount received for reissue of shares forfeited for non-payment of the call; all the shares involved were forfeited but only 320 were reissued.

[*Adapted from C.A.* (*Final*)]

Prepare Profit and Loss Account for the year ended 31st March, 2001 and Balance Sheet as on that date.

(*True Gross Profit Rs. 5,97,150; Net Profit Rs. 2,20,415; Proposed Equity Dividend Rs. 94,740; P. & L. Appr. A/c balance Rs. 48,901; Consignors' A/c Rs. 54,600; Shares Forfeited A/c Rs. 18,400; Balance Sheet Rs. 45,46,600*)

13. The book keeper of International Trading Corporation Ltd. hands you the following statement which he has prepared explaining that it is his attempt to prepare the Trial Balance as at 31st March, 2010. Without referring to the books and making such corrections as may be necessary (no journal entries are required), prepare the draft of Profit and Loss Account for the year ended 31st March, 2010 and Balance Sheet as at that date :

		Dr. Rs.	Cr. Rs.
Share Capital of Rs. 10 equity shares, fully paid			56,200
Forfeited Shares Account		2,500	
Balance due to Bank			25,900
Creditors			39,000
Cash in hand		500	
Sales			1,20,000
Stock at 31st March, 2009		18,000	
Purchases		92,000	
Carriage Out			1,600
Carriage In		2,200	
Discount allowed to Customers			1,500
Discount allowed by Creditors		4,000	
Rates and Insurance as per ledger	2,800		
Paid-in-advance	200	3,000	
Share Transfer Fee		10	
Advertising as per ledger	5,600		
Add: Accrued at 31st March, 2010	1,000	4,600	

		Dr. Rs.	Cr. Rs.
Wages			10,000
Profit and Loss Account at 31st March, 2009 (Profit)			24,843
Building at 1st April, 2009	80,000		
Add: Extension during the year	10,000	70,000	
Bad Debts Provision as on 31st March, 2009			1,200
Debtors		35,000	
Plant at 1st April, 2010	12,400		
Less: 5 per cent Depreciation	620	11,780	
Petty Expenses		400	
Telephone and Printing		5,810	
Stock at 31st March, 2009		27,000	
Plant Depreciation Account :			
Provision out of previous profits as at 31st March, 2009		10,000	
Dividend Paid		5,000	
Corporate Dividend Tax Paid		843	
		3,02,643	2,69,643

(*a*) The Authorised Share Capital is 10,000 equity shares of Rs. 10 each; 6,120 shares were issued. The final call of Rs. 5 on 500 shares was not paid and these shares were forfeited.

(*b*) Write off Rs. 1,500 as bad debt which is included in Debtors.

(*c*) Create a Provision for Bad Debts @ 5% on Debtors and a Provision for Discount @ 2%.

(*d*) At its meeting held on 15th July, 2009, the company declared a dividend of 10% for the year 2008-2009. It paid corporate dividend tax @ 10%.

(*e*) The stocks on 31st March, 2009 and on 31st March, 2010 were valued at 10% below cost. The Directors have not decided to show the stock at the end of the year at cost.

(*f*) Building as on April 1, 2009 was revalued at Rs. 1,50,000; Plant as on that date was revalued at Rs. 25,000. These values have to be brought into the books. Building is subject to depreciation @ 2.5%.

(*g*) In March 2010, part of the building was sold for Rs. 50,000; the final cost was Rs. 20,000 on which depreciation to the extent of Rs. 5,000 had been provided; in the revaluation, the value of this part of the building was put at Rs. 40,000. The transaction had not yet been recorded in the books.

(*h*) Make a Provision for Income Tax @ 35%. (*Adapted from C.A. First*)

(*Net Profit Rs. 6,135; Total of Balance Sheet, Rs. 2,57,638*)

Hint: There is unclaimed dividend, Rs. 620.

14. Sound Venture Private Limited was incorporated on 1st October, 2009 to take over a business as a going concern as from 1st April, 2009. The purchase price of the business for such acquisition was fixed on the basis of the Balance Sheet of the firm as at 31st March, 2009 but the agreement provided that the vendors would get 80 per cent of the profits earned prior to 1st October, 2009 as compensation. The company's accounts were made up to 31st March each year and the summarised Trading and Profit and Loss Accounts for the year ended 31st March, 2010 disclosed the following results:—

	Rs.		Rs.
To Materials consumed	1,86,000	By Net Sales	2,60,000
Manufacturing Wages	48,500	Stock:	
Misc. Expenses of Manufacture	18,600	Finished goods	49,000
Carriaage Inwards	6,300	Incomplete goods	6,000
Gross Profit c/d	55,600		
	3,15,000		3,15,000
To Salaries and establishment charges	18,300	By Gross Profit b/d	55,600

	Rs.		Rs.
Office expenses	2,750		
Directors' Fees	1,800		
Bad Debts	2,300		
Debentures Interest	1,250		
Commission and Discounts	7,800		
Carriage outwards	1,600		
Depreciation	10,300		
Net Profit for the year	9,500		
	55,600		55,600

Further information available was that sales made by the company amounted to Rs. 1,16,000. Bad debts amounting to Rs. 1,100 were written off prior to 1st October, 2009.

Prepare a statement showing the profits earned prior to and after incorporation. State also the amount of profits prior to 1st October, 2009 payable to the vendors.

How should the company deal with its share of profits in the year ending 31st March, 2010.

(Adapted C.A. Inter)

(Profit Prior to Incorporation, Rs. 8,813 before paying the vendor)

15. The promoters of proposed New Wave Ltd. purchased a running business on 1st April, 2009 from Mr. Altra Modern, New Wave Ltd. was incorporated on 1st August, 2009. The combined Profit and Loss Account of the company prior to and after the date of incorporation is as under:

Profit and Loss Account for year ended on 31st March, 2010

	Rs.		Rs.
To Rent, Rates, Insurance Electricity & Salaries	12,000	By Gross Profit	1,50,000
To Directors' Sitting Fees	3,600	By Discount Received from Creditors	6,000
To Preliminary Expenses	4,900		
To Carriage Outwards and Selling Expenses	5,500		
To Interest paid to Vendors	10,000		
To Net Profit	1,20,000		
	1,56,000		1,56,000

Following further information is available:

(1) Sales up to 31st July, 2009 were Rs. 3,00,000 out of total sales of Rs. 15,00,000 of the year.

(2) Purchases up to 31st July, 2009 were Rs. 3,00,000 out of total purchases of Rs. 9,00,000 of the year.

(3) Interest paid to vendors on 1st February, 2010 @ (12% p.a. on Rs. 1,00,000 being purchase consideration).

From the above information, prepare Profit and Loss Account for the year ended 31st March, 2010, showing the profit earned prior to and after incorporation and also show the transfer of the same to the appropriate accounts. *[Adapted C.W.A. (Inter.) Dec. 1985]*

(Profit : Pre-incorporation Rs. 22,900; Post-incorporation Rs. 97,100)

16. Adarsh Udyog Ltd., incorporated on 1st August, 2009, received the certificate to commence business on 31st August, 2009. It had acquired a running business from Gupta and Co. with effect from 1st April, 2009. The consideration was Rs. 50,00,000 of which Rs. 10,00,000 was to be paid in cash and Rs. 40,00,000 in the form of fully paid shares. The entire consideration was paid to vendors on 31st August, 2009.

The company also issued shares for Rs. 40,00,000 for cash. Machinery costing Rs. 25,00,000 was then installed. Assets acquired from the vendors were: machinery — Rs. 30,00,000; stock — Rs. 6,00,000; and patents — Rs. 4,00,000.

During the year ended 31st March, 2010 the total sales were Rs. 1,80,00,000, the sales per month in the first half-year being one-half of what they were in the latter half-year.

The net profit of the company, after charging the following expenses, was Rs. 10,00,000:

	Rs.
Depreciation	5,40,000
Audit fees	26,000
Directors' fees	60,000
Preliminary expenses	10,000
Office expenses	2,40,000
Selling expenses	1,98,000
Interest to vendors	50,000

Ascertain the pre-incorporation and post-incorporation amounts of profit and prepare the balance sheet of the company as on 31st March, 2010. The closing stock was valued at Rs. 7,00,000.

[*C.S. (Inter.) Dec., 1994 Modified*]

(*Treating audit fees as post-incorporation item, pre-incorporation profit Rs. 1,28,000 and post-incorporation profit Rs. 8,72,000. Total of balance sheet, Rs. 88,72,000*).

Hints: Goodwill = Consideration *less* value of tangible assets taken over and profit prior to incorporation = Rs. (50,00,000 – 40,00,000 – 1,28,000) = Rs. 8,72,000

Cash at Bank = Rs. (40,00,000 + 10,00,000 + 5,40,000 – 10,00,000 – 25,00,000 – 10,00,000) = Rs. 19,40,000.

17. Chaitanya Industries Pvt. Ltd. was incorporated on 1st May, 2009. It took over Chitanya's sole proprietary business with effect from 1st April, 2009. Chaitanya's balance sheet as at 31st March, 2010 is as follows:

Liabilities	*Rs.*	*Assets*	*Rs.*
Capital Account	43,15,000	Building	11,00,000
Loan	85,000	Machinery	30,00,000
Trade Creditors	1,70,000	Debtors	2,57,000
Creditors for Expenses	25,000	Profit and Loss Account	2,38,000
	45,95,000		45,95,000

It was agreed to pay Rs. 45 lakh in the form of equity shares to Chaitanya. The company decided to close its books of account for the first time as at 31st March, 2010. The following further details are furnished to you:—

	Rs.
Sales for full year	30,00,000
Purchases	14,00,000
Salaries and Wages	4,00,000
General Expenses	3,20,000
Carriage Inwards	47,000
Interest paid	80,000
Stock as at 31st March, 2010	2,20,000
Additions to Building	3,80,000

Depreciation is to be provided at 10% on assets including additions.

Make a Provision for Income Tax @ 35%.

The company requests you to:

(*i*) pass journal entries for the take over, and

(*ii*) prepare Profit & Loss Account showing separately pre-incorporation and post-incorporation profits. [*Adapted from C.A. (Inter) May, 1989*]

(*Goodwill on acquisition Rs. 4,23,000; Profits : Pre-incorporation Rs. 3,12,812; Post incorporation Rs. 28,437*)

Hint: Gross Profit and expenses have been apportioned in the time ratio due to lack of information i.e. 1 : 11.

18. From the following particulars, make out a Balance Sheet as at 31st March, 2010 and a Profit and Loss Account for the year 2009-2010 of the Mercantile Newspaper Co. Ltd. in accordance with the requirements of the Companies Act. The company was registered in 2005 with an authorised capital of 6,00,000 shares of Rs. 10 each and acquired the ownership of the Mercantile Gazette, paying the vendors Rs. 40 lakhs in fully paid shares; 20,000 shares were allotted to the public in 2005 and paid for at par, 20,000 shares were issued in March, 2009 and paid for at a premium of Rs. 2 per share.

Buildings were erected at a cost of Rs. 30,00,000. Plant and Machinery was purchased for Rs. 35,00,000 and Furniture and Fittings for Rs. 1,00,000. Depreciation written off up to 31st March, 2009 amounted to Rs. 5,56,481 on Buildings, Rs. 16,72,979 on Plant and Machinery and Rs. 34,390 on Furniture and Fittings. The directors wrote off on 31st March, 2010 5% on Buildings, 15% on Plant and Machinery and 10% on Furniture and Fittings, calculating the same on written down values. Provision for Doubtful Debts on 1st April, 2009 was Rs. 1,50,000. A sum of Rs. 84,000 was brought forward in 2009-2010 accounts from the Profit and Loss Account of the year 2009-2010 and an interim dividend for the half year ended 30th September, 2009 at 10% per annum was declared in November, 2009. Corporate dividend tax was paid @ 15%.

The Bank Loan raised on the security of the Buildings stood at Rs. 5,00,000 on 31st March, 2010. Interest for the year on the Bank Loan amounted to Rs. 90,000 of which one-third remained upaid. The company had Rs. 2,00,000 worth of paper at cost on 31st March, 2009; it bought in 2009-2010 paper for Rs. 10,00,000 one-half of which remained on hand at the end of the year.

	Rs.	Rs.
Subscriptions collected in 2009-2010		
on account of 2008-2009	1,50,000	
on account of 2009-2010	6,30,000	
on account of 2010-2011	1,00,000	8,80,000
Subscriptions in arrear on 31st March, 2010—		
on account of 2008-2009	60,000	
on account of 2009-2010	1,90,000	2,50,000
Collection in 2009-2010 on account of Advertisements—		
for 2008-2009	1,20,000	
for 2009-2010	11,10,000	
for 2010-2011	1,50,000	13,80,000
Uncollected on 31st March, 2010—		
on account of advertisement bills of 2009-2010	90,000	
on account of advertisement bills of 2009-2010	2,10,000	3,00,000
Printing done for customers in 2009-2010 and bills rendered out of which bills for 3,10,000 remained uncollected		8,35,000

The expenditure for 2009-2010 amounted in the Printing Department to Rs. 5,10,000 paid and Rs. 90,000 unpaid; Editorial Department to Rs. 2,00,000 paid and Rs. 80,000 unpaid; Manager's Department to Rs. 1,25,000 paid and Rs. 1,00,000 unpaid.

Cash in hand on 31st March, 2010	Rs. 3,850
Cash at Bank on 31st March, 2010	Rs. 8,38,000

5% of the Debts are doubtful.

Create Provision for Taxation equal to 35% of net profit.

(Net Profit Rs. 5,09,736 Balance Sheet Total Rs. 61,16,210)

19. B. Ltd. was formed on 1st August, 2009 to take over as from 1st April, 2009 the business of M/s. Slow and Sharp whose balance sheet on that date was as follows:—

	Rs.	*Rs.*		*Rs.*
Sundry Creditors		20,000	Freehold Land and Buildings	90,000
Capital:			Plant and Machinery	65,000

	Rs.	Rs.		Rs.
Slow	1,00,000		Trade marks and patents	10,000
Sharp	1,40,000	2,40,000	Stock — Materials	35,000
			— Finished Goods	10,000
			Sundry Debtors	40,000
			Cash at Bank	10,000
		2,60,000		2,60,000

The company did not take over the debtors and creditors but agreed, as agents, to collect the debts and pay the creditors, for a commission of 3% on amount collected and 2% on amounts paid. The company agreed to pay Rs. 3,00,000 in fully paid shares and decided to revalue the Freehold Land and Buildings at Rs. 1,20,000 and the Plant and Machinery at Rs. 60,000.The company issued 10,000 shares of Rs. 10 each to the public which were subscribed for and fully paid.

By 31st March, 2010 when the accounts were closed, the vendors' debtors had realised Rs. 32,000 and creditors had been paid off. The discounts allowed to debtors and received from creditors were Rs. 1,000 and Rs. 300 respectively. Included in the amount realised from debtors is a sum of Rs. 1,500 received against a debt previously written off. The vendors were paid the amount due to them. Apart from balances arising out of the above, the following other figures are supplied to you:—

	Rs.		Rs.
Sales	6,60,000	Salaries	39,000
Purchases	2,15,000	Audit Fees	500
Wages	1,80,000	Directors' Fees	5,500
Factory Lighting	400	Cash at Bank	1,15,800
Rent, Rates, etc. – factory	5,000	Cash in Hand	200
– office	2,600	Sundry Debtors (excluding Ventors' Debtors)	30,400
Carriage inwards	3,600		
Travellers' Salaries and Commission	15,000	Bad Debts (of which Rs. 200 were in respect of debts arising before 1st August)	600
Advertising	10,200		
Freight and Packing	4,200		
Advertising materials on hand	354	Investment (10% Government Bonds acquired on 1st October)	50,000
Sundry Creditors	10,300		
Bills Receivable	40,000	Advance against purchase of raw materials	13,300
Plant acquired on 1st October, 2009	50,000		

Stock on 31st march, 2010 was Raw materials Rs. 32,000 and Finished Goods Rs. 15,000. Raw materials worth Rs. 8,000 were received before 31st march, 2010 and taken into stock, but no entry had been passed in the accounts. Office rent and rates have been paid for 13 months up to 30th April, 2010. Rs. 400 out of the debtors are bad and a provision of 5% on debtors is required. Provision is to be made for directors' fees amounting to Rs. 500 still to be paid. There are two managing directors, each entitled to a commission of 5% of the revenue profits. The directors propose a dividend of 10%. Income-tax rate is to be taken at 35%. The rate of corporate dividend tax at 15%.

Prepare the Trading and Profit and Loss Account for the year ended 31st March, 2010 and Balance Sheet on that date, after charging depreciation of Plant and Machinery at 15% and Freehold Land and Buildings @5%. Sales up 1st August, 2009 were Rs. 1,65,000. Payments to vendors' creditors were made and payments from vendors' debtors were received evenly throughout the year.

(Profit : Pre-incorporation Rs. 23,438; Post-incorporation Rs. 69,758; Managing Directors' Remuneration Rs 11,925; Provision for taxation Rs. 50,183; Balance of Profit and Loss Appropriation Account Rs. 25,758; Total of Balance Sheet Rs. 5,82,604)

20. Fair Deal Retailers Ltd. was incorporated on 1st July, 2009 to take over an existing proprietary business from 1st April, 2009, its assets and liabilities then being:—

	Rs.
Leasehold Building	60,000
Furniture and Fixture	13,400
Debtors	84,000
Stock	36,000
Bank Balance	14,600
Creditors	26,000

The agreement provided that Debtors and Bank Balances are to be retained by the vendor but realisation of the Debtors is to be made by the company on a commission of 5% and cash collected, and creditors are to be paid by the vendor, and that the company shall give the vendor cash Rs. 20,000; 6,000 14% Redeemable preference shares of Rs. 10 each fully paid and 8,000 equity shares of Rs. 10 each as Rs. 7.50 per share paid up. It further provided that by 31st March, 2010 cash collected less expenses on account of the Debtors be paid to be vendor after adjusting Rs. 2.50 per share to make the equity shares fully paid up.

To provide the cash for payment to the vendor and for working capital, the company issued 10,000 14% Redeemable Preference Shares of Rs. 10 each at a premium of Re. 1 per share. The issue was underwritten in consideration of allotment of 100 equity shares of Rs. 10 each fully paid. The amount called up for preference shares issued to the public was Rs. 7.50 per share which was paid with the exception of Re. 1 per share on 1,200 shares and the amount received in advance of calls was at the rate of Rs. 2.50 per share on 800 shares.

The General Ledger of the company which had received Rs. 46,000 cash from vendors' debtors showed, in addition to the foregoing transactions, the following on 31st March, 2010:—

	Rs.
Purchases (net)	4,02,200
Sales (net)	4,81,800
Discount (Vendors' Debtors)	2,000
Discount (Company's Debtors)	6,000
Expenses Paid:—	
Preliminary	2,000
Directors' Fees	1,200
Management, General	23,000
Vendors' and company's Debtors	1,46,300
Creditors	43,600

Prepare the company's Cash Book Trading and Profit and Loss Account for the period to, and Balance Sheet as at 31st March, 2010 after taking into account Closing Stock, Rs. 49,980, and Depreciation on Leasehold Building and Furniture and Fixtures at 5% and 10% respectively.

Rate of Income Tax 35%. *(Adapted C.A. Final)*

(Pre-incorporation Profits Rs. 5,472; Post-incorporation Profits 29,708; Provision for Taxation Rs. 21,469; Total of Balance Sheet Rs. 3,57,577)

21. Hindustan Ltd. acquired an area of 10,000 square metres of freehold land, costing Rs. 1,00,000 on 1st April, 2009. During the year, the whole estate was developed, the area of road surface requiring 1,900 square metres while the remaining 8,100 sq. metres were divided into three equal portions, known as sites A, B and C respectively.

On site A four houses were erected, on site B two houses and on site C seven houses, each site being divided equally among the houses erected on it, except that site C was divided into eight equal plots, of which one was laid out as a croquet lawn. The houses on each of the respective sites were identical in construction and cost.

The company's operation during the year are summarised in the following Trial Balance as on 31st March, 2010:—

		Rs.	Rs.
Administrative Expenditure (including Directors' fees of Rs. 1,500)		41,650	..
Profit from croquet laws		..	200
Share Capital in shares of Rs. 10 each		..	1,50,000
Cost of Freehold Land		1,00,000	..
Road construction		30,000	..
Drainage and development of sites		44,100	..
Preliminary Expenses		5,700	..
Bank Overdraft (guaranteed by Directors)		..	24,100
Creditors		..	20,300
Debtors (including Rs. 500 unsecured loan to Secretary)		900	..
Cost of laying out croquet lawn		1,300	..
Loan to Householder (secured on freehold house)		1,000	..
Site A	– Cost of erecting four houses	48,000	
	– Rent from letting four houses	..	4,400
Site B	– Cost of erecting two houses	60,000	..
	– Sales Price of 99 years' lease of two houses	..	1,20,200
	– Ground Rent from two houses	..	150
Site C	– Cost of erecting seven houses	59,500	..
	– Sales Price of four freehold houses	..	72,800
		3,92,150	3,92,150

The directors decided:—

(*a*) to apportion drainage development, Rs. 44,100, to the 3 sites equally;

(*b*) to write off one-tenth of the total cost of roads;

(*c*) to depreciate the total cost of the site 'A' property by 5 per cent; and

(*d*) to write off administration expenditure wholly to Revenue Account.

Prepare Profit and Loss Account for the year to 31st March, 2001 and Balance Sheet as on that date.

(Adapted from C.A. Final)

(Net Loss, Rs. 10,885; Total of Balance Sheets, Rs. 1,94,400)

22. The Trial Balance of M. Ltd. for the year ended on 31st March, 2010 was as follows:—

Debit Balance	Rs.	*Credit Balance*	Rs.
Materials used	3,50,000	Sales (including 5% Sales Tax)	9,45,000
Cost of Labour	1,50,000	Sale of Scrap	100
Stock of Finished Goods and Word in Progress on 31st March, 2009	50,000	Rent received	2,000
		Discounts	2,750
Wages: Factory Staff	15,000	Recovered against fire claim regarding stock	5,000
Managerial Remuneration	50,000		
Salaries: Clerical Staff	75,000	Capital: Equity	25,000
Insurances: Workmen's Compensation	1,500	Preference-9%	8,000
General-Fire etc.	2,000	Creditors	1,56,000
Executive's Insurance	1,500	Provision for Taxation	55,000
Maintenance : Buildings	1,000	Profit and Loss Account	13,750
: Plant & Machinery	12,500	General Reserve	50,000
Rent and Rates of Premises and Hire of Plant	20,000		
Heat, Light and Power	15,000		
Experimental and Laboratory Expenses	10,000		
Canteen Expenses	5,000		
Staff Welfare Expenses	2,500		
Motor Expenses	12,500		

	Rs.	*Rs.*
Professional Charges (Accountancy and legal)	2,800	
Postage and Telephones	3,500	
Books, Printing and Stationery	11,000	
Sundry Expenses	10,000	
Carriage and Packing on Sales	3,300	
Discounts	5,000	
Debtors	1,78,000	
Freehold Property	50,000	
Plant and Machinery	12,500	
Fixtures and Fittings-offices	3,500	
Office machinery and Equipment	3,000	
Motor Car and Van	6,500	
Stock of Material at 31st March, 2010	1,20,000	
Bank	38,000	
Sales Tax Paid	42,000	
	12,62,600	12,62,600

Prepare:—

(*a*) an account showing the cost of manufacturing the products;

(*b*) Profit and Loss Account for the year ending 31st March, 2010; and

(*c*) Balance Sheet on that date.

Depreciation is to be provided at the following rates on written down values:—

Plant and Machinery	15%
Fixtures and Fittings	10%
Office Machinery, etc.	15%
Motor Car and Van	20%

The stock of finished goods and work in progress at 31st March, 2010 was Rs. 35,000. Provide for preference dividend and equity dividend at 10%. Provision for corporate dividend tax is also to be made @ 15%. The total taxation liability is estimated as Rs. 86,000 of which Rs. 44,000 relates to the current year.

Debtors include Rs. 10,000 deposited as security against Government contracts.

The Works Manager is paid partly by salary and partly by a commission; he is entitled to a commission of 5% on the amount by which the surplus in the factory cost exceeds 20% of the sales for the period. Charge the commission if any in the Profit and Loss Account.

(*Adapted from Incoorp. Acctts. Inter, England*)

(*Gross Profit, Rs. 3,06,725; Commission, 5% of (Rs. 3,06,725 – Rs. 1,80,000); Net Profit, Rs. 81,439; P. & L. App., Rs. 1,04,647; Total of Balance Sheet, Rs. 4,42,525*)

23. The following items appear in the Trial Balance extracted from the books of a limited company:—

	Dr. *Rs.*	*Cr.* *Rs.*
Plant and Machinery *less* depreciation	7,56,900	
Investment	2,50,000	
Capital Reserve		1,70,000
Income-tax	95,000	
14% Redeemable Preference Shares		6,00,000

You are required to state, in regard to each of the above items, the further information you would require to enable you to draft the final accounts of the company for publication.

(*Adapted from C.A. Final, England*)

24. Red Tape Ltd. carry on business as stationers. The following is the Trial Balance on 31st March, 2010:—

	Dr. Rs. '000	Cr. Rs. '000
Building	2,500	..
Shop Fittings	460	..
Motor Van	150	..
Stock	2,914	..
Sales Ledger	1,373	..
Purchases Ledger	..	1,368
Bank	915	..
Cash	36	..
Discount	..	27
Wages	..	20
Delivery Charges	18	..
Municipal Tax	9	..
Share Capital (shares of Rs. 10 each)	..	6,960
	8,375	8,375

The following are the cash abstract and totals of the Wages Book, and Day Books for the year ending 31st March, 2010:—

(*a*) Cash abstract for the year ended 31st March, 2010:

	Rs. '000	Discount Rs. '000		Rs. '000	Discount Rs. '000
To Bank Drawn	36,300		By Bank Lodged	3,52,60	
To Cash Sales	16,513		By Cash Purchases	42,01	
To Sales Ledger	21,276	98	By Purchases Ledger	2,87,74	110
			By Wages Pazdi	13,24	
			By Sundries	45,53	

(*b*) Total of Wages Book

Gross Wages	1,433
Employees P.F.	109
Employer P.F.	100
Net wages paid	1,320

(*c*) Purchases Day Book

Purchases	28,576	Purchases Returns Book	136
Delivery Charges	212	Trade Expenses	18
Trade Expenses	56		
	28,841		154

(*d*) Sales Day Book

Sales	21,664	Sales Returns Book	562
Rent	60		
	21,724		562

(*e*) Analysis of Miscellaneous Account of the Cash Book:

	Rs.
(*i*) Income-tax paid	1,035
(*ii*) Municipal tax	57
(*iii*) Delivery Charges	114
(*iv*) Motor Van purchased less Rs. 2 lakh proceeds of old van sold	600
(*v*) Trade Expenses	83
(*vi*) Repairs to property	46
(*vii*) Provident Fund Payment	218
(*viii*) Lodged in Fixed Deposit	2,400
	4,553

Stock on 31st March, 2010 was valued at Rs. 3,070 thousand. Bad debts amounting to Rs. 26 thousand have to be written off @2% of the Sales Ledger balances is to be provided as Provision for Discount.

Accrued Expenses on 31st March, 2010 were : (1) Wages Rs. 25 thousand and (2) Trade Expenses Rs. 20 thousand Prepaid Expenses were : (1) Delivery charges Rs. 15 thousand and Municipal Taxes Rs. 7 thousand. Depreciation on motor van @ 20% and on Shop Fittings @ 10% is to be provided. The Directors recommend a dividend of 10%. The company makes a provision for corporate dividend tax @15%.

Prepare the Profit and Loss Accounts for the year ended 31st march, 2001 and Balance Sheet as on that date. *(Adapted from C.A. First)*

(Gross Profit, Rs. 5,130 thousand Net Profit, Rs. 1,867 thousand; Total of Balance Sheet, Rs. 10,171 thousand)

24. You are required to prepare a Revenue Account and Balance Sheet from the following Trial Balance extracted from the books of the International Hotels Ltd. on 31st March, 2010:—

	Dr. *Rs.*	*Cr* *Rs.*
Authorised Capital-divided into 5,000 12% Preference Shares of Rs. 100 each and 10,000 Equity Shares of Rs. 100 each		15,00,000
Subscribed Capital:		
12% 5,000 Preference Shares of Rs. 100 each		5,00,000
Equity Capital		8,05,000
Purchases — Wines, Cigarettes, Cigars, etc.	45,800	
— Foodstuffs	36,200	
Wages and Salaries	28,300	
Rent, Rates and Taxes	8,900	
Laundry	750	
Sales — Wines, Cigarettes, Cigars, etc.		1,14,800
— Food		57,600
Coal and Firewood	3,290	
Carriage and Cooliage	810	
Sundry Expenses	5,840	
Advertising	8,360	
Repairs	4,250	
Rent of Rooms		48,000
Billiard		5,700
Miscellaneous Receipts		2,800
Discount Received		3,300
Transfer Fees		700
Income Tax on current income	16,400	
Freehold Land and Building, at cost	8,50,000	
Furniture and Fittings	86,300	
Stock on hand, 1st April, 2009:		
Wines, Cigarettes, Cigars, etc.	12,800	
Foodstuffs	5,260	
Cash in hand	2,200	
Cash with Bankers	1,06,380	
Preliminary and Foremation Expenses	8,000	
12% 2,000 Debentures of Rs. 100 each (issued on 1st October, 2009)		2,00,000
Profit and Loss Account		41,500
Sundry Creditors		42,000
Sundry Debtors	19,260	
Investments	2,72,300	

	Dr. Rs.	Cr Rs.
Goodwill, at cost	5,00,000	
General Reserve		2,00,000
	20,21,400	20,21,400
Wages and Salaries Outstanding	1,280	
Stock on 31st March, 2010		
Wines, Cigarettes and Cigars, etc.,	22,500	
Foodstuffs	16,400	

Depreciation at the following rates is to be provided as per Schedule XIV of the Companies Act, 1956.

Furniture and Fittings @ 10% p.a.: Land and Buildings @ 5% p.a.

The Equity Capital on 1st April, 2009 stood at Rs. 7,20,000 that is 6,000 shares fully paid and 2,000 shares, Rs. 60 paid. The directors made a call @ Rs. 40 per share on 1st October, 2009. A shareholder could not pay the call on 100 shares and his shares were then forteited and reissued @ Rs. 90 per share as fully paid.

The Directors propose a dividend of 8% on equity shares and create a provision for corporate dividend tax @ 15% transferring any amount that may be required from General Reserve.

(Adapted from C.A. Final)

(Net Profit, Rs. 30,430; Total of Balance Sheet, Rs. 18,32,210)

26. The following is the Trial Balance of the Choonabhatti Tea Co. Ltd. as on 31st March, 2010:—

Debit Balances	*Rs.*	*Credit Balance*	*Rs.*
Furniture	10,000	Equity Share Capital shares of Rs. 100 each, fully paid	4,00,000
Development Expenditure (cost)	2,40,000	14% Preference Share Capital in Shares of Rs. 100 each, fully paid	1,00,000
Land and Buildings	1,85,000	P. & L. A/c Balance	5,700
Workers' Houses	1,25,000	General Reserve	50,000
Plant and Machinery	45,000	Due for Excise Duty	5,000
Stocks of Manures, Packing Materials, etc.	11,000	Sundry Creditors	40,500
Manures Used	15,000	Due for Wages	15,000
Packing Materials used for Despatches	10,000	Due for Rates and Taxes	2,000
Sundry Stores	4,000	Sales (10,000 kg.)	3,75,000
Wages to Garden Workers	86,000		
Wages to Factory Workers	15,000		
Salaries	25,000		
Escise Duty (on sales)	15,000	Excluding a claim filed by a worker for Rs. 1,000 for alleged wrongful dismissal.	
Freight Inwards	2,500		
Freight on Sales	17,000		
Selling Brokerage	3,000		
Interest	5,500		
Cash in hand	400		
Directors' Fees	4,000		
Managing Director's Salary	10,000		
Rates and Taxes	4,100		
Preference Dividend paid for 2009-2010	14,000		
Corporate dividend Tax Paid	2,100		
Stock of tea on hand on 1st April 2009 (1,000 kg.)	35,000		
Insurance	8,000		
Cash at Bank	1,01,600		
	9,93,200		9,93,200

Half the manures, Rs. 10,000 of wages and Rs. 1,000 of stores were used for development of (new) areas not in bearing. It is estimated that the life of matured plants is 40 years.

Depreciation is to be provided @ 5% on Land and Buildings and Workers' Houses; @ 15% on Plant and Machinery and @ 10% on Furniture. Provision for Taxation is to be created @ 35%. The directors propose to delcare a dividend of 15% on equity shares after transfer of 10% of profit after tax to General Reserve. A provision for corporate dividend tax @ 15% is to be made.

Production during the year 2009-2010 totalled 10,500 kg.

(*Net Profit after tax Rs. 1,00,522; Balance of Profit and Loss Appropriation Account Rs. 14,069; Balance Sheet Total Rs. 7,56,750*)

Essay-type

1. Briefly describe the legal provisions regarding remuneration to directors of a joint stock company.
2. What is the maximum remuneration that can be legally paid to the manager of a joint stock company?
3. Write a note on the overall managerial remuneration that can be legally paid by a joint stock company?
4. What do you mean by Profits Prior to Incorporation? What is the nature of such profits? How are they calculated and treated in the books of account?
5. Explain 'divisible profits' fully.
6. What is meant by capital profits? Give five examples of capital profits which may arise in a joint stock company.
7. Distinguish between:—
   (*i*) Interim Dividend and Final Dividend.
   (*ii*) Preference Dividend and Equity Dividend.
8. What is Interest out of Capital? When is a company allowed to pay it?
9. Why are bonus shares issued? What are the conditions which have to be satisfied while making such an issue?
10. What are the circumstances in which bonus shares are generally issued? What profits can be used for such an issue?
11. Give a list of the major heads under which items appearing in the balance sheets of a joint stock company have to be arranged according to schedule VI part I of the Companies Act.
12. What is Vertical Form of balance sheet of a joint stock company?
13. What is directors' report? What important pieces of information does it provide?
14. What is auditors' report? Distinguish between qualified auditors' report and unqualified auditors' report.

20

VALUATION OF INTANGIBLE ASSETS, GOODWILL AND SHARES; REORGANISATION AND RECONSTRUCTION OF SHARE CAPITAL

SYNOPSIS

1. Valuation of intangible assets .. 20.1
   Meaning of intangible asset .. 20.1
   Valuation of intangible assets .. 20.2
   Recognition and initial measurement .. 20.3
   Separate acquisition of intangible assets ... 20.3
   Acquisition of intangible assets as part of an amalgamation .. 20.3
   Acquisition of intangible assets by way of a Government grant 20.4
   Internally generated intangible asset .. 20.4
   Research phase .. 20.4
   Development phase .. 20.4
   Cost of an internally generated intangible asset ... 20.5
   Recognition of an expense on intangible asset ... 20.5
   Subsequent expenditure on intangible asset .. 20.6
   Amortisation ... 20.6
   Amortisation period .. 20.6
   Amortisation method .. 20.6
   Residual value .. 20.6
   Review of amortisation period and amortisation method .. 20.6
   Impairement losses .. 20.7
   Retirements and disposals ... 20.7
2. Valuation of goodwill .. 20.7
   Need .. 20.8
   Components of goodwill .. 20.8
   General factors affecting value of goodwill .. 20.9
   Profitability .. 20.9
   Yield expected by investors .. 20.14
   Capital employed .. 20.15
   Methods for evaluating goodwill .. 20.16
   (*a*) Super profits method .. 20.17
   (*b*) Annuity method .. 20.22
   (*c*) Capitalisation method .. 20.25
3. Valuation of shares .. 20.27
   Need .. 20.27
   Methods .. 20.28
   Net assets method or intrinsic value .. 20.28
   Yield basis or market value .. 20.29
   Value based on earnings of company .. 20.33
4. Alteration of share capital .. 20.51
   Conversion into stock .. 20.51
   Increase or decrease of capital .. 20.52
   Reserve liability .. 20.52
5. Reduction of capital .. 20.53
   Variation of shareholders' rights .. 20.54
6. Schemes of reconstruction .. 20.88
   Internal vs. external reconstruction .. 20.90
   Legal position as regards external reconstruction .. 20.91

1. VALUATION OF INTANGIBLE ASSETS

Meaning of Intangible Asset

According to the Accounting Standard (AS) 26 'Intangible Assets' issued by the Institute of Chartered Accountants of India, an intangible asset is an identifiable non-monetary asset, without physical substance, held for use in the production or supply of goods or services, for rental to others, or for administrative purposes. An asset is a resource (*a*) rolled by an enterprise as a result of past events; and (*b*) from which future economic benefits are expected to flow to the enterprise. Monetary assets are money held and assets to be received in fixed or determinable amounts of money. Non-monetary assets are assets other than monetary assets.

An intangible asset must have: (*i*) identifiability, (*ii*) control over a resource; and (*iii*) expectation of future economic benefits flowing to be enterprise.

Enterprises often spend resources or incur liabilities on the acquisition, development, maintenance or enhancement of intangible resources such as scientific or technical knowledge, design and implementation of new processes or systems, licences, intellectual property, market knowledge and trademarks (including brand names and publishing titles). Computer software, patents, copyrights, motion picture films, customer lists, mortgage servicing rights, fishing licences, import quotas, franchises, customer or supplier relationships, customer loyalty, market share and marketing rights are common examples of items encompassed by these broad headings. Goodwill is another example of an item of intangible nature which either arises on acquisition or is internally generated.

Many items described in the above paragraph will not meet the definition of an intangible asset, that is, identifiability, control over a resource and expectation of future economic benefits flowing to the enterprise. Expenditure to acquire such an item or to generate it internally is recognised as an expense when it is incurred. However, if the item is acquired in an amalgamation in the nature of purchase, it forms part of the goodwill recognised at the date of amalgamation.

In some cases, intangible assets may be contained in or on a physical substance such as a compact disk (in the case of computer software), legal documentation (in the case of a licence or patent) or film (in the case of motion pictures). But where the cost of the physical substance containing the intangible asset is not significant, the physical substance containing an intangible asset, though tangible in nature, is treated as a part of the intangible asset containing in or on it.

Sometimes, an asset may incorporate both intangible and tangible elements that are, in practice, inseparable. In such cases, judgement is required to asses as to which element is prominent in determining whether such an asset should be treated as fixed asset or an intangible asset.

An intangible asset must be identifiable. It must be distinguished from goodwill. Goodwill arising on an amalgamation in the nature of purchase represents a payment made by the purchaser in anticipation of future economic benefits.

An intangible asset can be clearly distinguished from goodwill if the asset is separable. An asset is separable if the enterprise could rent, sell, exchange or distribute the specific future economic benefits attributable to the asset without also disposing of future economic benefits that flow from other assets used in the same revenue earning activity. However, separability is not a necessary condition for identifiability since an enterprise may be able to identify an asset in some other way.

An enterprise controls an asset if it has the power to obtain the future economic benefits flowing from the underlying resource and also can restrict the access of others to those benefits. Market and technical knowledge may give rise to future economic benefits. An enterprise controls those benefits if, for example, the knowledge is protected by legal rights such as copyrights, or a restraint of trade agreement, where permitted.

The future economic benefits flowing from an intangible asset may include revenue from the sale of products or services, cost savings, or other benefits resulting from the use of the asset by the enterprise.

Valuation of Intangible Assets

Valuation of intangible assets is a complex exercise. The non-physical form of intangible assets makes it difficult to identify the future economic benefits that the enterprise can expect to derive from the intangible assets. Many intangible assets do not have alternative use and cannot be **broken down into components or parts for resale.**

Further, intangible assets normally do not have an active market. Many times, they are not separable from the business and hence it becomes difficult to value them separately from the business.

There are three approaches used in valuing intangible assets, (*i*) cost approach, (*ii*) market value approach and (*iii*) economic value approach. The valuer has to select the approach after considering a number of factors like credibility, objectivity, relevance and practicality. The information available will also affect the selection.

In cost approach, expenditure incurred in developing the asset is aggregated. If the asset has been purchased recently, its purchase price may be taken to be the cost.

In market value approach, valuation is made by reference to transactions involving similar assets that have taken place recently in similar markets. The approach is possible if there is the existence of an active market of comparable intangible assets and adquate information in respect of transections that have taken place recently is available.

Economic value approach is based on the cash flows or earnings attributable to those assets and the capitalisation thereof, at an appropriate discount rate or multiple. The valuer has to identify the cash flows-earnings directly associated with the intangible assets like the cash flows arising from the exploitation of a patent or copyright, licensing of an intangible asset etc. It is possible only if cash flows from the intangible asset are identifiable from the management accounts and budgets, forecasts or plans of the enterprise.

Recognition and Initial Measurement

An intangible asset should be recognised if, and only if,

(*a*) it is probable that the future economic benefits that are attributable to the asset will flow to the enterprise; and

(*b*) the cost of the asset can be measured reliably.

Separate Acquisition of Intangible Assets

If an intangible asset is acquired separately, the cost of the intangible asset can usually be measured reliably. The cost comprises its purchase price, including any inport duties and other taxes and any directly attributable expenditure on making the asset ready for its intended use. Directly attributable expenditure includes, for example, professional fees for legal services. Any trade discounts and rebates are deducted in arriving at the cost. If an intangible asset is acquired in exchange for shares or other securities of the reporting enterprise, the asset is recorded at its fair value , or the fair value of the securities issued, whichever is more clearly evident.

Acquisition of Intangible Assets as part of an Amalgamation

An intangible asset acquired in an amalgamation in the nature of purchase is accounted for in accordance with Accounting Standard (AS) 14 – Accounting for Amalgamations.

Judgement is required to determine whether the cost (*i.e.* fair value) of an intangible asset acquired in an amalgamation can be measured with sufficient reliability for the purpose of separate recognition. Quoted market prices in an active market provide the most reliable measurement of fair value. If no active market exists for an asset; its cost reflects the amount that the enterprise would have paid, at the date of the acquisition, for the asset in an arm's length transaction between knowledgeable and willing parties, based on the best information available.

Certain enterprises that are regularly involved in the purchase and sale of unique intangible assets have developed techniques for estimating their fair values indirectly. These techniques include applying multiples reflecting current market transactions to certain indicators driving the profitability of the asset, such as revenue, market shares, operating profit etc.; or discounting estimated future net cash flows from the assets.

In amalgamation in the nature of purchase, a transferee recognises an intangible asset that meets the recognition crteria, even if that intangible asset had not been recognised in the financial statements of the transferor. If the cost (*i.e.*, fair value) of an intangible asset acquired cannot be measured reliably, that asset is not recognised as a separate intangible asset but is included in goodwill. Further, unless there is an active market for an intangible asset acquired, the cost initially recognised for the intangible asset is restricted to an amount that does not create or increase any capital reserve arising at the date of the amalgamation.

Acquisition of Intangible Assets by way of a Government Grant

An intangible asset may be acquired free of charge or for nominal consideration, by way of a government grant. This may happen when a government transfers or allocates to an enterprise intangible assets such as airport landing rights, licences to operate radio or television stations, import licences or quotas or rights to access other restricted resources. Such an intangible asset is recognised at a nominal value or at the acquisition cost, as appropriate. Any expenditure that is directly attributable to making the asset ready for its intended use is also included in the cost of the asset.

Internally Generated Intangible Asset

First of all, it should be remembered that internally generated goodwill should not be recognised as an asset.

To assess whether an internally generated intangible asset meets the criteria for recognition, an enterprise should classify the generation into (*a*) research phase and (*b*) development phase. If it is not possible to distinguish the research phase from the development phase, the enterprise should treat the entire expenditure as having been spent on research phase.

Research Phase

No intangible asset arising from research (or from the research phase of an internal project) should be recognised; such expenditure should be treated as an expense when it is incurred. Examples of research activities are activities aimed at obtaining new knowledge and the search for alternatives for materials, devices, products, processes, systems or services etc.

Development Phase:

An intangible asset arising from development (or from the development phase of an internal project) should be recognised if, and only if, an enterprise can demonstrate all of the following:

(*a*) the technical feasibility of completing the intangible asset so that it will be available for use or sale,

(*b*) its intention to complete the intangible asset and use or sell it,

(*c*) its ability to use or sell the intangible asset

(*b*) how the intangible asset will generate probable future economic benefits. For example, the enterprise should demonstrate the existence of a market for the output of the intangible asset or the intangible asset itself or if it is to used internally, the usefulness of the intangible asset.

(*e*) the availability of adequate technical, financial or other resources to complete the development and to use or sell the intangible asset, and

(*f*) its ability to measure the expenditure attributable to the intangible asset during its development reliably.

Examples of development activities are:

(*a*) the design, construction and testing of pre-production or pre-use prototypes and models.

(*b*) the design of tools, jigs, moulds and dies involving new technology,

(*c*) the design, construction and operation of a pilot plant that is not of a scale economically feasible for commercial production, and

(*d*) the design, construction and testing of a chosen alternative for new or improved materials, devices, products, processes, systems or services.

Internally generated brands, mastheads, publishing titles, customer lists and items similar in substance should not be recognised as intangible assets.

Cost of an Internally Generated Intangible Asset

The cost of an internally generated intangible asset is the sum of expenditure incurred from the **time when the intangible asset first meets the recognition criteria. Reinstatement of expenditure** recognised as an expense in previous annual financial statements or interim financial reports is prohibited.

The cost of an internally generated intangible asset comprises of all expenditure that can be directly attributed or allocated on a reasonable and consistent basis to creating, producing and making the asset ready for its intended use. The cost includes, if applicable:

(*a*) expenditure on materials and services used or consumed in generating the intangible asset;

(*b*) the salaries, wages and other employment related cost of personnel directly engaged in generating the asset;

(*c*) any expenditure that is directly attributable to generating the asset, such as fees to register a legal right and the amortisation of patents and licences that are used to generate the asset; and

(*d*) overheads that are necessary to generate the asset and that can be allocated on a reasonable and consistent basis to the asset (for example an allocation of the depreciation of fixed assets, insurance premium and rent). Allocations of overheads are made on bases similar to those used in allocating overheads to inventories. AS 16, Borrowing Costs, establishes criteria for the recognition of interest as a component of the cost of a qualifying asset. These criteria are also applied for the recognitation of interest as a component of the cost of an internally generated intangible asset.

The following are not components of the cost of an internally generated intangible asset:

(*a*) selling, administrative and other general overheads unless the expenditure can be directly attributed to making the asset ready for use.

(*b*) clearly identified inefficiencies and initial operating loss incurred before an asset achieves planned performance ; and

(*c*) expenditure on training the staff to operate the asset.

Recognition of an Expense on Intangible Asset

Expenditure on an intangible item should be recognised as an expense when it is incurred unless.

(*a*) it forms part of the cost of an intangible asset that meets the recognition criteria;

(*b*) the item is acquired in an amalgamation in the nature of purchase and cannot be recognised as an intangible asset. In this case, this expenditure (included in the cost of acquisition) should form part of the amount attributed to goodwill (capital reserve) at the date of acquisition.

In some cases, expenditure is incurred to provide future economic benefits to an enterprise, but no intangible asset or other asset is acquired or created that can be recognised. In these cases, the expenditure is recognised as an expense when it is incurred. Expenditure on research is always as an expense when it is incurred. A few other examples are:

(*a*) expenditure on start-up activities *i.e.*, start-up costs, unless this expenditure is included in the cost of a fixed asset. Start-up costs may consist of preliminary expenses incurred in establishing a legal entity;

(*b*) expenditure on training activities;

(*c*) expenditure on advertising and promotional activities; and

(*d*) expenditure on relocating or recognising part or all of an enterprise.

Subsequent Expenditure on Intangible Assets

Subsequent expenditure on an intangible asset after its purchase or its completion should be recognised as an expense when it is incurred unless

(*a*) it is probable that the expenditure will enable the asset to generate future economic benefits in excess of its originally assessed standard of economic performance; and

(*b*) the expenditure can be measured; and attributed to the asset reliably.

If the abovementioned conditions are fulfilled, the subsequent expenditure should be added to the cost of the intangible asset.

After initial recognition, an intangible asset should be carried at its cost less any accumulated amortisation and any accumulated impairment losses.

Amortisation

The depreciable amount of an intangible asset should be allocated on a systematic basis over the best estimate of its useful life.

Amortisation Period

There is a rebuttable presumption that the useful life of an intangible asset will not exceed ten years from the date when the asset is available for use. The cost of the asset less any residual value is allocated over the useful life as an expense following a systematic method.

Amortisation Method

The amortisation method should reflect the pattern in which the asset's economic benefits are consumed by the enterprise. If that pattern cannot be determined reliably, straight line method should be used. Sometimes, the economic benefits embodied in an asset are absorbed by the enterprise in producing other assets. In such cases, the amortisation charge forms part of the cost of the other asset. For example, the amortisation of intangible assets used in a production process is included in the carrying amount of inventories.

Residual Value

The residual value of an intangible asset should be assumed to be zero unless

(*a*) there is a commitment by a third party to purchase the asset at the end of its useful life, or

(*b*) there is an active market for the asset and

(*i*) residual value can be determined by reference to that market, and

(*ii*) it is probable that such a market will exist at the end of the asset's useful life.

Review of Amortisation Period and Amortisation Method

The amortisation period and the amortisation method should be reviewed at least at each financial year end. If the expected useful life is significantly different, the amortisation period should be changed accordingly. Similarly, if there has been a significant change in the expected pattern of economic benefits from the asset, the amortisation method should be changed to reflect the changed pattern. Such changes should be accounted for in accordance with AS-5, Net Profit or Loss for the Period ; Prior Period Items and Changes in Accounting Policies.

Impairement Losses:

To determine whether an intangible asset is impaired, an enterprise applies Accounting Standard on Impairement of Assets which explains how an enterprise reviews the carrying amount of its assets, how it determines the recoverable amount of an asset and when it recognises or reverses an impairement loss.

If an impairement loss occurs before the end of the first annual accounting period commencing after acquisition for an intangible asset acquired in an amalgamation in the nature of purchase, the impairement loss is recognised as an adjustment to both the amount assigned to the intangible asset and the goodwill (capital reserve) recognised at the date of the amalgamation, provided the loss does not relate to specific events or changes in circumstances occurring after the date of acquisition.

An enterprise should estimate the recoverable amount of the following intangible assets at least at each financial year and even if there is no indication that the asset is impaired:-

(*a*) an intangible asset that is not yet available for use; and

(*b*) an intangible asset that is amortised over a period exceeding ten years from the date when the asset is available for use.

Retirements and Disposals

An intangible asset should be derecognised (eliminated from the balance sheet) on disposal or when no future economic benefits are expected from its use and subsequent disposal.

Gains or losses arising from the retirement or disposal of an intangible asset should be recognised as income or expense, as the case may be, in the income statement of the accounting year in which the retirement or disposal takes place.

2. VALUATION OF GOODWILL

Goodwill is an intangible asset but not fictitious. Sometimes a tangible asset is less valuable than goodwill. A tramway company may have spent lakhs of rupees on laying the track and is justified in treating the expenditure as an asset. Yet, the realisable value of the track will only be a small fraction of the amounts spent unless the tram ways are profitable and unless the track is being sold as part of a going concern. It is so also with goodwill. Goodwill is a valuable asset if the concern is profitable; it is valueless if the concern is a losing concern. Goodwill is the value of the reputation of the firm judged in respect of its capacity to bring in, unaided, profits. Prof. Dicksee says, "When a man pays for goodwill he pays for something which places him in the position of being able to earn more money than he would be able to do by his own unaided efforts". Another authority says, "Thus given a business, the goodwill of which is for disposal, there would be no valuable goodwill if anyone could do just as well by establishing a business *de novo*." Goodwill *may be defined as the value of the reputation of a business house in respect of profits expected in future over and above the normal level of profits earned by undertakings belonging to the same class of business.*

A firm may enjoy better profits or even profitability than other firms in the industry because of numerous factors, some of which are stated below:—

(*i*) Favourable location in respect of source of raw materials or of markets or of both, enabling the firm to enjoy substantial economies through saving in freight or through facility in sales.

(*ii*) Favourable long-term contracts as regards supply of raw materials or components or as regards sales.

(*iii*) Exclusive use of patents or trade marks on the basis of which competition from similar products is avoided.

(*iv*) Know-how, *i.e.*, knowledge about the peculiar problems facing the industry (both in respect of production and marketing) and about how to overcome them. Often this knowledge is acquired through collaboration with foreign firms but it is also acquired through experience, well pondered, and through systematic research.

(*v*) Active, intelligent, dynamic and forward looking management.

Factors (*i*) to (*iii*) are rather temporary; factors (*iv*) and (*v*) are enduring in nature.

Strictly speaking, enduring goodwill should be in respect of know-how and management only—it comes about through the quality and calibre of the human resources at the disposal of the undertaking.

Here goodwill will be used in its wide meaning as including the value of future profits arising from whatever source or reason such as technical knowledge and experience (know-how), near-monopoly position, etc. It is, of course, possible to put a value on each major factor separately. In that case, the term goodwill will have a narrow meaning—value of the reputation only of the firm including that of its management.

Need

Goodwill is realisable only if the business is disposed of. No one would consider selling the goodwill, i.e., the firm's name and its special advantages while still trying to run the old business and no one will probably buy goodwill on the condition that the previous firm will continue to exist. Therefore, a question may arise as to the necessity of valuation of goodwill.

In case of a joint stock company, the need for evaluating goodwill may arise in the following cases:—

(*a*) When the company has previously written off goodwill and wants to write it back in order to wipe off or reduce the debit balance in the Profit and Loss Account.

(*b*) When the business of the company is to be sold to another company or when the company is to be amalgamated with another company.

(*c*) When, stock exchange quotations not being available, shares have to be valued for taxation purposes.

(*d*) When a large block of shares, such as to enable the holder to exercise control over the company concerned, has to be bought or sold.

(*e*) When one class of shares is to be converted into another.

Components of Goodwill

Conceptually, it is possible to analyse the super profits earned by a firm by the factors involved (see the previous page). Goodwill may therefore be broken up into various parts, related to:

(*i*) Know-how possessed by the firm;

(*ii*) Advantage enjoyed by it because of certain patents available to it:

(*iii*) Special locational advantage;

(*iv*) Special commercial advantages such as a long-term contract for supply of raw materials at a low price or for sale of finished goods at remunerative prices;

(*v*) Advantage because of prior entry specially if later entry is made difficult through a system of licensing that may be in force or some such other factor; and

(*vi*) Managerial superiority.

If it is possible to analyse profits in the manner mentioned above, the goodwill attaching each of the factors can be separately calculated. However, generally such an attempt is not made since it is difficult to disentangle the various forces leading to business results. Sometimes, however, such calculation becomes unavoidable — for example when compensation has to be paid for forcing a business firm to give up its present location.

General factors affecting the value of goodwill

The main factors affecting goodwill are the following:—

(*a*) Profits expected to be earned by the firm or company including those arising from its special advantages.

One must realise at the very outset that when one acquires a firm and its goodwill, one is hoping to earn good profits in the future. If, for any reason, it is evident that profits in the future will be low, one will not pay much for goodwill—perhaps one will decline to acquire the firm itself. Good past profits are not relevant except to the extent they point to the possibility of earning good profits in the future also.

(*b*) The yield expected by investors in the industry to which the firm or the company belongs.

(*c*) The amount of capital employed to earn the profit mentioned in (*a*) above.

(*d*) Special factors relevant to a particular situation, for instance those to be considered when the Government acquires control over a company by executive order.

Profitability

It is not well recognised that profitability of a concern is the chief factor in the valuation of goodwill. Investors invest money only to earn an income and the size of the income determines what they will pay for the asset concerned. The cost of the asset to the previous proprietor does not matter at all. The market value of a house does not depend on its cost but on the rent fetched by it. Suppose a business is for sale and proprietor demands Rs. 10,00,000 for the tangible assets and another Rs. 4,00,000 for goodwill, the profit earned in that business being Rs. 1,00,000 per year; no one will pay anything for goodwill if a new, similar, business started with Rs. 10,00,000 will also yield Rs. 1,00,000 profit. Goodwill is paid only for the extra profits. If, in the above example, the actual profits were Rs. 1,40,000 whereas a new business would earn with the same capital only Rs. 1,00,000, goodwill will arise in respect of the extra Rs. 40,000 profits.

One who pays for goodwill can look only to the future profits. Hence, the business will be thoroughly examined to see what special advantages it is in possession of and which of them are likely to continue with the change in ownership and passage of time. The attempt is to establish the future maintainable profits.

The following are the important factors that have a bearing on future profits, and therefore, the value of goodwill:—

(*a*) *Personal skill in management.* Reputation is built up by the skill displayed in management. Admittedly, in certain cases skill in management is much more important than in others. For example, a firm of architects, solicitors or chartered accountants depends much more on the skill possessed and reputation enjoyed by the proprietors for success than does a textile mill.

If the success of the firm whose goodwill is being valued depends on senior officials, continued service of such official is a point to remember. If they are unwilling to serve under new ownership, the value of goodwill cannot be much. For instance, if a newspaper has been built up by the editor and if the editor is unwilling to serve the new masters, the newspaper will suffer by the resignation and the continued success of the paper will not be assured.

(*b*) *Nature of business.* This covers many things. If it is difficult to enter an industry existing firms will enjoy a measure of goodwill by the mere fact of existence. Difficulties may arise, for proposed new entrants, due to the market having reached its saturation point or due to unduly heavy expenditure on fixed assets or due to legal difficulties. It is very difficult, due to exchange regulations and Import Control, for a new firm to enter import business. Existing firms, therefore will command goodwill which in ordinary times they would not. If a firm enjoys monopoly or near monopoly conditions, it also enjoys goodwill but not if the monopoly is due to case.

(c) *Favourable location or site.* It is well-known that certain cities or places are most suitable for particular industries and that in a city certain localities offer the most advantageous positions for particular trades. For example, in Delhi, Nai Sarak has acquired a reputation for being centre of the text-book trade. Existing shops, therefore, have an advantage which can be converted into cash by selling the goodwill. If ample space were available for newcomers, there would be no goodwill on account of location. Goodwill arises only because the newcomers find it hard to rent premises.

(d) *Access to supplies.* In these times of raw material shortages, a firm enjoying a favourable position regarding supplies of materials will possess goodwill. A firm holding large quotas for import of goods will be able to realise good money for goodwill as long as import restrictions continue. Favourable contracts with monopolist suppliers will have the same effect unless the contract is due to expire and is not likely to be renewed.

(e) *Patents and trade mark protection.* In most industries ownership of patents is necessary in order to carry on production. A firm enjoying the right to use the most valuable patents will have a valuable goodwill. If a firm has built up good reputation for its products by means of a trade mark, its possession will bring good profits and, therefore, goodwill will be worth a large sum of money. Similarly, a firm of publishers having good copyrights will enjoy goodwill but not if the copyrights are due to expire or if the book does not sell much.

(f) *Exceptional contracts.* Exceptionally favourable contracts for supply of goods or services to the customers will also raise the value of goodwill. If, however, the exceptional contracts were obtained only due to the personal skill and influence of the previous owner, and it is unlikely that such contracts will be obtained in future, the value of goodwill will not be influenced by such existing contracts. Pending contracts of recurring nature and likely to result in substantial profits will enhance the value of goodwill.

(g) *Capital requirements and arrangement of capital.* The amount of capital required will have much influence on the value of goodwill. If the capital required is large, considering the profits likely to be available, the value of goodwill will be small. If the business is highly profitable and the capital invested is relatively small, a high value may be placed on goodwill. In this connection, the sources of funds may have influence on profits available for equity shareholders. Suppose, there are two companies, *A* and *B*, both making a profit of, say Rs. 2,00,000 a year and both requiring Rs. 10,00,000 to produce the profit. Suppose further, that A's capital consists only of equity shares, whereas *B* has raised Rs. 2,00,000 by issuing 12% debentures, Rs. 3,00,000 by issuing 14% preference shares and Rs. 5,00,000 by issuing equity shares. The profits available for equity shareholders (who have the real stake in the profits of the companies) are as follows:

	Company A		*Company B*
	Rs.	*Rs.*	*Rs.*
Profit	2,00,000		2,00,000
Less: Debenture Interest	..	24,000	
Preference Dividend	..	42,000	66,000
Profit available for equity shareholders	2,00,000		1,34,000
Equity share capital	1,00,000		5,00,000
Percentage of profit available to equity share capital	20		26.8

B is said to be trading on equity.

Obviously, those who own equity shares in company *B* are favourably placed compared to the equity shareholders in company *A*. In other words, the existence of fixed interest or dividend bearing capital is advantageous to the equity shareholders if the profits are large. This advantage may have to be considered for valuation of the goodwill if the purchasing company continues to have advantage of the fixed interest or dividend bearing capital. But if the profits are small, the existence of such capital will have a depressing effect on the value of goodwill. If the profit is large, but if the debentures or preference shares have to be redeemed on transfer of ownership, there is no advantage left for the purchasing company and hence the value of goodwill will be correspondingly less. The logic behind the argument is that one can acquire control over the whole company by purchasing the majority of equity shares and that profit, after debenture interest and preference dividend have been paid, all belong to equity shareholders. Equity shareholders are, therefore, the main beneficiaries of any special advantage that a company enjoys.

It may be seen that a company may not be specially profitable (for example, company *B* in the example given above) and, therefore, not entitled to any goodwill as such. But, if, due to capital gearing arrangements, equity shareholders get a dividend higher than in other companies they will have a valuable right to be valued in terms of goodwill.

Note: It may be argued that in an industry a particular proportion of total funds required is likely to be raised by way of preference shares or debentures. Therefore, there may be no advantage to a company in this respect. In fact, a company which departs from the norms prevailing in the industry concerned is not looked upon with favour by investors.

Further, even if a company does have an advantage in the form of trading on equity, it is likely to be temporary. Therefore, it would be better not to attach too much weight to this point. It would be proper to consider the profitability of the company, considering profit earned (before interest and dividends but after tax) and total capital employed. However, the opinion so far is to exclude loans and debentures from capital employed and consider profits after interest.

The approach in this book will be to treat capital employed as equivalent to shareholders' funds, preference or equity, and consider profits available to shareholders.

The influence of all the factors discussed above works out in the figure of profits. These figures should be carefully examined to see how much of the profits are likely to be realised in future also, since (to repeat) the purchaser pays for goodwill on the expectation of earning good profits in the future. If in the past good profits have been earned due to

(*a*) the personality of the previous owner,
(*b*) the particularly favourable situation which is likely to be lost,
(*c*) short-lived monopoly conditions, or
(*d*) a temporary craze or fashion,

there will be no value attached to goodwill.

Future Maintainable Profit. It has been stated above that it is the future profits, likely to be earned, that are relevant for valuing goodwill. This is quite correct but the estimate for future profits will obviously be made on the basis of past profits. While estimating the future profits on the basis of past profits the points to be remembered are as under:

(*i*) All usual working expenses including interest to debentureholders and depreciation of the assets of the company should be provided for. If the fixed assets have to be revalued, depreciation should be based on the values arrived at as a result of the revaluation.

(*ii*) All necessary provisions for liabilities for, say, taxation or otherwise should be made. But transfer to general reserves, dividend equalization fund, or sinking fund for redemption of liabilities should not be taken note of, as such transfers merely transfer profits from one account to another, and the availability of profits is not affected.

(*iii*) In case non-trading assets have been excluded from the capital employed, the income derived from such assets should be excluded.

(*iv*) Profits for the past four or five years (during which conditions have remained normal) should be averaged since the average is more reliable than a single year's profit.

(*v*) Developments which have already taken place but whose results are likely to come in the future should be taken into account.

The whole idea is to arrive at a figure of profits which can be expected to be maintained in future.

Illustration 1:

Calculate Future Maintainable Profit for the year ending March 31, 2010 and the additional information :—

Year	*Profits after tax Rs.'000*	*Taxation Rs.'000*	*Transfer to general reserve Rs.'000*	*Managerial remuneration Rs.'000*
2005-2006	63,000	27,000	10,000	4,500
2006-2007	49,000	21,000	10,000	3,500
2007-2008	38,500	16,500	10,000	2,750
2008-2009	42,000	18,000	15,000	3,000
2009-2010	56,000	24,000	15,000	4,000

Depreciation on fixed assets has been provided @ 10% p.a.; Revaluation of the fixed assets shows an appreciation of Rs. 10 crore. Apart from equity share capital the company has 13% preference share capital of Rs. 10 crore. The rate of taxation is 30%.

Solution :

	Rs.
Total profits after tax	24,85,00,000
Add : Taxation	10,65,00,000
Managerial remuneration	1,77,50,000
Profit before tax and managerial remuneration for five years	37,27,50,000
Average profit before tax and managerial remunearion	7,45,50,000
Less : Additional depreciation on Rs. 10 crore @ 10%	1,00,00,000
Average profit before managerial remuneration and tax	6,45,50,000
Less : Managerial remuneration @ 5% on Rs. 6,45,50,000	32,27,500
Average profit before tax	6,13,22,500
Less : Income tax on Rs. 6,13,22,500 @ 30%	1,83,96,750
Future Maintaninable Profit	4,29,25,750

Markedly rising or falling profits: If the profits over the past four or five years have been falling or rising in a marked manner, it will be better to attach more importance to the profits of the last year and least importance to the profits of the first year. This is because conditions in say, 2009-2010 are more likely to be like those in 2008-09 than in 2005-06. This factor will be taken into account if the weighted average of profits is ascertained. Each year's profit is assigned a weight—the highest weight is attached to the profit of the most recent year. The profit is multiplied by the weight, the products are totalled and then divided by the total number of weights. If 5 years' profits are being averaged, the first year may be given a weight of one, the next one of two and so on. Thus

Year	*Profits Rs.'000*	*Weights*	*Products Rs.'000*
2005-2006	35,000	1	35,000
2006-2007	45,000	2	90,000
2007-2008	40,000	3	1,20,000
2008-2009	60,000	4	2,40,000
2010-2011	70,000	5	3,50,000
		15	8,35,000

Weighted average is = $\frac{\text{Rs. 8,35,000 thousand}}{15}$ = Rs. 55,667 thousand

One should not follow the practice suggested above, if there is a marked and continuous decline of profits. In that case, profits for the future should be estimated on the basis of the trend—they will be lower than the profits for the latest year.

Expected Developments. Results of development that have taken root, but are likely to bear fruit in future should be estimated and the past profits should be adjusted for this factor in order to arrive at the future maintainable profit. Suppose, as a result of research and development work in the past, a new product will soon be launched. The investment on this project should be added to capital employed and the expected profit to the estimate for future maintainable profit otherwise arrived at.

Illustration 2:

For the year ended 31st March 2010, a company reported a profit of Rs. 11,76,00,000 after paying income tax @ 30%. It was found that the year's income included Rs. 90 lakh for a claim lodged in 2007-08 for which no entry had been passed then. As far as trading conditions are concerned 2009-2010 was a normal year. The company expects to launch a new product and estimates in this respect are as follows :—

	Rs.
Sales	10,00,00,000
Expenditure on raw material, wages etc.	4,50,00,000
Share of fixed expenses (including an expected increase of Rs. 1 crore)	3,50,00,000

You are required to give an estimate of future maintainable profit.

Solution :

		Rs.
Profit before tax for the year ended 31st March, 2010		
$11,76,00,000 \times \frac{100}{70}$		16,80,00,000
Less : Income relating to the year 2007-08		90,00,000
Normal profit for the year 2009-2010		15,90,00,000
Add : Expected profit on the new product :	*Rs.*	
Sale	10,00,00,000	
Less : Expenditure on raw material, wages etc. and additional fixed expenses, Rs.(4,50,00,000 + 1,00,00,000)	5,50,00,000	4,50,00,000
Expected profit before tax		20,40,00,000
Less : Income tax @ 30%		6,12,00,000
Future Maintainable Profit		14,28,00,000

Illustration 3:

Wye Ltd. Shows the following summarised investment in its operations:—

	Rs.
Plant and machinery, at cost	50,00,000
Less: Depreciation till date	20,00,000
	30,00,000
Working Capital	20,00,000
	50,00,000

The nature of the industry is such that the plant, being of a sturdy nature, gives uniform service from year to year. The company makes a sale of Rs. 1,00,000 normally per annum and earns a profit of Rs. 20,00,000 before tax, the fixed expenses being 25% of the total cost. Tax is paid @ 30%.

Finding the sales to be good and the market expending, the company instals new plant costing Rs. 30 lakhs, 1/6 of the cost being due to price increases since the installation of the old plant. Increase in fixed expenses due to the new plant will be Rs. 6,00,000. Prepare an estimate of the future maintainable profit.

Solution:

		Rs.
Profit, as at present		20,00,000
Additional profit expected:		
Additional sale 1,00,000/2* Rs. 50,00,000		
(1/6 of the cost of the new plant of Rs. 30,00,000 is Rs. 5,00,000; therefore, the cost in terms of cost of the old plant would be Rs. 25,00,000. Thus, new plant has half the capacity of the old plant)		
Profit volume ratio = $\frac{\text{Profit} + \text{Fixed Expenses}}{\text{Sales}}$ = $\frac{20,00,000+20,00,000}{1,00,00,000}$ = 40%		
Increase in profit = 40% of Rs. 50,00,000 =	Rs. 20,00,000	
Less: Increase in fixed expenses	Rs. 6,00,000	14,00,000
		34,00,000
Tax @ 30%		10,20,000
Future Maintainable Profit		23,80,000

*Total cost is Rs. 80,00,000 i.e., sale minus profit 25% of this is Rs. 20,00,000.

Yield expected by investors

In valuation of goodwill, the expectation of investors plays an important role since it is this expectation that determines the normal level of profits. It is also called the average rate of return or the "normal rate of return". It means that return which will satisfy an ordinary investor (not very reluctant or eager to invest) in the industry concerned. Such a rate of return differs from one class of investment and business to another. An investor in government securities may feel satisfied with 10% yield on his outlay; he may expect, say, 20% if he invests in equity shares of a new company but, in case the company is old and well established, he may be content with only 18%.

Stock exchange quotations usually give a good indication of expectations of investors. If a share on which a dividend of Rs. 25 is paid and is expected to be paid sells for Rs. 125 the investors expect an yield of 20%, i.e., 25/125 × 100. Such a rate will be relevant to only the usual transactions on the stock exchange. It will have to be modified in view of the fact that valuation of goodwill envisages the transfer of a whole business or the majority of equity shares. Power itself being an advantage, the purchaser will have to pay for it by accepting a lower rate of return.

The yield expected by investors consists of three components:

(*i*) the pure interest — the interest which one can earn by parting with his funds without in any way incurring any risk, e.g., by buying government securities;

(*ii*) the business risk — a margin to cover to ordinary risks attendant in business; and

(*iii*) the financial risk — a margin to cover risks connected with the finances of the firm concerned.

If the pure interest is 12%, an investor in the shares of a company may want to add, say, 5% for ordinary business risks and 3% for the risks special to the company concerned — say, 20% in all.

The factors that affect the normal rate of return are the following:—

(*i*) the degree of risk attending investment — the risk may be because of the nature of the industry or of the situation in the company such as too much dependence on loans or debentures;

(*ii*) the period for which investment is to be made — longer the period, higher the expected rate of return;

(*iii*) the bank rate — any increase in the bank rate will lead to an all-round increase in expectation of investors; and

(*iv*) general economic and political situation — in case confidence is shaken there will be a sharp rise in the rate of return expected by investors. A boom, however, also may have the same effect because of a desire to share in the prosperity.

Capital employed

This is the third most important factor in valuation of goodwill, since the size of profits is significant only in relation to the capital used to earn it. Capital employed is now recognised to mean fixed assets (less depreciation written off) plus net working capital (that is, current assets minus current liabilities). This may also be expressed as aggregate of share capital, reserves and long-term loans. Non-trading assets, that is, assets acquired because of spare funds such as government securities, are excluded. Assets that must be acquired even if they are in the nature of shares, debentures, etc., cannot be treated as non-trading.

The abovementioned idea of capital employed, however, is not suitable for the purpose of valuing goodwill of individual companies where it is essentially the advantage accruing to the shareholders which has to be evaluated. *For this purpose, the amount of debentures or loans should also be excluded from capital.* (Of course, the profit considered for valuation of goodwill will also be after interest on debentures and loans Obviously goodwill is also excluded.)

An important point to note is the change in the value of fixed assets if these were acquired some years ago. Since profits are expressed in terms of current prices, it is proper that fixed assets should also be valued at current prices.

A refinement is that the figure of capital employed should be the average for the year concerned since the figure changes at least because of the profit or loss during the year.

Illustration 4:

The following is the balance sheet of Kajaria Ltd. as at 31st March, 2010:—

Liabilities	*Rs.*	*Assets*	*Rs.*	*Rs.*
Equity Shares of Rs. 10 each		Goodwill		75,000
fully paid up	5,00,000	Buildings, cost	80,000	
General reserve	1,50,000	*Less*: Depreciation Reserve	10,000	70,000
Profit & Loss Account	1,50,000	Plant & Machinery, cost	2,40,000	
14% Debentures	1,00,000	*Less*: Depreciation Reserve	40,000	20,00,000
Creditors	48,000	Furniture, cost	65,000	
Workman's Profit Sharing Reserve	45,000	*Less*: Depreciation Reserve	15,000	50,000
Workmen's Compensation Reserve	25,000	Trade Investments		
		(cost Rs. 1,00,000)		85,000
		Stock		1,50,000
		Debtors	3,00,000	
		Less: Provisions for Bad Debts	20,000	2,80,000
		Cash at Bank		88,000
		Preliminary Expreses		20,000
	10,18,000			10,18,000

Building are now worth Rs. 1,70,000 and Plant and Machinery is worth Rs. 1,80,000. Ascertain the Capital Employed.

Solution:

Assets		Rs.
Buildings		1,70,000
Plant and Machinery		1,80,000
Furniture		50,000
Investments		85,000
Stock		1,50,000
Debtors		2,80,000
Cash at Bank		88,000
		10,03,000*
Less: Liabilities	Rs.	
14% Debenture	1,00,000	
Creditors	48,000	
Workmen's Profit Sharing Reserve	45,000	1,93,000
Net Assets or Capital Employed		8,10,000

Alternatively, capital employed may be ascertained in the following manner:

Share Capital		5,00,000
General Reserve		1,50,000
Profit & Loss Account		1,50,000
Workmen's Compensation Reserve		25,000
Appreciation in the value of Buildings		1,00,000
		9,25,000
Less		
Goodwill**	75,000	
Preliminary Expenses	20,000	
Decrease in the value of Machinery	20,000	1,15,000
Capital Employed		8,10,000

Average capital employed means the mean of the capital employed at the end of the year and that employed in the beginning of the year. Thus, if the capital employed at the end of the year is Rs. 16,00,000, and capital employed in the beginning of the year is Rs. 10,00,000, the average capital employed in Rs. 13,00,000, *i.e.*, Rs. $\frac{16,00,000+10,00,000}{2}$.

Except for fresh capital, capital employed increases over a year mainly due to profits earned. If the capital employed in the beginning is Rs. 15,00,000 and the figure increases to Rs. 17,00,000 by the end of the year, the reasonable presumption is that during the year a profit of Rs. 2,00,000 has been earned. In this example, the average capital employed is Rs. 16,00,000, which figure can also be obtained by deducting from Rs. 17,00,000 half of the profit, viz., Rs. 1,00,000 (or adding Rs. 1,00,000 to the capital in the beginning). Thus if the capital employed in the beginning of the year is not given, average capital employed can be ascertained by deducting half the profits of the year from the capital employed at the end of the year. The assumption is that profits have been earned evenly over the year — that by the middle of the year half the profits were earned and thus used in business and that the profits have not yet been distributed. "Proposed Dividend" out of current year's profits, if it appears in balance sheet, should be treated as part of profits for this purpose.

METHODS FOR EVALUATING GOODWILL

Goodwill is sometimes valued on the basis of a certain number of years' purchase of the average profits of the past three or four or five years. For example, goodwill may have to be valued on the

* Goodwill is not to be included.

** To remove the effect of goodwill as given from capital employed.

basis of "three years' purchase of five years' profits." It means that the average profits of the immediately preceding five years should be ascertained and then the average should be multiplied by three. This method has nothing to recommend itself, since as already pointed out, goodwill attaches to profits over and above what one can earn by starting a new business and not to total profits. Therefore, this method is not followed in the business world. There are really only two methods for valuation of goodwill. These are the Super Profits Method and the Capitalsation Method. The Annuity Method is a variation of the Super Profits Method.

(*a*) **Super Profits Method.** In this case, the maintainable profits of the firm whose goodwill is for sale are compared with the "normal" profits for the firm, *i.e.*, profits, which would have been earned with the same capital by an average firm. If the estimated future profits are more than the normal profits, the difference is known as "Super Profits". This is the measure of the extra profits obtained by the firm. Goodwill is found by multiplying the super profits by a certain number, representing the number of years' purchase.

Normal profits are ascertained by multiplying the average capital employed by the rate of general expectation (*i.e.*, the rate of yield expected by investors in the industry concerned) and dividing by 100. To take a simplified example, suppose, (1) a firm employs Rs. 6,00,000 as capital (2) investors are not satisfied with an income of less than 20% and (3) the profits likely to be continued are Rs. 2,00,000. The super profits of the firm are as follows:—

	Rs.
Actual Profit	2,00,000
Less: Normal profit: Rs. 6,00,000 × 20/100	1,20,000
Super Profit	80,000

If goodwill is to be valued at three years' purchase, the value of goodwill will be Rs. 2,40,000 *i.e.*, Rs. 80,000 × 3.

Suppose, in the same firm, the profit actually is only Rs. 1,10,000. There is no super profit (because the actual profit is less than the normal profits) and hence no goodwill. It is only when actual profits exceed normal profits that goodwill arises.

In case of the super profits method, an important point to note is that the number of years of purchase of goodwill will also differ from industry to industry and from firm to firm. A business where the retiring proprietor was the main reason for success will have goodwill based on one or two years' purchase of goodwill. Three to five years' purchase is common. If the super profits are large, a large number of years' purchase is allowed. If the profits are declining, the number of years for purchase of goodwill will probably be only one or two. Theoretically, the number of years is to be determined with reference to the probability of a new business catching up with the old established business. Suppose, it is estimated that in four years' time a business, if started *de novo*, will be earning about the same profits as an old business is earning now, the purchaser of the business (old) will not pay for goodwill more than four or five times the super profits.

Illustration 5:

The following is the Balance Sheet of Jute Ltd. as at 31st March, 2010:—

Liabilities		*Rs.*	*Assets*	*Rs.*
Share Capital			Goodwill	3,72,000
5,000 14% Redeemable Preference			Premises and Land at cost	2,00,000
Shares of Rs. 100 each		5,00,000	Plant and Machinery at cost	15,00,000
1,00,000 Equity Shares of			Motor Vehicles at Cost (purchase	
Rs. 10 each		10,00,000	**on 1st October, 2008)**	20,000
General Reserve		3,50,000	Investments (to provide for replacement	
Profit and Loss Account:			of plant and machinery)	8,00,000
Balance as per previous			Raw materials at cost	2,60,000
Balance Sheet	16,000		Work in progress at cost (estimated)	65,000

		Rs.		Rs.
Profit for the year (after taxation)	5,50,000	5,66,000	Finished goods at cost	90,000
13% Debentures		10,00,000	Book debts	2,00,000
Secured Loans		1,00,000	Cash at bank and in hand	6,96,000
Sundry Creditors		1,50,000	Discount on Debentures	5,000
Provision for Taxation		5,50,000	Underwriting Commission	8,000
		38,16,000		38,16,000

The present value of premises and land is Rs. 6,00,000 and that of plant and machinery is Rs. 12,00,000. Market value of investments is Rs. 7,50,000. Book Debts are bad to the extent of 10%.

In a similar company, the market value of equity shares of the same denomination is Rs. 25 per share and in that company average dividend declared for the previous five years is 20% without any major fluctuations from year to year and without any marked upward or downward tendency. In the dividends of Jute Ltd. there have been fluctuations which are rather marked. Value the goodwill of the company. *(Adapted from C.A. Final)*

Solution:

1. *Calculation of capital employed:—*

	Rs.	Rs.
Present value of assets:		
Premises and Land		6,00,000
Plant and Machinery		12,00,000
Motor Vehicles [book value less depreciation for 1½ years @ 20% on original cost]		14,000
Raw materials		2,60,000
Work in Progress		65,000
Finished Goods		90,000
Book Debts (book value less 10%)		1,80,000
Investments (these have been included because the purpose is to replace plant and machinery)		7,50,000
Cash at Bank and in hand		6,96,000
		38,55,000
Less: Liabilities		
Provision for Taxation	5,50,000	
13% Debentures	10,00,000	
Secured loans	1,00,000	
Sundry creditors	4,50,000	18,00,000
Capital employed as on 31st March, 2010		20,55,000

Average capital employed: Rs. 20,55,000 less half of the profits for the year, viz., 2,16,500 [see (2) below] or Rs. 18,38,500. It is assumed that the profit has been earned evenly over the whole of the year.

2. *Profits earned by the company:—*

	Rs.	Rs.
Profits as given in the balance sheet		5,50,000
Less: Depreciation not provided for:		
On Premises and Land at (say) 5% on Rs. 6,00,000	30,000	
On Plant and Machinery at (say) 15% on Rs. 12,00,000	1,80,000	
On Motor Vehicles @ (say) 20% on Rs. 20,000	4,000	
Bad Debts	20,000	
	2,34,000	
Less: Tax-effect	1,17,000	1,17,000
		4,33,000

Depreciation has had to be deducted from the profits because the balance sheet shows the fixed assets at cost and does not mention any depreciation reserve. It has to be assumed, therefore, that depreciation was not provided.

3. *Calculation of General Expectation.*

20% dividend on Rs. 10, viz., a dividend of Rs. 2 per share enables a share to be quoted at Rs. 25 in the market. For a quotation at Rs. 100, a dividend of Rs. 8 will be required, *i.e.*, 2/25 × 100. Hence, the general expectation is 8%. But in this case, the company has a stable record as regards dividend which record Jute Ltd., does not possess. The expectation in case of Jute Ltd., will, therefore, be somewhat high, say, 10%.

4. *Super Profits*:

	Rs.
Maintainable Profits	4,33,000
Normal Profits : 10% on average capital employed	1,83,850
	2,49,150

5. Goodwill at 3 years' purchase (assumed) of the super profits come to Rs. 7,47,450.

Note. The problem gives profits only for one year. It would have been better it profits of some of the preceding years had also been given because the average of a few years' profits is a better basis than one year's profits.

Illustration 6:

On 31st March, 2010 A Ltd. proposes to purchase the business carried on by M/s X Ltd. Goodwill for this purpose is agreed to be valued at three years' purchase of the weighted average profits for the last four years. The appropriate weights to be used were decided as follows :

2006-2007	1
2007-2008	2
2008-2009	3
2009-2010	4

The profits for these years are :

2006-2007	Rs. 10,10,000;	2007-2008	Rs. 12,40,000;
2008-2009	Rs. 10,00,000 and	2009-2010	Rs. 14,00,000.

On a scrutiny of the accounts, the following facts are revealed :

(*i*) On 1st December, 2008 major repairs were carried out in respect of the plant, spending Rs. 3,00,000; the amount was charged to revenue. The said sum is agreed to be capitalised for the purpose of calculation of goodwill subject to the adjustment for depreciation @ 10% p.a. on reducing balance method.

(*ii*) The closing stock for the year 2007-2008 was overvalued by Rs. 1,20,000.

(*iii*) To cover management cost an annual charge of Rs. 2,40,000 is to be made while calculating goodwill.

Compute the value of goodwill of the transferor company.

[*Adapted B.Com. (Hons.) Delhi - 2000*]

Solution :

	2006-2007	2007-2008	2008-2009	2000-2010
	Rs.	*Rs.*	*Rs.*	*Rs.*
Profits, as given	10,10,000	12,40,000	10,00,000	14,00,000
(*i*) Increase in profit on rectification of error of principle made on 1st December, 2008			+ 3,00,000	
			13,00,000	
Decrease in profits due to depreciation in respect of abovementioned error				

	Rs.	Rs.	Rs.	Rs.
— Depreciation on Rs. 3,00,000 @10% p.a. for 4 months			– 10,000	
— Depreciation on Rs. 2,90,000 @10% p.a. for full year				– 29,000
			12,90,000	13,71,000
(*ii*) Adjustment of profits due to overvaluation of stock on 31.3.2008		– 1,20,000	+ 1,20,000	
Correct profits :	10,10,000	11,20,000	14,10,000	13,71,000

Calculation of weighted average :

Year	*Profits* *Rs.*	*Weight*	*Product* *Rs.*
2006-2007	10,10,000	1	10,10,000
2007-2008	11,20,000	2	22,40,000
2008-2009	14,10,000	3	42,30,000
2009-2010	13,71,000	4	54,84,000
		10	1,29,64,000

Weighted average = Rs. 1,29,64,000 / 10	12,96,400	
Less : Management cost		2,40,000
		10,56,400

Goodwill at 3 years' purchase = Rs. 10,56,400 × 3 = Rs. 31,69,200

Illustration 7:

The Balance Sheet of Abrasives Ltd. (a private limited company) discloses the following financial position as on 31st March, 2010:—

	Rs.		*Rs.*
Shareholders' Funds:—		Fixed Assets:—	
Paid up Capital —		Land and Building	1,00,000
2,000 14% Preference shares of Rs. 100 each	2,00,000	Plant and Machinery	7,00,000
10,000 Equity shares of Re. 1 each	10,000	Current Assets —	
General Reserve	9,000	Stock-in-Trade	4,00,000
Unappropriated Profits	31,000	Book Debts	2,00,000
Secured Loans		Cash at Bank	1,00,000
Mortgage Debentures	10,00,000		
Current Liabilities —			
Trade Creditors	2,50,000		
	15,00,000		15,00,000

It is proposed to convert the company into a public limited company and on that account you are asked to value goodwill of Abrasives Ltd. The following information is supplied:—

(*i*) Abrasives Ltd. was incorporated on 1st April, 2001.

(*ii*) The company manufactures abrasives material involving high technical skill.

(*iii*) The assets of the company have been adequately depreciated.

(*iv*) The item of Plant and Machinery of Rs. 7,00,000 is shown after charging adequate depreciation. The present market value of the asset is Rs. 8 lakh. Rate of depreciation on Plant and Machinery is 15% per annum.

(*v*) Noted below are the figures of (*a*) profits and losses arrived at after meeting all expenses including depreciation; and (*b*) sales for the various years:—

		Profit or loss before tax		Sales
		Rs.		Rs.
2001-02	..	24,000	..	1,17,000
2002-03	..	52,000	..	5,60,000
2003-04	..	1,50,000	..	10,70,000
2004-05	..	1,20,000	..	12,00,000
2005-06	.. (loss)	1,69,000 *	..	8,61,000
2006-07	..	1,90,000	..	7,18,000
2007-08	..	2,60,000	..	11,99,000
2008-09	..	2,95,000	..	13,17,000
2009-2010	..	3,35,000	..	18,22,000

*Due to exceptional circumstances.

The reasonable return on capital invested in the class of business done by Abrasives Ltd. is 18 per cent. It may be assumed that the company will be able to maintain its profits for the next few years on the same level as for the previous years.

Write a report to the directors stating what should be the value attached to goodwill of the company. State your reasons.

Solution:

Delhi
June 30, 2010

The Directors,
The Abrasive (Private) Ltd.,
Delhi

Dear Sirs,

We have examined the Balance Sheet as at March 31, 2010 submitted by you and other relevant data supplied to us for the purpose of valuation of goodwill of the Abrasives (Private) Ltd. In our opinion, the value to be placed on goodwill is Rs. 56,400. This is arrived at as under:

Capital employed:	Rs.	Rs.
Land and Building		3,00,000
Plant and Machinery		8,00,000
Stock-in-Trade		4,00,000
Book Debts		2,00,000
Cash at Bank		1,00,000
Total Assets		18,00,000
Less: Mortgage Debenture	10,00,000	
Trade Creditors	2,50,000	12,50,000
Capital employed		5,50,000

For calculating goodwill "average capital employed" is required. It appears the company has already made disbursements out of the profits for 2009-2010. This means that the figure of capital employed is more or less the same as in the beginning of the year. Hence we cannot deduct half the profits of the year (as is the usual practice) to arrive at average capital employed. An ad-hoc addition of Rs. 80,000 is made to the figure on 31st March, 2010, to arrive at the figure of average capital employed. Hence the average capital employed is taken to be Rs. 6,30,000.

2. The profits given are for nine years. In 2005-06, there was a heavy loss due to exceptional circumstances. It is desirable to take the average of the profits of the four years, 2006-07 to 2009-2010. This average may be taken to be a safe estimate of the profits expected to arise in future in view of the fact that, in the opinion of the directors, the company will be able to maintain its profits for the next few years.

The average profit for the last four years comes to Rs. 2,70,000. Becuase of increase in the value of Plant and machinery by Rs. 1,00,000, an additional amount of depreciation @ 15% p.a.

viz., Rs. 15,000 will be deducted so that the average becomes Rs. 2,55,000. Out of this, income tax has to be deducted. Taking income tax @ 50%, Rs. 1,27,500 is deducted, leaving Rs. 1,27,500. This is the measure of profits likely to be available for equity shareholders in future.

3. The super profits of the company will be Rs. 15,000 calculated as follows:—

	Rs.
Actual	1,27,500
Normal profits 18% of Rs. 6,30,000	1,13,400
	14,100

4. In view of the fact that both sales and profits have been increasing, it is reasonable to value goodwill on the basis of four years' purchase of the super profits. Hence the value of goodwill is Rs. 56,400.

We trust, you will find the calculation useful for the purpose.

Yours faithfully,

....

Chartered Accountant

(*b*) **The Annuity Method.** The idea behind super profit method is that the amount paid for goodwill be recouped during the next four or five years. If super profits are Rs. 1,00,000 and goodwill is calculated at 5 years purchase and is, therefore, valued at Rs. 5,00,000, the purchaser pays now Rs. 5,00,000 and will receive back Rs. 1,00,000 every year for 5 year as extra profits (which but for purchase of goodwill he would not receive). But in this case, there is a heavy loss of interest. Properly speaking what should be paid now is only the present value of Rs. 1,00,000 paid annually for 5 years at the proper rate of interest. The present value of Re. 1 paid annually can be calculated by the formula:

$$\frac{1-\left(1+\frac{r}{100}\right)^{-n}}{\frac{r}{100}} \text{ or } \frac{1-\left(\frac{100}{100+r}\right)^{n}}{\frac{r}{100}}$$

where r is the rate of interest per cent per annum and n is the number of years over which the payment is to be made. If the rate of interest is 20% and payment of one rupee is to be made for 3 years annually, the present value will be

$$\frac{1-\left(1+\frac{20}{100}\right)^{-3}}{\frac{20}{100}} \text{ or } \frac{1-(1.2)^{-3}}{0.2} \text{ or } \frac{1-\frac{1}{(1.2)^3}}{0.2} \text{ or } 2.106$$

If super profits are Rs. 1,00,000 and 3 years' purchase is to be allowed on annuity basis at 20%, the value of goodwill will be Rs. 1,00,000 × 2.106 or Rs. 2,10,600.

Illustration 8:

The following particulars are available in respect of the business of Lucky Ltd. :

(*i*) Profits earned for the years :

2007-2008	Rs. 5,00,000
2008-2009	Rs. 6,00,000
2009-2010	Rs. 5,50,000

(*ii*) Normal rate of return = 10%

(*iii*) Capital employed = Rs. 30,00,000

(*iv*) Present value of an annuity of one rupee for 5 years at 10% = Rs. 3.78

(*v*) The profits included non-recurring profits on an average basis of Rs. 30,000 a year.

You are required to calculate the value of goodwill of the company :

(*i*) as per five years purchase of super-profits;

(*ii*) as per capitalisation of super-profits method; and

(*iii*) as per annuity method. [*Adapted B.Com.(Hons.) Delhi, 2001*]

Solution :

	Rs.
Average profits for the last three years = Rs. (5,00,000 + 6,00,000 + 5,50,000) / 3	5,50,000
Less : Non-recurring profits	30,000
Recurring profits	5,20,000
Less : Normal profits = 10% of Rs. 30,00,000	3,00,000
Super profits	2,20,000

(*i*) Goodwill at five years' purchase of super profits = Rs. 2,20,000 × 5 = Rs. 11,00,000

(*ii*) Goodwill as per capitalisation of super profits @10% = Rs. 2,20,000 × 100/10 = Rs. 22,00,000

(*iii*) Goodwill as per annuity method = Rs. 2,20,000 × 3.78 = Rs. 8,31,600.

Illustration 9:

The summarised Balance Sheet of Jai Ltd. as at March 31, 2010 is as follows:

Liabilities	*Rs.*	*Assets*	*Rs.*	*Rs.*
Share Capital:		Fixed Assets		
1,500 14% Preference share of		Goodwill	45,000	
Rs. 100 each, fully paid	1,50,000	Freehold Property	3,75,000	
6,500 Equity Shares of		Plant and Machinery		
Rs. 100 each, fully paid	6,50,000	*Less*: Depreciation	3,50,000	7,70,000
Profit and Loss Account	4,50,000	Current Assets:		
12% Debentures – 2014-2015	3,00,000	Stock	3,75,000	
Sundry Creditors	2,39,250	Debtors (Net)	3,99,250	
		Cash at Bank	2,45,000	10,19,250
	17,89,250			17,89,250

Profits after tax for three years 2007-08, 2008-2009 and 2009-2010 after charging debenture interest, were Rs. 3,30,500; Rs. 4,22,500; and Rs. 3,40,000 respectively. Mr. Newrich is interested in buying all the equity shares and requests you to let him know the proper price. You are given the following information:—

(*i*) The normal rate of return @ 20% is on net assets attributed.

(*ii*) Goodwill may be calculated at three times the adjusted average super profits of the three years referred to above but loss of interest should be taken care of.

(*iii*) 12% Debentures will be immediately redeemed. The preference shares are also due to be redeemed but they are willing to exchange these for 14% Debentures.

(*iv*) The value of freehold property is to be ascertained on the basis of 16% return. The current rental value is Rs. 1,00,800.

(*v*) A claim of Rs. 8,250 was omitted to be provided in the year 2009-2010.

(*vi*) 10% of profits for 2008-2009 referred to above arose from a transaction of a non-recurring nature.

(*vii*) A provision of Rs. 15,750 on Sundry Debtors was made in 2009-2010 which is no longer required. Ascertain the value of goodwill of the company, the capital employed may be taken as on 31st March, 2010. [*Adapted from C.A. (Final)*]

Solution:

Assumptions:

(*i*) Since the present debentures are to be redeemed and the liquid resources of the company are not enough, it is assumed that the company will raise Rs. 2,00,000 from banks; as a term loan at 18 p.a.

(*ii*) The rate of tax applicable to the company is 50%.

Working Notes :

(1) Net assets of the company, taking into account the assumptions stated above:

		Rs.	Rs.
Freehold property at market value			
Rs. 1,00,000 × $\frac{100}{16}$			6,25,000
Plant and Machinery			3,50,000
Stock			3,75,000
Debtors		Rs.	4,15,000
Cash at Bank :	As stated	2,45,000	
	Loan [see (*i*) above]	2,00,000	
		4,45,000	
	Less: Payment to Debentureholders	3,00,000	1,45,000
			19,10,000
Less: Liabilities			
New Loan		2,00,000	
14% Debentures		1,50,000	
Sundry Creditors and Outstanding Claims		2,47,500	5,97,500
			13,12,500

(2) Additional interest payment in future:

	Rs.	
Interest on new debentures @ 14% on	1,50,000	21,000
Interest on term loans @ 18% on	2,00,000	36,000
		57,000
Less: Interest as at present @ 12% on	3,00,000	36,000
		21,000
Less: Tax effect thereof @ 50%		10,500
Additional after-tax burden of interest		10,500

(3) Future maintainable profit:

Average			
2007-08			3,30,500
2008-09		4,22,500	
Less: 10% non recurring profit		42,250	3,80,250
2009-2010		3,40,000	
Add : Provision on Sundry Debtors	15,750		
Less : Omission of Claim	8,250		
	7,500		
Less: Tax effect	3,750	3,750	3,43,750
			10,54,500
Average			3,51,500
Less: After-tax Interest (additional)			10,500
Future maintainable profits			3,41,000

Calculation of goodwill:

Future maintainable profit	3,41,000
Normal Profit, 20% on Rs. 13,12,500	2,62,500
Super Profit	78,500

	Rs.
Present value of Re. 1 per annum for three years @ 20% p.a.: 2.016	
Goodwill Rs. 78,500 × 2.016	1,58,256
Say	1,58,000

(*c*) **Capitalisation method.** In this case, the total value of the business is found out by capitalizing the actual (average) profits adjusted for any special circumstances on the basis of the normal expectation. The formula is:

$$\frac{\text{Estimated annual Profit}}{\text{Normal rate of return}} \times 100$$

For example, if a business is expected to yield a profit of Rs. 2,00,000 and the general expectation is 20%, the total value of the business is Rs. 2,00,000 × 100 ÷ 20 or Rs. 10,00,000. A reverse calculation of finding the income on Rs. 10,00,000 @ 20% will show that the profit is Rs. 2,00,000. Hence, those who want an income of 20% will pay Rs. 10,00,000 for a business yielding a profit of Rs. 2,00,000. The value of goodwill will be the total value of a business minus the net tangible assets of the firm. If in the above example the net assets amount to Rs. 8,50,000, goodwill be Rs. 1,50,000 *i.e.*, Rs. 10,00,000 – Rs. 8,50,000.

The value of goodwill under this method is generally much higher than that obtained under the method of super profits. In the example being discussed, the goodwill on super profits basis will be Rs. 90,000; thus:

	Rs.
Actual Profits (adjusted)	2,00,000
Normal profits : 20% on Rs. 8,50,000	1,70,000
Super Profit	30,000
Goodwill at three years' purchase	90,000

This is much less than the goodwill of Rs. 1,50,000 obtained under the capitalisation method which really means that goodwill is being valued on too many years' purchase of super profits. In this case, the number comes to 5, *i.e.*, 100 ÷ 20. If Rs. 30,000 (super profits) are multiplied by 5, goodwill comes to Rs. 1,50,000. Since the contention that super profits will continue for long (*i.e.*, a new firm will not be able to catch up with an old firm for a very long period) is unreasonable, the method is not a safe one to follow. But this is a proper method for valuing a business if the estimated future profit is less than the normal profit.

Note: Goodwill in case of professional people like chartered accountants is usually valued on the basis of one year's purchase of gross fees earned.

Illustration 10:

The balance sheets of X Ltd. are as follows :

(Rupees in lakhs)

Liabilities	*As at 31.3.2009*	*As at 31.3.2010*
Share Capital	1,000.0	1,000.0
General Reserve	800.0	850.0
Profit and Loss Account	120.0	175.0
Term Loans	370.0	330.0
Sundry Creditors	70.0	90.0
Provision for Tax	22.5	25.0
Proposed Dividend	200.0	250.0
	2,582.5	2,720.0
Assets		
Fixed Assets and Investment (Non-trading)	1,600.0	1,800.0
Stock	550.0	600.0
Debtors	340.0	220.0
Cash and Bank	92.5	100.0
	2,582.5	2,720.0

Other information :

(*i*) Current cost of fixed assets excluding non-trading investments on 31.3.2009 Rs. 2,200 lakh and on 31.3.2010 Rs. 2,532.8 lakh.

(*ii*) Current cost of stock on 31.3.2009 Rs. 670 lakh and on 31.3.2010 Rs. 750 lakh.

(*iii*) Face value of non-trading investments in 10% Government securities, Rs. 490 lakh.

(*iv*) Debtors include foreighn exchange debtors amounting to $ 70,000 recorded at the rate of $ 1= Rs. 17.50, but the closing exchange rate was $ 1 = Rs. 21.50.

(*v*) Creditors include foreign exchange creditors amounting to $ 1,20,000 recorded at the rate of $ 1= Rs. 16.50, but the closing exchange rate was $ 1 = Rs. 21.50.

(*vi*) Profit included Rs. 120 lakh being Government subsidy which is not likely to recur.

(*vii*) Rs. 247 lakh being the last instalment of R and D cost were written off the Profit and Loss Account. This expenditure is not likely to recur.

(*viii*) Tax rate during 2009-2010 was 50% effective future tax rate is estimated at 40%.

(*ix*) Normal rate of return is expected at 15%.

Based on the information furnished, Mr. Iral, a director, contends that the company does not have any goodwill. Examine his contention. Assume that there is no dividend tax.

[*Adapted C.A. (Final) Nov. 1997*]

Solution :

(*i*) *Calculation of average capital employed* : (*Rupees in lakhs*)

		As at 31.3.2009		As at 31.3.2010
Current cost of fixed assets other than non-trading investments		2,200.0		2,532.8
Current cost of stock		670.0		750.0
Debtors		340.0		222.8
Cash and Bank		92.5		100.0
		3,302.5		3,605.6
Less : Term loans	370.5		330.0	
Sundry creditors	70.0		96.0	
Provision for Tax	22.5	462.5	25.0	451.0
Capital employed		2,840.0		3,154.6

$$\text{Average capital employed at current value} = \text{Rs. } \frac{2{,}840.0 + 3{,}154.6}{2} \text{ lakh}$$

$$= \text{Rs. } 2{,}997.3 \text{ lakh}$$

(*ii*) *Calculation of future maintainable profit* :

	Rs. in lakhs	*Rs. in lakhs*
Increase in profit and loss account, Rs.(175.0 – 120.0) lakh		55.0
Increase in general reserve, Rs. (850.0 – 800.0) lakh		50.0
Proposed dividend on 31.3.2010		250.0
Profit after tax		355.0
Tax rate = 50%		
Hence, pre-tax profit = Rs. 355 lakh × 100 / 50		710.0
Less : Non-trading income, 10% of Rs. 490 lakh	49.0	
Exchange loss on creditors, [1.2 lakh × (21.5 – 16.5)]		6.0
Government Subsidy	120.0	175.0
		535.0
Add : Exchange gain on debotrs, [0.7 lakh × (21.5 – 17.5)]	2.8	
R & D Costs	247.0	
Stock adjustments	30.0	279.8

	Rs. in lakhs	*Rs. in lakhs*
Adjusted pre-tax profit		814.8
Less : Tax @ 40%		325.92
Future maintainable profit		488.88
Valuation of Goodwill		
(1) Capitalisation Method		
Capitalised Value of future maintainable profit (488.88 / 0.15)		3259.20
Less : Average Capital Employed		2997.30
Goodwill		261.90
(2) Super Profit Method		
Future Maintainable Profit		488.88
Normal Profit @ 15% on average capital employed		449.60
Goodwill		39.28

Under capitalisation method, the amount of goodwill is larger than the amount of goodwill computed under super profit method. In either case, the existence of goodwill cannot be doubted. **The director's contention is therefore unacceptable.**

Working Notes :

	Rs. in lakhs
(i) *Stock adjustments*	
Difference between current cost and historical cost of closing stock	150.0
Difference between current cost and historical cost of opening stock	120.0
	30.0
(*ii*) *Debtor's adjustment*	
Foreign exchange debtors at the closing exchange rate ($70,000 × 21.5)	15.05
Foreign exchange debtors at the original exchange rate ($70,000 × 17.5)	12.25
	2.80
(*iii*) *Creditor's adjustments*	
Foreign exchange creditors at the closing exchange rate ($ 1,20,000 × 21.5)	25.80
Foreign exchange creditors at the original exchange rate ($ 1,20,000 × 16.5)	19.80
	6.00

3. VALUATION OF SHARES

The Need

In most cases, shares are quoted on the stock exchange; and for ordinary transactions in shares or debentures or Government securities, the price prevailing on the stock exchange may be taken as the proper value. The stock exchange price does not hold good for very large lots. And not all shares are quoted on the stock exchange. Shares of private companies in any case will not be quoted. If, therefore, shares of such a company have to change hands, the value of such shares will have to be ascertained. In addition, in the following circumstances, need arises for valuation of shares of a company:—

(*a*) For formulating an amalgamation scheme.

(*b*) For purchase or sale of controlling shares (stock exchange quotations are valid only for regular lots).

(*c*) For the valuation of the assets of a finance or an investment trust company.

(*d*) For security purposes, *e.g.*, where loans are raised on the security of shares of a company.

(*e*) Where a company is reconstructed under section 494 of the Act and there are dissentient shareholders.

(*f*) Where a company acquires the shares in a company under section 395—that is when 9/10ths of shareholders in a company agree to transfer shares to another company and the transferee company decides to acquire the shares of dissentient shareholders also.

The factors that affect the value of shares of a company are similar to those that affect the value of goodwill of the company. In fact, valuation of goodwill and valuation of shares are inter-related.

The normal rate of return, though determined largely in the same way as in case of goodwill, has to be viewed in the light of some other factors also which are mentioned below:—

(*i*) Restrictions on transfer of shares — the normal rate of return will be increased, say, by ½%.

(*ii*) Disabilities attaching to the share will also cause the normal rate of return to go up — for instance, if the share is partly paid, the investors will expect a high yield from it (say, by ½% higher) than in case of fully paid shares.

(*iii*) Dividend performance — investors are satisfied with a comparatively low yield in case the company declares a uniform dividend from year to year and does not make a default. The normal rate of return is higher when the dividends have been fluctuating.

(*iv*) Financial prudence is also a factor. A company which distributes only a part of the profits will attract investors without having to offer high yield.

(*v*) Net asset backing is important from the point of view of sarfety. If tangible assets per share, after deduction of all liabilities, are twice or thrice the paid up value of the share, investors will be satisfied with a lower rate of return than if the net tangible assets are only a little more than the paid up capital.

Methods

Net Assets Basis or Intrinsic Value. In this case, the net assets of the company are determined and then the figure is divided by the number of shares. Care must be taken to value goodwill.* Non-trading assets will also be included. The assets will be put down at their market value. If there are preference shares, the preference capital will be deducted and only the remainder will be available for the equity shareholders. The figure will then be divided by the number of equity shares and the result will be the intrinsic value of the shares. For example, taking illustration, the intrinsic value of equity will be determined as follows:—

		Rs.
Net Assets:		
Goodwill (as ascertained)		56,400
Other assets (market value)		18,00,000
		18,56,400
	Rs.	
Less: Mortgage Debentures	10,00,000	
Trade Creditors	2,50,000	
Preference Capital	2,00,000	14,50,000
Assets available for Equity Shareholders		4,06,400
Number of Equity Shares : 10,000.		
Intrinsic value of one Equity Share Rs. $\frac{4,06,400}{10,000}$		40.64

Intrinsic value of shares is useful for formulating amalgamation schemes. Also, if some one wants to acquire controlling shares or if the company is about to go into liquidation, intrinsic value will be the price which will be paid.

*Some authorities state that goodwill need not be taken into account while valuing shares. Goodwill is as much an asset as any other and there seems to be no valid reason why goodwill should be ignored and other assets considered. However, in case of small lots, intrinsic value may be calculated ignoring goodwill because holders of small numbers of shares cannot force a company to realise its goodwill.

Illustration 11:

The following is the balance sheet of John Engineering Ltd. as on 31st March, 2010 :

Liabilities	*Rs.*
1,50,000 Equity Shares of Rs. 10 each, fully paid up	15,00,000
2,00,000 Equity Shares of Rs. 10 each, Rs. 6 paid up	12,00,000
60,000 12% Cumulative Preference Shares of Rs. 10 each, fully paid-up	6,00,000
Long Term Secured Loan	14,00,000
Sundry Creditors	6,50,000
	53,50,000

Assets	*Rs.*
Land and Buildings	23,00,000
Furniture, Fixtures and Fittings	3,90,000
Stock	8,30,000
Debtors	4,10,000
Cash at Bank	1,20,000
Profit and Loss Account	13,00,000
	53,50,000

The current value of land and buildings is Rs. 30,00,000 and that of furniture, fixtures and fittings is Rs. 2,50,000. Stock is valued at Rs. 9,11,000. Debtors are expected to realise only 90% of their book value. You are informed that preference dividend has not been paid for the last five years. Calculate the intrinsic value per equity share by the net assets method.

[*B.Com.(Hons.) Delhi, 2001- Modified*]

Solution :

		Rs.
Current value of land and buildings		30,00,000
Current value of furniture, fixtures and fittings		2,50,000
Value of stock		9,11,000
Debtors, 90% of Rs. 4,10,000		3,69,000
Cash at Bank		1,20,000
Notional call on 2 lakh equity shares @ Rs. 4 per share		8,00,000
	Rs.	54,50,000
Less : Long term loan	14,00,000	
Sundry creditors	6,50,000	20,50,000
Net assets		34,00,000
Less : Preference share capital		6,00,000
Intrinsic value of 3,50,000 equity shares		28,00,000

Intrinsic value of one fully paid equity share = Rs. 28,00,000 / 3,50,000 = Rs. 8

Intrinsic value of one equity share on which Rs. 6 have been paid up = Rs. 8 – Rs. 4 = Rs. 4

Yield Basis or Market Value. Investors are interested in income and hence the price they will be prepared to pay will depend upon the size of the dividends that can be expected. The formula for calculating market value, therefore, is:—

$$\frac{\text{Dividend in terms of rupees}}{\text{Normal rate of return}} \times 100$$

or
$$\frac{\text{Rate of Dividend}}{\text{Normal rate of return}} \times \text{the denomination to which the rate applies.}$$

Suppose, a company has issued shares of Rs. 100 each on which Rs. 40 have been paid. The company declares a dividend of 30%. The amount per share comes to Rs. 12. On the basis of normal rate of return of 20%, the market value of the share will be Rs. 60:—

Rs. $\frac{12}{20} \times 100$ = Rs. 60. Or, applying the other formula Rs. 40 × $\frac{30}{20}$ = Rs. 60.

The dividend on equity shares should be calculated, (*a*) by deducting from maintainable profits: (1) taxation, (2) transfers to reserves (3) transfers to debenture redemption fund and (4) preference dividend; and (*b*) dividing the remainder by the number of equity shares.

The market value of preference shares will also be calculated in the manner indicated above but the normal rate of return in case of preference shares will be lower than in the case of equity shares because there is priority both as regards dividend and as regards return of capital. If the net assets of the company are not ample to cover the preference capital, investors will expect a higher yield than ordinarily. Investors feel happy if the net assets are about three times the preference capital.

In order to give weightage to the part of profits not distributed, one-third or one-half of the undistributed profit may be added to the amount actually distributed and then the 'dividend' per share is ascertained. This will increase the value of shares of companies which build up reserves. However, the method of calculating value of shares on the basis of dividends declared will always put a premium on the shares of companies which distribute a larger part of their profits. This is clearly unsatisfactory, since it seems to reward lack of prudence. The method discussed below gives a better picture.

Illustration 12:

From the following information, calculate the value of an equity share :

(*i*) The subscribed share capital of a company consists of 10 lakh 13% preference shares of Rs. 10 each and 20 lakh equity shares of Rs. 10 each. All the shares are fully paid up.

(*ii*) The average annual profits of the company after providing depreciation but before taxation are Rs.1,80,00,000. It is considered necessary to transfer Rs. 34,50,000 to general reserve before declaring any dividend. Rate of taxation is 30%.

(*iii*) The normal return expected by investors on equity shares from the type of business carried on by the company is 20%.

Ignore corporate dividend tax.

Solution :

	Rs.
Average annual profits before tax	1,80,00,000
Less : Income tax @ 30%	54,00,000
	1,26,00,000
Less : Transfer to general reserve	34,50,000
Amount available for dividend	91,50,000*
Less : Preference dividend @ 13% on Rs. 1 crore	13,00,000
Amount available for equity dividend	78,50,000

$$\text{Rate of dividend} = \frac{\text{Rs. } 78,50,000}{\text{Rs. } 2,00,00,000} \times 100 = 39.25\ \%$$

Normal rate of dividend = 20 %

$$\text{Value of an equity share} = \text{Rs. } \frac{39.25}{20} \times 10 = \text{Rs. } 19.63$$

*If there is corporate dividend tax, say @ 10%, the amount available for dividend will be :

$$\text{Rs. } 91,50,000 \times \frac{100}{110} = \text{Rs. } 83,18,182$$

As a result, subsequent calculations will also change.

Illustration 13:

C. Ltd. started its business on 1st April, 2007. On 31st March, 2010, its balance sheet in a summarised form was as follows:—

Liabilities	*Rs.*	*Assets*	*Rs.*
Share Capital:		Fixed Assets (cost less depreciation)	30,00,000
10,000 14% Preference Shares of Rs. 100 each, fully paid	10,00,000	Current Assets	40,00,000
3,00,000 Equity Shares of Rs. 10 each, fully paid	30,00,000	Preliminary Expenses	50,000
Profit Prior to Incorporation	25,000		
Profit & Loss Account	5,50,000		
13% Debentures	5,00,000		
Sundry Creditors	18,00,000		
Provision for Income Tax	1,75,000		
	70,50,000		70,50,000

The company is yet to declare its maiden dividend. A revaluation reveals that the fixed assets as on 31st March, 2010 are really worth Rs. 32,00,000. Calculate the intrinsic worth of the two classes of shares. Ignore corporate dividend tax.

Solution:

	Rs.	
Net assets of the company:		
Fixed Assets as revalued		32,00,000
Current Assets		40,00,000
		72,00,000
Less: 13% Debentures	5,00,000	
Sundry Creditors	18,00,000	
Provision for Income Tax	1,75,000	24,75,000
		47,25,000
Alternatively, net assets may be calculated as follows:—		
Preference Share Capital		10,00,000
Equity Share Capital		30,00,000
Profit Prior to Incorporation		25,000
Profit & Loss Account		5,50,000
Appreciation in the value of Fixed Assets		2,00,000
		47,75,000
Less: Preliminary Expenses		50,000
		47,25,000
Preference Shares:		
Preference Share Capital		10,00,000
Add: Dividend @ 14% for 3 years		4,20,000
		14,20,000

$$\text{Value of one preference share} = \text{Rs. } \frac{14,20,000}{10,000}$$

$$= \text{Rs. } 142$$

Equity Shares

Net assets remaining, after satisfying preference shareholders' claim =
Rs. 47,25,000 – Rs. 14,20,000 = Rs. 33,05,000

$$\text{Value of one equity share} = \text{Rs. } \frac{33{,}05{,}000}{3{,}00{,}000}$$

$$= \text{Rs. } 11.02$$

Illustration 14:

From the following particulars, calculate the fair value of an equity share assuming that out of the total assets, those amounting to Rs. 41,00,000 are fictitious.

(*i*) Share capital :

5,50,000 10% preference shares of Rs. 100 each, fully paid

55,00,000 Equity shares of Rs. 10 each, fully paid.

(*ii*) Liability to outsiders = Rs. 75,00,000

(*iii*) Reserves and surplus = Rs. 45,00,000

(*iv*) The average normal profit after taxation earned every year by the Company during the last five years = Rs. 85,05,000

(*v*) The normal profit earned on the market value of fully paid equity shares of similar companies is 12%. **[*C.S.(Inter), June, 2001*]**

Solution :

Intrinsic value of shares :	*Rs.*	*Rs.*
Preference share capital		5,50,00,000
Equity share capital		5,50,00,000
Reserves & surplus		45,00,000
Liabilities to outsiders		75,00,000
Gross assets		12,20,00,000
Less : Fictitious assets	41,00,000	
Liabilities to outsiders	75,00,000	1,16,00,000
Assets available to shareholders		11,04,00,000
Less : Amount due to preference shareholders		5,50,00,000
Net assets available to equity shareholders		5,54,00,000

$$\text{Intrinsic value of an equity shares} = \frac{5{,}54{,}00{,}000}{55{,}00{,}000} = \text{Rs. } 10.07$$

Market value by capitalisation of profits :	*Rs.*
Average profits	85,05,000
Less : Preference dividend	55,00,000
Profit available to equity share holders	30,05,000
Profits capitalised at 12% = Rs. 30,05,000 × 100 / 12	2,50,41,667

Value of one equity share = Rs. 2,50,41,667 / 55,00,000 = Rs. 4.55

$$\text{Fair value} = \text{Rs. } \frac{10.07+4.55}{2} = \text{Rs. } 7.31$$

Illustration 15:

On March 31, 2010, the balance sheet of Harsh Ltd. disclosed the following position.

Liabilities	*Rs.'000*	*Assets*	*Rs. '000*
Subscribed Share Capital in shares of Rs. 10 each, fully paid	4,000	Goodwill	400
		Other Fixed Assets	5,000
General Reserve	1,900	Current Assets	4,000
Profit & Loss Account	1,200		
14% Debentures	1,000		
Current Liabilities	1,300		
	9,400		9,400

On the abovementioned date, the tangible fixed assets were independently valued at Rs. 3,500 thousand and goodwill at Rs. 500 thousand. The net profits for the three years were : 2007-08, Rs. 1,032 thousand; 1999-2000, Rs. 1,040 thousand; and 2000-2001, Rs. 1,033 thousand of which 20 per cent was placed to General Reserve, this proportion being considered reasonable in the industry in which the company is engaged and where a fair return on investment may be taken at 18 per cent. Compute the value of the company's share by (*a*) the net assets method and (*b*) the yield method. Ignore taxation. (*Adapted C.A. Inter*)

Solution:

(*a*) Net Assets Method

	Rs. '000	*Rs. '000*
Goodwill as revalued		500
Tangible Fixed Assets as revalued		3,500
Current Assets as per balance sheet		4,000
		8,000
Less: 14% Debenture	1,000	
Current Liabilities	1,300	2,300
Net Assets		5,700

$$\text{Value per share} = \frac{\text{Net Assets}}{\text{No.of shares}}$$

$$= \text{Rs. } \frac{5,700 \text{ thousand}}{400 \text{ thousand}}$$

$$= \text{Rs. } 14.25$$

(*b*) Yield Method

		Rs. '000
Total Profits for the last three years = Rs. (1,032 + 1,040 + 1,033) thousand	=	3,105
Average Profits for the last three years = Rs. $\frac{3,105 \text{ thousand}}{3}$	=	1,035
Less: Transfer to General Reserve @ 20%	=	207
Average profits after transfer to General Reserve	=	828

Expected return on equity share capital

$$= \frac{\text{Expected Profit}}{\text{Paid up Equity Share Capital}} \times 100$$

$$= \frac{828 \text{ thousand}}{4,000 \text{ thousand}} \times 100 = 20.7\%$$

$$\text{Value per share} = \frac{\text{Expected Rate}}{\text{Normal Rate}} \times \text{Paid up value of share}$$

$$= \frac{20.7}{8} \times 10 = \text{Rs. } 11.50$$

An alternative treatment. Another method of valuing shares is based on earning per share (EPS) or net profit per equity share multiplied by the price earning ratio (PE Ratio). The PE Ratio is really the converse of the normal rate of return applicable to the company. For example, if the normal rate of return is 20%, the PE Ratio will be 5 *i.e.* 100 ÷ 20. If the net profit per share or EPS is Rs. 7, the price of the share will be, for the PE Ratio of 5, Rs. 35.

The above is a simple way of stating the point made already except that instead of dividend per share net profit per share is taken. One can see that if either of the two factors, EPS or PE ratio changes, the price of the share will change. In the example given above, if the PE ratio becomes 4 i.e., normal rate of return is 25%, the share will be valued at Rs. 28.

The PE Ratio is high where risk is low and low when risk is high, say, when in the capital employed, loans preponderate.

Value based on earnings of the company. Often, the dividend declared by a company is much less than the rate of its earning. Since accumulated profits are likely to be distributed sooner or later, in the form of bonus shares, usually the market price is likely to be based on the earnings of the company rather than the dividend. This provides a firm basis for valuation of shares, since this relates the value to the real efficiency, as measured by profitability of the company. The formula is:

$$\frac{\text{Rate of earning}}{\text{Normal rate of return}} \times \text{paid up value of share.}$$

$$\text{Rate of return} = \frac{\text{Profit earned}}{\text{Capital employed}}$$

It should be based on total capital employed (including long-term borrowings) and the profit figure should be before debenture interest, preference dividend. etc., but after income-tax. This valuation is quite appropriate for large blocks of shares; also when the dividend is much more than the rate of earning on capital.

Illustration 16:

Mr. Aggarwal who desires to invest Rs. 33,000 in equity shares in a public limited company seeks your advice as to the fair value of the shares. The following information is made available.

	Rs.
Paid up share capital:	
14% Preference Shares of Rs. 100 each	5,50,000
Equity Shares of Rs. 10 each	8,50,000
	14,00,000

Average net profit of the business is Rs. 3,00,000. Expected normal yield is 20% in case of such equity shares. It is observed that the net tangible assets on revaluation are worth Rs. 1,00,000 more than the amounts at which they are stated in the books. Goodwill is to be valued at 3 years' purchase of the super profits, if any.

Give your workings of the fair value of equity shares and determine the number of shares which Mr. Aggarwal should purchase. Ignore income tax and corporate dividend tax.

Solution:

Computation of goodwill:	*Rs.*
Average net profits of the business	3,00,000
Less: Preference Dividend on Rs. 5,50,000 @ 14%	77,000
	2,23,000
Less: Normal Return @ 20% on Rs. 8,50,000 + Rs. 1,00,000 = Rs. 9,50,000	1,90,000
Super Profits	33,000

Goodwill = Rs. 33,000 × 3 = Rs. 99,000.

Intrinsic value of an equity share:	
Equity Share Capital	8,50,000
Add: Profit on revaluation of tangible fixed assets	1,00,000
Add: Goodwill	99,000
Value of 85,000 Equity Shares	10,49,000

Value of one Equity Share = Rs. 10,49,000 ÷ 85,000 = Rs. 12.34

Intrinsic Value (excluding goodwill) of one

$$\text{Equity Share} = \frac{9{,}50{,}000}{85{,}000} = \text{Rs. } 11.18$$

Value of an equity share on yield basis:	
Profit	3,00,000
Less: Preference Dividend	77,000
	2,23,000

$$\text{Earning per share} = \frac{2,23,000}{85,000} = \text{Rs. } 2.62$$

When expected normal yield is 20%, value of an equity share

$$= \frac{\text{Rs.}2.62}{2} \times 10 = \text{Rs. } 13.10$$

$$\text{Average of prices ascertained} = \frac{\text{Rs.}12.34 + \text{Rs.}11.18 + \text{Rs.}13.10}{3} = \text{Rs. } 12.21$$

$$\text{Number of shares to be purchased} = \frac{33,000}{12.21} = 2,702$$

Consider the following examples:

1. Two Companies *A* Ltd. and *B* Ltd. earn a profit of Rs. 2,00,000 each, the share capital consisting of 4,000 shares of Rs. 100 each. *A* Ltd. distributes 80% of the profit as dividend whereas *B* Ltd. distributes only 50% of the profits. The dividend per share in the two cases is Rs. 40 and Rs. 25 respectively. With an expectation of 20%, the market value of a share of *A* Ltd. would seem to be Rs. 200 *i.e.* 40/20 × 100 and that of *B* Ltd. Rs. 125 *i.e.*, 25/20 × 100. This is clearly unsatisfactory since *B* Ltd. is following a better financial course so that it will have better strength to meet adverse circumstances.

Even if part of the reserve created each year is added to the distributed profit, the result will not be satisfactory. Suppose, 1/3 of undistributed profit is added to the amount actually distributed, the amount per share will be:

$$A \text{ Ltd.} \quad \frac{\text{Rs.}1,60,000 + (1/3 \times \text{Rs.}40,000)}{4,000} = \text{Rs. } 43.33$$

$$B \text{ Ltd.} \quad \frac{\text{Rs.}1,00,000 + (1/3 \times \text{Rs.}1,00,000)}{4,000} = \text{Rs. } 33.33$$

The market value of the share of *A* Ltd. will still be much higher than that of *B* Ltd.

This could be rectified by taking the *earning* per share in each case and calculating the market value on that basis. The earning in each case is Rs. 50 per share and, on an expectation of 20%, the market value will be Rs. 250 per share. There are two qualifications.

(*a*) The market expectation on a cash dividend will always be lower than on mere earnings per share, since the latter only raises an expectation that later the shareholder will benefit from good earnings. It is quite possible that against 20% yield on the basis of cash dividend, the market may expect a yield of 25% on the basis of earning depending upon the estimate as to how soon the company will make a distribution of built up reserves.

(*b*) Financial prudence displayed by *B* Ltd. has still not been recognised — it will be recognised if the expected yield is raised in case of *A* Ltd. and lowered in case of *B* Ltd. — say 22% in case of *A* Ltd. and 18% for *B* Ltd.

2. *Zed* Ltd. has the following capital structure:

	Rs.
14% Preference Share Capital (Shares of Rs. 100 each)	5,00,000
Equity Share Capital (Shares of Rs. 100 each)	10,00,000
Reserves	5,00,000
12% Debentures	5,00,000

The profit of the company (after taxation but before debenture interest) is Rs. 4,00,000; equity share of companies in the same class of business yield is 20%.

Ignoring dividend tax, the rate of earning on equity capital is:

	Rs.	Rs.
Profit		4,00,000
Less: Debenture Interest	60,000	
Preference Dividend	70,000	1,30,000
		2,70,000
Equity Capital		10,00,000
Rate of earning on Equity Capital	27%	
Market Value based on this:		

$$\frac{27}{20} \times 100 = \text{Rs. } 135$$

However, the company is earning only 16% on the capital employed by it i.e.,

$$\frac{4{,}00{,}000}{25{,}00{,}000} \times 100$$

It is not likely therefore that the market will value the equity shares of the company on the basis of 27%, since it will not be safe to do so — the value is likely to be based on the earning ratio of 16% and may be Rs. 160, *i.e.*, 16/20 × 200. This will be the minimum — it may be slightly higher, since the peculiar advantage to the equity shareholders, because of gearing of capital, will be evaluated.

3. Two companies, *X* Ltd. and *Y* Ltd. are assumed to be exactly similar not only as to assets, liabilities and reserves but also as to all other factors except that the arrangement of the share capital differs.

The share capital of *X* Ltd. is Rs. 21,00,000 divided into 20,000 12% preference shares of Rs. 100 each and 1,000 equity shares of Rs. 100 each, fully paid up. The share capital of *Y* Ltd. is Rs. 21,00,000 divided into 2,000 12% preference shares of Rs. 100 each and 19,000 equity shares of Rs. 100 each fully paid up.

The equity shares of the companies may be taken to represent a somewhat speculative industrial risk and the market yield is 20 per cent. The companies' profits and distributions are:

2008-2009	Rs. 7,84,000
2009-2010	Rs. 2,52,000

There will be a greater fluctuation in the prices of equity shares of *X* Ltd. than in case of *Y* Ltd., as shown below:

	X Ltd.		*Y Ltd.*	
	2008-2009	*2009-2010*	*2008-2009*	*2000-2010*
	Rs.	*Rs.*	*Rs.*	*Rs.*
Profit	7,84,000	2,52,000	7,84,000	2,52,000
Less: Preference Dividend	2,40,000	2,40,000	24,000	24,000
Ignoring divided tax, profit available for equity shareholders	5,44,000	12,000	7,60,000	2,28,000
Ignoring dividend tax, dividend per equity share (available profits divided by the no. of shares	544	12	40	12
General expectation being 20% market value of share	2,720	60	200	60

This illustrates the effect which existence of preference shares has on the value of equity shares: (*i*) when the profits are high (*ii*) when they are low.

Illustration 17:

Tee Ltd. belongs to an industry in which equity shares sell at par on the basis of 18% yield provided the net tangible assets of the company are 250% of the paid up capital and provided the total distribution of profits does not exceed 50% of the profits. The dividend rate fluctuates from year to year in the industry. The balance sheet of Tee Ltd. stood as follows on 31st March, 2010:

Liabilities	*Rs.*	*Assets*	*Rs.*
14% 6,000 Preference Shares of Rs. 100 each, fully paid up	6,00,000	Goodwill	1,00,000
10,000 Equity Shares of Rs. 100 each, Rs. 80 paid up	8,00,000	Other Fixed Assets less depreciation	16,00,000
General Reserve	4,00,000	Government Securities	1,50,000
12% Debentures	4,00,000	Current Assets	11,30,000
Current Liabilities and Provisions	8,00,000	Preliminary Expenses	20,000
	30,00,000		30,00,000

The company has been earning on the average Rs. 8,00,000 as profit after interest but before taxation which is 50%. The rate of dividend on equity shares has been maintained at 25% in the past years and is expected to be maintained.

Determine the probable market value of the equity shares of the company. The tangible fixed assets may be taken to be worth Rs. 17,20,000. Ignore corporate dividend tax.

Solution:

	%
Adjustment of expected yield	
The yield as given	18
Add: For lower asset backing in case of Tee Ltd. as compared to the industry — 15% against 250% see note (*i*)	1
For higher proportion of profit distributed — 71% compared to 50% for the industry	½
For shares being partly paid up	½
	20
Less: For stability in dividend in Tee Ltd. as compared to fluctuating dividend in the industry	1
Probable appropriate yield for the equity shares in Tee Ltd.	19

Probable market value:

$$\text{Based on actual dividend} = \text{Rs. } \frac{80 \times 25}{19} = \text{Rs. } 105.26$$

$$\text{Based on earnings ratio} = \text{Rs. } \frac{80 \times 18.43}{19} = \text{Rs. } 77.60$$

[*See* note (*iii*)]

The two values set the maximum and minimum limits of the market price, the lower one being appropriate for the long run and the upper limit being appropriate for the immediate future.

Note:

(i) Net tangible assets backing for equity shares:	*Rs.*	*Rs.*
Fixed Assets *less* Depreciation		17,20,000
Government Securities		1,50,000
Current Assets		11,30,000
		30,00,000
Less: 12% Debentures	4,00,000	
Current liabilities and provisions	8,00,000	12,00,000
Net worth		18,00,000
Less: Preference Capital		6,00,000
Net tangible assets available for equity shares		12,00,000
Equity Share Capital		8,00,000

Ratio of net tangible assets to equity capital		150%
	Rs.	Rs.
(ii) *Ratio of distributed profits earned:*		
(a) Profit, as given		8,00,000
Less: Income Tax @ 50%		4,00,000
Available Profit		4,00,000
(b) Profit distributed		
Preference Dividend — 14% on Rs. 6,00,000	84,000	
Equity Dividend — 25% on Rs. 8,00,000	2,00,000	2,84,000
Ratio of (b) to (a)		71%
(iii) *Earnings ratio in Tee Ltd.*:		
Profit after tax		4,00,000
Add: Debenture Interest (after effect of income tax)		24,000
		4,24,000
Capital Employed:		
Preference Capital	6,00,000	
Equity Capital	8,00,000	
General Reserves less Preliminary Expenses	3,80,000	
Debentures	4,00,000	
Appreciation in tangible fixed assets	1,20,000	23,00,000

$$\text{Rate of return} = \frac{4,24,000}{23,00,000} \times 100$$

= 18.43% (subject to depreciation on appreciation in fixed assets)

Note: Goodwill is a valuable asset since profits are being earned.

Illustration 18:

Capital structure of Lot. Ltd. as at 31.3.2010 was as under :

	Rs. in lakhs
Equity share capital — fully paid shares of Rs. 10 each	10
10% preference share capital	5
15% debentures	8
Reserves	4

Lot Ltd. earns a profit of Rs. 5 lakhs annually on an average before deduction of interest on debentures and income-tax which works out to 40%.

Normal return on equity shares of companies similarly placed is 12% provided :

(a) Profit after tax covers fixed interest and fixed dividends at least 3 times.

(b) Capital gearing ratio is .75.

(c) Yield on share is calculated at 50% of profits distributed and at 5% on undistributed profits.

Lot Ltd. has been regularly paying equity dividend of 10%.

Compute the value per equity share of the company. [*C.A. (Final), Nov. 1998 Modified*]

Solution :

	Rs.
(i) Profit for calculation of interest and fixed dividend coverage :	
Average profit before interest and taxation	5,00,000
Less : Debenture interest, Rs. 8,00,000 × 15/100	1,20,000
	3,80,000
Less : Tax @ 40%	1,52,000
Profit after interest and taxation	2,28,000
Add back : Debenture interest	1,20,000
	3,48,000

(ii) *Calculation of interest and fixed dividend coverage* :

	Rs.
Fixed interest and fixed dividend :	
Debenture interest	1,20,000
Preference dividend	50,000
	1,70,000

$$\text{Fixed interest and fixed dividend coverage} = \frac{3,48,000}{1,70,000} = 2.05 \text{ times}$$

Interest and fixed dividend coverage 2.05 times is less than the prescribed three times.

(iii) *Capital gearing ratio* :

Equity Share Capital + Reserves = Rs. 10,00,000 + Rs. 4,00,000 = Rs. 14,00,000
Preference Share Capital + Debentures = Rs. 5,00,000 + Rs. 8,00,000 = Rs. 13,00,000
Capital Gearing Ratio = 13,00,000 / 14,00,000 = 0.93 (approximately)
Ratio 0.93 is more than the prescribed ratio of 0.75.

(iv) *Yield on equity shares* :

	Rs.	Rs.
Average profit after interest and tax		2,28,000
Less : Preference dividend	50,000	
Equity Dividend @ 10% on Rs. 10,00,000	1,00,000	1,50,000
Undistributed profit		78,000
50% of distributed profit (50% of Rs. 1,00,000)		50,000
5 % of undistributed profit (5% of Rs. 78,000)		3,900
		53,900

$$\text{Yield on equity shares} = \frac{53,900}{10,00,000} \times 100 = 5.39\ \%$$

(v) *Expected yield of equity shares* :

	%
Normal return	12.00
Add : For low coverage of fixed interest and fixed dividends (2.05 < 3), say	0.50*
Add : For high capital gearing ratio (0.93 > 0.75), say	0.50*
	13.00

* One may take some other reasonable per centage.

(vi) *Value per equity share* :

$$= \frac{5.19}{13.00} \times \text{Rs. } 10 = \text{Rs. } 4.15$$

Illustration 19:

Balance Sheet of *A* Ltd. as on 31.3.2010 was as under:—

Liabilities	*Rs.*	*Assets*	*Rs.*
Equity Share Capital (Rs. 10)		Buildings	2,00,000
Rs. 10 paid up per share	3,00,000	Plant & Machinery	4,00,000
Rs. 5 paid up per share	2,00,000	Sundry Debtors	2,10,000
14% Preference Share Capital		Stock	2,50,000
(Rs. 100)	1,00,000	Cash and Bank	40,000
Reserve	3,00,000		
Sundry creditors	2,00,000		
	11,00,000		11,00,000

Profit and dividend in last several years were as under:—

Year ended	*Profit before Tax* *Rs.*	*Equity Dividend*
31.3.2010	6,40,000	36%
31.3.2009	5,00,000	30%
31.3.2008	3,92,000	24%

Land and buildings are worth Rs. 4,00,000. Managerial remuneration is likely to go up by Rs. 40,000 p.a. Income tax may be provided at 50%. Equity shares of companies in the same industry with dividend rate of 20% are quoted at par.

Find the most appropriate value of an equity share assuming that:—

(*a*) Controlling interest is to be transferred.

(*b*) Only a few shares are to be transferred.

Ignore goodwill value, depreciation adjustment for revaluation corporate dividend tax and the need of transfer to General Reserve. [*Adapted C.A. (Final) May, 1998*]

Solution:

Calculation of Average Maintainable Profit:

Year ended	*Profit before Tax* Rs.	*Weight*	*Product* Rs.
31.3.2010	6,40,000	3	19,20,000
31.3.2009	5,00,000	2	10,00,000
31.3.2008	3,92,000	1	3,92,000
		6	33,12,000

Average Profit 33,12,000 ÷ 6	5,52,000
Less: Increase in Managerial remuneration	40,000
Profit before taxation	5,12,000
Less: Provision for taxation	2,56,000
Profit after taxation	2,56,000
Less: Preference dividend	14,000
Average Maintainable Profit	2,42,000

Valuation of Controlling Interest

	Rs.
Capitalization of maintainable profit @ 20%	
Capitalizated value of equity interest Rs. 2,42,000 × 5 =	12,10,000
Add: Notional Call on partly paid shares	2,00,000
	14,10,000
No. of fully paid shares after national call	70,000
Value of each fully paid share 14,10,000/70,000	20.10
Value of each partly paid share Rs. (20.10 – 5.00)	15.10

Net Assets Method

	Rs.	
Sundry Assets		13,00,000
Add: National Call on shares		2,00,000
		15,00,000
Less: Sundry Creditors	2,00,000	
14% Preference Share Capital	1,00,000	3,00,000
Net Assets		12,00,000

Value of fully paid share Rs. $\frac{12,00,000}{70,000}$ = Rs. 17.10

Value of partly paid share Rs. (17.10 – 5.00) = Rs. 12.10

Fair Value of fully paid share = Rs. $\frac{(20.10+17.10)}{2}$ = Rs. 18.60

Fair Value of partly paid share = Rs. $\frac{(15.10+12.10)}{2}$ = Rs. 13.60

Valuation of a few shares

A few shares can be valued on the basis of dividend paid say at the average rate

$$\frac{36+30+24}{3} = 30\%$$

As the normal rate of dividend is 20%, fully paid up share can be valued at Rs. 15 each and partly paid up share at Rs. 7.50 each.

Illustration 20:

Surya Ltd. and its subsidiary Chandra Ltd. get their supply of some Raw Material from Akash Ltd. To coordinate their production on a profitable basis, Surya Ltd. and Akash Ltd. agree between themselves each to acquire a quarter of shares in other's Authorised Capital by means of exchange of shares. The terms are as follows:—

(*i*) Surya Ltd.'s shares are quoted at Rs. 14 but for the purpose of exchange the value is to be taken at the higher of the two values, *i.e.*, (*a*) quoted; (*b*) on the basis of Balance Sheet valuation;

(*ii*) Akash Ltd.'s shares, which are unquoted are to be taken at the higher of the value as on (*a*) yield basis, and (*b*) the balance sheet basis. The future profits are estimated at Rs. 2,10,000 subject to one third to be retained for development purpose. Shares of similar companies yield 16%.

(*iii*) Freehold properties of Akash Ltd. are to be taken at Rs. 4,30,000.

(*iv*) No cash is to pass and the balance due on settlement is to be treated as loan between the two companies.

The summarised Balance Sheets of the Companies at the relevant dates stood as follows:—

	Surya Ltd. *Rs.*	*Chandra Ltd.* *Rs.*	*Akash Ltd.* *Rs.*
Authorised Share Capital	12,00,000	5,00,000	10,00,000
Equity Shares of Rs. 10 each, issued and fully paid	8,00,000	5,00,000	7,50,000
Share Premium	80,000	—	—
14% Debentures	3,00,000	—	—
Profit and Loss Account	4,60,000	4,20,000	4,00,000
Current Liabilities	2,80,000	1,80,000	2,10,000
Proposed Dividend	2,00,000	1,00,000	—
	21,20,000	12,00,000	13,60,000
Freehold Properties	6,60,000	2,90,000	3,30,000
Plant and machinery	4,50,000	4,10,000	4,40,000
Investment: 40,000 shares in Chandra Ltd.	4,70,000	—	—
Current Assets	5,40,000	5,00,000	5,90,000
	21,20,000	12,00,000	13,60,000

You are required to compute the values of shares according to the terms of the agreement and to present the final settlement showing all necessary workings. Ignore dividend tax.

[*Adapted C.A. (Final) and C.W.A. (Final) Dec. 1987*]

Solution:

	Surya Ltd. *Rs.*	*Chandra Ltd.* *Rs.*	*Akash Ltd.* *Rs.*
Assets			
Freehold Properties	6,60,000	2,90,000	4,30,000
Plant & Machinery	4,50,000	4,10,000	4,40,000
Investment in 40,000 shares in Chandra Ltd. (4/5ths of net assets of Chandra Ltd.)	7,36,000	—	—
Current Assets	5,40,000	5,00,000	5,90,000
Dividend receivable from Chandra Ltd.	80,000	—	—
(*A*)	24,66,000	12,00,000	14,60,000

		Rs.	Rs.	Rs.
Liabilities				
14% Debentures		3,00,000	—	—
Current Liabilities		2,80,000	1,80,000	2,10,000
Proposed Dividend		2,00,000	1,00,000	—
	(B)	7,80,000	2,80,000	2,10,000
Net Assets (A) — (B)		16,86,000	9,20,000	12,50,000
Number of shares		80,000	—	75,000
Book Value per share		21.08	—	16.67

Valuation of Akash Ltd.'s Shares on yield basis:

	Rs.
Estimated annual future profits	2,10,000
Less: 1/3rd profit retained for development	70,000
Profit available for dividend	1,40,000

Capitalised value of Akash Ltd.'s business @ 16% Rs. 1,40,000 $\times \frac{100}{16}$ = Rs. 8,75,000

Number of share = 75,000

Hence, Value of one share = Rs. $\frac{8,75,000}{75,000}$ = Rs. 11.67

Values taken for agreement to exchange shares between the two companies.

Surya Ltd.: Rs. 21.08 per share being the amount of Balance Sheet value which is higher than the quoted value of Rs. 14.00 per share.

Akash Ltd.: Rs. 16.67 per share being the amount to Balance Sheet value which is higher than the value calculated on yield basis, Rs. 11.67 per share.

Statement of Settlement	Rs.
Shares allotted by Surya Ltd. to Akash Ltd. — 30,000 shares @ Rs. 21.08	6,32,400
Shares allotted by Akash Ltd. to Surya Ltd. — 25,000 shares @ Rs. 16.67	4,16,750
Loan by Surya Ltd. to Akash Ltd.	2,15,650

Illustration 21:

You are asked to value shares as on 31st March, 2010 of a private company, engaged in engineering business, with a view to floating it as a public company. The following information is extracted from the audited accounts :

Year ended 31st March	*Net Profit before taxation* Rs.	*Salary of Managing Director* Rs.
2004	23,40,000	7,20,000
2005	32,40,000	7,20,000
2006	5,40,000 (Loss)	3,60,000
2007	7,20,000	5,40,000
2008	34,20,000	10,80,000
2009	45,00,000	10,80,000
2010	25,20,000	10,80,000

The audited balance sheet as at 31st March, 2010 showed the following position :

Shareholders' Funds :

	Rs.	Rs.
Capital		
Equity shares of Rs. 10 each	36,00,000	
Reserves	30,60,000	
Surplus in Profit and Loss Account	23,40,000	90,00,000
Current liabilities and provisions		1,26,00,000
		2,16,00,000

	Rs.	Rs.
Fixed Assets :		
Freehold Land and Building (at cost less depreciation)	64,80,000	
Plant and Machinery (at cost less depreciation)	72,00,000	
Factory and Office Fittings (at cost less depreciation)	18,00,000	1,36,80,000
Current Assets, Loans and Advances		79,20,000
		2,16,00,000

	Rs.
The various assets were valued by an independent valuer as on 31st March, 2010, as under :	
Freehold Land and Building	79,20,000
Plant and Machinery	72,00,000
Factory and Office Fittings	18,00,000
	1,69,20,000

In lieu of salary to Managing Director, the public company would incur directors' fees of Rs. 1,80,000 per annum. Income tax may be assumed at 30 per cent. Corporate dividend tax is payable @ 15%.

You are required to value the shares of the company. [*Adapted C.A. (Final) May, 1980*]

Solution :

(*i*) *Computation of value of shares on net assets basis* :

	Rs.
Fixed assets, as revalued	1,69,20,000
Current assets, loans and advances	79,20,000
	2,48,40,000
Less : Current liabilities and provisions	1,26,00,000
	1,22,40,000
Number of Equity shares	3,60,000
Value per equity share	34

(*ii*) *Computation of value based on earnings and dividends* :

Average Maintainable Profit Year ended 31st March	Profit before tax Rs.
2008	34,20,000
2009	45,00,000
2010	25,20,000
	1,04,40,000
Add back : Managing Director's salary for three years	32,40,000
	1,36,80,000

	Rs.	Rs.
Average Profits		45,60,000
Less : Directors' fees	1,80,000	
Additional Depreciation (on revaluation)		
5 % on Buildings (rate assumed)	72,000	
15% on Plant and Machinery (rate assumed)	2,70,000	5,22,000
		40,38,000
Income tax @ 30% on Rs. 40,38,000 *i.e.* Rs. 12,11,400		12,11,400
		28,26,600
Transfer to general reserve, say @ 10%		2,82,660
		25,43,940

Corporate dividend tax is payable @ 15% .

Hence, Profit available for dividend = Rs. 25,43,940 × 100/115 22,12,122

Profit per share = Rs. 22,12,122 / 3,60,000 = Rs. 6.14

If expected dividend is 20%, price = Rs 10× 6.14/2 = Rs 30.70

(*iii*) *Computation of value on the basis of capitalisation of profits* :

Average maintainable profit after tax 28,26,600

Capitalised value @ say 20% = Rs. 28,26,600 × 100 / 20 1,41,33,000

Value of one share = Rs. 1,41,33,000 / 3,60,000 = Rs. 39.25

For transactions involving a small number of shares, value based on earnings and dividend is irrelevant but for those who want to purchase a large number of shares as a long-term investment, value on the basis of capitalisation of profits will be more appropriate.

Illustration 22:

Below is given the Balance Sheet of Devta Ltd. as at 31st March, 2010:—

Liabilities		*Rs.*	*Assets*	*Rs.*
Share Capital			Fixed Assets:	
2,00,000 Equity Shares			Goodwill	2,00,000
of Rs. 10 each	20,00,000		Land and Buildings	12,00,000
Less: Calls in arrears			Machinery	11,00,000
2 for final call)	50,000	19,50,000	Furniture and Fixtures	6,00,000
10,000 14% Redeemable			Vehicles	8,00,000
Preference Shares of			Investments	8,00,000
Rs. 100 each			Current Assets: Loans and Advances	
Less: Calls in arrears	10,00,000		(*A*) Current Assets	
(Rs. 20 on final call)	10,000	9,90,000	Stock in Trade	5,50,000
Reserves and Surplus:			Sundry Debtors	9,00,000
General Reserve		8,00,000	Cash at Bank	1,00,000
Profit and Loss Account		1,60,000	(*B*) Loans and Advances	
Secured Loans:			Miscellaneous Expenditure	
Bank Loan		6,00,000	Preliminary Expenses	1,00,000
Current Liabilities and Provision				
(*A*) Current Liabilities				
Bills Payable		3,00,000		
Sundry Creditors		15,50,000		
(*B*) Provisions		Nil		
		63,50,000		63,50,000

Additional Information:

(*i*) For the purpose of valuation of shares, goodwill is to be considered on the basis of 2 years' purchase of the super profits based on average profits of last 4 years. Profits are as follows:

2006-2007	Rs. 8,00,000	2008-2009	Rs. 10,50,000
2007-2008	Rs. 9,00,000	2009-2010	Rs. 11,00,000

(*ii*) In a similar business normal return on capital employed is 20%.

(*iii*) Fixed assets are worth 30 per cent above their actual book value. Stock is overvalued by Rs. 50,000. Debtors are to be reduced by Rs. 10,000. All trade investments are to be valued at 10 per cent below cost.

(*iv*) Of the investments, 10 per cent is in trade and the balance non-trade. Trade investments were purchased on 1st April, 2009, 50 per cent of the non-trade investments on 1st April, 2008 and the rest on 1st April, 2009.

The following further information is relevant:

(*i*) In 2007-2008 a new machinery costing Rs. 1,00,000 was purchased but wrongly charged to revenue. No rectification has yet been made for above.

(*ii*) In 2008-2009, some old furniture (book value Rs. 50,000) was disposed of for Rs. 30,000.

You are required to value each fully paid and partly paid equity share. (Depreciation is charged on machinery @ 15 percent on reducing system. Ignore all types of tax and dividend).

[*Adapted C.A. (Final) May, 1982*]

Solution:

	Rs.
Value of net tangible assets as per working note no. (*i*)	40,01,836
Value of goodwill as per working note no. (*iii*)	95,444

		Rs.
Non-trading Investments		7,20,000
Calls in Arrear Rs. 50,000 + Rs. 10,000		60,000
		48,77,280
Less: Preference Share Capital		10,00,000
		38,77,280

Value of a fully paid Equity Share $= \text{Rs.} \dfrac{38,77,280}{2,00,000}$ = Rs. 19.39

Value of a partly paid Equity Share = Rs. 19.39 – Rs. 2 = Rs. 17.39

Working Notes:

(*i*) Net Tangible Operating Assets as on 31st March, 2010:—

	Rs.	Rs.
Fixed Assets		
Land & Buildings		12,00,000
Machinery (Rs. 11,00,000 + Rs. 1,00,000 – Rs. 15,000 – Rs. 12,750 – Rs. 10,838)		11,61,412
Furniture & Fixtures		6,00,000
Vehicles		8,00,000
		37,61,412
Add: Appreciation @ 30%		11,28,424
		48,89,836
Trade Investments [90/100 (10/100 × 8,00,000)]		72,000
Stock (Rs. 5,50,000 – Rs. 50,000)		5,00,000
Sundry Debtors (Rs. 9,00,000 – Rs. 10,000)		8,90,000
Cast at Bank		1,00,000
		64,51,836
Less: Bank Loan	6,00,000	
Bills Payable	3,00,000	
Sundry Creditors	15,50,000	24,50,000
		40,01,836

Alternatively, the figure may be arrived at in the following manner.

	Rs.	Rs.
Paid up Equity Share Capital		19,50,000
Paid up Preference Share Capital		9,90,000
General Reserve		8,00,000
Profit and Loss Account		1,60,000
Addition to Machinery Account by way of rectification of error		61,412
30% appreciation in fixed assets		11,28,424
		50,89,836
Less: Reduction in Trade Investments	8,000	
Reduction in Stock	50,000	
Reduction in Debtors	10,000	
Goodwill	2,00,000	
Preliminary Expenses	1,00,000	
Non-trading Investments	7,20,000	10,88,000
		40,01,836

Strictly the average of the four years should be taken but the net tangible operating assets may be taken as the capital employed. It is nearer the average since it appears that at least a major part of 2009-2010 profits have been disposed of making the capital employed in the beginning more or less the same as at the end.

(ii) *Calculation of average profits:*

	2006-07	2007-08	2008-2009	2009-2010
	Rs.	Rs.	Rs.	Rs.
Profits as per books of account	8,00,000	9,00,000	10,50,000	11,00,000
Add: Capital expenditure in respect of machinery charged to revenue	—	+ 1,00,000	—	—
Loss on sale of furniture (assumed extra ordinary item)	—	—	+ 20,000	—
	8,00,000	10,00,000	10,70,000	11,00,000
Less: Depreciation in respect of error in Machinery Account @ 15%	—	– 15,000	– 12,750	– 10,838
Dividend on non-trading investment @15%	—	– 54,000	– 1,08,000	– 1,08,000
Reduction in the value of stock	—	—	—	– 50,000
Bad debts	—	—	—	– 10,000
	8,00,000	9,31,000	9,49,250	9,21,162

Depreciation on addition to fixed assets, other than machinery on account of revaluation has not been taken into account for want of details.

(iii) *Computation of Goodwill:*

	Rs.
Total Profit for four years after adjustments	36,01,412
Average Profit	9,00,353
Less: Depreciation @ 15% on increase in the value of machinery Rs. 3,48,424	52,264
	8,48,089
Normal Profit: 20% of Rs. 40,01,836	8,00,367
Super Profits	47,722
Goodwill at two years purchase	95,444

Illustration 23:

Under the articles of a private company dealing in wines and tabacco, you as an auditor, have to fix annually the fair value of the shares. At 31st March, 2010 Company's position was as follows:—

Liabilities	Rs.	Rs.	*Assets*	Rs.	Rs.
1,000 14% Preference Shares of Rs. 100 each, fully paid up		1,00,000	Building at cost *less* depreciation		85,000
4,000 Equity Shares of Rs. 100 each, fully paid up		4,00,000	Furniture at cost less depreciation		3,000
General Reserve		1,00,000	Stock in Trade (at market value)		4,50,000
Profit and Loss Account			10% Government Securities at cost (face value Rs. 4,00,000)		3,75,000
Balance on 1st April, 2009	30,000		Book Debts	3,00,000	
Profit for 2009-2010 (Subject to tax)	5,30,000	5,60,000	*Less*: Provision for Bad and Doubtful Debts	20,000	2,80,000
Provision against:			Bank Balance		60,000
Buildings	10,000		Preliminary Expenses		10,000
Investment	45,000	55,000			
Creditors		48,000			
		12,63,000			12,63,000

You are given the following information:

(1) The company's prospects for 2001-2002 are equally good.

(2) The buildings are now worth Rs. 5,65,000.

(3) Public companies doing similar business show a profit earning capacity of 20 per cent on market value of their shares.

(4) Profits for the past three years have shown an increase of Rs. 50,000 annually.
(5) Rate of tax is 50%. *[Adapted from C.A. final and B.Com. Delhi]*

Solution:

For calculating the intrinsic value, goodwill will have to be valued. The average capital employed is calculated as under:

	Rs.	Rs.
Building		5,65,000
Furniture		3,000
Stock in Trade		4,50,000
Book Debts		2,80,000
Bank Balance		60,000
		13,58,000
Less: Creditors	48,000	
Provision for tax (50% on Rs. 5,30,000)	2,65,000	3,13,000
Capital employed on 31st March, 2010		10,45,000
Less: Half the profits after tax		1,32,500
Average capital employed.		9,12,500

(Investments have not been included for the purpose of finding out the value of goodwill because investments in this case seem to indicate that the company has surplus funds which, at least for the time being, cannot find employment).

The average profits of the company for the three years are Rs. 3,80,000, calculated as below:

	Rs.	
Profit for 2009-2010	5,30,000	
Profit for 2008-2009	4,80,000	(Rs. 50,000 less than for 2009-2010)
Profit for 2007-2008	4,30,000	(Rs. 50,000 less than for 2008-2009)

	Rs.	Rs.
Average		4,80,000
Less: Depreciation at 5% on increase in the value of the building	24,000	
Income from non-trading asset	40,000	64,000
		4,16,000
Less: Income tax @ 50%		2,08,000
		2,08,000
Normal Profits @ 20% on Rs. 9,12,500		1,82,500
Super Profits		25,500
Goodwill at 3 years' purchase		76,500
Say,		77,000

The net assets of the company on 31st March, 2010 are:

Goodwill		77,000
Buildings		5,65,000
Furniture		
Stock in Trade		4,50,000
Investments *less* Provision		3,30,000
Book debts *less* Provision		2,80,000
Bank Balance		60,000
		17,65,000
Less: Creditors	48,000	
Preference capital	1,00,000	
Provision for Taxation	2,65,000	4,13,000
Net Assets for Equity Shareholders		13,52,000

	Rs.	Rs.
Number of Equity Shares	4,000	
Intrinsic value per share Rs. 13,52,000/4,000 = Rs. 338		
The market value of the shares will be calculated as under if based on possible dividend on equity shares:—		
Average profits as calculated value		4,80,000
Less: Taxation @ 50%		2,40,000
		2,40,000
Less: Preference dividend		14,000
		2,26,000
Less: Transfer to General Reserve because dividend rate exceeds 20% of net profits		22,600
		2,03,400

Number of equity share being 4,000; the dividend per equity share = $\frac{2,03,400}{4,000}$ = 50.85

The market value is Rs. $\frac{50.85}{20} \times 100$ = Rs. 254.25 or Say Rs. 250.

Value on earning basis	Rs.
Capital employed	9,12,500
Profit earned (before preference dividend)*	2,08,000

Rate of earning = $\frac{2,08,000}{9,12,500} \times 100$ = 22.79%, say 23%

Value per share = $\frac{23}{20} \times 100$ = 115

The safest (long term) value that can be put on the equity shares is that on the basis of earnings ratio — the other two values have some unnatural elements. Intrinsic value is not relevant, since those who invest in shares do not have much interest in the assets behind the shares; they are interested in the income. The market value based on maximum possible dividends is also unnatural since few companies will distribute all the profit earned by them — probably they will distribute only what the capital has earned. Hence, the value based on earnings ratio seems to be the fairest.

The value of the preference shares is likely to be Rs. 100 as the assets available are more than sufficient to cover the shares and moreover, the company is earning good profits to ensure payment of dividend on the preference shares regularly.

Illustration 24:

The following is the summarised Balance Sheet of X & Co. Ltd. as at 31st March, 2010:—

		Rs. in lakhs
Share Capital		512.00
Reserves and Surplus		1,031.50
		1,543.50
Shareholders' Funds	Rs. In lakhs	
Loans: Secured	1,048.73	
Unsecured	382.77	1,431.50
Total		2,975.00
Fixed Assets (Groos Cost, Rs. 25 crores)		1,701.63
Current Assets	1,657.60	
Loans and Advances	719.50	
	2,377.10	
Less: Current liabilities and provisions	1,103.73	1,273.37
Total		2,975.00

***Excluding interest income *less* tax.**

The company has been granted an industrial licence for manufacturing a new product, the capital cost of which is expected to be around Rs. 9 crore. The company desires to finance the new project to the extent of Rs. 4 crore partly from internal resources and the balance of Rs. 5 crore by issue of fresh capital, *i.e.*, 2,00,000 Equity Shares of Rs. 100 each at a premium of Rs. 150 share.

You are required to make a report to the Directors of the company, stating your reasons whether or not the premium amount of Rs. 150 per share is, in your opinion, justified. You may also make other comments that you may wish to make. In order to enable you to issue the report, you are furnished the following additional information:

(1) Issued, Subscribed and Paid up Capital as on 31st march, 2010

	Rs.
5,00,000 Equity Shares of Rs. 100 each, fully paid	5,00,00,000
12,000 14% Redeemable Preference Shares of Rs. 100 each	12,00,000
	5,12,00,000

(2) Rate of Dividend on Equity shares for the last five years:

2009-2010	..	22%
2008-2009	..	22%
2007-2008	..	20%
2006-2007	..	20%
2005-2006	..	18%

(3) The normal earning capacity (net of tax) of the business may be presumed at 17%.

(4) Annual Turnover for the last 3 years:

2009-2010	..	Rs. 57 crore
2008-2009	..	Rs. 55 crore
2007-2008	..	Rs. 50 crore

(5) The net profit before tax had remained around 18% of the sales during the last three years. It is expected that the net profit would go up to 20% in the future on account of the internal savings and the new product sales. The figures of profit are subject to interest.

(6) The rate of tax may be presumed at 50%.

(7) The trend of market price of the equity shares of X & Co. Ltd., as per stock exchange quotations, was as follows:

	High	*Low*
2009-2010	450	350
2008-2009	435	320
2007-2008	425	300

Ignore corporate dividend tax. *(Adapted from C.A. Final)*

Delhi,
March, 31 2010

The Directors
X & Co. Ltd.
....

Dear Sirs,

Proposal to issue 2,00,000 equity shares of Rs. 100 each at a premium of Rs. 150 per share.

As requested by you vide your letter dated .... we have examined the question of the value that may be placed on the shares of your company, with particular reference to the desirability or otherwise of charging a premium of Rs. 150 per share. Our report is as follows:—

1. The value that the market is likely to place on any share, over a period of time, is always a function of (*i*) the profit likely to be earned by the company in the future, more particularly the profit per share or, to borrow American terminology, earings per share, and (*ii*) the yield that well informed investors will expect on the investment in the shares.
2. The following is an estimate of the profits likely to be earned after the new project becomes operational.

		Rs.
(*i*) Average Tumover (2007-2008, 2008-2009, 2009-2010)		54 crore
(*ii*) Gross Block		25 crore
(*iii*) Ratio of (*i*) to (*ii*)		2.16 crore
(*iv*) Gross Addition to Block		9 crore
(*v*) Total Gross Lock		34 crore
(*vi*) Expected Tumover after expansion 34 × 2.16		73 crore
Profit @ 20% of the sales as estimated by the Directors		1,460 lakh
Less: Interest at 20% (assumed) on borrowings		400 lakh
		1,060 lakh
Loans at present		1,431.50 lakh
Expected increase in borrowing to finance additional working capital, say	568.50 lakh	
		2,00.000 lakh

Profit before tax	1,060 lakh
Income tax @ 50%	530 lakh
Profit after tax	530 lakh

3. Estimated earnings per share:

Profit as above	530 lakh
Preference dividend	1.68 lakh
Balance of Profit	528.32 lakh
No. of equity shares 7,00,000	
Earning per share	
528.32 lakh divided by 7,00,000	= Rs. 75.47

4. The EPS at present:

18% profit on Rs. 54 crore (average tumover)	972.00 lakh
Less: Interest @ 20% on Rs. 14.31 crore	286.20 lakh
Profit after Interest	685.80 lakh
Net Profit after tax (50% of above)	342.90 lakh
Preference Dividend	1.68 lakh
Balance of Profit	341.22 lakh
No. of Shares 5,00,000	
EPS 341.22 lakh/5,00,000 = Rs. 68.24	

5. The PE ratio (price earning ratio) in 2000-2001 works out at 5.86 as shown below:—

Average price per share in 2000-2001	400.00
EPS	68.24
PE ratio 400/68.24	

This more or less tallies with the statement that the normal earning capacity (net of tax) may be presumed as 17%.

The PE Ratio is likely to be maintained if not improved due to the fact that the company's dividend record has shown a consistent improvement — 18% in 1984-85 to 20% in the next two years and to 22% in the next two years.

6. The price of the share after the project becomes operational is likely to be Rs. 75.47 × 5.86 or Rs. 450 (app.) on the average. The book value at present is Rs. 306.30.
7. **The price of the share in 2007-2008, 2008-2009 and 2009-2010 has moved up consistently. The new** project, if it proves profitable, should lead to a substantial improvement in the price of the share. Therefore, it may be taken that a valuation of Rs. 450 is rather safe. However, the calculations made above assume (*i*) an additional sale of Rs. 19 crore rising from the new project (maintaining the tumover ratio as hithertio) (*ii*) maintenance of present sales, and (*iii*) a profit margin of 20%. A failure of any of these assumptions will seriously affect share prices. However, the issue price of Rs. 250 per share appear's to be quite safe. The Controller of Capital Issues, may have no misgivings on the point of the premium of Rs. 150 per share.
8. Even though share prices should improve even according to the present plan, the company should seriously reconsider the scheme of financing. It would be better if the whole of the amount required from outside is raised by way of loans preferably from the financial institutions. There is enough debt

capacity, since loans can be easily twice the shareholders' funds. The income tax rate of 50% will bring the principle of 'trading on equity' into play powerfully. If Rs. 5 crore is raised by loans raised @ 20 the share prices are likely to be Rs. 560 as shown below:—

		Rs.
Profit as per area 2, after interest already taken into account	1,060	lakh
Interest @ 20% on Rs. 5 crore, additional borrowing	100	lakh
Profit before tax	960	lakh
Tax @ 50%	480	lakh
Profit after tax	480	lakh
EPS 480 lakhs/5,00,000	96	lakh
Price @ the present PE ratio of 5.86 :		
96 × 5.86	562.56	lakh
Say,	560	lakh

We would, therefore, urge that the financing plan be reconsidered. You are welcome to seek any clarification that you may need.

Yours faithfully

....

Chartered Accountants

4. ALTERATION OF SHARE CAPITAL

A company can alter its share capital, if it is empowered by its articles to do so. Alteration, as distinct from reduction (discussed later), may involve the following:

(1) Conversion of shares into stock;
(2) Increase in capital;
(3) Decrease (without reduction in the paid up amount) in share capital;
(4) Consolidation of shares of smaller denomination into shares of higher denomination or sub-division of shares into shares of smaller denomination.

Section 94 to 98 of the Companies Act, 1956 govern alteration of capital.

Conversion into Stock

Fully paid up shares can be converted into "stock", if the company is so authorised by its articles. "Stock" is not divided into equal and serially numbered parts and hence the members will hold so much amount of share capital after the shares have been converted into stock, rather that so many shares. Thus, if A held 20 shares of Rs. 100 each previously, after conversion into stock he will be said to hold Rs. 2,000 stock. He will then be able to transfer any amount even if it is odd. The position may be likened to cups of tea which would be "shares"; if all the cups of tea are poured into the tea pot the tea in the teapot would be "stock". Lord Cairns says, "The use of the term 'stock' merely denotes that the company has recognised the fact of the complete payment of the shares and that the time has come when these shares may be assigned in fragments, which for obvious reasons could not be permitted before, but that stock shall still be the qualification, e.g., of directors who must possess a certain number of shares and that the meeting shall be of persons entitled to this stock who meet and vote as shareholders in the proportion of shares which would entitle them to vote before the consolidation into stock".

After shares have been converted into stock, notice of the conversion must be filed with the Registrar within one month. Thereupon, those provisions of the Companies Act which apply only to shares cease to apply to so much of the share capital as is converted into stock. Also, the Register of Members, thereafter, will show the amount of stock held by each member instead of the number of shares.

The conversion of shares into stock is recorded in the books of account by the entry:

(Say) Equity Share Capital Account ...Dr.
To Equity Stock.

Stock can be reconverted into shares. The shares need not be of the same denomination as before.

Increase in capital

Increase in capital can be, of course, brought about of offering more shares for subscription. The only restriction is that the offer must first be made to the existing members (equity) in proportion to their holdings (unless the company has decided otherwise by a special resolution of by an ordinary resolution with the approval of the Central Government). A member must have at least 15 days to decide whether he will (or not) exercise the option to buy the new shares offered to him. If the members do not exercise the option, within the period allowed, the directors will be free to dispose of the shares as they think most beneficial to the company. The option is saleable in the market.

In case the capital is increased beyond the authorised capital, the notice of increase together with the particulars regarding class of shares and the conditions under which they are to be issued must be sent to the Registrar within thirty days of the passing of resolution making the increase.

Decrease in share capital

A company has the power to cancel the shares which, at the date of the passing of the necessary resolution, have not been subscribed or agreed to be subscribed by any person, and thus diminish the amount of its share capital. A company, however, cannot, without the sanction of the Court, cancel the amount unpaid on shares already issued or agreed to be subscribed.

Consolidation, etc. A company has the power to consolidate shares of smaller value into shares of bigger denomination or sub-divided shares of bigger denomination into shares of smaller denomination. Care must be exercised to see that in case of partly paid up shares, the amount paid up bears the same ratio to the nominal value after consolidation as before. For example, if shares of Rs. 1,000 each, Rs. 800 paid up (80%) are converted into shares of Rs. 100 each, the paid up amount must be Rs. 80 per share, *i.e.*, 80% of the nominal value. An entry is passed to record the changes. Suppose 1,000 shares of Rs. 1,000 fully paid are sub-divided into shares of Rs. 100 each, the entry will be:

		Rs.	*Rs.*
Share Capital A/c (Rs. 1,000)	... Dr.	10,00,000	
To Share Capital A/c (Rs. 100)			1,00,00,000

Notice in all cases of alteration discussed above must be sent to the Registrar within 30 days.

Reserve liability or reserve capital

According to section 99 of the Companies Act, a limited company may, by special resolution, determine that any portion of its share capital which has not already been called up shall not be called up except in the event and for the purposes of the company being would up. Such uncalled capital is known as "reserve capital".

In all the above-mentioned cases, no sanction of the Court is required. Speciel resolution of the company is enough.

Illustration 25:

Pass journal entries for the following:—

(*i*) conversion of fully paid equity share capital of Rs. 6,00,000 into equity stock.

(*ii*) cancellation of unpaid amount of Rs. 2,00,000 in respect of 1,00,000 equity shares of Rs. 10 each, Rs. 8 called and paid up.

(*iii*) sub-division of 20,000 fully paid equity shares of Rs. 100 each into 2,00,000 equity shares of Rs. 10 each fully paid.

(*iv*) consolidation of 40,000 14% preference shares of Rs. 25 each, fully paid up into 10,000 14% preference shares of Rs. 100 each.

(*v*) conversion of equity stock of Rs. 2,50,000 into 25,000 equity shares of Rs. 10 each.

Solution:

Journal

		Dr.	Cr.
		Rs.	Rs.
(*i*) Equity Share Capital Account To Equity Stock Account Conversion of fully paid equity share capital of Rs. 6,00,000 into equity stock.	Dr.	6,00,000	6,00,000
(*ii*) Equity Share Capital (Partly called) Account To Equity Share Capital (Fully called) Account Cancellation of unpaid amount of Rs. 2,00,000 in respect of 1,00,000 equity shares of Rs. 10 each, Rs. 8 called and paid up.	Dr.	8,00,000	8,00,000
(*iii*) Equity Share Capital (Rs. 100 each) Account To Equity Share Capital (Rs. 10 each) Account Sub-division of 20,000 fully paid equity shares of Rs. 100 each into 2,00,000 equity shares of Rs. 10 each, fully paid.	Dr.	20,00,000	20,00,000
(*iv*) 14% Preference Share Capital (Rs. 75 each) Account To 14% Preference Share Capital (Rs. 100 each) Account Consolidation of 40,000 14% preference shares of Rs. 25 each, fully paid up into 10,000 14% preference shares of Rs. 100 each.	Dr.	10,00,000	10,00,000
(*v*) Equity Stock Account To Equity Share Capital (Rs. 10) Account Conversion of equity stock of Rs. 2,50,000 into 25,000 equity shares of Rs. 10 each.	Dr.	2,50,000	2,50,000

5. REDUCTION OF CAPITAL

Reduction of capital means the following:—

(*a*) Extinguishing or reducing the liability on any of the shares in respect of the unpaid amount.

(*b*) Cancelling any paid up share capital (writing off) which is lost or unrepresented by available assets (together with or without extinguishing or reducing liability on shares).

(*c*) Paying off capital (already paid up) which is in excess of needs of the company (again together with or without extinguishing or reducing liability on shares).

Reduction of capital can be carried out by a company, if it is authorised by its articles and by special resolution and confirmation of the Court.

If the proposed reduction of the capital does not involve diminution of any liability in respect of paid up capital or the payment to any shareholder of any paid up share capital and if there are other special circumstances which, in the opinion of the Court, obviate the necessity of inviting objections from creditors or any class of them, the Court may confirm the proposed scheme without consulting the creditors.

But, normally, the Court will consult the creditors affected. For this purpose, a list of creditors entitled to object to the proposed scheme will be settled by the Court. The court may publish notices fixing the time before which creditors not already entered on the list may claim to be so entered.

The scheme of reduction involves either the consent of the creditors entered on the list or the settlement of their claims. The Court may dispense with the consent of a creditor it:

(*a*) the company admits the full amount of the debt or claim, or, though not admitting it, is willing to provide for it and secures the necessary amount; or

(*b*) if the company does not admit or is unwilling to provide for the amount, the company secures payment of the amount fixed by the Court.

After the consent of the creditors has been obtained or their claims discharged or the company has secured the payment of the dissenting creditors to the satisfaction of the Court, the Court may make an order confirming the reduction of capital on such terms and conditions as it thinks fit. The Court may direct the company to add the word, "And Reduced" to its name for such period as it thinks fit. The Court may also require the company to publish such statement, in the Press, in regard to the reduction, as the Court may think expedient, with a view to giving proper information to the public.

The order of the Court has to be registered with the Registrar. On such registration, the order takes effect. The Registrar has to certify the registration of the order and the minute. The certificate, is conclusive evidence that all requirements of the Act with respect to the share capital have been complied with. The relevant parts of the memorandum then stand amended.

Every copy of the memorandum and the articles issued after the alteration or reduction of capital must be a corrected copy.

If, at the time of winding up, a creditor cannot be paid and he proves that he was ignorant of the proceedings of reduction of capital and, therefore, his name was not entered on the list of creditors, the shareholders at the time of the reduction can be called upon by the Court to contribute with a view to settling the claims of such a creditor. Of course, they cannot be called upon to pay anything if they have already paid the full amount on their shares.

Variation of Shareholders' rights

If the share capital of a company consists of different classes, the memorandum or articles of association may contain provisions for the alteration of the rights attached to different classes of shares. This is subject to the following:—

(*a*) the consent of holders of at least three-fourths of the shares of the class concerned (or a higher proportion if so laid down in the articles or memorandum) must be obtained; and

(*b*) the consent should be obtained at a separate meeting of the affected class of shareholders by means of a resolution or in writing.

If the articles or memorandum are silent on the point, the variation will not be possible if prohibited by the terms of issue of shares of the concerned class. The holders of not less than 10 per cent of the issued shares of the class of shares, whose rights are being varied, may apply to the Court to have the variation cancelled; and if such an application is made, the variation will not have effect unless it is confirmed by the Court. The time limit for making the application is 21 days after the consent is obtained or the resolution is passed. The decision of the Court is final. Notice of the variation has to be filed with the Registrar within 15 days of the order of the Court.

Entries to record the reduction, etc.

I. If the uncalled capital on shares is cancelled, the paid up amount is not affected; only the partly paid shares become fully paid. To record this fact, the following entry will do:

Share Capital (Partly Paid)	Dr.	} with the amount credited
To Share Capital (Fully Paid)		} to share capital.

II. Sometimes a joint stock company has paid up share capital in excess of its requirements. In such a case, it may refund a part of the share capital to its shareholders after complying with the necessary legal formalities. The entries for such a refund may be as follows:

(*a*) Share Capital Account	Dr.	} with the amount to
To Sundry Shareholders		} be refunded
(*b*) Sundry Shareholders	Dr.	} Payment to shareholders
To Bank		} for refund

Illustration 28

Moti Ltd. with a subscribed equity share capital of Rs. 70,00,000 divided into fully paid shares

Rs. 10 each finds that its share capital is much in excess of its requirements and hence decides to refund Rs. 3 per share its shareholders. The necessary legal formalities are complied with. Pass journal entries.

Solution:

Journal

			Dr.	*Cr.*
			Rs.	*Rs.*
	Equity Share Capital (Rs. 10 each, fully paid) Account To Equity Share Capital (Rs. 7 each, fully paid)* Account To Sundry Equity Shareholders Account Reduction of equity share capital by means of refund to equity shareholders @ Rs. 3 per share, making 7,00,000 equity shares of Rs. 10 each fully paid 7,00,000 equity shares of Rs. 7 each fully paid.	Dr.	70,00,000	 49,00,000 21,00,000
	Sundry Equity Shareholders Account To Bank Refund made to sundry equity shareholders to reduce share capital	Dr.	21,00,000	 21,00,000

*Share may be partly paid up.

III. In the vast majority of cases, the reduction of share capital is necessitated by accumulated losses and the reduction is really another name for writing off the share capital. In a sole proprietorship concern or a partnership firm, any loss revealed by Profit and Loss Account is transferred to Capital Account or Capital Accounts respectively reducing the capital of the enterprise. But in the case of a joint stock company, the loss is not transferred to Share Capital Account; it is shown as a fictitious asset by way of the last item on the assets side of the Balance Sheet of the company and Share Capital is continued to be shown at paid up value. A joint stock company may incur heavy losses for a number of years and a fairly big portion of the share capital may thus be lost but the balance of Share Capital Account will not disclose this fact. The company may turn the corner and it may like to start on a clean state by writing off the past accumulated losses and show Share Capital at its real worth. It is done by reducing share capital under a scheme of reconsideration involving a number of legal formalities. In the books of the company, Capital Reduction Account, Reconganisation Account or Reconstruction Account is opened and with the amount of reduction in Share Capital Account, the following entry is passed:—

Share Capital Dr.
To Capital Reduction Account/
Reorganisation Account/
Reconstruction Account.

In the process of reduction, the description of the shares may be changed; in such a case, the old Share Capital Account should be closed and new Share Capital Account should be opened with the new amount crediting the amount of reduction made to Capital Reduction Account or Reorganisation Account or Reconstruction Account. For example 10,000 12% Preference Shares of Rs. 100 each are converted into 10,000 14% Preference Shares of Rs. 60 each, the journal entry will be as follows:—

		Rs.	*Rs.*
12% Preference Share Capital (Rs. 100 each) Account	Dr.	10,00,000	
To 14% Preference Share Capital (Rs. 60 each) Account			6,00,000
To Capital Reduction Account/Reorganisation Account / Reconstruction Account			4,00,000

The amount standing to the credit of Capital Reduction Account/Reorganisation Account/ Reconstruction Account is utilised to write off accumulated losses. The amount of reduction because of rounding of figures, be a little more than the amount of the accumulated losses; this extra reduction is credited to capital reserve. Thus, the entry may be:

Capital Reduction Account/Reorganisation Account/Reconstruction Account	Dr.	Amount of Capital Reduction
To Profit and Loss Account		Debit balance of Profit and Loss Account
To Capital Reserve		Balancing Figure

Illustration 27:

Following is the summarised balance sheet of Reckless Co. Ltd. as at 31st March, 2010:—

Liabilities	*Rs.*	*Assets*	*Rs.*
5,000 Equity Shares of Rs. 100 each, fully paid	5,00,000	Net Sundry Assets	2,02,800
		Profit and Loss Account	2,97,200
	5,00,000		5,00,000

The company feels that the worst is over and hence it adopts a scheme of reconstruction reducing all its equity shares into an equal number of fully paid equity shares of Rs. 40 each.

Pass journal entries and prepare the balance sheet immediately after the reconstruction.

Solution:

Journal

			Dr. Rs.	Cr. Rs.
	Equity Share Capital (Rs. 100 each) Account		5,00,000	
	To Equity Share Capital (Rs. 40 each) Account			2,00,000
	To Reconstruction Account			3,00,000
	Reduction of paid up value of 5,000 equity shares of Rs. 100 each, fully paid by Rs. 60 per share for purposes of reconstruction.			
	Reconstruction Account Dr.		3,00,000	
	To Profit and Loss Account			2,97,200
	To Capital Reserve			2,800
	Utilising the amount of Reconstruction Account to write off debit balance of Profit and Loss Account, the balance left in Reconstruction Account being transferred to Capital Reserve.			

Balance Sheet immediately after reconstruction as at 31st March, 2010

Liabilities	*Rs.*	*Assets*	*Rs.*
5,000 Equity Shares of Rs. 40 each, fully paid	2,00,000	Net Sundry Assets	2,02,800
Capital Reserve	2,800		
	2,02,800		2,02,800

Illustration 28:

The following is the Balance Sheet of Nav Bharat Co. Ltd. on 31st March 2010.

Liabilities	*Rs.*	*Assets*	*Rs.*
Authorised Share Capital—		Leasehold Premises	1,30,800
10,000 Preference Shares of		Plant and Machinery	42,200
Rs. 100 each	10,00,000	Patents at cost	8,50,000
10,000 Equity Shares of		Stocks-in-trade	55,000
Rs. 100 each	10,00,000	Sundry Debtors	76,500
	20,00,000	Cash in hand	500

	Rs.		*Rs.*
Subscribed Share Capital—		Preliminary Expenses	12,000
7,500 Preference Shares		Discount on Issue of Shares	18,000
Rs. 100 each, fully paid	7,50,000	Profit and Loss Account	1,15,000
5,000 Equity Share of			
Rs. 100 each fully paid	5,00,000		
Sundry Creditors	30,000		
Bank Overdraft	20,000		
	13,00,000		13,00,000

The company suffered losses and was not getting on well. The following scheme of reconstruction was adopted.

(*i*) The preference shares be reduced to an equal number of fully paid shares of Rs. 50 each.
(*ii*) The equity shares be reduced to an equal number of shares of Rs. 25 each.
(*iii*) The amount available be used to write off Rs. 30,800 off the Leasehold Premises, Rs. 15,000 off Stock, 20% off Plant and Machinery and Sundry Debtors and the balance available off Patents.

Journalise the transactions and prepare the Balance Sheet after the reconstruction has been carried out. (*Adapted from B.Com., Delhi*)

Solution:

Journal

				Dr.	*Cr.*
2010				*Rs.*	*Rs.*
Mar. 31	Preference Share Capital (Rs. 100 each) Account	Dr.		7,50,000	
	Equity Share Capital (Rs. 100 each) Account	Dr.		5,00,000	
	To Preference Share Capital (Rs. 50 each) Account				3,75,000
	To Equity Share Capital (Rs. 25 each) Account				1,25,000
	To Capital Reduction Account				7,50,000
	The reduction of Rs. 50 per share on 7,500 Preference Shares and Rs. 75 per share on 5,000 Equity Shares made pursuant to the Special Resolution No. .... dated .... and confirmed by the Court vide order dated				
Mar. 31	Capital Reduction Account	Dr.		7,50,000	
	To Profit and Loss Account				1,15,000
	To Preliminary Expenses Account				12,000
	To Discount on Issue of Shares Account				18,000
	To Leasehold Premises				30,800
	To Stock				15,000
	To Plant and Machinery				8,440
	To Provision for Doubtfull Debts				15,300
	To Patents				5,35,460
	The amount of capital reduction used to write off fictitious assets and losses, and to write off the various amounts as indicated in the special resolution.				

Balance Sheet of Nav Bharat Co. Ltd., as on March 31, 2010

Liabilities	*Rs.*	*Assets*	*Rs.*	*Rs.*
Share Capital		**Fixed Assets**		
Authorised:		Leasehold Premises	1,30,800	
10,000 Preference Shares of Rs. 50 each	5,00,000	*Less*: amount written off under Reconstruction Scheme dated	30,800	1,00,000
10,000 Equity Shares of Rs. 25 each	2,50,000			
	7,50,000	Plant and Machinery	42,200	
Issued and Subscribed:		*Less*: amount written off under Reconstruction Scheme dated	8,440	33,760
7,500 Preference Shares of Rs. 50 each, fully paid	3,75,000			
5,000 Equity shares of Rs. 25 each, fully paid	1,25,000	Patents	8,50,000	
Secured Loans	Nil	*Less*: amount written off under Reconstruction Scheme dated	5,35,460	3,14,540
Unsecured Loans				
Bank Overdraft	20,000	**Investments**		Nil
Current Liabilities and Provisions		**Current Assets, Loans & Advances**		
Sundry Creditors	30,000	(A) Current Assets		
Contingent Liabilities (not provided for)	Nil	Stock at market price		40,000
		Sundry Debtors	76,500	
		Less: Provision	15,300	61,200
		Cash in hand		500
		(B) Loans and Advances		Nil
		Miscellaneous Expenditure (not written off)		Nil
	5,50,000			5,50,000

In the case of reconstruction, the company may write off not only the debit balance of Profit & Loss account but may seize the opportunity to write off fictitious assets appearing under the broad heading of 'Miscellaneous Expenditure' also. Examples of such fictitious assets are Preliminary Expenses, Cost of Issue of Debentures and Underwriting Commission on Issue of Shares. The company may also bring down the values of other assets which are overstated in the balance sheet. Goodwill account appearing in the balance sheet is written off completely because a company which has been incurring losses cannot be said to be enjoying any goodwill. Certain unrecorded liabilities may also be recorded under the scheme of reconstruction.

When the losses are rather heavy, preference shareholders may also be made to make a sacrifice. To compensate them for their sercrifice to some extent, their rate of dividend for the future may be increased although as far as arrears of preference dividend are concerned, they may be made to forgo them.

If the losses to be written off are very heavy, even Trade Creditors and Debentureholders may be persuaded to make a sacrifice. In such case Capital Reduction Account is not opened; it must be either Reorganisation Account or Reconstruction Account.

Also, when assets are revalued, there may be appreciation in the value of a few assets. For example, usually there is an appreciation in the value of Land & Buildings. Such an appreciation is also available for writing off losses. Similarly, there may be capital profits like Profit Prior to Incorporation which may also be used to write off losses under a scheme of reconstruction.

Illustration 29:

The balance sheet of a joint stock company is as follows :

	Rs. in lakhs		*Rs. in lakhs*
12 lakh 13% Preference shares of Rs. 50 each, fully paid up	600	Goodwill	120
		Building	400
15 lakh Equity shares of Rs. 50 each, fully paid up	750	Plant	268
		Furniture	198
Loans	573	Stock	400
Sundry Creditors	242	Debtors	329
		Preliminary Expenses	10
		Profit and Loss Account	440
	2,165		2,165

Note : Preference dividend has been in arrear for five years.

The company had been incurring losses for a number of years. It is now earning profits. The following scheme of reconstruction has, therefore, been passed by the company and approved by the Court :—

(*i*) Equity shareholders have agreed that their Rs. 50 shares be reduced to Rs. 10 per share and they have agreed to subscribe in cash for three equity shares of Rs. 10 each for every share held.

(*ii*) The preference shareholders have agreed to cancel the arrears of preference dividend and to accept for each Rs. 50 preference share three new 14% preference shares of Rs. 10 each and two equity shares of Rs. 10 each, all credited as fully paid-up.

(*iii*) Lenders to the company amounting to Rs. 200 lakh have agreed to convert their loan into 10 lakh 14% preference shares of Rs. 10 each and an equal number of equity shares of Rs. 10 each, all credited as fully paid-up.

(iv) The directors have agreed to subscribe in cash for 10 lakh equity shares of Rs. 10 each in addition to any shares to be subscribed for by them under (i) above.

(v) 50% of the remaining amount of Loans and 50% of Sundry Creditors are discharged by payment of cash.

(vi) The reduction in equity share capital is to be applied to write off goodwill, preliminary expenses and debit balance of profit and loss account; the remaining amount of reduction is to be used to write down the value of plant.

You are required to :

(*i*) Pass journal entries to implement the above mentioned scheme;

(*ii*) show cash book and important ledger accounts; and

(*iii*) prepare the company's balance sheet immediately after the reconstruction.

Solution :

Journal

		Dr. *Rs. in lakhs*	*Cr.* *Rs. in lakhs*
Equity Share Capital (Rs. 50 each) Account	..Dr.	750	
To Equity Share Capital (Rs. 10 each) Account			150
To Capital Reduction Account			600
Reduction of equity share capital by converting 15 lakh fully paid equity shares of Rs. 50 each into 15 lakh fully paid equity shares of Rs. 10 each as per scheme of reconstruction dated			

		Rs. in lakhs	Rs. in lakhs
13% Preference Share Capital (Rs. 50 each) Account	..Dr.	600	
To 14% Preference Share Capital (Rs. 10 each) Account			360
To Equity Share Capital (Rs. 10 each) Account			240
Conversion of 12 lakh 13% fully paid preference shares of Rs. 50 each into 36 lakh 14% fully paid preference shares of Rs. 10 each and 24 lakh fully paid equity shares of Rs. 10 each.			
Loans	..Dr.	200	
To 14% Preference Share Capital (Rs. 10 each) Account			100
To Equity Share Capital (Rs. 10 each) Account			100
Loans amounting to Rs. 200 lakh being converted into 10 lakh fully paid 14% preference shares of Rs. 10 each and 10 lakh fully paid equity shares of Rs. 10 each.			
Bank	..Dr.	550	
To Equity Share Application & Allotment Account			550
Application money @ Rs. 10 per share received from equity shareholders for 45 lakh equity shares and from directors for 10 lakh equity shares.			
Equity Share Application & Allotment Account	..Dr.	550	
To Equity Share Capital (Rs. 10 each) Account			550
Allotment of 45 lakh equity shares to existing equity shareholders and 10 lakh equity shares to directors.			
Loans	..Dr.	186.50	
Sundry Creditor	..Dr.	121	
To Bank			307.50
Cash paid to discharge 50% of the remaining loans and 50% of Sundry Creditors.			
Capital Reduction Account	..Dr.	600	
To Goodwill			120
To Preliminary Expenses			10
To Profit and Loss Account			440
To Plant			30
The amount of capital reduction used to write off goodwill, preliminary expenses, debit balance of profit and loss account and plant (to the extent of balancing figure).			

Cash Book (Bank Columns)

Dr.	Rs. in lakhs	Cr.	Rs. in lakhs
To Equitys Share Application & Allotment Account	550	By Loans	186.5
		By Sundry Creditors	121
		By Balance c/d	242.5
	550		550
To Balance b/d	242.5		

Capital Reduction Account

Dr.	Rs. in lakhs	Cr.	Rs. in lakhs
To Goodwill	120	By Equity Share Capital (Rs. 50 each) Account	600
To Preliminary Expenses	10		
To Profit and Loss Account	440		
To Plant (balancing figure)	30		
	600		600

Loans Account

Dr.	Rs. in lakhs		Cr. Rs. in lakhs
To 14% Preference Share Capital (Rs. 10 each) Account	100	By Balance b/fd	573
To Equity Share Capital (Rs. 10 each) Account	100		
To Bank	186.5		
To Balance c/d	186.5		
	573		573
		By balance b/d	186.5

14% Preference Share Capital (Rs. 10 each) Account

Dr.	Rs. in lakhs		Cr. Rs. in lakhs
To Balance c/d	460	By 13% Preference Share Capital (Rs. 50 each) Account	360
		By Loans	100
	460		460
		By balance b/d	460

Equity Share Capital (Rs. 10 each) Account

Dr.	Rs. in lakhs		Cr. Rs. in lakhs
To Balance c/d	1,040	By Equity Share Capital (Rs. 50 each) Account	150
		By 13% Preference Share Capital (Rs. 50 each)Account	240
		By Loans	100
		By Equity Share Applications and Allotment Account	550
	1,040		1,040
		By Balance b/d	1,040

Balance Sheet (after reconstruction) as on ....

Liabilities	*Rs. in lakhs*	*Assets*	*Rs. in lakhs*	*Rs. in lakhs*
46 lakh 14% Preference Shares of Rs. 10 each, fully paid up	460	Goodwill	120	
		Less : Amount written off under scheme of reconstruction dated ...	120	Nil
1 crore 4 lakh Equity Shares of Rs. 10 each, fully paid up	1,040	Building		400
Loans	186.5	Plant	268	
Sundry Creditors	121	*Less* : Amount written off under scheme of reconstruction dated	30	238
		Furniture		198
		Stock		400
		Debtors		329
		Cash at Bank		242.5
	1,807.5			1,807.5

Illustration 30:

Following is the balance sheet of Downhill Ltd. as at 31st March, 2010:—

Liabilities	*Rs.*	*Assets*	*Rs.*
20,000 Equity Shares of Rs. 100 each	20,00,000	Goodwill	50,000
Profit Prior to Incorporation	25,000	Land and Buildings	1,50,000
12% Debentures	5,00,000	Plant and Machinery	3,00,000
Outstanding Debenture Interest	1,20,000	Furniture	80,000
Bank Loans	55,000	Stock	3,50,000
Trade Creditors	3,00,000	Debtors	60,000
		Cash at Bank	10,000
		Preliminary Expenses	20,000
		Profit & Loss Account	19,80,000
	30,00,000		30,00,000

The following scheme of reconstruction is executed:—

(*i*) Equity shares are reduced to Rs. 5 per share. They are, then, consolidated into 10,000 equity shares of Rs. 10 each.

(*ii*) Debentureholders agree to forgo outstanding debenture interest. As a compensation 12% Debentures are converted into 14% Debentures, the amount remaining Rs. 5,00,000.

(*iii*) Trade Creditors are given the options to either accept 50% of their claim in cash in full settlement or to convert their claims into equity shares of Rs. 10 each. Creditors for Rs. 2,00,000 opt for shares in satisfaction of their claims.

(*iv*) To make payment to trade creditors opting for cash payment, to repay bank loan and to augment working capital, the company issues 50,000 equity shares of Rs. 10 each at par, the entire amount being payable along with applications. The issue was fully subscribed.

(*v*) Land and buildings are revalued at Rs. 2,25,000 whereas plant and machinery is to be written down to Rs. 1,85,000. A provision amounting to Rs. 5,000 is to be made for doubtful debts.

Pass journal entries, prepare Reconstruction Account and redraft the company's balance sheet immediately after the reconstruction. *[B.Com. (Hons.) Delhi, 1990 Modified]*

Solution:

Journal

			Dr. *Rs.*	Cr. *Rs.*
	Equity Share Capital (Rs. 100 each) Account Dr. To Equity Share Capital (Rs. 5 each) Account To Reconstruction Account Reduction of equity share capital by Rs. 19,00,000 as per scheme of reconstruction.		20,00,000	1,00,000 19,00,000
	Equity Share Capital (Rs. 5 each) Account Dr. To Equity Share Capital (Rs. 10 each) Account Consolidation of 20,000 equity shares of Rs. 5 each into 20,000 equity shares of Rs. 10 each as per scheme of reconstruction.		1,00,000	1,00,000
	Outstanding Debenture Interest Account Dr. To Reconstruction Account Debentureholders forgo outstanding debenture interest as per scheme of reconstruction.		1,20,000	1,20,000
	12% Debentures Account Dr. To 14% Debentures Account Allotment of 14% Debentures in lieu of 12% Debentures as per scheme of reconstruction.		5,00,000	5,00,000

		Rs.	Rs.
Bank	Dr.	5,00,000	
To Equity Share Applications & Allotment Account			5,00,000
Receipt of application money in respect of 50,000 equity shares @ Rs. 10 per share.			
Equity Share Applications & Allotment Account	Dr.	5,00,000	
To Equity Share Capital (Rs. 10 each) Account			5,00,000
Allotment of 50,000 equity shares of Rs. 10 each.			
Trade Creditors	Dr.	2,00,000	
To Equity Share Capital (Rs. 10 each) Account			2,00,000
Allotment of equity shares in satisfaction of claims to trade creditors for Rs. 2,00,000.			
Trade Creditors	Dr.	1,00,000	
To Bank			50,000
To Reconstruction Account			50,000
Payment of cash equal to 50% of the claim in full and final settlement of the amount to trade creditors for Rs. 1,00,000.			
Bank Loan	Dr.	55,000	
To Bank			55,000
Discharge of bank loan.			
Profit Prior to Incorporation Account	Dr.	25,000	
To Reconstruction Account			25,000
Transfer of Profit Prior to Incorporation to Reconstruction Account.			
Land & Buildings Account	Dr.	75,000	
To Reconstruction Account			75,000
Appreciation in the value of Land & Buildings on revaluation.			
Reconstruction Account	Dr.	21,70,000	
To Profit & Loss Account			19,80,000
To Preliminary Expenses Account			20,000
To Goodwill Account			50,000
To Plant and Machinery Account			1,15,000
To Provision for Bad Debts Account			5,000
Account written off as per scheme of reconstruction.			

Reconstruction Account

	Rs.		Rs.
To Profit & Loss Account	19,80,000	By Equity Share Capital (Rs. 100 each)	19,00,000
To Preliminary Expenses Account	20,000	By Outstanding Debenture Interest	1,20,000
To Goodwill Account	50,000	By Trade Creditors	50,000
To Plant and Machinery Account	1,15,000	By Profit Prior to Incorporation Account	25,000
To Provision for Bad Debts Account	5,000	By Land & Buildings Account	75,000
	21,70,000		21,70,000

Balance Sheet as at ....

Liabilities	Rs.	*Assets*		Rs.
Share Capital		**Fixed Assets**		
Authorised		Goodwill	50,000	
80,000 Equity Shares of Rs. 10 each, fully paid	8,00,000	*Less*: amount written off under scheme of reconstruction dated —	50,000	Nil
Issued and subscribed:				

	Rs.		*Rs.*	*Rs.*
(Of the above shares 20,000 share are allotted as fully paid-up puronant a contract without payments being received in cash)		Land and Buildings	1,50,000	
		Add: amount of appreciation made under scheme of reconstruction dated—	75,000	2,25,000
Secured Loans				
14% Debentures	5,00,000	Plant and Machinery	3,00,000	
		Less: amount written off under scheme of reconstruction dated–	1,15,000	1,85,000
		Furniture		80,000
		Current assets, Loans and Advances		
		(A) Current Assets		
		Stock		3,50,000
		Debtors	60,000	
		Less: Provision for Doubtful Debts	5,000	55,000
		Cash at Bank		4,05,000
		(B) Loans and Advances		Nil
	13,00,000			13,00,000

Illustration 31:

The following is the summarised balance sheet of Greenfields Ltd. as at 31st March, 2010 :

	Rs. '000		*Rs. '000*
Share Capital :		Freehold Property	22,00
Fully paid equity shares of Rs. 10 each	30,00	Other Fixed Assets	31,60
Securities Premium	4,00	Cash at Bank	21,63
General Reserve	13,50	Other Current Assets	15,94
Debenture Redemption Reserve	10,00		
Profit and Loss (Appropriation) Account		9,82	
13% Debentures	15,00		
Current Liabilities	8,85		
	91,17		91,17

The company :

(*i*) has had the freehold property professionally valued and decides to include it in its balance sheet at its revalued amount of Rs. 35 lakh;

(*ii*) pays a dividend @ 10% and also pays tax on distributed profits @ 15% of the amount of dividend distributed;

(*iii*) redeems its debentures at a premium of 2%; the premium being provided for out of securities premium; and

(*iv*) distributes fully paid bonus shares of Rs. 10 each in the ratio of one share for every two shares held.

Pass journal entries for the above mentioned transactions and redraw the company's balance sheet recording effect of these transactions.

Solution :

Greenfield Ltd.
Journal

		Dr.	Cr.
		Rs.'000	Rs.'000
Freehold Property	..Dr.	13,00	
To Revaluation Reserve			13,00
Upward revision in the value of freehold property.			
Profit and Loss (Appropriation) Account	..Dr.	3,45	
To Dividend Payable			3,00
To Corporate Dividend Tax			45
Dividend declared @ 10% and corporate dividend tax payable @ 15%.			
Dividend Payable	..Dr.	3,00	
Corporate Dividend Tax	..Dr.	45	
To Bank			3,45
Payment of dividend and corporate dividend tax.			
Securities Premium	..Dr.	30	
To Premium on Redemption of Debentures			30
Premium payable on redemption of debentures provided for.			
13% Debentures	..Dr.	15,00	
Premium on Redemption of Debentures	..Dr.	30	
To Sundry Debentureholders			15,30
Amount payable to sundry debentureholders on redemption of debentures at a premium of 2%.			
Sundry Debentureholders	..Dr.	15,30	
To Bank			15,30
Payment made to sundry debentureholders.			
Debenture Redemption Reserve	..Dr.	10,00	
To General Reserve			10,00
Transfer of debenture redemption reserve to general reserve on redemption of debentures.			
General Reserve	..Dr.	15,00	
To Bonus to Equity Shareholders			15,00
Bonus shares to be distributed in the ratio of one share for every two shares held.			
Bonus to Equity Shareholders	..Dr.	15,00	
To Equity Share Capital Account			15,00
Distribution of bonus shares.			

(Redrafted) Balance Sheet of Greenfield Ltd. as on 31st March, 2010

	Rs.'000		Rs.'000
Share Capital :		Freehold Property	35,00
Fully paid equity shares of Rs. 10 each	45,00	Other Fixed Assets	31,60
(Of the above, shares for Rs. 15 lakh are allotted as fully paid-up by way of bonus shares)		Cash at Bank	2,88
Source : General Reserve		Other Current Assets	15,94
Securities Premium	3,70		
Revaluation Reserve	13,00		
General Reserve	8,50		
Profit and Loss (Appropriation) Account	6,37		
Current Liabilities	8,85		
	85,42		85,42

Working Notes :

(*i*) *Dr.* **Cash Book (Bank Columns)** *Cr.*

	Rs.'000		*Rs.'000*
To Balance b/fd	21,63	By Dividend Payable	3,00
		By Corporate Dividend Tax	45
		By Sundry Debentureholders	15,30
		By Balance c/d	2,88
	21,63		21,63
To Balance b/d	2,88		

Dr. **General Reserve** *Cr.*

	Rs.'000		*Rs.'000*
To Bonus to Equity Shareholders	15,00	By Balance b/fd	13,50
To Balance c/d	8,50	By Debenture Redemption Reserve	10,00
	23,50		23,50
		By Balance b/d	8,50

Dr. **Profit and Loss (Appropriation) Account** *Cr.*

	Rs.'000		*Rs.'000*
To Dividend Payable	3,00	By Balance b/fd	9,82
To Corporate Dividend Tax	45		
To Balance c/d	6,37		
	9,82		9,82
		By Balance b/d	6,37

Illustration 32:

The following is the Balance Sheet of Weak Ltd. as at 31st March 2010:—

Liabilities	*Rs.*	*Assets*	*Rs.*
Share Capital:		Buildings	2,00,000
20,000 Equity Shares of Rs. 10 each, fully paid up	2,00,000	Machinery	1,30,000
10% Cumulative Preference Shares of Rs. 100 each, fully paid up	50,000	Patents	40,000
8% Debentures	1,00,000	Inventories	80,000
Trade Creditors	3,30,000	Debtors	55,000
Creditors for Expenses	20,000	Preliminary Expenses	10,000
		Profit and Loss Account	1,85,000
	7,00,000		7,00,000

With a view to reconstructing the company, it is proposed:—

(*a*) to reduce (*i*) equity shares by Rs. 9 each, (*ii*) 10% preference shares by Rs. 40 each, (*iii*) 8% debentures by 10%, (*iv*) trade creditors' claims by one-third, (*v*) machinery to Rs. 70,000, and (*vi*) inventories by Rs. 10,000;

(*b*) to provide Rs. 15,000 for bad debts;

(*c*) to write off all the intangible assets; and

(*d*) to raise the rate of preference dividend to 14% and the rate of debenture interest to 12.5%.

Assuming that the aforesaid proposals are duly approved and sanctioned, pass the journal entries to give effect to the above, and show the company's post-reconstruction Balance Sheet.

[*Adapted from B.Com. (Hons.) Delhi, 1983*]

Solution:

Journal

			Dr.	Cr.
2010			*Rs.*	*Rs.*
Mar. 31	Equity Share Capital Account Dr.		1,80,000	
	To Reconstruction Account			1,80,000
	The reduction of Rs. 9 per share on 20,000 equity shares vide.....			
Mar. 31	10% Cumulative Preference Share Capital Account Dr.		50,000	
	To 14% Redeemable Preference Share Capital Account			30,000
	To Reconstruction Account			20,000
	The conversion of 500 10% cumulative preference shares of Rs. 100 each into 500 14% redeemable preference shares of Rs. 60 each vide			
	8% Debentures Account Dr.		1,00,000	
	To 12.5% Debentures Account			90,000
	To Reconstruction Account			10,000
	To conversion of 8% Debentures into 12.5% Debentures vide			
	Trade Creditors Dr.		1,10,000	
	To Reconstruction Account			1,10,000
	Reduction of Trade Creditors' claim by one-third.			
	Reconstruction Account Dr.		3,20,000	
	To Profit and Loss Account			1,85,000
	To Preliminary expenses			10,000
	To Machinery			60,000
	To Inventories			10,000
	To Provision for Bad debts			15,000
	To Patents			40,000
	The amount of Reconstruction Account used to write off the debit balance of Profit and Loss Account, intangible assets and to write down the value of various assets as indicated in the Resolution.......			

Balance Sheet of Weak Ltd. as at 31st March, 2010

Liabilities	*Rs.*	*Assets*	*Rs.*	*Rs.*
Share Capital		**Fixed Assets**		
20,000 Equity Shares of Rs. 1 each, fully padi	20,000	Buildings		2,00,000
500 14% Cumulative Preference shares of Rs. 60 each, fully paid	30,000	Machinery	1,30,000	
Secured Loans		*Less*: written off under Reconstruction Scheme dated.....	60,000	70,000
12.5% Debentures	90,000	Patents	40,000	
Current Liabilities and Provisions		*Less*: written of under Reconstruction Scheme dated	40,000	Nil
(*A*) Current Liabilities	Nil			
Trade Creditors	2,20,000	**Current Assets, Loans and Advances**		
Creditors for Expenses	20,000	(*A*) Current Assets		
(*B*) Provisions	Nil	Inventories at market value		70,000
		Debtors	55,000	
		Less: Provision	15,000	40,000
		(*B*) Loans and Advances		Nil
	3,80,000			3,80,000

Illustration 33:

The balance sheet of ABC Ltd. as on 31st March, 2010 is as follows :

Liabilities	*Rs. '000*	*Assets*	*Rs. '000*
Share Capital :		**Fixed Assets :**	
Issued and Subscribed :		Goodwill	10,000
20 lakh Equity Shares of		Land and Buildings	60,000
Rs. 100 each, Rs. 90 called		Machinery	80,000
and paid-up	1,80,000	Furniture, Fixtures and Fittings	10,000
6 lakh 12 % Preference Shares		**Current Assets, Loans**	
of Rs. 100 each, fully paid-up	60,000	**And Advances :**	
Secured Loans :		(*A*) Current Assets	
11% Debentures	50,000	Inventories	59,000
Unsecured Loans :	20,000	Sundry Debtors	30,000
Current Liabilities and		Cash at Bank	800
Provisions :		(*B*) Loans and Advances	Nil
(*A*) Current Liabilities		**Profit and Loss Account**	71,000
Sundry Creditors	8,000		
(*B*) Provisions			
Staff Provident Fund	2,800		
	3,20,800		3,20,800

The following scheme of reconstruction has been passed and approved by the court.

(*i*) Uncalled capital is to be called in full.

(*ii*) Every equity share of Rs. 100 each is to be subdivided into 10 equity share of Rs. 10 each. After subdivision, equity shareholders are to surrender 50% of their holdings for immediate cancellation.

(*iii*) Preference shareholders have aggreed to accept identical number of fully paid 12% preference shares of Rs. 75 each in lieu of their present holdings.

(*iv*) 11% debentureholder have aggreed to accept 12% debentures for Rs. 4 crore 50 lakh in full satisfaction of their claim on debentures for Rs. 5 crore.

(*v*) Unsecured loan for Rs. 2 crore is converted into 11.5% debentures for Rs. 1 crore 60 lakh.

(*vi*) Sundry Creditors have aggreed to surrender 30% of their claim in consideration of the balance being paid in cash forthwith.

(*vii*) Inventories are overvalued by Rs. 1 crore 20 lakh while machinery is to be depreciated by Rs. 3 crore.

(*viii*) A provision of Rs. 30 lakh is to be made for doubtful debts against trade debtors.

The scheme of reconstruction is fully implemented. You are required to pass journal entries for all the transactions concerning reconstruction and draw company's balance sheet immediately after the reconstruction. *[Adapted B.Com. (Hons.) Delhi, 1999]*

Solution :

Books of ABC Ltd.
Journal

		Dr.	*Cr.*
		Rs.'000	*Rs.'000*
Equity Share Final Call Account ..Dr. To Equity Share Capital Account Final call made on 20 lakh equity shares @ Rs. 10 per share.		20,000	20,000
Bank ..Dr. To Equity Share final Call Account Receipt of final call on equity shares @ Rs. 10 per share.		20,000	20,000

Particulars		Rs.'000	Rs.'000
Equity Share Capital (Rs. 100 each) Account	..Dr.	2,00,000	
To Equity Share Capital (Rs. 10 each) Account			2,00,000
Subdivision of 20 lakh equity share of Rs. 100 each into 2 crore equity shares of Rs. 10 each.			
Equity Share Capital (Rs. 10 each) Account	..Dr.	1,00,000	
To Reconstruction Account			1,00,000
Surrender of 1 Crore equity shares of Rs. 10 each by the equity shareholders for cancellation for purposes of reconstruction.			
12% Preference Share Capital (Rs. 100 each) Account	..Dr.	60,000	
To 14% Preference Share Capital (Rs. 75 each) A/c			45,000
To Reconstruction Account			15,000
Allotment of 6 lakh 14% fully paid preference shares of Rs. 75 each in lieu of identical number of 12% fully paid preference shares of Rs. 100 each; the amount of sacrifice being credited to reconstruction account.			
11% Debenture Account	..Dr.	50,000	
To 12% Debenture Account			45,000
To Reconstruction Account			5,000
Allotment of 12% debentures for Rs. 4,50,00,000 in lieu of 11% debentures for Rs. 5 crore under scheme of reconstruction.			
Unsecured Loan Account	..Dr.	20,000	
To 11.5 % Debentures Account			16,000
To Reconstruction Account			4,000
Allotment of 11.5% debentures for Rs. 1 crore 60 lakh in full satisfaction of unsecured loan amounting to Rs. 2 crore.			
Sundry Creditors Account	..Dr.	8,000	
To Reconstruction Account			2,400
To Bank			5,600
Surrender of 30% of the claim by sundry creditors, the balance being paid in cash forthwith under scheme of reconstruction.			
Reconstruction Account	..Dr.	1,26,000	
To Goodwill Account			10,000
To Machinery Account			30,000
To Inventories			12,000
To Provision for Bad Debts			3,000
To Profit and Loss Account			71,000
Transfer of goodwill account and profit & loss account to reconstruction account, writing down the book value of machineries and inventories and creation of provision of bad debts as per scheme of reconstruction.			
Reconstruction Account	..Dr.	400	
To Capital Reserve			400
Transfer of credit balance in Reconstruction Account to Capital Reserve.			

Reconstruction Account

	Rs. '000		Rs. '000
To Goodwill Account	10,000	By Equity Share Capital (Rs. 10 each) Account	1,00,000
To Machinery Account	30,000	By 12% Preference Share Capital Account	15,000
To Inventories Account	12,000		
To Provision for Bad			

	Rs. '000		Rs. '000
Debts Account	3,000	By 11% Debentures Account	5,000
To Profit and Loss Account	71,000	By Unsecured Loans Account	4,000
To Capital Reserve		By Trade Creditors Account	2,400
(balancing figure)	400		
	1,26,400		1,26,400

Balance Sheet of ABC Ltd. and Reduced as on 31st March, 2010

Liabilities	*Rs. '000*	*Assets*		*Rs. '000*
Share Capital :		**Fixed Assets :**		
Authorised	?	Goodwill	10,000	
		Less : Amount written off		
Issued and Subscribed :		under scheme of dated....	10,000	Nil
1 Crore Equity Shares of Rs. 10		Land and Buildings		60,000
each, fully paid-up	1,00,000	Machinery	80,000	
6 lakh 14 % Preference Shares		*Less* : Amount written off		
of Rs. 75 each, fully paid-up	45,000	under scheme of dated	30,000	50,000
Reserves and Surplus :		Furniture, Fixtures		
Capital Reserve	400	and Fittings		10,000
Secured Loans :		**Current Assets, Loans**		
12% Debentures	45,000	**And Advances :**		
11.5% Debentures	16,000	(*A*) Current Assets		
Current Liabilities and		Inventories		47,000
Provisions :		Sundry Debtors	30,000	
(*A*) Current Liabilities		*Less* : Provision for		
Sundry Creditors	Nil	Bad Debts	3,000	27,000
(*B*) Provisions		Cash at Bank		15,200
Staff Provident Fund	2,800	(*B*) Loans and Advances		Nil
	2,09,200			2,09,200

Illustration 34:

Having accumulated huge losses, Green Limited adopts a scheme of reconstruction on 31st March, 2010 on which date its balance sheet is as under :

Balance Sheet of Green Limited as on 31st March, 2010

Liabilities	*Rs.*	*Assets*	*Rs.*
Share Capital :		**Fixed Assets :**	
Authorised :		Goodwill	13,00,000
1,50,000 Equity shares of		Plant	10,00,000
Rs. 50 each	75,00,000	Computers	25,00,000
Subscribed and paid up :		Furniture	2,00,000
50,000 Equity shares of		**Current Assets :**	
Rs. 50 each	25,00,000	Stock	7,00,000
1,00,000 Equity shares of		Cash at Bank	1,00,000
Rs. 50 each,		**Profit and Loss Account**	27,00,000
Rs. 40 per share paid up	40,00,000		
Secured Loans :			
11.5% First Debentures	5,00,000		
12% Second Debentures	10,00,000		
Current Liabilities:			
Sundry Creditors	5,00,000		
	85,00,000		85,00,000

The following is the interest of Mr. X and Mr. Y in Green Limited :

	Mr. X *Rs.*	*Mr. Y* *Rs.*
11.5% First Debentures	3,00,000	2,00,000
12% Second Debentures	7,00,000	3,00,000
Sundry Creditors	2,00,000	1,00,000
	12,00,000	6,00,000
Fully paid up Rs. 50 Shares	3,00,000	2,00,000
Partly paid up Shares, Rs. 40 paid up	5,00,000	5,00,000

The following scheme of Reconstruction is approved by all parties interested and also by the Court :

(*a*) Uncalled capital is to be called up in full and such shares and also the fully paid up shares pertaining to the earlier issue be converted into equal number of fully paid up equity share of Rs. 20 each.

(*b*) Mr. X is to cancel Rs. 7,00,000 of his total debt (other than share amount), is to pay Rs. 2 lakh to the company and to receive new 13% First Debentures in full settlement.

(*c*) Mr. Y is to cancel Rs. 3,00,000 of his total debt (excluding shares) and to accept new 13% First Debentures for the balance.

(*d*) The amount thus rendered available by the scheme be utilized in writing off Goodwill, the debit balance of Profit and Loss Account and in reducing the book value of computers by Rs. 15,00,000.

You are required to pass the Journal Entries for all the above mentioned transactions and prepare the initial balance sheet of the reconstructed Company. [*Adapted C.A. (Inter), Nov. 2000*]

Solution :

Journal

			Dr. *Rs.'000*	*Cr.* *Rs.'000*
	Equity Share Final Call Account .. Dr.		10,00,000	
	To Equity Share Capital Account			10,00,000
	Final call on one lakh equity shares @ Rs. 10 each.			
	Bank .. Dr.		10,00,000	
	To Equity Share Final Call Account			10,00,000
	Receipt of final call on one lakh equity shares @Rs. 10 each, making them fully paid up.			
	Equity Share Capital (Rs. 50 each) Account .. Dr.		75,00,000	
	To Equity Share Capital (Rs. 20 each) Account			30,00,000
	To Reconstruction Account			45,00,000
	Conversion of 1,50,000 fully paid equity shares of Rs. 50 each into equal number of fully paid equity Shares of Rs. 20 each, gain being credited to reconstruction account.			
	11.5% First Debentures Account .. Dr.		3,00,000	
	12% Second Debentures Account .. Dr.		7,00,000	
	Sundry Creditors .. Dr.		2,00,000	
	Bank .. Dr.		2,00,000	
	To 13% New First Debentures Account			7,00,000
	To Reconstruction Account			7,00,000
	Cancellation of Rs. 7 lakh of total debt due to Mr. X, receipt of Rs. 2 lakh from him and issue of 13% new First debentures for Rs. 7 lakh in full settlement.			

		Rs.'000	Rs.'000
11.5% First Debentures Account	.. Dr.	2,00,000	
12% Second Debentures Account	.. Dr.	3,00,000	
Sundry Creditors	.. Dr.	1,00,000	
To 13% New First Debentures Account			3,00,000
To Reconstruction Account			3,00,000
Cancellation of Rs. 3 lakh of total debt due to Mr. Y, and issue of 13% new First debentures for the balance.			
Reconstruction Account	.. Dr.	55,00,000	
To Goodwill Account			13,00,000
To Profit and Loss Account			27,00,000
To Computers Account			15,00,000
Credit in reconstruction account used for writing off Goodwill, the debit balance of Profit and Loss A/c and for reducing the value of computers by Rs. 15 lakh.			

Balance Sheet of Green Limited (And Reduced) as on ______

Liabilities	Rs.	Assets		Rs.
Share Capital :		**Fixed Assets :**		
Authorised 3,75,000 equity shares of Rs. 20 each	75,00,000	Goodwill	13,00,000	
		Less : Amount written off under scheme of reconstruction as on 31st March, 2001	13,00,000	Nil
Issued and Subscribed :				
1,50,000 equity shares of Rs. 20 each fully paid up	30,00,000	Plant		10,00,000
Secured Loan :		Computers	25,00,000	
13% First Debentures	10,00,000	*Less* : Amount written off under scheme of reconstruction as on 31st March, 2001	15,00,000	10,00,000
Current Liabilities and Provisions:				
(*a*) *Current Liabilities* :				
Sundry Creditors	2,00,000			
(*b*) Provisions	Nil	Furniture		2,00,000
		Current Assets, Loans and Advances		
		(*a*) *Current Assets* :		
		Stock		7,00,000
		Cash at Bank		13,00,000
		(*b*) Loans and Advances		Nil
	42,00,000			42,00,000

Illustration 35:

The ledger-balance of J Company Ltd. as at 31st March, 2010 include: Fixed Assets Rs. 7,00,000, Investments Rs. 10,000, Inventories Rs. 3,90,000, Trade Debtors Rs. 4,60,000, Preliminary Expenses Rs. 20,000, Equity Share Capital (60% paid up) Rs. 6,00,000, 10% First Debentures Rs. 2,00,000, 12% Second Debentures Rs. 5,00,000, Bank Overdraft Rs. 50,000, Trade Creditors (including Y for Rs. 8,50,000) Rs. 11,50,000, Outstanding Interest for one year on Debenture Rs. 80,000.

The Company has incurred heavy losses. The following scheme of reconstruction is agreed upon:

(*a*) to make the existing Rs. 100 equity shares fully paid up, and then to reduce them to Rs. 20 each.

(*b*) to settle the claims of the holders of the First Debentures by issuing 2,000 12½% Debentures of Rs. 100 each;

(*c*) to discharge the claims of the holders of the Second Debentures by issuing 4,000 14%

Debentures of Rs. 100 each;

(*d*) to pay Rs. 3,00,000 to Y in full settlement of his account;

(*e*) to allot 15,000 fresh equity shares of Rs. 20 each to discharge the remaining Trade Creditors; and

(*f*) to write off the Fictitious Assets and to reduce the Fixed Assets.

Pass the necessary journal entries to give effect to the aforesaid scheme and show the post-reconstruction Balance Sheet. Assume that (*i*) all the formalities are duly complied with, and (*ii*) the Company has only one bank account to transact all the receipts and payments.

[*Adabted B.Com. (Hons.), Delhi, 1994 and 1996*]

Solution:

In order to know the amount of past losses and fictitious assets, we have to prepare the following Balance Sheet:—

Balance Sheet of J Ltd.

Liabilities	*Rs.*	*Assets*	*Rs.*
Equity Share Capital (60% paid up)		Fixed Assets	7,00,000
of Rs. 100 each	6,00,000	Investment	10,000
10% First Debenture	2,00,000	Inventories	3,90,000
12% Second Debentures	5,00,000	Trade Debtors	4,60,000
Bank Overdraft	50,000	Preliminary Expenses	20,000
Trade Creditors (including Y for		Fictitious Assets (balancing figure)	10,00,000
Rs. 8,50,000)	11,50,000		
Outstanding Interest on Debentures	80,000		
	25,80,000		25,80,000

Journal

			Dr.	*Cr.*
2010			*Rs.*	*Rs.*
March 31	Equity Share Final Call Account	Dr.	4,00,000	
	To Equity Share Capital Account			4,00,000
	The amount of final call due on 10,000 equity shares @ Rs. 40 per share.			
	Bank Account	Dr.	4,00,000	
	To Equity Share Final Call Account			4,00,000
	Receipt of Rs. 40 per share as final call on 10,000 shares.			
	Equity Share Capital Account	Dr.	8,00,000	
	To Reconstruction			8,00,000
	The reduction of Rs. 80 per share on 10,000 equity shares.			
	10% First Debentures Account	Dr.	2,00,000	
	Outstanding Interest on Debentures Account	Dr.	20,000	
	To 12.5% Debentures Account			2,00,000
	To Reconstruction Account			20,000
	Issue of 2,000 12.5% debentures of Rs. 100 each to settle the claims of the holders of the first debentures.			
	12% Second Debentures Account	Dr.	5,00,000	
	Outstanding Interest on Debentures Account	Dr.	60,000	
	To 14% Debentures Account			4,00,000
	To Reconstruction Account			1,60,000
	Issue of 4,000 14% Debentures of Rs. 100 each to discharge the claims of the holders of the second debentures.			

			Rs.	Rs.
2010				
March 31	Trade Creditors	Dr.	8,50,000	
	To Bank Account			3,00,000
	To Reconstruction Account			5,50,000
	The settlement of Y's claim.			
	Trade Creditors	Dr.	3,00,000	
	To Equity Share Capital			3,00,000
	Issue of 15,000 equity shares of Rs. 20 each to trade creditors in settlement of their claim.			
	Reconstruction Account	Dr.	15,30,000	
	To Fictitious Assets			10,00,000
	To Preliminary Expenses			20,000
	To Fixed Assets			5,10,000
	The Writing off fictitious assets, preliminary expenses and the transfer of balance in Reconstruction Account to Fixed Assets.			

Balance Sheet of J Company Ltd. as on 31st March, 2010

Liabilities	*Rs.*	*Assets*	*Rs.*	*Rs.*
Share Capital		**Fixed Assets**	7,00,000	
25,000 equity shares of Rs. 20 each	5,00,000	*Less*: written off under		
(Out of this 15,000 equity shares		Reconstruction Scheme		
of Rs. 20 each are issued to Trade		dated	5,10,000	1,90,000
Creditors)		**Investments**		10,000
Secured Loans		**Current Assets**		
12.5% Debentures	2,00,000	Inventories	3,90,000	
14% Debentures	4,00,000	Trade Debtors	4,60,000	
		Cash at Bank	50,000	9,00,000
	11,00,000			11,00,000

Illustration 36:

The following is the Balance Sheet of Sick Co. Ltd. as on 31st March, 2010:—

Liabilities	*Rs.*	*Assets*	*Rs.*
1,000 14% Redeemable Preference Shares of Rs. 100 each	1,00,000	Fixed Assets	15,00,000
		Current Assets	35,00,000
Equity Shares of Rs. 10 each	7,00,000	Profit and Loss Account	3,00,000
12% Debentures	3,00,000		
Current Liabilities	39,00,000		
Provision for Taxation	3,00,000		
	53,00,000		53,00,000

The following scheme of reorganisation is sanctioned:

(1) Fixed assets are to be written down by $33^1/_3$%.

(2) Current assets are to be revalued at Rs. 27,00,000.

(3) Preference shareholders decide to forego their right to arrears of dividend which are in arrears for three years.

(4) The taxation liabilitity of the company is settled at Rs. 4,00,000.

(5) One of the creditors of the company, to whom the company owes Rs. 25,00,000, decides to forego 50% of his claim. He is allotted 1,00,000 equity shares of Rs. 5 each in part satisfaction of the balance of his claim.

(6) The rate of interest on debentures is increased to 14%. The debentureholders surrender their existing debentures of Rs. 100 each and exchange the same for fresh debentures of Rs. 75 each.

(7) All existing equity shares are reduced to Rs. 5 each.

(8) All preference shares are reduced to Rs. 75 each.

Pass journal entries and show the balance sheet of the company after giving effect to the above.

[Adapted C.A. (Inter.) May 1978]
[Adapted C.S. (Inter.) June, 1987]

Solution:

Journal

			Dr.	Cr.
2010			*Rs.*	*Rs.*
March 31	14% Redeemable Preference Share Capital Account	Dr.	25,000	
	Equity Share Capital Account	Dr.	3,50,000	
	To Reconstruction Account			3,75,000
	The reduction of Rs. 25 per share on 1,000 14% cumulative preference shares and Rs. 5 per share on 70,000 equity shares vide Special Resolution No......... dated............. confirmed by the court vide order dated..........			
" "	12% Debentures Account	Dr.	3,00,000	
	To 14% Debentures Account			2,25,000
	To Reconstruction Account			75,000
	The conversion of 3,000 12% Debentures of Rs. 100 each into 3,000 14% Debentures of Rs. 75 each.			
" "	Creditors	Dr.	17,50,000	
	To Equity Share Capital Account			5,00,000
	To Reconstruction Account			12,50,000
	Sacrifice by a creditor for Rs. 25,00,000 of 50% of his claim and allotment to him of 1,00,000 equity shares of Rs. 5 each in part settlement of his dues vide reconstruction scheme dated			
" "	Reconstruction Account	Dr.	17,00,000	
	To Profit and Loss Account			3,00,000
	To Fixed Assets			5,00,000
	To Current Assets			8,00,000
	To Provision for Taxation			1,00,000
	The writing off of debit balance in Profit and Loss Account, increase in provision for taxation and to write off various amount as indicated in the Special Resolution.			
" "	Provision for Taxation Account	Dr.	4,00,000	
	To Liability for Taxation			4,00,000
	The conversion of provision for taxation into liability for taxation for settlement of amount due.			
" "	Liability for Taxation	Dr.	4,00,000	
	To Current Assets			4,00,000
	The settlement of liability for taxation by cash payment out of current assets.			

Balance Sheet of Sick Co. Ltd. as on 31st March, 2010

Liabilities	*Rs.*	*Assets*		*Rs.*
Share Capital		**Fixed Assets**	15,00,000	
1,000 14% Redeemable Preference		*Less*: amount written off		
Shares of Rs. 75 each, fully paid	75,000	under Reconstruction		
1,70,000 Equity Shares of Rs. 5 each	8,50,000	Scheme dated.....	5,00,000	10,00,000
(Out of this, 1,00,000 equity				

	Rs.		Rs.
shares of Rs. 5 were issued to creditors)		Current Assets (Rs. 35,00,000 – Rs. 8,00,000 – Rs. 4,00,000)	23,00,000
Secured Loans			
3,000 14% Debenture of Rs. 75 each, fully paid	2,25,000		
Current Liabilities			
(14,00,000 + 7,50,000)	21,50,000		
	33,00,000		33,00,000

Illustration 37:

The following is the Balance Sheet of R. Ltd. as at March 31, 2010:—

		Rs.		Rs.
Authorised, Issued and Subscribed Capital:			Delhi Works	16,00,000
			Nagpur Works	12,00,000
20,000 Equity Shares of Rs. 100 each, fully paid		20,00,000	Workmen's Compensation Fund Investment	30,000
18,000 11 % Preference Shares of Rs. 100 each, fully paid		18,00,000	Stock	9,00,000
			Debtors	5,00,000
"A" 10% Debentures (secured on Delhi Works)		3,00,000	Cash at Bank	1,00,000
			Profit and Loss Account	4,00,000
"B" 10% Debentures (secured on Nagpur Works)		3,50,000		
Workmen's Compensation Fund:				
Delhi	20,000			
Nagpur	10,000	30,000		
Creditors		2,50,000		
		47,30,000		47,30,000

A scheme was duly prepared and sanctioned whereby

(a) Equity shares were to be reduced to Rs. 10;

(b) Preference shares were to be reduced to Rs. 80, dividend being raised to 12%;

(c) Debentureholders to forgo their interest, Rs. 32,500, which is included among the Sundry Creditors;

(d) Directors refund Rs. 50,000 out of the fees previously received by them.

(e) "B" Debentureholders agreed to take over the Nagpur Works at Rs. 5,00,000 and to accept an allotment of 3,000 fully paid equity shares of Rs. 10 each at par; and upon their forming a company called R.P. Ltd. to take over the Nagpur Works, they allotted R. Ltd. 18,000 shares of Rs. 10 each fully paid at par;

(f) The Nagpur Workmen's Compensation Fund disclosed the fact that there were liabilities of Rs. 2,000. In consequence, the investments of the fund were realised to the extent of the balance, the investments realising a profit of 10% on book value and the proceeds used for part payment of the creditors; and

(g) Stock was to be written down by Rs. 4,00,000 and a provision for doubtful debts created to the extent of Rs. 44,800 on debtors. Any balance to be applied as to two-thirds to write down the value of Delhi Works and one-third to a capital reserve.

Show Journal entries covering these steps. Also show the important ledger accounts and the balance sheet after the scheme has been carried out.

Solution:

Journal

			Dr.	Cr.
2010			Rs.	Rs.
March 31	Equity Share Capital Account	Dr.	18,00,000	
	To Reconstruction Account			18,00,000
	The reduction of 20,000 shares of Rs. 100 each to Rs. 10 each.			
	11% Preference Share Capital Account	Dr.	18,00,000	
	To 12% Preference Share Capital Account			14,40,000
	To Reconstruction Account			3,60,000
	The conversion of 11% Preference Shares of Rs. 100 each into 12% Preference Shares of Rs. 80 each.			
	Bank	Dr.	8,800	
	To Workmen's Compensation Fund Investment			8,800
	Realisation of investments (surplus against liability at Nagpur) at a profit of 10%			
	Workmen's Compensation Fund Investment	Dr.	800	
	To Workmen's Compensation Fund			800
	Transfer of profit to Workmen's Compensation Fund.			
	Creditors (Debenture Interest)	Dr.	32,500	
	Bank	Dr.	50,000	
	Workmen's Compensation Fund	Dr.	8,800	
	To Reconstruction Account			91,300
	(1) Cancellation of debenture interest amounting to Rs. 32,500; (2) Refund of fees by directors amounting to Rs. 50,000; and (3) Surplus Workmen's Compensation Fund at Nagpur credited to Reconstruction Account under the scheme.			
	"B" Debentures	Dr.	3,50,000	
	To "B" Debentureholders			3,50,000
	The transfer of "B" debentures to the debentureholders.			
	"B" Debentureholders	Dr.	5,30,000	
	To Nagpur Works			5,00,000
	To Equity Share Capital Account			30,000
	The transfer of Nagpur Works valued at Rs. 5,00,000 and the allotment of 3,000 Equity Shares of Rs. 10 each fully paid to R.P. Ltd., formed by "B" Debentureholders.			
	Investment in R.P. Ltd.	Dr.	1,80,000	
	To "B" Debentureholders			1,80,000
	The receipt of 18,000 shares (in R.P. Ltd.) of Rs. 10 each, fully paid.			
	Creditors	Dr.	8,800	
	To Bank			8,800
	The payment of Rs. 8,800 (realised from sale of investment) to creditors in part payment.			
	Reconstruction Account	Dr.	22,51,300	
	To Profit and Loss Account			4,00,000
	To Nagpur Works			7,00,000
	To Stock			4,00,000
	To Provision for Doubtful Debts			44,800
	To Delhi Works			4,71,000
	To Capital Reserve			2,35,500
	The utilisation of the amount available in the reconstruction Account to write off the debit balance of the Profit and Loss Account and to, write down the value of various assets as per scheme.			

Workmen's Compensation Fund

Dr.	Delhi Rs.	Nagpur Rs.		Delhi Rs.	Nagpur Rs. Cr.
Reconstruction	—	8,800	By Balance b/fd	20,000	10,000
			By Workmen's Compensation	—	
To Balance c/d	20,000	2,000	Fund Investment Account		800
	20,000	10,800		20,000	10,800

Workmen's Compensation Fund Investment Account

Dr.	Delhi Rs.	Nagpur Rs.		Delhi Rs.	Nagpur Rs. Cr.
To Balance b/fd	20,000	10,000	By Bank	—	8,800
To Workmen's Compensation			By Balance c/d	20,000	2,000
Fund	—	800			
	20,000	10,800		20,000	10,800
To Balance b/d	20,000	2,000			

'B' Debentureholders Account

Dr.	Rs.		Rs. Cr.
To Nagpur Works	5,00,000	By 'B' Debentures	3,50,000
To Equity Share Capital Account	30,000	By Investment in R.P. Ltd.	1,80,000
	5,30,000		5,30,000

Creditors

Dr.	Rs.		Rs. Cr.
To Reconstruction Account		By Balance b/fd	2,50,000
(Debentures Interest)	32,500		
To Bank	8,800		
To Balance c/d	2,08,700		
	2,50,000		2,50,000
		By Balance b/d	1,89,200

Balance Sheet of R. Ltd. as on March 31, 2010

Liabilities	Rs.	Assets	Rs.	Rs.
Share Capital:		**Fixed Assets:**		
Authorised, Issued and Subscribed:		Delhi Works	16,00,000	
23,000 Equity Shares of Rs. 10 each, fully paid	2,30,000	*Less*: Amount written off as per Reconstructed Scheme dated......	4,71,000	11,29,000
18,000 12% Preference Shares of Rs. 80 each, fully paid	14,40,000	**Investments:**		
Reserve and Surplus:		Workmen's Compensation Fund Investment		22,000
Capital Reserve	2,35,500	Shares (fully paid) in R.P. Ltd.		1,80,000
Secured Loans:		**Current Assets, Loan and Advances**		
10% Debentures	3,00,000	(*A*) Current Assets		
Current Liabilities and Provisions:		Stock at market price		5,00,000
Creditors	2,08,700	Debtors	5,00,000	
Workmen's Compensation Fund	22,000	*Less*: Provision	44,800	4,55,200
Contingent Liabilities (not provided for)	Nil	(*B*) Loan and Advances		Nil
		Miscellaneous Expenditure		Nil
	24,36,200			24,36,200

Illustration 38:

The summarised assets and liabilities position of Hopeful Ltd. as on 1.4.2010 was as follows:—

Liabilities	*Rs.*
Authorised Capital:	
80,000 Equity Shares of Rs. 10 each	8,00,000
2,000 9% Preference Shares of Rs. 100 each	2,00,000
Issued and Paid-up Capital:	
40,000 Equity Shares of Rs. 10 each, Rs. 7.50 paid up	3,00,000
2,000 9% preference shares of Rs. 100 each, fully paid	2,00,000
Unsecured Loans	80,000
Trade Creditors	48,000
Bank Overdraft	16,800
	6,44,800
Assets	
Goodwill	20,000
Land and Buildings	1,60,000
Plant and Machinery	1,20,000
Investments	24,000
Stock	54,000
Debtors	1,18,000
Cash in Hand	6,000
Profit and Loss Account	1,42,800
	6,44,800

Notes:

(*a*) Dividend on Preference Shares has not been declared for 2 years.

(*b*) No provision has been made for sales tax liability of Rs. 9,600.

Following Scheme of Reconstruction has been approved by the court.

(*i*) Uncalled capital is to be called up in full and equity shares are to be reduced to Rs. 5 per share.

(*ii*) Sales tax liability of Rs. 9,000 is to be paid immediately.

(*iii*) Land and Buildings are to be shown in the balance sheet at full market value of Rs. 2,20,000 and Goodwill is to be written off.

(*iv*) Trade Creditors have consented for 25% of remission of liability on a condition that 25% of the net liability after remission is paid forthwith and the balance is paid within one year.

(*v*) Investments are to be taken over by Bank in full settlement of the overdraft balance.

(*vi*) Preference shareholders have agreed to give up their right for the two years' dividend and accept 12 fully paid equity shares of Rs. 5 each for each fully paid preference share.

You are required to:

(*i*) Pass necessary journal entries recording the above transactions; and

(*ii*) Draw up a fresh balance sheet after giving effect to the scheme of Reconstruction.

Working should form part of your answer. [*Adapted C.A.* (*Inter*) *Nov., 1988*]

Solution:

BOOK OF HOPEFUL LTD.
Journal

Particulars			Dr. Rs.	Cr. Rs.
Bank Account	Dr.		1,00,000	
To Equity Share Capital Account				1,00,000
Amount of call money received on 40,000 shares @ Rs. 2.50 per share, credited to share capital.				
Equity Share Capital (Rs. 10) Account	Dr.		4,00,000	
To Equity Share Capital (Rs. 5) Account				2,00,000
To Reconstruction Account				2,00,000
40,000 equity shares of Rs. 10 each fully paid reduced to 40,000 equity shares of Rs. 5 each, fully paid vide scheme of reconstruction dated.........., balance credited to Reconstruction Account.				
Land and Building Account	Dr.		60,000	
To Reconstruction Account				60,000
Appreciation in the value of Land & Buildings vide scheme of reconstruction dated.......... credited to Reconstruction Account.				
Reconstruction Account	Dr.		1,72,400	
To Goodwill Account				20,000
To Profit & Loss Account				1,42,800
To Sales Tax Payable Account				9,000
To Provision for Sales Tax				600
Amount of Goodwill, debit balance of Profit and Loss Account and Sales Tax Payable written off.				
Trade Creditors	Dr.		21,000	
To Reconstruction Account				12,000
To Bank Account				9,000
Amount paid to creditors Rs. 9,000, Rs. 12,000 sacrificed credited to Reconstruction Account vide scheme dated............				
Bank Overdraft Account	Dr.		16,800	
Reconstruction Account	Dr.		7,200	
To Investments Account				24,000
Investments having book value of Rs. 24,000 given in discharge of bank overdraft of Rs. 16,800, the difference debited to Reconstruction Account vide scheme dated				
9% Preference Share Capital Account	Dr.		2,00,000	
To Equity Share Capital (Rs. 5) Account				1,20,000
To Reconstruction Account				80,000
Amount of sacrifice by 9% Preference Share holders @ Rs. 40 per share on 2,000 share credited to Reconstruction Account, balance converted into Equity Shares of Rs. 5 each, fully paid vide scheme dated.............				
Sales Tax Payable	Dr.		9,000	
To Bank				9,000
Amount paid against Sales tax payable.				
Reconstruction Account	Dr.		1,72,400	
To Capital Reserve Account				1,72,400
Balance of Reconstruction Account transferred to Capital Reserve Account.				

Hopeful Ltd.
Balance Sheet as on 1st April, 2010 after reconstruction

Liabilities	*Rs.*	*Assets*	*Rs.*	*Rs.*
Share Capital		**Fixed Assets**		
Authorised:		Goodwill	20,000	
80,000 Equity Shares of Rs. 10		*Less*: Written off under		
each reduced to shares of Rs. 5		reconstruction scheme	20,000	Nil
each vide scheme of		Land and Buildings	1,60,000	
Reconstruction	4,00,000	*Add*: Appreciation under		
Issued, Subscribed and Paid up:		the reconstruction scheme	60,000	2,20,000
64,000 Equity Shares of Rs. 5		Plant & Machinery		1,20,000
each, fully paid (including		**Current Assets, Loans and Advances**		
24,000 shares issued for		(*A*)Current Assets		
consideration other than cash		Stock in trade		54,000
to preference shareholders)	3,20,000	Sundry Debtors		1,18,000
Reserve & Surplus		Cash in hand & at Bank		88,000
Capital Reserve	1,72,400	(*B*) Loans and Advances		Nil
Unsecured Loans	80,000			
Current Liabilities & Provisions				
(*A*) Current Liabilities				
Sundry Creditors*	27,000			
(*B*) Provision				
Provision for Sales Tax	600			
	6,00,000			6,00,000

Working Notes:

Dr. **Reconstruction Account** *Cr.*

	Rs.		*Rs.*
To Goodwill	20,000	By Equity Share Capital Account	2,00,000
To Profit & Loss Account	1,42,800	By Land & Building	60,000
To Sales Tax Payable Account	9,000	By Trade Creditors	12,000
To Provision for Sales Tax	600	By Preference Shares Capital Account	80,000
To Investment Account	7,200		
To Capital Reserve (balancing figure)	1,72,400		
	3,52,000		3,52,000

Cash / Bank Account *Cr.*

	Rs.		*Rs.*
To Balance b/fd	6,000	By Trade Creditors	9,000
To Equity Share Capital	1,00,000	By Sales Tax payable	9,000
		By Balance c/d	88,000
	1,06,000		1,06,000
To Balance b/d	88,000		

Surrender of shares

Sometimes for purposes of reconstruction, shares are sub-divided into shares of smaller denominations and then the shareholders are made to surrender some of them to the company. For example, suppose 10,000 equity share of Rs. 100 each are sub-divided into 1,00,000 equity shares of Rs. 100 each are sub-divided into 1,00,000 equity shares of Rs. 10 each and then the shareholders surrender 60% of the shares to the company. The entries will be:—

			Dr.	Cr.
			Rs.	Rs.
Equity Share Capital (Rs. 100 each) Account	Dr.		10,00,000	
To Equity Share Capital (Rs. 10 each) Account				10,00,000
Sub-division of 10,000 equity shares of Rs. 100 each into 1,00,000 equity shares of Rs. 10 each as per scheme of reconstruction.				
Equity Share Capital (Rs. 10 each) Account	Dr.		6,00,000	
To Shares Surrendered Account				6,00,000
Surrender of 60,000 equity shares of Rs. 10 each by the shareholders to the company for purposes of reconstruction.				

Shares so surrendered are usually reissued in favour of debentureholders and trade creditors to discharge liabilities partly or fully. The amount discharged by reissue is credited to Reconstruction Account or Reorganisation Account. For shares reissued, Shares Surrendered Account is debited and Share Capital Account is credited. Suppose, 14% Debentures for Rs. 2,00,000 are outstanding and debenture-interest for two years has not been paid. Further assume that the debentureholders agree to accept 30,000 surrendered equity shares of Rs. 10 each in full and final settlement of their claim. The entries will be as follows:—

			Dr.	Cr.
			Rs.	Rs.
14% Debentures Account	Dr.		2,00,000	
Outstanding Debenture Interest Account	Dr.		56,000	
To Reconstruction Account				2,56,000
Liability discharged by reissue of surrendered shares being transferred to Reconstruction Account.				
Shares Surrendered Account	Dr.		3,00,000	
To Equity Share Capital (Rs. 10 each) Account				3,00,000
Reissue of 30,000 surrendered equity shares of Rs. 10 each to satisfy the claims of all the debentureholders.				

Surrendered shares which are not reissued are cancelled, for which Shares Surrendered Account is debited and Reconstruction Account/Reorganisation Account is credited. Suppose 30,000 surrendered equity shares of Rs. 10 each are cancelled; the entry will be:

			Dr.	Cr.
			Rs.	Rs.
Shares Surrendered Account	Dr.		3,00,000	
To Reconstruction Account				3,00,000
Cancellation of 30,000 surrendered equity shares of Rs. 10 each.				

Illustration 39:

The abridged balance sheet of Z Ltd. as on 31st March, 2010 is given below :

Liabilities	*Rs.*	*Assets*	*Rs.*
30,000 Equity Shares of Rs. 100 each	30,00,000	Goodwill	5,00,000
10,000 11% Preference Shares of Rs. 100 each	10,00,000	Other Fixed Assets	30,00,000
15% Debentures	10,00,000	Current Assets	10,90,000
Interest Due on Debentures	3,00,000	Profit and Loss Account	15,50,000
Sundry Creditors	8,40,000		
	61,40,000		61,40,000

The following schemes of reconstruction has been passed by the company and sanctioned by the Court :

(*i*) The equity share are to be sub-divided into shares of Rs. 10 each, and each shareholders shall surrender 70 per cent of his holding.

(*ii*) Out of surrendered shares 50,000 shares shall be issued to preference shareholders in full settlement of their claims.

(*iii*) Debentureholders' total claim shall be reduced to Rs. 7,00,000 and shall be satisfied by issue of 70,000 equity shares, out of surrendered shares.

(*iv*) Creditors' claims are to be reduced by 50 per cent and in consideration the creditors the creditors shall receive 20,000 equity shares shall be cancelled.

(*v*) The remaining surrendered shares shall be cancelled.

(*vi*) Goodwill and Profit and Loss Account are to be written off completely and other fixed assets are to be depreciated by Rs. 10,00,000.

The scheme was duly implemented. You are required to :

(*a*) pass journal entries for all the transactions, and

(*b*) show Surrendered Shares Account and Reconstruction Account.

[*Adapted B. Com.(Hons.), Delhi 1998*]

Solution :

Journal

	Particulars		Dr. Rs.	Cr. Rs.
	Equity Share Capital (Rs. 100 each) Account	..Dr.	30,00,000	
	To Equity Share Capital (Rs. 10 each) Account			30,00,000
	Sub-division of 30,000 equity shares of Rs. 100 each into 3,00,000 equity shares of Rs. 10 each as per scheme of reconstruction.			
	Equity Share Capital (Rs. 10 each) Account	..Dr.	21,00,000	
	To Shares Surrendered Account			21,00,000
	Surrender of 70% of their holding by equity shareholders as per scheme of reconstruction.			
	Shares Surrendered Account	..Dr.	12,00,000	
	To Equity Share Capital (Rs. 10 each) Account			12,00,000
	Issue of 50,000 surrendered shares to preference shareholders and 70,000 surrendered shares to debentureholders in full satisfaction of their claims as per scheme of reconstruction.			
	11% Preference Share Capital Account	..Dr.	10,00,000	
	15% Debentures Account	..Dr.	10,00,000	
	Interest Due on Debentures Account	..Dr.	3,00,000	
	To Reconstruction Account			23,00,000
	Transfer of the liabilities towards preference shareholders and debentureholders to Reconstruction as these liabilities have been fully discharged by issue of surrendered shares as per scheme of reconstruction.			
	Shares Surrendered Account	..Dr.	2,00,000	
	To Equity Share Capital (Rs. 10 each) Account			2,00,000
	Issue of 20,000 surrendered shares to sundry creditors in lieu of reduction of their claims by 50% as per scheme of reconstruction.			
	Sundry Creditors Account	..Dr.	4,20,000	
	To Reconstruction Account			4,20,000
	Reduction of claims of sundry creditors by 50% as per scheme of reconstruction.			

		Rs.	Rs.
Shares Surrendered Account	..Dr.	7,00,000	
To Reconstruction Account			7,00,000
Cancellation of surrendered shares not reissued, as per scheme of reconstruction.			
Reconstruction Account	..Dr.	34,20,000	
To Goodwill Account			5,00,000
To Other fixed Assets Account			10,00,000
To Profit and Loss Account			15,50,000
To Capital Reserve			3,70,000
Reduction of the value of other Fixed Assets by Rs. 10,00,000 and writing off the fictitious assets; the balance in Reconstruction Account being transferred to Capital Reserve.			

Dr. **Surrendered Shares Account** Cr.

	Rs.		Rs.
To Equity Share Capital (Rs. 10 each) Account	12,00,000	By Equity Share Capital (Rs. 10 each) Account	21,00,000
To Equity Share Capital (Rs. 10 each) Account	2,00,000		
To Reconstruction Account (balancing figure)	7,00,000		
	21,00,000		21,00,000

Dr. **Reconstruction Account** Cr.

	Rs.		Rs.
To Goodwill A/c	5,00,000	By 11% Preference Share Capital A/c	10,00,000
To Other Fixed Assets A/c	10,00,000	By 15% Debentures A/c	10,00,000
To Profit and Loss A/c	15,50,000	By Interest Due on Debentures A/c	3,00,000
To Capital Reserve – balancing figure	3,70,000	By Sundry Creditors A/c	4,20,000
		By Shares Surrendered A/c	7,00,000
	34,20,000		34,20,000

Illustration 40:

The Balance Sheet of G. Ltd. as at March 31, 2010 is as follows:—

Liabilities	*Rs.*	*Rs.*	*Assets*	*Rs.*
Share Capital:			Land, Buildings, Machinery, etc.	14,30,000
Authorised and Issued:			Investments	17,000
8,000 shares of Rs. 100 each,			Stock-in-Trade	80,000
fully paid		8,00,000	Sundry Debtors	30,000
Debentures	14,00,000		Cash	1,03,000
Add: Interest			Profit and Loss Account	10,70,000
Outstanding	70,000	14,70,000		
Sundry Creditors:				
Income-tax	10,000			
Trade and General	4,50,000	4,60,000		
		27,30,000		27,30,000

The fixed assets are heavily overvalued. The debentureholders have a floating charge on the assets of the company. They are prepared to accept a modification of their claims in consideration of a substantial interest in the share capital. A scheme of reorganisation is accordingly prepared and confirmed by the Court. The salient points of the scheme are the following:—

(1) Each share shall be subdivided into twenty fully paid equity shares of Rs. 5 each.

(2) After sub-division, each shareholder shall surrender to the company 95% of his holding, for the purpose of reissue to debentureholders and creditors so far as may be required, and otherwise for cancellation.

(3) Of those surrendered 46,000 shares of Rs. 5 each shall be converted into 14% redeemable preference shares of Rs. 5 each fully paid.

(4) The debentureholders' total claim shall be reduced to Rs. 2,30,000. This will be satisfied by the issue to them of 46,000 redeemable preference shares of Rs. 5 each fully paid.

(5) The liability for income-tax is to be satisfied in full.

(6) The claims of unsecured creditors shall be reduced by 80% and the balance shall be satisfied by allotting them equity shares of Rs. 5 each, fully paid, from the shares surrendered.

(7) Shares surrendered and not reissued shall be cancelled.

Journalise the various entries to be made, assuming the tax liability is not yet paid. Also show Shares Surrendered Account and Reconstruction Account.

Solution:

Journal

			Dr.	*Cr.*
2010			*Rs.*	*Rs.*
March 31	Share Capital (Rs. 100 each) Account	Dr.	8,00,000	
	To Equity Share Capital (Rs. 5 each) Account			8,00,000
	The sub-division of 8,000 shares of Rs. 100 each into 1,60,000 shares of Rs. 5 each in accordance with the Special Resolution and Court Order.			
" "	Equity Share Capital (Rs. 5 each) Account	Dr.	7,60,000	
	To Shares Surrendered Account			7,60,000
	The surrender of 95% of the shares, viz., 1,52,000 shares of Rs. 5 each in accordance with the scheme.			
" "	Shares Surrendered Account	Dr.	2,30,000	
	To 14% Redeemable Preference Share Capital Account			2,30,000
	The conversion of 46,000 surrendered shares into 14% redemable preference shares of Rs. 5 each and issue of these shares to the debentureholders in full satisfaction of their claims in accordance with the scheme.			
" "	Shares Surrendered Account	Dr.	90,000	
	To Equity Share Capital Account			90,000
	The re-issue of shares worth Rs. 90,000 (20% of Rs. 4,50,000) to sundry creditors in full satisfaction of their claims in accordance with the scheme.			
" "	Debentures	Dr.	14,00,000	
	Interest	Dr.	70,000	
	Sundry Creditors	Dr.	4,50,000	
	To Reconstruction Account			19,20,000
	Transfer of the liabilities in respect of debentures, and creditors to the Reconstruction Account since these liabilities have been fully discharged by the issue of shares.			
" "	Shares Surrendered Account	Dr.	4,40,000	
	To Reconstruction Account			4,40,000
	Cancellation of the unissued surrendered shares (7,60,000 – 2,30,000 – 90,000) to Reconstruction Account.			
" "	Reconstruction Account	Dr.	23,60,000	
	To Profit and Loss Account			10,70,000
	To Land, Buildings, Machinery, etc.			12,90,000
	The writing off of the debit balance of the Profit and Loss Account and the transfer of the balance in the Reconstruction Account to fixed accets since these are overvalued.			

Shares Surrendered Account

Dr.	Rs.		*Cr.* Rs.
To 14% Redeembble Preference Share Capital	2,30,000	By Equity Share Capital Account	7,60,000
To Equity Share Capital Account	90,000		
To Reconstruction Account (balancing figure)	4,40,000		
	7,60,000		7,60,000

Reconstruction Account

Dr.	Rs.		*Cr.* Rs.
To Profit and Loss Account	10,70,000	By Shares Surrendered Account	4,40,000
To Land, Buildings, Machinery, etc.	12,90,000	By Debentures	14,00,000
		By Interest Outstanding Account	70,000
		By Sundry Creditors	4,50,000
	23,60,000		23,60,000

Note: The summarised balance sheet after reconstruction is as follows:

Liabilities	*Rs.*	*Assets*	*Rs.*
26,000 Equity Shares of Rs. 5 each fully paid	1,30,000	Land, Buildings, Machinery, etc.	14,30,000
		Less: amount written of under Reconstruction Scheme	12,90,000
46,000 14% Redeemable Preference Shares of Rs. 5 each, fully paid	2,30,000		1,40,000
Liability for Income-tax	10,000	Investments	17,000
		Stock-in-Trade	80,000
		Sundry Debtors	30,000
		Cash	1,03,000
	3,70,000		3,70,000

Illustration 41:

G. Ltd. is in the hands of a Receiver for debentureholders who hold a charge on all assets except uncalled capital. The following statement shows the position as regards creditors creditors as on 31st March, 2010:—

Liabilities	*Rs.*	*Assets*	*Rs.*
Share Capital, Rs. 3,60,000 in Shares of Rs. 60 each, Rs. 30 paid up	—	Cash in hand of the Receiver	2,70,000
		Property, Machinery & Plant, etc., cost Rs. 3,90,000 estimated at	1,50,000
First Debenture	3,00,000	Charged under Debentures	4,20,000
Second Debentures	6,00,000	Uncalled Capital	1,80,000
Unsecured Creditors	4,50,000	Deficiency	7,50,000
	13,50,000		13,50,000

A holds the First Debentures for Rs. 3,00,000 and Second Debentures for Rs. 3,00,000. He is also an unsecured creditor for Rs. 90,000. B holds Second Debentures for Rs. 3,00,000 and is an unsecured creditor for Rs. 60,000.

The following scheme of reconstruction is proposed and approved:—

(1) *A* is to cancel Rs. 2,10,000 of the total debt owing to him, to advance Rs. 30,000 in cash and to take First Debentures (in cancellation of those already issued to him) for Rs. 5,10,000 in satisfaction of all his claims.

(2) *B* is to accept Rs. 90,000 in cash in satisfaction of all claims by him.

(3) Unsecured creditors (other than *A* and *B*) are to accept four shares of Rs. 7.50 each, fully

paid in satisfaction of 75% of every Rs. 60 of their claim. The balance of 25% is to be postponed and to be payable at the end of three years from the date of the Court's approval of the scheme. The nominal share capital is to be increased accordingly.

(4) Uncalled capital is to be called up in full and Rs. 52.50 per share cancelled, thus making the shares of Rs. 7.50 each.

Assuming that the company keeps sectional ledgers, give necessary journal entries and the balance sheet of the company after the scheme has been carried into effect. (*Adapted C.A. Final*)

Solution:

Before passing journal entries, it would be advisable to make a regular balance sheet because the statement already given does not show the correct position. It does not include figure for share capital and, on the asset side, it includes "Uncalled Capital" which should not be included. The balance sheet given below gives the correct figure of deficiency.

Balance Sheet of G. Ltd. as on March 31, 2010

Liabilities	*Rs.*	*Assets*	*Rs.*
Share Capital		Property, Machinery and Plant, etc.	
6,000 shares of Rs. 60 each,		at cost	3,90,000
Rs. 30 paid up	1,80,000	Cash in hand	2,70,000
First Debentures	3,00,000	Deficiency (or Profit and Loss	
Second Debentures	6,00,000	Account)	8,70,000
Unsecured Creditors	4,50,000		
	15,30,000		15,30,000

Property, etc., has been shown at cost rather than at realisable value because the company will continue.

Journal

			Dr.	Cr.
2010			Rs.	Rs.
March 31	First Debentures	Dr.	3,00,000	
	Second Debentures	Dr.	3,00,000	
	Total Creditors Account	Dr.	90,000	
	To A			6,90,000
	The total amount due to *A*, transferred to his account.			
" "	Second Debentures	Dr.	3,00,000	
	Total Creditors Account	Dr.	60,000	
	To B			3,60,000
	To total amount due to *B*, transferred to his account.			
" "	Bank	Dr.	30,000	
	To A			30,000
	The amount paid by A under the scheme proposed by Special Resolution No..... dated.....confirmed by Court Order dated.......			
" "	A	Dr.	7,20,000	
	To First Debentures (New)			5,10,000
	To Reorganisation Account			2,10,000
	The issue of First Debentures worth Rs. 5,10,000 to A in full satisfaction of his claims, the balance of Rs. 2,10,000 credited to Reorganisation Account in accordance with the sanctioned scheme.			

			Rs.	Rs.
" "	B	Dr.	3,60,000	
	To Bank			90,000
	To Reorganisation Account			2,70,000
	The payment to B of Rs. 90,000 in full satisfaction of his claims in accordance with the sanctioned scheme.			
" "	Total Creditors Account	Dr.	2,25,000	
	To Share Capital Account			1,50,000
	To Reorganisation Account			75,000
	The issue of Rs. 7.50 fully paid shares to unsecured creditors, in accordance with the sanctioned scheme, thus: Four shares of Rs. 7.50 each fully paid (Rs. 30 in all) given to those who have claim of Rs. 60 each, *i.e.*, 50% is being paid in the form of shares, 25% is being postponed and 25% is being cancelled. Hence against a total claim of Rs. 3,00,000 (other than A & B) Rs. 1,50,000 will be given in the form of shares, Rs. 75,000 will be cancelled and Rs. 75,000 postponed. (No entry required for postponement).			
" "	Bank	Dr.	1,80,000	
	To Share Capital Account			1,80,000
	The balance on shares (Rs. 30 per share) called up in accordance with the sanctioned scheme.			
" "	Share Capital Account	Dr.	3,15,000	
	To Reorganisation Account			3,15,000
	The cancellation of Rs. 52.50 per share on 6,000 shares in accordance with the sanctioned scheme.			
" "	Reorganisation Account	Dr.	8,70,000	
	To Profit and Loss Account			8,70,000
	The debit balance in the Profit and Loss Account wiped off with the various reductions made.			

Balance Sheet of G. Ltd. as on March 31, 2010

Liabilities	*Rs.*	*Assets*	*Rs.*
Share Capital:		**Fixed Assets:**	
26,000 shares of Rs. 7.50 each, fully paid.	1,95,000	Property, Machinery, Plant, etc. at cost	3,90,000
Secured Loans:		**Current Assets:**	
First Debentures	5,10,000	Cash & Bank Balances	3,90,000
Current Liabilities and Provisions:			
Sundry Creditors	75,000		
	7,80,000		7,80,000

6. SCHEMES OF RECONSTRUCTION

The need for reconstruction arises when a company has accumulated losses or when a company finds itself overcapitalised which means either that the value placed on assets is too much as compared to their earning capacity or that the profits as a whole are insufficient to pay a proper dividend. In the previous section, the legal position and entries in respect of reduction of capital (which in other words means internal reconstruction) have been seen. The present section seeks to discuss how and on what basis, schemes should be formulated. Apart from clarity, wide acceptance and justice, the reconstruction scheme must take into account the following:—

The fundamental basis of any proposals is the earning power of the company. Even the interest to debentureholders cannot be paid unless the company's activities are profitable. A very careful estimate should, therefore, be made of the profits expected by the company in the future. Unless the profits are sufficient to meet all expenses including adequate depreciation, interest to debentureholders and other creditors, preference dividend, and a reasonable return to the equity shareholders, it would be useless to proceed with any reconstruction scheme because, otherwise the need for reconstruction will soon arise again.

Assuming that adequate profits can be expected, the reconstruction scheme should not adversely affect the rights of preference shareholders (not to speak of creditors and debentureholders) unless it is absolutely necessary. Suppose, the profits are such that after paying dividends to preference shareholders little remains for equity shareholders; the preference shareholders may be persuaded to accept a sacrifice either by reduction of capital or by reduction in the rate of dividend or both because the alternative to such acceptance of sacrifice may be the liquidation of the company (in which case, due to forced sale, the assets may not realise much and the preference shareholders may not be able to get back what they have invested). If the company is in a very bad position, even the debentureholders may be prevailed upon to accept a reduction of their claims. But, so far as is possible, contractual and legal rights and priorities should be maintained.

The equity shareholders will naturally have to bear the brunt of the losses and sacrifice. This is not as bad as it sounds because (*a*) the equity shareholders realise from the very beginning that if losses occur they have to bear them before anybody else can be called upon to do so, and (*b*) they must have already known that the value of their holding is small due to absence of dividends. The market price of shares is related to dividend and not to the face or nominal value of the shares. It really does not matter, therefore, whether the nominal value of an equity share in Re. 1 or Rs. 100 or Rs. 1,000 as long as it is not 0. (This does matter in case of preference shareholders and debentureholders whose earnings depend on the nominal value). In fact, a reconstruction scheme may be beneficial to the equity shareholders by enabling the payment of a dividend on such shares. On this ground, it would be unjust to ask the preference shareholders to accept a sacrifice when the equity shareholders improve their position.

There is, however, one important right which the equity shareholders enjoy. This is control over the affairs of the company. The equity shareholders will not easily give up this right, and hence the reconstruction scheme should keep this in mind. The equity shareholders may not agree to the conversion of preference shares or debentures into equity shares even if the holders of preference shares or debentures are willing to accept lower security for their holdings. The equity shareholders may agree to this only if there is a threat of the company being would up (in which case they will lose almost all). It should also be noted that, without the consent of the parties concerned, their liability cannot be increased. For instance, fully paid shares cannot be converted into partly paid shares without the consent of the shareholders.

The requirements of working capital must not be overlooked. Cash may be required to pay off certain dissenting creditors or even to pay arrears of preference dividend. Generally, therefore, a company under reconstruction will have to raise funds to enable it to pay off such dissenters and to carry on its work smoothly. Which of the various parties are willing to subscribe more shares will have to be seen. The equity shareholders may like to consolidate their position by buying more shares. Sometimes, outsiders are willing to subscribe to the shares but they will generally prefer to do so if they are given a controlling share.

Step. (1) First of all the total amount to be written off should be ascertained. This would mean totalling up the debit balance of the profit and loss account, all fictitious assets like goodwill, preliminary expenses, discount or commission on shares or debentures, any fall in the value of assets, any increase in liabilities and arrears of dividends on cumulative preference shares. If the value of any asset can be legitimately increased, the amount of the loss would then be reduced accordingly. The other way to get at the same figure would be to add up the present value, as a going concern, of all the assets and deduct therefrom the amount of liabilities and also the arrears of dividends on cumulative preference shares. What is left is "net assets". The share capital compared with net assets will show how much amount is to be written off.

(2) The question now arises as to who is to bear the loss. If the net assets are more than the preference share capital, it is obvious the whole of the loss will have to be borne by the equity shareholders—the nominal value of the equity shares should be reduced by a sufficient margin to cover the loss. If the net assets are not sufficient to cover the preference share capital (or if the net assets are just sufficient), the preference shareholders will have to accept a sacrifice, although their sacrifice will be smaller than that of the equity shareholders. (Equity shares must not be completely wiped off.) If the future earning power of the company permits, the dividend rate should be increased so that, in terms of rupees, the dividend remains unchanged. Thus if 10.5% preference shares of Rs. 100 are converted into preference shares of Rs. 75 each, the rate of dividend should be raised to 14%, if possible. In both cases then, the dividend will be Rs. 10.5 per share.

(3) Payment of arrears of dividend (question arises only in case of cumulative preference shares) in cash immediately may present difficulties. In such a case, a good method is to issue deposit certificates. This is prefereable to issuing shares because (*a*) it will not upset the voting power and (*b*) the certificates can be redeemed as soon as opportunity arises. The rate of interest need not be heavy; but, of course, it will depend on the future earning capacity of the company.

(4) Debentureholders and other creditors are affected by the reconstruction scheme only if the total assets of the company are insufficient to cover even the liabilities (although their consent will be necessary to any scheme that may be formulated). In such an eventuality, the creditors (including debentureholders) will have to accept sacrifice unless they think that by sending the company into liquidation they will be able to realise substantial portion of their claims. The shareholders, both preference and equity, will have to accept a heavy reduction in the value of shares but they cannot be expected to agree to a complete wiping off of the shares, in which case they will have no interest in keeping the company going. Generally, the sacrifice to be borne by the creditors will be as follows:—

Preferential Creditors (according to law)	Nil
Secured Creditors	Depending upon the value of the security
Unsecured Creditors	Heaviest.

In short, the whole scheme should broadly depend upon the expected earning power and upon the position as is likely to obtain if the company is sent into liquidation.

Internal vs. external reconstruction. Having decided who is to bear how much sacrifice or loss and having settled the broad details of the scheme, an important question remains to be decided. Will the reconstruction be internal or external? Internal reconstruction means that the scheme will be carried out by means of reduction of capital, *i.e.*, by getting the approval of the Court. External reconstruction means that the scheme will be carried out by liquidating the existing company and incorporating immediately another company (with the name only slightly changed such as A B (2009) Ltd. instead of A B Ltd. to take over the business of the outgoing company. There are advantages in both, but generally internal reconstruction is preferred. The advantages in its favour are:—

(*a*) Creditors, specially bank overdraft and debentureholders, may continue whereas they may not if the company is formally liquidated which will involve payment of claims to outsiders. If they do not continue, the company may suffer from want of financial assistance. This is, however, only academic since no reconstruction scheme, even internal, will be really formulated without the consent of the bank, debentureholders, etc.

(*b*) The company will be able to set off its past losses against future profits for income-tax purposes. This will materially reduce the income-tax liability depending on the losses suffered during the preceding eight years. Losses can be carried forward for eight years provided the business is carried on. The business will technically end where the company is liquidated. Hence, in case of external reconstruction, losses cannot be carried forward for income-tax purposes.

The arguments in favour of external reconstruction arè as under:—

(*a*) External reconstruction may be the only way to bring about speedy reconstruction because sometimes a few people hold up the scheme by delaying tactics by means of legal objections.

(*b*) It may help in raising more finance by issuing to the existing shareholders partly paid shares in the new company. It should be remembered that in internal reconstruction fully paid up shares cannot be converted into partly paid up shares unless every shareholder gives his assent in writing. This may prove cumbersome. However, it shareholders are willing to accept partly paid shares in the new company, there is not much reason why they should refuse to buy new shares under a scheme of internal reconstruction.

Legal position as regards external reconstruction :

Section 494 of the Companies Act permits the liquidator of a company to transfer the whole or any part of the company's business or property to another company and receive from the transferee company (by way of compensation or part compensation) shares etc. in the transferror company for distribution among the shareholders of the company under liquidation. The liquidator must obtain the sanction of the company by a special resolution. Any sale or arrangement it pursuance of this section is binding on the members of the transferror company.

But a shareholder who has not voted for the special resolution may, within seven days of the resolution, serve a notice on the liquidator expressing his dissent and requiring the liquidator either. (*a*) to abstain from carrying the resolution into effect, or (*b*) to purchase his interest at a price to be determined by agreement or by arbitration.

Illustration 42:

United Industries Ltd., which has suffered heavy losses in the past considers that the worst is over and that, on a sound reorganisation, it will be able to carry on business successfully, profits in future being expected to be between Rs. 2,25,000 and Rs. 2,70,000 (before providing for interest but after charging adequate depreciation). The Board of Directors of the company ask you (*i*) to draft a scheme of internal reconstruction which would be equitable to all the parties, (*ii*) to detail the journal entries to be made after all the formalities have been complied with, and (*iii*) to reframe the Balance Sheet. The following particulars are supplied to you:—

Balance Sheet as at 31st March, 2010

	Rs.		*Rs.*
Capital:		Sundry Fixed Assets (less depreciation)	20,00,000
30,000 12% Cumulative Preference		Sundry Floating Assets	10,20,000
Shares of Rs. 20 each, fully paid		Cash and Bank Balances	1,20,000
(Dividend in arrear for 2 years)	6,00,000	Profit and Loss Account	21,40,000
50,000 Equity Shares of Rs. 20 each	10,00,000		
10% Debentures of Rs. 100 each	26,80,000		
Interest due thereon	80,000		
Tax Liability	20,000		
Sundry Creditors (unsecured)	9,00,000		
	52,80,000		52,80,000

Debentures carry a floating charge on all assets. Sundry Fixed Assets are worth Rs. 10 lakhs and Sundry Floating Assets are worth Rs. 8,00,000. (*Adapted from C.A., Final*)

Solution:

Scheme of Reorganisation of United Industries Ltd.

The total assets of the company are:	Rs.
Fixed Assets	10,00,000
Floating Assets	8,00,000
Cash and Bank Balance	1,20,000
	19,20,000

Against these assets the liabilities amount to Rs. 36,80,000. If the company goes into liquidation, the tax liability will be payable in full, leaving Rs. 19,00,000 for debentureholders who have a floating charge. The debentureholders will suffer a loss of Rs. 8,60,000. Sundry creditors and the shareholders, both preference and equity, will get nothing. The loss suffered by the debentureholders may even be greater because, due to forced sale, the value of their security may be much less.

The debentureholders should agree to accept a substantial sacrifice in view of the loss that they will surely suffer if the company goes into liquidation. In view of expected profits in future, the rate of interest should be raised as a consideration for reduction in their claim. Sundry creditors who stand to get nothing, if the company goes into liquidation, should accept a heavy reduction in their claims. The heaviest sacrifices will have to be made by the shareholders.

The total amount to be written off is as follows:—

	Rs.
Profit and Loss Account (Dr. Balance)	21,40,000
Loss on Fixed Assets	10,00,000
Loss on Floating Assets	2,20,000
	33,60,000

To this, two years' dividend on Cumulative Preference Shares should have been added but in view of the heavy sacrifice that the preference shareholders have to make, they should agree to waive payment of arrears of dividend. It is recommended that the following reductions should be made:

	Rs.	
Sundry Creditors	7,20,000	80%
Interest on Debentures	80,000	100%
Debentureholders	11,80,000	44%
Preference Shareholders (Rs. 16 each)	4,80,000	80%
Equity Shareholders (Rs. 18 each)	9,00,000	90%
	33,60,000	

The rate of inte... on debentures should be raised to 12% and the dividend on preference shares to 14%. This will partly compensate the sacrifices made by them. If the scheme is accepted, the future distribution of profit on the basis of the minimum profits of Rs. 2,25,000 will be as follows:

	Rs.
12% Interest on Debentures of Rs. 15,00,000	1,80,000
14% Dividend on Cumulative Shares of Rs. 1,20,000	16,800
	1,96,800
Balance available for equity shareholders	28,200
Expected profits	2,25,000

This would enable a dividend of 28.2% to be paid on equity shares.

This seems rather unreasonable for the sundry creditors who have made a sacrifice of 80% of their claims (equal to the preference shareholders). They are the worst sufferers, since other parties have slightly improved their position in respect of yields. It is recommended that for five years at least a sum equal to the equity dividend should be set aside out of profits to restore the claims of sundry creditors partially.

Income-tax has been ignored, since, for at least a few years, the company will be able to avoid payment of tax due to past losses. Later, the company may be able to improve its earning power. There is also no need to take any steps to augment the working capital. The cash and bank balances of Rs. 1,20,000 should be sufficient.

An internal scheme should be adopted in order to take advantage of past losses for income-tax purposes.

The entries, if the scheme is accepted, will be as follows:

			Dr. Rs.	Cr. Rs.
	12% Cumulative Preference Share Capital Account	Dr.	6,00,000	
	To 14% Cumulative Preference Share Capital Account			1,20,000
	To Reorganisation Account			4,80,000
	The reduction of Preference shares by Rs. 16 each — dividend raised to 14%.			
	10% Debentures	Dr.	26,80,000	
	To 12% Debentures			15,00,000
	To Reorganisation Account			11,80,000
	The conversion of 10% Debentures of Rs. 26,80,000 into 12% Debentures of Rs. 15,00,000.			
	Equity Share Capital Account	Dr.	9,00,000	
	Interest on Debentures	Dr.	80,000	
	Sundry Creditors	Dr.	7,20,000	
	To Reorganisation Account			17,00,000
	The cancellation and reduction of the various items by amounts agreed upon.			
	Reorganisation Account	Dr.	33,60,000	
	To Profit and Loss Account			21,40,000
	To Floating Assets			2,20,000
	To Fixed Assets			10,00,000
	The balance in the Reorganisation Account utilised to wipe off the debit balance in the Profit and Loss Account and to write down the various assets to their proper value.			

The Balance Sheet of United Industries Ltd. will be as follows after the scheme has been put through.

Balance Sheet as at 31st March, 2010

Liabilities	*Rs.*	*Assets*	*Rs.*	*Rs.*
Share Capital:		Sundry Fixed Assets	20,00,000	
30,000 14% Cumulative Preference Shares of Rs. 4 each, fully paid	1,20,000	*Less*: Written off under Scheme of reconstruction dated....	10,00,000	10,00,000
50,000 Equity Shares of Rs. 2 each, fully paid	1,00,000	Sundry Floating Assets		8,00,000
12% Debentures	15,00,000	Cash and Bank Balances		1,20,000
Sundry Creditors	1,80,000			
Tax Liability	20,000			
	19,20,000			19,20,000

Illustration 43:

The Balance Sheet of Theta Ltd. as on 31st March, 2010 as follows:

	Rs.		Rs.
Share Capital: Authorised and Issued:		Goodwill, at cost	1,00,000
10,000 11% Cumulative Preference Shares of Rs. 100 each	10,00,000	Works and Plant, at cost (less depreciation)	16,00,000
13,000 Equity Shares of Rs. 100 each	13,00,000	Stock	2,00,000
10% Debenture	5,00,000	Debtors	1,50,000
Sundry Creditors	1,40,000	Cash	60,000
		Profit and Loss Account	8,30,000
	29,40,000		29,40,000

(Preference dividends are in arrear for two years and are payable on liquidation automatically).

It is believed that net profits in future will average 10% of the capital employed (after taxation). The Works and Plant is worth Rs. 15,00,000 (Rs. 10,00,000 if it has to be sold). Stock is worth its stated value but among the debtors there are doubtful debts to the extent of Rs. 30,000 (expected to realise 33.33%).

A recapitalisation being desired, you are requested to frame an external scheme of reconstruction.

Solution:

External Scheme of Reconstruction of Theta Ltd.

1. Assessment of the present position of Theta Ltd.:—

(*a*) The total assets of Theta Ltd. are as follow:—

	Rs.
Works and Plant	15,00,000
Stock	2,00,000
Debtors	1,30,000
Cash	60,000
	18,90,000

The assets cover the debentures and creditors amply and hence there is no question of their accepting any sacrifice. After paying the debentures and creditors, a surplus of Rs. 12,50,000 would remain which would cover the preference shareholders—but not if the company is forced into liquidation. Hence, the preference shareholders should agree to a reduction of their capital by 20% or Rs. 2,00,000 in all. They should accept preference shares of the total value of Rs. 8,00,000 in the new company.

(*b*) The total loss to be written off is Rs. 12,70,000 made up as follows:

	Rs.
Debit balance in the Profit and Loss A/c	8,30,000
Goodwill	1,00,000
Works and Plant	1,00,000
Debtors	20,000
Arrears of preference dividend (two years)	2,20,000
	12,70,000

As suggested above, the preference shareholders should agree to a sacrifice of Rs. 2,00,000. The remainder of the loss, viz., Rs. 10,70,000, *i.e.*, 12,70,000 – 2,00,000, will have to be borne by the equity shareholders. If the shares are reduced to Rs. 15 each, the equity share capital will be Rs. 1,95,000 and a sum of Rs. 11,05,000 will become available. After wiping off the various losses, a sum of Rs. 35,000 can then be placed to Capital Reserve.

The preference shareholders should be compensated by the rate of dividend being raised to

14%. It will mean yearly dividend Rs. 1,12,000, a little more than the existing yearly dividend of Rs. 1,10,000. The arrears of preference dividend, Rs. 1,20,000, will have to paid. Since Theta Ltd. does not have sufficient funds the liability will have to be taken over by the new company and then paid by it.

2. *The Scheme.*

(*a*) A new company, New Theta Ltd., should be floated with an authorised capital of 50,000 Equity Shares of Rs. 15 each and 10,000 14% Preference Shares of Rs. 100 each.

The company should take over the following assets of Theta Ltd. at the values stated:

	Rs.
Works and Plant	15,00,000
Stock	2,00,000
Debtors (*Less*: Provision of Rs. 20,000)	1,30,000
Cash	60,000
	18,90,000

It should assume the liability to sundry creditors and the liability to preference shareholders in respect of arrears of dividend, and issue the following:—

(*i*) 10% Debentures, Rs, 5,00,000 (in debentures of Rs. 100 each) for distribution amongst debentureholders of Theta Ltd.

(*ii*) 14% Preference Shares, of Rs. 8,00,000 (in shares of Rs. 100 each) for distribution amongst preference shareholders of Theta Ltd.

(*iii*) 13,000 Equity Shares of Rs. 15 each, fully paid for distribution amongst equity shareholders of Theta Ltd.

This will leave a capital reserve of Rs. 35,000.

(*b*) The company will require additional cash as follows:

	Rs.
To pay arrears of dividend to preferences shareholders to Theta Ltd.	2,20,000
Working capital (say)	50,000
	2,70,000
Less: cash balance already available	60,000
	2,10,000

The amount should be raised by issuing new 14,000 equity shares of Rs. 15 each to the existing equity shareholders. If the scheme is accepted, the balance sheet will be as follows:—

	Rs.		*Rs.*	*Rs.*
Share Capital:		Works and Plant		15,00,000
Authorised:		Current Assets		
10,000 14% Preference shares of		Stock		2,00,000
Rs. 100 each	10,00,000	Debtors	1,50,000	
50,000 Equity shares of Rs. 15 each	7,50,000	*Less*: Prov. for Bad Debts.	20,000	1,30,000
Issued Subscribed:		Cash		50,000
8,000 14% Cumulative Preference shares of Rs. 100 each, fully paid	8,00,000			
27,000 Equity Shares of Rs. 15 each, fully paid	4,05,000			
Capital Reserve	35,000			
10% Debentures	5,00,000			
Sundry Creditors	1,40,000			
	18,80,000			18,80,000

EXERCISE XX

VALUATION OF INTANGIBLE ASSETS, GOODWILL AND SHARES

Practical

1. The net profits of a company after providing for taxation for the past five years are Rs. 78 lakh, Rs. 82 lakh, Rs. 88 lakh, Rs. 93 lakh and Rs. 99 lakh. The capital employed in the business is Rs. 8 crore on which a reasonable rate of return of 10% is expected. It is expected that the company will be able to maintain its super profits for the next five years.

(*i*) Calculate the value of the goodwill of the business on the basis of an annuity of super-profits, taking the present value of an annuity of one rupee for the five years at 10% interest as Rs. 3.78.

(*ii*) How would your answer differ if the goodwill is valued by capitalising the excess of the annual profits over the resonable return on capital employed on the basis of the same return of 10% ?

Have you any comment to offer ? *[C.S. (Inter), 1995 Modified]*

[(i) Rs. 30,24,000; (ii) Rs. Rs. 80,00,000]

2. The following is the balance sheet of Bharat Manufacturing Co. Ltd., as at 31st March, 2010:—

Liabilities	*Rs.*	*Assets*	*Rs.*
3,00,000 Equity Shares of Rs. 10		Goodwill, at cost	2,50,000
each, fully paid	30,00,000	Plant & Machinery	
Capital Reserve	1,00,000	(cost *less*) depreciation)	8,50,000
General Reserve	6,95,000	Furniture & Fixture	
Profit & Loss Account	15,000	(cost *less* depreciation)	3,00,000
Sundry Creditors	12,85,000	Stock	16,00,000
Provision for Taxation	7,50,000	Debtors	10,00,000
Proposed Dividend	6,60,000	Cash at Bank	24,55,000
		Preliminary Expenses	50,000
	65,05,000		65,05,000

The following additional information is provided to you:—

(*i*) the reasonable return on capital employed in the industry in which Bharat Manufacturing Co. Ltd. is engaged is 18%.

(*ii*) the rate of tax is 50%. The balance in Provision for Taxation Account is in respect of profit for the year ended 31st March, 2010.

(*iii*) the year 2009-2010 was a normal year and the prospects for 2010-2011 are equally good.

Calculate value of goodwill at three years' purchase of the super profits of the company. Ignore corporate divided tax.

(*Hint*: As the company has proposed a dividend @ 22%, 10% of the profit has been transferred to General Reserve). *(Goodwill, Rs. 2,00,700)*

3. From the following particulars, calculate the intrinsic value of one equity share of Hilton Ltd.:—

Balance Sheet of Hilton Ltd. as at 31st March, 2010

Liabilities	*Rs.*	*Assets*	*Rs.*
2,00,000 Equity Shares of Rs. 10 each	20,00,000	Goodwill, at cost	2,00,000
General Reserve	7,00,000	Furniture, cost *less* depreciation	3,00,000
Profit & Loss Account	4,50,000	Investments, at cost (market value,	
14% Debenture	5,00,000	Rs. 5,50,000)	6,00,000
Sundry Creditors	5,50,000	Stock	22,00,000
Provision for Taxation	4,50,000	Debtors	6,00,000
Employees' Provident Fund	6,00,000	Bank Balance	13,00,000
		Expenses on Issue of Debentures	50,000
	52,50,000		52,50,000

Goodwill is revalued as on this date at Rs. 2,60,000 whereas debtors are subject to a provision for bad debts @ 5%. *(Rs. 15.40 per share)*

4. From the following particulars, calculate the value of an equity share :

2,000 9% Preference shares of Rs. 100 each	Rs. 2,00,000
50,000 Equity shares of Rs. 10 each, Rs. 8 per share paid up	Rs. 4,00,000
Expected profit per year before tax	Rs. 2,18,000
Rate of tax	40%
Transfer to general reserve every year	20% of profit
Normal rate of earning	15%

[C.S. (Inter) June, 1999]
[Rs. 11.55]

5. From the following information, calculate the value of an equity share:

(*i*) the paid up share capital of the company consists of 1,000 14% preference shares of Rs. 100 each and 20,000 equity shares of Rs. 10 each.

(*ii*) the annual profits of the company for the last four years after providing for depreciation but before taxation have been Rs. 1,90,000; Rs. 2,10,000; Rs. 2,05,000 and Rs. 2,15,000. The prospects of the company for the future are equally good. The rate of taxation is 50%.

(*iii*) the company transfers 20% of its profits remaining after tax to General Reserve before declaring any dividend; the transfer being considered as adequate.

(*iv*) the normal return expected by investors on equity shares from the type of business carried on by the company is 20 per cent. *(Rs. 17)*

6. X. Ltd. is to take over the business of Y. Ltd. on 1st April, 2010. For the purpose you are required to calculate the value of Y Ltd.'s goodwill on the basis of capitalization of earnings. The following is the balance sheet of Y Ltd. as at 31st March, 2010:—

Liabilities	*Rs.*	*Assets*	*Rs.*	*Rs.*
50,000 Equity Shares of Rs. 10 each	5,00,000	Goodwill, at cost		60,000
General Reserve	1,40,000	Plant and Machinery, cost *less* dep.		2,65,000
Profit and Loss Account	1,70,000	Furniture, cost *less* depreciation		35,000
Sundry Creditors	1,00,000	Stock		3,50,000
Provision for Taxation	1,70,000	Debtors	50,000	
		Less: Prov. for Bad Debts	1,000	49,000
		Cash at Bank		3,11,000
		Preliminary Expenses		10,000
	10,80,000			10,80,000

Y. Ltd.'s average profits before tax for the last five years have been Rs. 3,25,000 without any wide fluctuations. Future prospects are equally good. The normal rate of return is 20% while the rate of tax is 50%. *(Rs. 72.500)*

7. The following is the summarised balance sheet of Chandra Ltd. as at 31st March, 2010:—

Liabilities	*Rs.*	*Assets*	*Rs.*
50,000 Equity Shares of Rs. 10 each	5,00,000	Machinery	2,40,000
Securities Premium	1,00,000	Furniture	1,00,000
General Reserve	2,39,400	Stock	6,20,000
Profit and Loss Account	1,57,000	Debtors	2,06,000
Sundry Creditors	4,09,400	Cash in hand	3,400
Provision for Taxation	1,97,000	Cash at Bank	4,34,000
	16,03,400		16,03,400

The company transfers 20% of its profits (after tax) to General Reserve. Net profits before taxation for the last three years have been as follows:—

	Rs.
For the year ended 31st March, 2008	2,72,000
For the year ended 31st March, 2009	3,66,000
For the year ended 31st March, 2010	3,94,000

Machinery is valued at Rs. 3,20,000.

Average yield in this type of business is 20%. The rate of tax is 50%.

Calculate the value of one equity share on the basis of (*a*) intrinsic worth, (*b*) yield.

[(*a*) *Rs. 21.54* (*b*) *Rs. 13.76*]

8. The summarised balance sheet of BK Ltd. as at 31st March, 2010 is as follows :

Balance Sheet

Liabilities	*Rs. in lakhs*	*Assets*	*Rs. in lakhs*
30 lakh Equity Shares of Rs. 10 each, fully paid up	300	Goodwill	70
		Other Fixed Assets	450
10 lakh Equity Shares of Rs. 10 each, Rs. 8 paid up	80	Current Assets	220
		Preliminary Expenses	10
Reserves	180		
11% Debentures	100		
Current Liabilities	90		
	750		750

The goodwill is independently valued at Rs. 50 lakh and other fixed assets at Rs. 420 lakh. There was a contingent liability of Rs. 20 lakh which has become payable. Determine the value of both the shares under net assets method.

[*Adapted B.Com. (Hons.) Delhi, 1997*]

[*Fully paid, Rs. 12.50; Partly paid, Rs. 10.50; Alternatively, fully paid, Rs. 12.63; Partly paid, Rs. 10.11*]

9. The profits of a company, limited by shares, for the year ended 31st March, 2010 were Rs. 60 lakh. After setting apart amounts for interest on borrowings, taxation and other provisions, the net surplus available to shareholders is estimated at Rs. 15,00,000. The company's capital base consisted of:

(*a*) 10,00,000 equity shares of Rs. 10 each, Rs. 5 per share paid up; and

(*b*) 25,000 12% cumulative redeemable preference share of Rs. 100 each, fully paid up.

Enquiries in the stock market reveal that shares of companies engaged in similar business and declaring a dividend of 15% on equity shares are quoted at a premium of 10%. What do you expect the market value of the company's equity shares to be, basing your working on the yield method.

[*Adapted Co. Sec. (Final) Dec. 1995*] (*Rs. 8.80 per share*)

10. Ascertain the value of goodwill of the Prosperous Co. Ltd. carrying on business as Retail Traders from the following information supplied to you:—

Balance Sheet as on 31st March, 2010

	Rs. '000		*Rs. '000*
Share Capital: Share of Rs. 100 each, Fully paid	2,50,000	Goodwill, at cost	25,000
		Land and Buildings,	1,10,000
General Reserve	20,000	Plant and Machinery,	1,00,000
Profit and Loss Appropriation Account	36,650	Stock in Trade	1,50,000
Bank Overdraft	38,350	Book Debts *less* prov. for bad debts	90,000
Sundry Creditors	90,500		
Provision for Taxation	39,500		
	4,75,000		4,75,000

The company commenced operations in 2000 with a paid up capital of Rs. 2,50,000 thousand. Profit (after taxation) have been as follows for the recent years:

Year ending 31st March	*Rs. in thousands*
2006	20,000 (loss)
2007	44,000
2008	51,500
2009	58,500
2010	65,000

The loss in 2005-06 occurred due to a prolonged strike.

Income-tax paid so far has been at the average rate of 40% but is likely to be 50% from now onwards. Dividends were distributed at the rate of 10 per cent in 2007 and 2008 and at the rate of 15 per cent on the paid up capital in 2009 and 2010. (Ignore corporate dividend tax). The market price of the share is rolling at the end of the year ended 31st March, at Rs. 125. Profits till 2010 have been ascertained after debiting Rs. 20,000 thousand as remuneration to the manager. The company has approved a remuneration of Rs. 30,000 thousand with effect from 1st April, 2009. The company has been able to secure a contract for supply of materials at advantageous prices. The advantage has been valued at Rs. 20,000 thousand per annum for the next five years.

(At 3 years' purchase, Rs, 66,000 thousand)

11. The following is the Balance Sheet of X Ltd. as at March, 31, 2010:—

	Rs. in lakhs		*Rs. in lakhs*
Share Capital: 10,000 Share of Rs. 100 each, fully paid up	100	Land and Buildings	55
General Reserve	40	Plant and Machinery (at cost *less* depreciation)	65
Profit and Loss Appropriation Account	46	Trade Marks	10
Sundry Creditors	49	Stock	24
Workmen's Savings Account	15	Debtors	44
		Cash at Bank	46
		Preliminary Expenses	6
	250		250

The Plant and Machinery is worth Rs. 60 lakh and Land and Buildings have been valued at Rs. 120 lakh by an independent valuer. Rs. 4 lakh of the debts are bad. The profits of the company have been as follows:—

	Rs. in lakhs
2007-2008	40
2008-2009	45
2009-2010	53

It is the company's practice to transfer 25% of the profits to reserve. Ignoring taxation, find out the value of the shares. Similar companies give yield of 10% on the market value of their shares. Goodwill may be taken to be worth Rs. 60 lakh. (*Yield Basis, Rs. 29.19; Intrinsic Value Basis, Rs. 29.60*)

12. Richa wants to buy all the shares of Zed Ltd. whose balance sheet as at 31st March, 2010, is given below:—

Liabilities	*Rs.*	*Assets*		*Rs.*
Share Capital	6,00,000	Fixed Assets: Cost	10,00,000	
General Reserve	1,50,000	*Less*: Depreciation	2,70,000	7,30,000
Profit & Loss Account	75,000	10% Tax-free Govt. Securities		60,000
14% Debenture	1,00,000	Current Assets		3,70,000
Sundry Creditors	1,08,500	Preliminary Expenses		16,500
Provision for Taxation	1,43,000			
	11,76,500			11,76,500

The provision for taxation is only for the current year and is @ 50% of the net profits. The company transfers 10% of its profit after tax to its General Reserve. Other companies in the same industry show an income of 20% on capital employeed.

Richa seeks your advice as to the amount she should pay for the shares. What will be your advice? *(Rs. 7,45,000)*

		Rs.
Hindi:	Profit after tax	1,43,000
	Less: transfer to General Reserve @ 10%	14,300
		1,28,700
	Less: Profit & Loss Account balance	75,000
	Amount distributed as dividend	53,700

13. From the following information, prepare statements showing:—

(*i*) capital employed during each of three years;

(*ii*) goodwill on the basis of four years' purchase of the average super profits on a ten per cent yield basis; and

(*iii*) the real and marketable values of the business as a going concern.

Prosperous Company Ltd. — Balance Sheet as on 31st March ....

	2008	*2009*	*2010*
Capital and Liabilities:	*Rs.*	*Rs.*	*Rs.*
10,000 shares of Rs. 100 each, fully paid	10,00,000	10,00,000	10,00,000
General Reserve	5,00,000	6,00,000	7,00,000
Profit and Loss Account, balance	70,000	80,000	90,000
Creditors	3,00,000	4,00,000	5,00,000
	18,70,000	20,80,000	22,90,000
Property and Assets:			
Goodwill	5,00,000	4,00,000	3,00,000
Freehold Land, Factory Buildings, Machinery (cost less depreciation)	9,00,000	10,00,000	10,00,000
Stock-in-trade	4,00,000	5,00,000	6,00,000
Debtors	10,000	80,000	1,90,000
Cash and Bank Balance	60,000	1,00,000	2,00,000
	18,70,000	20,80,000	22,90,000

The following assets had been, by depreciation or otherwise, undervalued; their real worth to the business being:—

	Rs.	*Rs.*	*Rs.*
Freehold Land & Buildings & Machinery	10,00,000	11,00,000	12,00,000
Stock-in-trade	6,00,000	7,00,000	8,00,000
Net profits after writing off depreciation and making provision for taxation and general reserve were	4,10,000	5,10,000	6,10,000

As per articles of association, the directors have declared and paid dividends to the members in the month of March each year out of the profit of the relative year. The cost of the goodwill to the company was Rs. 5,00,000 and a sum of Rs. 10,000 was each year added to the balance of Profit and Loss Account to be carried forward. The capital employed on 1st April, 2007 was Rs. 14,60,000. *[Adapted C.A. Final]*

Hint: Assume in March, 1999, an addition of Rs. 50,000 was made to the reserve.

No adjustment as regards changes in value of stock is required in respect of profits, since undervaluation is uniform year by year.

(Average Capital Employed, Rs. 16,15,000, Rs. 17,25,000 and Rs. 20,35,000; Goodwill, Rs. 20,56,700, Real Value, Rs. 39,46,700; Market Value, Rs. 69,33,330.)

14. (*a*) Certain comparative figures for Company A and Company B both belonging to the same industry, are given below:

	Company A	*Company B*
Net tangible assets backing for equity shares	300%	200%
Profit earned to profit distributed as dividend	200%	150%
Dividend per equity share	Rs. 40	Rs. 60

If the market value of a share in Company A (considered representative of the industry) is Rs. 200, what should, in your opinion, be the value placed on a share in Company B? Give reasons for your answer. Ignore Corporate Dividend Tax.

(*b*) The capital structure of Exe Ltd. on 31st March, 2010 was as follows:

	Rs.
14% Preference Share Capital	4,00,000
Equity Share Capital	6,00,000
Reserves	2,00,000
14% Debentures	4,00,000

The company earns a profit of Rs. 6,00,000 on the average before debenture interest and income tax. The rate of income-tax on profits is 50%.

The market value of equity shares of similar companies indicates that the yield is 18% provided:

(*i*) The profit after tax covers the fixed interest and fixed dividend five times;

(*ii*) Equity capital and reserves are 150% of debentures and preference capital; and

(*iii*) Yield on shares is calculated as 60% of profit distributed and 50% of profit remaining undistributed.

Exe Ltd. pays a dividend of 25% p.a. regularly. Ascertain the probable market value of the equity shares of this company. Ignore Corporate Dividend Tax.

[(*a*) *Rs. 266.67 at adjusted normal yield of 22.5%*
(*b*) *Rs. 10.79 at adjusted yield of 20.5% and azt adjusted normal yield of 19%*)]

15. Two brothers, Preet and Meet, had worked for a number of years in a firm manufacturing swoozling rods. They decided that they would both leave, and set up separate companies to wholesale and retail these rods.

On 1st July, 2007 Preet formed a company, Preet Ltd., in which he held, with his wife, 100% of the share capital and he commenced trading in Delhi; Meet formed a company on a similar basis, Meet Ltd., and commenced trading in Bombay on the same date.

Both companies were successful and it was agreed that, with effect from 1st July, 2009, a holding company, Navin Ltd., would be formed to take over the shares in both the companies.

It was agreed that the accounts of Preet Ltd. for the two years ended 30th June, 2009 should be adjusted, as necessary, so as to conform to the accounting policies and conventions used by Meet Ltd. Navin Ltd. would then issue securities to the shareholders in Preet Ltd. and Meet Ltd. on the following basis:

(*a*) Rs. 10 of 9% Loan Stock 2000 for every Rs. 10 of net asset owned by each company, and

(*b*) Rs. 10 Equity Shares based on a two year purchase of the profits before taxation. These profits are to be the average profits of two years, with the second year weighted on the 2:1 basis.

The accounts of the two years ended 30th June, 2009 showed:

Balance Sheet as on 30th June, 2009

	2008 *Rs.*	*2009* *Rs.*	*2008* *Rs.*	*2009* *Rs.*
Fixed Assets:				
Furniture etc.	1,20,000	1,20,000	1,60,000	1,60,000
Less: Aggregate Depreciation	12,000	24,000	24,000	48,000
	1,08,000	96,000	1,36,000	1,12,000

	Rs.	Rs.	Rs.	Rs.
Trade Investments				3,00,000
Current Assets:				
Stock at cost	2,60,000	3,45,000	2,90,000	3,52,000
Debtors	2,92,500	4,24,000	3,24,000	4,32,000
Quoted Investments at cost (Market Value Rs. 1,40,000	—	1,00,000	—	—
Cash at Bank	10,000	—	35,000	—
	6,70,500	9,65,000	7,85,000	11,96,000
Share Capital:				
Rs. 10 Equity Shares fully paid	2,00,000	2,00,000	2,50,000	2,50,000
Reserves:				
Profit & Loss Account	1,28,000	2,70,000	1,39,000	3,02,000
Unrealised appreciation in investt.	—	—	—	80,000
Current Liabilities:				
Creditors	2,60,500	3,07,000	3,00,000	3,42,000
Bank Overdrawn	—	80,000	—	1,05,000
Taxation	82,000	1,08,000	96,000	1,17,000
	6,70,500	9,65,000	7,85,000	11,96,000

The following information is obtained:

(*a*) Both companies purchase the rods from the same supplier, who sells on a fixed price list. Preet Ltd. and Meet Ltd. themselves apply a 50% uplift on cost, to calculate their own selling prices. The suppliers' price list showed:

		Swoozling Rods
1st July 2007	—	Rs. 100 each
1st June 2008	—	Rs. 110 each
1st May 2009	—	Rs. 120 each

The number of rods purchased and sold in the periods after the price increased were:

	Preet Ltd.		*Meet Ltd.*	
	Purchased	*Sold*	*Purchased*	*Sold*
1st June — 30th June, 2008	1,000	800	1,200	900
1st May — 30th June, 2009	1,500	1,000	2,900	2,500

(*b*) Stock: Preet Ltd. calculates the cost price of stock on the "First in, first out" basis, whilst Meet Ltd. uses the "Last in first out" basis.

(*c*) Depreciation in both companies is provided on straight line method. There had been not material change in the fixed assets since 1st July, 2007 when the companies commenced trading. The fixed assets of the two companies are of a similar nature.

(*d*) Preet Ltd. deducts 1% from gross trade debtors, as a general provision against doubtful debts.

(*e*) Debtors comprise:

	Preet Ltd.		*Meet Ltd.*	
	2008	*2009*	*2009*	*2009*
	Rs.	*Rs.*	*Rs.*	*Rs.*
Trade Debtors	2,47,500	3,96,000	3,20,000	4,25,000
Prepaid Expenses	5,000	8,000	4,000	7,000
Advertising (see Note)	40,000	20,000	—	—
	2,92,500	4,24,000	3,24,000	4,32,000

Note: Preet Ltd. carried out an extensive advertising compaign when commencing to trade, and decided to write off this expense equally over three years. Meet Ltd. incurred similar expenditure which was however, written off as incurred.

(*f*) It was agreed by all parties that the directors' remuneration paid by Meet Ltd. is strictly or commercial basis, whereas that paid by Preet Ltd. contains a "distribution of profit" element of Rs. 30,000 in each year.

(*g*) The net profits, including the investment income, after provision for corporation tax were:

Preet Ltd.		Meet Ltd.	
2008	2009	2008	2009
1,28,000	1,42,000	1,39,000	1,63,000

You are required:

(*a*) to calculate the terms of the offer to be made to Preet Ltd. and Meet Ltd. by Navin Ltd. showing your working schedules, and

(*b*) to prepare the balance sheet of Navin Ltd. after the transaction has been completed.

(Navin Ltd.'s Share Capital Rs. 5,93,700; 9% Loan Stock Rs. 11,42,000
Value of Shares in : Preet Ltd. Rs. 7,93,700; Meet Ltd. Rs. 9,42,000)

INTERNAL RECONSTRUCTION

16. The following is the Balance Sheet of Weak Co. Ltd. as on 31.3.2010:

Liabilities	*Rs.*	*Assets*	*Rs.*
1,00,000 Equity Shares of Rs. 10 each	10,00,000	Land	1,00,000
Sundry Creditors	1,73,000	Plant and Machinery	2,30,000
		Furniture and Fittings	68,000
		Stock	1,50,000
		Debtors	70,000
		Cash at Bank	5,000
		Profit and Loss Account	5,50,000
	11,73,000		11,73,000

The approval of the court was obtained for the following scheme of reduction of capital:

(*a*) The equity shares to be reduced to Rs. 4 per share.

(*b*) Plant and Machinery to be written down to Rs. 1,50,000.

(*c*) Stock to be revalued at Rs. 1,40,000.

(*d*) The provision on debtors for doubtful debts to be created, Rs. 2,000.

(*e*) Land to be revalued at Rs. 1,42,000.

Pass journal entries to give effect to the above arrangement and also prepare Reconstruction Account. [*C.S. (Inter.), Dec. 1995 Modified*]

(Reconstruction Account, total Rs. 6,42,000)

17. The following is the summarised Balance Sheet of Notsowell Co. Ltd. as on 31st March, 2010:

Liabilities	*Rs.*	*Assets*	*Rs.*
5,000 10% Cumulative Preference		Goodwill	60,000
Shares of Rs. 100 each	5,00,000	Land and Building	5,40,000
1,00,000 Equity Shares of Rs. 10 each	10,00,000	Plant and Machinery	4,00,000
Creditors	3,00,000	Stock	70,000
Bills Payable	55,000	Debtors	1,30,000
Arrears of preference dividend,		Cash at Bank	35,000
Rs. 1,00,000		Preliminary Expenses	20,000
		Profit and Loss Account	6,00,000
	18,55,000		18,55,000

The scheme of reconstruction given below has been agreed to by all the affected parties and approved by the court. You are required to journalise the transactions given below and prepare the balance sheet of the company after completion of the scheme:

(*a*) The existing 10% cumulative preference shares of Rs. 100 each are to be converted into 14% redeemable preference share of Rs. 60 each.

(*b*) Arrears of preference dividend are to be cancelled.

(*c*) The equity shares are to reduced to Rs. 5 per share.

(*d*) Plant is to be written down by Rs. 20,000. *(Reconstruction Account, Rs. 7,00,000)*

18. X Co. Ltd. resolved to write off one-half of the subscribed capital by reducing each Rs. 100 share, both preference and equity, to Rs. 50 fully paid up and to reduce the book figures of its assets by an equivalent amount by wiping out the goodwill and the debit balance of the Profit and Loss Account and by writing down Land & Buildings by Rs. 15,000, Plant and Machinery by Rs. 10,000 and reserving the balance for bad debts.

The Balance Sheet of the company before the reduction of capital was as under:—

	Rs.		Rs.
Nominal Capital:—		Goodwill	1,00,000
3,000 Preference Shares of		Land and Buildings	1,10,000
Rs. 100 each	3,00,000	Plant and Machinery	90,000
5,000 Equity Shares of Rs. 100 each	5,00,000	Stock	80,000
	8,00,000	Sundry Debtors	90,000
Subscribed Capital:		Cash	10,000
2,000 Preference Shares of		Profit and Loss Account	1,20,000
Rs. 100 each	2,00,000		
3,000 Equity Shares of			
Rs. 100 each	3,00,000		
Sundry Creditors	1,00,000		
	6,00,000		6,00,000

Pass journal entries to give effect to the above resolution. Prepare the new balance sheet of the company. *(B.Com., Lucknow)*

(Total of Balance Sheet, Rs. 3,50,000)

19. M/s. Dalal & Co. promoted a joint stock company in 2005. The working of the company was not successful. On 31st March, 2010 the company's Balance Sheet stood as under:—

	Rs.		Rs.
Nominal Capital:—		Goodwill	2,00,000
20,000 shares of Rs. 100 each	20,00,000	Land and Buildings	1,00,000
Subscribed Capital:		Machinery	2,60,000
19,000 shares of Rs. 100 each,		Furniture	20,000
fully paid	19,00,000	Stock	3,70,000
Creditors	1,00,000	Debtors	1,80,000
Dalal & Co.	1,00,000	Profit and Loss Account	9,70,000
	21,00,000		21,00,000

The company is to be reconstructed on the basis of the following scheme:

(*a*) The 19,000 shares of Rs. 100 each are to be reduced to an equal number of fully paid shares of Rs. 40 each.

(*b*) The debt of Rs. 1,00,000 due to Dalal & Co. was also to be reduced, the remaining 1,000 unissued shares being issued to them as fully paid up shares of Rs. 40 each in full settlement of the amount due to them.

(*c*) The amount thus rendered available by the reduction of capital and by the above arrangement with Dalal & Co. is to be utilised in wiping off the Goodwill and the Profit and Loss

Account and in writing down the value of Machinery. (*B.Com., Agra*)

(*Machinery reduced By Rs. 30,000; Total of Balance Sheet Rs. 9,00,000*)

20. The following scheme of reconstruction has been approved for B Ltd.:—

(*i*) The shareholders to receive in lieu of their present holding of 50,000 shares of Rs. 10 each, the following:

(*a*) Fully paid equity shares equal to 2/5ths of their holding;

(*b*) 10% Preference shares, fully paid, to the extent of 1/5th of the above new equity shares; and

(*c*) Rs. 60,000 14% Second Debentures.

(*ii*) An issue of Rs. 50,000 12% First Debentures was made and allotted, payment for the same being received in cash forthwith.

(*iii*) Goodwill which stook at Rs. 1,50,000 was completely written off.

(*iv*) Plant and Machinery which stood at Rs. 1,00,000 was written down to Rs. 75,000.

(*v*) Freehold and Leasehold Premises which stood at Rs. 1,75,000 were written down to Rs. 1,50,000.

Give journal entries in the books of the company necessitated by the above reconstruction.

(*Adapted B.Com., Delhi*)

(*Total of Reconstruction Account, Rs. 2,00,000*)

21. The following was the Balance Sheet of Bharat Construction Ltd., as on 31st March 2010:—

Liabilities		*Rs.*	*Assets*	*Rs.*	*Rs.*
Authorised Capital:			Goodwill		10,000
20,000 Equity Shares of Rs. 10 each		2,00,000	Land and Buildings		20,500
Issued, Subscribed and Paid up Capital:			Machinery		50,850
12,000 Shares of Rs. 10 each	1,20,000		Stock		10,275
Less: Calls in arrear:			Book Debts		15,000
(Rs. 3 per share on			Cash at Bank		1,500
3,000 shares)	9,000	1,11,000	Preliminary Expenses		1,500
Sundry Creditors		15,425	Profit and Loss Account:		
Provision for Taxes		4,000	Balance as per last		
			Balance Sheet	22,000	
			Less: Profit for the year	1,200	20,800
		1,30,425			1,30,425

The directors have had a valuation made of the machinery and find it overvalued by Rs. 10,000. It is proposed to write down this asset to its true value and to extinguish the deficiency in the Profit and Loss Account and to write off Goodwill and Preliminary Expenses by the adoption of the following course:—

(*i*) Forfeit the shares on which the call is outstanding.

(*ii*) Reduce the paid up capital by Rs. 3 per share.

(*iii*) Reissue the forfeited shares at Rs. 5 per share.

(*iv*) Utilise the provision for taxes, if necessary.

The shares on which the calls were in arrear were duly forfeited and reissued as fully paid shares of Rs. 7 each on payment of Rs. 5 per share. You are requested to draft the journal entries necessary and the Balance Sheet of the company after carrying out the terms of the scheme as set above. (*Adapted C.A. First*)

(*Provision for Taxes Utilised, Rs. 300; Total of Balance Sheet, Rs. 1,03,125*)

22. Gloria and Swanson Ltd. had to pass to the hands of a receiver for debentureholders who held charge on all assets except uncalled capital. The following is the position as prepared by the receiver:

Share Capital:	*Rs.*
20,000 shares of Rs. 50 each fully paid up	10,00,000
1,00,000 shares of Rs. 50 each, Rs. 25 per share paid up	25,00,000

	Rs.
First Debentures	25,00,000
Second Debentures	50,00,000
Unsecured Creditors	40,00,000
Bank Balance	30,00,000
Building, Plant and Machinery (Estimated to realise Rs. 15,00,000).	40,00,000

The following is the interest of Gloria and Swanson in the company:—

	Gloria Rs.	Swanson Rs.
First Debentures	20,00,000	5,00,000
Second Debentures	30,00,000	20,00,000
Unsecured Creditors	6,00,000	9,00,000
	56,00,000	34,00,000
Share Capital:		
Fully Paid Shares	5,00,000	5,00,000
Parly Paid Shares	10,00,000	10,00,000

The following scheme of reconstruction is proposed:—

(*a*) Gloria is to cancel Rs. 31,00,000 of his total debt, pay cash Rs. 5,00,000 and he would be issued Rs. 30,00,000 First Debentures in lieu of First and Second Debentures to be cancelled.

(*b*) (*i*) Swanson is to cancel his total debt by accepting Rs. 5,00,000 in cash and Rs. 5,00,000 in First Debentures.

(*ii*) Swanson is to surrender for cancellation Rs. 5,00,000 worth of fully paid up shares.

(*c*) Unsecured creditors, other than Gloria and Swanson, agree to reduce their debt by 20% and accept in lieu thereof 1,00,000 shares of Rs. 10 each fully paid up and the balance in cash payable in five equal annual instalments.

(*d*) Uncalled capital is to be called up in full and Rs. 40 per share to be cancelled thus making shares of Rs. 10 each.

Assuming the scheme is duly approved by all parties interested and by the Court, show the reconstructed Balance Sheet and the journal entries in the books of the company. (*C.A. Final*)

(*Total of Balance Sheet, Rs. 70,00,000*)

Hint: Fist prepare balance sheet to ascertain debit balance of Profit and Loss Account which is Rs. 80,00,000. Reconstruction Account total, Rs. 1,05,00,000.

23. The business of Usha Limited was being carried on continuously at losses. The following are the extracts from the balance sheet of the company as on 31st March, 2010 :

Liabilities	*Rs.*	*Assets*	*Rs.*
Authorised, issued and subscribed capital :		Goodwill	1,00,000
60,000 equity shares of Rs. 10 each fully paid	6,00,000	Plant	6,00,000
4,000 10% cumulative preference shares of Rs. 100 each - fully paid	4,00,000	Furniture	90,000
Securities premium	1,80,000	Stock	5,00,000
Unsecured loan (from director)	1,00,000	Debtors	3,00,000
Sundry creditor	6,00,000	Bank	20,000
Outstanding expenses (including directors' remuneration, Rs. 40,000)	1,40,000	Preliminary expenses	10,000
		Profit & loss account	4,00,000
	20,20,000		20,20,000

Note : Dividend on cumulative preference shares are in arrears for the last three years.

The following scheme of reconstruction has been agreed upon and duly approved by the court:

(*i*) Equity shares to be converted into 3,00,000 equity shares of Rs. 2 each and then the equity shareholders are to surrender to the company 90% of their holding.

(*ii*) Preference shareholders agree to forego their right to arrears of dividend in consideration of which their 10% preference share are to be converted into equal number of 11% preference shares.

(*iii*) Sundry creditors agree to reduce their claim by 1/3rd in consideration of their getting shares of Rs. 1,50,000 out of the surrendered equity shares.

(*iv*) The directors agree to forego the amounts due on account of unsecured loan and directors' remuneration.

(*v*) The surrendered shares not utilised are to be cancelled.

(*vi*) Assets are to be reduced as under :

Goodwill by Rs. 1,00,000; Plant by Rs. 1,14,000; Furniture by Rs. 6,000;
Stock by Rs. 50,000; Debtors by Rs. 30,000;

(*vii*) Expenses of reconstruction amounted to Rs. 20,000.

(*viii*) Further, 1,20,000 equity shares of Rs. 2 each were issued to the existing members for increasing the working capital. The issue was fully subscribed and paid up. The authorised capital was suitably altered.

A member holding 100 equity shares opposed the scheme and his shares were taken over by a director on payment of Rs. 1,000 as fixed by the court.

You are required to pass the journal entries for giving effect to the above arrangement. Also draw up the balance sheet of the company immediately after the abovementioned transactions.

[*C.S. (Inter) June, 1997 Modified*]

(*Balance sheet total, Rs. 15,30,000*)

24. The following is the Balance Sheet of Bright Ltd. as at March 31, 2010:—

	Rs.		*Rs.*
Nominal Capital:		Goodwill	60,000
5,000 12% Preference Shares of		Land & Buildings	75,000
Rs. 100 each	5,00,000	Plant & Machinery	1,10,000
5,000 Equity Shares of Rs. 100		Patents & Trade Marks	25,000
each	5,00,000	Stock, at cost	80,000
Subscribed Capital:		Sundry Debtors	60,000
2,000 12% Preference Shares of		Cash at Bank	4,000
Rs. 100 each, fully paid	2,00,000	Preliminary Expenses	10,000
3,000 Equity Shares of Rs. 100		Profit & Loss Account	3,86,000
each, fully paid	3,00,000		
Profit Prior to Incorporation	15,000		
14% Debentures	1,00,000		
Sundry Creditors	1,50,000		
Provision for Income Tax	45,000		
Preference dividend			
in arrear, Rs, 48,000			
	8,10,000		8,10,000

It is believed that the worst is over and that the time has arrived to effect reconstruction. A revaluation of assets reveals the following:—

	Rs.
Land and Buildings	1,00,000
Plant & Machinery	80,000
Patents & Trade Marks	5,000

	Rs.
Stock	65,000
Debtors	55,000

The following scheme is framed and approved by the Court:—

(*a*) The Preference Shares be converted into fully paid 14% Preference Shares of Rs. 30 each.

(*b*) The arrears of preference dividend be cancelled.

(*c*) The Equity Shares be converted into fully paid shares of Rs. 5 each.

(*d*) The sundry creditors be given the option to either accept 50% of their claims in cash or to convert their claims into equity shares of Rs. 5 each.

(*e*) The revaluation of assets be adopted.

(*f*) The rate of interest on Debentures was to be reduced to 12%.

One-third (in value) of the creditors accepted equity shares for their claims. The rest were paid cash which was raised by issuing 17,000 fully paid equity shares of Rs. 5 each to the existing equity shareholders. All shares were then consolidated or subdivided into shares of Rs. 10 each.

Assuming that the necessary action was taken, journalise the steps and also give the balance sheet after the scheme is put into effect. The Provision for Taxation may be utilised, if necessary.

(*Provision for Taxation Utilised, Rs. 11,000; Reconstruction Account total, Rs. 5,26,000, Closing Bank Balance Rs. 39,000 total of Balance Sheet, Rs. 3,44,000*)

25. A company's position on 31st March, 2010 was as follows:—

	Rs.
20,000 Equity Shares of Rs. 100 each	20,00,000
1,000 12% Debentures of Rs. 1,000 each	10,00,000
Interest on above	1,20,000
Creditors for goods	5,00,000
The assets on that date were:	
Fixed Assets	20,00,000
Current Assets	6,50,000

The following scheme of reconstruction was implemented:

(*a*) The fixed assets were valued at Rs. 9,60,000 and the current assets at Rs. 4,80,000.

(*b*) The shares were sub-divided into shares of Rs. 5 each and 90% of the shares were surrendered.

(*c*) The total claims of the debentureholders were reduced to Rs. 4,90,000 and in consideration of this, they were allotted shares, out of the surrendered shares, amounting to Rs. 2,50,000.

(*d*) The creditors agreed to reduce their claims to Rs. 3,00,000, $^1/_3$ of which was to be satisfied by the issue of equity shares out of those surrendered.

(*e*) The shares surrendered but not reissued were cancelled.

Draft journal entries and give the Balance Sheet of the company after reconstruction.

(*Total of Balance Sheet, Rs. 14,40,000*)

Hint: First prepare balance sheet to ascertain debit balance of Profit and Loss Account which is Rs. 9,70,000; Rs. 6,30,000 of the claim of debentureholders should be credited to Reconstruction Account. Shares cancelled Rs. 14,50,000; Reconstruction Account total, Rs. 23,80,000; Transfer to Capital Reserve Rs. 2,00,000.

26. As on 31st March, 2010, $^1/_3$ of the capital of Zed Ltd. had been lost, not counting Goodwill. On that date, the position was as follows:

	Rs.	Rs.
Goodwill		2,00,000
Other Fixed Assets: Cost	20,00,000	
Less: Depreciation	5,00,000	15,00,000
Current Assets		4,50,000
		21,50,000

	Rs.	Rs.
Less: Current liabilities	6,00,000	
Bank Loan	4,50,000	10,50,000
		11,00,000

There are a capital reserve totalling Rs. 1,00,000. The capital consisted of equity shares and 10% preference shares in the ratio of 3 : 2, both shares being of Rs. 100 each fully paid.

It was found that the fixed assets needed further depreciation to the extent of Rs. 1,50,000 and the current assets were worth Rs. 4,00,000. A scheme of reconstruction was framed and received all requisitic approvals and sanction; the main features were the following:—

(*a*) The preference shares were to be converted into 14% redeemable preference shares, four new shares being issued for five old shares and 1/5 of the arrears of dividend which was last paid for the year ending 31st March, 1997 was to be paid in cash.

(*b*) Equity shares were to be reduced to Rs. 10 each, fully paid.

(*c*) For every two equity shares held, each equity shareholder was to subscribe for one equity share of Rs. 10 each fully paid.

(*d*) Of the profit earned in future, at least 50% would be retained by the company.

Pass journal entries and draft the balance sheet of the company after the scheme is implemented.

(Total of Capital Reduction Account Rs. 11,02,800; Capital Reserve, Rs. 20,200; Current Assets, Rs. 3,96,700; Preference Dividend Paid Rs. 52,800; Total of Balance Sheet, Rs. 17,46,700)

Hint: Suppose total loss is x, the capital loss is $x - 1{,}00{,}000$, since there is a capital reserve of Rs. 1,00,000. Capital of the company is $3\ (x - 1{,}00{,}000)$ or $3x - 3{,}00{,}000$.

Then,

$$11{,}00{,}000 + x - 1{,}00{,}000 = 3x - 3{,}00{,}000$$

The loss is Rs. 6,50,000 and the total capital of the company is Rs. 16,50,000.

27. With the approval of the court and sanction of the parties concerned, the Disappointed Ltd. decides upon a scheme of reconstruction as at March, 31, 2010:

The Balance Sheet of the Company at that date is as under:—

	Rs.		Rs.
10% Preference share of Rs. 10		Goodwill	3,79,460
each, fully paid	4,21,840	Land, Buildings, Plant and Machinery	9,43,200
Equity shares of Rs. 10 each		Investments	3,98,390
fully paid	8,19,330	Stock and Work in Progress	3,18,724
Capital Reserve	68,600	Debtors	1,80,391
9% 1st Mortgage Debentures	3,15,000	Discount and Expenses on Issue	
Interest due thereon less tax	5,950	of Debentures	31,735
12% Convertible Debentures	6,36,700	Profit & Loss Account	2,24,410
Interest due thereon less tax	15,120		
Bank Loan	1,00,000		
Creditors	93,770		
	24,76,310		24,76,310

The material points in the scheme are:—

(*i*) Each Rs. 100 of the convertible debentures is to be exchanged for Rs. 35 of non-convertible 14 debentures, Rs. 50 to 14% preference shares and Rs. 15 of equity shares.

(*ii*) Each existing 10% preference share is to be written down from Rs. 10 to Rs. 8 of which Rs. 5 will be represented by 14% preference shares and Rs. 3 by equity shares.

(*iii*) Each existing equity share will be written down from Rs. 10 to Rs. 3.

(*iv*) Both classes of shares will then be subdivided into shares of Re. 1 each.

(*v*) The B Finance Co. Ltd. will apply for Rs. 3,75,000 of equity shares paying cash in full on application.

(vi) The Bank Loan is to be paid off.

(vii) Capital reserves and the reduction of capital are to be applied in eliminating fictitious assets (including the whole of goodwill), and balance to be used in writing down the Land, Buildings, Plant and Machinery and Investments in the ratio of 3:1 respectively.

You are required to give the journal entries and the resultant balance sheet as at 1st April, 2001.

(Total of Balance Sheet, Rs. 20,24,811)

RECONSTRUCTION SCHEMES

28. The following is the Balance Sheet of Notsowell Co. Ltd. as on 31st March. 2010:—

	Rs.		Rs.
Capital:		Goodwill	3,00,000
Equity Shares: 1,25,000 of Rs. 10 each, Rs. 8 paid	10,00,000	Plant and Machinery	9,00,000
9% Cumulative Preference Shares:		Stock	2,90,000
2,000 shares of Rs. 100 each	2,00,000	Debtors	2,00,000
Sundry Liabilities	10,00,000	Cash at Bank	10,000
		Profit and Loss Account	5,00,000
	22,00,000		22,00,000

Preference Shares' dividends are two years in arrear. Draft a suitable scheme for reduction of capital which would help the company to reorganise on the following lines:—

(i) To write off the profit and loss account and goodwill.

(ii) To depreciate plant and machinery by 10%.

(iii) To satisfy the arrears of preference dividends.

(iv) To provide Rs. 1,00,000 as liquid funds.

Also give journal entries to implement the scheme and draft the final balance sheet.

(Total of Balance Sheet, Rs. 14,24,000)

Hint: Call @ Rs. 2 per share on equity shares be made.

29. The following is the balance sheet of N.D. Ltd. as at 31st March, 2010:—

Liabilities	Rs.	Assets	Rs.
Share Capital:		Goodwill	25,000
Authorised and Issued:		Freehold Property, at cost	90,000
10,000 12% Cumulative Preference		Plant and Machinery	
Shares of Rs. 10 each, fully paid	1,00,000	(cost *less* depreciation)	85,000
20,000 Equity Shares of Rs. 10		Investments (market value,	
each, fully paid	2,00,000	Rs. 88,000)	80,500
Creditors	75,000	Stock	35,000
Bank Overdraft	85,000	Debtors	40,000
		Cash at bank	10,500
		Profit and Loss Account	94,000
	4,60,000		4,60,000

Prepare an external scheme of reconstruction which in your opinion would be necessary for submission to the Board of Directors and redraft the Balance Sheet after incorporation of your proposals. The cumulative preference dividends are in arrears for two years.

30. The summarised Balance Sheet of Depressed Ltd. at March 31, 2010 was as under:—

	Rs.	Rs.
Share capital: 10.5% Preference Shares of Rs. 10 each	2,00,000	
Equity Shares of Rs. 10 each	4,00,000	
	6,00,000	
Less: Profit and loss Account	1,10,000	4,90,000
10% Debentures		3,00,000

		Rs.	Rs.
Current Liabilities:	Bank Loan	90,000	
	Creditors	89,000	
			1,79,000
			9,69,000
Tangible Fixed Assets at cost less depreciation			5,43,000
Current Assets			3,14,000
Goodwill			1,00,000
Discount on Issue of Debentures			12,000
			9,69,000

The tangible fixed assets are overvalued by Rs. 1,00,000 and the current assets include dead stock of the value of Rs. 25,000 and bad debts to the extent of 40,000. Plant and machinery has not been properly repaired in the past. It is estimated that an expenditure of Rs. 40,000 will necessary to put it in proper working order. In addition, a sum of Rs. 1,00,000 has to be spent on an advertising campaign and other sales promotion work.

The Bank is willing to continue the overdraft provided the company is reconstructed and measures mentioned above are put through.

An investment trust is willing to buy a substantial number of shares, provided the company is reorganised. The trust insists on all shareholders accepting suitable sacrifice. The debentureholders also desire an interest in the share capital. Draft a suitable scheme and redraft the balance sheet. Also state what profit should be earned to enable the scheme to work properly.

(Balance Sheet Total Rs. 8,92,000)

31. B. Ltd. has the following abridged Balance Sheet at 31st March, 2010:—

	Rs.		Rs.
Authorised, Issued & Subscribed Capital:		Goodwill	1,50,00,000
50 lakh 11% Cumulative Preference Share of Rs. 10 each	5,00,00,000	Other Fixed Assets	5,00,00,000
55 lakh Equity Shares of Rs. 10 each	5,50,00,000	Floating Assets	3,20,00,000
12% Debentures (with a charge on fixed assets)	2,00,00,000	Profit & Loss Account	5,80,00,000
Sundry Creditors	3,00,00,000		
	15,50,00,000		15,50,00,000

The last preference dividend was paid in respect of the year ended 31st March, 2006. **The fixed** assets are worth Rs. 4,50,00,000 as a going concern but only Rs. 2,00,00,000 it they have to be sold. The floating assets are worth the value stated.

It is estimated that the annual profit after taxation will be Rs. 1 crore. Do you think it is worthwhile to reconstruct the company? If so, draft a scheme of external reconstruction which is likely to be acceptable to all. Also draft the balance sheet according to your scheme.

32. Bright Ltd. has experienced difficulties. It is decided to reconstruct the company. The following is the Balance Sheet as at 31st March, 2010:—

	Rs.		Rs.
Capital:		Land	5,00,000
4 lakh 11% Preference shares of Rs. 10 each, fully paid	40,00,000	Buildings	10,00,000
3 lakh Equity shares of Rs. 10 each, fully paid	30,00,000	Plant and Machinery	30,00,000
10% Debentures	20,00,000	Patents	4,00,000
		Stock	19,00,000
		Debtors	7,00,000

	Rs.		*Rs.*
Trade Creditors	35,00,000	Bank Balance	1,50,000
Arrears of Preference Dividend, Rs. 13,20,000		Profit & Loss Account	48,50,000
	1,25,00,000		1,25,00,000

An analysis of causes leading to losses in the past reveals that certain processes are outdated and that sufficient credit is not allowed. Modernisation of plant will cost Rs. 20 lakh, Rs. 10 lakh worth of present plant being retired and sold for Rs. 2,00,000.

Two months' credit has to be allowed for sales to be maintained at their proper level of Rs. 1,20,00,000 leading to a profit, before tax, of Rs. 13,00,000.

Trade Creditors include Rs. 2,00,000 payable to preferential creditors. Land is valued at Rs. 10,00,000. Buildings at Rs. 8,00,000 and Patents are worth only Rs. 1,00,000.

Submit your proposal for reconstruction of the company.

Essay-type

1. Explain the meaning of an intagible asset.
2. What are the different approaches used in valuing intangible assets ?
3. What are the conditions for recognition of an intangible asset ?
4. How will you account for an intangible asset acquired in an amalgamation in the nature of purchase ?
5. How is an intangible asset acquired by way of a Government grant valued ?
6. Describe the way of dealing with the amount spent on (*i*) research phase and (*ii*) development phase of acquiring an intangible asset.
7. How is cost of an internally generated intangible asset calculated ?
8. Under what conditions is a review of amortisation period and amortisation method of an intangible asset done ?
9. How are impairement losses of intagible assets dealt with in the books of account ?
10. Define goodwill. When may the need for evaluating goodwill arise in the case of a joint stock company?
11. Discuss the main factors affecting the value of goodwill of a joint stock company?
12. What points will you keep in mind while estimating the future maintainable profit of a joint stock company?
13. Explain the term 'capital employed'?
14. What is Super Profits method of evaluating goodwill of a joint stock company?
15. Explain with the help of suitable illustration Capitalisation Method of evaluating goodwill of a joint stock company?
16. In what way is Annuity Method superior to Super Profits Method of evaluating goodwill from the point of view of a joint stock company selling its business?
17. What are the circumstances in which there may be a need for valuation of shares of a joint stock company? How will you determine the intrinstic value of one equity share of a joint stock company? Explain with the help of an illustration.
18. How will you determine the value of shares of a joint stock company on yield basis?
19. How is the share of a joint stick company valued on the basis of earning of the company? Explain with the help of suitable examples.
20. What is the effect of conversion of shares into stock? What are the conditions which must be fulfilled for such a conversion?
21. What is meant by internal reconstruction? Why is it resorted to?
22. Distinguish between internal reconstruction and external reconstruction.
23. Discuss the relative advantages of internal reconstruction and external reconstruction.
24. Describe the points you will keep in mind while formulating a scheme of reconstruction.

21

Amalgamation and External Reconstruction

SYNOPSIS

Meaning of amalgamation	...	21.1	Distribution between external reconstruction and amalgamation	...	21.56
Types of amalgamation	...	21.1	Dissenting shareholders	...	21.65
Distinction between merger and purchase	...	21.2	Inter-company owings	...	21.74
Methods of accounting for amalgamation	...	21.2	Unrealised profit on Stock	...	21.83
Disclosures	...	21.4	Inter-company holdings	...	21.96
Consideration	...	21.7	Amalgamation scheme	...	21.113
Accounting entries	...	21.10	Accounting standard (AS)-14: Accounting for Amalgamations	...	21.119
External reconstruction	...	21.56			

Meaning of Amalgamation

In order to reap the economies of scale and to reduce or eliminate competition, two or more than two joint stock companies may combine their undertakings and become one joint stock company. It may be done either by one of the existing joint stock companies taking over the other combining company or companies, the latter being dissolved or by starting a new joint stock company which takes over all the combining joint stock companies. Suppose, there are two joint stock companies A Ltd. and B Ltd. Now A Ltd. may take over the business of B Ltd. which is dissolved or B Ltd. may absorb A Ltd. There is another choice. Both *A* Ltd. and *B* Ltd. may be dissolved and the business of both the companies may be taken over by a newly formed joint stock company, say *C* Ltd. In all the three cases, we shall say that there is an amalgamation of *A* Ltd. and *B* Ltd. According to Halsbury's Laws of England, :"Amalgamation is a blending of two or more existing undertakings into one undertaking, the shareholders of each blending company becoming substantially the shareholders in the company which is to carry on the blended undertakings. There may be amalgamation either by transfer of two or more undertakings to a new company or by the transfer of one or more undertakings to an existing company."

The Institute of Chartered Accountants of India has issued Accounting Standard (AS) 14 on Accounting for Amalgamations. It has been made effective in respect of accounting periods commencing on or after Ist April, 1995. It is mandatory in nature. With the issue of this Standard, the guidance Note on Accounting Treatment of Reserves in Amalgamations issued by the Institute in 1993 stands withdrawn with effect from the abovementioned date.

According to AS-14, amalgamation means an amalgamation pursuant to the provisions of the Companies Act, 1956, or any other statute which may be applicable to companies. However, the Companies Act, 1956 has not specifically defined the term amalgamation. But it is noteworthy that the Accounting Standard 14 has done away with the distinction between merger and amalgamation. According to AS-14, merger is only a type of, and therefore, only a part of amalgamation.

Types of Amalgamation

Amalgamation may be in the nature of (*i*) merger or (*ii*) purchase. Amalgamation in the nature of merger is an amalgamation which satisfies **all** the following conditions:

(i) All the assets and liabilities of the transferor company become, after amalgamation, the assets and liabilities of the transferee company. The transferor company means the company which is amalgamated into another company while the transferee company means the company into which a transferor company is amalgamated.

(ii) Shareholders holding not less than 90% of the face value of the equity shares of the transferor company (other than the equity shares already held therein, immediately before the amalgamation, by the transferee company or its subsidiaries or their nominees) become equity shareholders of the transferee company by virtue of the amalgamation.

(iii) The consideration for the amalgamation receivable by those equity shareholders of the transferor company who agree to become equity shareholders of the transferee company is discharged by the transferee company wholly by the issue of equity shares in the transferee company, except that cash may be paid in respect of any fractional shares. Consideration for the amalgamation means the aggregate of the shares and other securities issued and the payment made in the form of cash or other assets by the transferee company to the shareholders of the transferor company.

(iv) The business of the transferor company is intended to be carried on, after the amalgamation, by the transferee company.

(v) No adjustment is intended to be made to the book values of the assets and liabilities of the transferor company when they are incorporated in the financial statements of the transferee company except to ensure uniformity of accounting policies.

An amalgamation is classified as an 'amalgamation in the nature of merger', when all the conditions listed above are satisfied. There are, however, differing views regarding the nature of any further conditions that may apply. Some believe that, in addition to an exchange of equity shares, it is necessary that the shareholders of the transferor company obtain a substantial share in the transferee company even to the extent that it should not be possible to identify any one party as dominant therein. This belief is based in part on the view that the exchange of control of one company for an insignificant share in a larger company does not amount to a mutual sharing of risk and benefits. Others believe that the substance of an amalgamation in the nature of merger is evidenced by meeting certain criteria regarding the relationship of the parties, such as the former independence of the amalgamating companies, the manner of their amalgamation, the absence of planned transactions that would undermine the effect of the amalgamation, and the continuing participation by the management of the transferor company in the management of the transferee company after the amalgamation.

Amalgamation in the nature of purchase is an amalgamation which does not satisfy any one or more of the five conditions mentioned above.

Distinction between merger and purchase

In an amalgamation which is in the nature of merger, there is a geniune pooling not merely of the assets and liabilities of the amalgamating companies but also of the shareholders' interest and of the businesses of these companies. The accounting treatment of such an amalgamation should ensure that the resultant figures of assets, liabilities, capital and reserves more or less represent the sum of the relevant figures of the amalgamating companies. An amalgamation in the nature of 'purchase' is in effect a mode by which one company acquires another company. As a consequence, the shareholders of the transferor company normally do not continue to have a proportionate share in the equity of the transferee company. Actually it may not be intended to continue the business of the transferor company.

Methods of accounting for amalgamations

There are two methods of accounting for amalgamations, namely *(i)* the pooling of interests method and *(ii)* the purchase method.

(*i*) *The pooling of interests method.* This method is followed in case of an amalgamation in the nature of merger. Under this method, the assets, liabilities and reserves of the transferor company are recorded by the transferee company at their existing carrying amounts and in the same form as at the date of the amalgamation. The balance of the Profit and Loss Account of the transferor company is aggregated with the balance of the Profit and Loss Account of the transferee company or transferred to the General Reserve, if any. The difference between the amount recorded as share capital issued plus any additional consideration in the form of cash or other assets on the one hand and the amount of share capital of the transferor company on the other hand is adjusted in reserves. If, at the time of the amalgamation, the transferor and transferee companies have conflicting accounting policies, a uniform set of accounting policies is adopted following the amalgamation. The effects on the financial statements of any changes in accounting policies are reported in accordance with Accounting Standard (AS) 5 (Revised)—'Net Profit or Loss for the Period, Prior Period Items and Changes in Accounting Policies'.

(*ii*) *The purchase method.* This method is followed in case of an amalgamation in the nature of purchase. Under this method, the transferee company accounts for the amalgamation either by incorporating the assets and liabilities of the transferor company at their existing carrying amounts or by allocating the consideration to individual identifiable assests and liabilities of the transferor company on the basis of their fair values at the date of amalgamation. The identifiable assets and liabilities may include assets and liabilities not recorded in the financial statements of the transferor company. Where assets and liabilities are restated on the basis of their fair values, the determination of fair values may be influenced by the intentions of the transferee company. For example, the transferee company may have a specialised use for an asset. Also, the transferee company may intend to effect changes in the activities of the transferor company which may necessitate the creation of specific provisions for the expected cost, for example, planned employee termination and plant relocation costs.

The reserves (whether capital or revenue or arising on revaluation) of the transferor company, other than the statutory reserves, are not included in the financial statements of the transferee company. To record the statutory reserves (such as Foreign Projects Reserve Account under sec. 80 HHB and Reserve created under sec. 80 HHD of the Income-tax Act) of the transferor company in the books of the transferee company, the relevant statutory reserve account is credited and the corresponding debit is given to a suitable account like **amalgamation adjustment account** which is disclosed as a part of 'miscellaneous expenditure' or other similar category in the balance sheet. When the identity of this statutory reserve is no longer required to be maintained, both the statutory reserves account and the corresponding debit account are reversed.

Any excess of the amount of the consideration over the value of the net assests of the transferor company acquired by the transferee company is recognised in the transferee company's books of account as goodwill arising on amalgamation. If the amount of the consideration is lower than the value of net assests acquired, the difference is credited to capital reserve.

The goodwill arising in amalgamation, as per Accounting Standard 14, should be amortised to income on a systematic basis over its useful life. The amortisation period should not exceed five years unless a somewhat longer period can be justified. The factors which may be considered in estimating the useful life of goodwill arising on amalgamation include:

(*a*) The foreseeable life of the business or industry;
(*b*) the effects of product obsolescence, changes in demand and other economic factors;
(*c*) the service life expectancies of key individuals or groups of employees;
(*d*) expected actions by competitors or potential competitors; and
(*e*) legal, regulatory or contractual provisions affecting the useful life.

The following points which are common to the two methods described above are also noteworthy :

The consideration for the amalgamation may include non-cash element at fair value. In case of issue of securities, the value fixed by the statutory authorities may be taken to be the fair value. In case of other assets, the fair value may be determined by reference to the market value of the assets given up. Where the market value of the assets given up cannot be reliably assessed, such assets are valued at their respective net book values.

Where the scheme of amalgamation provides for an adjustment to the consideration contingent on one or more future events, the amount of the additional payment is included in the consideration if payment is probable and a reasonable estimate of the amount can be made. In all other cases, the adjustment is recognised as soon as the amount is determinable. It is as per Accounting Standard (AS) 4 (Revised) on Contingencies and Events Occurring after the Balance Sheet Date.

Where the scheme of amalgamation sanctioned under a statute prescribes the treatment to be given to the reserve of the transferor company after amalgamation, the same has to be followed.

Distinction between the two methods

The following are the main points of distinction between the two methods of accounting for amalgamation:

(*i*) The pooling of interests method is applied in case of an amalgamation in the nature of merger whereas the purchase method is applied in case of an amalgamation in the nature of purchase.

(*ii*) In the pooling of interests method, not only the assests and liabilities but also the reserves of the transferor company are recorded by the transferee company in its books of account. However, in the purchase method, the transferee company records in its books of account only the assets and liabilities taken over; the reserves, except the statutory reserves, of the transferor company are not aggregated with those of the transferee company.

(*iii*) Under the pooling of interests method, the difference between the consideration paid and the share capital of the transferor company is adjusted in general reserve or other reserves of the transferee company. On the other hand, under the purchase method, the difference between the consideration paid and the net assets taken over is treated by the transferee company as goodwill or capital reserve, as the case may demand.

(*iv*) When for legal compliance, statutory reserve (such as Foreign Projects Reserve Account under sec. 80 HHB and Reserve created under sec. 80 HHD of the Income Tax Act) of the transferor company are incorporated in the books of the transferee company, in pooling of interests method these statutory reserves are recorded like all other reserves and no amalgamation adjustment account is required to be opened while in the purchase method, while incorporating the statutory reserves the transferee company has to open amalgamation adjustment account debiting it with the amount of the statutory reserves being incorported.

Disclosures

For all amalgamations, the following disclosures should be made in the first financial statements following the amalgamation:

(*a*) names and general nature of business of the amalgamating companies;

(*b*) effective date of amalgamation for accounting purposes;

(*c*) the method of accounting used to reflect the amalgamation; and

(d) particulars of the scheme sanctioned under a statute.

For amalgamations accounted for under the pooling of interests method, the following additional disclosures should be made in the first financial statements following the amalgamation:

(*a*) description and number of shares issued, together with the percentage of each company's equity shares exchanged to effect the amalgamation;

(*b*) the amount of any difference between the consideration and the value of net identifiable assets acquired, and the treatment thereof including the period of amortisation of any goodwill arising on amalgamation.

For amalgamations accounted for under the purchase method, the following additional disclosures should be made in the first financial statements following the amalgamation:

(*a*) consideration for the amalgamation and a description of the consideration paid or contingently payable; and

(*b*) the amount of any difference between the consideration and the value of net identifiable assets acquired, and the treatment thereof including the period of amortisation of any goodwill arising on amalgamation.

Amalgamation after the balance sheet date : When an amalgamation is effected after the balance sheet date but before the issuance of the financial statements of either party to the amalgamation, disclosure should be made in accordance with AS 4 (Revised), 'Contingencies and Events Occurring after the Balance Sheet Date', but the amalgamation should not be incorportated in the financial statements. In certain circumstances, the amalgamation may also provide additional information affecting the financial statements themselves, for instance, by allowing the going concern assumption to be maintained.

Now, study the following illustration carefully :

Illustration 1. The following are the balance sheets of P Ltd. and S Ltd. as on 31st March, 2010 :

	P Ltd.	S Ltd.
Liabilities	*Rs. '000*	*Rs. '000*
Equity Share Capital , Rs. 10 each, fully paid	72,000	30,000
11 % Preference Share Capital, Rs. 100 each, fully paid		17,000
General Reserve	8,000	4,500
Export Profit Reserve		2,000
Profit and Loss Account	7,500	4,000
9 % Debentures, Rs. 100 each, fully paid		5,000
Creditors	11,500	3,500
	99,000	66,000
Assets :		
Land and Buildings	25,000	
Plant and Machinery	32,500	29,000
Furniture and Fittings	5,750	9,410
Stock	21,500	17,390
Debtors	7,250	5,200
Cash at Bank	7,000	5,000
	99,000	66,000

P Ltd. takes over S Ltd. on 1st April, 2010 and discharges consideration for the business as follows :

(i) Issued 35 lakh fully paid equity shares of Rs. 10 each at par to the equity shareholders of S Ltd.

(ii) Issued fully paid 12% preference shares of Rs. 100 each to discharge the preference shareholders of S Ltd. at a premium of 10%.

It is agreed that the debentures of S Ltd. will be converted into equal number and amount of 10% debentures of P Ltd. The Statutory Reserve of S Ltd. is to be maintained for two more years.

You are required to show the balance sheet of P Ltd. assuming that :

(a) the amalgamation is in the nature of merger, and

(b) the amalgamation is in the nature of purchase.

[Adapted B.Com.(Hons.) Delhi - 2001]

Solution :

(a) *In case the amalgamation is in the nature of merger :*

Balance Sheet of P Ltd. as on 31st March, 2010

Liabilities	*Rs. '000*	*Assets*	*Rs. '000*
Share Capital		Fixed Assets	
Authorised	?	Land and Buildings	25,000
		Plant and Machinery	61,500
Issued and Subscribed :		Furniture and Fittings	15,160
1,07,00,000 Equity shares of		Current Assets, Loans and Advances	
Rs. 10 each, fully paid-up	1,07,000	A) Current Assets	
1,87,000 12% Preference shares		Stock	38,890
of Rs. 100 each, fully paid-up	18,700	Debtors	12,450
(Of the above shares, all the		Cash at Bank	12,000
preference shares and 35 lakh		B) Loans and Advances	Nil
equity shares are allotted as			
fully paid-up pursuant to a			
contract without payments			
being received in cash.)			
Reserves and Surplus			
General Reserve (as per working note)	9,800		
Export Profit Reserve	2,000		
Profit and Loss Account	7,500		
Secured Loans			
10% Debentures of Rs. 100			
each, fully paid-up	5,000		
Current Liabilities			
and Provisions			
A) Current Liabilities			
Creditors	15,000		
B) Provisions	Nil		
	1,65,000		1,65,000

Working Notes :

	Rs. '000	*Rs. '000*
(i) P Ltd.'s general reserve		8,000
Add : S Ltd.'s general reserve		4,500
S Ltd.'s profit and loss account		4,000
		16,500
Less : Consideration for equity shares	35,000	
Consideration for preference shares	18,700	
	53,700	
Less : S Ltd.'s share capital, Rs. (30,000 + 17,000) thousand	47,000	6,700
General reserve as appearing in P Ltd.'s balance sheet		9,800

(b) *In case the amalgamation is in the nature of purchase :*

Balance Sheet of P Ltd. as on 31st March, 2010

Liabilities	*Rs. '000*	*Assets*	*Rs. '000*
Share Capital		Fixed Assets	
Authorised	?	Land and Buildings	25,000
		Plant and Machinery	61,500
Issued and Subscribed :		Furniture and Fittings	15,160
1,70,00,000 Equity Shares of		Current Assets, Loans and Advances	
Rs. 10 each, fully paid-up	1,07,000	A) Current Assets	
1,87,000 12% Preference shares		Stock	38,890
of Rs. 100 each, fully paid-up	18,700	Debtors	12,450
(Of the above shares, all the		Cash at Bank	12,000
preference shares and 35 lakh		B) Loans and Advances	Nil
equity shares are allotted as		Miscellaneous Expenditure	
fully paid-up pursuant to a		Amalgamation Adjustment Account	2,000
contract without payments			
being received in cash.)			
Reserves and Surplus			
Capital Reserve, working note	3,800		
General Reserve	8,000		
Export Profit Reserve	2,000		
Profit and Loss Account	7,500		
Secured Loans			
10% Debentures of Rs. 100			
each, fully paid-up	5,000		
Current Liabilities			
and Provisions			
A) Current Liabilities			
Creditors	15,000		
B) Provisions	Nil		
	1,67,000		16,70,000

Working Notes :

	Rs. '000	*Rs. '000*
(i) Calculation of capital reserve arising on amalgamation		
Total assets of S Ltd. taken over		66,000
Less : 10% Debentures taken over	5,000	
Creditors taken over	3,500	8,500
Net assets taken over		57,500
Less : Consideration to equity shareholders	35,000	
Consideration to preference shareholders	18,700	53,700
Capital reserve arising on amalgamation		3,800

Consideration

For the purpose of accounting for amalgamation, Accounting Standard 14 (AS-14) defines the term 'consideration' as "the aggregate of the shares and other securities issued and the payment made in the form of cash or other assets by the transferee company to the shareholders of the transferor company". Consideration implies the value agreed upon for the net assets taken over. The amount depends on the terms of the contract between the transferor company and the transferee company.

The consideration for amalgamation may consist of shares and other securities, cash and other assets and the amount of consideration depends upon the fair value of its elements. In case of issue of securities, the value fixed by the statutory authorities may be taken to be the fair value. In case of other assets, the fair value may be determined by reference to the market value of the assets given up. Where the market value of the assets given up cannot be reliably assessed, such assets are valued at their respective net book values.

Where the scheme of amalgamation provides for an adjustment to the consideration contingent on one or more future events, the amount of the additonal payment it included in the consideration if payment is probable and a reasonable estimate of the amount can be made. In all other cases, the adjustment is recognised as soon as the amount is determinable.

Where the scheme of amalgamation sanctioned under a statute prescribes the treatment to be given to the reserves of the transferor company after amalgamation, the same has to be followed.

There are different methods in which consideration may be calculated:

(1) Lump-sum Method. It is the simplest method. In it, the consideration is stated as a lump-sum. For example, it may be stated that P Ltd. takes over the business of S Ltd. for Rs. 50,00,000. Here, the sum of Rs. 50,00,000 is the consideration.

(2) Net Assets Method. Under this method, the consideration is arrived at by adding the agreed values of all the assets taken over by the transferee company and deducting therefrom the agreed values of the liabilities taken over by the transfree company. The agreed value means the amount at which the transferor company has agreed to sell and the transferee company has agreed to take over a particular asset or a liablitity. In the absence of any statement to the contrary regarding the agreed value of an asset or a liablity, the amount at which the asset or the liability appears in the books of the transferor company is considered to be the agreed value. Fictitious assets (Preliminary Expenses, Underwriting Commission, Discount on Issue of Shares, Discount on Issue of Debentures, Expenses on Issue of Debentures, debit balance of Profits & Loss Account etc.) are not taken over.

The following is the balance sheet of A Ltd :

Liabilities	*Rs.*	*Assets*	*Rs.*
Share Capital: 6000 Equity Shares of Rs. 100 each, fully paid	6,00,000	Goodwill	70,000
		Plant and Machinery	4,60,000
General Reserve	2,50,000	Furniture and Fittings	1,02,000
Profit & Loss Appropriation A/c	80,000	Stock	4,36,000
Bills Payable	70,000	Debtors	1,34,000
Sundry Creditors	2,45,000	Cash at Bank	23,000
		Preliminary Expenses	20,000
	12,45,000		12,45,000

Suppose *(i)* B Ltd. purchases the business of A Ltd. *(ii)* Goodwill is valued at Rs. 2,00,000 while stock is valued at Rs. 4,16,000. Other assets are considered worth their book values. *(iii)* B Ltd. does not take over Cash at Bank *(iv)* Consideration is to be discharged in the form of 90,000 fully paid equity shares of Rs. 10 each, valued at par and the balance in cash.

In the abovementioned case, the consideration will be calculated as follows :

Agreed values of assets taken over by B Ltd :

		Rs.
Goodwill		2,00,000
Plant and Machinery		4,60,000
Furniture and Fittings		1,02,000
Stock		4,16,000
Debtors		1,34,000
		13,12,000
Less: Liabilities taken over :	*Rs.*	
Bills Payable	70,000	
Sundry Creditors	2,45,000	3,15,000
Consideration		9,97,000

B Ltd. will discharge the consideration as under :

90,000 equity shares of Rs. 10 each, fully paid, at par	9,00,000
Cash (balancing figure)	97,000
Total	9,97,000

One must remember:

(*a*) to add the values of the assets taken over by the transferee company, Goodwill is invariably taken over by the transferee company. Prepaid expenses should be added.

(*b*) not to add the assets not taken over. (*e.g.*, cash at bank in the above example) and the fictitious assets or expenses not written off. All items which appear in the balance sheet under the heading 'Miscellaneous Expenditure' like Preliminary Expenses, Discount or Commission on Issue of Shares or Debentures etc., and the debit balance of Profit and Loss Account, if any, should never be added.

(*c*) Not to deduct the liabilities not taken over by the transferee company but to deduct the agreed value of the liabilities taken over.

(*d*) Not to deduct such balances as Capital Reserve, Capital Redemption Reserve, Share Premium Account, General Reserve, Debenture Redemption Reserve, Credit balance of Profit and Loss Account etc.— in fact any account which denotes undistributed profits. All such items appear under the heading 'Reserves and Surplus'. However, if any, reserve or fund or a portion of any reserve and fund denotes liability to third parties, the same must be included in liabilities. Workmen Compensation Fund is an example. A company may credit regularly a certain amount to Workmen Compensation Fund so that it at any time a liability arises to pay compensation to a worker or workers, this fund may be used. At the time of the liquidation of the company, the credit balance of this fund will represent accumulated profit to be distributed among the equity shareholders. However, if at the time of liquidation there is a liability to pay a compensation to any worker, the liability will be recorded and the fund will be reduced to the extent of the liability; only the balance will be treated as accumulated profit. Insurance Reserve is another example. However, Employees Provident Fund or Staff Provident Fund denotes a liability towards the employees of the company.

(*e*) that the expression 'all assets' includes cash and the "the business" standing alone means assests including cash and all the liabilities to outsiders. Both the expressions exclude expenses or losses not written off.

(3) Net Payment Method. Under this method, consideration is ascertained by adding up the cash paid, agreed value of assets given and the agreed values of the securities allotted by the transferee company to the transferor company in discharge of consideration. Suppose, P Ltd. for business taken over from S Ltd. agrees to pay Rs. 5,00,000 in cash and allot to S Ltd. 4,00,000 equity shares of Rs.10 each fully paid at an agreed value of Rs. 15 per share. In this case, the consideration will be ascertained as follows :

	Rs.
Cash	5,00,000
4,00,000 equity shares of Rs. 10 each fully paid, at Rs.15 per share (4,00,000 × Rs.15)	60,00,000
Consideration	65,00,000

A modified method of indicating consideration is to say how much a shareholder will get per share on the transfer of the company's business to the transferee company. Consider the following balance sheet of S Ltd.

Liabilities	*Rs.*	*Assets*	*Rs.*
Share Capital :		Sundry Assets	2,10,00,000
20,000 11% Preference Shares of			
Rs. 100 each, fully paid up	20,00,000		
8,00,000 Equity Share			
of Rs. 10 each, fully paid up	80,00,000		
Reserves	50,00,000		
Sundry Liabiliities	60,00,000		
	2,10,00,000		2,10,00,000

Suppose P Ltd. takes over the business of S Ltd. and agrees to give for each 11% preference share in S Ltd. ten 12% preference shares of Rs.10 fully paid up at par and for each equity share in S Ltd. Re. 1 in cash and one fully paid equity share in P Ltd. of Rs. 10 valued at Rs. 15. The consideration will be computed as follows :

	Rs.
12% preference shares to be allotted by P Ltd.	
= Rs.10 × 20,000 × 10	20,00,000
Equity shares to be allotted by P Ltd.	
= Rs. 15 × 8,00,000	1,20,00,000
Cash to be paid by P Ltd.	
= Rs. 1 × 8,00,000	8,00,000
Consideration	1,48,00,000

4. Intrinsic Worth Method. Consideration may have to be calculated on the basis of the agreed value of shares of the transferor company. Shares are ownership securities; if the transferee company pays for all the shares of the transferor company, it can be said to have paid for the entire business of the transferor company. Suppose, the subscribed capital of S Ltd. consists of 6,00,000 equity shares of Rs. 10 each fully paid and there are no preference shares. Further suppose, P Ltd. takes over the business of S. Ltd. and it is agreed between S Ltd. and P. Ltd. that the value of one share of S Ltd. is Rs. 13; then the consideration will be Rs. 13 × 6,00,000 = Rs. 78,00,000. If the transferee company is to discharge the consideration in the form of its own equity shares, the agreed value of a share of transferee company also becomes relevant. The consideration, divided by the agreed value of one share of transferee company will give the number of shares to be allotted by the transferee company to transferor company to discharge consideration. In the abovementioned case, if P Ltd. is to discharge the consideration in the form of its own shares and if it is agreed between P Ltd. and S Ltd. that the value of one share of P Ltd. of the paid up value of Rs. 10 is Rs. 25, P Ltd. will allot 78,00,000/25=3,12,000 shares to S Ltd. to discharge the consideration. At the time of allotment, P Ltd will debit liquidator in S Ltd. with Rs. 78,00,000 (amount of consideration) and credit Equity Share Capital with Rs. 31,20,000 (paid up value of the shares allotted) and Securities Premium Account with Rs. 46,80,000 (the amount of securities premium charged @ Rs. 15 per share). The transferor company will debit Shares in Transferee Company Account and credit transferee company with the agreed value of shares received from transferee company.

ACCOUNTING ENTRIES

Entries or steps to close the books of the transferor company will be as under :

1. Open Realisation Account and transfer to this account all assets at book values.
   The entry is :
   Realisation Account Dr.
   To Various Assets (individually)

By this entry, the accounts of various assets will be closed.

Note : If the transferee company does not take over cash and bank balances, these should not be transferred to the Realisation Account. But other assets, even if they are not taken over by the transferee company, should be transferred. The term "assets" does not include expenses and losses appearing in the balance sheet not yet writeen off (In the balance sheet, these items appear under the heads 'Miscellaneous Expenditure' and Profit and Loss Account on the Assets side of the balance sheet of the transferor company) but includes prepaid expenses.

If there is a provision against an asset, such an asset is transferred to Realisation Account at gross figure; the related Provision Account is transferred to Realisation Account by means of another entry. Suppose there are Sundry Debtors amounting to Rs. 50,000 against which there is a Provision for Bad Debts @ 5% amounting to Rs. 2,500. In this case, Realisation Account will be debited and Sundry Debtors credited with Rs. 50,000; then Provision for Bad Debts Account will be debited and Realisation Account credited with Rs. 2,500.

2. Transfer those liabilities which the transferee company takes over to the credit of Realisation Account at *book figures*. The entry is:

Sundry Creditors	Dr.
Bills Payable	Dr.
etc. etc.	
To Realisation Account.	

The accounts of these liabilities will be closed in this manner.

Note : If any Fund or Reserve denotes liability, it should be transferred to the Realisation Account. If only a portion of it is a liability, that portion only should be transferred. For example, there may be an "Accident Compensation Fund". If there is no liability against it, it represents accumulated profit, but if there is a liability to workmen for an accident, the estimated amount of the liability should be transferred to the Realisation Account; the balance will represent accumulated profit and will be transferred to Equity Shareholders Account.

3. Debit the transferee company and credit Realisation Account with the consideration.

4. Debit what is received from the transferee company in discharge of the consideration and credit the transferee company. For example, the entry may be:

Bank	Dr.	with cash received
Equity Shares in Transferee Co.	Dr.	with agreed value of equity shares of transferee company received
Debentures in Transferee Co.	Dr.	with agreed value of debentures of transferee company received
To Transferee Company		with total consideration

5. If any asset is not taken over by the transferee company and is otherwise disposed of, debit Bank and credit Realisation Account with the amount realised.

6. Expenses of liquidation will be dealt with as follows :

(a) If the transferor company is to bear the expenses, debit Realisation Account and credit Bank with the amount paid.

(b) If the transferee company is to bear the expenses, then one of the following courses may be adopted :

(i) No entry may be passed for the expenses. It will happen when the transferee company pays the expenses of liquidation as and when they arise and the transferor company is never called upon to pay them.

(ii) Expenses of liquidation may first be paid by the transferor company to be reimbursed by the transferee company later. In such a case, the following entries will be passed :

On payment of expenses by the transferor company,

Transferee Company (by name)	Dr. with the amount of expenses
To Bank	

On receipt of reimbursement from the transferee company

Bank	Dr.

To Transferee Company

As an alternative, the following entries may by passed:

On payment of expenses by the transferor company:

Realisation Account	Dr.	with the amount of expenses
To Bank		
Transferee Company (by name)	Dr.	with the amount of expenses recoverable
To Realisation Account		

On receipt of reimbursement from the transferee company :

Bank	Dr.	
To Transferee Company		

7. If there are liabilities to be discharged by the transferor company (that is to say, liabilities other than those taken over by the transferee company), debit the liability account and credit Bank. If there is a difference in the book figure and the amount paid, the difference should be transferred to Realisation Account. Suppose, there are Debentures amounting to Rs. 1,00,000 and that they have to be discharged at a premium of 5%. This means that against the liability of Rs. 1,00,000, Rs. 1,05,000 is payable, Rs, 5,000 will be debited to Realisation Account. The entries will be :

(a)	Debentures	Dr.	1,00,000	
	Realisation Account	Dr.	5,000	
	To Debentureholders			1,05,000
(b)	Debentureholders	Dr.	1,05,000	
	To Bank			1,05,000

8. Transfer Preference Share Capital Account to Preference Shareholders Account. If it has been agreed to pay them more than the amount of the capital (*e.g.*, arrear of preference dividend), the additional amount concerned should be debited to Realisation Account and credited to Preference Shareholders Account. On the contrary, if the preference shareholders have agreed to accept something less than the amount of the capital, the amount 'saved' should be debited to Preference Shareholders Account, and credited to Realisation Account. The entries will be as follows :—

(a) It preference shareholders are to be paid more than the credit balance of Preference Share Capital :

Preference Share Capital Account	Dr.	credit balance
Realisation Account	Dr.	excess amount payable
To Preference Shareholders Account		total amount payable

However, if preference shareholders have agreed to accept less than the credit balance of Preference Share Capital, instead of the abovementioned entry, the following entry will be passed:

Preference Share Capital Account	Dr.	credit balance
To Preference Shareholders Account		amount actually payable
To Realisation Account		amount saved

(b) For payment to preference shareholders, the entry may be :

Preference Shareholders Account	Dr.	amount paid
To Bank		cash paid
To Debentures in Transferee Company		with agreed value
To Preference Shares in Transferee Company		" " "
To Equity Shares in Transferee Company		" " "

The preference share capital has to be repaid in priority to the equity share capital. Hence, if the amount available is not sufficient or barely sufficient to satisfy the preference shareholders, they will get the whole of the amount and the equity shareholders will get nothing.

9. Finally, the claim of the equity shareholders is to be determined and then paid. For this purpose, first of all Equity Shareholders Account is opened by transfer of Equity Share Capital Account; the entry being :

Equity Share Capital Account Dr.
To Equity Shareholders Account

Equity Shareholders are also entitled to all accumulated profits and reserves; hence all items appearing under the heading 'Reserves and Surplus' are also transferred to the credit of Equity Shareholders Account; the entry being :

Capital Reserve Dr.
Capital Redemption Reserve Dr.
Securities Premium Account Dr.
General Reserve Dr.
Profit and Loss Account (credit balance) Dr.
Sinking Fund etc. Dr.
To Equity Shareholders Account

But equity shareholders' claim is reduced by debit balance (if any) of Profit and Loss Account and expenses not written off *i.e.,* items appering under the heading 'Miscellaneous Expenditure'. Hence, the following entry may also have to be passed :

Equity Shareholders Account Dr.
To Preliminary Expenses Account
To Underwriting Commission Account
To Expenses on Issue of Shares Account
To Expenses on Issue of Debentures Account
To Discount on Issue of Shares Account
To Discount on Issue of Debentures Account etc.
To Profit and Loss Account (debit balance)

The balance in Realisation Account, indicating profit or loss on disposal of assets and discharge of liabilities of the company, should also be transferred to Equity Shareholders Account. The entry will be:

If Realisation Account shows a profit:

Realisation Account Dr. with the amount of profit
To Equity Shareholders Account

On the other hand, if Realisation Account reveals a loss, the entry will be:

Equity Shareholders Account Dr. with the amount of loss
To Realisation Account

The above mentioned entry will close Realisation Account.

10. At this stage, the credit balance of Equity Shareholders Account will reveal the net amount finally payable to equity shareholders. On payment of the amount to them, the entry will be:

Equity Shareholders Account	Dr.	total amount paid
To Bank		with cash paid
To Equity Shares in Transferee Company etc.		with agreed value of shares distributed

All the accounts in the books, and the books themselves, will thus be closed.

Entries in the books of the transferee company will be as follows :

(A) *In case the amalgamation is in the nature of purchase and hence purchase method is followed :*

1.	Business Purchase Account	Dr.	with consideration
	To Liquidator of Transferor Company		
2.	Various Assets (excluding Goodwill) taken over.	Dr.	with agreed values
	To Various Liabilities taken over		with agreed values
	To Business Purchase Account		with consideration

If in the abovementioned entry, the total credits exceed the total debits, such an excess is considered the value of Goodwill and hence debited to Goodwill Account, making the total debits equal to total credits. Then, the entry will be:

Goodwill Account	Dr.	balancing figure
Various other Assets taken over	Dr.	with agreed values
To Various Liabilities taken over		with agreed values
To Business Purchase Account		with consideration

On the other hand, if the total debits exceed the total credits, such an excess is a capital profit on acquisition of business and is credited to capital reserve. In such a case, the entry will change as follows:

Various Assets (excluding Goodwill) taken over	Dr.	with agreed values
To Various Liabilities taken over		with agreed values
To Business Purchase Account		with purchase consideration
To Capital Reserve		balancing figure

Normally, in an amalgamation in the nature of purchase, the identity of the reserve of the transferor company is not preserved. However, in order to get the advantage of provision of some statute, it may be necessary to retain the identity of statutory reserves of the transferor company in the books of the transferee company. Foreign Projects Reserve Account under Sec. 80 HHB and Reserve created under Sec. 80 HHD of the Income Tax Act are examples of statutory reserves. To record statutory reserves of the transferor company in the books of the transferee company, the following entry may be passed :—

Amalgamation Adjustment Account	Dr.	will the amount of
To Statutory Reserves	(individually)	statutory resreves of transferor company

It may be noted that later, when the identity of the statutory reserves of the transferor company is no longer required to be maintained, the abovementioned entry will be reversed.

One may not open Business Purchase Account. In that case, instead to two entries, one entry will do. For example, if there is no Goodwill or Capital Reserve on acquisition of business, the entry will be:

Various Assets (excluding Goodwill) taken over	Dr.	with agreed values
To Various Liabilities taken over		with agreed values
To Liquidator of Transferor Company		with consideration.

3. The transferee company may discharge the consideration in the form of cash and its own equity shares, preference shares and debentures. On payment to the transferor company, the entry will be:

Liquidator of Transferor Company	Dr.	with consideration
To Bank		with cash paid
To Equity Share Capital Account		with paid up value of equity shares allotted
To Preference Share Capital Account		with paid up value of preference shares allotted
To Debentures Account		with paid up value of debentures allotted

Shares or debentures may be allotted at a premium or at a discount.

(a) If the allotment is made at a premium, the entry will be:

Liquidator of Transferor Company	Dr.
To Equity Share Capital Account	

To Preference Share Capital Account
To Debentures Account
To Securities Premium Account — with premium charged on equity and preference shares and debentures

(*b*) If the allotment is made at a discount, the entry will be:

Liquidator on Transferor Company	Dr.	
Discount on Issue of Shares Account	Dr.	with discount allowed on shares
Discount of Issue of Debentures Account	Dr.	with discount allowed on debentures
To Equity Share Capital Account		
To Preference Share Capital Account		with paid-up values
To Debentures Account		

To illustrate the point, suppose a transferee company discharges the amount of the consideration amounting to Rs. 6,95,000 by allotment to transferor company 50,000 equity shares of Rs. 10 each at an agreed value of Rs.12 each and 14% debentures of Rs. 1,00,000 at a discount of 5%; the entry will be:

Liquidator of Transferor Company	Dr.	6,95,000	
Discount on issue of Debentures Account	Dr.	5,000	
To Equity Share Capital Account			5,00,000
To Securities Premium Account			1,00,000
To 14% Debentures Account			1,00,000

4. If the transferee company bears the expenses of liquidation of the transferor company the cost of business purchased increases with the amount of such expenses. Hence the entry is:

Goodwill Account or Capital Reserve Account Dr.
To Bank

(B) *In case the amalgamation is in the nature of merger and hence pooling of interets method is followed :*

1.	Business Purchase Account	Dr.	with amount of consideration
	To Liquidator of Transferor company		
2.	Various Assets taken over	Dr.	
	To Various Liabilities taken over		
	To Different Reserves of Transferor Company		
	To Business Purchase Account		with amount of consideration

Notes: (*i*) In an amalgamation in the nature of merger, all the assets, unwritten off expenses, debit balance of Profit and Loss Account, liabilities to outsiders and reserves of the transferor company have to be recorded in the books of the transferee company in the form and at the book values as they were appearing in the books of the transferor company on the date of amalgamation. However, there is an exception to this rule. If there is a conflict in the accounting policies of the transferee and transferor companies, changes in the book values may be made to ensure uniformity.

(*ii*) While passing the abovementioned entry, the difference between the amount of consideration payable by the transferee company to the transferor company and the amount of share capital of the transferor company is adjusted in the general reserves or other reserves. It is prudent that if reserves are to be decreased, revenue reserves should first be exhausted; then capital reserve and other reserves be also used. If reserves are to be increased, then if there is a debit balance of Profit and Loss Account, first that debit balance should be written off and the Capital Reserve should be credited with the remaining amount.

3. On discharge of consideration by the transferee company, the entry may be:

Liquidator of Transferor Company	Dr.	with consideration
To Bank		with cash paid
To Equity Share Capital Account		with paid-up value of equity shares allotted
To Preference Share Capital Account		with paid-up value of preference shares allotted
To Securities Premium Account		with premium charged, if any

If shares are allotted at a discount, 'Discount on Issue of Shares Account' will be debited with the amount of discount allowed. In a merger, the consideration receivable by those equity shareholders of the transferor company who agree to become equity shareholders of the transferee company is discharged by the transferee company wholly by the issue of equity shares in the transferee company, except that cash may be paid in respect of any fractional shares. But the transferee company may allot preference shares for the preference shares of the transferor company. Also, the transferee company may allot securities other than equity shares and give cash and other assets to satisfy the dissenting shareholders of the transferor company.

4. On discharge of a liability, say the debentures, of the transferor company by the transferee company directly, say, by allotment of its own debentures, the entry will be:

Debentures of Transferor Company	Dr.	with amount payable
To Debentures Account		with paid-up value of debentures allotted

5. If the transferee company bears the expenses of liquidation of the transferor company, the cost of business taken over increases by the amount of such expenses; the amount of such expenses is adjusted in the general reserve. The entry will be :

General Reserve	Dr.	with amount of expenses
To Bank		

6. The expenses incurred by the transferee company for its own formation are debited to Preliminary Expenses Account, the entry being :

Preliminary Expenses Account	Dr.	with the amount of preliminary expenses
To Bank		

Illustration 2. On 31st March, 2010 the balance sheet of X Ltd. stood as follows :

Liabilities.	*Rs.*	*Assets*	*Rs.*
Share Capital:		Plant and Machinery	16,10,000
1,50,000 Equity Shares of		Furniture and Fixtures	1,94,400
Rs. 10 each, fully paid	15,00,000	Stock	7,05,500
Securities Premium	1,50,000	Debtors	1,98,440
General Reserve	6,25,500	Cash at Bank	1,13,200
Profit & Loss Account	1,85,300		
Creditors	3,60,740		
	28,21,540		28,21,540

On this date, X Ltd. took over the business of Y Ltd. for Rs. 6,60,000 payable in the form of its fully paid equity shares of Rs. 10 each at par, shareholders of Y Ltd. getting 110 shares of X Ltd. for every 100 shares held in Y Ltd. The scheme of amalgamation also provided that 3,000 11% Debentures of Y Ltd. would be converted into equal number of 12% Debentures of X Ltd., of Rs. 100 each. The balance sheet of Y Ltd. on the date of the amalgamation was as follows :

Liabilities	*Rs.*	*Assets*	*Rs.*
Share Capital:		Machinery	5,50,000
60,000 Equity Shares of		Furniture	1,35,200
Rs. 10 each, fully paid	6,00,000	Stock	3,15,800
Capital Reserve	13,000	Debtors	1,29,300
Foreign Projects Reserve		Cash at Bank	68,260
(Statutory Reserve)	9,700	Preliminary Expenses	6,100
General Reserve	75,350		
Profit & Loss Account	24,130		
3,000 11% Debentures			
of Rs. 100 each	3,00,000		
Creditors	1,82,480		
	12,04,660		12,04,660

You are required to:

(*i*) pass journal entries in the books of X Ltd. and draw X Ltd.'s balance sheet immediately after the take over, assuming (*a*) the amalgamation is the the nature of merger, (*b*) the amalgamation is in the nature of purchase;

(*ii*) show journal entries and prepare important ledger accounts in the books of Y Ltd.

[*C.S. (Inter) Dec. 1998 Modified*]

Solution:

Books of X Ltd.

(*a*) *When the amalgamation is in the nature of merger:*

Journal

			Rs.	*Rs.*
2010 Mar. 31	Business Purchase Account	.. Dr.	6,60,000	
	To Liquidator of Y Ltd.			6,60,000
	Consideration payable to liquidator of Y Ltd. for business taken over			
" "	Machinery	.. Dr.	5,50,000	
	Furniture	.. Dr.	1,35,200	
	Stock	.. Dr.	3,15,800	
	Debtors	.. Dr.	1,29,300	
	Cash at Bank	.. Dr.	68,260	
	Preliminary Expenses	.. Dr.	6,100	
	To 11% Debentures (Y Ltd.) A/c			3,00,000
	To Creditors			1,82,480
	To Capital Reserve			13,000
	To Foreign Projects Reserve			9,700
	To General Reserve (balancing figure)			39,480
	To Business Purchase Account			6,60,000
	Incorporation of various assets and liabilities taken over from Y Ltd. and also the reserves of Y Ltd. adjusting the excess of consideration over share capital of Y Ltd. in the General Reserve.			
" "	Liquidator of Y Ltd.	.. Dr.	6,60,000	
	To Equity Share Capital Account			6,60,000
	Allotment of 66,000 equity shares of Rs.10 each fully paid at par to liquidator of Y Ltd. to discharge consideration for the business taken over			
" "	11% Debentures (Y Ltd.) Account	.. Dr.	3,00,000	
	To 12% Debentures Account			3,00,000
	Allotment of 3,000 12% debentures of Rs. 100 each in discharge of liability on 3,000 11% debentures of Y Ltd.			

Balance Sheet of X Ltd. as on 31st March, 2010

Liabilities	Rs.	Assets	Rs.
Share capital		**Fixed Assets**	
Authorised	?	Plant and Machinery	21,60,000
Issued and Subscribed:		Furniture and Fixtures	3,29,600
2,16,000 Equity Shares of		**Current Assets, Loans**	
Rs. 10 each, fully paid	21,60,000	**And Advances**	
(Of the above shares, 66,000		(A) Current Assets	
shares have been allotted		Stock	10,21,300
as fully paid up pursuant		Debtors	3,27,740
to a contract without		Cash at Bank	1,81,460
payments being received		(B) Loans and Advances	Nil
in cash)		**Miscellaneous Expenditure**	
Reserve and Surplus		Preliminary Expenses	6,100
Capital Reserve	13,000		
Securities Premium	1,50,000		
Foreign Project Reserve	9,700		
General Reserve	6,64,980		
Profit & Loss Account	1,85,300		
Secured Loans			
12% Debentures	3,00,000		
Current Liabilities and Provisions			
(A) Current Liabilities			
Creditors	5,43,220		
(B) Provisions	Nil		
	40,26,200		40,26,200

(b)When the amalgamation is in the nature of purchase:

Journal

				Rs.	Rs.
2010					
Mar. 31	Business Purchase Account ..	Dr.		6,60,00	
	To Liquidator of Y Ltd.				6,60,000
	Consideration payable to liquidator of Y Ltd. for business taken over.				
" "	Machinery ..	Dr.		5,50,000	
	Furniture ..	Dr.		1,35,200	
	Stock ..	Dr.		3,15,800	
	Debtors ..	Dr.		1,29,300	
	Cash at Bank ..	Dr.		68,260	
	To 11% Debentures (Y Ltd.) A/c				3,00,000
	To Creditors				1,82,480
	To Capital Reserve				56,080
	To Business Purchase Account				6,60,000
	Incorporation of various assets and liabilities taken over from Y. Ltd. for Rs.6,60,000; the balancing figure being credited to Capital Reserve.				
" "	Amalgamation Adjustment Account ..	Dr.		9,700	
	To Foreign Project Reserve				9,700
	Incorporation of Foreign Projects Reserve, a statutory reserve, of Y Ltd., debiting Amalgamation Adjustment Account with the amount.				

			Rs.	Rs.
" "	Liquidator of Y Ltd. .. Dr. To Equity Share Capital Account Allotment of 66,000 equity shares of Rs. 10 each fully paid at par to liquidator of Y Ltd. to discharge consideration for the business taken over.		6,60,000	6,60,000
" "	11% Debentures (Y Ltd.) Account .. Dr. To 12% Debentures Account Allotment of 3,000 12% debentures of Rs. 100 each in discharge of liability on 3,000 11% debentures of Y Ltd.		3,00,000	3,00,000

Balance Sheet of X Ltd. as on 31st March, 2010

Liabilities	*Rs.*	*Assets*	*Rs.*
Share Capital		**Fixed Assets**	
Authorised	?	Plant and Machinery	21,60,000
Issued and Subscribed:		Furniture and Fixtures	3,29,600
2,16,000 Equity Shares of Rs. 10 each, fully paid	21,60,000	**Current Assets, Loans and Advances**	
(Of the above shares, 66,000 shares have been allotted as fully paid up pursuant to a contract without payments being received in cash)		(A) Current Assets	
		Stock	10,21,300
		Debtors	3,27,740
		Cash at Bank	1,81,460
		(B) Loans and Advances	Nil
Reserves and Surplus		**Miscellaneous Expenditure**	
Capital Reserve	56,080	Amalgamation Adjustment Account	9,700
Securities Premium	1,50,000		
Foreign Projects Reserve	9,700		
General Reserve	6,25,500		
Profit and Loss Account	1,85,300		
Secured Loans			
12% Debentures	3,00,000		
Current Liabilities and Provisions			
(A) Current Liabilities			
Creditors	5,43,220		
(B) Provisions	Nil		
	40,29,800		40,29,800

Books of Y Ltd.
Journal

			Rs.	*Rs.*
2010 Mar. 31	Realisation Account .. Dr. To Machinery To Furniture To Stock To Debtors To Cash at Bank Transfer of all the assets to Realisation Account due to amalgamation.		11,98,560	 5,50,000 1,35,200 3,15,800 1,29,300 68,260
" "	11% Debentures Account .. Dr. Creditors .. Dr.		3,00,000 1,82,480	

Date	Particulars		Dr.	Cr.
	To Realisation Account Transfer of all the liabilities to Realisation Account due to amalgamation.			4,82,480
" "	X Ltd. .. Dr. To Realisation Account The amount of the consideration receivable from X Ltd. for the business sold to it as per agreement.		6,60,000	6,60,000
" "	Equity Shares in X Ltd. .. Dr. To X Ltd. Receipt of equity shares in X Ltd. in satisfaction of the consideration for the business sold to X Ltd. as per agreement.		6,60,000	6,60,000
" "	Equity Share Capital Account .. Dr. To Equity Shareholders Account Transfer of Equity Share Capital Account to Equity Shareholders Account.		6,00,000	6,00,000
" "	Equity Shareholders Account .. Dr. To Realisation Account Transfer of loss on realisation to Equity Shareholders Account.		56,080	56,080
" "	Capital Reserve .. Dr. Foreign Projects Reserve .. Dr. General Reserve .. Dr. Profit and Loss Account .. Dr. To Equity Shareholders Account Transfer of various reserves and credit balance of Profit and Loss Account to Equity Shareholders Account.		13,000 9,700 75,350 24,130	1,22,180
" "	Equity Shareholders Account .. Dr. To Preliminary Expenses Account Transfer of Preliminary Expenses Account to Equity Shareholders Account.		6,100	6,100
" "	Equity Shareholders Account .. Dr. To Equity Shares in X Ltd. Distribution of equity shares in X Ltd. among the equity shareholders to satisfy their final claim on liquidation of the company.		6,60,000	6,60,000

Ledger

Realisation Account

Dr.					*Cr.*
2010		*Rs.*	2010		*Rs.*
Mar. 31	To Machinery	5,50,000	Mar. 31	By 11% Debentures	3,00,000
	To Furniture	1,35,200		By Creditors	1,82,480
	To Stock	3,15,800		By X Ltd. (Consideration)	6,60,000
	To Debtors	1,29,300		By Equity Shareholders	
	To Cash at Bank	68,260		Account (Transfer of Loss)	56,080
		11,98,560			11,98,560

Equity Shareholders Account

Dr.					Cr.
2010		Rs.	2010		Rs.
Mar. 31	To Realisation Account	56,080	Mar. 31	By Equity Share Capital Account	6,00,000
	To Preliminary Expenses Account	6,100		By Capital Reserve	13,000
	To Equity Shares in X Ltd.	6,60,000		By Foreign Projects Reserve	9,700
				By General Reserve	75,350
				By Profit and Loss Account	24,130
		7,22,180			7,22,180

X Ltd.

Dr.					Cr.
2010		Rs.	2010		Rs.
Mar. 31	To Realisation Account	6,60,000	Mar. 31	By Equity Shares in X Ltd.	6,60,000

Equity Shares in X Ltd.

Dr.					Cr.
2010		Rs.	2010		Rs.
Mar. 31	To X Ltd.	6,60,000	Mar. 31	By Equity Shareholders	6,60,000

Illustration 3. The following are the balance sheets of X Ltd. and Y Ltd. as on 31st March, 2010 :

Liabilities	*Rs.*	*Assets*	*Rs.*
Share Capital in fully paid equity shares of Rs.10 each	15,00,000	Land and Buildings	5,60,000
Securities Premium	1,50,000	Plant and Machinery	9,42,000
General Reserve	4,70,000	Furniture	1,01,500
Profit & Loss Account	1,89,360	Stock	5,37,340
Sundry Creditors	2,33,070	Debtors	2,80,630
		Cash at Bank	1,10,960
		Cost of Issue of Shares Account	10,000
	25,42,430		25,42,430

Y Ltd.

Liabilities	*Rs.*	*Assets*	*Rs.*	*Rs.*
Share Capital:		Machinery		3,60,000
60,000 Equity Shares of Rs. 10 each, fully paid	6,00,000	Furniture and Fixtures		89.500
Capital Reserve	15,000	Stock		2,52,410
10% Debentures	2,00,000	Debtors	1,03,000	
Sundry Creditors	1,01,630	*Less:* Provision for Bad Debts	5,150	97,850
		Cash at Bank		20,340
		Profit and Loss Account		96,530
	9,16,630			9,16,630

The two companies agree to amalgamate and form a new company called Z Ltd. which takes over all the assets and liabilities of both the companies on 1st April, 2000. The consideration is agreed at Rs. 19,50,000 and Rs. 4,80,000 for X Ltd. and Y Ltd. respectively; and entire amount being payable by Z Ltd. in the form of its fully paid equity shares of Rs.10 each. Y Ltd.'s 10% debentures are converted into identical number of Z Ltd.'s 11% debentures for Rs. 2,00,000. Expenses of amalgamation amounting to Rs. 15,000 are borne by Z Ltd.

Pass journal entries and prepare important ledger accounts to close the books of X Ltd. and Y Ltd. Also pass journal entries in the books of Z Ltd. and prepare its balance sheet immediately after the amalgamation in the nature of merger.

Solution:

Books of X Ltd.

Journal

			Dr.	Cr.
			Rs.	Rs.
2010 Apr. 1	Realisation Account .. Dr. To Land and Buildings Account To Plant and Machinery Account To Furniture Account To Stock Account To Debtors To Cash of Bank Transfer of various assets at their book values of Realisation Account.		25,32,430	 5,60,000 9,42,000 1,01,500 5,37,340 2,80,630 1,10,960
" "	Sundry Creditors .. Dr. To Realisation Account Transfer of the accounts of sundry creditors to Realisation Account.		2,33,070	 2,33,070
" "	Z Ltd. .. Dr. To Realisation Account Consideration receivable from Z Ltd. for the business.		19,50,000	 19,50,000
" "	Equity Shares in Z Ltd. Account .. Dr. To Z Ltd. Receipt of fully paid 1,95,000 equity shares of Rs. 10 each from Z Ltd. in discharge of consideration for the business.		19,50,000	 19,50,000
" "	Equity Share Capital Account .. Dr. Securities Premium Account .. Dr. General Reserve Account .. Dr. Profit and Loss Account .. Dr. To Equity Shareholders Account Transfer of Equity Share Capital Account and all the reserves to Equity Shareholders Account.		15,00,000 1,50,000 4,70,000 1,89,360	 23,09,360
" "	Equity Shareholders Account .. Dr. To Cost of Issue of Shares Account Transfer of Cost of Issue of Share Account ot Equity Shareholders Account.		10,000	 10,000

			Dr.	Cr.
Apr. 1	Equity Shareholders Account .. Dr. To Realisation Account Transfer of loss on realisation to Equity Shareholders Account.		3,49,360	3,49,360
" "	Equity Shareholders Account .. Dr. To Equity Shares in Z Ltd. Account Distribution of equity shares in Z Ltd. among our shareholders.		19,50,000	19,50,000

Ledger

Realisation Account

Dr.					*Cr.*
2010		*Rs.*	2010		*Rs.*
Apr. 1	To Land and Building Account	5,60,000	Apr. 1	By Sundry Creditors	2,33,070
	To Plant and Machinery Account	9,42,000		By Z Ltd. (Consideration)	19,50,000
	To Furniture Account	1,01,500		By Equity Shareholders Account (Loss)	3,49,360
	To Stock Account	5,37,340			
	To Debtors	2,80,630			
	To Cash at Bank	1,10,960			
		25,32,430			25,32,430

Z Ltd.

Dr.					*Cr.*
2010		*Rs.*	2010		*Rs.*
Apr. 1	To Realisation Account (Consideration)	19,50,000	Apr. 1	By Equity Shares in Z Ltd. Account	19,50,000

Equity Shares in Z Ltd.

Dr.					*Cr.*
2010		*Rs.*	2010		*Rs.*
Apr. 1	To Z Ltd.	19,50,000	Apr. 1	By Equity Shareholders A/c	19,50,000

Equity Shareholders Account

Dr.					*Cr.*
2010		*Rs.*	2010		*Rs.*
Apr. 1	To Cost of Issue of Shares Account	10,000	Apr. 1	By Equity Share Capital Account	15,00,000
	To Realisation Account	3,49,360		By Securities Premium Account	1,50,000
	To Equity Shares in Z Ltd. Account	19,50,000		By General Reserve Account	4,70,000
				By Profit and Loss Account	1,89,360
		23,09,360			23,09,360

Books of Y Ltd.

Journal

Date	Particulars		L.F.	Dr.	Cr.
2010 Apr. 1	Realisation Account	.. Dr.		8,25,250	
	To Machinery Account				3,60,000
	To Furniture and Fixtures Account				89,500
	To Stock Account				2,52,410
	To Debtors				1,03,000
	To Cash at Bank				20,340
	Transfer of various assets to Realisation Account.				
" "	10% Debentures Account	.. Dr.		2,00,000	
	Sundry Creditors	.. Dr.		1,01,630	
	Provision for Bad Debts Account	.. Dr.		5,510	
	To Realisation Account				3,06,780
	Transfer of various liabilities and Provision for Bad Debts Account to Realisation Account.				
" "	Z Ltd.	.. Dr.		4,80,000	
	To Realisation Account				4,80,000
	Consideration for the business receivable from Z Ltd.				
" "	Equity Shares in Z Ltd.	.. Dr.		4,80,000	
	To Z Ltd.				4,80,000
	Equity shares in Z Ltd. recieved in satisfaction of consideration for the business.				
" "	Equity Share Capital Account	.. Dr.		6,00,000	
	Capital Reserve	.. Dr.		15,000	
	To Equity Shareholders Account				6,15,000
	Transfer of Equity Share Capital and Capital Reserve to Equity Shareholders Account.				
" "	Equity Shareholders Account	.. Dr.		96,530	
	To Profit and Loss Account				96,530
	Transfer of debit balance of Profit and Loss Account to Equity Shareholders Account.				
" "	Equity Shareholders Account	.. Dr.		38,470	
	To Realisation Account				38,470
	Transfer of loss on realisation to Equity Shareholders Account.				
" "	Equity Shareholders Account	.. Dr.		4,80,000	
	To Equity Shares in Z Ltd.				4,80,000
	Distribution of equity shares in Z Ltd. among the shareholders.				

Ledger

Realisation Account

Dr. | *Cr.*

Date	Particulars	Rs.	Date	Particulars	Rs.
2010 Apr. 1	To Machinery Account	3,60,000	2010 Apr. 1	By 10% Debentures Account	2,00,000
	To Furniture and Fixtures Account	89,500		By Sundry Creditors	1,01,630
	To Stock Account	2,52,410		By Provision for Bad Debts Account	5,150
	To Debtors	1,03,000		By Z Ltd. (Consideration)	4,80,000
	To Cash at Bank	20,340		By Equity Shareholders Account (Loss)	38,470
		8,25,250			8,25,250

Z Ltd.

Dr.					Cr.
2010		*Rs.*	2010		*Rs.*
Apr. 1	To Realisation Account (Consideration)	4,80,000	Apr. 1	By Equity Shares in Z Ltd.	4,80,000

Equity Shares in Z Ltd.

Dr.					Cr.
2010		*Rs.*	2010		*Rs.*
Apr. 1	To Z Ltd.	4,80,000	Apr. 1	By Equity Shareholders Account	4,80,000

Equity Shareholders Account

Dr.					Cr.
2010		*Rs.*	2010		*Rs.*
Apr. 1	To Profit and Loss Account	96,530	Apr. 1	By Equity Share Capital Account	6,00,000
	To Realisation Account (Loss)	38,470		By Capital Reserve Account	15,000
	To Equity Shares in Z Ltd. (Distribution)	4,80,000			
		6,15,000			6,15,000

Books of Z Ltd.

Journal

			Dr.	Cr.
2010			*Rs.*	*Rs.*
Apr. 1	Business Purchase Account .. Dr.		24,30,000	
	To Liquidator of X Ltd			19,50,000
	To Liquidator of Y Ltd.			4,80,000
	Consideration payable to liquidators of X Ltd. and Y Ltd.			
" "	Land and Buildings Account .. Dr.		5,60,000	
	Plant and Machinery Account .. Dr.		13,02,000	
	Furniture and Fixtures Account .. Dr.		1,91,000	
	Stock Account .. Dr.		7,89,750	
	Debtors .. Dr.		3,83,630	
	Cash at Bank .. Dr.		1,31,300	
	Cost of Issue of Shares Account .. Dr.		10,000	
	To 10% Debentures (Y Ltd.)			2,00,000
	To Sundry Creditors			3,34,700
	To Provision for Bad Debts Account			5,150
	To Capital Reserve Account			15,000
	To Securities Premium Account			1,50,000
	To General Reserve Account			2,32,830
	To Business Purchase Account			24,30,000
	Incorporation to assets, liabilities and reserves of X Ltd. and Y Ltd., excess of consideration over the share capitals of the transferor companies being adjusted in the general reserve.			
" "	Liquidator of X Ltd. .. Dr.		19,50,000	
	Liquidator of Y Ltd. .. Dr.		4,80,000	
	To Equity Share Capital Account			24,30,000
	Allotment of fully paid equity shares of Rs. 10 each in discharge of consideration for the net assets of X Ltd, and Y Ltd.			
" "	10% Debentures (Y Ltd.) Account .. Dr.		2,00,000	
	To 11% Debentures Account			2,00,000

			Dr.	Cr.
	Allotment of 11% debentures to discharge the liability on 10% debentures in Y Ltd.			
" "	General Reserve Account	.. Dr.	15,000	
	To Cash at Bank			15,000
	Payment of expenses relating to amalgamation.			

Balance Sheet of Z Ltd. as on 1st April, 2010

Liabilites	*Rs.*	*Assets*		*Rs.*
Share Capital		**Fixed Assets**		
Authorised	?	Land and Buildings		5,60,000
Issued and Subscribed:		Plant and Machinery		13,02,000
2,43,000 Equity Shares of Rs. 10 each fully paid (All of the above shares have been allotted as fully paid-up to vendors pursuant to a contract without payments being received in cash)	24,30,000	Furniture and Fixtures		1,91,000
		Current Assets, Loans and Advances		
		(A) Current Assets		
		Stock		7,89,750
		Debtors	3,83,630	
Reserve and Surplus		*Less:* Provision		
Capital Reserve	15,000	for Bad Debts	5,150	3,78,480
Securities Premium	1,50,000	Cash at Bank		1,16,300
General Reserve	2,17,830	(B) Loans and Advances		Nil
Secured Loans		**Miscellaneous Expenditure**		
11% Debentures	2,00,000	Cost of Issue of Shares		10,000
Current Liabilities and Provisions				
(A) Current Liablities				
Sundery Creditors	3,34,700			
(B) Provisions	Nil			
	33,47,530			33,47,530

Illustration 4. On 31st March, 2010, Thin Ltd. was absorbed by Thick Ltd., the latter taking over all the assets and liabilities of the former at book values. The consideration for the business was fixed at Rs. 40 crore to be discharged by the transferee company in the form of its fully paid equity shares of Rs. 10 each, to be distributed among the shareholders of the transferor company, each shareholder getting two shares for every share held in the transferor company. The balance sheets of the two companies as on 31st March, 2010 stood as under :

Liabilities	*Thick Ltd.*	*Thin Ltd.*	*Assets*	*Thick Ltd.*	*Thin Ltd.*
	Rs. '000	*Rs. '000*		*Rs. '000*	*Rs.'000*
Share Capital :			Goodwill	2,00,000	60,000
Authorised	15,00,000	5,00,000	Plant and Machinery	4,12,000	1,00,000
Issued and subscribed:			Furniture	80,000	30,000
Equity Shares of Rs. 10			Stock-in-trade	2,65,500	60,000
each, fully paid	9,00,000	2,00,000	Sundry Debtors	2,21,200	46,000
General Reserve	1,80,000	50,000	Prepaid Insurance	—	700
Profit & Loss A/c	20,502	12,900	Income-tax Refund		
Workmen Compensation			Claim	—	6,000
Fund	12,000	9,000	Cash in hand	869	356
Sundry Creditors	58,567	30,456	Cash at Bank	14,000	8,300
Staff Provident Fund	10,200	4,000			
Provision for Taxation	12,300	5,000			
	11,93,569	3,11,356		11,93,569	3,11,356

Amalgamation expenses amouting to Rs. 10 lakh were paid by Thick Ltd. You are required to:

(*i*) show the necessary ledger accounts in the books of Thin Ltd.,

(*ii*) show the necessary journal entries in the books of Thick Ltd., and

(*iii*) prepare the balance sheet of Thick Ltd. after the amalgamation.

[*Adatped(C.S. Inter) June 1998*]

Solution :

In Thin Ltd.'s Ledger

Realisation Account

Dr.					*Cr.*
2010		*Rs. '000*	2010		*Rs. '000*
Mar. 31	To Goodwill	60,000	Mar. 31	By Sundry Creditors	30,456
	To Plant and Machinery	1,00,000		By Staff Provident Fund	4,000
	To Furniture	30,000		By Provision for Taxation	5,000
	To Stock-in trade	60,000		By Thick Ltd. (Consideration)	4,00,000
	To Sundry Debtors	46,000			
	To Prepaid Insurance	700			
	To Income-Tax Refund Claim	6,000			
	To Cash in hand	356			
	To Cash at Bank	8,300			
	To Equity Shareholders Account—transfer of profit	1,28,100			
		4,39,456			4,39,456

Thick Ltd.

Dr.					*Cr.*
2010		*Rs. '000*	2010		*Rs. '000*
Mar. 31	To Realisation Account (Consideration)	4,00,000	Mar 31	By Equity Shares in Thick Ltd.	4,00,000

Equity Shares in Thick Ltd.

Dr.					*Cr.*
2010		*Rs. '000*	2010		*Rs. '000*
Mar. 31	To Thick Ltd.	4,00,000	Mar. 31	By Equity Shareholders A/c	4,00,000

Equity Shareholders Account

Dr.					*Cr.*
2010		*Rs. '000*	2010		*Rs. '000*
Mar. 31	To Equity Shares in Thick Ltd.	4,00,000	Mar. 31	By Equity Share Capital A/c	2,00,000
				By General Reserve	50,000
				By Profit and Loss A/c	12,900
				By Workmen Compensation Fund	9,000
				By Realisation A/c (Profit)	1,28,100
		4,00,000			4,00,000

Books of Thick Ltd

Journal

			Dr.	*Cr.*
2010			*Rs. '000*	*Rs. '000*
Mar. 31	Business Purchase Account .. Dr.		4,00,000	
	To Liquidator of Thin Ltd.			4,00,000
	Consideration payable for Thin Ltd.'s business taken over on amalgamation as per agreement dated....			

"	"	Goodwill ..	Dr.	60,000	
		Plant and Machinery ..	Dr.	1,00,000	
		Furniture ..	Dr.	30,000	
		Stock-in-trade ..	Dr.	60,000	
		Sundry Debtors ..	Dr.	46,000	
		Prepaid Insurance ..	Dr.	700	
		Income-tax Refund Claim ..	Dr.	6,000	
		Cash in hand ..	Dr.	356	
		Cash in Bank ..	Dr.	8,300	
		General Reserve ..	Dr.	1,37,100	
		To Workmen Compensation Fund			9,000
		To Sundry Creditors			30,456
		To Staff Provident Fund			4,000
		To Provision for Taxation			5,000
		To Business Purchase Account			4,00,000
		Incorporation of all the assets, liablities and reserve of Thin Ltd. at book values on amalgamation; the excess of consideration over the share capital of the transferor company being adjusted in general reserve.			
"	"	Liquidator of Thin Ltd. ..	Dr.	4,00,000	
		To Equity Share Capital Account			4,00,000
		Allotment of 40,000 equity shares of Rs. 10 each, fully paid in discharge of consideration for Thin Ltd.'s business taken over on amalgamation.			
"	"	General Reserve ..	Dr.	1,000	
		To Bank			1,000
		Payment of amalgamation expenses.			

Working Notes: (*i*) Calculation of the amount adjusted in general reserve of the transferee company:

	Rs. '000	*Rs. '000*
Consideration for Thin Ltd.'s business		4,00,000
Less: Equity Share Capital of Thin Ltd.		2,00,000
		2,00,000
Less: Thin Ltd.'s General Reserve	50,000	
Thin Ltd.'s Profit & Loss Account	12,900	62,900
Amount debited to Thick Ltd.'s General Reserve		1,37,100

(*ii*) Balance of Thick Ltd.'s General Reserve:

Balance before amalgamation		1,80,000
Less: Debit as per working note above	1,37,100	
Amalagmation expenses debited to General Reserve	1,000	1,38,100
Balance after amalgamation		41,900

(*iii*) Balance of Cash at Bank = Rs. (14,000 + 8,300 – 1,000) thousand

= Rs. 21,300 thousand

Balance Sheet of Thick Ltd. as on 31st March, 2010

Liabilities	*Rs. '000*	*Assets*	*Rs. '000*
Shares Capital		**Fixed Assets**	
Authorised	15,00,000	Goodwill	2,60,000
Issued and Subscribed:		Plant and Machinery	5,12,000
1,30,000 Equity Shares of Rs. 10 each, fully paid	13,00,000	Furniture	1,10,000
(Of the above shares, 40,000 equity shares have been allotted as fully paid-up pursuant to a contract without payments being received in cash)		**Currrent Assets, Loans and Advances**	
		(A) Current Assets	
		Stock-in-trade	3,25,500
		Sundry Debtors	2,67,200
		Cash in hand	1,225
Reserves and Surplus		Cash at Bank	21,300
General Reserve	41,900	(B) Loans and Advances	
Profit and Loss Account	20,502	Prepaid Insurance	700
Workmen Compensation Fund	21,000	Income-tax Refund Claim	6,000
Current Liabilities and Provisions			
(A) Current Liabilities			
Sundry Creditors	89,023		
(B) Provisions			
Provisions for Taxation	17,300		
Staff Provident Fund	14,200		
	15,03,925		15,03,925

Illustration 5. The balance sheets of B Ltd. and C Ltd. as on 31st March, 2010 were as follows:

(Rs. in '000)

	B Ltd. *Rs.*	*C Ltd.* *Rs.*		*B Ltd.* *Rs.*	*C Ltd.* *Rs.*
50,000 12 % Preference Shares of Rs. 100 each	5,000	—	Goodwill	—	150
			Land and Buildings	7,400	—
15,00,000 Equity Shares of Rs. 10 each	15,000	—	Plant and Machinery	16,380	—
			Furniture	270	500
4,00,000 Equity Shares of Rs.10 each	—	4,000	Patents	600	—
			Motor Vehicles	—	705
Capital Reserve	4,800	—	Stock	4,050	2,600
General Reserve	3,500	1,000	Debtors	800	1,290
Profit and Loss Account	600	150	Cash at Bank	100	155
Creditors	700	250			
	29,600	5,400		29,600	5,400

A new company, D Ltd. was formed with an authorised capital of Rs. 4 crore divided into 50,000 preference shares of Rs. 100 each and 35,00,000 equity shares of Rs. 10 each. B Ltd. and C Ltd. merged into D Ltd. on the following terms :

(*i*) D Ltd. allotted to B Ltd. 50,000 13% fully paid preference shares and 20 lakh fully paid equity shares to satisfy the claims of B Ltd.'s preference shareholders and equity shareholders respectively.

(*ii*) D Ltd. allotted to C Ltd. 4,40,000 fully paid equity shares to be distributed among C Ltd's shareholders in full satisfaction of their claims.

(*iii*) Mr. D. who mooted the scheme was allotted 5,000 fully paid equity shares in consideration of his services. The company debited the amount to Preliminary Expenses Account.

(*iv*) Expenses on the liquidation of B Ltd. and C Ltd. totalled Rs. 3,000 and were borne by D Ltd.

D Ltd. made a public issue of 2 lakh equity shares of Rs. 10 each at a premium of Rs. 2 per share. The issue was underwritten at a commission of 2 1/2% on the issue price of the shares. The issue was fully subscribed for by the public. D Ltd. paid Rs. 85,000 in cash as its preliminary expenses.

Show important ledger account to close the books of B Ltd., pass journal entries in the books of D Ltd. and prepare D Ltd.'s balance sheet immediately after all the abovementioned transactions have been recorded.

Solution:

B Ltd.'s Ledger

Realisation Account

Dr.	*Rs.* ('000)		*Cr.* *Rs.* ('000)
To Land and Buildings	7,400	By Creditors	700
To Plant and Machinery	16,380	By D Ltd.—consideration	25,000
To Furniture	270	By Equity Shareholders Account—transfer of loss	3,900
To Patents	600		
To Stock	4,050		
To Debtors	800		
To Bank	100		
	29,600		29,600

D Ltd.

Dr.	*Rs.* ('000)		*Cr.* *Rs.* ('000)
To Realisation Account—consideration	25,000	By 13% Preference Shares in D Ltd.	5,000
		By Equity Shares in D Ltd.	20,000
	25,000		25,000

13% Preference Share in D Ltd.

Dr.	*Rs.* ('000)		*Cr.* *Rs.* ('000)
To D Ltd.	5,000	By Preference Shareholders Account—distribution	5,000

Preference Shareholders Account

Dr.	*Rs.* ('000)		*Cr.* *Rs.* ('000)
To 13% Preference Shares in D Ltd.—settlement	5,000	By 12% Preference Shares Capital Account	5,000

Equity Shares in D Ltd.

Dr.	*Rs.* ('000)		*Cr.* *Rs.* ('000)
To D Ltd.	20,000	By Equity Shareholders Account—distribution	20,000

Equity Shareholders Account

Dr.	*Rs.* ('000)		*Cr.* *Rs.* ('000)
To Realisation Account—loss	3,900	By Equity Share Capital Account	15,000
To Equity Shares in D Ltd.—settlement	20,000	By Capital Reserve	4,800
		By General Reserve	3,500
		By Profit and Loss Account	600
	23,900		23,900

D Ltd.'s JOURNAL

(Rs. in '000)

		Rs.	Rs.
Business Purchase Account	.. Dr.	29,400	
To Liquidator of B Ltd.			25,000
To Liquidator of C Ltd.			4,400
Consideration payable for business of B Ltd. and C Ltd.			
Goodwill	.. Dr.	150	
Land and Buildings	.. Dr.	7,400	
Plant and Machinery	.. Dr.	16,380	
Furniture	.. Dr.	770	
Patents	.. Dr.	600	
Motor Vehicles	.. Dr.	705	
Stock	.. Dr.	6,650	
Debtors	.. Dr.	2,090	
Bank	.. Dr.	255	
To Creditors			950
To Capital Reserve			4,650
To Business Purchase Account			29,400
Incorporation of assets, liabilities and reserves of B Ltd. and C Ltd.; Rs. 5400 the excess of total consideration paid for the two companies over the total share capitals of the two companies being adjusted against the balances of General Reserve and Profit and Loss Account and then against the balance of Capital Reserve (as explained in Working Note).			
Liquidator of B Ltd.	.. Dr.	25,000	
Liquidator of C Ltd.	.. Dr.	4,400	
To 13% Preference Share Capital Account			5,000
To Equity Share Capital Account			24,400
Allotment of 50,000 13% preference shares of Rs. 100 each and 20,00,000 equity shares of Rs. 10 each to B Ltd. and of 4,40,000 equity shares of Rs. 10 each to C. Ltd. in discharge of consideration of their business.			
Bank	.. Dr.	2,400	
To Equity Share Applications and Allotment Account			2,400
Receipt of application money @ Rs. 12 per share in respect of 2 lakh equity shares of Rs. 10 each issued at a premium of Rs. 2 per share			
Equity Share Applications and Allotment Account	.. Dr.	2,400	
To Equity Share Capital Account			2,000
To Securities Premium Account			400
Allotment of 2 lakh equity shares of Rs. 10 each at a premium of Rs. 2 per share			
Underwriting Commission Account	.. Dr.	60	
To Underwriters			60
Underwriting commission @ 2 1/2% on the issue price of the shares underwritten payable to underwriters			
Underwriters	.. Dr.	60	
To Bank			60
Payment of underwriting commission to underwriters			

			Dr.	Cr.
	Preliminary Expenses Account .. Dr. To Equity Share Capital Account Allotment of 5,000 fully paid equity share of Rs, 10 each to Mr. D. in consideration of his services		50	50
	Preliminary Expenses Account .. Dr. To Bank Preliminary expenses paid in cash		85	85
	Expenses on Liquidation of B Ltd. and C Ltd. Account .. Dr. To Bank Payment of expenses incurred on Liquidation of B Ltd. and C Ltd.		3	3
	Profit and Loss Account .. Dr. To Expenses on Liquidation of B Ltd and C Ltd. Account Transfer of Expenses on Liquidation of B Ltd. and C Ltd. Account to Profit and Loss Account		3	3

Balance Sheet of D Ltd.
as at.......

Liabilities	Rs. ('000)	*Assets*	(*Rs.*'000)
Share Capital		**Fixed Assets**	
Authorised :		Goodwill	150
50,000 Preference Shares of		Land and Buildings	7,400
Rs. 100 each	5,000	Plant and Machinery	16,380
35,00,000 Equity Shares of		Furniture	700
Rs. 10 each	35,000	Patents	600
	40,000	Motor Vehicles	705
Issued and Subscribed:		**Current Assets, Loan and Advances**	
50,000 13% Preference Shares of		(A) *Current Assets*	
Rs. 100 each, fully paid	5,000	Stock	6,650
26,45,000 Equity Shares of Rs. 10 each, fully paid	26,450	Debtors	2,090
(Of the above shares, all he preference		Cash at Bank	2,507
shares and 24,45,000 equity shares		(B) *Loans and Advances*	Nil
have been allotted as fully paid-up		**Miscellaneous Expenditure**	
pursuant to contracts without		Preliminary Expenses	135
payments being received in cash)		Underwriting Commission	60
Reserves and Surplus		**Profit and Loss Account**	3
Capital Reserve	4,650		
Securities Premium	400		
Current Liablilities and Provisions			
Current Liablilities			
Creditors	950		
(B) *Provisions*	Nil		
	37,450		37,450

Working Notes:

	Rs. ('000)	Rs. ('000)
(*i*) Consideration for B Ltd.'s business		25,000
Consideration for C Ltd.'s business		4,400
Total consideration		29,400
Less: Share Capital of B Ltd.	20,000	
Share Capital of C Ltd.	4,000	24,000
Amount to be adjusted in reservess		5,400

	Combined amount	*Adjustment*	*Balance*
	Rs. ('000)	*Rs. ('000)*	*Rs.('000)*
General Reserve, 3,500+1,000	4,500	4,500	Nil
Profit and Loss Account	750	750	Nil
Capital Reserve	4,800	150	4,650
	10,050	5,400	4,650

(ii)

Cash Book (Bank Columns Only)

Dr.			*Cr.*
	Rs. ('000)		*Rs.* ('000)
To Business Purchase Account	255	By Underwriters	60
To Equity Share Applications and Allotment Account	2,400	By Preliminary Expenses Account	85
		By Expenses on Liquidation of B Ltd. and C Ltd. Account	3
		By Balance c/d	2,507
	2,655		2,655
To Balance b/d	2,507		

(iii)

	Rs. ('000)
Amount paid to D in the form of shares	50
Preliminary expenses paid in cash	85
Total preliminary expenses	135

Illustration 6. The following are the balance sheets of Pratiksha Ltd. and Nidhi Ltd. as on 31st March, 2010:—

Balance Sheet of Pratiksha Ltd. as on 31st March, 2010

Liabilities	*Rs.in lakhs*	*Assets*	*Rs.in lakhs*
Share Capital 20 lakh Shares of Rs. 10 each	200	Fixed Assets	350
General Reserve	250	Investments	250
Profit and Loss a/c	150	Current Assets	300
Debentures	175		
Current Liabilities	125		
	900		900

Balance Sheet of Nidhi Ltd. as on 31st March, 2010

Liabilities	*Rs. in lakhs*	*Assets*	*Rs. in lakhs*
Share Capital: 9 lakh Shares of Rs. 10 each	90	Fixed Assets	150
General Reserve	50	Current Assets	100
Profit and Loss a/c	40		
Current Liabilities:			
Creditors	50		
Bills payable	20		
	250		250

Pratiksha Ltd. agrees to take over Nidhi Ltd. Find out the ratio of exchange of shares on the basis of the book values. [*Adapted C.S. (Inter) Dec., 1998*]

Solution:

Calculation of value of one share of Pratiksha Ltd.:

	Rs. in lakhs	*Rs. in lakhs*
Total assets		900
Less: Liabilities		
Debentures	175	
Current liabilities	125	300
Value of 20 lakh shares		600

Value of 1 share = Rs. $\frac{600 \text{ lakh}}{20 \text{ lakh}}$ = Rs. 30

Calculation of value of one share of Nidhi Ltd.:

	Rs. in lakhs	*Rs. in lakhs*
Total assets		250
Less: Liabilities		
Creditors	50	
Bill Payable	20	70
Value of 9 lakh shares		180

Value of 1 share = Rs. $\frac{180 \text{ lakh}}{9 \text{ lakh}}$ = Rs. 20.

Value of shares of the two companies reveal that three shares of Nidhi Ltd. are worth two shares of Pratiksha Ltd. Thus for every three shares, the shareholders of Nidhi Ltd. will get two shares in Pratiksha Ltd.

It can also be arrived at in the following manner:—

Total worth of Nidhi Ltd. = Rs. 180 lakh.

Consideration is to be discharged by Pratiksha Ltd. in the form of its shares, each worth Rs.30.

Number of shares to be allotted by Pratiksha Ltd. = $\frac{180 \text{ lakh}}{30}$ = 6 lakh

Thus, shareholder of Nidhi Ltd. will get 6 lakh shares in Pratiksha Ltd. for their 9 lakh shares in Nidhi Ltd. Thus, for every 3 shares in Nidhi Ltd., they will get 2 shares in Pratiksha Ltd.

Illustration 7. The following is balance sheet of A Ltd. as on March 31, 2010: —

Liabilities	*Rs.*	*Assets*		*Rs.*
Equity Share Capital	10,00,000	Goodwill		1,90,000
General Reserve	1,10,000	Land and Buildings		2,00,000
Workmen's Accident Compensation Reserve	50,000	Plant and Machinery		4,40,000
Profit and Loss Account	70,000	Patents and Trade Marks		30,000
Sundry Creditors	1,60,000	Stock		2,10,000
		Surdry Debtors	1,80,000	
		Less: Provision for Bad Debts	12,000	1,68,000
		Cash at Bank		1,32,000
		Preliminary Expenses		20,000
	13,90,000			13,90,000

The company is acquired by X Ltd., which pays Rs. 14,00,000 in all — Rs. 12,00,000 in fully paid Rs. 10 shares and the balance in cash. There was a contingent liability in respect of a claim for compension under the Workmen's Compensation Act. The claim was not taken over by X Ltd. and A Ltd. had to pay ultimately a sum of Rs. 20,000 against the claim. The balance sheet of X Ltd. on 31st March, 2010 was as follows :

Liabilities	*Rs.*	*Assets*	*Rs.*
Share Capital :		Goodwill	2,20,000
2,00,000 Equity Shares of Rs. 10 each	20,00,000	Land and Buildings	6,00,000
General Reserve	2,00,000	Plant and Machinery	8,00,000
Profit and Loss Account	1,00,000	Stock	5,00,000
12% Debentures	3,50,000	Sundry Debtors	3,00,000
Sundry Creditors	2,10,000	Cash at Bank	4,40,000
	28,60,000		28,60,000

The expenses of liquidation of A Ltd. came to Rs. 10,000. Draft journal entries to close the books of A Ltd., and show the important accounts. Gove journal entries in the books of X Ltd. and redraft X Ltd.'s balance sheet after the amalgamation in the nature of purchase has been completed.

Solution:

Books of A Ltd.
Journal

				Dr.	Cr.
2010				*Rs.*	*Rs.*
Mar.	31	Realisation Account .. Dr.		13,82,000	
		To Goodwill			1,90,000
		To Land and Buildings			2,00,000
		To Plant and Machinery			4,40,000
		To Patents and Trade Marks			30,000
		To Stock			2,10,000
		To Sundry Debtors			1,80,000
		To Cash at Bank			1,32,000
		Transfer of the various assets to Realisation Account on sale of business to X Ltd.			
"	"	Sundry Creditors .. Dr.		1,60,000	
		Provision for Bad Debts Account .. Dr.		12,000	
		To Realisation Account			1,72,000
		Transfer of Sundry creditors and Provision for Bad Debts Account to Realisation Account.			
"	"	X Ltd. .. Dr.		14,00,000	
		To Realisation Account			14,00,000
		Amount receivable from X Ltd. for the business sold to it.			
"	"	Shares in X Ltd. .. Dr.		12,00,000	
		Bank .. Dr.		2,00,000	
		To X Ltd.			14,00,000
		Receipt of 1,20,000 shares of Rs. 10 each and Rs. 2,00,000 in cash from X Ltd. in full settlement of the consideration for the business sold to it.			
"	"	Realisation Account .. Dr.		10,000	
		To Bank			10,000
		Expenses of liquidation.			
"	"	Workmen's Accident Compensation Reserve .. Dr.		20,000	
		To Bank			20,000
		The claim for compensation for accident paid and debited to Workmen's Accident Compensation Reserve.			

				Rs.	Rs.
"	"	Equity Share Capital Account .. Dr. To Equity Shareholders Account Transfer to Equity Share Capital Account to Equity Shareholders Account.		10,00,000	10,00,000
"	"	General Reserve .. Dr. Workmen's Accident Compensation Reserve .. Dr. Profit and Loss Account .. Dr. To Equity Shareholders Account Transfer of General Reserve, Profit & Loss Account and the balance remaining in Workmen's Accident Compensation Reserve after meeting claim for accident to Equity Shareholders Account.		1,10,000 30,000 70,000	 2,10,000
"	"	Realisation Account .. Dr. To Equity Shareholders Account Profit on realisaton transferred to Equity Shareholders Account.		1,80,000	1,80,000
"	"	Equity Shareholders Account .. Dr. To Preliminary Expenses Account Transfer of Preliminary Expenses Account to Equity Shareholders Account.		20,000	20,000
"	"	Equity Shareholders Account .. Dr. To Equity Shares in X Ltd. To Bank Distribution of equity Shares in X Ltd. and cash to settle final claim of equity shareholders		13,70,000	 12,00,000 1,70,000

Ledger Accounts

Realisation Account

Dr. Cr.

2010			Rs.	2010			Rs.
Mar.	31	To Goodwill	1,90,000	Mar.	31	By Sundry Creditors	1,60,000
		To Land and Buildings	2,00,000			By Provision for Bad Debts	12,000
		To Plant and Machinery	4,40,000			By X Ltd.(consideration)	14,00,000
		To Patents and Trade Marks	30,000				
		To Stock	2,10,000				
		To Sundry Debtors	1,80,000				
		To Cash at Bank	1,32,000				
		To Bank (Expenses)	10,000				
		To Equity Shareholders Account (Transfer of Profit)	1,80,000				
			15,72,000				15,72,000

X Ltd.

2010			Rs.	2010			Rs.
Mar.	31	To Realisation	14,00,000	Mar.	31	By Shares in X Ltd.	12,00,000
						By Bank	2,00,000
			14,00,000				14,00,000

Cash Book (Bank Columns)

Dr.							Cr.
2010			Rs.	2010			Rs.
Mar.	31	To Balance b/fd	1,32,000	Mar.	31	By Realisation A/c (Transfer)	1,32,000
		To X Ltd.	2,00,000			By Realisation A/c (Expenses)	10,000
						By Workmen's Accident Compensation Reserve	20,000
						By Equity Shareholders Account	1,70,000
			2,00,000				2,00,000

Equity Shareholders Account

2010			Rs.	2010			Rs.
Mar.	31	To Preliminary Expenses	20,000	Mar.	31	By Equity Share Capital Account	10,00,000
		To Equity Shares in X Ltd.	12,00,000			By General Reserve	1,10,000
		To Bank	1,70,000			By Workmen's Accident Compensation Reserve	30,000
						By Profit and Loss Account	70,000
						By Realisation Account	1,80,000
			13,90,000				13,90,000

Books of X Ltd.
Journal

				Dr.	Cr.
2010				Rs.	Rs.
Mar.	31	Business Purchase Account .. Dr.		14,00,000	
		To Liquidator of A Ltd.			14,00,000
		The purchase price agreed to be paid for the business of A ltd.			
"	"	Land and Buildings ... Dr.		2,00,000	
		Plant and Machinery .. Dr.		4,40,000	
		Patents and Trademarks .. Dr.		30,000	
		Stock .. Dr.		2,10,000	
		Sundry Debtors .. Dr.		1,80,000	
		Bank .. Dr.		1,32,000	
		Goodwill .. Dr.		3,80,000	
		To Sundry Creditors			1,60,000
		To Provision for Bad Debts Account			12,000
		To Business Purchase Account			14,00,000
		The various assets and liablities taken over; Goodwill being the excess of the cost of acquisition over the value of net assets other than Goodwill.			
"	"	Liquidator of A Ltd. .. Dr.		14,00,000	
		To Equity Share Capital Account			12,00,000
		To Bank			2,00,000
		Allotment of equity shares and payment of cash in satisfaction of purchase consideration of business.			

Balance Sheet of X Ltd. as on 31st March, 2010

Liabilities	*Rs.*	*Assets*		*Rs.*
Share Capital		**Fixex Assets**		
Authorised	?	Goodwill		6,00,000
Issued & Subscribed :		Land and Buildings		8,00,000
3,20,000 Equity Shares of Rs. 10		Plant and Machinery		12,40,000
each fully, paid	32,00,000	Patents and Trademarks		30,000
(Of the above shares, 1,20,000 equity		**Current Assets, Loans and Advance**		
shares have been allotted as fully		(A) Current Assets		
paid up pursuant of a contract		Stock		7,10,000
without payment being received		Sundry Debtors	4,80,000	
in cash)		*Less* : Provision for Bad		
Reserves and Surplus		Debts	12,000	4,68,000
General Reserve	2,00,000	Cash at Bank		3,72,000
Profit & Loss Account	1,00,000	(B) Loans and Advances		Nil
Secured Loans				
12% Debentures	3,50,000			
Current Liabilities and Provisions				
(A) Current Liabilities				
Sundry Creditors	3,70,000			
(B) Provisions	Nil			
	42,20,000			42,20,000

Illustration 8. The following is the Balance Sheet of S Ltd. as on March 31, 2010:—

Liabilities	*Rs.*	*Assets*	*Rs.*
65,000 Equity Shares of Rs. 10 each	6,50,000	Furniture and Fittings	85,000
2,000 12% Preference Shares of		Stock	7,20,000
Rs. 100 each	2,00,000	Debtors	1,07,000
10% Debentures	1,50,000	Expenses of Issue of Debentures	7,500
Bank Overdraft	5,000	Profit and Loss Account	3,10,500
Sundry Creditors	2,25,000		
Preference dividend in arrears			
for 3 years			
	12,30,000		12,30,000

P Ltd. takes over the company on the terms that it would:

(i) take Furniture and Fittings after depreciating the same by 10%, Stock at Rs. 6,86,850 and Debtors subject to a Provision for Bad Debts @ 5%.

(ii) take 10% Debentures.

(iii) discharge the purchase consideration by allotment of 20,000 equity shares of Rs. 10 each at an agreed value of Rs. 12 each of S Ltd. and by the payment of the balance in cash.

(iv) bear the expenses of liquidation which came to be Rs. 8,000.

Preference shareholders of S Ltd. agreed to accept Rs. 1,80,000 in full settlement of their total claim. Close the books of S Ltd. and pass journal entries in the books of P Ltd.

Solution:

Calculation of the consideration :

Assets taken over :

	Rs.	*Rs.*
Furniture and Fittings	85,000	
Less : Depreciation @ 10%	8,500	76,500
Stock		6,86,850

Debtors	1,07,000	
Less : Provision for Bad Debts @ 5%	5,350	1,01,650
		8,65,000
Less : 10% Debentures		1,50,000
Consideration		7,15,000
The consideration will be discharged as follows :		
20,000 equity shares of Rs. 10 each, valued at Rs. 12 each		2,40,000
Cash, balancing figure		4,75,000
		7,15,000

Books of S Ltd.

Realisation Account

Dr. *Cr.*

2010		*Rs.*	2010		*Rs.*
Mar. 31	To Furniture and fittings	85,000	Mar. 31	By 10% Debentures	1,50,000
	To Stock	7,20,000		By P Ltd. (Consideration)	7,15,000
	To Debtors	1,07,000		By 12% Preference Share Capital	20,000
				By Equity Shareholders Account (Loss)	27,000
		9,12,000			9,12,000

Cash Book (Bank Columns)

Dr. *Cr.*

2010		*Rs.*	2010		*Rs.*
Mar. 31	To *P* Ltd.	4,75,000	Mar. 31	By Balance b/fd	5,000
				By Sundry Creditors	2,25,000
				By 12% Preference Shareholders	1,80,000
				By Equity Shareholders	65,000
		4,75,000			4,75,000

P Ltd.

Dr. *Cr.*

2010		*Rs.*	2010		*Rs.*
Mar. 31	To Realisation Account	7,15,000	Mar. 31	By Equity Shares in P Ltd.	2,40,000
				By Bank	4,75,000
		7,15,000			7,15,000

12% Preference Share Capital Account

Dr. *Cr.*

2010		*Rs.*	2010		*Rs.*
Mar. 31	To 12% Preference Shareholders Account	1,80,000	Mar. 31	By Balance b/fd	2,00,000
	To Realisation Account	20,000			
		2,00,000			2,00,000

12% Preference Shareholders Account

Dr. *Cr.*

2010		*Rs.*	2010		*Rs.*
Mar. 31	To Bank (payments of agreed amount)	1,80,000	Mar. 31	By 12% Preference Share Capital Account	1,80,000

Equity Shareholders Account

Dr.		Rs.			Cr. Rs.
2010 Mar. 31	To Expenses of Issue of Debentures	7,500	2010 Mar. 31	By Equity Share Capital Account	6,50,000
	To Profit and Loss Account	3,10,500			
	To Realisation Account (Loss)	27,000			
	To Shares in P Ltd.	2,40,000			
	To Bank	65,000			
		6,50,000			6,50,000

Books of P Ltd.

Journal

				Dr. Rs.	Cr. Rs.
2010 Mar.	31	Business Purchase Account ..	Dr.	7,15,000	
		To Liquidator of *S* Ltd.			7,15,000
		Amount payable to Liquidator of S Ltd. for the business purchased.			
"	"	Furniture and Fittings ..	Dr.	76,500	
		Stock ..	Dr.	6,86,850	
		Debtors ..	Dr.	1,07,000	
		To Provision for Bad Debts Account			5,350
		To 10% Debentures			1,50,000
		To Business Purchase Account			7,15,000
		Incorporation of assets and liablities taken over from S Ltd.			
"	"	Liquidator of S Ltd. ..	Dr.	7,15,000	
		To Equity Share Capital Account			2,00,000
		To Securities Premium Account			40,000
		To Bank			4,75,000
		Allotment of 20,000 equity shares of Rs. 10 each at a premium of Rs. 2 per share and payment of cash to satisfy consideration			
"	"	Goodwill Account ..	Dr.	8,000	
		To Bank			8,000
		Expenses of liquidation of S Ltd. met and debited to Goodwill Account.			

Illustration 9. White Ltd. agreed to acquire the business of Green Ltd. as on March 31, 2000. The summarised balance sheet of Green Ltd. at that date was as follows :

Liabilities	*Rs.*	*Assets*	*Rs.*
Share Capital in fully paid equity shares of Rs. 10 each	6,00,000	Goodwill	1,00,000
General Reserve	1,70,000	Land and Buildings	2,30,000
Profit and Loss Account	1,10,000	Plant and Machinery	4,10,000
12% Debentures	1,00,000	Stock in Trade	1,68,000
Creditors	20,000	Debtors	36,000
		Cash at Bank	56,000
	10,00,000		10,00,000

The consideration payable by White Ltd. was agreed as follows :

(1) A cash payment equivalent to Rs. 2.50 for every Rs. 10 share in Green Ltd.

(2) The issue of 90,000 Rs. 10 equity shares, fully paid in White Ltd. having an agreed value of Rs. 15 per share.

White Ltd. also agreed to discharge the 12% Debentures of Green Ltd. at a premium of 20% by allotment of its 14% Debentures at 96 per cent.

When computing the agreed consideration, the directors of White Ltd. valued the following assets at values noted against them :

	Rs.
Land and Buildings	7,50,000
Plant and Machinery	4,50,000
Stock in Trade	1,42,000
Debtors	Subject to an allowance of 5% to cover doubtful debts

The cost of liquidation of Green Ltd. came to Rs. 5,000 which was borne by White Ltd.

Give ledger accounts to close the books of the Green Ltd. and draft journal entries required in the books of White Ltd. [*Adapted from C.A. (Eng.) Inter*]

Solution:

Calculation of the consideration:

		Rs.
Cash	60,000 × *Rs.* 2,50	1,50,000
Shares	90,000 × *Rs.* 15	13,50,000
		15,00,000
Face value of shares alloted	90,000 × *Rs.* 10	9,00,000
Securities Premium	90,000 × *Rs.* 5	4,50,000
Agreed value of shares allotted		13,50,000

Books of Green Ltd.

Realisation Account

Dr. *Cr.*

2010		*Rs.*	2010		*Rs.*
Mar. 31	To Goodwill	1,00,000	Mar. 31	By 12% Debentures	1,00,000
	To Land and Buildings	2,30,000		By Creditors	20,000
	To Plant and Machinery	4,10,000		By White Ltd.	
	To Stock in Trade	1,68,000		(Consideration)	15,00,000
	To Debtors	36,000			
	To Bank	56,000			
	To Equity Shareholders Account (Profit)	6,20,000			
		16,20,000			16,20,000

White Ltd.

Dr. *Cr.*

2010		*Rs.*	2010		*Rs.*
Mar. 31	To Realisation Account	15,00,000	Mar. 31	By Bank	1,50,000
				By Shares in White Ltd.	13,50,000
		15,00,000			15,00,000

Equity Shareholders Account

Dr.					Cr.
2010		Rs.	2010		Rs.
Mar. 31	To Bank	1,50,000	Mar. 31	By Equity Share Capital Account	6,00,000
	To Shares in White Ltd.	13,50,000		By General Reserve	1,70,000
				By Profit and Loss Account	1,10,000
				By Realisation Account (profit)	6,20,000
		15,00,000			15,00,000

Cash Book (Bank Columns)

Dr.					Cr.
2010		Rs.	2010		Rs.
Mar. 31	To Balance b/fd	56,000	Mar. 31	By Realisation Account —transfer	56,000
	To White Ltd.	1,50,000		By Equity Shareholders Account	1,50,000

BOOKS OF WHITE LTD.

			Dr. Rs.	Cr. Rs.
2010 Mar. 31	Business Purchase Account	.. Dr.	15,00,000	
	To Liquidator of Green Ltd.			15,00,000
	The consideration payable for business purchased from Green Ltd.			
	Land and Buildings	.. Dr.	7,50,000	
	Plant and Machinery	.. Dr.	4,50,000	
	Stock	.. Dr.	1,42,000	
	Debtors	.. Dr.	36,000	
	Cash at Bank	.. Dr.	56,000	
	Goodwill	.. Dr.	2,07,800	
	To 12% Debentures (Green Ltd.) Account			1,20,000
	To Creditors			20,000
	To Provision for Bad and Doubtful Debts Account			1,800
	To Business Purchase Account			15,00,000
	Incorporation of assets and liablities taken over from Green Ltd.; Goodwill is the balancing figure.			
	Liquidator of Green Ltd.	.. Dr.	15,00,000	
	To Bank			1,50,000
	To Equity Share Capital Account			9,00,000
	To Securities Premium Account			4,50,000
	Payment of cash and allotment of shares at a premium in discharage of the consideration.			
	12% Debentures (Green Ltd.) Account	.. Dr.	1,20,000	
	Discount on Issue of Debentures Account	.. Dr.	5,000	
	To 14% Debentures Account			1,25,000
	Discharge of liablity of Rs. 1,20,000 in respect of 12% Debentures of Green Ltd. by issue of 14% Debentures of the face value of Rs, 1,25,000 at a discount of 4%.			
	Securities Premium Account	.. Dr.	5,000	
	To Discount on Issue of Debentures Account			5,000
	Use of Share Premium to write off Discount of Issue of Debentures.			
	Goodwill	.. Dr.	5,000	
	To Bank			5,000
	Payment of liquidation express of Green Ltd.			

Working Note : Calculation of face value of 14% Debentures issued = Rs. 1,20,000 × 100/96 = Rs. 1,25,000

Illustration 10. The balance Sheet of *A* Ltd. as at 31st March, 2010:—

Liabilities	*Rs.*	*Assets*	*Rs.*	*Rs.*
60,000 Equity Shares of Rs. 10 each	6,00,000	Freehold Premises		2,20,000
Profit Prior to Incorporation	21,000	Machinery		1,77,000
Contingency Reserve	1,35,000	Furniture and Fittings		90,800
Profit & Loss Appropriation Account	1,26,000	Stock		3,87,400
Acceptances	20,000	Sundry Debtors	80,000	
Creditors	1,13,000	*Less*: Provision of Doubtful		
Provision for Income Tax	1,10,000	Debts	4,000	76,000
		Cash in hand		2,300
		Cash at Bank		1,56,500
		Bills Receivable		15,000
	11,25,000			11,25,000

A Ltd. was wound up as at the date of the above-noted balance sheet. *B* Ltd. took over the following assets at values noted against them :

	Rs.
Freehold Premises	4,00,000
Machinery	1,60,000
Furniture and Fittings	80,000
Stock	3,45,000
Bills Receivable	15,000

One-fourth of the consideration was satisfied by the allotment of fully paid preference shares of Rs. 100 each at par which carried 13% dividend on cumulative basis. The balance was paid in the form of *B* Ltd.'s equity shares of Rs. 10 each, Rs. 8 paid up.

Sundry debtors realised Rs. 79,500. Acceptances were settled for Rs. 19,000. Income tax authorities fixed the taxation liability at Rs. 1,11,600. Creditors were finally settled with the cash remaining after meeting liquidation expenes amounting to Rs. 4,000.

You are required to

(i) calculate the number of equity shares and preference shares to be allotted by *B* Ltd. in discharge of consideration.

(ii) Prepare the important ledger accounts in the books of *A* Ltd., and

(iii) Pass journal entries in the books of *B* Ltd.

Solution:

Calculation of consideration

Agreed values of assets taken over :

	Rs.
Freehold premises	4,00,000
Machinery	1,60,000
Furnitures and fittings	80,000
Stock	3,45,000
Bills receivable	15,000
	10,00,000

Amount paid by allotment of preference shares $= \text{Rs.}10{,}00{,}000 \times \frac{1}{4}$

$= \text{Rs. } 2{,}50{,}000$

No. of preference shares allotted $= \frac{2{,}50{,}000}{100} = 2{,}500$

Amount paid by allotment of equity shares = Rs. 10,00,000 – Rs. 2,50,000 = Rs. 7,50,000

Paid up value of one equity share = Rs. 8

Hence, the number equity shares allotted $= \frac{7,50,000}{8} = 93,750$

In A Ltd.'s Ledger

Realisation Account

Dr.					*Cr.*
2010		*Rs.*	2010		*Rs.*
Mar. 31	To Freehold Premises	2,20,000	Mar. 31	By Provision for Doubtful Debts	4,000
	To Machinery	1,77,000		By B Ltd. (Consideration)	10,00,000
	To Furniture and Fittings	90,800		By Bank (Sundry Debtors)	79,500
	To Stock	3,87,400		By Acceptances (Gain)	1,000
	To Sundry Debtors	80,000		By Creditors (Gain)	9,300
	To Bill Receivable	15,000			
	To Provision for Income Tax	1,600			
	To Bank (Expenses)	4,000			
	To Equity Shareholders Account (Profit)	1,18,000			
		10,93,800			10,93,800

Cash Book (Bank Columns Only)

Dr.					*Cr.*
2010		*Rs.*	2010		*Rs.*
Mar. 31	To Balance b/fd.	1,56,500	Mar. 31	By Acceptances	19,000
	To Cash	2,300		By Provision for Income Tax	1,11,600
	To Realisation (Sundry Debtors)	79,500		By Realisation (Expenses)	4,000
				By Creditors (Balancing Figure)	1,03,700
		2,38,300			2,38,300

Equity Shareholders Account

Dr.					*Cr.*
2010		*Rs.*	2010		*Rs.*
Mar. 31	To 13% Cumulative Preference Shares in B Ltd.	2,50,000	Mar. 31	By Equity Share Capital	6,00,000
	To Equity Shares in B Ltd.	7,50,000		By Profit Prior to Incorportion	21,000
				By Contingency Reserve	1,35,000
				By Profit & Loss Appropriation Account	1,26,000
				By Realisation Account	1,18,000
		10,00,000			10,00,000

Acceptances

Dr.					*Cr.*
2010		*Rs.*	2010		*Rs.*
Mar. 31	To Bank	19,000	Mar. 31	By Balance b/fd	20,000
	To Realisation Account	1,000			
		20,000			20,000

Provision for Income Tax

Dr.					*Cr.*
2010		*Rs.*	2010		*Rs.*
Mar. 31	To Bank	1,11,600	Mar. 31	By Balance b/fd	1,10,000
				By Realisation	1,600
		1,11,600			1,11,600

Creditors

Dr.		Rs.			Cr. Rs.
2010 Mar. 31	To Bank	1,03,700	2010 Mar. 31	By Balance b/fd	1,13,000
	To Realisation Account	9,300			
		1,13,000			1,13,000

B Ltd.

Dr.		Rs.			Cr. Rs.
2010 Mar. 31	To Realisation Account	10,00,000	2010 Mar. 31	By 13% Cumulative Preference Shares in B Ltd.	2,50,000
				By Equity Shares in B Ltd.	7,50,000
		10,00,000			10,00,000

Ltd.'s Journal

				Dr. Rs.	Cr. Rs.
2010 Mar. 31	Business Purchase Account	Dr.		10,00,000	
	To Liquidator of A Ltd.				10,00,000
	Amount payable to Liquidator of A Ltd. for assets taken over				
	Freehold Premises	Dr.		4,00,000	
	Machinery	Dr.		1,60,000	
	Furniture and Fittings	Dr.		80,000	
	Stock	Dr.		3,45,000	
	Bills Receivable	Dr.		15,000	
	To Business Purchase Account				10,00,000
	Incorporation of assets taken over from A Ltd.				
	Liquidator of A Ltd.	Dr.		10,00,000	
	To 13% Cumulative Preference Share Capital Account				2,50,000
	To Equity Share Capital Account				7,50,000
	Allotment at par of 2,500 13% cumulative preference shares of Rs. 100 each fully paid-up and 93,750 equity shares of Rs. 10 each, Rs. 8 paid-up to liquidator of A Ltd. in discharge of purchase consideration of A Ltd.'s assets taken over.				

Illustration 11. The position of two companies is as follows :

Balance Sheet of *A* Ltd. as at 1st April 2010

	Rs.		Rs.
Nominal Capital:		Goodwill	1,00,000
50,000 Shares of Rs. 10 each	5,00,000	Other Fixed Assets	3,00,000
Issued and Subscribed Capital:		Debtors and Stocks	3,50,000
50,000 Shares of Rs. 10 each	5,00,000	Profit & Loss Account	1,50,000
12% Debentures	1,00,000		
Creditors	3,00,000		
	9,00,000		9,00,000

Balance Sheet of *B* Ltd. as at 1st April, 2010

	Rs.		Rs.
Nominal Capital :		Goodwill	3,50,000
1,00,000 Shares of Rs. 10 each	10,00,000	Other Fixed Assets	5,00,000
Issued and Subscribed Capital:		Debtors and Stock	1,00,000
70,000 Shares of Rs.10 each	7,00,000	Cash of Bank	1,00,000
Profit & Loss Account	1,50,000		
Creditors	2,00,000		
	10,50,000		10,50,000

B Ltd agreed to absorb *A* Ltd. upon the following terms :—

(a) the shares in *A* Ltd. are to be considered as worth Rs. 6 each (of which the shareholders are to be paid one-quarter in cash and the balance in shares in *B* Ltd.) and the share in *B* Ltd. @ Rs. 12.50 each.

(b) The debentureholders in *A* Ltd. agreed to take Rs. 95 of 14% Debentures in *B* Ltd. for every Rs. 100 of 12 per cent Debentures held in *A* Ltd.

(c) *A* Ltd. is to be wound up.

Show the journal entries necessary to record the above in the books of both the companies and draw up a balance sheet showing the position of *B* Ltd. after the amalgamtion Costs came to Rs. 6,000 which were paid by *B* Ltd. *[Adopted from Incorp. Acctts. (Inter.)]*

Solution:

Calculation of consideration :

	Rs.
Number of shares in A Ltd. = 50,000	
Total consideration = Rs. 6 × 50,000	3,00,000
Cash to be paid = Rs. 3,00,000 × 1/4	75,000
Value of shares to be allotted = Rs. 3,00,000–Rs. 75,000	2,25,000
Number of shares to be allotted = 2,25,000 × $\frac{2}{25}$ = 18,000	

Journal of *A* Ltd.

				Dr.	Cr.
2010				Rs.	Rs.
Mar. 31	Realisation Account	Dr		7,50,000	
	To Goodwill				1,00,000
	To Other Fixed Assest				3,00,000
	To Debtors and Stock				3,50,000
	Transfer of various assets to Realiation Account on winding up of the company.				
	12% Debentures	Dr.		1,00,000	
	Creditors	Dr.		3,00,000	
	To Realisation Account				4,00,000
	Transfer of liabilities to Realisation Account				
	B Ltd.	Dr.		3,00,000	
	To Realisation Account				3,00,000
	Consideration receivable from *B*. Ltd. for business sold to it as per agreement dated......				
	Bank	Dr.		75,000	
	Shares in *B* Ltd.	Dr.		2,25,000	
	To *B* Ltd.				3,00,000
	Receipt of cash and shares from *B* Ltd. in discharge of the consideration as per agreement dated......				

			Dr.	Cr.
Mar. 31	Share Capital Account To Sundry Shareholders Account Transfer of Share Capital Account to Sundry Shareholders Account	Dr.	5,00,000	5,00,000
	Sundry Shareholders Account To Profit & Loss Account Transfer of Profit & Loss Account to Sundry Shareholders Account.	Dr.	1,50,000	1,50,000
	Sundry Shareholders Account To Realisation Account Transfer of loss on realisation of Sundry Shareholders Account.	Dr.	50,000	50,000
	Sundry Shareholders Account To Shares in *B* Ltd. To Bank Distribution of Shares in *B*. Ltd. and cash among the shareholders.	Dr.	3,00,000	2,25,000 75,000

B Ltd.'s Journal

			Dr.	Cr.
2010			Rs.	Rs.
Mar. 31	Business Purchase Account To Liquidator of *A* Ltd. The consideration of the business taken over from A Ltd. as per agreement dated......	Dr.	3,00,000	3,00,000
	Goodwill Other Fixed Assets Debtors and Stock To Business Purchase Account To Creditors To 12% Debentures (*A* Ltd.) Account Incorporation of various assets and liabilities taken over, excess of the consideration over value of net assets debited to Goodwill Account.	Dr. Dr. Dr.	45,000 3,00,000 3,50,000	 3,00,000 3,00,000 95,000
	Liquidator of *A* Ltd. To Share Capital Account To Securities Premium Account To Bank Discharge of the consideration by paying cash and alloting shares at a premium of Rs. 2,50 per share.	Dr.	3,00,000	1,80,000 45,000 75,000
	12% Debentures (*A* Ltd.) Account To 14% Debentures Account Allotment of 14% debentures to discharge the liability on 12% debentures in *A* Ltd.	Dr.	95,000	95,000
	Goodwill To Bank Expenses of winding up of *A* Ltd. debited to Goodwill Account.	Dr.	6,000	6,000

Balance Sheet of B Ltd. as on 1st April 2010

	Rs.		Rs.
Share Capital:		**Fixed Assets:**	
Authorised:		Goodwill	4,01,000
1,00,000 shares of Rs. 10 each	10,00,000	Other Fixed Assets	8,00,000
Issued and Subscribed:		**Current Assets, Loans and Advances:**	
88,000 Shares of Rs. 10 each, fully called and paid up	8,80,000	(A) Current Assets	
(Of the above shares 18,000 shares have been allotted as fully paid-up pursuant to a contract without payment being received in cash).		Debtors and Stock	4,50,000
		Cash at Bank	19,000
		(B) Loans and Advances	Nil
Reserve and Surplus:			
Securities Premium	45,000		
Profit & Loss Account	1,50,000		
Secured Loans:			
14% Debentures	95,000		
Current Liabilities & Provisions:			
(A) Current Liabilities:			
Creditors	5,00,000		
(B) Provisions	Nil		
	16,70,000		16,70,000

Illustration 12. The following are the Balance Sheets of Big Ltd. and Small Ltd. for the year endng 31st March, 2010

(Figures in crores of rupees)

	Big Ltd.	Small Ltd.
Equity share capital in equity shares of Rs. 10 each	50	40
Preference share capital in 10% preference shares of Rs. 100 each	–	60
Reserve and surplus	200	150
	250	250
Loans–Secured	100	100
Total funds	350	350
Applied for: Fixed assets at cost *less* depreciation	150	150
Current assests *less* current liabilities	200	200
	350	350

The present worth of fixed assests of Big Ltd. is Rs. 200 crore and that of Small Ltd. is Rs. 429 crore. Goodwill of Big Ltd. is Rs. 40 crore and of Small Ltd. is 75 crore.

Small Ltd. absorbs Big Ltd. by issuing equity shares at par in such a way that intrinsic net worth is maintained.

Goodwill account is not to appear in the books. Fixed assets are to appear at old figures.

(*a*) Show the balance sheet after absorption.

(*b*) Draft a statement of valuation of shares on intrinsic value basis and prove the accuracy of your workings.

[*Adapted C.A. (Final) May, 1998*]

Solution:

(a)

Small Ltd.

Balance Sheet of B Ltd. as on 1st April 2010

	Schedule No.		(Rs. in crores)
I. Sources of funds			
(1) Sharehlder's funds:			
(*a*) Capital	1	125	
(*b*) Reserves and surplus	2	375	
			500
(2) Loan funds:			
Secured loans	3		200
	Total		700
II. Appliation of funds			
(1) Fixed assets:			
Net block	4		300
(2) Investment			Nill
(3) Net current assets	5		400
	Total		700

Schedules to Accounts (Rs. in crores)

		(Rs. in crores)
	Share Capital:	
	6.5 crore equity shares of Rs. 10 each	65
	(Of the above shares, 2.5 crore equity shares are allotted as fully paid-up persuant to a contract for consideration other than cash)	
	60 lakhs 10% prference shares of Rs. 100 each	60
		125
2.	Reserves and Surplus:	
	As per last balance sheet	150
	Add: Capital reserve on absorption of Big Ltd.	225
		375
3.	Secured Loans:	
	As per last balance sheet	100
	Taken over from Big Ltd.	100
		200
4.	Fixed Assests:	
	As per last balance sheet	150
	Taken over from Big Ltd.	150
		300
5.	Net Current Assests:	
	As per last Balance Sheet	200
	Taken over from Big Ltd.	200
		400

(b) **Valuation of shares on intrinsic value basis**

(*i*)	Big Ltd.	Small Ltd.
	(Rs. in crores)	
Equity share capital	50	40
Reserves and surplus	200	150
	250	190

Goodwill agreed upon	40	75
Increase in the value of fixed assests (Present worth less book value)	50	279
	340	544

	Big Ltd.	Small Ltd.
(*ii*) Number of equity shares	5 crore	4 crore
Intrinsic value per equity share	Rs. 68	Rs. 136
(*iii*) Ratio of intrinsic value of shares in the two companies	1 : 2	

Since the shares are to be issued at par, the number of equity shares of Rs. 10 each to be issued to maintain the intrinsic net worth = 5 crore/2 = 2.5 crore.

(*iv*) Statement to prove the accuracy of workings

		(Rs. in crores)
(1) Equity share capital, after absorption		65
Reserves and surplus. after absorption		375
		440
Add: Unrecorded value of goodwill, Rs. (40 + 75) crore		115
Add: Unrecorded increment of fixed assests, Rs. (50 + 279) crore		329
		884
(2) Number of equity shares	6.5 crore	
(3) Intrinsic value of an equity share (884/6.5)	Rs. 136	

Working Note:

Calclation of capital reserve on amalgamation:

	(Rs. in crore)
Fixed assests taken over	150
Net current assests taken over	200
	350
Less: Secured loans taken over	100
Net assests taken over	250
Less: Consideration	25
Capital reserve on amalgamation	225

Illustration 13: Given below is the Balance Sheet of H Ltd. as on 31st March, 2010:

(*Amounts in lakhs oj rupees*)

Equity share capital (in equity shares of Rs. 10 each)	4.00	Block assets *less* depreciation to date	6.00
10% preference share capital	3.00	Stock and debtors	5.30
General reserve	1.00	Cash and bank	0.70
Profit and loss account	1.00		
Creditors	3.00		
	12.00		12.00

M Ltd., another existing company holds 25% of equity share capital of H Ltd. purchased at Rs. 10 per share.

It was agreed that M Ltd. should take over the entire undertaking of H Ltd. on 30.9.2000 on which date the position of current assets (except cash and bank balances) and creditors was as follows:

Stock and debtors	4 lakh
Creditors	2 lakh

Profits earned for half year ended 30.9.2010 by H Ltd. was Rs. 70,500 after charging depreciation of Rs. 32,500 on block assets. H Ltd. declared 10% dividend for 2009-2010 on 30.8.2010 and the same was paid within a week. Ignore corporate dividend tax.

Goodwill of H Ltd. was valued at Rs. 80,000 and block assets were valued at 10% over their book value as on 31.3.2000 for purposes of take over. Preference shareholders of H Ltd. will be allotted 10% preference shares of Rs. 10 each by M Ltd. Equity shareholders of H Ltd. will receive requisite number of equity shares of Rs. 10 each from M Ltd. valued at Rs. 10 per share.

(*a*) Compute the consideration for the business taken over.

(*b*) Explain how the capital reserve or goodwill, if any, will appear in the balance sheet of M Ltd., after the amalgamation in the nature of purchase.

[*C.A. (Final), Nov., 1998 Modified*]

Solution:

(a) Calculation of consideration for the business taken over:

	Rs.
Assets taken over:	
Goodwill, as agreed	80,000
Block assets at 10% over their book value as on 31.3.2009	6,60,000
Stock and debtors	4,00,000
(*i*) Cash and bank, as per working note (*i*)	1,33,000
	12,73,000
Less: Liabilities taken over:	
Creditors	2,00,000
Consideration	10,73,000

(b) **Balance Sheet of M Ltd. as at 30th September, 2009**

(*Extract*)

	Rs.	Rs.
Reserves and Surplus		
Capital Reserve	93,250	
Less: Goodwill	80,000	13,250

Working Notes:

(*i*) *Ascertainment of cash and bank balances as on 30th September, 2010*

Balance Sheet as at 30th September, 2010

Liabilities	*Rs.*	*Rs.*	*Assets*	*Rs.*	*Rs.*
Equity share capital		4,00,000	Block assets	6,00,000	
10% preference share capital		3,00,000	*Less*: Depreciation	32,500	5,67,500
General reserve		1,00,000	Stock and debtors		4,00,000
Profit and loss account:			Cash and bank		
Balance b/fd	1,00,000		— balancing figure		1,33,000
Add: Profit for 6 months	70,500				
	1,70,500				
Less: Dividends paid					
Preference 30,000					
Equity 40,000	70,000	1,00,500			
Creditors		2,00,000			
		11,00,500			11,00,500

(*ii*) *Calculation of shars allotted:*

	Rs.
Consideration	10,73,000
Less: Preference shares allotted to preference shareholders	3,00,000
	7, 73,000
Less: 25% of Rs. 7,73,000 belonging to M Ltd.	1,93,250
Amount payable to other equity shareholders	5,79,750
Number of equity shares of Rs. 10 each to be issued	57,975

(iii) Calculation of capital reserve resulting on amalgamation

	Rs.	Rs.
Net assets; shares to be allotted		10,73,000
Less: Preference shares to be allotted	3,00,000	
Equity shares to be allotted	5,79,750	
Cost of investments	1,00,000	9,79,750
Capital reserve		93,250

Alternatively, capital reserve may be calculated as follows:—

	Rs.
Value of investments, 25% of Rs. 7,73,000	1,93,250
Less: Cost of investments	1,00,000
Capital reserve	93,250

Illustration 14. The balance sheets of 'S' Ltd. and 'H' Ltd. as on 30th June, 2010 were as follows:

(Rs. in crores)

		'S' Ltd.		'H' Ltd.
Liabilities				
Equity share capital in fully paid shares of Rs. 10 each		80		25
Reserves and surplus		400		75
10% 25 lakh debentures of Rs. 100 each		–		25
Other liabilities		120		–
		600		125
Assets				
Fixed assets, at cost	200		75	
Less: Depreciation	100	100	50	25
Investments in 'H' Ltd:				
2 crore equity shares of Rs. 10 each, at cost	32			
10% 25 lakh debentures of Rs. 100 each, at cost	24	56		
Current assets	800		300	
Less: Current liabilities	356	444	200	100
		600		125

In a scheme of absorption duly approved by the court, the fixed assets of 'H' Ltd. were taken over at an agreed value of Rs. 30 crore. The current assets and all the liabilities were taken over at par. Outside shareholders of 'H' Ltd. were allotted equity shares in 'S' Ltd. at a premium of Rs. 90 per share in satisfaction of their claims in 'H' Ltd. For record in the books of 'S' Ltd., fixed assets taken over from 'H' Ltd., were revalued at Rs. 40 crore.

The scheme was put through on 1st July, 2010

(*a*) Give journal entries in the books of 'S' Ltd. to record the transactions.

(*b*) Show the balance sheet of 'S' Ltd. after absorption of 'H' Ltd.

[*C.A. (Final) Nov. 1997 Modified*]

Solution:

Journal of S Ltd.

		Dr. Rs. in crores	Cr. Rs. in crores
Business Purchase Account	...Dr.	21.0	
To Liquidator of H Ltd.			21.0
Consideration payable to Liquidator of H Ltd. for business taken over.			

Fixed Assets	...Dr.	40.0	
Current Assets	...Dr.	300.0	
To Liability for debentures			25.0
To Current liabilities			200.0
To Investment in equity shares of H Ltd.			32.0
To Business purchase			21.0
To Capital reserve			62.0
Incorporation of assets and liabilities taken over from H Ltd., cancellation of investments in equity shares of H Ltd. on take-over; capital reserve being credited with balancing figure.			
Liability for debentures	...Dr.	25.0	
To Investments in debentures in H Ltd.			24.0
To Capital reserve			1.0
Cancellation of investments in debentures in H Ltd. against liability on debentures taken over from H Ltd.; capital reserve being credited with the profit on the cancellation.			
Liquidator of H Ltd.	...Dr.	21.0	
To Equity share capital			2.1
To Securities premium			18.9
Allotment of 21 lakh equity shares of Rs. 10 each at a premium of Rs. 90 each in discharge of consideration for H Ltd. business.			

Balance Sheet of S Ltd. as at 1st July, 2010

Liabilities	*Rs. in crores*	*Assets*		*Rs.in crores*
Share Capital		**Fixex Assets**		
Authorised	?	Fixed Assets	200.0	
Issued and subscribed		*Less:* Depreciation	100.0	
821 lakh equity shares of Rs. 10 each fully paid up	82.1	*Add:* Fixed assets taken over from H Ltd.	40.0	140.0
(Of the above shares, 21 lakh equity shares are allotted as fully paid up permanent to a contract without payment being received in cach)		**Current Assets, Loan and Advances**		
		Current Assets		1100.0
Reserves and Surplus				
As per last balance sheet	400.0			
Capital Reserve	63.0			
Securities Premium	18.9			
Other Liabilities	120.0			
Current Liabilities and Provision				
Current Liabilities	556.0			
	1240.0			1240.0

Working Note:

Calculation of consideration payable:	*Rs. in Crores*
Amount at which fixed assets were taken over	30
Add: Current assets	300
	330

	Rs. in crores	
Less: 10% debentures	25	
Current liabilities	200	225
		105
Less: S Ltd.'s share, 80% of Rs. 105 crore, as S Ltd. holds 2 crore shares out of 2.5 crore shares of H Ltd.		84
Payable for outside shareholders		21

As consideration is payable in the form S Ltd.'s shares of Rs. 10 each at a premium of Rs. 90 per share, number of shares to be allotted = $\frac{21 \text{ crore}}{100}$ = 21 lakh.

Illustration 15. X Ltd. was incorporated for taking over the business of Mr. X with effect from 1st April,2010. On 31st March,2010, the balance sheet of Mr. X was as follows :

Liabilities	*Rs.*	*Assets*	*Rs.*
Capital	5,04,000	Land and buildings	8,00,000
Loan Creditor	6,00,000	Plant and Machinery	2,80,000
Trade Creditor	3,56,000	Furniture	1,00,000
		Stock	70,400
		Trade Debtors	2,09,600
	14,60,000		14,60,000

The company took over the business on the following terms :

(i) The fixed assets be taken over at 90% of their book values.

(ii) Stock be valued at Rs. 56,000.

(iii) The company would realise trade debtors and pay to trade creditors on behalf of Mr. X for a commission @3% on the amount collected and 2% on the amount paid.

The company realised Rs. 1,90,000 from trade debtors as the agent of the vendor in full settlement and discharged all the trade creditors by paying Rs. 3,40,000 only. Necessary bank overdraft was arranged.

The loan creditor accepted from X Ltd. fully paid 12% preference shares of Rs. 100 each at par in discharge of his claim. After realisation of the debts and payment of the liabilities, the amount due to Mr. X was discharged by allotment of 35,000 fully paid equity shares of Rs. 10 each at par and payment of cash for the balance.

You are required to ascertain the consideration and pass journal entries in the books of the company. [*Co. Sec. (Inter) Dec. 2000*]

Solution :

(i) *Calculation of consideration :*

Assets taken over :	Rs.
Land and Buildings, 90% of Rs. 8,00,000	7,20,000
Plant and Machinery, 90% of Rs. 2,80,000	2,52,000
Furniture, 90% of Rs. 1,00,000	90,000
Stock	56,000
	11,18,000
Less : Loan creditor	6,00,000
	5,18,000

Working Notes :

(i) *Calculation of amount recoverable by X Ltd. on account of creditors etc.*	Rs.
Amount paid to creditors	3,40,000
Add : Commission @2% on Rs. 3,40,000	6,800
Commission @3% on Rs. 1,90,000 collected from debtors	5,700

	3,52,500
Less : Amount collected as agent from debtors	1,90,000
Net amount recoverable	1,62,500
(ii) *Calculation of cash paid to Mr. X in settlement :*	
Consideration	5,18,000
Less : Amount recoverable as per W.N. (i) above	1,62,500
	3,55,500
Less : Value of shares allotted to Mr.X : 35,000 ´ Rs. 10	3,50,000
	5,500

X's Journal

2010 Apr. 1	Business Purchase Account	..Dr.		5,18,000	
	To Mr. X				5,18,000
	Consideration payable to Mr. X for the business taken over from him.				
	Land and Buildings	.. Dr.		7,20,000	
	Plant and Machinery	.. Dr.		2,52,000	
	Furniture	.. Dr.		90,000	
	Stock	.. Dr.		56,000	
	To Loan Creditor				6,00,000
	To Business Purchase Account				5,18,000
	Incorporation of assets and liabilities taken over from Mr. X.				
	Vendor's Debtors	.. Dr.		2,09,600	
	To Vendor's Suspense Account				2,09,600
	Mr. X's debtors to be collected on his behalf.				
	Vendor's Suspense Account	.. Dr.		3,56,000	
	To Vendor's Creditors				3,56,000
	Mr. X's creditors to be paid on his behalf.				
	Loan Creditor	.. Dr.		6,00,000	
	To 12% Preference Share Capital A/c				6,00,000
	Allotment of 12% preference shares in satisfaction of claims by loan creditor.				
	Bank	.. Dr.		1,90,000	
	To Vendor's Debtors				1,90,000
	Amount collected from Mr. X's debtors.				
	Vendor's Suspense Account	.. Dr.		19,600	
	To Vendor's Debtors				19,600
	Amount of Mr. X's debtors not recovered being written back.				
	Vendor's Creditors	.. Dr.		3,40,000	
	To Bank				3,40,000
	Payment made to Mr. X's creditors.				
	Vendor's Creditors	.. Dr.		16,000	
	To Vendor's Suspense Account				16,000
	Gain on payment to Mr. X's creditors.				
	Vendor's Suspense Account	.. Dr.		12,500	
	To Commission / Profit and Loss Account				12,500
	Commission @2% on Rs. 3,40,000 and @3% on Rs. 1,90,000 receivable from Mr. X.				

Mr. X .. Dr.		1,62,500	
To Vendor's Suspense Account			1,62,500
Net amount recoverable form Mr. X on account of his debtors and creditors.			
Mr. X .. Dr.		3,55,000	
To Equity Share Capital Account			3,50,000
To Bank			5,500
Allotment of 35,000 fully paid equity shares of Rs. 10 each and payment of Rs. 5,500 in cash to Mr. X to clear his account.			

External Reconstruction

Reconstruction means reorganisation of a company's financial structure. In reconstruction of a company, usually the assets and liabilities of the company are revalued, the losses suffered by the company are written off by a deduction of the paid-up value of shares and/or varying of the rights attached to different classes of shares and compounding with the creditors. It may be done without liquidating the company and forming a new company in which case the process is called internal reconstruction which we have discussed in chapter 20. However, there may be external reconstruction in which case the undertaking being carried on by the company is transferred to a newly started company consisting substantially of the same shareholders with a view to the business of the transferor company being continued by the transferee company. An attempt is made that the newly started company has a sound financial structure and a good set of assets and liabilities recorded in the books of the transferee company at their fair values.

Distinction between external reconstruction and amalgamation:

From the point of view of an accountant, external reconstruction is similar to amalgamation in the nature of purchase; the books of the transferor company are closed and in the books of the transferee company, the purchase of the business is recorded. But otherwise external reconstruction and amalgamation differ as follows :

(i) In external reconstruction, only one existing company is involved whereas in amalgamation, there are at least two existing companies which amalgamate.

(ii) In external reconstruction, a new company is certainly formed whereas in amalgamation a new company may be formed or in the alternative one of the exiting companies may take over the other amalgamating company or companies and no new company may be formed.

(iii) The objective of external reconstruction is to reorganise the fianacial structure of the company. On the other hand, the objective of amalgamation is to cut competition and reap the economies of large scale.

Illustration 16. On 31st March, 2010 the balance sheet of H Ltd. was as follows :—

Liabilities	*Rs.*	*Assets*	*Rs.*
Share Capital		Goodwill	4,00,000
50,000 12% Cumulative		Plant and Machinery	7,00,000
Preference Shares of		Furniture and Fixtures	2,00,000
Rs. 10 each, fully paid	5,00,000	Patents	1,50,000
1,50,000 Equity Shares of Rs. 10		Stock	4,90,000
each, fully paid	15,00,000	Debtors	2,55,000
10% Debentures	3,00,000	Bank	5,000
Creditors	2,00,000	Preliminary Expenses	8,000
Preference dividends		Discount on Issue of Debentures	12,000
in arrear for 3 years		Profit and Loss Account	2,80,000
	25,00,000		25,00,000

The following scheme of external reconstruction was agreed upon:

(i) A new company to be formed called J Ltd. with an authorised capital of Rs. 32,50,000 in equity shares of Rs. 10 each.

(ii) One equity share, Rs. 5 paid up, in the new company to be allotted for each equity share in the old company.

(iii) Two equity shares, Rs. 5 paid-up, in the new company to be allotted for each preference share in the old company.

(iv) Arrears of preference dividends to be cancelled.

(v) Debentureholders to recieve 30,000 equity shares in the new company credited as fully paid.

(vi) Creditors to be taken over by the new company.

(vii) The remaining unissued shares to be taken up and paid for in full by the directors.

(viii) The new company to take over the old company's assets except patents, subject to writing down plant and machinery by Rs. 2,90,000 and stock by Rs. 60,000.

(ix) Patents were realised by H Ltd. for Rs. 10,000.

Show important ledger accounts in the books of H Ltd. and open the books of J Ltd. by means of journal entries and give the initial balance sheet of J Ltd. Expenses of H Ltd. came of Rs. 10,000.

(B.Com. Delhi 2004 Modified)

Solution:

Calculation of the consideration

	Number of shares allotted	*Amount credited as paid*	*Total Amount Rs.*
Allotment to:			
12% Cumulative Preference Shareholders (50,000 × 2)	1,00,000	5	5,00,000
Equity Shareholders (1,50,000 × 1)	1,50,000	5	7,50,000
Total	2,50,000		12,50,000

Books of H Ltd.

Realisation Account

Dr.					*Cr.*
2010		*Rs.*	**2010**		*Rs.*
Mar. 31	To Goodwill	4,00,000	Mar. 31	By 10% Debentures	3,00,000
	To Plant and Machinery	7,00,000		By Creditors	2,00,000
	To Furniture and Fixtures	2,00,000		By J Ltd. (consideration)	12,50,000
	To patents	1,50,000		By Bank (sale proceeds of patents)	10,000
	To Stock	4,90,000		By Equity Shareholders Account (loss)	4,50,000
	To Debtors	2,55,000			
	To Bank	5,000			
	To Bank (realisation expenses)	10,000			
		22,10,000			22,10,000

J Ltd.

Dr.					*Cr.*
2010		*Rs.*	2010		*Rs.*
Mar. 31	To Realisation Account	12,50,000	Mar. 31	By Equity Shares in J Ltd. (Rs.5 paid up)	12,50,000

Equity Shares in J Ltd. (Rs. 5 paid up)

Dr.					Cr.
2010		Rs.	2010		Rs.
Mar. 31	To J Ltd.	12,50,000	Mar. 31	By 12% Cumulative Preference Shareholders Account	5,00,000
				By Equity Shareholders Account	7,50,000
		12,50,000			12,50,000

12% Cumulative Preference Shareholders Account

Dr.					Cr.
2010		Rs.	2010		Rs.
Mar. 31	To Equity Shares in J Ltd. (Rs. 5 paid up)	5,00,000	Mar. 31	By 12% Cumulative Preference Share Capital Account	5,00,000

Cash Book (Bank Columns)

Dr.					Cr.
2010		Rs.	2010		Rs.
Mar. 31	To Balance b/fd	5,000	Mar. 31	By Realisation Account (transfer)	5,000
	To Realisation Account (patents)	10,000		By Realisation Account (expenses)	10,000

Equity Shareholders Account

Dr.					Cr.
2010		Rs.	2010		Rs.
Mar. 31	To Preliminary Expenese	8,000	Mar. 31	By Equity Share Capital Account	15,00,000
	To Discount on Issue of Shares	12,000			
	To Profit and Loss Account	2,80,000			
	To Realisation Account (loss)	4,50,000			
	To Equity Shares in J Ltd. (Rs. 5 paid up)	7,50,000			
		15,00,000			15,00,000

Books of J Ltd
Journal

Date		Particulars			Dr. Rs.	Cr. Rs.
2010 Mar.	31	Business Purchase Account	Dr.		12,50,000	
		To Liquidator of H Ltd.				12,50,000
		Amount payable to liquidator of H Ltd. for the business purchased.				
"	"	Plant and Machinery	Dr.		4,10,000	
		Furniture and Fixtures	Dr.		2,00,000	
		Stock	Dr.		4,30,000	
		Debtors	Dr.		2,55,000	
		Bank	Dr.		5,000	

				Rs.	Rs.
		Goodwill	Dr.	4,50,000	
		To 10% Debentures (H Ltd.) Account			3,00,000
		To Sundry Creditors			2,00,000
		To Business Purchase Account			12,50,000
		Incorporation of assets and liabilities taken over from H Ltd.			
Mar	31	Liquidator of H Ltd.	Dr.	12,50,000	
		To Equity Share Capital (Rs. 5 paid-up) Account			12,50,000
		Allotment of 2,50,000 equity shares of Rs. 10 each Rs. 5 paid up at par to discharge consideration.			
"	"	10% Debentures (H Ltd.) Account	Dr.	3,00,000	
		To Equity Share Capital (fully paid-up) Account			3,00,000
		Allotment of 30,000 equity shares Rs. 10 each fully paid-up at par to discharge the liability on 10% Debentures of H Ltd.			
"	"	Bank	Dr.	4,50,000	
		To Equity Share Capital Account			4,50,000
		Allotment of 45,000 equity shares of Rs. 10 each, fully paid-up to directors for cash.			

Balance Sheet of J Ltd. as on 31st March, 2010

Liabilities	*Rs.*	*Assets*	*Rs.*
Share Capital		**Fixed Assets**	
Authorised, Issued and Subscribed :		Goodwill	4,50,000
2,50,000 equity shares of Rs. 10 each		Plant and Machinery	4,10,000
Rs. 5 paid-up	12,50,000	Furniture and fixtures	2,00,000
75,000 equity shares of Rs. 10			
each, fully paid-up	7,50,000	**Current Assets, Loans and Advances**	
(Of the above shares, 30,000		(A) Current Assets	
shares have been allotted		Stock	4,30,000
as fully paid-up and 2,50,000		Debtors	2,55,000
equity shares have been alloted		Cash at Bank	4,55,000
as Rs. 5 paid up pursuant to a			
contract without payment being		(B) Loans and Advances	Nil
received in cash)			
Current Liabilities and Provisions			
(A) Current Liabilities			
Creditors	2,00,000		
(B) Provisions	Nil		
	22,00,000		22,00,000

Illustration 17. The abridged balance sheet of P Ltd. as at 31st March 2010 is as under:

Liabilities	*Rs.*	*Assets*	*Rs.*
5,000 Equity Shares of Rs. 100 each fully paid up	5,00,000	Freehold Premises	2,50,000
2,000 11% Preference Shares of Rs. 100 each, fully paid up	2,00,000	Machinery	1,35,000
15% Debentures	2,00,000	Patents	70,000
Outstanding Interest on Debentures	30,000	Stock	2,00,000
Unsecured Loan	1,00,000	Debtors	1,80,000
Creditors	1,50,000	Bank	50,000
		Profit and Loss Account	2,95,000
	11,80,000		11,80,000

The following scheme of reconstruction was passed by the company and approved by the Court:—

(i) A new company PK Ltd. to be formed to take over the entire business of P Ltd.

(ii) PK Ltd. to issue one equity share of Rs. 100, Rs. 60 paid up in exchange of every two shares in P Ltd. to the shareholders who agree with the scheme. Shareholders, who do not agree with the scheme, to be paid @ Rs. 20 per share in cash. Such shareholders hold 400 equity shares.

(iii) Preference shareholders to get fifteen 12% preference shares of Rs. 10 each in exchange of two preference shares of P Ltd.

(iv) Liability in respect of 15% debentures and outstanding interest thereon to be taken over and discharged directly by PK Ltd. by issue of equity shares of Rs. 100 each, fully paid uP

(v) PK Ltd. to discharge unsecured loan by allotment to lender 1000 fully paid equity shares of Rs. 100 each.

(vi) The creditors of P Ltd. to get from PK Ltd. 50% of their dues in cash and 25% in fully paid equity shares of Rs. 100 each and the balance to be forgone by them.

(vii) The freehold premises to be revalued at 20% more. The value of machinery to be reduced by $33\frac{1}{3}$% and that of debtors by 10%. The value of assets to be reduced to Rs. 1,60,000. Patents to have no value.

To facilitate the implementation of the reconstruction-scheme, PK Ltd. issued for cash 8,000 equity shares of Rs. 100 each, the entire amount being payable along with applications. The issue was fully subscribed for.

Preliminary expenses amounted is Rs. 5,000.

Show important ledger accounts in the boks of P Ltd. and pass journal entries in the books of PK Ltd. *[B.Com (Hons.) Delhi, 1997 Modified]*

Solution:

Calculation of consideration — *Rs.*

Paid-up value of equity shares issued

$= \text{Rs. } 60 \times \frac{(5{,}000 - 400)}{2} = \text{Rs. } 60 \times 2{,}300$ — 1,38,000

Paid-up value of 12% preference shares issued

$= \text{Rs. } 10 \times \left(\frac{2{,}000}{2} \times 15\right) = \text{Rs. } 10 \times 15{,}000$ — 1,50,000

2,88,000

In P Ltd.'s Ledger

Realisation Account

Dr.	Rs.		*Cr.* Rs.
To Freehold Premises	2,50,000	By 15% Debetors	2,00,000
To Machinery	1,35,000	By Outstanding Interest on Debtors	30,000
To Patents	70,000	By Unsecured Loan	1,00,000
To Stock	2,00,000	By Creditors	1,50,000
To Debtors	1,80,000	By PK Ltd. (consideration)	2,88,000
To Bank		By Dissentient Shareholders Account	32,000
(Rs. 50,000 – Rs. 8,000)	42,000	By 11% Preference Shareholders Account (Gain)	50,000
		By Equity Shareholders Account (Transfer of loss)	27,000
	8,77,000		8,77,000

PK Ltd.

Dr.	Rs.		Cr. Rs.
To Realisation Account (Consideration)	2,96,000	By Equity Shares in PK Ltd.	1,38,000
		By Bank (Cash for dissenting shareholders)	8,000
		By 12% Preference Shares in PK Ltd.	1,50,000
	2,96,000		2,96,000

11% Preference Shareholders Account

Dr.	Rs.		Cr. Rs.
To 12% Preference Shares in PK Ltd. (Distribution)	1,50,000	By 11% Preference Share Capital Account	2,00,000
To Realisation Account (Transfer of balance)	50,000		
	2,00,000		2,00,000

Dissentient Shareholders Account

Dr.	Rs.		Cr. Rs.
To Bank	8,000	By Equity Share Capital Account	40,000
To Realisation A/c-transfer	32,000		
	40,000		40,000

Equity Shareholders Account

Dr.	Rs.		Cr. Rs.
To Profit and Loss Account	2,95,000	By Equity Share Capital Account	4,60,000
To Realisation Account (Loss)	27,000		
To Equity Shares in PK Ltd. (Distribution)	1,38,000		
	4,60,000		4,60,000

PK Ltd.'s Journal

Dr.				Dr. Rs.	Cr. Rs.
2010 Mar.	31	Business Purchase Account	...Dr.	2,88,000	
		To Liquidator of P Ltd.			2,88,000
		Consideration payable for P Ltd. business			
		Freehold Premises	...Dr.	3,00,000	
		Machinery	...Dr.	90,000	
		Debtors	...Dr.	1,80,000	
		Stock	...Dr.	1,60,000	
		Bank	...Dr.	42,000	
		To Provision for bad debts account			18,000
		To 15% Debentures (P Ltd.) Account			2,00,000
		To Outstanding Interest on Debetures (P Ltd.) Account			30,000
		To Unsecured Loan (P Ltd.) Account			1,00,000
		To Creditors (P Ltd.)			1,12,500
		To Business Purchase Account			2,88,000
		To Capital Reserve			23,500
		Incorporation of various assets and liabilities taken over from P Ltd.; capital profit on take over being credited to Capital Reserve			

Particulars		Dr. (Rs.)	Cr. (Rs.)
Liquidator of P Ltd. ...Dr. To Equity Share Capital Account To 12% Preference Share Capital Allotment of 2,300 equity shares of Rs. 100 each, Rs. 60 per share paid-up and 15,000 12% preference shares of Rs. 10 each, fully paid up		2,88,000	 1,38,000 1,50,000
Bank ...Dr. To Equity share applications and allotment account Receipt of application money on 8,000 equity shares @ Rs. 100 per share		80,000	 80,000
Equity share applications and allotment account ...Dr. To Equity share capital account Allotment of 8,000 equity shares of Rs. 100 each on fully paid up		80,000	 80,000
15% Debentures (P Ltd.) account ...Dr. Outstanding interest on debentures (P Ltd.) account ...Dr. To Equity share capital account Allotment of 2,300 fully paid equity shares of Rs. 100 each in discharge of total liability in respect of 15% debentures in P Ltd.		2,00,000 30,000	 2,30,000
Unsecured loan (P Ltd.) account ...Dr. To Equity share capital account Discharge of unsecured loan taken over from P Ltd. by allotment to the lender 1,000 fully paid equity shares of Rs. 100 each		1,00,000	 1,00,000
Creditors (P Ltd.) ...Dr. To Bank To Equity share capital account Payment of Rs. 75,000 in cash and allotment of 375 fully paid equity shares of Rs. 100 each in discharge of liability towards creditors in P Ltd.		1,12,500	 75,000 37,500
Preliminary expenses account ...Dr. To Bank Payment of preliminary expenses		5,000	 5,000

Illustration 18. The following is the summarised balance sheet as on March 31, 2010 of Bharat Ltd:—

Liabilities	*Rs.*	*Rs.*	*Assets*	*Rs.*
Share Capital			Goodwill	2,00,000
Authorised, issued and fully paid-up :			Tangible Fixed Assets	12,00,000
25,000 12% Cumulative			Balance at Bank	10,000
Preference Shares of Rs. 20 each		5,00,000	Other Current Assets	4,60,000
60,000 Equity Shares of Rs. 20 each		12,00,000	Preliminary Expenses	20,000
10% Debentures	2,00,000		Profit and Loss Account	2,60,000
Interest thereon	20,000	2,20,000		
Creditors		2,30,000		
		21,50,000		21,50,000

Note: The dividend on the preference shares in arrears is Rs. 1,80,000.

The following scheme of external reconstruction was agreed to by all parties and the necessary sanction obtained:

A new company Navbharat Ltd. was to be registered with a capital of 1,50,000 shares of Rs. 10 each to acquire as from April 1, 2000 the undertaking and assets of the old company for a consideration to be satisfied partly in cash and partly in the shares of the new company to implement the following terms:

(1) The new company to assume the old company's debenture liability by issuing to the holders corresponding debentures in the new company, together with one fully paid equity share in the new company for every Rs. 10 of interest in arrears.

(2) The creditors of the old company agree to forego 10% of the amount due to them, the balance to be paid in cash by Navbharat Ltd. immediately.

(3) The preference shareholders in the old company to receive two fully paid equity shares in the new company for each share held in the old company; further the arrears of preference dividend to be satisfied by the issue of one fully paid equity share in the new company for every Rs. 50 due. (Ignore corporate dividend tax).

(4) The equity shareholders in the old company to receive one fully paid equity share in the new company for every three shares held.

(5) Costs amounting to Rs. 20,000 to be borne by the new company.

It was agreed that current assets should be taken into the new company's books at the values in the old company's books (except that stock was to be reduced by Rs. 10,000): goodwill was to be eliminated and the tangible fixed assets were valued at Rs. 7,23,000.

The new company allotted 30,000 equity shares at par for cash to some of the old shareholders of Bharat Ltd.

You are required to give:

(a) in the old company's books, necessary ledger accounts.

(b) in respect of the new company *(i)* journal entries to record all the transactions and *(ii)* a summarised balance sheet.

Solution:

Books of Bharat Ltd.

Realisation Account

Dr.					Cr.
2010		*Rs.*	2010		*Rs.*
Mar. 31	To Goodwill	2,00,000	Mar. 31	By 10% Debentures	2,00,000
	To Other Fixed Assets	12,00,000		By Outstanding Interest on Debentures	20,000
	To Balance at Bank	10,000		By Creditors	2,30,000
	To Other Current Assets	4,60,000		By New Bharat Ltd. —consideration	7,36,000
	To Preference Shareholders —settlement of arrears of preference dividend	36,000		By Equity Shareholders Accounts—loss	7,20,000
		19,06,00			19,06,000

Nav Bharat Ltd.

Dr.					Cr.
2010		*Rs.*	2010		*Rs.*
Mar. 31	To Realisation Account	7,36,000	Mar. 31	By Equity Shares in Nav Bharat Ltd.	7,36,000

Equity Shares in Nav Bharat Ltd.

Dr.					Cr.
2010		*Rs.*	2010		*Rs.*
Mar. 31	To Nav Bharat Ltd.	7,36,000	Mar. 31	By Preference Shareholders Account	5,36,000
				By Equity Shareholders Account	2,00,000
		7,36,000			7,36,000

Preference Shareholders Account

Dr.		Rs.			Cr. Rs.
2010 Mar. 31	To Equity Shares in Nav Bharat Ltd.	5,36,000	2010 Mar. 31	By 12% Cumulative Preference Share Capital Account	5,00,000
				By Realisation Account— for arrears of dividend	36,000
		5,36,000			5,36,000

Equity Shareholders Account

Dr.		Rs.			Cr. Rs.
2010 Mar. 31	To Preliminary Expenses	20,000	2010 Mar. 31	By Equity Share Capital Account	12,00,000
	To Profit and Loss Account	2,60,000			
	To Realisation Account (loss)	7,20.000			
	To Equity Shares in Nav Bharat Ltd.	2,00,000			
		12,00,000			12,00,000

Books of Nav Bharat Ltd.

Journal

Date		Particulars		Dr.	Cr.
2010 Mar.	31	Business Purchase Account .. Dr.		7,36,000	
		To Liquidator of Bharat Ltd.			7,36,000
		Consideration payable for the business taken over from Bharat Ltd.			
"	"	Tangible Fixed Assets .. Dr.		7,23,000	
		Balance at Bank .. Dr.		10,000	
		Other Current Assets .. Dr.		4,50,000	
		To 10% Debentures (Bharat Ltd.) Account			2,20,000
		To Creditors			2,07,000
		To Business Purchase Account			7,36,000
		To Capital Reserve			20,000
		Assets and liabilities taken over from Bharat Ltd., balance being credited to Capital Reserve.			
"	"	Liquidator of Bharat Ltd. .. Dr.		7,36,000	
		To Equity Share Capital Account			7,36,000
		Allotment of 73,600 equity shares of Rs. 10 each fully paid to Bharat Ltd. in discharge of consideration for the business taken over.			
"	"	10% Debentures (Bharat Ltd.) Account .. Dr.		2,20,000	
		To 10% Debentures Account			2,00,000
		To Equity Share Capital Account			20,000
		Allotment of 10% debentures in discharge of principal amount and 2,000 equity shares of Rs.10 each in discharge of outstanding interest amount regarding 10% debentures in Bharat Ltd.			
"	"	Bank .. Dr.		3,00,000	
		To Equity Share Capital Account			3,00,000
		Allotment for cash 30,000 Equity shares of Rs. 10 each at par			

"	"	Capital Reserve .. Dr. To Bank Payment of cost of the scheme.		20,000	20,000
"	"	Creditors .. Dr. To Bank Discharge of liability towards creditors		2,07,000	2,07,000

Balance Sheet of Nav Bharat Ltd. as on April 1, 2010.

Liabilities	*Rs.*	*Assets*		*Rs.*
Share Capital				
Authorised:		Tangible Fixed Assets		7,23,000
1,50,000 Equity Shares of Rs.10 each	15,00,000	Current Assets:		
Issued and Subscribed:		Balance at Bank	83,000	
1,05,600 Equity Shares of Rs.10 each, fully paid	10,56,000	Other Current Assets	4,50,000	5,33,000
(Of the above shares, 75,600 equity shares of Rs.10 each have been allotted as fully paid up pursuant to a contract for consideration other than cash)				
10% Debentures	2,00,000			
	12,56,000			12,56,000

Working Notes: (i) Calculation of consideration :

	Rs.
For 25,000 preference shares = 25,000 × 2 × Rs. 10	5,00,000
For arrears of preference dividend = $\frac{1,80,000}{50}$ × Rs. 10	36,000
For 60,000 equity shares = Rs. 10 × $\frac{60,000}{3}$	2,00,000
	7,36,000

Dr. **Cash Book (Bank Columns)** *Cr.*

	Rs.		*Rs.*
To Business Purchase Account	10,000	By Capital Reserve— expenses	20,000
To Equity Share Capital Account	3,00,000	By Creditors	2,07,000
		By Balance c/d	8,30,000
	3,10,000		3,10,000
To Balance b/d	8,30,000		

(iii)

	Amount Rs.
Equity shares issued to satisfy shareholders	7,36,000
Equity shares issued to discharge debenture interest liability	20,000
Equity shares issued for cash	3,00,000
Total	10,56,000

Dissenting Shareholders

In an amalgamation, some shareholders of the transferee company may not assent to the scheme of amalgamation and may refuse to transfer their shares to the transferee company in accordance with the scheme. Such shareholders are called dissenting shareholders. According to section

395 (5) (a) of the Companies Act, "dissenting shareholder" includes a shareholder who has not assented to the scheme or contract and any shareholder who has failed to transfer his shares to the transferee company in accordance with the scheme of contract. Here the terms scheme and contract refer to the scheme of amalgamation. According to section 395 (2) (*a*) and (*b*) of the Companies Act, the shares of dissenting shareholders may be acquired by the amalgamated company (transferee company) as follows:

(*i*) on the same terms on which the assenting shareholders transfered their shares; or

(*ii*) on other terms agreed upon between the amalgamated company and dissenting shareholders; or

(*iii*) on terms ordered by the court on an application made either by the amalgamated company or the dissenting shareholders.

In case where a separate settlement for dissenting shareholders is made, in the books of the transferor company, the paid up share capital held by the dissenting shareholders is transferred to a separate account called Dissenting Shareholders Account. Any premium the dissenting shareholders receive or discount they suffer as per agreement or order of the Court is also recorded in Dissenting Shareholders Account, the dual aspect being completed by the corresponding debit or credit to Realisation Account, as the case may require. Dissenting Shareholders Account will be closed on the satisfaction of the dissenting shareholders' claim. The profit or loss revealed by Realisation Account and all other accounts pertaining to accumulated profit and losses will be transferred as usual to Sundry Shareholders Account pertaining to assenting shareholders.

Illustration 19. The United Mills Limited took over the business of the Bharat Hosiery Ltd. with effect from 31st October, 2009. The following was the balance sheet of the Bharat Hosiery Ltd. as at the date:

Liabilities	*Rs.*	*Assets*		*Rs.*
12,000 Shares of Rs. 50 each, fully paid-up	6,00,000	Land and Buildings		1,80,000
		Plant and Machinery		1,00,000
Reserve	1,20,000	Furniture		25,000
Profit and Loss Account	65,000	Stock		2,50,000
Creditors	75,000	Debtors	2,90,000	
		Less : Provision for Bad Debts	10,000	2,80,000
		Cash at Bank		25,000
	8,60,000			8,60,000

The transferee company took over all the assets and liabilities of the transferor company except a sum of Rs. 10,000 to provide for the cost of liquidation and payment to dissentient shareholders, if any. The purchase price was discharged by the allotment to the shareholders of the transferor company of one share of Rs. 100 (Rs. 90 paid- up) of the United Mills Ltd. for every two shares in the Bharat Hosiery Ltd. The expenses of liquidation amounted to Rs. 3,000. Dissentient shareholders of 100 shares were paid at Rs.70 per share.

Pass the necessary journal entries in the books of the respective companies to give effect to the above transactions and show Realisation Account and Equity Shareholders Account in Bharat Hosiery Ltd.'s ledger.

[Adapted from B. Com., (Delhi)]

Solution :

Calculation of consideration :

Shares :

11,900 × 1/2 × Rs. 90 = Rs. 5,35,500

[One share to be allotted in United Mills Ltd. of Rs. 100 (Rs.90 paid-up) for every two shares held in Bharat Hosiery Ltd. to willing shareholders]

Books of Bharat Hosiery Ltd.
Journal

Date		Particulars		L.F.	Dr. Rs.	Cr. Rs.
2009 Oct.	31	Realisation Account	Dr.		8,60,000	
		To Land and Buildings				1,80,000
		To Plant and Machiery				1,00,000
		To Furniture				25,000
		To Stock				2,50,000
		To Debtors				2,90,000
		To Cash at Bank				15,000
		Transfer of all the assets except a sum of Rs. 10,000 to provide for cost of liquidation and payment to any dissentient shareholders to Realisation Account due to sale of the business to United Mills Ltd. as per agreement.				
"	"	Creditors	Dr.		75,000	
		Provision for Bad Debts	Dr.		10,000	
		To Realisation Account				85,000
		Transfer of Creditors and Provision for Bad Debts to Realisation Account as the same are taken over by United Mills as per agreement.				
"	"	United Mills Ltd.	Dr.		5,35,500	
		To Realisation Account				5,35,500
		The consideration receivable from United Mills Ltd.				
"	"	Shares in United Mills Ltd.	Dr.		5,35,500	
		To United Mills Ltd.				5,35,500
		Receipt of 5,950 equity shares of Rs. 100 each (Rs. 90 paid up) in United Mills Ltd. in satisfaction of the consideration.				
"	"	Realisation Account	Dr.		3,000	
		To Bank Account				3,000
		Payment of liquidation expenses.				
"	"	Share Capital Account	Dr.		5,000	
		Realisation Account	Dr.		2,000	
		To Dissentient Shareholders Account				7,000
		Amount payable to dissentient shareholders @ Rs. 70 per share for 100 shares, the loss on payment Rs. 2,000 being debited to Realisation Account.				
"	"	Dissentient Shareholders Account	Dr.		7,000	
		To Bank				7,000
		Payment to dissentient shareholders				
"	"	Realisation Account	Dr.		2,44,500	
		To Sundry Shareholders Account				2,44,500
		Transfer of loss on realisation to Sundry Shareholders Account				
"	"	Share Capital Account	Dr.		5,95,000	
		Reserve	Dr.		1,20,000	
		Profit and Loss Account			65,000	
		To Sundry Shareholders Account				7,80,000
		Transfer of balance of Share Capital, Reserves and Profit and Loss Account to Sundry Shareholders Account.				
"	"	Sundry Shareholders Account	Dr.		5,35,500	
		To Shares in United Mills ltd.				5,35,500
		Distribution of 5,950 shares of Rs. 100 (Rs. 90 paid-up) among the equity shareholders to satisfy their final claims on liquidation of the company.				

Books of United Mills Ltd.
Journal

				Rs.	Rs.
2009 Oct.	31	Business Purchase Account	Dr.	5,35,500	
		To Liquidator of Bharat Hosiery Ltd.			5,35,500
		The purchase of business of Bharat Hosiery Ltd. as per agreement dated.....			
"	"	Land and Buildings	Dr.	1,80,000	
		Plant and Machinery	Dr.	1,00,000	
		Furniture	Dr.	25,000	
		Stock	Dr.	2,50,000	
		Debtors	Dr.	2,90,000	
		Cash at Bank	Dr.	15,000	
		To Creditors			75,000
		To Provision for Bad Debts			10,000
		To Business Purchase Account			5,35,500
		To Capital Reserve			2,39,500
		The various assets and liabilities acquired from Bharat Hosiery Ltd., Capital Reserve being the difference.			
"	"	Liquidator of Bharat Hosiery Ltd.	Dr.	5,35,500	
		To Share Capital Account			5,35,500
		The allotment of 5,950 share of Rs. 100 each (Rs. 90 paid up) in satisfaction of the consideration.			

Illustration 20. Big Ltd. has agreed to acquuire all the assets excluding investments and bank balance of Small Ltd. as at 31st March, 2010. The balance sheet of Small Ltd. as at that date is as below :

Liabilities	*Rs. (in lacs)*	*Assets*	*Rs. (in lacs)*
Equity Share Capital (Rs.10)	160	Goodwill	50
General Reserve	25	Land and Buildings	80
Profit and Loss Account	18	Plant	80
12% Debtenture	60	Investments	30
Sundry Creditors	37	Stock	40
Provision for Taxation	20	Debtors	20
		Bank	20
	320		320

Big Ltd will :

(i) discharge the Debentures at 8% premium by issue of 14% Debentures in Big Ltd. at 10% discount,

(ii) issue 3 equity shares of Big Ltd. at a valuation of Rs. 11 for 2 equity shares of Small Ltd.,

(iii) pay Rs. 2 in cash for each share of Small Ltd., and

(iv) pay amalgamation expenses of Rs.3,00,000.

Small Ltd. sells investments for Rs. 32 lakh. One-third of the shares received from Big Ltd. are sold at Rs. 10.50 each. Tax liability was determined at Rs. 24 lakh. Before transfer, Small Ltd. declares and pays 10% dividend. Small Ltd. is then dissolved. Big Ltd. values land and buildings at Rs. 100 lakh, plant at 10% below book value, stock at Rs. 35 lakh and debtors subject to 10% provision for doubtful debts. Assume that there is no dividend tax.

Show *(a)* ledger accounts in the books of Small Ltd. *(b)* journal entries in the books of Big Ltd.

[Adapted Co. Sec. (Inter) Dec. 1982)

Solution :

Calculation of the consideration:

Form		*Amount* (Rs. in lacs)
Shares	Rs. 160 × 3/2 × 11/10	264
Cash	Rs.16 × 2	32
		296

Books of Small Ltd.

Realisation Account

Dr.					*Cr.*
2010		*Rs.* (in lacs)	2010		*Rs.* (in lacs)
Mar. 31	To Goodwill	50	Mar. 31	By 12% Debentures	60
	To Land and Building	80		By Big Ltd. (consideration)	296
	To Plant	80		By Bank (sale of investment)	32
	To Investments	30		By Big Ltd. (expenses)	3
	To Stock	40			
	To Debtors	20			
	To Bank (expenses)	3			
	To Shares in Big Ltd. (loss on sale)	4			
	To Equity Shareholdes Account (profit)	84			
		391			391

Big Ltd.

Dr.					*Cr.*
2010		*Rs.* (in lacs)	2010		*Rs.* (in lacs)
Mar. 31	To Realisation Account (consideration)	296	Mar. 31	By Shares in Big Ltd.	264
	To Realisation Account (expenses)	3		By Bank	35
		299			299

Cash Book (Bank Columns)

Dr.					*Cr.*
2010		*Rs.* (in lacs)	2010		*Rs.* (in lacs)
Mar. 31	To Balance b/fd	20	Mar. 31	By Dividend Payable Account	16
	To Big Ltd.	35		By Realisation Account (expenses)	3
	To Realisation Account (sale of investments)	32		By Tax Payable Account	24
	To Shares in Big Ltd. (sale of 8,00,000 shares @ Rs. 10.50 per share)	84		By Sundry Creditors	37
				By Equity Shareholders Account	91
		171			171

Provision for Tax

Dr.					*Cr.*
2010		*Rs.* (in lacs)	2010		*Rs.* (in lacs)
Mar. 31	To Tax Payable Account	24	Mar. 31	By Balance b/fd	20
				By Equity Shareholders Account (transfer)	4
		24			24

Tax Payable Account

		Rs. (in lacs)			Rs. (in lacs)
2010			2010		
Mar. 31	To Bank	24	Mar. 31	By Provision for Tax	24

Dividend Payable Account

		Rs. (in lacs)			Rs. (in lacs)
2010			2010		
Mar. 31	To Bank	16	Mar. 31	By Profit and Loss Account	16

Equity Shares in Big Ltd.

		Rs. (in lacs)			Rs. (in lacs)
2010			2010		
Mar. 31	To Big Ltd.	264	Mar. 31	By Bank (sale proceeds of 8,00,000 shares @ Rs. 10.50 per share)	84
				By Realisation Account (loss on sale)	4
				By Equity Shareholders Account	176
		264			264

Equity Shareholders Account

		Rs. (in lacs)			Rs. (in lacs)
2010			2010		
Mar. 31	To Provision for Tax	4	Mar. 31	By Equity Share Capital	160
	To Bank	91		By General Reserve	25
	To Equity Shares in Big Ltd.	176		By Profit and Loss Account	2
				By Realisation Account	84
		271			271

Books of Big Ltd. (Rs. in lakhs)

Journal

				Dr.	Cr.
2010				Rs.	Rs.
Mar.	31	Business Purchase Account	Dr.	296.00	
		To Liquidator of Small Ltd.			296.00
		Consideration agreed to be paid for the business of Small Ltd.			
"	"	Land and Buildings	Dr.	100.00	
		Plant	Dr.	72.00	
		Stock	Dr.	35.00	
		Debtors	Dr.	20.00	
		Goodwill	Dr.	135.00	
		To Business Purchase Account			296.00
		To Provision Doubtful Debts Account			2.00
		To Debentures (Small Ltd.) Account			64.80
		The various assets and liabilities taken over — goodwill being the excess of the cost of acquisition over the value of net assets other than goodwill.			
"	"	Liquidator of Small Ltd.	Dr.	296.00	
		To Equity Share Capital Account			240.00
		To Securities Premium Account			24.00
		To Bank			32.00

		Allotment of equity shares and payment of cash in satisfaction of the consideration.			
"	"	Debentures (Small Ltd.) Account	Dr.	64.80	
		Discount on Issue of Debentures Account	Dr.	7.20	
		To 10% Debentures Account			72.00
		Allotment of 14% debentures of the face value of 72 lakh at a discount of 10% to discharge the liability of Rs. 64.80 lakh on the debentures of Small Ltd.			
"	"	Goodwill	Dr.	3.00	
		To Bank			3.00
		Payment of expenses regarding amalgamation			

Illustration 21. The following are the balance sheets of *A* Ltd. and *B* Ltd. as on 31st March, 2010:—

	A Ltd (*Rs.*)	*B Ltd.* (*Rs.*)		*A Ltd.* (*Rs.*)	*B Ltd.* (*Rs.*)
Share Capital:			Goodwill	20,000	—
5,000 Shares of Rs. 100 each	5,00,000	—	Other Fixed Assets	8,30,000	16,00,000
80,000 Shares of Rs. 10 each	—	8,00,000	Investments	1,70,000	—
Capital Reserve	1,00,000	—	Current Assets	6,90,000	16,80,000
General Reserve	3,60,000	10,00,000			
Secured Loans	—	4,00,000			
Unsecured Loans	2,20,000	—			
Creditors	4,20,000	4,60,000			
Provision for Tax	1,10,000	5,20,000			
Proposed Dividend	—	1,00,000			
	17,10,000	32,80,000		17,10,000	32,80,000

B Ltd. took over *A* Ltd. with effect from 31st March, 2010.

For the purpose of purchase, the Goodwill of *A* Ltd. was considered valueless. *A* Ltd. had arrears of depreciation amounting to Rs. 40,000.

The shareholders of *A* Ltd. are allotted, in full satisfaction of their claims, shares in *B* Ltd. in the same proportion as the respective intrinsic value of the shares of the two companies bear to each other.

Close the books of *A* Ltd. by preparing the necessary ledger accounts and pass journal entries in the books of *B* Ltd. regarding purchase of *A* Ltd's. business. Ignore corporate dividend tax. *[Adapted B.Com. (Hons.) Delhi, 1988]*

Solution:

Intrinsic values of shares:	*Rs.*	*A Ltd.*		*B Ltd.*
Fixed assets		7,90,000		16,00,000
Investments		1,70,000		—
Current assets		6,90,000		16,80,000
		16,50,000		32,80,000
Less: Liabilities				
Secured loans	—		4,00,000	
Unsecured loans	2,20,000		—	
Creditors	4,20,000		4,60,000	
Provision of tax	1,10,000		5,20,000	
Proposed dividend	—	7,50,000	1,00,000	14,80,000
Total intrinsic values		9,00,000		18,00,000

Value of one share $\text{Rs. } \frac{9,00,000}{5,000} = \text{Rs. } 180$ $\quad \text{Rs. } \frac{18,00,000}{80,000} = \text{Rs. } 22.50$

For every share in *A* LTd. will allot eight shares.

Books of *A* Ltd.

Realisation Account

Dr.					Cr.
2010		Rs.	2010		Rs.
Mar. 31	To Goodwill	20,000	Mar.31	By Unsecured Loans	2,20,000
	To Other Fixed Assets	8,30,000		By Creditors	4,20,000
	To Investments	1,70,000		By Provision for Tax	1,10,000
	To Current Assets	6,90,000		By B Ltd — Consideration	9,00,000
				By Sundry Shareholders Account—Loss	60,000
		17,10,000			17,10,000

***B* Ltd.**

Dr.					Cr.
2010		Rs.	2010		Rs.
Mar. 31	To Realisation Account	9,00,000	Mar. 31	By Shares in B Ltd.	9,00,000

Shares in *B* Ltd.

Dr.					Cr.
2010		Rs.	2010		Rs.
Mar. 31	To B Ltd.	9,00,000	Mar. 31	By Sundry Shareholders Account	9,00,000

Sundry Shareholders Account

Dr.					Cr.
2010		Rs.	2010		Rs.
Mar. 31	To Realisation Account — Loss	60,000	Mar. 31	By Share Capital Account	5,00,000
	To Shares in B Ltd.	9,00,000		By Capital Reserve	1,00,000
				By General Reserve	3,60,000
		9,60,000			9,60,000

Books of *B* Ltd.

Journal

				Dr.	Cr.
2010				Rs.	Rs.
Mar.	31	Business Purchase Account	Dr.	9,00,000	
		To Liquidator of *A* Ltd.			9,00,000
		Amount payable to liquidator of *A* Ltd. for the business purchased.			
		Fixed Assets	Dr.	7,90,000	
		Investments	Dr.	1,70,000	
		Current Assets	Dr.	6,90,000	
		To Unsecured Loans			2,20,000
		To Creditors			4,20,000
		To Provision for Tax			1,10,000
		To Business Purchase Account			9,00,000
		Incorporation of assets and liabilities taken from *A* Ltd.			
		Liquidator of A Ltd.	Dr.	9,00,000	
		To Share Capital Account			4,00,000
		To Securities Premium Account			5,00,000
		Allotment of 40,000 shares of Rs. 10 each at a premium of Rs. 12.50 per share in discharge of consideration			

Illustration 22. The balance sheets of Rama Ltd. and Krishna (Pvt.) Ltd. as on 31 March, 2009 were as follows:

Liabilities	*Rama* *Rs.*	*Krishna* *Rs.*	*Assets*	*Rama* *Rs.*	*Krishna* *Rs.*
Share Capital :			Fixed Assets (other than		
Equity Shares of			goodwill)	5,00,000	3,50,000
Rs. 10 each	6,00,000	4,00,000	Stock-in-trade	95,000	75,000
Reserves	1,50,000	1,00,000	Debtors	1,40,000	1,00,000
Profit and Loss Account	75,000	60,000	Cash and Bank	1,17,500	60,000
Sundry Creditors	37,500	30,000	Preliminary Expenses	10,000	5,000
	8,62,500	5,90,000		8,62,500	5,90,000

Rama Ltd. took over Krishna (Pvt.) Ltd. as on 1st October, 2009. No balance sheet of Krishna (Pvt.) Ltd. was prepared on the date of take over. But the following information is made available to you:

(i) In the six months ended 30th September, 2009 Krishna (Pvt.) Ltd. made net profits of Rs. 60,000 after providing for depreciation at 10% per annum of fixed assets.

(ii) Rama Ltd., during that period had made net profits of Rs, 1,45,000 after providing for depreciation at 10% per annum on fixed assets.

(iii) Both the companies had distributed dividend of 10% on 1st July, 2009. Assume that there was no corporate dividend tax.

(iv) Goodwill of Krishna (Pvt.) Ltd., on the date of take over was estimated at Rs. 25,000 and it was agreed that the stocks of Krishna (Pvt.) Ltd. would be appreciated by Rs. 15,000 on the date of take over.

(v) Rama Ltd. to issue shares to shareholders of Krishna (Pvt.) Ltd. on the basis of the intrinsic values of the shares on the date of take over.

Draft the balance sheet of Rama Ltd. after the take over. *[Adapted C.A. (Inter,) Nov. 1981]*

Solution:

Balance Sheet of Rama Ltd. [after absorption of Krishna (Pvt.) Ltd.]
as at 1st October, 2009

	Rs.		*Rs.*	*Rs.*
Share Capital :		**Fixed Assets :**		
Issued & Subscribed		Goodwill		25,000
1,01,000 equity shares of Rs. 10 each,		Other Fixed Assets		
fully paid	10,10,000	Cost	5,00,000	
(Of the above, 41,000 shares have		Addition during the year	3,32,500	
been allotted as fully paid to vendor			8,32,500	
pursuant to a contract without		*Less* : Depreciation	25,000	8,07,500
payment being received in cash)				
Reserves and Surplus:		**Current Assets, Loans and Advances:**		
Securities Premium	2,05,000	(A) Current Assets		
Reserves	1,50,000	Stock-in-trade		1,85,000
Profit and Loss Account	1,60,000	Sundry Debtors		2,40,000
Current Liabilities & Provisions:		Cash in hand and at Bank		3,25,000
(A) Current Liabilities		(B) Loans and Advances		Nil
Sundry Creditors	67,500	**Miscellaneous Expenditure:**		
(B) Provisions	Nil	Preliminary Expenses		10,000
	15,92,500			15,92,500

Working Notes:

(i) Net assets of Rama Ltd. and Krishna Ltd. as on 30 September, 2009:—

	Rama Ltd. *Rs.*	*Krishna (Pvt.) Ltd.* *Rs.*
Goodwill	—	25,000
Other Fixed Assets	4,75,000	3,32,500
Debtors	1,40,000	1,00,000

Stock-in-trade	95,000	90,000
Cash & Bank*	2,27,500	97,500
	9,37,500	6,45,000
Less: Sundry Creditors	37,500	30,000
	9,00,000	6,15,000
(ii) Book value per share:		
Net Assets	9,00,000	6,15,000
No. of shares	60,000	40,000
Book value (Net Assets ÷ No. of shares)	15	15.125
(iii) Opening Cash & Bank Balance	1,17,500	60,000
Add : Net Profit	1,45,000	60,000
Add : Depreciation	25,000	17,500
	2,87,500	1,37,500
Less : Dividend paid	60,000	40,000
Closing Cash & Bank Balance*	2,27,500	97,500

In the absence of information about changes in other assets, it is assumed that the profit has resulted in cash only.

(iv) Net assets of Krishna (Pvt.) Ltd. as on 30th September, 2009 are worth Rs. 6,15,000. Rama Ltd. will issue 41,000 shares of Rs. 10 each at a premium of Rs. 5 per share in settlement of consideration.

Inter-company Owings

At the time of amalgamation, amounts owing by the transferee company to the transferor company, or *vice versa,* have to be eliminated. If P Ltd. acquires the business of S Ltd. and the latter company owes as a book debt Rs. 40,000 to the former company, then after the amalgamation, Sundry Debtors Account and Sundry Creditors Account should show the net figures after deduction of Rs. 40,000. Entries in case of S Ltd. are not affected and have to be passed as detailed earlier. Entries in case of P Ltd. would also be the same as discussed earlier but an additional entry is required. The entry is :

Sundry Creditors Account Dr.
  To Sundry Debtors Account

The treatment is exactly the same if the transferee company owed money to the transferor company.

Similar problem arises when at the time of amalgamation, the transferee company holds bills receivable accepted by the transferee company or *vice versa.* After amalgamation, such bills receivables have to be eliminated from the books of the transferee company by means of the following entry :

Bills Payable Account Dr.
  To Bills Receivable Account

No additional entry is required to be passed in the books of the transferor company.

Similarly if the transferee company has, as investments, certain debentures issued by the transferor company after amalgamation the same are to be eliminated from the books of the transferee company by means of the following entry:

Debentures Account Dr.
  To Investments in Debentures Account

If debentures were acquired as investment at above or below the amount at which the debentures have been recorded as liability by the transferee company at the time of amalgamation, while passing the entry for cancellation of Investment and Debentures in the books of transferee company, the difference between cost of Investment and recorded value of Debentures cancelled is adjusted as follows:

(i) In case of amalgamation in the nature of purchase

If debentures were purchased as investments at below the recorded value, the entry for cancellation would be:

Debentures Account	Dr.	recorded value
To Investments in Debentures Account		cost
To Goodwill/Capital Reserve		excess of recorded value over cost

On the other hand if debentures were acquired at above the recorded value the entry would be:

Debentures Account	Dr.	recorded value
Goodwill/Capital Reserve	Dr.	excess of cost over recorded value
To Investments in Debentues Account		cost

(ii) In case of amalgamation in the nature of merger: In case of amalgamation in the nature of merger, the recorded value of debentures in the books of the transferee company must be the same as the book value of the debentures in the books of the transferor company.

If debentures were purchased as investment at below the recorded (par) value, the entry for concellation would be:

Debentures Account	Dr.	recorded (par) value
To Investments in Debentures Account		cost
To Capital Reserve		excess of recorded (par) value over cost

If debentures were purchased as investment at above the recorded (par) value, the entry for cancellation would be:

Debentures Account	Dr.	recorded (par) value
General Reserve/Profit and Loss Account	Dr.	excess of cost over recorded (par) value
To Investments in Debentures Account		cost

Similarly, the transferor company may be holding as investment, debentures issued by the transferee company. On amalgamation, the transferee company will acquire from transferor company these debentrues as one of the assets. Again, in the books of the transferee company, the entry for cancellation will have to be passed.

(i) In case of amalgamation in the nature of purchase : If the par value of debentures of the transferee company to be cancelled is more than the value at which they have been recorded as investments in the books of the transferee company on amalgamation, the following entry for cancellation will be passed :—

Debentures Account	Dr.	par value
To Investments in Debentures Account		recorded value
To Capital Reserve/Goodwill Account		excess of par value over recorded value

On the other hand, if the value at which the debentures have been recorded as investments by the transferee company exceeds their par value, the entry for cancellation will be as follows:—

Debentures Account	Dr.	par value
Capital Reserve/Goodwill Account	Dr.	excess of recorded value over par value
To Investments in Debentures Account		recorded value

(ii) In case of amalgamation in the nature of merger : If the par value of debentures to be cancelled is more than the value at which they have been recorded as investments in the books of the transferee company, the entry for cancellation will be as follows :—

Debentures Account	Dr.	par value
To Investments in Debentures Account		recorded value
To Capital Reserve		excess of par value over recorded value

But if the value at which the debentures have been recorded as investments by the transferee company exceeds their par value, the entry will be as follows :—

Debentures	Dr.	par value
General Reserve/Profit and Loss Account	Dr.	excess of recorded value over par value
To Investments in Debentures Account		recorded value

The abovementioned entries are based on the assumption that in the books of the transferee company, Premium on Redemption of Debentures Account does not appear in respect of debentures to be cancelled. If Premium on Redemption of Debentures Account also exists in the books of the transferee company in respect of debentures to be cancelled, the amount of premium originally stipulated to be paid on redemption of the debentures now being cancelled will be debited to Premium on Redemption of Debentures Account while passing the entry for cancellation of debentures held as investments. It will also affect the resultant profit or loss on cancellation of debentures.

Illustration 23. The following are the summarised balance sheets of V Ltd. and P Ltd. as at 31st March, 2010:—

Balance Sheet of V Ltd.

Liabilities	*Rs.*	*Assets*	*Rs.*
Equity Share Capital	10,00,000	Sundry Fixed Assets	8,00,000
Reserve and Surplus	3,40,000	1,000 12% Debentures of P Ltd.	
Sundry Creditors	1,80,000	acquired at Rs. 95 each	95,000
		Stock	4,00,000
		Sundry Debtors	1,30,000
		Cash at Bank	55,000
		Bills Receivable	40,000
	15,20,000		15,20,000

Balance Sheet of P Ltd.

Liabilities	*Rs.*	*Assets*	*Rs.*
Equity Share Capital	25,00,000	Sundry Fixed Assets	29,50,000
Reserves and Surplus	7,75,000	Stock	11,60,000
12% Debentures of Rs. 100 each,		Sundry Debtors	5,20,000
fully paid	10,00,000	Cash at Bank	1,10,000
Bills Payable	25,000	Bills Receivable	50,000
Sundry Creditors	4,90,000		
	47,90,000		47,90,000

P Ltd. acquires the entire business of V Ltd. for Rs. 14,00,000 to be satisfied by allotment of equity shares at par. All the acceptances of P Ltd. are in the favour of V Ltd. and which are included in the figure of Rs. 40,000 in V Ltd.'s balance sheet. Debtors appearing in the balance sheet of V Ltd. include Rs, 10,000 due from P Ltd.

You are required to:

(a) prepare Realisation Account and Equity Shareholders Account in the books of V Ltd.

(b) pass journal entries in the books of P Ltd. and redraft P Ltd.'s balance sheet immediately after amalgamation assuming *(i)* it is an amalgamation in the nature of purchase and *(ii)* it is an amalgamation in the nature of marger.

Solution :

Books of V Ltd.

Realisation Account

Dr.					*Cr.*
2010		*Rs.*	2010		*Rs.*
Mar. 31	To Sundry Fixed Assets	8,00,000	Mar. 31	By Creditors	1,80,000
	To 12% Debentures of P Ltd.	95,000		By P Ltd.	14,00,000
	To Stock	4,00,000			
	To Debtors	1,30,000			
	To Cash at Bank	55,000			
	To Bills Receivable	40,000			
	To Equity Shareholders — transfer of profit	60,000			
		15,80,000			15,80,000

Equity Shareholders Account

Dr.					*Cr.*
2010		*Rs.*	2010		*Rs.*
Mar. 31	To Equity Shares in P Ltd.	14,00,000	Mar. 31	By Equity Share Capital Account	10,00,000
				By Reserves and Surplus	3,40,000
				By Realisation Account (Profit)	60,000
		14,00,000			14,00,000

(i) In case amalgamation is in the nature of purchase:

Books of P Ltd.

Journal

				Dr.	*Cr.*
2010				*Rs.*	*Rs.*
March	31	Business Purchase Account	Dr.	14,00,000	
		To Liquidator of V Ltd.			14,00,000
		Consideration payable to Liquidator of V Ltd. for V Ltd.'s business taken over.			
"	"	Sundry Fixed Assets	Dr.	8,00,000	
		Investments in Debentures of P Ltd.	Dr.	95,000	
		Stock	Dr.	4,00,000	
		Sundry Debtors	Dr.	1,30,000	
		Cash at Bank	Dr.	55,000	
		Bills Receivable	Dr.	40,000	
		Goodwill	Dr.	60,000	
		To Sundry Creditors			1,80,000
		To Business Purchase Account			14,00,000
		Assets and liabilities taken over from V Ltd., the amount of Goodwill being the balancing figure.			
"	"	Liquidator of V Ltd.	Dr.	14,00,000	
		To Equity Share Capital Account			14,00,000
		Payment of the consideration in the form of equity shares allotted at par			

				Rs.	Rs.
Mar.	31	Bills Payable Account To Bills Receivable Account Cancellation of bills of Rs. 25,000 earlier accepted in favour of V Ltd. and now received as part of V Ltd.'s business.	Dr.	25,000	25,000
"	"	Sundry Creditors To Sundry Debtors Elimination of inter company owings.	Dr.	10,000	10,000
"	"	12% Debentures To Investments in 12% Debentures of P Ltd. To Goodwill Account Cancellation of debentures held of business as investments, Goodwill on acquisition being reduced by excess of par value of debentures over cost of investments.	Dr.	1,00,000	95,000 5,000

Balance Sheet of P Ltd. as at 31st March, 2010

Liabilities	*Rs.*	*Assets*	*Rs.*
Equity Share Capital (Of the above shares, shares for Rs. 14,00,000 have been allotted to vendor pursuant to a contract without payment being recieved in cash)	39,00,000	Goodwill (Rs. 60,000–5,000)	55,000
		Other Fixed Assets	37,50,000
		Stock	15,60,000
		Sundry Debtors (Rs. 6,50,000– Rs. 10,000)	6,40,000
Reserves and Surplus	7,75,000	Cash at Bank	1,65,000
12% Debentures (Rs. 10,00,000 – Rs. 1,00,000)	9,00,000	Bills Receivable (Rs. 90,000–Rs. 25,000)	65,000
Sundry Creditors (Rs. 6,70,000 – Rs. 10,000)	6,60,000		
	62,35,000		62,35,000

(ii) In case amalgamation is in the nature of merger:

Books of P Ltd.
Journal

				Dr.	Cr.
				Rs.	Rs.
2010 Mar.	31	Business Purchase Account To Liquidator of V Ltd. Consideration payable to Liquidator of V Ltd. for V Ltd.'s business taken over.	Dr.	14,00,000	14,00,000
"	"	Sundry Fixed Assets	Dr.	8,00,000	
		Investments in Debentures of P Ltd.	Dr.	95,000	
		Stock	Dr.	4,00,000	
		Sundry Debtors	Dr.	1,30,000	
		Cash at Bank	Dr.	55,000	
		Bills Receivable	Dr.	40,000	
		Profit and Loss Account	Dr.	60,000	

			Rs.	Rs.
		To Sundry Creditors To Business Purchase Account Assets and liabilites taken over from P Ltd., the difference being debited to Profit and Loss Account.		1,80,000 14,00,000
"	"	Liquidator of V Ltd. Dr. To Equity Share Capital Account Payment of the consideration in the form of equity shares allotted at par.	14,00,000	14,00,000
"	"	Bills Payable Account Dr. To Bills Receivable Account Cancellation of bills of Rs. 25,000 earlier accepted in favour of V Ltd. and now received as part of V Ltd.'s business.	25,000	25,000
"	"	Sundry Creditors Dr. To Sundry Debtors Elimination of inter company owings.	10,000	10,000
"	"	12% Debentures Dr. To Investments in 12% Debentures of P Ltd. To Capital Reserve Cancellation of debentures against investments in debentures, gain being credited to capital Reserve.	1,00,000	95,000 5,000

Balance Sheet of P Ltd. as at 31st March, 2010

Liabilities	*Rs.*	*Assets*	*Rs.*
Equity Share Capital (Of the above shares, shares for Rs. 14,00,000 have been allotted to vendor pursuant to a contract without payment being received in cash	39,00,000	Fixed Assets	37,50,000
		Stock	15,60,000
		Sundry Debtors	6,40,000
		Cash at Bank	1,65,000
		Bills Receivable	65,000
Reserve and Surplus Rs. (7,75,000 + 5,000–60,000)	7,20,000		
12% Debentures	9,00,000		
Sundry Creditors	6,60,000		
	61,80,000		61,80,000

Illustration 24. The following were the balance sheets of P Ltd. and V Ltd. as at 31st March, 2010 :

Liabilities	*P Ltd.* (Rs. in lakhs)	*V Ltd.*	*Assets*	*P Ltd.* (Rs. in lakhs)	*V Ltd.*
Equity Share Capital (Fully paid shares of Rs. 10 each)	15,000	6,000	Land and Buildings	6,000	—
			Plant and Machinery	14,000	5,000
Securities Premium	3,000	—	Furniture, Fixtures and Fittings	2,304	1,700
Foreign Projects Reserve	—	310	Stock	7,862	4,041
General Reserve	9,500	3,200	Debtors	2,120	1,020

Profit and Loss Account	2,870	825	Cash at Bank	1,114	609
12% Debentures	—	1,000	Bills Receivable	—	80
Bills Payable	120	—	Cost of Issue of Debentures	—	50
Sundry Creditors	1,080	463			
Sundry Provisions	1,830	702			
	33,400	12,500		33,400	12,500

All the bills receivable held by V Ltd. were P Ltd.'s acceptances. On 1st April, 2010 P Ltd. took over V Ltd. in an amalgamation in the nature of merger. It was agreed that in discharge of consideration for the business, P Ltd. would allot three fully paid equity shares of Rs. 10 each at par for every two shares held in V Ltd. It was also agreed that 12% debentures in V Ltd. would be converted into 13% debentures in P Ltd. of the same amount and denomination. Expenses of amalgamation amounting to Rs. 1 lakh were borne by P Ltd.

You are required to : (i) pass journal entries in the books of P Ltd., and (ii) prepare P Ltd.'s balance sheet immediately after the merger. [*C.A. (Inter) May, 2001*]

Solution :

P Ltd.'s Journal

		Rs. in lakhs	*Rs. in lakhs*
Business Purchase Account	..Dr.	9,000	
To Liquidator of V Ltd.			9,000
Consideration payable for V Ltd.'s business taken over in an amalgamation in the nature of merger.			
Plant and Machinery	..Dr.	5,000	
Furniture, Fixtures and Fittings	..Dr.	1,700	
Stock	..Dr.	4,041	
Debtors	..Dr.	1,020	
Cash at Bank	..Dr.	609	
Bills Receivable	..Dr.	80	
Cost of Issue of Debentures	..Dr.	50	
To Foreign Projects Reserve			310
To General Reserve			200
To Profit and Loss Account			825
To 12% Debentures (V Ltd.)			1,000
To Sundry Creditors			463
To Sundry Provisions			702
To Business Purchase Account			9,000
Incorporation of assets, liabilities and reserves of V Ltd., the excess of consideration over paid up value of V Ltd.'s share capital being adjusted in V Ltd.'s General Reserve.			
Liquidator of V Ltd.	..Dr.	9,000	
To Equity Share Capital			9,000
Allotment of equity shares to discharge consideration for V Ltd.'s business.			
Bills Payable Account	..Dr.	80	
To Bills Receivable Account			80
Cancellation of mutual owing on account of bills.			

		Dr.	Cr.
General Reserve ..Dr.		1	
To Bank			1
Payment of expenses of amalgamation.			
12% Debentures (V Ltd.) ..Dr.		1,000	
To 13% Debentures			1,000
Allotment of 13% debentures in lieu of 12% debentures in V Ltd.			

Balance Sheet of P Ltd. as at 1st April, 2010

Liabilities	*Rs. in lakhs*	*Assets*	*Rs. in lakh*
Share Capital		**Fixed Assets**	
Authorised	?	Land and Buildings	6,000
Issued and Subscribed :		Plant and Machinery	19,000
24 crore Equity Shares of Rs. 10 each, fully called and paid up (Of the above shares, 9 crore shares have been allotted as fully paid up pursuant to a contract without payment being received in cash)	24,000	Furniture, Fixtures and Fittings	4,004
		Current Assets, Loans and Advances :	
		A) Current Assets :	
		Stock	11,903
		Debtors	3,140
		Cash at Bank	1,722
Reserves and Surplus :		B) Loans and Advances :	Nil
Security Premium	3,000	**Miscellaneous Expenditure :**	
Foreign Projects Reserve	310	Cost of issue of Debentures	50
General Reserve	9,699		
Profit and Loss Account	3,695		
Secured Loans :			
13% Debentures	1,000		
Current Liabilities and Provisions :			
A) Current Liabilities :			
Bills Paybale	40		
Sundry Creditors	1,543		
B) Provisions :			
Sundry Provisions	2,532		
	45,819		45,819

Illustration 25. Enterprise Ltd. has two divisions *A* and *B*. Division *A* has been making constant profits while division *B* has been invariably suffering losses. On 31st March 2010, its divisionwise balance sheet was as follows :

	(Rupees in crores)			(Rupees in crores)		
	A	*B*	Total	*A*	*B*	Total
Fixed assets, cost	250	500	750			
Less : Depreciation	225	400	625	25	100	125
Current assets	200	500	700			
Less : Current liabilities	25	400	425	175	100	275
				200	200	400
Financed by :						
Loan funds	—	300	300			
Capital : Equity shares of Rs. 10 each	25	—	25			
Surplus	175	–100	75	200	200	400

Division *B* along with its assets and liabilities was sold for Rs. 25 crores to Turnaround Ltd., a new company, which allotted 1 crore equity shares of Rs. 10 each at a premium of Rs. 15 per share to the members of Enterprise Ltd. in full settlement of the consideraiton, in proportion to their shareholdings in the company.

(a) Assuming that there are no other transactions, you are asked to :

(i) Pass journal entries in the books of Enterprise Ltd.

(ii) Prepare the balance sheet of Enterprise Ltd. after the entries in (i).

(iii) Prepare the balance sheet of Turnaround Ltd.

[*Adapted C.A.(Final) May,2000*]

(i) Enterprise Ltd.
Journal

Rupees in crores

			Dr.	*Cr.*
	Realisation Account	..Dr.	1,000	
	To Fixed Assets			500
	To Current Liabilities			500
	Transfer of all assets of Division *B* in view of sale to Turnaround Ltd.			
	Provision for Depreciation	..Dr.	400	
	Loan Funds	..Dr.	300	
	Current Liabilities	..Dr.	400	
	To Realisation Account			1,100
	Transfer of all liabilities of Division *B* in view of sale of division to Turnaround Ltd.			
	Turnaround Ltd.	..Dr.	25	
	To Realisation Account			25
	Consideration for Division *B* sold to Turnaround Ltd.			
	Realisation Account	..Dr.	125	
	To Capital Reserve			125
	Transfer of profits on sale of Division *B* to Capital Reserve.			
	Capital Reserve	..Dr.	25	
	To Turnaround Ltd.			25
	Allotment by Turnaround Ltd. of one crore equity shares of Rs. 10 each at a premium of Rs. 15 each to our shareholders in discharge of consideration for Division *B* sold to it.			

(ii) Balance Sheet of Enterprise Ltd.

(Rupees in crores)

	Before reconstruction	After reconstruction
Sources of Funds :		
Equity Share Capital :		
Shares of Rs. 10 each, fully paid	25	25
Reserves and Surplus :		
Capital Reserve	—	100
Surplus	75	75
Loan Funds	300	—
	400	200

Funds employed in :				
Fixed Assets, cost	750		250	
Less : Depreciation	625	125	225	25
Current assets	700		200	
Less : Current liabilities	425	275	25	175
		400		200

(iii) Balance Sheet of Turnaround Ltd.

Souces of Funds :		*Rs. in crores*
1 crore equity shares of Rs. 10 each, fully paid		10
Reserves and Surplus :		
Securities Premium		15
Loan Funds		300
		325
Funds Employed in :	*Rs. in crore*	
Fixed Assets - as revalued (balancing figure)		225
Current Assets	500	
Less : Current Liabilities	400	100
		325

Unrealised Profit on Stock

The question of the mutual owings on account of sale of goods may be connected with goods sold by the transferor company to the transferee company or *vice versa,* but still remaining unsold. It should be remembered that the transferee company will acquire all the stock of the transferor company, including the goods sold by it to the transferor company, and that, in the books of the transferor company, the stock will be recorded at invoice price (that is, including the profit charged by the transferee company). On re-acquisition of the goods, the profit must be eliminated. The method is simple. While making the entries for acquisition of the business of the transferor company, the figure of stock should be reduced by the profit charged by the transferee company —the figure of goodwill or capital reserve in the case of amalgamation in the nature of purchase and that of general reserve or profit and loss account in the case of amalgamation in the nature of merger will be automatically get adjusted.

But if it was the transferee company that had purchased goods from the transferor company, and the goods or part of them had remained unsold, the way to eliminate the unrealised profit charged by the transferor company is to debit Goodwill or Capital Reserve in the case of amalgamation in the nature of purchase and to debit General Reserve or Profit and Loss Account in the case of amalgamation in the nature of merger and to credit Stock Account by the amount of unrealised profit. Suppose P Ltd. had bought goods of the invoice value of Rs. 50,000 from S Ltd. which company invoices goods at cost plus 20%. Later, P Ltd. acquired the business of S Ltd., when out of the goods purchased, Rs, 30,000 were still in stock. The unrealised profit is:

$$\text{Rs. } 30{,}000 \times \frac{20}{120} \text{ or Rs. } 5{,}000.$$

In addition to the other purchase entries, P Ltd. must pass the following additional entry :

(i) If it is an amalgamation in the nature of purchase:

Goodwill Account (or Capital Reserve)	Dr.	Rs. 5,000	
To Stock Account			Rs. 5,000

(ii) If it is an amalgamation in the nature of meger:

General Reserve/Profit and Loss Account	Dr.	Rs. 5,000	
To Stock Account			Rs. 5,000

Illustration 26. The following are the balance sheets of P Ltd. and S Ltd. as at 31st March, 2010:—

	P Ltd.	*S Ltd.*		*P Ltd.*	*S Ltd.*
	Rs.	*Rs.*		*Rs.*	*Rs.*
Equity Share Capital	9,00,000	3,00,000	Plant	6,50,000	
Reserves	2,80,000	70,000	Furniture	75,000	30,000
Bills Payable	35,000	10,000	Stock	3,05,000	2,70,000
Sundry Creditors	1,05,000	80,000	Debtors	1,56,000	55,000
			Cash at Bank	1,14,000	75,000
			Bills Receivable	20,000	30,000
	13,20,000	4,60,000		13,20,000	4,60,000

P Ltd. takes over the business of S Ltd. for Rs. 3,00,000 payable in the form of equity shares allotted at par. Included in the Bills Payable of P Ltd. are bills amounting to Rs. 25,000 accepted in favour of S Ltd. for goods purchased; S Ltd. charging profit @ 25% on cost. On the date of amalgamation, goods purchased from S Ltd. of the invoice price of Rs. 12,500 still remain unsold in the stock of P Ltd. and of the above mentioned bills of Rs. 25,000, bills for Rs. 5,000 only still remain in S Ltd.'s hands, the rest having been endorsed in favour of creditors or got discounted with Bank. Expenses of liquidation of S Ltd. Rs. 6,000 were met by P Ltd.

Prepare Realisation Account and Equity Shareholders Accounts in S Ltd.'s ledger. Also pass journal entries in the books of P Ltd. and prepare its balance sheet assuming *(i)* it is an amalgamation in the nature of purchase and *(ii)* it is an amalgamation in the nature of merger.

Solution :

Book of S Ltd.

Realisation Account

Dr.					*Cr.*
2010		*Rs.*	2010		*Rs.*
Mar. 31	To Furniture	30,000	Mar. 31	By Bills Payable	10,000
	To Stock	2,70,000		By Sundry Creditors	80,000
	To Debtors	55,000		By P Ltd. (consideration)	3,00,000
	To Cash at Bank	75,000		By Equity Shareholders (loss)	70,000
	To Bills Receivable	30,000			
		4,60,000			4,60,000

Equity Shareholders Account

Dr.					*Cr.*
2010		*Rs.*	2010		*Rs.*
Mar. 31	To Realisation Account	70,000	Mar. 31	By Equity Share Capital	3,00,000
	To Equity Shares in P Ltd.	3,00,000		By Reserves	70,000
		3,70,000			3,70,000

Books of P Ltd.

(i) In case of amalgamation in the nature of purchase :

Journal

2010				*Rs.*	*Rs.*
Mar.	31	Business Purchase Account To Liquidator of S Ltd. The consideration payabale to Liquidator of S Ltd. for business purchased.	Dr.	3,00,000	3,00,000
"	"	Furniture Stock Debtors Cash at Bank Bills Receivable To Bills Payable To Sundry Creditors To Business Purchase Account To Capital Reserve Assets and liabilities taken over from S Ltd., the amount of Capital Reserve being the balancing figure.	Dr. Dr. Dr. Dr. Dr.	30,000 2,70,000 55,000 75,000 30,000	 10,000 80,000 3,00,000 70,000
"	"	Liquidator of S Ltd. To Equity Share Capital Account Amount of equity shares allotted at par to Liquidator of S Ltd. in discharge of the consideration.	Dr.	3,00,000	3,00,000
"	"	Bills Payable Account To Bills Receivable Account Cancellation of inter-company owings in the form of bills.	Dr.	5,000	5,000
"	"	Capital Reserve To Stock Elimination of unrealised profit in respect of unsold stock, (Rs. 12,500 × 25/125 = Rs. 2,500).	Dr.	2,500	2,500
"	"	Capital Reserve To Bank Expenses of liquidation of S Ltd. met as per agreement.	Dr.	6,000	6,000

Balance Sheet of P Ltd. as at 31st March, 2010

Liabilities	*Rs.*	*Assets*	*Rs.*
Share Capital		**Fixed Assets**	
Issued and Subscribed		Plant	6,50,000
Equity Share Capital	12,00,000	Furniture	1,05,000
(Of the above shares, shares of Rs. 3,00,000 have been allotted to vendors pursuant to a contract without payment being recieved in cash)		**Current Assets, Loans and Advances**	
		(A) Current Assets	
		Stock	5,72,500
		Debtors	2,11,000
		Cash at Bank	1,83,000
Reserves and Surplus		(B) Loans and Advances	
Capital Reserve	61,500	Bills Receivable	45,000
Other Reserve	2,80,000		

	Rs.		Rs.
Current Liabilities and Provision			
(A) Current Liabilities			
Bills Payable	40,000		
Sundry Creditors	1,85,000		
(B) Provisions	Nil		
	17,66,500		17,66,500

(ii) In case of amalgamation in the nature of merger:

Journal

				Dr.	Cr.
				Rs.	Rs.
2010 Mar.	31	Business Purchase Account To Liquidator of S Ltd. The consideration payable to Liquidator of S Ltd. for business purchased.	Dr.	3,00,000	3,00,000
"	"	Furniture Stock Debtors Cash at Bank Bills Receivable To Bills Payable To Sundry Creditors To Reserves To Business Purchase Account Incorporation of assets, liabilities and reserves pertaining to the business of S Ltd. takenover.	Dr. Dr. Dr. Dr Dr.	30,000 2,70,000 55,000 75,000 30,000	 10,000 80,000 70,000 3,00,000
"	"	Bills Payable Account To Bills Receivable Account Cancellation of inter-company owings in the form of bills.	Dr.	5,000	5,000
"	"	Reserves To Stock Elimination of unrealised profit in respect of unsold stock, (Rs. 12,500 × 25/125 = Rs. 2,500).	Dr.	2,500	2,500
"	"	Reserves To Bank Expenses of Liquidation of S Ltd., net as per agreement.	Dr.	6,000	6,000

Balance Sheet of P Ltd. as at 31st March, 2010

Liabilities	Rs.	*Assets*	Rs.
Share Capital		**Fixed Assets**	
Issued and Subscribed:		Plant	6,50,000
Equity Share Capital	12,00,000	Furuniture	1,05,000
(Of the above shares, shares of Rs, 3,00,000 have been allotted to vendors pursuant to a contract without payment being received in cash)		**Current Assets, Loans and Advances**	
		(A) Current Assets	
		Stock	5,72,500
		Debotrs	2,11,000
Reserves and Surplus		Cash at Bank	1,83,000
Reserves	3,41,500	(B) Loans and Advances	

Current Liabilities and Provisions	Rs.		Rs.
(A) Current Liabilities		Bills Receivable	45,000
Bills Payable	40,000		
Sundry Creditors	1,85,000		
(B) Provisions	Nil		
	17,66,500		17,66,500

Illustration 27. Wallace Ltd. is absorbed by Bharat Ltd. The consideration is as follows:

(i) taking over of liabilities

(ii) the payment of cost of amalgamation not exceeding Rs, 8,000;

(iii) a payment of Rs. 15 per share in cash and allotment of one 14% preference share of Rs. 100 each and 5 equity shares of Rs. 100 each fully paid for every 4 shares in Wallace Ltd.

The market value of the equity shares of Bharat Ltd. is Rs. 140 but it is desired that entries should be made on the basis of par value only. The actual cost of amalgamation came to Rs. 10,000.

The following is the balance sheet of Wallace Ltd. on the date of amalgamation:

Liabilities	*Rs.*	*Assets*		*Rs.*
Share Capital:		Land and Buildings		16,00,000
20,000 shares of Rs. 100 each,		Plant and Machinery		14,00,000
fully paid up	20,00,000	Patent Rights		3,50,000
General Reserve	13,00,000	Investment against Sinking Fund		1,00,000
Sinking Fund	1,00,000	Staff Provident Fund Investments		1,50,000
12% Loan	4,00,000	Stock		2,00,000
Sundry Creditors	1,40,000	Debtors	4,00,000	
Employees Profit Sharing Reserve	1,00,000	*Less* : Provision for Bad Debts	40,000	3,60,000
Staff Provident Fund	1,50,000	Cash at Bank		30,000
	41,90,000			41,90,000

Stock includes goods valued at Rs. 56,000 purchased from the Bharat Ltd. which company invoices goods at cost plus 16 2/3%. The creditors include Rs. 80,000 due by the Wallace Ltd. to the Bharat Ltd.

Journalise the closing entries of Wallace Ltd. and the opening entries of Bharat Ltd. Does it made any difference if the shares in Bharat Ltd. are valued at Rs. 140 but entries are made at par?

Solution :

Calculation of consideration:

Form	*Amount* Rs.
(i) Cash 20,000 × Rs. 15	3,00,000
(ii) Preference Shares $\frac{20,000}{4}$ × Rs. 100	5,00,000
(iii) Equity Shares $\frac{20,000}{4}$ × 5 × Rs.100	25,00,000
	33,00,000

Books of Wallace Ltd.

Realisation

Dr.	Rs.		Cr. Rs.
To Land and Buildings	16,00,000	By Provisions for Bad Debts	40,000
To Plant and Machinery	14,00,000	By 12% Loan	4,00,000
To Patents Rights	3,50,000	By Sundery Creditors	1,40,000
To Investment against Sinking Fund	1,00,000	By Employees' Profit Sharing Reserve	1,00,000

	Rs.		Rs.
To Staff Provident Fund Investment	1,50,000	By Staff Provident Fund	1,50,000
To Stock	2,00,000	By Bharat Ltd. (consideration)	33,00,000
To Debtors	4,00,000	By Bharat Ltd. (expenses)	8,000
To Cash at Bank	30,000	By Equity Shareholders Account (loss)	1,02,000
To Bank (expenses)	10,000		
	42,40,000		42,40,000

Bharat Ltd.

Dr.			Cr.
	Rs.		Rs.
To Realisation Account (consideration)	33,00,000	By Bank	3,00,000
To Realisation Account (for expenses)	8,000	By 14% Preference Shares in Bharat Ltd.	5,00,000
		By Equity Shares in Bharat Ltd.	25,00,000
		By Bank (for expenses)	8,000
	33,08,000		33,08,000

Cash Book (Bank Columns)

Dr.			Cr.
	Rs.		Rs.
To Balance b/fd	30,000	By Realisation Account (transfer)	30,000
To Bharat Ltd.	3,00,000	By Realisation Account (expenses)	10,000
To Bharat Ltd. (for expenses)	8,000	By Equity Shareholders Account (distribution)	2,98,000
	3,08,000		3,08,000

Equity Shareholders Account

Dr.			Cr.
	Rs.		Rs.
To Realisation (loss)	1,02,000	By Equity Share Capital Account	20,00,000
To Equity Shares in Bharat Ltd.	25,00,000	By General Reserve	13,00,000
To 14% Preference Shares in Bharat Ltd.	5,00,000	By Sinking Fund	1,00,000
To Bank	2,98,000		
	34,00,000		34,00,000

Books of Bharat Ltd.

Journal

		Dr.	Cr.
		Rs.	Rs.
Business Purchase Account To Liquidator of Wallace Ltd. The purchase price agreed to be paid for the business of Wallace Ltd.	Dr.	33,00,000	33,00,000
Land and Buildings	Dr.	16,00,000	
Plant and Machinery	Dr.	14,00,000	

Particulars			Dr. (Rs.)	Cr. (Rs.)
Patent Rights	Dr.		3,50,000	
Stock	Dr.		1,92,000	
Sundry Debtors	Dr.		4,00,000	
Investments against Sinking Fund	Dr.		1,00,000	
Investments against Staff Provident Fund	Dr.		1,50,000	
Cash at Bank	Dr.		30,000	
To Provision for Doubtful Debts				40,000
To 12% Loan				4,00,000
To Sundry Creditors				1,40,000
To Exployees Profit Sharing Reserve				1,00,000
To Staff Provident Fund				1,50,000
To Business Purchase Account				33,00,000
To Capital Reserve				1,00,000
Incorporation of assets and liabilities taken over from Wallace Ltd.—Credit to Capital Reserve being the balancing figure. A sum of Rs. 8,000 *i.e.* Rs. 56,000 × $\frac{16\frac{2}{3}}{116\frac{2}{3}}$ has been deducted from stock.				
Liquidator of Wallace Ltd.	Dr.		33,00,000	
To 14% Preference Share Capital Account				5,00,000
To Equity Share Capital Account				25,00,000
To Bank				3,00,000
Allotment of 14% Preference shares and equity shares and payment of cash in satisfaction of the consideration for business.				
Capital Reserve	Dr.		8,000	
To Bank				8,000
Reimbursement of expenses of Wallace Ltd. to the extent of Rs. 8,000.				
Sundry Creditors Account	Dr.		80,000	
To Sundry Debtors Account				80,000
Elimination of Rs. 80,000 included in creditors of Wallace Ltd. and in debtors of Bharat Ltd. being the sum owed by the former to the latter.				

Note : Whereas the market price of the equity shares in Bharat Ltd. is Rs. 140, making entries at par does not really make a difference. Had the entries been made at Rs. 140, the amount of goodwill would have been increased but, then, Rs. 40 per share would have been credited to Securities Premium Account. Shareholders of Wallace Ltd. have also not suffered at all because, although in the books the equity shares in Bharat Ltd. have been recorded at Rs. 100, they have in fact received shares worth Rs.140.

This shows that if a transferee company does not want to show both goodwill and premium on shares resulting from the acquisition of another company, it should record the issue of its shares at par. One should remember that once an amount is credited to Securities Premium Account, it cannot be used to write off assets like Goodwill.

Illustration 28. The following is the balance sheet of Weak Ltd. as on March 31, 2010:—

Liabilities	*Rs.*	*Assets*	*Rs.*
Share Capital :		Goodwill	35,000
2,000 shares of Rs. 100 each	2,00,000	Land and Buildings	85,000
General Reserve	20,000	Plant and Machinery	1,60,000
10% Debentures	1,00,000	Stock	55,000
Loan from A (a director)	40,000	Debtors	65,000
Sundry Creditors	80,000	Cash at Bank	34,000
		Discount on Issue of Debentures	6,000
	4,40,000		4,40,000

The business of the company is taken over by Strong Ltd. as on that date, on the following terms: (*a*) Strong Ltd. to take over all assets except cash, to value the assets at their book values less 10% except goodwill which was to be valued at 4 years' purchase of the excess of average (five years') profits over 8% of the combined amount of Share Capital and Reserves : (*b*) Strong Ltd. to take over trade creditors which were subject to a discount of five per cent; (*c*) the consideration was to be discharged in cash to the extent of Rs. 1,50,000 and the balance in fully paid equity shares of Rs. 10 each valued at Rs. 12.50 per share.

The average of the five years' profits was Rs, 30,100. The expenses of liquidation amounted to Rs. 4,000. Weak Ltd. had sold, prior to 31st March, 2000, goods costing Rs. 30,000 to Strong Ltd. for Rs. 40,000. Debtors include Rs. 20,000 still due from Strong Ltd. On the date of absorption, Rs, 25,000 worth of the goods were still in stock of Strong Ltd. Show the important ledger accounts in the books of Weak Ltd. and journal entries in the books of Strong Ltd.

Solution :

Calculation of the consideration :

		Rs.
Assets taken over:		
Land & Buildings		85,000
Plant & Machinery		1,60,000
Stock		55,000
Debtors		65,000
		3,65,000
Less : 10% reduction		36,500
		3,38,500
Goodwill*		50,000
		3,78,500
Less : Trade Creditors taken over	80,000	
Less : 5% Discount	4,000	76,000
Consideration		3,02,500

The consideration is to be discharged as to Rs, 1,50,000 in cash and the balance of Rs. 1,52,500 in shares valued at Rs. 12.50 each, *i.e.*, in 12,200 shares.

*Goodwill has been valued as follows :—

	Rs.
Average of the five years' profits	30,100
Less : Normal profits—8% of Rs. 2,20,000	17,600
Super Profits	12,500
Goodwill at four years' purchase = Rs. 12,500 × 4	50,000

Ledger of Weak Ltd.

Cash Book (Bank Columns)

Dr.					Cr.
2010		Rs.	2010		Rs.
Mar. 31	To Balance b/fd	34,000	Mar. 31	By Realisation Account	
	To Strong Ltd.	1,50,000		—expenses	4,000
				By 10% Debentures	1,00,000
				By A's Loan	40,000
				By Sundry Shareholders Account	40,000
		1,84,000			1,84,000

Realisation Account

Dr.					Cr.
2010		Rs.	2010		Rs.
Mar. 31	To Goodwill	35,000	Mar. 31	By Sundry Creditors	80,000
	To Land and Buildings	85,000		By Strong Ltd.—	
	To Plant and Machinery	1,60,000		consideration	3,02,500
	To Stock	55,000		By Sundry Shareholders —	
	To Debtors	65,000		transfer of loss	21,500
	To Bank—expenses	4,000			
		4,04,000			4,04,000

Sundry Shareholders Account

Dr.					Cr.
2010		Rs.	2010		Rs.
Mar. 31	To Discount of Issue of		Mar. 31	By Share Capital	2,00,000
	Debentures	6,000		By General Reserve	20,000
	To Realisation (loss)	21,500			
	To Bank	40,000			
	To Shares in Strong Ltd.	1,52,500			
		2,20,000			2,20,000

Shares in Strong Ltd.

Dr.					Cr.
2010		Rs.	2010		Rs.
Mar. 31	To Strong Ltd.	1,52,500	Mar. 31	By Sundry Shareholders	1,52,500

Books of Strong Ltd.

Journal

2010					Dr. Rs.	Cr. Rs.
Mar.	31	Business Purchase Account	Dr.		3,02,500	
		To Liquidator of Weak Ltd.				3,02,500
		The purchase price to be paid for the business of Weak Ltd. as per agreement dated......				
"	"	Land and Buildings	Dr.		76,500	
		Plant and Machinery	Dr.		1,44,000	
		Stock	Dr.		49,500	
		Debtors	Dr.		65,000	
		Goodwill	Dr.		50,000	
		Reserve for Discount on Creditors	Dr.		4,000	
		To Provision for Doubtful Debts				6,500
		To Sundry Creditors				80,000

				Rs.	Rs.
		To Business Purchase Account The various assets and liabilities taken over from Weak Ltd. in accordance with the agreement.			3,02,500
Mar.	31	Liquidator of Weak Ltd.	Dr.	3,02,500	
		To Bank			1,50,000
		To Equity Share Capital			1,22,000
		To Securities Premium Account			30,500
		The payment of cash of Rs.1,50,000 and the issue of 12,200 equity shares of Rs.10 each @ Rs. 12.50 in discharge of the consideration.			
"	"	Goodwill Account	Dr.	6,250	
		To Stock Account			6,250
		Elimination of unrealised profit on Rs. 25,000, goods bought from Weak Ltd. still unsold. Unrealised profit = Rs. 25,000 × 10,000/40,000.			
"	"	Sundry Creditors Account	Dr.	20,000	
		To Sundry Debtors Account			20,000
		Elimination of Rs.20,000 owed by Strong Ltd. to Weak Ltd., included respectively in the accounts relating to Sundry Creditors and Sundry Debtors.			

Passing entries at par value of shares

Sometimes the shares of the transferee company being allotted in discharge of consideration may be quoted above par in the market. But the companies may record the receipt and allotment of these shares at par value. In such a case, the consideration is recorded at suitably reduced figure and then the entry for shares is passed at par value.

Illustration 29. On 31st March, 2010 Varun Ltd. with an issued and subscribed capital of Rs. 7,00,000 divided into 70,000 fully paid equity shares of Rs.10 each had net tangible assets of Rs, 9,50,000 and Goodwill amounting to Rs. 50,000. On this date, Paul Ltd. took over Varun Ltd.'s business for Rs. 13,00,000 payable as to Rs. 1,00,00 in cash and Rs. 12,00,000 in 1,00,000 equity shares of Rs. 10 each, valued at Rs. 12 each; however, it was decided that the shares so allotted should be recorded by both the companies in the books of account at par value only.

On the date of purchase of business, Varun Ltd.'s debtors included Rs. 20,000 due from Paul Ltd. for goods sold to it at a profit for 25% on cost. Paul Ltd. had sold only one fourth of these goods by the date of absorption, the remaining goods lying unsold in stock.

Pass journal entries in the books of both the companies.

Solution:

Working Notes:

Summarised Balance Sheet of Varun Ltd. as at 31st March, 2010

	Rs.		Rs.
Share Capital		Goodwill	50,000
Issued and Subscribed:		Net Sundry Tangible Assets	9,50,000
70,000 Equity shares of Rs. 10 each, fully paid-up	7,00,000		
Reserves	3,00,000		
	10,00,000		10,00,000

The consideration on the basis of par value of shares:

	Rs.
Cash	1,00,000
1,00,000 Equity Shares of Rs.10 each	10,00,000
Total	11,00,000

Books of Varun Ltd.
Journal

				Dr.	*Cr.*
2010				*Rs.*	*Rs.*
Mar.	31	Realisation Account	Dr.	10,00,000	
		To Goodwill			50,000
		To Net Sundry Tangible Assets			9,50,000
		Transfer of Goodwill and net sundry tangible assets to Realisation Account.			
"	"	Paul Ltd.	Dr.	11,00,000	
		To Realisation Account			11,00,000
		Amount calculated on the basis of par value of shares due from Paul Ltd. for business sold to it.			
"	"	Bank	Dr.	1,00,000	
		Equity Shares in Paul Ltd.	Dr.	10,00,000	
		To Paul Ltd.			11,00,000
		Receipts of cash and equity shares in Paul Ltd. recorded at par from Paul Ltd. in discharge of purchase consideration for the business sold to it.			
"	"	Equity Share Capital Account	Dr.	7,00,000	
		Reserves	Dr.	3,00,000	
		Realisation Account	Dr.	1,00,000	
		To Equity Shareholders Account			11,00,000
		Transfer of Equity Share Capital Account, Reserves and profit on realisation to Equity Shareholders Account.			
"	"	Equity Shareholders Account	Dr.	11,00,000	
		To Bank			1,00,000
		To Equity Sheres in Paul Ltd.			10,00,000
		Distribution of cash and equity shares in Pual Ltd. among equity shareholders.			

Books of Paul Ltd.
Journal

				Dr.	*Cr.*
2010				*Rs.*	*Rs.*
Mar.	31	Business Purchase Account	Dr.	11,00,000	
		To Liquidator of Varun Ltd.			11,00,000
		Amount calculated on the basis of par value of shares payable to liquidator of Varun Ltd. for the business purchased.			
"	"	Goodwill	Dr.	1,50,000	
		Net sundry Tangible Assets	Dr.	9,50,000	
		To Business Purchase Account			11,00,000
		Incorporation of the net sundry tangible assets taken over and the amount paid for goodwill.			
"	"	Liquidator of Varun Ltd.	Dr.	11,00,00	
		To Bank			1,00,000
		To Equity Share Capital Account			10,00,000
		Payment of cash and allotment of 1,00,000 equity shares of Rs. 10 each (recorded at par) to liquidator of Varun Ltd. in discharge of the consideration.			

				Rs.	Rs.
Mar.	31	Sundry Creditors To Sundry Debtors Elimination of mutual owinG	Dr.	20,000	20,000
"	"	Goodwill To Stock Elimination of unrealised profit in respect of 3/4ths of goods purchased earlier from Varun Ltd. and remaining unsold on the date of absorption.	Dr.	3,000	3,000

Illustration 30. *A* Ltd. agreed to acquire the business of *B* Ltd. as on 31st March, 2009. On that date balance sheet of *B* Ltd. was summarised as follows:

Liabilities	*Rs.*	*Assets*	*Rs.*
Share Capital (fully paid shares of Rs. 10 each)	3,00,000	Goodwill	50,000
		Land, Buildings and Plant	3,20,000
General Reserve	1,35,000	Stock-in-trade	84,000
Profit and Loss Account	55,000	Debtors	18,000
Creditors	10,000	Cash and Bank balances	28,000
	5,00,000		5,00,000

The shareholders in *B* Ltd. were to receiver Rs. 2.50 in cash per share and 3 shares in *A* Ltd. for every two shares held — the shares in *A* Ltd. being considered as worth Rs. 12.50 each.

There were fractions equalling 50 shares of *A* Ltd. for which cash was paid. The directors of *A* Ltd. considered the various assets to be valued as follows:

	Rs.
Land	1,00,000
Buildings	2,50,000
Plant	3,50,000
Stock	80,000
Debtors	18,000

The cost of liquidation of *B* Ltd. ultimately was Rs. 5,000. Due to a technical hitch, the transaction could be completed only on 1st October, 2009. Till that date, *B* Ltd. carried on trading which resulted in a profit of Rs.20,000 (subject to interest) after providing Rs. 15,000 as depreciation. On October 1, 2009 stock was Rs. 90,000; Debtors were Rs. 25,000 and creditors were Rs, 15,000. There was no addition to or sale of fixed assets. It was agreed that the profit should belong to *A* Ltd.

You are requiued, as on Oct. 1, 2000 to:

(*i*) prepare Realisation Account and the Shareholders Account in the ledger of *B* Ltd., and

(*ii*) give journal entries in the books of *A* Ltd.

Solution :

Ledger of *B* Ltd.

Realisation Account

Dr. *Cr.*

		Rs.			*Rs.*
2009			2009		
Oct. 1	To Goodwill	50,000	Oct. 1	By Sundry Creditors	15,000
	To Land, Buildings, Plant, etc.	3,20,000		By Provision for Depreciation	15,000
	To Stock-in-trade	90,000		By *A* Ltd.—	
	To Debtors	25,000		consideration (*ii*)	6,37,500
	To Cash & Bank Balance (*i*)	55,000		By *A* Ltd. (for profit) (*iii*)	20,000
	To Shareholders — profit	1,47,500			
		6,87,500			6,87,500

Shareholders Account

Dr.					Cr.
2009		Rs.	2009		Rs.
Oct. 1	To Bank	75,625	Oct. 1	By Share Capital Account	3,00,000
	To Shares in *A* Ltd.	5,61,875		By General Reserve	1,35,000
				By Profit & Loss Account	55,000
				By Realisation Account	1,47,500
		6,37,500			6,37,500

Note : It is clear that the costs of liquidation will be payable by *A* Ltd. since amount payable to the shareholders has been specified.

			Rs.	Rs.
(i)	Cash and Bank balances as on April 1, 2009			28,000
	Add:	Profit earned		20,000
		Depreciation provided (no cash payment)		15,000
		Increase in Sundry Creditors		5,000
				68,000
	Less :	Increase in Stock	6,000	
		Increase in Debtors	7,000	13,000
				55,000

(*ii*) Consideration:

Form	*Amount* Rs.
Cash, Rs.2.50 × 30,000	75,000
Share, Rs.12.50 × (30,000 × 3/2 – 50)	5,61,875
Cash for fractions, Rs. 12.50 × 50	625
	6,37,500

(iii) Since the transfer of assets is as on 30th Sept. 2009, the profit of Rs.20,000 must be standing to the credit of *A* Ltd.

Journal of *A* Ltd.

2009					Dr. Rs.	Cr. Rs.
Oct.	1	Business Purchase Account.	Dr.		6,37,500	
		To Liquidator of *B* Ltd.				6,37,500
		The consideration settled as per agreement dated.....for the business of *B* Ltd.				
		Land	Dr.		1,00,000	
		Buildings	Dr.		2,50,000	
		Plant	Dr.		3,50,000	
		Stock	Dr.		86,000	
		Sundry Debtors	Dr.		25,000	
		Bank	Dr.		55,000	
		To Provision for Depreciation				15,000
		To Profit & Loss Suspense Account				20,000
		To Sundry Creditors				15,000
		To Business Purchase Account				6,37,500
		To Capital Reserve				58,500
		Various assets and liabilities taken over from *B* Ltd.—profit up to September 30, 2000 being credited to Profit and Loss Suspense Account				

				Rs.	Rs.
Oct	1	Liquidator of *B* Ltd.	Dr.	6,37,500	
		To Share Capital Account			4,49,500
		To Securities Premium Account			1,12,375
		To Bank			75,625
		Allotment of shares at a premium and payment of cash in discharge of consideration for the business taken over.			
"	"	Capital Reserve	Dr.	5,000	
		To Bank			5,000
		Expenses of liquidation.			

Note : It is assumed that the reduction in the value of stock as on April 1, 2009 still applies.

INTER-COMPANY HOLDINGS

We shall now discuss the situation arising when shares are already held by :

(i) the transferee company in the transferor company; or

(ii) the transferor company in the transferee company; or

(iii) the transferee company in the transferor company and the transferor company in the transferee company.

(a) Shares held by transferee company in the transferor company. In this case, the consideration has to be adjusted for the shares held. If P Ltd. acquires the business of S Ltd. on a valuation of Rs. 3,00,000 and if P Ltd. is holding 20% equity shares in S Ltd., the consideration should be treated as only Rs. 2,40,000 as 1/5th of Rs. 3,00,000 or Rs. 60,000 already belongs to P Ltd. The cost of the shares to P Ltd. is not relevant for this purpose. But while recording the acquisition entries, the account representing cost of shares acquired should be credited at cost to the transferee company.

The transferor company may treat the matter in either of two ways :

(i) The consideration may be computed only for outsiders and the Realisation Account credited and the transferee company debited accordingly. In this case, the paid-up value of the shares held by the transferee company should be debited to the Share Capital Account and credited to the Realisation Account. This is on the basis that no payment is to be made on account of such portion of the Share Capital.

(ii) The consideration may be computed ignoring the fact that some shares are held by the transferee company. Entries will then be passed and the Shareholders Account built up as shown in the previous sections of this chapter. Then the proportionate amount "due" to the transferee company for shares held by it should be debited to the Shareholders Account and credited to the account of the transferee company which company will square up its account by issuing shares and cash, etc., for the amount really due from it.

Illustration 31. The abridged balance sheet of Vidur Ltd. as at 31st March, 2010 was as follows:—

Liabilities	Rs.	*Assets*	Rs.
Share Capital:		Fixed Assets	13,10,000
2,00,000 Equity Shares of Rs.10		Current Assets	9,70,000
each, fully paid-up	20,00,000	Profit and Loss Account	70,000
Current Liabilities	3,50,000		
	23,50,000		23,50,000

On the above-mentioned date, Panchal Ltd. took over the business of Vidur Ltd. at balance sheet values. Winding up costs, Rs. 9,000 were also borne by Panchal Ltd. The summarised balance sheet of Panchal Ltd. at that date stood as follows:—

Liabilities	*Rs.*	*Assets*	*Rs.*
Share Capital		Fixed Assets	32,10,000
3,00,000 Equity Shares of Rs. 10 each	30,00,000	Investment in 50,000 Equity	
General Reserve	10,00,000	Shares of Vidur Ltd.	4,75,000
Current Liabilities	19,45,000	Current Assets	22,60,000
	59,45,000		59,45,000

Panchal Ltd. discharged the consideration by allotment to Vidur Ltd. 1,00,000 fully paid equity shares of Rs. 10 each at an agreed value of Rs. 12 each and by payment of cash for the balance. Panchal Ltd. had sufficient cash at bank for payment to Liquidator of Vidur Ltd.

Show important ledger accounts in the books of Vidur Ltd., pass journal entries in the books of Panchal Ltd. and draw Panchal Ltd.'s balance sheet immediately following the take over of the business.

Solution:

Calculation of consideration:

	Rs.
Fixed Assets	13,10,000
Current Assets	9,70,000
	22,80,000
Less : Current Liabilities	3,50,000
	19,30,000

However, 50,000 shares out of 2,00,000 shares of Vidur Ltd. are already with Panchal Ltd. It means 25% business has already been paid for.

$$\text{The amount to be paid now} = \text{Rs.}19{,}30{,}000 \times \frac{75}{100}$$
$$= \text{Rs.}14{,}47{,}500.$$

Books of Vidur Ltd.

Realisation Account

Dr. *Cr.*

2010		*Rs.*	2010		*Rs.*
Mar. 31	To Fixed Assets	13,10,000	Mar. 31	By Current Liabilities	3,50,000
	To Current Assets	9,70,000		By Panchal Ltd. (consideration)	14,47,500
	To Equity Shareholders Account (profit)	17,500		By Equity Share Capital Account	5,00,000
		22,97,500			22,97,500

Panchal Ltd.

Dr. *Cr.*

2010		*Rs.*	2010		Rs.
Mar. 31	To Realisation Account	14,47,500	Mar. 31	By Equity Shares in Panchal Ltd.	12,00,000
				By Bank	2,47,500
		14,47,500			14,47,500

Equity Shares in Panchal Ltd.

Dr. *Cr.*

2010		*Rs.*	2010		*Rs.*
Mar. 31	To Panchal Ltd.	12,00,000	Mar. 31	By Equity Shareholders	12,00,000

Equity Share Capital Account

Dr.					Cr.
2010		Rs.	2010		Rs.
Mar. 31	To Realisation Account	5,00,000	Mar. 31	By Balance b/fd	20,00,000
	To Equity Shareholders Account	15,00,000			
		20,00,000			20,00,000

Equity Shareholders Account

Dr.					Cr.
2010		Rs.	2010		Rs.
Mar. 31	To Profit & Loss Account	70,000	Mar. 31	By Equity Share Capital	15,00,000
	To Bank	2,47,500		By Realisation Account (profit)	17,500
	To Equity Shares in Panchal Ltd.	12,00,000			
		15,17,500			15,17,500

Books of Panchal Ltd.

Journal

Date		Particulars		Dr. Rs.	Cr. Rs.
2010 Mar.	31	Business Purchase Account	Dr.	14,47,500	
		To Liquidator of Vidur Ltd.			14,47,500
		Amount payable to Liquidator of Vidur Ltd. for the busines taken over.			
”	”	Fixed Assets	Dr.	13,10,000	
		Current Assets	Dr.	9,70,000	
		To Current Liabilities			3,50,000
		To Business Purchase Account			14,47,500
		To Investments in Equity Share of Vidur Ltd.			4,75,000
		To Capital Reserve			7,500
		Assets and liabilities of Vidur Ltd. taken over, consideration payable now, cancellation of shares of vendor company on take over and the resultant capital profit on acquisition credited to Capital Reserve			
”	”	Liquidator of Vidur Ltd.	Dr.	14,47,500	
		To Equity Share Capital Account			10,00,000
		To Securities Premium Account			2,00,000
		To Bank			2,47,500
		Allotment of 1,00,000 equity shares of Rs.10 each at a premium of Rs. 2 per share and payment of cash to liquidator of Vidur Ltd. in discharge of consideration.			
”	”	Capital Reserve	Dr.	7,500	
		Goodwill	Dr.	1,500	
		To Bank			9,000
		Payment of winding up cost in Vidur Ltd., Rs. 9,000 resulting in Goodwill of Rs. 1,500 after exhausting Rs. 7,500 of Capital Reserve on acquisition.			

Balance Sheet of Panchal Ltd.
as at 31st March, 2010

	Rs.		Rs.
Share Capital		**Fixed Assets**	
Authorised	?	Goodwill	1,500
Issued Subscribed		Other Fixed Assets	45,20,000
4,00,000 Equity Shares of		**Current Assets, Loans**	
Rs.10 each	40,00,000	**and Advances**	
(Of the above shares,		(A) Current Assets	29,73,500
1,00,000 equity share have		(B) Loans and Advances	Nil
been allotted as fully paid up			
pursuant to contract in that			
payment being recieved in cash)			
Reserves and Surplus			
Securities Premium	2,00,000		
General Reserve	10,00,000		
Current Liabilities and Provisions			
(A) Current Liabilities	22,95,000		
(B) Provisions	Nil		
	74,95,000		74,95,000

Working Notes :

Current Assets

	Rs.		Rs.
To Balance b/fd	22,60,000	By Liquidator of Vidur Ltd.	2,47,500
To Business Purchase Account	9,70,000	By Capital Reserve	7,500
		By Goodwill	1,500
		By Balance c/fd	29,73,500
	32,30,000		32,30,000

Illustration 32. The following are the summarized Balance Sheets of X Ltd. and Y Ltd. as on 31st March, 2010:—

X Ltd.

	Rs.		Rs.
Share Capital	40,000	Sundry Assets	50,000
Profit and Loss Account	5,000	Shares in Y Ltd.	
15% Debentures	10,000	(1,500 shares)	20,000
Creditors	15,000		
	70,000		70,000

Y Ltd.

	Rs.		Rs.
Share Capital		Sundry Assets	34,000
(of Rs. 10 each)	20,000		
Creditors	14,000		
	34,000		34,000

A new company, XY Ltd., is formed to a aquire the entire business of X Ltd. and Y Ltd. For this purpose, sundry assets of X Ltd. were valued at Rs.30,000 and sundry assets of Y Ltd. at Rs. 20,000. The consideration is to be discharged in shares of the new company.

Close the books of X Ltd. and Y Ltd.

Also give journal entries in the books of XY Ltd. for the purchase of business.

[Adapted B.,Com. (Hons.) Delhi, 1987]

Solution :

Books of X Ltd.

Realisation Account

Dr.					Cr.
2010		Rs.	2010		Rs.
Mar. 31	To Sundry Assets	50,000	Mar. 31	By Creditors	15,000
	To Shares in Y Ltd. (Loss)	15,500		By 15% Debentures	10,000
				By XY Ltd. (consideration)	5,000
				By Sundry Shareholders Account (loss)	35,500
		65,500			65,500

XY Ltd.

Dr.					Cr.
2010		Rs.	2010		Rs.
Mar. 31	To Realisation Account	5,000	Mar. 31	By Shares in XY Ltd.	5,000

Shares in Y Ltd.

Dr.					Cr.
2010		Rs.	2010		Rs.
Mar. 31	To balance b/fd	20,000	Mar. 31	By Shares in XY Ltd.	4,500
				By Realisation Account (loss)	15,500
		20,000			20,000

Shares in XY Ltd.

Dr.					Cr.
2010		Rs.	2010		Rs.
Mar. 31	To XY Ltd.	5,000	Mar. 31	By Sundry Shareholdres Account	9,500
	To Shares in Y Ltd.	4,500			
		9,500			9,500

Sundry Shareholders Account

Dr.					Cr.
2010		Rs.	2010		Rs.
Mar. 31	To Realisation Account—loss	35,500	Mar. 31	By Share Capital Account	40,000
	To Shares in XY Ltd.	9,500		By Profit and Loss Account	5,000
		45,000			45,000

Books of Y Ltd.

Realisation Account

Dr.					Cr.
2010		Rs.	2010		Rs.
Mar. 31	To Sundry Assets	34,000	Mar. 31	By Creditors	14,000
				By XY Ltd. (consideration)	6,000
				By Sundry Shareholders Account (loss)	14,000
		34,000			34,000

XY Ltd.

Dr.					*Cr.*
2010		*Rs.*	2010		*Rs.*
Mar. 31	To Realisation	6,000	Mar. 31	By Shares in XY Ltd.	6,000

Shares in XY Ltd.

Dr.					*Cr.*
2010		*Rs.*	2010		*Rs.*
Mar. 31	To XY Ltd.	6,000	Mar. 31	By Sundry Shareholders Account	6,000
		6,000			6,000

Sundry Shareholders Account

Dr.					*Cr.*
2010		*Rs.*	2010		*Rs.*
Mar. 31	To Realisation Account (loss)	14,000	Mar. 31	By Share Capital Account	20,000
	To Shares in XY Ltd.	6,000			
		20,000			20,000

Calculation of consideration:		X Ltd.		Y Ltd.
	Rs.	*Rs.*	*Rs.*	*Rs.*
Sundry Assets		30,000		20,000
Less : Liabilities taken over:				
Creditors	15,000		14,000	
15% Debentures	10,000	25,000	Nil	14,000
		5,000		6,000

As X Ltd. holds 1,500 shares *i.e.,* 3/4th shares of Y Ltd., it will get 3/4th share of Rs.6,000 = Rs. 4,500

Books of XY Ltd.

				Dr.	*Cr.*
2010				*Rs.*	*Rs.*
Mar.	31	Business Purchase Account	Dr.	11,000	
		To Liquidator of X Ltd.			5,000
		To Liquidator of Y Ltd.			6,000
		Amount payable to Liquidator of X Ltd. and Liquidator of Y Ltd. for the respective businesses purchased			
"	"	Sundry Assets	Dr.	50,000	
		To Creditors			29,000
		To 15% Debentures			10,000
		To Business Purchase Account			11,000
		Incorporation of assets and liabilities taken from X Ltd. and Y Ltd.			
"	"	Liquidator of X Ltd.	Dr.	5,000	
		Liquidator of Y Ltd.	Dr.	6,000	
		To Share Capital Account			11,000
		Allotment of 500 shares of Rs. 10 each at par to liquidator of X Ltd. and 600 shares of Rs. 10 each at par to liquidator of Y Ltd.			

Illustration 33. The following is the balance sheet of P Ltd. as on March 31, 2010 :—

Capital and Liabilities		*Rs.*	*Assets*	*Rs.*
Authorised & Issued Capital:			Land & Buildings	2,50,000
80,00,000 shares of Rs.10 each, fully			Plant & Machinery	6,00,000
paid		8,00,000	Stock and Work in Progress	2,35,000
Debentures (secured			Sundry Debtors	2,49,000
by a floating charge	5,00,000		Cash Balance	26,000
Accrued Interest	30,000	5,30,000	Profit and Loss Account	2,50,000
Sundry Creditors		2,80,000		
		16,10,000		16,10,000

The debentures are held by G Ltd. who also hold 20,000 shares acquired during the past two years at a total cost of Rs. 1,45,000.

Negotiations between the two companies resulted in an agreement for the absorption of P Ltd. by G Ltd. upon the following terms:

(a) That G Ltd. takes over the assets and liabilities of P Ltd. as on 31st March, 2010 at their book figures. subject to the revaluation of the Plant and Machinery at Rs, 4,50,000.

(b) That the amount due in respect of debentures be set off against the purchase consideration and that they be cancelled on the completion of the transaction.

(c) That the outside shareholders in P Ltd. be given Rs. 10 shares issued at par by G Ltd. on the basis of such shares being worth Rs. 15 each and the shares in P Ltd. being worth Rs. 5 each. (You are to assume that no fractional holding resulted).

The arrangement was approved by the necessary resolution of the shareholders in P Ltd.

Show journal entries required to close the books of P Ltd. and to record the transactions in the books of G Ltd. including the transfers required to close the accounts therein relating to the shares and debentures in P Ltd.

(Adapted C.A. Final and B.Com., Banaras)

Solution :

The consideration in the problem will be ascertained with reference to paragraph (c) of the arrangement. The outside shareholders (that is, shareholders other than G Ltd.) hold 60,000 shares. Each share is valued at Rs. 5 per share. Hence the total consideration is Rs. 3,00,000. This will be discharged by G Ltd. in the form of its own shares which are valued at Rs. 15 per share. Hence, total number of shares to be issued by G Ltd. to outside shareholders in P Ltd. is 20,000, *i.e.*, 3,00,000/15. The student should note that entries are to be made at par, that is, Rs, 10 per share. Hence, for the purpose of entries, the consideration comes to Rs. 2,00,000, *i.e.*, 2,00,000 × Rs. 10 although the real consideration is Rs. 3,00,000.

Books of P Ltd.

Journal

				Dr.	*Cr.*
2010				*Rs.*	*Rs.*
Mar.	31	Realisation Account	Dr.	13,60,000	
		To Land and Buildings			2,50,000
		To Plant and Machinery			6,00,000
		To Stock and Work in Progress			2,35,000
		To Sundry Debtors			2,49,000
		To Cash			26,000
		The transfer of various assets to Realisation Account on the sale of business to G Ltd., as per agreement.			
"	"	12% Debentures	Dr.	5,00,000	
		Interest Accrued	Dr.	30,000	
		Sundry Creditors	Dr.	2,80,000	
		To Realisation Account			8,10,000
		The transfer of various liabilities taken over by G Ltd.			

				Rs.	Rs.
Mar.	31	G Ltd.	Dr.	2,00,000	
		To Realisation Account			2,00,000
		The purchase price agreed to be paid by G Ltd. as per agreement			
"	"	Shares in G Ltd.	Dr.	2,00,000	
		To G Ltd.			2,00,000
		Receipt of shares in G Ltd. in discharge of consideration.			
"	"	Share Capital	Dr.	8,00,000	
		To Sundry (outside) Shareholders Account			6,00,000
		To Realisation Account			2,00,000
		Transfer of Share Capital to Outside Shareholders for shares held by them and to Realisation Account for shares held by G Ltd.			
"	"	Sundry (outside) Shareholders Account	Dr.	4,00,000	
		To Profit and Loss Account			2,50,000
		To Realisation Account			1,50,000
		Transfer of the debit balance in Profit and Loss Account and the loss on Realisation to Sundry Shareholders.			
"	"	Sundry (outside) Shareholders Account	Dr.	2,00,000	
		To Shares in G Ltd.			2,00,000
		Distribution of shares in G Ltd. amongst the shareholders.			

A more sophisticated treatment in the books of P Ltd. is as follows:

Consideration :

80,000 Shares @ Rs. 5 = Rs. 4,00,000

Number of shares to be issued by G Ltd. 4,00,000 ÷ 15 = 26,666 2/3.

Valued at par, Rs. 2,66,667.

Journal Entries (without narrations):

				Dr.	Cr.
2010				Rs.	Rs.
Mar.	31	Realisation Account	Dr.	13,60,000	
		To Land & Builidings			2,50,000
		To Plant & Machinery			6,00,000
		To Stock and Work in Progress			2,35,000
		To Sundry Debtors			2,49,000
		To Cash			26,000
"	"	Debentures	Dr.	5,00,000	
		Interest Accrued	Dr.	30,000	
		Sundry Creditors	Dr.	2,80,000	
		To Realisation Account			8,10,000
"	"	G Ltd.	Dr.	2,66,667	
		To Realisation Account			2,66,667
"	"	Share Capital	Dr.	8,00,000	
		To Sundry Members			8,00,000
"	"	Sundry Members	Dr.	5,33,333	
		To Profit & Loss Account			2,50,000
		To Realisation Account			2,83,333
"	"	Sundry Members	Dr.	66,667	
		To G Ltd.			66,667

				Rs.	Rs.
Mar.	31	Shares in GLtd.	Dr.	2,00,000	
		To G Ltd.			2,00,000
"	"	Sundery Members	Dr.	2,00,000	
		To Shares in G Ltd.			2,00,000

Journal of G Ltd.

				Dr.	Cr.
2010				Rs.	Rs.
Mar.	31	Business Purchase Account	Dr.	2,00,000	
		To Liquidator of P Ltd.			2,00,000
		The price agreed to be paid for the business of P Ltd. as per agreement dated.......			
"	"	Land and Buildings	Dr.	2,50,000	
		Plant and Machinery	Dr.	4,50,000	
		Stock and Work in Progress	Dr.	2,35,000	
		Sundry Debtors	Dr.	2,49,000	
		Bank	Dr.	26,000	
		To Sundry Creditors			2,80,000
		To Debentures in P Ltd.			5,00,000
		To Interest Accrued			30,000
		To Shares in P ltd.			1,45,000
		To Business Purchase Account			2,00,000
		To Capital Reserve Account			55,000
		Various assets and liabilities taken over from P Ltd. and the cancellation of accounts relating to debentures and shares in P Ltd. previously purchased.			
"	"	Liquidator of P Ltd.	Dr.	2,00,000	
		To Share Capital Account			2,00,000
		The allotment of 20,000 shares of Rs. 10 each fully paid is discharge of the consideration			

Illustration 34. The following are the Balance Sheets of *A* Ltd. and *B* Ltd. as on 31st March, 2010:—

A Ltd.

Liabilities	*Rs.*	*Assets*	*Rs.*
Share Capital		Fixed Assets	15,00,000
20,000 equity shares of Rs. 100 each, fully paid up	20,00,000	Investments	2,50,000
General Reserves	15,00,000	Current Assets	32,50,000
Current Liabilities	15,00,000		
	50,00,000		50,00,000

B Ltd.

Liabilities	*Rs.*	*Assets*	*Rs.*
Share Capital		Goodwill	1,00,000
10,000 Equity Shares of Rs. 100 each, fully paid-up	10,00,000	Other Fixed Assets	3,00,000
General Reserve	5,00,000	Current Assets	14,00,000
Current Liabilities	2,00,000		
Proposed Dividend	1,00,000		
	18,00,000		18,00,000

B Ltd. is to be taken over by *A* Ltd. on the following terms:

(*i*) *B* Ltd. declares a dividend of 10 per cent before absorption for the payment of which it is to retain sufficient amount of cash. (Ignore Corporate Dividend Tax)

(*ii*) The net worth of *B* Ltd. is valued at Rs. 14,50,000.

(*iii*) The consideration is satisfied by the allotment of fully paid shares of Rs. 100 each in *A* Ltd. The following further information is also to be taken into consideration:—

(*a*) *A* Ltd. holds 2,500 shares of *B* Ltd. at a cost of Rs. 2,00,000.

(*b*) The stocks of *B* Ltd. include items valued at Rs. 50,000 from *A* Ltd. (Cost to *A* Ltd., Rs. 37,500.)

(*c*) The creditors of *B* Ltd. include Rs. 45,000 due to *A* Ltd.

Show ledger accounts in the books of *B* Ltd. to give effect to the above and the balance sheet of *A* Ltd. after amalgamation. *[Adapted. C.A. (Inter.) and C.S. (Inter.)]*

Solution :

The total consideration (based on net worth of *B* Ltd.) is Rs. 14,50,000. Since *A* Ltd. already holds 2500 shares out of 10,000 shares allotted by *B* Ltd., it has now, to pay a net consideration 3/4 × Rs. 14,50,000 = Rs. 10,87,500.

Books of *B* Ltd.

Dr. **Realisation Account** *Cr.*

		Rs.			*Rs.*
2010			2010		
Mar. 31	To Goodwill	1,00,000	Mar. 31	By Current Liabilities	2,00,000
	To Fixed Assets	3,00,000		By *A* Ltd.	10,87,500
	To Current Assets	13,00,000		By Share Capital Account	2,50,000
				By Equity Shareholders Account (Loss)	1,62,500
		17,00,000			17,00,000

Dr. ***A* Ltd.** *Cr.*

		Rs.			*Rs.*
2010			2010		
Mar. 31	To Realisation Account (Consideration)	10,87,500	Mar. 31	By Shares in *A* Ltd.	10,87,500
		10,87,500			10,87,500

Dr. **Proposed Dividend Account** *Cr.*

		Rs.			*Rs.*
2010			2010		
Mar. 31	To Dividend Payable Account	1,00,000	Mar. 31	By Balance b/fd	1,00,000

Dr. **Dividend Payable Account** *Cr.*

		Rs.			*Rs.*
2010			2010		
Mar. 31	To Bank	1,00,000	Mar. 31	By Proposed Dividend Account	1,00,000

Dr. **Shares in *A* Ltd.** *Cr.*

		Rs.			*Rs.*
2010			2010		
Mar. 31	To A Ltd.	10,87,500	Mar. 31	By Equity Shareholders (outside) Account	10,87,500

Dr. **Equity Shareholders (outside) Account** Cr.

		Rs.			Rs.
2010			2010		
Mar. 31	To Realisation Account (Loss)	1,62,500	Mar. 31	By Share Capital	7,50,000
	To Shares in *A* Ltd.	10,87,500		By General Reserve	5,00,000
		12,50,000			12,50,000

Balance Sheet of *A* Ltd. as on 31st March, 2010.

Liabilities	Rs.	*Assets*	Rs.	Rs.
Share Capital		**Fixed Assets**		
30,875 equity shares	30,87,500	A Ltd.	15,00,000	
of Rs.100 each, fully paid-up		B Ltd.	3,00,000	18,00,000
(Out of these 10,875 equity		**Investments**		50,000
shares have been issued to		**Current Assets, Loans & Advances**		
vendors pursuant to a contract for		(A) Current Assets		45,17,500
consideration other than cash)		(B) Loans and Advances		Nil
Reserves & Surpluse				
Capital Reserve	1,00,000			
General Reserve	15,00,000			
Profit & Loss A/c	25,000			
(Divident from B Ltd.)				
Current Liabilities & Provisions				
(A) Current Liabilities	16,55,000			
(B) Provisions	Nil			
	63,67,500			63,67,500

Notes:

(i) Rs. 2,00,000 has been deducted from Investments being cost of shares held in B Ltd.

	Rs.
(ii) Current Assets:	
(a) Current Assets of *A* Ltd.	32,50,000
Add: Dividend received from *B* Ltd.	25,000
	32,75,000
Less: Inter company owings	45,000
	32,30,000
(b) Current Assets of *B* Ltd. Rs. (14,00,000 – 1,00,000)	13,00,000
Less: Unrealised profits on stock Rs. (50,000 – 37,500)	12,500
	12,87,500
Total Current Assets:	
A Ltd.	32,30,000
B Ltd.	12,87,500
	45,17,500
(iii) Current Liabilities	
(a) A Ltd.	15,00,000
(b) B Ltd.	2,00,000

	Rs.	
	17,00,000	
Less: Inter-company Owings	45,000	
	16,55,000	

(iv) Calculation of Capital Reserve:	Rs.	Rs.
Assets taken over from *B* Ltd.		
Fixed Assets		3,00,000
Current Assets	13,00,000	
Less: Unrealised profit on stock	12,500	12,87,500
		15,87,500
Less:		
Investment in *B* Ltd.	2,00,000	
Current Liabilities	2,00,000	
Consideration	10,87,500	14,87,500
Capital Reserve		1,00,000

(b) Shares held by the transferor company in the transferee company. The proper treatment in a case like this is to deduct from the number of shares, that would have been otherwise allotted to the transferor company, the shares already held by it in the transferee company. Suppose, S Ltd. holds 1,000 shares in P Ltd., P Ltd. acquires the business of S Ltd. allotting 2 shares for every three held in S Ltd., and the total number of shares in S Ltd. is 15,000. In all, the shareholders of S Ltd. will get 10,000 shares in P Ltd., *i.e.,* 15,000 × 2/3. Since S Ltd. already has got 1,000 shares in P Ltd., it will get from that company additional 9,000 shares. P Ltd. will calculate the consideration on the basis of 9,000 shares.

While closing the books of the transferor company, it would be proper to revalue the shares already held by it in the transferee company, debiting or crediting the Realisation Account as the case may be. The account representing the shares should not be transferred to the Realisation Account.

Illustration 35. P Ltd. takes over the business of V Ltd. for Rs. 16,00,000 on 31st March, 2010 on which date the balance sheets of the two companies stand as follows:—

P Ltd.

Liabilities	*Rs.*	*Assets*	*Rs.*
Equity Shares of		Goodwill	2,00,000
Rs. 10 each, fully paid	36,00,000	Other Fixed Assets	28,00,000
General Reserve	8,50,000	Cash at Bank	5,00,000
Current Liabilities	10,50,000	Other Current Assets	20,00,000
	55,00,000		55,00,000

V Ltd.

Liabilities	*Rs.*	*Assets*	*Rs.*
Equity Shares		Fixed Assets	12,00,000
of Rs.10 each, fully paid	20,00,000	2,500 Shares in P Ltd. (at cost)	30,000
Current Liabilities	3,00,000	Cash at Bank	10,000
		Other Current Assets	8,60,000
		Profit and Loss Account	2,00,000
	23,00,000		23,00,000

The cosideration is to be discharged by a cash payment of Rs, 1,00,000 and allotment of sufficient number of fully paid equity shares in P Ltd. of the face value of Rs. 10 each valued at Rs. 12.50 each. Expenses of winding up, Rs. 10,000 are borne by P Ltd.

You are required to

(*i*) prepare important ledger accounts and pass journal entries in the books of V Ltd;

(*ii*) pass journal entries in the books of P Ltd.; and

(*iii*) draw P Ltd.'s balance sheet immediately following the absorption.

Solution :

The consideration to be discharged in the form of shares	=	Rs.16,00,000 – Rs.1,00,000
	=	Rs.15,00,000
Agreed value of one share of P Ltd.	=	Rs. 12.50
Hence the number of shares of be allotted	=	15,00,000 × 2/25 = 1,20,000
Shares already held by V Ltd.	=	2,500
Agreed value of 1,17,500 shares	=	1,17,500 × Rs.12.50
	=	Rs. 14,68,750
Adding Rs. 1,00,000 of cash to be paid, entries are to be passed with Rs. 14,68,750 + Rs. 1,00,000	=	Rs. 15,68,750

Books of V Ltd.

Realisation Account

Dr.					Cr.
2010		*Rs.*	2010		*Rs.*
Mar. 31	To Fixed Assets	12,00,000	Mar. 31	By Current Liabilities	3,00,000
	To Cash at Bank	10,000		By P Ltd. (reduced consideration)	15,68,750
	To Other Current Assets	8,60,000		By Shares in P Ltd. (revaluation profit)	1,250
				By Sundry Shareholders Account (loss)	2,00,000
		20,70,000			20,70,000

P Ltd.

Dr.					Cr.
2010		*Rs.*	2010		*Rs.*
Mar. 31	To Realisation Account	15,68,750	Mar. 31	By Bank	1,00,000
				By Shares in P Ltd.	14,68,750
		15,68,750			15,68,750

Shares in P Ltd.

Dr.					Cr.
2010		*Rs.*	2010		*Rs.*
Mar. 31	To Balance b/fd	30,000	Mar. 31	By Sundry Shareholders Account (distribution)	15,00,000
	To Realisation Account (profit on revaluation)	1,250			
	To P Ltd.	14,68,750			
		15,00,000			15,00,000

Cash Book (Bank Columns)

Dr.					Cr.
2010		*Rs.*	2010		*Rs.*
Mar. 31	To Balance b/f	10,000	Mar. 31	By Realisation Account - transfer	10,000
	To P Ltd.	1,00,000		By Sundry Shareholders Account	1,00,000

Sundry Shareholders Account

Dr.					Cr.
2010		*Rs.*	2010		*Rs.*
Mar. 31	To Profit & Loss Account	2,00,000	Mar. 31	By Equity Share Capital Account	20,00,000
	To Realisation Account (loss)	2,00,000			
	To Bank	1,00,000			
	To Shares in P Ltd.	15,00,000			
		20,00,000			20,00,000

Journal

			Dr.	*Cr.*
2010			*Rs.*	*Rs.*
Mar. 31	Realisation Account	Dr.	20,70,000	
	To Fixed Assets			12,00,000
	To Cash at Bank			10,000
	To Other Current Assets			8,60,000
	Transfer of all the assets (except shares in P Ltd.) to Realisation Account on winding up of the company.			
	Current Liabilities	Dr.	3,00,000	
	To Realisation Account			3,00,000
	Current liabilities transferred to Realisation Account as they are being taken over by P Ltd.			
	P Ltd.	Dr.	15,68,750	
	To Realisation Account			15,68,750
	The reduced amount of consideration now receivable from P Ltd. for the business sold to it.			
	Bank	Dr.	1,00,000	
	Shares in P Ltd.	Dr.	14,68,750	
	To P Ltd.			15,68,750
	Cash and value of 1,17,500 shares received from P Ltd. in discharge of the consideration.			
	Shares in P Ltd.	Dr.	1,250	
	To Realisation Account			1,250
	Appreciation in the value of 2,500 shares (now valued at Rs. 12.50 each) credited to Realisation Account			
	Equity Share Capital Account	Dr.	20,00,000	
	To Sundry Shareholders Account			20,00,000
	Transfer of Equity Share Capital Account to Sundry Shareholders Account.			
	Sundry Shareholders Account	Dr.	4,00,000	
	To Profit & Loss Account			2,00,000
	To Realisation Account			2,00,000
	Transfer of Profit & Loss Account and loss on realisation to Shareholders Account.			
	Sundry Shareholders Account	Dr.	16,00,000	
	To Bank			1,00,000
	To Shares in P Ltd.			15,00,000
	Distribution of cash and shares in P Ltd. among sundry shareholders to satisfy their claim.			

Books of P Ltd.
Journal

			Dr.	Cr.
2010			Rs.	Rs.
Mar. 31	Business Purchase Account	Dr.	15,68,750	
	To Liquidator of V Ltd.			15,68,750
	Amount payable to liquidator of V Ltd.			
	Fixed Assets	Dr.	12,00,000	
	Cash at Bank	Dr.	10,000	
	Other Current Assets	Dr.	8,60,000	
	To Current Liabilities			3,00,000
	To Business Purchase Account			15,68,750
	To Capital Reserve			2,01,250
	Assets and liabilities taken over from V Ltd. and capital profit resulting from take-over.			
	Liquidator of V Ltd.	Dr.	15,68,750	
	To Bank			1,00,000
	To Equity Share Capital Account			11,75,000
	To Securities Premium Account			2,93,750
	Payment of cash and allotment of 1,17,500 equity shares of Rs. 10 each at a premium of Rs. 2,50 P per share to liquidator of V Ltd. in discharge of consideration.			
	Capital Reserve	Dr.	10,000	
	To Bank			10,000
	Cost of winding up of V Ltd. being paid up resulting in the reducation of capital reserve on acquisition of business.			

Balance Sheet of P Ltd. as on 31st March, 2010

	Rs.		Rs.
Share Capital		**Fixed Assets**	
Authorised, Issued & Subscribed:		Goodwill	2,00,000
4,77,500 Equity Shares of		Other Fixed Assets	40,00,000
Rs. 10 each, fully paid	47,75,000	**Current Assets, Loans and Advances**	
(Of the above shares,		(*A*) Current Assets	
1,17,500 shares have been		Cash of Bank	4,00,000
allotted to vendors pursuant		Other Current Assets	28,60,000
to a contract without payment		(*B*) Loans and Advances	Nil
being received in cash).			
Reserves and Surplus			
Capital Reserve	1,91,250		
Securities Premium	2,93,750		
General Reserve	8,50,000		
Current Liabilities and Provisions			
(*A*) Current Liabilities	13,50,000		
(*B*) Provisions	Nil		
	74,60,000		74,60,000

(*c*) *Shares held by both companies in one another.* The main point in such a case is to determine the value of shares of both the compaines, since the value of one share will influence the value of the other. If C Ltd. holds shares in D Ltd. and D Ltd. holds shares in C Ltd., the value of a share in D Ltd. will obviously be influenced by the value of a share in *C* Ltd., and *vice versa.* The total value is ascertained by means of an algebraical equation. Consider the following balance sheets:

	C Ltd.	D Ltd.		C Ltd.	D Ltd.
	Rs.	*Rs.*		*Rs.*	*Rs.*
Share Capital (shares of Rs. 100 each, fully paid)	10,00,000	5,00,000	Sundry Assets	10,80,000	7,00,000
			1,000 Shares in D Ltd.	1,20,000	
Reserves	2,00,000	3,00,000	1,000 Shares in C Ltd.		1,00,000
	12,00,000	8,00,000		12,00,000	8,00,000

Assuming the assets to be of the value stated in the balance sheets, the value of shares in D Ltd. is Rs. 7,00,000 plus 1/10 of the value of the shares in C Ltd; similarly the value of shares of C Ltd. is Rs. 10,80,000 plus 1/5 of the value of shares in D Ltd. Let *c* denote the value of shares in C Ltd. and *d* denote the value of shares in D Ltd. Then :

$c \quad = \quad 10{,}80{,}000 + 1/5\ d$; and

$d \quad = \quad 7{,}00{,}000 + 1/10\ c.$

Substituting the value of *c*,

$d \quad = \quad 7{,}00{,}000 + 1/10\ (10{,}80{,}000 + 1/5\ d)$

$\quad = \quad 7{,}00{,}00 + 1{,}08{,}000 + 1/50\ d$

$\quad = \quad 8{,}08{,}000 + 1/50\ d$

Multiplying both sides by 50,

$50d \quad = \quad 4{,}04{,}00{,}000 + d$

$49d \quad = \quad 4{,}04{,}00{,}000$

$d \quad = \quad 8{,}24{,}490$

$c \quad = \quad 10{,}80{,}000 + 1/5 \times 8{,}24{,}490$

$\quad = \quad 12{,}44{,}898$

Value of each share:

D Ltd. Rs. 8,24,490/5,000 = Rs.164.90

C Ltd. Rs. 12,44,989/10,000 = Rs. 124. 49

If C Ltd. acquires the business of D Ltd. it will determine the total purchase price at 4,000 shares (held outside) @ Rs. 164.90 or Rs. 6,59,592 in all. The number of shares to be issued will be : 6,59,592/124.49 less 1,000 shares already held by D Ltd.

It the two companies are amalgamated with another company, the total consideration will be Rs. 17,80,000 to be divided by the outside shareholders in the two companies as follows:

	C Ltd.	D Ltd.
	Rs.	*Rs.*
Total value of shares as determined above	12,44,898	8,24,490
Less: 1/10 for shares held by D Ltd.	1,24,490	
1/5 for shares held by C Ltd.		1,64,898
Amount due to outsiders	11,20,408	6,59,592

Illustration 36. The following are the summarised balance sheets of two companies, P Ltd. and N Ltd. as on 31st March, 2010:—

Liabilities	P Ltd. *Rs.*	N Ltd. *Rs.*	*Assets*	P Ltd. *Rs.*	N Ltd. *Rs.*
Share Capital :			Shares in P Ltd (10,000)		1,00,000
(Shares of Rs. 10 each)	5,00,000	1,80,000	Shares in N Ltd. (4,500)	30,000	
Reserves	1,45,000	...	Debentures in N Ltd.	1,00,000	
Debentures	...	2,00,000	Sundry Assets	8,15,000	4,60,000
Trade Creditors	3,00,000	2,00,000	Profit and Loss A/c	...	20,000
	9,45,000	5,80,000		9,45,000	5,80,000

The two companies agreed that *P* should take over N Ltd. The debentureholders in N Ltd. agreed to the conversion of their debentures into 14% Redeemable Preference Shares of Rs. 100 each. Prior to the absorption, P Ltd. declared a dividend of 20% — the dividend had not yet been paid. Shareholders in *N* Ltd. were to receive shares in P Ltd. on the basis of the intrinsic value of the shares. The sundry assets of N Ltd. had to be written up by Rs. 40,000 and those of P Ltd. reduced by Rs. 15,000. Assume the absence of corporate dividend tax.

Draw up the Balance Sheet of P Ltd. after the absorption is completed.

Solution :

Balance Sheet of P Ltd. as on March 31, 2010

Liabilities	*Rs.*	*Assets*	*Rs.*
Share Capital		Sundry Assets	13,00,000
Equity: 55,563 fully paid shares of Rs. 10 each	5,55,630		
14% Redeemable Preference Shares of Rs. 100 each	1,00,000		
	6,55,630		
(Of the above shares 5,563 equity shares and all the preference shares have been issued for consideration other than cash)			
Securities Premium	6,453		
Reserves — Capital	12,917		
— General	45,000		
Trade Creditors	5,00,000		
Dividend Payable	80,000		
	13,00,000		13,00,000

Working Notes:

(*i*) Intrinsic value (without taking into account shares held)

	P Ltd.	N Ltd.
	Rs.	*Rs.*
Sundry Assets as valued	8,00,000	5,00,000
Debentures in N Ltd.	1,00,000	
Add : Dividend Receivable from P Ltd.		20,000
	9,00,000	5,20,000
Less : Liabilities and Dividend Payable	4,00,000	4,00,000
	5,00,000	1,20,000

Total = Rs. 5,00,000 + Rs. 1,20,000 = Rs. 6,20,000.

(*ii*) Division of Rs. 6,20,000 between P Ltd. and N Ltd.:

Let *P* Stand for the shares of P Ltd. and *n* for that of N Ltd.

Then :

p = 5,00,000 + 1/4 n

n = 1,20,000 + 1/5 p

= 1,20,000 + 1/5 (5,00,000+1/4n) substituting the value of P

= 1,20,000 + 1,00,000+1/20 n = 2,20,000 + 1/20 n

20 n = 44,00,000 + n

19 n = 44,00,000

n = 2,31,579

p = 5,00,000 + 1/4 × 3,21,579 = 5,57,895.

(*iii*) Intrinsic value of one share of P Ltd. 5,57,895/50,000 = Rs. 11.16

(*iv*) Amount to be paid to outsiders in N Ltd. = Rs. 1,73,684.

(*v*) Number of shares in P Ltd. to be issued = 15,563 *i.e.,* 1,73,684 ÷ 11.16

Shares already with N Ltd. = 10,000

Additional shares to be issued 5,563

Amount : Share Capital @ Rs. 10 — Rs. 55,630

Securities Premium @ Rs. 1.16 — Rs.6,453

(*vi*) P Ltd. will not convert Own Debentures in N Ltd. into preference shares.

			Rs.
(*vii*)	Goodwill / Capital Reserve		
	Assets taken over from N Ltd.		5,00,000
	Add : Cancellation of Dividend Payable		20,000
			5,20,000
	Less: Intrinisc value of shares held in N Ltd. 2,31,579 × 1/4	57,895	
	Liabilities taken over	4,00,000	
	Instrinsic value of 5,563 shares now issued	62,083	5,19,978
	Capital Profit		22
(*viii*)	Capital Reserve :		
	Instrinsic value of 4,500 shares in N Ltd.		57,895
	Purchase price of these shares		30,000
			27,895
	Add : Capital Profit as in (*vii*) above		22
			27,917
	Less : Loss on revaluation of assets		15,000
			12,917

Amalgamation Scheme

While formulating schemes of amalgamation of two companies, the main point to remember is to evaluate the special advantage enjoyed by the companies. In other words, first of all goodwill of the companies should be valued (as discussed in the previous chapter). This will determine the shareholders' equity and the amount they can claim in the new amalgamated company. This is illustrated below :

Illustration 37. The following are the agreed balance sheets of A Ltd. and B Ltd. as on 31st March, 2010:

Liabilities		*A* Rs.	*B* Rs.	*Assets*	*A* Rs.	*B* Rs.
Share Capital :				Sundry Assets		
14% Preference		—	4,00,000	(worth the book value)	14,20,000	14,20,000
Equity		10,00,000	4,00,000			
14% Debentures		—	2,00,000			
General Reserves		1,00,000	1,00,000			
Sundry Creditors		50,000	50,000			
Profit & Loss Account						
Balance from 1998-99	20,000					
Profit for 1999-2000						
(before deb. intt.)	2,50,000	2,70,000	2,70,000			
		14,20,000	14,20,000		14,20,000	14,20,000

Negotiations are going on for the amalgamation of the two companies. Suggest a suitable scheme. Ignore income tax and corporate dividend tax. *(Adapted from C.A., Final)*

Solution : It is clear from the balance sheets that the two companies are equal in all respects except the capital structure. The assets of the two companies are of the same value. The profits earned (subject to preference dividend and debenture interest) are also equal. However, the difference in the constitution of funds will make an important difference as regards yield to equity shareholders as the following figures show.

		A	B
		Rs.	*Rs.*
Profit for 2009-2010		2,50,000	2,50,000
Less Interest on Debentures	28,000		
Preference Dividend	56,000	—	84,000
Profit available for equity shareholders		2,50,000	1,66,000
Ignoring corporate dividend tax, rate of dividend possible on equity shares		25%	41.5%

Since the market value of shares depends on the dividend paid, it is clear, the market value of one share in company B will be almost double the market value of one share in company A. Thus, the present arrangement in company B gives an important advantage to the equity shareholders of that company. They will not, therefore, consent to any scheme that does not compensate them for this advantage which they have to share with the shareholders of company A on amalgamation. The exact valuation of the advantage will depend upon the general expectation. Supposing the general expectation is 25%, the shares of company A will be valued at par and the equity shares shares of company B will be worth, in all, Rs. 1,66,000 × 100/25 or Rs. 6,64,000. The par value being Rs. 4,00,000, the equity shareholders of company B are entitled to an additional payment of Rs. 2,64,000. Hence, goodwill to the extent of this amount should be created and the interest of the equity shareholders in company B accordingly increased. The scheme, therefore, is to issue equity shares in the amalgamated company, say, C Ltd. as follows :

	Company A	*Company B*
	Rs.	*Rs.*
Equity Share Capital	10,00,000	4,00,000
General Reserves	1,00,000	1,00,000
Profit and Loss A/c Balance (Debenture interest and preference dividend deducted in case of company *B*)	2,70,000	1,86,000
Goodwill	—	2,64,000
Total	13,70,000	9,50,000

In addition, the debentureholders in *B* Ltd. should receive debentures in the new company and, similarly, the preference shareholders in *B* Ltd. should receive preferece shares in the new company. The debentureholders and preference shareholders should have no objection because in the new company their security will be even greater. If the scheme is carried out, the balance sheet of the amalgamated company, say, C Ltd., will be as follows:

Balance Sheet of C Ltd.

Liabilities	*Rs.*	*Assets*	*Rs.*
Share Capital : Issued		Goodwill	2,64,000
14% Preference Shares of Rs...each	4,00,000	Sundry Assets	28,40,000
Equity Shares of Rs...each	23,20,000		
14% Debentures	2,00,000		
Sundry Creditors	1,00,000		
Liability for Debenture Interest	28,000		
Liability for Preference Dividend	56,000		
	31,04,000		31,04,000

Illustration 38. The following are the balance sheets of *A* Ltd. and *B* Ltd as on **31st March, 2010:–**

Liabilities	*A Ltd.*	*B Ltd.*	*Assets*	*A Ltd.*	*B Ltd.*
	Rs.	*Rs.*		*Rs.*	*Rs.*
Share Capital			**Fixed Assets**	6,00,000	3,50,000
Equity Shares of Rs. 10 each	5,00,00	2,00,000	**Investments**		
10% Preference			4,000 Shares in B Ltd.	60,0000	
shares of Rs. 100 each	1,00,000	1,00,000	3,000 Shares in A Ltd.		80,000

Reserves and Surplus	2,00,000	1,50,000	**Current Assets**		
Secured Loans			Stock	3,00,000	1,70,000
12% Debentures	1,00,000	1,00,000	Debtors	1,60,000	90,000
Current Liabilities			Cash and Bank	90,000	30,0900
Bills Payable	20,000	20,000	**Loans and Advances**		
Sundry Creditors	3,40,000	1,60,000	Bills Receivable	50,000	10,000
	12,60,000	7,30,000		12,60,000	7,30,000

Contingent Liability: For bills receivable discounted, Rs. 20,000.

Fixed Assets of both the companies are to be revalued at 20% above book value. Both the companies are to pay 10% equity dividend; preference dividend having been already paid.

After the above transactions are given effect to, *A* Ltd. will take over *B* Ltd. on the following terms:

(*i*) 6 equity shares of Rs. 10 each will be issued by *A* Ltd. as par against 5 shares of *B* Ltd.

(*ii*) 10% preference shareholders of *B* Ltd. will be paid at 10% discount by issue of 11% preference shares of Rs. 100 each at par in *A* Ltd.

(*iii*) 12% debentureholders of *B* Ltd. are to be paid at 8% premium by 13% debentures in *A* Ltd. issued at 10% discount.

(*iv*) Rs. 20,000 is to paid by *A* Ltd. to *B* Ltd. for liquidation expenses.

Sundry Creditors of *B* ltd. include Rs. 30,000 due to *A* Ltd. Bills Receivable discounted by *A* Ltd. were all accepted by *B* Ltd.

(*a*) Prepare Journal entries, Vendors Account and Investment in *B* Ltd. Account in the books of *A* Ltd.

(*b*) Realisation Account, Equity Shareholders Account, *A* Ltd. Account and Investment in *A* Ltd. Account in the books of *B* Ltd; and

(*c*) Balance Sheet of *A* Ltd. after the amalgamation. *[Adapted C.A.(Final) May, 1988]*

Solution :

Working Notes :

	Rs.
(*i*) *Total number of shares in B Ltd.*	20,000
Less: already held by *A* Ltd.	4,000
Held by outsiders	16,000
Number of shares to be issued to outsiders 16,000 × 6/5	19,200
Less: already held by *B* Ltd.	3,000
Additional shares to be issued	16,200

(*ii*) *Calculation of consideration :*

	Amount Rs.	Form
(*a*) For equity shareholders	1,62,000	Equity shares
(*b*) For preferences shareholders	90,000	11% preference shares
	2,52,000	

(*iii*) *B Ltd.'s Cash and Bank balance:*	Rs.
As per its balance sheet	1,50,000
Add: Dividend received by *B* Ltd.	3,000
	1,53,000
Less : Dividend paid by *B* Ltd.	20,000
Balance taken over by *A* Ltd.	1,33,000

Books of *A* Ltd.
Journal

Date	Particulars		L.F.	Dr. Rs.	Cr. Rs.
2010 Mar. 31	Fixed Assets	Dr.		1,20,000	
	To Revaluation Reserve				1,20,000
	Revaluation of fixed assets at 20% above book value.				
	Bank	Dr.		4,000	
	To Surplus				4,000
	Dividend received from *B* Ltd. on 4,000 shares.				
	Surplus	Dr.		50,000	
	To Equity Dividend				50,000
	Declaration of equity dividend @ 10%.				
	Equity Dividend	Dr.		50,000	
	To Bank				50,000
	Distribution of equity dividend.				
	Business Purchase Account	Dr.		2,52,000	
	To *B* Ltd.				2,52,000
	Consideration payable to *B* Ltd. for business taken over.				
	Fixed Assets	Dr.		4,20,000	
	Stock	Dr.		1,70,000	
	Debtors	Dr.		90,000	
	Cash at Bank	Dr.		13,000	
	Bills Receivable	Dr.		10,000	
	To Debentures (*B* Ltd.)				1,08,000
	To Bills Payable				20,000
	To Sundry Creditors				1,60,000
	To Inverstment in *B* Ltd.				60,000
	To Business Purchase Account				2,52,000
	To Capital Reserve				1,03,000
	Incorporation of assets and liabilities taken over and cancellation of Investment in *B* Ltd. Account; Capital Reserve being credited with balancing figure.				
	B Ltd.	Dr.		2,52,000	
	To Equity Share Capital Account				1,62,000
	To 11% Preference share Capital Account				90,000
	Allotment of equity and 11% preference shares to discharge consideration for the business taken over.				
	Sundry Creditors	Dr.		30,000	
	To Debtors				30,000
	Cancellation of mutual owing.				
	Capital Reserve	Dr.		20,000	
	To *B* Ltd.				20,000
	Amount payable to *B* Ltd. for liquidation expenses.				
	B Ltd.	Dr.		20,000	
	To Bank				20,000
	Payment of liquidation expenses due to *B* Ltd.				

				Rs.	Rs.
Mar. 31	Debentures (*B* Ltd.)	Dr.		1,08,000	
	Discount on Issue of Debentures Account	Dr.		12,000	
	To 13% Debentures Account				
	Allotment of 13% debentures of the face value of Rs. 1,20,000 at a discount jof 10% to discharge the liability on *B* Ltd. debentures				1,20,000

Ledger

B Ltd.

Dr.					Cr.
2010		*Rs.*	2010		*Rs.*
Mar. 31	To Equity Share Capital Account	1,62,000	Mar. 31	By Business Purchase Account	2,52,000
	To 11% Preference Share Capital Account	90,000		By Capital Reserve (liquidation expenses)	20,000
	To Bank (for liquidation expenses)	20,000			
		2,72,000			2,72,000

Investment in B Ltd.

Dr.					Cr.
2010		*Rs.*	2010		*Rs.*
Mar. 31	To Balance b/fd	60,000	Mar. 31	By Business Purchase Account	60,000

Books of B Ltd.

Ledger

Realisation Account

Dr.					Cr.
2010		*Rs.*	2010		*Rs.*
Mar. 31	To Fixed Assets	4,20,000	Mar. 31	By 12% Debentures	1,00,000
	To Stock	1,70,000		By Bills Payable	20,000
	To Debtors	90,000		By Sundry Creditors	1,60,000
	To Cash and Bank	13,000		By *A* Ltd.(consideration)	2,52,000
	To Bills Receivable	10,000		By Preference shareholders Account (sacrifice)	10,000
	To Investment in *A* Ltd. (loss on revaluation)	50,000		By Equity share Capital Account (held by *A* Ltd.)	40,000
	To Bank (liquidation expenses)	20,000		By *A* Ltd. (for liquidation expenses)	20,000
				By Equity Shareholders Account (loss)	1,71,000
		7,73,000			7,73,000

Equity Shareholders (Outsiders) Account

Dr.					Cr.
2010		*Rs.*	2010		*Rs.*
Mar. 31	To Realisation Account—Loss	1,71,000	Mar. 31	By Share Capital Account	1,60,000
	To Shares in *A* Ltd.	1,92,000		By Reserves and Surplus*	1,33,000
				By Revaluation Reserve	70,000
		3,63,000			3,63,000

	Rs.
*Opening Balance	1.50,000
Add: Dividend received	3,000
	1,53,000
Less: Dividend paid	20,000
Closing Balance	1,33,000

A Ltd.

Dr.		Rs.		Cr.	Rs.
2010 Mar. 31	To Realisation Account (consideration)	2,52,000	2010 Mar. 31	By Equity Shares in *A* Ltd.	1,62,000
	To Realisation Account (for liquidation expenses)	20,000		By 11% Preference Shares in *A* Ltd.	90,000
				By Bank (for liquidation expenses)	20,000
		2,72,000			2,72,000

Investment in *A* Ltd. Accounts.

Dr.		Rs.		Cr.	Rs.
2010 Mar. 31	To Balance b/fd	80,000	2010 Mar. 31	By Realisation Account (loss on revaluation)	50,000
	To *A* Ltd.	1,62,000		By Shareholders Account	1,92,000
		2,42,000			2,42,000

To discharge consideration, *A* Ltd. is to allot to *B* Ltd. shares at par *i.e.* Rs. 10 each. The shares already with *B* Ltd. are to be revalued at par. The par value of 3,000 shares is Rs. 30,000 whereas their cost is Rs, 80,000. Hence, there is a loss of Rs. 50,000 on revaluation.

Balance Sheet of *A* Ltd. as at 31st March, 2010

Liabilities	*Amount*	*Assets*	*Amount*
	Rs.		Rs.
Share Capital :		**Fixed Assets:**	
Issued and subscribed :		(7,20,000 + 4,20,000)	11,40,000
66,200 Equity Shares of Rs. 10 each, fully paid	6,62,000	**Current Assets, Loans and Advances:**	
		(A) Current Assets	4,70,000
10% Preference Shares of Rs. 100 each, fully paid	1,00,000	Stock in trade (3,00,000 + 1,70,000)	
		Sundry Debtors (1,30,000 + 90,000)	2,20,000
11% Preference Shares of Rs. 100 each, fully paid	90,000	Cash and Bank (24,000 + 13,000)	37,000
		(B) Loans and Advances	1,20,000
(Of the above shares, 16,200 equity shares and all the 11% preference shares are allotted as fully paid up pursuant to a contract without payment being received in cash)		Bills Receivable (50,000 + 10,000)	60,000
		Miscellaneous Expenditure	
		Discount or Issue of Debentures	12,000
Reserves and Surplus			
Capital Reserve	83,000		
Revaluation Reserve	1,20,000		

Other Reserves and Surplus (2,00,000 – 50,000 + 4,000)	1,54,000		
Secured Loans:			
13% Debentures	1,20,000		
12% Debentures	1,00,000		
Current Liabilities and Provisions:			
(A) Current Liabilities			
Bills Payable	40,000		
Sundry Creditors (3,40,000+1,30,000)	4,70,000		
(B) Provisions	Nil		
	19,39,000		19,39,000

ACCOUNTING STANDARD (AS)-14

Accounting for Amalgamations

The following is the text of Accounting Standard (AS)-14, Accounting for Amalgamations, issued by the Institute of Chartered Accountants of India. This standard will come into effect in respect of accounting periods commencing on or after 1.4.1995 and will be mandatory in nature. The Guidance Note on Accounting Treatment of Reserves in Amalgamations issued by the Institute in 1983 will stand withdrawn from the aforesaid date.

INTRODUCTION

1. This statement deals with accounting for amalgamations and the treatment of any resultant goodwill or reserves. This statement is directed principally to companies although some of its requirements also apply to financial statements of other enterprises.
2. This statement does not deal with cases of acquisitions which arise when there is a purchase by one company (referred to as the acquiring company) of the whole or part of the shares, or the whole or part of the assets of another company (referred to as the acquired company) in consideration for payment in cash or by issue of shares or other securities in the acquiring company or partly in one form and partly in the other. The distinguishing feature of acquisition is that the acquired company is not dissolved and its separate entity continues to exist.

DEFINITIONS

3. The following terms are used in this statement with the meaning specified:
   (*a*) ***Amalgamation*** means an amalgamation pursuant to the provisions of the Companies Act, 1956, or any other statute which may be applicable to companies.
   (*b*) ***Transferor company*** means the company which is amalgamated into another company.
   (*c*) ***Transferee company*** means the company into which a transferor company is amalgamated.
   (*d*) ***Reserve*** means the portion of earnings, receipts or other surplus of an enterprise (whether capital or revenue) appropriated by the management for a general or a specific purpose other than a provision for depreciation or diminution in the value of assets or for a known liability.
   (*e*) ***Amalgamation in the nature of merger*** is an amalgamation which satisfies all the following conditions:
      (*i*) All the assets and liabilities of the transferor company become, after amalgamation, the assets and liabilities of the transferee company.
      (*ii*) Shareholders holding not less than 90% of the face value of the equity shares of the transferor company (other than the equity shares already held therein, immediately before the amalgamation, by the transferee company or its subsidiaries or their nominees) become equity shareholders of the transferee company by virtue of the amalgamation.

(*iii*) The consideration for the amalgamation receivable by those equity shareholders of the transferor company who agree to become equity shareholders of the transferee company is discharged by the transferee company **wholly** by the issue of equity shares in the transferee company, except that **cash** may be paid in respect of any fractional shares.

(*iv*) The business of the transferor company is intended to be carried on, after the amalgamation, by the transferee company.

(*v*) No adjustment is intended to be made to the book values of the assets and liabilities of the transferor company when they are incorporated in the financial statements of the transferee company except to ensure uniformity of accounting policies.

(*f*) **Amalgamation in the nature of purchase** is an amalgamation which does not satisfy any one or more of the conditions specified in **sub-paragraph (e)** above.

(*g*) ***Consideration*** for the amalgamation means the aggregate of the shares and other seurities issued and the payment made in the form of cash or other assets by the transferee company to the shareholders of the transferor company.

(*h*) ***Fair value*** is the amount for which an asset could be exchanged between a knowledgeable, willing buyer and a knowledgeable, willing seller in an arm's length transaction.

(*i*) ***Pooling of interests is a method of accounting*** for amalgamations the object of which is to account for the amalgamation as if the separate businesses of the amalgamating companies were intended to be continued by the transferee company. Accordingly, only minimal changes are made in aggregating the individual financial statements of the amalgamating companies.

EXPLANATION

Types of Amalgamations

4. Generally speaking, amalgamations fall into two broad categories. In the first category are those amalgamations where there is a genuine pooling not merely of the assets and liabilities of the amalgamating companies but also of the shareholders' interests and of the businesses of these companies. Such amalgamations are amalgamations which are in the nature of **'merger'** and the accounting treatment of such amalgamations should ensure that the resultant figures of assets, liabilities, capital and reserves more or less represent the sum of the relevant figures of the amalgamating companies. In the **second** category are those amalgamations which are in effect a mode by which one company acquires another company and, as a consequence, the shareholders of the company which is acquired normally do not continue to have a proportionate share in the equity of the combined company, or the business of the company which is acquired is not intended to be continued. Such amalgamations are amalgamations in the nature of **'purchase'**.

5. An amalgamation is classified as an **'amalgamation in the nature of merger'** when all the conditions listed in paragraph 3 (*e*) are satisfied. There are, however, differing views regarding the nature of any further conditions that may apply. Some believe that, in addition to an exchange of equity shares, it is necessary that the shareholders of the transferor company obtain a substantial share in the transferee company even to the extent that it should not be possible to identify any one party as dominant therein. This belief is based in part on the view that the exchange of control of one company for an insignificant share in a larger company does not amount to a mutual sharing of risks and benefits.

6. Others believe that substance of an amalgamation in the nature of merger is evidenced by meeting certain criteria regarding the relationship of the parties, such as the former independence of the amalgamating companies, the manner of their amalgamation, the absence of planned transactions that would undermine the effect of the amalgamation, and the

continuing participation by the management of the transferor company in the management of the transferee company after the amalgamation.

Methods of Accounting for Amalgamations

7. There are **two main methods** of accounting for amalgamations:
   (*a*) the pooling of interests method; and
   (*b*) the purchase method.
8. The use of the pooling of interests method is confined to circumstances which meet the criteria referred to in paragraph 3 (*e*) for an amalgamation in the nature of merger.
9. The object of the purchase method is to account for the amalgamation by applying the same principles as are applied in the normal purchase of assets. This method is used in accounting for amalgamations in the nature of purchase.

The Pooling of Interests Method

10. Under the pooling of interests method, the assets, liabilities and reserves of the transferor company are recorded by the transferee company at their existing carrying amounts (after making the adjustments required in paragraph 11).
11. If, at the time of the amalgamation, the transferor and the transferee companies have conflicting accounting policies, **a uniform set** of accounting policies is adopted following the amalgamation. The effects on the financial statements of any changes in accounting policies are reported in accordance with **Accounting Standard (AS)-5, 'Prior Period and Extraordinary Items and Changes in Accounting Policies'.**

The Purchase Method

12. Under the purchase method, the transferee company accounts for the amalgamation either by incorporating the assets and liabilities at their existing carrying amounts or by allocating the consideration to individual indentifiable assets and liabilities of the transferor company on the basis of their fair values at the date of amalgamation. The identifiable assets and liabilities may include assets and liabilities not recorded in the financial statements of the transferor company.
13. Where assets and liabilities are restated on the basis of their fair values, the determination of fair values may be influenced by the intentions of the transferee company. For example, the transferee company may have a specialised use for an asset, which is not available to other potential buyers. The transferee company may intend to effect changes in the activities of the transferor company which necessitate the creation of specific provisions for the expected costs, *e.G*, planned employee termination and plant relocation costs.

Consideration

14. The consideration for the amalgamation may consist of securities, cash or other assets. In determining the value of the consideration, an assessment is made of the fair value of its elements. A variety of techniques is applied in arriving at fair values. For example, when the consideration includes securities, the value fixed by the statutory authorities may be taken to be the fair value. In case of other assets, the fair value may be determined by reference to the market value of the assets given uP Where the market value of the assets given up cannot be reliably assessed, such assets may be valued at their respective net book values.
15. Many amalgamations recognize that adjustments may have to be made to the consideration in the light of one or more future events. When the additional payment is probable and can reasonably be estimated at the date of amalgamation, it is included in the calculation of the consideration. In all other cases, the adjustment is recognised as soon as the amount is determinable **[see Accounting Standard (AS) 4, Contingencies and Events Occurring after the Balance Sheet Date].**

Treatment of Reserves on Amalgamation

16. If the amalgamation is an 'amalgamation in the nature of merger', the identity of the reserves is preserved and they appear in the financial statements of the transferee company in the same form in which they appeared in the financial statements of the transferor company. Thus, for example, the General Reserve of the transferor company becomes the General Reserve of the transferee company, the Capital Reserve of the transferor company becomes the Capital Reserve of the transferee company and the Revaluation Reserve of the transferor company becomes the Revaluation Reserve of the transferee company. As a result of preserving the identify, reserves which are available for distribution as dividend before the amalgamation would also be available for distribution as dividend after the amalgamation. The difference between the amount recorded as share capital issued (plus any additional consideration in the form of cash or other assets) and the amount of share capital of the transferor company is adjusted in reserves in the financial statements of the transferee company.

17. If the amalgamation is an **'amalgamation in the nature of purchase'**, the identity of the reserves, other than the statutory reserves dealt within paragraph 1, is not preserved. The amount of the consideration is deducted from the value of the net assets of the transferor company acquired by the transferee company. If the result of the computation is negative, the difference is debited to goodwill arising on amalgamation and dealt with in the manner stated in paragraphs 19-20. If the result of the computation is positive, the difference is credited to **Capital Reserve**.

18. Certain reserves may have been created by the transferor company pursuant to the requirements of, or to avail of the benefits under, the Income-tax Act, 1961; for example, Development Allowance Reserve, or Investment Allowance Reserve. The Act requires that the identity of the reserves should be preserved for a specified period. Likewise, certain other reserves may have been created in the financial statements of the transferor company in terms of the requirements of other statutes. Though, normally, in an amalgamation in the nature of purchase, the identity of reserves is not preserved, an exception is made in respect of reserves of the aforesaid nature (referred to hereinafter as 'statutory reserves') and such reserves retain their identity in the financial statements of the transferee company, so long as their identity is required to be maintained to comply with the relevant statute. This exception is made only in those amalgamations where the requirements of the relevant statute for recording the statutory reserves in the books of the transferee company are complied with. In such cases, the statutory reserves are recorded in the financial statements of the transferee company by a corresponding debit to a suitable account head (*e.G,* **'Amalgamation Adjustment Account'**) which is disclosed as a part of **"miscellaneous expenditure"** or other similar category in the balance sheet. When the identity of the statutory reserves is no longer required to be maintained, both the reserves and the aforesaid account are reversed.

Treatment of Goodwill Arising on Amalgamation

19. Goodwill arising on amalgamation represents a payment made in anticipation of future income and it is appropriate to treat it as an asset to be amortised to income on a systematic basis over its useful life. Due to the nature of goodwill, it is frequently difficult to estimate its useful life with reasonable certainty. Such estimation is, however, made on a prudent basis. Accordingly, it is considered appropriate to amortise goodwill over a period not exceeding five years unless a somewhat longer period can be justified.

20. Factors which may be considered in estimating the useful life of goodwill arising on amalgamation include:
    - the foreseeable life of the business or industry;
    - the effects of product obsolescence, changes in demand and other economic factors;
    - the service life expectancies of key individuals or groups of employees;
    - expected actions by competitors or potential competitors; and
    - legal, regulatory or contractual provisions affecting the useful life.

Balance of Profit and Loss Account

21. In the case of an 'amalgamation in the nature of merger', the balance of the Profit and Loss Account appearing in the financial statement of the transferor company is aggregated with the corresponding balance appearing in the financial statements of the transferee company. Alternatively, it is transferred to the General Reserve, if any.

22. In the case of an 'amalgamation in the nature of purchase', the balance of the Profit and Loss Account appearing in the financial statements of the transferor company, whether debit or credit, loses its identity.

Treatment of Reserves Specified in a Scheme of Amalgamation

23. The scheme of amalgamation sanctioned under the provisions of the Companies Act, 1956, or any other statute may prescribe the treatment to be given to the reserves of the transferor company after its amalgamation. Where the treatment is so prescribed, the same is followed.

Disclosure

24. For all amalgamations, the following disclosures are considered appropriate in the first financial statements following the amalgamation:
    (*a*) names and general nature of business of the amalgamating companies;
    (*b*) effective date of amalgamation for accounting purposes;
    (*c*) the method of accounting used to reflect the amalgamation; and
    (*d*) particulars of the scheme sanctioned under a statute.

25. For amalgamations accounted for under the **pooling of interests method,** the following **additional disclosures** are considered **appropriate in the first financial** statements following the amalgamation:
    (*a*) description and number of shares issued, together with the percentage of each company's equity shares exchanged to effect the amalgamation;
    (*b*) the amount of any difference between the consideration and the value of net identifiable assets acquired, and the treatment thereof.

26. For amalgamations accounted for under the purchase method, the following additional disclosures are considered appropriate in the first financial statements following the amalgamation:
    (*a*) consideration for the amalgamation and a description of the consideration paid or contingently payable; and
    (*b*) the amount of any difference between the consideration and the value of net indentifiable assets acquired, and the treatment thereof including the period of amortisation of any goodwill arising on amalgamation.

Amalgamation after the Balance Sheet Date

27. When an amalgamation is effected after the balance sheet date but before the issuance of the financial statements of either party to the amalgamation, disclosure is made in accordance with **AS-4, 'Contingencies and Events Occurring after the Balance Sheet Date',** but the amalgamation is not incorporated in the financial statement. In certain circumstances, the amalgamation may also provide additional information affecting the financial statements themselves, for instance, by allowing the going concern assumption to be maintained.

ACCOUNTING STANDARD

The Accounting Standard comprises paragraphs 28 to 46 of this statement. The Standard should be read in the context of paragraphs 1 to 27 of this Standard and of the Preface to the Statements of Accounting Standards.

28. An amalgamation may be either:
    (*a*) an amalgamation in the nature of merger, or
    (*b*) an amalgamation in the nature of purchase.

29. An amalgamation should be considered to be an **amalgamation in the nature of merger when all the following conditions are satisfied:**
    (*i*) All the assets and liabilities of the transferor company become, after amalgamation, the assets and liabilities of the transferee company.
    (*ii*) Shareholders holding not less than 90% of the face value of the equity shares of the transferor company (other than the equity shares already held therein, immediately before the amalgamation, by the transferee company or its subsidiaries or their nominees) become equity shareholders of the transferee company be virtue of the amalgamation.
    (*iii*) The consideration for the amalgamation receivable by those equity shareholders of the transferor company who agree to become equity shareholders of the transferee company is discharged by the transferee company wholly by the issue of equity shares in the transferee company, except that cash may be paid in respect of any fractional shares.
    (*iv*) The business of the transferor company is intended to be carried on, after the amalgamation, by the transferee company.
    (*v*) No adjustment is intended to be made to the book values of the assets and liabilities of the transferor company when they are incorporated in the financial statements of the transferee company except to ensure uniformity of accounting policies.
30. An amalgamation should be considered to be an amalgamation in the nature of purchase, when any one or more of the conditions specified in paragraph 29 is not satisfied.
31. When an amalgamation is considered to be an amalgamation in the nature of merger, it should be accounted for under the pooling of interests method described in paragraphs 33-35.
32. When an amalgamation is considered to be an amalgamation in the nature of purchase, it should be accounted for under the purchase method described in paragraphs 36-39.

The Pooling of Interests Method

33. In preparing the transferee company's financial statements, the assets, liabilities and reserve (whether capital or revenue or arising on revaluation) of the transferor company should be recorded at their existing carrying amounts and in the same form as at the date of the amalgamation. The balance of the Profit and Loss Account of the transferor company should be aggregated with corresponding balance of the transferee company or transferred to the General Reserve, if any.
34. If, at the time of the amalgamation, the transferor and the transferee companies have conflicting accounting policies, a uniform set of accounting policies should be adopted following the amalgamation. The effects on the financial statements of any changes in accounting policies should be reported in accordance with **Accounting Standard (AS)-5, 'Prior Period and Extraordinary Items and Changes in Accounting Policies'.**
35. The difference between the amount recorded as share capital issued (plus any additional consideration in the form of cash or other assets) and the amount of share capital of the transferor company should be adjusted in reserves.

The Purchase Method

36. In preparing the transferee company's financial statements, the assets and liabilities of the transferor company should be incorporated at their existing carrying amounts or, alternatively, the consideration should be allocated to individual indentifiable assets and liabilities on the basis of their fair values at the date of amalgamation. The reserves (whether capital or revenue or arising on revaluation) of the transferor company, other than the statutory reserves, should not be included in the financial statements of the transferee company except as stated in paragraph 39.
37. Any excess of the amount of the consideration over the value of the net assets of the transferor company acquired by the transferee company should be recognised in the transferee company's financial statements as goodwill arising on amalgamation. If the amount of the

consideration is lower than the value of the net assets acquired, the difference should be treated as Capital Reserve.

38. The goodwill arising on amalgamation should be amortised to income on a systematic basis over its useful life. The amortisation period **should not exceed five years unless a somewhat longer period can be justified.**

39. Where the requirements of the relevant statute for recording the statutory reserves in the books of the transferee company are complied with, statutory reserves of the transferor company should be recorded in the financial statements of the transferee company. The corresponding **debit** should be given to a suitable account head (*e.G,* 'Amalgamation Adjustment Account') which should be disclosed as a part of "miscellaneous expenditure" or other similar category in the balance sheet. When identity of the statutory reserves is no longer required to be maintained, both the reserves and the aforesaid account should be reversed.

Common Procedures

40. The consideration for the amalgamation should include any non-cash element at fair value. In case of issue of securities, the value fixed by the statutory authorities may be taken to be the fair value. In cash of other assets, the fair value may be determine by reference to the market value of the assets given uP Where the market value of the assets given up cannot be reliably assessed, such assets may be valued at their respective net book values.

41. Where the scheme of amalgamation provides for an adjustment to the consideration contingent on one or more future events, the amount of the additional payment should be included in the consideration if payment is probable and a reasonable estimate of the amount can be made. In all other cases, the adjustment should be recognised as soon as the amount is determinable **[See Accounting Standard (AS)-4, Contingencies and Events Occurring after the Balance Sheet Date].**

Treatment of Reserves Specified in a Scheme of Amalgamation

42. Where the scheme of amalgamation sanctioned under a statute prescribe the treatment to be given to the reserves of the transferor company after amalgamation, the same should be followed.

Disclosure

43. For all amalgamations, the following disclosures should be made in the first financial statements following the amalgamation:
   (*a*) names and general nature of business of the amalgamating companies;
   (*b*) effective date of amalgamation for accounting purposes;
   (*c*) the method of accounting used to reflect the amalgamation; and
   (*d*) particulars of the scheme sanctioned under a statute.

44. For amalgamations accounted for under the pooling of interests method, the following additional disclosures should be made in the first financial statements following the amalgamation:
   (*a*) description and number of shares issued, together with the percentage of each company's equity shares exchanged to effect the amalgamation;
   (*b*) the amount of any difference between the consideration and the value of net indentifiable assets acquired, and the treatment thereof.

45. For amalgamations accounted for under the purchase method, the following additional disclosures should be made in the first financial statements following the amalgamation:
   (*a*) consideration for the amalgamation and a description of the consideration paid or contingently payable; and
   (*b*) the amount of any difference between the consideration and the value of net identifiable assets acquired, and the treatment thereof including the period of amortisation of any goodwill arising on amalgamation.

Amalgamation after the Balance Sheet Date

46. When an amalgamation is effected after the balance sheet date but before the issuance of the financial statements of either party to the amalgamation, disclosure should be made in accordance with **AS-4, 'Contingencies and Events Occurring after the Balance Sheet Date',** but the amalgamation should not be incorporated in the financial statements. In certain circumstances, the amalgamation may also provide additional information, affecting the financial statement themselves, for instance, by allowing the going concern assumption to be maintained.

EXERCISE XXI

1. The following are the abridged balance sheets of P Ltd. and V Ltd. as at **31st March, 2010:—**

Liabilities	*P Ltd.* Rs.in '000	*V Ltd.* Rs.in '000	*Assets*	*P Ltd.* Rs. in '000	*V Ltd.* Rs. in '000
Equity Share Capital (Rs. 10 each)	90,00	40,00	Fixed Assets	1,16,50	71,42
13% Preference Share Capital (Rs.100 each)	—	15,00	Current Assets	42,23	23,64
General Reserve	43,20	21,90	Miscellaneous Expenditure	3,00	—
Statutory Reserve	2,70	1,20			
Profit and Loss Account	7,45	4,15			
11% Debentures	—	3,00			
Current Liabilities	18,38	9.81			
	1,61,73	95,06		1,61,73	95,06

On 1st April, 2010 P Ltd. takes over V Ltd. on the following terms :

(i) P Ltd will allot 5,00,000 fully paid equity shares of Rs. 10 each at par to the equity shareholders of V Ltd.

(ii) P Ltd. will allot 16,500 fully paid 13% preference shares of Rs. 100 each to the preference shareholders of V Ltd.

(iii) The debentures in V Ltd. will be converted into an equal number of 12% debentures in P Ltd. of the same denomination.

You are informed that the statutory reserves of V Ltd. are still to be maintained. You are required to show the balance sheet of P Ltd. immediately after the abovementioned scheme of amalgamation has been implemented assuming that:

(a) the amalgamation is in the nature of a merger; and

(b) the amalgamation is in the nature of a purchase.

[(a) General Reserve Rs. 53,60 thousand; Balance Sheet Rs. 2,56,79 thousand (b) Capital Reserve Rs. 15,75 thousand; Amalgamation Adjustment Account Rs. 1,20 thousand; Balance Sheet Rs. 2,57,99 thousand]

2. The balance sheets of Big Ltd. and Small Ltd. as on 31st March, 2010 stood as follows :

Liabilities	*Big Ltd.* *Rs.*	*Small Ltd.* *Rs.*	*Assets*	*Big Ltd.* *Rs.*	*Small Ltd.* *Rs.*
Authorised Share Capital	30,00,000	10,00,000	Goodwill	80,000	15,000
Issued and Subscribed Share Capital :			Machinery	9,10,000	2,85,000
			Furniture	92,500	60,000
Equity Shares of Rs. 10 each, fully paid	10,00,000	4,00,000	Investments	75,000	24,000
Securities Premium	1,00,000	—	Stock	2,61,000	1,01,800
Exports Projects Reserve	17,000	8,000	Debtors	93,630	62,310
Investments Fluctuation Reserve	8,000	3,000	Cash at Bank	53,320	32,230
			Cost of Issue of Shares	—	6,000

General Reserve	2,50,000	1,00,000			
Profit and Loss Account	48,800	23,500			
Sundry Creditors	83,650	32,840			
Provision for Taxation	43,000	13,000			
Staff Provident Fund	15,000	6,000			
	15,65,450	5,86,340		15,65,450	5,86,340

Small Ltd. merged into Big Ltd. as on the abovementioned date. Big Ltd. allotted at par 44,000 fully paid equity shares of Rs. 10 each to be distributed among the shareholderes of Small Ltd. Expenses which amounted to Rs. 7,000 were borne by Big Ltd. You are required to:

(i) prepare important ledger accounts to close the books of Small Ltd.,
(ii) pass the journal entries in the books of Big Ltd; and
(iii) draw the balance sheet of Big Ltd. after the merger.

[*Loss on realisation Rs. 88,500; Balance Sheet Rs. 21,44,790*]

3. The following were the balance sheets of *B* Ltd. and *D* Ltd. as on 31st March, 2010:

(Rs. in'000)

Liabilities	*B Ltd.* *Rs.*	*D Ltd* *Rs.*	*Assets*	*B Ltd* *Rs.*	*D Ltd* *Rs.*
75,000 13% Preference shares of Rs. 100 each	7,500	—	Goodwill	—	250
			Freehold Premises	12,000	—
30,00,000 Equity Shares of Rs. 10 each	30,000	—	Machinery	34,510	—
			Furniture and Fixtures	1,120	750
5,00,000 Equity Share of Rs. 10 each	—	5,000	Trade Marks	100	—
			Stock	12,800	5,010
Capital Reserve	9,600	—	Debtors	4,340	1,170
General Reserve	12,400	1,450	Cash at Bank	2,230	220
Profit and Loss Account	1,150	220	Bills Receivable	—	100
12% Debentures	5,000	—			
Creditors	1,450	830			
	67,100	7,500		67,100	7,500

On the abovementioned date, *B* Ltd. and *D* Ltd. agreed to amalgamate their business units and formed a new company named *BD* Ltd. for the purpose. The merger took place on the following terms:

(i) *BD* Ltd. allotted to *B* Ltd. 75,000 14% fully paid preference shares of Rs. 100 each and 45 lakh fully paid equity shares of Rs. 10 each to satisfy the claims of *B* Ltd.'s preference shareholders and equity shareholders respectively. It also agreed to convert 12% debentures of *B* Ltd. into 13% debentures of identical amount.

(ii) *BD* Ltd. allotted to *D* Ltd. 5,50,000 fully paid equity shares of Rs. 10 each to be distributed among *D* Ltd.'s shareholders in full satisfaction of their claims.

Expenses on the liquidation of the two companies Rs. 10,000 were borne by *BD* Ltd. In addition to this, the preliminary expenses of *BD* Ltd. totalled Rs. 88,000.

You are required to :

(i) prepare in columnar form important ledger accounts pertaining to B Ltd. and D Ltd;
(ii) pass journal entries in the books of *BD* Ltd; and
(iii) draw *BD* Ltd.'s balance sheet after all the transactions have been recorded.

(Loss on realisation, B Ltd. Rs.8,150 thousand; D Ltd. Rs. 1,170 thousand; Balance Sheet, Rs. 74,590 thousand)

4. The balance sheets of *A* Ltd. and *B* Ltd. as on 31st March 2010:—

(Rs. in'000)

Liabilities	*A Ltd.* Rs.	*B Ltd.* Rs.	*Assets*	*A Ltd.* Rs.	*B Ltd.* Rs.
Share capital:			Goodwill	—	700
50,000 Preference shares			Land and buildings	6,000	—
of Rs. 100 each	5,000	—	Plant and machinery	15,000	—
15,00,000 Equity shares of			Furniture	500	250
Rs. 10 each	15,000	—	Patents	2,000	—
4,00,000 Equity shares of			Motor vehicles	—	400
Rs. 10 each	—	4,000	Investment	1,150	—
			Stock	3,500	2,390
	20,000	4,000	Debtors	800	620
General reserve	8,000	—	Cash at bank	450	170
Profit and loss account	900	320			
Creditors	500	210			
	29,400	4,530		29,400	4,530

A new company, *C* Ltd. was formed to acquire the assets and liabilities of *A* Ltd. and *B* Ltd. The terms of the amalgamation in the nature of merge were as under:

(*i*) *C* Ltd. to have an authorised capital of Rs. 3,50,00,000 divided into 50,000 13% preference shares of Rs. 100 each and 30,00,000 equity shares of Rs. 10 each.

(*ii*) Business of *A* Ltd. valued at Rs. 3,00,00,000; settlement being Rs. 60,00,000 in cash and balance by issue of fully-paid equity shares at Rs. 12.

(*iii*) Business of *B* Ltd. valued at Rs. 48,00,000 to be satisfied by issue of fully-paid equity shares at Rs. 12.

(*iv*) Preference shares of *A* Ltd. were redeemed.

(*v*) *C* Ltd. made a public issue of 30,000 preference shares at par and 3,00,000 equity shares at Rs. 12. The issue was underwritten at the commission allowed by law and was fully subscribed. All obligation were met.

(*vi*) D, who mooted the scheme, was allotted 40,000 equity shares (fully-paid) at Rs. 12 in consideration of his services.

You are required to :

(*a*) prepare in columnar form (*i*) realisation account, (*ii*) equity shareholders account and (*iii*) the account of *C* Ltd. in the books of *A* Ltd. and *B* Ltd,

(*b*) show *A* Ltd.'s cash book,

(*c*) pass journal entries in the books of *C* Ltd., and

(*d*) draw *C* Ltd.'s balance sheet after the abovementioned transaction have been recorded.

[*C.S. (Inter) Dec., 1994 Modified*]

5. The Indo-Gulf Co. Ltd. sells its business to the Continental Co. Ltd. as on 31st March, 2010, on which date its Balance Sheet was as under :—

Liabilities	*Rs.*	*Assets*	*Rs.*
Paid up Capital:		Goodwill	50,000
2,000 Shares of Rs. 100 each	2,00,000	Freehold Property	1,50,000
General Reserve	50,000	Plant and Tools	83,000
Profit and Loss Account	20,000	Stock	35,000
Debentures	1,00,000	Sundry Debtors	27,500
Trade Creditors	30,000	Cash at Bank	50,000
		Bills Receivable	4,500
	4,00,000		4,00,000

The Continental Co. Ltd. agreed to take over the assets (exclusive of cash at bank and goodwill) at 10 per cent less than the book value, to pay Rs. 75,000 for goodwill, and to take over the debentures.

The consideration was to be discharged by the allotment to the Indo-Gulf Co. Ltd. of 1,500 shares of Rs.100 each at a premium of Rs. 10 per share and the balance in cash.

The cost of the liquidation amounted to Rs. 3,000. Show the necessary accounts in the books of the Indo-Gulf Co. Ltd. and show the necessary journal entries recording the transactions in the books of the Continental Co. Ltd. *[Adapted C.A. (Inter) May 1986]*

(Consideration Rs. 2,45,000; Loss on Realisation Rs. 8,000; goodwill on acquisition of business Rs. 75,000)

6. The following are the balance sheet of P Ltd. and S Ltd. as at 31st March, 2010 :

	P Ltd. *(Rs. in lakhs)*	S Ltd. *(Rs. in lakhs)*
Liabilities		
Fully paid equity shares of Rs. 10 each	300	300
Fully paid 11% preference shares of Rs. 100 each		150
General Reserve	150	
Profit and Loss Account	25	
10% Debentures of Rs. 100 each, fully paid up		100
Sundry Creditors	37	45
	512	545
Assets		
Plant and Machinery	240	350
Furniture and Fixtures	110	50
Stock	70	30
Sundry Debtors	60	25
Cash at Bank	32	20
Profit and Loss Account		70
	512	545

On the abovementioned date, P Ltd. took over S Ltd. by way of amalgamation in the nature of purchase on the following conditions :-

(i) The preference shareholders would be allotted four fully paid 12% preference shares in P Ltd. for every five preference shares held in S Ltd.; the nominal value remaining Rs. 100 per share.

(ii) The debentureholders would be discharged by P Ltd. by issue to them an equal number of fully paid 10.5% debentures of Rs. 100 each.

(iii) The fixed assets were valued at 90% of their book values, value of stock was reduced by 2.5 % while a provision for doubtful debts was created at 2%.

(iv) The equity shareholders were paid the amount due to them in the form of fully paid equity shares of Rs. 10 each allotted at a premium of Rs. 5 per share.

(v) Expenses of amalgamation amounting to Rs. 1 lakh were borne by P Ltd.

You are required to :

(i) calculate the consideration;

(ii) prepare realisation account, preference shareholders account and equity shareholders account in S Ltd.'s ledger; and

(iii) pass journal entries for all the transactions in the books of P Ltd.
Observe provisions of Accounting Standard 14.

[Adapted C.S. (Inter), June, 2001]

[Consideration : Rs. 288.75 lakh;No. of equity shares allotted : 11.25 lakh; Loss on realisation: Rs. 11.25 lakh;]

7. Star Ltd. and Moon Ltd. had been carrying on business independently. They agreed to amalgamate and form a new company Neptune Ltd. with an authorised share capital of Rs. 5,00,000 divided into 50,000 equity shares of Rs. 10 each.

On 31st March, 2010 the abridged balance sheets of Star Ltd. and Moon Ltd. were as follows:

	Star Ltd. Rs.	*Moon Ltd.* Rs.
Fixed Assets	3,17,500	2,62,500
Current Assets	3,46,000	1,80,125
	6,63,500	4,42,625
Less: Current Liabilities	2,98,500	90,125
Representing Capital	3,65,000	3,52,500

The following additional information is provided to you:

(*a*) Revalued figures of fixed and current assets were as follows:

	Star Ltd. Rs.	*Moon Ltd.* Rs.
Fixed Assets	3,82,600	2,86,750
Current Assets	3,28,400	1,70,875

(*b*) The debtors and creditors include Rs. 40,000 owed by Star Ltd. to Moon Ltd.

The consideration to be satisfied by issue of the following shares and debentures :

(*i*) 30,000 equity shares of Neptune Ltd. to Star Ltd. and Moon Ltd. in the proportion to the profitability of their respective business based on the average net profit during the last three years which were as follows:—

Star Ltd. Rs.	*Moon Ltd.* Rs.
4,49,576	2,73,900
(2,500)	3,42,100
3,77,924	3,59,000

(*ii*) 15% debentures in Neptune Ltd. at par to provide an income equivalent to 8% return on capital employed in their respective business as on 31st March, 1998 after revaluation of assets.

You are required to-

(1) Compute the amount of shares and debentures to be issued to Star Ltd and Moon Ltd.

(2) Balance Sheet of Neptune Ltd., showing the position immediately after amalgamation.

(Adapted C.A. Inter, May, 1996)

(Shares : Star Ltd. Rs, 1,37,500 Moon Ltd. Rs. 1,62,500; Debentures : Star Ltd. Rs. 2,20,000 Moon Ltd. Rs. 1,96,000; Balance Sheet Rs. 11,28,625).

8. The assets of the National Steel Co. Ltd. (NASCO) are purchased by the Hindustan Iron & Steel Co. Ltd. (HISCO). The consideration was as follows:

(*a*) A payment in cash at Rs. 90 for every equity share in NASCO.

(*b*) An exchange of six shares of the HISCO of Rs. 75 each for every share in NASCO.

It was also agreed that the debentures in the NASCO would be converted into debentures in the HISCO for identical amount issued at par.

Out of the cash received by it, the NASCO paid to its Sundry Creditors at a discount of 5%. Workmen's savings were returned at par. The remaining cash was distributed among the shareholders.

The balance sheet of the National Steel Co. Ltd. stood as follows when given over:—

	Rs.		Rs.
Capital:			
6,000 Equity Shares of Rs. 500 each	30,00,000	Land and Buildings	11,00,000
General Reserve	2,75,000	Plant and Machinery	15,50,000
Profit & Loss Account	60,000	Furniture and Fittings	2,60,000
Exports Projects Reserve	65,000	Patents	2,40,000
1,300 Debentures of Rs. 500 each	6,50,000	Stock of Goods	1,85,000
Sundry Creditors	2,50,000	Work-in-Progress	8,15,000
Workmen's Savings Bank	2,00,000	Sundry Debtors	2,65,000
		Cash at Bank	85,000
	45,00,000		45,00,000

Make the necessary closing and opening entries in the journals of the transferor and transferee companies respectively. *[Adapted C.S. (Inter.) Dec. 1985]*

(Consideration Rs. 32,40,000; Loss on Realisation, Rs.5,97,500; Amalgamation Adjustment Account Rs. 65,000; Capital Reserve on purchase of business Rs. 6,10,000).

9. The following is the Balance Sheet of Ashok Limited as at 31st March, 2010:—

	Rs.		Rs.
Subscried Capital:		Fixed Assets:	
36,000 Equity Shares of Rs. 10		Goodwill	50,000
each, fully paid	3,60,000	Land and Buildings	1,40,000
Reserves and Surplus:		Plant and Machinery	2,20,700
General Reserve	70,000	Furniture	20,800
Profit and Loss Account	14,500	Current Assets:	
Statutory Reserve	1,500	Stock	72,800
Secured Loans:		Debtors	60,000
12% Debentures	1,00,000	Cash at Bank	16,700
Current Liabilities and Provisions:		Miscellaneous Expenditure:	
Sundry Creditors	40,000	Discount on issue of Debentures	5,000
	5,86,000		5,86,000

Bharat Limited, a newly formed company took over the assets of Ashok Limited with the exception of books debts. It took over no liabilities. However, it agreed to collect the book debts and pay the liabilities on behalf of Ashok Limited.

In discharge of the consideration, the equity shareholders of Ashok Limited were to be alloted six equity shares of Rs. 10 each in Bharat Limited for every five shares held. The debentureholders of Ashok Limited were to be allotted 14% Debentures in Bharat Limited so as to give them a premium of 10 per cent.

The expenses of liquidation amounted to Rs. 3,250.

Of the debtors, Rs. 3,000 proved bad and a cash discount of 2 per cent was allowed on settlement. The creditors were paid subject to a discount of 3 per cent. The Bharat Limited were allowed a commission of one per cent on gross debtors collected by it.

Show the ledger accounts necessary to close the books of Ashok Ltd. and give journal entries to record the purchase of business in the books of Bharat Ltd. *[Adapted B.Com. Bombay]*

(Consideration Rs. 4,32,000; Profit on Realisation, Rs. 4,240; Amalgamation Adjustment Account Rs. 1,500' Goodwill on acquisition of business Rs. 71,000).

10. The books of S Ltd. contained the following balances as on 31st March, 2010 :—

	Debit Rs.	Credit Rs.
Equity share capital (of Rs. 10 each)		12,00,000
Creditors		14,00,000
Patents and trade marks	12,00,000	
Plant and machinery	4,00,000	
Stock	3,00,000	
Debtors	5,00,000	
Cash	12,500	
Preliminary expenses	72,500	
Profit and loss account	1,15,000	
	26,00,000	26,00,000

The patents and trade marks are considerably overvalued. The company is also not in a position to raise any further capital. The following scheme of reconstruction has, therefore, been framed:

(*a*) The company will go into voluntary liquidation. A new company S.S. Ltd. will be formed with an authorised capital of Rs. 20,00,000 to take over the assets and liabilities.

(*b*) After the take over, the new company will discharge the liability to the creditors by payment of 25 p. in a rupee in cash and 50 p. in a rupee by issue of 14% debentures.

(*c*) 1,20,000 shares of Rs. 10 each (Rs. 5 per share paid up) will be issued to the shareholders of S Ltd., the balance of Rs. 5 per share to be paid on allotment.

(*d*) Expenses of liquidation amounting to Rs. 17,500 will be paid by S.S. Ltd.

The scheme was approved by all concerned.

You are required to:

(*i*) Close the ledger of S Ltd.

(*ii*) Give the journal entries to in the books of S.S. Ltd.

(*iii*) Prepare the balance sheet of S.S. Ltd. after implementation of the scheme

[Adapted Co. Sec, (Inter.) June, 1978]

(Loss on Realisation Rs. 4,12,500; Balance Sheet of S.S. Ltd. Rs. 19,00,000)

11. The Balance Sheet of V Ltd. as at March 31, 2010 is as under:—

Liabilities	*Rs.*	*Assets*	*Rs.*
Share Capital		Fixed Assets	3,20,000
40,000 equity shares of Rs. 10		Current Assets	1,68,000
each, fully paid-up	4,00,000	Preliminary Expenses	24,000
Workmen Compensation Reserve	30,000	Profit and Loss Account	88,000
Current Liabilities	1,70,000		
	6,00,000		6,00,000

The shareholders of the company resolve to take the company into voluntary liquidation and to form a new company, named P Ltd. with an authorised share capital of Rs.10,00,000 divided into 1,00,000 equity shares of Rs. 10 each, to take over V Ltd. Shareholders in V Ltd. are allotted one share in the new company of Rs. 10 each, Rs, 5 paid up for every existing share held by them. Preferential creditors of Rs. 20,000 included in the above current liabilities are to be paid in full by P Ltd. Unsecured creditors amounting to Rs. 1,50,000 are given the option to receive either:

(*a*) 50 per cent of the claim in cash, or

(*b*) 100 per cent amount of the claim in 14 per cent debentures of Rs. 100 each in P Ltd. at par.

Half of the unsecured creditors in value opt to be paid in cash. P Ltd. takes over the creditors at the revised value and pays to them as per agreement.

The cost of winding up of V Ltd. amounting to Rs. 7,000 is also paid by P Ltd.

Show ledger accounts in the books of V Ltd. Also give journal entries in the books of P Ltd. and draft P Ltd.'s balance sheet after the external reconstruction has been completed,

(Consideration, Rs, 2,00,000; Loss on Realisation, Rs. 1,18,000; Capital Reserve Rs. 1,48,500; Balance Sheet, Rs. 4,23,5000).

12. On 31st March, 2010, the balance sheet of Varun Ltd. was as under:—

Liabilities	*Rs.*	*Rs.*	*Assets*	*Rs.*
Share Capital:			Sundry Assets	15,70,000
7,500 14% Redeemable Preference			Profit and Loss Account	5,14,000
Shares of Rs. 100 each, fully paid up		7,50,000		
1,00,000 Equity Shares of Rs. 10 each, fully paid-up		10,00,000		
14% Debentures	2,00,000			
Accrued Interest for 6 months	14,000	2,14,000		
Sundry Creditors		1,20,000		
		20,84,000		20,84,000

No dividend has been paid on the preference shares for the past two years. It is proposed that a new company, Stores Ltd., be formed to take over the whole of the assets. The capital of the new company is to consist of equity shares of Rs. 10 each.

The following scheme has been duly adopted and sanctioned:

(i) Shares in the new company to be issued in exchange for shares in the old company on the following basis:

Equity shareholders to receive one new share for every five shares held by them;

Preference shareholders to receive six new shares for every share held and a further one new share for every five shares held in satisfaction of the arrears of preference dividend.

(ii) The debentureholders to be paid by the new company the amount due to them in respect of principal; any claim for arrears of interest was to be waived.

(iii) The other creditors to be paid 25% of their claims by the new company in cash and to be allotted shares in the new company to the extent of one half of the balance.

(iv) The new company issues 25,000 shares of Rs. 10 each. These shares are fully taken over by the public.

You are required to close the books of the old company assuming that the cost of winding up Rs. 10,000 is to be borne by the new company and that no fractional holdings result from the scheme.

Also give the Balance Sheet of Stores Ltd.

(Consideration Rs. 6,65,000; Loss on Realisation Rs. 2,86,000; Balance Sheet total of Stores Ltd. Rs. 15,80,000)

13. The following are the Balance Sheets of *A* Ltd. and *B* Ltd. as at March 31,2010:

A Ltd.

Liabilities	*Rs.*	*Assets*	*Rs.*
Shares Capital :		Fixed Assets	15,00,000
2,00,000 equity shares of Rs. 10		Investments	2,50,000
each, fully paid-up	20,00,000	Current Assets	32,50,000
General Reserve	15,00,000		
Current Liabilities	15,00,000		
	50,00,000		50,00,000

B Ltd.

Liabilities	*Rs.*	*Assets*	*Rs.*
Share Capital :		Goodwill	25,000
50,000 Equity Shares of Rs. 10 each,		Other Fixed Assets	1,75,000
fully paid-up	5,00,000	Cash at Bank	50,000
General Reserve	2,50,000	Other Current Assets	6,50,000
Current Liabilities	1,00,000		
Proposed Dividend	50,000		
	9,00,000		9,00,000

B Ltd. is to be absorbed by *A* Ltd. on the following terms:

(i) *B* Ltd. pays a dividend of 10 per cent before absorption. Assume there is no corporate dividend tax.

(ii) *A* Ltd. takes over the assets (excluding cash at bank) and liabilities of *B* Ltd. at 10% less than book values.

(iii) The consideration is to be discharged by *A* Ltd. in the form of equity shares of Rs. 10 per share at a premium of Rs. 5 per share.

Show ledger accounts in the books of *B* Ltd. Also give journal entries in the books of *A* Ltd. and redraft A Ltd.'s balance sheet after the amalgamation has been completed.

(Consideration Rs. 6,75,000; Loss on Realisation Rs. 75,000; Balance Sheet of A Ltd. Rs. 57,65,000)

14. The following are the summarised balance sheets of Exe Ltd. and Wye Ltd. as on March 31, 2010:

	Exe.Ltd. Rs.	*Wye Ltd.* Rs.
Authorised Capital in Rs. 10 shares	10,00,000	4,00,000
Issued Share Capital	5,00,000	4,00,000
General Reserve	1,00,000	50,000
Profit & Loss Account	56,290	38,650
Current Liabilities:		
Accounts Payable	1,12,100	39,480
Taxation Provision	75,000	48,000
	8,43,390	5,76,130
Freehold Premises	1,94,280	—
Leasehold Premises	—	1,56,240
Plant & Machinery	2,34,280	1,07,630
Fixtures & Fittings	21,720	10,470
Stock & Work in Progress	1,52,290	98,670
Account Receivable	1,26,410	94,330
Unexpired Payments	2,980	1,400
Cash at Bank	1,11,430	1,07,390
	8,43,390	5,76,130

Exe Ltd. took over the fixed assets and stock and work in progress of Wye Ltd. as from 1st April, 1998 for a sum of Rs. 4,50,000 to be satisfied by a allotment of shares, the transferor company to pay the necessary costs of sale amounting to Rs.10,000. The accounts receivable realise Rs. 91,000. The transactions having been completed, you are required to show:

(1) The necessary journal entries in the books of Exe Ltd. and to prepare the balance sheet after completion; and

(2) The Realisation Account, Sundry Members Account and Cash Book in the books of Wye Ltd. assuming the final taxation liability of the company to be Rs. 37,000.

(Adapted from Incorp. Acctts. Inter.)

(Profit on Realisation, Rs. 63,660; Total of Balance Sheet of Wye Ltd. Rs. 12,93,390)

Hint: Exe Ltd will pay cash for Unexpired Payments of Wye Ltd. Surplus taxation provision, Rs. 11,000 to be transferred to Sundry Members' Account.

15. The summarised balance sheets of two companies on 31st March, 2010 were as follows:—

***A* Ltd.**

Liabilities	*Rs*	*Assets*	*Rs*
Authorised Capital:		Fixed Assets	1,00,000
15,000 Equity Shares of Rs. 10 each	1,50,000	Floating Assets	50,000
Issued Capital:			
12,500 Equity Shares of Rs. 10 each	1,25,000		
Trade Creditors	15,000		
Profit and Loss Account	10,000		
	1,50,000		1,50,000

***B* Ltd.**

Liabilities	*Rs.*	*Assets*	*Rs.*
Authorised Capital:		Goodwill, at cost	27,000
12,500 Equity Shares of Rs. 10 each	1,25,000	Other Fixed Assets	45,000
Issued Capital:		Floating Assets	35,000
10,000 Equity Shares of Rs. 10 each	1,00,000	Profit and Loss Account	23,000
Trade Creditors	30,000		
	1,30,000		1,30,000

On 1st April, 2010, A Ltd decided to take over the business of *B* Ltd. as from that date. The shareholders of *B* Ltd. agreed to accept shares in *A* Ltd. the agreed basis being that such shares were worth Rs. 12 each and that shares of *B* Ltd. were worth Rs. 6 each on 31st March, 2010.

Give journal entries recording the transactions in the books of the transferee company and draw up Balance Sheet showing the effect of the merger. Assume that the authorised capital of *A* Ltd. was increased to the required extent.

(Adapted from C.A. Final)

(Consideration, Rs. 60,000; Total of Balance Sheet of A Ltd. Rs. 2,57,000)

16. *B* Ltd. and *C* Ltd. were competing companies both of which had incurred losses in recent years. Their respective balance sheets as on 31st March, 2010 were as follows:

Balance Sheet of *B* Ltd.

Liabilities	*Rs.*	*Assets*	*Rs.*
Issued Capital:		Patents	2,500
10,000 shares of Rs. 10 each,		Plant	40,000
fully-paid	1,00,000	Furniture & Fittings	4,600
Creditors	18,560	Stock	42,460
Bank Overdraft	6,050	Debtors	15,630
		Profit & Loss Account	19,420
	1,24,610		1,24,610

Balance Sheet of *C* Ltd.

Liabilities	Rs.	*Assets*	Rs.
Issued Capital:		Goodwill	10,000
12,000 shares of Rs. 5 each	60,000	Patents	8,000
Creditors	8,310	Plant	21,000
Profit & Loss Account	640	Furniture & Fittings	3,280
		Stock	16,990
		Debtors	9,550
		Cash	130
	68,950		68,950

In order to eliminate competition and provide for more economical working as well as to make it possible ot introduce fresh capital, the following arrangements were made and carried into effect:

(a) Both companies were to be wound up , a new company, *A* Ltd., being formed to take over both businesses.

(b) *A* Ltd. took over the floating assets of both companies at book values (but not *C* Ltd.'s cash) and the fixed assets at the following valuations:

	B Ltd. Rs.	*C Ltd.* Rs.
Goodwill	1,000	1,000
Patents	500	2,000
Plant	27,000	11,000
Furniture & Fittings	3,000	2,300
	31,500	16,300

(c) The consideration for the assets of *B* Ltd. was satisfied by the issue of 1,200 13% preference shares of Rs. 10 each and Rs. 64,490 in Rs. 10 equity shares of *A* Ltd. fully paid and the balance in cash; and for the assets of *C* Ltd. Rs. 34,300 in Rs. 10 equity shares of *A* Ltd. and the balance in cash.

(d) The liquidator of *B* Ltd. transferred the preference shares to a loan creditor for Rs. 12,000 in satisfaction of his claim and the equity shares were distributed *pro rata* among the shareholders of each of the original companies, the cash being just sufficient to satisfy the creditors of each company and the expenses of liquidation which amount to Rs. 500 and Rs. 300 respectively for *B* Ltd. and *C* Ltd.

(e) In order to provide the necessary cash, *A* Ltd. issued 100 12 1/2% debentures of Rs. 100 each at a discount of 5% and 1,800 13% preference shares of Rs. 10 each at par; these were fully paid. You are required *(i)* to prepare the Balance Sheet of *A* Ltd. showing the position after the completion of purchase, *(ii)* to prepare statements showing cash paid and received by *A* Ltd. and by the liquidators of *B* Ltd. and *C* Ltd. and *(iii)* to prepare the shareholders accounts in the books of *B* Ltd. and *C* Ltd. *[Adatped B. Com. Agra)*

(Tatal of Balance Sheet of A Ltd. Rs. 1,38,790; B Ltd. Consideration Rs. 89,590, Loss on Realisation Rs. 16,090; C Ltd. Consideration Rs. 42,840; Loss on Realisation Rs. 26,340)

17. The balance sheets of X Co. Ltd. and Y Co Ltd. as on 31 March, 2010 are as follows:—

Balance Sheet of X Co. Ltd.

Liabilities		Rs.	*Assets*		Rs.
Share Capital:			Fixed Assets:		
Authorised Capital :			Goodwill	80,000	
10,000 shares of Rs. 100 each		10,00,000	Other Fixed Assets	8,00,000	8,80,000
Issued Capital:			Current Assets, Loans and Advances		9,00,000
10,000 Shares of Rs. 100 each, fully paid		10,00,000			
Reserves and Surplus:					
Capital Reserve	2,00,000				
General Reserve	70,000	2,70,000			
Unsecured Loans		2,00,000			
Current Liabilities and Provisions:					
Sundry Creditors		3,10,000			
		17,80,000			17,80,000

Balance Sheet of Y Co. Ltd.

Liabilities	*Rs.*	*Assets*		*Rs.*
Share Capital:		Fixed Assets		16,00,000
Authorised :		Current Assets, Loans and		
2,00,000 share of Rs. 10 each	20,00,000	Advances:		
Issued :		Bank	2,00,000	
80,000 Shares of Rs. 10 each,		Other Current Assets	6,60,000	8,60,000
fully paid	8,00,000			
Reserves and Surplus:				
General Reserve	8,00,000			
Secured Loans	5,00,000			
Current Liabilities and Provisions:				
Sundry Creditors	3,60,000			
	24,60,000			24,60,000

It was proposed that X Co. Ltd. should be taken over by Y Co. Ltd. The following arrangement was accepted by both the companies:

(*a*) Goodwill of X Co. Ltd. is considered valueless.

(*b*) Arrears of depreciation in X Co. Ltd. amounted to Rs. 40,000.

(*c*) The holder of every 2 shares in X Co. Ltd. was to receive:

(*i*) as fully paid, 10 shares in Y Co. Ltd. and

(*ii*) so much cash as is necessary to adjust the rights of shareholders of both the companies in accordance with the intrinsic value of the shares as per their balance sheets subject to necessary adjustmetns with regard to goodwill and depreciation in X Co. Ltd.s' balance sheet.

You are required to:

(*a*) determine the composition of consideration; and

(*b*) show the Balance Sheet after absorption.

[Adapted C.A. (Inter.) Nov. 1982]

(Consideration Rs. 11,50,000; Shares Rs. 10,00,000 and Cash Rs. 1,50,000; Balance Sheet Total Rs. 39,70,000)

18. *A* Ltd. agreed to acquire the business of *B* Ltd. as on March 31, 2010 The Balance Sheet of B Ltd. as on that date was as under:

Liabilities	*Rs.*	*Assets*	*Rs.*
Paid-up Capital:		Fixed Assets:	
10,000 12% preference		Land and Buildings	2,00,000
shares of Rs. 10 each	1,00,000	Machinery	1,00,000
20,000 equity shares of		Current Asssts:	
Rs. 10 each	2,00,000	Stock	2,00,000
General Reserve	20,000	Debtors	50,000
Profit & Loss Account	30,000	Cash and Bank balances	35,000
11% Debentures	1,00,000	Miscellaneous Expenditure:	
Sundry Creditors	1,50,000	Preliminary Expenses	10,000
		Discount on Issue of Debentures	5,000
	6,00,000		6,00,000

The consideration payable by A Ltd. was agreed as under :—

(*i*) The preference shareholders of B Ltd. were to be allotted 14% preference shares of Rs. 1,10,000.

(*ii*) Equity shareholders to be allotted six equity shares of Rs. 10 each issued at a premium of 10% and Rs. 3 cash against every five shares held.

11% debentureholders of *B* Ltd. to be paid at 8% premium by 14% debentures at 10% discount.

While arriving at the agreed consideration the liquidator of *A* Ltd. valued land the buildings at Rs. 2,50,000; stock at Rs. 2,20,000; and debtors at their book value, subject to an allowance of Rs. 2,000 to cover doubtful debts. Debtors of *B* Ltd. include Rs. 10,000 due from *A* Ltd. The machinery was valued at book value.

It was agreed that before acquisition, *B* Ltd. will pay a dividend of 10% on equity shares (preference dividend having been paid already). Liquidation expenses amounted to Rs. 5,000 and were borne by *A* Ltd.

Draft journal entries necessary to close the books of *B* Ltd. and to record acquisition in the books of *A* Ltd. Assume the absence of corporate dividend tax.

[Adapted Co. Sec.(Inter.) Dec. 1984]

(Consideration Rs. 3,86,000; Profit on Realisation Rs. 61,000; Goodwill on purchase of business Rs. 16,000 including Rs. 5,000 for liquidation expenses.)

19. *A* Ltd. and *B* Ltd. are two independent companies engaged respectively in the manufacture and distribution of a certain commodity. The balance sheets of the two companies, both drawn up as on 31st March, 2010 were as follows:

Balance Sheet of *A* Ltd.

	Rs.		Rs.
Capital, issued and fully paid:		Freehold Land & Buildings	6,00,000
50,000 10% Redeemable Preference		Plant amd Machinery	15,50,000
Shares of Rs. 10 each	5,00,000	Patent Rights	2,00,000
1,50,000 Equity Shares of Rs. 10 each	15,00,000	10,000 Shares in *B* Ltd.	1,15,000
	20,00,000	Stock	3,50,000
General Reserve	8,00,000	Sundry Debtors	80,000
Profit and Loss Account	90,000	Cash and Bank balances	45,000
Sundry Creditors	50,000		
	29,40,000		29,40,000

Balance Sheet of *B* Ltd.

	Rs.		Rs.
Capital issued and fully paid:		Goodwill	70,000
40,000 shares of Rs. 10 each	4,00,000	Furniture and Fittings	25,000
Profit and Loss Account	32,000	Motor Vehicles	40,000
Sundry Creditors	21,000	Stocks	2,39,000
		Sundry Debtors	62,000
		Cash & Bank Balances	17,000
	4,53,000		4,53,000

It has been agreed between the two boards of directors that both companies should be wound up and a new company, *C* Ltd., would be formed to acquire the assets of both companies on the following terms:

(i) *C* Ltd. is to have an authorised capital of Rs. 35,00,000 divided into 50,000 14% redeemable preference shares of Rs. 10 each and 3,00,000 equity shares of Rs. 10 each.

(ii) The business of *A* Ltd. was valued at Rs. 30,00,000: the settlement being Rs. 6,00,000 in cash and the balance in the form of fully paid equity shares valued at Rs. 12 each.

(iii) The business of *B* Ltd. was valued at Rs. 4,80,000 to be satisfied by issue of fully paid equity shares valued at Rs. 12 per share.

(iv) The preference shareholders in *A* Ltd. were paid cash.

(v) *C* Ltd. made a public issue of 50,000 preference shares at par and 30,000 equity shares at Rs. 12 per share. The issue was underwritten for the maximum commission allowed by law. All obligations were fulfilled.

(vi) To D, who mooted the scheme and got it accepted, 4,000 equity shares (fully paid) were allotted at Rs. 12 in consideration of his work.

The scheme has been carried through in its entirety. You are required to:

(a) Set out the closing entries in the books of *A* Ltd. in the form of journal entries together with the closing cash book entries; and

(b) Draw up the initial balance sheet of *C* Ltd.

(Profit on Realisation of A Ltd., Rs. 1,10,000; Total of Balance Sheet of C. Ltd., Rs, 37,39,000)

(Hint: As out of 40,000 shares of *B* Ltd; 10,000 shares are now with *C* Ltd., due to purchase of business of *A* Ltd.; *A* Ltd. will have to pay only for 30,000 shares of *B* Ltd. Hence, it will issue to *B* Ltd. shares worth Rs. 3,60,000.)

20. Flying Saucers Ltd. was just recovering out of great financial stress and consequently went into voluntary liquidation. Its summarised Balance Sheet on 31st March, 2010 was as follows:

Liabilities	*Rs.*	*Assets*	*Rs.*
Preference Shares	5,20,000	Skyscraper	4,13,400
Equity Shares	7,80,000	Other Fixed Assets	2,22,560
Profit Prior to Incorporation	15,730	Floating Assets	2,79,370
Liabilities	1,36,110	Profit and Loss Account	5,36,510
There is a contingent liability in respect of a pending suit to the extent of Rs. 18,840			
	14,51,840		14,51,840

Flying Cups Ltd. was incorporated on 15th April, 2010 to take over some of the assets of the Flying Saucers Ltd., at agreed valuation as under :

		Rs.
Skyscraper	..	2,60,000
Plant and Machinery	..	1,56,000
Motor Lorries	..	5,200
Stock in Trade	..	98,800
		5,20,000

The consideration was satisfied by the allotment of preference and equity shares in the new company in the ratio of 3 : 2. The preference shares carried 14% dividend, whereas the equity shares of Rs. 30 each were issued as partly paid to the extent of Rs. 20 per share. The new company also agreed to take over the contingent liability which ultimately materialised. The claimant was allotted equity shares as fully paid.

The book debts of the old company realised Rs. 1,65,425 and the trade creditors were settled for Rs. 1,14,842. The liabilities were discharged. The cost of voluntary winding up came to Rs. 13,923. The preference shareholders in the old company agreed to accept, in full satisfaction of their claims, the preference shares in the new company and all the available cash.

You are required to (*i*) close the books of Flying Saucers Ltd., and (*ii*) give journal entries for opening the books of Flying Cups Ltd.

[Adapted from C.A., Final]

(Consideration Rs, 5,20,000; Loss an Realisation, Rs, 51,220)

Hint: The transferee company will debit the amount paid for contingent liabilities to Goodwill Account.

21. A. Ltd. had acquired, as a current asset, 60,000 shares in B Ltd., for Rs. 60,000 on 1st November, 2008. On 1st April, 2010 it agreed to absorb B Ltd., the consideration being:

(i) the assumption of its liabilities;

(ii) a payment in cash of Re. 0.50 per share in *B* Ltd., and

(iii) the issue of shares of Re. 1 each in *A* Ltd., credited as fully paid, to the members of *B* Ltd. on the basis of:

Two equity shares (valued at Rs. 1.60 each) and one 14% redeemable preference share (valued at Rs. 1.10) for every five shares held in *B* Ltd.

A Ltd. also agreed to discharge Rs, 40,000 debentures in *B* Ltd., held outside the company at a premium of 10 per cent by the issue of its 13% debentures carrying a full six months' interest payable on 1st October, 2010.

The summarised Balance Sheet of *B* Ltd. as on 31st March, 2010 was as follows:—

Liabilities	*Rs.*	*Assets*		*Rs.*
Share Capital		Goodwill		20,000
1,60,000 shares of Re. 1 each,		Fixed Assets, at cost *less* accumulated		
Re. 0.75 paid	1,20,000	depreciation :		
General Reserve	75,000	Land		11,000
Profit & Loss Account	21,550	Buildings		22,000
Insurance Fund*	10,000	Plant		40,000
10% Debentures	45,000			93,000
Creditors	17,800	Investments:	*Rs.*	
*The company had been carrying its own insurance risk crediting amounts equivalent to premium to the fund and charging losses threreto.		On account of Insurance Fund	10,000	
		General, Rs. 5,000 10% Debentures in B Ltd.	4,800	14,800
		Stock		85,800
		Debtors		45,000
		Bank Balance		50,750
	2,89,350			2,89,350

It was agreed that for amalgamation purposes, 5 per cent should be written off stocks and provision of 2 1/2% made for doubtful debts. The remaining assets, other than goodwill, are considered to be properly valued for the purpose of amalgamation.

Before passing entries in respect of the amalgamation, A. Ltd.decided to revalue the shares in B Ltd. on the same basis as that of the amalgamation.

The amalgamation was completed on 1st June, 2010.

Expenses amounted to Rs. 750 and were paid by A Ltd.

You are required to draft the journal entries (to include cash items) to record:

(*a*) the closing entries in the books of B Ltd.

(*b*) the entries in the books of A Ltd. in respect of the amalgamation and the public issue.

(Consideration Rs. 1,36,000 Loss on Realisation of B Ltd., Rs. 45,550; Goodwill in A Ltd. Rs. 21,015)

Hint: The following entry is passed for cancellation of own debentures

10% Debentures	Dr.	5,000	
To Own Debentures Account			4,800
To Realisation Account			200

22. The abridged balance sheet of P Ltd. as at 31st March, 2010 is as under:

Liabilities	*Rs.*	*Assets*	*Rs.*
24,000 Equity Shares of Rs. 10 each	2,40,000	Goodwill	5,000
5,000 12% Cumulative Preference		Tangible Fixed Assets	2,57,000
Shares of Rs. 10 each	50,000	Stock	50,000
12% Debentures	1,00,000	Debtors	58,000
Outstanding Interest on Debentures	6,000	Bank	1,000
Creditors	1,00,000	Preliminary Expenses	15,000
		Profit and Loss Account	1,10,000
	4,96,000		4,96,000

The following scheme is passed and sanctioned by the Court :

1. A new company PK Ltd. is formed with Rs. 3,00,000 dividend into 30,000 equity shares of Rs. 10 each

2. The new company will acquire the assets and liabilities of P Ltd. on the following terms:-

(*a*) Old company's debentures are paid by similar debentures in new company and for outstanding debentures interest, shares of equal amount are issued at par.

(*b*) The creditors are paid for every Rs. 100 Rs. 16 in cash and 10 shares issued at par.

(*c*) Preference shareholders are to get equal number of equity shares at par. For arrears of dividend amounting to Rs. 12,000, 5 shares are issued at par for each Rs. 100 in full satisfaction.

(*d*) Equity shareholders are issued one share at par for 3 shares held.

(*e*) Expenses Rs. 8,000 are to be borne by the new company.

3. Current assets are to taken at book values (except stock which is to be reduced by Rs. 3,000) Goodwill to be eliminated and Tangible Fixed Assets be valued at Rs. 2,60,000.

4. Remaining shares of the new company are issued at par and are fully paid.

You are required to show :

(*a*) In the old company's books.

(*i*) New Company's Account.

(*ii*) Realisation and Reconstruction (combined) Account.

(*b*) In the new company's books.

(*i*) Bank Account.

(*ii*) Equity Share Capital Account.

(*iii*) Summarised Balance Sheet.

[Adapted C.A. Final Nov. 1986]

(Consideration Rs. 1,36,000; Loss on Realisation Rs. 29,000; Loss on Reconstruction; Rs. 1,60,000; Shares issued for cash, Rs. 58.000; Balance Sheet total, Rs. 3,98,000)

23. The following are the balance sheets of two companies, Wye Ltd. and Zed Ltd. as at March 31, 2010.

Wye Ltd.

	Rs.		Rs.
Share Capital :		Sundry Assets	7,50,000
5,000 equity shares of Rs. 100 each fully paid	5,00,000		
Reserves	1,00,000		
Creditors	1,50,000		
	7,50,000		7,50,000

Zed Ltd.

	Rs.		Rs.
Share Capital:		1,000 shares in Wye Ltd.	1.00,000
3,000 equity shares of Rs. 100 each fully paid-up	3,00,000	Sundry Assets	3,50,000
Reserves	55,000		
Creditors	95,000		
	4,50,000		4,50,000

Wye Ltd. was to absorb Zed Ltd. on the basis of intrinsic value of the shares — the consideration was to be discharged in the form of fully paid shares, entries to be made at par value only. A sum of Rs. 20,000 is owed by Wye Ltd. to Zed Ltd. Also included in the stocks of Wye Ltd. is Rs. 30,000 goods supplied by Zed Ltd. @ cost plus 20%. Give journal entries in the books of both the companies. Also show Realisation Account and Sundry Equity Shareholders Account in Zed Ltd.'s ledger.

(Realisation Loss, Rs. 42,500; Wye Ltd. will allot 2,125 shares @ Rs. 100 per share to Zed Ltd.)

24. The balance sheet of Y Ltd. as on 31st March 2010 was as follows :—

Liabilities	*Rs.*	*Assets*	*Rs.*
15,000 equity shares of Rs. 100		Goodwill	1,00,000
each, fully paid	15,00,000	Other Fixed Assets	15,00,000
12% Debentures	5,00,000	Current Assets	4,00,000
Sundry Creditors	3,00,000	Profit and Loss Account	3,00,000
	23,00,000		23,00,000

Of the shares 5,000 were held by Z Ltd.which had paid Rs. 3,50,000 for them. Z Ltd. agreed to acquire the business of Y Ltd., valuing the shares in Y Ltd. at Rs. 60 each. The consideration was to be discharged in the form of fully paid equity shares of Z Ltd. at the agreed valuation of Rs. 12 per share but entries were made only at par value of Rs. 10 per share. The claims of debentureholders in Y Ltd. were satisfied at a discount of 5% by issue at par 14% Debentures in Z Ltd. Y Ltd.'s. Sundry Creditors also agreed to be discharged in cash by Z Ltd. at a discount of 5%. Z Ltd. agreed to bear the liquidation expenses which totalled Rs. 10,000.

Z Ltd. decided first to revalue shares in Y Ltd. and then to record the acquisition of business. State the journal entries to be passed in the books of the two companies.

(Consideration Rs. 5,00,000; Loss on Realisation Rs. 2,00,000)

25. On 31st March, 2010, the balance sheet of the Asbestos Company Ltd. was as follows:—

Liabilities	*Rs.*	*Assets*	*Rs.*
Share Capital:		Freehold Land & Buildings	2,00,000
Authorised and Issued:		Benefit of Pending Contracts	1,50,000
4,000 12% Cumulative Preference		Machinery & Plant	2,00,000
Shares of Rs. 100 each	4,00,000	Stock as valued and certified	
12,000 Equity Shares of Rs. 50 each	6,00,000	by Manager	3,00,000
	10,00,000	Sundry Debtors (of which considered	
12 per cent Debentures of Rs. 500 each	1,50,000	doubtful Rs. 2,43,170)	3,00,000
Debenture Interest Outstanding	9,000	Balance at Bank	1,570
Trade Creditors	1,00,000	Profit and Loss Account	2,82,430
Liabilities for Expenses	1,75,000		
	14,34,000		14,34,000

The company's creditors were pressing. The dividend on preference shares was in arrear for one year, and additional working capital was badly needed. The company had a very valuable property which stood highly understated in the books and which it was not in a position to sell, being required for use in business.

Meetings of the debentureholders, the two classes of shareholders and the creditors were held, and the following scheme was agreed to by all the parties and sanctioned by the Court:

(i) A new company was to be registered as Asbestos (2010) Ltd. with a capital of 3,00,000 shares of Rs. 10 each for the purpose of purchasing the business.

(ii) 13% Debentures were to be issued in exchange for 12 per cent Debentures in the old company.

(iii) Twenty shares of Rs. 10 each were to be issued as fully paid to the holder of each preference share of Rs. 100 each in the old company.

(iv) The arrears of preference dividend were to be satisfied by the issue of 20 fully paid shares of Rs. 10 each in the new company for every Rs. 100 of the arrears.

(v) The debentureholders were to accept fully paid shares of Rs.10 each in the new company in satisfaction of the outstanding interest.

(vi) The creditors were to be satisfied by a cash payment of fifty paise in the rupee and by the issue of fully paid shares in the new company for the balance of fifty paise.

(vii) Five fully paid shares of Rs. 10 in the new company were to be issued in respect of every Rs. 50 equity share in the old company.

The balance of the capital of the new company fully subscribed for and paid-up by the directors. The amount made available under the reconstruction scheme was to be utilised as follows:

Benefit of pending contracts and the debit balance of Profit and Loss Account were to be written off; Machinery and Plant was to be increased by Rs. 6,850; and

Stock to be reduced by Rs. 1,50,000 and Freehold Land and Buildings to be adjusted by the balance available.

You are required to prepare :

(*a*) A statement showing the shares to be allotted as fully paid by the new company.

(*b*) The journal entries necessary to record the above in the books of the old company.

(*c*) The initial Balance Sheet of Asbestors (2010) Ltd. *[Adapted C.A., Final]*

(Consideration Rs. 14,96,000; Profit on Realisation Account, Rs. 2,82,430; Total of Balance Sheet of new company, Rs. 31,50,000)

Hint : Value of Freehold Land and Buildings is arrived at as follows:

	Rs.	Rs.	Rs.
Consideration			14,96,000
Add: Liabilities taken over:			
Debentures		1,50,000	
Outstanding Debenture Interest		9,000	
Trade Creditors		1,00,000	
Liabilites for Expenses		1,75,000	4,34,000
			19,30,000
Less: Total value of other assets acquired:			
Machinery and Plant		2,06,850	
Stock		1,50,000	
Debtors	3,00,000		
Less: Provision	2,43,170	56,830	
Bank		1,570	
Benefit of Pending Contracts		Nil	4,15,250
Balance, being the value of Freehold Land & Buildings.			15,14,750

26. The following is the summarised balance sheet as on March, 31, 2010 of J More Ltd., a company:

	Rs.		Rs.	Rs.
Share Capital: Authorised, issued and fully paid:		Goodwill		2,00,000
50,000 12% Cum-Preference Shares of Rs. 10 each	5,00,000	Other Fixed Assets		15,00,000
1,20,000 Equity Shares of Rs. 10 each	12,00,000	Current Assets:		
12% Debentures	2,00,000	Stock	1,09,000	
Interest thereon	12,000	Debtors	60,000	
Creditors	2,40,000	Balance at Bank	3,000	1,72,000
		Preliminary Expenses		30,000
		Profit and Loss Account		2,50,000.
	21,52,000			21,52,000

Note. The dividend in arrear on the Preference Shares is Rs. 90,000.

The following scheme of reconstruction was agreed to by all parties and the necessary sanctions obtained:

A new company J. More (2010) Ltd. was to be registered with a capital of 2,50,000 shares of Rs. 5 each to acquire as from April 1, 2010 the undertaking on the following terms :

(1) The new company to assume the old company's debenture liability by issuing to the holders corresponding debentures in the new company together with two fully paid shares in the new company for every Rs. 10 of interest in arrear.

(2) The creditors of the old company to accept, for every Rs. 10 due to them, Rs. 2.50 in cash (to be provided by the new company) and two fully paid shares in the new company.

(3) The preference shareholders in the old company to receive two fully paid shares in the new company for each share held in the old company; further, the arrears of preference dividend company to be satisfied by the issue of one fully paid share in the new company for every Rs. 10 due. Assume there is no corporate dividend tax.

(4) The equity shareholders in the old company to receive one fully paid share in the new company for every three shares held.

(5) Costs amounting to Rs. 36,000 to be borne by the new company.

It was agreed that current assets should be taken into the new company's books at the values in the old company's books (except, that stock was to be reduced by Rs. 10,000); goodwill was to be eliminated and Other Fixed Assets were valued at Rs. 11,31,000.

The balance of shares in the new company was issued to and paid for in full by certain of the old shareholders.

You are required to give:

(a) in the old company's books :*(i)* the Realisation Account, *(ii)* the account with the new company; and *(iii)* Sundry Eqity Shareholders Account; and

(b) in respect of the new company : *(i)* Equity Share Capital Account, *(ii)* The Cash Book, and *(iii)* A summarised opening Balance Sheet.

[Adapted from C.A. (Eng.), Final]

(Consideration Rs. 7,45,000; Loss on Realisation, Rs. 7,20,000; Total of Balance Sheet of new company, Rs. 14,52,000)

27. It has been agreed that Body Ltd. should purchase as on March 31, 2010 the undertaking of Leg Ltd., and Arm Ltd. the price paid in each case being *(a)* the book value of the net assets excluding goodwill, plus *(b)* goodwill, valued at four years' purchase of the excess of the average of the profits earned during the last three years over 8 per cent of *(a)*. The purchase price is to be settled in each case by the issue of Rs. 10 equity shares in Body Ltd. at par. Thereafter, Leg Ltd. and Arm Ltd. are to be liquidated by the distribution in specie to their shareholders of the shares in Body Ltd.

The balance sheets of Leg Ltd. and Arm Ltd. as on March 31, 2010 were as follows:

	Leg Ltd.	*Arm Ltd.*
	Rs.	*Rs.*
Issued Equity Capital	1,50,000	2,00,000
General Reserve	1,60,000	...
Profit and Loss Account	1,20,000	70,000
Current Liabilities	2,00,000	1,40,000
	6,30,000	4,10,000
Goodwill	...	90,000
Fixed Assets	4,00,000	1,00,000
Current Assets	2,30,000	2,20,000
	6,30,000	4,10,000

The profits have been:

Year ended March 31, 2008	44,900	22,600
Year ended March 31, 2009	51,100	15,500
Year ended March 31, 2010	40,200	24,600

Show the journal entries in the books of Leg Ltd. and Arm Ltd. necessary to record the sale, of assets and the distribution of the shares in the Body Ltd. to the respective shareholders. Ignore. the costs of liquidation.

[Adapted from Incorp. Accts., Inter]

(Leg Ltd : Consideration Rs. 4,74,000; Goodwill Rs. 44,000. Arm Ltd. : Consideration Rs. 2,06,000; Goodwill Rs. 26,000)

28. The Balance Sheets of Gonne Ltd. and Drie Ltd. as on 31st March, 2010 contain the following:—

	Gonne	*Drie*
	Rs.	*Rs*
Authorised and Issued Capital—Shares of Rs. 10 each	5,00,000	3,00,000
Creditors	1,40,000	1,60,000
Debentures, 12 per cent	1,00,000	—
Debenture Redemption Reserve	50,000	—
Profit and Loss Account	(Cr.) 90,000	(Dr.) 70,000

Fixed Assets	5,10,000	3,70,000
Current Assets	3,34,000	50,000
Leasehold Redemption Reserve	—	30,000
Investment in Drie Ltd., 3,000 Shares at cost	36,000	

Gonne and Drie Ltd. is formed to amalgamate the two businesses. The consideration for assets, payable in cash, is agreed at Rs. 10,00,000 for Gonne Ltd. (excluding the shares of Drie Ltd.) and Rs. 4,50,000 for Drie Ltd. In addition. the new company agrees to issue Rs. 1,00,000 14% Debentures in exchange for the Debentures in Gonne Ltd. The creditors of Gonne Ltd. and Drie Ltd. were paid Rs. 1,35,000 and Rs. 1,58,000 respectively. Close the books of the transferor companies.

(Profit on Realisation Accounts : Gonne Ltd., 2,54,200; Drie Ltd., Rs. 62,000)

Hint : The total amount avaiable for 30,000 shares in Drie Ltd. Rs. 2,92,000; 3,000 shares are held by Gonne Ltd. Hence 1/10 of Rs. 2,92,000 or Rs. 29,200 will be received from the liquidator of Drie Ltd.

29. The Wet Ltd. was unsuccessful and had to be reconstructed. For this purpose, Dry Ltd. was incorporated with an authorised capital of 50,000 shares of Rs. 10 each. The shareholders in Wet Ltd. were to receive two shares of Rs. 10 each credited as Rs. 6 paid for every three shares held. The balance of Rs. 4 was to be paid as final call money. The Trial Balance of Wet Ltd. on the date of reconstruction was as follows :

	Dr. *Rs.*	*Cr.* *Rs.*
Share Capital 50,000 shares of Rs.10 each, full paid		5,00,000
Creditors		1,50,000
Patent Rights	2,50,000	
Sundry Debtors	1,45,000	
Stock	70,000	
Cash at Bank	15,000	
Preliminary Expenses	20,000	
Profit and Loss Account	1,50,000	
	6,50,000	6,50,000

The creditors were to be discharged by the new company on the following basis :

	Rs.	
Preferential Creditors	20,000	in full in cash
Creditors for Rs.80,000	50,000	in cash
Creditors for Rs. 50,000	50,000	in Debentures.

The cost of liquidation amounted to Rs 3,000 which was also met by Dry Ltd. Fractions of shares in all amounted to 133 1/3 shares in terms of shares of Dry Ltd. for which cash was paid. The other shares were duly allotted and all payment due in respect of them received by Dry Ltd. 5,000 of the unissued shares were offered to the public and were underwritten by M/s. Bulls and Bears for a commission of 2 per cent. All the shares offered were taken up and paid for in cash.

Close the books of Wet Ltd. nad prepare the books of Dry. Ltd. Give is Balance Sheet, the value of patent rights being adjusted to the required extent.

(Considersation Rs. 2,00,000; Cash for fractional shares 133 1/3 @ Rs. 6 per share = Rs. 800; Loss on Realisation of Wet Ltd. Rs. 1,30,000; Total of Balance Sheet of Dry Ltd. Rs. 4,32,000)

30. Go Ltd. and Ready Ltd. decide to amalgamate themselves into Go Ready Ltd. on the basis of the following balance sheets as on March 31, 2010—

	Go Ltd. *Rs.*	*Ready Ltd.* *Rs.*		*Go Ltd.* *Rs.*	*Ready Ltd.* *Rs.*
Share Capital (shares of Rs. 100 each)	5,00,000	4,00,000	Investment :		
Reserve	2,00,000	1,00,000	1,000 shares in Ready Ltd.	1,30,000	
Creditors	2,00,000	1,50,000	2,000 shares in Go Ltd.		2,10,000
			Sundry Assets	7,70,000	4,40,000
	9,00,000	6,50,000		9,00,000	6,50,000

Show how much is payable to outside shareholders of the two companies.

(Rs. 4,28,333 to shareholders of Go Ltd. and Rs. 4,31,667 to shareholders of Ready Ltd.)

31. The following Balance Sheets of *B* Ltd. and *A* Ltd. as on March 31, 2010 are given :—

	B Ltd. Rs.	*A Ltd.* Rs.		*B Ltd.* Rs.	*A Ltd.* Rs.
Share Capital (Shares of Rs. 100 each fully paid)	15,00,000	5,00,000	Fixed Assets	12,60,000	20,000
Reserves	3,78,000	1,10,000	Sundry Debtors	2,30,000	1,80,000
12% Debentures	...	3,00,000	Stock	3,80,000	2,10,000
Sundry Creditors	2,00,000	90,000	1,000 shares in *A* Ltd.	90,000	...
			3,000 shares in *B* Ltd.	...	5,00,000
			Cash at Bank	1,18,000	90,000
	20,78,000	10,00,000		20,78,000	10,00,000

A Ltd. traded in raw materials which were required by *B* Ltd. Of the stock held by *B* Ltd. as shown above, Rs. 1,00,000 represented purchase from *A* Ltd. which company had a normal margin of 20%. *B* Ltd. owed Rs. 50,000 to *A* Ltd. in this regard.

It was decided that B Ltd. should absorb *A* Ltd. on the basis of the intrinsic values of the shares of the two companies. Before absorption, *B* Ltd. declared a dividend of 8% on which tax on distributed profits @ 15% (including surcharge) was paid. *B* Ltd. were holding the shares in *A* Ltd. as a current asset.

Prepare the balance sheet of *B* Ltd. after the acquisition is complete.

(Total of Balance Sheet, Rs. 23,99,915)

ESSAY-TYPE

1. What do you mean by amalgamation in the light of the Accounting Standard 14 on Accounting for Amalgamations issued by the Institute of Chartered Accountants of India? What are the two types of amalgamations?
2. Describe the conditions which must be fulfilled for an amalgamation in the nature of merger.
3. What is the distinction between (*i*) an amalgamation in the nature of merger and (*ii*) an amalgamation in the nature of purchase?
4. What do you mean by external reconstruction? Is it correct to say that external reconstruction is covered under the category of an amalgamation in the nature of purchase?
5. Distinguish between external reconstruction and amalgamation in the nature of purchase.
6. Briefly describe the methods of accounting for amalgamation.
7. What is the pooling of interests method of accounting for amalgamation? How does it differ from the purchase method?
8. Explain the term consideration in the context of amalgamations.
9. In case of an amalgamation, how are reserves of the transferor company treated in the books of the transferee company?
10. How is goodwill arising on an amalgamation treated in the books of the transferee company? What period will you suggest over which such goodwill should be amortised?
11. Describe the factors which may be considered in estimating the useful life of goodwill arising on an amalgamation.
12. In an amalgamation, how will you treat the balance of Profit and Loss Account of the transferor company in the books of the transferee company?
13. What are the disclosures which are considered appropriate in the first financial statemets in the transferee company following an amalgamation?
14. Distinguish between internal reconstruction and external reconstruction.

22

HOLDING COMPANIES

SYNOPSIS

1.	General	.. 22.1
	Definitions	.. 22.1
	Advantages of holding companies	.. 22.2
	Disadvantages of holding companies	.. 22.2
2.	Legal definition and requirements	.. 22.2
	Accounts	.. 22.4
3.	AS-21: Consolidated Financial Statements	.. 22.7
	Consolidation of balance sheets and profit and loss accounts	.. 22.12
	Treatment of dividend	.. 22.12
	Debiting the subsidiary with profits etc...	22.14
	Preparation of consolidated balance sheet	.. 22.15
	Cost of control and capital reserve	.. 22.15
	Minority interest	.. 22.17
	Capital profits and revenue profits	.. 22.22
	Controlling interest acquired during the course of the year	.. 22.26
	Treatment relating to preference shares of the subsidiary	.. 22.29
	Unrealised profits	.. 22.31
	Mutual owings	.. 22.33
	Dividend out of preacquisition profits	.. 22.36
	Dividend out of post acquisition profits	.. 22.37
	Error relating to dividend from subsidiary company	.. 22.37
	Interim dividend	.. 22.39
	Proposed dividend	.. 22.41
	Change in value of fixed assets	.. 22.47
	Successive purchases of shares	.. 22.66
	Bonus Shares	... 22.54
	Consolidation of profit and loss accounts	.. 22.73
	Inter-company holdings	.. 22.93
	Foreign subsidiaries	.. 22.95
	Associated Companies	.. 22.99

1. GENERAL

Definitions:

A holding company is a company which controls another company known as subsidiary company by owning its majority of the shares carrying voting rights or controlling the composition of its board of directors. Accounting Standard 21 on Consolidated Financial Statements gives the following definitions :

A *subsidiary* is an enterprise that is controlled by another enterprise (known as the parent).

A *parent* is an enterprise that has one or more subsidiaries.

A *group* is a parent and all its subsidiaries.

Thus , the Accoutning Standard calls the holding company, a parent.

Advantages of holding companies :

Holding companies have been used extensively to further the combination movement. Particularly in the United States of America, the holding company device was found to be useful in bringing a number of companies under one control, and it is only when the combination movement gathered momentum that holding companies became popular. The advantages of holding companies are as under :—

1. Subsidiary companies maintain their separate identities and as such they maintain their goodwill.

2. The public may not be aware of the existence of combination among the various companies and, therefore, the fruits of monopoly or near monopoly may be enjoyed without resentment in the minds of the people.

   This, however, is clearly a disadvantage from the social point of view, because, if there is a monopoly, the public ought to know.

3. The persons controlling the holding company need invest a comparatively small amount in order to control the subsidiary companies. If, for example, A, a holding company, has two subsidiaries, B and C and if B and C in turn have three subsidiaries each, the persons who have the majority of shares in A will be able to control eight other companies. Had these companies been amalgamated, a much larger amount would have been required in order to control the concerns.

   This, again, is a disadvantage from the social point of view, because it may lead to irresponsibility.

4. By maintaining the separate identities of various companies, it would be possible to carry forward losses for income tax purposes.
5. Each subsidiary company has to prepare its own accounts and, therefore, the financial position and profitability of each undertaking is known.
6. Should it be found desirable that the control of the holding company be given up, it can be easily arranged; all that is required is that the shares in the subsidiary companies should be disposed of in the market.

Disadvantages of holding companies :

The disadvantages of holding companies are the following :—

1. There is a possibility of fraudulent manipulation of accounts, specially if the accounts of various companies are made up to different dates.
2. Inter-company transactions are often entered at fanciful or unduly low prices in order to suit those who control the holding companies.
3. There is the danger of the oppression of minority shareholders.
4. There may be accounting difficulties in appraising the financial position of companies due to inter-company transactions carried on at too high or too low prices.
5. The shareholders in the holding company may not be aware of the true financial position of the subsidiary companies.
6. Similarly, the creditors and outside shareholders in the subsidiary companies may not also be aware of the true financial position.
7. The subsidiary companies may be forced to appoint persons of the choosing of holding companies as directors or other officers at unduly high remuneration.

Whatever the advantages and disadvantages, the holding company has come to stay and the law now wisely tries to regulate its working. The law has defined a holding company and a subsidiary company. Private companies, subsidiary to a public company, do not enjoy the privileges given to private companies. Also, the law compels the holding company to give information about the subsidiary companies.

2. LEGAL DEFINITION AND REQUIREMENTS

Section 4 of the Companies Act, 1956 defines a subsidiary company. A company is a subsidiary of another if and only if—

"(*a*) that other company controls the composition of its Board of Directors; or

(*b*) that other—

(*i*) where the first mentioned company is an existing company in respect of which the holders of preference shares issued before the commencement of this Act have the same voting rights in all respects as the holders of equity shares, exercises or controls more than half of the total voting power of such company;

(*ii*) where the first mentioned company is any other company, holds more than half in nominal value of its equity share capital; or

(*c*) the company is a subsidiary of any company which is that other company's subsidiary".

(*Illustration*. Company *B* is a subsidiary of Company *A* and Company *C* is a subsidiary of Company *B*, Company *C* is a subsidiary of Company *A*. If Company *D* is a subsidiary of Company *C*, Company *D* will also be subsidiary of Company *B* and consequently also of Company *A*.)

The composition of a company's Board of Directors will be treated as controlled by another company if, by the exercise of some power exercisable by it at its sole discretion (without the consent or concurrence of any other person), that other company can appoint or remove all or the majority of the directors. Such a power will be deemed to exist when any one of the following conditions are satisfied :—

(*a*) a person cannot be appointed as director without the exercise in his favour of the powers vested in that other company;

(*b*) a person's appointment as director follows necessarily from his appointment as director, or manager of, or to any other office or employment in that other company; and

(*c*) the directorship is held by an individual nominated by that other company itself or subsidiary of it.

In determining whether one company is a subsidiary of another the following should be kept in mind :-

(*a*) any shares held or power exercisable by that other company in a fiduciary capacity should be ignored, *i.e.*, treated as not really held by that other company;

(*b*) any shares held or power exercisable by any person by virtue of the provisions of any debentures or of a trust deed for securing any issue of such debentures should be disregarded;

(*c*) any shares held or power exercisable by, or by a nominee for, that other or its subsidiary [except as mentioned in (*b*) above] should be treated as not held or exercisable by that other if the ordinary business of that other (or its subsidiary, as the case may be) includes the lending of money and the shares are held or the power is exercisable by way of security only for the purpose of a transaction entered into in the ordinary course of that business.

(This is to say that a finance or a banking company will not be treated as a holding company if, as security for a loan granted by it, it holds the majority of equity shares or has the power to nominate the majority of directors.)

(*d*) Any shares held or power exercisable—

(*i*) by any person as a nominee for that other company (except where that other is concerned only in a fiduciary capacity), or

(*ii*) by, or by a nominee for, a subsidiary of that company, not being a subsidiary which is concerned only in fiduciary capacity,

shall be treated as held or exercisable by that other company, unless (b) and (c) above apply.

In case a company is incorporated in a foreign country, the laws of that country will determine whether a company is a holding or a subsidiary company.

The substance of the above definition is that a company is a holding company if (1) it is able to appoint or dismiss the majority of directors of another company without consulting any one; but such a power exercised by it in a fiduciary capacity (*i.e.*, in its capacity as a trustee or by virtue of debentures held by it or by virtue of a loan given by it (if its ordinary business is to lend money) will not make a company holding company; (2) it holds the majority of voting power or equity shares in another company (unless the shares are held in a fiduciary capacity or, if it is a lending company, by way of security for a loan granted); and (3) a company is a subsidiary of one of its subsidiaries. Shares held or power to appoint majority of directors on behalf of a company by a nominee really belongs to the company.

Accounts :

Sections 212 to 214 of the Companies Act govern the presentation of accounts of subsidiary companies by the holding companies. It should be remembered that the various sections relating to the preparation of the profit and loss account and the balance sheet apply to the holding as well as subsidiary companies.

Under section 212, the following must be attached to the balance sheet of a company :-

(*a*) a copy of the recent balance sheet of the subsidiary company (or companies);

(*b*) a copy of the recent profit and loss account of the subsidiary (or subsidiaries);

(*c*) a copy of the recent report of the Board of Directors of the subsidiary;

(*d*) a copy of the recent report of the auditors of the subsidiary (or subsidiaries);

(*e*) a statement showing :—

(*i*) the extent of the holding company's interest in the subsidiary (or subsidiaries) at the end of the financial year of the subsidiary (or subsidiaries);

(*ii*) the profits (after deduction of losses) of the subsidiary (or subsidiaries) so far as they concern the holding company separately for the current financial year and for previous financial years and separately for profits already dealt with in the books of the holding company and not so dealt with.

(The term "profits" means profits of a revenue nature and earned after the date of the acquisition of the shares by the holding company.)

(*f*) Where the financial year of the subsidiary company does not coincide with the financial year of the holding company, a statement showing the following :—

(*i*) whether and to what extent there has been a change in the holding company's interest in the subsidiary company since the close of the financial year of the subsidiary company;

(*ii*) details of any material changes which have occurred between the end of the financial year of the subsidiary company and the end of the financial year of the holding company in respect of :—

the subsidiary's fixed assets;

its investments;

the money lent by it; and

the moneys borrowed by it for any purpose other than that of meeting current liabilities.

(g) If for any reason the Board of Directors of the holding company is unable to obtain information on the subject of revenue or capital profits [subject of statement (*e*) above], a report in writing to that effect.

Under the same section, the interval between the close of the financial year of the subsidiary company and that of the holding company cannot be more than six months for the purpose of the section. This means that the information to be attached to the balance sheet of a holding company in respect of the subsidiary companies cannot be more than 6 months old. Under section 213, the Central Government has the power to declare that the financial year of the subsidiary shall end with that of the holding company. This power will be exercised either at the request or with the consent of the Board of Directors of the company whose financial year is to be extended. This will naturally postpone the preparation of the final accounts and the holding of the general meeting and submission of the various returns.

However, many of the provisions of the Companies Act relating to holding company and subsidiary company have become redundant due to the amendment in the Income-tax Act which now requires that every assessee shall have a uniform financial year beginning on 1st April and ending on 31st March of the subaequent year.

Section 212 is reproduced below :

"(1) There shall be attached to the balance sheet of a holding company having a subsidiary or subsidiaries at the end of the financial year as at which the holding company's balance sheet is made out, the following documents in respect of such subsidiary or of each subsidiary, as the case may be :—

(*a*) a copy of the balance sheet of the subsidiary;
(*b*) a copy of its profits and loss account;
(*c*) a copy of the report of its Board of Directors;
(*d*) a copy of the report of its auditors;
(*e*) a statement of the holding company's interest in the subsidiary as specified in sub-section (3);
(*f*) the statement referred to in sub-section (5), if any; and
(*g*) the report referred to in sub-section (6), if any.

(2) (*a*) The balance sheet referred to in clause (*a*) of sub-section (1) shall be made out in accordance with requirements of this Act—

(*i*) as at the end of the financial year of the subsidiary, where such financial year coincides with the financial year of the holding company;

(*ii*) as at the end of the financial year of the subsidiary last before that of the holding company where the financial year of the subsidiary does not coincide with that of the holding company.

(*b*) The profit and loss account and the reports of the Board of Directors and of the auditors, referred to in clauses (*b*), (*c*) and (*d*) of sub-section (1), shall be made out, in accordance with the requirements of this Act, for the financial year of the subsidiary referred to in clause (*a*).

(*c*) Where the financial year of the subsidiary does not coincide with that of the holding company, the financial year aforesaid of the subsidiary shall not end on a day which precedes the day on which the holding company's financial year ends by more than six months.

(*d*) Where the financial year of a subsidiary is shorter in duration than that of its holding company, references to the financial year of the subsidiary in clauses (*a*), (*b*) and (*c*) shall be construed as references to two or more financial years of the subsidiary the duration of which, in the aggregate, is not less than the duration of the holding company's year.

(3) The statement referred to in clause (*e*) of sub-section (1) shall specify—

(*a*) the extent of the holding company's interest in the subsidiary at the end of the financial year or of the last of the financial years of the subsidiary referred to in sub-section(2);

(*b*) the net aggregate amount, so far as it concerns members of the holding company and is not dealt with in the company's accounts, of the subsidiary's profits after deducting its losses or *vice versa*—

(*i*) for the financial year or years of the subsidiary aforesaid; and

(*ii*) for the previous financial years of the subsidiary since it became the holding company's subsidiary;

(*c*) the net aggregate amount of the profits of the subsidiary after deducting its losses or *vice versa*—

(*i*) for the financial year or years of the subsidiary aforesaid; and

(*ii*) for the previous financial years of the subsidiary since it became the holding company's subsidiary;

so far as those profits are dealt with or a provision is made for those losses, in the company's accounts

(4) Clauses (*b*) and (*c*) of sub-section (3) shall apply only to profits and losses of the subsidiary which may properly be treated in the holding company's accounts as revenue profits or losses, and the profits or losses attributable to any shares in a subsidiary for the time being held by the holding company or any other of its subsidiaries shall not (for that or any other purpose) be treated as aforesaid so far as they are profits or losses for the period before the date on or as from which the shares were acquired by the company or any of its subsidiaries, except that they may in a proper case be so treated where—

(*a*) the company is itself the subsidiary of another body corporate; and

(*b*) the shares were acquired from that body corporate or a subsidiary of it;

and for the purpose of determining whether any profits or losses are to be treated as profits or losses for the said period, the profit or loss for any financial year of the subsidiary may, if it is not practicable to apportion it with reasonable accuracy by reference to the facts be treated as accruing from day to day during that year and be apportioned accordingly.

(5) Where the financial year or years of a subsidiary referred to in sub-section (2) do not coincide with the financial year of the holding company, a statement containing information on the following matters shall also be attached to the balance sheet of the holding company :-

(*a*) whether there has been any, and, if so, what change in the holding company's interest in the subsidiary between the end of the financial year or of the last of the financial years of the subsidiary and the end of the holding company's financial year;

(*b*) details of any material changes which have occurred between the end of the financial year or of the last of the financial years of the subsidiary and the end of holding company's financial year in respect of-

(*i*) the subsidiary's fixed assets;

(*ii*) its investments;

(*iii*) the moneys lent by it;

(*iv*) the moneys borrowed by it for any purpose other than that for meeting current liabilities.

(6) If, for any reason, the Board of Directors of the holding company is unable to obtain information on any of the matters required to be specified by sub-section (4), a report in writing to that effect shall be attached to the balance sheet of the holding company.

(7) The documents referred to in clauses (*e*), (*f*) and (*g*) of sub-section (1) shall be signed by the persons by whom the balance sheet of the holding company is required to be signed.

(8) The Central Government may, on the application or with the consent of the Board of Directors of the company, direct that in relation to any subsidiary, the provisions of this section shall not apply, or shall apply only to such extent as may be specified in the direction.

(9) If any such person as is referred to in sub-section (6) of section 209 fails to take all reasonable steps to comply with the provisions of this section, he shall in respect of each offence, be punishable with imprisonment for a term which may extend to six months, or with fine which may extend to one thousand rupees, or with both;

Provided that in any proceeding against a person in respect of an offence under this section, it shall be a defence to prove that a competent and reliable person was charged with the duty of seeing that the provisions of this section were complied with and was in a position to discharge that duty :

Provided that in any proceeding against a person in respect of an offence under this section, it shall be a defence to prove that a competent and reliable person was charged with the duty of seeing that the provisions of this section were complied with and was in a position to discharge that duty :

Provided further that no person shall be sentenced to imprisonment for any such offence unless it was committed wilfully.

(10) If any person, not being a person referred to in sub-section (6) of Section 209 having been charged by the Board of Directors as the case may be, with the duty of seeing that the provisions of this section are complied with, makes default in doing so, he shall, in respect of each offence, be punishable with imprisonment for a term which may extend to six months, or with fine which may extend to ten thousand rupees, or with both :

Provided that no person shall be sentenced to imprisonment for any such offence unless it was committed wilfully."

AS-21 CONSOLIDATED FINANCIAL STATEMENTS *

Accounting Standard (AS-21), 'Consolidated Financial Statements', issued by the Council of the Institute of Chartered Accountants of India, comes into effect in respect of accounting periods commencing on or after 1.4.2001. An enterprise that presents consolidated financial statements should prepare and present these statements in accordance with this Standard. The accounting standard does not mandate an enterprise to present consolidated financial statements but, if the enterprise presents consolidated financial statements for complying with the requirements of any statute or otherwise, it should prepare and present consolidated financial statements in accordance with AS 21. In this Accounting Standard, the standard portions have been set in **bold** type. These should be read in the context of the background material which has been set in normal type, and in the context of the 'Preface to the Statements of Accounting Standards'. Attention is specifically drawn to para 4.3 of the preface, according to which accounting standards are intended to apply only to material items.

OBJECTIVE

The objective of this Statement is to lay down principles and procedures for preparation and presentation of consolidated financial statements. Consolidated financial statements are presented by a parent (also known as holding enterprise) to provide financial information about the economic activities of its group. These statements are intended to present financial information about a parent and its subsidiary (ies) as a single economic entity to show the economic resources controlled by the group, the obligations of the group and results the group achieves with its resources.

SCOPE

1. This Statement should be applied in the preparation and presentation of consolidated financial statements for a group of enterprises under the control of a parent.

2. This Statement should also be applied in accounting for investments in subsidiaries in the separate financial statements of a parent.

3. In the preparation of consolidated financial statements, other Accounting Standards also apply in the same manner as they apply to the separate financial statements.

4. This Statement does not deal with :

(*a*) methods of accounting for amalgamations and their effects on consolidation, including goodwill arising on amalgamation (see AS 14, Accounting for Amalgamations);

(*b*) accounting for investments in associates (at present governed by AS 13, Accounting for Investments*);

(*c*) accounting for investments in joint ventures (at present governed by AS 13, Accounting for Investments**).

DEFINITIONS

5. For the purpose of this Statement, the following terms are used with the meanings specified :

Control

(*a*) the ownership, directly or indirectly through susbsidiary(ies), of more than one-half of the voting power of an enterprise; or

(*b*) control of the composition of the board of directors in the case of a compnay or of the composition of the corresponding governing body in case of any other enterprise so as to obtain economic benefits from its activities.

A *Subsidiary* is an enterprise that is controlled by another enterprise (known as the parent).

A *parent* is an enterprise that has one or more subsidiaries.

A *group* is a parent and all its subsidiaries.

* AS 23 on 'Accounting for Investments in Associates in Consolidated Financial Statements' specifies the requirements relating to accounting for investments in associates.

** AS-27 on 'Financial Reporting of Interests in Joint Ventures' specifies the requirements relating to accounting for investments in joint ventures.

Consolidated financial statements **are the financial statements of a group presented as those of a single enterprise.**

Equity **is the residual interest in the assets of an enterprise after deducting all its liabilities.**

Minority interest **is that part of the net results of operations and of the net assets of a subsidiary attributable to interests which are not owned, directly or indirectly through subsidairy(ies), by the parent.**

6. Consolidated financial statements normally include consolidated balance sheet, consolidated statement of profit and loss, and notes, other statements and explanatory material that form an integral part thereof. Consolidated cash flow statement is presented in case a parent presents its own cash flow statement. The consolidated financial statements are presented, to the extent possible, in the same format as that adopted by the parent for its separate financial statements.

PRESENTATION OF CONSOLIDATED FINANCIAL STATEMENTS

7. A parent which presents consolidated financial statements should present these statements in addition to its separate financial statement.

8. Users of the financial statements of a parent are usually concerned with, and need to be informed about, the financial position and rsults of operations of not only the enterprise itself but also of the group as a whole. This need is served by providing the users -----

(*a*) separate financial statements of the parent; and

(*b*) consolidated financial statements, which present financial information about the group as that of a single enterprise without regard to the legal boundaries of the separate legal entities.

SCOPE OF CONSOLIDATED FINANCIAL STATEMENTS

9. A parent which presents consolidated financial statements should consolidate all subsidiaries, domestic as well as foreign, other than those referred to in paragraph 11.

10. The consolidated financial statements are prepared on the basis of financial statements of parent and all enterprise that are controlled by the parent, other than those subsidiaries excluded for the reasons set out in paragraph 11. Control exists when the parent owns, directly or indirectly through subsidiary(ies), more than one-half of the voting power of an enterprise. Control also exists when an enterprise controls the composition of the board of directors (in the case of a company) or of the corresponding governing body (in case of an enterprise not being a company) so as to obtain economic benefits from its activities. An enterprise may control the composition of the governing bodies of entities such as gratuity trust, provident fund trust etc. Since the objective of control oversuch entities is not considered for the purpose of preparation of consolidated financial statements. For the purpose of this Statement, an enterprise is considered to control of the composition of ;

(*i*) the Board of directors of a company, if it has the power, without the consent or concurrence of any other person, to appoint or remove all or a majority of directors of that company. An enterprise is deemed to have the power to appoint a director, if any of the following conditions is satisfied :

   (*a*) a person cannot be appointed as director without the exercise in his favour by that enterprise of such a power as aforesaid; or

   (*b*) a person's appointment as director follows necessarily from his appointment to a position held by him in that enterprise; or

   (*c*) the director is nominated by that enterprise or a subsidiary thereof,

(*ii*) the governing body of an enterprise that is not a company, if it has the power, without the consent or the concurrence of any other person, to appoint or remove all or a majority of members of the governing body of that other enterprise. An enterprise is deemd to have the power to appoint a member, if any of the following conditions is satisfied :

(*a*) a person cannot be appointed as member of the governing body without the exercise in his favour by that other enterprise of such a power as aforesaid; or

(*b*) a person's appointment as member of the governing body follows necessarily form his appointment to a position held by him in that enterprise; or

(*c*) the member of the governing body is nominated by that other enterprise.

11. A subsidiary should be excluded from consolidation when :

(*a*) control is intended to be temporary because the susbsidiary is acquired and held exclusively with a view to its subsequent disposal in the near future; or

(*b*) it operates under severe long-term rest~i~ctions which significantly impair its ability to transfer funds to the parent.

In consolidated financial statements, such subsidiaries should be accounted for investments in accordance with Accounting Standard (AS) 13, Accounting for investments. The reasons for not consolidatting a subsidairy should be disclosed in the consolidated financial statements.

12. Exclusion of a subsidiary from consolidation on the ground that its business activities are dissimilar from those of the other enterprises within the group is not justified because better information is provided by consolidating such subsidiaries and disclosing additional information in the consolidated financial statements about the different business activities of subsidiaries. For example, the disclosures required by Accounting Standard (AS) 17, Segment Reporting, help to explain the significance of different business activities within the group.

CONSOLIDATION PROCEDURES

13. In preparing consolidated financial statements, the financial statements of the parent and its subsidiaries should be combined on a line by line basis by adding together like items of assets, liabilities, income and expenses. In order that the consolidated financial statements present financial information about the group as that of a single enterprise, the following steps should be taken:

(*a*) the cost to the parent of its investment in each subsidiary and tne parent's portion of equity of each subsidiary, at the date on which investment in each subsidiary is made should be eliminated.

(*b*) any excess of the cost to the parent of its investment in a subsidiary over the parent's portion of equity of the subsidairy, at the date on which investment in the subsidiary is made, should be described as goodwill to be recognised as an asset in the consolidated financial statements;

(*c*) when the cost to the parent of its investment in a subsidiary is less than the parent's portion of equity of the subsidiary, at the date on which investment in the subsidiary is made, the difference should be treated as a capital reserve in the consolidated financial statements;

(*d*) minority interests in the net income of consolidated subsidiaries for the reporting period should be identified and adjusted against the income of the group in order to arrive at the net income attiributable to the owners of the parent; and

(*e*) minority interests in the net assets of consolidated subsidiaries should be identified and presented in the consolidated balance sheet separately from liabilities and the equity of the parent's shareholders. Minority interests in the net assets consist of :

(*i*) the amount of equity attributable to minorities at the date on which investment in a subsidiary is made; and

(*ii*) the minorities' share of movements in equity since the date the parent-subsidiary relationship came in existence.

Where the carrying amount of the investment in the subsidiary is different from its cost, the carrying amount is considered for the purpose of above computations.

14. The parent's portion of equity in a subsidiary, at the date on which investment is made, is determined on the basis of information contained in the financial statements of the subsidiary as on

the date of investment. However, if the financial statements of a subsidiary, as on the date of investment, are not available and if it is impracticable to draw the financial statements of the subsidiary as on that date, financial statements of the subsidary for the immediately preceding period are used as a basis for consolidation. Adjustments are made to these financial statements for the effects of significant transactions or other events that occur between the date of such financial statements and the date of investment in the subsidiary.

15. If an enterprise makes two or more investments in another enterprise at different dates and eventually obtains control of the other enterprise, the consolidated financial statements are presented only from the date on which holding-subsidiary relationship comes in existence. If two or more investments are made over a period of time, the equity of the subsidairy at the date of investment, for the purpose of paragraph 13 above, is generally determined on a step-by-step basis; however, if small investments are made over a period of time and then an investment is made that results in control, the date of the latest investment, as a practicable measure, may be considered as the date of investment.

16. Intragroup balances and intragroup transactions and resulting unrealised profits should be eliminated in full. Unrealised losses resulting from intragroup transactions should be eliminated unless cost cannot be recovered.

17. Intragroup balances and intragroup transactions, including sales, expenses and dividends, are eliminated in full. Unrealised profits resulting from intragroup transactions that are included in the carrying amount of assets, such as inventory and fixed assets, are eliminated in full. Unrealised losses resulting from intragroup transactions that are deducted in arriving at the carrying amount of assets are also eliminated unless cost cannot be recovered.

18. The financial statements used in the consolidations should be drawn up to the same reporting date. If it is not practicable to draw up the financial statements of one or more subsidiaries to such date and accordingly, those financial statements are drawn up to different reporting dates, adjustments should be made for the effects of significant transactions or other events that occur between those dates and the date of parent's financial statements. In any case, the difference between reporting dates should not be more than six months.

19. The financial statements of the parent and its subsidiaries used in the preparation of the consolidated financial statements are usually drawn up to the same date. When the reporting dates are different, the subsidiary often prepares, for consolidation purposes, statements as at the same date as that of the parent. When it is impracticable to do this, financial statements drawn up to different reporting dates may be used provided the difference in reporting dates is not more than six months. The consistency principle requires that the length of the reporting periods and any difference in the reporting dates should be the same from period to period.

20. Consolidated financial statements should be prepared using uniform accounting policies for like transactions and other events in similar circumstances. If it is not practicable to use uniform accounting policies in preparing the consolidated financial statements, that fact should be disclosed together with the proportions of the items in the consolidated financial statements to which the different accounting policies have been applied.

21. If a member of the group uses accounting policies other than those adopted in the consolidated financial statements for like transactions and events in similar circumstances, appropriate adjustments are made to its financial statements when they are used in preparing the consolidated financial statements.

22. The results of operations of a subsidiary are included in the consolidated financial statements as from the date on which parent-subsidiary relationship came in existence. The results of operations of a subsidiary with which parent-subsidiary relationship ceases to exist are included in the consolidated statement of profit and loss until the date of cessation of the relationship. The difference between the proceeds from the disposal of investment in a subsidiary and the carrying amount of its assets less liabilities as of the date of disposal is recognised in the consolidated state-

ment of profit and loss as the profit or loss on the disposal of the investment in the subsidiary. In order to ensure the comparability of the financial statements from one accounting period to the next, supplementary information is often provided about the effect of the acquisition and disposal of subsidiaries on the financial position at the reporting date and the results for the reporting period and on the corresponding amounts for the preceeding period.

23. An investment in an enterprise should be accounted for in accordance with Accounting Standard (AS) 13, Accounting for Investments, from the date that the enterprise ceases to be a subsidiary and does not become an associate.*

24. The carrying amount of the investment at the date that it ceases to be a subsidiary is regarded as cost thereafter.

25. Minority interests should be presented in the consolidated balance sheet separately from liabilities and the equity of the parent's shareholders. Minority interests in the income of the group should also be separately presented.

26. The losses applicable to the minority in a consolidated subsidiary may exceed the minority interest in the equity of the subsidiary. The excess, and any further losses applicable to the minority, are adjusted against the majority interest except to the extent that the minority has a binding obligation to, and is able to, make good the losses. If the subsidiary subsequently reports profits, all such profits are allocated to the majority interest until the minority's share of losses previously absorbed by the majority has been recovered.

27. If a subsidiary has outstanding cumulative preference shares which are held outside the group, the parent computes its share of profits or losses after adjusting for the subsidiary's preference dividends, whether or not dividends have been declared.

ACCOUNTING FOR INVESTMENTS IN SUBSIDIARIES IN A PARENT'S SEPARATE FINANCIAL STATEMENTS

28. In a parent's separate financial standards, investments in subsidiaries should be accounted for in accordance with Accounting Standard (AS) 13, Accounting for Investments.

DISCLOSURE

29. In addition to disclosures required by paragraph 11 and 20, following disclosures should be made :

- **(*a*) in consolidated financial statements a list of all subsidiaries including the name, country of incorporation or residence, proportion of ownership interest and, if different, proportion of voting power held;**
- **(*b*) in consolidated financial statements, where applicable :**
  - **(*i*) the nature of the relationship between the parent and a subsidiary, if the parent does not own, directly or indirectly through subsidiaries, more than one-half of the voting power of the subsidiary;**
  - **(*ii*) the effect of the acquisition and disposal of subsidiaries on the financial position at the reporting date, the results for the reporting period and on the corrsponding amounts for the preceeding period; and**
  - **(*iii*) the names of the subsidiary(ies) of which reporting date(s) is/are different from that of the parent and the difference in reporting dates.**

TRANSITIONAL PROVISIONS

30. On the first occasion that consolidated financial statemetns are presented, comparative figures for the previous period need not be presented. In all subsequent years full comparative figures for the previous period should be presented in the consolidated financial statements.

---

* AS 23 on 'Accounting for Investments in Associates in Consolidated Financial Statements' (mandatory with effect from accounting period beginning on 1-4-2002) defines the term 'associate' and specifies the requirements relating to accounting for investments in associates.

CONSOLIDATION OF BALANCE SHEETS AND PROFIT AND LOSS ACCOUNTS

In England the holding company is required to present, in addition to its normal balance sheet, a consolidated balance sheet covering the holding company and its subsidiaries and a consolidated profit and loss account. In India, the law does not insist on consolidated accounts but there is no doubt that for a clear picture, it is desirable to present one single balance sheet of the holding and subsidiary companies and a single profit and loss account.

Before the rules for consolidation are discussed, it is necessary to see how dividend received from the subsidiary is treated in the books of the holding company.

Treatment of dividend :

It has been pointed out above that the profits already earned and accumulated by the subsidiary company, up to the date of acquisition of the shares by the holding company, are capital profits. If shares are acquired during the course of a year, the profit should be treated as accruing from day to day (in the absence of any other indication) and, therefore, should be apportioned on the time basis. Take the following example :

Balance Sheet of Small Ltd. as on 31st March, 2010

		Rs.		*Rs.*
Share Capital :			Sundry Assets	4,60,000
3,000 Shares of Rs. 100 each		3,00,000		
General Reserve on 1st April, 2009		50,000		
P. and L. Account :	*Rs.*			
Balance on 1st April, 2009	10,000			
Profits for 2009-2010	60,000	70,000		
Sundry Creditors		40,000		
		4,60,000		4,60,000

Suppose, Big Ltd. acquires 2,010 shares in Small Ltd. on 1st January, 2010. The capital profits will then be as follows :—

	Rs.
General Reserve on 1st April, 2009	50,000
Profit and Loss Account—Balance on 1st April, 2009	10,000
9 months' profits up to 31st December, 2009 (apportioned according to time)	45,000
	1,05,000

Rs. 15,000, that is, three months' profits (after 1st January, 2010) will be revenue profit; all trading profits earned after 1st January, 2010 will be revenue profits.

The distinction between capital profits and revenue profits is most important from the point of view of the holding company. Dividends received out of capital profits must be credited to "*Investment Account" since the cash received is against the price of shares paid at the time of the acquisition.* Only dividends received out of revenue profits can be treated as income and credited to the Profit and Loss Account. Study the following example :

On 1st November, 2009, H Ltd. acquired 3,000 equity shares of Rs. 100 each (at a cost of Rs. 150 per share) in S Ltd. whose total share capital consisted of 5,000 equity shares of Rs. 100 each, fully paid. The balance in the Profit and Loss Account of S Ltd. on 31st March, 2010 was Rs. 4,40,000 made up as :

	Rs.
Balance brought forward on 1st April, 2009	1,40,000
Profit (after meeting all expenses and taxation)	3,00,000
	4,40,000

S Ltd. declared a dividend of 40% and issued bonus shares in the ratio of one share for every four held.

First of all capital profits should be ascertained. These are :

	Rs.
Balance in Profit and Loss Account on 1st April, 2009	1,40,000
Profit for seven months up to 1st November, 2009 (7/12 of 3,00,000)	1,75,000
Total	3,15,000
Revenue Profits are (5/12 of 3,00,000)	1,25,000

Since H Ltd. holds 3,000 shares out of 5,000, three-fifths of the profits belong to H Ltd.

Hence, capital profit, as far as H Ltd. is concerned, is three-fifths of Rs. 3,15,000 or Rs. 1,89,000; Revenue Profit, as far as H Ltd. is concerned, is Rs. 75,000. Total dividend received by H Ltd. is 40% on Rs. 3,00,000 or Rs. 1,20,000. The question now arises : which profit has been utilised first to pay the dividend ? There are four possibilities :—

1. The dividend has been paid first out of latest profits and then out of the previous profits.
2. The profits of the current year as a whole have been used first to pay the dividend.
3. The dividend has been paid first out of previous profits and then out of current profits.
4. The two profits have been utilised proportionately.

The journal entries to be made in each of the cases are :

		Rs.	*Rs.*
I. Bank	Dr.	1,20,000	
To Investments			45,000
To Dividend Received			75,000
[Being the total dividend of Rs. 1,20,000 received from S Ltd. having been declared first out of current profits (Rs. 75,000) and then out of previous (capital) profits, Rs. 45,000, *i.e.*, 1,20,000—75,000]			
II. Bank	Dr.	1,20,000	
To Investments			70,000
To Dividend Received			50,000

[Total Dividend received Rs. 1,20,000.

Treated as capital receipt $\left(1{,}20{,}000 \times \dfrac{1{,}75{,}000}{3{,}00{,}000}\right)$ and

revenue receipt $\left(1{,}20{,}000 \times \dfrac{1{,}25{,}000}{3{,}00{,}000}\right)$, in the proportion

of current year's profit upto and after 1st November, 1999.

III. Bank	Dr.	1,20,000	
To Investments			1,20,000
[Being the dividend of Rs. 1,20,000 received from S Ltd. credited to investments being out of previous (capital) profits only].			
IV. Bank	Dr.	1,20,000	
To Investments			85,909
To Dividend Received			34,091
[Being the dividend of Rs. 1,20,000 received from S Ltd. split into two parts in the ratio of previous profits, viz., Rs. 1,89,000, and current profits, viz., Rs. 75,000—the portion applicable to current profits credited to dividend received].			

There will be no entries in the books of H Ltd. for the receipt of bonus shares, since no extra payment has been made and the possibility of a gain is uncertain.

Note : In the absence of information, one should assume that the dividend is out of the profits for the year for which the dividend is being paid.

A Ltd. purchased 1,600 shares in B Ltd. on 1st April, 2009, and another 200 shares on 30th November, 2009. The share capital of B Ltd. is Rs. 2,00,000 divided into shares of Rs. 100 each. The company had Rs. 1,20,000 to the credit of Profit and Loss Account on April 1, 2009, and earned a profit of Rs. 75,000 during the 2009-2010 out of which in March, 2010 it paid a dividend of 15%. How should A Ltd. treat the dividend received and what is its share of capital profits ?

The dividend received by A Ltd. will be Rs. 27,000 – Rs. 24,000 for 1,600 shares bought on April 1, 2009 and Rs. 3,000 for 200 shares bought on November 30, 2009. Out of the latter amount, eight months' dividend, Rs. 2,000, is capital receipt and hence should be credited to Investments Account. The remaining amount of Rs. 25,000 is revenue income to be credited to the Profit and Loss Account.

The capital profit as regards A Ltd. is Rs. 1,20,000 the balance on 1st April, 2009. Since 90% shares are held by A Ltd., Rs. 1,08,000 is the share of A Ltd. Further, out of the profits earned in 2009-2010, Rs. 45,000 remains after dividend. Out of this eight months' profit in respect of 200 shares purchased on 30.11.2009 is also capital profit; the amount is Rs. 3,000. Hence, total capital profit for A Ltd. is Rs. 1,11,000.

Debiting the subsidiary with profits, etc. :

If the holding company holds the entire share capital in the subsidiary company, it would be possible to treat the subsidiary as a debtor for profits earned by it; to do so, it should debit the "Subsidiary Company (Profits) Account" and credit "Profits and Losses of Subsidiaries Account" or "Subsidiary Companies' Revenue Account". The entry in case of a loss is just the reverse of it. The "Subsidiary Company (Profits) Account" is in the nature of a personal account. This account is opened to distinguish it from the usual account with the subsidiary. When dividend is received, cash is debited and the "Subsidiary Company (Profits) Account" is credited. The balance in the account will represent what the subsidiary company owes to the holding company in respect of profits earned by it. "The Profits and Losses of Subsidiaries Account" is closed by transfer to the holding company's profit and loss account.

The law does not require a holding company to follow the practice outlined above. And the practice is also not desirable from the accountancy point of view also. But it would be quite proper for the holding company to make a provision in its books for its share of the loss suffered by its subsidiary or subsidiaries.

Illustration 1:

H Ltd. holds the entire share capital of S Ltd. which made a loss of Rs. 50,000 in its first year and a profit of Rs. 1,10,000 in its second year. In the second year S Ltd. paid a dividend of Rs. 40,000. Show journal entries in the books of the holding company assuming that the latter company brings into account all the losses and profits of the subsidiary company.

			Dr. *Rs.*	*Cr.* *Rs.*
Year 1	Profits and Losses of Subsidiaries	Dr.	50,000	
	To S Ltd. (Profits)			50,000
	Losses incurred by S Ltd. and hence credited to S Ltd. (Profits) A/c.			
Year 2	S Ltd. (Profits)	Dr.	1,10,000	
	To Profits and Losses of Subsidiaries			1,10,000
	Profit earned by S Ltd. debited to S Ltd. (Profits) A/c.			
	Bank	Dr.	40,000	
	To S Ltd. (Profits)			40,000
	Dividend received from S Ltd.—credited to S Ltd. (Profits).			

S Ltd. (Profits) Account stands debited to the extent of Rs. 20,000. This presents what S Ltd. owes to H Ltd. in respect of profits.

Preparation of Consolidated Balance Sheet

The basic point to understand in the preparation of consolidated balance sheet is that the shares in the subsidiary company held by the holding company represent the assets and liabilities of the subsidiary company. Shares are ownership securities. Suppose H Ltd. owns 100% shares of S Ltd. we may as well say that H Ltd. owns 100% of the net assets i.e., the assets and liabilities of S Ltd. The consolidated balance sheet shows, instead of the shares of the subsidiary company, the net assets of the subsidiary company in addition to those of holding company.

Illustration 2:

H Ltd. acquires all the shares of S Ltd. on 31st March, 2010 on which date the balance sheets of the two companies are as under :

Liabilities	*H Ltd.* *Rs.*	*S Ltd.* *Rs.*	*Assets*	*H Ltd.* *Rs.*	*S Ltd.* *Rs.*
Share Capital:			Sundry Assets	4,80,000	2,60,000
Shares of Rs. 10 each,			100% Shares in S Ltd.	**2,00,000**	—
fully paid	5,00,000	**2,00,000**			
Reserves	1,00,000	—			
Creditors	80,000	60,000			
	6,80,000	2,60,000		6,80,000	2,60,000

Prepare a Consolidated Balance Sheet as at 31st March, 2010.

Solution :

100% shares in S Ltd. represent assets of Rs. 2,60,000 minus the liabilities of Rs. 60,000. Hence, while preparing the consolidated balance sheet of H Ltd. and S Ltd. the assets and liabilities of both the companies will be added; the share capital of S Ltd. being cancelled against 'Shares in S Ltd.' shown as an asset by H Ltd. The consolidated balance sheet will appear as under :

Consolidated Balance Sheet of H Ltd. and its Subsidiary S Ltd. as at 31st March, 2010

Liabilities	*Rs.*	*Rs.*	*Assets*	*Rs.*	*Rs.*
Share Capital :			Sundry Assets :		
Shares of Rs. 10 each,			H Ltd.	4,80,000	
fully paid		5,00,000	S Ltd.	2,60,000	7,40,000
Reserves		1,00,000			
Creditors : H Ltd.	80,000				
S Ltd.	60,000	1,40,000			
		7,40,000			7,40,000

The journal entry that H Ltd. may pass is :

		Rs.	*Rs.*
Sundry Assets	Dr.	2,60,000	
To Creditors			60,000
To Shares in S Ltd.			2,00,000

Cost of Control/Capital Reserve

In the abovementioned example, the shares held by H Ltd. represent S Ltd's net assets of Rs. 2,00,000 and H Ltd. acquires the shares for exactly Rs. 2,00,000. But H Ltd. may pay for the shares an amount which either is more or is less than Rs. 2,00,000. If it pays more, the excess amount paid is considered the payment for goodwill or cost of control. On the other hand if H Ltd. pays less than Rs. 2,00,000 the excess of S Ltd.'s net assets (excluding Goodwill) out the cost of shares to H Ltd. is a capital profit and is shown as Capital Reserve in the consolidated balance sheet.

Illustration 3:

The following are the balance sheets of H Ltd and S Ltd as at 31st March, 2010:—

Liabilities	*H Ltd.* Rs.	*S Ltd.* Rs.	*Assets*	*H Ltd.* Rs.	*S Ltd.* Rs.
Share Capital :			Sundry Assets	4,70,000	2,60,000
Shares of Rs. 10 each,			100% Shares in S Ltd.		
fully paid	5,00,000	**2,00,000**	(at cost)	**2,10,000**	
Reserves	1,00,000				
Creditors	80,000	60,000			
	6,80,000	2,60,000		6,80,000	2,60,000

Prepare a consolidated balance sheet as at 31st March, 2010.

Solution:

In this case, H Ltd. has paid Rs. 10,000 for goodwill. The consolidated balance sheet will appear as follows :—

Consolidated Balance Sheet of H Ltd and its subsidiary S Ltd. as at 31st March, 2010

Liabilities	*Rs.*	*Rs.*	*Assets*	*Rs.*	*Rs.*
			Goodwill or cost of control		**10,000**
Share Capital :			Other Assets :		
Shares of Rs. 10 each, fully paid		5,00,000	H Ltd.	4,70,000	
Reserves		1,00,000	S Ltd.	2,60,000	7,30,000
Creditors :					
H Ltd.	80,000				
S Ltd.	60,000	1,40,000			
		7,40,000			7,40,000

Illustration 4:

The following are the balance sheets of H Ltd. and S Ltd. as at 31st March, 2010:—

Liabilities	*H Ltd.* Rs.	*S Ltd.* Rs.	*Assets*	*H Ltd.* Rs.	*S Ltd.* Rs.
Share Capital :			Sundry Assets	4,90,000	2,60,000
Shares of Rs. 10 each,			100% Shares in S Ltd.		
fully paid	5,00,000	**2,00,000**	(at cost)	**1,90,000**	
Reserves	1,00,000				
Creditors	80,000	60,000			
	6,80,000	2,60,000		6,80,000	2,60,000

Prepare a consolidated balance sheet as at 31st March, 2010.

Solution :

In this case, H Ltd. has acquired shares worth Rs. 2,00,000 for Rs. 1,90,000 only. It has thus earned a capital profit of Rs. 10,000. The consolidated balance sheet will appear as under :—

Consolidated Balance Sheet of H Ltd. and its subsidiary S Ltd. as at 31st March 2010.

Liabilities	*Rs.*	*Rs.*	*Assets*	*Rs.*	*Rs.*
Share Capital :			Sundry Assets :		
Shares of Rs. 10 each, fully paid		5,00,000	H Ltd.	4,90,000	
Capital Reserve		**10,000**	S Ltd.	2,60,000	7,50,000
Other Reserves		1,00,000			
Creditors:					
H Ltd.	80,000				
S Ltd.	60,000	1,40,000			
		7,50,000			7,50,000

Minority Interest

The holding company may not hold 100% shares of the subsidiary company. In other words, the subsidiary company may not be wholly owned by the holding company. Suppose H Ltd. purchases only 70% of the shares in S Ltd. the remaining 30% shares continuing to be held by outsiders. S Ltd. thus becomes a partly owned as opposed to wholly owned subsidiary with a minority interest of 30%. In the consolidated balance sheet, the fact that H Ltd. owns S Ltd. partly has to be reflected.

In theory two possible approaches could be :

(1) to include 70% of the respective items i.e. stock, debtors, cash, creditors etc. relating to S Ltd., or

(2) to include 100% of all such items and show 30% outside ownership on the liabilities side as a compensating adjustment.

In actual practice, the second approach is adopted. Thus even when the subsidiary company is only partly owned, the method of consolidation is to include in the consolidated balance sheet, the whole of the assets and liabilities of the holding and subsidiary companies i.e. both the proportion owned by the holding company and the proportion attributable to the shareholders other than the holding company who are known as minority shareholders. The interest of the minority shareholders in the net assets of the subsidiary company is registered and shown as 'Minority Interest' on the liabilities side of the consolidated balance sheet.

Illustration 5:

The following are the balance sheets of H Ltd and S Ltd. as at 31st March, 2010:—

Liabilities	*H Ltd.* Rs.	*S Ltd.* Rs.	*Assets*	*H Ltd.* Rs.	*S Ltd.* Rs.
Share Capital :			Sundry Assets	5,60,000	2,60,000
Shares of Rs. 10 each,			60% Shares in S Ltd.		
fully paid	5,00,000	**2,00,000**	(at cost)	**1,20,000**	
Reserves	1,00,000				
Creditors	80,000	60,000			
	6,80,000	2,60,000		6,80,000	2,60,000

Prepare a consolidated balance sheet as at 31st March, 2010.

Solution :

Consolidated Balance Sheet of H Ltd. and its subsidiary S Ltd. as at 31st March, 2010

Liabilities	*Rs.*	*Rs.*	*Assets*	*Rs.*	*Rs.*
Share Capital:			Sundry Assets:		
Shares of Rs. 10 each, fully paid		5,00,000	H Ltd.	5,60,000	
Minority Interest			S Ltd.	2,60,000	8,20,000
Rs. 2,00,000 × 40/100 = Rs. 80,000		**80,000**			
Reserves		1,00,000			
Creditors:					
H Ltd.	80,000				
S Ltd.	60,000	1,40,000			
		8,20,000			8,20,000

Illustration 6:

The following are the balance sheets of H Ltd and S Ltd. as at 31st March, 2010:—

Balance Sheets as at 31st March, 2000

Liabilities	*H Ltd.* Rs.	*S Ltd.* Rs.	*Assets*	*H Ltd.* Rs.	*S Ltd.* Rs.
Share Capital:			Sundry Assets	5,50,000	2,60,000
Shares of Rs. 10 each,			60% Shares in S Ltd.		
fully paid	5,00,000	**2,00,000**	(at cost)	**1,30,000**	
Reserves	1,00,000				
Creditors	80,000	60,000			
	6,80,000	2,60,000		6,80,000	2,60,000

Prepare a consolidated balance sheet as at 31st March, 2010.

Solution :

Consolidated Balance Sheet of H Ltd. and its subsidiary S Ltd. as at 31st March, 2010

Liabilities	*Rs.*	*Rs.*	*Assets*	*Rs.*	*Rs.*
Share Capital:			Goodwill		**10,000**
Shares of Rs. 10 each, fully paid		5,00,000	Other Assets:		
Minority Interest		**80,000**	H Ltd.	5,50,000	
Reserves		1,00,000	S Ltd.	2,60,000	8,10,000
Creditors:					
H Ltd.	80,000				
S Ltd.	60,000	1,40,000			
		8,20,000			8,20,000

Illustration 7:

The following are the balance sheets of H Ltd and S Ltd. as at 31st March, 2010:—

Balance Sheets as at 31st March, 2010

Liabilities	*H Ltd.* Rs.	*S Ltd.* Rs.	*Assets*	*H Ltd.* Rs.	*S Ltd.* Rs.
Share Capital:			Sundry Assets	5,70,000	2,60,000
Shares of Rs. 10 each,			60% Shares in S Ltd.		
fully paid	5,00,000	**2,00,000**	(at cost)	**1,10,000**	
Reserves	1,00,000				
Creditors	80,000	60,000			
	6,80,000	2,60,000		6,80,000	2,60,000

Prepare a consolidated balance sheet as at 31st March, 2010.

Solution :

Consolidated Balance Sheet of H Ltd. and its subsidiary S Ltd. as at 31st March 2010

Liabilities	*Rs.*	*Rs.*	*Assets*	*Rs.*	*Rs.*
Share Capital:			Sundry Assets:		
Shares of Rs. 10 each, fully paid		5,00,000	H Ltd.	5,70,000	
Minority Interest		**80,000**	S Ltd.	2,60,000	8,30,000
Capital Reserve		**10,000**			
Other Reserves		1,00,000			
Creditors:					
H Ltd.	80,000				
S Ltd.	60,000	1,40,000			
		8,30,000			8,30,000

The holding company, while acquiring the shares of the subsidiary company, pays not only for the paid up value of the shares acquired but also for the profits that the subsidiary company has accumulated till the date of acquisition. By the same logic, the worth of the shares of the subsidiary company decreases if on the date of acquisition of its shares by the holding company, the subsidiary company has some accumulated losses or expenses which have not been written off till that date.

Illustration 8:

The following are the balance sheets of H Ltd and S Ltd. as at 31st March, 2010:—

Liabilities	*H Ltd.* *Rs.*	*S Ltd.* *Rs.*	*Assets*	*H Ltd.* *Rs.*	*S Ltd.* *Rs.*
Share Capital:			Sundry Assets	4,36,000	3,04,000
Shares of Rs. 10 each,			100% Shares in S Ltd.		
fully paid	5,00,000	**2,00,000**	acquired on 31st		
Reserves	1,00,000	**50,000**	March, 2000 (cost)	**2,44,000**	
Creditors	80,000	60,000	Preliminary Expenses		**6,000**
	6,80,000	3,10,000		6,80,000	3,10,000

Prepare a consolidated balance sheet as at 31st March, 2010.

Solution :

Working Notes :

	Rs.
Paid up value of 100% shares in S Ltd.	2,00,000
Add : Reserves of S Ltd.	50,000
	2,50,000
Less : Preliminary Expenses	6,000
	2,44,000
Amount paid by H Ltd. for acquiring 100% shares in S Ltd.	2,44,000

Thus, there is no cost of control or capital reserve on acquisition of shares.

Consolidated Balance Sheet of H Ltd. and its subsidiary S Ltd. as at 31st March, 2010

Liabilities	*Rs.*	*Rs.*	*Assets*	*Rs.*	*Rs.*
Share Capital:			Sundry Assets:		
Shares of Rs. 10 each, fully paid		5,00,000	H Ltd.	4,36,000	
Reserves		1,00,000	S Ltd.	3,04,000	7,40,000
Creditors:					
H Ltd	80,000				
S Ltd.	60,000	1,40,000			
		7,40,000			7,40,000.

Illustration 9:

The following are the balance sheets of H Ltd and S Ltd. as at 31st. March, 2010:—

Liabilities	*H Ltd.* *Rs.*	*S Ltd.* *Rs.*	*Assets*	*H Ltd.* *Rs.*	*S Ltd.* *Rs.*
Share Capital:			Sundry Assets	4,26,000	3,04,000
Shares of Rs. 10 each,			100% Shares in S Ltd.		
fully paid	5,00,000	**2,00,000**	acquired on 31st March,		
Reserves	1,00,000	**50,000**	2000 (cost)	**2,54,000**	
Creditors	80,000	60,000	Preliminary Expenses		**6,000**
	6,80,000	3,10,000		6,80,000	3,10,000

Prepare a consolidated balance sheet as at 31st March, 2010. [*CS.* (*Inter.*) *Dec.* 1996 *Modified*]

Solution :

Calculation of Goodwill or Cost of Control :		Rs.
Amount paid for 100% shares in S Ltd.	Rs.	2,54.000
Less : Paid up value of 100% shares in S Ltd.	2,00,000	
Add : 100% of Reserves of S Ltd. on the date of acquisition	50,000	
	2,50,000	
Less: 100% of unwritten off Preliminary Expenses of S Ltd. as on the date of acquisition	6,000	2,44,000
Goodwill or Cost of Control		10,000

Consolidated Balance Sheet of H Ltd. and its subsidiary S Ltd. as at 31st March, 2010

Liabilities	*Rs.*	*Rs.*	*Assets*	*Rs.*	*Rs.*
Share Capital:			Cost of Control or Goodwill		**10,000**
Shares of Rs 10 each, fully paid		5,00,000	Other Assets :		
Reserves		1,00,000	H Ltd.	4,26,000	
Creditors:			S Ltd.	3,04,000	7,30,000
H Ltd.	80,000				
S Ltd.	60,000	1,40,000			
		7,40,000			7,40,000

Illustration 10:

The following are the balance sheets of H Ltd and S Ltd. as at 31st March, 2010:—

Liabilities	*H Ltd.* *Rs.*	*S Ltd.* *Rs.*	*Assets*	*H Ltd.* *Rs.*	*S Ltd.* *Rs.*
Share Capital:			Sundry Assets	4,46,000	3,04,000
Shares of Rs. 10 each, fully paid	5,00,000	**2,00,000**	100% Shares in S Ltd. acquired on 31st March, 2000 (cost)	**2,34,000**	
Reserves	1,00,000	**50,000**			
Creditors	80,000	60,000	Preliminary Expenses		**6,000**
	6,80,000	3,10,000		6,80,000	3,10,000

(C.S. (Inter.) Dec. 1996 Modified)

Prepare a consolidated balance sheet as at 31st March, 2010.

Solution:

Calculation of Capital Reserve on acquisition of shares :—	Rs.
Paid up value of 100% shares in S Ltd.	2,00,000
Add: 100% of Reserves of S Ltd. on the date of acquisition	50,000
	2,50,000
Less: 100% of unwritten off Preliminary Expenses of S Ltd. as on the date of acquisition	6,000
	2,44,000
Less: Amount paid for 100% shares of S Ltd.	2,34,000
Capital Reserve	10,000

Consolidated Balance Sheet of H Ltd. and its subsidiary S Ltd. as at 31st March, 2010

Liabilities	*Rs.*	*Rs.*	*Assets*	*Rs.*	*Rs.*
Share Capital:			Sundry Assets		
Shares of Rs. 10 each, fully paid		5,00,000	H Ltd.	4,46,000	
Capital Reserve		**10,000**	S Ltd.	3,04,000	7,50,000
Other Reserves		1,00,000			
Creditors:					
H Ltd.	80,000				
S Ltd.	60,000	1,40,000			
		7,50,000			7,50,000

The minority shareholders are also entitled to their proportionate share of the profits and reserves of the subsidiary company and have to bear their share of losses suffered by the subsidiary company. Thus the minority interest is increased by the profits and decreased by the losses of the subsidiary company.

Illustration 11:

The following are the balance sneets of H Ltd and S Ltd. as at 31st March, 2010:—

Liabilities	*H Ltd.* *Rs.*	*S Ltd.* *Rs.*	*Assets*	*H Ltd.* *Rs.*	*S Ltd.* *Rs.*
Share Capital:			Sundry Assets	5,17,600	3,04,000
Shares of Rs. 10 each,			60% Shares in S Ltd.		
fully paid	5,00,000	**2,00,000**	acquired on 31st		
Reserves	1,00,000	**50,000**	March, 2000 (cost)	**1,62,400**	
Creditors	80,000	60,000	Preliminary Expenses		**6,000**
	6,80,000	3,10,000		6,80,000	3,10,000

Prepare a consolidated balance sheet as at 31st March, 2010.

Solution:

Working Notes

(*i*) *Calculation of Goodwill or Cost of Control :*

	Rs.	*Rs.*
Amount paid for 60% shares in S Ltd.		1,62,400
Less: Paid up value of 60% shares in S Ltd.	1,20,000	
Add: 60% of Reserves of S Ltd. as on the date of acquisition, Rs. 50,000 × 60/100	30,000	
	1,50,000	
Less: 60% of Preliminary Expenses of S Ltd. as on the date of acquisition, Rs. 6,000 × 60/100	3,600	1,46,400
Goodwill or Cost of Control		16,000

(*ii*) *Calculation of minority interest :*

Paid up value of 40% Shares of S Ltd. held by minority shareholders	80,000
Add: 40% of Reserves of S Ltd. as on the date of consolidation Rs. 50,000 × 40/100	20,000
	1,00,000
Less : 40% of Preliminary Expenses, Rs. 6,000 × 40/100	2,400
	97,600

Consolidated Balance Sheet of H Ltd. and its subsidiary S Ltd. as at 31s March, 2010

Liabilities	*Rs.*	*Rs.*	*Assets*	*Rs.*	*Rs.*
Share Capital:			Goodwill or Cost of Control		**16,000**
Shares of Rs. 10 each, fully paid		5,00,000	Other Assets :		
Minority Interest		**97,600**	H Ltd.	5,17,600	
Reserves		1,00,000	S Ltd.	3,04,000	8,21,600
Creditors:					
H Ltd.	80,000				
S Ltd.	60,000	1,40,000			
		8,37,600			8,37,600

Revaluation of fixed assets of the subsidiary company also has an effect on the cost of control (or capital reserve) and minority interest.

Illustration 12:

The following are the balance sheets of H Ltd and S Ltd. as at 31st, March, 2010:—

Liabilities	*H Ltd.* *Rs.*	*S Ltd.* *Rs.*	*Assets*	*H Ltd.* *Rs.*	*S Ltd.* *Rs.*
Share Capital:			Fixed Assets	3,00,000	1,00,000
Shares of Rs. 10 each,			60% Shares in S Ltd.		
fully paid	5,00,000	2,00,000	acquired on 31st		
Reserves	1,00,000	50,000	March, 2000 (cost)	1,62,400	
Creditors	80,000	60,000	Current Assets	2,17,600	2,04,000
			Preliminary Expenses		6,000
	6,80,000	3,10,000		6,80,000	3,10,000

On 31st March 2010 S Ltd. revalued its fixed assets at Rs. 1,10,000. Prepare the consolidated balance sheet of H Ltd. and its subsidiary S Ltd. as at 31st March, 2010.

Solution :

Working Notes :

(i) *Calculation of Goodwill or Cost of Control :*

	Rs.	*Rs.*
Amount paid for 60% Shares in S Ltd.		1,62,400
Less: Paid up value of 60% Shares in S Ltd.	1,20,000	
Add: 60% Reserves of S Ltd. as on the date of acquisition Rs. 50,000 × 60/100	30,000	
60% of appreciation in the value of fixed assets on revaluation (Rs. 1,10,000 – Rs. 1,00,000) × 60/100	6,000	
	1,56,000	
Less: 60% of Preliminary Expenses Rs. 6,000 × 60/100	3,600	1,52,400
		10,000

(ii) *Calculation of minority interest :*

	Rs.
Paid up value of 40% shares of S Ltd.	80,000
Add: 40% of Reserves of S Ltd. as on the date of consolidation Rs. 50,000 × 40/100	20,000
40% of appreciation in the value of fixed assets of S Ltd. Rs. 10,000 × 40/100	4,000
	1,04,000
Less: 40% of Preliminary Expenses Rs. 6,000 × 40/100	2,400
	1,01,600

Consolidated Balance Sheet of H Ltd. and its subsidiary S Ltd. as at 31st March, 2010

Liabilities	*Rs.*	*Rs.*	*Assets*	*Rs.*	*Rs.*
Share Capital:			Goodwill		10,000
Shares of Rs. 10 each, fully paid		5,00,000	Other Fixed Assets .		
Minority Interest		1,01,600	H Ltd.	3,00,000	
Reserves		1,00,000	S Ltd.	1,10,000	4,10,000
Creditors:			Current Assets:		
H Ltd.	80,000		H Ltd.	2,17,600	
S Ltd.	60,000	1,40,000	S Ltd.	2,04,000	4,21,600
		8,41,600			8,41,600

Capital Profits and Revenue Profits :

So far profits and losses of the subsidiary company pertaining to pre-acquisition period only have been dealt with; they are capital profits and losses for purposes of preparation of consolidated balance sheets. It must be understood that the term 'capital profit' in this context, apart from the generic meaning of the term, connotes profit earned by the subsidiary company till the date of acquisition. As a result, profits which may be of revenue nature for the subsidiary company, may be capital profits so far as the holding company is concerned. Profit arising out of appreciation of fixed assets on their revaluation even in the post acquisition period is also a capital profit and is treated like profits pertaining to preacquisition period.

The profits earned and losses incurred by the subsidiary in the post acquisition period are treated as revenue profits and revenue losses respectively. Holding company's share of such profits and losses are shown in the consolidated balance sheet as increase or decrease as the case may be in Profit and Loss Account. Minority shareholders' share of post acquisition profits increases the minority interest and their share of post acquisition loss decreases the minority interest.

Illustration 13:

The following are the balance sheets of H Ltd and S Ltd. as at 31st March, 2010:—

Liabilities	*H Ltd.* Rs.	*S Ltd.* Rs.	*Assets*	*H Ltd.* Rs.	*S Ltd.* Rs.
Share Capital:			Fixed Assets	3,00,000	1,00,000
Shares of Rs. 10 each,			60% Shares in S Ltd.,		
fully paid	5,00,000	2,00,000	at cost	1,62,400	
General Reserves	1,00,000	50,000	Current Assets	2,77,600	2,39,000
Profit and Loss Account	60,000	35,000	Preliminary Expenses		6,000
Creditors	80,000	60,000			
	7,40,000	3,45,000		7,40,000	3,45,000

H Ltd. acquired the shares on 1st April, 2009 on which date General Reserve and Profit and Loss Account of S Ltd. showed balances of Rs. 40,000 and Rs. 8,000 respectively. No part of Preliminary Expenses was written off during the year ending 31st March, 2010.

Prepare the consolidated balance sheet of H Ltd. and its subsidiary S Ltd. as at 31st March, 2010.

Solution :

(*i*) *Capital Profits of the subsidiary i.e. profits earned prior to acquisition of shares :*

	Rs.
General Reserve	40,000
Profit & Loss Account	8,000
	48,000
Less : Preliminary Expenses	6,000
	42,000

(*ii*) *Revenue profits of the subsidiary i.e. profits earned after the acquisition of shares :*

Profit & Loss Account

	Rs.		Rs.
To General Reserve (Rs. 50,000 – Rs. 40,000)	10,000	By Balance b/fd	8,000
To Balance c/d	35,000	By Net Profit for the year (balancing figure)	37,000
	45,000		45,000

(*iii*) *Calculation of Cost of Control or Goodwill :*

	Rs.	Rs.
Amount paid for 60% Shares of S Ltd.		1,62,400
Less : Paid up value of 60% Shares of S Ltd.	1,20,000	
Add : 60% of Capital Profits *i.e.* profits prior to acquisition, Rs. 42,000 × 60/100	25,200	1,45,200
		17,200

(*iv*) *Calculation of minority interest:*

Paid up value of 40% shares of S Ltd.	80,000
Add : 40% of Capital Profits = Rs. 42,000 × 40/100	16,800
Add : 40% of Revenue Profits = Rs. 37,000 × 40/100	14,800
	1,11,600

Alternatively, minority interest may be calculated as follows :—

	Rs.
Paid up value of 40% shares of S Ltd.	80,000
Add : 40% of General Reserve as on 31.3.2000 Rs. 50,000 × 40/100	20,000
Add : 40% of Profit & Loss Account as on 31.3.2000 Rs. 35,000 × 40/100	14,000
	1,14,000
Less : 40% of Preliminary Expenses Rs. 6,000 × 40/100	2,400
	1,11,600

Consolidated Balance Sheet of H Ltd. and its subsidiary S Ltd. as at 31st March, 2010

Liabilities	Rs.	Rs.	*Assets*	Rs.	Rs.
Share Capital:			Goodwill		17,200
Shares of Rs. 10 each, fully paid		5,00,000	Other Fixed Assets :		
Minority Interest		1,11,600	H Ltd.	3,00,000	
General Reserve		1,00,000	S Ltd.	1,00,000	4,00,000
Profit & Loss Account :			Current Assets :		
H Ltd.	60,000		H Ltd.	2,77,600	
Add : H Ltd.'s share of revenue profits of S Ltd, Rs. 37,000 × 60/100	22,200	82,200	S Ltd.	2,39,000	5,16,600
Creditors :					
H Ltd.	80,000				
S Ltd.	60,000	1,40,000			
		9,33,800			9,33,800

Illustration 14:

From the balance sheets given below, prepare a consolidated balance sheet of X Ltd. and its subsidiary Y Ltd. The interest of minority shareholders in Y Ltd. is to be shown as a separate item in the consolidated balance sheet.

Balance Sheet of X Ltd. as on 31st March, 2010

Liabilities	Rs.	*Assets*	Rs.	Rs.
Share Capital :		Freehold Building, at cost		8,00,000
Authorised, Issued and Subscribed :		Plant and Machinery		
1,20,000 Shares of Rs. 10 each	12,00,000	Cost	4,00,000	
General Reserve	2,50,000	*Less*: Depreciation	1,00,000	3,00,000
Profit and Loss Account	1,20,000	Furniture		
Trade Creditors	1,50,000	Cost	1,20,000	
		Less: Depreciation	20,000	1,00,000
		Shares in Y Ltd., at cost (20,000 shares of Rs. 10 each)		2,50,000
		Stock		1,40,000
		Trade Debtors		90,000
		Bank Balance		40,000
	17,20,000			17,20,000

Balance Sheet of Y Ltd. as on 31st March, 2010

Liabilities	Rs.	*Assets*	Rs.	Rs.
Share Capital :		Leasehold Property		
Authorised, Issued and Subscribed :		Cost		3,00,000
30,000 Shares of Rs. 10 each	3,00,000	*Less* : Depreciation	50,000	2,50,000
General Reserve as on 1.4.2000	60,000	Plant and Machinery		
Profit and Loss Account	90,000	Cost	1,50,000	

	Rs.		Rs.	Rs.
Trade Creditors	50,000	*Less* : Depreciation	50,000	1,00,000
		Furniture		
		Cost		65,000
		Less : Depreication	15,000	50,000
		Stock		65,000
		Trade Debtors		20,000
		Bank Balance		5,000
	5,00,000			5,00,000

On the 1st April, 2009, the date of acquisition by X Ltd. of its holding of 20,000 shares in Y Ltd., the latter company had a credit balance of Rs. 60,000 in its profit and loss account.

[*Adapted C.S. (Inter) Dec. 1995*]

Solution :

Consolidated Balance Sheet of X Ltd. and its subsidiary Y Ltd. as on 31st March, 2009

Liabilities	*Rs.*	*Rs.*	*Assets*	*Rs.*	*Rs.*	*Rs.*
Share Capital			**Fixed Assets**			
Authorised :			Freehold Premises			
1,20,000 Shares of Rs. 10 each		12,00,000	X Ltd :			
Issued and Subscribed :			Cost			8,00,000
1,20,000 Shares of Rs. 10 each,			Leasehold Property			
fully paid-up		12,00,000	Y Ltd.			
Minority Interest		1,50,000	Cost		3,00,000	
Reserves and Surplus			*Less* : Depreciation		50,000	2,50,000
Capital Reserve, on acquisition			Plant and Machinery			
of shares in Y Ltd.		30,000	X Ltd.			
General Reserve		2,50,000	Cost	4,00,000		
Profit and Loss Account:			*Less* : Depreciation	1,00,000	3,00,000	
X Ltd.	1,20,000		Y Ltd.			
Add : X Ltd.'s share			Cost	1,50,000		
in Y Ltd.'s revenue			*Less* : Depreciation	50,000	1,00,000	4,00,000
profits	20,000	1,40,000	Furniture			
Current Liabilities and			X Ltd.			
Provisions			Cost	1,20,000		
(A) Current Liabilites			*Less* : Depreciation	20,000	1,00,000	
Trade Creditors			Y Ltd.			
X Ltd.	1,50,000		Cost	65,000		
Y Ltd.	50,000	2,00,000	*Less* : Depreciation	15,000	50,000	1,50,000
(B) Provisions		Nil	**Current Assets, Loans and Advances :**			
			(A) Current Assets			
			Stock			
			X Ltd.		1,40,000	
			Y Ltd.		65,000	2,05,000
			Trade Debtors			
			X Ltd.		90,000	
			Y Ltd.		20,000	1,10,000
			Bank Balance			
			X Ltd.		40,000	
			Y Ltd.		15,000	55,000
			(B) Loans and Advances			Nil
		19,70,000				19,70,000

Working Notes :

(*i*) *Calculation of capital profits* :

	Rs.
Y Ltd.'s general reserve on 1.4.2009	60,000
Y Ltd.'s profit and loss account on 1.4.2009	60,000
	1,20,000

X Ltd.'s share = Rs. 1,20,000 × 20,000 / 30,000 = Rs. 80,000

Minority shareholders's share = Rs. 1,20,000 – Rs. 80,000 = Rs. 40,000

(*ii*) *Calculation of revenue profits* :

Y Ltd.'s profit and loss account on 31.3.2010	90,000
Less : Y Ltd.'s profit and loss account on 1.4.2009	60,000
	30,000

X Ltd.'s share = Rs. 30,000 × 20,000 / 30,000 = Rs. 20,000

Minority shareholders's share = Rs. 30,000 – Rs. 20,000 = Rs. 10,000

(*iii*) *Calculation of capital reserve on acquisition of shares* :

Paid up value of 20,000 shares acquired by X Ltd.	2,00,000
Add : X Ltd.'s share in capital profits	80,000
	2,80,000
Less : Cost of shares	2,50,000
Capital reserve on acquisition of shares	30,000

(*iv*) *Calculation of minority interest* :

Paid up value of 10,000 shares held by minority shareholders	1,00,000
Add : Minority shareholders' share in capital profits	40,000
Add : Minority shareholders' share in revenue profits	10,000
	1,50,000

Controlling Interest Acquired During the Course of the year

Holding Company may not acquire shares of the subsidiary company on a date on which the subsidiary company prepares its final accounts. It may acquire shares in the course of a financial year; in such a case all reserves and the profit and loss account balance up to the beginning of the year will naturally be capital profits, but, in addition, current year's profit up to the date of acquisition will also be treated as capital profits. In the absence of any indication to the contrary, profits should be treated as accruing from day to day, that is to say, the apportionment should be made on time basis.

Illustration 15:

The following are the balance sheets of H Ltd. and its subsidiary S Ltd. as at 31st March, 2010:—

Liabilities	*H Ltd.* Rs.	*S Ltd.* Rs.	*Assets*	*H Ltd.* Rs.	*S Ltd.* Rs.
Share Capital :			Machinery	3,00,000	1,00,000
Shares of Rs. 10 each,			Furniture	70,000	45,000
fully paid	6,00,000	2,00,000	70% Shares in S Ltd.,		
General Reserve	1,50,000	70,000	at cost	2,60,000	
Profit and Loss Account	70,000	50,000	Stock	1,75,000	1,89,000
Creditors	90,000	60,000	Debtors	55,000	30,000
			Cash at Bank	50,000	10,000
			Preliminary Expenses	—	6,000
	9,10,000	3,80,000		9,10,000	3,80,000

H Ltd. acquired the shares of S Ltd. on 30th June, 2009. On 1st April, 2009 S Ltd.'s General Reserve and Profit and Loss Account stood at Rs. 60,000 and Rs. 20,000 respectively. No part of Preliminary Expenses was written off during the year ended 31st March, 2009.

Prepare the consolidated balance sheet of H Ltd. and its subsidiary S Ltd. as at 31st March, 2010.

[*C.S.* (*Inter.*) *June, 1995 Modified*]

Solution :

Working Notes :

(*i*) In the books of S Ltd.

Profit and Loss Appropriation Account for the year ended 31st March, 2010

	Rs.		*Rs.*
To General Reserve (Rs. 70,000 – Rs. 60,000)	10,000	By Balance b/fd	20,000
To Balance c/d	50,000	By Net Profit for the year (Balancing figure)	40,000
	60,000		60,000
		By Balance b/d	50,000

Assuming that the profits during the current year have been evenly earned.

Profit for the first three months

i.e. up to 30th June, 2009, the date of acquisition
= Rs. 40,000 × 3/12 = Rs. 10,000.

Profits for the remaining nine months
= Rs. 40,000 – Rs. 10,000 = Rs. 30,000.

Hence, revenue profits of S Ltd. *i.e.* profits earned after the acquisition of shares by H Ltd. = Rs. 30,000

H Ltd.'s share = Rs. 30,000 × 70/100 = Rs. 21,000

Minority shareholders' share = Rs. 30,000 × 30/100 = Rs. 9,000

(*ii*) *Capital Profits*

	Rs.
General Reserve on 1st April, 2009	60,000
Profit & Loss Account on 1st April, 2009	20,000
Profits earned upto 30th June, 2009	10,000
	90,000
Less: Preliminary Expenses	6,000
	84,000

H Ltd.'s share = Rs. 84,000 × 70/100 = Rs. 58,800

Minority shareholders' share = Rs. 84,000 × 30/100 = Rs. 25,200

(*iii*) *Calculation of cost of control :*

Amount paid for 70% shares of S Ltd.		2,60,000
Less:		
Paid up value of 70% shares of S Ltd.	1,40,000	
Add: H Ltd.'s share of capital profits	58,800	1,98,800
		61,200

(*iv*) *Calculation of minority interest :*

Paid up value of 30% shares	60,000
Add: minority shareholders' share of capital profits	25,200
Add: minority shareholders' share of revenue profits	9,000
	94,200

Alternatively :

Paid up value of 30% shares	60,000
30% of General Reserve, Rs. 70,000 × 30/100	21,000
30% of Profit & Loss Account, Rs. 50,000 × 30/100	15,000
	96,000
Less: 30% of Preliminary Expenses, Rs. 6,000 × 30/100	1,800
	94,200

Consolidated Balance Sheet of H Ltd. and its subsidiary S Ltd. as at 31st March, 2010

Liabilities	*Rs.*	*Rs.*	*Assets*	*Rs.*	*Rs.*
Share Capital :			Goodwill		61,200
60,000 Shares of Rs.10 each.		6,00,000	Machinery :		
fully paid			H Ltd.	3,00,000	
Minority Interest		94,200	S Ltd.	1,00,000	4,00,000
General Reserve		1,50,000	Furniture :		
Profits & Loss Account:			H Ltd.	70,000	
H Ltd.	70,000		S Ltd.	45,000	1,15,000
Add: Share in			Stock :		
S Ltd."s profits	21,000	91,000	H Ltd.	1,75,000	
Creditors :			S Ltd.	1,89,000	3,64,000
H Ltd.	90,000		Debtors :		
S Ltd.	60,000	1,50,000	H Ltd.	55,000	
			S Ltd.	30,000	85,000
			Cash at Bank :		
			H Ltd.	50,000	
			S Ltd.	10,000	60,000
		10,85,200			10,85,200

Illustration 16:

From the following balance sheets of H Ltd. and its subsidiary S Ltd. as at 31st March, 2010 and the additional information provided thereafter, prepare a Consolidated Balance Sheet of the two companies as at that date:

Liabilities	*H Ltd.* *Rs.*	*S Ltd.* *Rs.*	*Assets*	*H Ltd.* *Rs.*	*S Ltd.* *Rs.*
Share Capital:			Fixed Assets	11,62,000	1,80,000
Shares of Rs. 10 each,			70% Shares of S Ltd.,		
fully paid	10,00,000	2,00,000	at cost	1,42,000	
General Reserve	3,10,000	—	Current Assets	3,86,000	1,24,000
Profit & Loss Account	1,50,000	40,000	Preliminary Expenses		5,000
Creditors	2,30,000	69,000			
	16,90,000	3,09,000		16,90,000	3,09,000

H Ltd. acquired the shares on 31st December, 2009. On 1st April, 2009 S Ltd.'s Profit and Loss Account showed a debit balance of Rs. 8,000. On 31st March, 2010 S Ltd. decided to revalue its Fixed Assets at Rs. 2,00,000.

Solution :

Working Notes :

(*i*) S Ltd.'s Profit & Loss Appropriation Account

	Rs.		*Rs.*
To Balance b/fd	8,000	By Net Profit for the year	48,000
To Balance c/fd	40,000		
	48,000		48,000

Profit up to 31st December, 2009 = Rs. 48,000 × 9/12 = Rs. 36,000

Profit for the subsequent three months = Rs. 48,000 × 3/12 = Rs. 12,000.

Thus, revenue profits = Rs. 12,000

H Ltd.'s share = Rs. 12,000 × 70/100 = Rs. 8,400

Minority Shareholders' share = Rs. 12,000 × 30/100 = Rs. 3,600

(*ii*) *Capital Profits :*

	Rs.
Appreciation in the value of fixed assets (Rs. 2,00,000 – Rs. 1,80,000)	20,000
Current year's profit till 31st December, 2009	36,000

	Rs.	Rs.
		56,000
Less: Preliminary Expenses	5,000	
Debit balance of Profit & Loss Account on 1st April, 2009	8,000	13,000
		43,000

H Ltd.'s share = Rs. 43,000 × 70/100 = Rs. 30,100
Minority shareholders' share = Rs. 43,000 × 30/100 = Rs. 12,900

(*iii*) *Calculation of Capital Reserve on acquisition of shares :*

	Rs.
Paid up value of 70% shares	1,40,000
Add : H Ltd.'s share of capital profits	30,100
	1,70,100
Less : Amount paid for acquiring shares	1,42,000
	28,100

(*iv*) *Calculation of minority interest :*

Paid up value of 30% shares	60,000
30% of revenue profits	3,600
30% of capital profits	12,900
	76,500

Consolidated Balance Sheet of H Ltd. and its subsidiary S Ltd. as at 31st March, 2010

Liabilities	*Rs.*	*Rs.*	*Assets*	*Rs.*	*Rs.*
Equity Shares of Rs. 10 each, fully paid		10,00,000	Fixed Assets :		
			H Ltd.	11,62,000	
Minority Interest		76,500	S Ltd.	2,00,000	13,62,000
Capital Reserve		28,100	Current Assets :		
General Reserve		3,10,000	H Ltd.	3,86,000	
Profit & Loss Account :			S Ltd.	1,24,000	5,10,000
H Ltd.	1,50,000				
Share in S Ltd.	8,400	1,58,400			
Creditors :					
H Ltd.	2,30,000				
S Ltd.	69,000	2,99,000			
		18,72,000			18,72,000

Treatment Relating to Preference Shares of the Subsidiary

A subsidiary company may have issued equity shares as well as preference shares. In such a case, irrespective of the percentage of preference shares held by outsiders, the minority interest will include the paid up value of the preference shares held by the outsiders plus the dividend accrued thereon to the date of consolidation. Out of the profits of the subsidiary company, first preference dividend accrued (remember preference shares are always cumulative) on all the preference shares will be deducted (and apportioned between holding company's share and minority shareholders' share depending upon the percentage of preference shares held by the two parties) and the remaining profit will be apportioned between the minority shareholders and the holding company in the ratio of equity shares held by them. If the subsidiary company's Profit and Loss Account shows a debit balance, no provision will be made for arrears of preference dividend. Preference shareholders are not called upon to bear any part of the loss; the whole debit balance is apportioned between minority interest and holding company's share in the ratio of equity shares held by them.

Excess of amount paid by the holding company for acquiring preference shares over their paid up value is treated as cost of control.

Illustration 17:

On 1st April 2009 H Ltd. acquired 80% equity shares and 30% preference shares of S Ltd. for Rs. 1,95,000 and Rs. 30,500 respectively on which date S Ltd.'s General Reserve and Profit and Loss Account showed balances of Rs. 30,000 and Rs. 4,000 respectively. On 31st March, 2010 the balance sheets of the two companies stood as follows:—

Liabilities	H Ltd. *Rs.*	S Ltd. *Rs.*	*Asset*	H Ltd. *Rs.*	S. Ltd. *Rs.*
Equity Share Capital	10,00,000	2,00,000	Sundry Assets	13,54,500	4,76,000
10% Preference Share Capital	—	1,00,000	80% Equity Shares in S Ltd.	1,95,000	
General Reserve	3,00,000	40,000	30% Preference Shares in S Ltd.	30,500	
Profit and Loss Account	1,00,000	39,000			
Creditors	1,80,000	97,000			
	15,80,000	4,76,000		15,80,000	4,76,000

You are required to draw the consolidated balance sheet as at 31st March, 2010 assuming that on 1st April, 2009 there were no arrears of preference dividend.

Solution :

(*i*) In S Ltd.'s Ledger

Profit and Loss Appropriation Account

	Rs.		*Rs.*
To General Reserve (Rs. 40,000 – Rs. 30,000)	10,000	By Balance b/fd	4,000
To Balance c/d	39,000	By Net Profit for the year (balancing figure)	45,000
	49,000		49,000

	Rs.
Revenue Profit	45,000
Less: Preference Dividend on Rs. 1,00,000 @ 10% per annum for 1 year	10,000
Remaining profit	35,000

Holding company's share = Rs. 35,000 × 80/100 = Rs. 28,000
Minority shareholders' share = Rs. 35,000 × 20/100 = Rs. 7,000
Holding company's share in preference dividend
= Rs. 10,000 × 30/100 = Rs. 3,000
Minority shareholders' share in preference dividend
= Rs. 10,000 × 70/100 = Rs. 7,000
Holding company's total share = Rs. 28,000 + Rs. 3,000 = Rs. 31,000

(*ii*) *Capital Profits :*

	Rs.
General Reserve as on 1st April, 2009	30,000
Profit & Loss Account as on 1st April, 2009	4,000
	34,000

H Ltd.'s share = Rs. 34,000 × 80/100 = Rs. 27,200
Minority interest = Rs. 34,000 × 20/100 = Rs. 6,800

(*iii*) *Calculation of Cost of Control or Goodwill :*

	Rs.	
Amount paid for acquiring equity shares		1,95,000
Amount paid for acquiring preference shares		30,500
		2,25,500
Less: Paid up value of 80% equity shares	1,60,000	
Paid up value of 30% preference shares	30,000	
H Ltd.'s share of capital profits	27,200	2,17,200
		8,300

(iv) *Calculation of minority interest :*

	Rs.
Paid up value of 20% equity shares	40,000
Share in capital profits	6,800
Share in revenue profits in addition to preference dividend	7,000
Paid up value of 70% preference shares	70,000
Share in preference dividend	7,000
	1,30,800

Consolidated Balance Sheet of H Ltd. and its subsidiary S Ltd. as at 31st March, 2010

Liabilities	*Rs.*	*Rs.*	*Assets*	*Rs.*	*Rs.*
Equity Share Capital		10,00,000	Goodwill		8,300
Minority Interest		1,30,800	Other Assets		
General Reserve		3,00,000	H Ltd.	13,54,500	
Profit and Loss Account :			S Ltd.	4,76,000	18,30,500
H Ltd.	1,00,000				
Add: Share in S Ltd.'s profits	31,000	1,31,000			
Creditors :					
H Ltd.	1,80,000				
S Ltd.	97,000	2,77,000			
		18,38,800			18,38,800

Unrealised Profits

Usually, there will be transactions between the holding company and the subsidiary company involving profits and losses. Suppose, H Ltd. (the holding company) buys from S Ltd. (the subsidiary company) goods of the value of Rs. 20,000 on which S Ltd. has put a profit of 25% on selling price. It means that S Ltd. has made a profit of Rs. 5,000 on goods sold to H. Ltd. If H Ltd. is able to sell these goods, it does not matter because the whole profit—the Rs. 5,000 charged by S. Ltd. and whatever profit H Ltd. makes—is realised. But if the goods remain unsold and are taken in stock at the close of the financial year, the profit charged by S Ltd. remains unrealised and it will not be proper to credit the Profit and Loss Account with such a profit. Either a reserve should be created or the value of closing stock written down. If a portion of the goods has been sold, proportionate reserve should be created for unrealised profit on unsold goods.

But if there are outside shareholders in the subsidiary company, they will treat the profit made by the subsidiary company as realised. Similarly, if the holding company sells goods to S Ltd. and the goods remain unsold, the holding company can treat the profits as realised so far as the outside shareholders are concerned. This means that the reserve to be created in respect of unrealised profit should be reduced by the share applicable to the outside shareholders. Suppose, H Ltd. holds 3,000 shares in S Ltd. out of the total 4,000 shares. During the year, S Ltd. sold goods costing Rs. 50,000 to H Ltd. at a profit of 20% on cost. At the end of the year, H Ltd. has still in stock a portion of these goods and this was valued by H Ltd. at Rs. 30,000 (cost to H Ltd.). The total unrealised profit is Rs. 30,000 × 20/120 or Rs. 5,000. Since the outside shareholders have one-fourth interest, Rs. 1,250, *i.e.*, 5000/4 may be treated as realised and a reserve of the remaining balance, *viz.*, Rs. 3,750 created by debit to the Profit and Loss Account.

The point will also arise when fixed assets are transferred at a profit or loss. It will have to be treated exactly in the same way in which sale of goods is treated.

The modern practice is to create the whole of the profit mentioned in these paragraphs as unrealised without adjustment for minority interest. Hence, a reserve equal to the total unrealised profit may be created.

Illustration 18:

On 31st March, 2010 the Balance Sheets of H Ltd. and its subsidiary S Ltd. stood as follows:—

Liabilities	*H Ltd.* Rs.	*S Ltd.* Rs.	*Assets*	*H Ltd.* Rs.	*S Ltd.* Rs.
Equity Share Capital	8,00,000	2,00,000	Fixed Assets	5,50,000	1,00,000
General Reserve	1,50,000	70,000	75% Shares in S Ltd. (at cost)	2,80,000	—
Profit and Loss Account	90,000	55,000	Stock	1,05,000	1,77,000
Creditors	1,20,000	80,000	Other Current Assets	2,25,000	1,28,000
	11,60,000	4,05,000		11,60,000	4,05,000

Draw a consolidated balance sheet as at 31st March, 2010 after taking into consideration the following information also :—

(i) H Ltd. acquired the shares on 31st July 2009.

(ii) S Ltd. earned a profit of Rs. 45,000 for the year ended 31st March, 2010.

(iii) In January, 2010 S Ltd. sold to H Ltd. goods costing Rs. 15,000 for Rs. 20,000. On 31st March, 2010 half of these goods were lying as unsold in the godowns of H Ltd.

[*C.S. (Inter.) June, 1996 Modified*]

Solution :

Working Notes :

(i) *Capital Profits :*

	Rs.
General Reserve	70,000
Profit & Loss Account as on 31st March, 2009 (Rs. 55,000 – Rs. 45,000)	10,000
Current year's profit up to 31st July 2009, the date of acquisition of shares Rs. 45,000 × 4/12 = Rs. 15,000	15,000
	95,000

H Ltd.'s share = Rs. 95,000 × 75/100 = Rs. 71,250

Minority shareholders' share = Rs. 95,000 × 25/100 = Rs. 23,750

(ii) *Revenue Profits :*

Profits from 1st August, 2009 to 31st March, 2010

i.e., for 8 months = Rs. 45,000 × 8/12 = Rs. 30,000

H Ltd's share = Rs. 30,000 × 75/100 = Rs. 22,500

Minority shareholders' share = Rs. 30,000 × 25/100 = Rs. 7,500

(iii) *Unrealised profit in respect of stock with H Ltd. :*

Total profit charged by S Ltd. = Rs. 20,000 – Rs. 15,000 = Rs. 5,000

Since only half of the goods remained unsold as on 31st March, 2000, the unrealised profit = Rs. 5,000 × 1/2 = Rs. 2,500

(iv) *Cost of control or goodwill :*

	Rs.	
Amount paid for acquiring 75% shares of S Ltd.		2,80,000
Less: Paid up value of 75% shares of S Ltd.	1,50,000	
H Ltd.'s share of capital profits	71,250	2,21,250
Cost of control		58,750

(v) *Minority Interest :*

	Rs.
Paid up value of 25% shares of S Ltd.	50,000
Add : Share in capital profits	23,750
Add : Share in reserve profits	7,500
	81,250

Or

Paid up value of 25% shares in S Ltd.	50,000
25% of General Reserve as on 31st March, 2000 = Rs. 70,000 × 25/100	17,500
25% of Balance of Profit & Loss Account as on 31st March, 2000 = Rs. 55,000 × 25/100	13,750
	81,250

Consolidated Balance Sheet of H Ltd. and its subsidiary S Ltd. as at 31st March, 2010

Liabilities	*Rs.*	*Rs.*	*Assets*	*Rs.*	*Rs.*
Equity Share Capital		8,00,000	Goodwill		58,750
Minority Interest		81,250	Other Fixed Assets :		
General Reserve		1,50,000	H Ltd.	5,50,000	
Profits & Loss Account :			S Ltd.	1,00,000	6,50,000
H Ltd.	90,000		Stock :		
Add : Share in			H Ltd.	1,05,000	
S Ltd.'s profits	22,500		S Ltd.	1,77,000	
	1,12,500			2,82,000	
Less : Unrealised profit	2,500	1,10,000	*Less* : Unrealised profit	2,500	2,79,500
Creditors :			Other Current Assets :		
H Ltd.	1,20,000		H Ltd.	2,25,000	
S Ltd.	80,000	2,00,000	S Ltd.	1,28,000	3,53,000
		13,41,250			13,41,250

Mutual Owings

In preparing consolidated balance sheet, sums owed by holding company to its subsidiary and *vice versa* have to be eliminated. For instance if holding company owes Rs. 1,00,000 to its subsidiary, this sum will be deducted both from the total debtors and total creditors in the consolidated balance sheet. The same applies to bills accepted by either of them and held by the other as bills receivable. However, bills receivable which have been got discounted or which have been endorsed in favour of creditors will not be eliminated and will appear in the balance sheet as a liability, since the company which has accepted the bills will have to pay on the due dates to the outsiders *i.e.* the banks who discounted the bills or endorsees in whose favour the bills have been endorsed. Likewise, debentures issued by either company and held by the other company as investments will also be eliminated from debentures on the liabilities side and from investments on the assets side. But in such a case, the difference in the purchase price of debentures and the paid up value of the same is shown as cost of control or capital reserve. Also, internal contingent liabilities, that is, sums that may have to be paid by the holding company to the subsidiary company or *vice versa* are not shown by way of a note in the consolidated balance sheet.

Illustration 19:

H Ltd. acquired as investment 15,000 shares in S Ltd. for Rs. 1,55,000 on 1st July, 2009. The balance sheets of the two companies on 31st March, 2010 were as follows :—

Liabilities	*H Ltd.* Rs.	*S Ltd.* Rs.	*Assets*	*H Ltd.* Rs.	*S Ltd.* Rs.
Equity Shares of Rs. 10 each			Machinery	7,00,000	1,50,000
fully paid	9,00,000	2,50,000	Furniture	1,00,000	70,000
General Reserve	1,60,000	40,000	Investment	1,55,000	—
Profit & Loss Account	80,000	25,000	Stock	1,00,000	50,000
Bills Payable	40,000	20,000	Debtors	60,000	35,000
Creditors	50,000	30,000	Cash at Bank	90,000	40,000
			Bills Receivable	25,000	20,000
	12,30,000	3,65,000		12,30,000	3,65,000

The following additional information is provided to you :—

(*i*) General Reserve appearing in the balance sheet of S Ltd. has remained unchanged since 31st March, 2009.

(*ii*) Profit earned by S Ltd. for the year ended 31st March, 2010 amounted to Rs. 20,000.

(*iii*) On 1st February, 2010 H Ltd. sold to S Ltd. goods costing Rs. 8,000 for Rs. 10,000. 25%

of these goods remained unsold with S Ltd. on 31st March, 2010. Creditors of S Ltd. include Rs. 4,000 due to H Ltd. on account of these goods.

(*iv*) Out of S Ltd.'s acceptances, Rs. 15,000 are those which have been accepted in favour of H Ltd. Out of these, H Ltd. had endorsed by 31st March, 2010 Rs. 8,000 worth of bills receivable in favour of its creditors.

You are required to draw a consolidated balance sheet as at 31st March, 2010.

[*C.S (Inter) June, 2002*]

Solution :

(*i*) *Capital Profits* :

	Rs.
General Reserve	40,000
Profit & Loss Account balance as on 31st March, 2009 (Rs. 25,000 – Rs. 20,000)	5,000
Profit earned during the current year up to the date of acquisition of shares Rs. 20,000 × 3/12 = Rs. 5,000	5,000
	50,000

H Ltd.'s share = Rs. 50,000 × (15,000/25,000) = Rs. 30,000.

Minority shareholders' share = Rs. 50,000 – Rs. 30,000 = Rs. 20,000.

(*ii*) *Revenue Profit* :

Profit earned during the current year subsequent to the acquisition of shares = Rs. 20,000 × 9/12 = Rs. 15,000

H Ltd.'s share = Rs. 15,000 × (15,000/25,000) = Rs. 9,000

Minority shareholders' share = Rs. 15,000 – Rs. 9,000 = Rs. 6,000.

(*iii*) *Capital Reserve on acquisition of shares* :

Paid up value of 15,000 shares of S Ltd.	1,50,000
H Ltd.'s share of capital profits	30,000
	1,80,000
Less: Cost of shares	1,55,000
Capital Reserve	25,000

(*iv*) *Minority Interest* :

Paid up value of 10,000 shares held by minority shareholders	1,00,000
Capital Profits	20,000
Revenue Profits	6,000
	1,26,000

Alternatively :

Paid up value of 10,000 shares	1,00,000
General Reserve Rs. 40,000 × (10,000/25,000)	16,000
Profit & Loss Account Rs. 25,000 × (10,000/25,000)	10,000
	1,26,000

(*v*) *Unrealised profit in respect of stock* :

=(Rs. 10,000 – Rs. 8,000) × 25/100 = Rs. 500.

Consolidated Balance Sheet of H Ltd. and its subsidiary S Ltd. as at 31st March, 2010

Liabilities	*Rs.*	*Rs.*	*Assets*	*Rs.*	*Rs.*
Equity Shares Capital		9,00,000	Machinery :		
Minority Interest		1,26,000	H Ltd.	7,00,000	
Capital Reserve		25,000	S Ltd.	1,50,000	8,50,000
General Reserve		1,60,000	Furniture :		
Profit & Loss Account			H Ltd.	1,00,000	
H Ltd.	80,000		S Ltd.	70,000	1,70,000
Add: H Ltd.'s share of			Stock :		
S Ltd.'s post			H Ltd.	1,00,000	
acquisition profits	9,000		S Ltd.	50,000	
	89,000			1,50,000	
Less: Unrealised profit	500	88,500	*Less*: Unrealised Profit	500	1,49,500

	Rs.	Rs.		Rs.	Rs.
Bills Payable :			Debtors :		
H Ltd.	40,000		H Ltd.	60,000	
S Ltd.	20,000		S Ltd.	35,000	
	60,000			95,000	
Less : Mutual Owings	7,000	53,000	*Less:* Mutual Owings	4,000	91,000
Creditors :			Cash at Bank :		
H Ltd.	50,000		H Ltd.	90,000	
S Ltd.	30,000		S Ltd.	40,000	1,30,000
	80,000		Bills Receivable :		
Less: Mutual Owings	4,000	76,000	H Ltd.	25,000	
			S Ltd.	20,000	
				45,000	
			Less: Mutual Owings	7,000	38,000
		14,28,500			14,28,500

Illustration 20:

The balance sheets of H Ltd. and S Ltd. at 31st March, 2010 were as under :—

Liabilities	*H Ltd.* Rs.	*S Ltd.* Rs.	*Assets*	*H Ltd.* Rs.	*S Ltd.* Rs.
Share Capital:			Land & Buildings	60,000	—
Shares of Rs. 10 each,			Plant & Machinery	2,00,000	—
fully paid	2,00,000	50,000	3,000 Shares in S Ltd.,		
General Reserve	30,000	10,000	at cost	65,000	—
Profit and Loss Account :			Stock	40,000	85,000
Balance as on 1st April, 1999	40,000	20,000	Sundry Debtors	10,000	30,000
Profit for 1999-2000	50,000	25,000	Bank Balances	10,000	10,000
Bills Payable	15,000	—	Bills Receivable	—	10,000
Creditors	30,000	30,000			
Bank Overdraft	20,000	—			
	3,85,000	1,35,000		3,85,000	1,35,000

Shares were acquired by H Ltd. on 1st October, 2009. Bills receivable held by S Ltd. are all accepted by H Ltd. Included in the Sundry Debtors of S Ltd. is a sum of Rs. 6,000 owing by H Ltd. in respect of goods supplied.

Prepare the consolidated balance sheet as at 31st March, 2010.

Solution :

Workings :

	Rs.
(*i*) *Capital Profits* :	
General Reserve	10,000
Profit & Loss Account :	
Balance as on 1st April, 2009	20,000
Profit for 1999-2000 up to October 1, 2009 = Rs. 25,000 × 6/12	12,500
	42,500
(*ii*) *Current Interest* :	
Profits after 1st October, 2009 = Rs. 25,000 × 6/12	12,500
Share of H Ltd. = Rs. 12,500 × 3000/5000	7,500
Minority shareholders' share = Rs. 12,500 – Rs. 7,500	5,000
(*iii*) *Minority Interest* :	
2,000 shares of Rs. 10 each	20,000
Add : Share of capital profits	17,000
Share of current profits	5,000
	42,000

(iv) *Goodwill* :

		Rs.
Amount paid		65,000
Less : Paid up value of 3,000 shares	Rs. 30,000	
H Ltd.'s share of capital profits	Rs. 25,500	55,500
Goodwill		9,500

(v) *Profit & Loss Account :*

Balance as on 1st April, 2009	40,000
H Ltd.'s profits for 2009–2010	50,000
H Ltd.'s share in S Ltd.'s current profits	7,500
	97,500

(vi) *Sundry Debtors :*

H Ltd.	10,000
S Ltd.	30,000
	40,000
Less: Mutual Owing	6,000
	34,000

(vii) *Creditors :*

H Ltd.	30,000
S Ltd.	30,000
	60,000
Less: Mutual Owing	6,000
	54,000

(viii) *Bills Payable :*

H Ltd.	15,000
Less: Mutual Owing	10,000
	5,000

(ix) *Bills Receivable :*

S Ltd.	10,000
Less: Mutual Owing	10,000
	Nil

(x) Bank Overdraft need not be deducted from Bank Balances appearing on the Assets-side as the appropriate assumption is that they are separate bank accounts.

Consolidated Balance Sheet of H Ltd. and its subsidiary S Ltd. as at 31st March, 2009

Liabilities	*Rs.*	*Assets*	*Rs.*
Share Capital :		Goodwill	9,500
Shares of Rs. 10 each, fully paid	2,00,000	Land & Buildings	60,000
Minority Interest	42,000	Plant & Machinery	2,00,000
General Reserve	30,000	Stock	1,25,000
Profit and Loss Account	97,500	Sundry Debtors	34,000
Bills Payable	5,000	Bank Balances	20,000
Creditors	54,000		
Bank Overdraft	20,000		
	4,48,500		4,48,500

Dividend from Subsidiary Company out of Preacquisition Profits :

Dividend received by the holding company from its subsidiary out of preacquisition profits is treated as capital receipt; the journal entry for its record being as follows :—

Bank Dr.
To Shares in Subsidiary Company
Dividend received from the subsidiary company out of pre-acquisition profits.

Its effect on the holding company's balance sheet is as follows :—

Balance Sheet of the Holding Company

Liabilities	*Assets*
	Shares in Subsidiary Company (Decrease) Cash at Bank (Increase)

Thus the holding company deducts the amount of dividend received out of preacquisition profits from the balance of shares in subsidiary company account. But it does not alter the amount of cost of control or capital reserve arising out of acquisition of shares; the reason being that although the cost of investment in the subsidiary company is reduced, the holding company's share in the capital profits is also reduced by an identical amount.

Dividend from Subsidiary Company out of Post-acquisition Profits

Dividend received out of post acquisition profits is treated as a revenue receipt; the journal entries regarding it being as follows :—

(*i*) Bank Dr.
To Dividend from Subsidiary Company
Dividend received from subsidiary company out of post-acquisition profits.

(*ii*) Dividend from Subsidiary Company Dr.
To Profit & Loss Account
Transfer of Dividend from Subsidiary Company Account to Profit & Loss Account.

The final effect on the holding company's balance sheet is as follows :

Balance Sheet of the Holding Company

Liabilities	*Assets*
Profit & Loss Account (Increase)	Cash at Bank (Increase)

Because such a dividend does not effect the cost of shares of the subsidiary company and the holding company's share of capital profits, it will also not alter the cost of control or capital reserve on acquisition of shares.

Rectification of error relating to dividend from Subsidiary Company

In a question on consolidation of balance sheets, it may be given that the holding company has received dividend from the subsidiary company out of pre-acquisition profits and has credited its Profit & Loss Account with the amount so received. It means an error has been committed in as much as a capital receipt has been treated as an income. The correct journal entry for receipt of dividend out of preacquisition profits is as follows :—

Bank Dr.
To Shares in Subsidiary Company

But by mistake, the following entry has been passed :—

Bank Dr.
To Profit & Loss Account

From the above, it is clear that there is no error in Bank Account. The error lies in the fact that instead of crediting shares is Subsidiary Company, Profit & Loss Account has been credited. The rectifying journal entry, therefore, will be as follows :—

Profit & Loss Account Dr.
To Shares in Subsidiary Company

The effect on the balance sheet will be that the credit balance of Profit and Loss Account will be decreased and the debit balance of shares in Subsidiary Company will also be decreased as shown below :—

Balance Sheet of the Holding Company

Liabilities	*Assets*
Profit & Loss Account (Decrease)	Shares in Subsidiary Company (Decrease)

Illustration 21:

H Ltd. acquired 12,000 shares of S Ltd. for Rs. 1,70,000 on April 1, 2009 on which date S Ltd's Profit & Loss Account showed a credit balance of Rs. 53,000. In August, 2009 S Ltd. declared a dividend of 10% for the year ended 31st March, 2009. This dividend was credited by H Ltd. to its Profit & Loss Account. Assume corporate dividend tax was paid @ 15%. On 31st March, 2000 the balance sheets of the two companies appeared as follows :—

Liabilities	*H Ltd.* *Rs.*	*S Ltd.* *Rs.*	*Assets*	*H Ltd.* *Rs.*	*S Ltd.* *Rs.*
Share Capital :			Goodwill	30,000	20,000
Equity Shares of			Machinery	2,50,000	—
Rs. 10 each, fully paid	5,00,000	2,00,000	Furniture	85,000	50,000
General Reserve as at		12,000	Shares in S Ltd.	1,70,000	
31st March 2009	1,30,000	55,000	Stock	2,10,000	2,30,000
Profit & Loss Account	1,60,000	65,000	Debtors	65,000	58,000
Sundry Creditors	1,00,000	75,000	Cash at Bank	80,000	37,000
	8,90,000	3,95,000		8,90,000	3,95,000

You are required to prepare a consolidated balance sheet as at 31st March, 2000.

Solution :

Working Notes :

(i) *In S Ltd.'s Ledger*

Profit & Loss Appropriation Account

	Rs.		*Rs.*
To Dividend	20,000	By Balance b/fd	53,000
To Corporate Dividend Tax	3,000		
To Balance c/d	65,000	By Net Profit for the year (Balancing figure)	35,000
	88,000		88,000

H Ltd.'s share in current year's profit = Rs. 35,000 × 12,000/20,000 = Rs. 21,000.

Minority shareholders' share = Rs. 35,000 – Rs. 21,000 = Rs. 14,000

(ii) Dividend received by H Ltd. out of pre-acquisition profits

= Rs. 1,20,000 × 10/100 = Rs. 12,000.

The dividend has been wrongly credited to profit and loss account.

It should have been credited to Shares in S Ltd. Account.

Rectifying the error :

Shares in S Ltd. Account

	Rs.		*Rs.*
To Balance b/fd	1,70,000	By Profit & Loss Account (Rectification of error)	12,000
		By Balance c/d	1,58,000
	1,70,000		1,70,000
To Balance b/d	1,58,000		

H Ltd.'s Profit & Loss Account

	Rs.		*Rs.*
To Shares in S Ltd. (Rectification of error)	12,000	By Balance b/fd	1,60,000
To Balance c/d	1,48,000		
	1,60,000		1,60,000
		By Balance b/d	1,48,000

	Rs.
(*iii*) *Capital Profits :*	
General Reserve	55,000
Profit & Loss account Rs. 52,000 – Rs. 2,00,000 × 10/100 – 2000	30,000
	85,000

H Ltd.'s share = Rs. 85,000 × 12,000/20,000 = Rs. 51,000
Minority shareholders' share = Rs. 85,000 – Rs. 51,000 = Rs. 34,000.

(*iv*) *Capital Profit on acquisition of shares :*	
Paid up value of 12,000 shares	1,20,000
Add: H Ltd.'s share of capital profits	51,000
	1,71,000
Less: Balance of Shares in S Ltd. Account after deduction of dividend received out of pre-acquisition profits	1,58,000
	13,000
(*v*) *Minority Interest :*	
Paid up value of 8,000 shares	80,000
Capital Profits	34,000
Current year's profit	14,000
	1,28,000

Consolidated Balance Sheet of H Ltd. and its subsidiary S Ltd. as at 31st March, 2010

Liabilities	*Rs.*	*Rs.*	*Assets*	*Rs.*	*Rs.*
Share Capital :			Goodwill :		
Shares of Rs. 10 each, fully paid		5,00,000	H Ltd.	30,000	
Minority Interest		1,28,000	S Ltd.	20,000	
General Reserve		1,30,000		50,000	
Profit & Loss Account :			*Less*: Capital Reserve on		
H Ltd.(after rectification)	1,48,000		acquisition of shares	13,000	37,000
Share in S Ltd.'s profits	21,000	1,69,000	Machinery :		
Sundry Creditors :			H Ltd.	2,50,000	
H Ltd.	1,00,000		S Ltd.	Nil	2,50,000
S Ltd.	75,000	1,75,000	Furniture :		
			H Ltd.	85,000	
			S Ltd.	50,000	1,35,000
			Stock :		
			H Ltd.	2,10,000	
			S Ltd.	2,30,000	4,40,000
			Debtors :		
			H Ltd.	65,000	
			S Ltd.	58,000	1,23,000
			Cash at Bank :		
			H Ltd.	80,000	
			S Ltd.	37,000	1,17,000
		11,02,000			11,02,000

Interim Dividend from the Subsidiary Company

The holding company may receive interim dividend from the subsidiary company; if such an interim dividend is to be apportioned between pre-acquisition period and post acquisition period, it should be assumed that the interim dividend has been earned evenly throughout the year.

Illustration 22:

H Ltd. acquired 80% shares in S Ltd. on 30th September, 2009 at a total cost of Rs. 3,60,000. The balance sheets at 31st March, 2010 when the accounts of both the companies were prepared were as under :—

Balance Sheet of H Ltd. as at 31st March, 2010

Liabilities	*Rs.*	*Assets*	*Rs.*
Equity Share Capital	7,50,000	Land and Buildings	4,15,000
Security Premium	50,000	Plant and Machinery	2,25,000
General Reserve	4,00,000	Furniture and Fittings	1,50,000
Profit & Loss Account	2,40,000	80% Shares in S Ltd.	3,60,000
Creditors	60,000	Stock	1,45,000
		Debtors	85,000
		Cash at Bank	1,20,000
	15,00,000		15,00,000

Profit & Loss Account balance of Rs. 2,40,000 includes interim dividend @ 10% per annum received from S Ltd.

Balance Sheet of S Ltd. as at 31st March, 2010

Liabilities	*Rs.*	*Assets*	*Rs.*
Share Capital :		Plant and Machinery	1,50,000
25,000 Equity Shares of		Furniture and Fittings	65,000
Rs. 10 each, fully paid	2,50,000	Stock	1,61,000
General Reserve as on 1st April, 2009	1,10,000	Debtors	79,000
Profit & Loss Account	80,000	Cash at Bank	55,000
Creditors	70,000		
	5,10,000		5,10,000

On 1st April, 2009 S Ltd.'s Profit & Loss Account showed a credit balance of Rs. 40,000. S Ltd. declared the interim dividend on 1st January, 2010. Assume the absence of corporate dividend tax.

You are required to prepare a consolidated sheet balance of H Ltd. and its subsidiary S Ltd. as at 31st March, 2010.

Solution :

Working Notes :

(i) S Ltd.'s Profit & Loss Appropriation Account for the year ended 31st March, 2010

	Rs.		*Rs.*
To Interim Dividend @ 10% on Rs. 2,50,000	25,000	By Balance b/fd	40,000
To Balance c/d	80,000	By Net Profit for the year (Balancing figure)	65,000
	1,05,000		1,05,000
		By Balance b/d	80,000

Profit up to 30th September, 2009 = Rs. 65,000 × 6/12 = Rs. 32,500

Profit after the acquisition of shares = Rs. 65,000 – Rs. 32,500 = Rs. 32,500

(ii) Interim Dividend received by H Ltd. = Rs. 25,000 × 80/100 = Rs. 20,000

Interim Dividend pertaining to pre-acquisition period = Rs. 20,000 × 6/12 = Rs. 10,000

(iii) ***Capital Profits :***

		Rs.
General Reserve		1,10,000
Profit & Loss Account as on 1st April, 2009		40,000
Profit for the current year upto the date of acquisition *i.e.* 30th September, 2009	Rs. 32,500	
Less: ½ of interim dividend	Rs. 12,500	20,000
		1,70,000

H Ltd.'s share = Rs. 1,70,000 × 80/100 = Rs. 1,36,000

Minority shareholders' share = Rs. 1,70,000 – Rs. 1,36,000 = Rs. 34,000.

(iv) ***Revenue Profits :***

Profit after the acquisition of shares	32,500
Less: ½ of interim dividend	12,500
	20,000

			Rs.
	H Ltd.'s share Rs. 20,000 × 80/100 = Rs. 16,000.		
	Minority shareholders' share = Rs. 20,000 – Rs. 16,000 = Rs. 4,000.		
(v)	*Cost of Control :*		
	Amount paid for acquiring 80% shares in S Ltd.		3,60,000
	Less: Interim dividend pertaining to pre-acquisition period		10,000
			3,50,000
	Less: Paid up value of 80% shares in S Ltd.	2,00,000	
	Add: H Ltd.'s share of Capital Profits	1,36,000	3,36,000
			14,000
(vi)	*Minority Interest :*		
	Paid up value of 20% shares in S Ltd.		50,000
	Add: Minority shareholders' share in Capital Profits		34,000
	Add: Minority shareholders' share in Revenue Profits		4,000
			88,000

Consolidated Balance Sheet of H Ltd. and its subsidiary S Ltd. as at 31st March, 2010

Liabilities	*Rs.*	*Rs.*	*Assets*	*Rs.*	*Rs.*
Equity Share Capital		7,50,000	Goodwill		14,000
Minority Interest		88,000	Land and Buildings		4,15,000
Security Premium		50,000	Plant and Machinery :		
General Reserve		4,00,000	H Ltd.	2,25,000	
Profit and Loss Account :			S Ltd.	1,50,000	3,75,000
H Ltd.	2,40,000		Furniture & Fittings :		
Less: 1/2 of Interim			H Ltd.	1,50,000	
Dividend	10,000		S Ltd.	65,000	2,15,000
	2,30,000		Stock :		
Add: H Ltd.'s share in			H Ltd.	1,45,000	
S Ltd.'s profits	16,000	2,46,000	S Ltd.	1,61,000	3,06,000
Creditors :			Debtors :		
H Ltd.	60,000		H Ltd.	85,000	
S Ltd.	70,000	1,30,000	S Ltd.	79,000	1,64,000
			Cash at Bank :		
			H Ltd.	1,20,000	
			S Ltd.	55,000	1,75,000
		16,64,000			16,64,000

Proposed Dividend

On the liabilities side of the balance sheet of the subsidiary company, proposed dividend may appear. Unless the facts of the case point otherwise, it should be assumed that proposed dividend is out of post acquisition profits. Hence, holding company's share of proposed dividend will be added to the holding company's Profit and Loss Account whereas minority shareholders' share will be added to minority interest.

Illustration 23:

On 1st April, 2009 H Ltd. acquired 70% shares in S Ltd. for Rs. 3,40,000. S Ltd.'s General Reserve and Profit and Loss Account on that date showed balances of Rs. 80,000 and Rs. 50,000 respectively. On 10th July, 2009 S Ltd. declared the final dividend of 10% per annum for the year ended 31st March, 2009. On 10th January, 2010 it declared an interim dividend @ 8% per annum for full year. H Ltd. credited the final dividend of 10% as well as interim dividend of 8% to its Profit and Loss Account. Ignore corporate dividend tax.

On 31st March, 2010 the balance sheets of the two companies stood as follows :—

Liabilities	*H Ltd.* Rs.	*S Ltd.* Rs.	*Assets*	*H Ltd.* Rs.	*S Ltd.* Rs.
Share Capital :			Machinery	6,25,000	1,80,000
Shares of Rs. 10 each,			Furniture	85,000	50,000
fully paid	8,00,000	3,00,000	Shares in S Ltd. (at cost)	3,40,000	—
General Reserve	5,00,000	1,50,000	Stock	4,10,000	1,90,000
Profit and Loss Account	2,10,000	90,000	Debtors	1,00,000	80,000
Creditors	82,000	47,000	Cash at Bank	1,20,000	1,11,000
Unclaimed Dividend		1,000	Preliminary Expenses		10,000
Proposed Dividend @ 11%	88,000	33,000			
	16,80,000	6,21,000		16,80,000	6,21,000

Obviously, the entire unclaimed dividend appearing in the balance sheet of S Ltd. belongs to minority shareholders.

Prepare the consolidated balance sheet as at 31st March, 2010.

Solution :

(i) *S Ltd.'s Profit & Loss Appropriation Account for the year ended 31st March, 2010*

	Rs.		Rs.
To Final Dividend @ 10% per annum for the year ended 31st March, 1999	30,000	By Balance b/fd	50,000
To Interim Dividend @ 8% per annum for full year	24,000	By Net Profit for the year (Balancing figure)	1,97,000
To General Reserve (Rs. 1,50,000 – Rs. 80,000)	70,000		
To Proposed Dividend @ 11%	33,000		
To Balance c/d	90,000		
	2,47,000		2,47,000
		By Balance b/d	90,000

(ii) Final dividend for the year ended 31st March, 2009 received by H Ltd. = Rs. 30,000 × 70/100 = Rs. 21,000

(iii) *Capital Profits* :

	Rs.	Rs.
General Reserve		80,000
Profit and Loss Account balance as on 31st March, 2009	50,000	
Less: Final Dividend for the year ended 31st March, 2009	30,000	20,000
		1,00,000
Less: Preliminary Expenses		10,000
		90,000

H Ltd.'s share Rs. 90,000 × 70/100 = Rs. 63,000

Minority shareholders' share = Rs. 90,000 – Rs. 63,000 = Rs. 27,000

(iv) *Cost of Control* :

Amount paid for 70% shares		3,40,000
Less: Dividend received out of pre-acquisition profits		21,000
		3,19,000
Less: Paid up value of 70% shares	2,10,000	
H Ltd.'s share in capital profits	63,000	2,73,000
		46,000

(v) *Revenue Profits :*

Net Profit for the year	1,97,000

	Rs.
Less: Interim Dividend	24,000
	1,73,000

H Ltd.'s share = Rs. 1,73,000 × 70/100 = Rs. 1,21,100
Minority shareholders' share = Rs. 1,73,000 – Rs. 1,21,100 = Rs. 51,900

(*vi*) *Minority Interest :*

Paid up value of 30% shares	90,000
Add: Capital Profits	27,000
Add: Revenue Profits	51,900
Add: Unclaimed Dividend	1,000
	1,69,900

Consolidated Balance Sheet of H Ltd. and its subsidiary S Ltd. as at 31st March, 2000

Liabilities	*Rs.*	*Rs.*	*Assets*	*Rs.*	*Rs.*
Share Capital :			Goodwill		46,000
Shares of Rs. 10 each,			Machinery :		
fully paid		8,00,000	H Ltd.	6,25,000	
Minority Interest		1,69,900	S Ltd.	1,80,000	8,05,000
General Reserve		5,00,000	Furniture :		
Profit and Loss Account :			H Ltd.	85,000	
H Ltd.	2,10,000		S Ltd.	50,000	1,35,000
Less: Final dividend			Stock :		
wrongly credited	21,000		H Ltd.	4,10,000	
	1,89,000		S Ltd.	1,90,000	6,00,000
Add: H Ltd.'s Share of			Debtors :		
S Ltd.'s profits	1,21,100	3,10,100	H Ltd.	1,00,000	
Creditors :			S Ltd.	80,000	1,80,000
H Ltd.	82,000		Cash at Bank :		
S Ltd.	47,000	1,29,000	H Ltd.	1,20,000	
Proposed Dividend		88,000	S Ltd.	1,11,000	2,31,000
		19,97,000			19,97,000

Illustration 24:

H Ltd. acquired 90 per cent of the equity shares in S Ltd. on September 30, 2009 at a cost of Rs. 6,00,000. No balance sheet was prepared on the date of acquisition. The balance sheets of S Ltd. as at 31st March, 2009 and 31st March, 2010 were as follows :—

Liabilities	*As at 31.3.2009 Rs.*	*As at 31.3.2010 Rs.*	*Assets*	*As at 31.3.2009 Rs.*	*As at 31.3.2010 Rs.*
Issued & Subscribed			Goodwill	1,00,000	1,00,000
Share Capital :			Tangible Assets	6,80,000	8,56,000
20,000 Equity Shares					
of Rs. 10 each	2,00,000	2,00,000			
General Reserve	4,00,000	4,40,000			
Profit and Loss Account	1,00,000	1,74,000			
Creditors	80,000	1,00,000			
Proposed Dividend		42,000			
	7,80,000	9,56,000		7,80,000	9,56,000

The balance sheet of H Ltd. as at 31st March, 2010 was as under :—

Liabilities	Rs.	Assets	Rs.
Issued & Subscribed Share Capital :		Sundry Assets	33,00,000
2,00,000 Equity Shares of Rs. 10 each	20,00,000	18,000 Equity Shares of Rs. 10 each in S Ltd.	6,00,000
Securities Premium	2,00,000		
General Reserve	10,00,000		
Profit and Loss Account	4,00,000		
Creditors	3,00,000		
	39,00,000		39,00,000

H Ltd. has not yet passed entries for the dividend proposed by S Ltd. Prepare the consolidated balance sheet as at 31st March, 2010. Assume the absence of corporate dividend tax.

(Adapted from Incorp. Acctts. Final)

Solutions :

Workings :

	Rs.
(i) Current Profits :	
Balance of Profit & Loss Account as on 31.3.2010	1,74,000
Add: Transfer to General Reserve (Rs. 4,40,000 – Rs. 4,00,000)	40,000
Proposed Dividend	42,000
	2,56,000
Less : Balance of Profit & Loss Account as on 31.3.2010	1,00,000
Profits for the year ended 31.3.2010	1,56,000
Half Year's profits = Rs. 1,56,000 × ½	78,000

Assuming transfer to General Reserve is out of profits of the year as a whole, Rs. 20,000 of increase in General Reserve and half of the remaining profits are Capital Profits.

	Rs.
(ii) Capital Profits :	
General Reserve Balance as on 1st April, 2009	4,00,000
Profit & Loss Account Balance as on 1st April, 2009	1,00,000
Half of increase in General Reserve	20,000
Half year's profit after transfer to General Reserve Rs. 78,000 – Rs. 20,000	58,000
	5,78,000
H Ltd.'s share = Rs. 5,78,000 × 90/100	5,20,200
Minority Shareholders' share = Rs. 5,78,000 × 10/100	57,800
(iii) Cost of Control/Capital Reserve :	
Paid up value of 18,000 Equity Shares	1,80,000
H Ltd.'s share of Capital Profits	5,20,200
	7,00,200
Less: Amount paid for 18,000 Equity Shares	6,00,000
Capital Reserve on acquisition	1,00,200
(iv) Minority Interest :	
Paid up value of 2,000 Equity Shares	20,000
Add: 1/10th of Capital Profits	57,800
1/10th of increase in General Reserve	2,000
1/10th of profits after 1st October, 2009 remaining after transfer to General Reserve	5,800
	85,600

Consolidated Balance Sheet of H Ltd. and its subsidiary S Ltd. as at March 31, 2010

Liabilities	*Rs.*	*Rs.*	*Assets*	*Rs.*	*Rs.*
Share Capital :			Sundry Assets :		
Issued & Subscribed :			H Ltd.	33,00,000	
2,00,000 Equity Shares of			S Ltd.	8,56,000	41,56,000
Rs. 10 each, fully paid		20,00,000			
Minority Interest		85,600			
Securities Preimum		2,00,000			
Capital Reserve					
Add: Capital Reserve on acquisition minus Goodwill of S Ltd. (Rs. 1,00,200–Rs. 1,00,000)		200			
General Reserve	10,00,000				
Add : 9/10ths increase in General Reserve in S Ltd. after acquisition (Rs. 20,000 × 9/10)	18,000	10,18,000			
Profit & Loss Account	4,00,000				
Add; 9/10ths of Profits of S Ltd. after acquisition remaining after transfer to General Reserve 9/10 (78,000 – 20,000)	52,200	4,52,200			
Creditors :					
H Ltd.	3,00,000				
S Ltd.	1,00,000	4,00,000			
		41,56,000			41,56,000

Illustration 25:

H Ltd. acquired 80 per cent of both classes of shares in S Ltd. as on 1st April, 2009 at a total cost of Rs. 5,60,000. The balance sheets of both the companies as at 31st March, 2010 were as follows :—

Balance Sheet of H Ltd. as at 31st March, 2010

Liabilities	*Rs.*	*Assets*	*Rs.*
Share Capital Authorised	7,50,000	Plant and Machinery	5,15,000
Issued & Subscribed :		Furniture, Fixtures and Fittings	1,50,000
75,000 Shares of Rs. 10 each	7,50,000	Investments	5,60,000
General Reserve	4,75,000	Stock (*iii*)	1,70,000
Profit and Loss Account (*i*)	4,00,000	Debtors	1,40,000
Creditors (*ii*)	75,000	Cash at Bank	1,65,000
	17,00,000		17,00,000

(*i*) Includes dividend @ 16% per annum from S Ltd. The dividend was for the year ended 31st March, 2009.

(*ii*) Includes Rs. 30,000 for purchases from S Ltd. on which the latter company made a profit of Rs. 7,500.

(*iii*) Includes Rs. 15,000 of stock at cost purchased from S Ltd. part of the Rs. 30,000 purchases mentioned in (*ii*) above.

Balance Sheet of S Ltd. as at 31st March, 2010

Liabilities	Rs.	Assets	Rs.
Share Capital :		Plant and Machinery	1,50,000
1,000 14% Preference Shares of Rs. 100 each, fully paid	1,00,000	Furniture, Fixtures and Fittings	1,35,500
15,000 Equity Shares of Rs. 10 each, fully paid	1,50,000	Stock	1,01,000
General Reserve as on 1st April, 2009	10,000	Debtors	79,000
Profit & Loss Account	1,80,000	Cash at Bank	55,000
Creditors	80,500		
	5,20,500		5,20,500

The balance in Profit and Loss Account of S Ltd. on 1st April, 2009 was Rs. 80,000 out of which dividend @ 16% per annum for full year ended 31st March, 2009 was paid on fully paid equity shares of Rs. 1,50,000. The dividend in respect of preference shares for the year 2009-2010 was still payable as on 31st March, 2010. Ignore dividend tax.

Prepare Consolidated Balance Sheet as at 31st March, 2010.

Solution :

Workings :

	Rs.	Rs.
(i) Capital Profits :		
General Reserve as on 1st April, 2009		10,000
Balance of Profit and Loss Account as on 1st April, 2009	80,000	
Less : Dividend @ 16% on Rs. 1,50,000	24,000	56,000
		66,000
H Ltd.'s share = Rs. 66,000 × 80/100		52,800
Minority shareholders' share = Rs. 66,000 × 20/100		13,200
(ii) Current Profits :		
Balance of Profit and Loss Account as on 31st March, 2010		1,80,000
Less : Balance of Profit & Loss Account as on 1st April, 2009	80,000	
Less : Dividend Paid	24,000	56,000
		1,24,000
Less : Preference Dividend Payable for the year 2009-2010 @ 14% on Rs. 1,00,000		14,000
Amount available for equity shareholders		1,10,000

H Ltd's share of current profits
= Rs. (1,10,000 × 80/100) + Rs. (14,000 × 80/100)
= Rs. 88,000 + Rs. 11,200
= Rs. 99,200

Minority shareholders' share of current profits
= Rs. 1,24,000 – Rs. 99,200 = Rs. 24,800

Out of it, a sum of Rs. 2,800 is for preference dividend.

(iii) Minority Interest :	Rs.	Rs.
Preference Shares :		
Paid up value of 20% preference shares	20,000	
Add : Dividend due thereon @ 14%	2,800	22,800
Equity Shares :		
Paid up value of 20% equity shares	30,000	
Add : 20% of Capital Profits	13,200	
20% of Current Profits after preference dividend	22,000	65,200
		88,000

(iv) Goodwill or Cost of Control :	
Amount paid for all the shares	5,60,000

Less : Dividend @ 16% received for the year ended 31st March, 2009, being a capital receipt Rs. 1,20,000 × 16/100			19,200
			5,40,800
Less : Paid up value of preference shares held		80,000	
Paid up value of equity shares held	1,20,000		
H Ltd.'s share of Capital Profits		52,800	2,52,800
Goodwill on Cost of Control			2,88,000

(*v*) Unrealised profit in respect of stock = Rs. 7,500 × 15,000/30,000 = Rs. 3,750

Consolidated Balance Sheet of H Ltd. and its subsidiary S Ltd. as at 31st March, 2010

Liabilities	*Rs.*	*Rs.*	*Assets*	*Rs.*	*Rs.*
Share Capital :			Goodwill		2,88,000
Authorised		7,50,000	Plant and Machinery :		
Issued & Subscribed :			H Ltd.	5,15,000	
75,000 Shares of Rs. 10 each,			S Ltd.	1,50,000	6,65,000
fully paid		7,50,000	Furniture, Fixtures and Fittings:		
Minority Interest		88,000	H Ltd.	1,50,000	
General Reserve		4,75,000	S Ltd.	1,35,500	2,85,500
Profit and Loss Account :	4,00,000		Stock :		
Less : Dividend of a capital			H Ltd.	1,70,000	
nature wrongly credited			S Ltd.	1,01,000	
earlier	19,200			2,71,000	
	3,80,800		*Less* : Unrealised Profit	3,750	2,67,250
Less : Unrealised Profit			Debtors :		
on stock	3,750		H Ltd.	1,40,000	
	3,77,050		S Ltd.	79,000	
Add : H Ltd.'s share of				2,19,000	
S Ltd.'s profits	99,200	4,76,250	*Less* : Mutual Owing	30,000	1,89,000
Creditors :			Cash at Bank :		
H Ltd.	75,000		H Ltd.	1,65,000	
S Ltd.	80,500		S Ltd.	55,000	2,20,000
	1,55,500				
Less : Mutual Owing	30,000	1,25,500			
		19,14,750			19,14,750

Treatment of Depreciation in Respect of a Change in the Value of a Fixed Asset of the Subsidiary

If the value of a fixed asset of the subsidiary company is changed with retrospective effect after depreciation has been provided for full year, depreciation in respect of increase or decrease in the value of the fixed asset has to be adjusted as a revenue profit or loss.

Illustration 26:

H Ltd. acquired 30,000 equity shares in S Ltd. on 1st October, 2009. On 31st March, 2010 the balance sheet of S Ltd. stood as follows :—

Liabilities	*Rs.*	*Rs.*	*Assets*	*Rs.*	*Rs.*
50,000 Equity Shares of Rs. 10			Land and Buildings, at cost		2,50,000
each, fully paid		5,00,000	Machinery :		
1,000 14% Redeemable Preference			Balance as on		
Shares of Rs. 100 each, fully paid		1,00,000	1st April, 2009	2,50,000	
General Reserve		1,50,000	*Less* : Depreciation	37,500	2,12,500
Profit & Loss Account :			Furniture :		
Balance as on			Cost, *less* depreciation		81,000
1st April, 2009	30,000		Stock, at cost		1,56,500

	Rs.	Rs.		Rs.
Add: Profit for the year ended 31st March, 2010	90,000	1,20,000	Sundry Debtors	1,10,000
Trade Creditors		80,000	Cash at Bank	1,00,000
			Preliminary Expenses	40,000
		9,50,000		9,50,000

As on the date of acquisition, H Ltd. found the Land and Buildings undervalued by Rs. 50,000 and the value of Machinery to be Rs. 2,00,000. In preparing the consolidated balance sheet, it decided to use the proper values of assets and to eliminate Preliminary Expenses. Ascertain Capital Profits, Revenue Profits and Minority Interest.

Solution :

	Rs.
Book value of Machinery as on 1st April, 2009	2,50,000
Less: Depreciation Rs. 37,500 × 6/12	18,750
	2,31,250
Less: Revised value as on 1st October, 2009	2,00,000
Decrease in the value of machinery	31,250
Profit for the year ended 31st March, 2010	90,000
Less: Preference Dividend @ 14% on Rs. 1,00,000	14,000
Profit for the year available to equity shareholders	76,000

Profit for 6 months i.e., upto 1st October, 2009 = Rs. 76,000 × 6/12 = Rs. 38,000.

(i) *Calculation of Capital Profits*

Increase in the value of Land and Buildings		50,000
General Reserve		1,50,000
Profit & Loss Account as on 1st April, 2009		30,000
Current year's profit upto 1st October, 2009		38,000
		2,68,000
Less: Reduction in the value of machinery	31,250	
Preliminary Expenses	40,000	71,250
		1,96,750

Holding Company's share of capital profits

$$= \text{Rs. } 1,96,750 \times \frac{30,000}{50,000} = \text{Rs. } 1,18,050$$

Minority shareholders' share

= Rs. 1,96,750 × Rs. 1,18,050 = Rs. 78,700.

(ii) *Revenue Profits :*

Current year's profit available to equity shareholders after 1st October, 2009	38,000
Add: Depreciation @ 15% for 6 months on the decrease in the value of Machinery = Rs. 31,250 × $\frac{15}{100} \times \frac{6}{12}$	2,343.75
	40,343.75

Holding company's share = Rs. 35,656.25 × $\frac{30,000}{50,000}$ = Rs. 24,206,25

Minority shareholders' share = Rs. 35,656.25 – Rs. 21,393.75 = Rs. 14,262.50

(iii) *Minority Interest :*

	Rs.	Rs.
Paid up value of 1,000 Preference Shares	1,00,000	
Add: Preference Dividend for the current year	14,000	1,14,000
Paid up value of 20,000 Equity Shares	2,00,000	
Share of Capital Profits	78,700	
Share of Revenue Profits	16,137.50	2,94,835.50
		4,08,837.50

Illustration 27:

The following are the balance sheets of H Ltd. and its subsidiary S Ltd. as at 31st March, 2010:—

Liabilities	*H Ltd.* Rs.	*S Ltd.* Rs.	*Assets*	*H Ltd.* Rs.	*S Ltd.* Rs.
Equity Share Capital			Plant and Machinery	3,90,000	1,35,000
Shares of Rs. 10 each, fully paid	6,00,000	2,00,000	Furniture	80,000	40,000
General Reserve	3,40,000	80,000	80% Shares in S Ltd. (at cost)	3,40,000	
Profit & Loss Account	1,00,000	60,000	Stock	1,80,000	1,20,000
Creditors	70,000	35,000	Debtors	50,000	30,000
			Cash at Bank	70,000	50,000
	11,10,000	3,75,000		11,10,000	3,75,000

Additional information :

(*i*) Profit and Loss Account of S Ltd. stood at Rs. 30,000 on 1st April, 2009 whereas General Reserve stood at Rs. 80,000 even on this date.

(*ii*) H Ltd. acquired 80% shares in S Ltd. on 1st October, 2009.

(*iii*) S Ltd.'s Plant and Machinery which stood at Rs. 1,50,000 on 1st April, 2009 was considered worth Rs. 1,80,000 as on 1st October, 2009; this figure is to be considered while consolidating the balance sheets.

You are required to prepare consolidated balance sheet as at 31st March, 2010.

Solution:

Workings:

	Rs.
(*i*) Book value of S Ltd.'s Plant and Machinery as on 1st April, 2009	1,50,000
Less: Book value of Plant and Machinery as on 31st March, 2010	1,35,000
Depreciation for full year	15,000

Rate of depreciation = $\frac{15,000}{1,50,000} \times 100 = 10\%$

Depreciation for six months i.e. up to 30th September, 2009 = Rs. 15,000 × 6/12 = Rs. 7,500

Book value as on 1st October, 2009 = Rs. 1,50,000 – Rs. 7,500 = Rs. 1,42,500

Appreciation made = Rs. 1,80,000 – Rs. 1,42,500 = Rs. 37,500

	Rs.
Book value as on 31st March, 2010	1,35,000
Appreciation	37,500
	1,72,500
Less: Depreciation on Rs. 37,500 for 6 months @ 10% per annum. $\frac{\text{Rs.}37,500 \times 6 \times 10}{100 \times 12}$	1,875
Revised value as on 31 March, 2010	1,70,625

(*ii*) *Capital Profits:*	Rs.
General Revenue	80,000
Profit & Loss Account as on 1st April 2009	30,000
Current years's profit upto 1st October, 2009 = 6/12 (60,000 – 30,000)	15,000
Appreciation in the value of Plant & Machinery	37,500
	1,62,500

H Ltd.'s share = 1,62,500 × 80/100 = Rs. 130,000

Minority shareholders' share = Rs. 1,62,500 – Rs. 1,30,000 = Rs. 32,500

(iii) Cost of Control:

	Rs.	Rs.
Amount paid for 80% shares in S Ltd.		3,40,000
Less:		
Paid up value of 80% shares in S Ltd.	1,60,000	
Add: H Ltd.'s share of capital profits	1,30,000	2,90,000
		50,000

(iv) Revenue Profits:

Profit after 1st October 2009 = Rs. 6/12 (60,000 – 30,000)	15,000
Less: Depreciation in respect of increase in the value of Plant and Machinery for six months	1,875
	13,125

H Ltd.'s share = Rs. $13{,}125 \times \frac{80}{100}$ = Rs. 10,500

Minority shareholders' share = Rs. 13,125 – Rs. 10,500 = Rs. 2,625

(v) Minority Interest:

Paid up value of 20% shares	40,000
Add: Capital Profits	32,500
Revenue Profits	2,625
	75,125

Consolidated Balance Sheet of H Ltd. and its subsidiary S Ltd. as at 31st March, 2010

Liabilities	Rs.	Rs.	*Assets*	Rs.	Rs.
Equity Share Capital :			Goodwill		50,000
Shares of Rs. 10 each, fully paid		6,00,000	Plant & Machinery		
Minority Interest		75,125	H Ltd.	3,90,0000	
General Reserve		3,40,000	S Ltd.	1,70,625	5,60,625
Profit & Loss Account :			Furniture :		
Add: H Ltd.'s	1,00,000		H Ltd.	80,000	
Share in S Ltd.'s Revenue			S Ltd.	40,000	1,20,000
Profits	10,500	1,10,500	Stock :		
Creditors :			H Ltd.	1,80,000	
H Ltd.	70,000		S Ltd.	1,20,000	3,00,000
S Ltd.	35,000	1,05,000	Debtors :		
			H Ltd.	50,000	
			S Ltd.	30,000	80,000
			Cash at Bank :		
			H Ltd.	70,000	
			S Ltd.	50,000	1,20,000
		12,30,625			12,30,625

Illustration 28:

The following are the balance sheets of Sun Ltd. and Moon Ltd. as on 31st March, 2010 :

Liabilities	*Sun Ltd.* Rs.	*Moon Ltd.* Rs.
Equity share capital (Rs. 100 each)	2,50,000	1,00,000
Capital reserve		60,000
General reserve	1,20,000	
Profit and loss account	28,600	18,000
Loan from bank	50,000	
Bills payable (including Rs. 1,500 to Sun Ltd.)		4,200
Creditors	23,550	4,500
	4,72,150	1,86,700

	Rs.	Rs.
Assets		
Building	75,000	90,000
Plant	1,20,000	54,700
Furniture	10,000	5,000
800 shares in Moon Ltd.	1,70,000	—
Stock	70,000	18,000
Debtors	11,000	15,000
Bank	8,450	4,000
Bills receivable (including Rs. 1,500 from Moon Ltd.)	7,700	
	4,72,150	1,86,700

Sun Ltd. acquired 800 shares of Moon Ltd. on 1st July, 2009. Prepare a consolidated balance sheet as at 31st March, 2010 taking into account the following :

(*i*) Creditors of Sun Ltd. include Rs. 6,000 due to Moon Ltd.

(*ii*) On 31st March, 2010, buildings of Moon Ltd. are found undervalued by Rs. 10,000 and the plant of the same company is found overvalued by Rs. 5,000. The new values are to be incorporated.

(*iii*) The balance of profit and loss account of Moon Ltd. Rs. 18,000 represents the profit earned by the company during the year ended 31st March, 2010.

[*C.S. (Inter) June, 1998 Modified*]

Solution :

Consolidated Balance Sheet of Sun Ltd. and its Subsidiariy Moon Ltd. as on 31st March, 2010

Liabilities	*Rs.*	*Rs.*	*Assets*	*Rs.*	*Rs.*
Share Capital			Fixed Assets		
Authorised		?	Goodwill		34,400
Issued and Subscribed			Building :		
2,500 Equity shares of Rs. 100			Sun Ltd.	75,000	
each, fully paid up		2,50,000	Moon Ltd.	1,00,000	1,75,000
Minority Interest		36,600	Plant :		
Reserves and Surplus			Sun Ltd.	1,20,000	
General Reserve		1,20,000	Moon Ltd.	49,700	1,69,700
Profit and Loss Account :			Furniture :		
Sun Ltd.	28,600		Sun Ltd.	10,000	
Add : Share in Moon Ltd.'s			Moon Ltd.	5,000	15,000
revenue profits	10,800	39,400	Current Assets, Loans		
Secured Loan :			and Advances :		
Loan from Bank		50,000	(A) Current Assets		
Current Liabilities and Provisions :			Stock :		
(A) Current Liabilities			Sun Ltd.	70,000	
Bills Payable :			Moon Ltd.	18,000	88,000
Moon Ltd.	4,200		Debtors :		
Less: In favour of Sun Ltd.	1,500	2,700	Sun Ltd.	11,000	
Creditors :			Moon Ltd.	15,000	
Sun Ltd.	23,550			26,000	
Moon Ltd.	4,500		*Less* : Mututal owing	6,000	20,000
	28,050		Bank :		
Less: Mututal owing	6,000	22,050	Sun Ltd.	8,450	
(B) Provisions		Nil	Moon Ltd.	4,000	12,450
			(B) Loans and Advances		
			Bills Receivable :		
			Sun Ltd.	7,700	
			Moon Ltd.	1,500	6,200
		5,20,750			5,20,750

Working Notes :

(i) *Calculation of capital profits* :

	Rs.
Profit for 3 months till 1st July, 2009 = Rs. 18,000 × 3/12	4,500
Capital reserve	60,000
Appreciation in the value of buildings	10,000
	74,500
Less: Decrease in the value of plant	5,000
	69,500

Sun Ltd.'s share = Rs. 69,500 × 80 / 100 = Rs. 55,600

Minority shareholders' share = Rs. 69.500 × 20 / 100 = Rs. 13,900

(ii) *Calculation of revenue profits* :

Profit from 1st July, 2009 to 31st March, 2010 = Rs. 18,000 × 9 / 12 = Rs. 13,500

Sun Ltd.'s share = Rs. 13,500 × 80 / 100 = Rs. 10,800

Minority shareholders' share = Rs. 13,500 × 20 / 100 = Rs. 2,700

(iii) *Calculation of cost of control/goodwill* :

	Rs.	Rs.
Cost of 800 shares acquired by Sun Ltd.		1,70,000
Less : Paid up value of 800 shars	80,000	
Sun Ltd.'s share in capital profits	55,600	1,35,600
		34,400

(iv) *Calculation of minority interest* :

	Rs.
Paid up value of 200 shares	20,000
Add : Share in capital profits	13,900
Share in revenue profits	2,700
	36,600

Illustration 29;

From the following balance sheets and the additional information given thereafter, prepare consolidated balance sheet of H Ltd. and its subsidiary S Ltd. as on 31st March, 2010 :

Balance Sheet as on 31st March, 2010

Liabilities	*H Ltd.* *Rs.*	*S Ltd.* *Rs.*
Equity Share Capital, fully paid shares of Rs. 100 each	12,00,000	4,00,000
12% Preference Share Capital	2,00,000	1,00,000
General Reserve	4,50,000	2,10,000
Profit and Loss Account	2,80,000	1,29,000
Creditors	1,90,000	1,00,000
	23,20,000	9,39,000
Assets		
Land and Building	5,00,000	3,20,000
Plant and Machinery	7,10,000	1,90,000
Furniture and Fittings	1,34,000	85,000
3,000 Equity Shares in S Ltd., purchased on 30.9.2000	5,10,000	—
Stock	2,96,000	2,04,000
Debtors	1,30,000	1,10,000
Cash at Bank	40,000	30,000
	23,20,000	9,39,000

Additional information :

(i) On 1st April, 2009 S Ltd.'s General Reserve and Profit and Loss Account showed balances of Rs. 1,30,000 and Rs. 1,24,000 respectively.

(ii) In October, 2009 S Ltd. declared and paid full year's preference dividend and equity dividend @22 % for the year ended 31st March, 2009. It also paid Corporate Dividend Tax @15%. H Ltd. credited the dividend received by it to its Profit and Loss Account.

(*iii*) Included in Creditors of S Ltd. is a sum of Rs. 30,000 for goods supplied by H Ltd. On 31st March, 2010 half of these goods were lying unsold in S Ltd.'s godown. H Ltd. charged profit @ 25% on cost.

(*iv*) S Ltd. has a contingent liability of Rs. 2,500 in a suit pending in a court of law.

Solution :

Consolidated Balance Sheet of H Ltd. and its Subsidiary S Ltd. as on 31st March, 2010

Liabilities	*Rs.*	*Rs.*	*Assets*	*Rs.*	*Rs.*
Share Capital			Fixed Assets		
Authorised		?	Land and Buildings :		
12,000 Equity Shares of			H Ltd.	5,00,000	
Rs. 100 each, fully paid-up		12,00,000	S Ltd.	3,20,000	8,20,000
12% Preference Share Capital		2,00,000	Plant and Machinery :		
Minority Interest		2,93,750	H Ltd.	7,10,000	
Reserves and Surplus			S Ltd.	1,90,000	9,00,000
Capital Reserve		30,750	Furniture and Fittings :		
General Reserve		4,50,000	H Ltd.	1,34,000	
Profit and Loss Account :			S Ltd.	85,000	2,19,000
H Ltd.	2,80,000		**Current Assets, Loans and Advances :**		
Less : Dividend wrongly credited	66,000		(A) Current Assets		
	2,14,000		Stock :		
Add : Share in S Ltd.'s			H Ltd.	2,96,000	
revenue profit	70,500		S Ltd.	2,04,000	
	2,84,500			5,00,000	
Less : Unrealised profit	3,000	2,81,500	*Less* : Unrealised profit	3,000	4,97,000
Current Liabilities and Provisions :			Debtors :		
(A) Current Liabilities			H Ltd.	1,30,000	
Creditors			S Ltd.	1,10,000	
				2,40,000	
H Ltd.	1,90,000		*Less* : Mutual owing	30,000	2,10,000
S Ltd.	1,00,000		Cash at Bank :		
	2,90,000		H Ltd.	40,000	
Less : Mutual owing	30,000	2,60,000	S Ltd.	30,000	70,000
(B) Provisions		Nil	(B) Loans and Advances		Nil
		27,16,000			27,16,000

Note : There is a contingent liability of S Ltd. amounting to Rs. 2,500 in a law-suit.

Working Notes :

(*i*) *Calculation of revenue profit :*

S Ltd.'s Profit and Loss (Appropriation) Account

	Rs.		*Rs.*
To General Reserve, Rs. 2,10,000 – Rs. 1,30,000	80,000	By Balance b/fd	1,24,000
To Preference Dividend @ 12% on Rs. 1,00,000	12,000	By Net Profit for the year — balancing figure	2,00,000
To Equity Dividend @ 22% on Rs. 4,00,000	88,000		
To Corporate Dividend Tax	15,000		
To Balance c/fd	1,29,000		
	3,24,000		3,24,000

Profit for preacquisition period = Rs. 2,00,000 × 6 / 12 = Rs. 1,00,000
Post-acquisition profit *i.e.* revenue profit = Rs. 2,00,000 – Rs. 1,00,000 = Rs. 1,00,000
Revenue profit after deduction of preference dividend for
6 months = Rs. 1,00,000 – Rs. 6,000 = Rs. 94,000
H Ltd.'s share = Rs. 94,000 × 3,000 / 4,000 = Rs. 70,500
Minority equity shareholders' share = Rs. 94,000 × 1,000 / 4,000 = Rs. 23,500

(*ii*) *Calculation of capital profit* :

	Rs.
General Reserve on 1st April, 2009	1,30,000
Profit and Loss Account on 1st April, 2009	1,24,000
Current year's profit till date of acquisition	1,00,000
	3,54,000
Less : Dividend and Corporate Dividend Tax paid	1,15,000
	2,39,000

(*iii*) *Distribution of capital profit* :

Capital profit	2,39,000
Less : Preference dividend for 6 months to minority shareholders	6,000
Amount available to equity shareholders	2,33,000

H Ltd.'s share = Rs. 2,33,000 × 3 / 4 = Rs. 1,74,750
Minority equity shareholders' share = Rs. 2,33,000 × 1 / 4 = Rs. 58,250

(*iv*) *Calculation of capital reserve on acquisition of shares* :

	Rs.	Rs.
Paid up value of 3,000 equity shares		3,00,000
Add : H Ltd.'s share of capital profit		1,74,750
		4,74,750
Less : Amount paid for shares	5,10,000	
Less : Dividend out of preacquisition profits	66,000	4,44,000
Capital reserve		30,750

(*v*) *Calculation of minority interest* :

12% Preference share capital	1,00,000	
Add : Preference dividend for one year	12,000	1,12,000
Paid up value of 1,000 equity shares	1,00,000	
Add : Share in capital profit	58,250	
Share in revenue profit	23,500	1,81,750
		2,93,750

(*vi*) Unrealised profit = Rs. 15,000 × 25 / 125 = Rs. 3,000

Bonus Shares :

Issue of bonus shares by the subsidiary company increases the number of shares held by the holding company without changing the cost of investment. While preparing a consolidated balance sheet, its treatment will differ depending upon the source from where the bonus shares have been issued by the subsidiary company.

(*i*) *Bonus Shares out of Pre-acquisition Profits.* If the subsidiary company issues bonus shares out of pre-acquisition profits, such an issue will not alter the consolidated balance sheet. Cost of control or capital reserve on acquisition of shares does not change because although the paid up value of the shares held by the holding company increases, the holding company's share in the pre-acquisition is reduced by an identical amount because of transfer of pre-acquisition profits to Equity Share Capital Account. Thus, the total of paid up value of shares held by holding company and share in capital profits of the subsidiary company remains unaltered; the holding company gets the bonus shares without any fresh payment hence the cost of investment also remains unaltered. The result is that there is no change in the cost of control or capital reserve on acquisition of shares. Minority interest also remains the same because although the paid up value of the shares held by minority shareholders increases, minority shareholders' share in the pre-acquisition profits decreases by an identical amount because of the reduction in the pre-acquisition profits due to issue of bonus shares.

Illustration 30:

On 1st April 2009, S Ltd. had a subscribed share capital of Rs. 5,00,000 divided into 50,000 fully paid equity shares of Rs. 10 each. It had accumulated capital and revenue profits to the tune of Rs. 3,90,000 by that date when H Ltd. acquired 80% of its shares for Rs. 9,00,000. The profit earned by S Ltd. amounted to Rs. 2,60,000 for the year ended 31st March, 2010 on which date S Ltd. issued, by way of bonus, one fully paid equity share of Rs. 10 for every five equity shares held out of its pre-acquisition profits.

Calculate as on 31st March, 2010 cost of control and minority interest :

(*i*) just before issue of bonus shares and

(*ii*) immediately after issue of bonus shares.

Solution:

(*i*) *Calculation of cost of control just before issue of bonus shares :*	*Rs.*	*Rs.*
Amount paid for 80% *i.e.* 40,000 shares		9,00,000
Less:		
Paid up value of 40,000 shares	4,00,000	
Add : H Ltd.'s share of pre-acquisition profits		
Rs. 3,90,000 × 80/100	3,12,000	7,12,000
Cost of control		1,88,000
Minority Interest just before issue of bonus shares :		
Paid up value of 10,000 shares		1,00,000
Share in pre-acquisition profits Rs. 3,90,000 × 20/100		78,000
Share in post-acquisition profits Rs. 2,60,000 × 20/100		52,000
		2,30,000

(*ii*) *Calculations immediately after issue of bonus shares:*

Total share capital of the subsidiary company is increased by Rs. 5,00,000 × 1/5 = Rs. 1,00,000

Out of it, H Ltd. gets shares for Rs. 1,00,000 × 80/100 = Rs. 80,000 and the minority shareholders get remaining shares for Rs. 20,000.

Pre-acquisition profits remaining after issue of bonus shares = Rs. 3,90,000 – Rs. 1,00,000 = Rs. 2,90,000.

Cost of Control:		
Amount paid for 40,000 shares		9,00,000
Amount paid for 8,000 bonus shares		Nil
Amount paid for 48,000 shares		9,00,000
Less: Paid up value of 48,000 shares	4,80,000	
Add: H Ltd.'s share in pre-acquisition profits remaining after issue of bonus shares Rs. 2,90,000 × 80/100	2,32,000	7,12,000
Cost of Control		1,88,000
Minority interest:		
Paid up value of 12,000 shares		1,20,000
Share in pre-acquisition profits remaining after issue of bonus shares Rs. 2,90,000 × 20/100		58,000
Share in post acquisition profits Rs 2,60,000 × 20/100		52,000
		2,30,000

Illustration 31:

H Ltd. acquired 30,000 equity shares of Rs. 10 each in S Ltd. on 31st March, 2010. The balance sheets of H Ltd. and S Ltd. as at that date were as under ·

Liabilities	H Ltd. Rs.	S Ltd. Rs.	Assets	H Ltd. Rs.	S Ltd. Rs.
Share Capital :			Machinery	5,80,000	3,00,000
Equity Shares of Rs. 10			Furniture	1,10,000	50,000
each, fully paid	10,00,000	4,00,000	30,000 Shares in		
Securities Premium	2,00,000	—	S Ltd. (at cost)	6,00,000	
General Reserve	5,00,000	3,70,000	Stock	4,43,000	3,80,000
Profit & Loss Account	38,000	1,60,000	Debtors	1,20,000	1,70,000
Creditors	1,65,000	85,000	Cash at Bank	2,00,000	1,15,000
Proposed Dividend	1,50,000	—			
	20,53,000	10,15,000		20,53,000	10,15,000

On 31st March, 2010 the Board of Directors of S Ltd. proposed a dividend of 10% on the share capital of Rs. 4,00,000 and made a bonus issue of one equity share for every four equity shares held using General Reserve. Effect of bonus issue is to be incorporated in the abovementioned balance sheets. Ignore corporate divided tax.

Prepare a consolidated balance sheet as at 31st March, 2010.

Solution :

Working Notes :

	Rs.
(*i*) Balance of General Reserve of S Ltd. as appearing in the Balance Sheet	3,70,000
Less: Amount used for issue of bonus shares = Rs. 4,00,000 × 1/4	1,00,000
Balance remaining after issue of bonus shares	2,70,000
(*ii*) Balance of Profit & Loss Account of S Ltd. as appearing in the Balance Sheet	1,60,000
Less: Proposed Dividend Rs. 4,00,000 × 10/100	40,000
Balance of Profit & Loss Account after proposed dividend	1,20,000
(*iii*) *Capital Profits:*	
General Reserve after issue of bonus shares	2,70,000
Profit & Loss Account after debit for Proposed Dividend	1,20,000
Proposed Dividend	40,000*
	4,30,000

* Proposed Dividend has been shown separately to pinpoint that it is not to be treated like dividend declared out of pre-acquisition profits; it is as good as a part of Profit & Loss Account.

	Rs.
(*iv*) ***Capital Reserve on acquisition of shares:***	
Paid up value of 30,000 + 7,500 = 37,500 shares	3,75,000
Add: H Co.'s share of Capital Profits = Rs. 4,30,000 × 75/100	3,22,500
	6,97,500
Less: Cost of investment	6,00,000
Capital Reserve on acquisition of shares	97,500
(*v*) ***Minority Interest:***	
Paid up value of 10,000 + 2,500 = 12,500 shares	1,25,000
Add: Minority shareholders' share of Capital Profits = Rs. 4,30,000 × 25/100	1,07,500
	2,32,500

Consolidated Balance Sheet of H Ltd. and its subsidiary S Ltd. as at 31st March 2010

Liabilities	Rs.	Assets	Rs.	Rs.
Share Capital :				
Equity Shares of Rs. 10		Machinery:		
each, fully paid	10,00,000	H Ltd.	5,80,000	
Minority Interest	2,32,500	S Ltd.	3,00,000	8,80,000
Capital Reserve	97,500	Furniture :		
Securities Premium	2,00,000	H Ltd.	1,10,000	

	Rs.	Rs.		Rs.	Rs.
General Reserve		5,00,000	S Ltd.	50,000	1,60,000
Profit & Loss Account		38,000	Stock :		
Creditors :			H Ltd.	4,43,000	
H Ltd.	1,65,000		S Ltd.	3,80,000	8,23,000
S Ltd.	85,000	2,50,000	Debtors :		
Proposed Dividend		1,50,000	H Ltd.	1,20,000	
			S Ltd.	1,70,000	2,90,000
			Cash at Bank :		
			H Ltd.	2,00,000	
			S Ltd.	1,15,000	3,15,000
		24,68,000			24,68,000

(ii) *Bonus Shares out of Post-acquisition Profits.* If the subsidiary company issues bonus shares out of post-acquisition profits, it will reduce cost of control or increase capital reserve. It happens because such an issue of bonus shares increases the paid up value of shares held by the holding company without a change in the cost of investment and the holding company's share in pre-acquisition profits.

Such an issue of bonus shares reduces the post-acquisition profits. Hence holding company's share in post-acquisition profits also goes down.

Minority Interest does not change by the issue of such shares. Although minority shareholders' share in post acquisition profits decreases, the paid up value of shares held by the minority shareholders increases by an identical amount. The result is that minority interest remains unchanged.

Illustration 32:

On 31st March, 2008 H Ltd. acquired 70,000 equity shares of S Ltd. for Rs. 8,00,000 when S Ltd.'s summarised balance sheet stood as follows :—

Liabilities	*Rs.*	*Assets*	*Rs.*
Subscribed Share Capital :		Fixed Assets	7,00,000
Fully paid equity shares of		Current Assets	4,30,000
Rs. 10 each	10,00,000		
Profit Prior to Incorporation	20,000		
Profit & Loss Account	40,000		
Creditors	70,000		
	11,30,000		11,30,000

On 31st March, 2010 the balance sheets of the two companies were as follows:—

Liabilities	*H Ltd.* Rs.	*S Ltd.* Rs.	*Assets*	*H Ltd.* Rs.	*S Ltd.* Rs.
Share Capital :			Fixed Assets	52,80,000	15,40,000
Equity Shares of Rs. 10			70,000 shares in S Ltd.		
each, fully paid	30,00,000	10,00,000	(at cost)	8,00,000	—
Securities Premium	6,00,000	—	Current Assets	29,40,000	11,70,000
Profit Prior to					
Incorporation	—	20,000			
	40,00,000	12,70,000			
General Reserve	10,50,000	2,80,000			
Profit & Loss Account	3,70,000	1,40,000			
Creditors	90,20,000	27,10,000		90,20,000	27,10,000

The Board of Directors of S Ltd. made a bonus issue in the ratio of one fully paid equity share of Rs. 10 for every two shares held.

You are required to calculate as on 31st March, 2010 (*i*) Cost of Control/Capital Reserve and (*ii*) Minority Interest and (*iii*) Consolidated Profit & Loss Account in each of the following situations :—

(*a*) Just before issue of bonus shares.

(*b*) Immediately after issue of bonus shares assuming that bonus shares were issued wholly out of post acquisition profits by using General Reserve.

Also prepare a consolidated balance sheet as at 31st March, 2010 after the bonus issue.

Solution :

(*a*) *Before Issue of Bonus Shares:*

(*i*) *Capital Profits :*

		Rs.
Profit Prior to Incorporation		20,000
Profit and Loss Account		40,000*
		60,000

* Pre-acquisition profit as on 31st March, 2008 has remained intact even on 31st March, 2010. In the balance sheet of H Ltd. as on 31st March, 2010 shares in S Ltd. continue to appear at Rs. 8,00,000 which indicates that S Ltd. has not distributed any part of pre-acquisition profits. H Ltd.'s share of Capital Profits = Rs. 60,000 × 70/100 = Rs. 42,000

Minority shareholders' share = Rs. 60,000 × 30/100 = Rs. 18,000

(*ii*) *Revenue Profits :*

General Reserve		12,70,000
Profit & Loss Account (Rs. 2,80,000 – Rs. 40,000)		2,40,000
		15,10,000

H Ltd.'s share = Rs. 15,10,000 × 70/100 = Rs. 10,57,000

Minority shareholders' share = Rs. 15,10,000 × 30/100 = Rs. 4,53,000

(*iii*) *Cost of Control :*

Amount paid for 70% shares		8,00,000
Less: Paid up value of 70,000 shares	Rs. 7,00,000	
H Ltd.'s share of Capital Profits	Rs. 42,000	7,42,000
		58,000

(*iv*) *Minority Interest :*

Paid up value of 30,000 shares	3,00,000
Share in Capital Profits	18,000
Share in Revenue Profits	4,53,000
	7,71,000

(*v*) *Consolidated Profit & Loss Account :*

H Ltd.	10,50,000
Add: H Ltd.'s share in revenue profits of S Ltd.	10,57,000
	21,07,000

(*b*) *After issue of Bonus Shares :*

(*i*) *Capital Profits*

Profit Prior to Incorporation	20,000
Profit and Loss Account	40,000
	60,000

H Ltd.'s share = Rs. 60,000 × 70/100 = Rs. 42,000

Minority shareholders' share = Rs. 60,000 × 30/100 = Rs. 18,000

(*ii*) *Revenue Profits :*

General Reserve	Rs. 12,70,000	
Less: Amount used for issue of bonus shares = Rs. 10,00,000 × 1/2	Rs. 5,00,000	7,70,000
Profit & Loss Account (Rs. 2,80,000 – Rs. 40,000)		2,40,000
		10,10,000

H Ltd.'s share = Rs. 10,10,000 × 70/100 = Rs. 7,07,000

Minority shareholders' share = Rs. 10,10,000 × 30/100 = Rs. 3,03,000

	Rs.
(iii) *Capital Reserve on acquisition of shares :*	
Paid up value of 70,000 + 35,000 = 1,05,000 shares	10,50,000
Add : H Ltd.'s share of Capital Profits	42,000
	10,92,000
Less : Amount paid for shares of S Ltd.	8,00,000
Capital Reserve	2,92,000
(iv) *Minority Interest :*	
Paid up value of 30,000 + 15,000 = 45,000 shares	4,50,000
Share in Capital Profits	18,000
Share in Reserve Profits	3,03,000
	7,71,000
(v) *Consolidated Profit & Loss Account :*	
H Ltd.	10,50,000
Add : H Ltd.'s share in Revenue Profits	7,07,000
	17,07,000

Consolidated Balance Sheet of H Ltd. and its subsidiary S Ltd. as at 31st March, 2010

Liabilities	*Rs.*	*Rs.*	*Assets*	*Rs.*	*Rs.*
Share Capital :					
Equity Shares of Rs. 10 each,			Fixed Assets:		
fully paid		30,00,000	H Ltd.	52,80,000	
Minority Interest		7,71,000	S Ltd.	15,40,000	68,20,000
Capital Reserve		2,92,000	Current Assets :		
Securities Premium		6,00,000	H Ltd.	29,40,000	
General Reserve		40,00,000	S Ltd.	11,70,000	41,10,000
Profit & Loss Account :					
H Ltd.	10,50,000				
Add: Share in S Ltd.	7,07,000	17,57,000			
Creditors :					
H Ltd.	3,70,000				
S Ltd.	1,40,000	5,10,000			
		1,09,30,000			1,09,30,000

Illustration 33:

The balance sheets of H Ltd. and its subsidiary S Ltd. as on 31st March, 2010 are as follows :

Liabilities	*H Ltd.* *Rs.*	*S Ltd.* *Rs.*	*Assets*	*H Ltd.* *Rs.*	*S Ltd.* *Rs.*
13% Preference Share Capital		2,00,000	Freehold Premises	7,00,000	1,00,000
			Machinery	8,30,000	1,20,000
Equity Share Capital			Furniture and fittings	2,10,000	67,100
(Fully paid shares of			Investment in 12,000		
Rs. 10 each)	10,00,000	2,10,000	equity shares of		
Revaluation Reserve		30,000	S Ltd. on 1.4.2009	1,95,000	
General Reserve	6,80,000	26,000	Stock	4,72,000	80,400
Profit and Loss Account	7,10,000	1,10,000	Debtors	2,50,000	50,600
Creditors	2,20,000	68,300	Cash at Bank	1,53,000	26,200
	28,10,000	4,44,300		28,10,000	4,44,300

The following additional information is provided to you :

(*a*) Profit and Loss Account of H Ltd. includes Rs. 12,000 received from S Ltd. in October, 2009 as interim dividend.

(*b*) On 1st April, 2009 S Ltd.'s General Reserve and Profit and Loss Account showed balances of Rs. 66,000 and Rs. 86,500. S Ltd. earned a profit of Rs. 60,750 for the year ended 31st

March, 2010 out of which it paid interim dividend of Rs. 15,000 and corporate dividend tax Rs. 2,250.

(c) In January, 2010 S Ltd. made an upward revision of the book value of its Freehold Premises by Rs. 30,000 crediting the amount to Revaluation Reserve.

(d) In February, 2010 S Ltd. issued fully paid shares amounting to Rs. 60,000 out of pre-acquisition profits, giving two shares for every five shares held. The company has used only General Reserve for the purpose. Receipt of the bonus shares by H Ltd. has not been recorded in the abovementioned balance sheet of H Ltd.

Prepare a consolidated balance sheet of H Ltd. and its subsidiary S Ltd. as on 31st March, 2010. Show all your working notes clearly, preparing S Ltd.'s General Reserve and Profit and Loss Account also.

Solution:

Consolidated Balance Sheet of H Ltd. and its subsidiary S Ltd. as at 31st March, 2010

Liabilities	*Rs.*	*Rs.*	*Aseets*	*Rs.*	*Rs.*
Share Capital			**Fixed Assets**		
Authorised		?	Freehold Premises		
Subscribed:			H Ltd.	7,00,000	
13% Preference Share Capital		2,00,000	S Ltd.	1,00,000	8,00,000
Equity Share Capital:			Machinery:		
1,00,000 Equity Shares of			H Ltd.	8,30,000	
Rs. 10 each, fully paid-up		10,00,000	S Ltd.	1,20,000	9,50,000
Minority Interest		75,200	Furniture and Fittings:		
Reserves and Surplus:			H Ltd.	2,10,000	
Capital Reserve		71,000	S Ltd.	67,100	2,77,100
General Reserve		6,80,000	**Current Assets, Loans and Advances:**		
Profit and Loss Account			(A) Current Assets		
H Ltd.	7,10,000		Stock:		
Add: H Ltd.'s share in			H Ltd.	4,72,000	
S Ltd.'s revenue profit	34,800	7,44,800	S Ltd.	80,400	5,52,400
Current Liabilities and			Debtors:		
Provisions:			H Ltd.	2,50,000	
(A) Current Liabialities			S Ltd.	50,600	3,00,600
Creditors:			Cash at Bank:		
H Ltd.	2,20,000		H Ltd.	1,53,000	
S Ltd.	68,300	2,88,300	S Ltd.	26,200	1,79,200
(B) Provisions		Nil	(B) Loans and Advances		Nil
		30,59,300			30,59,300

Working Notes:

(i) *Calculation of equity shares in S Ltd. held by H Ltd.*:

	Rs.
Number of shares purchased on 1.4.2009	12,000
Add: Bonus shares received in the ratio of 2 shares for every 5 shares held, 2/5 × 12,000	4,800
	16,800

Out of 21,000 shares of S Ltd., H Ltd. holds 16,800 shares.

Thus, H Ltd. holds 80% shares in S Ltd.

(ii) *Dr.* **S Ltd.'s General Reserve** *Cr.*

	Rs.		*Rs.*
To Bonus to Equity Shareholders	60,000	By Balance b/fd	66,000
To Balance c/d	26,000	By Profit and Loss Account	

	Rs.		Rs.
		— balancing figure	20,000
	86,000		86,000
		By Balance b/d	26,000

Dr. **S Ltd.'s Profit and Loss Account** Cr.

	Rs.		Rs.
To Interim Dividend	15,000	By Balance b/fd	86,500
To Corporate Dividend Tax	2,250	By Net Profit for the year	60,750
To General Reserve — balancing figure	20,000		
To Balance c/d	1,10,000		
	1,47,250		1,47,250
		By Balance b/d	1,10,000

Calculation of undistributed revenue profit :

	Rs.	Rs.
Net profit for the year		60,750
Less : Interim dividend paid	15,000	
Corporate dividend tax paid @ 10%	2,250	17,250
		43,500

S Ltd.'s share = Rs. 43,500 × 80 / 100 = Rs. 34,800
Minority shareholders' share = Rs. 43,500 – Rs. 34,800 = Rs. 8,700

(iii) *Calculation of capital profits :*

General reserve on 1.4.2009	66,000	
Less : Bonus issue	60,000	6,000
Profit and Loss Account on 1.4.2009		86,500
Upward revision of Freehold Premises		30,000
		1,22,500

H Ltd.'s share = Rs. 1,22,500 × 80 / 100 = Rs. 98,000
Minority shareholders share = Rs. 1,22,500 – Rs. 98,000 = Rs. 24,500

(iv) *Calculation of capital reserve on acquisition* :

Paid up value of 16,800 shares held by H Ltd.	1,68,000
H Ltd.'s share in capital profits	98,000
	2,66,000
Amount paid for the shares	1,95,000
	71,000

(v) *Calculation of minority interest* :

Paid up value of 4,200 shares	42,000
Add : Share in revenue profit	8,700
Share in Capital profit	24,500
	75,200

Illustration 34:

The balance sheets of H Ltd. and S Ltd. as on 31st March, 2010 are as follows :

Liabilities	*H Ltd.* Rs.	*S Ltd.* Rs.	*Assets*	*H Ltd.* Rs.	*S Ltd.* Rs.
Equity Share Capital (Fully paid shares of Rs. 100 each)	9,00,000	4,00,000	Goodwill	70,000	60,000
			Land and Buildings	6,00,000	2,60,000
15% Preference Share Capital	3,00,000	40,000	Plant and Machinery	3,30,000	1,80,000
General Reserve as on 1.4.2009	2,00,000	1,20,000	Investments :		
Profit and Loss Account	2,80,000	1,80,000	3,000 Equity Shares in S Ltd. purchased on 30.9.2009	4,80,000	—
Bills Payable	—	40,000			
Creditors	1,60,000	1,00,000	Stock	2,00,000	1,80,000
			Debtors	40,000	1,50,000
			Cash at Bank	1,20,000	40,000
			Preliminary Expenses	—	10,000
	18,40,000	8,80,000		18,40,000	8,80,000

The following informationis also given to you :-

(*i*) 15% dividend on both types of shares was paid by S Ltd. in October, 2009 for the year ended 31st March, 2009. Tax on Distributed Profits @ 15% was also paid in the same month. H Ltd. credited the dividend received to its Profit and Loss Account.

(*ii*) S Ltd.'s Plant and Machinery Account showed a balance of Rs. 2,00,000 on 1st April, 2009. At the time of purchase of shares in S Ltd., H Ltd. revalued S Ltd.'s plant and machinery upward by Rs. 1,00,000.

(*iii*) There was a bonus issue of equity shares amounting to Rs. 40,000 out of post-acquisition profits by S Ltd. which has not been recorded in the books of account as yet.

(*iv*) Credit balance of Profit and Loss Account on 1st April, 2010 was Rs. 1,09,900.

(*v*) Included in creditors of S Ltd. are Rs. 40,000 for goods supplied by H Ltd. Also included in S Ltd.'s stock are goods of Rs. 16,000 which were supplied by H Ltd. at a profit of 25% on sales.

Prepare a Conslidated Balance Sheet of H Ltd. and its subsidiary S Ltd. as on 31st March, 2010 giving working notes. [*Adapted B.Com.(Hons.) Delhi, 1998*]

Solution :

Consolidated Balance Sheet of H Ltd. and its Subsidiary S Ltd. as on 31st March, 2010

Liabilities	*Rs.*	*Rs.*	*Assets*	*Rs.*	*Rs.*
Share Capital :			Fixed Assets		
Equity Share Capital :			Land and Buildings		
9,000 Equitys Shares of			H Ltd.	6,00,000	
Rs. 100 each, fully paid-up		9,00,000	S Ltd.	2,60,000	8,60,000
Preference Share Capital		3,00,000	Plant and Machinery		
Minority Interest		2,36,250	H Ltd.	3,30,000	
Reserves and Surplus			S Ltd.	2,75,000	6,05,000
Capital Reserve	1,32,750		Current Assets, Loans		
Less : Goodwill	1,30,000	2,750	and Advances :		
General Reserve		2,00,000	(A) Current Assets		
Profit and Loss Account			Stock		
Balance b/fd	2,80,000		H Ltd.	2,00,000	
Less : Capital receipt			S Ltd.	1,80,000	
wrongly credited	45,000			3,80,000	
	2,35,000		*Less* : Unrealised Profit	4,000	3,76,000
Add : Share in S Ltd.'s			Debtors		
revenue profits	21,000		H Ltd.	40,000	
	2,56,000		S Ltd.	1,50,000	
Less : Unrealised profit	4,000	2,52,000		1,90,000	
Current Liabilities and			*Less* : Mutual owing	40,000	1,50,000
Provisions :			Cash at Bank		
(A) Current Liabilities			H Ltd.	1,20,000	
Bills Payable – S Ltd.		40,000	S Ltd.	40,000	1,60,000
Creditors			(B) Loans and Advances		Nil
H Ltd.	1,60,000				
S Ltd.	1,00,000				
	2,60,000				
Less : Mututal owing	40,000	2,20,000			
(B) Provisions		Nil			
		21,51,000			21,51,000

Working Notes :

(*i*) *Calculation of revenue profits :*

S Ltd.'s Profit and Loss Account

Dr.			*Cr.*
	Rs.		*Rs.*
To Preference Dividend		By Balance b/fd	1,09,900
— 15% of Rs. 40,000	6,000	By Net Profit for the year	
To Equity Dividend		— balancing figure	1,46,000
— 15% of Rs. 4,00,000	60,000		
To Tax on Distributed Profits			
— 15% of Rs. 66,000	9,900		
To Balance c/fd	1,80,000		
	2,55,900		2,55,900

Depreciation provided on Plant and Machinery
= Rs. 2,00,000 – Rs. 1,80,000 = Rs. 20,000

	Rs.	*Rs.*
Hence, rate of depreciation = $\frac{20,000}{2,00,000} \times 100 = 10$		
Profit earned after 30th September, 2009 = Rs. 1,46,000 × 6 / 12		73,000
Less : Additional depreciation on Plant and Machinery @ 10% per annum for 6 months on Rs. 1,00,000 = Rs. 1,00,000 × 10/100 × 6/12	5,000	
Bonus issue	40,000	45,000
Revenue profit		28,000
H Ltd.'s share = 75% of Rs. 28,000		21,000
Minority interest = Rs. 28,000 – Rs. 21,000		7,000

(*ii*) *Calculation of captial profits* :

Profit and Loss Account as on 1st April, 2009	1,06,600	
Less : Dividend paid, Rs. 6,000 + Rs. 60,000	66,000	
Tax paid	6,600	
Preliminary Expeneses	10,000	82,600
		24,000
Add: General Reserve as on 1st April, 2009	1,20,000	
Profit earned till 30th September, 2009		73,000
Profit on revaluation of Plant and Machinery		1,00,000
Capital profit		3,17,000

H Ltd.'s share = 75% of Rs. 3,17,000 = Rs. 2,37,750
Minority Interest = 25% of Rs. 3,17,000 = Rs. 79,250

(*iii*) *Calculation of cost of control / capital reserve* :

Paid-up value of 3,300 equity shares		3,30,000
Add: Share in capital profits, [Working Note (*ii*)]		2,37,750
		5,67,750
Amount paid to acquire the equity shares	4,80,000	
Less : Dividend received out of pre-acquisition profits		45,000
		4,35,000

Capital Reserve = Rs. 5,67,750 – Rs. 4,35,000 = Rs. 1,32,750

(*iv*) *Calculation of minority interest* :

Paid-up value of preeference shares	40,000
Paid-up value of 1,100 equity shares	1,10,000
Share in revenue profits, [Working Note (*i*)]	7,000
Share in Capital profits, [Working Note (*ii*)]	79,250
	2,36,250

(*v*) Unrealised profit = Rs. 16,000 × 25 / 100 = Rs. 4,000

Illustration 35:

The balance sheets of Sun Ltd. and Moon Ltd. as on 31.3.2010 are given below:

Liabilities	*Sun Ltd.* *Rs.*	*Moon Ltd.* *Rs.*	*Assets*	*Sun Ltd.* *Rs.*	*Moon Ltd.* *Rs.*
Share Capital			Fixed Assets	44,000	84,000
Rs. 10 each,			Investments in		
fully paid up	1,20,000	1,00,000	Moon Ltd :		
General Reserve	20,000	36,000	8,000 shares		
Profit and Loss A/c	12,000	20,000	@ Rs. 11 each	88,000	—
Bills Payable	2,000	5,000	Stock in trade	10,000	40,000
Sundry Creditors	4,000	7,000	Sundry Debtors	6,000	15,000
			Cash at Bank	6,000	13,000
			Bills receivable	4,000	16,000
	1,58,000	1,68,000		1,58,000	1,68,000

Contingent liability of Sun Ltd. : Bills discounted not yet matured, Rs. 2,500.

Sun Ltd. purchased the share on 1.4.2007. When the shares were purchased, General Reserve and Profit and Loss Account of Moon Ltd. stood at Rs. 30,000 and Rs. 16,000 respectively. Dividends have been paid @10% every year after acquisition of shares, first dividend being paid out of preacquisition profits. No dividend has been proposed for 2009-2010 as yet and no provision need be made in consolidated balance sheet. Sun Ltd. has credited all dividends received to Profit and Loss Account.

On 31.3.2010, Moon Ltd. declared bonus shares @1 fully paid shares for every 5 shares held. However, no effect has been given to bonus shares in the above accounts. The bonus was declared out of profits earned prior to 1.4.2007 from General Reserve.

When the shares were purchased agreed valuation of fixed assets of Moon Ltd. was Rs. 1,08,000. No effect has been given with regard to revaluation of fixed assets in the abovementioned accounts. Depreciation has been charged @10% p.a. on straight line method on the book value as on 1.4.2007; there has been no addition or sale since then.

Every year a sum of Rs. 2,000 has been transfered out of current profits to General Reserve.

Bills receivable of Sun Ltd. include Rs. 2,000 due to Moon Ltd. whereas Sundry Debtors of Moon Ltd. include Rs. 4,000 due from Sun Ltd. It is found that Sun Ltd. has remitted a cheque of Rs. 2,000, which has not yet been recieved by Moon Ltd.

Prepare consolidated balance sheet as at 31.3.2010 of Sun Ltd., and its subsidiary.

[*Adapted C.A.(Final) May, 2000*]

Solution :

Working Notes :

(*i*) Book value of fixed assets on 31.3.2010 = Rs. 84,000

Depreciation has been provided on straight line basis @10% p.a. on book value as on 1.4.2007.

Hence, book value of fixed assets on 1.4.2007 = Rs. 84,000 × 100/70 = Rs. 1,20,000

Fixed assets are revalued on 1.4.2007 at Rs. 1,08,000.

Hence, loss on revaluation of fixed assets = Rs. (1,20,000 – 1,08,000) = Rs. 12,000

Excess depreciation provided @105 p.a. for three years = Rs. 12,000 × $\frac{10}{100}$ × 3 = Rs. 3,600

(*ii*) *Capital Profits* :

	Rs.	Rs.
General Reserve on 1.4.2007	30,000	
Less : Bonus shares =1/5 of Rs. 1,00,000	20,000	10,000
Profit and Loss Account on 1.4.2007	16,000	
Less : First dividend, 10% of Rs. 1,00,000	10,000	6,000
		16,000

	Rs.	Rs.
Less : Loss on revaluation of fixed assets as per W.N. (*i*)		12,000
		4,000

Sun Ltd.'s share = 80% of Rs, 4,000 = Rs. 3,200

Minority shareholders' share = 20% of Rs. 4,000 = Rs. 800

(*iii*) *Revenue Profits :*

	Rs.	Rs.
Balance of Profit and Loss Account on 31.3.2010, as given		20,000
Less : Balance on 1.4.1997 minus dividend for 2007-08, Rs. 16,000 – Rs. 10,000		6,000
		14,000
Add : Excess depreciation on fixed assets as per W.N. (*i*)		3,600
Add : Increase in General Reserve since date of acquisition		6,000
		23,600

Sun Ltd.'s share = 80% of Rs. 23,600 = Rs. 18,880

Minority shareholders' share = 20% of Rs. 23,600 = Rs. 4,720

(*iv*) *Cost of control / capital reserve on acquisition of shares* :

Paid up value of shares acquired on 1.4.2007		80,000
Add : Bonus shares = 1/5th of Rs. 80,000		16,000
Add : Share in capital profits as per W.N. (*ii*)		3,200
		99,200
Less : Cost of shares	88,000	
Less : Dividend out of pre-acquisition profits	8,000	80,000
Capital reserve on acquisition of shares		19,200

(*v*) *Minority interest* :

Paid up value of shares held before bonus issue, 20% of Rs. 1,00,000	20,000
Add : Bonus shares, 1/5th of Rs. 20,000	4,000
Add : Share in capital profits as per W.N. (*ii*)	800
Add : Share in revenue profits as per W.N. (*iii*)	4,720
	29,520

(*vi*) *Sun Ltd.'s Profit and Loss Account* :

Balance on 31.3.2010, as given	12,000
Less : Dividend wrongly credited	8,000
Add : Share in Moon Ltd.'s revenue profits as per W.N. (*iii*)	18,880
	22,880

(*vii*) Bills Payable :

Sun Ltd.	2,000
Moon Ltd.	5,000
	7,000
Less : Mutual indebtedness	2,000
	5,000

(*ix*) Sundry Debtors :

Sun Ltd.	6,000
Moon Ltd.	15,000
	21,000
Less : Mutual indebtedness	2,000
	19,000
Less : Cash in transit	2,000
	17,000

(*x*) Bills Receivable :

Sun Ltd.	4,000
Moon Ltd.	16,000
	20,000
Less : Mutual indebtedness	2,000
	18,000

	Rs.	Rs.
(*xi*) Fixed Assets :		
Sun Ltd.		44,000
Moon Ltd.	84,000	
Less : Loss on revaluation	12,000	
	72,000	
Add : Excess depreciation	3,600	75,600
		1,19,600

Consolidated Balance Sheet of Sun Ltd. and its subsidiary Moon Ltd. as at 31st March, 2010

Liabilities	*Rs.*	*Assets*	*Rs.*	*Rs.*
Share Capital :		Fixed Assets, W.N. (*xi*)		1,19,600
Authorised	?	Current Assets, Loans and Advances		
Issued and subscribed :		A) Current Assets		
12,000 shares of Rs. 10 each,		Stock		
fully paid up	1,20,000	Sun Ltd.	10,000	
Minority Interest, W.N.(v)	29,520	Moon Ltd.	40,000	50,000
Reserves and Surplus		Sundry Debtors, W.N. (*ix*)		17,000
Capital Reserve	19,200	Cash at Bank:		
General Reserve	20,000	Sun Ltd.	6,000	
Profit and Loss Account, W.N. (*vi*)	22,880	Moon Ltd	13,000	19,000
Current Liabilities and Provisions		Cash in transit		2,000
A) Current Liabilities		B) Loans and Advances		
Bills Payable, W.N. (*vii*)	5,000	Bills receivable, W.N. (*x*)		18,000
Sundry Creditors, W.N. (*viii*)	9,000			
B) Provisiions	Nil			
	2,25,600			2,25,600

Contingent Liabilities of Sun Ltd. : Bills discounted but not yet matured, Rs. 1,000.

Note : As regards bills receivable, one may take total bills receivable of Sun Ltd. as accepted by Moon Ltd. as Rs. 2,000 out of which Rs. 1,500 have been discounted. If this assumption is made only Rs. 500 will be deducted as mutual indebtedness regarding bills receivable and bills payable. Consequently net bills receivable will be Rs. 19,500 while net bills payable will be Rs. 6,500 and the balance sheet total will be Rs. 2,27,100.

Successive Purchases of Shares :

So far, we have dealt with cases where the holding company purchases shares of the subsidiary company once only. Actually, a company may make a succession of purchases of the shares of another company till it acquires the status of the holding company. Also, even though a company may already be enjoying controlling interest, it may still buy more shares of its subsidiary. Where a holding company has purchased shares of the subsidiary company more than once, the cost of control will have to be calculated by taking into account the cost of shares acquired on different dates and the holding company's share of capital profits of the subsidiary company on those different dates.

Illustration 36:

On 1st April, 2008 S Ltd. had an issued and subscribed share capital of Rs. 5,00,000 divided into 50,000 fully paid equity shares of Rs. 10 each. H Ltd. made a succession of purchases of the shares of S Ltd. as detailed below:—

Date of purchase	*No. of shares purchased* Rs.	*Amount paid for share* Rs.	*S Ltd.'s accumulated profits on the date of purchase* Rs.
1st April, 2008	20,000	2,90,000	1,70,000
1st April, 2009	10,000	1,60,000	2,00,000
1st April, 2010	5,000	1,05,000	2,40,000

Calculate Cost of Control as on different dates of purchases.

Solution:

	Rs.	Rs.
1st April, 2008		
Amount paid for 20,000 shares		2,90,000
Less : Paid up value of 20,000 shares	2,00,000	
H Ltd.'s share in S Ltd.'s Capital Profits		
$= \text{Rs. } 1{,}70{,}000 \times \frac{20{,}000}{50{,}000}$	68,000	2,68,000
Cost of Control		22,000
1st April, 2009		
Amount paid for additional 10,000 shares		1,60,000
Less : Paid up value of 10,000 shares	1,00,000	
H Ltd.'s share in S Ltd.'s Capital Profits		
for 10,000 shares $= \text{Rs. } 2{,}00{,}000 \times \frac{10{,}000}{50{,}000}$	40,000	1,40,000
Cost of Control		20,000
Add: Earlier Cost of Control		22,000
Total Cost of Control		42,000
1st April, 2010		
Amount paid for additional 5,000 shares		1,05,000
Less : Paid up value of 5,000 shares	50,000	
H Ltd.'s share in S Ltd.'s Capital Profits for		
5,000 shares $= \text{Rs. } 2{,}40{,}000 \times \frac{5000}{50{,}000}$	24,000	74,000
Cost of Control		31,000
Add: Earlier Cost of Control		42,000
Total Cost of Control		73,000

Disposal of Shares

Holding Company may dispose of some of the shares held by it in the subsidiary company. If there is a loss on disposal, it will be debited to cost of control. On the other hand, if there is a profit on sale, it may be credited to either cost of control or Investment Fluctuation Reserve. Minority interest and cost of control will be calculated on the basis of shares left with the holding company on the date of consolidation.

Illustration 37:

On 1st April, 2008 H Ltd. purchased 85% equity shares of S Ltd. for Rs. 2,60,000 when S Ltd.'s accumulated reserves and profits amounted to Rs. 70,000. On 31st March, 2010 the summarised balance sheets of H Ltd. and S Ltd. stood as follows :—

Liabilities	*H Ltd.* *Rs.*	*S Ltd.* *Rs.*	*Assets*	*H Ltd.* *Rs.*	*S Ltd.* *Rs.*
Equity Shares of Rs. 10			Fixed Assets	3,05,500	1,87,000
each, fully paid	5,00,000	2,00,000	17,000 Shares in S Ltd.		
General Reserve	1,20,000	90,000	at cost	2,60,000	—
Profit & Loss Account	70,000	30,000	Current Assets	2,20,000	1,90,000
Creditors	95,500	57,000			
	7,85,500	3,77,000		7,85,500	3,77,000

On 31st March, 2010 H Ltd. disposed of 1,000 shares for Rs. 20,000. After taking into account this sale of shares, prepare consolidated balance sheet as at 31st March, 2010.

Solution :

Working Notes :

(*i*) *Cost of Control :*

	Rs.	Rs.
Cost of 17,000 shares		2,60,000
Less: Sale proceeds of 1,000 shares		20,000
Cost of 16,000 shares		2,40,000
Less: Paid up value of 16,000 shares	1,60,000	
H Ltd.'s share in capital profits = Rs. 70,000 × $\frac{16,000}{20,000}$	56,000	2,16,000
Cost of Control		24,000

(*ii*) *Current Assets of H Ltd :*

	Rs.
Balance as given	2,20,000
Add: Sale proceeds of shares	20,000
	2,40,000

(*iii*) *Minority Interest :*

	Rs.
Paid up value of 4,000 shares	40.000
Share in General Reserve = Rs. 90,000 × $\frac{4,000}{20,000}$	18,000
Share in Profit & Loss Account = Rs. 30,000 × $\frac{4,000}{20,000}$	6,000
	64,000

(*iv*) *Revenue Reserve*

	Rs.
General Reserve as on 31st March, 2010	90,000
Profit & Loss Account as on 31st March, 2010	30,000
	1,20,000
Less : Accumulated reserves and profits as on the date of acquisition	70,000
	50,000

H Ltd.'s share = Rs. 50,000 × $\frac{16,000}{20,000}$ Rs. 40,000

Consolidated Balance Sheet of H Ltd. and its subsidiary S Ltd. as at 31st March, 2010

Liabilities	*Rs.*	*Assets*	*Rs.*	*Rs.*
Share Capital :		Goodwill		24,000
Fully paid Equity share of		Other Fixed Assets:		
Rs. 10 each	5,00,000	H Ltd.	3,05,500	
Minority Interest	64,000	S Ltd.	1,87,000	4,92,500
General Reserve	1,20,000	Current Assets:		
Profit & Loss Account :		H Ltd.	2,40,000	

	Rs.	Rs.		Rs.	Rs.
H Ltd.	70,000		S Ltd.	1,90,000	4,30,000
Shares in S Ltd.	40,000	1,10,000			
Creditors :					
H Ltd.	95,500				
S Ltd.	57,000	1,52,500			
		9,46,500			9,46,500

Illustration 38:

The following are the Balance Sheets of H Ltd. and S Ltd. as at 31st march, 2010:

Liabilities	*H Ltd.*	*S Ltd.*
	Rs.	*Rs.*
Equity Share Capital (Rs. 10 each)	10,00,000	7,00,000
General Reserve	2,00,000	3,00,000
Profit and Loss Account	3,00,000	3,00,000
Current Liabilities	5,00,000	9,00,000
	20,00,000	22,00,000
Assets		
Fixed Assets	8,00,000	9,00,000
Investments in S Ltd.	5,00,000	—
Current Assets	7,00,000	13,00,000
	20,00,000	22,00,000

The following further information is furnished :

(1) H Ltd. acquired 30,000 shares in S Ltd. on 1.4.2009 when Reserves and Profit and Loss Position was as follows:
   (*a*) General Reserve—Rs. 5,00,000
   (*b*) Profit and Loss Account—Rs. 2,00,000

(2) On 1.10.2009, S Ltd. issued 2 shares for every 5 shares held, as bonus shares at a face value of Rs. 10 per share. No entry is made in the books of H Ltd. for the receipt of these bonus shares.

(3) On 30.6.2009, S Ltd. declared a dividend, out of pre-acquisition profits @ 20% and H Ltd. credited the receipt of dividend to its profit and loss account. Assume that there was no dividend tax in force.

(4) S Ltd. owed H Ltd. Rs. 1,20,000 for purchase of stock from H Ltd. The entire stock is held by S Ltd. on 31.3.2010. H Ltd. made a profit of 20% on cost.

(5) H Ltd. transferred a machinery to S Ltd. for Rs. 1,00,000. The book value of machine to H Ltd. was Rs. 75,000. Prepare consolidated balance sheet as at 31st March, 2010.

[*Adapted C.A.* (*Final*)]

Solution :

Working Notes :

(*i*) *In S Ltd.'s Books*

Profit & Loss Account

	Rs.		Rs.
To Dividend on Rs. 5,00,000 @ 20%	1,00,000	By Balance b/fd	2,00,000
To Balance c/d	3,00,000	By Net Profit for the year 2009-2010 (Balancing figure)	2,00,000
	4,00,000		4,00,000
		By Balance b/d	3,00,000

General Reserve

	Rs.		*Rs.*
To Bonus to Equity Shareholders Account Rs. 5,00,000 × 2/5	2,00,000	By Balance b/fd	5,00,000
To Balance c/d	3,00,000		
	5,00,000		5,00,000
		By Balance b/d3,00,000	

(*ii*) *Capital Profits:*

	Rs.
General Reserve as on 1.4.2009 less amount used for issue of bonus shares	3,00,000
Profit & Loss Account as on 1.4.2009 less amount used for payment of dividend	1,00,000
	4,00,000
H Ltd.'s share = Rs. 4,00,000 × 60/100	2,40,000

Minority shareholders' share = Rs. 4,00,000 – Rs, 2,40,000 = Rs. 1,60,000

(*iii*) *Capital Reserve on acquisition of shares :*

Paid up value of 60% shares in S Ltd.		4,20,000
Add: H Ltd.'s share of Capital Profits		2,40,000
		6,60,000
Less: Amount paid for acquiring shares	5,00,000	
Less: Dividend on Rs. 3,00,000 @ 20%, being a capital receipt	60,000	4,40,000
Capital Reserve		2,20,000

(*iv*) *Minority Interest :*

Paid up value of 40% shares in S Ltd.	2,80,000
40% of General Reserve as on 31.3.2010	1,20,000
40% of Profit & Loss Account as on 31.3.2010	1,20,000
	5,20,000

(*v*) *Unrealised profit in respect of stock :*
= Rs. 1,20,000 × 20/100 = Rs. 20,000

Consolidated Balance Sheet of H Ltd. and its subsidiary S Ltd. as at 1st March, 2010

Liabilities	*Rs.*	*Rs.*	*Assets*	*Rs.*	*Rs.*
Equity Share Capital (Rs. 10 each)		10,00,000	Fixed Assets :		
Minority Interest		5,20,000	H Ltd.	8,00,000	
Capital Reserve		2,20,000	S Ltd.	9,00,000	
General Reserve		2,00,000		17,00,000	
Profit & Loss Account :			*Less :* Unrealised Profit	25,000	16,75,000
H Ltd. 3,00,000			Current Assets :		
Less : Dividend wrongly			H Ltd.	7,00,000	
credited	60,000		S Ltd.	13,00,000	
	2,40,000			20,00,000	
Add : H Ltd.'s share in			*Less*: Internal Debt 1,20,000		
S Ltd.'s current profits			Unrealised Profit		
Rs. 2,00,000 ×			on stock 20,000	1,40,000	18,60,000
(60/100)	1,20,000				
	3,60,000				
Less: Unrealised Profit :					
(*i*) on machine 25,000					
(*ii*) on stock 20,000	45,000	3,15,000			

	Rs.	Rs.		Rs.
Current Liabilties :				
H Ltd.	5,00,000			
S Ltd.	9,00,000			
	14,00,000			
Less : Internal Debt	1,20,000	12,80,000		
		35,35,000		35,35,000

Illustration 39:

H Ltd. purchased on 1.4.2005 8,000 equity shares of Rs. 100 each in S Ltd. when S Ltd. had Rs. 10,00,000 share capital.

It sold 500 such shares on 1.4.2006 and purchased 1,000 shares on 1.4.2007.

S Ltd. paid 15% dividend each year in September and there was no change in Share Capital Account upto 31.3.2008.

Profit and Loss Account balances in S Ltd. and Investments of H Ltd. in S Ltd. on different dates were as under:—

	Profit and Loss Account Balance of S Ltd. Rs.	*Investments of H Ltd. in S Ltd.* Rs.
1st April, 2005	5,00,000	12,80,000
31st March, 2006	6,20,000	12,80,000
31st March, 2007	7,00,000	11,90,000
31st March, 2008	8,00,000	14,00,000

The amounts shown as investments represent cost price as reduced by sales and increased by further purchase without making any adjustment for profit or loss on sale or for dividend.

Prepare statements to show the relevant figures as on 31st March, 2006, 2007 and 2008 for preparation of Consolidated Accounts in respect of:

(*a*) Goodwill or Cost of Control

(*b*) Revenue Profit *(Adapted C.A. Final, May 1988)*

Solution:

Working Notes :

(1) *Calculation of correct Cost of investment :*

Dr. **Investment in Shares in S Ltd. Account** *Cr.*

		Rs.			Rs.
2005			2006		
April 1	To Bank (8,000 shares)	12,80,000	March 31	By Profit & Loss Account— Rectification regarding pre-acquisition dividend — Rs. 8,00,000 × 15/100	1,20,000
				By Balance c/d (8,000 shares)	11,60,000
		12,80,000			12,80,000
2006			2006		
April 1	To Balance b/d (8,000 shares)	11,60,000	April 1,	By Bank (Sale proceeds of 500 shares Rs.12,80,000 – Rs.11,90,000)	90,000
" "	To Profit & Loss Account — Profit on sale: Rs. 90,000 — (11,60,000 × 500/8,000)	17,500	2007		
			March 31	By Balance c/d (7,500 shares)	10,87,500
		11,77,500			11,77,500

2007		Rs.	2008		Rs.
April 1	To Balance b/d (7,500 shares)	10,87,500	March 31	By Profit & Loss Account— Rectification regarding pre-acquisition dividend on 1,000 shares	15,000
April 1	To Bank (1,000 shares purchased)	2,10,000	March 31	By Balance c/d (8,500 shares)	12,82,500
		12,97,500			12,97,500
2008					
April 1	To Balance b/d	12,82,500			

(ii) *Capital Profits :*

	Rs.
31st March, 2006 :	
Balance of Profit & Loss Account as on 31.3.2005	5,00,000
Less : Dividend on Rs. 10,00,000 @ 15%	1,50,000
	3,50,000

$$\text{H Ltd.'s share} = \text{Rs. } 3{,}50{,}000 \times \frac{8{,}000}{10{,}000} = 2{,}80{,}000$$

31st March, 2007 :

As H Ltd. has sold 500 shares, its share of capital profits is reduced.

$$\text{H Ltd.'s share} = \frac{\text{Rs.}3{,}50{,}000 \times 7{,}500}{10{,}000} = \text{Rs. } 2{,}62{,}500$$

	Rs.
31st March, 2008 :	
Balance of Profit & Loss Account as on 31.3.2007	7,00,000
Less : Dividend on Rs. 10,00,000 @ 15%	1,50,000
	5,50,000
H Ltd.'s share in respect of 1,000 shares purchased on 1.4.2007 = $\frac{\text{Rs.}5{,}50{,}000 \times 1{,}000}{10{,}000}$	
H Ltd.'s share of Capital Profits in respect of 7,500 shares purchased on 31.3.2005 as calculated above	2,62,500
Total	3,17,500

(a) *Goodwill or Cost of Control :*

	31.3.2006 Rs.	31.3.2007 Rs	31.3.2008 Rs.
Correct Cost of Investment as per working notes no (*i*)	11,60,000	10,87,500	12,82,500
Less : Paid up value of shares in hand	8,00,000	7,50,000	8,50,000
	3,60,000	3,37,500	4,32,500
Less : H Ltd.'s share of Capital profits as per working notes no (*ii*)	2,80,000	2,62,500	3,17,500
Goodwill or Cost of Control	80,000		

(b) *Revenue Profit :*

Balance of Profit & Loss Account	6,20,000	7,00,000
Less: Capital Profits		
Balance of Profit & Loss Account as on 1st April, 2005 after deducting dividend for the year 2004-05 @ 15%	3,50,000	3,50,000
	2,70,000	3,50,000
Less: Minority Interest		
20% on 31.3.2006	54,000	
20% on 31.3.2007		87,500
H Ltd.'s share	2,16,000	2,62,500

		31.3.2008
	Rs.	Rs.
Balance of Profit & Loss Account		8,00,000
Less: Capital Profits as mentioned above		3,50,000
		4,50,000
Less: Minority Interest @ 15%		67,500
But for 10% shares acquired on 1.4.2007, there are additional Capital Profits		3,82,500
Balance of Profits & Loss Account as an 31.3.2007	7,00,000	
Less: Dividend for the year ended 31.3.2007 @ 15%	1,50,000	
	5,50,000	
Less: Capital Profit already taken into account above	3,50,000	
Additional Capital Profit	2,00,000	
H Ltd.'s share = Rs.2,00,000 × 10/100		20,000
		3,62,500

Consolidation of profit and loss accounts :

Apart from the usual items of gains, incomes, losses and expenses which will appear in the profit and loss accounts of both the holding and the subsidiary companies and which will therefore be aggregated, some adjustments will be required. The following are the most important :—

(1) The profit of the subsidiary company arising before the date of acquisition of shares in the subsidiary company and belonging to the holding company should be debited to the Consolidated Profit and Loss Account and credited to Capital Reserve or Goodwill as the case may be. In case there is a loss, the Consolidated Profit and Loss Account will be credited and Capital Reserve or Goodwill debited.

(2) In respect of the proportion of the profits of the subsidiary company which belongs to the minority shareholders, their account should be credited by debit to the Consolidated Profit and Loss Account. In case of loss, the Minority Shareholders Suspense Account should be debited and the Consolidated Profit and Loss Account credited.

(3) All items internal to the holding and subsidiary companies should be eliminated. If the subsidiary company has passed entries for proposed dividend and the holding company has also taken credit for its share of the dividends, there will be a cancellation from both sides of the Consolidated Profit and Loss Account. If the proposed dividend has not been passed through the holding company's books, the debit in respect of proposed dividend will be reduced by the holding company's share in the Consolidated Profit and Loss Account; the corresponding liability in the Balance Sheet will also be reduced.

(4) Reserve for unrealised profit in respect of inter-company transactions relating to goods will have to be created by debit to the Consolidated Profit and Loss Account and credit to Stock Reserve Account.

The transfer of goods between the holding company and the subsidiary company should be eliminated both from the purchases and sales appearing in the Consolidated Profit and Loss Account.

(5) Debenture interest or dividends received by the holding company from the subsidiary will have to be eliminated from both sides of the Consolidated Profit and Loss Account.

No adjustment is required in respect of tax on dividends or on interest on debentures paid by the subsidiary company to the holding company. In case of interest outstanding or accruing, care should be taken to see that both the holding and subsidiary companies pass entries. Then the debenture interest will be cancelled from both sides of the Consolidated Profit and Loss Account, so far as it relates to the debentures held by the holding company.

(6) In case Cumulative Preference Shares are held by outsiders and in case the dividend is in arrear, such arrear may be shown by way of a note in the Consolidated Balance Sheet. Alternatively, the amount due by way of dividends should be debited to the Consolidated Profit and Loss Account and credited to the Minority Shareholders Account and shown as a liability in the Consolidated Balance Sheet.

Illustration 40:

H Ltd. holds 7,500 equity shares of Rs. 10 each in S Ltd. whose capital consists of 10,000 equity shares of Rs. 10 each and 14% 1,000 cumulative preference shares of Rs. 100 each. S Ltd. has also issued 14% debentures to the extent of Rs. 2,00,000 out of which H Ltd. holds Rs. 1,00,000. The following are the profit and loss accounts of the two companies for the year ending 31st March, 2009 :—

Particulars	*H Ltd.* *Rs.*	*S Ltd.* *Rs.*	*Particulars*	*H Ltd.* *Rs.*	*S Ltd.* *Rs.*
To Adjusted Purchases	15,00,000	6,00,000	By Sales	19,00,000	15,00,000
To Manufacturing Expenses		4,00,000			
To Gross Profit	4,00,000	5,00,000			
	19,00,000	15,00,000		19,00,000	15,00,000
To Sundry Expenses	1,58,000	1,84,000	By Gross Profit	4,00,000	5,00,000
To Debenture Interest		28,000	By Debenture Interest	14,000	
To Net Profit c/d	2,98,000	2,88,000	By Interim Dividend (gross)	42,000	
	4,56,000	5,00,000		4,56,000	5,00,000
To Income-tax	1,40,000	1,12,000	By Net Profit b/d	2,98,000	2,88,000
To Preference Dividends		14,000			
To Interim Dividend		56,000			
To Proposed Dividend	1,00,000	84,000			
To Balance c/d	58,000	22,000			
	2,98,000	2,88,000		2,98,000	2,88,000

The following further information is given :—

(1) The shares were acquired by H Ltd. on 1st July 2008 but the debentures were acquired on 1st April 2008, S Ltd. was incorporated on 1st April, 2008.

(2) During the year, S Ltd. sold to H Ltd. goods costing Rs. 1,00,000 at the selling price of Rs. 1,50,000. One-fourth of the goods remained unsold on 31st March, 2009. The goods were valued at cost to the holding company for closing stock purposes.

Prepare Consolidated Profit and Loss Account. Assume the absence of corporate dividend tax.

Solution :

H Ltd. & S Ltd.

Consolidated Profit and Loss Account for the year ended 31st March, 2009

Particulars	*Aggregate of* *Rs.*	*Adjust-ments H. & S.* *Rs.*	*Total* *Rs.*	*Particulars*	*Aggregate* *Rs.*	*Adjust-of* *Rs.*	*Total ment H & S* *Rs.*
To Adjusted Purchases	21,00,000	-1,50,000	19,50,000	By Sales	34,00,000	−1,50,000	32,50,000
To Manufacturing Expenses	4,00,000	. . .	4,00,000				
To Gross Profit c/d	9,00,000	. . .	9,00,000				
	34,00,000	−1,50,000	32,50,000		34,00,000	−1,50,000	32,50,000

	Rs.	Rs.	Rs.		Rs.	Rs.	Rs.
To Sundry Expenses	3,42,000	...	3,42,000	By Gross Profit b/d	9,00,000	...	9,00,000
To Debenture Interest	28,000	– 14,000	14,000	By Debenture Intt.	14,000	–14,000	...
To Profit c/d	5,86,000	– 42,000	5,44,000	By Dividends Recd. (1)	42,000	– 42,000	...
	9,56,000	– 56,000	9,00,000		9,56,000	– 56,000	9,00,000
To Income Tax	2,52,000	...	2,52,000	By Net Profit b/d	5,86,000	– 42,000	5,44,000
To Preference Dividend	14,000	...	14,000				
To Interim Dividend	56,000	– 42,000	14,000				
To Proposed Dividend (2)	1,84,000	– 63,000	1,21,000				
To Capital Profits (3)	...	+ 30,375	30,375				
To Reserve against unsold stock (4)	...	+ 12,500	12,500				
To Share of Outside Shareholders (¼th of Rs. 22,000)		+ 5,500	5,500				
To Balance carried to Balance Sheet	80,000	+ 14,625	94,625				
	5,86,000	– 42,000	5,44,000		5,86,000	– 42,000	5,44,000

Notes: (1) The dividend received has been eliminated against interim dividend paid.

(2) The proposed dividend includes Rs. 63,000 payable to H Ltd. by S Ltd. This has been eliminated. The corresponding elimination on the other side will be from the liability for Proposed Dividend in the Balance Sheet, since H Ltd. has not yet taken credit for the proposed dividend.

(3) The total capital profits—up to 1st June 2008—are 1/4 of Rs. 1,62,000 or Rs. 40,500, *i.e.*, 1/4 (2,88,000 – 1,12,000 – 14,000). Three fourths of this—the holding company's share—is capital profit.

(4) The reserve against profits on unsold stock has been calculated as under : The total profit made was Rs. 50,000 but since only one-fourth of the goods remain unsold, only one-fourth of the profit, *viz.*, Rs. 12,500 is unrealised.

(5) It has been assumed that the dividends have been paid or proposed out of current (post-acquisition) profits.

Illustration 41:

Air Ltd., Sea Ltd. and Rail Ltd. are members of a group. Air Ltd. bought 70% of the shares of Sea Ltd. on October 1, 2007 and 30% of the shares of Rail Ltd., on 1st January 2009. Sea Ltd. bought 60% of the shares of Rail Ltd. on October 1, 2008. The following information is available:

Profit and Loss Account

	Balance, April 1, 2009 Rs.	*Profit (Loss) for 2008-09 Rs.*	*Balance, Mar. 31, 2009 Rs.*	*Company Formed*
Air Ltd.	55,000	25,000	80,000	April 1, 2006
Sea Ltd.	20,000 (Dr)	47,500	27,500	April 1, 2007
Rail Ltd.	—	24,000 (loss)	24,000(Dr)	April 1, 2008

State how the profits (losses) will be reflected in the consolidated balance sheet.

[*Adapted from C.A. (Final), Eng.*]

Solution:

Rail Ltd.:

	Capital Profit Rs.	*Revenue Profit Rs.*
Loss for the year (assumed accruing evenly)	12,000	12,000
Less : Due to Minority Interest (10%)	1,200	1,200
	10,800	10,800

	Rs.	Rs.
Due to Sea Ltd. (60%)	7,200	7,200
Share of Air Ltd. (30%)	3,600	3,600
Revenue loss pertaining to further 3 months to be treated as capital, since shares are acquired on Jan. 1, 2009	+1,800	–1,800
Loss:	5,400	1,800
Sea Ltd. :		
Profit from Rail Ltd.	–7,200	–7,200
Profit as on April 1, 2008	–10,000	–10,000
Profit during 2008-09	—	47,500
	–17,200	30,300
Due to Outsiders, 30%	5,160	19,090
Due to Air Ltd.	–12,040	21,210
Air Ltd. :		
Profit from Rail Ltd.	– 5,400	–1,800
Profit from Sea Ltd.	–12,040	21,210
Own Profit	—	80,000
	–17,440	99,410
Share of Minority Shareholders :		
Capital Loss in Rail Ltd.		1,200
Revenue Loss in Rail Ltd.		1,200
Capital Loss in Sea Ltd.		5,160
Total 'Profit'		–7,560
Revenue Profit in Sea Ltd.		9,090
Share of Outsiders		1,530

Illustration 42:

Flower Ltd. is a trading company which has owned 100% of the share capital of Pot Ltd. for many years. On 1st December, 2008 Flower Ltd. acquired 80% of the equity share capital of Shed Ltd. but did not acquire any of the Rs. 1,00,000 14% preference shares.

The draft Profit and Loss Accounts of three companies for the year ended 31st March, 2009 showed :—

	Flower Ltd.		*Pot Ltd.*		*Shed Ltd.*	
	Rs.	*Rs.*	*Rs.*	*Rs.*	*Rs.*	*Rs.*
Profit after charging or crediting the items below :		2,00,000		40,000		85,000
Directors' remuneration :	20,000		8,000		9,000	
Director's compensation for loss of office :	. . .		. . .		5,000	
Depreciation	34,000		12,000		7,000	
Audit fees	3,500		1,100		2,000	
Interest receivable	24,000		. . .		. . .	
Dividends receivable	21,000		1,000		. . .	
Provision for taxation		51,000		15,000		36,000
		1,49,000		25,000		49,000
Dividend paid (1-10-2008) :						
Preference				. . .	7,000	
Dividend proposed :						
Equity	70,000		12,000		5,000	
Preference	14,000		. . .		7,000	
		84,000		12,000		19,000
		65,000		13,000		30,000
Balance brought forward from previous year		3,23,000		88,000		96,000
		3,88,000		1,01,000		1,26,000

The following information is ascertained :

(1) The equity dividend proposed by Shed Ltd. has not been brought into credit by Flower Ltd. in the draft accounts.

(2) In all three companies, the trading profits are deemed to occur evenly over the year.

(3) Included in the stock of Flower Ltd. at cost is Rs. 18,000 for goods which were purchased subsequent to December from Shed Ltd., which had added its usual margin of 33 1/3% to cost but then allowed a special sales discount of 10%.

(4) On 1st May, Flower Ltd. sold a machine in the ordinary course of its trade to Pot Ltd., which capitalized this item as part of Plant and Machinery. Pot Ltd. paid Rs. 10,000, the cost to Flower Ltd. being Rs. 6,000.

(5) Throughout the group, depreciation on fixed assets is charged at 1% per month calculated on cost.

(6) The holding company believes in a policy of decentralized management. The only director common to all companies is the chairman of Flower Ltd. who received fees of Rs. 500 from Pot Ltd. and Rs. 200 from Shed Ltd.

(7) The compensation for loss of office was paid by Shed Ltd. in June 2008 and was an exceptional item of expense, not connected with the acquisition of control by Flower Ltd.

(8) In general, in all three companies the taxable profits approximate to the accounting profits. However, in 2008 when the rate of corporation tax is taken as 50%, Flower Ltd. is to provide Rs. 30,000 as additional provision for taxation.

(9) Rs. 20,000 of the interest receivable by Flower Ltd. was from a bank deposit account, the balance being from a mortgage loan repayable in 2013.

You are required to prepare the consolidated profit and loss statement for the year ended 31st March, 2009. Ignore corporate dividend tax. [*Adapted from C.A. (Eng.) Final*]

Solution :

FLOWER LTD. AND ITS SUBSIDIARIES POT LTD. AND SHED LTD.
Consolidated Profit and Loss Statement year ended March 31, 2009

	Rs.	*Rs.*	*Rs.*
Profit Before Taxation after accounting for :			3,06,440
Directors' remuneration		37,000	
Depreciation		52,560	
Audit fees		6,600	
Bank deposit interest receivable	20,000		
Other interest receivable	4,000	24,000	
Dividends receivable		10,000	
Provision for taxation based on profits for the year :			1,32,000
			1,75,040
Deduct Minority Interests			14,600
			1,60,440
Deduct pre-acquisition profits		20,000	
Dividends proposed :			
Equity	70,000		
Preference	7,000	77,000	97,000
			63,440
Balance brought forward from previous year			4,11,000
Balance carried forward			4,74,440

Working Notes :

(1) Profit before taxation :

	Flower Ltd. Rs.	Rs.	*Pot Ltd.* Rs.	Rs.	*Shed Ltd* Rs.	*Total* Rs.	*Total* Rs.
Profit per question :		2,00,000	40,000		85,000		3,25,000
Add Depreciation over-provided, 1 per cent on Rs. 4,000 for 11 months			440				440
		2,00,000	40,440		85,000		3,25,440
Deduct inter-company Dividend:	12,000					12,000	
Stock Profit : Rs. 3,000*				3,000		3,000	
Plant Profit :	4,000					4,000	
		16,000			3,000		19,000
		1,84,000	40,440		82,000		3,06,440

(2) Provision for Taxation Flower Ltd.

	Rs.	Rs.
Flower Ltd.		
Per own accounts	51,000	
Additional taxation	30,000	81,000
Pot Ltd :		
Per own accounts		15,000
Shed Ltd. per own accounts		36,000
		1,32,000

	Rs.	Rs.
(3) Minority interest		14,000
Preference dividends—Shed Ltd. :		
Equity shareholders Shed Ltd.	49,000	
Profit after tax per Shed Ltd.'s accounts :		
Less: Preference dividends :	14,000	
	35,000	
One-fifth thereof		7,000
		21,000
		49,000
(4) Pre-acquisition profits—Shed Ltd. :		
Profit for year ended March 31, 2009	21,000	
Deduct Minority interests	2,400	23,400
Stock profit		25,600
Add: Back Director's compensation for loss of office paid June, 2008		4,000
		29,600
Pre-acquisition profits, 2/3rds of Rs. 29,600		19,734
Deduct Director's compensation for loss of office (4/5ths)		4,000
		15,734

Illustration 41:

From the following balance sheets of a group of companies and the other information provided, draw up the consolidated Balance Sheets as on 31.3.2010. Figures given are in lakhs of rupees.

Balance Sheet as on 31.3.2010

	X	Y	Z		X	Y	Z
Share capital (in shares of Rs. 100 each)	300	200	100	Fixed assets less depreciation	130	150	100
Reserves	50	40	30	Cost of investment			

*Suppose cost is Rs. 300, normal sales price is Rs. 400; discount being Rs. 40, the invoice price will be Rs. 360. Unrealised profit in closing stock is one-sixth of invoice price.

	X	Y	Z		X	Y	Z
Profit and loss account balance	60	50	40	in Y Ltd.	180	—	—
Bills payables	10	—	5	Cost of investment in Z Ltd.	40	—	—
Creditors	30	10	10	Cost of investment in Z Ltd.	—	80	—
Y Ltd. balance	—	—	15	Stock 50 20	20		
Z Ltd. balance	50	—	—	Debtors 70	10	20	
				Bills receivables	—	10	20
				Z Ltd. balance	—	10	—
				X Ltd. balance	—	—	30
				Cash and bank balance	30	20	10
	500	300	200		500	300	200

Additional information :

(*i*) X Ltd. holds, 1,60,000 shares and 30,000 shares respectively in Y Ltd. and Z Ltd.; Y Ltd. holds 60,000shares in Z Ltd. These investments were made on 1.7.2009 on which date the position was as follows :

	Y Ltd.	Z Ltd.
Reserves	20	10
Profit and loss account	30	16

(*ii*) In December, 2009 Y Ltd. invoiced to X Ltd. for Rs. 40 lakhs at cost plus 25%. The closing stock of X Ltd. includes such goods valued at Rs. 5 lakhs.

(*iii*) Z Ltd. sold to Y Lyd. an equipment costing Rs. 24 lakhs at a profit of 25% on selling price on 1.1.2010. Depreciation at 10% per annum was provided by Y Ltd. on this equipment.

(*iv*) Bills payables of Z Ltd. represent acceptances given to Y Ltd. out of which Y Ltd. had discounted bills worth Rs. 3 lakhs.

(*v*) Debtors of X Ltd. include Rs. 5 lakhs being the amount due from Y Ltd.

(*vi*) X Ltd. proposes dividend at 10%. [*Adpated C.A. (Final) May. 1998*]

Solution :

Consolidated Balance Sheet of X Ltd. and its subsidiaries Y Ltd. and Z Ltd. as at 31st March, 2010

(*Rs. in lakhs*)

Liabilities	*Rs.*	*Rs.*	*Assets*	*Rs.*	*Rs.*
Share Capital			Fixed Assets		
Authorised		?	X Ltd.	130.00	
Issued and Subscribed :			Y Ltd.	150.00	
3 lakh shares of Rs. 100			Z Ltd.	100.00	
each, fully paid up		300.00		380.00	
Minority Interest			*Less* : Unrealised profit	7.80	372.20
Y Ltd.	63.28		Current Assets, Loans		
Z Ltd.	17.00	80.28	and Advances :		
Reserves and Surplus			(A) Current Assets		
Capital Reserve		13.40	Stock		
Other Reserves		50.00	X Ltd.	50.00	
Profit and Loss Account			Y Ltd.	20.00	
[Working Note (vii)]		87.52	Z Ltd.	20.00	
Current Liabilities and				90.00	
Provisions			*Less* : Unrealised profit	1.00	89.00
(A) Current Liabilities			Debtors		

	Rs.	Rs.		Rs.	Rs.
			X Ltd.	70.00	
Bills Payable			Y Ltd.	10.00	
X Ltd.	10.00		Z Ltd.	20.00	
Z Ltd.	5.00			100.00	
	15.00		*Less* : Unrealised profit	5.00	95.00
Less : Mutual owing	2.00	13.00	Cash and Bank Balances		
Creditors			X Ltd.	30.00	
X Ltd.	30.00		Y Ltd.	20.00	
Y Ltd.	10.00		Z Ltd.	10.00	60.00
Z Ltd.	10.00		(B) Loans and Advances		
	50.00		Y Ltd.	10.00	
Less : Mutual owing	5.00	45.00	Z Ltd.	20.00	
Current Account Balances				30.00	
X Ltd.	50.00		*Less* : Mutual owing	2.00	28.00
Z Ltd.	15.00				
	65.00				
Less : Mutual owing, Rs.(10 + 30) lakhs	40.00	25.00			
(B) Provisions					
Proposed Dividend		30.00			
		644.20			644.20

Working Notes :

(i) *Analysis of profits of Z Ltd.*

Rs. in lakhs

	Capital profit	*Revenue Reserve*	*Revenue Profit*
Reserves on 1.7.2009	10.00		
Profit and Loss Account balance on 1.7.2009	16.00		
Increase in reserves		20.00	
Increase in profit			24.00
	26.00	20.00	24.00
Less : Minority Interest (10%)	2.60	2.00	2.40
	23.40	18.00	21.60
Shares of X Ltd.	7.80	6.00	7.20
Shares of Y Ltd.	15.60	12.00	14.40

(ii) *Analysis of profits of Y Ltd.*

	Capital profit	*Revenue Reserve*	*Revenue Profit*
Reserves on 1.7.2009	20.00		
Profit and Loss Account balance on 1.7.2009	30.00		
Increase in reserves		20.00	
Increase in profit			20.00
	50.00	20.00	20.00
Share in Z Ltd.		12.00	14.40
	50.00	32.00	34.40
Less . Minority Interest (20%)	10.00	6.40	6.88
	40.00	25.60	27.52

(iii) *Cost of Control* :

Investment in Y Ltd.			180.00
Investment in Z Ltd.			120.00
			300.00
Less : Paid up value of investments			
in Y Ltd.	160.00		
in Z Ltd.	90.00	250.00	
Capital profit			
in Y Ltd.	40.00		
in Z Ltd.	23.40	63.40	313.40
Capital Reserve			13.40

Rs. in lakhs

	Capital profit	*Revenue Reserve*	*Revenue Profit*
(*iv*) *Minority interest :*		*Y Ltd.*	*Z Ltd.*
Share capital		40.00	10.00
Capital profit		10.00	2.60
Revenue reserves		6.40	2.00
Reveneue profits		6.88	2.40
		63.28	17.00

(*v*) *Unrealised profit on sale of equipment* :

Cost	24.00
Profit	8.00
Selling price	32.00

$$\text{Unrealised profit} = 8 - 8 \times \frac{10}{100} \times \frac{3}{12} = 8.00 - 0.20 = 7.80$$

(*vi*) Unrealised profit on stock = 5 × 25 / 125 = 1.00

(*vii*) *X Ltd.'s Profit and Loss Account :*

Balance, as given		60.00
Less : Proposed dividend		30.00
		30.00
Add : Share in Z Ltd.'s revenue reserve		6.00
Share in Z Ltd.'s revenue profit		7.20
Share in Y Ltd.'s revenue reserve		25.60
Share in Y Ltd.'s revenue profit		27.52
		96.32
Less : Unrealised profit on :		
Equipment	7.80	
Stock	1.00	8.80
Amount appearing in consolidated balance sheet		87.52

Illustration 43:

The following are the Balance Sheets as on 31st March, 2010 of two cigarette companies :—

		Union *Rs.*		*Hind* *Rs.*
Share Capital	(*g*)	1,00,00,000	(*g*)	30,00,000
General Reserve		24,00,000	(*h*)	5,00,000
Profit and Loss Account	(*i*)	12,10,000	(*i*)	4,40,000
		1,36,10,000		39,40,000
Bills Payable		1,50,000		—
Sundry Creditors	(*j*)	33,50,000		8,00,000
		1,71,10,000		47,40,000
Goodwill		20,00,000		4,40,000
Land and Buildings		24,00,000	(*b*)	10,00,000
Plant and Machinery		52,00,000	(*b*)	19,00,000
Investments	(*a*)	28,80,000		—
Stocks	(*c*)	14,00,000		5,00,000
Debtors	(*d*)	24,00,000		5,60,000
Bills Receivable		—	(*e*)	1,00,000
Cash and Bank Balance		8,30,000	(*f*)	2,40,000
		1,71,10,000		47,40,000

Ignoring corporate dividend tax prepare a consolidated balance sheet taking into account the following particulars, detailed working being shown therein or in a separate statement : —

(*a*) The investment consists of 2,40,000 shares of Rs. 10 each fully paid in Hind Co., which were acquired on 1st July, 2009.

(b) Land and Buildings and Plant and Machinery of Hind Company on revaluation on 1st April, 2009 came to Rs. 11,60,000 and Rs. 20,40,000 respectively, which should be taken in the Consolidated Balance Sheet.

(c) Stocks include goods which cost Union Co., Rs. 4,80,000 but which were received from Hind Company, their cost being Rs. 4,41,600.

(d) Debtors include (i) Loan of Rs. 60,000 to Hind Co., and (ii) Dividend of Rs. 2,40,000 from Hind Co.

(e) Bills Receivable, all accepted by Union Co., were for Rs. 1,50,000 of which Bills for Rs. 50,000 had been discounted but had not till 31st March, 2010 matured.

(f) Cash and Bank Balance of Rs. 2,40,000 were arrived at after sending a cheque for Rs. 60,000 to repay the Loan from Union Co., which, however, had not been received by it by 31st March, 2010.

(g) Share Capital of Union Co., consists of 20,000 14% Preference Shares of Rs. 100 each and 8,00,000 equity shares of Rs. 10 each. Share Capital of Hind Co. consists of 3,00,000 equity shares of Rs. 10 each.

(h) General Reserve of Hind Co., was Rs. 4,00,000 on 1st April, 2009.

(i) The details making up the balances of Profit and Loss Accounts are :—

	Union Rs.	Hind Rs.
1st April, 2009	1,60,000	1,20,000
Profit for the year	9,50,000	3,20,000
	11,10,000	4,40,000
Dividend Receivable from Hind Co.	2,40,000	—
	13,50,000	4,40,000
Less: Dividend Paid on Preference Shares	1,40,000	—
	12,10,000	4,40,000

(j) Sundry Creditors include Rs. 3,20,000 due to Hind Co. for goods supplied. (*C.A. Final*)

Solution:

In this problem, the main point to note is that the figure given as "Profit for the year" in note (i) for Hind Co., does not represent the full profit for the year but only the balance left after transfer to General Reserve of Rs. 1,00,000 (since the Reserve on 31st March, 2009 is Rs. 5,00,000, whereas, according to note (b), it was only Rs. 4,00,000 on 1st April 2009) and payment of dividend which must have been Rs. 3,00,000 (since Union Company, holding 2,40,000 shares, has received Rs. 2,40,000 which means outsiders, holding 60,000 shares, must have received Rs. 60,000). The total profits for the year, therefore, are Rs. 3,20,000 plus Rs. 1,00,000, transferred to General Reserve plus Rs. 3,00,000 declared as dividend, *viz.*, Rs. 7,20,000. Assuming that the dividend for the year as a whole, the figure comes down to Rs. 3,20,000. One-fourth of this (i.e., profits up to 1st July) is capital profit.

Capital Profits :

	Rs.
General Reserve on 1st July, 2009	4,25,000
Profit and Loss Account Balance on 1st April, 2009	1,20,000
Profit up to 1st July, 2009 i.e. 1/4 of total profit for the year*	80,000
Increase in the value of Land and Buildings	1,60,000
Increase in the value of Plant and Machinery	1,40,000
	9,25,000
Less: 1/5 share to outsiders	1,85,000
Share of the Union Co.	7,40,000

*General Reserve will be Rs. 4,00,000 (on 1st April, 2009) plus Rs. 25,000, 3/12 of increase. Profits up to Ist July, 2009 will be 3/12 of Rs. 3,20,000.

	Rs.	Rs.
Current Profits :		
Balance in P. L. Account		4,40,000
Less: Treated as Capital Profit—	Rs.	
Balance on 1st April, 2009	1,20,000	
Profits up to 1st July, 2009	80,000	2,00,000
Balance remaining of current profits		2,40,000
Less: 1/5 share to outsiders		48,000
		1,92,000
Less: Unrealised profit on stock ex-sale from Hind Co. to Union Company : 4/5 (4,80,000 × 4,41,600)		30,720
		1,61,280
Minority interest :		
60,000 shares of Rs. 10 each		6,00,000
1/5 share of Capital Profits		1,85,000
1/5 share of Current Profits		48,000
1/5 share of increase in General Reserve (5,00,000 — 4,25,000)		15,000
		8,48,000
Goodwill		
Amount paid for the shares in Hind Co.	Rs.	28,80,000
Less : par value of shares	24,00,000	
4/5 share of Capital Profits	7,40,000	
1/4 of dividend received from Hind Co.*	60,000	32,00,000
Capital Reserve (to be set off against other goodwill)		3,20,000

Consolidated Balance Sheet of Union Co., Ltd. and its subsidiary, Hind Co. Ltd., as on 31st March 2010

Liabilities	Rs.	Rs.	*Assets*	Rs.	Rs.
Share Capital			Goodwill :		
20,00 14% Preference			Union Co.	20,00,000	
Shares of Rs. 10 each		20,00,000	Hind Co.	4,40,000	
8,00,000 Equity Shares of				24,40,000	
Rs. 10 each		80,00,000	*Less:* Capital Reserve on		
General Reserve :			consolidation	3,20,000	21,20,000
Union Co.	24,00,000		Land and Buildings:		
4/5 Share of increase in			Union Co.	24,00,000	
General Reserve of			Hind Co.	11,60,000	35,60,000
Hind Co.	60,000	24,60,000	Plant and Machinery:		
Profit and Loss Account :			Union Co.	52,00,000	
Balance of Union Co.	12,10,000		Hind Co.	20,40,000	
Less: Treated as Capital			Stock:		
Receipt	60,000		Union Co.	14,00,000	
	11,50,000		Hind Co.	5,00,000	
Current Profit of Hind Co.	1,61,280	13,11,280		19,00,000	
Bills Payable	1,50,000		*Less:* Unrealised Profit	30,720	18,69,280
Less: held by Hind Co.	1,00,000	50,000	Debtors:		
Sundry Creditors :			Union Co.	24,00,000	
Union Co.	33,50,000		Hind Co.	5,60,000	
Hind Co. (increase for				29,60,000	
cash in transit)	8,60,000		*Less:* Internal debts	6,20,000	23,40,000
	42,10,000		Cash in Transit		60,000
Less: Internal credits	6,20,000	35,90,000	Cash and Bank		
Minority Interest		8,48,000	Balance : Union Co.	8,30,000	
			Hind Co.	2,40,000	10,70,000
		1,82,59,280			1,82,59,280

*The dividend received is assumed to be for the year 2009–10 out of the profits for the year. Hence, dividend for the three months up to 1st July is capital receipt to be deducted from the value of investments.

Illustration 44:

Ack Ltd. acquired control of Tick Ltd. and Tock Ltd. on 1st April, 2009. The respective Balance Sheets on March 31, 2010 were :

	Ack Ltd. *Rs.*	*Tick Ltd.* *Rs.*	*Tock Ltd.* *Rs.*
Share Capital :			
Equity Shares of Rs. 10 each	1,50,000	80,000	50,00
General Reserve	10,000	—	—
Profit & Loss Account	45,000	13,000	11,000
Creditors :			
Trade	24,000	18,000	12,000
Loan from Ack Ltd.	—	4,000	—
Bills Payable to Ack Ltd.	—	—	3,000
	2,29,000	1,15,000	76,000
Fixed Assets :	31,000	36,000	22,000
Investments in Subsidiaries :			
6,000 shares in Tick Ltd.	75,000	—	—
4,000 shares in Tock Ltd.	50,000	—	—
Loan to Tick Ltd.	4,000	—	—
Current Assets :			
Stock	26,000	24,000	16,000
Debtors	28,000	48,000	27,000
Bill Receivable from Tock Ltd.	2,000	—	—
Bank	13,000	7,000	11,000
	2,29,000	1,15,000	76,000

Notes : (*i*) Balance on P. & L. A/c 1st April, 2009 — Ack Ltd. 26,000; Tick Ltd. 9,000; Tock Ltd. 8,000
Dividends proposed for 2009-2010 — Ack Ltd. 20%; Tick Ltd. 12%; Tock Ltd. 15%

(*ii*) The Fixed Assets of Tick Ltd. include plant purchased in September 2009 from Tock Ltd. for Rs. 1,000. The cost to Tock Ltd., who are plant manufacturers, was Rs. 750 and credit for the profit has been taken by that company.

(*iii*) Tick Ltd. held on March 31, 2010 stock, of Rs. 2,000 purchased from Ack Ltd. who invoiced the goods at cost plus 25%.

(*iv*) The loan by Ack Ltd. was made on October 1, 2009 and carried 15 per cent interest for which no entry has been made in the books.

Prepare a Consolidated Balance Sheet on March 31, 2010, ignoring taxation.

(Adapted from Incorp. Acctts., Final)

Solution:

	Tick Ltd. *Rs.*	*Tock Ltd.* *Rs.*
(*i*) *Current Profits :*		
P. & L. Account Balance (less brought forward from previous year)	4,000	3,000
Less: Interest due to Ack Ltd. on Loan	300	—
	3,700	3,000
Less: Due to minority shareholders :		
Tick Ltd. – one-fourth	925	—
Tock Ltd. – one-fifth	—	600
Share of Ack Ltd.	2,775	2,400

(*ii*) ***P. & L. A/c of Ack Ltd. (consolidated) :***

	Rs.
Balance as per Balance Sheet	45,000
Add: Interest on Loan for 6 months	300
	45,300

	Rs.	Rs.
Profit from Tick Ltd.		2,775
Profit from Tock Ltd.		2,400
		50,475
Less: Unrealised Profit on sale of Plant by Tock Ltd. to Tick Ltd. 3/4 of 4/5 of Rs. 250	150	
Unrealised Profit on Sale of Stock—3/4 of Rs. 400	300	
Proposed Dividend of Ack Ltd. @ 10%	30,000	30,450
Balance to Balance Sheet		20,025

(iii) *Minority Interest*

Face value of shares held	20,000	10,000
Add: Proportionate share of profit brought forward from the previous year	2,250	1,600
Proportionate share of current year's profits*	925	600
	23,175	12,200

(iv) *Goodwill or Cost of Control :*

Amount paid	75,000	50,000
Less: Face value of shares	60,000	40,000
	15,000	10,000
Less: Proportionate profits brought forward from 1997-98	6,750	6,400
	8,250	3,600

Consolidated Balance Sheet of Ack Ltd. and its subsidiaries, Tick Ltd. and Tock Ltd., as on March 31, 2010

Liabilities	*Rs.*	*Assets*	*Rs.*	*Rs.*
Share Capital :				
Equity shares of Rs. 10 each	1,50,000	Goodwill on Consolidation		11,850
Minority Interest	35,375	Other Fixed Assets	89,000	
General Reserve	10,000	*Less:* Unrealised profit	150	88,850
Profit & Loss Account	20,025	Current Assets :		
Creditors :		Stock	66,000	
Trade	54,000	*Less:* Unrealised Profit	300	65,700
Bills payable	1,000	Debtors		1,03,000
Proposed Dividend	30,000	Bank		31,000
	3,00,400			3,00,400

Illustration 45:

You are requested to prepare from the following data the Consolidated Balance Sheet of a group of companies :—

Balance Sheets as on 31st March, 2009

Liabilities	*A Ltd.* *Rs.*	*B Ltd* *Rs.*	*C Ltd.* *Rs.*	*Assets*	*A Ltd.* *Rs.*	*B Ltd.* *Rs.*	*C Ltd.* *Rs.*
Share Capital	1,25,000	1,00,000	60,000	Fixed Assets	28,000	55,000	37,500
Reserves	18,000	10,000	7,200	Investments : (at cost)			
Profit and Loss A/c	16,000	2,000	5,100	Shares in :			
C Ltd. Balance	3,300	—	—	*B* Ltd.	85,000	—	—
Sundry Creditors	7,000	5,000	—	*C* Ltd.	18,000	53,000	—
A Ltd. Balance	—	7,000	—	Stock-in-trade	12,000	—	—
				B Ltd. Balance	8,000	—	—
				Sundry Debtors	18,300	16,000	31,500
				A Ltd. Balance	—	—	3,300
	1,69,300	1,24,000	72,300		1,69,300	1,24,000	72,300

*If desired, the figure can be split into "proposed dividend" and the balance.

Notes :
(i) The share capital of all companies is divided into shares of Rs. 100 each.
(ii) A Ltd. held 750 shares of B Ltd. and 150 shares of C Ltd.
(iii) B Ltd. held 400 shares of C Ltd.
(iv) All investments were made on 30th September, 2009.
(v) The following balances were there on 1st April, 2010 :

	B Ltd. Rs.	C Ltd. Rs.
Reserves	9,000	6,000
Profit and Loss A/c	1,000	840

(vi) Dividends have not been declared by any company during the year, nor are any proposed.
(vii) B Ltd. sold goods costing Rs. 4,000 to A Ltd. at the price of Rs. 4,400. These goods were still unsold on 31st March, 2009.
(viii) Included in the current account of B Ltd. is an amount of Rs. 320 being interest credited to A Ltd. *(Adapted from C.A. Final)*

Solution :

Workings
Analysis of Profits : C. Ltd.

	Capital Profits Rs.	Revenue Reserves Rs.	Current Profits Rs.
Reserve	6,600	600	—
P. & L. A/c on 1st April, 2008	840	—	—
Profit for 2008-09	2,130	—	2,130
Total	9,570	600	2,130
Less: 1/4 to A Ltd.	2,392	150	533
	7,178	450	1,597
Less: 1/12 (of total) to outsiders	798	50	177
To B Ltd.	6,380	400	1,420
B Ltd.			
Reserves	9,500	500	—
P. & L. A/c on 1st April, 2008	1,000	—	—
Profit for 2008-09	500	—	500
Total for B Ltd.	17,380	900	1,920
Less: 1/4 to outsiders	4,345	225	480
	13,035	675	1,440
Less: unrealised profit : 400 × 3/4			300
			1,140

Cost of Control :

Total Cost of Shares		1,56,000
Less : Face Value of Shares	1,30,000	
Capital Profit :		
from B Ltd.	13,035	
from C Ltd.	2,392	1,45,427
Cost of Control or Goodwill		10,573

Minority Interest :

	B Ltd. Rs.	C Ltd. Rs.
Face value of shares	25,000	5,000
Share of capital profits	4,345	798
Share of revenue reserves	225	50
Share of current profits	480	177
Total	30,050	6,025

Consolidated Balance Sheet as on 31st March, 2009

Liabilities	*Rs.*	*Rs.*	*Assets*	*Rs.*	*Rs.*
Share Capital		1,25,000	Goodwill on consolidation		10,573
Reserves :	18,000		Fixed Assets		1,20,500
Add: Reserve from *C* Ltd.	150		Current Assets		
B Ltd.	675	18,825	Stock-in-Trade	12,000	
Profit & Loss A/c :	16,000		*Less:* Stock Reserve	300	11,700
Add: Profit from *C* Ltd.	533		Sundry Debtors		65,800
B Ltd.	1,140	17,673	Cash in Transit*		1,000
Sundry Creditors		12,000	*Difference between the amount owned by B Ltd. to A Ltd. and the amount shown by A Ltd. in its balance sheet as owing from B Ltd.		
Minitority Interest:					
B Ltd.	30,050				
C Ltd.	6,025	36,075			
		2,09,573			2,09,573

Illustration 46:

The following figures were extracted from three companies' records for the year ended 31st March, 2009 :–

	A Ltd. Rs.	*D Ltd.* Rs.	*P Ltd.* Rs.
Revenue Reserve on 31st March, 2008	29,690	42,000	64,000
Stock on hand on 31st March, 2008	90,270	1,67,230	96,540
Sales	11,51,250	9,38,000	7,56,000
Purchases	7,10,970	4,99,620	3,08,200
Overhead Expenses	1,42,900	87,200	75,000
Distribution Expenses	27,600	54,800	81,000
Interim Dividend paid on 1st October, 2008 :			
Equity Shares	48,000	25,000	20,000
Preference Shares		6,000	
Capital — Equity Shares of Rs. 10 each	4,00,000	2,50,000	2,00,000
10% Preference shares of Rs. 10 each		1,20,000	

You also obtain the following information :

(1) On 1st November, 2008 A Ltd. purchased 20,000 equity shares and 8,000 Preference shares in D Ltd. on 1st April, 2008.

(2) On 1st December, 2008 A Ltd. purchased 15,000 Equity Shares in P Ltd.

(3) The profits of D Ltd. and P Ltd. are deemed to accrue evenly throughout the year.

(4) A Ltd. buys goods for resale from D Ltd. at a price which yields a profit to D Ltd. of 33 1/3% on selling price.

A Ltd. also sells goods to P Ltd. at a price which yields a profit to A Ltd. of 25% on selling price. In the stocks in hand as on 31st March, 2009 A Ltd. held stocks purchased from D Ltd. for Rs. 36,000; P Ltd. held stocks purchased from A Ltd. for Rs. 20,000—the latter were out of goods purchased by A Ltd. from D Ltd.

(5) Stocks on hand as on 31st March, 2009 were A Ltd. Rs. 1,10,490; D Ltd. Rs. 84,740.

(6) Provision for corporation tax based on the profits for the year is to be made as to A Ltd. Rs. 1,50,000; D Ltd. Rs. 1,30,000 and P Ltd. Rs. 1,45,000.

(7) A Ltd. proposes to pay a final dividend on Equity shares of 33% D Ltd. a half year's dividend on Preference shares and final dividend on Equity shares of 30% and P Ltd. a final dividend of 40%.

You are required to prepare a profit and loss account of A Ltd. and its subsidiary companies for the year ended 31st March, 2009. (Separate profit & loss accounts need not be given). Ignore taxation.

Solution :

Consolidated Profit & Loss Account of A Ltd. and its subsidiaries, D Ltd. & P Ltd., for the year ending March 31, 2009

	Aggre Rs.	Adjust. Rs.	Net Rs.		Aggre.. Rs.	Adjust. Rs.	Net Rs.
To Cost of Sales	15,56,750	56,000*	15,00,750	By Sales	28,45,250	56,000*	27,89,250
To Overhead Expenses	3,05,100		3,05,100				
To Distribution Expenses	1,63,400		1,63,400				
To Provision for taxation	4,25,000		4,25,000				
To Profit after tax	3,95,000		3,95,000				
	28,45,250	56,000	27,89,250		28,45,250	56,000	27,89,250
To Interim Dividend	99,000	—	99,000	By Profit after tax	3,95,000		3,95,000
To Proposed Equity Dividend	2,87,000	1,20,000	1,67,000	By Proposed Dividend—D Ltd.	60,000	60,000	—
Proposed Dividend				P Ltd.	60,000	60,000	—
(Preference)-D Ltd.	6,000	4,000	2,000	D Ltd. (Preference)	4,000	4,000	—
To Minority Interest	10,350		10,350				
To Capital Profits	96,234		96,234				
To Stock Reserve	17,350		17,350				
To Balance c/d	3,066		3,066				
	5,19,000	1,24,000	3,95,000		5,19,000	1,24,000	3,95,000

*Assumed equal to stocks in hand.

Working Notes :

(1) *Consolidation Schedule*

	A Ltd.. Rs.	Rs.	D Ltd. Rs.	Rs.	P Ltd. Rs.	Rs.
Sale		11,51,250		9,38,000		7,56,000
Less: Cost of sales						
Opening stock	90,270		1,67,230		96,540	
Purchases	7,10,970		4,99,620		3,08,200	
	8,01,240		6,66,850		4,04,740	
Less: Closing stock	1,10,490	6,90,750	1,20,850	5,46,000	84,740	3,20,000
Gross Profit		4,60,500		3,92,000		4,36,000
Less: Expenses :						
Overhead	1,42,900		87,200		75,000	
Distribution	27,600	1,70,500	54,800	1,42,000	81,000	1,56,000
		2,90,000		2,50,000		2,80,000
Taxation		1,50,000		1,30,000		1,45,000
Profit after taxation		1,40,000		1,20,000		1,35,000

(2) **Profit & Loss A/c-D Ltd.**

	Capital 7/12 Rs.	Revenue 5/12 Rs.		Capital 7/12 Rs.	Revenue 5/12 Rs.
Div. Paid or Proposed 1,00,000 (7 : 5)	58,333	41,667	By Balance after Dividend Preference	63,000	45,000
Minority Interest (1/5 of balance)	933	667			
Share of A Ltd.	3,734	2,666			
	63,000	45,000		63,000	45,000

(3) **Profit & Loss A/c-P Ltd.**

		2/3	1/3		2/3	1/3
Div. Paid or proposed				By Balance	90,000	45,000
Paid	20,000					
Proposed	80,000	66,667	33,333			
	1,00,000					
Minority Interest (1/4)		5,833	2,917			
Share of A Ltd.		17,500	8,750			
		90,000	45,000		90,000	45,000

(4) *Dividends*

Equity	*Interim*	*Proposed*
A Ltd.	48,000	1,32,000
D Ltd.	25,000	75,000
P Ltd.	20,000	80,000
	93,000	2,87,000
Add: Preference Dividend	6,000	6,000*
	99,000	2,93,000

* Shown separately.

(5) *Capital Profits*

	D Ltd. Rs.	*P Ltd.* Rs.	*Total* Rs.
Proposed Dividend	75,000	80,000	1,55,000
Share of Minority Interest 1/5 and 1/4	15,000	20,000	35,000
	60,000	60,000	1,20,000
"Capital" portion, pertaining to pre-acquisition period	35,000	40,000	75,000
"Capital" portion of balance in P. & L. A/c	3,734	27,500	21,234
	38,734	57,500	96,234

(6) *Stock Reserve*

	A Ltd's Share Rs.	Rs.
Stock with A Ltd. ex D Ltd.	36,000	
Total Profit @ 33 1/3%	12,000	9,600
Stock with P Ltd.	20,000	
Profit of A Ltd. 25%	5,000	3,750
"Cost" to A ex-D	15,000	
Profit @ 33 1/3%	5,000	4,000
		17,350

Illustration 47:

Whole Ltd. purchased 8,000 shares in Fragment Ltd. 2004-05, and a further 2,000 shares in 2006-07. In 2004-05 Fragment Ltd. had no capital reserve and a balance on revenue reserve of Rs. 15,000; in 2006-07 the balances on capital and revenue reserves were Rs. 60,000 and Rs. 30,000 respectively.

Whole Ltd. purchased 12,000 shares in Part Ltd. in 2005-06 when there had been an adverse balance on reserves of Rs. 40,000.

As on 31st March, 2009 the balance sheets of the three companies showed the following position :

	Whole Ltd.		Fragment Ltd.		Part Ltd.	
	Rs.	Rs.	Rs.	Rs.	Rs.	Rs.
Fixed Assets						
Freehold land*		89,000		30,000		65,000
Buildings*	1,00,000		1,20,000		40,000	
Less: aggregate depreciation	36,000	64,000	40,000	80,000	16,400	23,600
Plant and equipment*	1,02,900		1,70,000		92,000	
Less: aggregate depreciation	69,900	33,000	86,000	84,000	48,200	43,800
Investments						
Shares in Fragment Ltd.*	1,35,000					
Share in Part Ltd.*	75,000	2,10,000				
Current Assets						
Stock in hand	68,740		76,490		81,070	
Debtors	1,96,420		1,23,732		45,660	
Balance at Bank	81,520	3,46,680	42,760	2,42,982	31,470	1,58,200
	7,42,680		4,36,982		2,90,600	
Deduct Current Liabilities						
Creditors	1,60,014		1,13,722		59,638	
Provision for taxation	56,900		47,620		22,490	
Proposed dividends	90,000	3,06,914	48,000	2,09,342	16,000	98,128
		4,35,766		2,27,640		1,92,472
Financed By :						
Share capital : authorised and issued share of Rs. 10 each, fully paid		3,00,000		1,20,000		1,60,000
Capital reserve		70,000		60,000		—
Revenue reserve		65,766		47,640		32,472
		4,35,766		2,27,640		1,92,472

*at cost

You are also given the following additional information :

(1) The proposed dividends from subsidiary companies have been included in the figure for debtors in the accounts of the parent company.

(2) On 1st April, 2008 Part Ltd. had purchased a warehouse from Whole Ltd. for Rs. 50,000 apportioned as to Rs. 30,000 for land. Whole Ltd. had originally acquired the warehouse on 1st April, 2004 for Rs. 30,000 (building Rs. 15,000 and land Rs. 15,000). The group policy is to depreciate buildings on a straight line basis over fifty years. The surplus over cost on the sale of the land and building has been credited to capital reserve.

You are required to prepare the consolidated balance sheet of Whole Ltd. and its subsidiaries as on 31st March, 2009.

Solution :

Consolidated Balance Sheet of Whole Ltd. and its subsidiaries, Fragment Ltd. and Part Ltd., as on 31st March, 2009

Liabilities	*Rs.*	*Assets*	*Rs.*	*Rs.*
Share Capital		Fixed Assets		
Authorised, Issued & Subscribed:		Freehold land at cost		1,69,000
30,000 shares of Rs. 10 each		Buildings at cost	2,55,000	
fully paid	3,00,000	*Less:* Depreciation	93,500	1,61,500
Reserves & Surplus		Plant & Equipment		
Capital Reserve	90,000	at cost	3,64,900	
Capital Reserve on Consolidation	5,000	*Less*: Depreciation	2,04,100	1,60,800

	Rs.		Rs.
Revenue Reserve*	1,43,695	Investment	—
Secured Loans	—	Current Assets	
Unsecured Loans	—	Stock in Trade	2,26,300
Current liabilities & Provisions		Sundry Debtors	3,13,812
Sundry Creditors	3,33,374	Cash at Bank	1,55,750
Provision for Income tax	1,27,010		
Proposed Dividends	1,02,000		
Minority Interest	86,083		
	11,87,162		11,87,162

* Out of Revenue Reserve Rs. 30,000 may not be available for dividend.

Working Notes :

(i) *Part Ltd.—Analysis of profits:*	*Capital Profits* Rs.	*Post-acquisition Capital Reserve* Rs.	*Revenue Reserve* Rs.
Balance in 2005-06	– 40,000		
Profit earned since acquisition			72,472
Add: back excess depreciation			100
	– 40,000		72,572
Minority Interest (1/4)	– 10,000		18,143
Share of Whole Ltd.	– 30,000		54,429
(ii) *Fragment Ltd.—Analysis of profits:*			
Balance in 2004-05 (Revenue Reserve)	15,000		
Increase during 2005-06 and 2006-07		60,000	15,000
Increase during 2007-08 and 2008-09			17,640
	15,000	60,000	32,640
Minority Interest (1/6)	2,500	– 10,000	– 5,440
Share of Whole Ltd.	12,500	50,000	27,000
Part of Revenue Profit treated as Capital on acquisition in 2006-07 (1/6 of Rs. 60,000 and Rs. 15,000 respectively)	+ 12,500	-10,000	-2,500
	25,000	40,000	24,700

(iii) *Cost of Control/Capital Reserve :*

Cost of Investments in Fragment Ltd.		1,35,000
Cost of Investments in Part Ltd.		75,000
		2,10,000
Paid up value of shares in Fragment Ltd.	1,00,000	
Paid up value of shares in Part Ltd.	1,20,000	
Capital Profits in Fragment Ltd.	25,000	
	2,45,000	
Less: Capital Loss in Part Ltd.	30,000	2,15,000
Capital Reserve		5,000

(iv) *Minority Interest :*	*Fragment Ltd.* Rs.	*Part Ltd.* Rs.
Share Capital	20,000	40,000
Post-acquisiton Capital Profits	2,500	–10,000
Capital Reserve	10,000	—
Revenue Reserve	5,440	18,143
	37,940	48,143

(v) *Whole Ltd.'s Retained Profits :*	*Capital Reserve Rs.*	*Revenue Reserve Rs.*
Balance as per Books	70,000	65,766
Less: Capital profit on sale of warehouse and depreciation for four years written back (300 × 4)	– 20,000	– 1,200
	50,000	64,566
Share in Fragment Ltd.	40,000	24,700
Share in Part Ltd.	—	54,429
	90,000	1,43,695

(vi) *Sundry Debtors* — *Whole*		1,96,420
— Fragment		1,23,732
— Part		45,660
		3,65,812
Less : Dividends receivable by Whole Ltd.		
5/6 × 48,000	40,000	
3/4 × 16,000	12,000	52,000
		3,13,812

(vii) *Fixed Assets Transfer :*	
Land : Sale price	30,000
Cost	15,000
Profit	15,000
Buildings: Sale price	20,000
Cost	15,000
Profit	5,000
(viii) *Dividend payable :* Whole Ltd.	90,000
Minority shareholders in subsidiaries	12,000
	1,02,000

Some Alternative Workings Notes :—

1. *Acquisition of Fragment Ltd.*

	Capital Reserve Rs.	*Revenue Reserve Rs.*
2004-05 8,000 shares (2/3)	NIL	15,000
2006-07 2,000 shares (1/6)	60,000	30,000

2. *Acquisition of Part Ltd.*

2005-06 12,000 shares (3/4)		(40,000)

3. *Cost of Control Account*

	Rs.		*Rs.*
Cost of investment	2,10,000	Shares of Fragment	1,00,000
Part Ltd. Reserves	30,000	Share of Part	1,20,000
	2,40,000	Fragment Ltd, Capital Res.	10,000
Capital Reserve	5,000	Fragment Revenue Res.	5,000
	2,45,000		2,45,000

4. *Consolidated Capital Reserve*

	Rs.		*Rs.*
Land	15,000	Whole Ltd.	70,000
Buildings	5,000	Fragment Ltd.	40,000
Balance c/d	90,000		
	1,10,000		1,10,000

5. *Consolidated Revenue Reserve*

	Rs.		Rs.
Depreciation on buildings*	1,200	Whole Ltd.	65,766
Balance c/cd	1,43,695	Fragment Ltd.	21,760
		Fragment Ltd.	2,940
		Part Ltd.	54,429
	1,44,895		1,44,895

* On sale of Building, an amount equal to the provision for depreciation must have been added back to revenue which has now been restored to provision for depreciation.

6. *Minority Interests*

	Rs.		Rs.
Balance	86,083	Shares in Fragment Ltd.	20,000
		Shares in Part Ltd.	40,000
		Capital Res. of Fragment Ltd.	10,000
		Revenue Res. of Fragment Ltd.	7,940
		Part Ltd. Revenue Res.	8,143
	86,083		86,083

7. *Capital Reserves of Fragment Ltd.*

	Rs.		Rs.
Cost of Control (1/6 × 60,000)		Capital Reserve b/d	60,000
Consolidated	10,000		
Capital Reserve (2/3 × 60,000)	40,000		
Minority Interest (1/6 × 60,000)	10,000		
	60,000		60,000

Revenue Reserve of Fragment Ltd.

	Rs.		Rs.
Cost of Control (2/3 of 15,000)	10,000	Revenue Reserve b/d	47,640
Cost of Control (1/6 of 30,000)			
Consolidated	5,000		
Revenue Reserve (1/6 of 17,640)	21,760		
Revenue Reserve (1/6 of 17,640)	2,940		
Minority Interest (1/6 of 47,640)	7,940		
	47,640		47,640

8. *Reserves of Part Ltd.*

	Rs.		Rs.
Consolidated Revenue Reserve			
(3/4 × 72,472)	54,354	Revenue Reserves b/d	32,472
Minority Interest (1/4 of 32,472)	8,118	Cost of Control (3/4 × 40,000)	30,000
	62,472		62,472

Inter-company holdings :

In India, a subsidiary company is not allowed to acquire shares in its holding company. But if the subsidiary company had acquired shares in the holding company before it became the subsidiary or before the commencement of the Companies Act, 1956, the company can continue to hold the shares [section 42 (3)]. However, the subsidiary company will not be able to exercise any voting rights at the meetings of the members of the holding company.

From the accounts point of view, the profits belonging to the subsidiary company will have to be calculated taking into consideration the fact that it will have a right on the profit of the holding company also which, in turn, will claim its share of the profits of the subsidiary company. A proper calculation of the subsidiary company's profit is obviously necessary for ascertaining minority interest. But, as has been pointed out already, cost of control cannot be calculated without ascertaining the holding company's share of capital profits of the subsidiary company. This will again require taking into account profits of the holding company up to the date the holding company acquired control over the subsidiary company. It will be remembered that profits of the subsidiary company, even if revenue in nature up to the date of acquisition of control, are capital from the point of view of the holding company. This will include that part of profits also which the subsidiary company claims from the holding company. Calculations of profits mentioned above will require algebraical equations; these are illustrated below.

While consolidating the balance sheets, paid up value of shares held by the subsidiary company will be deducted from the share capital of the holding company. Any excess amount paid (over the paid up amount) should be added to Cost of Control or Goodwill.

Illustration 49:

Following are the balance sheets of two companies H Ltd. and S Ltd. as on March, 2009 :—

	H Ltd. *Rs.*	*S Ltd.* *Rs.*		*H Ltd.* *Rs.*	*S Ltd.* *Rs.*
Share Capital (Shares of Rs. 100 each, fully paid)	10,00,000	5,00,000	Sundry Assets	9,00,000	6,90,000
			Investments 4,000 shares in S. Ltd.	5,00,000	
Reserves	3,00,000	2,00,000	1,000 shares in H. Ltd.		1,10,000
Creditors	1,00,000	1,00,000			
	14,00,000	8,00,000		14,00,000	8,00,000

H Ltd. acquired the shares in S Ltd. on 1st April, 2008 when reserves in S Ltd. stood at Rs. 1,20,000 and in H Ltd. at Rs. 1,80,000. S Ltd. had acquired the shares in H Ltd. on 1st April 2007. Prepare the consolidated balance sheet of the two companies.

Solution :

(*i*) *Capital Profit of S Ltd.* :

Let Capital profits of S Ltd. be X and that of H Ltd. Y. Then

$$X = 1,20,000 + 1/10Y; \text{ and}$$
$$Y = 1,80,000 + 4/5X;$$
$$Y = 1,80,000 + 4/5(1,20,000 + 1/10Y), \text{ substituting the value of X}$$
$$Y = 1,80,000 + 96,000 + 2/25Y$$
$$= 2,76,000 + 2/25Y$$
$$25Y = 69,00,000 + 2Y$$
$$23Y = 69,00,000$$
$$Y = 3,00,000$$
$$X = 1,20,000 + 1/10 \times 3,00,000 + \text{Rs. } 1,50,000$$

Share of Minority Shareholders : 1,50,000 × 1/5 Rs. 30,000

Share of H Ltd. Rs. 1,20,000

Since the capital profit in the balance sheet of S Ltd. is only Rs. 1,20,000 in all, Rs. 30,000 (to make it Rs. 1,50,000) will have to be transferred from the Reserves of H Ltd.-

(*ii*) *Revenue Profit of S Ltd.*

Let the Revenue Profits of S Ltd. be x and that of H Ltd. y.

Then—

$$x = 80,000 + 1/10y; \text{ and}$$
$$y = 1,20,000 + 4/5x$$
$$x = 80,000 + 1/10(1,20,000 + 4/5x), \text{ substituting the value of y}$$
$$= 80,000 + 12,000 + 2/25x$$
$$= 92,000 + 2/25x$$
$$25x = 23,00,000 + 2x$$
$$23x = 23,00,000$$
$$x = 1,00,000$$

Share of Minority Shareholders : Rs. 1,00,000 × 1/5 = Rs. 20,000

Total profit of S Ltd. being Rs. 80,000, the share of H Ltd. is Rs. 60,000.

	Rs.	Rs.
(iii) *Cost of Control :*		
Amount paid for 4,000 shares		5,00,000
Less : Face value	4,00,000	
Capital Profit	1,20,000	5,20,000
Capital Reserve		20,000
Less : Excess amount paid by S Ltd. (over face value of 1,000 shares)		10,000
Capital Reserve		10,000
(iv) *Minority Interest :*		
Face value of shares		1,00,000
Add Share of Capital Profit		30,000
Share of Revenue Profits		20,000
		1,50,000

Consolidated Balance Sheet of H Ltd. and its subsidiary S Ltd. as on March 31, 2009

Liabilities	*Rs.*	*Rs.*	*Assets*	*Rs.*
Share Capital 10,000 on shares of			Sundry Assets	15,90,000
Rs. 100 each, fully paid		10,00,000		
Less: Shares held by S Ltd.		1,00,000		
		9,00,000		
Capital Reserve		10,000		
Reserves	3,00,000			
Less: treated as Capital Profit	30,000			
	2,70,000			
Add: share of H Ltd. in Revenue Reserve of S Ltd.	60,000	3,30,000		
Creditors :				
H Ltd.	1,00,000			
S Ltd.	1,00,000	2,00,000		
Minority Interest		1,50,000		
		15,90,000		15,90,000

Foreign Subsidiaries :

Foreign subsidiary companies should be consolidated along with other subsidiary companies in the usual manner. This will be possible only if the trial balance of the foreign subsidiary is first converted into 'home' currency. The rules for conversion are the same as for foreign branches.

There may, however, be subsidiary companies in some countries where the political or economic conditions do not permit free transactions, specially remittance of profits to the holding company. Severe exchange restrictions will lead to such a state of affairs. In the case of such foreign subsidiaries, consolidation is not recommended. Instead, the equity method should be followed. This is discussed under "Associated Companies".

Illustration 49:

The following summarised balance sheets as on March, 2009 are given :—

	A Ltd. Rs.	*B Ltd.* Rs.	*C Ltd.* T sh.
Share Capital (fully paid shares of Rs. 100/T sh. 100 each)	20,00,000	5,00,000	5,00,000
Reserves & Surplus	6,00,000	2,50,000	3,50,000
Loan from B Ltd. (Including interest)	2,25,000	—	—
Bank Overdraft	—	1,40,000	—
Sundry Creditors	2,40,000	2,10,000	1,60,000
	30,65,000	11,00,000	10,10,000

	Rs.	Rs.	T. sh
Fixed Assets	16,00,000	5,00,000	6,00,000
Investment :			
In B Ltd.	4,72,500		
In C Ltd.	5,25,000		
Other		45,000	30,000
Loan to A Ltd.	—	2,00,000	—
Cash at Bank	1,20,000	16,000	60,000
Other Current Assets	3,02,500	3,84,000	3,20,000
	30,65,000	11,00,000	10,10,000

The following other information is available :—

(1) The reserves of the various companies as on April 1, 2008 were :
A Ltd. Rs. 4,30,000; B Ltd. Rs. 2,00,000; C Ltd. TSh. 1,70,000.

(2) B Ltd. had advanced the loan to A Ltd. on April 1,2008.

(3) On October 1, 2008, B Ltd. issued fully paid bonus shares at the rate of one share for every four held. On the same date, a dividend of 10% was paid for 2007-08.

(4) A Ltd. had purchased 3,500 shares in B Ltd. on July 1, 2008 but had disposed of 375 shares on January 31, 2009 at Rs. 140, the sale proceeds being credited to the concerned Investment Account which so far has only this entry in addition to that made on the acquisition of the shares.

(5) 3,500 shares were acquired in C Ltd. on September 30, 2008 @ Rs. 150 per share. C Ltd. is a Tanzanian company; the currency of Tanzania is "Shilling".

(6) Stock of C Ltd. include goods costing Rs. 10,000 sent by A Ltd. at the invoice value of Rs. 12,500 which were recorded in the books of C Ltd. at T Sh. 11,625.

(7) There has been no movement in the fixed assets or share capital of C Ltd. during the year.

(8) C Ltd. paid in January, 2009 an interim dividend @ 6% p.a. for six months. C Ltd. remitted the amount due to A Ltd. when Rs. 100 was equal to T Sh. 94.

(9) The exchange rates between India and Tanzania during 2008 were as follows :-

April 1, 2008	Rs. 100 = 92 Sh.
September 30, 2008	Rs. 100 = 90 Sh.
March 31, 2009	Rs. 100 = 93 Sh.
Average	Rs. 100 = 91 Sh.

Prepare the consolidated balance sheet of the group.

Solution :

Consolidated Balance Sheet of A Ltd. and its subsidiaries B Ltd. and C Ltd. as on March 31, 2009

	Rs.		Rs.
Share Capital	20,00,000	Fixed Assets	27,66,667
Reserves & Surplus (Revenue)	7,50,583	Investments	78,333
Capital Reserve	10,500	Cash at Bank	2,00,516
Capital Reserve on Consolidation	1,14,448	Other current assets	10,28,045
Minority Interest	4,35,942		
Bank Overdraft	1,40,000		
Sundry Creditors	6,22,088		
	40,73,561		40,73,561

Working Notes :

(1) *Conversion of figures relating to C Ltd. :-*

	Dr. T. Sh.	Cr. T. Sh.	Rate (Sh.=Rs. 100)	Dr. Rs.	Cr. Rs.
Share Capital		5,00,000	90		5,55,556
Reserves & Surplus :					
As on September 30, 2008		2,52,500	90		2,80,556
Remaining		97,500	91		1,07,143
Sundry Creditors		1,60,000	93		1,72,088
Fixed Assets	6,00,000		90	6,66,667	
Investments	30,000		90	33,333	
Cash at Bank	60,000		93	63,516	
Stock, ex A Ltd.	11,625		Actual	12,500	
Other current assets	3,08,375		93	3,31,545	
Difference in exchange	—	—	—	6,782	
	10,10,000	10,10,000		11,15,343	11,15,343

	No.	Rs.	
(2) *Shares acquired on 1st July, 2008*	3,500	5,25,000	(Original cost, balancing figure)
Bonus Shares	875	—	
Total	4,375	5,25,000	
Shares disposed of	375	52,500	
Shares held at present	4,000	4,72,500	(as per Balance Sheet)
Cost of Shares	4,375	5,25,000	
Less: Dividend received in respect of 2007-08		35,000	
	4,375	4,90,000	

(3) *Cost per share 4,90,000 ÷ 4,375*	112
Sale price	140
Profit per share	28
Total profit on 375 shares	10,500

(4) *Profit earned by B Ltd. in 2008-09*

	Rs.	Rs.	Rs.
Reserves and Surplus as shown in Balance Sheet			2,50,000
Add: Interest on Loan to A Ltd.			25,000
			2,75,000
Less : Reserves as on 1st April, 2008		2,00,000	
Less : Utilised for bonus shares	1,00,000		
Dividend for 2007-08	40,000	1,40,000	60,000
			2,15,000

	T. Sh.	T. Sh.
*Reserve Surplus as on April 1, 2008		17,000
Profit for 2008-09 (3,50,000–1,70,000)	1,80,000	
Add: Interim dividend paid	15,000	
	1,95,000	
Profit up to September 30, 2008	97,500	
Less: Interim Dividend paid	15,000	82,500
		2,52,500

(5) *Analysis of Profits*

	B Ltd. Capital Rs.	B Ltd. Revenue Rs.	C Ltd. Capital Rs.	C Ltd. Revenue Rs.
Reserves and Surplus as on April 1, 2008	60,000			
Profit earned up to the date of acquisition	53,750		2,80,556	
Profit earned after the date of acquisition		1,61,250		1,07,143
Less : Loss on Exchange		—		6,782
	1,13,750	1,61,250	2,80,556	1,00,361
Minority Interest(20% and 30%)	22,750	32,250	84,167	30,108
Share of A Ltd.	91,000	1,29,000	1,96,389	70,253

(6) *Reserves and Surplus of A Ltd. :*

Balance as given		6,00,000
Less: Dividend from		
B Ltd. (On 3,500 shares)	35,000	
C Ltd. (T. Sh. 10,500 @ Sh. 94 = Rs. 100)	11,170	46,170
		5,53,830
Add: Revenue Profit from : B Ltd.		1,29,000
C Ltd.		70,253
		7,53,083
Less : Stock Reserve		2,500
		7,50,583

(7) *Minority Interest*

	B Ltd. Rs.	C Ltd. Rs.
Share Capital	1,00,000	1,66,667
Capital Profits	22,750	84,167
Revenue Profits	32,250	30,108
	1,55,000	2,80,942

Total Rs. 4,35,942.

(8) *Cost of Capital/Capital Reserve :*

			B Ltd. Rs.	C Ltd. Rs.
Cost of Shares acquired			4,72,500	5,25,000
Less : Dividend Received			35,000	11,170
			4,37,500	5,13,830
Add : Profit on sale of shares			10,500	—
			4.48,000	5,13,830
	B Ltd.	C Ltd.		
Face value of shares	4,00,000	3,88,889		
Capital Profits	91,000	1,96,389	4,91,000	5,85,278
Capital reserve Total Rs. 1,14,448			43,000	71,448

(9) *Current Assets :*

		Rs.
A Ltd.		3,02,500
B Ltd.		3,84,000
C Ltd. —	Stock	12,500
	Others	3,31,545
		10,30,545
Less : Stock Reserve*		2,500
		10,28,045

* It would also be permissible to deduct only 70% (A. Ltd.'s share) of this amount.

Associated Companies :

The Institute of Chartered Accountants of India issued Accounting Standard 23 on 'Accounting for Investments in Associates in Consolidated Financial Statement' effective in respect of accounting periods commencing on or after 1.4.2002. The accounting standard sets out principles and procedures on recognising, in the consolidated financial statements the effect of investment in associates on the financial positions and operating results of the group. An associated company is one in which the investor has significant influence but which is neither a subsidiary nor a joint venture of the investor. Significant influence is the power to participate in the finanical and/or operating policy decisions of the investee but not control over those policies. Broadly, it may be stated that if the investor holds 20% or more of the voting power, it will have the power to exercise significant influence over the investee company. The interest should be a long-term one–temporary acquisition of shares will not make the investee company an associated company.

Equity Method : In the equity method of accounting, the investment is initially recorded at cost, identifying any goodwill or capital reserve arising at the time of acquisition. The carrying amount of investment is adjusted thereafter for the post-acquisition change in the investor's share of net assets of the investee. In the consolidated profit and loss account, investor's share of the results of operations of the investee is shown.

Dividends received from an investee reduce the carrying amount of the investment. But dividend proposed by the associate company will not affect the carrying amount of the investment in the books of the investor. Adjustments to the carrying amount may also be necessary for alterations in the investor's proportionate interest in the investee arising from changes in the investee's equity that have not been included in the income statement. For example revaluation of fixed assets of the investee company may require such an adjustment; an appreciation in the value of fixed assets being recorded through revaluation reserve.

Illustration 50:

Harry Ltd., which has an authorised and issued Share Capital of 10 crore equity shares of Rs. 10 each fully paid, has a balance of revenue reserve of Rs. 1,62,000 thousand on 31st March, 2008, after paying a dividend for the year ended on that date.

You are also given the following information :

(1) On 1st April, 2008, Harry Ltd. purchased 90 lakh of the 4 crore issued equity shares of Rs. 10 each fully paid in Anoop Ltd. for Rs. 1,42,500 thousand. The balance on revenue reserve of Anoop Ltd. as on 31st March, 2008 was Rs. 3,45,000 thousand after paying a dividend for the year ended on that date.

(2) For the year ended 31st March 2009, Harry Ltd. made a trading profit of Rs. 1,84,000 thousand and paid a dividend of 15% whilst Anoop Ltd. made a trading profit of Rs. 1,40,000 thousand and paid a dividend of 20%.

(3) For the year ended 31st March, 2010, Harry Ltd. made a trading profit of Rs. 2,65,400 thousand and paid a dividend of 20% whilst Anoop Ltd. incurred a trading loss of Rs. 1,41,000 thousand and no dividend was paid.

(4) During the year ended 31st March, 2010, Anoop Ltd. had manufactured and sold to Harry Ltd. an item of plant for Rs. 80,000 thousand which included a profit on selling price to Anoop Ltd. thousand of 25%. The plant had been included in the fixed assets of Harry Ltd. and a full year's depreciation had been provided thereon at 20% on cost.

You are required to show how the above items would be reflected in the Balance Sheet of Harry Ltd. as on 31st March, 2010, together with the corresponding figures for the preceeding year.

Solution :

Balance Sheet of Harry Ltd. as on March 31, 2010

Figures on 31-3-09 *Rs.* '000		*Rs. '000*	*Figures* on 31-3-09 Rs. '000		*Rs. '000*
	Share Capital : 10 crore Equity Shares of			Investment in Anoop Ltd. Cost	1,42,500
10,00,000	Rs. 10 each fully paid	10,00,000	1,42,500	Share of Profit (loss)	
			13,500	(Post-acquisition)	(18,225)
2,09,500	Profit & Loss A/c	2,43,175			
77,625	Investment Suspense A/c (9/40 of pre-acquisition profits)	77,625	77,625	Anoop Ltd. Suspense (Share of Pre-acquisition profits)	77,625

Workings :

Profit and Loss Account Balances

	Harry Ltd. *Rs.'000*	*Anoop Ltd.* *Rs. '000*
Balance as on April 1, 2008	1,62,000	3,45,000
Profit for 2008-09	1,84,000	1,40,000
	3,46,000	4,85,000
Less: Dividend, 15% and 20%	1,50,000	80,000
Balances as on April 1, 2009	1,96,000	4,05,000
Profit (Loss) for 2009-10	2,65,400	(1,41,000)
	4,61,400	2,64,000
Dividend for 2009-10	2,00,000	—
Balance as on March 31, 2010	2,61,400	2,64,000
Share of Net loss (Rs. 81,000) for Harry Ltd. in Anoop Ltd. (9/40) for 2008-09 and 2009-2010	18,225	
	2,43,175	

Illustration 51:

R Ltd. acquired on October 1, 2008, 30 lakh shares of Rs. 100 each in V Ltd. paying Rs. 4,90,000 thousand for the shares. The issued share capital of V Ltd. consisted of 1 crore shares. In 2008-09, it earned a profit of Rs. 2,50,000 thousand and on June 16, 2009 it paid a dividend of 15%. During 2009-2010, it suffered a loss of Rs. 90,000 thousand.

Show the Investment Account in the books of R Ltd. and also show by means of a memorandum account the value at which the investment account may be shown in the Balance Sheet of R Ltd. on 31st March, 2010 assuming V Ltd. is member of a group.

Solution :

Investment in V Ltd. Account

		No.'000	*Rs.'000*			*No.'000*	*Rs.'000*
2008				2009			
October 1	To Bank	3,000	4,90,000	March 31	By Balance c/d	3,000	4,90,000
2009				2009			
April 1	To Balance b/d	3,000	4,90,000	June 16	By Bank-Dividend for half of 2002-03		22,500
				2010 March 31	By Balance c/d	3,000	4,67,500
		3,000	4,90,000			3,000	4,90,000
2010							
April	To Balance b/d	3,000	4,67,500				

Memorandum Investment in V Ltd. Account

		No. '000	Rs. '000			No. '000	Rs. '000
2008				2009			
October 1	To Bank	3,000	4,90,000	March 31	By Balance b/d	3,000	5,27,500
2009			37,500				
March 31	To P. & L. A/c*	3,000	5,27,500			3,000	5,27,500
2009				2009			
April 1	To Balance b/d	3,000	5,27,500	June 16	By Bank–Out of profits for first 6 months		22,500
				2010 March 31	By P. & L. A/c 3/10 × Rs. 90,000 thousand		27,000
					By Balance c/d	3,000	4,55,500
		3,000	5,27,500			3,000	5,27,500
2010							
April 1	To Balance b/d	3,000	4,55,500				

*Profit for the six months after the date of acquisition, 3/10 × Rs. 1,25,000.

Exercise XXII

Practical

1. From the balance sheets given below, prepare a consolidated balance sheet of A Ltd. and its subsidiary company B Ltd. :

Balance Sheets as at 31st March, 2010

Liabilities	*A Ltd.* *Rs.*	*B Ltd.* *Rs.*
Share Capital :		
Equity shares of Rs. 10 each	25,00,000	6,00,000
General reserve	3,60,000	1,20,000
Profit and loss account	2,40,000	1,80,000
Trade creditors	3,50,000	1,00,000
	34,50,000	10,00,000
Assets		
Land and building	6,40,000	2,00,000
Machinery	12,60,000	3,40,000
Furniture	1,40,000	60,000
40,000 Equity shares in B Ltd.	5,00,000	—
Stock in hand	4,10,000	2,50,000
Debtors	3,80,000	1,00,000
Bank balance	1,20,000	50,000
	34,50,000	10,00,000

At the date of acquisition by A Ltd. of its holding of 40,000 equity share in B Ltd., the latter company had undistributed profit and reserve amounting to Rs. 1,00,000, none of which has been distributed since then. *[Adapted C.S. (Inter) June, 1999]*

[Goodwill Rs. 33,333; Minority Interest Rs. 3,00,000; Total of Balance Sheet Rs. 39,83,333]

2. On April, 2008 S Ltd. issued at par 10% Preference Shares for Rs. 1,00,000. On this date, S Ltd.'s General Reserve and Profit and Loss Account showed balances of Rs. 80,000 and Rs. 35,400 respectively. On July 5, 2008 S Ltd. paid a final dividend of 12% equity shares for the year ended 31st March, 2008. S Ltd. also paid tax on Distributed Profits @ 15%. H Ltd. credited the dividend received to its Profit and Loss Account.

On April 1, 2008 H Ltd. acquired 80% equity shares in S Ltd. for Rs. 3,00,000. On this date, Machinery of S Ltd. was revalued at Rs. 2,50,000. No entry for this was made in the books of S Ltd.

On March 31, 2009, the summarised balance sheets of H Ltd. and its subsidiary S Ltd. stood as follows :-

Liabilities	H. Ltd. Rs.	S. Ltd. Rs.	Assets	H. Ltd. Rs.	S. Ltd. Rs.
Equity Share Capital	8,00,000	3,00,000	Machinery	6,25,000	2,70,000
10% Preference Share Capital	—	1,00,000	Furniture	85,000	50,000
General Reserve	4,00,000	1,50,000	Shares in S Ltd.	3,00,000	
Profit and Loss Account	2,00,000	90,000	Stock	4,00,000	1,90,000
Loans	1,10,000		Loan to H Ltd.		10,000
Bills Payable	—	4,000	Debtors	1,50,000	80,000
Creditors	1,70,000	76,000	Bank	1,20,000	1,10,000
			Preliminary Expenses	—	10,000
	16,80,000	7,20,000		16,80,000	7,20,000

The following further information is furnished :

(*i*) S Ltd. provides depreciation on Machinery @10% on written down value. No machine was sold or purchased during the year.

(*ii*) H Ltd. remitted a cheque of Rs. 10,000 to S Ltd. on 27th March, 2009 for repayment of loan, which was received by S Ltd. in April, 2009.

(*iii*) No part of preliminary expenses was written off during the year.

Prepare consolidated balance sheet of H Ltd. and S Ltd. as at 31st March, 2009.

[*B.Com.(Hons.) Delhi, 1997 Modified*]

[*Loss on Revaluation of Machinery Rs. 50,000; H Ltd.'s Profit and Loss Account Rs. 2,84,000; Goodwill Rs. 4,000; Minority Interest Rs. 2,05,000; Total of Balance Sheet Rs. 20,49,000*]

3. The balance sheets of H Ltd. and its subsidiary S Ltd. on 31st March, 2010 were as under:

Liabilities	H Ltd. Rs.	S Ltd. Rs.	Assets	H Ltd. Rs.	S Ltd. Rs.
Share Capital			Land and Buildings	6,00,000	—
Equity Shares of Rs. 10			Plant and Machinery	20,00,000	
each, fully paid	20,00,000	5,00,000	Furniture and Fixtures	90,000	1,00,000
General Reserve	3,00,000	1,00,000	30,000 Shares in		
Profit and Loss Account,			S Ltd. at cost	6,50,000	
Balance on 1st April, 2009	4,00,000	2,00,000	Stock	4,00,000	7,50,000
Profit for the year ended			Debtors	1,00,000	2,80,000
31st March, 2010	5,00,000	2,50,000	Cash in hand	10,000	15,000
Bills Payable	1,50,000		Cash at Dena Bank		1,05,000
Creditors	3,00,000	3,00,000	Bills Receivable		1,00,000
Canara Bank - overdraft	2,00,000	—			
	38,50,000	13,50,000		38,50,000	13,50,000

All the 30,000 shares in S Ltd. were acquired by H Ltd. on 1st October, 2009. Bills receivable held by S Ltd. are all accepted by H Ltd. included in debtors of S Ltd. is a sum of Rs. 60,000 owing by H Ltd. in respect of goods supplied by S Ltd.

You are required to prepare a consolidated balance sheet of H Ltd. and its subsidiary S Ltd. as at 31st March, 2010. Give all your working notes clearly. [*B.Com.(Hons.) Delhi, 1991 Modified*]

[*Revenue Profit Rs. 1,25,000; Capital Profit Rs. 4,25,000; Cost of Control Rs. 95,000; Minority Interest Rs. 4,20,000; Total of Balance Sheet Rs. 44,85,000*]

4. The balance sheets of H Ltd. and its subsidiary S Ltd. as on 31st March, 2010 are as follows:-

Liabilities	H Ltd. Rs.	S Ltd. Rs.
Equity Share Capital (Shares of Rs. 100 each, fully paid)	30,00,000	15,00,000
General Reserve, as on 1st April, 2009	8,00,000	4,00,000

	Rs.	Rs.
Profit and Loss Account, as on 1st April, 2009	2,00,000	2,50,000
Net Profit, for the year 2009-2010	6,00,000	4,00,000
15% Debentures	10,00,000	—
Creditors	4,00,000	2,70,000
Bills Payable	60,000	30,000
	60,60,000	28,50,000
Assets		
Premises	14,00,000	9,00,000
Machinery	12,00,000	7,00,000
Investment in shares of S Ltd.	17,00,000	—
Inventories	7,00,000	4,50,000
Debtors	5,00,000	4,20,000
Cash and Bank	3,80,000	2,00,000
Bills Receivable	1,80,000	80,000
Miscellaneous Expenditue, as on 1st April, 2009	—	1,00,000
	60,60,000	28,50,000

The following is the additional information :

(*i*) H Ltd. acquired 12,000 equity shares in S Ltd. on 1st April, 2009.

(*ii*) Bills receivable of H Ltd. include Rs. 30,000 accepted by S Ltd.

(*iii*) Accounts receivable of H Ltd. include Rs. 1,00,000 due from S Ltd.

(*iv*) Inventories of S Ltd. include goods purchased from H Ltd. for Rs. 1,25,000 which invoiced by H Ltd. at a profit of 25% on cost.

(*v*) Both H Ltd. and S Ltd. have proposed 10% dividend for the year 2009-2010, but no effect has been given in the balance sheets.

Prepare a consolidated balance sheet of H Ltd. and its susbsidiary S Ltd. as on 31st March, 2010, giving proper working notes. Ignore corporate dividend tax.

[*Adapted B.Com.(Hons.) Delhi, 1999*]

[*Goodwill Rs. 60,000; Minority Interest Rs. 4,90,000; Total of Balance Sheet Rs. 70,15,000*]

5. The Balance Sheet of Hari Ltd. and its subsidiary Suri Ltd. as at 31st March, 2010 are as follows :

Liabilities	*Hari Ltd.* Rs.	*Suri Ltd.* Rs.	*Assets*	*Hari Ltd.* Rs.	*Suri Ltd.* Rs.
Share Capital :			Plant and Machinery	4,80,000	90,000
Equity Shares of Rs. 10			Furniture	15,000	27,000
each, fully paid	4,00,000	1,00,000	Investments	2,00,000	
General Reserve			Stock	95,000	42,000
(on 1.4.2009)	2,80,000	34,000	Debtors	60,000	32,000
Profit and Loss Account	1,70,000	42,000	Cash at Bank	70,000	20,000
Creditors	70,000	35,000			
	9,20,000	2,11,000		9,20,000	2,11,000

The following information is also given to you :

(*i*) Hari Ltd. acquired 8,000 equity shares in Suri Ltd., as at 1st July, 2009 at a cost of Rs. 2,00,000.

(*ii*) Stock of Hari Ltd. includes Rs. 6,000 relating to stock purchased from Suri Ltd. which follows the practice of charging 25% extra on the cost for determining the sale price.

(*iii*) Creditors of Hari Ltd. include Rs. 10,000 on account of purchases from Suri Ltd.

(*iv*) Profit and Loss Account of Hari Ltd. includes dividend @ 10% for the year 2008-09 received from Suri Ltd. which declared and paid it in August, 2009.

(*v*) Balance in Suri Ltd.'s Profit and Loss Account on 1st April, 2009 was Rs. 27,500.

Dividend @10% for the year 2008-09 was declared out of this balance in August, 1998. Suri Ltd. also paid Rs. 1,500 as tax on distributed profit in August, 2009.

(*vi*) Profits during the year 2009-2010 have been earned on uniform basis throughout the year.

Prepare a consolidated balance sheet of Hari Ltd. and its subsidiary Suri Ltd. as at 31st March, 2010. Submit all your working notes neatly. [*B.Com. (Hons.) Delhi, 1992 Modified*]

[*Cost of Control Rs. 66,800; Minority Interest Rs. 35,200; Unrealised Profit Rs. 1,200; Total of Balance Sheet Rs. 9,86,600*]

6. The following are the balance sheets of RM Ltd. and its subsidiary GM Ltd. as at 31st March, 2010 :

Liabilities	*RM Ltd.*	*GM Ltd.*
	Rs.	*Rs.*
Fully paid equity shares of Rs. 10 each	6,00,000	2,00,000
General Reserve	3,40,000	80,000
Profit and Loss Account	1,00,000	60,000
Creditors	70,000	35,000
	11,10,000	3,75,000
Assets		
Machinery	3,90,000	1,35,000
Furniture	80,000	40,000
80% Shares in GM Ltd., at cost	3,40,000	
Stock	1,80,000	1,20,000
Debtors	50,000	30,000
Cash at Bank	70,000	50,000
	11,10,000	3,75,000

The following additional information is provided to you :

(*i*) Profit and Loss Account of GM Ltd. stood at Rs. 30,000 on 1st April, 2009 whereas General Reserve has remained unchanged since that date.

(*ii*) RM Ltd. acquired 80% shares in GM Ltd. on 1st October, 2009 for Rs. 3,40,000 as mentioned above.

(*iii*) Included in Debtors of GM Ltd. is a sum of Rs. 10,000 due from RM Ltd. for goods sold at a profit of 25% on cost price. Till 31st March, 2010 only one half of the goods had been sold while the remaining goods were lying in the godown of RM Ltd. as on that date.

Prepare consolidated balance sheet as at 31st March, 2009. Show all calculations clearly. [*B.Com.(Hons.) Delhi, 1990 and 1994 - Modified*]

[*Revenue Profit Rs. 15,000; Capital Profit Rs. 1,25,000; Cost of Control Rs. 80,000; Minority Interest Rs. 68,000; Unrealised Profit Rs. 1,000; Total of Balance Sheet Rs. 12,14,000*]

7. A Ltd. acquired 8,000 equity shares of B Ltd. on 1st April, 2009. The following are the balance sheets of the two companies as at 31.3.2010 :–

Liabilities	*A Ltd.*	*B Ltd.*
	Rs.	*Rs.*
Equity shares of Rs. 100 each	20,00,000	10,00,000
General reserve (1.4.2009)	4,00,000	2,00,000
Profit and loss account (1.4.2009)	1,00,000	60,000
Profit for the year 2009-2010	2,00,000	80,000
Sundry creditors	1,00,000	1,00,000
Bills payable	30,000	10,000
	28,30,000	14,50,000
Assets	*Rs.*	*Rs.*
Land and buildings	5,00,000	3,00,000
Plant and machinery	5,00,000	6,00,000

	Rs.	Rs.
Stock	1,50,000	1,00,000
Sundry debtors	1,00,000	1,20,000
Investment in shares of B Ltd., at cost	10,00,000	
Bills receivable	80,000	10,000
Cash and bank balances	5,00,000	3,20,000
	28,30,000	14,50,000

(*i*) Bills receivable of A Ltd. include Rs. 10,000 accepted by B Ltd.

(*ii*) Sundry debtors of A Ltd. include Rs. 50,000 due from B Ltd.

(*iii*) Stock of B Ltd. includes goods purchased from A Ltd. for Rs. 60,000 which were invoiced by A Ltd. at a profit of 25% on cost.

Prepare a consolidated balance sheet of A Ltd. and its subsidiary B Ltd.

[*Adapted Co. Sec. (Inter) O.S. Dec. 1985*]

(*Capital Reserve Rs. 8,000; Minority Interest Rs. 2,68,000; Total of Balance Sheet Rs. 32,08,000)*

8. The balance sheets of H Ltd. and its subsidiary S Ltd., as on 31st March, 2010 were as follows:

Liabilities	*H Ltd. Rs. '000*	*S Ltd. Rs. '000*	*Assets*	*H Ltd. Rs. '000*	*S Ltd. Rs. '000*
Share Capital			Sundry Assets	16,000	10,000
(Shares of Rs. 10 each)	10,000	6,000	Investments —		
General Reserve	4,000	—	400 Thousand Shares in S Ltd.	4,000	—
Profit and Loss Account	4,000	1,800			
Creditors	2,000	2,200			
	20,000	10,000		20,000	10,000

The shares were purchased by H Ltd. in S Ltd. on 30th September, 2009.

On 1st April 2009, the Profit and Loss Account of S Ltd. showed a loss of Rs. 30 lakh which was written off from out of the profits earned during the year. Profits are earned uniformly over the year 2009-2010.

Prepare a Consolidated Balance Sheet of H Ltd. and S Ltd. as on 31st March, 2010 giving all workings. [*Adapted B.Com (Hons.) Delhi, 1987*]

(*Goodwill Rs. 400 thousand; Minority Interest Rs. 2,600 thousand; Total of Balance Sheet Rs. 26,400 thousnad*)

9. The summarised balance sheets of P Ltd. and S Ltd. on 31st March, 2010 were as follows:

Liabilities	*P Ltd. Rs. '000*	*S Ltd. Rs. '000*	*Assets*	*P Ltd. Rs. '000*	*S Ltd. Rs. '000*
Share Capital :			Fixed Assets	1,50,00	2,44,70
30 lakh shares of			Investments in S Ltd., at cost	1,70,00	—
Rs. 10 each	3,00,00	—	Stock	40,00	20,00
10 lakh shares of			Loan to P Ltd.	—	2,00
Rs. 10 each	—	1,00,00	Bills Receivable (including		
Capital Reserve	—	55,00	Rs. 20,000 from S Ltd.)	1,20	—
General Reserve	30,00	1,05,00	Debtors	20,00	15,00
Profit and Loss			Cash	7,00	5,00
Account	38,20	18,00			
Loan from S Ltd.	2,10	—			
Bills Payable (including					
Rs. 50,000 to P Ltd.)	—	1,70			
Creditors	17,90	7,00			
	3,88,20	2,86,70		3,88,20	2,86,70

There is a contingent liability of Rs. 1 lakh for bills discounted appearing in the balance sheet of P Ltd. S Ltd. acquired 8 lakh shares of Rs. 10 each in S Ltd., on 31st March, 2010.

You are given the following additional information :

(*i*) S Ltd. made a bonus issue on 31st March, 2010 of one share for every two shares held, reducing General Reserve by an equivalent amount, but the transaction is not shown in the balance sheets.

(*ii*) Interest receivable amounting to Rs. 10,000 in respect of loan due by P Ltd. has not been credited in the accounts of S Ltd.

(*iii*) The directors decided that the fixed assets of S Ltd. were overvalued and should be written down by Rs. 5,00,000.

Prepare a Consolidated Balance Sheet of the two Companies on 31st March, 2001 giving all workings. *[Adapted B.Com. (Hons.) Delhi 1988]*

(Capital Reserve Rs. 48,480; Minority Interest Rs. 54,620; Total of Balance Sheet of Rs. 4,97,700)

10. The following are the Balance Sheets of R Ltd. and S Ltd. as at 31st March, 2010 :

Liabilities	*P Ltd.* *Rs. '000*	*S Ltd.* *Rs. '000*	*Assets*	*P Ltd.* *Rs. '000*	*S Ltd.* *Rs. '000*
Share Capital :			Fixed Assets	5,00,00	2,40,00
Equity Shares of Rs. 10 each, fully paid up	4,00,00	1,50,00	Investment in 15,000 equity shares in S Ltd. on April, 1, 2008	2,00,00	—
14% Preference Shares of Rs. 100 each, fully paid up	—	1,00,00	Current Assets (including Rs. 10,000 stock-in-trade purchased from R Ltd.)	3,00,00	2,60,00
General Reserve	50,00	40,00			
Profit and Loss A/c (before appropriation for dividends)	30,00	25,00			
14% Debentures	2,00,00	—			
Current Liabilities and Provisions	3,20,00	1,85,00			
	10,00,00	5,00,00		10,00,00	5,00,00

Prepare the consolidated balance sheet as at 31st March, 2010, assuming that (*a*) S Ltd.'s General Reserve and Profit and Loss Account (after appropriation for dividends) stood at Rs. 25 lakh and Rs. 10 lakh respectively on April 1, 2009, and (*b*) R Ltd. sells goods at a profit of 25% on cost. *[Adapted B.Com, (Hons.) Delhi, 1983]*

(Goodwill Rs. 15 lakh; Minority Interest Rs. 1 crore 14 lakh; Unrealised Profit on Stock Rs. 2 lakh; Total of Balance Sheet Rs. 13 crore 13 lakh)

Hint: Preference Share Capital alongwith dividend will appear as Minority Interest.

11. The following are the Balance Sheets of M Ltd. and N Ltd. as at 31st March, 2010:

Liabilities	*M Ltd.* Rs.	*N Ltd.* Rs.
Equity Shares of Rs. 10 each, fully paid	3,00,000	2,00,000
Capital Redemption Reserve	1,20,000	—
Capital Reserve	1,00,000	30,000
Profit and Loss Account (before any appropriation)	60,000	40,000
Debentures	2,00,000	1,00,000
Oustanding Interest on Debentures for one year	30,000	15,000
Other Liabilities	1,90,000	1,15,000
Total	10,00,000	5,00,000

Assets	*M Ltd.* Rs.	*N Ltd.* Rs.
Fixed Assets	6,00,000	3,40,000
Investments in : 15,000 Equity Shares in N Ltd. on 30.9.2009	2,00,000	—
Debentures of N Ltd. at par	50,000	—
Debentures of M Ltd. at par	—	60,000
Current Assets	1,50,000	1,00,000
Total	10,00,000	5,00,000

Prepare the consolidated balance sheet as at 31st March, 2010 assuming that N Ltd. has earned uniformly in 2009-2010 and its Profit and Loss Account showed a debit balance of Rs. 20,000 on April 1, 2009. *[Adapted B.Com., (Hons.) Delhi, 1984]*

(Goodwill Rs. 20,00,000; Minority Interest Rs. 67,50,000; Total of Balance Sheet Rs. 11,93,50,000)

Hint: Current Assets of M Ltd. and N Ltd. include interest on investments in debentures, earned but not yet received, Rs. 7,50,000 and Rs. 9,00,000 respectively; these amounts alongwith cost of debentures held as investments will be eliminated as mutual owings while preparing consolidated balance sheet.

12. The following are the Balance Sheets of X Ltd. and Y Ltd. as at 31st March, 2010 :

Liabilities	*X Ltd.* Rs.'000	*Y Ltd.* Rs.'000	*Assets*	*X Ltd.* Rs.'000	*Y Ltd.* Rs.'000
Equity Share Capital, (Rs. 10 each)	4,00,00	1,00,00	Equipment	2,50,00	95,00
Profit and Loss Account	50,00	20,00	Investment : 9,000 Equity Shares in Y Ltd. acquired on April 1, 2009	1,40,00	—
External Liabilities	7,50,00	4,80,00	Other Assets	8,10,00	5,05,00
	12,00,00	6,00,00		12,00,00	6,00,00

On April 1, 2009, Profit and Loss Account of Y Ltd. showed a credit balance of Rs. 8 lakh and Equipment of Y Ltd. was revalued by X Ltd. at 20% above its book value of Rs. 1 crore (but no such adjustment effected in the books of Y Ltd.)

Prepare the consolidated balance sheet as at 31st March, 2010.

[Adapted B.Com (Hons.) Delhi, 1985]

(Goodwill Rs. 24,80,000; Minority Interest Rs. 13,90,000; Total of Balance Sheet Rs. 17,03,80,000)

Hint: Capital Profit on revaluation Rs. 20 lakh additional depreciation Rs. 1 lakh will reduce the current year's profits to Rs. 11 lakhs.

13. A Ltd. acquired 20,000 equity shares of Rs. 10 each in B Ltd. as at 31st March, 2009. The summarised balance sheets of the two companies as at 31st March, 2010 were as follows :

Liabilities	*A Ltd.* Rs.	*B Ltd.* Rs.
Equity Share Capital (Shares of Rs. 10 each)	8,00,000	2,50,000
General Reserve	3,00,000	50,000
Profit and Loss Account	1,00,000	2,00,000
Creditors	2,00,000	50,000
	14,00,000	5,50,000
Assets		
Fixed Assets	7,00,000	2,50,000
20,000 Shares in B Ltd., at cost	3,00,000	—
Current Assets	4,00,000	3,00,000
	14,00,000	5,50,000

B Ltd. had a credit balance of Rs. 50,000 in General Reserve and Rs. 20,000 in Profit and Loss Account when A Ltd. acquired shares in B Ltd.

B Ltd. issued bonus shares in the ratio of one for every five shares held out of the profits earned during 2009-2010. This is not shown in the above balance sheet of B Ltd.

Prepare a consolidated balance sheet of A Ltd. and its subsidiary as at 31st March, 2001.

[*Adapted B.Com. (Hons.) Delhi, 1986*]

(*Goodwill Rs. 4,000; Minority Interest Rs. 1,00,000; Total of Balance Sheet Rs. 16,54,000*)

14. From the balance sheets given below, prepare a consolidated balance sheet of Moti Ltd. and its subsidiary company, Chhoti Ltd. :-

Balance Sheet of Moti Limited as on 31st March, 2010

Liabilities	*Rs.*	*Assets*	*Rs.*	*Rs.*
Share Capital :		Freeholding Building		7,20,000
Authorised and Issued :		Plant & Machinery	4,00,000	
12,000 shares of Rs. 10 each	12,00,000	*Less:* Depreciation	1,00,000	3,00,000
General Reserves	2,50,000	Shares in Chhoti Ltd. at cost,		
Profit & Loss Account	1,20,000	2,000 shares of Rs. 10 each		2,50,000
Trade Creditors	1,50,000	Stock, at cost		1,80,000
		Trade Debtors		2,20,000
		Bank Balance		50,000
	17,20,000			17,20,000

Balance Sheet of Chhoti Ltd. as on 31st March, 2010

Liabilities	*Rs.*	*Assets*	*Rs.*	*Rs.*
Share Capital :		Leasehold Property	3,00,000	
Authorised & Issued—		*Less* : Depreciation	50,000	2,50,000
30,000 shares of Rs. 10 each	3,00,000	Plant & Machinery	1,50,000	
General Reserve	60,000	*Less* : Depreciation	50,000	1,00,000
Profit and Loss Account	90,000	Stock, at cost		30,000
Trade Creditors	50,000	Trade Debtors		70,000
		Bank Balance		50,000
	5,00,000			5,00,000

At the date of acquisition (1-4-2009) by Moti Ltd. of its holding of 20,000 shares in Chhoti Ltd. the latter company had undistributed profits and reserve amounting to Rs. 50,000, none of which has been distributed since the date of acquisition. (*Adapted C.A. Final*)

[*Goodwill Rs. 16,667; Minority Interest Rs. 1,50,000; Total of Balance Sheet Rs. 19,86,667*]

15. Following are the balance sheets of H Ltd. and S Ltd. as at March 31, 2010 :

Liabilities	*H Ltd. Rs.*	*S Ltd. Rs.*	*Assets*	*H Ltd. Rs.*	*S Ltd. Rs.*
Share Capital :			Goodwill	40,000	30,000
Shares of Rs. 100 each	5,00,000	2,00,000	Other Fixed Assets	3,60,000	2,20,000
General Reserve as on			Stock	1,00,000	90,000
1st April, 2009	1,00,000	60,000	Debtors	20,000	75,000
Profit & Loss Account	1,40,000	90,000	1,500 shares in S Ltd.,		
Bills Payable	—	40,000	at cost	2,40,000	—
Creditors	80,000	50,000	Cash at Bank	60,000	25,000
	8,20,000	4,40,000		8,20,000	4,40,000

The Profit and Loss Account of S Ltd. showed a balance of Rs. 54,500 on 1st April, 2009. A dividend of 15 per cent was paid on 15th October, 2009 for the year 2009-2010. Corporate Dividend tax @ 15% was also paid on the dividend paid. The dividend was credited by H Ltd. to its Profit and Loss Account. H Ltd. acquired the shares on 1st October, 2009. The bills payable of S

Ltd. were all issued in favour of H Ltd. which company got the bills discounted. Included in the creditors of S Ltd. is Rs. 20,000 for goods supplied by H Ltd. The stock of S Ltd. includes goods to the value of Rs. 8,000 which were supplied by H Ltd. at a profit of 33 1/3% on cost.

Prepare consolidated balance sheet of H Ltd. as on 31st March, 2010.

[*Capital Reserve on Consolidation Rs. 18,750; Minority Interest Rs. 87,500; Total of Balance Sheet Rs. 9,79,250*]

16. The following are the balance sheets of H Ltd. and S Ltd. as on 31st March, 2010 :

Liabilities	*H Ltd.* *Rs. in lakhs*	*S Ltd.* *Rs. in lakhs*
Share capital :		
Equity shares of Rs. 10 each, fully paid up	1,000	800
General reserve	192	230
Profit and loss account	365	270
Current liabilities	243	200
	1,800	1,500
Assets :		
Fixed Assets	814	973
Investment in shares in S Ltd.	500	—
Current assets	486	527
	1,800	1,500

The following further information is furnished :

(*i*) H Ltd. acquired 30 lakh shares in S Ltd. on 1st April, 2009 when the reserve and surplus of S Ltd. were as under :

(*a*) General reserve Rs. 5 crore

(*b*) Profit and loss account credit balance, Rs. 2,15,00,000.

(*ii*) On 1st October, 2009 S Ltd. issued 3 fully paid up shares for every 5 shares held, as bonus shares out of pre-acquisition general reserve. No entry has yet been mad in the books of H Ltd. for the receipt of these bonus shares.

(*iii*) On 30th June, 2009 S Ltd. declared 20% dividend out of pre-acquisition profits and paid corporate dividend tax @15%. H Ltd credited the receipt of the dividend to its profit and loss account.

(*iv*) On 31st March, 2010 S Ltd. owed Rs. 10 lakh to H Ltd. for purchase of stock from H Ltd; the entire stock is held by S Ltd. on 31st March, 2010. H Ltd. made a profit of 25% on cost.

(*v*) On 31st March, 2010 H Ltd. transferred for cash payment a machine to S Ltd. for Rs. 9 lakh. The book value of the machine to H Ltd. was Rs. 8 lakh.

Prepare a consolidated balance sheet of H Ltd. and its subsidiary S Ltd. as on 31st March, 2010.

[*Adapted B.Com.(Hons.) Delhi*]

[*Capital Reserve Rs. 220 lakh; Minority Interest Rs. 520 lakh; Total of Balance Sheet Rs. 2,787 lakh*]

17. The balance sheets of Ashis Ltd. and Anand Ltd. as on 31st March, 2010 are as follows :

Liabilities	*Ashish Ltd.* *Rs. in thousand*	*Anand Ltd.* *Rs. in thousand*
Equity share capital,		
Fully paid shares of Rs. 10 each	40,000	10,000
General reserve, as on 1.4.2009	28,000	400
Profit and loss account	17,000	7,200
Sundry creditors	7,000	3,500
	92,000	21,100

Assets	Rs. '000	Rs. '000
Buildings	28,000	5,800
Plant and machinery	20,000	5,200
Furniture and fittings	1,500	700
Investments	20,000	—
Stock	7,500	4,200
Sundry Debtors	8,000	3,200
Cash at bank	7,000	2,000
	92,000	21,100

Prepare a consolidated balance sheet after considering the following :

(i) Ashish Ltd. acquired 8 lakh equity shares of Anand Ltd. on 1st July, 2009 at Rs. 2 crore.

(ii) Stock of Ashish Ltd. includes Rs. 6 lakh relating to stock purchased from Ashish Ltd. which sells goods at cost plus 25%.

(iii) Sundry creditors of Ashish Ltd. includes Rs. 10 lakh due to Anand Ltd.

(iv) Profit and loss account of Ashish Ltd. includes interim dividend received from Anand Ltd. on 1st August, 2009.

(v) On 1st April, 2009 balance of profit and loss account in Anand Ltd.'s ledger stood at Rs. 57,50,000. Out of this balance an interim dividend @ 10% was paid on 1st August, 2009. Corporate dividend tax @ 15% was also paid on the amount of interim dividend.

(vi) Profits during the year 2009-2010 have been earned by Anand Ltd. on a uniform basis throughout the year. *[C.S. (Inter) Dec. 1998 Modified]*

[Goodwill Rs. 6,680 thousand; Minority Interest Rs. 3,520 thousand; Total of Balance Sheet Rs. 98,660 thousand or 98,684 thousand]

18. The following balance sheets are presented to you:

Balance Sheets on 31st March, 2010

Liabilities	H Ltd. Rs.'000	S Ltd. Rs.'000	Assets	H Ltd. Rs.'000	S Ltd. Rs.'000
Share Capital :			Fixed Assets	3,500	1,500
Shares of Rs. 10 each	5,000	2,000	Stock-in-trade	900	400
General Reserve	1,000		Debtors	600	300
P. and L. Account	800		14% Debentures in S Ltd., acquired at par	600	
14% Debentures		1,000			
Trade Creditors	750	450	Shares in S Ltd., 1,50,000 @ Rs. 80	1,200	
			Cash at Bank	750	250
			Profit and Loss Account		1,000
	7,550	3,450		7,550	3,450

H Ltd. acquired the shares on 1st August 2009. The Profit and Loss Account of *S* Ltd. showed a debit balance of Rs. 15 lakh on 1st April, 2009. During June 2009, goods costing Rs. 60,000 were destroyed against which the insurer paid only Rs. 20,000. Trade creditors of *S* Ltd. include Rs. 2 lakh for goods supplied by *H* Ltd. on which *H* Ltd. made a profit of Rs. 20,000. Half of the goods were still in stock on 31st March, 2010.

Prepare the consolidated balance sheet. *{Adapted B.Com (Hons.), Delhi, 2002}*

[Goodwill Rs. 7,20,000; Minority Interest Rs. 2,50,000; Total of Balance Sheet Rs. 87,10,000]

19. On 1st April, 2009 H Ltd. acquired 40 lakh fully paid equity shares of Rs. 10 each in S Ltd. for Rs. 7.5 crore. The balance sheets of the two companies as at 31st March, 2010 are given below:

Liabilities :	*H Ltd.* *Rs. in lakhs*	*S Ltd.* *Rs. in lakhs*
Share Capital, fully paid equity shares of Rs. 10 each	1,000	500
Securities Premium	100	—
General Reserve	120	280
Profit and Loss Account	460	150
Creditors	190	170
Unclaimed Dividend	—	3
Proposed Dividend	150	—
	2,020	1,103
Assets :		
Land and Buildings	175	160
Plant and Machinery	425	270
Furniture and Fixtures	200	57
Shares in S Ltd.	750	—
Stock	220	286
Debtors	150	170
Cash at Bank	100	140
Preliminary Expenses	—	20
	2,020	1,103

The following additional information is given to you :

(*i*) The balances of general reserve and profit and loss account on the date of acquisition of shares by H Ltd. were Rs. 2 crore and Rs. 30 lakh respectively.

(*ii*) In July, 2009 S Ltd. distributed 10% dividend for the year 2009-2010. H Ltd. credited the entire amount of dividend received to its profit and loss account.

(*iii*) On 31st March, 2010, S Ltd. owed Rs. 60 lakh to H Ltd. for goods purchased from it. H Ltd. sold goods to S Ltd. at cost plus 25%. Goods costing Rs. 15 lakh to S Ltd. were still lying unsold with S Ltd. on the abovementioned date of balance sheet.

(*iv*) As expected, the entire amount of unclaimed dividend appearing in the balance sheet of S Ltd. belonged to the minority shareholders.

(*v*) No part of preliminary expenses has been written off during the year.

You are required to prepare consolidated balance sheet of H Ltd. and its subsidiary S Ltd. as at 31st March, 2010. [*Goodwill Rs. 182 lakh; Minority Interest Rs. 185 lakh; Total of Balance Sheet Rs. 2,472 lakh*]

20. On 1st July, 2009, H Ltd. acquired a controlling interest in S Ltd. by acquiring 72,000 fully paid equity shares of Rs. 10 each for Rs. 8,00,000. On 31st March,2010, the following were the balance sheets of H Ltd. and its subsidiary S Ltd. :

Balance sheet of H Ltd. as on 31st March, 2010

Liabilities	*Rs.*	*Assets*	*Rs.*
Share Capital	22,00,000	Goodwill	3,50,000
Securities Premium	1,20,000	Plant and Machinery	7,00,000
General Reserve	1,75,000	Furniture and fittings	1,20,000
Profit and loss account		Shares in S Ltd.	8,00,000
(including interim dividend		Stock	4,50,000
received from S Ltd., Rs. 36,000)	3,05,000	Debtors	3,40,000
Creditors	1,95,000	S Ltd.	75,000
		Bank balance	1,10,000
		Bills receivable	50,000
	29,95,000		29,95,000

Balance Sheet of S Ltd. as on 31st March,2010

Liabilities:	*Rs.*	*Rs.*
Share Capital :		
80,000 equity shares of Rs. 10 each, fully paid-up		8,00,000
General Reserve		90,000
Profit and Loss Account :		
Balance as on 1.4.2009	10,000	
Add : Profit for the year 2009-2010	3,20,000	
	3,30,000	
Less : Transfer to General Reserve	40,000	
	2,90,000	
Less : Interim dividend paid	40,000	2,50,000
Bills Payable		80,000
Creditors		1,10,000
H Ltd.		70,000
		14,00,000
Assets :		
Plant and Machinery		6,30,000
Furniture and Fixtures		1,60,000
Stock		3,10,000
Debtors		2,05,000
Bank balance		95,000
		14,00,000

The following additional information is provided to you :

(*i*) S Ltd. remitted a cheque for Rs. 5,000 to H Ltd. on 30th March, 2010, which was received by H Ltd. on 1st April, 2010.

(*ii*) Bills accepted by S Ltd. were all drawn by H Ltd. and H Ltd. had got bills amounting to Rs. 30,000 discounted with the Bank.

(*iii*) S Ltd. had purchased goods from H Ltd. of which goods invoiced at Rs. 50,000 were in stock on 31st March, 2010. H Ltd. added 25% to cost to arrive at the invoice price.

Prepare a consolidated balance sheet of H Ltd. and its subsidiary S Ltd. as on 31st March,2000.

[C. S. (Inter) Dec. 2000]

[Capital Reserve Rs. 46,000; Minority Interest Rs. 1,14,000; Total of Balance Sheet Rs. 34,19,000]

21. The balance sheets of Harry Ltd. and its subsidiary Suman Ltd. as at 31st March, 2010 are as follows :—

Balance Sheet of Harry Ltd. as on 31st March, 2010

Liabilities	*Rs.*	*Assets*	*Rs.*
Share Capital	10,00,000	Goodwill	2,00,000
General Reserve	3,40,000	Land & Buildings	7,60,000
Profit & Loss A/c	1,11,000	Investments*	2,88,000
Bills Payable	4,10,000	Stock	5,20,000
Sundry Creditors	6,39,000	Sundry Debtors & advances (including loan to Suman Ltd. : Rs. 10,000)	5,80,000
		Cash and Bank	1,52,000
	25,00,000		25,00,000

*The investment consists of 24,000 shares of Rs. 10 each fully paid in its subsidiary Suman Ltd. which were acquired on 1st July, 2009.

Balance Sheet of Suman Ltd. as on 31st March, 2010

Liabilities	*Rs.*	*Assets*	*Rs.*
Share Capital (d)	3,00,000	Goodwill	44,000
General Reserve (e)	50,000	Plant & Machinery (a)	2,90,000
Profit & Loss A/c (e)	44,000	Stock	60,000
Loan	2,10,000	Sundry Debtors	1,25,000
Sundry Creditors	2,84,000	Bills Receivable (b)	3,00,000
		Cash and Bank (c)	69,000
	8,88,000		8,88,000

(*a*) On 1st April, 2009 the plant and machinery were revalued at Rs. 3,20,000 which should be taken in the consolidated balance sheet. Ignore depreciation. There were no additions or deletions to plant during the year.

(*b*) Total bills receivable were Rs. 4,10,000 (all accepted by Harry Ltd.) of which bills for Rs. 1,10,000 had been discounted with the banker and were yet to mature.

(*c*) Cash and bank balances were arrived at after sending a cheque for Rs. 10,000 to Harry Ltd. on account of repayment of loan.

(*d*) Share capital of Suman Ltd. consists of 30,000 equity shares of Rs. 10 each.

(*e*) Balances as on 1st April, 2009 :

Profit & Loss Account	Rs. 12,000
General Reserve	Rs. 40,000

Prepare a consolidated balance sheet as on 31st March, 2010. Workings will be part of your answer. [*Adapted Co. Sec. (Inter) O.S. June 1987*]

[*Cash in transit Rs. 10,000; Capital Reserve on consolidation Rs. 26,000; Minority Interest Rs. 84,800; Total of Balance Sheet Rs. 28,04,000*]

22. A Ltd. acquired the whole of the shares in B Ltd. as on 1st October, 2009 at a total cost of Rs. 5,60,000. The Balance sheets at 31st March, 2010, when accounts of both companies were prepared and audited, were as under :—

Balance Sheet of A Ltd. as on 31st March, 2010

	Rs.		*Rs.*
Share Capital :		Land & Buildings	5,15,000
Shares of Rs. 10 each	7,50,000	Plant & Machinery	1,50,000
General Reserve	4,75,000	Investments	5,60,000
Profit & Loss Account (*x*)	4,00,000	Stock (*z*)	1,70,000
Creditors (*y*)	75,000	Debtors	1,40,000
		Cash at Bank	1,65,000
	17,00,000		17,00,000

(*x*) Includes interim dividend at the rate of 16% per annum from B Ltd.

(*y*) Includes Rs. 30,000 for purchases from B Ltd. on which the latter company made a profit of Rs. 7,500.

(*z*) Includes Rs. 15,000 stock at cost purchased from B Ltd. part of Rs. 30,000 purchases [see note (y)].

Balance Sheet of B Ltd. as on 31st March, 2010

	Rs.		*Rs.*
Share Capital :		Land & Buildings	1,50,000
Shares of Rs. 5 each	2,50,000	Plant & Machinery	1,35,000
General Reserve as at 1st April, 2009	20,000	Stock	1,01,000
Profit & Loss Account	1,70,000	Debtors	79,000
Creditors	80,500	Cash at Bank	55,000
	5,20,500		5,20,500

Note. The balance of Profit and Loss Account and General Reserve on 1st April, 2009 was Rs. 1,40,000 and Rs. 10,000 respectively.

Make the necessary adjustments and show a consolidated balance sheet as on 31st March, 2010. *(Adapted from C.A. Final)*

[Goodwill Rs. 1,20,000; Total of Balance Sheet Rs. 17,46,750]

23. M Ltd. acquired 12,000 shares in D Ltd. for Rs. 1,70,000 on July 1, 2009. The balance sheets of the two companies on 31st March, 2010 were as follows :—

Liabilities	*H Ltd.* Rs.	*S Ltd.* Rs.	*Assets*	*H Ltd.* Rs.	*S Ltd.* Rs.
Share Capital :			Goodwill	3,00,000	70,000
(Shares of Rs. 10 each)	10,00,000	3,00,000	Land and Buildings	4,00,000	1,00,000
General Reserve	4,20,000	50,000	Plant and Machinery	5,00,000	1,00,000
Profit and Loss Account	2,60,000	85,000	Investments	1,70,000	—
Loan from D. Ltd.			Stock	2,00,000	40,000
(incl. interest)	57,500	—	Book Debts	3,00,000	85,000
Bills Payable	80,000	60,000	Cash and Bank Balances	80,000	62,000
Sundry Creditors	1,82,500	42,000	Bills Receivable	50,000	30,000
			Loan to M. Ltd.	—	50,000
	20,00,000	5,37,000		20,00,000	5,37,000

On April 1, 2009, the Profit and Loss Account of *D* Ltd. stood at Rs. 44,500 out of which a dividend of 15% on the then capital of Rs. 2,00,000 was paid in September 2009. Corporate dividend tax @ 15% was also paid on the dividend. At the same time, a bonus issue of one share (fully paid) for every two shares held, was also made out of General Reserve. Bills Payable of *D* Ltd. represent bills issued in favour of *M* Ltd. which company still held Rs. 40,000 of the bills accepted by *D* Ltd. The entire closing stock of *D* Ltd. represents goods supplied by *M* Ltd. at cost plus 20%.

M Ltd. and *D* Ltd. agreed that for services rendered *M* Ltd. should charge Rs. 500 p.m. from *D* Ltd. Entries for this were not made when the accounts were drawn up. The loan to *M* Ltd. was made by *D* Ltd. on April 1, 2009.

Prepare the consolidated balance sheet of the two companies as at 31st March, 2010.

[Capital Reserve Rs. 76,375; Minority Interest Rs. 1,75,200; Total of Balance Sheet Rs. 21,93,958]

24. The Balance Sheets of X Ltd. and Y Ltd. as on 31st March, 2008 were as under :—

Liabilities	*X Ltd.* Rs.	*Y Ltd.* Rs.	*Assets*	*X Ltd.* Rs.	*Y Ltd.* Rs.
Share Capital :			Land & Buildings	5,33,780	1,35,000
Paid up shares of			Plant & Machinery	11,15,720	4,27,600
Rs. 100 each	15,00,000	5,00,000	Stocks	6,42,390	3,91,930
Reserves	9,50,000	1,50,000	Sundry Debtors	7,37,410	2,69,850
Profit & Loss			Cash at Bank	2,17,900	1,18,420
Appropriation A/c	85,870	1,04,880	Bills Receivable	46,350	—
Sundry Creditors	4,37,760	3,82,710	Prepaid Expenses	32,750	5,790
Provision for Taxation	3,52,670	2,11,000			
	33,26,300	13,48,590		33,26,300	13,48,590

As on 31st March, 2008, X Ltd. acquired all the shares of Y Ltd. in exchange for 14% Debentures of the face value of Rs. 10,00,000 repayable after 7 years. The excess cost of acquisition is to be amortised in the books of X Ltd. over this period.

For the years 2008-2009 and 2009-2010, X Ltd. made a profit of Rs. 2,10,000 and Rs. 3,90,000 respectively after making provision for taxation and Y Ltd. incurred losses of Rs. 52,300 and Rs. 16,500 respectively. X Ltd. provided a reserve in its books by charge to income for the losses of its subsidiary. The profits of X Ltd. as shown above are before provision for amortisation of the excess cost of acquisition and for the losses of the subsidiary. Dividends of Rs. 1,50,000 were paid by X Ltd. in each of the years 2008-2009 and 2009-2010.

The assets and liabilities, except cash and those arising out of above, of the two companies at end of 2008-2009 and 2009-2010 were as under :—

	X Ltd.		*Y Ltd.*	
	2008-2009	2009-2010	2008-2009	2009-2010
	Rs.	*Rs.*	*Rs.*	*Rs.*
Land & Buildings	5,72,890	6,31,400	1,42,000	1,45,000
Plant & Machinery	11,70,810	12,28,980	4,37,500	4,42,000
Stocks	4,75,890	5,72,800	3,42,600	3,47,890
Sundry Debtors	8,37,420	8,45,360	3,37,890	4,15,680
Advances to Y Ltd.	1,25,000	2,75,000	—	—
Prepaid Expenses	28,750	47,650	11,620	15,670
Reserves	9,50,000	11,50,000	1,50,000	1,50,000
Sundry Creditors	6,06,590	6,39,040	6,19,670	5,90,880
Advances from X Ltd.	—	—	1,25,000	2,50,000
Provision for Taxation	2,50,000	4,15,000	—	—

You are required to prepare the consolidated balance sheet as on 31st March, 2010.

(Adapted from C.A. Final)

(Goodwill on consolidation Rs. 1,75,086; Total of Consolidated Balance Sheet, Rs. 53,41,956)

25. The following are the summarised balance sheets of three companies, F. Ltd., S. Ltd. and D. Ltd. as on March 31st, 2010 :—

Particulars	*F. Ltd.* *Rs.*	*S. Ltd.* *Rs.*	*D. Ltd.* *Rs.*		*F. Ltd.* *Rs.*	*S. Ltd.* *Rs.*	*D. Ltd.* *Rs.*
Share Capital :				Goodwill	30,000		
(Shares of Rs. 10 each)	5,00,000	4,00,000	1,50,000	Fixed Assets	2,80,000	2,70,000	1,42,000
Profit & Loss Account	1,20,000	1,00,000	30,000	Investments :			
Creditors	2,00,000	2,50,000	1,02,000	30,000 shares in S. Ltd.	3,50,000		
				12,000 Shares in D. Ltd.		1,40,000	
				Stock	60,000	1,40,000	80,000
				Other Current Assets	1,00,000	2,00,000	60,000
	8,20,000	7,50,000	2,82,000		8,20,000	7,50,000	2,82,000

The investments were all acquired on 1st October, 2009. On April 1, 2009 the Profit and Loss Accounts showed the following balances :

	Rs.
F. Ltd.	80,000
S. Ltd.	48,000
D. Ltd.	10,000 (Debit balance)

The proposed dividends for 2009-2010 are : F. Ltd. 16%; S. Ltd. 15% and D. Ltd. 10% after transfer of Rs. 8,000 and Rs. 3,000 from Profit and Loss Account to General Reserve by F. Ltd. and S. Ltd. respectively.

Prepare the consolidated balance sheet of the group as on March 31, 2010.

[Cost of Control Rs. 8,500; Minority Interest: S. Ltd. Rs. 1,31,000 D. Ltd. Rs. 36,000; Balance Sheet Rs. 13,70,500]

26. On 1st April, 2009, X. Limited acquired 90 per cent of the shares of Y. Limited and 80 per cent of the shares of Z. Limited. With a view to increasing its holdings in Z. Limited, X. Limited disposed of 4,000 shares in Y. Limited at price of Rs. 16 per share on 30th September, 2009 and on the said date purchased further 10 per cent of the shares of Z. Limited in exchange for the proceeds received on the sale of shares of Y. Limited.

The following are the Balance Sheets of the three companies as at 31st March, 2010 in a condensed form :—

	X. Ltd.	*Y. Ltd.*	*Z. Ltd.*
Assets	*Rs.*	*Rs.*	*Rs.*
Fixed Assets	1,20,000	3,80,000	3,40,000
Investments :—			
Shares in Y. Ltd.	4,40,000		
Shares in Z. Ltd.	4,28,000		
Current Assets	2,27,000	2,40,000	4,10,000
Loans and Advances	95,000	25,000	—
	13,10,000	6,45,000	7,50,000
Liabilities			
Share Capital			
Equity Shares of Rs. 10 each	7,00,000	4,00,000	2,00,000
Profit & Loss Account	2,33,000	1,10,000	3,50,000
Creditors	3,77,000	1,35,000	2,00,000
	13,10,000	6,45,000	7,50,000

Each of the companies has maintained a consolidated Profit and Loss Account which shows the following position:—

	X. Ltd.	*Y. Ltd.*	*Z. Ltd.*
	Rs.	*Rs.*	*Rs.*
Balance as on 1st April, 2009	2,63,000	1,20,000	2,90,000
Net Profit for the year 2009-2010	40,000	30,000	80,000
	3,03,000	1,50,000	3,70,000
Less : Dividend	70,000	40,000	20,000
	2,33,000	1,10,000	3,50,000

The investment accounts in the books of Z. Ltd. are carried at cost except that the account representing the investment in Y. Ltd. which has been credited with the proceeds of the 4,000 shares sold, viz., Rs. 64,000.

You are required to prepare (1) the consolidated balance sheet as at 31st March, 2010, and (2) the supporting work sheet. Ignore corporate dividend tax. . *(Adapted C.A. Final)*

[Cost of Control Rs. 15,000; Minority Interest : Y Ltd. Rs. 1,02,000, Z Ltd. Rs. 55,000; Total of Balance Sheet Rs. 18,52,000]

27. You are given the following balance sheets as on March 31, 2010 :—

	P. Ltd.	*Q. Ltd.*	*R. Ltd.*
	Rs.	*Rs.*	*Rs.*
Liabilities Side :—			
Share Capital (Shares of Rs. 10 each fully paid)	20,00,000	10,00,000	8,00,000
Securities Premium Account	2,00,000	50,000	—
General Reserve	6,00,000	3,00,000	2,00,000
Profit and Loss Account	2,50,000	1,80,000	1,20,000
Creditors	3,00,000	2,00,000	1,40,000
P. Ltd.	—	50,000	30,000
	33,50,000	17,80,000	12,90,000
Assets Side :—			
Fixed Assets (cost *less* depreciation)	15,00,000	9,00,000	9,70,000
Investments	13,00,000	5,80,000	—

	Rs.	*Rs.*	*Rs.*
Current Assets	4,50,000	3,00,000	3,00,000
Q Ltd.	70,000	—	—
R Ltd.	30,000	—	—
Preliminary Expenses	—	—	20,000
	33,50,000	17,80,000	12,90,000

P Ltd. had acquired 80,000 shares in Q Ltd. at a total cost of Rs. 11,00,000 on 1st October, 2008. On 1st April 2009, P Ltd. and Q Ltd. purchased respectively 10,000 and 50,000 shares in R Ltd. at Rs. 11.60 per share.

Particulars about General Reserve and the Profit and Loss Account are as given below :—

Assets	*P. Ltd.* *Rs.*	*Q. Ltd.* *Rs.*	*R. Ltd.* *Rs.*
General Reserve as on April 1, 2008	5,50,000	2,50,000	2,00,000
Profit and Loss Account balance on April 1, 2008	50,000	40,000	20,000
Profit during 2008-2009	1,70,000	1,00,000	1,00,000
Dividend paid in November 2009 in respect of 2008-2009	10%	12%	10%

P Ltd. and Q Ltd. have credited the dividends received by them to their Profit and Loss Accounts. Increases in reserves were made in 2009-2010.

On 31st March 2010 R Ltd. sold goods costing Rs. 20,000 to Q Ltd. for Rs. 25,000; these were immediately sold for Rs. 28,000 to P Ltd.

Prepare the consolidated balance sheet of the group as on 31st March, 2010. Ignore corporate dividend tax. *[Capital Reserve Rs. 1,13,500; Minority Interest: Q Ltd. Rs. 3,23,500, R. Ltd. Rs. 2,75,000; Total of Balance Sheet Rs. 45,16,000]*

28. Greater Combinations Ltd. and its subsidiary Cooperative Ltd., have produced the following summarised balance sheets as on 31st March, 2010 and Profit and Loss Accounts for the year ended on that date.

Summarised Balance Sheets as on 31st March, 2010 :

	Greater Comb-nation Ltd. *Rs. ('000)*	*Cooperative Ltd.* *Rs. ('000)*
Issued Share Capital:		
Equity shares of Rs. 10	500	100
Reserves and unapportioned profits	800	260
Plant Replacement Reserve	100	90
	1,400	450
Fixed assets	675	120
Shares in subsidiary 7,500 shares of Re. 10	25	—
Net current assets	700	330
	1,400	450

Summarised Profit and Loss Accounts for the year ended 31st March, 2010 :

		Greater Comb-nation Ltd. *Rs. ('000)*	*Cooperative Ltd.* *Rs. ('000)*
Trading Profit		300	80
Taxation @ 50%	165	44	
		135	36
Proposed Dividends	75	20	
Retained		60	16

You have ascertained that :—

(1) The entire issued share capital of Cooperative Ltd. was acquired on 1st November, 2005 at Rs. 10 per share. At this date total reserves and unappropriated profits of Cooperative Ltd. were equivalent to Rs. 8 per share. There have not been any changes in the share capital account since that date.

(2) On 30th September 2009, 2,500 shares of Cooperative Ltd. were sold at Rs. 30 per share. The sale had been recorded in the books of Greater Combinations Ltd. by crediting the receipt against the cost of purchase.

(3) Trading profits of Cooperative Ltd. arise evenly throughout the year.

(4) Greater Combinations Ltd. sells to Cooperative Ltd. on the normal trade terms of cost plus 25%, goods to the value of Rs. 1,00,000 per month. Stocks held by Cooperative Ltd. at the end of the year represents one month's purchases.

(5) Greater Combinations Ltd. does not take credit in its own accounts for dividends until they have been received.

You are required to prepare a consolidated balance sheet as at 31st March, 2010 which complies with the current practice in so far as the information provided will allow. Assume absence of corporate dividend tax. *[Adapted from C.A. (Eng.) Prof. Exam. II]*

[Capital Reserve on consolidation Rs. 60,000; Minority Interest Rs. 95,000; Total of Balance Sheet Rs. 19,00,000]

29. As on 31st March, 2009, the Balance Sheets of three companies showed the following position:

	Fig Ltd.		*Run Ltd.*		*Trot Ltd.*	
	Rs.	*Rs.*	*Rs.*	*Rs.*	*Rs.*	*Rs.*
Fixed Assets :						
Freehold Land and Buildings at Cost		4,00,000		10,00,000		6,50,000
Plant and Machinery, at cost	13,00,000		5,60,000		8,70,000	
Less : aggregate depreciation	5,00,000	8,00,000	2,20,000	3,40,000	6,00,000	2,70,000
		12,00,000		13,40,000		9,20,000
Investments:						
Shares in Run Ltd. at cost	11,50,000					
Shares in Trot Ltd., at cost	7,00,000	18,50,000				
Current Assets :						
Stocks on hand	5,70,000		6,80,000		5,41,400	
Debtors	9,63,400		4,32,450		4,21,900	
Balance at Bank	4,42,500	19,75,900	11,04,250	22,16,700	1,14,090	10,77,390
		50,25,900		35,56,700		19,97,390
Deduct Current Liabilities						
Creditors	3,23,960		6,17,100		3,42,870	
Income Tax	7,24,500		5,20,000		2,44,000	
Proposed Dividends	12,00,000	22,48,460	8,00,000	19,37,100	1,00,000	6,86,870
		27,77,440		16,19,600		13,10,520
Financed by :						
Share Capital, authorised and issued : Equity shares of Rs. 10/- each fully paid		20,00,000		8,00,000		10,00,000
Capital Reserve		2,00,000		4,00,000		—
Revenue Reserve		5,77,440		4,19,600		3,10,520
		27,77,440		16,19,600		13,10,520

You are also given the following information :

(1) Fig Ltd. acquired 50,000 shares in Run Ltd. in 2003-04 when the balance on capital reserve had been Rs. 2,00,000 and on revenue reserve Rs. 1,60,000. A further 20,000

shares, were purchased in 2005-06 when the balance on capital reserve and revenue reserve had been Rs. 4,00,000 and Rs. 2,40,000 respectively.

(2) Fig Ltd. had purchased 75,000 shares in Trot Ltd. in 2004-05 when there had been an adverse balance on revenue reserve of Rs. 60,000.

(3) During the year ended 31st March, 2009, Fig Ltd. had purchased a machine from Run Ltd. for Rs. 1,00,000 which had yielded a profit on selling price of 30% to that company. Depreciation on the machine had been charged in the accounts at 20% on cost.

(4) Run Ltd. purchases goods from Fig Ltd. providing Fig Ltd. with a standard gross profit on invoice price of 33 $^1/_3$%. On 31st March, 2009 the stock valuation of Run Ltd. included an amount of Rs. 1,60,000 being goods purchased from Fig Ltd. for Rs. 1,80,000.

(5) The proposed dividends from subsidiary companies have been included in the figure for debtors in the accounts of the parent company. Assume there was no corporate divident tax.

You are required to prepare the Consolidated Balance Sheet of Fig Ltd. and its subsidiaries as on 31st March, 2009, together with your consolidation schedules.

[Adapted from C.A. (Eng.) Prof. Exam. I]

[Capital Reserve on consolidation Rs. 65,000; Minority Interest : Run Ltd. Rs. 3,02,450, Trot Ltd. Rs. 3,52,630; Total of Balance Sheet Rs. 78,98,990]

30. The balance sheets of S Ltd. and J Ltd. as on March 31, 2010 are given below :—

Liabilities	*S Ltd.* *Rs.*	*J Ltd.* *Rs.*	*Assets*	*S Ltd.* *Rs.*	*J Ltd.* *Rs.*
Share Capital :			Goodwill	1,26,000	46,000
Equity (Rs. 10 shares)	1,80,000	1,00,000	Land & Buildings	95,000	47,000
14% Preference	1,50,000	80,000	Plant & Machinery	45,000	50,400
Share Premium			Fixtures	1,000	500
(Equity Shares)	36,000	—	Government Securities	26,000	—
Reserve	26,000	30,000	9,000 Equity Shares in		
Profit & Loss Account	71,250	25,200	J Ltd.	1,20,000	—
14% Debentures	40,000	50,000	2,000 Equity Shares in		
Creditors	19,000	34,000	S. Ltd.	—	24,000
			Stock	48,000	1,14,000
			Book Debts	55,000	35,000
			Cash	6,000	3,100
	5,22,000	3,20,000		5,22,000	3,20,000

J Ltd. acquired the shares in S Ltd. on 1st April, 2009 when it made a fresh issue of shares. S Ltd. acquired the shares in J Ltd. on 1st October, 2009. Some of the figures on 1st April, 2009 were:

	S Ltd. *Rs.*	*J Ltd.* *Rs.*
Reserve	26,000	30,000
Profit and Loss Account	15,000 (Dr.)	8,000
Plant and Machinery	50,000	56,000

As on the date of acquisition of control, S Ltd. valued the Plant and Machinery of J Ltd. at Rs. 60,000. Creditors of S Ltd. include Rs. 15,000 due to J Ltd. the stock of S Ltd. includes goods of the value of Rs. 33,000 supplied by J Ltd. at cost plus 10%.

Prepare the consolidated balance sheet of the group as on 31st March, 2010, taking into account the enhanced value of Plant and Machinery of J Ltd. *(Adapted from C.A. Final)*

[Capital Reserve Rs. 18,634; Minority Interest Rs. 1,07,745; Total of Balance Sheet Rs. 6,67,826]

31. The following are the balance sheets of Mumbai Ltd., Delhi Ltd., Amritsar Ltd. and Kanpur Ltd. as at 31st March, 2010 :—

Liabilities	*Mumbai Ltd.*	*Delhi Ltd.*	*Amritsar Ltd.*	*Kanpur Ltd.*
	Rs.	*Rs.*	*Rs.*	*Rs.*
Share Capital (fully paid shares of Rs. 10 each)	50,00,000	40,00,000	20,00,000	60,00,000
General Reserve	20,00,000	4,00,000	2,50,000	10,00,000
Profit and Loss Account	10,00,000	4,00,000	2,50,000	3,20,000
Sundry Creditors	3,00,000	1,00,000	50,000	80,000
	83,00,000	49,00,000	25,50,000	74,00,000
Assets				
Fixed Assets	—	20,00,000	15,00,000	70,00,000
Current Assets	1,00,000	6,00,000	4,50,000	4,00,000
Investments :				
3,00,000 shares in Delhi Ltd.	35,00,000	—	—	—
1,00,000 shares in Amritsar Ltd.	11,00,000	—	—	—
50,000 shares in Amritsar Ltd.	—	5,00,000	—	—
Shares in Kanpur Ltd. @ Rs. 12	36,00,000	18,00,000	6,00,000	—
	83,00,000	49,00,000	25,50,000	74,00,000

Balance in General Reserve Account and Profit and Loss Account, when shares were purchased in different companies were :

	Mumbai Ltd.	*Delhi Ltd.*	*Amritsar Ltd.*	*Kanpur Ltd.*
	Rs.	*Rs.*	*Rs.*	*Rs.*
General Reserve Account	10,00,000	2,00,000	1,00,000	6,00,000
Profit and Loss Account	6,00,000	2,00,000	50,000	60,000

You are required to prepare the consolidated balance sheet of the group as at 31st March, 2010. Calculations may be rounded off to the nearest rupee. *[Adapted C.A. (Final) May, 2007]*

[Goodwill Rs. 6,55,834 ; Minority interest Rs. 30,81,668 ; General reserve Rs. 20 lakh, Profit and loss account Rs. 20,94,166; Minority interest Rs. 30,81,668; Total of balance sheet Rs. 1,27,05,834]

Essay-type

1. What do you mean by holding companies? What are their advantages and disadvantages?
2. Define (*i*) a parent, (*ii*) a subsidiary and (*iii*) a group as per Accounting Standard 21?
3. Explain the following terms : —
   (*i*) Minority Interest, (*ii*) Cost of control, (*iii*) Mutual Owings.
4. What is meant by mutual owings between the holding company and the subsidiary company? How are they treated while preparing a consolidated balance sheet?
5. What is an associated company? How does it differ from a holding company?

23

CASH AND FUNDS FLOW STATEMENTS, CASH BUDGET AND WORKING CAPITAL

SYNOPSIS

1. Cash Flow Statement .. 23.1
   Introduction .. 23.1
   Definition .. 23.2
   Classification of activities .. 23.2
   Non-cash transactions .. 23.5
   The direct method .. 23.9
   The indirect method .. 23.13
   Advantages .. 23.30
   Limitations .. 23.30
   Distinction between Cash Flow Statement and Income Statement .. 23.30
   AS-3 (Revised): Cash Flow Statements .. 23.31
2. Funds Flow Statement .. 23.43
   Rules for drawing Funds Flow Statement .. 23.44
   Advantages .. 23.46
   Limitations .. 23.46
   Distinction between Funds Flow Statement and Cash Flow Statement .. 23.46
   Distinction between Funds Flow Statement and Income Statement .. 23.46
   Distinction between Statement Showing Changes in Working Capital and Funds Flow Statement .. 23.47
3. Cash Budget .. 23.66
4. Working Capital .. 23.68
   Concept of Working Capital .. 23.68
   Factors determining working capital requirements .. 23.70
   Estimating working capital requirements .. 23.72

1. Cash Flow Statement

Introduction

Income Statement and Balance Sheet are the financial statements most sought after. But many of those who study these statements are, for different reasons, also interested in knowing the inflows and outflows of cash or working capital. For example, the creditors may be interested in this information to assess the short term ability of the enterprise to pay to its creditors. Hence, many companies presented along with the final accounts, a statement called Funds Flow Statement showing changes in financial position. In June, 1981 the Institute of Chartered Accounts of India issued Accounting Standard-3: Changes in Financial Position. This accounting standard dealt with the financial statement that summarised, for the period convered by it, the changes in financial position showing the sources from which funds were obtained by the enterprise and the specific uses to which funds were applied. Funds were defined as cash or cash equivalents or working capital (*i.e.*, current assets minus current liabilities). But funds flow statements suffered from certain limitations. A funds flow statement showed flows of working capital which included items like stock of goods and prepaid expenses which did not contribute to the short term ability of the enterprise to pay its debts. Flows were not classified under the heads of operating, financial and investing activities. There was no standard format of the statement. There was the need of a cash flow statement in a standard format classifying flows from different activities. In June, 1995 the Securities and Exchange Board of India (SEBI) amended clause 32 of the Listing Agreement requiring every listed company to give along with its balance sheet and profit and loss account, a cash flow statement prepared in the prescribed format, showing separately cash flows from operating activities, investing activities and financing activities. In March, 1997 the Institute of Chartered Accountants of India issued AS-3 (Revised): Cash Flow Statements. The revised accounting standard supersedes AS-3: Changes in Financial Position, issued in June, 1981. Cash Flow Statement has replaced Statement of Changes in Financial Position.

Definition

Cash Flow Statement is a statement which shows inflows (receipts) and outflows (payments) of cash and its equivalents in an enterprise during a specified period of time. According to the revised accounting standard 3, an enterprise should prepare a cash flow statement and should present it for each period for which financial statements are presented. In this context, the terms cash, cash equivalents and cash flows mean the following:

(*i*) **Cash** comprises cash on hand and demand deposits with banks. A demand deposit with a bank is a deposit which is repayable by bank on demand by the depositor.

(*ii*) **Cash equivalents** are short term, highly liquid investments that are readily convertible into known amounts of cash and which are subject to an insignificant risk of changes in value. An investment normally qualifies as a cash equivalent only when it has a short maturity of, say, three months or less from the date of acquisition. Investments in shares are excluded from cash equivalents unless they are, in substance, cash equivalents; for example, preference shares of a company acquired shortly before their specific redemption date (provided there is only an insignificant risk of failure of the company to repay the amount at maturity). Cash equivalents are held for the purpose of meeting short-term cash commitments rather than for investment or other purposes.

(*iii*) **Cash flows** are inflows and outflows of cash and cash equivalents. An inflow increases the total cash and cash equivalents at the disposal of the enterprise whereas an outflow decreases them. The difference between the cash inflows and cash outflows is known as net cash flow which can be either a net cash inflow or a net cash outflow. Cash flows exclude movements between items that constitute cash or cash equivalents because these components are part of the cash management of an enterprise rather than part of its operating, investing and financing activities. Cash management includes the investment of excess cash in cash equivalents.

Classification of Activities

According to AS-3 (Revised), the cash flow statement should report cash flows during the period classified by operating, investing and financing activities. This classification of activities is described below:

(*i*) **Operating Activities:** Operating activities are the principal revenue-producing activities of the enterprise and other activities that are not investing or financing activities. The amount of cash flows arising from operating activities is a key indicator of the extent to which the operations of the enterprise have generated sufficient cash flows to maintain the operating capability of the enterprise to pay dividends, repay loans and make investments without recourse to external sources of financing. Information about the specific components of historical operating cash flows is also useful in forecasting future operating cash flows.

Cash flows from operating activities generally result from the transactions and other events that enter into the determination of net profit or loss. Examples of cash flows from operating activities are:

(*a*) cash receipts from the sale of goods and the rendering of services, usually forming a major share of cash inflow;

(*b*) cash receipts from royalties, fees, commissions, and other revenue;

(*c*) cash payments to suppliers for goods and services such as payment of rent, electricity bill, fire-insurance premium, printing charges etc.

(*d*) cash payments of salaries and wages to employees and also cash payments made on behalf of employees to others like those of life insurance premium and tax deducted at source.

(*e*) cash payments or refunds of income taxes unless they can be specifically identified with financing and investing activities.

(*f*) cash receipts and payments relating to future contracts, forward contracts, option contracts and swap contracts when the contracts are held for dealing or trading purposes.

(*g*) cash receipts and payments arising from the purchase and sale of dealing or trading securities.

Some transactions, such as the sale of an item of plant, may give rise to a gain or loss which is included in the determination of net profit or loss. However, the cash flows relating to such transactions are cash flows from investing activities.

(*ii*) **Investing Activities:** Investing activities are the acquisition and disposal of long-term assets (such as land, buildings, plant, machinery, furniture, fixtures etc.) and other investments not included in cash equivalents. It is important to make a separate disclosure of cash flows arising from investing activities because the cash flows represent the extent to which expenditures have been made for resources intended to generate future income and cash flows. Examples of cash flows arising from investing activities are:

(*a*) cash payments to acquire fixed assets (including intangibles) like payments made to purchase goodwill, land, buildings, plant, machinery, furniture, fixtures, fittings, trade marks, copy rights etc. These payments include those relating to self-constructed fixed assets;

(*b*) cash payments relating to capitalised research and development costs;

(*c*) cash receipts from disposal of fixed assets (including intangibles);

(*d*) cash payments to acquire shares, warrants, or debt instruments of other enterprises and interests in joint ventures (other than payments for those instruments considered to be cash equivalents and those held for dealing or trading purposes);

(*e*) cash receipts from disposal of shares, warrants, of debt instruments of other enterprises and interests in joint ventures (other than receipts from those instruments considered to be cash equivalents and those held for dealing or trading purposes);

(*f*) cash advances and loans made to third parties (other than advances and loans made by a financial enterprise);

(*g*) cash receipts from the repayment of advances and loans made to third parties (other than advances and loans of a financial enterprise);

(*h*) cash payment for and cash receipts from futures contracts, forward contracts, option contracts, and swap contracts except when the contracts are held for dealing or trading purposes, or the payments are classified as financing activities.

When a contract is accounted for as a hedge of an identifiable position, the cash flows of the contract are classified in the same manner as the cash flows of the position being hedged.

(*iii*) **Financing Activities:** Financing activities are activities that result in changes in the size and composition of the owners' capital (including preference share capital in the case of a company) and borrowings of the enterprise. The separate disclosure of cash flows from financing activities is important because it is useful in predicting claims on future cash flows by providers of funds (both capital and borrowings) to the enterprise. Examples of cash flows arising from financing activities are:

(*a*) cash proceeds from issuing shares other similar instruments;

(*b*) cash proceeds from issuing debentures, loans, notes, bonds, and other short or long-term borrowings; and

(*c*) cash repayments of amounts borrowed,

(*d*) cash payments to redeem preference shares.

Other Items: In addition to the cash flows described, AS-3 (Revised) also deals with certain other items as outlined below:—

(*a*) **Interest and Dividends:** Treatment of cash flows from interest and dividends can be described under two heads:

(*i*) In case of a financial enterprise, cash flows arising from interest paid and interest and dividends received should be classified as cash flows from operating activities. Dividends paid should be classified as cash flows from financing activities.

(*ii*) In the case of other enterprises, cash flows arising from interest and dividends paid should be classified as cash flows from financing activities while interest and dividends received should be classified as cash flows from investing activities.

In all cases, cash flows from interest and dividends received and paid should each be disclosed separately. Also, the total amount of interest paid during the period is disclosed in the cash flow statement whether it has been recognised as an expense in the statement of profit and loss or capitalised in accordance with AS-10: Accounting for Fixed Assets.

The following excerpt taken from an annexture to a letter issued by SEBI lists the requirements laid down by SEBI regarding treatment of interest and dividends in cash flow statement:

Interest and dividends

35. Cash flows from interest and dividends received and paid should each be disclosed separately. Each should be classified in a consistent manner from period to period as either operating, investing or financing activities.
36. The total amount of interest paid during the period is disclosed in the cash flow statement whether it has been recognised as an expense in the income statement or capitalised.
37. Interest paid and interest and dividends received are usually classified as operating cash flows for a financial institution. However, there is no consensus on the classification of these cash flows for other companies. Interest paid and interest and dividends received may be classified as operating cash flows because they enter into the determination of net profit or loss. Alternatively, interest paid and interest and dividends received may be classified as financing cash flows and investing cash flows, respectively, because they are costs of obtaining financing resources or returns on investments.
38. Dividends paid may be classified as financing cash flows because they are cost of obtaining financial resources. Alternatively, dividends paid may be classified as a component of cash flows from operating activities in order to assist users to determine the ability of a company to pay dividends out of operating cash flows.

It may be noted that although SEBI allows dividends paid to be classified as a component of cash flows from operating activities, companies invariably treat dividends paid as a component of cash flows from financing activities.

(*b*) **Taxes on Income:** Cash flows arising from taxes on income should be separately disclosed and should be classified as cash flows from operating activities unless they can be specifically identified with financing and investing activities. Taxes on income arise on transactions that give rise to cash flows that are classified as operating, investing or financing activities in a cash flow statement. While tax expense may be readily identifiable with investing or financing activities, the related tax cash flows are often impracticable to identify and may arise in a different period from the cash flows of the underlying transactions. Therefore, taxes paid are usually classified as cash flows from operating activities. However, when it is practicable to identify the tax cash flow with an individual transaction that gives rise to cash flows that are classified as investing or financing activities, the tax cash flow is classified as an investing or financing activity as appropriate. For example, capital gain tax on the sale of land and building is identifiable with the investing activities and hence in the cash flow statement, it should be shown as outflow from investing activities.

When the flows are allocated over more than one class of activity, the total amount of taxes is disclosed.

(*c*) **Extraordinary Items:** The cash flows associated with extraordinary items should be classified as arising from operating, investing or financing activities as appropriate and separately disclosed, winning of a law suit or a lottery and receipt of claim from an insurance company are examples of extraordinary items.

The cash flows associated with extraordinary items are disclosed separately as arising from operating, investing or financing activities in the cash flow statement, to enable users to understand their nature and effect on the present and future cash flows of the enterprise. These disclosures are in addition to the separate disclosures of the nature and amount of extraordinary items required by AS 5, Net Profit Or Loss For The Period, Prior Period Items, and Changes In Accounting Policies.

(*d*) **Investments in Subsidiaries, Associates and Joint Ventures:** When accounting for an investment in a subsidiary, an associate or a joint venture, the investor should restrict its reporting in the cash flow statement to the cash flows between itself and the investee/joint venture, for example, cash flows relating to dividends and advances.

(*e*) **Aquisitions and Disposals of Subsidiaries and other Business Units:** The aggregate cash flows arising from acquisitions and from disposals of subsidiaries or other business units should be presented separately and classified as investing activities. An enterprise should disclose, in aggregate, in respect of both acquisition and disposal of subsidiaries or other business units during the period each of the following.

(*i*) the total purchase or disposal consideration, and

(*ii*) the portion of the purchase or disposal consideration discharged by means of cash and cash equivalents.

The separate presentation of the cash flow effects of acquisitions and disposals of subsidiaries and other business units as single line items helps to distinguish those cash flows from other cash flows. The cash flow effects of disposals are not deducted from those of acquisitions.

(*f*) **Foreign Currency Cash Flows:** Cash flows arising from transactions in a foreign currency should be recorded in an enterprise's reporting currency by applying to the foreign currency amount the exchange rate between the reporting currency and the foreign currency at the date of the cash flow. A rate that approximates the actual rate may be used if the result is substantially the same as would arise if the rates at the dates of the cash flows were used. For example, a weighted average exchange rate for a period may be used for recording foreign currency transactions. The effect of changes in exchange rates on cash and cash equivalents held in a foreign currency should be reported as a separate part of the reconciliation of the changes in cash and cash equivalents during the period.

Unrealised gains and losses arising from changes in foreign exchange rates are not cash flows. However, the effect of exchange rate changes on cash and cash equivalents held or due in a foreign currency is reported in the cash flow statement in order to reconcile cash and cash equivalents at the beginning and the end of the period. This amount is presented separately from cash flows from operating, investing and financing activities and includes the differences, if any, had those cash flows been reported at the end-of-period exchange rates.

Non-cash Transactions: Transactions which do not involve inflow or outflow of cash or cash equivalents are, for obvious reasons, excluded from a cash flow statement. But significant non-cash investing and financing transactions should be reported in a separate schedule to the cash flow statement. Examples of non-cash transactions are:

(*i*) the acquisition of an enterprise by means of issue of shares;

(*ii*) the acquisition of a fixed asset, say machinery, on credit; and

(*iii*) the conversion of convertible debentures into equity shares.

Format: AS-3 (Revised) has not prescribed any specific format of cash flow statement. However, suggested format can be inferred from the illustrations appearing in the appendices to the accounting standard. A widely used format is outlined below:

...Co. Ltd. (Name of the Company)

Cash Flow Statement for the (period for which the statement has been prepared)

	Rs.	*Rs.*
Cash flows from operating activities		
Either:		
Individual items of cash inflows and outflows from operating activities	***	
Net cash from (used in) operating activities		***
Or:		
Net profit (loss) before taxation and extraordinary items	***	
Adjustments for non-cash and non-operating items and for gains and losses on sale of fixed assets and investments	***	
Operating profit (loss) before working capital changes	***	
Adjustments for changes in current assets (except cash and cash equivalents) and current liabilities	***	
Cash generated from (used in) operations before tax	***	
Income-tax paid	***	
Cash flow before extraordinary items	***	
Extraordinary items	***	
Net cash from (used in) operating activities		***
Cash flows from investing activities		
Individual items of cash inflows and outflows from investing activities	***	
Net cash from (used in) investing activities		***
Cash flows from financing activities		
Individual items of cash inflows and outflows from financing activities	***	
Net cash from (used in) financing activities		***
Net increase (decrease) in cash and cash equivalents		***
Cash and cash equivalents at the beginning of the period		***
Cash and cash equivalents at the end of the period		***

Significant non-cash investing and financing transactions mentioned by way of a note.

In the light of the abovementioned format, study the following cash flow statements prepared with imaginary figures:

XYZ Co. Ltd.

Cash Flow Statement

for the year ended 31st March, 2010

	(Rs. '000)	*(Rs. '000)*
Cash flows from operating activities		
Cash receipts from customers	23,470	
Cash paid to suppliers and employees	(18,355)	
	5,115	
Income-tax paid	(2,100)	
Net cash from operating activities		3,015
Cash flows from investing activities		
Purchase of machinery	(6,200)	
Sale of furniture	12	
Net cash used in investing activities		(6,188)
Cash flows from financing activities		
Proceeds from issuance of equity capital	6,000	
Redemption of debentures	(1,000)	

	(Rs. '000)	(Rs. '000)
Dividends paid	(1,800)	
Net cash from financing activities		3,200
Net increase in cash and cash equivalents		27
Cash and cash equivalents as on 1st April, 2009		894
Cash and cash equivalents as on 31st March, 2010		921

Significant non-cash transaction:
Debentures were converted into equity shares, Rs. 15 lakh.

XYZ Ltd.
Cash Flow Statement
for the year ended 31st March, 2010

	(Rs. '000)	(Rs. '000)
Cash flow from operating activities		
Net profit before taxation	4,450	
Adjustments for:		
Depreciation	840	
Loss on sale of furniture	2	
Operating profit before working capital changes	5,292	
Decrease in debtors	15	
Increase in stock	(164)	
Decrease in creditors	(28)	
Cash generated from operations	5,115	
Income-tax paid	(2,100)	
Net cash from operating activities		3,015
Cash flows from investing activities		
Purchase of machinery	(6,200)	
Sale of furniture	12	
Net cash used in investing activities		(6,188)
Cash flows from financing activities		
Proceeds from issuance of equity share capital	6,000	
Redemption of debentures	(1,000)	
Dividends paid	(1,800)	
Net cash from financing activities		3,200
Net increase in cash and cash equivalents		27
Cash and cash equivalents on 1st April, 2009		894
Cash and cash equivalents on 31st March, 2010		921

Significant non-cash transactions:
Debentures were converted into equity shares, Rs. 15 lakh

The Securities and Exchange Board of India (SEBI) amended in 1995 clause 32 of the Listing Agreement requiring all listed companies/entities to give a cash flow statement (prepared as per requirements prescribed by SEBI) in their annual report. It requires the cash flow statement to be prepared in the following format:—

ABC Limited
Cash flow statement for..........

A. Cash flow from operating activities:

Net profit before tax and extraordinary items

Adjustments for:

Depreciation

Foreign exchange

Investments
Interest/dividend
Operating profit before working capital changes
Adjustments for:
Trade and other receivables
Inventories
Trade payables
Cash generated from operations
Interest paid
Direct taxes paid
Cash flow before extraordinary items
Extraordinary items
Net cash from operating activities

B. Cash flow from investing activities:
Purchase of fixed assets
Sale of fixed assets
Acquisition of companies
(As per annexure)
Purchase of investments
Sale of investments
Interest received
Dividend received
Net cash used in investing activities

C. Cash flow from financing activities:
Proceeds from issue of share capital
Proceeds from long-term borrowings
Repayments of finance lease liabilities
Dividends paid
Net cash used in financing activities
Net increase in cash and cash equivalents
Cash and cash equivalents as at.........
(opening balance)
Cash and cash equivalents as at..........
(closing balance).

As a sepecimen, the following is the cash flow statement published by the Tata Iron and Steel Co. Ltd. in its annual report for the year 1997-98:

Cash Flow Statement for the year ended 31st March, 1998

		Year Ended 31-3-1998 Rs. Crores		*Year Ended 31-3-1997 Rs. Crores*
A. Cash Flow from Operating Activities:				
Net Profit before tax and Extraordinary Items		363.33		542.21
Adjustments for:				
Depreciation	343.23		326.83	
(Profit)/Loss on sale of Assets/ Discarded Assets written off	(11.29)		(8.07)	
(Profit)/Loss on sale of investments and provision for diminution in value of investments	(12.17)		(3.13)	
Interest income	(93.23)		(136.00)	
Dividend income	(26.65)		(25.49)	
Interest on borrowings	323.42		389.08	
Miscellaneous Expenditure (Amortised)	112.19		84.35	
Miscellaneous Expenditure paid	(80.64)		(100.41)	

Provision for Wealth Tax	0.40		0.75	
		556.26		527.91
Operating Profit before Working Capital Changes		919.59		1,070.12
Adjustments for:				
Trade and Other Receivables	(9.38)		(229.92)	
Inventories	(17.92)		51.51	
Trade Payables and Other Liabilities	(11.85)		(10.41)	
		(39.15)		(188.82)
		880.44		881.30
Cash Generated from Operations				
Interest paid	(323.15)		(392.75)	
Direct Taxes paid	(63.23)		(57.35)	
		(386.38)		(450.10)
Net Cash from Operating Activities ...A		494.06		431.20
B. Cash Flow from Investing Activities:				
Purchase of fixed assets	(1,119.44)		(756.37)	
Sale of fixed assets	13.86		304.77	
Purchase of investments	(101.98)		(469.31)	
Sale of investments	168.51		208.82	
Intercorporate deposits	259.90		(153.10)	
Interest received	101.89		136.97	
Dividend received	26.65	(650.61)	25.49	(702.73)
Net Cash used in Investing Activities: ....B		(650.61)		(702.73)
C. Cash Flow from Financing Activities:				
Proceeds from issue of share capital	1.45		1.22	
Capital contributions received	2.30		—	
Borrowings (net)	496.49		241.57	
Dividends paid	(165.66)	334.58	(156.97)	85.82
Net Cash from Financing Activities C		334.58		85.82
Net increase/(decrease) in Cash and Cash equivalents (A + B + C)		178.03		(185.71)
Cash and Cash equivalents as at 1st April, 1997 (Opening Balance)		251.38		437.09
Cash and Cash equivalents as at 31st March, 1998 (Closing Balance)		429.41		251.38

Note: (*i*) Figures in brackets represent outflows.

(*ii*) Cash and cash equivalents is net of exchange rate difference of Rs. 4.72 crores (31.3.1997: Rs. 0.67 crore).

Cash Provided (Used) by Operating Activities: A very important piece of information that is made available by cash flow statement is the net cash provided (used) by operating activities. Income statement is prepared on the accrual basis of accounting meaning thereby that revenues are recorded when earned and the expenses are recorded when incurred. In most cases, earned revenues include credit sales. At the end of the accounting period, there are trade debtors from whom cash is yet to be collected for credit sales. Also, at the end of the accounting period, there are at least some expenses which have been incurred but which have not yet been paid for. Thus, net profit disclosed by the income statement does not indicate the net cash provided by operating activities. In order to calculate the net cash provided by (used in) operating activities, revenues and expenses are replaced by actual receipts and payments in cash. There are two methods of converting net income into net cash flows from operating activities: the direct method and the indirect method.

The Direct Method: Under the direct method, cash receipts from operating revenues and cash payments for operating expenses are calculated and shown in the cash flow statement in a summarised form. The difference between the total cash receipts and the total cash payments is shown as the net cash provided by (or used in) operating activities.

The following are some examples of usual cash receipts and cash payments resulting from operating activities:

(*i*) Cash sales of goods and services,
(*ii*) Cash collected from credit customers,
(*iii*) Cash receipts on account of royalties, fees, commissions and other revenues,
(*iv*) Cash payments for purchase of inventories,
(*v*) Cash payments for various operating expenses like rent, power, electricity etc.,
(*vi*) Cash payments of wages and salaries to employees,
(*vii*) Cash payment of income tax to Government.

Amounts which appear in the income statement are accrual based. Various adjustments have to be made to them to convert them into cash-based items. The necessary information required to make these adjustments may be available from balance sheet in the beginning of the accounting period, the balance sheet at the end of the accounting period or some other source. Some calculations with imaginary figures are given below to illustrate the point.

	Rs.
(*i*) Credit Purchases for the year ended 31st March, 2010 as per Trading Account	13,80,000
Add: Trade Creditors as on 1st April, 2009 as per opening Balance Sheet	1,07,000
	14,87,000
Less: Trade Creditors as on 31st March, 2010 as per closing Balance Sheet	1,32,000
Cash payments to credit suppliers	13,55,000
(*ii*) Salary expense for the year ended 31st March, 2010 as per Profit and Loss Account	1,28,000
Add: Outstanding Salaries as on 1st April, 2009 as per opening Balance Sheet	10,000
	1,38,000
Less: Outstanding Salaries as on 31st March, 2010 as per closing Balance Sheet	11,000
Payments on account of Salaries	1,27,000
(*iii*) Fire Insurance expense for the year ended 31st March, 2010 as per Profit and Loss Account	2,700
Add: Unexpired Fire Insurance as on 31st March, 2010 as per closing Balance Sheet	700
	3,400
Less: Unexpired Fire Insurance as on 1st April, 2009 as per opening Balance Sheet	600
Payment of Fire Insurance premium during the year	2,800
(*iv*) Commission income for the year ended 31st March, 2010 as per Profit and Loss Account	8,700
Add: Commission Earned but not Received as on 1st April, 2009 as per opening Balance Sheet	300
	9,000
Less: Commission Earned but not Received as on 31st March, 2010 on per closing Balance Sheet	350
Cash receipt on account of Commission	8,650
(*v*) Credit Sales for the year ended 31st March, 2010 as per Trading Account	23,56,000

	Rs.
Add: Trade Debtors as on 1st April, 2009 as per opening Balance Sheet	25,600
	23,81,600
Less: Trade Debtors as on 31st March, 2010 as per closing Balance Sheet	27,200
Cash collections from credit customers	23,54,400

Illustrations 1:

From the following particulars, prepare a cash flow statement for the year ended 31st March, 2010, using direct method:

Profit and Loss Account
for the year ended 31st March, 2010

	Rs. '000		Rs. '000
To Opening Stock	3,150	By Sales	18,480
To Purchases	12,820	By Closing Stock	3,490
To Gross Profit c/d	6,000		
	21,970		21,970
To Rent	1,200	By Gross Profit b/d	6,000
To Salaries	2,140		
To Advertising	300		
To Sundry Trade Expenses	130		
To Depreciation on Furniture	270		
To Provision for Income Tax	980		
To Net Profit c/d	980		
	6,000		6,000
To Transfer to General Reserve	200	By Balance b/fd.	180
To Proposed Dividend with corporate divident tax	575	By Net Profit for the year b/d	980
To Balance carried to Balance Sheet	385		
	1,160		1,160

Balance Sheets

Liabilities	As on 31.3.2009 Rs '000.	As on 31.3.2010 Rs. '000	Assets	As on 31.3.2009 Rs. '000	As on 31.3.2010 Rs. '000
Issued and Subscribed			Furniture	3,000	2,700
Share Capital	5,000	5,000	*Less:* Depreciation	300	270
General Reserve	1,000	1,200		2,700	2,430
Profit and Loss A/c	180	385	Stock	3,150	3,490
Trade Creditors	663	842	Trade Debtors	830	810
Outstanding Expenses	17	18	Cash on hand	20	55
Provision for Taxation	940	980	Cash at Bank	725	1,200
Proposed Dividend (with			Prepaid Expenses	—	15
corporate dividend tax)	575	575	Advance Payment of Income Tax	950	1,000
	8,375	9,000		8,375	9,000

You are also informed that during the year, dividend for the year 2008-2009 and corporate dividend tax together amounting to Rs. 575 thousand was paid. A tax refund of Rs. 10 thousand for the accounting year 2008-2009 was received. Advance payment of tax amounting to Rs. 1,000 thousand was made during the year.

Solution:

Cash Flow Statement
for the year ended 31st March, 2010

	(Rs. '000)	(Rs. '000)
Cash Flows from Operating Activities		
Cash receipts from customers [Working Note (i)]	18,500	
Cash paid to suppliers and employees [Working Note (ii)]	(16,425)	
Cash inflows from operations	2,075	
Income tax paid	(990)	
Net cash provided by operating activities		1,085
Cash flows from Financing Activities		
Dividends and corporate dividend tax paid	(575)	
Net cash used in financing activities		(575)
Net increase in cash and cash equivalents		510
Cash and cash equivalents at the beginning		745
Cash and cash equivalents at the end		1,255

Working Notes:

		Rs. '000
(i) *Calculations of cash receipts from customers:*		
Sales for the year as per Trading Account		18,480
Add: Trade Debtors as on 31st March, 2009		830
		19,310
Less: Trade Debtors as on 31st March, 2010		810
Cash receipts from customers		18,500
(ii) *Calculation of cash paid to suppliers and employees:*		
Purchases for the year as per Trading Account		12,820
Add: Trade Creditors as on 31st March, 2009		663
		13,483
Less: Trade Creditors as on 31st March, 2010		842
Cash paid for goods	(a)	12,641
Expenses as per Profit and Loss Account:		
Rent		1,200
Salaries		2,140
Advertising		300
Sundry Trade Expenses		130
		3,770
Add: Outstanding Expenses as on 31.3.2009		17
Prepaid Expenses as on 31.3.2010		15
		3,802
Less: Outstanding Expenses as on 31.3.2010		18
Cash paid for services	(b)	3,784
Cash paid to suppliers and employees	(a) + (b)	16,425
(iii) Tax paid as advance		1,000
Less: Refund of tax		10
Net amount of tax paid		990
(iv) Cash on hand on 31.3.2009		20
Cash at Bank on 31.3.2010		700
Cash and Cash equivalents in the beginning		720

	Rs. '000
(v) Cash on hand on 31.3.2010	55
Cash at Bank on 31.3.2010	1,200
Cash and cash equivalents at the end	1,255

The Indirect Method: Under the indirect method, the necessary adjustments are made to the figure of net profit (loss) as disclosed by the profit and loss account to arrive at the figure of net cash flow from operating activities. It involves a reconciliation of the net profit with net cash flow from operating activities, and hence this method may as well be called reconciliation method. The process of reconciliation (making adjustments) may be undertaken as outlined below:

(a) Take net profit before tax and extra-ordinary items.

(b) Make adjustments for non-cash and non-operating items.
- *(i)* Add depreciation on fixed assets
- *(ii)* Add amount of goodwill written off
- *(iii)* Add amount of preliminary expenses, discount on issue of shares, discount on issue of debentures, underwriting commission and brokerage on issue of shares and debenture, cost of issue of shares and debentures and such similar accounts, written off
- *(iv)* Add or deduct, as the case may require, other non-operating items.

(c) Make adjustments for gains and losses on sale of fixed assets and investments.
- *(i)* Deduct gains on sale of fixed assets
- *(ii)* Deduct gains on sale of investments
- *(iii)* Add losses on sale of fixed assets
- *(iv)* Add losses on sale of investments

(d) Make adjustments for changes in current operating assets (except cash and cash equivalents) and current operating liabilities (except bank overdraft).
- *(i)* Add decrease in the accounts of current operating assets (except cash and cash equivalents) like Trade Debtors, Bills Receivable, Stock-in-trade and Prepaid Expenses.
- *(ii)* Deduct increases in the abovementioned accounts.
- *(iii)* Add increases in the accounts of currents operating liabilities (except Bank Overdraft) like Creditors, Bill Payable and Outstanding Expenses.
- *(iv)* Deduct decreases in the abovementioned accounts.

(e) Deduct income-tax paid

(f) Make adjustments for extraordinary items, if any.

The result will be the figure of net cash provided by (used in) operating activities.

Illustration 2:

From the following particulars, prepare cash flow statements for the year ended 31st March, 2010 using the indirect method:

Profit and Loss Account
for the year ended 31st March, 2010

	Rs. '000		*Rs. '000*
To Opening Stock	2,900	By Sale	18,930
To Purchases	9,530	By Closing Stock	3,110
To Wages	2,870		
To Power	240		
To Gross Profit c/d	6,500		
	22,040		22,040

	Rs. '000		Rs. '000
To Rent	1,500	By Gross Profit b/d	6,500
To Salaries	2,140		
To Electricity	100		
To Petty Office Expenses	95		
To Loss on Disposal of Furniture	40		
To Depreciation on Machinery	405		
To Depreciation on Furniture	120		
To Goodwill written off	200		
To Preliminary Expenses written off	100		
To Provision for Income Tax	900		
To Net Profit c/d	900		
	6,500		6,500
To Proposed Dividend and Corporate Dividend Tax	740	By Net Profit b/d	900
To Transfer to General Reserve	160		
	900		900

Balance Sheets

Liabilities	*As on 31.3.2009*	*As on 31.3.2010*	*Assets*	*As on 31.3.2009*	*As on 31.3.2010*
	Rs.'000	*Rs.'000*		*Rs.'000*	*Rs.'000*
Equity Share Capital	6,000	6,500	Goodwill	600	400
General Reserve	1,000	1,160	Machinery	1,700	2,295
Creditors	650	622	Furniture	1,350	1,080
Outstanding Expenses	20	38	Stock	2,900	3,110
Provision for Taxation	800	900	Debtors	800	830
Proposed Dividend and Corporate Dividend Tax	690	740	Cash on hand	30	40
			Cash at Bank	780	1,130
			Prepaid Expenses	—	25
			Advance Payment of Income Tax	800	950
			Preliminary Expenses	200	100
	9,160	9,960		9,160	9,960

The following additional information is provided to you:

(i) During the year, Furniture of the book value of Rs. 150 thousand was sold for Rs. 110 thousand and new Machinery costing Rs. 1,000 thousand was purchased and put into operation.

(ii) New equity shares were allotted at par for Rs. 500 thousand.

(iii) Taxation liability for the accounting year 1999-2000 was settled at Rs. 800 thousand, the amount having already been paid. For the year 2000-2001 an advance tax of Rs. 950 thousand was paid.

(iv) During the year, dividend with the corporate dividend tax thereon for the year 1999-2000, Rs. 690 thousand was paid.

Solution:

Cash Flow Statement for the year ended 31st March, 2010

	Rs. '000	*Rs. '000*
Cash Flow from Operating Activities		
Net profit before tax	1,800	
Adjustments for:		
Depreciation	525	
Goodwill and preliminary expenses, amortized	300	
Loss on disposal of furniture	40	
Operating profit before working capital changes	2,665	
Adjustments for:		
Increase in stock	(210)	
Increase in debtors	(30)	
Increase in prepaid expenses	(25)	
Decrease in creditors	(28)	
Increase in outstanding expenses	18	
Cash generated from operations	2,390	
Tax paid	(950)	
Net cash from operating activities		1,440
Cash Flows from Investing Activities		
Proceeds from sale of furniture	110	
Purchase of machinery	(1,000)	
Net cash used in investing activities		(890)
Cash Flows from Financing Activities		
Proceeds from issue of equity share capital	500	
Dividends paid	(690)	
Net cash used in financing activities		(190)
Net Increase in Cash and Cash Equivalents		360
Cash and Cash Equivalents (Opening Balance)		810
Cash and Cash Equivalents (Closing Balance)		1,170

Working Notes:

		Rs.'000
(*i*)	Depreciation on Machinery	405
	Depreciation on Furniture	120
	Total depreciation	525
(*ii*)	Goodwill, written off	200
	Preliminary Expenses, written off	100
	Total	300
(*iii*)	Stock on 31st March, 2010	3,110
	Stock on 31st March 2009	2,900
	Increase in Stock	210

(*iv*) Increase in Debtors = Rs. 830 thousand – Rs. 800 thousand = Rs. 30 thousand

(*v*) Decrease in Creditors = Rs. 650 thousand – Rs. 622 thousand = Rs. 28 thousand

(*vi*) Increase in Outstanding Expenses = Rs. 38 thousand – Rs. 20 thousand = Rs. 18 thousand

Illustration 3:

The following particulars pertain to Cee Ltd.:

Income Statement for the year ended 31st March, 2010

		Rs.
Sales revenue		32,00,000
Less: Cost of goods sold		20,00,000
		12,00,000
Add: Government compensation for loss in riots		50,000
		12,50,000
	Rs.	
Less: Operating expenses	7,90,000	
Interest on debentures	15,000	
Depreciation on fixed assets	2,10,000	
Cost of issue of debentures, written off	1,000	10,16,000
Profit before tax		2,34,000
Less: Provision for Income tax		92,000
Profit after tax		1,42,000

	Year Ended 31st March, 2009	*Year Ended 31st March, 2010*
	Rs.	*Rs.*
Inventories	1,80,000	2,20,000
Debtors	40,000	38,000
Bills receivable	30,000	55,000
Cash in hand and at bank	1,17,000	2,48,000
Creditors	78,000	95,000
Bills payable	20,000	15,000
Outstanding expenses	31,000	44,000

You are also informed that the following important transactions have taken place during the year ended 31st March, 2010:

(*i*) Fully paid equity shares of the face value of Rs. 2,00,000 were allotted at a premium of 20%.

(*ii*) 10% debentures for Rs. 3,00,000 were redeemed at a premium of 2%.

(*iii*) Land was purchased for Rs. 1,50,000 and the consideration was discharged by the allotment to the vendor of zero per cent convertible debentures for the amount.

(*iv*) Dividend and corporate dividend tax thereon for the year ended 31st March, 2009 amounting to Rs. 1,15,000 was paid.

(*v*) Income tax paid during the year totalled Rs. 95,000.

You are required to prepare cash flow statement for the year ended 31st March, 2001 using (*i*) the direct method and (*ii*) the indirect method.

Solution:

(*i*) *By Direct Method:*

Cash Flow Statement for the year ended 31st March, 2010

	Rs.	*Rs.*
Cash Flows from Operating Activities		
Cash receipts from customers	31,77,000	
Cash payments to suppliers and employees	(28,05,000)	
Cash inflow from operations	3,72,000	

	Rs.	Rs.
Income tax paid	(95,000)	
	2,77,000	
Cash flow from extraordinary item:		
Government compensation for loss in riots	50,000	
Net cash from operating activities		3,27,000
Cash Flows from Financing Activities		
Issue of equity share capital at a premium	2,40,000	
Redemption of 10% debentures at a premium	(3,06,000)	
Debenture-interest paid*	(15,000)	
Dividend and corporate dividend tax thereon paid	(1,15,000)	
Net cash used in financing activities		(1,96,000)
Net increase in cash and cash equivalents		1,31,000
Cash and cash equivalents in the beginning		1,17,000
Cash and cash equivalents at the end		2,48,000

Significant Non-cash Transaction:

Land was purchased by issuing at par, zero per cent convertible debentures of Rs. 1,50,000

*Alternatively, debenture interest paid may be treated as a flow from operating activities.

Working Notes:

		Rs.	Rs.
(*i*) Sales revenue			32,00,000
Add:	Debtors on 31.3.2009		40,000
	Bills receivable on 31.3.2009		30,000
			32,70,000
Less:	Debtors on 31.3.2010	38,000	
	Bills receivable on 31.3.2010	55,000	93,000
Cash receipts from customers			31,77,000
(*ii*) Cost of goods sold			20,00,000
Operating expenses			7,90,000
			27,90,000
Add:	Inventories on 31.3.2010		2,20,000
	Creditors on 31.3.2009		78,000
	Bills payable on 31.3.2009		20,000
	Outstanding expenses on 31.3.2009		31,000
			31,39,000
Less:	Inventories on 31.3.2009	1,80,000	
	Creditors on 31.3.2010	95,000	
	Bills payable on 31.3.2010	15,000	
	Outstanding expenses on 31.3.2010	44,000	3,34,000
Cash paid to suppliers and employees			28,05,000

(*ii*) *By Indirect Method:*

Cash Flow Statement for the year ended 31st March, 2010

Cash Flows from Operating Activities	Rs.	Rs.
Net profit before tax and extraordinary item	1,84,000	
Adjustments for:		
Interest on debentures	15,000	
Depreciation on fixed assets	2,10,000	

	Rs.	Rs.
Cost of issue of debentures amortized	1,000	
Operating profit before working capital changes	4,10,000	
Adjustments for:		
Increase in inventories	(40,000)	
Decrease in debtors	2,000	
Increase in bills receivable	(25,000)	
Increase in creditors	17,000	
Decrease in bills payable	(5,000)	
Increase in outstanding expenses	13,000	
Cash generated from operations	3,72,000	
Income tax paid	(95,000)	
	2,77,000	
Cash flow from extraordinary item:		
Government compensation for loss in riots	50,000	
Net cash from operating activities		3,27,000
Cash Flows from Financing Activities		
Issue of equity share capital at a premium	2,40,000	
Redemption of 10% debentures at a premium	(3,06,000)	
Debenture - interest paid*	(15,000)	
Dividend and corporate dividend tax thereon paid	(1,15,000)	
Net cash used in financing activities		(1,96,000)
Net increase in cash and cash equivalents		1,31,000
Cash and cash equivalents in the beginning		1,17,000
Cash and cash equivalents at the end		2,48,000

Significant Non-cash Transaction:
Land was purchased by issuing at par, zero per cent convertible debentures of Rs. 1,50,000

*Alternatively, debenture – interest paid may be treated as a flow from operating activities.

Illustration 4:

Zed Ltd. presents to you the following balance sheet and income statement:

Balance Sheets

	As on 31st March, 2009 Rs.	As on 31st March, 2010 Rs.
Equity Share Capital	10,00,000	10,00,000
Retained Earnings	8,60,000	9,46,000
12% Debentures	6,00,000	5,00,000
Trade Creditors	1,02,500	1,21,700
Outstanding Expenses	21,800	27,400
	25,84,300	25,95,100
Fixed Assets, at cost	24,00,000	26,00,000
Provision for Depreciation	(8,00,000)	(9,80,000)
Investments	2,50,000	1,00,000
Inventories	4,13,300	5,07,100
Trade Debtors	1,60,000	1,80,000
Provision for Bad Debts	(8,000)	(9,000)
Cash in hand and at Bank	1,64,200	1,93,400
Underwriting Commission	4,800	3,600
	25,84,300	25,95,100

Profit and Loss Account for the year Ended 31st March, 2010

	Rs.
Sales	36,40,200
Cost of Goods Sold	(18,60,000)
Compensation Received in Lawsuit	55,000
Interest received on Investments	21,000
Profit on Sale of Investments	7,500
Sundry Operating Expenses	(7,83,500)
Interest on Debentures	(66,000)
Provision for Bad Debts	(1,000)
Provision for Depreciation	(1,80,000)
Underwriting Commission, written off	(1,200)
Net Profit before Tax	8,32,000
Tax for the year, paid	4,16,000
Net Profit after Tax	4,16,000

Prepare Zed Ltd.'s Cash flow statement for the year ended 31st March, 2010 using (*i*) the direct method and (*ii*) the indirect method. Zed Ltd. informs you that debentures have been redeemed at par.

Solution:

(*i*) *Direct Method:*

Zed Ltd.
Cash Flow Statement for the year ended 31st March, 2010

	Rs.	*Rs.*
Cash Flows from Operating Activities		
Cash receipts from customers	36,20,200	
Cash paid to suppliers and employees	(27,12,500)	
Cash inflow from operations	9,07,700	
Income tax paid	(4,16,000)	
	4,91,700	
Cash flow from extraordinary item:		
Compensation received in law suit	55,000	
Net cash from operarting activities		5,46,700
Cash Flows from Investing Activities		
Puchase of fixed assets	(2,00,000)	
Sale proceeds of investments	1,57,500	
Interest received on investment*	21,000	
Net cash used in investing activities		(21,500)
Cash Flows from Financing Activities		
Redenption of debentures at par	(1,00,000)	
Interest on debentures paid*	(66,000)	
Dividends and corporate dividend tax paid	(3,30,000)	
Net cash used in financing activities		(4,96,000)
Net increase in cash and cash equivalents		29,200
Cash and cash equivalents as on 31st March, 2009 (Opening Balance)		1,64,200
Cash and cash equivalents as on 31st March 2010 (Closing Balance)		1,93,400

*Alternatively, interest received on investments and interest paid on debentures may be treated as flows from operating activities.

Working Notes:

(i) *Calculation of cash receipts from customers:*

		Rs.
Sales		36,40,200
Add: Trade Debtors as on 31st March, 2009		1,60,000
		38,00,200
Less: Trade Debtors as on 31st March, 2010		1,80,000
		36,20,200

(ii) *Calculation of cash paid to suppliers and employees:*

	Rs.	Rs.
Cost of Goods Sold		18,60,000
Add: Sundry Operating Expenses		7,83,500
		26,43,500
Add: Inventory as on 31st March, 2010		5,07,100
Trade Creditors as on 31st March, 2009		1,02,500
Outstanding Expenses as on 31st March, 2009		21,800
		32,74,900
Less: Inventory as on 31st March, 2009	4,13,300	
Trade Creditors as on 31st March, 2010	1,21,700	
Outstanding Expenses as on 31st March, 2010	27,400	5,62,400
		27,12,500

(iii) *Fixed Assets purchased during the year:*

Fixed Assets, at cost, on 31st March, 2010	26,00,000
Less: Fixed Assets, at cost, on 31st March, 2009	24,00,000
	2,00,000

(iv) *Sale proceeds of Investments:*

Cost of Investments sold (Rs. 2,50,000 – Rs. 1,00,000)	1,50,000
Add: Profit on sale of Investments	7,500
	1,57,500

(v) *Calculation of dividends and corporate dividend tax thereon paid:*

Retained Earnings on 31st March, 2009	8,60,000
Add: Net Profit for the year ended 31st March, 2010	4,16,000
	12,76,000
Less: Retained Earnings as on 31st March, 2010	9,46,000
Dividends and corporate dividend tax paid	3,30,000

(ii) *Indirect Method:*

Zed Ltd.

Cash Flow Statement for the year ended 31st March, 2010

	Rs.	Rs.
Cash Flows from Operating Activities		
Net profit before income tax and extra-ordinary item:	7,77,000	
Adjustments for:		
Depreciation	1,80,000	
Provision for bad debts	1,000	
Underwriting commission amortised	1,200	
Profit on sale of investments	(7,500)	
Income from investments	(21,000)	
Interest on debentures	66,000	
Operating profit before working capital changes	9,96,700	
Adjustments for:		
Increase in inventory	(93,800)	

	Rs.	Rs.
Increase in trade debtors	(20,000)	
Increase in trade creditors	19,200	
Increase in outstanding expenses	5,600	
Cash inflow from operations	9,07,700	
Income tax paid	(4,16,000)	
	4,91,700	
Cash flow from extraordinary item:		
Compensation received in lawsuit	55,000	
Net cash from operating activities		5,46,700
Cash Flows from Investing Activities		
Purchase of fixed assets	(2,00,000)	
Sale proceeds of investments	1,57,500	
Interest received on investments*	21,000	
Net cash used in investing activities		(21,500)
Cash Flows from Financing Activities		
Redemption of debentures at par	(1,00,000)	
Interest on debentures paid*	(66,000)	
Dividends and corporate dividend tax paid	(3,30,000)	
Net cash used in financing activities		(4,96,000)
Net increase in cash and cash equivalents		29,200
Cash and cash equivalents as on **31st March, 2009 (Opening Balance)**		1,64,200
Cash and Cash equivalents as on 31st March, 2010 (Closing Balance)		1,93,400

*Alternatively, interest received on investments and interest paid on debentures may be treated as flows from operating activities.

Working Notes:

(*i*) ***Net profit before income-tax and extraordinary item:***

	Rs.
Net profit before income tax	8,32,000
Less: Compensation received in lawsuit	55,000
	7,77,000

Working notes (*iii*), (*iv*) and (*v*) as prepared under the direct method are also relevant under the indirect method.

Illustration 5:

Moon Ltd. gives you the following information for the year ended 31st March, 2010:—

(*i*) Sales for the year totalled Rs. 96,00,000. The company sells goods for cash only.

(*ii*) Cost of goods sold was 60% of sales. Closing inventory was higher than opening inventory by Rs. 43,000. Trade creditors on 31st March, 2010 exceeded those on 31st March, 2009 by Rs. 23,000.

(*iii*) Net profit before tax was Rs. 13,80,000. Tax paid amounted to Rs. 7,00,000. Depreciation on fixed assets for the year was Rs. 3,15,000 whereas other expenses totalled Rs. 21,45,000. Outstanding expenses on 31st March, 2009 and 31st March, 2010 totalled Rs. 82,000 and Rs. 91,000 respectively.

(*iv*) New machinery and furniture costing Rs. 10,27,500 in all were purchased.

(*v*) A rights issue was made of 50,000 equity shares of Rs. 10 each at a premium of Rs. 3 per share. The entire money was received with applications.

(*vi*) Dividends and corporate dividend tax totalling Rs. 4,14,000 were paid.

(*vii*) Cash in hand and at bank as at 31st March, 2000 totalled Rs. 2,13,800.

You are requested to prepare a cash flow statement using *(a)* the direct method and *(b)* the indirect method.

Solution:

(a) Direct Method:

Moon Ltd.
Cash Flow Statement for the year ended 31st March, 2001

	Rs.	Rs.
Cash Flows from Operating Activities		
Cash receipts from customers	96,00,000	
Cash paid to suppliers and employees	(79,16,000)	
Cash inflow from operations	16,84,000	
Tax paid	(7,00,000)	
Net cash from operating activities		9,84,000
Cash Flows from Investing Activities		
Purchase of fixed assets	(10,27,500)	
Net cash used in investing activities		(10,27,500)
Cash Flows from Financing Activities		
Proceeds from issue of share capital	6,50,000	
Dividends and corporate dividend tax paid	(4,14,000)	
Net cash from financing activities		2,36,000
Net increase in cash and cash equivalents		1,92,500
Cash and cash equivalents as at 31st March, 2000 (Opening Balance)		2,13,800
Cash and cash equivalents as at 31st March, 2001 (Closing Balance)		4,06,300

Working Notes:

(i) Calculation of cash paid to suppliers and employees:

		Rs.
Cost of sales, 60% of Rs. 96,00,000		57,60,000
Add: Expenses incurred		21,45,000
Outstanding expenses on 31st March, 2009		82,000
Excess of closing inventory over opening inventory		43,000
		80,30,000
	Rs.	
Less: Excess of closing creditors over opening creditors	23,000	
Outstanding expenses on 31st March, 2010	91,000	1,14,000
		79,16,000

(ii) Proceeds from issue of share capital:
Issue price of one share = Rs. 10 + Rs. 3 = Rs. 13
Proceeds from issue of 50,000 shares = Rs. 13 × 50,000 = Rs. 6,50,000

(b) Indirect Method:

Moon Ltd.
Cash Flow Statement for the year ended 31st March, 2010

	Rs.	Rs.
Cash Flows from Operating Activities		
Net profit before tax	13,80,000	
Adjustment for:		
Depreciation	3,15,000	
Operating profit before working capital changes	16,95,000	

	Rs.	Rs.
Adjustments for:		
Increase in inventory	(43,000)	
Increase in trade creditors	23,000	
Increase in outstanding expenses	9,000	
Cash generated from operations	16,84,000	
Tax paid	(7,00,000)	
Net cash from operating activities		9,84,000
Cash Flows from Investing Activities		
Purchase of fixed assets	(10,27,500)	
Net cash used in investing activities		(10,27,500)
Cash Flows from Financing Activities		
Proceeds from issue of share capital	6,50,000	
Dividends and corporate dividend tax paid	(4,14,000)	
Net cash from financing activities		2,36,600
Net increase in cash and cash equivalents		1,92,500
Cash and cash equivalents as at 31st March, 2000 (Opening Balance)		2,13,800
Cash and cash equivalents as at 31st March, 2001 (Closing Balance)		4,06,300

Working Notes:

(*i*) Increase in outstanding expenses = Rs. 91,000 – Rs. 82,000 = Rs. 9,000

(*i*) Proceeds from issue of share capital = 50,000 × (Rs. 10 + Rs. 3) = Rs. 6,50,000

Illustration 6:

Ms. Jyothi of Star Oils Limited has collected the following information for the preparation of cash flow statement for the year ended 31st March, 2010:

	(*Rs. in lakhs*)
Net profit	25,000
Dividend and corporate dividentd tax thereon paid	8,535
Provision for income-tax	5,000
Income-tax paid during the year	4,248
Loss on sale of fixed assets (net)	40
Book value of the fixed assets sold	185
Depreciation charged to Profit & Loss Account	20,000
Amortisation of capital grant	6
Profit on sale of investments	100
Carrying amount of investments sold	27,765
Interest income on investments	2,506
Interest expenses	10,000
Interest paid during the year	10,520
Increase in working capital (excluding cash and bank balances)	56,075
Purchase of fixed assets	14,560
Investment in joint venture	3,850
Expenditure on construction, work-in-progress	34,740
Proceeds from calls in arrear	2
Receipt of grant for capital projects	12
Proceeds from long-term borrowings	25,980
Proceeds from short-term borrowings	20,575
Opening cash and Bank balances	5,003
Closing cash and bank balances	6,988

Required:

Prepare the cash flow statement in accordance with AS-3, Cash Flow Statements issued by the Institute of Chartered Accountants of India. Make necessary assumptions.

[*Adapted C.A.* (*Final*), *May, 2001*]

Solution:

Star Oils Limited
Cash Flow Statement for the year ended 31st March, 2010

	Rs. in lakhs	*Rs. in lakhs*
Cash Flow from Operating Activities		
Net profit before tax, Rs. (25 + 5) lakh	30,000	
Adjustments for:		
Depreciation	20,000	
Loss on sale of fixed assets (net)	40	
Amortisation of capital grant	(6)	
Profit on sale of investments	(100)	
Interest income on investments	(2,506)	
Interest expenses	10,000	
Operating profit before working capital changes	57,428	
Adjustment for increase in working capital, (excluding cash and bank balances)	(56,075)	
Cash generated from operations	1,353	
Tax paid	(4,248)	
Net cash used in operating activities		(2,895)
Cash Flows from Investing Activities		
Sale of fixed assets, Rs. (185 – 40) lakh	145	
Sale of investment, Rs. (27,765 + 100) lakh	27,865	
Interest income on investments	2,506	
Purchase of fixed assets	(14,560)	
Investment in joint venture	(3,850)	
Expenditure on construction, work-in-profits	(34,740)	
Net Cash used in investing activities		(22,634)
Cash Flows from Financing Activities		
Proceeds from calls in area	2	
Receipt of grant for capital projects	12	
Proceeds from long-term borrowing	25,980	
Proceeds from short-term borrowings	20,575	
Interest paid during the year	(10,520)	
Dividend and corporate dividend tax thereon paid	(8,535)	
Net cash from financing activities		27,514
Net increase in cash and cash equivalents		1,985
Cash and cash equivalents as on 1st April, 2009 (Opening Balance)		5,003
Cash and cash equivalents as on 31st March, 2010 (Closing Balance)		6,988

Illustration 7:

The following are the changes in the account balances taken from the Balance Sheets of PQ Ltd. as at the beginning and end of the year:

	Changes in Rupees in debit or (credit)
Equity share capital 30,000 shares of Rs. 10 each issued and fully paid	0
Capital reserve	(49,200)
8% debentures	(50,000)
Debenture discount	1,000
Freehold property at cost/revaluation	43,000
Plant and machinery at cost	60,000
Depreciation on plant and machinery	(14,400)
Debtors	50,000

	Changes in Rupees in debit or (credit)
Stock and work-in-progress	38,500
Creditors	(11,800)
Net profit for the year	(76,500)
Dividend paid in respect of earlier year	30,000
Provision for doubtful debts	(3,300)
Trade investments at cost	47,000
Bank	(64,300)
	0

You are informed that:

(*a*) Capital reserve as at the end of the year represented realised profits on sale of one freehold property together with surplus arising on the revaluation of balance of freehold properties.

(*b*) During the year plant costing Rs. 18,000 against which depreciation provision of Rs. 13,500 was lying was sold for Rs. 7,000.

(*c*) During the middle of the year Rs. 50,000 debentures were issued for cash at a discount of Rs. 1,000.

(*d*) The net profit for the year was after crediting the profit on sale of plant and charging debenture interest.

You are required to prepare a statement which will explain, why bank borrowing has increased by Rs. 64,300 during the year end. Ignore taxation. [*C.A. (Final), Nov., 1998*]

Solution:

PQ Ltd.
Cash Flow Statement for the year ended ....

	Rs.	*Rs.*
Cash flows from operating activities	76,500	
Net profit		
Adjustments for		
Depreciation [Working Note (*iv*)]	27,900	
Profit on sale of plant	(2,500)	
Interest expense	2,000	
Operating profit before working capital changes	1,03,900	
Adjustments for:		
Increase in debtors (less provision)	(46,700)	
Increase in stock and work-in-progress	(38,500)	
Increase in creditors	11,800	
Net cash from operating activities		30,500
Cash flows from investing activities		
Purchase of plant and machinery	(78,000)	
Proceeds from sale of plant	7,000	
Proceeds from sale of freehold property	6,200	
Increase in trade investments	(47,000)	
Net cash used in investing activities		(1,11,800)
Cash flows from financing activities		
Proceeds from issuance of debentures at discount	49,000	
Debenture interest paid	(2,000)	
Dividend paid in respect of earlier year	(30,000)	
Net cash from financing activities		17,000
Excess of outflows over inflows		64,300

Thus, the shortfall of Rs. 64,300 was made up through borrowings from bank.

Working Notes:

	Rs.
(*i*) *Acquisition of plant and machinery*:	
Amount of increase, at cost	60,000
Add: Cost of plant disposed of	18,000
Cost of plant and machinery purchased	78,000

(*ii*) Profit on sale of plant = Rs. 7,000 – (Rs. 18,000 – Rs. 13,500)
= Rs. 7,000 – Rs. 4,500 = Rs. 2,500

	Rs.
(*iii*) *Proceeds from sale of freehold property:*	
Capital reserve	49,200
Less : Increase in freehold property (given)	43,000
Proceeds from sale	6,200
(*iv*) *Depreciation on Plant and Machinery provided for the year*:	
Increase in Provision for Depreciation (given)	14,400
Add: Accumulated depreciation on plant sold	13,500
Depreciation for the year	27,900

(*v*) Due to the absence of relevant information, income from investments has been ignored.

Illustration 8:

Given below are the condensed balance sheets of Lambakadi Ltd. for two years and the statement of profit and loss for one year.

(Figures in Rs. Lakhs)

As at 31st March	*2010*	*2009*
Share Capital :		
Equity shares of Rs. 100 each	150	110
10% redeemable preference shares of Rs. 100 each	10	40
Capital redemption reserve	10	—
General reserve	15	10
Profit and loss account balance	30	20
8% debentures with convertible option	20	40
Other term loans	15	30
	250	250
Fixed assets less depreciation	130	100
Long term investments	40	50
Working capital	80	100
	250	250

Statement of Profit and Loss for the year ended 31st March, 2010

(Figures in Rs. lakhs)

Sales		600
Less: Cost of sales		400
		200
Establishment charges	30	
Selling and distribution expenses	60	
Interest expenses	5	
Loss on sale of equipment (Book value, Rs. 40 lakhs)	15	110
		90
Interest income	4	
Dividend income	2	

Foreign exchange gain	10	
Damages received for loss of reputation	14	30
		120
Depreciation		50
		70
Taxes		30
		40
Dividends		15
Net profit carried to balance sheet		25

You are informed by the accountant that ledgers relating to debtors, creditors and stock for both the years were seized by the income-tax authorities and it would take at least two months to obtain copies of the same. However, he is able to furnish the following data:

	(Figures in Rs. lakhs) 31.3.2010	31.3.2009
Dividend receivable	2	4
Interest receivable	3	2
Cash on hand and with bank	7	10
Investments maturing within two months	3	2
	15	18
Interest payable	4	5
Taxes payable	6	3
	10	8
Current ratio	1.5	1.4
Acid test ratio	1.1	0.8

It is also gathered that debenture-holders owning 50% of the debentures outstanding as on 31.3.2009 exercised the option for conversion into equity shares during the financial year and the same was put through.

You are required to prepare a direct method cash flow statement for the financial year ended 31st March, 2010 in accordance with para 18(*a*) of Accounting Standard (*AS*) 3 revised.

[*Adapted C.A.* (*Final*)]

Solution:

Lambakadi Ltd.
Direct Method Cash Flow Statement for the year ended 31st March, 2010

(*Rs. in lakhs*)

Cash Flows from Operating Activities		
Cash receipts from customers	621	
Cash paid to suppliers and employees	(496)	
Cash generated from operations	125	
Taxes paid	(27)	
Cash flow before extraordinary item	98	
Damages received for loss of reputation	14	
Net cash from operating activities		112
Cash Flows from Investing Activities		
Purchase of fixed assets	(120)	
Proceeds from sale of equipment	25	
Proceeds from sale of long term investments	10	
Interest received	3	
Dividend received	4	
Net cash used in investing activities		(78)

Cash Flows from Financing Activities		
Proceeds from issuance of share capital	20	
Redemption of preference share capital	(30)	
Repayments of term loans	(15)	
Interest paid	(6)	
Dividend paid	(15)	
Net cash used in financing activities		(46)
Net increase in cash and cash equivalents		(12)
Cash and cash equivalents at beginning of period (See Note to the Cash Flow Statement)		12
Cash and cash equivalents at end of the period (See Note to the Cash Flow Statement)		NIL

Significant Non-cash Transaction:
Debentures amounting to Rs. 20 lakh were converted into equity shares.

Note to the Cash Flow Statement

(Rs. in lakhs)

	31.3.2001	31.3.2000
Cash and cash equivalents :		
Cash on hand and with bank	7	10
Short-term investments	3	2
	10	12
Effect of exchange rate changes	(10)	—
Cash and cash equivalents	Nil	12

Working Notes:

(Rs. in lakhs)

	31.3.2001	**31.3.2000**
(*i*) *Calculation of debtors, creditors and stock*:		
(*a*) Current ratio	1.5:1	1.4:1
Working capital to current liabilities ratio	0.5:1	0.4:1
Working capital (Rs. in lakhs)	80	100
Current assets (Rs. in lakhs)	$\frac{80\times1.5}{0.5}$ = 240	$\frac{100\times1.4}{0.4}$ = 350
Current liabilities (Rs. in lakhs)	240–80 = 160	350 – 100 = 250
(*b*) Current ratio	1.5	1.4
Less: Acid test ratio	1.1	0.8
	0.4	0.6
Stock: Current liabilities	0.4:1	0.6:1
Stock (Rs. in lakhs)	160 × 0.4 = 64	250 × 0.6 = 150
(*c*) *Break-up of current assets:*		
Stock	64	150
Debtors (balancing figure)	161	182
Other current assets	15	18
	240	350
(*d*) *Break-up of current liabilities*		
Creditors (balancing figure)	150	242
Others	10	8
	160	250

(ii) *Cash receipts from customers:*

		(Rupees in lakhs)
Sales		600
Add: Debtors on 31.3.2009		182
		782
Less: Debtors on 31.3.2010		161
Receipts		621

(iii) *Cash paid to suppliers and employees*:

Cost of sales		400
Add: Establishment charges		30
Add: Selling and distribution expenses		60
		490
Add: Creditors on 31.3.2009	242	
Stock on 31.3.2010	64	306
		796
Less: Creditors on 31.3.2010	150	
Stock on 31.3.2009	150	300
Payment made		496

(iv) *Taxes paid*:

Tax expense for the year	30
Add: Tax liability on 31.3.2009	3
	33
Less: Tax liability on 31.3.2010	6
Payment made	27

(v) *Fixed assets acquired during the year:*

Book value of fixed assets on 31.3.2010	130
Add: Depreciation for the year	50
Disposals	40
	220
Less: Book value of fixed assets on 31.3.2009	100
Fixed assets acquired during the year	120

(vi) *Interest paid*:

Interest expense for the year	5
Add: Interest payable on 31.3.2009	5
Disposals	10
	10
Less: Interest payable on 31.3.2010	4
Payment	6

(vii) *Interest received*:

Interest income for the year	4
Add: Interest receivable on 31.3.2009	2
	6
Less: Interest receivable on 31.3.2010	3
Receipt	3

(viii) *Dividend received*:

Dividend income for the year	2
Add: Dividend receivable on 31.3.2009	4
	6
Less: Dividend receivable on 31.3.2010	2
Receipt	4

(Rs. in lakhs)

(ix) *Cash received on issue of shares*:	
Equity share capital on 31.3.2010	150
Add: Equity share capital on 31.3.2009	110
Disposals	40
Less: Equity shares issued by way of Conversion of debentures	20
Shares issued for cash	20

(x) It has been assumed that foreign exchange gain represents the effect of charges in exchange rates on cash and cash equivalents held in a foreign currency.

Advantages: The following are the main advantages of cash flow statement:

(i) Cash flow statement enhances the comparability of the reported performance by different enterprises because it eliminates the effects of using different accounting treatments for the same transactions and events. Since it gives the figure of cash inflow from operations, it gives much more reliable picture of the results of operations than the usual profit and loss account. The figure of profit can be easily changed by changing the amount of depreciation. Higher depreciation will mean lower profit and *vice versa*. The amount to be charged in respect of depreciation often depends on the management's decisions and hence the figure of profit revealed in the profit and loss account may sometimes be unreliable. This is not the case with the inflow of cash from operations—this figure is not subject to manipulation though the figure can be marginably increased by postponing payments for goods and services to a certain extent.

(ii) It is useful in checking the accuracy of past assessments of future cash flows. Comparison of cash budget and cash flow statement for the same period will show the extent to which cash budget has been followed.

(iii) It is often used as an indicator of the amount, timing and certainty of future cash flows. It is thus helpful in preparing cash budgets for a subsequent period.

(iv) A study of cash flow statement with other financial statements gives an idea about the ability of the enterprise to meet its short-term commitments in time and to pay dividends.

(v) Cash flow statement provides information of all the investing and financing cash transactions which have taken place during the year. It explains most of the changes in financial statements. Thus, it enables the users to evaluate changes in net assets of an enterprise and its financial structure.

(vi) Cash flow statement, prepared by the indirect method lists reasons for the difference between net profit before tax and net cash generated from operations. Thus, it shows the relationship between profitability and net cash flow.

Limitations: The following may be said to be the limitations of cash flow statement:

(i) It ignores non-cash charges. For judging the profitability of an enterprise, non-cash charges will also have to be taken into account.

(ii) It ignores one of the basic accounting concepts namely accrual concept.

Distinction between Cash Flow Statement and Income Statement: The following are the points of distinction between Cash Flow Statement and Income Statement (*i.e.* Profit and Loss Account):

(i) Cash Flow Statement shows cash inflows and cash outflows while Income Statement shows incomes and expenses for a particular period.

(ii) Cash Flow Statement reveals the net increase or decrease in cash and cash equivalents whereas Income Statement reveals the net profit or net loss for a period.

(iii) Cash Flow Statement deals with revenue as well as capital items whereas Income Statement deals with revenue items only.

(*iv*) In order to prepare Cash Flow Statement, Income Statement is required because information contained in the Income Statement forms the basis of some of the items appearing in Cash Flow Statement. On the other hand, Income Statement can be prepared without any reference to Cash Flow Statement.

(*v*) Preparation of Cash Flow Statement except for listed companies is optional. Preparation of Income Statement, barring for very small businessmen, is a must.

(*vi*) Different forms have not been prescribed for different types of companies for the presentation of Cash Flow Statement. But different forms have been prescribed for different companies like insurance companies, banking companies and electricity companies in which Income Statement has to be prepared.

ACCOUNTING STANDARD 3

Accounting Standard 3 was originally issued in June 1981 and was titled 'Changes in Financial Position. The Standard was revised in March, 1997. In the initial years, it was recommendatory for all types of enterprises. But this Standard was made mandatory with effect from accounting period on or after 1-4-2001 in respect of enterprises which fell in any one or more of the specified categories.

At present, this standard is mandatory in nature in respect of accounting periods commencing on or after 1-4-2004 for the enterprises which fall in any one or more of the specified categories, at any time during the according period.

ACCOUNTING STANDARD (AS) 3* (Revised 1997)
CASH FLOW STATEMENTS

(*This Accounting Standard includes paragraphs set in* ***bold italic*** *type and plain type, which have equal authority. Paragraphs in bold italic type indicate the main principles. This Accounting Standard should be read in the context of its objective and the Preface to the Statements of Accounting Standards.*)

Accounting Standard (AS)3, 'Cash Flow Statements' (revised 1997), issued by the Council of the Institute of Chartered Accountants of India, comes into effect in respect of accounting periods commencing on or after 1-4-1997. This Standard supersedes Accounting Standard (AS)3, 'Changes in Financial Position', issued in June 1981. This Standard is mandatory in nature in respect of accounting periods commencing on or after 1-4-2004[1] for the enterprises which fall in any one or more of the following categories, at any time during the accounting period :

(*i*) Enterprises whose equity or debt securities are listed whether in India or outside India.

(*ii*) Enterprises which are in the process of listing their equity or debt securities as evidenced by the board of directors' resolution in this regard.

(*iii*) Banks including co-operative banks.

(*iv*) Financial institutions.

(*v*) Enterprises carrying on insurance business.

(*vi*) All commercial, industrial and business reporting enterprises, whose turnover for the immediately preceding accounting period on the basis of audited financial statements exceeds Rs. 50 crore. Turnover does not include 'other income'.

(*vii*) All commercial, industrial and business reporting enterprises having borrowings, including public deposits, in excess of Rs. 10 crore at any time during the accounting period.

(*viii*) Holding and subsidiary enterprises of any one of the above at any time during the accounting period.

The enterprises which do not fall in any of the above categories are encouraged, but are not required, to apply this Standard.

* Revised in March, 1997

1. AS 3 was originally made mandatory in respect of accounting periods commencing on or after 1-4-2001, for the following:
   (*i*) Enterprises whose equity or debt securities are listed on a recognised stock exchange in India, and enterprises that are in the process of issuing equity or debt securities that will be listed on a recognised stock exchange in India as evidenced by the board of directors' resolution in this regard.
   (*ii*) All other commercial, industrial and business reporting enterprises, whose turnover for the accounting period exceeds Rs. 50 crores.

Where an enterprise has been covered in any one or more of the above categories and subsequently, ceases to be so covered, the enterprise will not qualify for exemption from application of this Standard, until the enterprise ceases to be covered in any of the above categories for two consecutive years.

Where an enterprise has previously qualified for exemption from application of this Standard (being not covered by any of the above categories) but no longer qualifies for exemption in the current accounting period, this Standard becomes applicable from the current period. However, the corresponding previous period figures need not be disclosed.

An enterprise, which, pursuant to the above provisions, does not present a cash flow statement, should disclose the fact.

OBJECTIVE

Information about the cash flows of an enterprise is useful in providing users of financial statements with a basis to assess the ability of the enterprise to generate cash and cash equivalents and the needs of the enterprise to utilise those cash flows. The economic decisions that are taken by users require an evaluation of the ability of an enterprise to generate cash and cash equivalents and the timing and certainty of their generation.

The Statement deals with the provision of information about the historical changes in cash and cash equivalents of an enterprise by means of a cash flow statement which classifies cash flows during the period from operating, investing and financing activities.

SCOPE

1. An enterprise should prepare a cash flow statement and should present it for each period for which financial statements are presented.

2. Users of an enterprise's financial statements are interested in how the enterprise generates and uses cash and cash equivalents. This is the case regardless of the nature of the enterprise's activities and irrespective of whether cash can be viewed as the product of the enterprise, as may be the case with a financial enterprise. Enterprises need cash for essentially the same reasons, however, different their principal revenue-producing activities might be. They need cash to conduct their operations, to pay their obligations, and to provide returns to their investors.

BENEFITS OF CASH FLOW INFORMATION

3. A cash flow statement, when used in conjunction with the other financial statements, provides information that enables users to evaluate the changes in net assets of an enterprise, its financial structure (including its liquidity and solvency), and its ability to affect the amounts and timing of cash flows in order to adapt to changing circumstances and opportunities. Cash flows information is useful in assessing the ability of the enterprise to generate cash and cash equivalents and enables users to develop models to assess and compare the present value of the future cash flows of different enterprises. It also enhances the comparability of the reporting of operating performance by different enterprises because it eliminates the effects of using different accounting treatments for the same transactions and events.

4. Historical cash flow information is often used as an indicator of the amount, timing and certainty of future cash flows. It is also useful in checking the accuracy of past assessments of future cash flows and in examining the relationship between profitability and net cash flows and the impact of changing prices.

DEFINITIONS

5. The following terms are used in this Statement with the meanings specified:

Cash comprises cash on hand and demand deposits with banks.

Cash equivalents are short term, highly liquid investments that are readily convertible into known amounts of cash and which are subject to an insignificant risk of changes in value.

Cash flows are inflows and outflow of cash and cash equivalents.

Operating activities are the principal revenue-producing activities of the enterprise and other activities that are not investing or financing activities.

Investing activities are the acquisition and disposal of long-term assets and other investments not included in cash equivalents.

Financing activities are activities that result in changes in the size and composition of the owners' capital (including preference share capital in the case of a company) and borrowings of the enterprise.

CASH AND CASH EQUIVALENTS

6. Cash equivalents are held for the purpose of meeting short-term cash commitments rather than for investment or other purposes. For an investment to qualify as a cash equivalent, it must be readily convertible to a known amount of cash and be subject to an insignificant risk of changes in value. Therefore, an investment normally qualifies as a cash equivalent only when it has a short maturity of, say, three months or less from the date of acquisition. Investments in shares are excluded from cash equivalents unless they are, in substance, cash equivalents; for example, preference shares of a company acquired shortly before their specified redemption date (provided there is only an insignificant risk of failure of the company to repay the amount at maturity).

7. Cash flows exclude movements between items that constitute cash or cash equivalents because these components are part of the cash management of an enterprise rather than part of its operating, investing and financing activities. Cash management includes the investment of excess cash and cash equivalents.

PRESENTATION OF A CASH FLOW STATEMENT

8. The cash flow statement should report cash flows during the period classified by operating, investing and financing activities.

9. An enterprise presents its cash flows from operating, investing and financing activities in a manner which is most appropriate to its business. Classification by activities provides information that allows users to assess the impact of those activities on the financial position of the enterprise and the amount of its cash and cash equivalents. This information may also be used to evaluate the relationship among those activities.

10. A single transaction may include cash flows that are classified differently. For example, when the instalment paid in respect of a fixed asset acquired on deferred payment basis includes both intererst and loan, the interest element is classified under financing activities and the loan element is classified under investing activities.

OPERATING ACTIVITIES

11. The amount of cash flows arising from operating activities is a key indicator of the extent to which the operations of the enterprise have generated sufficient cash flows to maintain the operating capability of the enterprise, pay dividends, repay loans, and make new investments without recourse to external sources of financing. Information about the specific components of historical operating cash flows is useful, in conjunction with other information, in forecasting future operating cash flows.

12. Cash flows from operating activities are primarily derived from the principal revenue-producing activities of the enterprise. Therefore, they generally result from the transactions and other events that enter into the determination of net profit or loss. Examples of cash flows from operating activities are:

(*a*) cash receipts from the sale of goods and the rendering of services:
(*b*) cash receipts from royalties, fees, commissions, and other revenue;
(*c*) cash payment to suppliers for goods and services;
(*d*) cash payments to and on behalf of employees;
(*e*) cash receipts and cash payments of an insurance enterprise for premiums and claims, annuities and other policy benefits;
(*f*) cash payments or refunds of income taxes unless they can be specifically identified with financing and investing activities; and
(*g*) cash receipts and payments relating to future contracts, forward contracts, option contracts, and swap contracts when the contracts are held for dealing or trading purposes.

13. Some transactions, such as the sale of an item of plant, may give rise to a gain or loss which is included in the determination of net profit or loss. However, the cash flows relating to such transactions are cash flows from investing activities.

14. An enterprise may hold securities and loans for dealing or trading purposes, in which case they are similar to inventory acquired specifically for resale. Therefore, cash flows arising from the purchase and sale of dealing or trading securities are classified as operating activities. Similarly, cash advances and loans made by financial enterprises are usually classified as operating activities since they relate to the main revenue-producing activity of that enterprise.

INVESTING ACTIVITIES

15. The separate disclosure of cash flows arising from investing activities is important because the cash flows represent the extent to which expenditures have been made for resources intended to generate future income and cash flows. Examples of cash flows arising from investing activities are:

(a) cash payments to acquire fixed assets (including intangibles). These payments include those relating to capitalised research and development costs and self-constructed fixed assets;
(b) cash receipts from disposal of fixed assets (including intangibles);
(c) cash payments to acquire shares, warrants, or debt instruments of other enterprises and interests in joint ventures (other than payments for those instruments considered to be cash equivalents and those held for dealing or trading purposes);
(d) cash receipts from disposal of shares, warrants, or debt instruments of other enterprises and interests in joint ventures (other than receipts from those instruments considered to be cash equivalents and those held for dealing or trading purposes);
(e) cash advances and loans made to third parties (other than advances and loans made by a financial enterprise);
(f) cash receipts from the repayment of advances and loans made to third parties (other than advances and loans of a financial enterprise);
(g) cash payments for future contracts, forward contracts, option contracts, and swap contracts except when the contracts are held for dealing or trading purposes, or the payments are classified as financing activities; and
(h) cash receipts from future contracts, forward contracts, option contracts, and swap contracts except when the contracts are held for dealing or trading purposes, or the receipts are classified as financing activities.

16. When a contract is accounted for as a hedge of an identifiable position, the cash flows of the contract are classified in the same manner as the cash flows of the postion being hedged.

FINANCING ACTIVITIES

17. The separate disclosure of cash flows arising from financing activities is important because it is useful in predicting claims on future cash flows by providers of funds (both capital and borrowings) to the enterprise. Examples of cash flows arising from financing activities are:

(a) cash proceeds from issuing shares or other similar instruments;
(b) cash proceeds from issuing debentures, loans, notes, bonds, and other short or long-term borrowings; and
(c) cash repayments of amounts borrowed.

REPORTING CASH FLOWS FROM OPERATING ACTIVITIES

18. An enterprise should report cash flows from operating activities using either:

***(a)* the direct method, whereby major classes of gross cash receipts and gross cash payments are disclosed; or**
***(b)* the indirect method, whereby net profit or loss is adjusted for the effect of transactions of a non-cash nature, any deferrals or accruals of past or future operating cash receipts or payments, and items of income or expense associated with investing or financing cash flows.**

19. The direct method provides information which may be useful in estimating future cash flows and which is not available under the indirect method and is, therefore, considered more appropriate than the indirect method. Under the direct method, information about major classes of gross cash receipts and gross cash payments may be obtained either:

(a) from the accounting records of the enterprise; or
(b) by adjusting sales, cost of sales (interest and similar income and interest expense and similar charges for a financial enterprise) and other items in the statement of profit and loss for:
   (i) changes during the period in inventories and operating receivables and payables;
   (ii) other non-cash items; and
   (iii) other items for which the cash effects are investing or financing cash flows.

20. Under the indirect method, the net cash flow from operating activities is determined by adjusting net profit or loss for the effects of:

(a) changes during the period in inventories and operating receivables and payables;
(b) non-cash items such as depreciation, provisions, deferred taxes, and unrealised foreign exchange gains and losses; and

(*c*) all other items for which the cash effects are investing or financing cash flows.

Alternatively, the net cash from operating activities may be presented under the indirect method by showing the operating revenues and expenses, excluding non-cash items disclosed in the statement of profit and loss and the changes during the period in inventories and operating receivables and payables.

REPORTING CASH FLOWS FROM INVESTING AND FINANCING ACTIVITIES

21. An enterprise should report separately major classes of gross cash receipt and gross cash payments arising from investing and financing activities, except to the extent that cash flows described in Paragraphs 22 and 24 are reported on a net basis.

REPORTING CASH FLOWS ON A NET BASIS

22. Cash flows arising from the following operating, investing or financing activities may be reported on a net basis:

(*a*) **cash receipts and payments on behalf of customers when the cash flows reflect the activities of the customer rather than those of the enterprise; and**

(*b*) **cash receipts and payments for items in which the turnover is quick, the amounts are large, and the maturities are short.**

23. Examples of cash receipts and payments referred to in Paragraph 22(*a*) are:

(*a*) the acceptance and repayment of demand deposits by a bank;

(*b*) funds held for customers by an investment enterprise; and

(*c*) rents collected on behalf of, and paid over to, the owners of properties.

Examples of cash receipts and payments referred to in Paragraph 22(*b*) are advances made for, and the repayments of:

(*a*) principal amounts relating to credit card customers;

(*b*) the purchase and sale of investments; and

(*c*) other short-term borrowings, for example, those which have a maturity period of three months or less.

24. Cash flows arising from each of the following activities of a financial enterprise may be reported on a net basis:

(*a*) **Cash receipts and payments for the acceptance and repayment of deposits with a fixed maturity date;**

(*b*) **the placement of deposits with and withdrawal of deposits from other financial enterprises; and**

(*c*) **cash advances and loans made to customers and the repayment of those advances and loans.**

FOREIGN CURRENCY CASH FLOWS

25. Cash flows arising from transactions in a foreign currency should be recorded in an enterprise's reporting currency by applying to the foreign currency amount the exchange rate between the reporting currency and the foreign currency at the date of the cash flow. A rate that approximates the actual rate may be used if the result is substantially the same as would arise if the rates at the dates of the cash flows were used. The effect of changes in exchange rates on cash and cash equivalents held in a foreign currency should be reported as a separate part of the reconciliation of the changes in cash and cash equivalents during the period.

26. Cash flows denominated in foreign currency are reported in a manner consistent with Accounting Standard (AS) 11, Accounting For the The Effects of Changes In Foreign Exchange Rates. This permits the use of an exchange rate that approximates the actual rate. For example, a weighted average exchange rate for a period may be used for recording foreign currency transactions.

27. Unrealised gains and losses arising from changes in foreign exchange rates are not cash flows. However, the effect of exchange rate changes on cash and cash equivalents held or due in a foreign currency is reported in the cash flow statement in order to reconcile cash and cash equivalents at the beginning and the end of the period. This amount is presented separately from cash flows from operating, investing and financing activities and includes the differences, if any, had those cash flows been reported at the end-of-period exchange rates.

EXTRAORDINARY ITEMS

28. The cash flows associated with extraordinary items should be classified as arising from operating, investing or financing activities as appropriate and separately disclosed.

29. The cash flows associated with extraordinary items should be classified as arising from operating, investing or financing activities in the cash flow statement, to enable users to understand their nature and effect on the present and future cash flows of the enterprise. These disclosures are in addition to the separate disclosures of the nature and amount of extraordinary items required by AS 5, Net Profit Or Loss For The Period, Prior Period Items, and Changes In Accounting Policies.

INTEREST AND DIVIDENDS

30. Cash flows from interest and dividends received and paid should each be disclosed separately. Cash flows arising from interest paid and interest and dividends received in the case of a financial enterprise should be classified as cash flows arising from operating activities. In the case of other enterprises, cash flows arising from interest paid should be classified as cash flows from financing activities while interest and dividends received should be classified as cash flows from investing activities. Dividends paid should be classified as cash flows from financing activities.

31. The total amount of interest paid during the period is disclosed in the cash flow statement whether it has been recognised as an expense in the statement of profit and loss or capitalised in accordance with AS 10, Accounting For Fixed Assets.

32. Interest paid and interest and dividends received are usually classified as operating cash flows for a financing enterprise. However, there is no consensus on the classification of these cash flows for other enterprises. Some argue that interest paid and interest and dividends received may be classified as operating cash flows because they enter into the determination of net profit or loss. However, it is more appropriate that interest paid and interest and dividends received are classified as financing cash flows and investing cash flows respectively, because they are cost of obtaining financial resources or returns on investments.

33. Some argue that dividends paid may be classified as a component of cash flows from operating activities in order to assist users to determine the ability of an enterprise to pay dividends out of operating cash flows. However, it is considered more appropriate that dividends paid should be classified as cash flows from financing activities because they are cost of obtaining financial resources.

TAXES ON INCOME

34. Cash flows arising from taxes on income should be separately disclosed and should be classified as cash flows from operating activities unless they can be specifically identified with financing and investing activities.

35. Taxes on income arise on transactions that give rise to cash flows that are classified as operating, investing or financing activities in a cash flow statement. While tax expense may be readily identifiable with investing or financing activities, the related tax cash flows are often impracticable to identify and may arise in a different period from the cash flows of the underlying transactions. Therefore, taxes paid are usually classified as cash flows from operating activities. However, when it is practicable to identify the tax cash flow with an individual transaction that gives rise to cash flows that are classified as investing or financing activities, the tax cash flow is classified as an investing or financing activities as appropriate. When tax cash flows are allocated over more than one class of activity, the total amount of taxes paid is disclosed.

INVESTMENT IN SUBSIDIARIES, ASSOCIATES AND JOINT VENTURES

36. When accounting for an investment in an associate or a subsidiary or a joint venture, an investor restricts its reporting in the cash flow statement to the cash flow between itself and the investee/joint venture, for example, cash flows relating to dividends and advances.

ACQUISITIONS AND DISPOSALS OF SUBSIDIARIES AND OTHER BUSINESS UNITS

37. The aggregate cash flows arising from acquisitions and from disposals of subsidiaries

or other business units should be presented separately and classified as investing activities.

38. An enterprise should disclose, in aggregate, in respect of both acquisition and disposal of subsidiaries or other business units during the period each of the following:

(*a*) **the total purchase or disposal consideration; and**

(*b*) **the portion of the purchase or disposal consideration discharged by means of cash and cash equivalents.**

39. The separate presentation of the cash flow effects of acquisitions and disposals of subsidiaries and other business units as single line items helps to distinguish those cash flows from other cash flows. The cash flow effects of disposals are not deducted from those of acquisitions.

NON-CASH TRANSACTIONS

40. Investing and financing transactions that do not require the use of cash or cash equivalents should be excluded from a cash flow statement. Such transactions should be disclosed elsewhere in the financial statements in a way that provides all the relevant information about these investing and financing activities.

41. Many investing and financing activities do not have a direct impact on current cash flows although they do affect the capital and asset structure of an enterprise. The exclusion of non-cash transactions from the cash flow statement is consistent with the objective of a cash flow statement as these items do not involve cash flow in the current period. Examples of non-cash transactions are:

(*a*) the acquisition of assets by assuming directly related liabilities;

(*b*) the acquisition of an enterprise by means of issue of shares; and

(*c*) the conversion of debt to equity.

COMPONENTS OF CASH AND CASH EQUIVALENTS

42. An enterprise should disclose the components of cash and cash equivalents and should present a reconciliation of the amounts in its cash flow statement with the equivalent items reported in the balance sheet.

43. In view of the variety of cash management practices, an enterprise discloses the policy which it adopts in determining the composition of cash and cash equivalents.

44. The effect of any change in the policy for determining components of cash and cash equivalents is reported in accordance with Accounting Standard (AS) 5, Net Profit or Loss for the Period, Prior Period Items, and Changes in Accounting Policies.

OTHER DISCLOSURES

45. An enterprise should disclose, together with a commentary by management, the amount of significant cash and cash equivalent balances held by the enterprise that are not available for use by it.

46. There are various circumstances in which cash and cash equivalent balances held by an enterprise are not available for use by it. Examples include cash and cash equivalent balances held by a branch of the enterprise that operates in a country where exchange controls or other legal restrictions apply as a result of which the balances are not available for use by the enterprise.

47. Additional information may be relevant to users in understanding the financial position and liquidity of an enterprise. Disclosure of this information, together with a commentary by management, is encouraged and may include:

(*a*) the amount of undrawn borrowing facilities that may be available for future operating activities and to settle capital commitments, indicating any restrictions on the use of these facilities; and

(*b*) the aggregate amount of cash flows that represent increase in operating capacity separately from those cash flows that are required to maintain operating capacity.

48. The separate disclosure of cash flows that represent increases in operating capacity and cash flows that are required to maintain operating capacity is useful in enabling the user to determine whether the enterprise is investing adequately in the maintenance of its operating capacity. An enterprise that does not invest adequately in the maintenance of its operating capacity may be prejudicing future profitability for the sake of current liquidity and distributions to owners.

APPENDIX I

CASH FLOW STATEMENT FOR AN ENTERPRISE OTHER THAN A FINANCIAL ENTERPRISE

The appendix is illustrative only and does not form part of the accounting standard. The purpose of this appendix is to illustrate the application of the accounting standard.

1. The example shows only current period amounts.

2. Information from the statement of profit and loss and balance sheet is provided to show how the statements of cash flows under the direct method and the indirect method have been derived. Neither the statement of profit and loss nor the balance sheet is presented in conformity with the disclosure and presentation requirements of applicable laws and accounting standards. The working notes given towards the end of this appendix are intended to assist in understanding the manner in which the various figures appearing in the cash flow statement have been derived. These working notes do not form part of the cash flow statement and, accordingly, need not be published.

3. The following additional information is also relevant for the preparation of the statement of cash flows (figures are in Rs. '000).

(*a*) An amount of 250 was raised from the issue of share capital and a further 250 was raised from long-term borrowings.

(*b*) Interest expense was 400 of which 170 was paid during the period. 100 relating to interest expense of the prior period was also paid during the period.

(*c*) Dividends paid were 1,200.

(*d*) Tax deducted at source on dividends received (included in the tax expense of 300 for the year) amounted to 40.

(*e*) During the period, the enterprise acquired fixed assets for 350. The payment was made in cash.

(*f*) Plant with original cost of 80 and accumulated depreciation of 60 was sold for 20.

(*g*) Foreign exchange loss of 40 represents the reduction in the carrying amount of a short-term investment in foreign currency designated bonds arising out of a change in exchange rate between the date of acquisition of the investment and the balance sheet date.

(*h*) Sundry debtors and sundry creditors include amounts relating to credit sales and credit purchases only.

Balance Sheet as at 31.12.1996

(Rs. '000)

		1996		1995
Assets				
Cash on hand and balances with banks		200		25
Short-term investments		670		135
Sundry debtors		1,700		1,200
Interest receivable		100		—
Inventories		900		1,950
Long-term investments		2,500		2,500
Fixed assets at cost	2,180		1,910	
Accumulated depreciation	(1,450)		(1,060)	
Fixed assets (net)		730		850
Total Assets		6,800		6,660

	1996	(Rs. '000) 1995
Liabilities		
Sundry creditors	150	1,890
Interest payable	230	100
Income taxes payable	400	1,000
Long-term debt	1,110	1,040
Total liabilities	1,890	4,030
Shareholders' Funds		
Share capital	1,500	1,250
Reserves	3,410	1,380
Total shareholders' funds	4,910	2,630
TOTAL LIABILITIES AND SHAREHOLDERS' FUND	6,800	6,660

Statement of Profit and Loss
for the period ended 31.12.1996

	(Rs. '000)
Sales	30,650
Cost of sales	(26,000)
Gross profit	4,650
Depreciation	(450)
Administrative and selling expenses	(910)
Interest expense	(400)
Interest income	300
Dividend income	200
Foreign exchange loss	(40)
Net profit before taxation and extraordinary item	3,350
Extraordinary item:	
Insurance proceed from earthquake disaster settlement	180
Net profit after extraordinary item	3,530
Income tax	(300)
NET PROFIT	3,230

Direct Method Cash Flow Statement [Paragraph 18(a)]

		(Rs. '000) 1996
Cash flows from operating activities		
Cash receipts from customers	30,150	
Cash paid to suppliers and employees	(27,600)	
Cash generated from operations	2,550	
Income taxes paid	(860)	
Cash flow before extraordinary item	1,690	
Proceeds from earthquake disaster settlement	180	
Net cash from operating activities		1,870
Cash flows from investing activities		
Purchase of fixed assets	(350)	
Proceeds from sale of equipment	20	
Interest received	200	
Dividend received	160	
Net cash from investing activities		30

		(Rs. '000) 1996
Cash flows from financing activities		
Proceeds from issuance of share capital	250	
Proceeds from long-term borrowings	250	
Repayments of long-term borrowings	(180)	
Interest paid	(270)	
Dividend paid	(1,200)	
Net cash used in financing activities		(1,150)
Net increase in cash and cash equivalents		750
Cash and cash equivalents at beginning of period (See Note 1)		160
Cash and cash equivalents at end of the period (See Note 1)		910

Indirect Method Cash Flow Statement (Paragraph 18 (b)]

		(Rs. '000) 1996
Cash flows from operating activities		
Net profit before taxation, and extraordinary item	3,350	
Adjustments for:		
Depreciation	450	
Foreign exchange loss	40	
Interest income	(300)	
Dividend income	(200)	
Interest expense	400	
Operating profit before working capital changes	3,740	
Increase in sundry debtors	(500)	
Decrease in inventories	1,050	
Decrease in sundry creditors	(1,740)	
Cash generated from operations	2,550	
Income taxes paid	(860)	
Cash flow before extraordinary item	1,690	
Proceeds from earthquake disaster settlement	180	
Net cash from operating activities		1,870
Cash flows from investing activities		
Purchase of fixed assets	(350)	
Proceeds from sale of equipment	20	
Interest received	200	
Dividends received	160	
Net cash from investing activities		30
Cash flows from financing activities		
Proceeds from issuance of share capital	250	
Proceeds from long-term borrowings	250	
Repayment of long-term borrowings	(180)	
Interest paid	(270)	
Dividends paid	(1,200)	
Net cash used in financing activities		(1,150)
Net increase in cash and cash equivalents		750
Cash and cash equivalents at beginning of period (See Note 1)		160
Cash and cash equivalents at end of period (See Note 1)		910

NOTE TO THE CASH FLOW STATEMENT
(Direct & Indirect Method)

1. Cash and Cash Equivalents

Cash and cash equivalents consist of cash on hand and balances with banks, and investments in money-market instruments. Cash and cash equivalents included in the cash flow statement comprise the following balance sheet amounts.

	(Rs.'000) 1996	1995
Cash on hand and balances with banks	200	25
Short-term investments	670	135
Cash and cash equivalents	870	160
Effect of exchange rate changes	40	—
Cash and cash equivalents as restated	910	160

Cash and cash equivalents at the end of the period include deposits with banks of 100 held by a branch which are not freely remissible to the company because of currency exchange restrictions.

The company has undrawn borrowing facilities of 2,000 of which 700 may be used only for future expansion.

2. Total tax paid during the year (including tax deducted at source on dividends received) amounted to 900.

ALTERNATIVE PRESENTATION

(Indirect Method)

As an alternative, in an indirect method cash flow statement, operating profit before working capital changes is sometimes presented as follows:

	(Rs.'000)	
Revenues excluding investment income	30,650	
Operating expense excluding depreciation	(26,910)	
Operating profit before working capital changes		3,740

Working Notes

The working notes given below do not form part of the cash flow statement and, accordingly need not be published. The purpose of these working notes is merely to assist in understanding the manner in which various figures in the cash flow statement have been derived.

(Figures are in Rs. '000)

1. Cash receipts from customers		
Sales		30,650
Add: Sundry debtors at the beginning of the year		1,200
		31,850
Less: Sundry debtors at the end of the year		1,700
		30,150
2. Cash paid to suppliers and employees		
Cost of sales		26,000
Administrative & selling expenses		910
		26,910
Add: Sundry creditors at the beginning of the year	1,890	
Inventories at the end of the year	900	2,790
		29,700
Less: Sundry creditors at the end of the year	150	
Inventories at the beginning of the year	1,950	2,100
		27,600

(Figures are in Rs. '000)

3. Income taxes paid (including tax deducted at source from dividends received)

Income tax expense for the year (including tax deducted at source from dividends received)	300
Add: Income tax liability at the beginning of the year	1,000
	1,300
Less: Income tax liability at the end of the year	400
	900

Out of 900, tax deducted at source on dividends received (amounting to 40) is included in cash flows from investing activities and the balance of 860 is included in cash flows from operating activities (See Paragraph 34).

4. Repayment of long-term borrowings

Long-term debt at the beginning of the year	1,040
Add: Long-term borrowings made during the year	250
	1,290
Less: Long-term borrowings at the end of the year	1,110
	180

5. Interest paid

Interest expense for the year	400
Add: Interest payable at the beginning of the year	100
	500
Less: Interest payable at the end of the year	230
	270

APPENDIX II
CASH FLOW STATEMENT FOR A FINANCIAL ENTERPRISE

The appendix is illustrative only and does not form part of the accounting standard. The purpose of this appendix is to illustrate the application of the accounting standard.

1. The example shows only current period amounts.
2. The example is presented using the direct method.

		(Rs. '000) 1996
Cash flows from operating activities		
Interest and commission receipts	28,447	
Interest payments	(23,463)	
Recoveries on loans previously written off	237	
Cash payments to employees and suppliers	(997)	
Operating profit before changes in operatings assets	4,224	
(Increase) decrease in operating assets:		
Short-term funds	(650)	
Deposits held for regulatory or monetary control purposes	234	
Funds advanced to customers	(288)	
Net increase in credit card receivables	(360)	
Other short-term securities	(120)	
Increase (decrease) in operating liabilities:		
Deposits from customers	600	
Certificates of deposit	(200)	
Net cash from operating activities before income tax	3,440	
Income taxes paid	(100)	
Net cash from operating activities		3,340

		(Rs. '000)
		1996
Cash flows from investing activities		
Dividends received	250	
Interest received	300	
Proceeds from sales of permanent investments	1,200	
Purchase of permanent investments	(600)	
Purchase of fixed assets	(500)	
Net cash from investing activities		650
Cash flows from financing activities		
Issue of shares	1,800	
Repayment of long-term borrowings	(200)	
Net decrease in other borrowings	(1,000)	
Dividends paid	(400)	
Net cash from financing activities		200
Net increase in cash and cash equivalents		4,190
Cash and cash equivalents at beginning of period		4,650
Cash and cash equivalents at end of the period		8,840

2. FUNDS FLOW STATEMENT

Accounting Standard (Revised)-3 has made Funds Flow Statement obsolete. Hence, the following description is meant only for those who may, for some reasons, still be required to prepare a Funds Flow Statement.

Funds mean the net working capital *i.e.,* current assets minus current liabilities. Funds Flow Statement is a statement which lists first all the sources of funds and then all the applications of funds that have taken place in a business enterprise during the particular period of time for which the statement has been prepared. The statement finally shows the net increase or net decrease in the working capital that has taken place over the period of time. This statement is also called "Statement of Sources and Applications of Funds" or even "How Come Where Gone Statement".

Usually along with Funds Flow Statement a "Statement Showing Changes in Working Capital" also called "Working Capital Statement" is also prepared for the same period for which Funds Flow Statement is prepared. In this statement, all the individual current assets and current liabilities in the beginning as well as at the end of the period are first noted. Then increase or decrease in working capital due to increase or decrease in each such item is recorded. Finally, the overall net increase or decrease in working capital over the period is found out. This figure is the same as the one that appears by way of net increase or decrease in working capital in Funds Flow Statement.

The following is an example of Funds Flow Statement and Statement Showing Changes in Working Capital :

Funds Flow Statement
for the year ended 31st March, 1996

Sources		*Rs.*	*Applications*	*Rs.*
Flow from trading Operations:			Purchase of machinery	6,15,000
Net profit for	Rs.		Redemption of debentures	3,00,000
the year	4,80,000		Income tax paid	5,00,000
Add: Non-cash charges:			Dividends paid	4,00,000
Provision for taxation	4,80,000		Increase in working capital	79,000
Depreciation on fixed assets	1,35,000			

		Rs.		Rs.
Preliminary expenses, written off	15,000			
Loss on sale of furniture	12,000			
	11,22,000			
Less: Gain on sale of investments	17,000	11,39,000		
Sale of furniture		38,000		
Sale of investments		2,17,000		
Issue of shares		5,00,000		
		18,94,000		18,94,000

Statement Showing Charges in Working Capital

		As on 31.3.1995	*As on 31.3.1996*	*Increase in Working Capital*	*Decrease in Working Capital*
		Rs.	*Rs.*	*Rs.*	*Rs.*
Current Assets :					
Stock		4,86,000	5,21,000	35,000	
Debtors		97,000	1,15,000	18,000	
Cash in hand		13,500	12,100		1,400
Cash at Bank		1,34,000	1,48,000	14,000	
	(*a*)	7,30,500	7,86,100		
Current Liabilities :					
Bill Payable		50,000	40,000	10,000	
Creditors		1,13,700	1,05,300	8,400	
Outstanding Expenses		23,000	28,000		5,000
	(*b*)	1,96,700	1,73,300	85,400	6,400
Working Capital	(*a*)—(*b*)	5,33,800	6,12,800		

Increase in working capital = Rs. 85,400 – Rs. 6,400 = Rs. 79,000

Rules for drawing up the Funds Flow Statement

To prepare a Funds Flow Statement, sources and applications of funds have to be ascertained. The usual sources of funds for a joint stock company are as follows:

(*i*) *Funds from Trading Operations:* It is an internal source of funds. To ascertain it, take the figure of net profit for the year as per Profit & Loss Account. This is the figure of net profit after depreciation and provision of income tax for the year but before any appropriations for the year like transfer to General Reserve, Debenture Redemption Reserve etc. To this figure of net profit, add the following amounts:

(*a*) Depreciation on fixed assets

(*b*) Goodwill, Preliminary Expenses, Cost of Issue of Debentures etc., written off during the year.

(*c*) Loss on sale of fixed assets.

(*d*) Loss on sale of investments.

From the total, deduct the following amounts:

(*a*) Profit on sale of fixed assets

(*b*) Profit on sale of investments

(*c*) Profit on revaluation of fixed assets

(*d*) Non-operating incomes.

(*ii*) *Issue of Shares:* Issue of shares for cash or for any other current asset or in discharge of a current liability is another source of funds. However, shares allotted in consideration of some fixed assets will not result in funds. However, it is recommended that such purchase of fixed assets as well as issue of securities to pay for them be revealed in Funds Flow Statement.

Actual collection on issue of shares should be recorded. For example, if shares have been partly called up, only that part which has actually been received will be shown as a source of funds. If shares have been issued at a premium, the amount of share premium collected will also be included. If on the other hand, shares have been issued at a discount, the amount of the discount will be deducted to ascertain the amount collected. Also, shares might have been allotted in an earlier period, and in the period for which Funds Flow Statement is prepared only a call might have been made. In such a case, the amount of the call collected will be a source of funds.

(*iii*) *Issue of Debentures:* Whatever has been said about shares in *(ii)* above holds good for debentures also.

(*iv*) *Raising of long-term loans from financial institutions :* Like debentures, long-term loans from financial institutions form a source of funds.

(*v*) *Sale proceeds of fixed assets and long-term investments:* As sale proceeds of fixed assets and long-term investments are noted as separate items of sources of funds, the effect of any profit or loss on their disposal is removed from the figure of net profit as per Profit & Loss Account before noting it as a source of funds from trading operations so that there may be no double counting.

(*vi*) Non-operating incomes are also a source of funds.

The usual applications of funds are as follows:

(*i*) *Purchae of Fixed Assets:* Purchase of fixed assets for cash or some other current asset or on short-term credit causes reduction of funds.

(*ii*) *Purchase of Long-Term Investments:* Such a purchase is mostly for cash and hence an application of funds.

(*iii*) *Redemption of Preference Shares and/or Debentures:* Payment made to redeem these securities is an application of funds. However, if prepference share or debentures are converted into equity shares, it will not result in an application of funds. But for the sake of disclosure, issue of shares on such a conversion as well as redemption of the securities by conversion should be shown in Funds Flow Stetement.

(*iv*) *Repayment of Long-term Loans* also entails applications of funds.

(*v*) *Payment of Dividend*-It is a very frequent application of funds.

(*vi*) *Payment of Income Tax*-Amount paid by way of income tax will be shown as an application of funds if Provision for Income Tax is treated as an apropriation of profits rather than as a current liability. In the Income Statement of a joint stock company, Provision for Income Tax is shown above the line and not in the Profit & Loss Appropriation Account. Hence, Provision for Income Tax may be treated as a current liability. In such a case, payments of income tax will not appear as an application of funds. However, if one takes the view that as income tax is a tax on income, Provision for Income Tax should be treated as an appropriation of profits for purposes of preparation of Funds Flow Statements. In that case, while ascertaining Funds from Trading Operations, Provision for Income Tax should be added to the figure of net profit after tax. Provision for Income Tax will not appear in the Schedule of Changes in Working Capital and the amount of income tax paid will be shown as an application of funds.

It is to be borne in mind that the statement should bring out the significant factors which have led to the change in the funds position of the company or the firm without giving too many details, for details often hide the important factors from view. Taking the above into account, the statement should show up all new features if they are of significance. For instance, if a company has newly resorted to bank overdrafts, these should be shown as a separate source; this will also be the case if there is a big increase in it or a similar other source. But if bank overdraft is a normal feature and the amount does not change much from year to year, it may not be shown separately; the working capital figure will be adjusted for the purpose.

Advantages: The following are the main advantages of Funds Flow Statement :

(*i*) It gives the figure of flow of funds from operations which is, in one way, more reliable than the figure of net profit revealed by profit and loss account. The amount to be charged in respect of depreciation often depends on the management's decisions and hence the figure of profit revealed by the profit and loss account may sometimes be unrealiable. In the funds flow statement, the effect of depreciation and other non-cash charges is eliminated.

(*ii*) Comparison of the figures of working capital budget with the figures of sources and applications of funds in the funds flow statement enables the management to ascertain how for the budget has been implemented. It also helps in the preparation of the budget for the subsequent period.

Limitations: Funds flow statement shows flows of net working capital which includes items like stock of goods and prepaid expenses which do not contribute to the short term ability of the enterprise to pay its debts. Because of its limitations, AS (Revised)-3 has done away with it and has recommended the preparation of cash flow statement. SEBI also requires the listed companies to prepare cash flow statement.

Distinction between Funds Flow Statement and Cash Flow Statement:

The following are the points of distinction between Funds Flow Statement and Cash Flow Statement:

(*i*) Funds Flow Statement deals with the change in the working capital position while Cash Flow Statement deals with the change in the cash position between two points of time.

(*ii*) Funds Flow Statement does not contain any opening and closing balances but in the Cash Flow Statement, opening as well as closing balances of cash and cash equivalents are given.

(*iii*) Funds Flow Statement records sources of funds on one hand and applications of funds on the other hand. If sources of funds exceed applications of funds, the result is an increase in the working capital. If sources of funds fall short of applications of funds, the final figure is a decrease in the working capital. Cash Flow Statement records inflows and outflows of cash. The difference between total inflows and total outflows is the net increase or decrease in cash and cash equivalents

(*iv*) A statement showing changes in working capital is usually prepared along with Funds Flow Statement. No such statement is prepared along with Cash Flow Statement.

(*v*) One can prepare Funds Flow Statement if Cash Flow Statement prepared by the indirect method is made available. But one cannot prepare Cash Flow Statement if Funds Flow Statement is made available. To prepare Cash Flow Statement by the indirect method, one will also require Statement Showing Charges in Working Capital. To prepare Cash Flow Statement by the direct method, one requires the figures of cash collected from customers and cash payments to suppliers and employees which are not available in Funds Flow Statement and Statement Showing Changes in Working Capital.

(*vi*) Funds Flow Statement is more relevant in estimating the firm's ability to meet its long-term liabilities. However, Cash Flow Statement is more relevant in estimating the firm's capacity to meet its liabilities after a short period of time.

(*vii*) Funds Flow Statement is not required to be prepared by any business enterprise; it has rather become obsolete. On the other hand, SEBI requires every listed company to prepare Cash Flow Statement in the form prescribed by it.

Distinction between Funds Flow Statement and Income Statement:

The following are the points of distinction between Funds Flow Statement and Income Statement (*i.e.*, Profit and Loss Account):

(*i*) Funds Flow Statement matches the funds raised during a period with the funds applied during that time whereas Income Statement matches the incomes and expenditure of a particular period.

(*ii*) Funds Flow Statement tells us the increase or decrease in net working capital during a period of time whereas Income Statement reveals the net profit earned or net loss incurred during a period of time.

(*iii*) Funds Flow Statement deals with revenue as well as capital items whereas Income Statement deals with only revenue items.

(*iv*) In order to prepare Funds Flow Statement, Income Statement is required because information contained in the Income Statement forms the basis of a few items appearing in Funds Flow Statement Income Statement can be prepared without any reference to Funds Flow Statement.

(*v*) Preparation of Funds Flow Statement, though advantageous, is optional, Preparation of Income Statement, barring for very small businessmen, is a must.

(*vi*) No concern is required to prepare Funds Flow Statement in any particular form. But certain companies like insurance companies, banking companies and electricity companies have to prepare Income Statement in a prescribed form.

Distinction between Statement Showing Changes in Working Capital and Funds Flow Statement:

The following are the points of distinction between Statement Showing Changes in Working Capital and Funds Flow Statement:

(*i*) Statement Showing Changes in Working Capital notes the effect of changes in each one of the current assets and current liabilities on working capital. (An increase in a current asset or a decrease in a current liability means an increase in working capital whereas a decrease in a current asset or an increase in a current liability means a decrease in working capital). On the other hand, Funds Flow Statement notes the effect of items other than current assets and current liabilities on working capital.

(*ii*) Items like cash, stock, debtors, bills payable, creditors etc., appearing in Statement Showing Changes in Working Capital are constituents of working capital whereas items appearing in Funds Flow Statement are not constituents of working capital.

(*iii*) Only balance sheets are required to prepare a Statement Showing Changes in Working Capital whereas in order to prepare a Funds Flow Statement, income statement as well as balance sheets are required.

(*iv*) Statement Showing Changes in Working Capital is not presented in T form whereas Funds Flow Statement may be presented in T form.

Illustration 9:

On the basis of the following balance sheet of Nakul Ltd. as at 31st March, 1996 and additional information provided thereafter, prepare:

(*i*) Statement of Changes in Working Capital, and

(*ii*) Funds Flow Statement.

Balance Sheet of Nakul Ltd. as at 31st March, 1996

As at 31.3.1995 Rs.	*Liabilities*	*As at 31.3.1996 Rs.*	*As at 31.3.1995 Rs.*	*Assets*	*As at 31.3.1996 Rs.*
3,00,000	Equity Share Capital	4,50,000	2,00,000	Machinery	2,21,000
1,00,000	14% Preference Share Capital	—	80,000	Furniture	72,000
30,000	Share (Securities) Premium*	50,000	2,72,000	Stock	3,50,000
1,00,000	General Reserve	1,30,000	80,000	Debtors	79,000
50,000	Profit and Loss Account	30,000	20,000	Cash in hand	15,000
1,07,000	Trade Creditors	84,500	1,05,000	Cash at Bank	1,15,000
60,000	Provision for Taxation	77,500	20,000	Preliminary Expense	15,000
30,000	Proposed Final Equity Dividend	45,000			
7,77,000		8,67,000	7,77,000		8,67,000

*Now, the account is called Securities Premium Account. On 31.3.1995 and 31.3.1996, it used to be called Share Premium Account.

Additional information:

(*i*) On 1.4.1995 a machine with a book value of Rs. 40,000 was sold for Rs. 55,000 and a new machine was installed at a total cost of Rs. 1,00,000. Depreciation on machinery is provided @ 15% per annum.

(*ii*) In April, 1995 equity shares of the face value of Rs. 1,50,000 were issued at a premium of 20% and preference shares of Rs. 1,00,000 were redeemed at a premium of 10%. In September, 1995 an interim dividend of Rs. 22,500 was distributed.

(*iii*) The company provides depreciation @ 10% on Furniture.

Solution:

Working Notes:

(*i*) **Profit and Loss Account**

	Rs.		Rs.
To Interim Dividend	22,500	By Balance b/fd	50,000
To General Reserve	30,000	By Net Profit for the year (Balancing Figure)	77,500
To Proposed Equity Dividend	45,000		
To Balance c/d	30,000		
	1,27,500		1,27,500
		By Balance b/d	30,000

(*ii*) **Machinery Account**

		Rs.		Rs.
To Balance b/fd		2,00,000	By Bank	55,000
To Profit and Loss Account (Profit on disposal of machine)	15,000		By Depreciation on Rs. 2,60,000 @ 15%	39,000
To Bank (Purchase of new machine)		1,00,000	By Balance c/d	2,21,000
		3,15,000		3,15,000
To Balance b/d		2,21,000		

(*iii*) *Calculation of fund from trading operations*:

	Rs.
Net Profit of the year	77,500
Less: Profit on disposal of machine	15,000
Trading Profit	62,500
Add: Depreciation on Machinery	39,000
Depreciation on Furniture	8,000
Preliminary Expenses written off	5,000
Fund from trading operations	1,14,500

Statement of Changes in Working Capital

	As at 31.3.1995	*As at 31.3.1996*	*Increase in working capital*	*Decrease in working capital*
	Rs.	*Rs.*	*Rs.*	*Rs.*
Current Assets:				
Stock	2,72,000	3,50,000	78,000	
Debtors	80,000	79,000		1,000
Cush in hand	20,000	15,000		5,000
Cash at Bank	1,05,000	1,15,000	10,000	
(*a*)	4,77,000	5,59,000		

	Rs.	*Rs.*	*Rs.*	*Rs.*
Current Liabilities:				
Trade creditors	1,07,000	84,500	22,500	
Provision for taxation	60,000	77,500		17,500
(*b*)	1,67,000	1,62,000	1,10,500	23,500
Working capital (*a*) – (*b*)	3,10,000	3,97,000		

Net increase in working capital = Rs. 1,10,500 – Rs. 23,500 = Rs. 87,000.

Funds Flow Statement

Sources	*Rs.*	*Applications*	*Rs.*
Fund from trading operations as per working note no. (*iii*)	1,14,500	Redemption of preference at a Premium	1,10,000
Issue of equity shares at a premium	1,80,000	Purchase of machinery	1,00,000
Sale proceeds of machinery	55,000	Final equity dividend for 1994-95	30,000
		Interim dividend	22,500
		Net increase in working capital	87,000
	3,49,500		3,49,500

Illustration 10:

The following is the balance sheet of Chandrabala Ltd. as at 31st March, 1996:

As at 31.3.1995 Rs.	*Liabilities*	*As at 31.3.1996 Rs.*	*As at 31.3.1995 Rs.*	*Assets*	*As at 31.3.1996 Rs.*
5,00,000	Equity Share Capital	7,50,000	2,50,000	Land	2,50,000
	14% Preference		3,30,000	Plant and Machinery	3,40,000
2,00,000	Share Capital	—	70,000	Furniture and Fixtures	63,000
—	Capital Redemption		4,55,000	Stock	4,74,000
	Reserve	2,00,000	1,30,000	Debtors	1,20,000
—	Share (Securities) Premium	20,000	3,80,000	Cash at Bank	4,15,000
3,00,000	General Reserve	1,25,000	30,000	Bill Receivable	35,000
50,000	Profit & Loss Account	60,000	25,000	Underwriting Commission	20,000
3,00,000	11% Debentures	—			
—	14% Debentures	2,00,000			
30,000	Bills Payable	40,000			
65,000	Trade Creditors	60,000			
1,500	Outstanding Expenses	2,000			
1,20,500	Provision for Taxation	1,47,500			
28,000	Proposed Preference Dividend*	—			
75,000	Proposed Equity Dividend*	1,12,500			
16,70,000		17,17,000	16,70,000		17,17,000

(*i*) 11% Debentures were convertible into equity shares at par at the option of debentureholders during the year. Debentureholders for Rs. 2,00,000 opted for conversion; others were paid cash.

(*ii*) A machine was purchased for Rs. 70,000; the supplier accepted equity shares of the face value of Rs. 50,000 at a premium of Rs. 20,000 in discharge of purchase consideration.

You are required to prepare

(*a*) Statement of Changes in Working Capital and

(*b*) Funds Flow Statement.

* Corporate dividend tax has not been provided for because on 31.3.1995 and 31.3.1996 there was no such tax.

Solution: (*i*)

Equity Share Capital Account

	Rs.		Rs.
To Balance c/d	7,50,000	By Balance b/d	5,00,000
		By 11% Debentureholders	2,00,000
		By Supplier of Machine	50,000
	7,50,000		7,50,000
		By Balance b/d	7,50,000

Plant and Machinery Account

	Rs.		Rs.
To Balance	3,30,000	By Depreciation (Balancing Figure)	60,000
To Supplier of Machine	70,000	By Balance c/d	3,40,000
	4,00,000		4,00,000
To Balance b/d	3,40,000		

General Reserve

	Rs.		Rs.
To Capital Redemption Reserve	2,00,000	By Balance b/fd	3,00,000
To Balance c/d	1,25,000	By Profit & Loss (Appropriation) Account	25,000
	3,25,000		3,25,000
		By Balance b/d	1,25,000

Profit & Loss Appropriation Account

	Rs.		Rs.
To General Reserve	25,000	By Balance b/fd	50,000
To Proposed Equity Dividend	1,12,500	By Net Profit for the year (Balancing Figure)	1,47,500
To Balance c/fd	60,000		
	1,97,500		1,97,500

Calculation of Fund from Trading Operations

	Rs.
Net Profit for the year	1,47,500
Add: Non-cash charges	
Depreciation on Plant and Machinery	60,000
Depreciation on Furniture and Fixtures	7,000
Underwriting Commission written off	5,000
	2,19,500

Statement of Changes in Working Capital

	As at 31.3.1995	*As at 31.3.1996*	*Increase in working capital*	*Decrease in working capital*
	Rs.	*Rs.*	*Rs.*	*Rs.*
Current Assets:				
Stock	4,55,000	4,74,000	19,000	
Debtors	1,30,000	1,20,000		10,000
Cush in Band	3,80,000	4,15,000	35,000	
Bills Receivable	30,000	35,000	5,000	
(*a*)	9,95,000	10,44,000		

	Rs.	Rs.	Rs.	Rs.
Current Liabilities:				
Bills Payable	30,000	40,000		10,000
Trade Creditors	65,000	60,000	5,000	
Outstanding Expenses	1,500	2,000		500
Provision for Taxation	1,20,500	1,47,500		27,000
(*b*)	2,17,000	2,49,500	64,000	47,500
Working Capital	7,78,000	7,94,500		

Increase in Working Capital = Rs. 64,000 – Rs. 47,500 = Rs. 16,500.

Funds Flow Statement

Sources	*Rs.*	*Applications*	*Rs.*
Flow from Trading Operations	2,19,500	Redemption of 11% Debentures	3,00,000
Issue of Equity Shares to 11% Debentureholders	2,00,000	Redemption of 14% Preference Shares	2,00,000
Issue of Equity Shares to Supplier of Machine	70,000	Purchase of Machine	70,000
		Preference Dividend Paid	28,000
Issue of 14% Debentures	2,00,000	Equity Dividend Paid	75,000
		Increase in Working Capital	16,500
	6,89,500		6,89,500

Illustration 11:

From the figures given below, prepare a statement showing applications and sources of funds during the year 1995-96:

	March 31, 1995	March 31 1996
Assets	*Rs.*	*Rs.*
Fixed Assets (Net)	5,10,000	6,20,000
Investments	30,000	80,000
Current Assets	2,40,000	3,75,000
Discount on Issue of Debentures	10,000	5,000
	7,90,000	10,80,000
Liabilities and Capital		
Equity Share Capital	3,00,000	3,50,000
14% Preference Share Capital	2,00,000	1,00,000
14% Debentures	1,00,000	2,00,000
Reserves	1,10,000	2,70,000
Provision for Doubtful Debts	10,000	15,000
Current Liabilities	70,000	1,45,000
	7,90,000	10,80,000

The provision for depreciation stood at 1,50,000 on 31st March, 1995 and at Rs. 1,90,000 on 31st March, 1996.

During the year:

(*i*) a machine costing Rs. 70,000 (book value Rs. 40,000) was disposed of for Rs. 25,000;

(*ii*) preference share redemption was carried out at a premium of 5% on 1st April, 1995; and

(*iii*) dividend @ 15% was paid on equity shares for the year 1994-95.

Solution:

Statement of Sources and Applications of Funds for the year ended 31st March, 1996

Sources	*Rs.*	*Rs.*	*Applications*	*Rs.*	*Rs.*
Profit earned during 1995-96	2,34,000		Purchase of Fixed Assets		2,20,000
Add: Non-cash Charges:			Purchase of Investments		50,000
Depreciation	70,000		Redemption of Preference Shares		1,05,000
Discount on Issue of			Payment of Dividend:		
Debentures written off	5,000	3,09,000	Preference	9,000	
Issue of Shares		50,000	Equity	45,000	54,000
Issue of Debentures		1,00,000	Increase in Working Capital		55,000
Sale of Machine		25,000			
		4,84,000			4,84,000

Working Notes:

(*i*) *Working Capital*

	31.3.1995	31.3.1996
	Rs.	*Rs.*
Current Assets	2,40,000	3,75,000
Less: Provision for Doubtful Debts	10,000	15,000
	2,30,000	3,60,000
Current Liabilities	70,000	1,45,000
Working Capital	1,60,000	2,15,000
Increase	55,000	—
	2,15,000	2,15,000

(*ii*) *Depreciation provided during the years*:

Provision as on 31.3.1995	1,50,000
Less: Provision relating to the machine sold during the year (Cost Rs. 70,000; book value Rs. 40,000)	30,000
	1,20,000
Provision as on 31.3.1996	1,90,000
Fresh provision made during the year	70,000

(*iii*) *Profit earned during the year*:

Reserves

	Rs.		*Rs.*
To Loss on Sale of Machine	15,000	By Balance b/fd	1,10,000
To Premium on Redemption of Preference Shares	5,000	By Profit earned during the year (balancing figure)	2,34,000
To Preference Dividend	9,000		
To Equity Dividend	45,000		
To Balance c/fd	2,70,000		
	3,44,000		3,44,000

(*iv*) *Fixed Assets acquired*:

	Rs.
Book value of fixed assets on 31.3.1995	5,10,000
Add: Provision for Depreciation on 31.3.1995	1,50,000
Cost of Fixed Assets on 31.3.1995	6,60,000
Less: Cost of machine disposed of	70,000
	5,90,000
New assets acquired during 1995-96 (balancing figure)	2,20,000
Cost of fixed assets as on 31.3.1996, (Rs. 6,20,000 + Rs. 1,90,000)	8,10,000

Illustration 12:

The balance sheet of Bharat Mills Ltd. as at 31st March, 1995 was as follows:

Liabilities	*Rs.*	*Assets*	*Rs.*	*Rs.*
Equity Share Capital	10,00,000	Plant and Machinery (cost)	6,00,000	
General Reserve	1,50,000	*Less*: Depreciation	2,21,050	3,78,950
Profit & Loss Account	2,50,000	Furniture, Fittings and		
Trade Creditors	1,62,850	Fixtures (*cost*)	1,00,000	
Provision for Income Tax	1,95,000	*Less*: Depreciation	27,100	72,900
		Long-term Investment		2,00,000
		Stock		4,50,000
		Debtors	80,000	
		Less: Provision for Bad Debts	4,000	76,000
		Cash at Bank		3,80,000
		Advance Payment of Income Tax		2,00,000
	17,57,850			17,57,850

On 1st April, 1995 the company took over a business for Rs. 5,00,000. The consideration was satisfied by allotment to vendor 27,000 equity shares of Rs. 10 each at par and a cash payment of Rs. 2,30,000 which was raised by sale of all the long-term investments. The assets and liabilities taken over and their agreed values were as follows:

Plant and Machinery	3,00,000
Furniture, Fittings and Fixtures	40,000
Stock	1,05,000
Trade Debtors	45,000
Trade Creditors	15,000

In July 1995, the company paid a dividend @ 20% per annum for the year ended 31st March, 1995.

In December, 1995 the income tax officer made a demand of Rs. 5,000 in respect of income tax liability for the accounting year ended 31st March, 1995. During 1995-96 advance payment of tax amounting to Rs. 2,50,000 was made.

In February, 1996 the company made a public issue of 1,00,000 equity shares of Rs. 10 each at par, the whole amount being payable along with applications. The issue was got underwritten at a commission of 2½% of the issue price. The purpose of the issue was to finance a new plant which was acquired to Rs. 9,00,000 in the last week of March, 1996.

The balance sheet of Bharat Mills Ltd. as at March, 1996 stood as follows:

Balance Sheet of Bharat Mills Ltd., as at 31st March, 1996

Liabilities	*Rs.*	*Assets*	*Rs.*	*Rs.*
Equity Share Capital	22,70,000	Goodwill	25,000	25,000
(Of the above shares, 27,000		Plant and Machinery (cost)	18,00,000	
shares of Rs. 10 each have		*Less*: Depreciation	3,21,893	14,78,107
been allotted as fully paid up		Furniture, Fittings and		
pursuant to a contract without		Fixtures (cost	1,40,000	
payment being received in cash)		*Less*: Depreciation	38,390	1,01,610
General Reserve	2,00,000	Stock		5,05,283
Profit and Loss Account	3,00,000	Debtors	98,000	
Trade Creditors	1,43,100	*Less*: Provision for Bad Debts	4,900	93,100
Provision for Income Tax	3,10,000	Cash at Bank		6,95,000
		Advance Payment of Income tax		3,00,000
		Underwritten Commission		25,000
	32,23,100			32,23,100

You are required to prepare:

(*i*) Statement ‹f Changes in Working Capital, and

(*ii*) Funds Flow Statement.

Solution:

Working Notes:

(*i*) *Calculation of Goodwill*:

		Rs.
Assets taken over:		
Plant and Machinery		3,00,000
Furniture, Fittings and Fixtures		40,000
Stock		1,05,000
Trade Debtors		45,000
		4,90,000
Less: Trade Creditors taken over		15,000
Net tangible assets taken over		4,75,000
Consideration		5,00,000

Hence, goodwill is Rs. 5,00,000 – Rs. 4,75,000 = Rs. 25,000

(*ii*) Dividend paid = Rs. 10,00,000 × 20/100 = Rs. 2,00,000

(*iii*) Underwriting Commission = Rs. 10,00,000 × $^5/_2$ × 100 = Rs. 25,000

(*iv*) *Calculation of Flow from Trading Operations*

		Rs.
Balance of Profit & Loss Account as at 31.3.1996		3,00,000
Add: Transfer to General Reserve		50,000
Dividend paid		2,00,000
Depreciation on Plant & Machinery (Rs. 3,21,893 – 2,21,050)		1,00,843
Depreciation of Furniture, Fittings and Fixtures (Rs. 38,390 – Rs. 27,100)		11,290
		6,62,133
Less : Profit on sale of investments	30,000	
Balance of Profit & Loss Account as at 31.3.1995	2,50,000	2,80,000
		3,82,133

Statement of Changes in Working Capital

Particulars	*As at 31.3.1995* Rs.	*As at 31.3.1996* Rs.	*Increase in working capital* Rs.	*Decrease in working capital* Rs.
Current Assets:				
Stock		4,50,000	5,05,283	55,283
Debtors	76,000	93,100	17,100	
Cush in Band	3,80,000	6,95,000	3,15,000	
Advance Payment of Tax	2,00,000	3,00,000	1,00,000	
(*a*)	11,06,000	15,93,383		
Current Liabilities:				
Trade Creditors	1,62,850	1,43,100	19,750	
Provision for Income tax	1,95,000	3,10,000		1,15,000
(*b*)	3,57,850	4,78,100	5,07,133	1,15,000
Working capital (*a*) – (*b*)	7,48,150	11,40,283		

Increase in Working Capital = Rs. 11,40,283 – Rs. 7,48,150 = Rs. 3,92,133

Funds Flow Statement

Sources	*Rs.*	*Applications*	*Rs.*
Flow from Trading Operations	3,82,133	Purchase of Goodwill	25,000
Issue of Shares	12,70,000	Purchase of Plant and Machinery	12,00,000
Sale of Long-term Investments	2,30,000	Purchase of Furniture	40,000
		Underwriting Commission	25,000
		Dividend Paid	2,00,000
		Increase in Working Capital	3,92,133
	18,82,133		18,82,133

Illustration 13:

The summarised balance sheets of Exe. etc. as on 31st March, 1995 and 1996 are as follows:

	March 31, 1995 *Rs.*	March 31 1996 *Rs.*
Fixed Assets: Cost	8,00,000	9,50,000
Less: Depreciation	2,30,000	2,90,000
	5,70,000	6,60,000
Trade Investments	1,00,000	80,000
Current Assets	2,80,000	3,30,000
Preliminary Expenses	20,000	10,000
	9,70,000	10,80,000
Share Capital	3,00,000	4,00,000
Capital Reserve	—	10,000
Debentures Redemption Reserve	1,70,000	2,00,000
Profit & Loss Account	60,000	75,000
Debentures	2,00,000	1,40,000
Liabilities for Goods and Services	1,20,000	1,30,000
Provision for Income Tax	90,000	85,000
Proposed Dividend	30,000	36,000
Unpaid Dividend	—	4,000
	9,70,000	10,80,000

During 1995-96, the company:

(*i*) sold one machine for Rs. 25,000; the cost of the machine was Rs. 50,000 and the depreciation provided on it amounted to Rs. 21,000;

(*ii*) provided Rs. 95,000 as depreciation;

(*iii*) redeemed 30% of the Debentures @ 103;

(*iv*) sold some trade investments at a profit credited to Capital Reserve; and

(*v*) decided to value the stock at cost whereas previously the practice was to value stock at cost *less* 10%. The stock according to books on 31.3.1995 was Rs. 54,000; the stock on 31.3.1996, Rs. 75,000, was correctly valued at cost.

You are required to prepare the statement of sources and applications of funds during 1995-96.

Solution:

Statement of Sources and Applications of Funds of Exe Ltd. for the year ended 31st March, 1995

Sources	*Rs.*	*Rs.*	*Applications*	*Rs.*
Profit earned	80,800		Purchase of Fixed Assets	2,14,000
Add: Non-cash charges:			Redemption of Debentures	61,800
Depreciation	95,000		Payment of Dividend	30,000
Preliminary Expenses	10,000	1,85,800	Increase in Working Capital	35,000

	Rs.		Rs.
Issue of Shares	1,00,000		
Sale of Trade Investments	30,000		
Sale of Machine	25,000		
	3,40,800		3,40,800

Working Notes:

(*iii*) *Profit earned during the year*:

Profit & Loss Account for 1995-96

	Rs.		Rs.
To Loss on Redemption of Debenture (3% on Rs. 60,000)	1,800	By Balance b/fd	60,000
To Loss on Sale of Machine	4,000	By Opening Stock written up (54,000 × 10/90)	6,000
To Redemption Debenture Reserve	30,000	By Net Profit earned (balancing figure)	80,800
To Proposed Dividend	36,000		
To Balance c/d	75,000		
	1,46,800		1,46,800

	Rs.	Rs.
(2) (*i*) *Working Capital on 31.3.1995*		
Current Assets on 31.3.1995		2,80,000
Add: Write-up for Opening Stock		6,000
		2,86,000
Less: Current Liabilities:		
Liabilities for Goods and Services	1,20,000	
Provision for Income-tax	90,000	2,10,000
		76,000
(*ii*) *Working Capital on 31.3.1996*:		
Current Assets on 31.3.1996		3,30,000
Less: Liabilities for Goods and Services	1,30,000	
Provision for Income-tax	85,000	
Unpaid Dividend	4,000	2,19,000
		1,11,000
(*iii*) Income [(*ii*) – (*i*)]		35,000
(3) *Depreciation Provision*:		
Balance on 31.3.1995		2,30,000
Less: Depreciation on machine sold		21,000
		2,09,000
Add: Amount provided in 1995-96		95,000
Total that should be on 31.3.1996		3,04,000
Less: Amount shown in the Balance Sheet		2,90,000
Difference, presumably the provision in respect of a discarded machine		14,000
(4) *Fixed Assets acquired during 1995-96*:		
Cost as on 31.3.1995		8,00,000
Less: Cost of Machine sold	50,000	
Discarded [see (3) above]	14,000	64,000
		7,36,000
Cost as per Balance Sheet as on 31.3.1996		9,50,000
∴ addition, Rs. (9,50,000 – 7,36,000)		2,14,000

(5) Trade investments have declined by Rs. 20,000 (book value); in addition there is profit of Rs. 10,000, credited to Capital Reserve, Hence, total amount realised is Rs. 30,000.

Illustration 14:

The following are the balance sheets of K. Ltd. as on 31st March, 2000 and 31st March 2001:

Liabilities	31.3.2000 *Rs.*	31.3.2001 *Rs.*
Share Capital	12,00,000	15,00,000
General Reserve	2,00,000	2,50,000
Debenture Redemption Reserve	3,00,000	3,00,000
Profit and Loss (Appropriation) Account	1,00,000	1,48,500
14% Debentures	6,00,000	4,00,000
Creditors	4,90,000	5,60,000
Provision for Taxation	1,00,000	1,30,000
Proposed Dividend	1,08,000	1,65,000
Provision for Corporate Dividend tax	10,800	16,500
	31,08,800	34,70,000

Assets	31.3.2000 *Rs.*	31.3.2001 *Rs.*
Buildings	10,00,000	9,60,000
Machinery	5,00,000	7,20,000
Short-term Investments	3,00,000	4,50,000
Inventories	4,00,000	4,70,000
Debtors	6,70,000	5,30,000
Cash at Bank	2,18,800	3,30,000
Prepaid Expenses	20,000	10,000
	31,08,800	34,70,000

The following additional information is given to you:

(*i*) Debentures were redeemed at a premium of 10%.

(*ii*) Taxes paid during the year amounted to Rs. 1,40,000.

(*iii*) A machine which appeared at a written down value of Rs. 80,000 was sold for Rs. 1,30,000 and new machines worth Rs. 3,60,000 were acquired during the year.

Prepare Funds Flow Statement and Statement showing changes in working capital.

[*Adapted B.Com. (Hons.) Delhi, 1999*]

Solution:

Funds Flow Statement of K. Ltd. for the year ended 31st March, 2001

Sources	*Rs.*	*Applications*	*Rs.*
Flow of Funds from Trading Operations — [Working Note (*iii*)]	3,50,000	Purchase of Machines	3,60,000
		Redemption of Debentures at a Premium	2,20,000
Issue of Shares	3,00,000	Dividends Paid During the Year	1,08,000
Sale Proceeds of Machine	1,30,000	Corporate Dividend Tax Paid	10,800
		Increase in Working Capital	81,200
	7,80,000		7,80,000

Statement Showing Changes in Working Capital

	As at 31.3.2000 *Rs.*	*As at 31.3.2001* *Rs.*	*Increase in working capital* *Rs.*	*Decrease in working capital* *Rs.*
Current Assets:				
Short-term Investments	3,00,00	4,50,000	1,50,000	
Inventories	4,00,000	4,70,000	70,000	
Debtors	6,70,000	5,30,000		1,40,000
Cash at Bank	2,18,800	3,30,000	1,11,200	
Prepaid Expenses	20,000	10,000		10,000
(*x*)	16,08,800	17,90,000		

	Rs.	Rs.	Rs.	Rs.
Current Liabilities:				
Creditors	4,90,000	5,60,000		70,000
Provision for taxation	1,00,000	1,30,000		30,000
(y)	5,90,000	6,90,000	3,31,200	2,50,000
Working capital (x) – (y)	10,18,800	11,00,000		

Increase in Working Capital = Rs. 3,31,200 – Rs. 2,50,000 = Rs. 81,200.

Working Notes:

(*i*) *Dr.* **Profit & Loss (Appropriation) Account** *Cr.*

	Rs.		Rs.
To General Reserve, (Rs. 2,50,000 – Rs. 2,00,000)	50,000	By Balance b/fd	1,00,000
To Proposed Dividend	1,65,000	By Net Profit for the year (Balancing Figure)	2,80,000
To Provision of Corporate Dividend Tax	16,500		
To Balance c/d	1,48,500		
	3,80,000		3,80,000

(*ii*) *Dr.* **Machinery Account** *Cr.*

	Rs.		Rs.
To Balance b/fd	5,00,000	By Bank (Sale)	1,30,000
To Profit on Sale of Machine Account (Rs. 1,30,000 – Rs. 80,000)	50,000	By Depreciation (Balancing Figure)	60,000
To Bank (Addition)	3,60,000	By Balance c/fd	7,20,000
	9,10,000		9,10,000

(*iii*) *Funds from Trading Operations*:

	Rs.
Net Profit, as per working note (*i*)	2,80,000
Add: Depreciation on Buildings, Rs. 10,00,000 – Rs. 9,60,000	40,000
Depreciation on Machinery as per working note (*ii*)	60,000
Premium on Redemption of Debentures	20,000
	4,00,000
Less: Profit on Sale of Machine	50,000
Fund from Trading Operations	3,50,000

Illustration 15:

The following are the balance sheets of Z Ltd. as on 31st March, 2000 and 2001.

Liabilities	*2000* *Rs.*	*2001* *Rs.*	*Assets*	*2000* *Rs.*	*2001* *Rs.*
Equity Share Capital	5,00,000	7,20,000	Building	6,00,000	5,80,000
Securities Premium	—	1,10,000	Machinery	3,00,000	3,65,000
General Reserve	1,50,000	2,70,000	Furniture	1,00,000	1,04,500
Debenture Redemption Reserve	1,00,000	—	Stock	3,00,000	3,22,000
			Debtors	1,20,000	1,05,200
Profit and Loss Account	61,000	82,300	Cash at Bank	13,500	11,300
12% Debentures	2,00,000	—	Advance Payment of Income Tax	75,500	62,000
Creditors	4,24,000	3,05,700			
Unclaimed Dividends	—	1,000	Cost of Issue of Debentures	1,000	—
Provision for Income Tax	75,000	61,000			
	15,10,000	15,50,000		15,10,000	15,50,000

The following additional information is provided to you:

(*i*) Dividend paid in cash during are year 2000-01, Rs. 49,000, Corporate Dividends Tax amounting to Rs. 5,500 on dividend declared was also paid at the same time.

(*ii*) Machinery for Rs. 1,00,000 and stock for Rs. 80,000 were acquired in consideration of allotment of fully paid 12,000 equity shares of Rs. 10 each at a premium of Rs. 5 per share.

(*iii*) The face value of every fully paid 12% debenture was Rs. 200. During the year, each debenture was converted into 10 fully paid equity shares of Rs. 10 each at a premium of Rs. 5 per share and tax balance of Rs. 50 per debenture was paid in cash.

(*iv*) Furniture purchased during the year for cash, Rs. 10,000.

Prepare Funds Flow Statement and Schedule of changes in working capital for the year ended 31st March, 2001.

Solution:

Funds Flow Statement for the year ended 31st March, 2001

Sources	*Rs.*	*Rs.*	*Applications*	*Rs.*
Flow from trading Operations:			Purchase of furniture	10,000
Net profit for the year	96,800		Machinery purchased for shares	1,00,000
Add: Non-cash charges:			Part conversion of debentures into shares	1,50,000
Depreciation on:			Redemption of debentures in cash	50,000
Building	20,000		Payment of dividends	49,000
Machinery	35,000		Payment of corporate dividend tax	5,500
Furniture	5,500		Increase in working capital	1,23,800
Cost of Issue of Debentures, written off	1,000	1,58,300		
Issue of shares in considertion of:				
Machinery	1,00,000			
Stock	80,000	1,80,000		
Issue of shares in part convension of debentures		1,50,000		
		4,88,300		4,88,300

Schedule of Changes in Working Capital for the year ended 31st March, 2001

	As at 31.3.2000 Rs.	*As at 31.3.2001* Rs.	*Increase in working capital* Rs.	*Decrease in working capital* Rs.
Current Assets:				
Stock	3,00,000	3,22,000	22,000	
Debtors	1,20,000	1,05,200		14,800
Cash at Bank	13,500	11,300		2,200
Advance Payment of Income Tax	75,500	62,000		13.500
(*a*)	5,09,000	5,00,500		
Current Liabilities:				
Creditors	4,24,000	3,05,700	1,18,300	
Provision for Income tax	75,000	61,000	14,000	
(*b*)	4,99,000	3,66,700	1,54,300	30,500
Working capital (*a*) – (*b*)	10,000	1,33,800		

Increase in Working Capital = Rs. 1,54,300 – Rs. 30,500 = Rs. 1,23,800.

Note: Unclaimed Dividend has not been shown as a current liability because in the Funds Flow Statement, actual payment of dividends (and not dividends declared) has been shown as an application.

Working Notes:

(*i*) *Dr.* **General Reserve** *Cr.*

	Rs.		*Rs.*
To Balance c/fd	2,70,000	By Balance b/fd	1,50,000
		By Debenture Redemption Reserve	1,00,000
		By Profit & Loss (Appropriation) Account — Balancing Figure	20,000
	2,70,000		2,70,000

(*ii*) *Dr.* **Profit and Loss (Appropriation) Account** *Cr.*

	Rs.		*Rs.*
To General Reserve	20,000	By Balance b/fd	61,000
To Dividends Declared, Rs. (49,000 + 1,000)	50,000	By Net Profit for the year — Balancing Figure	96,800
To Corporation Dividend Tax	5,500		
To Balance c/fd	82,300		
	1,57,800		1,57,800

(*iii*) Depreciation on Building = Rs. (6,00,000 – 5,80,000) = Rs. 20,000.

(*iv*) *Depreciation on Machinery*:

	Rs.
Opening balance of Machinary Account	3,00,000
Add: Purchase for shares	1,00,000
Total	4,00,000
Less: Closing balance of Machinery Account	3,65,000
Depreciation for the year	35,000

(*v*) *Depreciation on Furniture*:

	Rs.
Opening balance of Furniture Account	1,00,000
Add: Purchase for cash	10,000
Total	1,10,000
Less: Closing balance of Furniture Account	1,04,500
Depreciation for the year	5,500

Illustration 16:

The balance sheet of A Ltd. as at 31st March, 2009 and the consolidated balance sheet of A Ltd. and its subsidinary *B* Ltd. as at 31st March, 2010 were as follows:

Liabilities	*As at 31.3.2000*	*(Rs. in lakhs)* *As at 31.3.2001*
Equity Share Capital (of Rs. 10 per share)	500.0	675.0
Reserves and Surplus	850.0	1,175.0
Term Loans	300.0	425.0
Minority Interest	—	175.0
Creditors	275.0	600.0
Bank Overdraft	—	67.5
	1,925.0	3,117.5

Assets:		
Goodwill	—	50.00
Land and Buildings	650.0	650.0
Plant and Machinery	625.0	1,617.5
Stock	275.0	375.0
Debtors	225.0	420.0
Cash	150.0	5.0
	1,925.0	3,117.5

Further information:

A Ltd. had acquired 75% of the equity shares of *B* Ltd. on 01.09.2009. At that date, assets and liabilities of *B* Ltd. were:

	(*Rs. in lakhs*)
Fixed Assets	625
Stock	75
Debtors	100
Cash	125
Term Loans	125
Creditors	200

A Ltd. had paid Rs. 500 lakhs to acquire the shares in *B* Ltd. This was made up of an issue of shares valued at 437.5 lakhs. Balance consideration was met from cash. The premium on the issue of shares stood included in the reserves.

Depreciation charged in the consolidated accounts amounted to Rs. 125 lakhs, as to building Rs. 25 lakhs and as to plant and machinery Rs. 100 lakhs.

A Ltd. paid an interim dividend of Rs. 50 lakhs on 01.03.2001. On the same date *B* Ltd. paid on interim dividend of Rs. 25 lakhs.

Prepare a consolidated statement of sources and application of funds with relevant workings. Ignore corporate dividend tax. [*Adapted C.A.* (*Final*) *Nov., 1997*]

Solution:

Consolidated Funds Flow Statement for the year ended 31st March, 2010

	Rs. in lakhs
Sources:	
Fund from operations	268.75
Issue of shares at a premium	437.50
Loans	125.00
Minority interest	150.00
Decrease in working capital	242.50
	1223.75
Applications:	
Purchase of fixed assets	1117.50
Payment of dividend by *A* Ltd.	50.00
Payment of dividend to minority shareholders in *B* Ltd.	6.25
Goodwill	50.00
	1223.75

Statement Showing Changes in Working Capital

Particulars	*As on 31.3.2009* *Rs. in lakhs*	*As on 31.3.2010* *Rs. in lakhs*	*Increase in working capital* *Rs. in lakhs*	*Decrease in working capital* *Rs. in lakhs*
Current Assets:				
Stock	275.0	375.0	100.0	
Debtors	225.0	420.0	195.0	
Cash	150.0	5.0		145.0
(*x*)	650.0	800.0		
Current Liabilities:				
Creditors	275.0	600.0		325.0
Bank overdraft	—	67.5		67.5
(*y*)	275.0	667.5	295.0	537.5
Working Capital (*x*) – (*y*)	375.0	132.5		

Increase in Working Capital = Rs. (537.5 – 295.0) lakhs = Rs. 242.5 lakhs.

Working Notes:

		Rs. in lakhs
(*i*) Consideration for 75% shares in *B* Ltd.		500.00
Less: Face value of shares issued	175.00	
Premium on shares issued	262.50	437.50
Consideration paid in cash		62.50

(*ii*) *Calculation of goodwill on acquisition of shares*:

	Rs. in lakhs	
Assets:		
Fixed	625	
Stock	75	
Debtors	100	
Cash	125	925
Less: *Liabilities*:		
Term loans	125	
Creditors	200	325
Equity on 1.9.2009		600
Less: Minority interest on 1.9.2000, Rs. $\left(600 \times \frac{25}{100}\right)$ lakhs		150
A Ltd.'s share in *B* Ltd.'s share capital and capital profits		450
Consideration		500
Goodwill, Rs. (500 – 450) lakhs		50

(*iii*) Minority interest on the date of consolidation	175
Less: Minority interest on the date of acquisition shown as source	150
Minority shareholders' share in port-acquisition profit of *B* Ltd. treated as part of fund from operations	25

(*iv*) *Fund from operation*:

Increase in reserves and surplus,. Rs. (1175 – 850) lakhs	325.00
Less: Increase on account of premium	262.50
	62.50
Add: Depreciation	125.00
Dividend paid by *A* Ltd., shown as application	50.00
Dividend paid by *B* Ltd. to minority shareholders, shown as application,	

	Rs. in lakhs
Rs. $\left(25 \times \frac{25}{100}\right)$ lakhs	6.25
	243.75
Add: Share of minority shareholders of *B* Ltd. in its port-acquisition profits	25.00
	268.75

(*v*) *Purchase of fixed assets:*

Rs. in lakhs

	Land and Building	*Plant and Mechinery*
Closing balance	650.0	1617.5
Add: Depreciation	25.0	100.0
	675.0	1717.5
Less: Opening balance	650.0	625.0
Addition during the year	25.0	1092.5

Illustration 17:

The Directors of Chintamani Ltd. present you with the Balance Sheets as on 31st March, 1995 and 1996 and ask you to prepare statements which will show them what has happened to the money which came into the business during the year 1995-96:

Liabilities	31st March, 1995 *Rs.*	31st March, 1996 *Rs.*
Authorised capital 15,000 shares of Rs. 100 each	15,00,000	15,00,000
Paid up capital	10,00,000	14,00,000
Debentures (1996)	4,00,000	—
General reserves	60,000	40,000
Profit and loss appropriation account	36,000	38,000
Provision for purpose of final dividends	78,000	72,000
Sundry trade creditors	76,000	1,12,000
Banks overdraft	69,260	1,29,780
Bills payable	40,000	38,000
Loans on mortgage	—	5,60,000
	17,59,260	23,89,780
Assets		
Land and freehold buildings	9,00,000	9,76,000
Machinery and plant	1,44,000	5,94,000
Fixtures and fittings	6,000	5,500
Cash in hand	1,560	1,280
Sundry trade debtors	1,25,600	1,04,400
Bills receivable	7,600	6,400
Stock	2,44,000	2,38,000
Prepayments	4,500	6,200
Shares in other companies	80,000	2,34,000
Goodwill	2,40,000	2,20,000
Preliminary expenses	6,000	4,000
	17,59,260	23,89,780

You are given the following additional information:

(*a*) Depreciation has been charged (*i*) on Freehold Building @ 5% on written-down value. (*ii*) on Machinery and Plant Rs. 32.000. (*iii*) on Fixtures and Fittings @ 10% on written-down value basis Rs. 10,000. No depreciation has been written off on newly acquired Buildings and Plant and Machinery.

(*b*) A piece of land was sold on 1st April, 1995 for Rs. 2,50,000 (W.D.V. Rs. 1,00,000). The sale proceeds were all credited to Land and Buildings Accounts.

(*c*) Shares in other companies were purchased and dividends amounting to Rs. 6,000 declared out of profits made prior to purchase has been received and used to write down the investments in shares in other companies.

(*d*) Goodwill has been written down against General Reserves.

(*e*) The proposed dividend for the year 31st March, 1995 was paid and, in addition, an interim dividend, Rs. 52,000 was paid. (*Adapted from C.A. Final*)

Solution:

Working — (*a*) Ascertainment of net profit earned:

Profit and Loss Account

	Rs.		*Rs.*
To Interim Dividend	52,000	By Balance b/fd	36,000
To Proposed Dividend	72,000	By Net Profit earned	
To Balance c/fd	38,000	(balancing figure)	1,26,000
	1,62,000		1,62,000

(*b*) Amounts written off against Profit and Loss Account (before the net profit as shown above):

	Rs.
Freehold Buildings	40,000
Machinery and Plant	32,000
Fixtures and Fittings	600
Preliminary Expenses	2,000
	59,500

(*c*) *Working Capital*:

		On 31st March, 1995		*On 31st March, 1996*
	Rs.	*Rs.*	*Rs.*	*Rs.*
Cash in Hand		1,560		1,280
Sundry Tradce Debtors		1,25,600		1,04,400
Bills Receivable		7,600		6,400
Stock		2,44,000		2,38,000
Prepayments		4,500		6,200
		3,83,260		3,56,280
Less: Sundry Trade Creditors	76,000		1,12,000	
Bills Payable	40,000	1,16,000	38,000	1,50,000
		2,67,260		2,06,280

Release of working capital : Rs. 2,67,260 – 2,06,280 = Rs. 60,980.

Funds Flow Statement for the year ended March 31, 1996

Sources of Funds:	*Rs.*	*Rs.*
Cash Inflow from Operations:		
Net Profit	1,26,000	
Dividend from Investments	6,000	
Amounts written off	59,500	1,91,500
Issue of Share Capital, Rs. (14,00,000 – 10,00,000)		4,00,000
Loan on Mortgage		5,60,000
Bank Overdraft, Rs. (1,29,780 – 69,260)		60,520
Sale of Land		2,50,000
Release of Working Capital		60,950
Total		15,23,000

Applications of Funds:	*Rs.*	*Rs.*
Purchase of Fixed Assets:		
Land and Freehold Buildings*	3,51,000	
Machinery and Plant, Rs. [5,94,000 – (1,44,000 – 32,000)]	4,82,000	8,33,000
Redemption of Debentures		4,00,000
Purchase of Shares in Other Companies Rs. (2,23,000 + 6,000 – 80,000)		1,60,000
Payment of Dividends:		
Final for year up to 31st March, 1995	78,000	
Interim	52,000	1,30,000
		15,23,000

Alternative ways of preparation: The solution to the illustration given above can also be presented in the following manner:—

(1) Funds Flow Statement for the year ended March 31,1996

Sources:		*Rs.*	*Rs.*
Working Capital on April 1, 1995			2,67,260
Cash inflow from operations:			
Profit		1,26,000	
Non-operating profit		6,000	
Non-cash charges		59,500	1,91,500
Sale of Land			2,50,000
Loan on Mortgage			5,60,000
Bank Overdraft			60,520
Issue of Shares			4,00,000
			17,29,280
Applications:			
Purchase of: Land and Freehold Buildings		3,51,000	
Machinery and Plant		4,82,000	
		8,33,000	
Investments		1,60,000	
Redemption of Debentures		4,00,000	
Payment of Dividends:	*Rs.*		
Final	78,000		
Interim	52,000	1,30,000	15,23,000
Working Capital on 31st March, 1996			2,06,280

* The real balance in Land and Freehold Buildings is Rs. 12,26,000, *i.e.*, Rs. 9,76,000 plus Rs. 2,50,000 credit for sale proceeds. Additional outlay is Rs. 3,51,000, *i.e.*, Rs. 12,26,000 less Rs. 8,75,000 *i.e.*, Rs. 9,00,000 less depreciation Rs. 25,000.

(2) Another very useful way to present the statement would be the following:

Funds Flow Statement for the year ended March 31,1996

Sources:	*Rs.*	*Rs.*
Working Capital on April 1, 1995		2,67,260
Inflow from Operations:		1,91,500
Financing Decisions:		
Loan of Mortgage	5,60,000	
Bank Overdraft	60,520	
Issue of Shares	4,00,000	
	10,20,520	
Less: Redemption of Debentures	4,00,000	6,20,520

	Rs.	Rs.	Rs.
Investment Decision:			
Investment in Fixed Assets:			
Land and Buildings	3,51,000		
Machinery and Plant	4,82,000	8,33,000	
Investments		1,60,000	
		9,93,000	
Less: Sale proceeds of land		2,50,000	– 7,43,000
Dividend Payments			– 1,30,000
Working Capital on March 31, 1996			2,06,280

The statement as presented above brings into bold relief the main features of the financial operations during the year as is the main objective of the Funds Flow Statement.

3. CASH BUDGET

Cash Flow Statements mostly portray how cash was received and spent in the past period. This is of only limited use as far as the coming periods are concerned. Most firms, therefore, prepare statements, on an estimated basis, showing how much cash is likely to be received during each of the next three or four months and what will be the demands to be met. The statement will show the likely cash balance at the end of each month. The firm can then decide whether the balance is just enough, whether there will be surplus cash to be temporarily invested or whether arrangements should be made for a bank overdraft, etc.

The technique for preparing the statement (called Cash Budget) is quite simple. For estimating receipts, one must know the percentage of sales that will be made for cash and the average period after which cash is collected from credit customers. Suppose, 20% sales are made for cash and on the balance two months credit is allowed to customers. If, in January, the sales are Rs. 80,000, Rs. 16,000 or 20% will be collected in January itself and the balance, Rs. 64,000, will be collected in March. In January, the collection from credit customers will be in respect of sales made in November. On the same basis, the timing of payments has to be determined. For each month, the amount to be paid will be determined — the payments should not only be the regular ones but also those which are not regular, *e.g.*, advance payment of tax, hire purchase instalments, dividend, etc.

Illustration 18:

Pearl Manufactures start manufacture on 1st April, 2010. The prime cost of a unit is expected to be Rs. 200, out of which Rs. 80 is for materials and Rs. 120 for labour. In addition, variable expenses per unit are expected to be Rs. 40 and fixed expenses per month will be Rs. 15 lakh. Payment for materials is to be made in the month following the purchase. One-third of sales will be for cash and the rest on credit to be settled in the following month. Expenses are payable in the month in which they are incurred.

The selling price is fixed at Rs. 400 per unit. The number of units manufactured and sold are expected to be as under:

April	9,000	July	21,000
May	12,000	August	21,000
June	18,000	September	24,000

Draw up a statement showing requirements of working capital from month to month, ignoring the question of stocks.

Solution:

Cash Budget

	April Rs. '000	May Rs. '000	June Rs. '000	July Rs. '000	August Rs. '000	September Rs. '000
Requirements:						
Wages	1,080	1,440	2,160	2,520	2,520	2,880
Materials	—	720	960	1,440	1,680	1,680
Expenses:						
Fixed	1,500	1,500	1,500	1,500	1,500	1,500
Variable	360	480	720	840	840	960
Total:	2,940	4,140	5,340	6,300	6,540	7,020
Receipts:						
Cash Sales	1,200	1,600	2,400	2,800	2,800	3,200
Collection from debtors	—	2,400	3,200	4,800	5,600	5,600
Total:	1,200	4,000	5,600	7,600	8,400	8,800
Cash required	1,740	140	—	—	—	—
Surplus	—	—	260	1,300	1,860	1,780
Cumulative requirement	1,740	1,880	1,620	320	—	—
Surplus	—	—	—	—	1,540	3,320

Illustration 19:

Bittoo Ltd. wants you to prepare the cash budget of the company for the three months, April to June, 2010. You are given the following information:

(1) "Operation":

2000	*Sales Rs. '000*	*Purchases Rs. '000*	*Wages Rs. '000*	*Other Rs. '000*
April	600	200	150	100
May	500	200	150	100
June	800	400	150	150
July	1,000	500	250	200
August	1,400	700	250	200
September	1,600	600	300	200

(2) Sales are 20% cash and the balance at two months credit; purchases are at one month's credit subject to a cash discount of 5%.

(3) Wages are paid 1/2 month in arrear and other expenses are paid one month in arrear.

(4) During August, the company pays a dividend of 10% on its equity capital of Rs. 2,000 thousand and during September deferred payment instalment (quarterly) of Rs. 250 thousand will fall due. The company paid corporate dividend tax @ 15% on the dividend paid.

(5) It is expected that at the end of June, 2000 there will be cash balance of Rs. 140 thousand.

Prepare the cash budget as requested.

Solution:

Cash Budget of Bittoo Ltd. for the Quarter ending June 30, 2010

Receipts:	*July Rs. '000*	*August Rs. '000*	*Septemter Rs. '000*
Opening Cash Balance	140	10	—225
Cash Sales	200	280	320
Collection from Debtors	400	640	800
Total	740	930	895

	July Rs. '000	August Rs. '000	September Rs. '000
Receipts:			
Payments:			
Payment to Creditors	380	475	665
Wages	200	250	275
Other Expenses	150	200	200
Payment of Dividend	—	200	—
Corporate Dividend Tax paid	—	30	—
Deferred Payment Installment	—	—	250
Total	730	1,155	1,390
Closing Balance	10	— 225	— 495

Working Notes:

(1) Cash collected from Debtors will be for 80% of sales made two months previously. For example in July the credit sale made in May (80% of Rs. 500 thousand) will be collected.

(2) Payment to creditors is for the previous month's purchases less 5%. For instance in July the payment is for purchases in June Rs. 400 thousand less 5%.

(3) Payment in respect of wages is 1/2 for the current month and 1/2 for the previous month. In September it is Rs. 150 thousand for wages relating to September and Rs. 125 thousand for wages relating to August.

4. WORKING CAPITAL

Working capital is that part of a firm's capital which is required to hold current assets of the firm. Examples of current assets are raw material, semi-finished goods, finished goods, debtors, bills receivable, prepaid expenses, cash at bank and cash in hand. The firm requires cash to pay various expenses like wages, salaries, rent, advertising etc. current assets have a short life span. They are swiftly transformed into other current-asset forms and ultimately in cash. In other words, funds invested in current assets are constantly converted into cash. This cash again flows out in exchange for other current assets. There is an operating cycle. Cash is used to buy raw material. Various manufacturing expenses are incurred to convert raw material into semi-finished goods and then into finished goods. On sale of finished goods on credit, trade debtors or bills receivable result. On receipt of payment, trade debtors and bills receivable are converted into cash and a cycle of working capital is completed. In case of cash sales, finished goods will directly be converted into cash. The cash is once again used to buy raw material to start another cycle. It can be shown by means of the following diagram:—

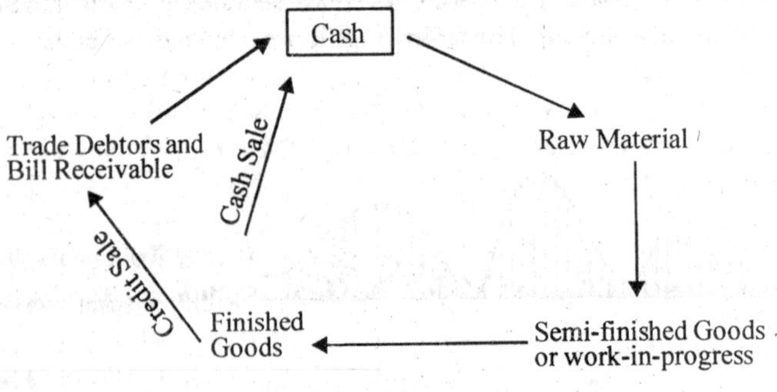

Working Capital Cycle

As current assets keep circulating or revolving fast, working capital is also called circulating capital, revolving capital or short-term capital.

Concepts of Working Capital. There are two concepts of working capital namely gross working capital and net working capital.

(*i*) **Gross Working Capital**. It is also called simply 'working capital'. It refers to the total of all the current assets of the firm. Current assets are the assets which are meant to be converted into cash within a year or an operating cycle. Stock of raw materials, stock of semi-finished goods, stock of finished goods, trade debtors, bills receivable, prepaid expenses, cash at bank and cash in hand are examples of current assets.

(*ii*) **Net Working Capital**. For financing current assets, long-term funds as well as short term funds are used. Short-term funds are provided by current liabilities i.e. claims of outsiders which are expected to mature for payment within a year. Trade creditors, bills payable and outstanding expenses are examples of current liabilities. Net working capital refers to the excess of current assets over current liabilities. Suppose, the total current assets and total current liabilities of a firm amount to Rs. 90,000 and Rs. 40,000 respectively. Then, gross working capital of the firm is Rs. 90,000 while net working capital of the firm is Rs. 50,000 and this sum of Rs. 50,000 will be financed by long-term funds. Thus, net working capital is that part of the working capital which is financed by long-term funds.

Generally, current assets far exceed current liabilities. It is considered ideal that current asset are twice as much as current liabilities. Even in unfavourable situations, current assets are likely to be more than current liabilities. In a very rare case, current liabilities may be more than current assets. It means that there is a negative net working capital. It is a very serious situation indicating that short-term funds are being used to meet a part of the long-term capital requirements.

Permanent and Temporary Working Capital. From the point of view of the period for which capital is required, working capital can be divided into two categories namely permanent working capital and temporary working capital.

(*i*) **Permanent Working Capital**. It refers to that minimum amount of investment in current assets that has always to be true. It is the working capital required to carry out the minimum level of activities of the business. It is also called core working capital, regular working capital or fixed working capital.

(*ii*) **Temporary Working Capital**. It refers to that part of total working capital which is required by a firm over and above its permanent working capital. It is required because the actual level of activities of the business most of the time exceeds the minimum level of activities. As the level of business activities fluctuates, the volume of temporary working capital also may keep fluctuating. Temporary working capital is also known as flunctuating or variable or circulating working capital.

The management has to provide for both kinds of working capital—permanent working capital and temporary working capital. But the period for which temporary working capital is required is rather short and the amount is also fluctuating whereas the amount of permanent working capital is stable and it is permanently needed. The following figure shows these facts:—

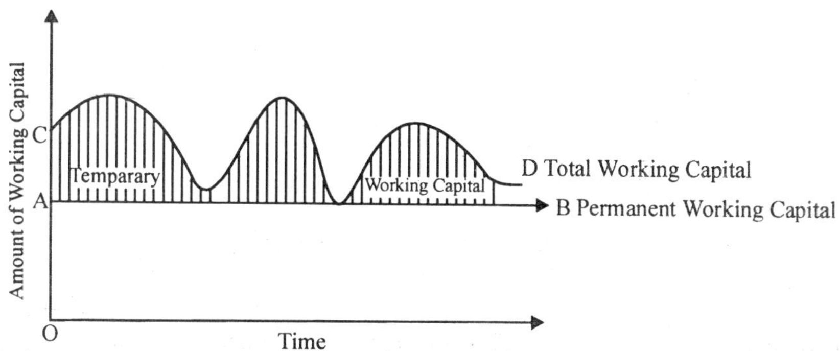

OA is the amount of permanent working capital. Straight line AB shows that the amount remains the same over a period of time. Curve CD shows the total working capital requirement which varies from time to time because temporary working capital goes on changing. Requirement over and above the permanent working capital requirement is the temporary working capital requirement and has been marked as such in the figure.

It should be noted that as the business of a firm grows, the amount of its permanent working capital will also increase. Thus for a growing business firm, the difference between permanent working capital and temporary working capital may appear as follows:—

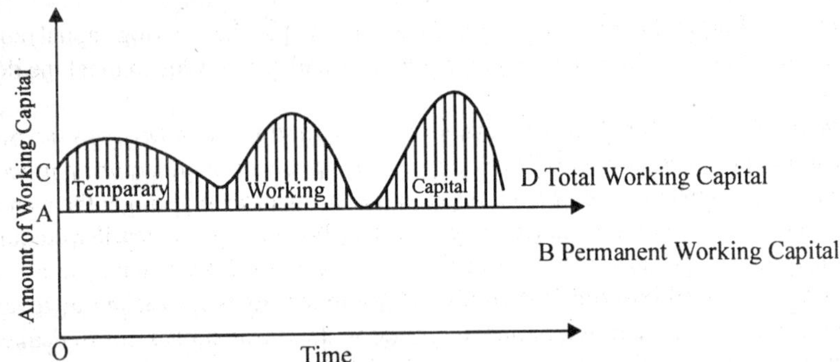

Working Capital to be Adequate but Not Excessive. The management is to ensure that the firm has adequate working capital to run its business operations smoothly. Inadequate working capital results in inefficiency and consequently decreased profitability. The following are the disadvantages of inadequate working capital:—

(*i*) It renders the firm unable to avail itself of attractive discounts from suppliers.

(*ii*) As the firm is found unable to honour its short-term obligations in time, it loses some of its creditworthiness. As a result it faces tight credit terms.

(*iii*) The firm finds it difficult to grow, profitable projects are not undertaken due to paucity of working capital.

(*iv*) Fixed assets are not fully and efficiently utilised because of inadequacy of working capital. It decreases firm's profitability.

(*v*) Operating inefficiencies creep in. There may be interruptions in production. The result is that the profit targets are not met.

But excessive working capital has also to be avoided. Excessive working capital means idle funds earning no profits for the firm. It also lowers profitability. The following are the disadvantages of excessive working capital:—

(*i*) It may mean unnecessary accumulation of inventories which increases the chances of inventory mishandling, waste, theft and accumulation of old items which are ultimately disposed of at low prices or just discarded.

(*ii*) It may be an indication of excessively liberal credit policy and slack collection from customers resulting in higher incidence of bad debts.

(*iii*) Excessive working capital makes management complacent ultimately resulting in managerial inefficiency.

(*iv*) It may also lead to speculative transactions.

Factors Determining Working Capital Requirements. There are a number of factors which determine the working capital requirements of a firm. These factors are of different importance. The influence of an individual factor may also change for a firm over time. An analysis of the relevant factors has to be made in order to determine total investment in working capital. The following is a brief description of important factors which determine the working capital requirements of a firm:—

Nature of Business. The working capital requirements are significantly influenced by the nature of the business carried on by the firm. Public utility undertakings like road-transport corporations or electricity supply undertakings need very small working capital because they offer services rather than products and offer mostly cash sales with the result that very small amount of capital remains invested in inventory and receivables. In manufacturing enterprises, the working capital requirements are fairly large. The requirements differ from industry to industry. For example, the working capital requirements of an edible oil mill or a building construction company will be more that those of an iron and steel mill. The working capital requirements of trading and financial enterprises are the maximum as they have to maintain a sufficiently large amount of cash, inventories and receivables.

Size of Business. Larger the size of business, the greater will be the working capital requirements of the firm as more funds will be looked up in inventories and receivables to meet the demands of bigger size of business.

Manufacturing Cycle. Manufacturing cycle refers to the time-span between the purchase of raw-materials and their conversion into finished goods by means of manufacturing process. Funds remain tied up in semi-finished goods during the manufacturing process. Longer the manufacturing cycle the larger the working capital needed and *vice versa*. For example, a distillery requires heavy investment in inventories because it has an ageing process. On the other hand, in a bakery, raw materials are soon converted into finished goods and not much funds are looked up inventories.

Production Policy. In certain industries, there are wide seasonal changes in demand for the product manufactured by the firm. In such a case, if the firm adopts a steady production policy, inventories of finished goods will accumulate during the off-season periods requiring a higher amount of working capital. If the firm opts to vary its production schedules in accordance with changing demand, there may be serious production problems. During the slack season, the firm will have to maintain its working force and fixed assets without adequate production and sale. During the peak period, it will have to operate at full capacity. This arrangement may be a costly affair. One namely is to manufacture some other product during the off-season and concentrate on the main line during the season of the main product. But it may not be feasible in all the cases.

Business Cycles. There are business cycles resulting in marked variations in business conditions. There is an upward swing of business conditions leading to a boom when the business activities are at their peak. It is followed by a downward phase called recession when business activities decline. The downward phase ends in a depression, completing the business cycle. Then again, there is a recovery to start a new business cycle. During the recovery, the working capital requirements increase while during the stock period, the working capital requirements decrease.

Conditions of Supply of Raw Material. In an industry where raw material is available only in a particular season and the firm has to buy raw material in bulk in that reason to enoure uninterempted production of finished goods, the working capital requirements will be more. When in cases where the supply of raw material is unpredictable, the firm may have to accumulate stock of raw material requiring more working capital.

Terms of Credit to Customers. The terms of credit granted to customers normally depend upon the norms followed in the industry in which the firm is engages. But the firm has some flexibility within the norms. Ideally, the firm should be use discretion in granting credit to its customers. Different terms of credit should be offered to different types of customers. A liberal credit policy without caring much for the creditworthiness of the customers will land the firm in trouble and the requirements of working capital will also unnecessarily increase.

Credit from Suppliers. If the firm is able to procure liberal terms of credit from suppliers of raw material, its net working capital requirements will be reduced.

Stock Turnover Ratio. Stock turnover ratio refers to the speed with which finished goods are converted into sales. If a firm has a high stock turnover ratio as in the case of a bakery, its working capital requirements will be less. On the other hand, if a firm has a low stock turnover ratio as in the case of fancy jewellery shop, its working capital requirements will be high.

Price Level Changes. Price level changes also affect the working capital requirements. In times of rising prices, a firm will require a larger amount of working capital to maintain the same quantity of inventory and credit sales. But the effect will be different for different firms. If the firm increases the price of its products promptly, the requirements of working capital will not be high.

Income Tax. Out of the profits, income tax has to be paid. Mostly, advance payment of income-tax has to be made on the estimated income of the current year. The management has no discretion in the matter. If level of income-tax is increased by the government, the working capital requirement will increase.

Operating Efficiency. The working capital requirement can be reduced by management by means of operating efficiency. Management can ensure the efficient utilisation of resources by minimising wastages, improving coordinations and accelerating the pace of cash cycle.

Estimating Working Capital Requirements

Working capital means the difference between current assets and current liabilities. At any time, therefore, the working capital required may be estimated by:

(*i*) totalling current assets (excluding cash) that have to be maintained for efficient operations;

(*ii*) adding to it the cash balance that has to be maintained to take advantage of any profitable opportunity that may arise as well as to see that there is no hindrance in day-to-day operations. The cash budget illustrated earlier in this chapter is an exercise in estimating requirements of cash on account of the day to day operations. For instance, in the illustration given there, in August an additional sum of Rs. 3,25,000 will be required; and

(*iii*) deducting therefrom the amounts due to suppliers of goods and services (expenses outstanding).

Care must be taken to make all calculations in terms of "cash" costs. For estimating working capital requirements, sale value should not be considered. To the calculations thus made, a margin for safety may be added. This margin should in any case include the payment to be made for administrative and selling expenses during the period commencing from commencement of production and realisation of sale proceeds. Suppose, the production cycle is one month, finished goods are carried in stock on the average for one month and credit period allowed to customers is also one month. In that case, administrative and selling expenses, not included in cost as such, for 3 months should be capable of being met out of the cash balance.

Illustration 20:

R & V Ltd. gives you the following abridged Profit and Loss Account:

	Rs.		*Rs.*
To Materials Consumed	14,00,000	By Sales	24,00,000
To Wages	2,10,000		
To Manufacturing Expenses (Including depreciation, Rs. 72,000)	2,70,000		
To Office & Administrative Expenses	1,80,000		
To Selling Expenses	1,20,000		
To Advertisement & Sales Promotion Expenses	90,000		
To Provision for Income Tax	52,000		
To Net Profit	78,000		
	24,00,000		24,00,000

It is the company's policy to extend two months' credit to customers and maintain the undermentioned stocks:

Finished Goods	One month's sale
Materials	1½ months' consumption

Work in progress is equal to 1½ months' production in terms of materials and ½ months' wages and manufacturing expenses.

The company receives three months' credit from suppliers and pays all expenses and wages one month in arrear except that advertisement and sales promotion expenses are paid two months in advance. Income-tax is payable in advance in three instalments of 20% and 50% of the estimated tax payable in the 6th, 9th and 12th month of the accounting year.

The company would like to maintain Rs. 90,000 in cash always to cover expenses not included in cost of finished goods and work in progress. A safety margin of 10% on total current assets in desirable.

Estimate the requirements of working capital for the company.

Solution:

Current assets to the maintained in terms of cash cost:	*Rs.*	*Rs.*
Stock of: Finished goods	1,50,500	
Materials	1,75,000	
Work-in-progress	1,92,000	5,17,500
Sundry debtors		3,01,500
Advance payment of advertising, etc.		15,000
Cash balance		90,000
		9,24,000
Add: 10%		92,400
		10,16,400
Less: Due to creditors	3,50,000	
Expenses outstanding	59,000	4,09,000
Estimated requirement of working capital		6,07,400

Working Notes:

(1) The cash cost of the sales is:

	Rs.
Materials used	14,00,000
Wages	2,10,000
Manufacturing expenses *less* depreciation	1,98,000
	18,08,000

(2) Sales outstanding against debtors will be Rs. 4,00,000, *i.e.*, 24,00,000 × 2/12 but the cash costs incurred will be Rs. 18,08,000 × 2/12 or Rs. 3,01,333 or say Rs. 3,01,500.

(3) Similarly the cash cost incurred for one month's production for finished goods stock will be Rs. 1,50,667 or say Rs. 1,50,000.

(4) The stock of materials will be Rs. 14,00,000 × 1 1/1/12 or Rs. 1,75,000.

(5) Work-in-progress will be:

Material	1,75,000
Watges + Manufacturing Expenses (cash), for 1/2 month, *i.e.*, $\frac{2,10,000+1,98,000}{12 \times 2}$	17,000
	1,92,000

(6) Total cash expenses incurred are:

Wages	2,10,000
Manufacturing expenses	1,98,000
Office expenses	1,80,000
Selling expenses	1,20,000
	7,08,000
Outstanding @ 1/12	59,000

(7) No treatment for income-tax is necessary, since payment will relate to the current year.

EXERCISE XXIII

Practical

1. Classify the following into cash flows from (*a*) operating activities, (*b*) investing activities and (*c*) financing activities:

(*i*) Cash sales of goods-in-trade,
(*ii*) Cash paid to suppliers of raw materials,
(*iii*) Cash payments of salaries and wages to employees,
(*iv*) Cash payment to acquire a fixed asset, say, machinery,
(*v*) Cash proceeds from issuing shares at a premium,
(*vi*) Payment of dividends,
(*vii*) Interest received on investments,
(*viii*) Interest paid on debentures,
(*ix*) Dividends received on shares of other companies held as investments,
(*x*) Cash repayment of a long-term loan,
(*xi*) Payment of income tax.

[*Cash flows from operating activities,* (*i*), (*ii*), (*iii*) *and* (*xi*); *cash flows from investing activities,* (*iv*), (*vii*) *and* (*ix*); *cash flows from financing activities,* (*v*), (*vi*), (*viii*) *and* (*x*)].

2. From the following particulars, prepare a cash flow statement for the year ended 31st March, 2010:

(*i*) Total sales for the year were Rs. 98,49,000 out of which cash sales totalled Rs. 65,86,000.
(*ii*) Cash collections from credit customers during the year amounted to Rs. 33,23,400.
(*iii*) Cash paid to suppliers and employees was Rs. 79,36,810.
(*iv*) Rs. 9,20,000 were paid by way of income tax.
(*v*) Fully paid debentures of the face-value of Rs. 3,00,000 were redeemed at a premium of 2%. Interest on debentures, Rs. 84,000 was also paid.
(*vi*) Furniture of the book value of Rs. 18,500 was disposed of for Rs. 11,100 and new furniture costing Rs. 83,160 was purchased.
(*vii*) Dividends, Rs. 4,50,000 for the year ended 31st March, 2009 were distributed in August, 2009. Corporate dividend tax @ 15% was also paid.
(*viii*) On 31st March, 2010 cash in hand and at bank totalled Rs. 1,80,000.

(*Net increase in cash and cash equivalents, Rs. 73,030, Cash and cash equivalents as at 31st March, 2009, Rs. 1,06,970*).

3. The following data have been extracted from *P* Ltd.'s books of account for the year ended 31st March 2010:

(*i*) Net profit before income tax, Rs. 21,90,700 taking into account the following items also:
  (*a*) Depreciation on fixed assets, Rs. 5,76,000;
  (*b*) Discount on issue of debentures written off, Rs. 40,000;
  (*c*) Interest on debentures paid, Rs. 3,60,000;
  (*d*) Profit on sale of investments, Rs. 11,000;
  (*e*) Interest received on investments, Rs. 50,000; and
  (*f*) Compensation received in a lawsuit, Rs. 80,000.
(*ii*) Income tax paid during the year, Rs. 9,80,000.
(*iii*) Book value of investments sold, Rs. 2,45,000.
(*iv*) Preference shares of Rs. 15,00,000 were redeemed at a premium of 5% after issuing equity shares of Rs. 5,00,000 at a premium of 20%.
(*v*) Dividends paid for the year 2008-09, Rs. 6,00,000. Interim dividends paid for 1997-98, Rs. 2,00,000. Corporate dividend tax @ 15% was also paid.
(*vi*) Land was purchased for Rs. 4,80,000 for which payment was made in the form of 40,000 equity shares of Rs. 10 each issued at a premium of 20%.
(*vii*) Different current assets and current liabilities in the beginning and at the end of the year:

		As on 31st March, 1997 *Rs.*	*As on 31st March, 1998* *Rs.*
Stock		12,43,000	13,61,000
Debtors		2,08,500	2,14,600
Cash in hand	19,000	25,300	
Cash at Bank		1,87,000	?
Bills receivable		70,000	60,000
Bills payable	55,000	50,000	
Creditors		1,67,100	1,72,400
Outstanding expenses		76,400	83,200

Prepare cash flow statement for the year ended 31st March, 2010

(Net increase in cash and cash equivalents Rs. 69,700; cash and cash equivalents on 31st March, 2010, Rs. 2,75,700).

4. Dee Ltd. provides the following data to you:

Profit and Loss Account for the year ended 31st March, 2010

	Rs.
Sales	43,37,200
Cost of Good Sold	(34,21,200)
Gross Profit	9,16,000
Sundry Operating Expenses	(3,17,500)
Depreciation on Land and Buildings	(45,000)
Depreciation on Furniture, Fixtures & Fittings	(8,500)
Loss on Disposal of Furniture	(2,000)
Preliminary Expenses, amortized	(7,000)
Net profit before Income Tax	5,36,000
Provision for Income Tax	(2,68,000)
Net Profit after Income Tax	2,68,000
Provision for Income Tax (2008-09)	(2,000)
Interim Dividend	(55,000)
Proposed Dividend and Corporate Dividend Tax thereon	(1,10,000)
Transfer to General Reserve	(1,01,000)
	Nil

Balance Sheets

		As on 31.3.2009 *Rs.*	*As on 31.3.2010* *Rs.*
Land and Buildings		8,00,000	8,55,000
Furniture, Fixtures and Fittings		90,000	76,500
Stock		5,32,500	5,96,300
Debtors		1,87,300	1,84,200
Cash in hand		18,200	13,400
Cash at Bank		1,15,200	1,62,000
Bills Receivable		30,000	50,000
Advance Payment of Income Tax		2,55,000	2,70,000
Preliminary Expenses		21,000	14,000
		20,49,200	22,21,400
Equity Share Capital		10,00,000	11,00,000
Securities Premium		—	30,000
General Reserve		4,00,000	5,01,000
Bills Payable	60,000	20,000	

	Rs.	Rs.
Creditors	2,07,200	1,57,400
Outstanding Expenses	30,000	35,000
Provision for Income Tax	2,52,000	2,68,000
Proposed Dividend and Corporate Dividend Tax thereon	1,00,000	1,10,000
	20,49,200	22,21,400

Additional information:

(*i*) Liability for income tax for the accounting year 2008-09 was fixed at Rs. 2,54,000 and hence a refund of Rs. 1,000 was received out of advance tax paid for that year.

(*ii*) book value of furniture sold during the year was Rs. 5,000.

You are required to prepare a cash flow statement using (*i*) the direct method and (*ii*) the indirect method.

(Net cash from operating activities, Rs. 1,64,000; net cash used in investing activities, Rs. 97,000; net cash used in financing activities, Rs. 25,000; and net increase in cash and cash equivalents, Rs. 42,000).

5. Privileges Ltd's summerised balance sheets as at 31.3.2009 and 31.3.2010 are given below:

Liabilities		*31.3.2009*	*31.3.2010*
		Rs.	*Rs.*
Equity Share Capital		5,00,000	12,00,000
Securities Premium		—	3,50,000
General Reserve		2,80,000	3,30,000
Profit & Loss Account		60,000	59,750
13% Convertible Debentures		3,00,000	—
Bills Payable	50,000	30,000	
Sundry Creditors		1,90,000	1,95,000
Provision for Taxation		1,32,000	1,51,400
Proposed Dividend		70,000	99,000
Provision for Corporate Dividend Tax		10,500	14,850
		15,92,500	24,30,000

Assets		
Plant and Machinery	7,00,000	9,00,000
Furniture and Fixtures	90,000	81,000
Stock	4,25,000	6,19,000
Debtors	1,20,000	2,30,000
Cash at Bank	2,52,500	5,80,000
Share Issue Expenses	—	20,000
Cost of Issue of Debentures	5,000	—
	15,92,500	24,30,000

The following additional information is provided to you:

(*i*) On 1st April, 2009 13% Convertible Debentures of the face value of Rs. 3,00,000 were converted into 20,000 equity shares of Rs. 10 each issued at a premium of Rs. 5 each.

(*ii*) Plant was purchased during the year for Rs. 3,00,000; half of the consideration was discharged by issue to the vendor 10,000 equity shares of Rs. 10 each at a premium of Rs. 5 each while the balance was paid in cash.

(*iii*) Tax liability for the accounting year 2008-09, Rs. 1,32,000 was discharged in May, 2009.

(*iv*) Proposed dividend and corporate dividend tax thereon for 2008-09 was paid in August, 2009. You are required to prepare a cash flow statement for the year ended 31st March, 2010.

(Net cash used in operating activities, Rs. 22,000; net cash used in investing activities, Rs. 1,50,000; and net cash from financing activities, Rs. 4,99,500).

6. Progressive Ltd. presents you the following balance sheet as on March 31, 2009 and 2010.

Liabilities	*As on March 31, 2009* Rs.	*As on March 31, 2010* Rs.
Equity Share Capital	5,00,000	6,00,000
14% Redeemable Preference Share Capital	2,00,000	—
Capital Redemption Reserve Amount	—	1,00,000
Securities Premium	50,000	50,000
General Reserve	1,00,000	1,30,000
Profit & Loss Account	1,40,000	2,63,75
Provision for Depreciation	1,80,000	2,30,000
Sundry Creditors	1,40,000	1,80,000
Provision for Taxation	70,000	90,000
Proposed Dividend (on Equity Shares)	50,000	60,000
Provision for Corporate Dividend Tax	7,500	9,000
	14,37,500	17,12,975
Assets		
Fixed Assets	8,50,000	10,40,000
Investments	1,00,000	80,000
Cash in hand and at Bank	97,500	1,52,975
Other Current Assets	3,50,000	4,10,000
Preliminary Expenses	40,000	30,000
	14,37,500	17,12,975

During 2009-2010, the proposed dividend was paid in addition to the preference dividend up to 30th September, 2009 on which date the preference shares were redeemed at a premium of 5%. The premium has been provided out of Securities Premium Account. Tax liability in respect of 2008-09 came to Rs. 55,000; the balance in the Provision for Taxation as on 31st March, 2009, was transferred to General Reserve.

During the year, a fixed asset costing Rs. 30,000 (depreciation provided for Rs. 16,000) was sold for Rs. 10,000. Investments costing Rs. 20,000 were realised at Rs. 16,000. Interest on investments received during the year amounted to Rs. 10,000. There was no accrued interest either at the beginning or at the end of the year. These matters have been adjusted in the Profit and Loss Account.

Prepare a cash flow statement for the year ended 31st March, 2010. The rate of corporate dividend tax is 15%.

(*Net cash provided by operating activities, Rs. 4,13,075; net cash used in investing activities, Rs. 1,84,000; net cash used in financing activities, Rs. 1,73,600*).

7. Wee Ltd. had the following figures as on 1st April, 2009:—

	Rs.
Fixed Assets — Cost	6,00,000
Less: Depreciation	2,10,000
	3,90,000
Bank Balance	35,000
Current Assets, Other than Bank Balance	2,50,000
Current Liabilities	1,00,000
Capital (Shares of Rs. 10 each)	4,00,000

The company made the following estimates for 2009-2010:

(*i*) The profit would be Rs. 58,000 after depreciation of Rs. 60,000.

(*ii*) The company will acquire fixed assets costing Rs. 1,00,000 after selling one machine for Rs. 20,000 costing Rs. 50,000 and on which depreciation provided will amount to Rs. 35,000.

(*iii*) Current assets and current liabilities, other than bank balance, at the end of March, 2010 are expected to be Rs. 2,95,000 and Rs. 1,30,000 respectively.

(*iv*) The company will pay a dividend @ 10% and corporate dividend tax thereon @ 15%.

At the end of the accounting year, the company sends all the cash in hand to the bank.

Prepare a cash flow statement for the year ended 31st March, 2010 and estimate the bank balance or overdraft as on that date.

(Net cash provided by operating activities Rs. 98,000; net cash used in investing activities Rs. 80,000; net cash used in financing activities Rs. 46,000 bank balance as on 31st March, 2010 Rs. 7,000).

8. The following are the final accounts of Gen. Ltd. for the year ended 31st March, 2010.

Profit and Loss Account for the year ended 31st March, 2010

	Rs. in lakhs
Sale	149.72
Interest on investments	0.28
	150.00
Raw materials consumed	(59.31)
Sundry operating expenses	(53.00)
Interest on debentures	(1.80)
Loss on sale of investments	(0.10)
Depreciation on plant and machinery	(8.25)
Depreciation on furniture and fittings	(1.50)
Cost of issue of debentures (amortized)	(0.08)
Net profit before income tax	25.96
Provision for income tax	12.98
Net profit after income tax	12.98
Balance of account on 31.3.2009 b/fd	1.05
	14.03
Appropriations:	
Preference dividend paid	(0.70)
Capital redemption reserve	(3.00)
Debenture redemption reserve	(1.50)
General reserve	(1.25)
Proposed dividends and provision for corporate dividend tax thereon	(6,16)
Balance carried to balance sheet	1.42

Balance Sheet as at 31st March, 2010

	As on 31.3.2010 (Rs. in lakhs)	*As on 31.3.2009 (Rs. in lakhs)*
Equity share capital	42.00	35.00
14% preference share capital	—	10.00
Capital redemption reserve	3.00	—
Securities premium	1.40	—
Debenture redemption reserve	7.50	6.00
General reserve	23.35	22.10
Profit and loss account	1.42	1.05
12% debentures	15.00	15.00
Creditors for goods and operating expenses	13.97	12.82
Provision for income tax	12.98	12.00
Proposed dividends	6.16	6.65
	126.78	120.62

	(Rs. in lakhs)	*(Rs. in lakhs)*
Plant and machinery	51.75	50.00
Furniture and fittings	13.50	15.00
Investments	—	5.00
Stock	28.14	22.75
Debtors	16.04	13.76
Cash in hand and at bank	4.35	2.03
Advance payment of income tax	13.00	12.00
Cost of issue of debentures	—	0.08
	126.78	120.62

The following additional information is provided to you:

(*i*) During the year, all the preference shares were redeemed at par. For the purpose, fully paid equity shares of the nominal value of Rs. 7 lakh were issued at a premium of 20% to the existing equity shareholder on rights basis. At the time of redemption of preference shares, preference dividend for six months till 30th September, 2009 was also paid.

(*ii*) Proposed dividends for the year 2008-09 and corporate dividend tax thereon were paid in July, 2009.

(*iii*) Income tax liability for the accounting year 2008-09 was settled at Rs. 12 lakh.

(*iv*) Interest on debentures is paid every six months on 30th September and 31st March.

(*v*) New machinery was acquired by the company on 1st October, 2009.

You are required to prepared cash flow statement for the year ended 31st March, 2010 using (*i*) the direct method and (*ii*) the indirect method. Ignore corporation dividend tax.

(*Net cash provided by operating activities, Rs. 17.89 lakh; net cash used in investing activities, Rs. 4.82 lakh; net cash used in financing activities, Rs. 10.75 lakh and net increase in cash and cash equivalents, Rs. 2.32 lakh*).

9. State which of the following items indicate:

(*i*) Source of fund (*ii*) use of fund (*iii*) neither source nor use of fund:

(*a*) Cash collected from debtors Rs. 9,000;

(*b*) Bill receivable amounting to Rs. 5,000 from Joy, a customer has been dishonoured;

(*c*) Conversion of 12% convertible debentures of Rs. 7,50,000 into equity shares of the face value of Rs. 5,00,000 at a premium of 50%.

(*d*) Purchase of machinery amounting to Rs. 3,30,000 from Esskay Ltd. The vendor is allotted 30,000 equity shares of Rs. 10 each at a premium of Re. 1 per share;

(*e*) Recovery of Rs. 1,000 from Zed previously written off a bad debt.

(*f*) Purchase of machinery from Excellent Machinery Mart on credit for Rs. 80,000.

[*Source*: (*e*); *Use* (*f*); *Neither Source nor Use*; (*a*); (*b*); (*c*) and (*d*)]

10. The net profit after providing for income tax Rs. 3,30,000 of Moon Ltd. for the year ending 31st March, 1996 amounts to Rs. 4,00,000. The figure of the net profits has been arrived at after taking into account the following items:

	Rs.	*Rs.*
(*a*) Depreciation provided on:		
Plant and Machinery	30,000	
Furniture and Fixtures	15,000	
Motor Vans	20,000	65,000
(*b*) Preliminary Expenses written off		3,000
(*c*) Bad debts		1,000
(*d*) Loss on sale of furniture		1,500
(*e*) Discount allowed to customers		19,000
(*f*) Discount of Issue of Debentures written off		4,000
(*g*) Profit on sale of long-term investments		5,000
(*h*) Discount received from trade creditors		14,000

Calculate Funds from Operations.

(*Rs. 4,68,500*)

11. Calculate 'Funds from Operations' of Jaypee Ltd. from the following details:

Profit and Loss Account

	Rs.	Rs.		Rs.
To Salaries	1,10,000		By Gross Profit b/fd	9,62,500
Add: Outstanding Salaries	10,000	1,20,000	By Discount Received from Suppliers	6,000
To Rent, Rates & Taxes		60,000	By Profit on sale of Land	70,000
To Insurance	40,000			
Less: Prepaid Insurance	5,000	35,000		
To Printing & Stationary	24,000			
Less: amount paid for last year	3,000	21,000		
To Directors' Fees		15,000		
To Debenture Interest		42,000		
To Provision for Bad Debts		17,000		
To Provision for Discount on Debtors		5,500		
To Depreciation:				
Plant & Machinery	30,000			
Furniture	6,000	36,000		
To Cost of Issue of Shares written off		11,000		
To Preliminary Expenses written off		8,000		
To Provision for Income tax		3,10,000		
To General Reserve		80,000		
To Proposed Dividends:				
Preference		28,000		
Equity		50,000		
To Provision for Corporate Dividend Tax		7,800		
To Balance of Profit		1,92,200		
		10,38,500		10,38,500

(*Rs. 3,43,000*)

12. The following are the summarised Balance Sheets of XYZ Ltd., as on 31st March, 1995 and 1996.

	1995 Rs.	1996 Rs.		1995 Rs.	1996 Rs.
Share Capital:			Fixed Assets, cost	41,000	40,000
14% Redeemable Preference Shares	—	10,000	*Less*: Depreciation	11,000	15,000
Equity Shares	40,000	40,000		30,000	25,000
	40,000	50,000	Current Assets:		
General Reserve	2,000	2,000	Debtors	20,000	24,000
Profit & Loss Account	1,000	1,200	Stock	30,000	35,000
Debentures	6,000	7,000	Cash	1,200	3,500
Current Liabilities:			Prepaid Expenses	300	500
Creditors	12,000	11,000			
Provision for Taxation	3,000	4,200			
Proposed Dividends	5,000	5,800			
Bank Overdraft	12,500	6,800			
	81,500	88,000		81,500	88,000

You are required to prepare: (*i*) statement showing changes in the working capital, and (*ii*) a statement of sources and applications of funds. [*Adapted B. Com. (Hons.) Delhi*]

(*Funds from Operations Rs. 10,000; Increase in Working Capital Rs. 17,000; Total of Funds Flow Statement Rs. 22,000. Provision for taxation has been treated as a current liability*)

13. From the following information, prepare a Statement Showing Changes in Working Capital and a Funds Flow Statement for the year ended 31st March, 1996:

Balance Sheet of Asian Steels Ltd.

Liabilities	*As on 31.3.1996 Rs.*	*As on 31.3.1995 Rs.*
Equity Share Capital	9,00,000	6,00,000
13% Preference Share Capital	—	2,00,000
Profit and Loss Account	1,10,000	75,000
12% Debentures	2,50,000	3,00,000
Bank Loan	75,000	1,00,000
Bills Payable	45,000	40,000
Trade Creditors	1,50,000	1,15,000
Outstanding Expenses	18,000	19,000
Provision for Taxation	95,000	85,000
	16,43,000	15,34,000
Assets		
Furniture and Fittings	1,17,000	1,30,000
Motor Vans	1,54,000	80,000
Long-term Investments	3,00,000	2,60,000
Stock	8,29,000	8,00,000
Debtors	90,000	1,09,000
Cash at Bank	1,43,000	1,40,000
Preliminary Expenses	10,000	15,000
	16,43,000	15,34,000

(Funds from Operations Rs. 53,000; Decrease in Working Capital Rs. 36,000; Total of Funds Flow Statement Rs. 3,89,000; Provision for Taxation has been treated as a current liability).

14. From the following balance sheets of A Ltd. make out (*i*) Statement of changes in the working capital and (*ii*) Funds flow statement.

Liabilities	*31.3.1995 Rs.*	*31.3.1996 Rs.*	*Asset*	*31.3.1995 Rs.*	*31.3.1996 Rs.*
Equity Share Capital	3,00,000	4,00,000	Goodwill	1,15,000	90,000
14% Redeembable			Land and Buildings	2,00,000	1,70,000
Preference Share Capital	1,50,000	1,00,000	Plant	80,000	2,00,000
General Reserve	40,000	70,000	Debtors	1,60,000	2,00,000
Profit and Loss Account	30,000	48,000	Stocks	77,000	1,09,000
Proposed Dividend	42,000	50,000	Bills Receivable	20,000	30,000
Creditors	55,000	83,000	Cash in hand	15,000	10,000
Bills Payable	20,000	16,000	Cash at Bank	10,000	8,000
Provision for Taxation	40,000	50,000			
	6,77,000	8,17,000		6,77,000	8,17,000

Additional information: (*i*) Depreciation of Rs. 10,000 and Rs. 20,000 has been charged on plant and land and buildings respectively in 1995-96, (*ii*) An interim dividend of Rs. 20,000 has been paid in 1995-96, (*iii*) Income-tax Rs. 35,000 has been paid during the year 1995-96.

[*Adapted B. Com. (Hones.) Delhi*]

[*Funds from operations Rs. 1,73,000; Increase in Working Capital Rs. 41,000; Total of Funds Flow Statement Rs. 2,83,000 if provision for taxation is treated as a current liability. The respective figures will be Rs. 2,18,000, Rs. 51,000 and Rs. 3,28,000 respectively if provision for taxation is treated as a non-current liability*).

15. The following particulars pertain to Hitesh Ltd.:

	As at 31.3.1995	As at 31.3.1996
Liabilities	Rs.	Rs.
Equity Share Capital Shares of Rs. 10 each, fully paid up	10,00,000	15,00,000
General Reserve	12,00,000	8,00,000
Debenture Redemption Reserve	—	3,00,000
Profit and Loss Account	5,00,000	3,00,000
14% Debentures	6,00,000	4,00,000
Bills Payable	50,000	40,000
Trade Creditors	2,80,000	3,20,000
Provision for Taxation	4,50,000	5,50,000
	40,80,000	42,10,000
Assets		
Fixed Assets, cost	25,00,000	25,00,000
Less: Depreciation	7,50,000	10,00,000
	17,50,000	15,00,000
Inventors	9,70,000	8,90,000
Sundry Debtors	2,00,000	2,30,000
Cash and Bank Balance	10,80,000	15,30,000
Preliminary Expenses	80,000	60,000
	40,80,000	42,10,000

During the accounting year ended 31st March, 1996 the company distributed dividend @ 35% on the then share capital of Rs. 10,00,000 and later distributed bonus shares in the ratio of 1:2 capitalising Rs. 5,00,000 out of General Reserve. The company also redeemed debentures of Rs. 2,00,000 at par by draw of lots.

Treating Provision for Taxation as a current liability, you are required to prepare for the year ended 31st March 1996 the following statements:

(*i*) Statement Showing Changes in Working Capital.

(*ii*) Funds Flow Statement.

(Funds from Operations Rs. 8,20,000; Increase in Working Capital Rs. 2,70,000; total of Funds Flow Statement Rs. 8,20,000).

16. Prepare Funds Flow Statement from the following balance sheets of Jupiter Ltd. for the years ending 31st March, 1996 and 31st March, 1995 respectively:

		March 31, 1996 (Rs. in lacs)		March 31, 1995 (Rs. in lacs)
I. Sources of Funds				
1. Shareholders' Funds				
(*a*) Capital		500		300
(*b*) Reserves and Surplus		750		400
2. Loan Funds:				
(*a*) Secured Loans		1,000		900
(*b*) Unsecured Loans		200		200
		2,450		1,800
II. Application of Funds		(Rs. in lacs)		(Rs. in lacs)
1. Fixed Assets				
(*a*) Gross Block	1,947		1,551	
(*b*) *Less*: Depreciation	177	1,770	141	1,410
		30		10
2. Investments				
3. Current Assets, Loans & Advances:				
(*a*) Current Assets:				

		(Rs. in lacs)		(Rs. in lacs)
(i) Inventories	400		200	
(ii) Sundry Debtors	300		200	
(iii) Cash and Bank Balances	120		80	
(b) Loans and Advances:				
(i) Bills Receiable	60		95	
(ii) Prepaid Expenses	10		5	
	890		580	
Less: Current Liabilities and Provisions				
(i) Current Liabilities	170		180	
(ii) Provisions	110		80	
	280		260	
Net Working Capital		610		320
4. Miscellaneous Expenditure to the extent not written off or adjusted		40		60
Total		2,450		1,800

(*Funds from Operations Rs. 406 lacs; Increase in Working Capital Rs. 290 lacs; Total of Funds Flow Statement Rs. 706 lacs*)

17. From the figures given below, prepare statement showing application and sources of funds for the year ending 31st March, 1996.

	As at 31.3.1995 Rs.	*As at 31.3.1996* Rs.
Assets:		
Fixed Assets	5,10,000	6,20,000
Investments	30,000	80,000
Current Assets	2,40,000	3,75,000
Discount on Issue of Debentures	5,000	—
Total	7,85,000	10,75,000
Liabilities:		
Share Capital	3,00,000	3,50,000
Debentures	1,00,000	2,00,000
General Reserve	1,50,000	2,00,000
Profit and Loss Account	60,000	70,000
Provision for Depreciation	90,000	1,30,000
Provision for Doubtful Debts	10,000	15,000
Current Liabilities	75,000	1,10,000
	7,85,000	10,75,000

During the year, a dividend of 15% was paid for 1994-95. A fixed asset costing Rs. 40,000 (depreciation provided Rs. 17,000) was disposed of for Rs. 25,000.

(*Funds from Operation Rs. 1,65,000; Increase in Working Capital Rs. 95,000; total of Funds Flow Statement Rs. 3,40,000*).

18. Nakul Ltd. gives the following summarised balance sheets as on 31st March, 1995 and 31st March, 1996:

Liabilities	*On 31.3.1995* Rs.	*On 31.3.1996* Rs.	*Asset*	*On 31.3.1995* Rs.	*On 31.3.1996* Rs.
Equity Share Capital	5,00,000	6,00,000	Sundry Fixed Asset		
Preference Share Capital	2,00,000	—	(at cost)	10,00,000	11,50,000
Redemption Reserve	—	1,00,000	*Less*: Provision for		
General Reserve	3,00,000	3,30,000	Depreciation	4,50,000	5,30,000
Profit and Loss Account	40,000	30,000		5,50,000	6,20,000

	Rs.	Rs.		Rs.	Rs.
Debentures	1,50,000	2,00,000	Long-term Investment	80,000	60,000
Sundry Creditors	1,20,000	1,60,000	Stock	4,50,000	3,80,000
Provision for Income Tax	1,10,000	1,90,000	Debtors	2,30,000	2,80,000
Proposed Preference Dividend	25,000	—	Cash at Bank	1,80,000	3,40,000
Proposed Equity Dividend	75,000	90,000	Preliminary Expenses	30,000	20,000
	15,20,000	17,00,000		15,20,000	17,00,000

During 1995-96, investments costing Rs. 20,000 were sold for Rs. 25,000 income tax for 1994-95 Rs. 1,10,000 was paid. Preference and equity dividends for 1994-95 amounting to Rs. 25,000 and Rs. 75.000 respectively were distributed. Tax amounting to Rs. 10,000 on distributed profit was also paid.

You are required to prepare—

(*a*) a schedule of changes in working capital, and

(*b*) a statement showing sources and uses of funds, *i.e.* a funds flow statement.

Show all calculations clearly. *[B.Com. (Hons.) Delhi, 1989 Modified]*

(Net increase in working Capital, Rs. 20,000)

19. From the following summarised balance sheets as at 31.3.1996 and 31.3.1995 of A Products Ltd. and other information, prepare a statement showing the sources and application of funds during 1995-96:

	31.3.1996	*31.3.1995*
	Rs.	*Rs.*
Cash in hand and at bank	2,87,800	1,70,600
Sundry Debtors	1,53,000	1,38,800
Inventories	2,87,700	2,35,800
Prepaid Expenses	4,600	3,200
Total Current Assets	7,33,100	5,48,400
Investments	25,000	1,05,000
Debenture Discount	5,000	7,000
Patents	34,000	30,000
Goodwill	75,000	85,000
Property, Plant, etc.	4,92,900	4,25,900
	13,65,000	12,01,300
Sundry Creditors	2,93,000	1,12,000
Dividends Payable	25,000	—
Provision for Taxation	10,000	50,000
Accrued Interest on Debentures	3,000	4,300
Total Current Liabilities	3,31,000	1,66,300
14% Debentures (redeemable at a premium of 5%)	1,00,000	1,50,000
Share Capital	6,00,000	5,00,000
Reserve	2,52,000	2,00,000
Profit & Loss Account	82,000	1,85,000
	13,65,000	12,01,300

Other information:

(*i*) Depreciation written off on property, plant, etc., till 31.3.1995 was Rs. 4,25,000. During 1995-96, the depreciation on this group of assets was Rs. 80,000. For the assets in use on 31.3.1996 depreciation so far provided totalled Rs. 4,40,000.

(*ii*) During the year, a machine costing Rs. 70,000 (depreciation written off Rs. 30,000) was sold for Rs. 32,000.

(*iii*) Investments costing Rs. 80,000 were sold for Rs. 90,000 in 1995-96.

(*iv*) The Profit & Loss Account stood as under:

	Rs.	*Rs.*
Balance brought forward from 1994-95		1,84,800
Less: Dividend declared	50,000	
Loss during 1995-96 (after all write offs)	52,800	1,02,800
		82,000

[*Funds from operations Rs. 97,700; Increase in working capital Rs. 20,200*]

20. Narain & Co. Ltd. gives you its Balance Sheet as on 31st March, 1995, and its projected Profit and Loss Account (summarised) for the year ending 31st March, 1996:

Balance Sheet

	Rs.		*Rs.*	*Rs.*
Share Capital:		Goodwill		1,50,000
(Fully paid shares of Rs. 10 each)		Plant & Equipment	10,50,000	
12% Redeemable Preference	3,00,000	*Less*: Depreciation	2,70,000	7,80,000
Equity	5,00,000	Patents		50,000
General Reserve	50,000	Stock		2,70,000
Debenture Redemption Reserve	1,30,000	Book Debts		2,50,000
14% Debentures	2,50,000	Cash		90,000
Creditors for Goods	1,20,000	Underwriting Commission		15,000
Outstanding Expenses	20,000			
Provision for Taxation	1,55,000			
Proposed Dividend (Equity)	80,000			
	16,05,000			16,05,000

Projected Profit and Loss Account

	Rs.		*Rs.*
Opening Stock	2,70,000	Sales—Cash	3,50,000
Purchases	15,00,000	Credit	21,00,000
Wages	1,70,000		24,50,000
Manufacturing Expenses	1,30,000	Stock	2,90,000
Depreciation	1,05,000	Miscellaneous Income	10,000
Selling Expenses	1,10,000	Profit on Sale of Machinery	6,000
Office and Administration Expenses	75,000		
Interest	35,000		
Goodwill	20,000		
Patents	10,000		
Provision for Taxation	1,70,000		
General Reserve	10,000		
Preference Dividend	36,000		
Proposed Dividend (Equity)	75,000		
Balance of Profit	40,000		
	27,56,000		27,56,000

Both the preference shares and debentures are due for redemption on 31st March, 1995. Half the debentureholders in value will accept new 14% redeemable preference shares; also the company proposes to issue equity capital with a nominal value of Rs. 2,00,000 at a premium of 20%.

Fixed assets will be acquired for Rs. 1,60,000. The cost of the fixed asset to be sold in 1995-96 is Rs. 60,000 with a depreciation of Rs. 35,000. It is expected that:

(*i*) Tax liability up to 31.3.1995 will be settled for Rs. 1,40,000;

(*ii*) Book debts will be 10% more than warranted by the credit period of 1½ months; and

(*iii*) Creditors for goods will continue to extend one month's credit and expenses outstanding and prepaid as on 31st March, 1996 will be Rs. 25,000 and Rs. 2,000 respectively.

You are required to

(*i*) Prepare the statement showing sources and applications of funds for the year ending 31st March, 1996; and

(*ii*) draft the company's projected balance sheet as on March 31, 1996.

(Flow from Trading Operations Rs. 3,05,000; Decrease in Working Capital Rs. 1,25,000; Total of Funds Flow Statement Rs. 8,26,000; Total of Projected Balance Sheet Rs. 15,75,000; Total of cash Flow Statement Rs. 8,86,750).

21. A company commencing business on 1st April, 2000 has the undermentioned projected Profit and Loss Account:

	Rs.	*Rs.*
Sales		21,00,000
Cost of goods sold		15,30,000
Gross Profit		5,70,000
Administrative Expenses	1,40,000	
Selling Expenses	1,30,000	2,70,000
Profit before tax		3,00,000
Provision for tax		1,50,000
Profit after tax		1,50,000

The cost of goods sold has been arrived at as follows:

Materials Used	8,40,000
Wages and Manufacturing Expenses	6,25,000
Depreciation	2,35,000
	17,00,000
Less: Stock of Finished Goods (10% goods produced, not yet sold)	1,70,000
	15,30,000

The figures given above relate only to the goods that have been finished and not work in progress. Goods equal to 15% of the year's productions (in terms of physical units) are in process on the average, requiring full materials but only 40% of the other expenses. The company believes in keeping two months consumption of materials in stock.

All expenses are paid one month in arrear; suppliers of materials extend 1½ months' credit; sales are 20% cash and the rest at two months' credit; 70% of the income tax has to be paid in advance in quarterly instalments.

The company wants you to prepare an estimate of the requirement of working capital. What other information do you require for the purpose? Making your own assumptions in this respect, prepare a statement showing how much working capital will be required. Work to the nearest hundred.

[*Rs. 4,01,200 not counting cash and safety margins*]

22. Tee Ltd. sells goods in the domestic market on a gross profit of 25%, not counting depreciation as part of the cost of goods sold.

Its annual figures are as follows:	*Rs.*
Sales — home at one month's credit	12,00,000
— export, at three months' credit — sale price 10% below home price	5,40,00
Materials used, suppliers extend two months' credit	4,50,000
Wages paid 1/2 month in arrear	3,60,000
Manufacturing expenses (cash), paid one month in arrear	5,40,000
Administrative Expenses, paid one month in arrear	1,20,000
Sales Promotion Expenses payable quarterly in advance	60,000
Income Tax payable in four instalments of which one falls in the next financial year	1,50,000

The company keeps one month's stock of each of raw materials and finished goods and believes in keeping Rs. 1,00,000 available to it, including the overdraft limit of Rs. 50,000 not yet utilised by the company.

Assuming a 15% safety margin, ascertain the requirement of the working capital of the company. Ignore work in progress. [*Rs. 3,22,000*]

23. Ess Ltd. has seasonal sales; it sells its goods at Rs. 50 per unit. Sales are 25% cash and the remainder at 1½ months' credit. The cost of the goods in terms of percentages of the selling price is as follows:

Materials	20%
Wages	25%
Expenses	20%
Depreciation	10%
	75%

In addition, each month a sum of Rs. 1,00,000 has to be paid in respect of fixed factory and administrative expenses. Income tax, Rs. 60,000 is payable on 15th March, 2010. The company pays dividend on equity shares in February, totalling Rs. 75,000.

The company purchases materials a month before the one in which it is required. Payment is made to suppliers after one month and in respect of expenses fortnightly, unless otherwise indicated.

The sales in units for various months are as following:

October, 2009	3,000	January, 2010	8,000
November, 2009	5,000	February, 2010	8,000
December, 2009	6,000	March, 2010	10,000

Sales in each month are spread uniformly over the month.

On 1st January, 2010 the company expected to have an overdraft of Rs. 54,000. Prepare the Cash Budget for the three months ending March 31, 2010.

[*Overdraft on, 31.3.2001, Rs. 85,250; 28.2.2001, Rs. 1,57,750 and 31.3.2001, Rs. 1,98,250*]

24. Prepare cash budgets from the following information for the months of January to March 2010.

(1) Overdraft on 1st January, 2010

(2) Sales (actual and estimated)

Actual	*Rs.*	*Estimated*	*Rs.*
October, 2009	1,00,000	January, 2010	1,00,000
November, 2009	1,10,000	February, 2010	1,20,000
December, 2009	90,000	March, 2010	90,000

(3) Purchases (actual and estimated)

Actual	*Rs.*	*Estimated*	*Rs.*
October, 2009	50,000	January, 2010	50,000
November, 2009	60,000	February, 2010	70,000
December, 2009	50,000	March, 2010	50,000

(4) Wages and Expenses (actual and estimated)

	Actual			*Estimated*	
	Wages	*Expenses*		*Wages*	*Expenses*
	Rs.	*Rs.*			*Rs.*
November, 2009	16,000	8,000	January, 2010	15,000	9,000
December, 2009	12,000	9,000	February, 2010	18,000	10,000
			March, 2010	12,000	10,000

(5) A machine to be purchased in January, 2010 Rs. 1,50,000, with a down payment of Rs. 30,000; subsequently, starting with 31st March, 2010, a quarterly payment of Rs. 20,000 is to be made together with interest @ 12% p.a. with quarterly rests.

(6) Income tax to be paid on 15th March, 2010 Rs. 30,000.

(7) Time lag: Credit sales — 2 months
Credit purchases — 1 months
Wages purchases — ½ months
Expenses — ¼ months

(8) Net interest income to be received in January, 2010, Rs. 11,700.

(*Overdraft on 31st January 2010, Rs. 10,800; balance on 28th February 2010, Rs. 2,950 and overdraft on 31st March 2010, Rs. 45,650*).

Essay-Type

1. What is a cash flow statement? What is meant by the terms cash, cash equivalents and cash flows in the context of cash flow statements?

2. What do you mean by operating activities, investing activities and financing activities? Give four examples of cash flows from each one class of these activities.

3. What are the recommendations of Accounting Standard-3 (Revised) regarding classification of cash flows arising from interest and dividends received and paid? Is there any controversy regarding these cash flows? Clarify the position.

4. While preparing a cash flow statement, how will you deal with non-cash transactions?

5. Explain (*i*) the direct method and (*ii*) the indirect method of calculating cash provided or used by operating activities.

6. How does the direct method of calculating cash provided or used by operating activities differ from the indirect method of making this calculation?

7. Describe the advantages of cash flow statement. Are there any limitations also?

8. Enumerate the points of distinction between cash flow statement and income statement.

9. What do you mean by the term 'Funds'?

[**Hint:** The term generally refers to (*i*) cash, (*ii*) cash and cash equivalents like marketable securities, or (*iii*) net working capital *i.e.* current assets minus current liabilities. Of these, the third definition whereby funds mean net working capital is most widely accepted.]

10. How are funds from trading operations calculated? Explain with the help of imaginary figures.

11. How does a Funds Flow Statement differ from a Cash Flow Statement?

12. What is a Funds Flow statement? What are its advantages? Does it suffer from some limitations also?

13. Distinguish between:

(*i*) Income Statement and Funds Flow Statement

(*ii*) Statement Showing Changes in Working Capital and Funds Flow Statement.

14. Explain the term 'Working Capital'.

[**Hint:** Two concepts of working capital. Gross concept refers to firm's investment in current assets. Net concept refers to excess of current assets over current liabilities. Net concept is more widely accepted.]

15. What is a Cash Budget? Why is it prepared?

16. How will you estimate the working capital requirements of a concern?

24

ACCOUNTING RATIOS

SYNOPSIS

Importance of Accounting Ratios	...24.1	Turnover, Performance or Activity Ratios	...24.23
Limitations	...24.2	Ratios to judge financial position and policies	...24.26
Various Accounting Ratios	...24.3	Predictability of insolvency on the basis of ratios	...24.65
Profitability Ratios	...24.5		
AS-20: Earnings Per Share	...24.9		

Importance of Accounting Ratios :

The importance of accounting ratios, that is, relationships worked out among various accounting data which are mutually interdependent and which influence each other in a significant manner, arises from the fact that often absolute figures standing alone convey no meaning. They become significant only when considered along with other figures. A firm earns a profit of Rs. 1,00,000. This information is meaningless unless either the figure of capital employed to earn it or of sales affected is available. Even if an absolute figure is considered significant, one may be subconsciously aware of the other relevant figures. When we say that so and so is fat, what we are trying to say is that considering the age and height of the person, he is overweight. Ratio may be expressed as a rational figure or as a percentage. For example, the ratio of 3,00,000 to 2,00,000 may be expressed as 1.5 or 150%.

For purposes of analysis, accounting ratios are indispensable. Suppose, sales have increased but profit has fallen. One may be vaguely aware of the causes, but for precise knowledge it will be necessary to analyse all the figures completely. For example, one will have to ascertain the contribution to higher sales by change in prices and by increased or lower sales volume ; the consumption of materials will also be analysed both for changes in prices and in quantities consumed. Such analysis is greatly facilitated by accounting ratios. In fact, a meaningful analysis of the financial situation and performance is the first great advantage of accounting ratios. This requires ratios and their comparison which may be :

(*i*) for the same firm over a period of years, or

(*ii*) for one firm against another, or

(*iii*) for one firm against the industry as a whole or against predetermined standards, or

(*iv*) for one division or department of a firm against other divisions or departments of the same firm.

Inter-firm comparison and intra-firm comparison are, thus, both possible on the basis of accounting ratios; this can also be attempted in other ways but accounting ratios are indispensable in this respect. For example, to judge which firm has the best overall efficiency, one should compare the rate of profit on capital employed for the firms concerned—the size of the profit as such is not relevant.

Accounting ratios not only indicate the present position, they also indicate the causes leading up to the position to a large extent. For instance, accounting ratios may indicate not only that financial position is precarious but also the past policies or actions which have caused it. Best results are obtained when ratios for a number of years are put in a tabular form so that the figures for one year can be easily compared with those of other years.

Accounting ratios tabulated for a number of years indicate the trend of the change. This helps in preparation of estimates for the future. Ratios also help in ascertaining other figures if one figure is available. Suppose it is known that the ratio of wages to sales is 15%; it is then easy to calculate the amount to be spent on wages if the amount of expected sales is known.

Limitations :

Ratio analysis is very fashionable these days and is useful but one should be aware of its limitations also. The following are the chief limitations of accounting ratios :—

(*i*) Accounting ratios can be only as correct as the data on which they are based. For instance, if inventory values are inflated, not only will one have an exaggerated view of profitability of the concern, but also of its financial position. The basic data must be absolutely reliable, if the ratios worked out on its basis are to be relied upon.

(*ii*) When two firms' results are being compared, it should be remembered that the firms may follow different accounting policies ; for instance, one firm may charge depreciation on the straight line basis and the other on diminishing value. Such differences will not make some of the accounting ratios strictly comparable.

(*iii*) Changes in price levels often make comparison of figures for various years difficult. For instance, the ratio of sale to fixed assets in 2001 would be much higher than in 1984 due to rising prices, fixed assets being expressed still on the basis of cost.

(*iv*) Accounting ratios may be worked out for any two figures even if they are not significantly related. For example, a ratio may be worked out for sales and investments in government securities. Such ratios will only be misleading. Care should be exercised to work out ratios between only such figures as have a cause and effect relationship. One should also be reasonably clear as to what is cause and what is effect.

(*v*) Ratios sometimes give a misleading picture. One company produces 1,000 units in one year and 2,000 units next year ; the progress is 100%. Another firm raises production from 6,000 units to 8,000 units—the progress is only 33 1/3%. The second firm will appear to be less active than the first firm if only the rate of increase is compared. It is, therefore, useful if, along with ratios, absolute figures are also studied—unless the firms being studied are equal in all respects. In fact, one should be extremely careful while comparing the results of one firm with those of another if the two firms differ in any significant manner, say, in size, location, degree of automation or mechanisation, etc.

(*vi*) Accounting ratios are expressed in precise figures and that may be misleading unless one remembers that the figures on which they are based are often only estimates and that different figures could also have been worked out legitimately. One should also remember that often the basis of accounting is changed; this will mean that ratios of one period and those of another may not be comparable. In a nutshell, before one works out the ratios, one should be sure of the figures leading to the ratios.

(*vii*) Another important point to keep in mind is that there is almost no single standard ratio against which the actual ratio is measurable. Circumstances differ from firm to firm and the nature of each industry is different. Therefore, the standard will differ for each industry and the circumstances of each firm will have to be kept in mind. For instance, while comparing the rate of return of electricity companies with that in other industries, one must remember that, by law, electricity companies are precluded from making high profits. One industry may have to invest heavily in fixed assets and another industry may have to keep large stocks of raw materials and finished goods. For these reasons, the performance of one industry may not be properly comparable with that of another. For each industry, standard ratios will have to be worked out separately, mostly on the basis of actuals for a few representative companies which may be considered as reasonably sound and competent. The performance of firms in the industry may then be compared but still remembering the circumstances of each firm.

Even when the ratios are worked out correctly, it should be remembered that they can at best be used as a doctor uses symptoms—indications that something is wrong somewhere. Just as the doctor will try to get to the real reason, in the same manner the analyst should try to locate the real factor leading to the present state of affairs. Suppose, the ratio of gross profit to sales is low. The reasons may be poor sales, bad purchasing, defective pricing policy, wastages and losses, etc. Ratios thus point out the area that needs investigation—they are only a tool in the hands of the person trying to get at the truth.

Various Accounting Ratios :

Ratios may be based on figures in the balance sheet, in the profit and loss account or in both. Briefly, ratios indicating financial position are calculated on the basis of the balance sheet; those indicating profitability and efficiency of control over expenses are calculated on the basis of the profit and loss account and those which throw light on operating efficiency or effective use of facilities and resources are calculated on the basis of figures in both statements. We have stated above that profitability is of the utmost importance. If a concern goes on losing, its financial condition will definitely be bad sooner or later. Profits enable a firm to improve its financial strength. Therefore, ratios based on profitability are termed "causal" ratios, indicating the causes of the present or repeated financial position.

Return on Investment :

Profitability or the Return on Investment is the basic casual ratio. It is ascertained by a comparison of profit earned and capital employed to earn it. The resultant ratio, usually expressed as a percentage, is called Rate of Return or *Net Profit to Capital employed* or, more commonly, Return on Investment. The purpose is to ascertain how much income, use of Rs. 100 of capital generates. Therefore, for this purpose :—

(*i*) Capital employed means total capital including that borrowed from outsiders but excluding non-trading assets; in other words, it means the total of net fixed assets (that is, fixed assets *less* depreciation) and working capital (that is, current assets *less* current liabilities). Taking the liabilities side, it would include share capital, both equity and preference, reserves and debentures less non-trading and fictitious assets [See Note (1) below].

(*ii*) Net profit should mean operating profit before interest, tax on profits and dividends; income-tax is not considered because its incidence is not at all certain—the income-tax rates can be changed almost at will by the Government. However, most authorities calculate the Rate of Return on the basis of profit after tax.

The ratio is calculated as :

$$\frac{\text{Net Profit before interest, tax and dividends}}{\text{Net fixed assests + working capital}} \times 100$$

or

$$\frac{\text{Net Profit before interest, but after tax}}{\text{Net fixed assests + working capital}} \times 100$$

[*Notes :* (1) There is no unanimity about the term, 'capital employed' or even the profit earned. Capital employed may mean any one of the following :—

(*i*) Net fixed assets + working capital.

(*ii*) Net fixed assets + current assets.

(*iii*) Gross fixed assets + current assets.

(*iv*) Gross fixed assets + working capital.

Most people use (*i*) as the meaning of capital employed but one must always specify how capital employed has been arrived at. Similarly one must state what the figure of profit used really signifies.

(2) The ratio judges the overall performance of the concern. The rate of return from the point of view of equity shareholders, however, is different since for them profit including non-operating income, after income-tax and preference dividend, is relevant. They are interested in the following ratio:

$$\left. \frac{\text{Net Profit before interest, taxes and preference dividends}}{\text{Equity capital plus reserves}} \times 100 \right]$$

In this chapter, "profit" will mean net profit before interest but after tax and "capital" will mean net fixed assets plus working capital. To summarise, the return on investment will be measured by

$$\frac{\text{Profit}}{\text{Capital}} \times 100$$

This ratio can be easily stated as

$$\frac{\text{Net Profit}}{\text{Sales}} \times \frac{\text{Sales}}{\text{Capital}} \times 100$$

The chart given below shows the return on investment and its analysis :

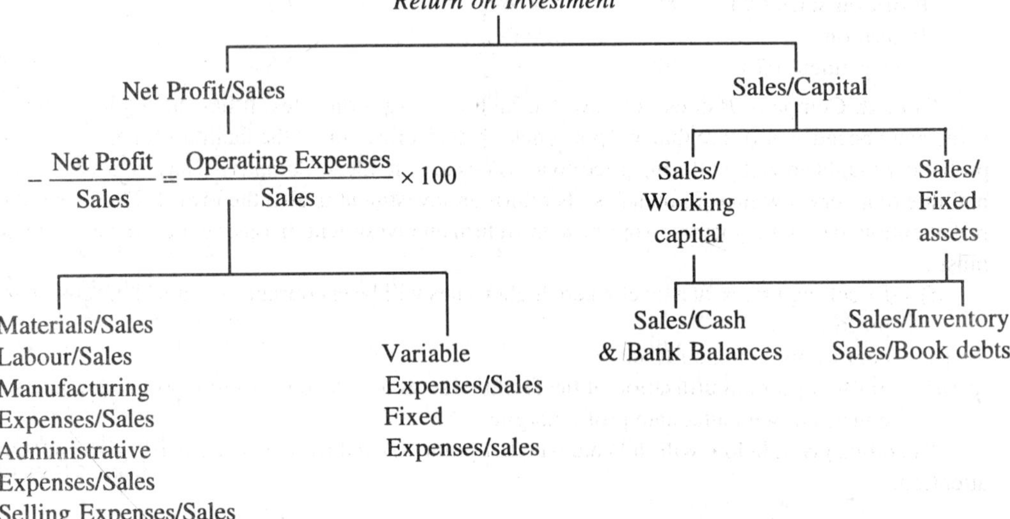

Net Profit/Sales is the net margin on sales; and Sales/Capital is the turnover of capital. Using commonsense also, one can see that the total profit earned is a function of both the factors—the difference between selling price and the costs as well as the quantum and rapidity of sales. Hence, the return on investment may be expressed as net margin on sales (percentage) x rate of turnover of capital (showing the effectiveness with which the resources at the disposal of the firm are being used). Consider the following figures :—

	Rs.
Sales	50,00,000
Capital employed	40,00,000
Profit earned	6,00,000

The turnover of capital is 1.25, i.e., $\frac{50,00,000}{40,00,000}$

The margin on sales is 12%, i.e., $\frac{6,00,000}{50,00,000} \times 100$

The rate of return is 15%, i.e., $\frac{6,00,000}{40,00,000} \times 100$

This may also be expressed as $\frac{6,00,000}{50,00,000} \times \frac{50,00,000}{40,00,000} \times 100$

Or, $12\% \times 1.25 = 15\%$

This method of calculating the rate of return has the advantage of showing that both factors, margin on sales and the turnover rate of capital, are important in earning profits. Study the following figures relating to three companies, equal in size :

	Company A	*Company B*	*Company C*
	Rs.	*Rs.*	*Rs.*
Capital	10,00,000	10,00,000	10,00,000
Sales	25,00,000	30,00,000	35,00,000
Profit	2,00,000	2,25,000	1,75,000
The figures yield the following ratios :			
Sales/capital	2.5	3.0	3.5
Profit on sales (%)	8%	7.5%	5.0%
Return on investment (%)	20%	22.5%	17.5%

Through Company *B* does not have the highest margin on sales, it has the highest return on investment because of (more than proportionate) better utilisation of the facilities for effecting sales, probably brought about by offering price concessions to customers. Company *C* has the best utilisation but, due to a very low margin on sales, its return on investment is also the lowest. Thus, one has to pay attention to both the factors to optimise the return on investment. In other words, the management must :

(*i*) fix selling prices, at a level where higher sales will be encouraged but not at the cost of total profit ;

(*ii*) control operating cost; and

(*iii*) ensure optimum utilisation of the facilities so as to ensure maximum production and sales consistent with adequate profit margins.

The ratios given below will indicate whether points (i) and (ii) above are being given adequate attention.

Profitability Ratios :

The figures in the Profit and Loss Account (including the Trading Account) enable one to calculate a number of ratios. The most important of these are the following :—

(*i*) *Gross Profit Ratio*. This is the most common ratio calculated. The method is Gross Profit x 100/Sales. A major change in this ratio over a period of years should be investigated—the change may be due to a change in the economic situation (changes in costs without a change in selling price or vice versa) or due to errors or due to a change in the basis of accounting—say, valuing stock on a different basis. For comparison over a number of years, the method of calculating gross profit should not change and, if the figures for a number of firms are to be compared, the firms should follow the same accounting system and practice. Of course, higher the gross profit ratio, the better.

(*ii*) *Net Profit Ratio* (*or Margin*). This measures the rate of net profit earned on sales. The profit is usually only the operating profit, that is, income from non-trading assets and expenses, which do not relate to trading or manufacturing, are not included. The ratio is calculated as :

$$\frac{\text{Net Operating Profit}}{\text{Sales}} \times 100$$

Higher the ratio the better it is, but what has been said above in regard to gross profit ratio should be kept in mind.

Some firms calculate the ratio on the basis of net profit after deducting the tax payable on the profit but this is not the usual practice.

(*iii*) *Operating Ratio.* This ratio measures the extent of costs incurred for making the sale. It is ascertained as :

$$\frac{\begin{array}{c}\text{Cost of goods sold plus all other operating expenses,}\\ \text{i.e., manufacturing, administrative and selling expenses}\\ \text{(but excluding financial expenses like interest)}\end{array}}{\text{Sales}} \times 100$$

Operating ratio plus net profit ratio is 100 — obviously the two ratios are interrelated. A rise in the operating ratio indicates a decline in efficiency; lower the ratio, the better it is.

Operating ratio should be analysed further—in fact such an analysis will throw good light on the levels of efficiency prevailing in different aspects of the work. The ratios that analyse the operating ratio are the following —

1. Materials Consumed Ratio — $\frac{\text{Material Consumed}}{\text{Sales}} \times 100$
2. Conversion Cost (or Manufacturing Expenses) Ratio— $\frac{\text{Manufacturing Expenses (excluding materials)}}{\text{Sales}} \times 100$
3. Administrative Expenses Ratio— $\frac{\text{Administrative Expenses}}{\text{Sales}} \times 100$
4. Selling Expenses Ratio— $\frac{\text{Selling and Distribution Expenses}}{\text{Sales}} \times 100$

The total of these four ratios will be equal to the operating ratio. Since revenue expenditure may be either fixed or variable, it is also useful to work out ratios of fixed and variable expenses to sales separately. The ratio of variable cost to sales will and should remain constant—a reduction in it indicates efficiency and a rise in it is a sign of declining efficiency unless it is due to changes in prices such as material prices and wage rates.

It should be noted that the ratio 1—Variable costs/Sales is the same as cost-volume profit ratio, measuring the effect on profit of a given change in sales. Suppose, the figures for a firm for the year ended 31st March, 2001 are as follows :—

	Rs.
Sales	50,00,000
Variable costs	30,00,000
Fixed costs	15,00,000
Net Profit	5,00,000

The ratio of variable costs to sales is 0.6, i.e., 30,00,000/50,00,000. The cost-volume profit ratio is 0.4, i.e., 1 - 0.6, indicating that out of every rupee of sale, 40 paise will be left for meeting fixed expenses and for profit since 60 paise will be spent for producing the sale of one rupee. If sales increase by Rs. 5 lakh, the profit will be Rs. 7,00,000, as shown below :

	Rs.
Sales	55,00,000
Variable Cost Rs. (55,00,000 x 0.6)	33,00,000
	22,00,000
Fixed Cost	15,00,000
Net Profit	7,00,000

The increase in profit is Rs. 2,00,000 which is equal to Rs. 5,00,000 (the increase in sales) x 0.4. That is why this ratio is called the cost-volume profit ratio.

The ratio of fixed expenses to sales should decline when sales increase, since an increase in sales should not lead to an increase in fixed expenses. Also, since a fall in sales cannot result in a saving in fixed expenses, a reduction in sales will be accompanied by an increase in the fixed expenses ratio. There is inefficiency if the fixed expenses ratio does not decline when sales go up and there is efficiency when a decline in sales is not accompanied by a rise in the fixed expenses ratio.

Return on Proprietors' Funds :

This ratio is also called Return on Shareholders' Funds or Return on Shareholders' Investment. It shows the relationship between net profits after interest and tax and the proprietors' funds or shareholders' funds. Proprietors' funds include equity share capital, preference share capital, all the reserves (capital redemption reserve, capital reserve, securities premium account, general reserve, credit balance of profit and loss appropriation account etc.) less accumulated losses and miscellaneous expenditure not yet written off (preliminary expenses, underwriting commission, discount on issue of shares or debentures, interest paid out capital etc.).

The formula to calculate this ratio is as follows :-

$$\text{Return on Proprietors' Funds} = \frac{\text{Net Profit after Interest and Tax}}{\text{Proprietors' Funds}} \times 100$$

In this ratio, the net profits which are taken into consideration are the net profits arrived at after deducting interest on the borrowings and income tax. These are the net profits which are available to the shareholders. This ratio tells us the rate at which net profits have been earned on proprietors' funds.

Return on Equity Capital :

In a joint stock company, equity shareholders bear the greatest risks. Preference shareholders enjoy a preference over the equity shareholders both in the payment of dividend and return of capital. However, they are entitled to a fixed rate of dividend even when the company earns profits at a very high rate. High profitability of the company's business benefits the equity shareholders only. The performance of the company will be judged by the equity shareholders on the basis of the return on equity capital of the company. Return on equity capital is calculated as follows :

$$\frac{\text{Net Profit after Tax} - \text{Preference Dividend}}{\text{Paid} - \text{up Equity Share Capital}}$$

Return on Shareholders' Total Equity

Return on equity capital considers only paid-up equity share capital and ignores reserves, surplus etc. which belong to equity shareholders and are used to earn profits. An issue of bonus shares will bring down the return on equity capital without a decline in the profitability of the company's business. Return on Shareholders' Total Equity does not suffer from this defect. Shareholders' total equity means paid-up equity share capital plus reserves and surplus minus accumulated losses and miscellaneous expenditure not yet written off. Return on Shareholders' Total Equity is worked out as follows :-

$$\frac{\text{Net Profit after Tax} - \text{Preference Dividend}}{\text{Shareholders' Total Equity}}$$

where Shareholders' Total Equity = Paid-up Equity Share Capital + Reserves + Surplus - Debit balance of Profit and Loss Account (if any) - Miscellaneous Expenditure not yet written off (if any). Thus, to the paid up equity share capital all items under Reserves and Surplus are added and from the total all items under 'Miscellaneous Expenditure' and debit balance of Profit and Loss Account is deducted to ascertain Shareholders' Total Equity.

Earnings Per Share (E.P.S.)

This ratio measures profit after tax and preference dividend per equity share. It serves the same purpose as is served by return on equity capital whereas return on equity capital reveals profit on total paid-up equity share capital, earnings per share is another version of return on equity capital. The formula to calculate earnings per share may be expressed as follows :

Earnings Per Share =

$$\frac{\text{Net Profit after Tax} - \text{Preference Dividend} - \text{Corporate Dividend Tax on Pref. Dividend}}{\text{Number of Equity Shares}}$$

The Council of Institute of Chartered Accountants of India has issued Accounting Standard (AS) 20, 'Earnings Per Share'. It is effective in respect of accounting periods commencing on or after 1.4.2001 and is mandatory in nature. According to it , an enterprise should show basic and diluted earnings per share in its income statement for each class of its equity shares. Basic earnings per share is calculated by dividing the net profit for the year which is available to the equity shareholders by the weighted average number of equity shares outstanding during the year.

Basic earnings = Net profit for the year after tax – preference dividend which pertains to the preference shareholders for the year – corporate dividend tax at the existing rate on the preference dividend so calculated .

Weighted number of equity shares has to be calculated if new equity shares have been allotted during the year or there has been buyback of shares during the course of the year. Suppose, in the beginning of an accounting year there are 18 lakh fully paid equity shares of Rs. 10 each and after 4 months, 6 lakh fully paid equity shares of Rs. 10 each are allotted for cash; then weighted average number of shares will have to be calculated which will be 18 lakh + (6 lakh × 8 / 12) = 22 lakh. If on the other hand instead of issuing fresh shares, the company buys back 3 lakh equity shares 4 months after the beginning of the accounting year, the weighted average number of shares will be 18 lakh – (3 lakh × 8 / 12) = 16 lakh.

If a company has issued convertible debentures or convertible preference shares, it will also be required to calculate diluted earnings per share. Let us assume a company has issued 1 lakh 12% debentures of Rs. 100 each, each debenture being convertible into 10 equity shares of Rs. 10 each. It should be noted that before conversion, the company would incur an expenditure of Rs. 12 lakh by way of interest on debentures and will not be paying income tax on the amount of interest, it being an allowable expense in Income Tax Act. No dividend is payable in respect of such debentures. After conversion, the company will save interest on debentures but will pay income tax on the amount of interest saved. However, after conversion, dividend will have to be paid on 10 lakh equity shares resulting due to conversion. Such debentures are recognised as potential equity shares. In such a case, diluted earnings per share has also to be calculated and shown in the profit and loss account. The concept and the procedure of this calculation has been explained in detail with the help of illustrations in the accounting standard 20 which is reproduced in full in the following pages.

ACCOUNTING STANDARD (AS)20*
(issued 2001)

EARNING PER SHARE

*(This Accounting Standard includes paragraphs set in **bold italic** type and plain type, which have equal authority. Paragraphs in bold type indicate the main principles. This Accounting Standard should be read in the context of its objective and the Preface to the Statements of Accounting Standards*[1]*.)*

Accounting Standard (AS) 20, 'Earnings Per Share', issued by the Council of the Institute of Chartered Accountants of India, comes into effect in respect of accounting periods commencing on or after 1-4-2001 and is mandatory in nature from that date, in respect of enterprises whose equity shares or potential equity shares are listed on a recognised stock exchange in India.

An enterprise which has neither equity shares nor potential equity shares which are so listed but which discloses earnings per share, should calculate and disclose earnings per share in accordance with this Standard from the aforesaid date. However, in respect of accounting periods commencing on or after 1-4-2004, if any such enterprise does not fall in any of the following categories, it need not disclose diluted earnings per share (both including and excluding extraordinary items) and information required by paragraph 48(ii) of this Standard[2]:

(*i*) Enterprises whose equity securities or potential equity securities are listed outside India and enterprises whose debt securities (other than potential equity securities) are listed whether in India or outside India.

(*ii*) Enterprises which are in the process of listing their equity or debt securities as evidenced by the board of directors' resolution in this regard.

(*iii*) Banks including co-operative banks.

(*iv*) Financial institutions.

(*v*) Enterprises carrying on insurance business.

(*vi*) All commercial, industrial and business reporting enterprises, whose turnover for the immediately preceding accounting period on the basis of audited financial statements exceeds Rs. 50 crore. Turnover does not include 'other income'.

(*vii*) All commercial, industrial and business reporting enterprises having borrowings, including public deposits, in excess of Rs. 10 crore at any time during the accounting period.

(*viii*) Holding and subsidiary enterprises of any one of the above at any time during the accounting period.

Where an enterprise (which has neither equity shares nor potential equity shares which are listed on a recognised stock exchange in India but which discloses earning per share) has been

---

* A limited revision to this Standard has been made in 2004, pursuant to which paragraphs 48 and 51 of this Standard were revised. The Standard presented in this book contains the revised version of the paragraphs.

1 Attention is specifically drawn to paragraph 4.3 of the Preface, according to which Accounting Standards are intended to apply only to items which are material.

2. Originally, no exemption was available to an enterprise, which had neither equity shares nor potential equity shares which were listed on a recognised stock exchange in India, but which disclosed earning per share. It is clarified that no exemption is available even in respect of accounting periods commencing on or after 1-4-2004 to enterprises whose equity shares or potential equity shares are listed on a recognised stock exchange in India. It is also clarified that this Standard is not applicable to an enterprise which has neither equity shares nor potential equity shares which are listed on a recognised stock exchange in India and which also does not disclose earnings per share.

covered in any one or more of the above categories and subsequently, ceases to be so covered, the enterprise will not qualify for exemption from the disclosure of diluted earnings per share (both including and excluding extraordinary items) and paragraph 48 (ii) of this Standard, until the enterprise ceases to be covered in any of the above categories for two consecutive years.

Where an enterprise (which has neither equity shares nor potential equity shares which are listed on a recognised stock exchange in India but which discloses earnings per share) has previously qualified for exemption from the disclosure of diluted earnings per share (both including and excluding extraordinary items) and paragraph 48 (ii) of this Standard (being not covered by any of the above categories) but no longer qualifies for exemption in the current accounting period, this Standard becomes applicable, in its entirety, from the current period. However, the relevant corresponding previous period figures need not be disclosed.

If an enterprise (which has neither equity shares nor potential equity shares which are listed on a recognised stock exchange in India but which discloses earnings per share), pursuant to the above provisions, does not disclose the diluted earnings per share (both including and excluding extraordinary items) and information required by paragraph 48 (ii), it should disclose the fact.

The following is the text of the Accounting Standard.

OBJECTIVE

The objective of this Statement is to prescribe principles for the determination and presentation of earnings per share which will improve comparison of performance among different enterprises for the same period and among different accounting periods for the same enterprise. The focus of this Statement is on the denominator of the earnings per share calculation. Even though earnings per share data has limitations because of different accounting policies used for determining 'earnings', a consistently determined denominator enchances the quality of financial reporting.

SCOPE

1. This Statement should be applied by enterprises whose equity shares or potential equity shares are listed on a recognised stock exchange in India. An enterprise which has neither equity shares nor potential equity shares which are so listed but which discloses earnings per share should calculate and disclose earnings per share in accordance with this Statement.

2. In consolidated financial statements, the information required by this Statement should be presented on the basis of consolidated information.*

3. This Statement applies to enterprises whose equity or potential equity shares are listed on a recognised stock exchange in India. An enterprise which has neither equity shares nor potential equity shares which are so listed is not required to disclose earnings per share. However, comparatively in financial reporting among enterprises is enhanced if such an enterprise that is required to disclose by any statute or chooses to disclose earnings per share calculates earnings per share in accordance with the principles laid down in this Statement. In the case of a parent (holding enterprise), users of financial statements are usually concerned with, and need to be informed about, the results of operations of both the enterprise itself as well as of the group as a whole. Accordingly, in the case of such enterprises, this Statement requires the presentation of earnings per share information on the basis of consolidated financial statements as well as individual financial statements of the parent. In consolidated financial statements, such information is presented on the basis of consolidated information.

* Accounting Standard (AS) 21, 'Consolidated Financial Statements' specifies the requirements relating to consolidated financial statements.

DEFINITIONS

4. For the purpose of this Statements, the following terms are used with the meanings specified :

An *equity share* is a share other than a preference share.

A *preference share* is a share carrying preferential rights to dividends and repayment of capital.

A *financial instrument* is any contract that gives rise to both a financial asset of one enterprise and a financial liability or equity shares of another enterprise.

A *potential equity share* is a financial instrument or other contract that entitles, or may entitle, its holder to equity shares.

***Share warrants* or *options* are financial instruments that give the holder the right to acquire equity shares.**

***Fair value* is the amount for which an asset could be exchanged, or a liability settled, between knowledgeable, willing parties in an arm's length transaction.**

5. Equity shares participate in the net profit for the period only after preference shares. An enterprise may have more than one class of equity shares. Equity shares of the same class have the same rights to receive dividends.

6. A financial instrument is any contract that gives rise to both a financial asset of one enterprise and a financial liability or equity shares of another enterprise. For this purpose, a financial asset is any asset that is

(a) cash;

(b) a contractual right to receive cash or another financial asset from another enterprise;

(c) a contractual right to exchange financial instruments with another enterprise under conditions that are potentially favourable; or

(d) an equity share of another enterprise.

A financial liability is any liability that is a contractual obligation to deliver cash or to exchange financial instruments with another enterprise under conditions that are potentially unfavourable.

7. Examples of potential equity shares are :

(a) debt instruments or preference shares, that are convertible into equity shares;

(b) share warrants;

(c) options including employee stock option plans under which employees of an enterprise are entitled to receive equity shares as part of their remuneration and other similar plans; and

(d) shares which would be issued upon the satisfaction of certain conditions resulting from contractual arrangements (contingently issuable shares), such as the acquisition of a business or other assets, or shares issuable under a loan contract upon default of payment of principal or interest, if the contract so provides.

PRESENTATION

8. An enterprise should present basic and diluted earnings per share on the face of the statement of profit and loss for each class of equity shares that has a different right to share in the net profit for the period. An enterprise should present basic and diluted earnings per share with equal prominence for all periods presented.

9. This Statement requires an enterprise to present basic and diluted earnings per share, even if the amounts disclosed are negative (a loss per share).

MEASUREMENT

Basic Earnings Per Share

10. Basic earnings per share should be calculated by dividing the net profit or loss for the period attributable to equity shareholders by the weighted average number of equity shares outstanding during the period.

EARNINGS—BASIC

11. For the purpose of calculating basic earnings per share, the net profit or loss for the period attributable to equity shareholders should be the net profit or loss for the period after deducting preference dividends and any attributable tax thereto for the period.

12. All items of income and expense which are recognised in a period, including tax expense and extraordinary items, are included in the determination of the net profit or loss for the period unless an Accounting Standard requires or permits otherwise (see Accounting Standard (AS) 5, Net Profit or Loss for the period, Prior Period Items and Changes in Accounting Policies). The amount of preference dividends and any attributable tax thereto for the period is deducted from the net profit for the period (or added to the net loss for the period) in order to calculate the net profit or loss for the period attributable to equity shareholders.

13. The amount of preference dividends for the period that is deducted from the net profit for the period is :

(a) the amount of any preference dividends on non-cumulative preference shares provided for in respect of the period; and

(b) the full amount of the required preference dividends for cumulative preference shares for the period, whether or not the dividends have been provided for. The amount of preference dividends for the period does not include the amount of any preference dividends for cumulative preference shares paid or declared during the current period in respect of previous period.

14. If an enterprise has more than one class of equity shares, net profit or loss for the period is apportioned over the different classes of shares in accordance with their dividend rights.

PER SHARE—BASIC

15. For the purpose of calculating basic earnings per share, the number of equity shares should be the weighted average number of equity shares outstanding during the period.

16. The weighted average number of equity shares outstanding during the period reflects the fact that the amount of shareholders' capital may have varied during the period as a result of a larger or lesser number of shares outstanding at the beginning of the period, adjusted by the number of equity shares bought back or issued during the period multiplied by the time-weighting factor. The time-weighting factor is the number of days for which the specific shares are outstanding as a proportion of the total number of days in the period; a reasonable approximation of the weighted average is adequate in many circumstances.

Appendix I illustrates the computation of weighted average number of shares.

17. In most cases, share are included in the weighted average number of shares from the date the consideration is receivable, for example :

(a) equity shares issued in exchange for cash are included when cash is receivable;

(b) equity shares issued as a result of the conversion of a debt instruement to equity share are included as of the date of conversion;

(c) equity shares issued in lieu of interest or principal on other financial instruments are included as of the date interest ceases to accrue;

(d) equity shares issued in exchange for the settlement of a liability of the enterprise are included as of the date the settlement becomes effective;

(e) equity shares issued as consideration for the acquisition of an asset other than cash are included as of the date on which the acquisition is recognised; and

(f) equity shares issued for the rendering of services to the enterprise are included as of the date on which the services are rendered.

In these and other cases, the timing of the inclusion of equity shares is determined by the specific terms and conditions attaching to their issue. Due consideration should be given to the substance of any contract associated with the issue.

18. Equity shares issued as part of the consideration in an amalgamation in the nature of purchase are included in the weighted average number of shares as of the date of the acquisition because the transferree incorporates the results of the operations of the transferor into its statement of profit and loss as from the date of acquisition. Equity shares issued during the reporting period as part of the consideration in an amalgamation in the nature of merger are included in the calculation of the weighted average number of shares from the beginning of the reporting period because the financial statements of the combined enterprise for the reporting period are prepared as if the combined entity had existed from the beginning of the reporting period. Therefore, the number of equity shares used in an amalgamation in the nature of merger is the aggregate of the weighted average number of shares of the combined enterprises, adjusted to equivalent shares of the enterprise whose shares are outstanding after the amalgamation.

19. Partly paid equity shares are treated as a fraction of an equity share to the extent that they were entitled to participate in dividends relative to a fully paid equity share during the reporting period.

Appendix II illustrates the computations in respect of partly paid equity shares.

20. Where an enterprise has equity shares of different nominal values but with the same dividend rights, the number of equity shares is calculated by converting all such equity shares into equivalent number of shares of the same nominal value.

21. Equity shares which are issuable upon the satisfaction of certain conditions resulting from contractual arrangements (contingently issuable shares) are considered outstanding, and included in the computation of basic earnings per share from the date when all necessary conditions under the contract have been satisfied.

22. The weighted average number of equity shares outstanding during the period and for all periods presented should be adjusted for events, other than the conversion of potential equity shares, that have changed the number of equity shares outstanding, without a corresponding change in resources.

23. Equity shares may be issued, or the number of shares outstanding may be reduced, without a corresponding change in resources, Examples include :

(a) a bonus issue ;

(b) a bonus element in any other issue, for example a bonus element in a rights issue to existing shareholders;

(c) a share split; and

(d) a reverse share split (consolidation of shares).

24. In case of a bonus issue or a share split, equity shares are issued to existing shareholders for no additional consideration. Therefore, the number of equity shares outstanding is increased without an increase in resources. The number of equity shares outstanding before the event is adjusted for the proportionate change in the number of equity shares outstanding as if the event had occurred at the beginning of the earliest period reported. For example, upon a two-for-one bonus issue, the number

of shares outstanding prior to the issue is multiplied by a factor of three to obtain the new total number of shares, or by a factor of two to obtain the number of additional shares.

Appendix III illustrates the computation of weighted average number of equity shares in case of a bonus issue during the period.

25. The issue of equity shares at the time of exercise or conversion of potential equity shares will not usually give rise to a bonus element, since the potential equity shares will usually have been issued for full value, resulting in a proportionate change in the resources available to the enterprise. In a rights issue, on the other hand, the exercise price is often less than the fair value of the shares. Therefore, a rights issue usually includes a bonus element. The number of equity shares to be used in calculating basic earnings per share for all periods prior to the rights issue is the number of equity shares outstanding prior to the issue, multiplied by the following factor :

$$\frac{\text{Fair value per share immediately prior to the exercise of rights}}{\text{Theoretical ex-rights fair value per share}}$$

The theoretical ex-rights fair value per share is calculated by adding the aggregate fair value of the shares immediately prior to the exercise of the rights to the proceeds from the exercise of the rights, and dividing by the number of shares outstanding after the exercise of the rights. Where the rights themselves are to be publicly traded separately from the shares prior to the exercise date, fair value for the purposes of this calculation is established at the close of the last day on which the shares are traded together with the rights.

Appendix IV illustrates the computation of weighted average number of equity shares in case of a rights issue during the period.

DILUTED EARNINGS PER SHARE

26. For the purpose of calculating diluted earnings per share, the net profit or loss for the period attributable to equity shareholders and the weighted average number of shares outstanding during the period should be adjusted for the effects of all dilutive potential equity shares.

27. In calculating diluted earnings per share, effect is given to all dilutive potential equity shares that were outstanding during the period, that is :

(a) the net profit for the period attributable to equity shares is :

  (i) increased by the amount of dividends recognised in the period in respect of the dilutive potential equity shares as adjusted for any attributable change in tax expense for the period;

  (ii) increased by the amount of interest recognised in the period in respect of the dilutive potential equity shares as adjusted for any attributable change in tax expense for the period; and

  (iii) adjusted for the after-tax amount of any other changes in expenses or income that would result from the conversion of the dilutive potential equity shares.

(b) the weighted average number of equity shares outstanding during the period is increased by the weighted average number of additional equity shares which would have been outstanding assuming the conversion of all dilutive potential equity shares.

28. For the purpose of this Statement, share application money pending allotment or any advance share application money as at the balance sheet date, which is not statutorily required to be kept separately and is being utilised in the business of the enterprise, is treated in the same manner as dilutive potential equity shares for the purpose of calculation of diluted earnings per share.

EARNINGS—DILUTED

29. For the purpose of calculating diluted earnings per share, the amount of net profit or loss for the period attributable to equity shareholders, as calculated in accordance with paragraph 11, should be adjusted by the following, after taking into account any attributable change in tax

expense for the period :

(a) **any dividends on dilutive potential equity shares which have been deducted in arriving at the net profit attributable to equity shareholders as calculated in accordance with paragraph 11;**

(b) **interest recognised in the period for the dilutive potential equity shares; and**

(c) **any other changes in expenses or income that would result from the conversion of the dilutive potential equity shares.**

30. After the potential equity share are converted into equity shares, the dividends, interest and other expenses or income associated with those potential equity shares will no longer be incurred (or earned). Instead, the new equity shares will be entitled to participate in the net profit attributable to equity shareholders. Therefore, the net profit for the period attributable to equity shareholders calculated in accordance with paragraph 11 is increased by the amount of dividends , interest and other expenses that will be saved, and reduced by the amount of income that will cease to accrue, on the conversion of the dilutive potential equity shares into equity shares. The amount of dividends, interest and other expenses or income are adjusted for any attributable taxes.

Appendix V illustrates the computation of diluted earnings in case of convertible debentures.

31. The conversion of some potential equity shares may lead to consequential changes in other items of income or expense. For example, the reduction of interest expense related to potential equity shares and the resulting increase in net profit for the period may lead to an increase in the expense relating to a non-discretionary employee profit sharing plan. For the purpose of calculating diluted earnings per share, the net profit or loss for the period is adjusted for any such consequential changes in income or expenses.

PER SHARE—DILUTED

32. For the purpose of calculating diluted earnings per share, the number of equity shares should be the aggregate of the weighted average number of equity shares calculated in accordance with paragraphs 15 and 22, and the weighted average number of equity shares which would be issued on the conversion of all the dilutive potential equity shares into equity shares. Dilutive potential equity shares should be deemed to have been converted into equity shares at the beginning of the period or, if issued later, the date of the issue of the potential equity shares.

33. The number of equity shares which would be issued on the conversion of dilutive potential equity shares is determined from the terms of the potential equity shares. The computation assumes the most advantageous conversion rate or exercise price from the standpoint of the holder of the potential equity shares.

34. Equity shares which are issuable upon the satisfaction of certain conditions resulting from contractual arrangements (contingently issuable shares) are considered outstanding and included in the computation of both the basic earnings per share and diluted earnings per share from the date when the conditions under a contract are met. If the conditions have not been met, for computing the diluted earnings per share, contingently issuable shares are included as of the beginning of the period (or as of the date of the contingent share agreement, if later). The number of contingently issuable shares included in this case in computing the diluted earnings per share is based on the number of shares that would be issuable if the end of the reporting period was the end of the contingency period. Restatement is not permitted if the conditions are not met when the contingency period actually expires subsequent to the end of the reporting period. The provisions of this paragraph apply equally to potential equity shares that are issuable upon the satisfaction of certain conditions (contingently issuable potential equity shares).

35. For the purpose of calculating diluted earnings per share, an enterprise should assume the exercise of dilutive options and other dilutive potential equity shares of the enterprise. The assumed proceeds from these issues should be considered to have been received from the issue of shares at fair value. The difference between the number of shares issuable and the number of shares that would have been issued at fair value should be treated as an issue of equity shares for no consideration.

36. Fair value for this purpose is the average price of the equity shares during the period. Theoretically, every market transaction for an enterprise's equity shares could be included in determining the average price. As a practical manner, however, a simple average of last six months weekly closing prices are usually adequate for use in computing the average price.

37. Options and other share purchase arrangements are dilutive when they would result in the issue of equity shares for less than fair value. The amount of the dilution is fair value less the issue price. Therefore, in order to calculate diluted earnings per share, each such arrangement is treated as consisting of :

(a) a contract to issue a certain number of equity shares at their average fair value during the period. The shares to be so issued are fairly priced and are assumed to be neither dilutive nor anti-dilutive. They are ignored in the computation of diluted earnings per share; and

(b) a contract to issue the remaining equity shares for no consideration. Such equity shares generate no proceeds and have no effect on the net profit attributable to equity shares outstanding. Therefore, such shares are dilutive and are added to the number of equity shares outstanding in the computation of diluted earnings per share.

Appendix VI illustrates the effects of share options on diluted earnings per share.

38. To the extent that partly paid shares are not entitled to participate in dividends during the reporting period they are considered the equivalent of warrants or options.

DILUTIVE POTENTIAL EQUITY SHARES

39. Potential equity shares should be treated as dilutive when, and only when, their conversion to equity shares would decrease net profit per share from continuing ordinary operations.

40. An enterprise uses net profit from continuing ordinary activities as "the control figure" that is used to establish whether potential equity shares are dilutive or anti-dilutive. The net profit from continuing ordinary activities is the net profit from ordinary activities (as defined in AS 5) after deducting preference dividends and any attributable tax thereto and after excluding items relating to discontinued operations.*

41. Potential equity shares are anti-dilutive when their conversion to equity shares would increase earnings per share from continuing ordinary activities. The effects of anti-dilutive potential equity shares are ignored in calculating diluted earnings per share.

42. In considering whether potential equity shares are dilutive or anti-dilutive, each issue or series of potential equity shares is considered separately rather than in aggregate. The sequence in which potential equity shares are considered may affect whether or not they are dilutive. Therefore, in order to maximise the dilution of basic earnings per share, each issue or series of potential equity shares is considered in sequence from the most dilutive to the least dilutive. For the purpose of determining the sequence from most dilutive to least dilutive potential equity shares, the earnings per incremental equity shares is calculated. Where the earnings per incremental share is the least, the potential equity share is considered most dilutive and vice-versa.

Appendix VII illustrates the manner of determining the order in which dilutive securities should be included in the computation of weighted average number of shares.

43. Potential equity shares are weighted for the period they were outstanding. Potential equity shares that were cancelled or allowed to lapse during the reporting period are included in the computation of diluted earnings per share only for the portion of the period during which they were outstanding. Potential equity shares that have been converted into equity shares during the reporting period are included in the calculation of diluted earnings per share from the beginning of the period to the date of conversion; from the date of conversion, the resulting equity shares are included in computing both basic and diluted earnings per share.

---

* A separate accounting standard 'Discontinuing Operations', which is being formulated, will specify the requirements in respect of discontinued operations.

RESTATEMENT

44. If the number of equity or potential equity shares outstanding increases as a result of a bonus issue or share split or decreases as a result of a reverse share split (consolidation of shares), the calculation of basic and diluted earnings per share should be adjusted for all the periods presented. If these changes occur after the balance sheet date but before the date on which the financial statements are approved by the board of directors, the per share calculations for those financial statements and any prior period financial statements presented should be based on the new number of shares. When per share calculations reflect such changes in the number of shares, that fact should be disclosed.

45. An enterprise does not restate diluted earnings per share of any prior period presented for changes in the assumptions used or for the conversion of potential equity shares into equity shares outstanding.

46. An enterprise is encouraged to provide a description of equity share transactions or potential equity share transactions, other than bonus issues, share splits and reverse share splits (consolidation of shares) which occur after the balance sheet date when they are of such importance that non-disclosure would affect the ability of the users of the financial statements to make proper evaluations and decisions. Examples of such transactions include :

(a) the issue of shares for cash;

(b) the issue of shares when the proceeds are used to repay debt or preference shares outstanding at the balance sheet date;

(c) the cancellation of equity shares outstanding at the balance sheet date;

(d) the conversion or exercise of potential equity shares, outstanding at the balance sheet date, into equity shares;

(e) the issue of warrants, options or convertible securities; and

(f) the satisfaction of conditions that would result in the issue of contingently issuable shares.

47. Earnings per share amounts are not adjusted for such transactions occurring after the balance sheet date because such transactions do not affect the amount of capital used to produce the net profit or loss for the period.

After the limited revision of AS 20, paragraphs 48 to 51 of the Standard appear as follows:–

DISCLOSURE

48. *In addition to disclosures as required by paragraphs 8,9 and 44 of this Statement, an enterprise should disclose the following:

(i) where the statement of profit and loss includes extraordinary items (within the meaning of AS 5, Net Profit or Loss for the Period, Prior Period Items and Changes in Accounting Policies), the enterprise should disclose basic and diluted earnings per share

---

* As a limited revision to AS 20, the Council of the Institute decided to revise this paragraph in 2004. This revision comes into effect in respect of accounting periods commencing on or after 1.4.2004. General Clarification (GC) - 10/2002, on AS 20 issued by the Accounting Standards Board, in October 2002, stands withdrawn from that date. The erstwhile paragraph was as under:

"*48. In addition to disclosures as required by paragraphs 8, 9 and 44 of this Statement, an enterprise should disclose the following:*

(a) the amounts used as the numerators in calculating basic and diluted earnings per share, and a reconciliation of those amounts to the net profit or loss for the period;

(b) the weighted average number of equity shares used as the denominator in calculating basic and diluted earnings per share, and a reconciliation of these denominators to each other; and

(c) the nominal value of shares along with the earning per share figures."

computed on the basis of earnings excluding extraordinary items (net of tax expense); and

(*ii*) (*a*) **the amount used as the numerators in calculating basic and diluted earnings per share, and a reconciliation of those amounts to the net profit or loss for the period;**

(*b*) **the weighted average number of equity shares used as the denominator in calculating basic and diluted earnings per share, and a reconciliation of these denominators to each other; and**

(*c*) **the nominal value of shares along with the earnings per share figures[3].**

49. Contracts generating potential equity shares may incorporate terms and conditions which affect the measurement of basic and diluted earnings per share. These terms and conditions may determine whether or not any potential equity shares are dilutive and, if so, the effect on the weighted average number of shares outstanding and any consequent adjustments to the net profit attributable to equity shareholders. Disclosure of the terms and conditions of such contracts is encouraged by this Statement.

50. If an enterprise discloses, in addition to basic and diluted earnings per share, per share amounts using a reported component of net profit other than net profit or loss for the period attributable to equity shareholders, such amounts should be calculated using the weighted average number of equity shares determined in accordance with this Statement. If a component of net profit is used which is not reported as a line item in the statement of profit and loss, a reconciliation should be provided between the component used and a line item which is reported in the statement of profit and loss. Basic and diluted per share amounts should be disclosed with equal prominence.

51. *An enterprise may wish to disclose more information than this Statement requires. Such information may help the users to evaluate the performance of the enterprise and may take the form of per share amounts for various components of net profit. Such disclosures are encouraged. However, when such amounts are disclosed, the denominators need to be calculated in accordance with this Statement in order to ensure the comparability of the per share amounts disclosed.[4]

APPENDICES

Note : These appendices are illustrative only and do not form part of the Accounting Standard. The purpose of the appendices is to illustrate the application of the Accounting Standard.

Appendix 1

Example -- Weighted Average Number of Shares

(Accounting year 01-01-20X1 to 31-12-20X1)

		No. of Shares issued	*No. of Shares Bought Back*	*No. of Shares Outstanding*
1st January, 20X1	Balance at beginning of year	1,800	—	1,800

* As a limited revision to AS 20, the Council of the Institute decided to revise this paragraph in 2004. This revision comes into effect in respect of accounting periods commencing on or after 1.4.2004. General Clarification (GC) - 10/2002, on AS 20 issued by the Accounting Standards Board, in October 2002, stands withdrawn from that date. The erstwhile paragraph was as under:

"51. *An enterprise may wish to disclose more information than this Statement requires. Such information may help the users to evaluate the performance of the enterprise and may take the form of per share amounts for various components of net profit, e.g., profit from ordinary activities. Such disclosures are encouraged. However, when such amounts are disclosed, the denominators need to be calculated in accordance with this Statement in order to ensure the comparability of the per share amounts disclosed."*

31st May, 20X1	Issue of shares for cash	600	—	2,400
1st November, 20X1	Buy Back of Shares	—	300	2,100
31st December, 20X1	Balance at end of year	2,400	300	2,100

Computation of Weighted Average :

$(1,800 \times 5/12) + (2,400 \times 5/12) + (2,100 \times 2/12) = 2,100$ shares

The weighted average number of shares can alternatively be computed as follows :

$(1,800 \times 12/12) + (600 \times 7/12) - (300 \times 2/12) = 2,100$ shares.

Appendix II

Example -- Partly Paid Shares

(Accounting year 01-01-20X1 to 31-12-20X1)

		No. of Shares issued	*Nominal value of shares*	*Amount Paid*
1st Januray, 20X1	Balance at beginning of year	1,800	Rs. 10	Rs. 10
31st October, 20X1	Issue of shares	600	Rs. 10	Rs. 5

Assuming the partly paid shares are entitled to participate in the dividend to the extent of amount paid, number of partly paid equity shares would be taken as 300 for the purpose of calculation of earnings per share.

Computation of weighted average would be as follows :

$(1,800 \times 12/12) + (300 \times 2/12) = 1,850$ shares

Appendix III

Example -- Bonus Issue

(Accounting year 01-01-20XX to 31-12-20XX)

Net profit for the year 20X0	Rs. 18,00,000
Net profit for the year 20X1	Rs. 60,00,000
No. of equity shares outstanding until 30th September 20X1	20,00,000
Bonus issue 1st October, 20X1	2 equity shares for each equity share outstanding at 30th September, 20X1 $20,00,000 \times 2 = 40,00,000$
Earnings per share for the year 20X1	$\frac{\text{Rs. } 60,00,000}{(20,00,000 + 40,00,000)} = \text{Re. } 1$
Adjusted earnings per share for the year 20X0	$\frac{\text{Rs. } 18,00,000}{(20,00,000 + 40,00,000)} = \text{Re. } 0.30$

Since the bonus issue is an issue without consideration the issue is treated as if it had occured prior to the beginning of the year 20X0, the earliest period reported.

Appendix IV

Example -- Rights Issue

(Accounting year 01-01-20XX to 31-12-20XX)

Net Profit	Year 20X0 : Rs. 11,00,000 Year 20X1 : Rs. 15,00,000
No. of shares outstanding prior to rights issue	5,00,000 shares
Rights issue	One new share for each five outstanding (i.e. 1,00,000 new shares) Rights issue price : Rs. 15.00 Last date of exercise rights 1st March 20X1
Fair value of one equity share immediately prior to exercise of rights on 1st March 20X1	Rs. 21.00

Computation of theoretical ex-rights fair value per share

$$\frac{\text{Fair value of all outstanding shares immediately prior to exercise of rights + total amount received from exercise}}{\text{Number of shares outstanding prior to exercise + numebr of shares issued in the exercise}}$$

$$\frac{(\text{Rs. } 21.00 \times 5{,}00{,}000 \text{ shares}) + (\text{Rs. } 15.00 \times 1{,}00{,}000 \text{ shares})}{5{,}00{,}000 \text{ shares} + 1{,}00{,}000 \text{ shares}}$$

Theoretical ex-rights fair value per share = Rs. 20.00

Computation of adjustment factor

$$\frac{\text{Fair value per share prior to exercise of rights}}{\text{Theoretical ex - rights value per share}} = \frac{\text{Rs.}(21.00)}{\text{Rs.}(20.00)} = 1.05$$

Computation of earnings per share	Year 20X0	Year 20X1
EPS for the year 20X0 as originally reported : Rs. 11,00,000 / 5,00,000 shares	Rs. 2.20	
EPS for the year 20X0 restated for rights issue : Rs. 11,00,000 /(5,00,000 shares × 1.05)	Rs. 2.10	
EPS for the year 20X1 including effects of rights issue $\frac{\text{Rs. } 15{,}00{,}000}{(5{,}00{,}000 \times 1.05 \times 2/12) + (6{,}00{,}000 \times 10/12)}$		Rs. 2.55

Appendix V

Example -Convertible Debentures

(Accounting year 01-01-20XX to 31-12-20XX)

Net profit for the current year	Rs. 1,00,00,000
No. of equity shares outstanding	50,00,000
Basic earnings per share	Rs. 2.00
No. of 12% convertible debentures of Rs. 100 each	1,00,000
Each debenture is convertible into 10 equity shares	
Interest expense for the current year	Rs. 12,00,000
Tax relating to interest expense (30%)	Rs. 3,60,000
Adjusted net profit for the current year	Rs.(1,00,00,000 + 12,00,000 – 3,60,000) = Rs. 1,08,40,000
No. of equity shares resulting from conversion of debentures	10,00,000
No. of equity shares used to compute diluted earnings per share	50,00,000 + 10,00,000 = 60,00,000
Diluted earnings per share	1,08,40,000 / 60,00,000 = Rs. 1.81

Appendix VI

Example -- Effects of Share Options on Diluted Earnings Per Share

(Accounting year 01-01-20XX to 31-12-20XX)

Net profit for the year 20X1	Rs. 12,00,000
Weighted average number of equity shares outstanding during the year 20X1	5,00,000 shares
Average fair value of one equity share during the year 20X1	Rs. 20.00
Weighted average number of shares under option during the year 20X1	1,00,000 shares
Exercise price for shares under option during the year 20X1	Rs. 15.00

Computation of earnings per share

	Earnings	*Shares*	*Earnings per share*
Net profit for the year 20X1	Rs. 12,00,000		
Weighted average number of shares outstanding during the year 20X1		5,00,000	
Basic earnings per share			Rs. 2.40
Numbers of shares under option		1,00,000	
Number of shares that would have been issued at fair value (1,00,000 × 15.00) / 20.00	*	(75,000)	
Diluted earnings per share	Rs. 12,00,000	5,25,000	Rs. 2.29

Appendix VII

Example -- Determining the Order in Which to Include Dilutive Securities in the Computation of Weighted Average Number of Shares

(Accounting year 01-01-20XX to 31-12-20XX)

Earnings, i.e. Net profit attributable to equity shareholders	Rs. 1,00,00,000
No. of equity shares outstanding	20,00,000
Average fair value of one equity share during the year	Rs. 75.00
Potential Equity Shares	
Options	1,00,000 with exercise price of Rs. 60.
Convertible Preference Shares	8,00,000 shares entitled to a cummulative dividend of Rs. 8 per share. Each preference share is convertible into 2 equity shares.
Attributable tax, e.g., corporate dividend tax	10 %
12% Convertible Debentures of Rs. 100 each	Nominal amount of Rs. 10,00,00,000. Each debenture is convertible into 4 equity shares.
Tax rate	30 %

Increase in Earnings Attributable to Equity Shareholders on Conversion of Potential Equity Shares

	Increase in Earnings	*Increase in number of Equity Shares*	*Earnings per Incremental Share*
Options			
Increase in earnings	Nil		
No. of incremental shares issued for no consideration {1,00,000 × (75 – 60) / 75}		20,000	Nil

*The earnings have not been increased as the total number of shares has been increased only by the number of shares (25,000) deemed for the purpose of the computation to have been issued for no consideration {see para 37(b)}

Convertible Preference Shares			
Increase in net profit attributable to equity share holders as adjusted by attributable tax [(Rs. 8 × 8,00,000) + 10% (8 × 8,00,000)]	Rs. 70,40,000		
No. of incremental shares (2 × 8,00,000)		16,00,000	Rs. 4.40
12% Convertible Debentures			
Increase in net profit, {Rs. 10,00,00,000 × 0.12 × (1-0.30)}	Rs. 84,00,000		
No. of incremental shares (10,00,000 × 4)		40,00,000	Rs. 2.10

It may be noted form the above that options are most dilutive as their earnings per incremental shares is nil. Hence, for the purpose of computation of diluted earnings per share, options will be considered first. 12% convertible debentures being second most dilutive will be considered next and thereafter convertible preference shares will be considered (see para 42).

Computation of Diluted Earnings Per Share

	Net Profit Attributable (Rs.)	No. of Equity Shares	Net profit attributable Per Share (Rs.)	
As reported	1,00,00,000	20,00,000	5.00	
Options		20,000		
	1,00,00,000	20,20,000	4.95	Dilutive
12% Convertible Debentures	84,00,000	40,00,000		
	1,84,00,000	60,20,000	3.06	Dilutive
Convertible Preference Shares	70,40,000	16,00,000		
	2,54,40,000	76,20,000	3.34	Anti-Dilutive

Since diluted earnings per share is increased when taking the convertible preference shares into account (form Rs. 3.06 to Rs. 3.34), the convertible preference shares are anti-dilutive and are ignored in the calculation of diluted earnings per share. Therefore, diluted earnings per share is Rs. 3.06.

Cover : Two ratios called fixed charges cover and fixed dividends cover show the effect of financial policies followed. These ratios may not be strictly called profitability ratios but they are based on figures in Profit and Loss Account.

Fixed Charges Cover is calculated as :

$$\frac{\text{Net Profit before interest and tax}}{\text{Interest on long - term loans and debentures}}$$

Interest being paid periodically, usually half yearly, it will take second place to other expenses which are paid monthly or weekly. This is the reason why the ratio is calculated using profit after other usual expenses. The ratio indicates how many times the profit covers the fixed interest—it measures the margin of safety for the lenders. If profit just equals interest, it is a bad position for the company (since nothing will be left for shareholders) and an unsafe one for the lenders.

Fixed Dividends Cover indicates how many times the fixed (preference) dividend is covered by profits after tax; it measures the margin of safety of preference shareholders. The method of calculation is :

$$\frac{\text{Profit after tax and other necessary prior apportunities, such as transfer to Development Reserve}}{\text{Fixed (or Preference) Dividend}}$$

Equity shareholders can expect a safe dividend only if the fixed dividends cover is substantial, say, when available profit is four or five times the preference dividend.

Two more ratios may be calculated.

(*a*) *Net Profit to Net Worth*, measuring profit earned, usually after interest but before tax, to net worth, that is, total of all assets less total of all liability or total of equity share capital and reserves. It roughly serves the same purpose as rate of return.

(*b*) *Net Profit to Fixed Assets*, measures the operating profit (before interest and tax) against the amount invested in fixed assets. The purpose is to ascertain whether fixed assets are being used properly but that purpose will be better served by working out turnover ratios, discussed below.

Note : One should remember that rise in prices of fixed assets will inflate the rate of return if only the historical cost of the assets is considered. Suppose, a company was started in 1980 with a capital of Rs. 1,00,000, acquiring fixed assets for the amount. The value of the assets in 2010 may be, say, Rs. 10,00,000. If the company earns a profit of Rs. 80,000, it will appear that the rate of return is 80%, i.e., 100 x 80,000/1,00,000, if only the historical cost is considered. The rate of return is only 8% since Rs. 80,000 is earned on the effective capital of Rs. 10,00,000, that too ignoring depreciation. Therefore, if values of fixed assets have changed materially, rate of return calculated on the basis of historical cost will not reflect the true picture.

Turnover (Performance or Activity) Ratios :

Performance or activity ratios judge how well the facilities at the disposal of the concern are being used. The ratios are usually calculated on the basis of cost of sales. The ratios are also known as turnover ratios as they express the rapidity with which a unit of capital invested in fixed assets, stock, etc. produces sales. The following are the important turnover or performance ratios :—

(*i*) *Total Capital Turnover Ratio* takes into account both long-term and short-term capital and is calculated as :

$$\frac{\text{Sales or Cost of Sales}}{\text{Capital Employed}}$$

(*ii*) *Fixed Assets Turnover Ratio* shows how well the fixed assets are being utilised. The way to ascertain the ratio is :

$$\frac{\text{Sales or Cost of Sales}}{\text{Net Fixed Assets (i.e., fixed assets less depreciation)}}$$

In manufacturing concerns, the ratio is important and appropriate, since sales are produced not only by use of working capital but also by the capital invested in fixed assets. An improvement in the ratio indicates better performance and a decline in it would show a declining efficiency or improvident investment. Suppose, the figures are :

	20098-2009 *Rs.*	2009-2010 *Rs.*
Fixed Assets	50,00,000	70,00,000
Sales	1,20,00,000	1,40,00,000
Fixed Assets Turnover Ratio	2.4	2.0

The figures indicate that the additional investment in fixed assets (Rs. 20,00,000) has not yielded good results—since the increase in sales is not as much as warranted by the 2009-2009.

(*iii*) *Working Capital Turnover Ratio* expresses the number of times a unit invested in working capital produces sale. The ratio is ascertained as :—

$$\frac{\text{Sales or Cost of Sales}}{\text{Net Working Capital (that is, current assets — current liabilities)}}$$

The ratio is better than the Stock Turnover Ratio, since it shows up efficiency or inefficiency in the use of the whole of working capital and not merely a part of it, viz., that invested in stocks—it is the whole of the working capital that leads to sales.

(iv) *Stock Turnover Ratio* (or Inventory Turnover Ratio). It is calculated as :—

$$\frac{\text{Cost of Sales}}{\text{Average Stock Carried or Inventory}}$$

The term stock may include all types of stock (raw materials, work in process and finished goods) but since sales are of finished goods, it is better to calculate the ratio on the basis of stock of finished goods only. Higher the ratio, the better it is, since it indicates that more sales are being produced by a unit of investment in stocks. Industries in which the stock turnover ratio is high usually work on a comparatively low margin of profit—the rate of profit on sales must be high if the stock turnover ratio is low.

It may be noted that this ratio may also be calculated as

$$\frac{\text{Sales}}{\text{Average 'Inventory'}}$$

even though the inventory figure will be at cost and sales at the selling price. This has the advantage that for a given figure of sale, the inventory level required can be easily ascertained. Suppose, the ratio is 5 and it is expected that next year the sales will be Rs. 75,00,000. Then the inventory to be carried will be around Rs. 15 lakh, i.e., Rs. 75,00,000 / 5.

(v) Debtors Turnover Ratio : It is also called Receivables Turnover Ratio or Debtors Velocity. It shows the relationship between credit sales and accounts receivable. Its formula is as follows :-

$$\text{Debtors Turnover Ratio} = \frac{\text{Net Credit Annual Sales}}{\text{Average Accounts Receivable}}$$

Net Credit Annual Sales = Credit Sales for the year – Sales Returns for the year.

$$\text{Average Accounts Receivable} = \frac{\text{Opening Accounts Receivable + Closing Accounts Receivable}}{2}$$

Accounts Receivable = Trade Debtors + Bills Receivable from Customers

Trade debtors and bills receivable are taken at gross values. It means that for purposes of calculation of this ratio provision for bad debts and provision for discount on debtors are not deducted from trade debtors and bills receivable. When the information regarding credit sales and opening and closing balances of accounts receivable is not available, debtors turnover ratio may be calculated by dividing the total sales by the balance of accounts receivable as known.

Allowing credit to customers is one of methods of sales promotion. A liberal credit policy increases sales but results in tying up funds in the form of accounts receivable. If trade debtors are collected as scheduled, the firm is able to meet its short-term obligations comfortably. Thus, quality of trade debtors is important for sound liquidity position of the firm. Thus, a good debtors turnover ratio is important. Higher the value of debtors turnover ratio , the better it is as it shows efficient collection of trade debtors. There is no standard debtors turnover ratio. What a good debtors turnover ratio is will depend upon the nature of the business. The ratio of a firm should be compared with the ratio of other firms doing the same or similar business. Trend of the ratio in the firm should be studied to judge the efficiency or otherwise of the collection department.

Debtors Ratio or Debt Collection Period : It may be calculated for the same purpose for which Debtors Turnover Ratio is calculated. The formula for the calculation of Debt Collection Period is as follows :-

$$\text{Debt Collection Period} = \frac{\text{Average Accounts Receivable}}{\text{Average Daily Credit Sales}}$$

$$\text{Average Accounts Receivable} = \frac{\text{Opening Accounts Receivable + Closing Accounts Receivable}}{2}$$

$$\text{Average Daily Credit Sales} = \frac{\text{Credit Sales for the year} - \text{Sales Returns for the year}}{365}$$

Debt Collection Period shows the number of days' sales that remain uncollected on the average. On comparison with the official credit period allowed by the firm, it would show whether debts are being collected on time or not. If net credit sales for a year total Rs. 73 lakh or Rs. 20,000 per day and the accounts receivable total Rs. 10 lakh, the debt collection period is 50 days. If the firm allows 30 days' credit to its customers, debt collection period of 50 days will indicate slackness in collection.

To ascertain average daily credit sales accurately net credit sales for the year may be divided by the working days in the year. Hence some authors divide the yearly net credit sales by 300, taking 300 to be the number of working days. However, the customary figure is 365.

(vi) Creditors Turnover Ratio : It is also called Payable Turnover Ratio or Creditors Velocity. It shows the relationship between credit purchases and accounts payable. Its formula is as follows :-

$$\text{Creditors Turnover Ratio} = \frac{\text{Net Credit Annual Purchases}}{\text{Average Accounts Payable}}$$

Net Credit Annual Purchases = Credit Purchases for the year - Purchases Returns for the year.

$$\text{Average Accounts Payable} = \frac{\text{Opening Accounts Payable} + \text{Closing Accounts Payable}}{2}$$

Accounts Payable = Trade Creditors + Bills Payable accepted in favour of Suppliers.

Trade Creditors are taken at gross values. It means that for purposes of calculation of this ratio, reserve for discount on creditors, if any, is not deducted from trade creditors. When the information regarding credit purchases and opening and closing balances of accounts payable is not available, creditors turnover ratio may be calculated by dividing the total purchases by the balance of accounts payable as known.

Creditors Turnover Ratio will depend on the period of credit allowed by the suppliers and the firm's ability to meet its liability in respect of accounts payable on time. Thus this ratio of the firm should be compared with the ratio of other firms doing the same or similar business. Trend of the ratio in the firm should also be studied to determine the soundness of the policy followed by the firm in the matter of payment to suppliers.

Creditors Ratio or Average Payment Period : May be calculated for the same purpose for which Creditors Turnover Ratio is calculated. The formula for the calculation of Average Payment Period is as follows :-

$$\text{Average Payment Period} = \frac{\text{Average Accounts Payable}}{\text{Average Daily Credit Purchases}}$$

$$\text{Average Accounts Payable} = \frac{\text{Opening Accounts Payable} + \text{Closing Accounts Payable}}{2}$$

Accounts Payable = Trade Creditors + Bills Payable accepted in favour of Suppliers

$$\text{Average Daily Credit Purchases} = \frac{\text{Credit Purchases for the year} - \text{Purchases Returns for the year}}{365}$$

Average Payment Period shows the number of days' purchases that remain unpaid on the average. In other words, it shows the average number of days taken by the firm to pay to its suppliers of goods. On comparison with the credit period allowed by the suppliers, it will show whether the firm has been paying to its suppliers on time or not. A low ratio may mean sound liquidity position of the firm with the result that the firm is able to take advantage of cash discounts allowed by the supplier. A higher ratio may imply less discount facilities availed or higher prices paid for the goods. A comparison of the ratio with the ratio of different other firms in the same industry and study of the trend of this ratio in the firm itself is very important.

(*vii*) *Raw Materials Stock Turnover Ratio* indicates whether stock of raw materials is too much, adequate or inadequate. It is calculated as :

$$\frac{\text{Stock of raw materials}}{\text{Average monthly consumption of raw materials}}$$

The figure will indicate the number of months' consumption that the actual stock is equal to. The figure compared with the average delivery period will indicate over-stocking or under-stocking. Suppose, the stock of materials at the end of the year is Rs. 3,00,000 whereas the consumption during the year was Rs. 9,60,000 or Rs. 80,000 per month. Then the firm has stock of raw materials equal to consumption for 3.75 months. There is over-stocking if the stock can be acquired on reasonable prices, say, in six or seven weeks; but if the supply of material is seasonal and the next season is to start after, say, six months, the present stock is not adequate.

Ratios to judge financial position and policies :

Most of the ratios to judge the soundness of financial position and policies are based on the balance sheet. Basically, two ratios, viz., the debt-equity ratio showing the long-term financial policy followed by the concern, and the current ratio showing the short-term financial policy should throw enough light on the financial position of the concern. We discuss below these and the other connected ratios.

(*i*) *Debt-Equity Ratio.* This is the ratio between long-term loans and total funds. Lower the ratio, more comfortable is the position of creditors, because it means that they can be called upon to suffer losses only if the losses are exceptionally heavy. It is worked out as :

$$\frac{\text{Long term Debt}}{\text{Shareholders' Funds + Long-term Debt}}$$

Redeemable preference shares are also treated as part of debt.

This ratio portrays the proportion of total funds acquired by a firm by way of debt. The ratio considered appropriate goes on changing; at one time it was thought that not more than half the long term requirements should be raised by way of long-term loans but now the proportion can be 2/3rds or even 3/4ths. In other words, 67% to 75% of the long term funds required by an industrial concern may be raised by way of loans—the proportion may be higher in the case of public utility concerns where sales and profit more or less remain stable. Diversified concerns may also have a higher proportion of loans for the same reason.

Example : The debt-equity ratio of a company is 0.67:1. How will each one of the following events affect the ratio ?

(*i*) issue of equity shares ;
(*ii*) redemption of preference shares ;
(*iii*) conversion of debentures into equity shares ;
(*iv*) cash received from debtors ;
(*v*) equity shares allotted to vendor against purchase of machinery.

In events (*i*), (*ii*), (*iii*) and (*v*), the debt equity ratio would decrease. Event (*iv*) will not affect the debt-equity ratio.

The ratio may be calculated also as:

$$\frac{\text{Long term Debt}}{\text{Shareholders' Funds}}$$

In this case, the ratio may be "2", indicating that long-term loans may be twice the shareholders' funds.

The main reason why concerns go in for loans is "trading on equity", i.e., the advantage of paying interest (which is treated as an expense by income-tax authorities) at a fixed rate, generally much lower than the yield, for the use of the funds. But since profits do fluctuate a great deal, too big a dependence on loans may mean an intolerable burden of interest when recession comes. Hence good concerns keep the debt equity ratio round acceptable norms only. The ratio indicates the soundness of the long-term financial policy. (See also Fixed Charges Cover on page 24.20). In a way, it is this cover which will show up the capacity of the firm to borrow. If profits before interest are many times the interest to be paid, the firm can safely borrow an additional amount. But, for this purpose a single year's profit is no guide. The average of past few years, adjusted for expected changes in business environment and profits, should be used as the basis to determine the amount of interest burden that may be assumed and thus to arrive at the amount of the loans that may be raised.

(*ii*) *Ratio of Capital and Long-term Funds to Fixed Assets or Fixed Assets Ratio.* The debt-equity ratio indicates the way finances have been raised; the proper investment of funds is also important from the point of view of long-term financial soundness. The ratio of long-term loans to fixed assets is therefore important and another aspect of long-term financial policy. The ratio should be worked out as :

$$\frac{\text{Shareholders' Fund + Long-term Debt}}{\text{Net Fixed Assets}}$$

It is well established that fixed assets should be acquired only out of long-term funds; this ratio shows whether this is so. The ratio will be 1 if the two are equal but if the ratio is less than 1, it means that the company has followed the imprudent policy of using short terms funds (like bank overdraft or amounts due to suppliers) for acquiring fixed assets.

But a good company always provides part of the working (or short-term) capital out of long-term funds since, at all times, a substantial amount must remain invested in current assets. Hence, the ratio should properly be 1.5 or thereabouts and not less. A very high ratio would indicate that long-term funds are being used for short-term purposes to an extent larger than necessary. Since it is usually more difficult to raise long-term funds, the practice may not be best from the company's point of view.

Another way to calculate this ratio is :

$$\frac{\text{Fixed Assets}}{\text{Net Worth}}$$

The ratio of fixed assets to net worth should be only about 1.0, not more. If it is more, it would indicate tight short-term position.

(*iii*) *Current Ratio or Working Capital Ratio.* This is the ratio of current assets to current liabilities and should be about 2, indicating that current assets are twice the current liabilities. Care should be taken to see that current assets are not unduly inflated by over-valuation. Also sale proceeds of fixed assets received shortly before the close of the year should be excluded for the purpose of calculating the ratio; if it is included, it will amount to window dressing. One must always be careful about window dressing and, therefore, the various assets should be carefully scrutinised. Sundry debtors may, for example, include advances to employees (which will be recoverable over a long period) or advances to suppliers of machinery or just doubtful debts. Stocks may include obsolete or slow moving items. Only those assets which can be and are meant to be converted into cash (or equivalent) quickly should be included. Readily saleable securities, if acquired only because funds were surplus, should be included but not securities which either cannot be sold readily (shares in private companies, for example) or which were acquired for long-term investment (for instance, shares in subsidiary companies).

Current liabilities will include *all* sums payable within one year, including such long-term liabilities as are payable within the year.

As a normal rule, current assets should be twice the current liabilities as then on payment of the liabilities, there will be no adverse effect on business operations. But the emphasis is on running the business smoothly. If the concern can quickly lay its hands on additional funds, say, because of arrangement with a bank, the current ratio may well be less than 2 without any damage to the company. But it should not be too low; that will indicate over-trading. A very high ratio will result from idleness of funds only and, therefore, is not a good sign.

One should also remember that the figure 2 is accepted only as a general guide—the figure for a particular industry may be more or less depending upon circumstances; it is usually more in case of seasonal industries.

(iv) Liquidity Ratio. This is a part of current ratio really and is found by comparing liquid resources, i.e., cash and bank balance, readily saleable securities (securities which have to be kept intact for the purpose of the business should be excluded) and book debts with current liabilities. This ratio is of great importance for banks and financial institutions but not for ordinary trading and manufacturing concerns. Some people call this ratio Acid Test or Quick Ratio. It is calculated as :

$$\frac{\text{Quick Assets}}{\text{Current Liabilities}}$$

Quick assets can be ascertained by deducting stock and prepaid expenses from current assets.

Note. A decline in the current ratio and the liquidity ratio indicates overtrading which, if serious, may land the company in difficulties.

A good current ratio accompanied by a low quick ratio will indicate a disproportionately high investment in stocks.

However, for industrial concerns monthly cash budgets will be more useful, since they will indicate the estimated cash position during each month.

Shortcomings of current ratio and quick ratio as measures of liquidity:

The following are the shortcomings of current ratio and quick ratio as measures of liquidity :

(i) These ratio are calculated at the date of the balance sheet and hence indicate the position only on that date. It is possible to manage to show a much better ratio at the end whereas throughout the year the firm may have faced difficulties.

(ii) Quick ratio is calculated on the basis of quick assets and quick liabilities which are not well-defined. Inventories may not essentially be non-liquid assets if the firm holds them for less than the credit period. Also, provisions for taxation and proposed dividend are created only at the end of the year and hence are not usual current liabilities.

(v) Stock to Working Capital Ratio : This ratio indicates the proportion of stock of raw materials, semi-finished goods and finished goods in the working capital of the concern. The following is the formula to calculate this ratio :-

$$\text{Stock to Working Capital Ratio} = \frac{\text{Stock - in - trade or Inventory}}{\text{Working Capital}}$$

where Stock-in-trade = Stock of raw material, semi-finished goods and finished goods; and

Working Capital = Current Assets – Current Liabilities

If stock to working capital ratio is 1, it means that total working capital is comprised of stock and current assets other than stock are sufficient to meet current liabilities. It also means that working capital has been financed by long-term sources of finance. It provides comfort in the fact that if due to some reason the firm is not able to dispose of stock in the anticipated period of time, there will be no difficulty in meeting obligations on current labilities in time.

(vi) Fixed Assets to Current Assets. The ratio will differ from industry to industry and even from company to company and, therefore, no standard can be laid down. An increase in the ratio may mean either (*a*) that trading is slack, or (*b*) a measure of mechanisation has been put through. A decline in the ratio may mean (*a*) that stock and debtors have unduly increased, or (*b*) the fixed assets are being more intensively used. Increase in current assets if accompanied by increase in profit, shows that business is expanding. The ratio is worked out as :

$$\frac{\text{Fixed Assets}}{\text{Current Assets}}$$

(vii) Proprietary Ratio. It is the ratio of funds belonging to shareholders to the total assets of the company. 'Funds belonging to shareholders' means share capital plus reserves and surpluses, both of capital and revenue nature. Losses should be deducted. Funds payable to others should not be added. Higher the ratio, better it is for all concerned. It is worked out as :

$$\frac{\text{Proprietors' Funds}}{\text{Total Assets}}$$

(viii) Reserves to Capital. The ratio of reserves created out of revenue profit to share capital indicates the financial position of the company. Higher the ratio, better it is, because that means that any future loss can be easily absorbed. It is worked out by dividing capital by reserves

(ix) Dividend Pay-out Ratio : Another name of this ratio is Pay-out Ratio. This ratio shows the extent to which earnings per equity share have been distributed by the company as equity dividend. It is calculated as follows :

$$\frac{\text{Dividend per equity share}}{\text{Earnings per share}}$$

High pay-out ratio will keep the equity shareholders happy. But ploughing back of profits is also a very good source of corporate finance and enables the company to increase earnings per share in future. Hence, a very high pay-out ratio may not be in the long-term interests of the company. The Board of Directors has to strike a balance between short-term interests of the equity shareholders and long-term interests of the company while deciding the pay-out ratio.

(x) Price Earning Ratio : Price Earning Ratio is the ratio between market price per equity share and the earnings per equity share. Thus,

$$\text{Price Earning Ratio} = \frac{\text{Market Price per Equity Share}}{\text{Earnings per Share}}$$

The ratio shows a relationship between market price per equity share and earnings per equity share. Investors frequently consider this ratio to decide whether or not to pay equity shares of a particular company. Higher the ratio, the better for the company.

(xi) Earnings Yield Ratio : This ratio is calculated for the same reason for which Price Earnings Ratio is calculated. The ratio can be expressed as follows :

$$\text{Earnings Yield Ratio} = \frac{\text{Earnings per share}}{\text{Market price per equity share}} \times 100$$

Suppose a joint stock company has an issued and subscribed share capital of 10,00,000 fully paid-up equity shares of Rs. 10 each and for a particular accounting year, the profits after tax are Rs. 30,00,000. Then,

$$\text{Earning per share} = \frac{\text{Profits available for equity shareholders}}{\text{Number of equity shares}}$$

$$= \text{Rs.}\frac{30,00,000}{10,00,000} = \text{Rs.}3$$

If the market price of the above mentioned share is Rs. 60, the earnings yield ratio will be 5%, calculated as follows :-

$$\text{Earnings Yield Ratio} = \frac{\text{Earning per share}}{\text{Market price per share}} \times 100$$

$$= \frac{3}{60} \times 100 = 5\%$$

(xii) Debt Service Ratio : This ratio is also known as Interest Coverage Ratio or simply Coverage Ratio or Fixed Charges Cover or Times Interest Earned. It is calculated to ascertain the capacity of the firm to pay interest on its debts out of its profits before interest and tax. The formula for calculation of this ratio is as follows :-

$$\text{Debt Service Ratio} = \frac{\text{Net Profit before Interest and Tax}}{\text{Fixed Interest Charge}}$$

Suppose, yearly interest liability of a company on its long-term borrowings is Rs. 50 lakh and the company's net profit before interest and tax is Rs. 6 crore. Then, the Debt Service Ratio for the Company is 12 times as calculated below :-

$$\text{Debt Service Ratio} = \frac{6{,}00{,}00{,}000}{50{,}00{,}000} = 12 \text{ times.}$$

Higher this ratio, the better it is for the firm as well as for the lender. A high ratio means that the firm will be able to pay interest out of profits comfortably. It is time that interest has to be paid even if there are losses but in the case of losses, the chances of delayed payment and even of default increase.

(xii) Capital Gearing Ratio : The funds employed by a joint stock company can be dividend into the following two groups :-

1. Long-term loans carrying interest at a fixed rate and preference share capital carrying dividend at a fixed rate with the difference that interest has to be paid even if there are losses whereas preference dividend is paid only out of divisible profits.

2. Equity Share Capital, reserves and surplus i.e. equity shareholders' funds which do not bear fixed dividends.

Capital gearing ratio shows the relationship between that above mentioned two groups of funds i.e. funds bearing fixed interest or fixed dividends and equity shareholders' funds which do not bear fixed dividends. This ratio can be calculated as follows :-

$$\frac{\text{Funds bearing fixed interest or fixed dividends}}{\text{Total capital employed}}$$

or

$$\frac{\text{Funds bearing fixed interest or fixed dividends}}{\text{Equity shareholders funds}}$$

If funds bearing fixed interest or fixed dividends exceed the equity shareholders funds, the company is said to be highly geared. On the other hand, if the equity shareholders funds are more than the funds bearing fixed interest or fixed dividends, then the company is said to be low-geared. If the two types of funds are equal, the company is said to be evenly-geared.

If a company pays interest on loans and dividends on preference share capital at a rate lower than the rate at which it earns on its total funds, then it is advantageous to the equity shareholders as it enables them to earn on their funds at a rate higher than the rate at which the company earns on its total funds. In such a case, a highly-geared company is at a greater advantage. Suppose a company has the following capital structure :-

	Rs.
Equity Share Capital	20,00,000
Reserves	20,00,000
12% Preference Share Capital	15,00,000
10% Debentures	35,00,000
11% Long-term Loan	10,00,000

Suppose the company earns a profit of Rs. 40 lakh before interest and taxation and the rate of income-tax is 40%. Then, the return on equity shareholders' funds can be calculated as follows :-

	Rs.	*Rs.*
Profits before interest and taxation		40,00,000
Less : Interest on 10% Debentures	3,50,000	
Interest on 11% Long-term Loan	1,00,000	4,50,000

	35,50,000
Less : Income-tax @ 40%	14,20,000
	21,30,000
Less : Preference -dividend	1,80,000
	19,50,000

$$\text{Return on equity shareholders' funds} = \frac{19,50,000}{40,00,000} \times 100 = 48.75\%$$

$$\text{General rate of return} = \frac{\text{Profit before interest and taxation} - \text{Income tax}}{\text{Total funds}} \times 100$$

$$\text{General rate of return} = \frac{40,00,000 - 14,20,000}{1,00,00,000} \times 100 = \frac{35,80,000}{1,00,00,000} \times 100 = 35.8\%$$

Thus against the general rate of return of 35.8 % return on equity shareholders' funds is 48.75%. This is called Trading on Equity or Financial Leverage. A Company may enjoy the benefit of financial leverage even when it is evenly geared or low-geared if the following factors are favourable :-

(*a*) the overall profitability

(*b*) the rate of fixed interest and fixed dividends

(*c*) the rate of income-tax.

Trading on equity results in extra profits for the equity shareholders for the risk undertaken by them. If the company's rate of return on funds falls below the fixed rate of interest and fixed dividends, the return on equity shareholders' funds will be lower than the general rate of return.

There is a similarity between capital gearing ratio and debt equity ratio. But in the case of capital gearing ratio, the classification of funds is based on the return on the funds while in the case of debt-equity ratio, the classification was members funds and outsiders funds.

Illustration 1. From the following annual statements of Pioneer Ltd., calculate the following ratios :

(*a*) Gross Profit Ratio,

(*b*) Current Ratio,

(*c*) Liquid Ratio,

(*d*) Return on Investment Ratio.

Trading and Profit and Loss Account for the year ended 31st March, 2010

	Rs.	*Rs.*		*Rs.*
To Materials Consumed :			By Sales	8,50,000
Opening Stock	90,500		By Profit on Sale of Investments	6,000
Purchases	5,45,250		By Interest on Investments	3,000
	6,35,750			
Less: Closing Stock	1,40,000	4,95,750		
To Carriage Inwards		14,250		
To Office Expenses		1,50,000		
To Sales Expenses		30,000		
To Financial Expenses		15,000		
To Loss on Sale of Fixed Asset		4,000		
To Net Profit		1,50,000		
		8,59,000		8,59,000

Balance Sheet as at 31st March, 2010

	Rs.	*Rs.*		*Rs.*	*Rs.*
Share Capital :			Fixed Assets :		
20,000 Equity Shares of			Buildings	1,50,000	
Rs. 10 each, fully paid up		2,00,000	Plant	80,000	2,30,000
General Reserve		90,000	Current Assets :		
Profit and Loss Account		60,000	Stock in Trade	1,40,000	

Bank Overdraft		30,000	Debtors	70,000	
Sundry Creditors :			Bill Receivable	10,000	
For Expenses	20,000		Bank Balances	30,000	2,50,000
For Others	80,000	1,00,000			
		4,80,000			4,80,000

[*Adapted C.A. (Inter) May 1986*]

Solution :

(*a*) Gross Profit Ratio = $\frac{\text{Gross Profit}}{\text{Sales}} \times 100$

Gross Profit = Sales – Materials Consumed – Carriage Inwards
= Rs. 8,50,000 – Rs. 4,95,750 – Rs. 14,250
= Rs. 3,40,000

Sales = Rs. 8,50,000

Gross Profit Ratio = $\frac{\text{Rs. } 3{,}40{,}000}{\text{Rs. } 8{,}50{,}000} \times 100$
= 40%

(*b*) Current Ratio = $\frac{\text{Current Assets}}{\text{Current Liabilities}}$

Current Assets = Stock + Debtors + Bills Receivable + Bank
= Rs. (1,40,000 + 70,000 + 10,000 + 30,000)
= Rs. 2,50,000

Current Liabilities = Sundry Creditors + Bank Overdraft
= Rs. (1,00,000 + 30,000)
= Rs. 1,30,000

Current Ratio = $\frac{\text{Rs. } 2{,}50{,}000}{\text{Rs. } 1{,}30{,}000}$ = 1.92:

(*c*) Liquid Ratio = $\frac{\text{Liquid Assets}}{\text{Current Liabilities}}$

Liquid Assets = Debtors + Bills Receivable + Bank
= Rs. (70,000 + 10,000 + 30,000)
= Rs. 1,10,000

Current Liabilities = Rs. 1,30,000

Liquid Ratio = $\frac{\text{Rs. } 1{,}10{,}000}{\text{Rs. } 1{,}30{,}000}$ = 0.84:1

(*d*) Return on Investment Ratio = $\frac{\text{Net Profit}}{\text{Capital employed}} \times 100$

Net Profit = Rs.1,50,000

Capital employed = Share Capital + General Reserve + Profit and Loss Account
= Rs. (2,00,000 + 90,000 + 60,000)
= Rs. 3,50,000

= $\frac{\text{Rs. } 1{,}50{,}000}{\text{Rs. } 3{,}50{,}000} \times 100$
= 42.86%

Illustration 2. Following is the Balance Sheet of M/s. Weldone Ltd as on 31.3.2010:

	Rs.		*Rs.*
Equity Share Capital	30,00,000	Land	5,00,000
Preference Share Capital	40,00,000	Building	30,00,000
General Reserve	5,00,000	Plant and Machinery	30,00,000

Profit and Loss Account	5,00,000	Furniture	4,00,000
12% Debentures	20,00,000	Debtors	20,00,000
Trade Creditors	6,00,000	Stock	15,00,000
Outstanding Expenses	1,50,000	Cash	4,00,000
Provision for Taxation	2,00,000	Prepaid Expenses	1,00,000
Proposed Dividends	3,00,000	Preliminary Expenses	3,50,000
	1,12,50,000		1,12,50,000

From the above particulars, you are required to calculate :—

(*i*) Current Ratio
(*ii*) Debt Equity Ratio
(*iii*) Capital Gearing Ratio
(*iv*) Liquid Ratio

[*Adapted C.W.A. (Inter) Dec. 1984*]

Solution :

(*i*) $\text{Current Ratio} = \dfrac{\text{Current Assets}}{\text{Current Liabilities}}$

Current Assets = Debtors + Stock + Cash + Prepaid Expenses
= Rs. (20,00,000 + 15,00,000 + 4,00,000 + 1,00,000)
= Rs. 40,00,000

Current Liabilities = Trade Creditors + Outstanding Expenses + Provision for Taxation + Proposed Dividend
= Rs. (6,00,000 + 1,50,000 + 2,00,000 + 3,00,000)
= Rs. 12,50,000

$\text{Current Ratio} = \dfrac{\text{Rs. } 40{,}00{,}000}{\text{Rs. } 12{,}50{,}000} = 3.2 : 1$

(*ii*) $\text{Debt Equity Ratio} = \dfrac{\text{Long term Debt}}{\text{Shareholders' Funds + Long term Debt}}$

Long term Debt = Preference Share Capital + 12% Debentures
= Rs. 40,00,000 + Rs. 20,00,000
= Rs. 60,00,000

Shareholders' Funds = Equity Share Capital + General Reserve + Profit and Loss Account – Preliminary Expenses
= Rs. 30,00,000 + Rs. 5,00,000 + Rs. 5,00,000 – Rs. 3,50,000
= Rs. 36,50,000

$= \dfrac{\text{Rs. } 60{,}00{,}000}{\text{Rs. } 36{,}50{,}000 + \text{Rs. } 60{,}00{,}000} = 0.62 : 1$

(*iii*) $\text{Capital Gearing Ratio} = \dfrac{\text{Preference Capital + Debentures}}{\text{Equity Share Capital + Reserves and Surplus}}$

$= \dfrac{\text{Rs. } 40{,}00{,}000 + \text{Rs. } 20{,}00{,}000}{\text{Rs. } 30{,}00{,}000 + \text{Rs. } 5{,}00{,}000 + \text{Rs. } 5{,}00{,}000}$

= 1.5 : 1

(*iv*) $\text{Liquid Ratio} = \dfrac{\text{Liquid Assets}}{\text{Current Liabilities}}$

Liquid Assets = Debtors + Cash
= Rs. (20,00,000 + 4,00,000)
= Rs. 24,00,000

Current Liabilities = Trade Creditors + Outstanding Expenses + Provision for Taxation + Proposed Dividend

$= \text{Rs. } (6,00,000 + 1,50,000 + 2,00,000 + 3,00,000)$
$= \text{Rs. } 12,50,000$

$$\text{Liquid Ratio} = \frac{\text{Rs. } 24,00,000}{\text{Rs. } 12,50,000} = 1.92 : 1$$

Illustration 3. The following extracts of financial information relate to Curious Ltd. :

(Rs. in lakhs)

Balance Sheet as at 31st March,		2010		2009
Share Capital		10		10
Reserves and Surplus		30		10
Loan Funds		60		70
		100		90
Fixed Assets (Net)		30		30
Current Assets :				
Stocks	30		20	
Debtors	30		30	
Cash and Bank Balances	10		20	
Other Current Assets	30		10	
	100		80	
Less : Current Liabilities	30		20	
Net		70		60
Total Assets		100		90
Sales		270		300

(*i*) Calculate, for the two years. Debt-Equity Ratio, Quick Ratio, and Working Capital Turnover Ratio; and

(*ii*) Find the sales volume that should have been generated in the year 2009-2010 if the company were to have maintained its Working Capital Turnover Ratio.

[*C.A. (Inter) Nov. 1996 Modified*]

Solution :

(*i*) Debt Equity Ratio — 2000-2001 | 1999-2000

$$= \frac{\text{Debt}}{\text{Equity}} = \frac{\text{Loan Funds}}{\text{Share Capital + Reserves}} = \frac{60}{40} \quad \frac{70}{20}$$

$= 1.5 \text{ times} \quad 3.5 \text{ times}$

Quick Ratio

$$= \frac{\text{Quick Ratio}}{\text{Quick Liabilities}} = \frac{\text{Debtors + Cash}}{\text{Quick Liabilities}} = \frac{30 + 10}{30} \quad \frac{30 + 20}{20}$$

$= 1.33 : 1 \quad 2.5 : 1$

(Assumed that all current liabilities are quick liabilities)

Working Capital Turnover Ratio

$$= \frac{\text{Sales}}{\text{Working Capital}} = \frac{270}{70} \quad \frac{300}{60}$$

$= 3.86 \text{ times} \quad 5 \text{ times}$

(Working Capital = Current Assets – Current Liabilities)

(*ii*) Sales Volume to be maintained

$$5 = \frac{\text{Required Sales}}{70}$$

Sales required for the year 2000-2001 = Rs. 350 lakhs.

Illustration 4. The Balance Sheet of Y Ltd. stood as follows as on :

(Rs. in lakhs)

Liabilities	31.3.2010	31.3.2009	*Assets*	31.3.2010		31.3.2009	
Capital	250	250	Fixed Assets	400		300	
Reserves	116	100	*Less* : Depreciation	140	260	100	200
Loans	100	120	Investment		40		30
			Stock		120		100
Creditors and other			Debtors		70		50
current liabilities	129	25	Cash / Bank		20		20
			Other current assets		25		25
			Miscellaneous expenditure		60		70
	595	495			595		495

You are given the following information for the year 2009-2010 :

	Rs. in lakhs
Sales	600
PBIT	150
Interest	24
Provision for tax	60
Proposed dividend	50

From the above particulars, calculate for the year 2009-2010 :

(*a*) Return on capital employed ratio.
(*b*) Stock turnover ratio.
(*c*) Return on net worth ratio.
(*d*) Current ratio.
(*e*) Proprietary ratio. [*C.A. (Inter) Nov. 1995 Modified*]

Solution :

(*a*) Return on capital employed ratio $= \dfrac{\text{PBIT}}{\text{Average capital employed}} \times 100$

$$= \frac{150}{403} \times 100 = 37.22\%$$

(*b*) Stock turnover ratio $= \dfrac{\text{Sales}}{\text{Average stock}} = \dfrac{600}{110} = 5.45$ times

(*c*) Return on net worth ratio $= \dfrac{\text{PAT}}{\text{Average net worth}} \times 100 = \dfrac{66}{293} \times 100 = 22.53\%$

(*d*) Current ratio $= \dfrac{\text{Current assets}}{\text{Current liabilities}} = \dfrac{235}{129} = 1.82$ times

(*e*) Proprietary ratio $= \dfrac{\text{Proprietary funds}}{\text{Total assets} - \text{miscellaneous expenditure}}$

$$= \frac{306}{595-60} = \frac{306}{535} = 0.57$$

Working Notes :

(*i*) *Average capital employed :*

	31.3.2010	31.3.2009
	(Rupees in lakhs)	
Total assets excluding miscellaneous expenditure	535	425
Less : Creditors and other current liabilities	129	25
	406	400

Average = Rs. (406 + 400) lakh / 2 = Rs. 806 lakh / 2 = Rs. 403 lakh

(ii) *Average net worth* :

Share capital	250	250
Reserves	116	100
	366	350
Less : Miscellaneous expenditure	60	70
	306	280

Average = Rs. (306 + 280) lakh / 2 = Rs. 586 / 2 = Rs. 293 lakh

Proprietary funds as on 31.3.2010 mean net worth as on that date.

(iii) Average stock = Rs. (120 + 100) lakh / 2 = Rs. 110 lakh

(iv) *Profit after tax* :

	Rs. in lakhs
P B I T	150
Less : Interest	24
	126
Less : Tax	60
	66

(v) *Current assets as on 31st March, 2010* :

Stock	120
Debtors	70
Cash / Bank	20
Other current assets	25
	235

Illustration 5 . The directors of Bharucha Enterprises Ltd. ask you to ascertain :-

(*a*) Proprietors' funds
(*b*) Fixed assets
(*c*) Closing debtors
(*d*) Closing creditors
(*e*) Closing stock
(*f*) Share capital
(*g*) Cash and bank balances

The following information is provided to you :

(i) Inventory turnover ratio is 6 times.
Year end debtors are outstanding for 2 months.
Year end creditors are outstanding for 73 days.

(ii) Ratios of cost of goods sold to :
(a) Proprietors' funds is 2:1
(b) Fixed assets is 4 :1.

(iii) Ratio of gross profit to sales is 20%.

(iv) Closing stock is greater than the opening stock by Rs. 10,000.

(v) The gross profit for the year is Rs. 1,20,000.

(vi) Reserves and surplus appearing in the balance sheet at the end of the year total to Rs. 40,000. [*C.A. (Inter) May, 1998 Modified*]

Solution :

(*a*) Ratio of cost of goods sold to proprietors' funds is 2:1.

$$\text{Proprietors' funds} = \frac{\text{Cost of goods sold}}{2}$$

Cost of goods sold = Rs. 4,80,000 [Working note (ii)]

$$\text{Hence, proprietors' funds} = \frac{4{,}80{,}000}{2} = \text{Rs.}2{,}40{,}000$$

(*b*) Ratio of cost of goods sold to fixed assets is 4:1.

$$\text{Fixed assets} = \frac{\text{Cost of goods sold}}{4}$$

Cost of goods sold = Rs. 4,80,000

Hence, fixed assets = Rs. 4,80,000 / 4 = Rs. 1,20,000

(*c*) Year end debtors are outstanding for 2 months *i.e* they represent 2/12ths of annual sales.
Annual sales = Rs. 6,00,000 [Working note (i)]
Hence closing debtors = Rs. 6,00,000 x 2 /12 = Rs. 1,00,000

(*d*) Year end creditors are outstanding for 73 days *i.e* they represent 73/365ths or 1/5th of the purchases for the year.
Purchases = Rs. 4,90,000 [Working note (iii)]
Hence, closing creditors = Rs. 4,90,000 × 1/5 = Rs. 98,000

(*e*) Inventory turnover ratio is 6 times.

$$\text{Average inventory} = \frac{\text{Cost of goods sold}}{\text{Inventory turnover ratio}}$$

$$= \frac{4,80,000}{6} = \text{Rs.}80,000$$

Let the opening stock be x

Then, closing stock = x + Rs. 10,000

$$\text{Average inventory} = \frac{\text{Opening stock + Closing stock}}{2}$$

$$\text{Rs. } 80,000 = \frac{2x + \text{Rs. } 10,000}{2}$$

Multiplying the two sides by 2, we get

Rs. 1,60,000 = 2 x + Rs. 10,000

or Rs. 1,60,000 – Rs. 10,000 = 2 x

or 2 x = Rs. 1,50,000

or x = Rs. 75,000

Thus, opening stock = Rs. 75,000

Hence, closing stock = Rs. 75,000 + Rs. 10,000
= Rs. 85,000

(*f*) Proprietors' funds = Share capital + Reserves and surplus
Share Capital = Proprietors' funds - Reserves and surplus
Hence, share capital = Rs. 2,40,000 - Rs. 40,000
= Rs. 2,00,000

(*g*) Fixed assets + Stock + Debtors + Cash and bank balances = Proprietors' funds + Creditors
Cash and bank balances = Proprietors' funds + Creditors – Fixed assets – Stock – Debtors
Hence, cash and bank balances = Rs. 2,40,000 + Rs. 98,000 – Rs. 1,20,000 – Rs. 85,000 – Rs. 1,00,000 = Rs. 33,000

Working Notes :

(*i*) Ratio of gross profit to sales is 20%.
Gross profit for the year = Rs. 1,20,000
Hence, sales = Rs. 1,20,000 x 100 / 20 = Rs. 6,00,000

(*ii*) Cost of goods sold = Sales - Gross profit
= Rs. 6,00,000 - Rs. 1,20,000
= Rs. 4,80,000

(*iii*) Purchases = Cost of goods sold + Closing stock - Opening stock
= Rs. 4,80,000 + Rs. 10,000
= Rs. 4,90,000

Illustration 6. The following table gives comparative figures of ratios for the actual condition for a given period and the standard selected. Give, in few words, your general conclusions on examination of the several ratios :

Particulars	Actual condition	Standard selected
1. Current Assets/Current Liabilities	6.5	2.5
2. Cash/Current Liabilities	0.6	0.2
3. Fixed Assets/Net Worth	0.4	0.5
4. Trade Debtors/Sales	0.08	0.1
5. Stock/Sales	6.0	4.0
6. Sales/Net Worth	1.3	2.0
7. Liabilities/Net Worth	0.7	0.1
8. Sales/Fixed Assets	0.3	0.4
9. Net Profits/Net Worth	0.3	0.7

Solution :

1. The ratio of current assets to current liabilities is far higher than the standard. It is very comfortable for the creditors but, for the company, it indicates idle funds and a certain lack of enthusiasm for work.
2. The above is also true of the second ratio—cash to current liabilities.
3. This ratio of fixed assets to net worth shows that the company is not as mechanised as other companies—or it may be because of idle funds.
4. The ratio of trade debtors to sales is lower than the standard. It is comforting to note that debts are collected more promptly; but in view of comments in (1) above, the ratio may be favourable because of low activity rather than prompt collection. Further, the company may be insisting more on cash sales and thus missing sales opportunities.
5. The ratio of stocks to sales clearly shows that the company is not rapidly turning over the stock. Sales are low. Ratio Nos. 6, 8 and 9 confirm this. The facilities of the company are not being fully utilised.
6. Liabilities to net worth ratio is more favourable than the standard but in view of the extremely high current ratio, this ratio is rather high. It indicates that long-term liabilities preponderate and perhaps working capital needs have also been raised by issue of long-term loans.

On the whole, it is clear the company seems to be missing its opportunities and is not as active as it ought to be; there is under-trading. It must use its facilities fully.

Illustration 7. Assume that a firm has owners' equity of Rs. 1 crore. and the ratios for the firm are :

Short-term debt to total debt	= 0.40
Total debt to owners' equity	= 0.60
Fixed assets to owners' equity	= 0.60
Total assets turnover	= 2 times
Inventory turnover	= 8 times

From the information given above, complete the following balance sheet :—

Capital & Liabilities	*Rs.*	*Assets*	*Rs.*
Short-term Debt	....	Cash	....
Long-term Debt	....	Inventory	....
Total Debt	....	Total Current Assets	....
Owners' Equity	....	Fixed Assets	....
Total Capital and Liabilities	....	Total Assets	....

[*Co. Sec. (Inter) June, 1987 Modified*]

Solution :

Balance Sheet as at ....

Liabilities	*Rs. in lakhs*	*Assets*	*Rs. in lakhs*
Short-term Debt	24	Cash	60
Long-term Debt	36	Inventory	40
Total Debt	60	Total Current Assets	100
Owners' Equity	100	Fixed Assets	60
Total Capital and Liabilities	160	Total Assets	160

Working Notes :

(*i*) *Owners' Equity* = Rs. 1 crore; hence,
Total Debts = Rs. 1 crore × 0.60 = Rs. 60 lakh, and
Fixed Assets = Rs. 1 crore × 0.60 = Rs. 60 lakh

(*ii*) Total Capital and Liabilities = Total Debt + Owners' Equity
= Rs. 60 lakh + Rs. 1 crore
= Rs. 160 lakh

(*iii*) Total Assets = Total Capital and Liabilities = Rs. 1,60,000

(*iv*) Current Assets = Total Assets – Fixed Assets
= Rs. 160 lakh – Rs. 60 lakh
= Rs. 100 lakh

(*v*) Sales are twice as much as total assets i.e
= Rs. 160 lakh × 2
= Rs. 320 lakh

(*vi*) Inventory is 1/8th of sales i.e.
= Rs. 320 lakh × 1/8
= Rs. 40 lakh

(*vii*) Cash = Current Assets – Inventory
= Rs. 100 lakh – Rs. 40 lakh
= Rs. 60 lakh

(*viii*) If total debt = Rs. 60 lakh
Then, short-term debt = Rs. 60 lakh × 0.40 = Rs. 24 lakh

(*ix*) Long-term debt = Total debt – Short-term debt
= Rs. 60 lakh – Rs. 24 lakh
= Rs. 36 lakh

Illustration 8. From the following information, relating to a limited company, prepare a Statement of Proprietors' Funds :

(*i*)	Current Ratio	2
(*ii*)	Liquid Ratio	1.5
(*iii*)	Fixed Assets/Proprietary Fund	3/4
(*iv*)	Working Capital	Rs. 75 lakh
(*v*)	Reserves and Surplus	Rs. 50 lakh
(*vi*)	Bank Overdraft	Rs. 10 lakh

There were no long-term loans or fictitious assets. [*Adapted C.A.* (*Inter*) *Nov.* 1987]

Solution :

Statement of Proprietors' Funds

I	*Sources of Funds :*	*Rs. in lakhs*	*Rs. in lakhs*	*Rs. in lakhs*
	Share Capital		250	
	Reserves and Surplus		50	300

		Rs. in lakhs			
II	*Application of Funds :*				
	Fixed Assets			225	
	Current Assets :	*Rs. in lakhs*			
	Stock	37.5			
	Liquid Assets	112.5			
			150		
	Less: Current Liabilities :				
	Bank Overdraft	10			
	Other Current Liabilities	65	75		
	Working Capital			75	300

Working Notes :

(*i*) Let the current liabilities be x
then current assets are $2x$
and working capital is x (current assets minus current liabilities)
It is given that working capital is Rs. 75 lakh. Hence,
the current assets are Rs. 75 lakh × 2 = Rs. 150 lakh
the liquid assets are Rs. 75 lakh × 3/2 = Rs. 112.5 lakh, and
the current liabilities are Rs. 75 lakh × 1 = Rs. 75 lakh
Further, it is given that bank overdraft is Rs. 10 lakh. Therefore, the amount of other current liabilities is the balancing figure i.e. Rs. 75 lakh – Rs. 10 lakh = Rs. 65 lakh and
Stock is (current assets - liquid assets) = Rs. 150 lakh – Rs. 112.5 lakh = Rs. 37.5 lakh

(*ii*) Let the proprietary funds be x,
then fixed assets are $3/4\ x$
As there are no long-term loans or fictitious assets, the following equation may be formulated:
Proprietary Funds + Current Liabilities = Fixed Assets + Current Assets

x + Rs. 75 lakh = $3/4\ x$ + Rs. 150 lakh
or $x - 3/4\ x$ = Rs. 150 lakh – Rs. 75 lakh
$1/4\ x$ = Rs. 75 lakh

Multiplying both the sides by 4, we get x i.e. Proprietary Funds = Rs. 300 lakh

(*iii*) Fixed assets are 3/4ths of proprietary funds; hence
Fixed Assets = Rs. 300 lakh × 3/4
= Rs. 225 lakh

(*iv*) Share Capital = Proprietary Fund – Reserves
= Rs. 300 lakh – Rs. 50 lakh
= Rs. 250 lakh

Illustration 9. Following are the ratios relating to the trading activities of an organisation :

Debtors' Velocity	3 months
Stock Velocity	6 months
Creditors' Velocity	2 months
Gross Profit Ratio	20%

Gross profit for the year ended 31st March, 2010 was Rs. 500 lakh. Stock as on 31st March, 2010 was Rs. 20 lakh more than it was on 1st April, 2009. Bills payable and bills receivable were Rs. 36.667 lakh and Rs. 60 lakh respectively.

You are to ascertain the figures of :

(*i*) Sales
(ii) Debtors
(*iii*) Creditors; and
(iv) Stock

[*Adapted C.A.* (*Inter*) *May,* 1987]

Solution :

		Rs.
(*i*)	Gross Profit	500 lakh
	Rate of Gross Profit	20%
	∴ Sales Rs. 500 lakh × 100 / 20	2,500 lakh
(*ii*)	Sales	2,500 lakh
	Debtors' Velocity	3 months
	Accounts Receivable as on 31st March, 2010 :	
	Rs. 2,500 lakh/4	625 lakh
	Less: Bills Receivable	60 lakh
	∴ Trade Debtors	565 lakh
(*iii*)	Purchases :	
	Cost of Sales = (Sales – Gross Profit)	
	= Rs. 2,500 lakh – Rs. 500 lakh	2,000 lakh
	Increase in Stock	20 lakh
	Purchases for the year	2,020 lakh
	Accounts Payable as on 31st March 2010	
	Rs. 2020 lakh/6	336.667 lakh
	Less: Bills Payable	36.667 lakh
		300 lakh
(*iv*)	Cost of Goods sold	2,000 lakh
	Stock Velocity	6 months
	∴ Average Stock = Rs. 2,000 lakh/2	1,000 lakh

Let opening stock be = x
then, closing stock = x + Rs. 20 lakh
Twice the average stock or Rs. 1,000 lakh × 2 = 2 x + Rs. 20 lakh
or $2x$ = Rs. 1,980 lakh
x = Rs. 990 lakh
Opening Stock = Rs. 990 lakh
Closing Stock = Rs. 990 lakh + Rs. 20 lakh = Rs. 1,010 lakh

Illustration 10. Shri Devdas asks you to prepare his balance sheet from the particulars furnished hereunder :

Stock velocity : 6
Gross profit margin : 20%
Capital turnover ratio : 2
Fixed assets turnover ratio : 4
Debt collection period : 2 months
Creditors payment period : 73 days
Gross profit was Rs. 60,000
Excess of closing stock over opening stock was Rs. 5,000
Difference in Balance Sheet represents bank balance.

[*C.A. (Inter) May, 1999*]

Solution :

Balance Sheet of Shri Devdas as on ________

Liabilities	*Rs.*	*Assets*	*Rs.*
Capital	1,50,000	Fixed Assets	75,000
Creditors	49,000	Stock	42,500
		Debtors	50,000
		Bank balance	31,500
	1,99,000		1,99,000

Working Notes :

(*i*) Gross profit = Rs. 60,000
Gross profit margin = 20%
Hence, sales = Rs. 60,000 x 100 / 20 = Rs. 3,00,000
Cost of goods sold = Sales – Gross profit
= Rs. (3,00,000 - 60,000)
= Rs. 2,40,000
Purchases = Cost of goods sold + Increase in stock
= Rs. (2,40,000 + 5,000) = Rs. 2,45,000

$$\text{Average stock} = \frac{\text{Cost of goods sold}}{\text{Stock velocity}} = \text{Rs.}\ \frac{2,40,000}{6} = \text{Rs. } 40,000$$

(*ii*) *Capital* :
Capital turnover ratio = 2

$$\frac{\text{Sales}}{\text{Capital}} = 2$$

$$\text{Hence, capital} = \frac{\text{Rs. } 3,00,000}{2} = \text{Rs. } 1,50,000$$

or

$$\frac{\text{Cost of goods sold}}{\text{Capital}} = 2$$

$$\text{Hence, capital} = \frac{2,40,000}{2} = \text{Rs. } 1,20,000$$

(*iii*) *Creditors :*
Creditors payment period = 73 days
Hence, creditors = Purchases x 73 / 365 = Rs. 2,45,000 × 1 / 5 = Rs. 49,000

(*iv*) *Fixed assets* :
Fixed assets turnover ratio = 4
Hence, fixed assets = Sales / 4 = Rs. 3,00,00 / 4 = Rs. 75,000

(*v*) *Closing stock* :
As closing stock is Rs. 5,000 more than opening stock, it is Rs. 2,500 more than average stock.
Hence, closing stock = Average stock + Rs. 2,500
= Rs. 40,000 + Rs. 2,500 = Rs. 42,500

(*vi*) *Debtors :*
Debt collection period = 2 months
Hence, debtors = Sales × 2 /12 = Rs. 3,00,000 × 1/6 = Rs. 50,000

(*vii*) Bank balance is the balancing figure.
If capital is shown at Rs. 1,20,000, bank balance will appear at Rs. 1,500.

Illustration 11. From the following information, prepare the balance sheet of XYZ Co. Ltd., showing the details of working :—

		Rs.
Paid-up capital		50 lakh
Plant and machinery		125 lakh
Total sales (annual)		500 lakh
Gross profit margin	25%	
Annual credit sales	80% of net sales	
Current ratio	2	

Inventory turnover	4
Fixed assets turnover	2
Sales returns	20% of sales
Average collection period	73 days
Bank credit to trade credit	2
Cash to inventory	1 :15
Total debt to current liabilities	3

[*Adapted C.A.* (*Final*) *May,* 1985]

Solution :

Balance Sheet of XYZ Co. Ltd. as at ....

Liabilities	*Rs. in lakhs*	*Rs. in lakhs*	*Assets*	*Rs. in lakhs*	*Rs. in lakhs*
Share Capital		50	Fixed Assets :		
Reserves & Surplus		78	Plant & Machinery	125	
Long-term Debt		144	Other Fixed Assets	75	200
Current Liabilities :			Current Assets :		
Bank Credit	48		Inventory	75	
Trade Credit	24	72	Receivables	64	
			Cash	5	144
		344			344

Working Notes :

			Rs. in lakh
(*i*)	Net Sales = (Sales - Sales Returns) = (Rs. 500 lakh – Rs. 100 lakh)	=	400
	Credit Sales, being 80% of Net Sales	=	320
	Gross Profit, being 25% of Net Sales	=	100
(*ii*)	Cost of Sales = (Net Sales - Gross Profit) = (Rs. 400 lakh – Rs. 100 lakh)	=	300
(*iii*)	Inventory : Cost of Sales / 4 i.e. Rs. 300 lakh/4	=	75
(*iv*)	Receivable Turnover : 365 days / 73 days i.e. 5		
	Receivables : Credit Sales/5 i.e. Rs. 320 lakh/5	=	64
(*v*)	Cash : 1/15 of inventory i.e. Rs. 75 lakh × 1/15	=	5
(*vi*)	Total Current Assets i.e., Cash + Receivable + Inventory are	=	144
	The current ratio being 2, current liabilities will be Rs. 72 lakh		
(*vii*)	Total Current Liabilities being Rs. 72 lakh of which 2/3rd i.e. Rs. 48 lakh are Bank Credit and 1/3rd i.e. Rs. 24 lakh are Trade Credit.		
(*viii*)	Total Debts : Current Liabilities × 3 i.e. Rs. 72 lakh × 3	=	216
(*ix*)	Fixed Assets turnover is 2 per annum. Hence, the total of Fixed Assets is Rs. 400 lakh/2	=	200
(*x*)	Other Fixed Assets : Total Fixed Assets – Plant & Machinery = Rs. 200 lakh – Rs. 125 lakh	=	75
(*xi*)	Total Assets : (Fixed Assets + Current Assets) = (Rs. 200 lakh + Rs. 144 lakh)	=	344
(*xii*)	Net worth : (Total Assets – Total debts) = (Rs. 344 lakh – Rs. 216 lakh)	=	128
(*xiii*)	Reserves & Surplus : Net worth – Paid up Capital = (Rs. 128 lakh – Rs. 50 lakh)	=	78

Illustration 12. You are given the following figures worked out from the Profit and Loss Account and Balance Sheet of Zed Ltd. relating to the year 2009-2010. Prepare the Balance Sheet.

	Rs.
Fixed Assets (net, after writing off 30%)	10,50,000
Fixed Assets Turnover Ratio (Cost of sales basis)	2

Finished Goods Turnover Ratio	6
Rate of Gross Profit to Sales	25%
Net Profit (before interest) to Sales	16%
Fixed Charges Cover (Debenture Interest, 14%)	8
Debt Collection Period	1½ months
Materials consumed to Sales	30%
Stock of raw materials (in terms of number of months' consumption)	3
Current Ratio	2.4
Quick Ratio	1.0
Reserves to Capital	0.21

Solution :

Balance Sheet of Zed Ltd. as on 31st March 2010

Liabilities	*Rs.*	*Assets*	*Rs.*	*Rs.*
Share Capital	10,00,000	Fixed Assets, at cost	15,00,000	
General Reserve	2,10,000	*Less:* Depreciation	4,50,000	10,50,000
14% Debentures	4,00,000	Current Assets :		
Current Liabilities	4,00,000	Stock of Raw Materials	2,10,000	
		Stock of Finished Goods	3,50,000	5,60,000
		Book Debts		3,50,000
		Cash		50,000
Total	20,10,000	Total		20,10,000

Working Notes :

(*i*) Cost of sales : Fixed assets (net) × 2 = Rs. 10,50,000 × 2 = Rs. 21,00,000

(*ii*) Finished goods stock : (Cost of sales/6) = Rs. 21,00,000/6 = Rs.Rs. 3,50,000

(*iii*) Total sales : Rs. $21,00,000 \times \frac{100}{75}$ = Rs. 28,00,000

(*iv*) Book debts : $\frac{28,00,000}{12} \times 1.5$ = Rs. 3,50,000

(*v*) Materials consumed : 30% of Rs. 28,00,000 or Rs. 8,40,000

(*vi*) Stock of raw materials : 3 months' consumption = $\frac{8,40,000}{12} \times 3$ or Rs. 2,10,000

(*vii*) Ratio of stock to current liabilities is 1.4, i.e., 2.4—1.0; stocks of finished goods and of raw materials total Rs. 5,60,000. Hence, current liabilities are Rs. 5,60,000/1.4 = Rs. 4,00,000. Quick assets ratio being 1, quick assets (book debts and cash) are equal to the current liabilities *i.e.* Rs. 4,00,000. Book debts are Rs. 3,50,000; therefore cash in hand is Rs. 50,000.

(*viii*) Net profit on sales is 16%; total profit is Rs. 4,48,000; this covers the debenture interest 8 times, hence debenture interest is Rs. 56,000. At 14%, the debentures must be Rs. 4,00,000.

(*ix*) Capital and reserves are the balancing figures in total; capital and reserves are in the ratio of 100 : 21.

(*x*) Fixed assets are after writing of 30% depreciation; the total cost is Rs. $10,50,000 \times \frac{100}{70}$ = Rs. 15,00,000.

Illustration 13. Exe Limited is a dealer in automobile components. While preparing the financial statements for the year ended 31.3.2010, it was discovered that a substantial portion of the record was missing. However, the accountant was able to gather the following data :

	Rs.	Rs.		Rs.	Rs.
Share Capital			Fixed Assets		
Authorised and subscribed :			Land		1,20,000
20,000 equity shares			Plant and Machinery		
of Rs. 10 each, fully			At cost	?	
paid up		2,00,000	*Less* : Depreciation	?	?
Reserves and Surplus			Current Assets		
General Reserve :			Stock	?	
Balance on 1.4.2009	60,000		Debtors	?	
Add : Transfer during			Cash and Bank	?	?
the year	?	?			
Secured Loans					
15% Loan		?			
Current Liabilities					
Creditors	?				
Provision for tax	?				
Proposed Dividend	?	2,00,000			
		?			?

The following additional information is provided to you :

(i)	Current ratio	2 times
(ii)	Cash and Bank	30% of total current assets
(iii)	Debtors velocity (Sales/Debtors)	12 times
(iv)	Stock velocity (Cost of goods sold/Stock)	12 times
(v)	Creditors velocity (Cost of goods sold/Creditors)	12 times
(vi)	Gross profit/sales	25%
(vii)	Proposed dividend	20%
(viii)	Tax rate	33 1/3%
(ix)	Debt service coverage ratio	1 time
(x)	Interest coverage ratio	3 times interest on the balance of loan outstanding on 1.4.2000
(xi)	Selling and distribution expenses	Rs. 1,80,000
(xii)	Depreciation rate	40%.
(xiii)	Cost of goods sold does not include depreciation.	

On the basis of the above–mentioned information, you are required to complete the balance sheet as on 31.3.2010. It is assumed that there is no corporate dividend tax.

Solution :

Working Notes :

(i) Creditors are Rs. 2,00,000 and current ratio is 2 times.
Hence, total current assets = 2 × Rs. 2,00,000 = Rs. 4,00,000

(ii) Cash and bank = 30% of total current assets = 30% of Rs. 4,00,000 = Rs. 1,20,000

(iii) Stock + debtors = Total current assets – cash and bank = Rs. 4,00,000 – Rs. 1,20,000 = Rs. 2,80,000
Since gross profit is 25% on sales and since debtors velocity and stock velocity are 12 times, their ratio will be 4:3 in terms of sales and cost of goods sold.
Hence, debtors = Rs. 2,80,000 × 4/7 = Rs. 1,60,000;
and stock = Rs. 2,80,000 × 3/7 = Rs. 1,20,000

(iv) Since stock velocity and creditors velocity are the same, creditors will be equal to stock.
Hence, creditors = Rs. 1,20,000

(v) Proposed dividend = 20% of Rs. 2,00,000 = Rs. 40,000
Provision for tax = Current liabilities – creditors – proposed dividend
= Rs. (2,00,000 – 1,20,000 - 40,000) = Rs. Rs. 40,000

(vi) Tax rate = 33 1/3%
Hence, profit before tax = Rs. 40,000 × 300/100 = Rs. 1,20,000
Profit after tax = Rs. 1,20,000 – Rs. 40,000 = Rs. 80,000

(vii) Amount transferred to general reserve = Profit after tax – proposed dividend
= Rs. 80,000 - Rs. 40,000 = Rs. 40,000.

(viii) Interest coverage ratio = Profit before interest and tax / interest
Profit before interest and tax = Profit before tax + Interest = 3 times of interest
Profit before tax = 2 times interest
Hence, interest = Profit before tax / 2 = Rs. 1,20,000 /2 = Rs. 60,000
Profit before interest and tax = 3 × Rs. 60,000 = Rs. 1,80,000

(ix) Gross profit is 12 times the difference between debtors and stock.
Hence, gross profit = 12 × Rs. (1,60,000 – 1,20,000) = Rs. 4,80,000

(x) Profit before interest, depreciation and tax = Gross profit – selling and distribution expenses
= Rs. 4,80,000 – Rs, 1,80,000 = Rs. 3,00,000

(xi) Depreciation = Profit before interest, depreciation and tax - profit before interest and tax
= Rs. 3,00,000 – Rs. 1,80,000 = Rs. 1,20,000

(xii) Opening value of plant and machinery = Rs. 1,20,000 × 100/40 = Rs. 3,00,000
Closing value of plant and machinery = Rs. 3,00,000 – Rs. 1,20,000 = Rs. 1,80,000

(xiii) Debt service ratio,
(profit after tax + depreciation + interest) / interest and installments = 1 time
Rs. (80,000+1,20,000+60,000) = installments + Rs.60,000

or installments = Rs. 2,60,000 - Rs. 60,000 = Rs. 2,00,000

(xiv) Opening amount of loan = Rs. 60,000 × 100 / 15 = Rs. 4,00,000
Closing balance = Opening balance – installments = Rs. 4,00,000 – Rs. 2,00,000 = Rs. 2,00,000.

Balance Sheet of Exe Limited as on 31st March. 2010

Liabilities	*Rs.*	*Rs.*	*Assets*	*Rs.*	*Rs.*
Share Capital			Fixed Assets		
Authorised and subscribed :			Land		1,20,000
20,000 equity shares			Plant and Machinery :		
of Rs. 10 each, fully			At cost	3,00,000	
paid up		2,00,000	*Less* : Depreciation	1,20,000	1,80,000
Reserves and Surplus			Current Assets		
General Reserve :			Stock	1,20,000	
Balance on 1.4.2000	60,000		Debtors	1,60,000	
Add : Transfer during			Cash and Bank	1,20,000	4,00,000
the year	40,000	1,00,000			
Secured Loans					
15% Loan		2,00,000			
Current Liabilities					
Creditors	1,20,000				
Provision for tax	40,000				
Proposed Dividend	40,000	2,00,000			
		7,00,000			7,00,000

Illustration 14. From the following information and ratios, prepare the Profit and Loss Account for the year ended 31st March, 2010, and the Balance Sheet as on that date of M/s Stan & Co., an export company :

Current Assets to Stock	3 : 2
Current Ratio	3.00
Acid Test Ratio	1.00
Financial Leverage	2.20
Earnings per Share (each of Rs. 10)	10.00
Book Value per Share (Rs.)	40.00
Average Collection Period (assume 360 days in a year)	30 days
Stock Turnover Ratio	5.00
Fixed Assets, Turnover Ratio	1.20
Total Liabilities to Net Worth	2.75
Net working Capital	Rs. 10.00 lakh
Net Profit to Sales	10%
Variable Cost	60%
Long-term Loan Interest	12%
Taxation	Nil

[*Adapted C.A. (Inter) Nov. 1994*]

Solution :

M/s Stan & Co.
Profit and Loss Account for the year ended 31st March, 2010

	Rs.
Sales	50,00,000
Less : Variable costs	30,00,000
	20,00,000
Less : Fixed costs (excluding interest)	9,00,000
Earnings before interest and tax	11,00,000
Less : Interest	6,00,000
Earnings before tax	5,00,000
Less : Tax	0
Profit after tax	5,00,000

Balance Sheet as at 31st March, 2010

	Rs.	Rs.
Sources		
Shareholders' Funds		20,00,000
Long-term Liabilities		50,00,000
		70,00,000
Applications		
Fixed Assets		41,66,667
Current Assets:		
Stock	10,00,000	
Debtors	4,16,667	
Other Current Assets	83,333	
	15,00,000	
Less : Current Liabilities	5,00,000	
Net Current Assets		10,00,000
Other Assets (balancing figure)		18,33,333
		70,00,000

Working Notes :

(*i*) Net working capital = Rs. 10,00,000 or current assets – current liabilities = Rs. 10,00,000
Current ratio = 3
If current liabilities are x, current assets = 3x.
Then 3x – x = Rs. 10,00,000 or 2 x = Rs. 10,00,000 or x = Rs. 5,00,000
Current liabilities = Rs. 5,00,000
Current assets = 3 × Rs. 5,00,000 = Rs. 15,00,000

(*ii*) Current assets to stock = 3 : 2
Stock = Rs. 15,00,000 × 2 /3 = Rs. 10,00,000

(*iii*) Stock turnover ratio = 5
Turnover = 5 × Rs. 10,00,000 = Rs. 50,00,000

(*iv*) Variable cost = 60% of sales = 60% of Rs. 50,00,000
= Rs. 30,00,000
Contribution = Rs. 50,00,000 – Rs. 30,00,000 = Rs. 20,00,000

(*v*) E B T = 10% of sales = Rs. 5,00,000

(*vi*) Financial leverage = 2.2
E B I T / E B T = 2.2
E B I T = 2.2 × Rs. 5,00,000 = Rs. 11,00,000

(*vii*) Interest on long-term loan = Rs. 11,00,000 – Rs. 5,00,000
= Rs. 6,00,000

(*viii*) Long-term loan = Rs. 6,00,000 / 0.12 = Rs. 50,00,000

(*ix*) Total liabilities to net worth = 2.75
Total liabilities = Long-term loan × Current liabilities
= Rs. 50,00,000 + Rs. 5,00,000 = Rs. 55,00,000
Net worth = Rs. 55,00,000 / 2.75 = Rs. 20,00,000
Book value per share = Rs. 10
Number of shares = 20,00,000 / 40 = 50,000

(*x*) Fixed assets turnover ratio = 1.2
Sales / Fixed assets = 1.2 or 50,00,000 / Fixed assets = 1.2
Fixed assets = Rs. 50,00,000 / 1.2 = Rs. 41,66,667

(*xi*) Average collection period = 30 days
Debtors = Rs. 50,00,000 × 30 / 360 = Rs. 4,16,667

(*xii*) Other current assets = Total current assets – stock – debtors
= Rs. 15,00,000 – Rs. 10,00,000 – Rs. 4,16,667
= Rs. 83,333

(*xiii*) Fixed cost, excluding interest = Contribution --- E B I T = Rs. 20,00,000 -- Rs. 11,00,000
= Rs. 9,00,000

(*xiv*) The difference in the balance sheet, prepared on the basis of given information has been shown as other assets.

Illustration 15. The following is the balance sheet of Sanjay, a small trader as on 31.3.2009 :

Rs. in '000

Liabilities	*Rs.*	*Assets*	*Rs.*
Capital	200	Fixed Assets	145
Creditors	50	Stock	40
		Debtors	50
		Cash in Hand	5
		Cash at Bank	10
	250		250

A fire destroyed the accounting records as well as the closing cash of the trader on 31.3.2010. However, the following information was available :

(a) Debtors and creditors on 31.3.2010 showed an income of 20% as compared to 31.3.2009.

(b) Credit Period :

Debtors – 1 month   Creditors – 2 months

(c) Stock was maintained at the same level throughout the year.

(d) Cash sales constituted 20% of total sales.

(e) All purchases were for credit only.

(f) Current ratio as on 31.3.2010 was exactly 2.

(g) Total expenses excluding depreciation for the year amounted to Rs. 2,50,000.

(h) Depreciation was provided at 10% on the closing value of fixed assets.

(i) Bank and cash transactions :

  (i) Payments to creditors included Rs. 50,000 by cash.

  (ii) Receipts from debtors included Rs. 5,90,000 by way of cheques.

  (iii) Cash deposited with the bank Rs. 1,20,000.

  (iv) Personal drawings from bank Rs. 50,000.

  (v) Fixed assets purchased and paid by cheques Rs. 2,25,000.

You are required to prepare :

(a) Trading and profit and loss account of Sanjay for the year ended 31.3.2010; and

(b) A balance sheet on that date.

For your exercise, assume cash destroyed by fire is written off in the Profit and Loss Account.

[*C.A. (Inter.) May, 1997 Modified*]

Solution :

Dr. **Trading and Profit and Loss Account of Sanjay for the year ended 31st March, 2010** *Cr.*

	Rs. '000		*Rs. '000*	*Rs. '000*
To Opening Stock	40	By Sales :		
To Purchases	360	Cash	180	
To Gross Profit c/d	540	Credit	720	900
		By Closing Stock		40
	940			940
To Expenses	250	By Gross Profit b/d		540
To Cash Destroyed - Working Note	10			
To Depreciation	37			
To Net Profit transferred to Capital A/c	243			
	540			540

Balance Sheet as on 31st March, 2010

Liabilities	*Rs. '000*	*Rs. '000*	*Assets*	*Rs. '000*	*Rs. '000*
Capital Account	200		Fixed Assets	145	
Less : Drawings	50		*Add* : Additions during		
	150		the year	225	
Add : Net Profit for the year	243	393		370	
Creditors		60	*Less* : Depreciation for the year		
			@ 10% on closing balance	37	333
			Stock		40
			Debtors		60
			Cash at Bank		20
		453			453

Working Notes :

(i) Dr. **Debtors** Cr.

	Rs. in '000		Rs. in '000
To Balance b/fd	50	By Bank – given	590
To Credit Sales – 12 times closing debtors i.e. (12 × Rs. 60) thousand	720	By Cash – balancing figure	120
		By Balance c/fd – 20% more than opening balance	60
	770		770

Total sales = Rs. (720 × 100 / 80) thousand = Rs. 900 thousand

Cash sales = Rs. (900 × 20 / 100) thousand = Rs. 180 thousand

(ii) Dr. **Creditors** Cr.

	Rs. in '000		Rs. in '000
To Cash – given	50	By Balance b/fd	50
To Bank – balancing figure	300	By Credit Purchases – 6 times closing creditors i.e. (6 × Rs. 60) thousand	360
To Balance c/fd – 20% more than opening balance	60		
	410		410

(*iii*) Creditors i.e. Current Liability = Rs. 60 thousand

As Current ratio is 2, Current Assets = Rs. (60 × 2) thousand = Rs. 120 thousand

Bank balance = Current Assets - Stock - Debtors

= Rs. (120 – 40 – 60) thousand = Rs. 20 thousand

(iv) Dr. **Cash Book** Cr.

(Rs. in'000)

	Cash	Bank		Cash	Bank
To Baalance b/fd	5	10	By Creditors - Working Note (*ii*)	50	300
To Debtors – Working Note (*i*)	120	590	By Drawings		50
To Cash Sales – Working Note (*i*)	180		By Bank (C)	120	
To Cash (C)		120	By Fixed Assets		225
			By Expenses – Payment by cheques being balancing figure	125	125
			By Cash Destroyed – balancing figure	10	
			By Balance c/fd – Working Note (*iii*)		20
	305	720		305	720

Illustration 16. Following is the abridged Balance Sheet of the Everest Co. Ltd. as at 31st March, 2009 :

	Rs.		Rs.	Rs.
Paid up Share Capital	5,00,000	Free-hold Property		4,00,000
Profit and Loss Account	85,000	Plant and Machinery	2,50,000	
Current Liabilities	2,00,000	*Less:* Depreciation	75,000	1,75,000
		Stock	1,05,000	
		Debtors	1,00,000	
		Bank	5,000	2,10,000
	7,85,000			7,85,000

From the following information, you are required to prepare Profit and Loss Account for the year ended 31st March, 2010 and Balance Sheet as at that date :

(a) The composition of the total of the 'Liabilities' side of the company's Balance Sheet as at 31st March, 2010 (the paid up share capital remaining the same as at 31st March, 2009) was :

Share Capital	50 per cent
Profit and Loss Account	15 per cent
14 per cent Debentures	10 per cent
Creditors	25 per cent

The debentures were issued on 1st October, 2009 interest being payable on 30th September and 31st March every year. Interest was duly paid on 31st March, 2010.

(b) During the year ended on 31st March, 2010, additional Plant and Machinery had been bought and a further Rs. 25,000 depreciation written off. Freehold property remained unchanged. The total fixed assets then constituted 60 per cent of total fixed and xurrent assets.

(c) The current ratio was 1.6 : 1. The quick ratio was 1 : 1.

(d) The debtors (four-fifths of the quick assets) to sales ratio revealed a credit period of two months.

(e) Gross profit was at the rate of 15 per cent of selling price and Return on Net worth as at 31st March, 2010 was 10 per cent.

Ignore taxation. [*C.A. (Inter) Nov. 1997, Modified*]

Solution :

Dr. **Profit and Loss Account of Everest Co. Ltd. for the year ended March 31, 2010** *Cr.*

	Rs.		*Rs.*
To Opening Stock	1,05,000	By Sales	12,00,000
To Purchases (balancing figure)	10,65,000	By Closing Stock	1,50,000
To Gross Profit c/d	1,80,000		
	13,50,000		13,50,000
To Sundry Expenses (balancing figure)	83,000	By Gross Profit b/d	1,80,000
To Debenture Interest	7,000		
To Depreciation	25,000		
To Net Profit carried to balance sheet	65,000		
	1,80,000		1,80,000

Balance Sheet of Everest Co. Ltd. as at 31st March, 2010

Liabilities	*Rs.*	*Assets*	*Rs.*	*Rs.*
Share Capital	5,00,000	Fixed Assets :		
Reserves and Surplus :		Freehold Property		4,00,000
Profit and Loss Account	1,50,000	Plant and Machinery	3,00,000	
Secured Loans :		*Less* : Depreciation	1,00,000	2,00,000
14% Debentures	1,00,000	Current Assets, Loans and Advances :		
Current Liabilities and Provisions :				
(A) Current Liabilities :		(A) Current Assets :		
Creditors	2,50,000	Stock		1,50,000
(B) Provisions	Nil	Debtors		2,00,000
		Cash at Bank		50,000
		(B) Loans and Advances		Nil
	10,00,000			10,00,000

Working Notes :

(*i*) Share Capital, Rs. 5,00,000 is 50% of the total of the liabilities side.
Hence, total of the liabilities side = Rs. 5,00,000 × 100 / 50 = Rs. 10,00,000

(*ii*) Profit and Loss Account = 15% of Rs. 10,00,000 = Rs. 1,50,000

(*iii*) 14% Debentures = 10% of Rs. 10,00,000 = Rs. 1,00,000

(*iv*) Creditors = 25% of Rs. 10,00,000 = Rs. 2,50,000

(*v*) Total fixed and current assets = Rs. 10,00,000
Fixed assets = 60% of Rs. 10,00,000 = Rs. 6,00,000
As Freehold Property is Rs. 4,00,000
Plant and Machinery = Rs. 6,00,000 – Rs. 4,00,000 = Rs. 2,00,000
Total depreciation on plant and machinery = Rs. 75,000 + Rs. 25,000 = Rs. 1,00,000
Cost price of plant and machinery in use = Rs. 2,00,000 + Rs. 1,00,000 = Rs. 3,00,000

(*vi*) Current liabilities (creditors) = Rs. 2,50,000
Current assets = 1.6 × Rs. 2,50,000 = Rs. 4,00,000
As quick assets are equal to current liabilities,
Stock = Rs. 4,00,000 – Rs. 2,50,000 = Rs. 1,50,000

(*vii*) Debtors = 4/5ths of Rs. 2,50,000 = Rs. 2,00,000

(*viii*) Cash at Bank = Rs. 4,00,000 – Rs. 1,50,000 – Rs. 2,00,000 = Rs. 50,000

(*ix*) According to the debtors to sales ratio, sales are 6 times the amount of debtors.
Hence, Sales = Rs. 2,00,000 × 6 = Rs. 12,00,000

(*x*) Gross Profit = 15% of Rs. 12,00,000 = Rs. 1,80,000

(*xi*) Debenture Interest paid = Rs. 1,00,000 × 14/100 × 6/12 = Rs. 7,000

(*xii*) Net profit is 10% of net worth.
Net worth = Share Capital + Profit and Loss Account
= Rs. 5,00,000 + Rs. 1,50,000 = Rs. 6,50,000
Net Profit = 10% of Rs. 6,50,000 = Rs. 65,000

Illustration 17. The following is the balance sheet of D Ltd. on March 31,2009 :

Balance Sheet of D Ltd. as on 31st March, 2009

Liabilities	*Rs.*	*Assets*	*Rs.*	*Rs.*
Equity Shares of Rs. 10 each	10,000	Fixed Assets	1,10,000	
Additional money received on shares	30,000	*Less* : Accumulated depreciation	30,000	80,000
Retained earnings	13,250	Inventories		11,000
Bonds	30,000	Accounts receivable		3,000
Accounts payable	11,580	Cash		600
		Prepaid expenses		230
	94,830			94,830

The company did not buy or sell any fixed assets nor issue any shares during the year ended 31st March, 2010. On 31st March, 2010 the company's accountant obtained the following ratios and other data based on the operations during the year 2009-2010 :

Current ratio	—	2.0 times
Acid-test ratio	—	0.8 times
Turnover of average inventory	—	5.0 times
Turnover of average receivables	—	25.0 times
Equity ratio	—	58.8 %
Debt ratio	—	41.2 %
Times interest earned	—	6.0 times
Percentage of profit after tax on sales	—	7.0 %

Gross margin percentage	—	52.0%
Book value per share	—	Rs. 58.80
Market value per share	—	Rs. 64.00
Earnings per share	—	Rs. 8.75
Dividend yield	—	5.0%
Corporate income tax rate	—	30%
Depreciation rate	—	4 % on original cost

Required : Use the above data to prepare the company's balance sheet on March 31, 2010 and income statement for the year ended March 31, 2010.

Ignore corporate dividend tax. [*Adapted C.A. (Final) May, 2000*]

Solution :

Working Notes :

(i) Earnings per share = Rs. 8.75. Number of shares = 1,000
Hence, profit after tax = 1,000 × Rs. 8.75 = Rs. 8,750

(ii) Percentage of profit after tax on sales = 7 %
Hence, sales = Rs. 8,750 × 100/7 = Rs. 1,25,000

(iii) Turnover of average receivables = 25 times. Turnover = Rs. 1,25,000
Hence, average receivables = Rs. 1,25,000 / 25 = Rs. 5,000
Opening receivables as given Rs. 3,000
Hence, closing receivables = Rs. (5,000 × 2) – Rs. 3,000 = Rs. 7,000

(iv) As margin percentage is 52%, cost of goods sold is 48% of turnover.
Hence, cost of goods sold = Rs. 1,25,000 × 48 / 100 = Rs. 60,000
Turnover average inventory = 5 times
Hence, average inventory = Rs. 60,000 / 5 = Rs. 12,000
Opening inventory = Rs. 11,000
Hence, closing inventory = Rs. (12,000 × 2) – Rs. 11,000 = Rs. 13,000

(v) Depreciation on Rs. 1,10,000 @ 4% for one year = Rs. 4,400
Hence, accumulated depreciation on 31st March, 2010 = Rs.(30,000 + 3,400) = Rs.33,400
Net fixed assets = Rs. (1,10,000 – 34,400) = Rs. 75,600

(vi) Dividend yield = 5% of market value of Rs. 64 = Rs. 3.20 per share
Total dividend = 1,000 × Rs. 3.20 = Rs. 3,200

(vii) Retained earnings = Profit after tax – dividend = Rs. 8,750 – Rs. 3,200 = Rs. 5,550
Total retained earnings as on 31.3.2010 = Rs. 13,250 + Rs. 5,550 = Rs. 18,800

(viii) Shareholders' fund as on 31st March, 2010 :

	Rs.
Equity shares	10,000
Additional money received on shares	30,000
Retained earnings	18,800
Total	58,800

Book value per share Rs. 58,800/1,000 = Rs. 58.80 which tallies with the amount given in the question.
Equity ratio is 58.8% and debt ratio is 41.2%.
Hence, total debts (bonds + accounts payable) on 31.3.2010 = Rs. 41,200.

(ix) Total of liability side = Shareholders' fund + total debts = Rs. 58,800 + Rs. 41,200 = Rs. 1,00,000
Total of assets side will also be Rs. 1,00,000.
Current assets = Total assets – Fixed assets = Rs. (1,00,000 – 75,600) = Rs. 24,400

(x) Current ratio = 2 times
Hence, current liabilities as on 31.3.2010 = Rs. 24,400 / 2 = Rs.12,200

(xi) Bonds payable = Total debts – Current liabilities = Rs. (41,200 –12,200) = Rs. 29,000

(xii) Acid-test ratio = 0.8

$$\frac{\text{Cost} + \text{Accounts receivable}}{\text{Accounts payable}} = 0.8$$

Accounts payable = Rs. 12,200 and accounts receivable = Rs. 7,000 [W.N. (iii)]
Hence, cash = Rs. (12,200 × 0.8) – Rs. 7,000 = Rs. 2,760
Prepaid expenses = Total current assets – inventories – accounts receivable – cash
= Rs. (24,400 – 13,000 – 7,000 – 2,760) = Rs. 1,640

(xiii) Profit after tax = Rs. 8,750 [W.N. (i)]
Corporate income tax rate = 30%
Hence, profit before tax = Rs. 8,750 × 100/70 = Rs. 12,500
Times interest earned = 6 times

$$\frac{\text{Profit before tax} + \text{interest}}{\text{Interest}} = 6$$

Hence, $$\frac{\text{Rs. } 12{,}500 + \text{interest}}{\text{Interest}} = 6$$

or 5 times interest = Rs. 12,500
Hence, interest = Rs. 2,500

Income Statement of D Ltd. for the year ended 31st March, 2010

	Rs.	Rs.
Sales		1,25,000
Less : Cost of goods sold		60,000
Gross margin (52% of sales)		65,000
Less : Expenses		
Depreciation	4,400	
Interest	2,500	
Others	45,600	52,500
Profit before tax	12,500	
Less : Income tax @ 30%	3,750	
Profit after tax		8,750
Less : Dividend @ Rs. 3.20 per share		3,200
Retained earnings		5,550

Balance Sheet of D Ltd. as on 31st March, 2010

Liabilities	*Rs.*	*Assets*	*Rs.*	*Rs.*
Equity share capital	10,000	Fixed assets	1,10,000	
Additional money received on shares	30,000	*Less* : Depreciation	34,400	75,600
		Inventories		13,000
Retained earnings	18,800	Accounts receivable		7,000
Bonds	29,000	Cash		2,760
Accounts payable	12,200	Prepaid expenses		1,640
	1,00,000			1,00,000

Illustration 18. X and Y who are software engineers, commenced practice on 1.4.2009 with an initial capital of Rs. 5 lakh. On the same date, they borrowed Rs. 5 lakh repayable in flexible installments. With the amount borrowed they purchased office furniture and personal computers on 1.4.2000 for Rs. 5 lakh. They also took on lease, office accommodation by paying Rs. 60,000 being rental advance for three months.

Details of other information furnished by X and Y are as follows :

(a) An amount of Rs. 1 lakh being the fees receivable as on 31.3.2010 represented one month's billing on an average.
(b) Rent for one month was outstanding as on 31.3.2010. [Rent is payable apart from the advance.]
(c) Office expenses [excluding rent, interest and depreciation] constituted 30% of total billings.
(d) Entire tax on income for the year was paid in advance and the tax rate was 30%.
(e) Depreciation on furniture and computers is to be allowed at 15%.
(f) Partners have drawn Rs. 10,000 each per month.
(g) Debt service coverage ratio is 3 times.
(h) Interest coverage ratio is 7 times.
(i) Acid test ratio as on 31.3.2010 is 3 times.
(j) Partners invested firm's excess cash in 5 year 8% government bonds.

You are required to prepare :

A. The financial statements of the firm for the year ended 31.3.2010.
B. The cash account summary to quantify the amount invested in government bonds.

For your exercise treat the provision for tax and advance tax paid separately as current liability and current asset. *[C.A. (Final) Nov. 1998 Modified]*

Solution :

(A) **Balance Sheet of X and Y as at 31st March, 2010**

Liabilities	*Rs.*	*Rs.*	*Assets*	*Rs.*	*Rs.*
Capital	5,00,000		Furniture and Computers	5,00,000	
Less : Drawings	2,40,000		Less : Depreciation	75,000	4,25,000
	2,60,000		Investment in Government		
Add : Profit	3,15,000	5,75,000	Bonds		2,60,000
Loan	5,00,000		Fees Receivable		1,00,000
Less : Repayment	80,000	4,20,000	Rental Advance		60,000
Outstanding Rent		20,000	Advance Tax		1,35,000
Provision for Tax		1,35,000	Cash		1,70,000
		11,50,000			11,50,000

Profit and Loss Account for the year ended 31st March, 2010

	Rs.
Fees / Billings, Rs. 1 lakh × 12	12,00,000
Rent, Rs. 60,000 × 12 / 3	(2,40,000)
Office Expenses, 30% of Rs. 12 lakhs	(3,60,000)
Profit before Depreciation, Interest and Tax	6,00,000
Depreciation	(75,000)
Profit before Interest and Tax	5,25,000
Interest	(75,000)
Profit before Tax	4,50,000
Provision for Tax @ 30%	(1,35,000)
Profit after Tax	3,15,000

(B) Dr. **Cash Account** *Cr.*

	Rs.		*Rs.*
To Capital	5,00,000	By Fixed Assets	5,00,000
To Loan	5,00,000	By Rental Advance	60,000
To Fees	11,00,000	By Rent	2,20,000
		By Office Expenses	3,60,000
		By Advance Tax	1,35,000

		By Drawings	2,40,000
		By Interest	75,000
		By Loan (Repayment)	80,000
		By Bonds (Balancing Figure)	2,60,000
		By Balance c/fd [W.N. (iii)]	1,70,000
	21,00,000		21,00,000

Working Notes :

(*i*) Interest Coverage Ratio = Profit before Interest and Tax / Interest = 7 times
Hence, Interest on loan = Profit before Interest and Tax / 7 = Rs. 5,25,000 / 7
= Rs, 75,000

(*ii*) Debt Service Coverage Ratio $= \frac{\text{Profit after Tax + Depreciation + Interest}}{\text{Loan Instalment + Interest}} = 3$ times

$= \frac{\text{Rs. (3,15,000 + 75,000 + 75,000)}}{\text{Loan Instalment + Rs. 75,000}} = 3$ times

$= \frac{\text{Rs. 4,65,000}}{\text{Loan Interest + Rs. 75,000}} = 3$ times

Hence, Loan Instalment $= \text{Rs. } \frac{4,65,000}{3} - \text{Rs. } 75,000$
= Rs. 1,55,000 – Rs. 75,000 = Rs. 80,000

(*iii*) Acid Test Ratio = Quick Assets / Quick Liabilities = 3 times
Quick Assets = Fees Receivable + Rental Advance + Advance Tax + Cash
= Rs. 1,00,000 + Rs. 60,000 + Rs. 1,35,000 + Cash
= Rs. 2,95,000 + Cash
Quick Liabilities = Outstanding Rent + Provision for Tax
= Rs. 20,000 + Rs. 1,35,000
= Rs. 1,55,000

$\frac{\text{Quick Assets}}{\text{Quick Liabilities}} = \frac{\text{Rs. 2,95,000 + Cash}}{\text{Rs. 1,55,000}} = 3$ times

Hence, Cash = Rs. 1,55,000 × 3 – Rs. 2,95,000
= Rs. 4,65,000 – Rs. 2,95,000
= Rs. 1,70,000

(*iv*) For calculating the amount of tax provision, the amount of depreciation as charged in the profit and loss account has been considered as eligible for income tax purposes.

(*v*) One may not consider Rental Advance (Rs. 60,000) as quick asset for the purposes of 'Acid test ratio'. In such a case, the cash balance will be Rs. 2,30,000 and consequently, the investment in government bonds will amount to Rs. 2,00,000.

(*vi*) It has been assumed that investment in government bonds was made at the year end.

Illustration 19. A company has maintained the following relationships in recent years :

(*i*) Gross profit to net sales	40%
(*ii*) Net profit to net sales	10%
(*iii*) Selling expenses to net sales	20%
(*iv*) Book debts turnover	8 per annum
(*v*) Inventory turnover	6 per annum
(*vi*) Quick ratio	2
(*vii*) Current ratio	3

(*viii*)	Assets turnover (sales basis)	2 per annum
(*ix*)	Total assets to intangible assets	20
(*x*)	Accumulated depreciation to cost of fixed assets	1/3
(*xi*)	Book debts to sundry creditors (for goods)	1.5
(*xii*)	Shareholders' funds to working capital	1.6
(*xiii*)	Total debt to shareholders' funds	0.5

Quick assets comprise 25% cash, 15% marketable securities and 60% book debts.

During 2009-2010, the company earned Rs. 1,20,000 or Rs. 4.68 per equity share; the market value of one equity share was Rs. 78. The capital consisted of equity shares issued at a premium of 10% and 12% preference shares of Rs. 100 each. Interest was earned 17 times in 2009-2010; many years ago, the company had issued 10% debentures due for redemption in 2011. During 2009-2010 there was no change in the level of inventory, book debts, debentures and shareholders' funds. All purchases and sales were on account. Preference dividend paid in 2009-2010, in full, was Rs. 3,000.

You are required to prepare the balance sheet and the profit and loss account relating to 2009-2010. Ignore taxation including corporate dividend tax.

Solution :

Balance Sheet of ....Ltd. as on March 31, 2010

Liabilities	*Rs. in lakhs*	*Assets*	*Rs. in lakhs*	*Rs. in lakhs*
Share Capital, Issued & Subscribed :		Fixed Assets :		
25 lakh Equity Shares of Rs. 10		Cost	292.5	
each, fully paid	250	*Less* Depreciation	97.5	195
12% Preference Shares of Rs. 100		Investments		37.5
each, fully paid	25	Current Assets :		
Reserves & Surplus :		Stock	120	
Securities Premium	25	Book Debts	150	
Profit and Loss Account	100	Cash	62.5	
Secured Loans :		Prepaid expenses	5	337.5
10% Debentures, due for		Intangible Assets		30
redemption in 2002	75			
Current Liabilities & Provisions :				
Sundry Creditors for Goods	100			
Outstanding Expenses	25			
	600			600

Dr. **Profit and Loss Account of ...... Ltd. for the year ended March 31, 2010** *Cr.*

	Rs. in lakhs		*Rs. in lakhs*
To Cost of Goods sold	720	By Sales	1200
To Selling Expenses	240		
To Administrative Expenses	112.5		
To Interest	7.5		
To Net Profit	120		
	1200		1200

Working Notes :

(*i*) Sales will be Rs. 1,200 lakh, since net profit given as Rs. 120 lakh is 10% of sales.

(*ii*) Gross profit being 40% of sales, cost of goods sold will be 60% of sales or Rs. 720 lakh.

(*iii*) Selling expenses : 20% of Rs. 1200 lakh or Rs. 240 lakh.

(*iv*) Interest, suppose, interest = i. Interest has been earned 17 times.

$\therefore 17i = 120$ lakh $+ i$

or $16i = 120$ lakh

or $i = 7.5$ lakh

(*v*) Administrative expenses is the balancing figure

(*vi*) Book debts : 1,200 lakh/8 or Rs. 150 lakh.

(*vii*) Inventory : Cost of sale/6, i.e. 720 lakh/6 or Rs. 120 lakh

(*viii*) Book debts : Cash : : 60 : 25
Therefore, cash = 150 lakh × 25/60 = 62.5 lakh

(*ix*) Similarly, marketable securities = 62.5 lakh/25 × 15 = 37.5 lakh.

(*x*) Total quick assets, i.e., cash + marketable securities + book debts are Rs. 250 lakh. The quick ratio being 2, current liabilities will be Rs. 125 lakh, i.e., 250 lakh/2.

(*xi*) Total current assets, 125 lakh × 3 = 375 lakh

(*xii*) The total of quick assets and inventory being Rs. 370 lakh, the balance must be prepaid expenses.

(*xiii*) Sundry creditors for goods : Book debts are 1.5 times sundry creditors for goods, hence the latter must be 150 lakh/1.5 or Rs. 100 lakh.

(*xiv*) Total current liabilities being Rs. 125 lakh of which Rs. 100 lakh are for goods, the balance of Rs. 25 lakh must be for outstanding expenses.

(*xv*) Total asset turnover is 2 p.a. Hence, the total of assets is Rs. 600 lakh, i.e., 1200 lakh/2.

(*xvi*) Intangible assets are 1/20 of the total; hence, these must be Rs. 30 lakh.

(*xvii*) The balance of assets, i.e., excluding current and intangible assets, must be net fixed assets—the figure is Rs. 195 lakh. Since depreciation has accumulated up to 1/3 of the cost or 1/2 of the w.d.v., the accumulated depreciation is Rs. 97.5 lakh, giving Rs. 292.5 lakh as the original cost.

(*xviii*) Interest on debentures being Rs. 7.5 lakh @ 10%; the principal must be Rs. 75 lakh.

(*xix*) Total debt is current liabilities plus debentures or Rs. 200 lakh. It is 1/2 of shareholders' funds; the latter must be Rs. 400 lakh.

(*xx*) Preference dividend being Rs. 3 lakh @ 12%, the preference capital must be Rs. 25 lakh; the balance Rs. 375 lakh is accounted for by equity share capital and reserves.

(*xxi*) After paying preference dividend, the balance of profit is Rs. 117 lakh; the earning per share is Rs. 4.68. The total number of shares, therefore, is 117 lakh/4.68 or 25 lakh.

(*xxii*) Equity capital, therefore, is Rs. 250 lakh; the premium @ 10% is Rs. 25 lakh; the balance of equity funds must be the credit balance in the Profit and Loss Account.

Illustration 20. From the following details, prepare comparative balance sheets in vertical form showing sources and employment of fund with broad break-up of the components of working capital :—

	31.3.2009	31.3.2010
Current Ratio	2.50	1.80
Liquid Ratio	1.20	0.60
Fixed Assets to Proprietary Fund	0.70	0.80
Bank, Overdraft	Rs. 80,000	Rs. 1,20,000
Working Capital	Rs. 2,25,000	Rs. 2,40,000

There was no term loan or intangible asset.

[*Adapted C.A. (Final) Nov.* 1988]

Solution :

Balance Sheet of . . . .

		Rs.	Rs.	31st March, 2010 Rs.	Rs.	Rs.	31st March, 2009 Rs.
I	*Sources of Funds*						
	Proprietary Funds			12,00,000			7,50,000

II *Application of Funds*						
(1) Fixed Assets			9,60,000			5,25,000
(2) Current Assets, Loans and Advances:						
Stock		3,60,000			1,95,000	
Other Current Assets		1,80,000			1,80,000	
		5,40,000			3,75,000	
Less: Current Liabilities:						
Bank Overdraft	1,20,000			80,000		
Other Current Liabilities	1,80,000	3,00,000	2,40,000	70,000	1,50,000	2,25,000
			12,00,000			7,50,000

Working Notes :

	31st March, 2010	31st March, 2009
(*i*) Let the current liabilities be	x	x
then, current assets are	1.8 x	2.5 x
and working capital is	0.8 x	1.5 x
The amount of working capital as given	Rs. 2,40,000	Rs, 2,25,000
Hence, current assets	= Rs. 2,40,000 × 1.8x/0.8x	= Rs.2,25,000 × 2.5x/1.5x
	= Rs. 5,40,000	= Rs. 3,75,000
Liquid assets	= Rs. 2,40,000 × 0.6x/0.8x	= Rs. 2,25,000 × 1.2x/1.5x
	= Rs. 1,80,000	= Rs. 1,80,000
Current liabilities	= Rs. 2,40,000 × x/0.8x	= Rs. 2,25,000 × x/1.5x
	= Rs. 3,00,000	= Rs. 1,50,000
Bank overdraft as given	= Rs. 1,20,000	= Rs. 80,000
Hence, other current liabilities, balancing figure	= Rs. 1,80,000	= Rs. 70,000
Stock = current assets – liquid assets	= Rs. 5,40,000 – Rs. 1,80,000	= Rs. 3,75,000 –Rs. 1,80,000
	= Rs. 3,60,000	= Rs. 1,95,000
(*ii*) Let thc proprietary fund be	x	x
then, fixed assets are	0.8 x	0.7 x
As there are no long – term loans or fictitious assets,		
Proprietary funds + current liabilities = Fixed assets + current assets	x + Rs. 3,00,000 = 0.8 x + Rs. 5,40,000	x + Rs. 1,50,000 = 0.7x + Rs. 3,75,000
	or x - 0.8 x	or x-0.7 x =
	= Rs. 5,40,000 – Rs. 3,00,000	Rs.3,75,000 – Rs. 1,50,000
	or 0.2 x = Rs. 2,40,000	or 0.3 x = Rs. 2,25,000
Proprietary funds	∴ x = Rs. 12,00,000	∴ x = Rs. 7,50,000
Fixed assets	and 0.8 x = Rs. 9,60,000	and 0.7 x = Rs. 5,25,000

Illustration 21. The balance sheet of A company Ltd., as on 31.3.2009 is as under :—

Liabilities	*Rs. in lakhs*	*Assets*	*Rs. in lakhs*	*Rs. in lakhs*
Share Capital :		Fixed Assets :		
Equity Shares	100	At cost	250	
14% Preference Shares	50	*Less:* Depreciation	80	170
General Reserve	20	Stock in Trade		30
12% Debentures	30	Sundry Debtors		40
Current Liabilities	50	Bank		10
	250			250

The company wishes to forecast the balance sheet as on 31.3.2010.

The following additional particulars are available :—

(*i*) Fixed assets costing Rs. 50 lakh have been installed on 1.4.2009, but the payment will be made on 31.3.2010.

(*ii*) The Fixed Assets Turnover Ratio on the basis of gross value of fixed assets would be 1.5.

(*iii*) The Stock Turnover Ratio would be 14.4 (calculated on the basis of average stock).

(*iv*) The break-up of cost profit would be as follows :-

Materials	40%
Labour	25%
Manufacturing Expenses	10%
Office and Selling Expenses	10%
Depreciation	5%
Profit	10%
	100%

The profit is subject to interest and taxation @ 50%.

(*v*) Debtors would be 1/9 of sales.

(*vi*) Creditors would be 1/5 of material consumed.

(*vii*) In March 2010, a dividend @ 9% on equity capital would be paid. Corporate dividend tax @ 15% would also be paid.

(*viii*) Rs. 25 lakh, 12% debentures have been issued on 1.4.2010.

Prepare the forecast balance sheet as on 31.3.2010 and show the following resultant ratios :—

(*a*) Current Ratio,

(*b*) Fixed Assets/Net Worth Ratio, and

(*c*) Debt Equity Ratio.

[*Adapted C.A.* (*Final*) *Nov.* 1986]

Solution :

Forecast Balance Sheet of A Company Ltd. as on 31st March, 2001

Liabilities	*Rs. in lakhs*	*Assets*	*Rs. in lakhs*	*Rs. in lakhs*
Share Capital :		**Fixed Assets :**		
Equity	100	Cost	300	
14% Preference		*Less:* Depreciation	102.5	197.5
(Redemption on 1.1.2003)	50	**Current Assets :**		
Reserves and Surplus :		Stock in Trade		20
General Reserve	20	Sundry Debtors		50
Profit & Loss Account	0.8	Cash at Bank		13.5
Secured Loans :				
12% Debentures	55			
Current Liabilities & Provisions :				
Sundry Creditors	36			
Provisions for Taxation	19.2			
	281			281

Ratios :

(*a*) *Current Ratio* = $\frac{\text{Current Assets}}{\text{Current Liabilities}} = \frac{\text{Rs. 84.9 lakh}}{\text{Rs. 55.2 lakh}} = 1.54 : 1$

(*b*) *Fixed Assets/Net Worth Ratio* $= \frac{\text{Net fixed Assets}}{\text{Net Worth}}$

Net Fixed Assets	=	Rs. 197.5 lakh
and Net Worth	=	Equity Share Capital + General Reserve + Profit Loss Account
	=	Rs. (100 + 20 + 0.5) lakh
	=	Rs. 120.5 lakh
	=	$\frac{\text{Rs. 197.5 lakh}}{\text{Rs. 120.5 lakh}} = 1.64 : 1$

(*c*) *Debt-equity Ratio* $= \frac{\text{Long term Loans}}{\text{Shareholder Funds + Long term Loans}}$

Long-term Loans	=	12% Debentures + !4% Preference Share Capital
	=	Rs. 55 lakh + Rs. 50 lakh
	=	Rs. 105 lakh
and Shareholders' Funds	=	Equity Share Capital + General Reserve + Profit Loss Account
	=	Rs. (100 + 20 + 0.5) lakh
	=	Rs, 120.5 lakh
	=	$\frac{\text{Rs. 105 lakh}}{\text{Rs. 120.5 lakh + Rs. 105 lakh}}$
	=	$\frac{\text{Rs. 105 lakh}}{\text{Rs. 225.5 lakh}}$
	=	0.47 :1

Working Notes :

(*i*) Fixed Assets as on 31.3.2001 (cost) Rs. 250 lakh
Addition on 1.4.2001 Rs. 50 lakh
Rs. 300 lakh

(*ii*) Sales : 300 lakh × 1.5 = Rs. 450 lakh

(*iii*) Cost of goods sold = Material + Labour + Mfg. Exp. + Depreciation (80% of Sales)

$= \frac{450 \text{ lakh} \times 80}{100} = \text{Rs. } 360 \text{ lakh}$

(*iv*) Depreciation included in (*iii*) above $= \frac{450 \text{ lakh} \times 5}{100} = \text{Rs. } 220.5 \text{ lakh}$

Hence, total depreciation upto 31.3.2010 = Rs. (80 + 22.5) lakh = Rs. 102.5 lakh

(*v*) Average Stock $= \frac{3.60 \text{ lakh}}{14.4} =$ **Rs. 25 lakh**

(*vi*) Stock on 31.3.2010 = Rs. 30 lakh + 2 (25 lakh – 30 lakh) = Rs. 20 lakh

(*vii*) Debtors on 31.3.2010 = Rs. 450 lakh × 1/9 = Rs. 50 lakh

(*viii*) Creditors on 31.3.2010 : Materials Consumed = 40% of Rs. 450 lakh = Rs. 36 lakh
Creditors = 1/5 of Material Consumed = 1/5 × 180 lakh = 36 lakh

(ix) Bank Balance :

Bank

	Rs. in lakhs		*Rs.in lakhs*
Opening Balance	10	Sundry Debtors – Increase	10
Debentures	^25	Creditors	14
Profit @ 15% on Sales		Interest on Debentures, 12% on Rs. 55 lakh	6.6
before depreciation	67.5	Fixed Assets	50
Stock—Decrease	10	Preference Dividend	7
		Equity Dividend	9

		Corporate Dividend tax @ 15%	2.4
		Closing Balance	13.5
	112.5		112.5

(x) Profit for the year :

Profit and Loss Account

	Rs. in lakh		*Rs. in lakh*
To Debentures Interest	6.6	By Profit before Interest & Income Tax	45
To Preference Dividend	7		
To Equity Dividend	9		
To Corporate Dividend Tax @ 15%	2.4		
To Provision for Income Tax @ 50%, 1/2 (45 – 6.6) lakh	19.2		
To Balance c/fd	0.8		
	45		45

Illustration 22. You are given the following summarised figures relating to Tee Ltd. for two years :—

	2008-2009 Rs.	2009-2010 Rs.
Fixed Assets : Gross	50,00,000	70,00,000
Less: Depreciation	20,00,000	27,00,000
Net Block	30,00,000	43,00,000
Investments, in 10% govt. securities	1,00,000	1,00,000
Current Assets	20,00,000	30,00,000
	51,00,000	74,00,000
Less: Current Liabilities	12,00,000	12,00,000
	39,00,000	62,00,000
Less: Loan @ 15%	20,00,000	40,00,000
Shareholders' Funds	19,00,000	22,00,000
Represented by :		
Equity Share Capital	10,00,000	12,00,000
Reserves (Fully paid shares of Rs. 100 each)	9,00,000	10,00,000
	19,00,000	22,00,000
Turnover	1,00,00,000	1,10,00,000
Materials	40,00,000	46,00,000
Labour	30,00,000	34,00,000
Other Costs	20,00,000	22,00,000
Interest	3,00,000	6,00,000
Profit	7,00,000	2,00,000
Dividend Paid	1,00,000	1,20,000

Using ratio analysis, comment on the performance and financial policies of the company during 2009-2010. The fixed assets were operational throughout the year concerned and their efficiency does not decline with age.

Solution :

		2008-09 Rs.	2009-2010 Rs.
1.	Capital Employed :		
	(i) Fixed Assets, gross	50,00,000	70,00,000
	(ii) Working Capital	8,00,000	18,00,000
		58,00,000	88,00,000

2.	Profit before interest	10,00,000	8,00,000
3.	Turnover	1,00,00,000	1,10,000
		Ratios	Ratios
4.	Net Margin or Profit/Turnover	10%	7.27%
5.	Turnover Ratio, i.e., Turnover/Capital	1.72	1.25
6.	Return on Investment Profit/Capital (or 4x5)	17.25%	9.09%
	Analysis and other Ratios :		
	(*a*) Turnover of Fixed assets [3/1(i)]	2.00	1.57
	(*b*) Turnover of Working Capital [3/1(ii)]	12.50	6.11
7.	Operating Ratio 100—Net Margin	90.00%	92.73%
	(*i*) Materials/Turnover	40.00%	41.82%
	(*ii*) Labour/Turnover	30.00%	30.91%
	(*iii*) Other Costs/Turnover	20.00%	20.00%
8.	Interest/Turnover	3%	5.45
9.	Pay out Ratio	14.28%	60.00%

Comments :

In 2009-2010, the performance has been poor : the ROI has fallen from 17.25% to 9.09%. There has been an increase of Rs. 20 lakh in investment in fixed assets but it has led to an increase in sale to the extent of Rs. 10 lakh only, whereas, taking the 2008-2009 performance as the basis, the increase should have been Rs. 40 lakh, i.e., 20 lakh multiplied by 2, the fixed assets turnover ratio in 2008-09. This shortfall in sales has led to poor performance in 2009-2010; the additional interest that has been paid is probably due to the loan that was necessary to finance the new assets installed.

Besides the decline in the turnover ratio, the net margin on sales has also declined because of higher expenditure on all items of cost. There are some other disquieting features also. The current ratio has increased from 1.67 in 2008-2009 to 2.50 in 2009-2010. The increase in current assets is 10 lakhs, financed by depreciation (Rs. 7 lakh), fresh capital issued (Rs. 2 lakh) and retained profits (Rs. 1 lakh). In view of this availability of funds, borrowing of additional Rs. 20 lakh could have been substantially reduced. If borrowing became necessary, there will be a doubt about the reliability of the current assets—perhaps there is a big accumulation of inventories or book debts not readily capable of being realised into cash.

Another point against the company is the high pay out ratio in 2009-2010. Since the financial position is deteriorating, the need is to conserve resources and, therefore, dividends could have been avoided. Further, the company now has a debt-equity ratio of 0.65 which means the debt capacity has been almost exhausted. It is necessary for the company to build up its equity base—for this purpose it is desirable to retain as much profits as possible.

Illustration 23. Zed Ltd., whose order book is full and has been full for about three years, is suffering from an acute shortage of working capital. The current ratio, bad at the end of March 2009, was only 0.8 at the end of March, 2010. Payments to suppliers are overdue to the extent of Rs. 4 lakhs and this led to stoppage of certain essential supplies. The company has approached a bank for accommodation. The bank has obtained the following information :—

	2007-2008	2008-2009	2009-2010
	Rs.	*Rs.*	*Rs.*
Sales	50,00,000	63,00,000	69,30,000
Materials Consumed	20,00,000	26,40,000	30,36,000
Wages	20,00,000	24,00,000	28,80,000
Factory Expenses	6,00,000	7,00,000	7,50,000
Administrative Expenses	2,50,000	3,20,000	3,50,000
Selling Expenses	50,000	2,00,000	2,50,000

Interest	—	60,000	1,00,000
Total Costs	49,00,000	63,20,000	73,66,000
Profit (Loss)	1,00,000	(20,000)	(4,36,000)

The following index numbers have been worked out and are applicable to the whole of the year concerned :

	2007-2008	2008-2009	2009-2010
Sale Price	100	105	105
Price of Raw Materials	100	110	120
Wages	100	120	144

The bank requests you to analyse these figures and advise it whether accommodation should be extended to the company.

Solution :

1. Efficiency in Operations (at constant prices)

	2007-2008		2008-2009		2009-2010	
	Rs.	%	*Rs.*	%	*Rs.*	%
Sales	50,00,000	100.00	60,00,000	100.00	66,00,000	100.00
Materials	20,00,000	40.00	24,00,000	40.00	25,30,000	38.33
Wages	20,00,000	40.00	20,00,000	33.33	20,00,000	30.30
Factory Expenses	6,00,000	12.00	7,00,000	11.67	7,50,000	11.38
Administrative Expenses	2,50,000	5.00	3,20,000	5.33	3,50,000	5.30
Selling Expenses	50,000	1.00	2,00,000	3.33	2,50,000	3.79
Total Operating Costs	49,00,000	98.00	56,20,000	93.66	58,80,000	89.10
Operating Profit	1,00,000	2.00	3,80,000	6.34	7,20,000	10.90

2. Effect of price changes—increases

	2008-2009	2009-2010
	Rs.	*Rs.*
Sales	3,00,000	3,30,000
Materials	2,40,000	5,06,000
Wages	4,00,000	8,80,000
Increase in Costs	6,40,000	13,86,000
Loss due to increase in costs	3,40,000	10,56,000
Interest (extra, now paid)	60,000	1,00,000
	4,00,000	11,56,000
Profit as per (1) above	3,80,000	7,20,000
Loss as reported	20,000	4,36,000

Comments:

It is quite clear that it is the pricing policy of the company that has led to the huge loss that the company has suffered. The sale price over 2007-08 has increased by 5% only, whereas other costs have gone up by a much higher margin. Since the order book of the company is full, it is probably using its facilities to the full but that is not enough—the selling price should have been raised suitably as indicated below, using 2007-08 costs as the basis:

	2008-2009	2009-2010
Materials : (40 x 110%, 40 x 120%)	44.00	48.00
Labour (40 x 120%, 40 x 144%)	48.00	57.60
Factory Expenses	12.00	12.00
Administrative Expenses	5.00	5.00
Selling Expenses	1.00	1.00
	110.00	123.60
Profit Margin	2.00	2.00
	112.00	125.60

Properly, prices in 2008-2009 should have risen by 12% and in 2009-2010 by 25.6% above 2007-08 prices, even ignoring the increase in expenses other than materials and labour. A proper increase on account of this factor is also called for.

The company resorted to borrowing in 2008-2009 and 2009-2010; for this there would have been no necessity had the company taken care to revise its selling price. In fact, this is the central point; further accommodation to the company without a proper change in the selling price will be merely a palliative; and the additional funds will also be lost soon and put the company in an even greater difficulty.

The company is to be complemented, however, on the efficiency of use of materials in 2009-2010 but it should watch the other expenses--there is a tendency for them to increase. It has a big advantage in that labour is fixed and has done the additional work without an increase in the number of men employed. The company's only weak point appears to be neglect of proper pricing.

Working Notes:

Note: 2008-2009 and 2009-2010 figures on the basis of 2007-2008 prices

	2008-2009 *Rs.*	2009-2010 *Rs.*
Sales	$63,00,000 \times \frac{100}{105} = 60,00,000$	$69,00,000 \times \frac{100}{105} = 66,00,000$
Materials	$24,40,000 \times \frac{100}{110} = 24,00,000$	$30,36,000 \times \frac{100}{120} = 25,30,000$
Wages	$24,00,000 \times \frac{100}{120} = 20,00,000$	$28,80,000 \times \frac{100}{144} = 20,00,000$

Predictability of insolvency on the basis of ratios

Edward I. Altman of U.S.A. has developed a model on the basis of which insolvency of a firm can be predicted— this has been developed on the basis of empirical research conducted by him. In Altman's view, the 'Z' value of the firm under study should be computed on the basis of the following:

$$Z = .012\,x_1 + .014x_2 + .033x_3 + .006x_4 + .999x_5$$

where

x_1 = Working capital/Total assets

x_2 = Retained earnings/Total assets

x_3 = Earnings before interest and taxes/Total assets

x_4 = Market value of equity/Book value of total debt

x_5 = Sales/Total assets.

If Z, or the overall index, comes to more than 2.99, there is no danger of insolvency of the concerned firm, firms having a Z value below 1.81 face imminent insolvency; those having Z between 1.81 and 2.99 are in the grey area—there is a danger of insolvency.

The relevance of the ratios mentioned above will be apparent after a little thought. The ratio of working capital to total assets will indicate the liquidity of the firm; if the ratio is very small, it will mean lack of liquid funds to enable the firm to carry on its day to day work. Insolvent firms generally have a minus working capital and that poses great danger as any fresh cash coming in will be used to pay off pressing claims—it will not be available for operating purposes.

Retained earnings to total assets indicates the wisdom of the management in disposing of or rather retaining profits. Retained earnings are a cushion against losses—the danger is great if the cushion is weak—in insolvent firms the cushion is non-existent as, usually, there are accumulated losses. Earnings before interests and taxes to total assets (a form or ROI) shows at what rate fresh cash is flowing into the firm. Solvent firms have a sizeable stream of fresh funds; insolvent firms lose cash steadily—for them the ratio is usually minus.

Market value of all the shares compared with the amount of total liabilities of the firm will indicate the extent to which the debt is covered. It shows to what extent asset values may decline and still leave the firm in a position to cover the debt. If the value of equity is Rs. 1,00,000 and liabilities total Rs. 2,00,000 the total assets will be Rs. 3,00,000. If asset values decline by more than 1/3, debt will cease to be fully covered and the firm will be entering insolvency.

Ratio of sales to total assets is important since it is sales that will produce profits—a persistent ratio will lead the firm towards insolvency sooner or later.

In addition to the ratios stated above, another figure that is important is the "Net Credit Interval" indicating the period in which fresh funds must be raised if the firm is to continue to operate. It may be calculated as

$$\frac{\text{Immediate cash assets} - \text{Immediate current liabilities}}{\text{Monthly cash operating costs}}$$

The figure will indicate the period in months for which the firm has sufficient funds before the expiry of which it must raise fresh funds. If the period is much short than the period of the operating cycle—commencement of the production process and receipt of cash against sale—there is great danger of the firm being caught short of cash.

Cash Loss: The ratios mentioned above were all developed in the western countries and, therefore, they may not have automatic application in India. But they do point to one more important factor—cash. All ratios emphasise the continued availability of cash and, therefore, insolvency (or sickness) can be easily predicted if cash flows are drying up. The Reserve Bank of India is of the opinion that a firm is sick if it has a cash loss in the previous year and in the current year and is expected to incur a cash loss in the next year also. In other words, cash losses continuing for three years means sickness. Cash loss, of course, means loss before depreciation and other write-offs. It means that the current cash costs exceed revenues. Cash loss for a firm is like loss of blood for an individual—both must be stopped immediately as otherwise death may occur.

Illustration 24. Zed Ltd. presents the following summarised statements relating to 2009-2010:-

Balance Sheet

	Rs.		*Rs.*
Share Capital (Fully paid shares of Rs. 10 each	20,00,000	Fixed Assets: Cost	50,00,000
		Less: Depreciation (upto 31.3.2008)	15,00,000
Loans from Financial Institutions	25,00,000		35,00,000
Bank Overdraft	10,00,000	Inventories	16,50,000
Sundry Creditors for goods	15,00,000	Book Debts:	
		More than 6 months, considered doubtful	5,00,000
		Others	9,00,000
		Cash	50,000
		Profit and Loss Accounts	4,00,000
	70,00,000		70,00,000

Profit and Loss Account

	Rs.		*Rs.*
Materials consumed	20,00,000	Sales (adjusted for inventories)	43,00,000
Wages, Salaries	9,00,000	Loss	3,00,000
Manufacturing Expenses	6,00,000		
Administrative and Selling Expenses	7,00,000		
Interest	4,00,000		
	46,00,000		46,00,000

Assuming the figures to be indicative of the firm's situation, comment on the position in which it is placed.

Solution:

(*i*) Working capital/Total assets

		Rs.
Working capital: Inventories (assumed all usable)		16,50,000
Book debts (good)		9,00,000
Cash		50,000
Total current assets		26,00,000
Less: Sundry creditors	15,00,000	
Bank overdraft	10,00,000	25,00,000
Working capital		1,00,000
Total assets: Fixed assets, as above		35,00,000
Less: Two years's depreciation (assumed)		10,00,000
		25,00,000
Current assets as shown above		26,00,000
Total assets		51,00,000

Rate of working capital to total assets:

1,00,000/51,00,000 or 0.2

(*ii*) Retained earnings/total assets

Loss as shown in the balance sheet	4,00,000
Add: Two years' depreciation not yet provided	10,00,000
Doubtful debts	5,00,000
	19,00,000

Ratio = 19,00,000/51,00,000 or –0.37

(*iii*) Earnings before interest and taxes/Total assets

Loss for the year as per Profit and Loss Account	3,00,000
Add: Depreciation for one year	5,00,000
Bad debts arising during the year (assumed)	1,00,000
	9,00,000
Less: Interest	4,00,000
	5,00,000

Ratio = –5,00,000/51,00,000 or –0.10

(*iv*) Market value of equity/Total debt

Assuming the shares to be valued at Rs. 50 in the market, ratio comes to 10,00,000/50,00,000 or 0.20

(*v*) Sales/Total assets

43,00,000/51,00,000 or 0.84

Overall index or 'Z'

$= .012 \times .02 + .014 \times -.37 + 0.33 \times -.10 + .006 \times .20 + .999 \times .84$

$= .80242$ or $.80$

This figure shows that the company is in great danger. The net credit interval may also be calculated—it will confirm this conclusion.

		Rs.
Net credit interval	Immediate cash assets:	
	Book debts (good)	2,00,000
	Cash	50,000
	Inventories (assuming half are readily saleable)	8,25,000
		17,75,000

Immediate requirements:	
Sundry creditors for goods	15,00,000
Cash likely to be available	2,75,000
Monthly cash costs 46,00,000/12	3,83,333
Net credit interval 2,75,000/3,83,333 or 0.72 months or 22 days	

Fresh funds are, therefore, sorely needed as 22 days is too short a period during which the firm may continue without additional funds.

EXERCISE XXIV

1. In a firm, debt-equity ratio is 0.7. State, giving reasons whether the ratio will increase or decrease or remain unchanged in each one of the following cases:

(*i*) Sale of land having book value of Rs. 7 lakh for Rs. 9 lakh.
(*ii*) Issue of equity shares for Rs. 20 lakh to vendors for purchase of plant.
(*iii*) Collection of trade debts amounting to Rs. 1 lakh.
(*iv*) Redemption of debentures of Rs. 25 lakh at a premium of 1%.
(*v*) Payment of Rs. 80,000 for bills payable on their maturity.

[*Decrease: (i), (ii) and (iv); Unchanged: (iii) and (v)*]

2. Following is the Trading and Profit and Loss Account of Adarsh Trading House for the year ended 31st March, 2010:

Trading and Profit and Loss Account

	Rs. in lakhs		*Rs. in lakhs*
To Stock on 1.4.2009	75	By Sales	500
To Purchases	310	By Stock on 31.3.2010	100
To Freight	15		
To Gross Profit c/d	200		
	600		600
To Administrative Expenses	85	By Gross Profit b/d	200
To Selling and Distribution Expenses	40	By Interests on Investments	5
To Financial Expenses	6		
To Other Non-operating Expenses	3		
To Net Profit	71		
	205		205

You are required to calculate:

(*i*) Gross Profit Ratio
(*ii*) Net Operating Profit Ratio
(*iii*) Operating Ratio
(*iv*) Administrative Expenses Ratio
(*v*) Selling and Distribution Expenses Ratio

[*B.Com. (Hons) Delhi, 1992, modified*]

[(*i*) 40% (*ii*) 15% (*iii*) 85% (*iv*) 17% (*v*) 8%]

3. From the follwoing information, calculate :
(i) Current ratio and (ii) Net profit ratio (iii) Debt-equity ratio.

	Rs. '000
Net Profit	1,200
Bills receivable	40
Debtors	160
Stock	195
Cash	120
Creditors	209
Bills payable	47
Debentures	5,000

Long-term bank loan	1,000
Net sales	28,000
Share capital	8,000
Reserves and surplus	2,000

[*(i)* : 2.012; *(ii)* : 42.86%; *(iii)* : 0.375]

4. Calculate Debt Equity Ratio from the balance sheet of Prestige Ltd. as at 31st March, 2010:

Liabilities	*Rs. in lakhs*	*Assets*	*Rs. in lakhs*
80 lakh Equity Shares of Rs. 10 each, fully paid up	800	Land and Buildings	620
4,000 11% Redeemable Preference Shares of Rs. 100 each, fully paid up	400	Plant and Machinery	1,200
Securities Premium Account	80	Furniture and Fittings	180
General Reserve	580	Stock	530
Profit and Loss Account	140	Trade Debtors	470
10 lakh 12.5% Convertible Debentures of Rs. 100 each, fully paid up	1,000	Cash in hand	65
Bills Payable	80	Cash at Bank	300
Trade Creditors	140	Bills Receivable	135
Outstanding Expenses	60		
Provision for Tax	220		
	3,500		3,500

(0.47 : 1 or 0.88 : 1)

5. You are required to calculate Return on Investment from the following details of Rahu Ltd. for the year ending 31st March, 2010:

	Rs. in lakhs
Net profit after tax	65
Rate of income tax, 50%	
12.5% convertible debentures of Rs. 100 each, fully paid up	80
Fixed assets, at cost	246
Depreciation up to date	46
Current assets	150
Current liabilities	70

(50%)

Hint: $$\frac{\text{Net profit before interest and tax}}{\text{Net fixed assets + Net working capital}} \times 100$$

6. Compute Return on Capital Employed from the following details:

	Rs. in lakhs
Net profit after tax	43
Rate of income tax, 50%	
14% Debentures	100
Share capital	250
Profit and loss account	158
Loss on issue of debentures	8

(20%)

Hint: $$\frac{\text{Net profit before interest and tax}}{\text{Shareholder's funds + Long-term funds}} \times 100$$

7. M/s Jupiter Ltd. intends to supply goods on credit to M/s Pluto Ltd. and M/s Mars Ltd. The relevant details for the year ending 31st March, 2010 are as follows:

	M/s Pluto Ltd. *Rs. in lakhs*	M/s Mars Ltd. *Rs. in lakhs*
Trade Creditors	30	16
Total Purchases	93	66
Cash Purchases	3	2

Advise with reasons as to which company he should prefer to deal with.

(Creditors Turnover Ratio: M/s Pluto Ltd. 3 times; M/s Mars Ltd. 4 times; M/s Mars Ltd. is better).

8. Compute the amount of capital employed from the balance sheet of Mars Ltd. as at 31st March, 2010:

Liabilities	*Rs. in lakhs*	*Assets*	*Rs. in lakhs*
Equity Shares Capital	700	Land and Buildings	500
12% Preference share Capital	260	Plant and Machinery	600
General Reserve	320	Furniture and Fittings	100
Profit and Loss Account	160	Investments (Non-trading)	100
11% Debentures	200	Stock	400
Bills Payable	192	Sundry Debtors	300
Sundry Creditors	360	Cash in hand	80
Income Tax Payable	160	Cash at Bank	200
Outstanding Expenses	48	Bills Receivable	90
		Prepaid Expenses	10
		Preliminary Expenses	20
	2,400		2,400

(Rs. 1,520 lakh)

9. The balance sheet of Star Ltd. as at 31st March, 2010 is given below:

Liabilities	*Rs. in lakhs*	*Assets*	*Rs. in lakhs*
Equity Share Capital	60	Plant and Machinery	45
Reserves	18	Furniture	5
Creditors	12	Stock	18
		Debtors	12
		Cash at Bank	10
	90		90

The other details are as follows:

(*i*) Total sales during the year have been Rs. 100 lakh out of which cash sales amounted to Rs. 20 lakhs.

(*ii*) The gross profit has been earned @ 20%.

(*iii*) Amounts as on 1.4.2009:

	Rs. in lakhs
Debtors	8
Stock	14
Creditors	3

(*iv*) Cash paid to creditors during the year, Rs. 21 lakh.

You are required to calculate the following ratios:

(*i*) Debtors Turnover Ratio;

(*ii*) Creditors Turnover Ratio;

(*iii*) Stock Turnover Ratio.

[(i) 8 times; (ii) 4 times; (iii) 5 times or 6.25 times]

10. (*a*) Calculate Debt Collection Period of Confident Ltd. for the year ending 31st March, 2010:

	Rs. in lakhs
Sales during the year	3,650
Debtors as on 31.3.2010	425
Bills receivable as on 31.3.2010	75

(*b*) Compute Debtors Turnover Ratio and Average Collection Period of Prosperous Ltd. for the year ending 31st March, 2010:

	Rs. in lakhs
Net Credit Sales	80
Opening Trade Debtors	18
Closing Trade Debtors	14

The sixty days credit is common to the industry to which the company belongs. State whether the debts are being collected efficiently or not.

[*(a) 50 days; (b) debt collection in unsatisfactory*]

11. Calculate the following ratios from the financial statements given below for AB Ltd.

(*a*) Current Ratio;
(*b*) Acid Test Ratio;
(*c*) Stock Turnover Ratio;
(*d*) Debt Equity Ratio;
(*e*) Interest Coverage Ratio.

Income Statement of AB Ltd. for the year ending 31st March, 2010:

	Rs. in lakhs	*Rs. in lakhs*
Sales		500
Cost of Goods Sold:		
Stock, April 1, 2009	40	
Add: Purchases	245	
Direct Expenses	25	
	310	
Less: Stock, March 31, 2010	60	250
Gross Profit		250
Operating Expenses	110	
Interest Expenses	20	130
Net Profit before Tax		120
Provision for Income Tax		60
Net Profit		60

Balance Sheet of AB Ltd. as at 31st March, 2010

Assets	*Rs. in lakhs*	*Rs. in lakhs*
Fixed Assets (cost)	540	
Less: Accumulated Depreciation	140	400
Stock		60
Debtors		230
Cash at Bank		155
B. Receivable		43
Prepaid Expenses		12
Total Assets		900
Liabilities		
Equity Share Capital		150
Reserves and Surplus		300
10% Debentures		200
Creditors		180
Bills Payable		70
Total Liabilities		900

[*(a) 2:1; (b) 1.71:1; (c) 5 times; (a) 0.31:1 or 0.44:1; (e) 7 times*]

12. The following data have been abstracted from the annual accounts of a company:

	Rs. in lakhs
Share Capital:	
20,00,000 Equity Shares of Rs. 10 each	200
General Reserve	150
Investment Allowance Reserve	50

	Rs. in lakhs
15% Long-term Loan	300
Profit before Tax	140
Provision for Tax	84
Proposed Dividend	10

Calculate, from the above, the following ratios:

(*i*) Return on Capital Employed

(*ii*) Return on Net Worth [*C.A. (Inter) May 1985*]

[*(i) 26.4% (ii) 14%*]

13. Mr. T Munim is made an offer by the promoters of S Enterprises Ltd. to invest in the project of the company by purchasing a substantial portion of the share capital. He is promised good returns by way of dividends and capital appreciation.

Mr. Munim desires you to compute the following ratios for financial analysis. Workings should form part of your answer.

(*i*) Return on Investment Ratio

(*ii*) Net Profit Ratio

(*iii*) Stock Turnover Ratio

(*iv*) Current Ratio

(*v*) Debt Equity Ratio.

The figures given to him are as under:

	Rs.'000
Sales	16,000
Raw Materials Consumed	7,800
Consumable	800
Direct Labour	750
Other Direct Expenses	480
Administrative Expenses	1,200
Selling Expenses	260
Interest	1,440
Fixed Assets	14,000
Income tax	50
Depreciation	700
Share Capital	5,000
Reserves and Surplus	1,500
Secured Term Loans	12,000
Unsecured Term Loans	1,500
Trade Creditors	3,350
Investments	400
Inventories	6,000
Receivables	3,700
Cash in hand and at Bank	100
Provisions	650
Other Current Liabilities	200

[*C.A. (Inter) Nov. 1988*]

[*(i) 20.05%; (ii) 25.06%; (iii) 1.64 times; (iv) 2.33:1; (v) 0.675:1* ***by applying the formula Long-term Loans— (Shareholders' Funds + Long term Debts)***]

14. Fine Products Ltd. presents to you the following Balance Sheet as at March 31, 2010:–

Liabilities	*Rs. in lakhs*	*Assets*		*Rs. in lakhs*
Equity Shares Capital	50	Fixed Assets	120	
14% Debentures (Due for redemption on 31.3.2011	20	*Less:* Depreciation	30	90
General Reserve	10	Stock		13
Profit and Loss Account	5	Debtors		16
Sundry Creditors	35	Cash at Bank		1
	120			120

Comment upon the financial policies of the company.

[Current Ratio 0.55:1; Acid Test Ratio 0.31:1; Fixed Assets Ratio 1.38:1]

15. New Ltd. was floated on 1st July, 2009 taking over a running business. The vendors were paid 50% of the consideration in cash and remaining in the form of shares. The Balance Sheet on 31st March, 2010 was as under:–

Liabilities	*Rs. in lakhs*	*Assets*	*Rs. in lakhs*	*Rs. in lakhs*
Equity Shares Capital	50	Goodwill		12
14% Debentures	20	Other Fixed Assets		45
Sundry Creditors	15	Current Assets:		
		Stock		10
		Book Debts:		
		More than 6 months	4	
		Others	5	9
		Cash at Bank		4
		Profit and Loss Account		5
	85			85

The company approaches you for more funds either as loan or as participation in capital. Give your decision together with reasons.

16. Some years ago, the sales manager of a company persuaded the management to increase the stocks of finished goods (to improve delivery period) and to sell more on credit (terms being 6 weeks). The following figures are given to you:

Year	*Sales*	*Finished Goods Stock*	*Debtors at end*	*Gross Profit*
	Rs.	*Rs.*	*Rs.*	*Rs.*
2006-2007	5,00,000	50,000	40,000	60,000
2007-2008	5,50,000	54,000	45,000	65,000
2008-2009	7,00,000	90,000	90,000	75,000
2009-2010	7,50,000	1,00,000	1,00,000	80,000

Assuming the stock levels and debtors to be true for the whole year, comment upon the wisdom of the decision taken. The company financed working capital by borrowing from banks. What remedial action do you suggest?

17. Y Ltd. presents to you the following Balance Sheet as on March 31, 2010:

Liabilities	*Rs. in lakhs*	*Rs. in lakhs*	*Assets*	*Rs. in lakh*	*Rs. in lakhs*
Equity Shares Capital		500	Fixed Assets	1,150	
14% Preference Share Capital		100	*Less:* Depreciation	275	875
General Reserve		400			
Profit and Loss Account:			Investments in subsidiaries		300
Balance b/fd	10		Stock		250
Profit for current year	200	210	Debtors	150	
14% Debentures		200	*Less:* Provision	15	135
Creditors		300	Bank		65
			Preliminary Expenses		85
		1,710			1,710

It was found that the profit for the current year was before provision for taxation @ 50%. The company has been declaring dividends @ 15% p.a. on equity shares, that being the normal rate in the industry concerned. The subsidiary companies are not producing profits.

(*a*) Calculate the ratios affecting creditors, shareholders, and prospective investors.

(*b*) What will be your reaction to a request for participation in the equity share capital of the company?

(*c*) Show how the shareholders' funds are employed.

(*d*) If sales of the company are Rs. 2,000 lakh producing a gross profit of Rs. 400 lakh, calculate the inventory ratio and the average collection period.

(Current Ratio 1.13:1; Quick Ratio 0.5:1; Current liabilities include provision for tax Rs. 1,00,000; Debt Equity Ratio 0.27 : 1).

18. Some of the ratios in case of Z Ltd. together with the desirable standards are given below. Assess the efficiency of the company.

	For Z Ltd.	*Standard*
Current Ratio	1.90	2.50
Gross Profit Ratio	.35	.30
Fixed Expenses to Sales Ratio	.20	.15
Variable Expenses to Sales Ratio	.08	.10
Sales/Capital	4.00	3.00
Fixed Assets/Long Term Funds	.90	1.00
Rate of Return on Capital	20%	15%

19. State the effect of the following on the current ratio and the liquidity ratio:–

(*i*) Payment of an amount due to a supplier.

(*ii*) Collection of an amount due from a customer.

(*iii*) Sale of goods for cash at the normal profit.

(*iv*) Repayment of fixed deposits raised 3 years ago; the repayment being made before time at the special request of the deposit-holder.

(*v*) Purchase of machinery on deferred payment system; installments being payable half yearly.

(*vi*) Sale of long-term investments.

[*Increase (i) (iii) (vi); Decrease (iv) and (v); No effect (ii)*]

20. You are given the following figures:–

Current Ratio	2.5
Liquidity Ratio	1.5
Net Working Capital	Rs. 3 crore
Stock Turnover Ratio	6
Ratio of Gross Profit to Sales	20%
Ratio of Turnover to Fixed Assets (net)	2
Average Debt Collection Period	2 months
Fixed Assets to Net Worth	0.80
Reserves and Surplus to Capital	.5

Draw up the Balance sheet of the concern to which the figures relate.

(*Total of Balance Sheet, Rs. 11 crore; Capital Rs. 5 crore*)

21. The assets of ABC Ltd. consist of fixed assets and current assets while it current liabilities comprises back credit and trade credit in the ratio of 2:1. From the following figures relating to the company for the year 2009-2010, prepare its balance sheet showing the details of working:–

Share Capital	Rs. 1,99,50,000
Working Capital i.e. Current Assets – Current Liabilities	Rs. 4,50,000
Gross Margin	20%
Inventory Turnover	6
Average Collection Period	2 months
Current Ratio	1.5
Quick Ratio	0.9
Reserves and Surplus to Cash	3

[*Adapted C.A. (Final) May, 1986*]

[*Balance Sheet Total Rs. 3 crore 30 lakh*]

Hint: [*Sales Rs. 4 crore 5 lakh; Inventory Rs. 54 lakh*]

22. You are advised by the management of ABC Ltd. to project a Trading and Profit and Loss Account and the Balance Sheet on the basis of the following estimated figures and ratios, for the next financial year ending March 31, 2010:

Ratio of Gross Profit	25%
Stock Turnover Ratio	5 times
Average Debt Collection Period	3 months
Creditors Velocity	3 months
Current Ratio	2
Proprietory Ratio (Fixed Assets to Capital Employed)	80%
Capital Gearing Ratio (Pref. shares and Debentures to Equity)	30%

Net Profit to Issued Capital (Equity)	10%
General Reserve and Profit and Loss to Issued Capital Equity)	25%
Preference Share Capital to Debentures	2

Cost of sales consists of 50% for materials

Gross Profit Rs. 1,250 lakh

Working notes should be clearly shown.

[*Adapted C.A. (Final) Nov. 1985*]

[*Net Profit Rs. 280 lakh; Balance Sheet Total Rs. 6,000 lakh*]

Hint: Total Current Assets Rs. 2,000 lakh, Bank Overdraft Rs. 531.25 lakh; Working Capital Rs. 1,000 lakh; Fixed Assets Rs. 4,000 lakh; Net Worth Rs. 3,500 lakh; Equity Capital Rs. 2,800 lakh.

23. From the following figures relating to the accounts of Alpha Ltd., comment upon the present state and trend in respect of profitability, solvency and capitalisation of the company.

Consider only two significant ratios under each head:–

	2008-2009 *Rs. in '000*	2009-2010 *Rs. in '000*
Sales	12,000	15,000
Net Block	5,000	8,000
Receivables	2,000	2,950
Payables	1,000	2,000
Cash and Bank	500	200
Closing Stock	2,000	4,000
Bank Overdraft	1,000	2,500
Purchases	9,000	12,000
Expenses	1,000	1,500
Depreciation	750	1,200
Interest on Bank Overdraft	150	400
Loan	—	2,000
Interest on Loan	—	350
Share Capital	4,000	4,000
Reserve and Surplus	1,900	2,075
Provision for Income Tax	1,200	1,975
Proposed Dividend	400	600
Stock on 1.4.2009	1,800	

[*Adapted C.A. (Final) Nov. 1987*]

Profitability:

Gross Profit Ratio 26.67%; 33.33%; Return on Capital Employed: 22.03%; 23.53%

Solvency:

Current Ratio: 1.25:1; 1.01:1; Liquid Ratio: 0.69:1; 0.45:1

Capitalisation:

Debt Equity Ratio: Nil, 0.25:1; Capital Gearing: Nil, 0.25:1

24. From the following information, prepare the projected Trading and Profit and Loss Account for the next financial year ending March 31, 2010 and the projected Balance Sheet as on that date:–

Gross Profit Ratio	25%
Net Profit to Equity Capital	10%
Stock Turnover Ratio	5 times
Average Debt Collection Period	2 months
Creditors Velocity	3 months
Current Ration	2
Proprietary Ratio (Fixed Assets to Capital Employed)	80%
Capital Gearing Ratio (Preference Shares and Debentures to Equity)	30%
General Reserve and Profit and Loss to issued Equity Capital	25%
Preference Share Capital to Debentures	2

Cost of Sales consists of 40% for materials and balance for Wages and Overheads. Gross Profit Rs. 60 lakh. Working notes should be clearly shown.

[*Adapted C.A. (Final) May 1985*]

[*Net Profit Rs. 10.64 lakh; Balance Sheet Total Rs. 228 lakh*]

[**Hint:** Cost of Sales Rs. 180 lakh; Stock Rs. 36 lakh; Debtors Rs. 40 lakh; Trade Creditors Rs. 18 lakh; Working Capital Rs. 38 lakh; Equity Capital Rs. 106.4 lakh; General Reserve and Profit and Loss Account Balance being 25% of equity capital i.e., 1/5 of Rs. 133 lakh].

25. Prepare a trading account and a balance sheet from the particulars furnished hereunder :

Stock velocity	:	6
Gross profit margin	:	20%
Capital turnover ratio	:	2
Fixed assets turnover ratio	:	4
Debt collection period	:	2 months
Creditors payment period	:	73 days
Gross profit	:	Rs. 60,00,000
Excess of closing stock over opening stock	:	Rs. 5,00,000

All the purchases and the sales have been on credit. Treat the difference in the balance sheet as bank balance.

[*Adapted B.Com. (Hons.) Delhi, 2001*]

[*Total of Balance Sheet : Rs. 1.69 crore*]

Hints : Sales : 3 crore, Cost of sales : 2.4 crore; Closing stock : Rs. 42,50,000; Purchases and cash are balancing figures of trading account and balance sheet respectively.

26. Using the following data, complete the balance sheet of X Limited as at 31.3.2010

(*a*) Gross profit is 25% of sales
(*b*) Gross profit = Rs. 1,20,00,000
(*c*) Shareholders equity = Rs. 20,00,000
(*d*) Credit sales to total sales = 80%
(*e*) Total turnover to total assets is 4 times
(*f*) Cost of sales to inventory is 10 times
(*g*) Average collection period is 30 days
(*h*) Long-term debt = ?
(*i*) Current ratio is 1.5
(*j*) Sundry creditors are Rs. 60,00,000

Balance Sheet of X Limited as at 31.3.2010

Liabilities	*Rs.*	*Assets*	*Rs.*
Sundry Creditors		Cash	
Long-term Debt		Sundry Debtors	
Share Capital		Inventory	
		Fixed Assets	

[*Adapted C.A. (Inter) Nov. 2000*]

[*Balance Sheet Total : Rs. 1.2 crore*]

27. Certain items of the annual accounts of ABC Ltd. are missing as shown below:–

Trading and Profit and Loss Account for the year ended 31st March, 2010

	Rs.'000		*Rs. '000*
To Opening Stock	3,500	By Sales	—
To Purchase	—	By Closing Stock	—
To Other Expenses	875		
To Gross Profits c/d	—		
To Office and Other Expenses	3,700	By Gross Profit b/d	—
To Interest on Debentures	300	By Commission	500

To Provision for Taxation	—		
To Net Profit for the year c/d	—		
To Proposed Dividends	—	By Balance brought Forward	700
To Transfer to General Reserves	—	By Net Profit for	—
To Balance transferred to Balance Sheet	—		

Balance Sheet as on 31st March, 2010

Liabilities	*Rs.'000*	*Assets*	*Rs. '000*
Paid up Capital	5,000	Fixed Assets:	
General Reserves:		Plant and Machinery	7,000
Balance at the beginning of the year	—	Other Fixed Assets	—
Proposed Addition	—	Current Assets:	
Profit and Loss Appropriation Account	—	Stock-in-trade	—
10% Debentures	—	Sundry Debtors	—
Current Liabilities	—	Bank Balance	625

You are required to supply the missing figures with the help of the following information:–

(*i*) Current Ratio 2:1

(*ii*) Closing stock is 25% of sales

(*iii*) Proposed dividends are 40% of the paid-up capital

(*iv*) Gross profit ratio is 60%

(*v*) Ratio of current liabilities to debentures is 2:1

(*vi*) Transfer to General Reserves is equal to proposed dividends

(*vii*) Profits carried forward are 10% of the proposed dividends

(*viii*) Provision for taxation is 50% of profits

(*ix*) Balance to the credit of General Reserves at the beginning of the year is twice the amount transferred to that account from the current profits.

Working should form part of your answer.

[*Adapted C.A. (Final) May 1987*]

[*Net Profit Rs. 3,50,000; Balance Sheet Total Rs. 20,20,000*]

[**Hint:** Net Profit for the year: (Proposed dividends + Transfer to General Reserve + Profits carried forward – Profit brought forward) = Rs. (2,000 + 2,000 + 200 – 700) thousand = 3,500 thousand; Gross Profit Rs. 10,500 thousand, Sales Rs. 17,500 thousand; Debentures Rs. 3,000 thousand; Sundry Debtors Rs. 7,000 thousand].

28. Below are given some figures (ratios and percentages) relating to three companies carrying on the same type of business, for the year 2009-2010 which year may be treated as representative. State which company, in your opinion, has put in the best performance and has followed the best financial policies:–

	A. Ltd.	B Ltd.	C Ltd.
Net Block to Net Worth	1.70	0.83	0.90
Current Assets to Current Liabilities	0.94	1.32	1.03
Quick Assets to Current Liabilities	0.75	0.68	0.22
Gross Profit to Net Sales (%)	20	15	12
Net Sales to Capital	1.50	2.50	3.50
Dividends to Profit earned (%)	40	25	50
Net Profits to Net Sales (%)	8	6	3

29. Towards the end of March, 2009 the directors of Wholesale Merchants Ltd. decided to expand their business. The annual accounts of the company for 2008-2009 and 2009-2010 may be summarised as follows:–

	Year 2008-2009		Year 2009-2010	
	Rs. in lakhs	*Rs. in lakhs*	*Rs. in lakhs*	*Rs. in lakhs*
Sales				
Cash	30		32	
Credit	270		342	
		300		374
Cost of Sales		236		298
Gross margin		64		76
Expenses:				
Warehousing	13		14	
Transport	6		8	
Administration	19		19	
Selling	11		14	
Debenture Interest	—	49	3	59
Net Profit		15		17

	Rs. in lakhs	*Rs. in lakh*	*Rs. in lakh*	*Rs. in lakhs*
Fixed assets (*less* depreciation)		30		40
Current assets				
Stock	60		94	
Debtors	50		82	
Cash	10	120	7	183
Less: Current Liabilities:				
—Trade creditors		50		76
Net Current Assets		70		107
Capital Employed		100		147
Share Capital		75		75
Reserves and undistributed profits		25		42
Debentures		—		30
		100		147

You are informed that:

(1) All sales were from stocks in the company's warehouse. (2) The range of merchandise was not changed and buying prices remained steady throughout the two years. (3) Budgeted total sales for 2009-2010 were Rs. 39 lakh. (4) The debenture loan was received on 1st April, 2009 and additional fixed assets were purchased on that date.

You are required to state the internal accounting ratios that you would use in this type business to assists the management of the company in measuring the efficiency of its operation, including its use of capital.

Your answer should name the ratios and give the figures (calculated to one decimal place) for 2008-2009 and 2009-2010, together with possible reason for changes in the ratios for the two years. Ratios relating to capital employed should be based on the capital at the two years' end. Ignore taxation. [*Adapted C.A. Final*]

Essay Type

1. Define accounting ratios. What is their importance? Describe their limitations also.
2. What do you mean by (*i*) profitability ratios and (*ii*) turnover ratios?
3. What are the ways in which debt-equity ration may be calculated? What does this ratio signify? What, in your view, is the ideal debt-equity ratio?
4. Distinguish between current ratio and quick ratio. Also describe the shortcomings of these two ratios as measures of liquidity.
5. How is debtors turnover ratio helpful to credit collection department of a business concern?
6. Write short notes on:
   (*i*) Stock turnover ratio; (*ii*) Working capital turnover ratio; (*iii*) Operating ratio
   (*iv*) Net profit ratio; (*v*) Pay out Ratio and (*vi*) Return on investment ratio

25

Insurance Companies

SYNOPSIS

1. General	... 25.1
Various types of insurance	... 25.1
Various terms	...25.2
2. Regulation of Insurance Business	...25.3
3. Final Accounts	...25.3
A. Life Insurance Business	...25.3
B. General Insurance Business	...25.25
Reserve for Unexpired Risks	...25.25

1. GENERAL

Under a contract of insurance, one party, known as the 'insurer', undertakes to indemnify the loss suffered (due to specified causes) by the other party, known as the 'insured', in consideration for a fixed sum of money, known as 'premium'. Since the amount of premium is generally small, insurance contracts spread the loss suffered by one person over a large number of persons. Everyone pays a premium; those who suffer a loss are paid a sum equivalent to the loss (or loss according to terms of the contract) and those who do not suffer a loss lose only the premium paid. Thus, protection against unforeseen events is purchased through a contract of insurance. The document containing the terms of an insurance contract is known as 'policy'.

Various types of insurance :

Insurance contracts are of many types. Life insurance guarantees that on the policyholder (or insured) reaching a certain age, or on his death, a certain sum of money will be paid by the insurer. Throughout the terms of the policy, the insured has to pay regularly a sum of money (the premium). Life Insurance is also known as assurance because ultimately the amount of the policy must be paid. A policyholder not only buys protection but also makes an investment since the amounts paid by him will, sooner or later, come back to him. Insurance is available against most risks that befall man or business as shown below :

Risk	*Type of Insurance*
Loss through fire	Fire
Risks of sea transport to goods, ship and freight	Marine
Accidents	Accidents or Motor Vehicles
Loss by theft	Burglary
Dishonesty of employees	Fidelity
Damage to third parties	Third Parties

Injury (including sickness) or death of workers caused at work	Workmen Compensation
Loss of profits due to fire or natural causes	Consequential Loss.

Almost anything can be insured if only one is prepared to pay a sufficient premium.

Various terms:

Besides the terms used above, the following are some other terms commonly in use :—

Annuity is an annual payment. A life insurance office guarantees to pay a sum of money regularly, as long as one lives, in consideration of a lump sum money received in the beginning. The amount payable depends upon the age of the person concerned (called the annuitant) and the prevailing rate of interest. The annual (or regular) payment is called annuity; the lump sum received in the beginning is called "consideration for annuities granted". The former is an expense; the latter, an income.

Whole Life Policy is a policy which matures only on the death of the insured.

Endowment Policy is a policy which matures on the policyholder reaching a certain age or on his death, whichever is earlier.

With Profit Policies are those on which, in addition to a guaranteed sum payable on maturity, a share of profits of the life office will be payable.

Without Profit Policies are those which entitle the policyholder to get only a fixed sum of money on maturity.

Bonus is the share of profit which a policyholder gets from the life insurance company. *Reversionary Bonus* is that which is payable only on the maturity of the policy. *Bonus in Cash* is payable immediately. *Bonus in Reduction* of Premium *is bonus* which is payable in cash but which is utilised by the policyholder to adjust premium due from him. *Interim Bonus* is a bonus payable on the maturity of a policy pending the ascertainment of profit.

Reinsurance means insurance effected by an insurance company in order to cover itself against a large risk. Suppose a building is insured with company *A* for Rs. 50,00,000. Company *A*, in order to reduce its risk, can get the same building insured with company *B*. The contract between company *A* and company *B* will be reinsurance. If company *A* wants to reduce its risk, it can get the same building insured with company *C*; in this case it will be called *retrocession*. *Reinsurance* can be for part of the amount or for some of the risks. The reinsurance company will pay a commission on the premium received. In the above example, company B will pay commission to company *A*. For company *B* it will be "commission on reinsurance accepted"—it will be a debit balance and an expense. For company *A* it will be a gain and will be called "commission on reinsurance ceded".

First Year's Premium is premium paid by the policyholder in the first year of the life policy. Premiums paid in later years are known as Renewal Premiums. When a policyholder pays all the premiums in a lump sum in the beginning, it is called *Single Premium*.

Surrender Value is the amount which a policyholder can get immediately in cash from the life insurance company if he stops paying premium. It is the present cash value of the policy. The other option to the policyholder is to get the policy *Paid Up*. In this case, no further premiums are payable. The amount of the policy is reduced proportionately to the number of premiums already paid having regard to total number of premiums payable. The policy will mature in its normal course.

Claim means the amount payable by the insurance company. If the policy is a whole life policy, the amount is payable on the death of the policyholder (in which case it is known *as claim by death*). In case of an endowment policy, the amount is payable earlier—on the policyholder reaching the stipulated age but the amount will be paid immediately if the policyholder dies before reaching the particular age. Claims paid upon the policyholder reaching the age mentioned in the policy are known as *claims by maturity* (*or survivance*). Claims include reversionary bonus and interim bonus.

2. REGULATION OF INSURANCE BUSINESS

Insurance business in India is regulated by the provisions of the Insurance Regulatory and Development Authority Act, 1999. Here, the following points may be noted :

(*i*) By means of amendment to the Life Insurance Corporation Act, 1956 and to the General Insurance Business (Nationalisation) Act, 1972, the insurance business has been thrown open to the private sector also.

(*ii*) Every insurer is required at all times, the on or after the commencement of the Insurance Regulatory and Development Act, 1999 to maintain a minimum amount of excess of the value of his assets over the amount of his liabilities. This minimum amount is called 'required ovluency margin' and has to be calculated as per rules laid down in the Insurance Regulatory and Development Authority Act.

(*iii*) Every year, the accounting year of every insurance company is to end on 31st March.

3. FINAL ACCOUNTS

The insurance companies are required to prepare their financial statements *i.e.* Revenue Account, Profit and Loss Account and Balance Sheet according to the Insurance Regulatory and Development Authority (Preparation of Financial Statements and Auditors' Report of Insurance Companies) Regulations, 2002.

Insurers carrying on Life Insurance Business should comply with the requirements of Schedule A of the Regulations which among other things, gives the following Forms:

Revenue Account	–	Form A – RA
Profit and Loss Account	–	Form A – PL
Balance Sheet	–	Form A – BS

Insurers doing General Insurance Business should comply with requirements of Schedule B of the Regulations which among other things, gives the following Forms:

Revenue Account	–	Form B – RA
Profit and Loss Account	–	Form B – PL
Balance Sheet	–	Form B – BS

In both cases, Revenue Account and Balance Sheet are given in summary form. There are 15 Schedules in each case, the first four schedules relate to Revenue Account and the remaining eleven schedules relate to Balance Sheet which give details of the summary heads. In both Schedules A and B, Profit and Loss Appropriation Account is dispensed with and appropriations are accommodated in the Profit and Loss Account.

A. LIFE INSURANCE BUSINESS

The chief peculiarity of the life insurance business is that the life insurance contracts are for a long term and that, on a particular date, the future implications of a contract must be considered before profit can be ascertained. Under an annuity contract, the life insurance office does not receive any amount after the initial payment but has to go on paying till the annuitant dies. On a particular date, therefore, there is a liability in respect of future payments to be made. Under a life insurance policy, also, there is liability because against a policy, the premiums expected to be received in future will generally be much less than the amount payable by way of the claim. Suppose, *A* took out a policy for Rs. 10,000 on 5th July, 1987 for twenty years, the premium being Rs. 500 per annum. On 31st March, 2003, the life insurance company is faced with the position that only four premiums (in 2003-04, 2004-05, 2005-06, 2006-07) can be expected, amounting in all to Rs. 2,000. The company will have to pay Rs. 10,000 latest, on 5th July, 2008. There is a gap of Rs. 8,000. In terms of 31st March, 2003 the gap is slightly less because of interest. The possibility of *A*'s death must be kept in mind because death means stoppage of payment of premium and hastening the payment of the claim leading to loss of interest. The chief point to remember is that in respect of policies already issued and still in force, there is a deficiency of claims that are expected to arise over premiums that are expected to be received. This deficiency is known as "net liability". A company cannot be said to have made profits unless it has reserves equal to the net liability. The calculation is made only by actuaries, mathematicians well versed in the intricacies of life insurance. The valuation has to be got done by the insurance company every year.

In case of life insurance, Revenue Account (Policyholders' Account), Profit and Loss Account (Shareholders' Account) and Balance Sheet are prepared as per Form A-RA, Form A-PL and Form A-BS respectively.

FORM A-RA

Name of the Insurer :
Registration No. and Date of Registration with the IRDA

REVENUE ACCOUNT FOR THE YEAR ENDED 31ST MARCH, 20___

Policyholders' Account (Technical Account)

Particulars	*Schedule*	*Current Year*	*Previous Year*
		(Rs.'000)	*(Rs.'000)*
Premiums earned – net (*a*) Premium (*b*) Reinsurance ceded (*c*) Reinsurance accepted	1		
Income from Investments (*a*) Interest, Dividends & Rent – Gross (*b*) Profit on sale/redemption of investments (*c*) (Loss on sale/redemption of investments) (*d*) Transfer/Gain on revaluation/change in fair value*			
Other Income (to be specified)			
TOTAL (A)			
Commission	2		
Operating Expenses related to Insurance Business	3		
Provision for doubtful debts			
Bad debts written off			
Provision for Tax			
Provisions (other than taxation) (*a*) For diminution in the value of investments (Net) (*b*) Others (to be specified)			
TOTAL (B)			

Benefits Paid (Net)	4		
Interim Bonuses Paid			
Change in valuation of liability in respect of life policies (*a*) Gross** (*b*) Amount ceded in Reinsurance (*c*) Amount accepted in Reinsurance			
TOTAL (C)			
SURPLUS/(DEFICIT) (D) = (A)-(B)-(C)			
APPROPRIATIONS			
Transfer to Shareholders' Account			
Transfer to Other Reserves (to be specified)			
Balance being Funds for Future Appropriations			
TOTAL (D)			

Notes :

* *Represents the deemed realised gain as per norms specified by the Authority.*

** *represents Mathematical Reserves after allocation of bonus*

The total surplus shall be disclosed separately with the following details:

(*a*) Interim Bonuses Paid:

(*b*) Allocation of Bonus to policyholders:

(*c*) Surplus shown in the Revenue Account:

(*d*) Total Surplus: [(*a*)+(*b*)+(*c*)].

See Notes appended at the end of Form A-PL

FORM A-PL

Name of the Insurer :
Registration No. and Date of Registration with the IRDA

PROFIT & LOSS ACCOUNT FOR THE YEAR ENDED 31ST MARCH, 20____.

Shareholders' Account (Non-technical Account)

Particulars	*Schedule*	*Current Year*	*Previous Year*
		(Rs.'000)	*(Rs.'000)*
Amounts transferred from/to the Policyholders Account (Technical Account)			
Income From Investments			
(*a*) Interest, Dividends & Rent – Gross (*b*) Profit on sale/redemption of investments (*c*) (Loss on sale/redemption of investments)			
Other Income (to be specified)			
TOTAL (A)			
Expenses other than those directly related to the insurance business			
Bad debts written off			
Provisions (Other than taxation)			
(*a*) For diminution in the value of investments (Net) (*b*) Provisions for doubtful debts (*c*) Others (to be specified)			
TOTAL (B)			

Profit/(Loss) before tax			
Provision for Taxation			
Profit/(Loss) after tax			
APPROPRIATIONS			
(*a*) Balance at the beginning of the year. (*b*) Interim dividends paid during the year (*c*) Proposed final dividend (*d*) Dividend distribution tax (*e*) Transfer to reserves/other accounts (to be specified)			
Profit carried to the Balance Sheet			

Notes to Form A-RA and A-PL.

(*a*) Premium income received from business concluded in and outside India shall be separately disclosed.

(*b*) Reinsurance premiums whether on business ceded or accepted are to be brought into account gross (i.e. before deducting commissions) under the head reinsurance premiums.

(*c*) Claims incurred shall comprise claims paid, specific claims settlement costs wherever applicable and change in the outstanding provision for claims at the year-end.

(*d*) Items of expenses and income in excess of one percent of the total premiums (less reinsurance) or Rs. 5,00,000 whichever is higher, shall be shown as a separate line item.

(*e*) Fees and expenses connected with claims shall be included in claims.

(*f*) Under the sub-head "others" shall be included items like foreign exchange gains or losses and other items.

(*g*) Interest, dividends and rentals receivable in connection with an investment should be stated as gross amount, the amount of income tax deducted at source being included under "advance taxes paid and taxes deducted at source".

(*h*) Income from rent shall include only the realised rent. It shall not include any notional rent.

FORM A-BS

Name of the Insurer :
Registration No. and Date of Registration with the IRDA

BALANCE SHEET AS AT 31ST MARCH, 20______.

	Schedule	*Current Year*	*Previous Year*
		(Rs.'000)	*(Rs.'000)*
SOURCES OF FUNDS			
SHAREHOLDERS' FUNDS:			
SHARE CAPITAL	**5**		
RESERVES AND SURPLUS	**6**		
CREDIT/[DEBIT] FAIR VALUE CHANGE ACCOUNT			
Sub-Total			
BORROWINGS	**7**		
POLICYHOLDERS' FUNDS:			
CREDIT/[DEBIT] FAIR VALUE CHANGE ACCOUNT			
POLICY LIABILITIES			

INSURANCE RESERVES			
PROVISION FOR LINKED LIABILITIES			
Sub-Total			
FUNDS FOR FUTURE APPROPRIATIONS			
TOTAL			
APPLICATION OF FUNDS			
INVESTMENTS			
Shareholders'	**8**		
Policyholders'	**8A**		
ASSETS HELD TO COVER LINKED LIABILITIES	**8B**		
LOANS	**9**		
FIXED ASSETS	**10**		
CURRENT ASSETS			
Cash and Bank Balances	11		
Advances and Other Assets	12		
Sub-Total (A)			
CURRENT LIABILITIES	13		
PROVISIONS	14		
Sub-Total (B)			
NET CURRENT ASSETS (C) = (A) – (B)			
MISCELLANEOUS EXPENDITURE (to the extent not written off or adjusted)	15		
DEBIT BALANCE IN PROFIT & LOSS ACCOUNT (Shareholders' Account)			
TOTAL			

CONTINGENT LIABILITIES

	Particulars	*Current Year*	*Previous Year*
		(Rs.'000)	*(Rs.'000)*
1.	Partly paid-up investments		
2.	Claims, other than against policies, not acknowledged as debts by the company		
3.	Underwriting commitments outstanding (in respect of shares and securities)		
4.	Guarantees given by or on behalf of the Company		
5.	Statutory demands/liabilities in dispute, not provided for		
6.	Reinsurance obligations to the extent not provided for in accounts		
7.	Others (to be specified)		
	TOTAL		

SCHEDULES FORMING PART OF FINANCIAL STATEMENTS

SCHEDULE – 1
PREMIUM

	Particulars	Current Year	Previous Year
		(Rs.' 000)	(Rs.'000)
1	First Year Premiums		
2	Renewal Premiums		
3	Single Premiums		
	TOTAL PREMIUM		

SCHEDULE – 2
COMMISSION EXPENSES

Particulars	Current Year	Previous Year
	(Rs.' 000)	(Rs.'000)
Commission paid		
Direct – First year premiums – Renewal premiums – Single premiums Add: Commission on Re-insurance Accepted Less: Commission on Re-insurance Ceded		
Net Commission		

SCHEDULE – 3
OPERATING EXPENSES RELATED TO INSURANCE BUSINESS

	Particulars	Current Year	Previous Year
		(Rs.'000)	(Rs.'000)
1.	Employees' remuneration & welfare benefits		
2.	Travel, conveyance and vehicle running expenses		
3.	Training expenses		
4.	Rents, rates & taxes		
5.	Repairs		
6.	Printing & stationery		
7.	Communication expenses		
8.	Legal & professional charges		
9.	Medical fees		
10.	Auditors' fees, expenses etc.		
	(a) as auditor (b) as adviser or in any other capacity, in respect of (i) Taxation matters (ii) Insurance matters (iii) Management services; and (c) in any other capacity		

11.	Advertisement and publicity		
12.	Interest & Bank Charges		
13.	Others (to be specified)		
14.	Depreciation		
	TOTAL		

SCHEDULE – 4

BENEFITS PAID [NET]

	Particulars	*Current Year*	*Previous Year*
		(*Rs.'000*)	(*Rs.'000*)
1.	Insurance Claims (*a*) Claims by Death, (*b*) Claims by Maturity, (*c*) Annuities/Pension payment, (*d*) Other benefits, specify		
2.	(Amount ceded in reinsurance): (*a*) Claims by Death, (*b*) Claims by Maturity, (*c*) Annuities/Pension payment, (*d*) Other benefits, specify		
3.	Amount accepted in reinsurance: (*a*) Claims by Death, (*b*) Claims by Maturity, (*c*) Annuities/Pension payment, (*d*) Other benefits, specify		
	TOTAL		

Notes : (*a*) Claims include specific claims settlement costs, wherever applicable.
(*b*) Legal and other fees and expenses shall also form part of the claims cost, wherever applicable.

SCHEDULE – 5

SHARE CAPITAL

	Particulars	*Current Year*	*Previous Year*
		(*Rs.'000*)	(*Rs.'000*)
1.	Authorised Capital		
	.....Equity Shares of Rs....each		
2.	Issued Capital		
	....Equity Shares of Rs...each		
3.	Subscribed Capital		
	......Equity Shares of Rs...each		
4.	Called-up Capital		
	Equity Shares of Rs....each		
	Less : Calls unpaid		
	Add : Shares forfeited (Amount originally paid up)		

Less : Par Value of Equity Shares bought back		
Less : Preliminary Expenses Expenses including commission or brokerage on underwriting or subscription of shares		
TOTAL		

Notes: (*a*) Particulars of the different classes of capital should be separately stated.
(*b*) The amount capitalised on account of issue of bonus shares should be disclosed.
(*c*) In case any part of the capital is held by a holding company, the same should be separately disclosed.

SCHEDULE – 5 A

PATTERN OF SHAREHOLDING

[As certified by the Management]

Shareholders	*Current Year*		*Previous Year*	
	Number of shares	*% of Holding*	*Number of Shares*	*% of Holding*
Promoters • Indian • Foreign				
Others				
TOTAL				

SCHEDULE – 6

RESERVES AND SURPLUS

	Particulars	*Current Year (Rs.'000)*	*Previous Year (Rs.'000)*
1.	Capital Reserve		
2.	Capital Redemption Reserve		
3.	Securities Premium		
4.	Revaluation Reserve		
5.	General Reserves *Less*: Debit balance in Profit and Loss Account, If any *Less*: Amount utilized for Buy-back		
6.	Catastrophe Reserve		
7.	Other Reserves (to be specified)		
8.	Balance of profit in Profit and Loss Account		
	TOTAL		

Note: Additions to and deductions from the reserves shall be disclosed under each of the specified heads.

SCHEDULE – 7

BORROWINGS

	Particulars	*Current Year (Rs.'000)*	*Previous Year (Rs.'000)*
1.	Debentures/Bonds		
2.	Banks		
3.	Financial Institutions		
4.	Others (to be specified)		
	TOTAL		

Notes:(*a*) The extent to which the borrowings are secured shall be separately disclosed stating the nature of the security under each sub-head.

(*b*) Amounts due within 12 months from the date of Balance Sheet should be shown separately.

SCHEDULE – 8

INVESTMENTS–SHAREHOLDERS

	Particulars	*Current Year*	*Previous Year*
		(Rs.'000)	*(Rs.'000)*
	LONG TERM INVESTMENTS		
1.	Government securities and Government guaranteed bonds including Treasury Bills		
2.	Other Approved Securities		
3.	Other Investments		
	(*a*) Shares (*aa*) Equity (*bb*) Preference (*b*) Mutual Funds (*c*) Derivative Instruments (*d*) Debentures/Bonds (*e*) Other Securities (to be specified) (*f*) Subsidiaries Investment Properties-Real Estate		
4.	Investments in Infrastructure and Social Sector		
5.	Other than Approved Investments		
	SHORT TERM INVESTMENTS		
1.	Government securities and Government guaranteed bonds including Treasury Bills		
2.	Other Approved Securities		
3.	Other Investments		
	(*a*) Shares (*aa*) Equity (*bb*) Preference (*b*) Mutual Funds (*c*) Derivative Instruments (*d*) Debentures/Bonds (*e*) Other Securities (to be specified) (*f*) Subsidiaries (*g*) Investment Properties-Real Estate		
4.	Investments in Infrastructure and Social Sector		
5.	Other than Approved Investments		
	TOTAL		

Note: *See Notes appended at the end of Schedule-8B*

SCHEDULE – 8A

INVESTMENTS-POLICYHOLDERS

	Particulars	*Current Year*	*Previous Year*
		(Rs.'000)	*(Rs.'000)*
	LONG TERM INVESTMENTS		
1.	Government securities and Government guaranteed bonds including Treasury Bills		
2.	Other Approved Securities		
3.	(*a*) Shares (*aa*) Equity (*bb*) Preference (*b*) Mutual Funds (*c*) Derivative Instruments (*d*) Debentures/Bonds (*e*) Other Securities (to be specified) (*f*) Subsidiaries (*g*) Investment Properties-Real Estate		
4.	Investments in Infrastructure and Social Sector		
5.	Other than Approved Investments		
	SHORT TERM INVESTMENTS		
1.	Government securities and Government guaranteed bonds including Treasury Bills		
2.	Other Approved Securities		
3.	(*a*) Shares (*aa*) Equity (*bb*) Preference (*b*) Mutual Funds (*c*) Derivative Instruments (*d*) Debentures/Bonds (*e*) Other Securities (to be specified) (*f*) Subsidiaries (*g*) Investment Properties-Real Estate		
4.	Investments in Infrastructure and Social Sector		
5.	Other than Approved Investments		
	TOTAL		

Note: *See Notes appended at the end of Schedule-8B*

SCHEDULE – 8B

ASSETS HELD TO COVER LINKED LIABILITIES

	Particulars	*Current Year*	*Previous Year*
		(Rs.'000)	*(Rs.'000)*
	LONG TERM INVESTMENTS		
1.	Government securities and Government guaranteed bonds including Treasury Bills		

2.	Other Approved Securities		
3.	(*a*) Shares (*aa*) Equity (*bb*) Preference (*b*) Mutual Funds (*c*) Derivative Instruments (*d*) Debentures/Bonds (*e*) Other Securities (to be specified) (*f*) Subsidiaries (*g*) Investment Properties-Real Estate		
4.	Investments in Infrastructure and Social Sector		
5.	Other than Approved Investments		
	SHORT TERM INVESTMENTS		
1.	Government securities and Government guaranteed bonds including Treasury Bills		
2.	Other Approved Securities		
3.	(*a*) Shares (*aa*) Equity (*bb*) Preference (*b*) Mutual Funds (*c*) Derivative Instruments (*d*) Debentures/Bonds (*e*) Other securities (to be specified) (*f*) Subsidiaries (*g*) Investment Properties-Real Estate		
4.	Investments in Infrastructure and Social Sector		
5.	Other than Approved Investments		
	TOTAL		

Notes : (*applicable to Schedules 8 and 8A & 8B*):

(*a*) Investments in subsidiary/holding companies, joint ventures and associates shall be separately disclosed, at cost.

(*i*) Holding company and subsidiary shall be construed as defined in the Companies Act, 1956:

(*ii*) Joint Venture is a contractual arrangement whereby two or more parties undertake an economic activity, which is subject to joint control.

(*iii*) Joint control is the contractually agreed sharing of power to govern the financial and operating policies of an economic activity to obtain benefits from it.

(*iv*) Associate is an enterprise in which the company has significant influence and which is neither a subsidiary nor a joint venture of the company.

(*v*) Significant influence (for the purpose of this schedule) – means participation in the financial and operating policy decisions of a company, but not control of those policies. Significant influence may be exercised in several ways, for example, by representation on the board of directors, participation in the policy making process, material intercompany transactions, interchange of managerial personnel or dependence on technical information. Significant influence may be gained by share ownership statute or agreement. As regards share ownership, if an investor holds, directly or indirectly through subsidiaries, 20 percent or more of the voting power of the investee, it is presumed that the investor does have significant influence, unless it can be clearly demonstrated that this is not the case. Conversely, if the investor holds, directly or indirectly through subsidiaries, less than 20 percent of the voting power of the investee, it is presumed that the investor does not have significant influence, unless such influence is clearly demonstrated. A substantial or majority ownership by another investor does not necessarily preclude an investor from having significant influence.

(*b*) Aggregate amount of company's investments other than listed equity securities and derivative instruments and also the market value thereof shall be disclosed.

(*c*) Investment made out of Catastrophe Reserve should be shown separately.

(*d*) Debt securities will be considered as "held to maturity" securities and will be measured at historical costs subject to amortisation.

(*e*) Investment Property means a property [land or building or part of a building or both] held to earn rental income or for capital appreciation or for both, rather than for use in services or for administrative purposes.

(*f*) Investments maturing within twelve months from balance sheet date and investments made with the specific intention to dispose them of within twelve months from balance sheet date shall be classified as short-term investments.

SCHEDULE – 9

LOANS

	Particulars	*Current Year*	*Previous Year*
		(Rs.'000)	*(Rs.'000)*
1.	SECURITY-WISE CLASSIFICATION		
	Secured		
	(*a*) On Mortgage of property (*aa*) In India (*bb*) Outside India		
	(*b*) On Shares, Bonds, Govt. Securities, etc.		
	(*c*) Loans against policies		
	(*d*) Others (to be specified)		
	Unsecured		
	TOTAL		
2.	BORROWER-WISE CLASSIFICATION		
	(*a*) Central and State Governments		
	(*b*) Banks and Financial Institutions		
	(*c*) Subsidiaries		
	(*d*) Companies		
	(*e*) Loans against policies		
	(*f*) Others (to be specified)		
	TOTAL		
3.	PERFORMANCE-WISE CLASSIFICATION		
	(*a*) Loans classified as standard (*aa*) In India (*bb*) Outside India (*b*) Non-standard loans less provisions (*aa*) In India (*bb*) Outside India		
	TOTAL		

4.	MATURITY-WISE CLASSIFICATION		
	(*a*) Short Term		
	(*b*) Long Term		
	TOTAL		

Notes:

(*a*) Short-term loans shall include those, which are repayable within 12 months from the date of balance sheet. Long term loans shall be the loans other than short-term loans.

(*b*) Provisions against non-preforming loans shall be shown separately.

(*c*) The nature of the security in case of all long term secured loans shall be specified in each case. Secured loans for the purposes of this schedule, mean loans secured wholly or partly against an asset of the company.

(*d*) Loans considered doubtful and the amount of provision created against such loans shall be disclosed.

SCHEDULE – 10

FIXED ASSETS

(Rs.'000)

Particulars	*Cost/Gross Block*				*Depreciation*				*Net Block*	
	Opening	*Additions*	*Deductions*	*Closing*	*Up to Last Year*	*For the Year*	*On Sales/ Adjustments*	*To Date*	*As at Year end*	*Previous Year*
Goodwill										
Intangibles (specify)										
Land-Freehold										
Leasehold Property										
Buildings										
Furniture & Fittings										
Information Technology										
Equipment										
Vehicles										
Office Equipment										
Others (Specify nature)										
TOTAL										
Work in progress										
Grand Total										
PREVIOUS YEAR										

Note: *Assets included in land property and building above exclude Investment Properties as defined in note (e) to Schedule 8.*

SCHEDULE – 11

CASH AND BANK BALANCES

	Particulars	*Current Year*	*Previous Year*
		(Rs.'000)	*(Rs.'000)*
1.	Cash (including cheques, drafts, and stamps)		
2.	Bank Balances		
	(*a*) Deposit Accounts (*aa*) Short-term (due within 12 months of the date of Balance Sheet) (*bb*) Others (*b*) Current Accounts (*c*) Others (to be specified)		
3.	Money at Call and Short Notice		
	(*a*) With Banks (*b*) With Other Institutions		
4.	Others (to be specified)		
	TOTAL		
	Balances with non-scheduled banks included in 2 and 3 above		
	CASH & BANK BALANCES		
1.	In India		
2.	Outside India		
	TOTAL		

Note: *Bank balance may include remittances in transit. If so, the nature and amount shall be separately stated.*

SCHEDULE – 12

ADVANCES AND OTHER ASSETS

	Particulars	*Current Year*	*Previous Year*
		(Rs.'000)	*(Rs.'000)*
	ADVANCES		
1.	Reserve deposits with ceding companies		
2.	Application money for investments		
3.	Prepayments		
4.	Advances to Directors/Officers		
5.	Advance tax paid and taxes deducted at source (Net of provision for taxation)		
6.	Others (to be specified)		
	TOTAL (A)		
	OTHER ASSETS		

1.	Income accrued on investments		
2.	Outstanding Premiums		
3.	Agents' Balances		
4.	Foreign Agencies Balances		
5.	Due from other entities carrying on insurance business (including reinsures)		
6.	Due from subsidiaries/holding company		
7.	Deposit with Reserve Bank of India [Pursuant to section 7 of Insurance Act, 1938]		
8.	Others (to be specified)		
	TOTAL (B)		
	TOTAL (A) + (B)		

Notes:

(*a*) The items under the above heads shall not be shown net of provisions for doubtful amounts. The amount of provision against each head should be shown separately.

(*b*) The term 'officer' should conform to the definition of that term as given under the Companies Act, 1956.

(*c*) Sundry debtors will be shown under item 8 (Others)

SCHEDULE – 13

CURRENT LIABILITIES

	Particulars	*Current Year*	*Previous Year*
		(Rs.'000)	*(Rs.'000)*
1.	Agents' Balances		
2.	Balances due to other insurance companies		
3.	Deposits held on reinsurance ceded		
4.	Premiums received in advance		
5.	Unallocated premium		
6.	Sundry creditors		
7.	Due to subsidiaries/holding company		
8.	Claims Outstanding		
9.	Annuities Due		
10.	Due to Officers/Directors		
11.	Others (to be specified)		
	TOTAL		

SCHEDULE – 14

PROVISIONS

	Particulars	*Current Year*	*Previous Year*
		(Rs.'000)	*(Rs.'000)*
1.	For taxation (less payments and taxes deducted at source)		
2.	For proposed dividends		
3.	For dividend distribution tax		
4.	Others (to be specified)		
	TOTAL		

SCHEDULE – 15

MISCELLANEOUS EXPENDITURE
(To the extent not written off or adjusted)

	Particulars	*Current Year*	*Previous Year*
		(Rs.'000)	*(Rs.'000)*
1.	Discount Allowed in issue of shares/debentures		
2.	Others (to be specified)		
	TOTAL		

Notes :

(*a*) No item shall be included under the head "Miscellaneous Expenditure" and carried forward unless:
1. some benefit from the expenditure can reasonably be expected to be received in future, and
2. the amount of such benefit is reasonably determinable.

(*b*) The amount to be carried forward in respect of any item included under the head "Miscellaneous Expenditure" shall not exceed the expected future revenue/other benefits related to the expenditure.

Illustration 1. The undermentioned balances form part of the Trial Balance of the All People's Assurance Co. Ltd., as on 31st March, 2009 :—

Amount of Life Assurance Fund at the beginning of the year, Rs. 14,70,562 thousand; claims by death Rs. 76,980 thousand; claims by maturity, Rs. 56,420 thousand; premiums, Rs. 2,10,572 thousand; expenses of management, Rs. 19,890 thousand; commission, Rs. 26,541 thousand; consideration for annuities granted Rs. 10,712 thousand; interests, dividends and rents, Rs. 52,461 thousand; income tax paid on profits Rs. 3,060 thousand; surrenders, Rs. 21,860 thousand; annuities, Rs. 29,420 thousand; bonus paid in cash, Rs. 9,450 thousand; bonus paid in reduction of premiums, Rs. 2,500 thousand; preliminary expenses balance, Rs. 600 thousand; claims admitted but not paid at the end of year, Rs. 10,034 thousand; annuities due but not paid, Rs. 2,380 thousand; capital paid up, Rs. 14,00,000 thousand; Government securities, Rs. 24,90,890 thousand; Sundry Fixed Assets, Rs. 4,19,110 thousand.

Prepare Revenue Account and the Balance Sheet after taking into account the following :—

(*a*) Claims covered under reinsurance, Rs. 10,000 thousand } by death;
(*b*) Further claims intimated, Rs. 8,000 thousand } by death;
(*c*) Further bonus utilised in reduction of premium, Rs. 1,500 thousand
(*d*) Interest Accrued, Rs. 15,400 thousand;
(*e*) Premiums Outstanding, Rs. 7,400 thousand.

Solution:

All People's Co. Ltd.
Revenue Account for the year ended 31st March, 2009

Particulars	*Schedule*	*Rs. '000*
Premiums earned – net	1	2,19,472
Income from Investments		67,861
Other Income :		
Consideration for Annuities granted		10,712
Total (A)		2,98,045
Commission	2	26,541
Operating Expenses related to Insurance Business	3	19,890
Provision for Tax		3,060
Total (B)		49,491
Benefits Paid (Net)	4	1,96,130
Total (C)		1,96,130
Surplus (D) = (A) – (B) – (C)		52,424
Balance being Funds for Future Appropriations		52,424
Total (D)		52,424

Balance Sheet as at 31st March, 2009

	Schedule	*Rs.'000*
Sources of Funds		
Share Capital	5	13,99,400
Policyholders' Funds		
Life Assurance Fund		14,70,562
		28,69962
Funds for Future Appropriations		52,424
Total		29,22,386
Application of Funds		
Investments	8	24,90,890
Fixed Assets	10	4,19,110
Current Assets:		
Advances and Other Assets	12	32,800
Sub Total (A)		32,800
Current Liabilities	13	20,414
Sub Total (B)		20,414
Net Current Assets (C) = (A) – (B)		12,386
Total		29,22,386

SCHEDULE – 1

Premium

Premiums earned-net	2,19,472

SCHEDULE – 2

Commission Expenses	26,541

SCHEDULE – 3

Operating Expenses Related to Insurance Business	19,890

SCHEDULE – 4

Benefits Paid (Net)

1. Insurance Claims	
(a) Claims by Death	84,980
(b) Claims by Maturity	56,420
(c) Annuities	29,420
(d) Surrenders	21,860
Bonus in cash	9,450
Bonus in reduction of Premiums	4,000
2. (Amount ceded in reinsurance)	
(a) Claims by Death	(10,000)
Total	1,96,130

SCHEDULE – 5

Share Capital

Called up and paid-up Capital	20,00,000
Less: Preliminary Expenses	600
Total	19,99,400

SCHEDULE – 8

Investments

Government Securities	24,90,890
Total	24,90,890

SCHEDULE – 10

Fixed Assets	4,19,110
Total	4,19,110

SCHEDULE -12

Advances and Other Assets

Other Assets

Interest accrued on investments	15,400
Outstanding premiums	7,400
Due from Reinsurers	10,000
Total	32,800

SCHEDULE – 13

Current Liabilities

Claims Outstanding	20,414
Total	20,414

Working Notes :

(*i*) Premiums received	2,10,572
Add : Outstanding	7,400
Covered by bonus utilised for reduction of premium	1,500
Premiums earned (net)	2,19,472
(*ii*) Interest dividends and rents	52,461
Add: Interest accrued	15,400
Income from Investments	67,861

Illustration 2. The following balances appeared in the books of the Happy Life-Assurance Co. Ltd., as on 31st March, 2009:–

	Rs. in lakhs
Claims *less* reassurances paid during the year :	
By Death	2,200
By Maturity	1,500
Annuities	6
Furniture and Office Equipment at cost (including Rs. 40 lakh bought during the year)	250
Printed Stationery	77
Cash with Bank on Current Account	1,350
Cash and Stamps in hand	30
Surrenders	40
Commission	250
Expenses of Management	3,100
Sundry deposits with Electricity Companies etc.	1
Advance Payment of Income-tax	50
Sundry Debtors	50
Agents' Balances	100
Income-tax	450
Income-tax on Interest, Dividends and Rents	500
Loans and Mortgages	150
Loans on Policies	3,250
Sundry Investments (Rs. 250 lakh deposited with the Reserve Bank of India)	52,000
Building at cost (including Rs. 85 lakh added during the year)	5,400
	70,754
Share Capital	10,000
Life Assurance Fund at the beginning of the year	40,000
Premiums *less* reassurances	15,000
Claims *less* reassurances outstanding at the beginning of the year :	
By Death	900
By Maturity	600
Credit balances pending adjustment	60
Consideration for annuities granted	2
Interest, Dividends and Rents	1,800
Registration and other fees	2
Sundry Deposits	100
Taxation Provision	300
Premium Deposits	1,150
Sundry Creditors	350
Contingency Reserve	150
Furniture and Office Equipment Depreciation Account	40
Building Depreciation Account	300
	70,754

From the foregoing balances and the following information, prepare the company's Balance Sheet as on 31st March, 2009 and its Revenue Account for the year ended on that date :

(*a*) Claims *less* reassurances outstanding at the end of the year : By Death Rs. 600 lakh; By Maturity, Rs. 400 lakh.

(*b*) Expenses outstanding Rs. 60 lakh and prepaid Rs. 15 lakh.

(*c*) Provide Rs. 45 lakh for depreciation of buildings, Rs. 15 lakh for depreciation of furniture and office equipment and Rs. 110 lakh for taxation.

(*d*) Premium outstanding Rs. 2,028 lakh; commission thereon Rs. 65 lakh.

(*e*) Interests, Dividends and Rents outstanding (net) Rs. 30 lakhs and interest and rents accrued (net) Rs. 350 lakh. *(Adapted C. Sec. (Inter) Dec. 2002)*

Solution :

Happy Life Assurance Co. Ltd.

Revenue Account for the year ended 31st March, 2009

Particulars	*Schedule*	*Rs. in lakhs*
Premiums earned - net	1	17,028
Income from Investments:		
Interest, Dividends & Rent (gross)		2,180
Other Income :		
Consideration for annuities granted		2
Registration and other fees		2
Total (A)		19,212
Commission	2	315
Operating Expenses related to Insurance Business	3	3,282
Provision for tax		760
Total (B)		4,357
Benefits paid (net)	4	3,246
Total (C)		3,246
Surplus (D) = (A) – (B) – (C)		11,609
Appropriations :		
Balance being Funds for Future Appropriations		11,609
Total (D)		11,609

Balance Sheet as on 31st March, 2009

Particulars	*Schedule*	*Rs. in lakhs*
Sources of Funds		
Share Capital	5	10,000
Reserves and Surplus	6	150
Borrowings	7	1,250
Life Assurance Fund		40,000
Funds for Future Appropriations		11,609
Total		63,009
Application of Funds		
Investments	8	51,750
Loans	9	3,400
Fixed Assets	10	5,250
Current Assets :		
Cash and Bank Balance	11	1,380
Advances and Other Assets	12	2,874
Sub-Total (A)		4,254
Current Liabilities	13	1,535
Provisions	14	110
Sub-Total (B)		1,645
Net Current Assets C = (A) – (B)		2,609
Total		63,009

SCHEDULE – 1

	Rs. in lakhs
Premium	
Premium received	15,000
Add : Outstanding premium	2,028
	17,028

SCHEDULE – 2

Commission Expenses	
Commission Paid	250
Add : Commission on reinasurance accepted	65
	315

SCHEDULE – 3

Operating Expenses Related to Insurance Business	
Expenses of management paid	3,100
Add : Outstanding expenses	60
	3,160
Less : Prepaid expenses	15
	3,145
Printing and Stationery	77
Depreciation on :	
Building	45
Furniture	15
	3,282

SCHEDULE – 4

	Rs. in lakhs	
Benefits Paid (Net)		
Insurance claims :		
Claims by Death		
Paid	2,200	
Add : Outstanding at the end of the year	600	
	2,800	
Less : Outstanding in the beginning	900	1,900
Claims by Maturity		
Paid	1,500	
Add : Outstanding at the end of the year	400	
	1,900	
Less : Outstanding in the beginning	600	1,300
Annuities		6
Surrenders		40
		3,246

SCHEDULE – 5

Share Capital	10,000

SCHEDULE – 6

Reserves and Surplus	
Contingency Reserve	150
	150

SCHEDULE – 7

Borrowings	
Premium Deposits	1,150
Sundry Deposits	100
	1,250

SCHEDULE – 8

Investments	
Sundry Investments	51,750

SCHEDULE – 9

Loans	
On mortgage of property	150
Loans against policies	3,250
	3,400

SCHEDULE – 10

Fixed Assets	*Rs. in lakhs*	
Building, at cost	5,315	
Additions during the year	85	
	5,400	
Less : Depreciation	345	5,055
Furniture and Office Equipment, at cost	210	
Additions during the year	40	
	250	
Less : Depreciation	55	195
		5,250

SCHEDULE – 11

Cash and Bank Balances	
Cash (including stamps)	30
Bank Balance on Current Account	1,350
	1,380

SCHEDULE – 12

Advances and Other Assets	
Prepaid expenses	15
Interest, dividends and rent outstanding	30
Interest, dividends and rent accrued	350
Advance payment of income-tax	50
Outstanding premium	2,028
Agents' balances	100
Deposit with Reserve Bank of India	250
Deposits with electricity companies	1
Sundry debtors	50
	2,874

SCHEDULE – 13

Current Liabilities	
Sundry creditors	350
Claims outstanding	1,000
Expenses outstanding	60
Commission due but not yet paid	65
Credit balances pending adjustment	60
	1,535

SCHEDULE – 14

Provisions	
For taxation	110

B. GENERAL INSURANCE BUSINESS

Insurance other than life insurance is called general insurance. Fire insurance against loss of property due to fire and marine insurance against loss of cargo, freight and ship are examples of general insurance

Reserve for Unexpired Risks : An insurance company issues general insurance policies throughout the accounting year. Premium is received at the time of issue of the policy. But the period for which the policy is issued may cover part of the current accounting year and a part of the next accounting year. It means the company may be required to pay for losses which may take place next year in respect of at least some of the policies issued in the current accounting year. It is, therefore, wrong to consider the premium received in an accounting year to be income of the insurance company without taking into account a reserve for unexpired risks. Schedule II B of the Insurance Regulatory and Development Authority (Assets, Liabilities and Solvency Margin of Insurance) Regulation 2000 lays down that the reserve for unexpired risks, shall be, in respect of :

(*i*) Fire business, 50 per cent,
(*ii*) Miscellaneous business, 50 per cent
(*iii*) Marine business other than marine hull business, 50 per cent, and
(*iv*) Marine hull business, 100 per cent

of the premium, net of reinsurances, received or receivable during the preceding twelve months.

To ascertain the amount of surplus for which a general insurance company can take credit in respect of a particular type of general insurance business, in the relevant Revenue Account, net premium earned is adjusted for Reserve for Unexpired Risks as in the beginning and as at the end of the accounting year concerned.

Illustration 3. Indian Insurance Co. Ltd. furnishes you with the following information :

(*i*) On 31.3.2009 it had reserve for unexpired risks to the tune of Rs. 40 crore. It comprised of Rs. 15 crore in respect of marine insurance business; Rs. 20 crore in respect of fire insurance business and Rs. 5 crore in respect of miscellaneous insurance business.

(*ii*) It is the practice of Indian Insurance Co. Ltd. to create reserve at 100% of net premium income in respect of marine insurance policies and at 50% of net premium income in respect of fire and miscellaneous insurance policies.

(*iii*) During the year ended 31st March, 2010, the following business was conducted :

	Marine *Rs. crores*	*Fire* *Rs. crores*	*Miscellaneous* *Rs. crores*
Premia collected from :			
(*a*) Insured (other than insurance companies) in respect of policies issued	18	43	12
(*b*) Other insurance companies in respect of risks undertaken	7	5	4
Premia paid/payable to other insurance companies on business ceded	6.7	4.3	7

Indian Insurance Co. Ltd. asks you to :

(a) Pass journal entries relating to "unexpired risks reserve'.

(*b*) Show in columnar form Unexpired Risks Reserve Account for the year ended 31st March, 2010.

[*C.A. (Inter) May, 1998 Modified*]

Solution :

Journal

Date		Particulars	L.F.	Dr. Rs. crore	Cr. Rs. crore
2010 Mar.	31	Marine Revenue Account ..Dr.		3.30	
		To Unexpired Risks Reserve Account			3.30
		Excess of closing provision for unexpired risks of Rs. 18.3 crore over opening provision of Rs. 15 crore charged to Marine Revenue Account.			

Mar.	31	Fire Revenue Account To Unexpired risks Reserve Account Excess of closing provision for unexpired risks of Rs. 21.85 crore over opening provision of Rs. 20 crore charged to Fire Revenue Account.	..Dr.	1.85	1.85
"	"	Unexpired Risks Revenue Account To Miscellaneous Revenue Account Excess of opening provision for unexpired risks of Rs. 5 crore over the required closing balance of Rs. 4.5 crore in the provision account credited to Miscellaneous Revenue Account.	..Dr.	0.50	0.50

Working Notes :

Required closing balances in Unexpired Risks Reserve accounts :-

For marine business = Rs. (18 + 7 - 6.7) crore = Rs. 18.3 crore

$$\text{For fire business} = \frac{\text{Rs. }(43+5-4.3)}{2}\text{ crore} = \text{Rs. } 21.85 \text{ crore}$$

$$\text{For miscellaneous business} = \frac{\text{Rs. }(12+4-7)}{2}\text{ crore} = \text{Rs. } 4.5 \text{ crore}$$

Dr. **Unexpired Risks Reserve Account** *Cr.*

Date	*Particulars*	*Marine*	*Fire*	*Misc.*	Date	*Particulars*	*Marine*	*Fire*	*Misc.*
2010		(Rupees	in crores)		**2009**		(Rupees	in crores)	
Mar. 31	To Revenue A/c	--	--	0.50	Apr. 1	By Balance b/fd	15.00	20.00	5.00
" "	To Balance c/fd	18.30	21.85	4.50	**2010**				
					Mar. 31	By Revenue A/c	3.30	1.85	--
		18.30	21.85	5.00			18.30	21.85	5.00

Note : Alternatively, the opening balances of unexpired risk reserves may be reversed in the beginning of year by transfer to Revenue account and fresh reserve of full required amount may be created at the end of the year which will be carried forward as closing balances.

In case of general insurance, the insurer should prepare the Revenue Account, Profit and Loss Account (Shareholders' Account) and Balance Sheet in Form B-RA, Form B-PL and Form B-BS respectively.

The insurer should prepare Revenue Account separately for fire, marine and miscellaneous business and separate schedules should be prepared for marine cargo, marine other than marine cargo and the following classes of miscellaneous insurance business: 1. Motor 2. Workmen's Compensation/Employers' Liability, 3. Public/Product Liability, 4. Engineering 5. Aviation, 6. Personal Accident, 7. Health Insurance, 8. Others.

FORM B-RA

Name of the Insurer :

Registration No. and Date of Registration with the IRDA

REVENUE ACCOUNTS FOR THE YEAR ENDED 31ST MARCH, 20______.

	Particulars	*Schedule*	*Current Year*	*Previous Year*
			(Rs.'000)	*(Rs.'000)*
1.	Premiums earned (Net)	**1**		
2.	Profit/Loss on sale/redemption of Investments			
3.	Others (to be specified)			
4.	Interest, Dividend & Rent-Gross			
	TOTAL (A)			

1.	Claims Incurred (Net)	2		
2.	Commission	3		
3.	Operating Expenses related to Insurance Business	4		
	TOTAL (B)			
	Operating Profit/(Loss) from Fire/Marine/ Miscellaneous Business (C) = (A) – (B)			
	APPROPRIATIONS			
	Transfer to Shareholders' Account			
	Transfer to Catastrophe Reserve			
	Transfer to other Reserves (to be specified)			
	TOTAL (C)			

Note : See Notes appended at the end of Form B-PL

FORM B-PL

Name of the Insurer :

Registration No. and Date of Registration with the IRDA

PROFIT AND LOSS ACCOUNT FOR THE YEAR ENDED 31ST MARCH, 20______.

	Particulars	*Schedule*	*Current Year*	*Previous Year*
			(Rs.'000)	*(Rs.'000)*
1.	OPERATING PROFIT/(LOSS)			
	(*a*) Fire Insurance			
	(*b*) Marine Insurance			
	(*c*) Miscellaneous Insurance			
2.	INCOME FROM INVESTMENTS			
	(*a*) Interest, Dividend & Rent-Gross			
	(*b*) Profit on sale of investments			
	Less : Loss on sale of investments			
3.	OTHER INCOME (to be specified)			
	TOTAL (A)			
4.	Provisions (other than taxation)			
	(*a*) For diminution in the value of investments (*b*) For doubtful debts (*c*) Others (to be specified)			
5.	OTHER EXPENSES (*a*) Expenses other than those related to Insurance Business (*b*) Bad debts written off (*c*) Others (to be specified)			
	TOTAL (B)			

	Profit before Tax			
	Provision for Taxation			
	APPROPRIATIONS			
	(*a*) Interim dividend paid during the year (*b*) Proposed final dividend (*c*) Dividend distribution tax (*d*) Transfer to any Reserves or Other Accounts (to be specified)			
	Balance of profit/loss brought forward from last year			
	Balance carried forward to Balance Sheet			

Notes : to forms B-RA and B-PL

(*a*) Premium income received from business concluded in and outside India shall be separately disclosed.

(*b*) Reinsurance premiums whether on business ceded or accepted are to be brought into account gross (i.e. before deducting commissions) under the head reinsurance premiums.

(*c*) Claims incurred shall comprise claims paid, specific claims settlement costs wherever applicable and change in the outstanding provision for claims at the year-end.

(*d*) Items of expenses and income in excess of one percent of the total premiums (less reinsurance) or Rs. 5,00,000 whichever is higher, shall be shown as a separate line item.

(*e*) Fees and expenses connected with claims shall be included in claims.

(*f*) Under the sub-head "others" shall be included items like foreign exchange gains or losses and other items.

(*g*) Interest dividends and rentals receivable in connection with an investment should be stated as gross amount, the amount of income tax deducted at source being included under 'advance taxes paid and taxes deducted at source".

(h) Income from rent shall include only the realised rent. It shall not include any notional rent.

FORM B-BS

Name of the Insurer :
Registration No. and Date of Registration with the IRDA

BALANCE SHEET AS AT 31ST MARCH, 20_____.

Particulars	*Schedule*	*Current Year*	*Previous Year*
		(Rs.'000)	*(Rs.'000)*
SOURCES OF FUNDS			
SHARE CAPITAL	5		
RESERVES AND SURPLUS	6		
FAIR VALUE CHANGE ACCOUNT			
BORROWINGS	7		
TOTAL			
APPLICATION OF FUNDS			
INVESTMENTS	8		
LOANS	9		
FIXED ASSETS	10		

CURRENT ASSETS

Cash and Bank Balances	11		
Advances and Other Assets	12		
Sub-Total (A)			
CURRENT LIABILITIES	13		
PROVISIONS	14		
Sub-Total (B)			
NET CURRENT ASSETS (C) = (A) – (B)			
MISCELLANEOUS EXPENDITURE (to the extent not written off or adjusted)	15		
DEBIT BALANCE IN PROFIT AND LOSS ACCOUNT			
TOTAL			

CONTINGENT LIABILITIES

	Particulars	*Current Year*	*Previous Year*
		(Rs.'000)	*(Rs.'000)*
1.	Partly paid-up investments		
2.	Claims, other than against policies, not acknowledged as debts by the company		
3.	Underwriting commitments outstanding (in respect of shares and securities)		
4.	Guarantees given by or on behalf of the Company		
5.	Statutory demands/liabilities in dispute, not provided for		
6.	Reinsurance obligations to the extent not provided for in accounts		
7.	Others (to be specified)		
	TOTAL		

SCHEDULES FORMING PART OF FINANCIAL STATEMENTS

SCHEDULE – 1

PREMIUM EARNED [NET]

Particulars	*Current Year*	*Previous Year*
	(Rs.'000)	*(Rs.'000)*
Premium from direct business		
Add : Premium on reinsurance accepted		
Less : Premium on reinsurance ceded		
Net Premium		

Adjustment for change in reserve for unexpired risks		
Total Premium Earned (Net)		

Note: Reinsurance premiums whether on business ceded or accepted are to be brought into account, before deducting commission, under the head of reinsurance premiums.

SCHEDULE – 2

CLAIMS INCURRED [NET]

Particulars	*Current Year*	*Previous Year*
	(Rs.'000)	*(Rs.'000)*
Claims paid		
Direct		
Add : Reinsurance accepted		
Less : Reinsurance ceded		
Net Claims paid		
Add : Claims Outstanding at the end of the year		
Less : Claims Outstanding at the beginning		
Total Claims Incurred		

Notes:

(*a*) Incurred But Not Reported (IBNR), Incurred But Not Enough Reported [IBNER] claims should be included in the amount for outstanding claims.

(*b*) Claims include specific claims settlement cost but not expenses of management.

(*c*) The surveyor fees, legal and other expenses shall also form part of claims cost.

(*d*) Claims cost should be adjusted for estimated salvage value if there is a sufficient certainty of its realisation.

SCHEDULE – 3

COMMISSION

Particulars	*Current Year*	*Previous Year*
	(Rs.'000)	*(Rs.'000)*
Commission paid		
Direct		
Add: Re-insurance accepted		
Less: Commission on re-insurance ceded		
Net Commission		

Note : The profit/commission, if any, are to be combined with the re-insurance accepted or re-insurance ceded figures.

SCHEDULE – 4

OPERATING EXPENSES RELATED TO INSURANCE BUSINESS

	Particulars	*Current Year*	*Previous Year*
		(Rs.'000)	*(Rs.'000)*
1.	Employees' remuneration & welfare benefits		
2.	Travel, conveyance and vehicle running expenses		
3.	Training expenses		
4.	Rents, rates & taxes		
5.	Repairs		
6.	Printing & stationery		
7.	Communication		
8.	Legal & professional charges		
9.	Auditors' fees, expenses etc.		
	(*a*) as auditor (*b*) as adviser or in any other capacity, in respect of (*i*) Taxation matters (*ii*) Insurance matters (*iii*) Management services; and (*c*) in any other capacity		
10.	Advertisement and publicity		
11.	Interest & Bank Charges		
12.	Others (to be specified)		
13.	Depreciation		
	TOTAL		

Note : Items of expenses and income in excess of one percent of the total premiums (less reinsurance) or Rs. 5,00,000 whichever is higher, shall be shown as a separate line item.

SCHEDULE – 5

SHARE CAPITAL

	Particulars	*Current Year*	*Previous Year*
		(Rs.'000)	*(Rs.'000)*
1.	Authorised Capital		
	... Equity Shares of Rs....each		
2.	Issued Capital		
	...Equity Shares of Rs...each		
3.	Subscribed Capital		
	...Equity Shares of Rs...each		
4.	Called-up Capital		

	.... Equity Shares of Rs...each		
	Less : Calles unpaid		
	Add : Equity Shares Forfeited (Amount originally paid up) *Less* : Par value of Equity Shares bought back		
	Less : Preliminary Expenses Expenses including commission or brokerage on underwriting or subscription of shares		
	TOTAL		

Notes:

(*a*) Particulars of the different classes of capital should be separately stated.

(*b*) The amount capitalised on account of issue of bonus shares should be disclosed.

(*c*) In case any part of the capital is held by a holding company, the same should be separately disclosed.

SCHEDULE–5A

SHARE CAPITAL

PATTERN OF SHAREHOLDING

[As certified by the Management]

Shareholder	*Current Year*		*Previous Year*	
	Number of Shares	*% of Holding*	*Number of Shares*	*% of Holding*
Promoters • Indian • Foreign				
Others				
TOTAL				

SCHEDULE – 6

RESERVES AND SURPLUS

	Particulars	*Current Year*	*Previous Year*
		(Rs.'000)	*(Rs.'000)*
1.	Capital Reserve		
2.	Capital Redemption Reserve		
3.	Securities Premium		
4.	General Reserve *Less* : Debit balance in Profit and Loss Account *Less* : Amount utilized for Buy-back		
5.	Catastrophe Reserve		
6.	Other Reserves (to be specified)		
7.	Balance of profit in Profit & Loss Account		
	TOTAL		

Note : Additions to and deductions from the reserves should be disclosed under each of the specified heads.

SCHEDULE – 7

BORROWINGS

	Particulars	*Current Year*	*Previous Year*
		(Rs.'000)	*(Rs.'000)*
1.	Debentures/Bonds		
2.	Banks		
3.	Financial Institutions		
4.	Others (to be specified)		
	TOTAL		

Notes:

(*a*) The extent to which the borrowings are secured shall be separately disclosed stating the nature of the security under each sub-head.

(*b*) Amounts due within 12 months from the date of Balance Sheet should be shown separately

SCHEDULE – 8

INVESTMENTS

	Particulars	*Current Year*	*Previous Year*
		(Rs.'000)	*(Rs.'000)*
	LONG TERM INVESTMENTS		
1.	Government securities and Government guaranteed bonds including Treasury Bills		
2.	Other Approved Securities		
3.	Other Investments		
	(*a*) Shares (*aa*) Equity (*bb*) Preference (*b*) Mutual Funds (*c*) Derivative Instruments (*d*) Debentures/Bonds (*e*) Other Securities (to be specified) (*f*) Subsidiaries (*g*) Investment Properties-Real Estate		
4.	Investments in infrastructure and Social Sector		
5.	Other than Approved Investments		
	SHORT TERM INVESTMENTS		
1.	Government securities and Government guaranteed bonds including Treasury Bills		
2.	Other Approved Securities		
3.	Other Investments		
	(*a*) Shares (*aa*) Equity (*bb*) Preference		

	(*b*) Mutual Funds (*c*) Derivative Instruments (*d*) Debentures/Bonds (*e*) Other Securities (to be specified) (*f*) Subsidiaries (*g*) Investment Properties-Real Estate		
4.	Investments in Infrastructure and Social Sector		
5.	Other than Approved Investments		
	TOTAL		

Notes :

(*a*) Investments in subsidiary/holding companies, joint ventures and associates shall be separately disclosed, at cost.

(*i*) Holding company and subsidiary shall be construed as defined in the Companies Act, 1956.

(*ii*) Joint Venture is a contractual arrangement whereby two or more parties undertake an economic activity, which is subject to joint control.

(*iii*) Joint control is the contractually agreed sharing of power to govern the financial and operating policies of an economic activity to obtain benefits from it.

(*iv*) Associate is an enterprise in which the company has significant influence and which is neither a subsidiary nor a joint venture of the company.

(*v*) Significant influence (for the purpose of this schedule) means participation in the financial and operating policy decisions of a company, but not control of those policies. Significant influence may be exercised in several ways, for example, by representation on the board of directors, participation in the policy making process, material inter-company transactions, interchange of managerial personnel or dependence on technical information. Significant influence may be gained by share ownership, statute or agreement. As regards share ownership, if an investor holds, directly or indirectly through subsidiaries, 20 percent or more of the voting power of the voting power of the investee, it is presumed that the investor does have significant influence unless it can be clearly demonstrated that this is not the case. Conversely, if the investor holds, directly or indirectly through subsidiaries, less than 20 percent of the voting power of the investee, it is presumed that the investor does not have significant influence, unless such influence is clearly demonstrated. A substantial or majority ownership by another investor does not necessarily preclude an investor for having significant influence.

(*b*) Aggregate amount of company's investments other than listed equity securities and derivative instruments and also the market value thereof shall be disclosed.

(*c*) Investments made out of Catastrophe Reserve should be shown separately.

(*d*) Debt securities will be considered as "held to maturity" securities and will be measured at historical cost subject to amortisation.

(*e*) Investment Property means a property [land or building or part of a building or both] held to earn rental income or for capital appreciation or for both, rather than for use in services or for administrative purposes.

(*f*) Investments maturing within twelve months from balance sheet date and investments made with the specific intention to dispose of within twelve months from balance sheet date shall be classified as short-term investments.

SCHEDULE – 9

LOANS

	Particulars	*Current Year*	*Previous Year*
		(Rs.'000)	*(Rs.'000)*
1.	SECURITY-WISE CLASSIFICATION		
	Secured		
	(*a*) On mortgage of property (*aa*) In India (*bb*) Outside India (*b*) On Shares, Bonds, Govt. Securities (*c*) Others (to be specified)		
	Unsecured		
	TOTAL		
2.	BORROWER-WISE CLASSIFICATION		
	(*a*) Central and State Governments (*b*) Banks and Financial Institutions (*c*) Subsidiaries (*d*) Industrial Undertakings (*e*) Others (to be specified)		
	TOTAL		
3.	PERFORMANCE-WISE CLASSIFICATION		
	(*a*) Loans classified as standard (*aa*) In India (*bb*) Outside India (*b*) Non-performing loans less provisions (*aa*) In India (*bb*) Outside India		
	TOTAL		
4.	MATURITY-WISE CLASSIFICATION		
	(*a*) Short-Term (*b*) Long Term		
	TOTAL		

Notes:

(*a*) Short-term loans shall include those, which are repayable within 12 months from the date of balance sheet. Long term loans shall be the loans other than short-term loans.

(*b*) Provisions against non-preforming loans shall be shown separately.

(*c*) The nature of the security in case of all long term secured loans shall be specified in each case. Secured loans for the purposes of this schedule, means loans secured wholly or partly against an asset of the company.

(*d*) Loans considered doubtful and the amount of provision created against such loans shall be disclosed.

SCHEDULE – 10

FIXED ASSETS

(*Rs.'000*)

Particulars	*Cost/Gross Block*				*Depreciation*				*Net Block*	
	Opening	*Additions*	*Deductions*	*Closing*	*Up to Last Year*	*For the Year*	*On Sales/ Adjustments*	*To Date*	*As at Year end*	*Previous Year*
Goodwill										
Intangibles (specify)										
Land–Freehold										
Leasehold Property										
Buildings										
Furniture & Fittings										
Information										
Technology										
Equipment										
Vehicles										
Office Equipment										
Others (Specify nature)										
TOTAL										
Work in progress										
Grand Total										
PREVIOUS YEAR										

Note: *Assets included in land, building and property above exclude Investment Properties as defined in note (e) to Schedule 8.*

SCHEDULE – 11

CASH AND BANK BALANCES

	Particulars	*Current Year*	*Previous Year*
		(Rs.'000)	*(Rs.'000)*
1.	Cash (including cheques, drafts and stamps)		

2.	Bank Balances		
	(*a*) Deposit Accounts (*aa*) Short-term (due within 12 months) (*bb*) Others (*b*) Current Accounts (*c*) Others (to be specified)		
3.	Money at Call and Short Notice		
	(*a*) With Banks (*b*) With other Institutions		
4.	Others (to be specified)		
	TOTAL		
	Balances with non-scheduled banks included in 2 and 3 above		

Note : Bank balance may include remittances in transit. If so, the nature and amount should be separately stated.

SCHEDLE – 12

ADVANCES AND OTHER ASSETS

	Particulars	*Current Year*	*Previous Year*
		(Rs.'000)	*(Rs.'000)*
	ADVANCES		
1.	Reserve deposits with ceding companies		
2.	Application money for investments		
3.	Prepayments		
4.	Advances to Directors/Officers		
5.	Advance tax paid and taxes deducted at source (Net of provision for taxation)		
6.	Others (to be specified)		
	TOTAL (A)		
	OTHER ASSETS		
1.	Income accrued on investments		
2.	Outstanding Premiums		
3.	Agents' Balances		
4.	Foreign Agencies Balances		
5.	Due from other entities carrying on insurance business (including reinsurers)		

6.	Due from subsidiaries/holding		
7.	Deposit with Reserve Bank of India [Pursuant to section 7 of Insurance Act, 1938]		
8.	Others (to be specified)		
	TOTAL (B)		
	TOTAL (A) + (B)		

Notes:

(*a*) The items under the above heads shall not be shown net of provisions for doubtful amounts. The amount of provision against each head should be shown separately.

(*b*) The term 'Officer' should conform to the definition of that term as given under the Companies Act, 1956.

(*c*) Sundry Debtors will be shown under item 9 (others)

SCHEDULE – 13

CURRENT LIABILITIES

	Particulars	*Current Year*	*Previous Year*
		(Rs.'000)	*(Rs.'000)*
1.	Agents' Balances		
2.	Balances due to other insurance companies		
3.	Deposits held on re-insurance ceded		
4.	Premiums received in advance		
5.	Unallocated Premium		
6.	Sundry creditors		
7.	Due to subsidiaries/holding company		
8.	Claims Outstanding		
9.	Due to Officers/Directors		
10.	Others (to be specified)		
	TOTAL		

SCHEDULE – 14

PROVISIONS

	Particulars	*Current Year*	*Previous Year*
		(Rs.'000)	*(Rs.'000)*
1.	Reserve for Unexpired Risk		
2.	For taxation (less advance tax paid and taxes deducted at source)		
3.	For proposed dividends		
4.	For dividend distribution tax		
5.	Others (to be specified)		
	TOTAL		

SCHEDULE – 15

MISCELLANEOUS EXPENDITURE
(To the extent not written off or adjusted)

	Particulars	*Current Year*	*Previous Year*
		(Rs.'000)	*(Rs.'000)*
1.	Discount Allowed in issue of shares/debentures		
2.	Others (to be specified)		
	TOTAL		

Notes:

(*a*) No item shall be included under the head "Miscellaneous Expenditure" and carried forward unless:
1. some benefit from the expenditure can reasonably be expected to be received in future, and
2. the amount to be carried forward in respect of any item included under the head "Miscellaneous Expenditure" shall not exceed the expected future revenue/other benefits related to the expenditure.

(*b*) The amount to be carried forward in respect of any item included under the head "Miscellaneous Expenditure" shall not exceed the expected future revenue/other benefits related to the expenditure.

Illustration 4. From the following particulars, prepare the Fire Revenue Account for 2009 - 2010:—

	Rs in lakhs
Claims paid	235
Legal expenses regarding claims	5
Premiums received	600
Reinsurance premiums	60
Commission	100
Expenses of management	150
Provision against unexpired risk on April 1, 2009	260
Claims unpaid on April 1, 2009	20
Claims unpaid on March 31, 2010	35

Solution:

Revenue Account for the year ended 31st March, 2010

Particulars	*Schedule*	*Current Year Rs. in lakhs*
Premiums earned (Net)	1	530
Total (A)		530
Claims incurred (Net)	2	255
Commission	3	100
Operating Expenses related to Insurance Business	4	150
Total (B)		505
Operating Profit from Fire Business C = (A) – (B)		25
Appropriations :		
Transfer to Shareholders' Account		25
Total (C)		25

SCHEDULE -1

Premiums Earned (Net)

Particulars		*Current Year Rs. in lakhs*
Premiums received		600
Less : Premium on reinsurance ceded		60
Net Premium		540
Adjustment for change in reserve for unexpired risks :	*Rs. in lakhs*	
Opening provision	260	
Closing provision, 50% of Rs. 540 lakh	(270)	(10)
Total Premium Earned (Net)		530

SCHEDULE -2

Claims Incurred (Net)

	Rs. in lakhs
Net claims paid (including legal expenses regarding claims)	240
Add : Claims outstanding at the end of the year	35
	275
Less : Claims outstanding at the beginning	20
	255

SCHEDULE -3

Commission	*Rs. in lakhs*
Net Commission	100

SCHEDULE - 4

Operating Expenses Related to Insurance Business	*Rs. in lakhs*
Expenses of Management	150

Illustration 5. From the following figures taken from the books of New Asia Insurance Co. Ltd. doing fire underwriting business, prepare the set of final accounts for the year 2009-2010:

	Rs.'000		*Rs.'000*
Fire Fund (as on 1-4-2009)	11,80,000	Commission on Direct Business	2,99,777
General Reserve	4,50,000	Commission on reinsurance accepted	60,038
Investments	36,00,000	Outstanding Premium	22,300
Premium	26,01,533	Claims intimated but not paid (1.4.2009)	60,000
Claims Paid	6,02,815	Expenses on Management	4,31,947
Share Capital — Divided into Equity		Audit fees	36,000
Shares of Rs. 100 each	10,00,000	Rates and Taxes	5,804
Profit and Loss Account (Cr.)	25,000	Rents	67,500
Re-insurance Premium	1,12,525	Income from Investments	1,53,000
Claim recovered from re-insurers	21,119	Sundry Creditors	22,500
Commission on reinsurance ceded	48,016	Agents Balance (Dr.)	20,000
Advance income tax paid	2,50,000	Cash in Hand and Bank Balance	1,32,462

The following further information may also be noted:

(*a*) Expenses of management include survey fees and legal expenses of Rs. 36,000 thousand and Rs. 20,000 thousand relating to claims.

(*b*) Claims intimated but not paid on 31st March 2010, Rs. 1,04,000 thousand.

(*c*) Income-tax to be provided at 40%.

(*d*) Transfer of Rs. 2,25,000 thousand to be made from current profit to General Reserve.

(*e*) The company maintains a reserve for unexpired risk @ 50% of net premium income.

(*f*) The directors propose a dividend @ 30 %. Dividend distribution tax is payable @ 15%.

[*Adapted C.A. (Inter) May, 1987*]

Solution :

New Asia Insurance Co. Ltd.

Revenue Account for the year ended 31st March, 2010

Particulars	*Schedule*	*Current Year Rs. '000*
Premiums earned (Net)	1	24,24,504
Total (A)		24,24,505
Claims Incurred (Net)	2	6,81,696
Commission	3	3,11,799
Operating Expenses related to Insurance Business	4	3,75,947
Total (B)		13,69,442
Operating Profit from Fire Business (C) = (A) – (B)		10,55,062
Appropriations :		
Transfer to Shareholders' Account		10,55,062
Total (C)		1055,062

Profit and Loss Account for the year ended 31st March, 2003

Particulars	Current Year Rs. '000
Operating Profit from Fire Insurance	10.55.062
Income from Investments	1.53.000
Total (A)	12.08.062
Expenses other than those related to Insurance Business:	
Rent	67.500
Rates and taxes	5,804
Andit fee	36,000
Total (B)	1.09.304
Profit before Tax, (A) – (B)	10.98.758
Provision for Taxation @ 40%	4.39.503
	6.59.255
Appropriations :	
Proposed Final Dividend @ 30%	3.00.000
Dividend Distribution Tax @ 15%	45.000
Transfer to General Reserve	2.25.000
	89.255
Balance of profit brought forward from last year	25,000
Balance carried forward to Balance Sheet	1,14,255

Balance Sheet as on 31st March, 2003

Particulars	Schedule	Current Year Rs. '000
Sources of Funds		
Share Capital	5	10.00.000
Reserves and Surplus	6	9.19.255
Total		19,19,255
Application of Funds		
Investments	8	31.30.000
Current Assets		
Cash and Bank Balances	11	4,82,462
Advances and Other Assets	12	42,300
Sub-Total (A)		5.24.762
Current Liabilities	13	1.26.500
Provisions	14	16.09.007
Sub-Total (B)		17.35.507
Net Current Assets (C) = (A) – (B)		11.86.745
Total		19.19.255

SCHEDULE -1

Premiums Earned (Net)

	Rs. '000
Premiums	26,01,533
Less : Premium on reinsurance ceded	(1,12,525)
	24,89,008
Adjustment for increase in reserve for unexpired risks, Rs. (12,44,504 – 11,80,000) thousand	(64,504)
	24,24,504

SCHEDULE -2

Claims Incurred (Net)

	Rs. '000
Claims paid, Rs. (6,02,815 + 36,00 + 20,000) thousand	6,58,815
Less : Reinsurance ceded	(21,119)
	6,37,696
Add : Claims outstanding at the end of the year	1,04,000
	7,41,696
Less : Claims outstanding at the beginning	(60,000)
	6,81,696

SCHEDULE -3

Commission

	Rs. '000
Commission paid on :	
Direct Business	2,99,777
Add : Reinsurance accepted	60,038
	3,59,815
Less : Reinsurance ceded	48,016
	3,11,799

SCHEDULE -4

Operating Expenses Related to Insurance Business

	Rs. '000
Expenses of Management, (Rs. 4,31,947 – 36,000 – 20,000 thousand	3,75,947

SCHEDULE-5

Share Capital	10,00,000

SCHEDULE -6

Reserves and Surplus	*Rs. '000*	*Rs. '000*
General Reserve	5,80,000	
Addition during the year	2,25,000	
		8,05,000
Credit balance of Profit and loss Account		1,14,255
		9.19.255

SCHEDULE-8

	Rs. '000
Investments	31,30,000

SCHEDULE-11

	Rs. '000
Cash and Bank Balances	4,82,462

SCHEDULE-12

	Rs. '000
Advances and other Assets	
Outstanding Premiums	22,300
Agents Balances	20,000
	42,300

SCHEDULE-13

	Rs, '000
Current Liabilitis	
Sundry Creditors	22,500
Claims Outstanding	1,04,000
	1,26,500

SCHEDULE-14

	Rs, '000	Rs, '000
Provisions		
Reserve for Unexpired Risk		12,44,504
For Taxation	4,39,503	
Less : Advance Tax Paid	4,20,000	19,503
For Proposed Dividend		3,00,000
For Dividend Distribution Tax		45,000
		16,09,007

EXERCISE XXV

1. From the following trial balance, prepare the Revenue Account and the Balance Sheet of the Imaginary Assurance Co. Ltd.

Trial Balance as on 31st March, 2010

	Rs. in lakhs		Rs. in lakhs
Expenses of Management	18,241	Premiums	3,65,982
Deposit with Reserve Bank of India	3,42,520	Profit on sale of investments	10,824
Commission	9,872	Claims admitted but not paid.	15,421
Investment Properties-Real Estate	1,68,421	Sundry trade creditors	724
Bonuses in cash	4,222	Life Assurance Fund at the beginning of the year 2009-2010	28,00,510
Surrenders	21,104	Consideration for annuities granted	12,272
Claims by Maturity	1,04,728	Interest, dividends and rents — gross	1,20,682
Claims by Death	1,72,681	Share capital	1,00,000
Annuities Paid	7,681	General reserve	50,000
Outstanding Premiums	21,641		
Income-tax Paid	7,139		
Agents' Balances	6,824		
Port Trust Debentures, interest and principle guaranteed by Government	5,28,241		
Cash at Bank, Current Account	13,178		
Office Furniture	1,500		

Fully paid up shares in limited liability companies registered in India	1,81,509	
Stock of policy stamps in hand	68	
Mortgages in India	8,67,911	
Loans on Government securities	7,19,961	
Loans on company's policies	1,78,973	
	33,76,415	33,76,415

(Surplus, Rs. 1,64,092 lakh; Balance Sheet Rs. 30,14,602 lakh)

2. The following trial balance was extracted from the books of the Goodluck Life Assurance Company Ltd. as on 31st March, 2010 :

	Dr. *Rs. in crores*	*Cr.* *Rs. in crores*
Paid-up capital - 200 crore shares of Rs. 10 each	—	2,000
Life Assurance Fund as on 1st April, 2009		59,446
Bonus to policyholders	630	
Premium received		3,230
Claims paid	3,940	
Commission paid	186	
Management expenses	646	
Mortgages in India	9,844	
Interest and dividends and rents		2,254
Agents' balances	186	
Investment properties – real estate	800	
Investments	46,100	
Loan on company's policies	3,472	
Cash on deposit	540	
Cash in hand and on current account	46	
Surrenders	140	
	66,930	66,930

You are required to prepare the company's revenue account for the year ended 31st March, 2010 and its balance sheet as on that date after taking the following matters also into consideration :

		Rs. in crores
(*i*)	Claims admitted but not paid	186
(*ii*)	Management expenses due	4
(*iii*)	Interest accured	386
(*iv*)	Premiums outstanding	240

[Adapted C.S. (Inter), June, 1996]
[Surplus, Rs. 378 crore, Balance Sheet Rs. 61,824 crore)

3. The books of Jai Hind Insurance Co. Ltd. contained the following information in respect of personal accidents insurance as on 31st March, 2010:—

	Rs. in crores
Provision for unexpired risks on 1st April 2009	800
Estimated liability in respect of outstanding claims:	
On 1st April, 2009	100
On 31st March, 2009	150
Medical expenses regarding claims	10
Claims paid	700
Reinsurance premiums	140
Reinsurance recoveries	15
Premiums	1,900
Commission on direct business	250

Commission on reinsurance ceded	30
Management expenses	550
Interests and dividends	80
Legal expenses regarding claims	15
Profit on sale of investments for the year ended 31st March, 2010.	17

Prepare the Revenue Account for the year ended 31st March, 2010.

(Operating Profit Rs. 237 crore)

Hint: Reinsurance recoveries to be deducted from claims.

4. Zaldi Pay Insurance Co. Ltd. has furnished the following information for preparation of revenue account for fire insurance business for the year ended 31st March, 2010:—

	Rs. in crores
Claims admitted but not paid	150
Commission paid	500
Commission on reinsurance ceded	120
Expenses of management	780
Claims paid	1,423
Premiums received	5,520
Reserve for unexpired risks as on 1.4.2009	2,300
Claims outstanding as on 1.4.2009	270

The following further information has also to be considered :—

(*i*) Premiums outstanding at the end of the year: Rs. 400 crore.

(*ii*) It is the policy of the company to maintain 50% of premium towards reserve for unexpired risks.

[*Adapted C.A. (Inter) May 1989*]

(Operating Profit, Rs. 2,797 crore)

5. The following balances as at 31st March, 2010 have been extracted from the books of New Insurance Co. Ltd. which carries on only Fire Insurance Business:—

	Rs. in crores
Claims less reinsurances	2,500
Provision for unexpired risks on 31.3.2009	2,000
Premiums less reinsurances	4,500
Commission on:	
Direct business	350
Reinsurance accepted	150
Reinsurance ceded	200
Claims outstanding on 1.4.2009	50
Bad Debts	10
Expenses of management	895
Share Capital (shares of Rs. 10 each)	5,000
General Reserve	2,000
Cash in hand and at Bank	3,060
Investments	5,500
Furniture & Equipments	200
Sundry Creditors	500
Investment Reserve	100
Agents' Balances (Debit)	510

Profit and Loss Appropriation Account on 1.4.2009	800
Amounts due from other insurers	250
Interests, dividends and rents (Fire)	625

Prepare Revenue Account, Profit and Loss Account and Balance Sheet after taking into consideration the following:

(*i*) Claims outstanding on 31.3.2009 were Rs. 100 crore.

(*ii*) Provision for taxation is to be made at 35%.

(*iii*) The company's directors propose a dividend@ 10% on share capital after transfer of Rs. 150 crore to General Reserve. Dividend tax is payable @ 15%.

(*Operating profit, Rs. 1,130 crore; Profit after tax Rs. 728 crore, Balance Sheet, Rs. 8,053 crore)*

Essay Type

1. What do you understand by a contract of insurance ? What are its advantages to the insured especially a businessman ?
2. Enumerate the risks against which insurance policies are normally issued by general insurance companies.
3. What is an annuity granted by a life insurance company ?
4. What is meant by a whole-life policy ? How does it differ from an endowment policy ?
5. How do With Profit Life Policies differ from Without Profit Life Policies ?
6. Explain the following terms as used in connection with life insurance :--
   (*i*) Bonus,
   (*ii*) Interim Bonus,
   (*iii*) Reversionary Bonus, and
   (*iv*) Bonus in Reduction of Premium.
7. What is meant by reinsurance ? How is it helpful to insurance companies ?
   (**Hint :** An insurance company can share heavy risk with other insurance companies with the help of reinsurance policies).
8. What is 'double insurance'? Can an insured take a number of endowment policies on his own life and recover full amounts on all such policies on their maturity ? What will be your answer in case a person takes a number of fire insurance policies in respect of his house, the total amount of all the policies far exceeding the total value of the subject matter insured which is subsequently destroyed completely due to fire during the currency of those fire insurance policies.
   (**Hint :** In fire insurance, the insured cannot recover in all more than the amount of his loss)
9. Distinguish between reinsurance and double insurance.
10. What is meant by surrender value of a life insurance policy ? How does it differ from paid up value of such a policy ? Of the surrender value and paid up value of a life insurance policy, which will be higher at any point of time and why ?
    (**Hint :** Paid up value will be more than surrender value because whereas surrender value is to be paid immediately, payment of paid up value is postponed to a later date.)
11. How are the provisions of surrender value and paid up value of a life insurance policy helpful to the assured ?
12. Is there a surrender value of general insurance policy also ? (Hint : No.)
13. Distinguish between surrender value and paid up value of a life insurance policy.
14. What is meant by an insurance claim ? In life insurance business, there are claims by death and claims by maturity or survivance. How will you distinguish between these two types of claim ?
15. What is meant by Single Premium Life Policy ?

16. Distinguish between First Year's Premium and Renewal Premium of a life insurance policy.

17. Clearly distinguish between life insurance on one hand and fire and marine insurance on the other hand.

Hints :

(*i*) In life insurance, the claim must arise either at the expiry of the term of the policy or on the death of the subject matter. In fire insurance and marine, a claim may arise or may not arise and the loss due to the risk insured against is not certain.

(*ii*) A contract of life insurance is not a contract of indemnity whereas other contracts of insurance are contracts of indemnity

(*iii*) In life insurance, insurable interest is required only at the time of contract of insurance, it need not exist when the policy matures. In marine insurance, insurable interest must be present at the time of loss; it may not be present at the time of taking the policy. In fire insurance, insurable interest must be present both at the time of the policy and at the time of loss.

(*iv*) In life insurance, insurable interest may not be measurable. In other types of insurance, it is always measurable in terms of money.

(*v*) A contract of life insurance is a continuing contract. A contract of any other type of insurance can be, at the most, for one year at a time.

18. "A contract of insurance is a contract of indemnity". Discuss. How far does the statement apply to life insurance policies ?

19. To what extent is it correct to say that even policyholders get a share of the profits of a life insurance company ?

20. Clearly distinguish :

(*i*) Commission on reinsurance accepted,

(*ii*) Commission on reinsurance ceded.

21. What is the purpose of maintaining Reserve for Unexpired Risks in respect of general insurance business ?

22. In general insurance business, what is meant by Reserve for Unexpired Risks ? What is the minimum percentage of net premium income that must be maintained as reserve of Unexpired Risks in respect of (*i*) fire insurance business and (*ii*) marine insurance business while preparing revenue accounts ?

23. Distinguish between Revenue Account and Profit and Loss Account as prepared by a general insurance company.

24. Distinguish between (*i*) direct business and (*ii*) reinsurance business as accepted by an insurance company.

26

BANK

SYNOPSIS

1. Legal Provisions .. 26.1
Forms of Business .. 26.1
Non-banking Assets .. 26.2
Management .. 26.3
Minimum Capital and Reserves .. 26.3
Floating Charge .. 26.4
Restrictions on Dividends .. 26.4
Statutory Reserve .. 26.4
Cash Reserves and Statutory Liquidity Reserve .. 26.4
Restrictions on Loans and Advances .. 26.5
Subsidiary Companies .. 26.5
Control .. 26.5
2. Accounts and Books .. 26 5
Demand Drafts and Telegraphic Transfers .. 26.6
Travellers Cheques and Letters of Credit .. 26.6
Acceptances, Endorsements and Other Obligations .. 26.6
Bills for Collection .. 26.7
Bills Purchased and Discounted .. 26.7
Rebate on Bills Discounted .. 26.7
Books Required .. 26.10
Accounting Year .. 26.11
3. Final Accounts .. 25.11
Form of Balance Sheet .. 26.13
Form of Profit and Loss Account .. 26.17
Guidelines of RBI .. 26.19
Notes on Accounts and Disclosure of Accounting Policies .. 26.28
Capital Adequacy Norms .. 26.30
Income from Non-performing Assets .. 26.35
Classification of Advances - 26.37
Specimen of Final Accounts - 26.39

1. LEGAL PROVISIONS

The Banking Regulation Act, 1949 defines banking as "the accepting, for the purpose of lending or investment, of deposits of money from the public, repayable on demand or otherwise and withdrawable by cheque, draft, order or otherwise." Till 1949, there was no special legislation to regulate banking companies but since that year the Banking Regulation Act applies to corporate entities carrying on the business of banking in India. Such companies are also subject to the Companies Act, 1956. The nationalised banks are also subject to the Banking Regulation Act except in regard to appointment of directors and disposal of profit etc. But the Act is not applicable to a primary agricultural society, a cooperative land mortgage bank and any other cooperative society, except in the manner and to the extent specified in Part V of the Act.

Forms of Business :

Section 6 (1) of the Act lays down that in addition to the usual banking business, the following business may also be carried on by a banking company :—

(*i*) borrowing, raising or taking up of money;
(*ii*) lending or advancing of money;
(*iii*) drawing, making, accepting, discounting, buying, selling, collecting and dealing in bills of exchange, hundis, promissory notes and other instruments;
(*iv*) granting and issuing of letters of credit, travellers' cheques and circular notes;

(*v*) buying, selling and dealing in bullion and specie;
(*vi*) buying and selling, on commission, underwriting and dealing in stock, shares, debentures, bonds etc;
(*vii*) receiving of all kinds of scrips or valuables on deposit or for safe custody;
(*viii*) providing of safe deposit vaults;
(*ix*) collecting and transmitting of money and securities;
(*x*) acting as agents for any Government or local authority or any other person or persons; the carrying on of agency business of any description including the clearing and forwarding of goods, giving of receipts and discharges and otherwise acting as an attorney on behalf of customers, but excluding the business of a managing agent or secretary and treasures of a company;
(*xi*) contracting for public and private loans and negotiating and issuing the same;
(*xii*) effecting, insuring, guaranteeing, underwriting, participating in managing and carrying out of any issue, public or private, of State, municipal or other loans or of shares, stock, debentures, or debenture stock of any company, corporation or association and of lending of money for the purpose of any such issue;
(*xiii*) carrying on and transacting every kind of guarantee and indemnity business;
(*xiv*) managing, selling and realising any property which may come into the possession of the company in satisfaction or part satisfaction of any of its claims;
(*xv*) acquiring and holding and generally dealing with any property or any right title or interest in any such property which may form the security or part of the security for any loans or advances or which may be connected with any such security;
(*xvi*) undertaking and executing trusts;
(*xvii*) undertaking and administration of estates as executor, trustee or otherwise;
(*xviii*) establishing and supporting associations, funds, trusts, and conveniences for the benefit of employees, their dependants and the general public;
(*xix*) acquiring, constructing, maintaining and altering any building or works necessary for the purposes of the banking company;
(*xx*) selling, improving, managing, developing, exchanging, leasing, mortgaging, disposing of or turning into account or otherwise dealing with all or any part of the property and rights of the company;
(*xxi*) acquiring and undertaking the whole or any part of the business of any person or company when such business is of a nature enumerated or described in this sub-section;
(*xxii*) doing all such things as are incidental or conducive to the promotion or advancement of the business of the company;
(*xxiii*) any other form of business which the Central Government may notify in the Official Gazette.

Other types of business are prohibited for a banking company. No banking company can directly or indirectly deal in the buying or selling or bartering of goods, except in connection with the realisation of security given to or held by it, or engage in any trade or buy or sell or barter goods for others otherwise than in connection with bills of exchange. Immovable property, except that required for its own use, however acquired, must be disposed of within seven years from the date of acquisition. However, the Reserve Bank may in any particular case extend the aforesaid period of seven years by such period not exceeding five years.

Non-banking Assets :

As mentioned in the previous paragraph, a bank cannot acquire certain assets but it can always lend against the security of such assets. This means that sometimes, in case of failure on the part of the loanee to repay the loans, the bank may have to take possession of such assets. In that case, the assets are shown as "non-banking assets." These must be disposed of within seven years.

It may be noted that should the bank lend against such assets as are allowed to be held by a bank, say, government securities, it can continue to hold them if the loanee fails to meet his obligations. Such assets cannot be treated as non-banking assets.

Management. A banking company must have a whole-time chairman appointed for five years at a time. He may become a director of a subsidiary of the banking company or of a guarantee company registered under section 25 of the Companies Act but cannot take up any other appointment. The chairman is appointed by the Board of Directors but, in the case of nationalised banks, he is appointed by the Central Government.

At least 51% of the directors of a banking company must be such persons as have specialised knowledge, or practical experience, in respect of accountancy, agriculture, rural economy, banking, co-operation, economics, finance, law or any other matter which is approved by the Reserve Bank as useful to the banking company. Directors must not be proprietors of any trading, commercial or industrial concerns (other than small industrial concerns) and also must not have substantial interest in, or be connected with (as employee or manager, etc.), any commercial company except a guarantee company incorporated under section 25 of the Companies Act and except a small-scale industrial concern.

The Reserve Bank of India has the power to order the removal of a director or the chairman,

Minimum Capital and Reserves :

Sections 11 lays down the following minimum limit of paid up capital and reserves :—

(*a*) Banking companies incorporated outside India :—

If it has a place of business in Mumbai or Kolkata or both . . . . . Rs. 20 lakhs

If it does not have a place of business in Mumbai or Kolkata . . . . . Rs. 15 lakhs

Further, every year 20% of the profits earned in India must be added to the sums specified above.

The sum must be kept deposited with the Reserve Bank either in cash or in the form of unencumbered approved securities.

(*b*) Banking companies incorporated in India :—

(*i*) If the places of business are in more than one State and if any places of business is in Mumbai or Kolkata. ..Rs. 10 lakhs

(*ii*) If the places of business are in more than one State but none of the places of business is in Mumbai or Kolkata. .. Rs. 5 lakhs

(*iii*) If the places of business are only in one State, none of the places of business being in Mumbai or Kolkata. .. Rs. 1 lakh for the principal places plus Rs. 10,000 for each additional place of business in the same district and Rs. 25,000 for a place of business outside the district. The total need not exceed Rs. 5 lakhs, or Rs. 50,000 in case there is only one place of business.

[But companies which commence business after the commencement of the Banking (companies) Amendment Act of 1962, a minimum of rupees five lakhs is required.]

(*iv*) If the places of business are only in one State and if the places of business are also in Mumbai or Kolkata. .. Rs. 5 lakhs Plus Rs. 25,000 for each place of business situated outside Mumbai and Kolkata. The total need not exceed Rs. 10 lakhs.

Banking companies carrying on business in India must see to it that—

(*a*) the subscribed capital is not less than half the authorised capital;

(*b*) the paid up capital is not less than half the subscribed capital; and

(*c*) the capital of the company consists only of ordinary or equity shares and such preference shares as may have been issued before July, 1,1944.

A shareholder cannot exercise more than one per cent of the total voting rights of the company. A chairman, managing director or chief executive of a banking company must declare his full holdings in the capital of the company. Underwriting commission or brokerage or discount on shares issued by a banking company cannot exceed $2^1/_2\%$ of the paid up value of the shares. A charge on unpaid capital cannot be created. No dividend can be declared unless expenses not represented by tangible assets have been completely written off.

Floating Charge :

Section 14A lays down that a banking company shall not create a floating charge on the undertaking or any property of the company or any part thereof except upon a certificate from the Reserve Bank that such a charge is not detrimental to the interests of the depositors of the company. A floating charge created without such a certificate is invalid. A charge on un-called capital is invalid.

Restrictions of Dividends :

Under section 15, a banking company cannot pay dividends unless all of its capitalised expenses (including preliminary expenses, organisation expenses, share selling commission, brokerage, amounts of losses incurred and any other item of expenditure not represented by tangible assets) have been completely written off.

But a banking company need not

(*a*) write off depreciation in the value of its investments in approved securities (except in 'current' investments) in any case where such depreciation has not actually been capitalised or otherwise accounted for as a loss ;

(*b*) write off depreciation in the value of its investments in shares, debentures or bonds (other than approved securities) in any case where adequate provision for such depreciation has been made to the satisfaction of the auditor ;

(*c*) write off bad debts in any case where adequate provision for such debts has been made to the satisfaction of the auditors of the banking company.

Statutory Reserve :

Section 17 of the Act lays down that at least 20 per cent of the profits prior to declaration of dividend must be transferred to the Reserve Fund. The Reserve Fund thus built up has to be shown separately from other reserves. The Central Government may, on the recommendation of the Reserve Bank and having regard to the adequacy of the paid up capital and reserves of the bank in relation to its deposit liabilities, exempt the bank for a period of time from the obligation of transfer of profits to the Reserve Fund. But the Central Government shall not pass such an order unless the amount in the statutory reserve fund together with the amount in the securities premium account is at least equal to the paid-up capital of the bank.

Cash Reserves and Statutory Liquidity Reserve :

Section 18 of the Banking Regulation Act requires that every banking company, not being a scheduled bank, shall maintain in India by way of cash reserve with itself, or by way of balance in a current account with the Reserve Bank, or by way of net balance in current accounts, or in one or more of the aforesaid ways, a sum equivalent to at least three per cent of the total of its demand and time liabilities in India as on the last Friday of the second preceding fortnight.

Every scheduled Bank is required, by virtue of the provisions of section 42(1) of the Reserve Bank of India Act, to maintain with the Reserve Bank an average daily balance the amount of which shall not be less than three per cent of the total of its demand and time liabilities in India. The said rate may, however, be increased by the Reserve Bank of India by notification up to 15% of the total of demand and time liabilities in India.

Section 24 of the Banking Regulation Act requires that every banking company shall maintain in India in cash, gold or unencumbered approved securities an amount which shall not, at the close of business on any day, be less than thirty five per cent, or such other percentage not exceeding forty, as the Reserve Bank of India may from time to time specify, of the total of its demand and time liabilities in India as on the last Friday of the second preceding fortnight. This is known as Statutorary Liquidity Ratio (SLR).

The Term 'demand liabilities' means liabilities which must be met on demand. The term 'liabilities' means liabilities which are not demand liabilities.

Restrictions on Loans and Advances :

After the amendment of the law in 1968, a bank cannot : (*i*) grant loans or advances on the security of its own shares; and (*ii*) grant or agree to grant loan or advance to or on behalf of : (*a*) any of its directors; (*b*) any firm in which any of its directors is interested as partner, manager or guarantor; (*c*) any company of which any of its directors is a director, manager, employee guarantor or in which he holds substantial interest; or (*d*) any individual in respect of whom any of its directors is a partner or guarantor.

Note : (*ii*) (*c*) does not apply to subsidiaries of the banking company, registered under section 25 of the Companies Act or a government company.

Subsidiary Companies :

A banking company is allowed to form a subsidiary company (*a*) only for the purpose of undertaking of any business laid down in section 6 (1) of the Banking Regulation Act, 1949; or (*b*) with the written permission of the Reserve Bank to carry on the banking business exclusively outside India. or (*c*) to undertake such other business which the Reserve Bank may, with the prior approval of the Central Government, consider conducive to the spread of banking in India or useful or necessary in the public interest.

Control :

The Reserve Bank of India has the authority to exercise general supervision of banks. A bank has to obtain the prior permission of the Reserve Bank for opening a new place of business or for transfer of an existing place of business either in India or abroad. The Reserve Bank is authorised to determine the policy in relation to advances to be followed by banks. For example, it may give direction to banks regarding the purposes for which advances may or may not be made. It may lay down the margins to be maintained in respect of secured advances. It may prescribe the maximum amount of advances that may be made to any one company, firm or an individual. It may determine the rate of interest and other conditions on which advances or other financial accommodation may be made or guarantees may be given.

2. ACCOUNTS AND BOOKS

Because of the peculiar nature of its business, a bank has to keep its ledger accounts especially those of its customers always up-to-date. A customer may present a cheque to the bank for payment at any moment. Unless the accounts of the customers are kept up-to-date, it would not be possible to decide correctly whether to honour or dishonour a cheque. A bank may be liable to pay exemplary damages if it wrongfully dishonours a cheque. And, of course, the bank will not like to unknowingly pay a cheque on an account whose balance is inadequate. Hence, a bank has to enter into the ledger every transaction as soon as it takes place. To do so, banks resort to what is called 'Voucher Posting'

Posting' or 'Slip System of Ledger Posting'. Under this system, entries in the personal ledgers are made directly from vouchers instead of being posted from the Day Book. Pay-in-slips used by the customers at the time of making deposits and the cheques are the slips which form the basis of most of the transactions directly recorded in the accounts of the customers. As the slips are mostly filled up by the customers themselves, this system saves a lot of time and labour of the bank staff. The vouchers entered into different personal ledgers are summarised on summary sheets every day, totals of which are posted to the different control accounts which are maintained in the general ledger.

For every transaction which does not involve cash, two vouchers are prepared — one debit voucher and another credit voucher. The vouchers are sent to the different clerks who make entries in books under their charge.

Let us now discuss a few peculiar types of transactions.

Demand Drafts and Telegraphic Transfers :

People find demand drafts and telegraphic transfers to be safe vehicles of transmitting money specially to distant place; telegraphic transfers being quicker. When a customer requests his bank to issue a demand draft in favour of the party to whom he wants to make payment, he has to pay to the bank the amount of the demand draft and the bank charges for the service. The demand draft is drawn on the appropriate branch of the bank which is required to make the payment. If the bank issuing the demand draft does not have its own branch at the desired place, it may draw the demand draft on another bank having a branch there if there is an agreement for this purpose with that bank. The customer sends the demand draft to the payee who collects the amount from the branch on which the demand draft has been drawn.

In a telegraphic transfer, the bank telegraphically informs the relevant branch to credit the requisite amount to the account of the payee, making the transmission of money rather quick.

Travellers Cheques and Letters of Credit :

To avoid the risk of losing cash in travel, a customer while going on a travel may take with him travellers cheques rather than cash. The customer pays to the bank the amount for which he wants travellers cheques to be issued. The bank issues travellers cheques of the desired denominations, crediting Travellers Cheques Account. Every cheque carries the specimen signatures of the customer. Travellers cheques can be encashed at the different branches of the bank. To encash a travellers cheque, the customer has to sign the cheque again; the signatures must tally with the specimen signatures on the travellers cheque. The customer may present the unused cheques for cancellation; he will get back the full amount of the cheques cancelled. The bank may even pay interest in respect of the travellers cheques for the period for which the amounts have remained with it before payment. On payment, the bank debits Travellers Cheques Account.

Any Time Money (ATM) Cards have Made Traveller Cheques :

A customer may request his bank to issue a Letter of Credit for which he has to deposit cash for the required amount; the bank issues the letter of credit, crediting Letters of Credit Account. When the bill of exchange drawn against the letter of credit is received for payment, the amount is debited to Letters of Credit Account.

If a bank is requested to issue travellers cheques or letter of credit in a foreign currency, the bank collects from the customer the equivalent value in home currency and purchases immediately the amount of the foreign currency equal to the value of travellers cheques or letter of credit issued.

Acceptances, Endorsements and Other Obligations :

Credit of a bank is more acceptable than that of its customers. Hence, a bank is often requested by a customer to accept or endorse a bill of exchange on his behalf or give a guarantee of repayment of a loan raised by the customer. Suppose, *A* makes a purchase from *B* and wants credit. *B* is willing to extend credit provided he is satisfied that on the due date, payment will be forthcoming. To assure *B*, *A* can do one of the following things :—

(*a*) he may request his bank to stand as a guarantor ;

(*b*) he may send a promissory note in favour of the bank and the bank may then endorse it in favour of *B* ; and

(*c*) he may request the bank to send its own acceptance to *B*.

Guarantee and endorsement are on the same footing and will stand cancelled when A makes the payment. If *A* does not pay, the bank will pay to *B* and debit *A's* account. In case the bank accepts a bill of exchanger, the bank will have to pay to *B* recovering the amount from *A*. In this case "acceptances on behalf of customers" will equal "customers' liability for acceptances."

To safeguard its interests, the bank may require the customer to deposit a security for an appropriate amount against a guarantee, or an acceptance or endorsement by the bank on behalf of the customer. A record of the guarantee given or the particulars of the bill accepted or endorsed as well as the particulars of the security collected from the customer will have to be recorded in different registers.

Outstanding amount of acceptances, endorsements and other obligations at the end of the year has to be shown as Contingent Liabilities in Schedule-12 of the Balance Sheet of the bank.

Bills for Collection :

A bank receives a large number of bills receivable from its customers for collection on the due dates of the bills. The bank keeps these bills with itself till maturity and, on realisation, credits the amounts to the clients concerned. Similarly, businessmen having sold goods to outstation customers hand over documentary bills to the bank to be handed over to the purchasers on payment of the concerned bills. Here also, the amounts collected for the documentary bills are credited to the clients submitting such bills. The bank keeps a systematic records of all such bills in a separate register which is called Bills for Collection Register (see page 26.12 for ruling). The total amount of all the bills lying with the bank for collection at the end of the year is shown separately at the foot of the Balance Sheet of the bank.

Bills Purchased and Discounted :

Customers offer to a bank bills receivable for outright purchase or discounting. When the bank purchases or discounts the bill, the amount of the bill less discount charge is credited to the account of the customer, the discount charged is credited to the Discount Account and the full amount of bill is debited to Discounted Bills Account. At the end of the year, the outstanding amount of all such bills is shown as Bills Purchased and Discounted in Schedule-9 of the Balance Sheet.

Rebate on Bills Discounted :

This means unearned discount for those bills that will mature after the date of closing of accounts, that is, that portion of the discount which relates to the period falling after the close of the accounting year. When a customer gets a bill discounted, the bank credits the Discount Account with the total amount of the discount the bank will earn in respect of the discounted bill. The credit of the Discount Account represents the bank's earning. If a bill matures after the close of the accounting year, the discount on the bill from the date of closing to the date of maturity of the bill is unearned and hence it will be wrong to credit the Profit and Loss Account with the full discount on the bill. The unearned discount is known as" Rebate on Bills Discounted".

With effect from the accounting year ended 31st March, 1992, 'Rebate on Bills Discounted' is not to be shown as a separate item in the Balance Sheet or any of its Schedules. The amount of Rebate on Bills Discounted is included in the item 'Other Liabilities and Provisions' in Schedule-5 attached to the Balance Sheet.

Illustration 1:

On 31st March 2005, the New Bank Ltd. held the following bills :

Date of Bill 2005	*Amount* *Rs.*	*Term* *Months*	*Discounted* *@ % p.a.*
Feb. 9	1,00,000	4	9
Feb 17	1,20,000	3	7.5
Mar. 6	80,000	4	8.25

Calculate the Rebate on Bills Discounted and give the necessary journal entry.

Solution :

Date of Bill 2005	*Date of Maturity* 2005	*No. of Days after March 31, 2005*
Feb. 9	June 12	73
Feb. 17	May 20	50
Mar. 6	July 9	100

Amount Rs.	*Rate % p.a.*	*Total Annual Discount* Rs.	*Proportionate Discount for Days after 31st March* Rs. P.
1,00,000	9	9,000	1,800.00
1,20,000	7.5	9,000	1,232.88
80,000	8.25	6,600	1,808.22
		Total Rs.	4841.10

THE JOURNAL ENTRY REQUIRED :

		Rs. P.	Rs. P.
Discount Account	Dr.	4,841.10	
To Rebate on Bills Discounted Account			4,841.10
Discount not yet earned on discounted bills			

In the beginning of the next year, this entry will be reversed.

Illustration 2:

The following particulars are extracted from the (Trial Balance) Books of the M/s. Sound Bank Ltd., for the year ending 31st March, 2010 :

	Rs.
(1) Interest and Discount	1,96,62,400
(2) Rebate on Bills Discounted (balance on 1-4-2009)	65,040
(3) Bills Discounted and Purchased	67,45,400

It is ascertained that proportionate discount not yet earned on the bills discounted which will mature during 2009-2010 amounted to Rs. 92,760..

Pass the necessary journal entries adjusting the above and show in the ledger of the Bank :

(*a*) Rebate on Bills Discounted Account and

(*b*) Interest and Discount Account. *[Adapted C.A., Final]*

Solution :

BOOKS OF M/S SOUND BANK LTD.

Journal

				Rs.	Rs.
2009					
April	1	Rebate on Bills Discounted Account	Dr.	65,040	
		To Interest and Discount Account			65,040
		(Opening balance of Rebate on Bills Discounted, being the income of the current year credited to Interest and Discount Account)			

2010			*Rs.*	*Rs.*
Mar.	31	Interest and Discount Account Dr.	92,760	
		To Rebate on Bills Discounted Account		92,760
		(Interest and discount received this year, but not yet earned transferred to Rebate on Bills Discounted Account to be carried forward to the next accounting year)		

Dr. **Rebate on Bills Discounted Account** *Cr.*

2009		*Rs.*	2009		*Rs.*
April 1	To Interest and Discount A/c—transfer	65,040	April 1	By Balance b/fd	65,040
2010			2010		
Mar. 31	To Balance c/d	92,760	Mar. 31	By Interest and Discount Account	92,760
			2010		
			April 1	By Balance b/d	92,760

Dr. **Interest and Discount Account** *Cr.*

2010		*Rs.*	2009		*Rs.*
Mar. 31	To Rebate on Bills Discounted Account	92,760	April 1	By Rebate on Bills Discounted A/c (Opening Balance)	65,040
,, ,,	To Profit and Loss Account — transfer	1,96,34,680	2009-2010 Apr. 1 to Mar. 31	By Bills Purchased and Discounted A/c	1,96,62,400
		1,97,27,440			1,97,27,440

Illustration 3:

On 31st March, 2009, Uncertain Bank Ltd. had a balances of Rs. 9 crores in 'rebate on bills discounted' account. During the year ended 31st March, 2010, Uncertain Bank Ltd. discounted bills of exchange of Rs. 8,000 crores charging interest at 9% per annum, the average period of discount being 73 days. Of these, bills of exchange of Rs. 1,200 crores were due for realisation from the acceptors/customers after 31st March, 2010, the average period outstanding after 31st March, 2010 being 36.5 days.

Uncertain Bank Ltd. asks you to pass journal entries and show the ledger accounts pertaining to:

(*i*) discounting of bills of exchange, and

(*ii*) rebate on bills discounted. [*C.A. (Inter) May, 1998_Modified*]

Solution :

Uncertain Bank Ltd.
Journal

		Rs. (*in crores*)	*Rs.* (*in crores*)
2009 Apr. 1	Rebate on bills Discounted Account Dr.	9.00	
	To Discount on Bills Account		9.00
	Transfer of opening balance in Rebate on Bills Discounted Account to Discount on Bills Account.		
Apr. 1, 2009 to	Bills Purchased and Discounted Account Dr.	8,000	
	To Discount on Bills Account		144.00
	To Clients		7,856.00

			Rs. (in crores)	Rs. (in crores)
Mar. 31, 2010	Discounting of bills of exchange during the year [See working note (i)]			
2010 Mar. 31	Discount on Bills Account To Rebate on Bills Discounted Account Unexpired portion of discount in respect of the discounted bills of exchange carried forward [See working note (ii)]	Dr.	10.80	10.80
,, ,,	Discount on Bills Account To Profit and Loss Account Amount of income for the year from discounting of bills of exchange transferred to Profit and Loss Account.	Dr.	142.20	142.20

Working Notes :

(i) Discount on bills discounted during the year
= Rs. 8,000 crores × 9/100 × 73/365 = Rs. 144 crores

(ii) Unexpired portion of discount in respect of the discounted bills
= Rs. 1,200 crores × 9/100 × 36.5/365
= Rs. 10.80 crores

Ledger

Discount on Bills Account

Dr.				Cr.	
2010		Rs. in crores	2009		Rs. in crores
Mar.31	To Rebate on Bills Discounted Account	10.80	Apr. 1	By Rebate on Bills Discounted Account	9.00
,, ,,	To Profit and Loss Account — transfer	142.20	Apr. 1 2009 to Mar.31, 2010	By Bills Purchased and Discounted Account	144.00
		153.00			153.00

Rebate on Bills Discounted Account

Dr.				Cr.	
2009		Rs. in crores	2009		Rs. in crores
Apr. 1	To Discount on Bills Account — transfer	9.00	Apr. 1	By Balance b/fd	9.00
2010 Mar. 31	To Balance c/d	10.80	2010 Mar. 31	By Discount on Bills Account	10.80
			2010 Apr. 1	By Balance b/d	10.80

Books Required :

A bank has to maintain a large number of subsidiary books ; the following being the more prominent ones :

(a) Receiving Cashier's Counter Cash Book,

(b) Paying Cashier's Counter Cash Book,

(c) Current Accounts Ledger,

(d) Savings Bank Accounts Ledger,

(e) Fixed Deposit Accounts Ledger,

(f) Recurring Deposit Accounts Ledger,

(*g*) Investment Ledger,

(*h*) Loan Ledger,

(*i*) Bills Discounted and Purchased Ledger,

(*j*) Customers' Acceptances, Endorsements and Guarantee Ledger.

The principal books are (1) the Cash Book into which are summarised the results disclosed by the Receiving Cashier's Counter Cash Book and the Paying Cashier's Counter Cash Book; and (2) the General Ledger which contains control accounts for the subsidiary ledgers, revenue accounts and the accounts of the assets not covered by the subsidiary ledgers.

In every bank, ledgers are maintained on self-balancing system. In the General Ledger, there is a separate Control Account for each subsidiary ledger. Periodically, usually every two weeks, the total of the balances of all the individual accounts of each subsidiary ledger is compared with the balance of the relevant Control Account in the General Ledger; in other words, a trial balance of the personal ledgers is prepared and agreed with the general ledger control accounts. This is in addition to the preparation of the daily trial balance of the general ledger.

Besides the abovementioned books, there are a number of registers and memorandum books which are maintained by a bank, their actual number depending on the individual needs of the bank. The following is the list of some such registers :-

(1) Bills for Collection Register,

(2) Demand Draft Register,

(3) Share Security Register,

(4) Jewellery Register,

(5) Safe Custody Register,

(6) Letters of Credit Register,

(7) Safe Deposit Vault Register,

(8) Standing Orders Register.

The rulings of the Bills for Collection Register, the Share Security Register and the Loan Ledger are given on the following page.

Accounting Year :

Every bank closes its books each year on 31st March. Banks usually close books, for internal purposes, on 30th September also.

3. FINAL ACCOUNTS

According to section 29 of the Banking Regulation Act, 1949 a banking company is required to prepare its Balance Sheet and Profit and Loss Account in the forms set out in the third Schedule of Act. The formats have been revised effective from the accounting year ended 31st March, 1992. The following are the revised formats which include Form A for Balance Sheet, Form B for Profit and Loss Account and sixteen schedules out of which the first twelve schedules pertain to Balance Sheet while the remaining four schedules concern Profit and Loss Account.

Bills for Collection (or D.D.) Register

Date	D.D or (B.C.) No.	From whom Received	Drawn by	Drawee and Station	Bill or R/R		Favbouring	Amount Rs.	Date of Realisation	Remarks
					Date	No.				

Share Security Register

Name of Party .... Limit Rs. ....
Address .... Margin ....

Serial No.	Date of Pledge	Name of Company	Share Scrip No.	Distinctive Numbers		Number of Shares Received	Paid up Value Rs.	Market Value Rs.	Class of Shares	Disposal	Remarks
				From	To						

Loan Ledger

Name .... Date ....
Address .... Security .... Rate of Interest .... % per annum.

Date	Particulars	Debit Rs.	Credit Rs.	Dr. Balance Rs.	Days	Product	Interest Rs.

Form 'A'
FORM OF BALANCE SHEET

Balance Sheet of .... (here enter name of the Banking company)
as on 31st March (*year*)

(000's omitted)

CAPITAL AND LIABILITIES	Schedule	As on 31.3.... (Current Year)	As on 31.3...... (Previous Year)
Capital	1		
Reserves & Surplus	2		
Deposits	3		
Borrowings	4		
Other liabilities and provisions	5		
Total :			
ASSETS			
Cash and balances with Reserve Bank of India	6		
Balances with banks and money at call and short notice	7		
Investments	8		
Advances	9		
Fixed Assets	10		
Other Assets	11		
Total :			
Contingent Liabilities	12		
Bills for Collection			

SCHEDULE 1—CAPITAL

	As on 31.3.... (Current Year)	As on 31.3.... (Previous Year)
I. **For Nationalised Banks**		
Capital (Fully owned by Central Government)		
II. **For Banks Incorporated Outside India**		
Capital		
(*i*) (The amount brought in by banks by way of start-up capital as prescribed by RBI should be shown under this head)		
(*ii*) Amount of deposit kept with the RBI under Section 11 (2) of the Banking Regulation Act, 1949		
Total :		
III. **For Other Banks**		
Authorised Capital		
(Shares of Rs. each)		
Issued Capital		
Shares of Rs. each)		
Subscribed Capital		
(Shares of Rs. each)		
Called-up Capital		
(Shares of Rs. each)		
Less : Calls unpiad		
Add : Forfeited Shares		

SCHEDULE 2 — RESERVES & SURPLUS

	As on 31.3.... (Current Year)	As on 31.3.... (Previous Year)
I. Statutory Reserves		
Opening Balance		
Additions during the year		
Deductions during the year		
II. Capital Reserves		
Opening Balance		
Additions during the year		
Deductions during the year		
III. Securities Premium		
Opening Balance		
Additions during the year		
Deductions during the year		
IV. Revenue and other Reserves		
Opening Balance		
Additions during the year		
Deductions during the year		
V. Balance in Profit and Loss Account		
Total : (I, II, III, IV and V)		

SCHEDULE 3 — DEPOSITS

	As on 31.3.... (Current Year)	As on 31.3.... (Previous Year)
A. I. Demand Deposits		
(*i*) From Banks		
(*ii*) From others		
II. Saving Bank Deposits		
III. Term Deposits		
(*i*) From Banks		
(*ii*) From others		
Total (I, II and III)		
B. (*i*) Deposits of branches in India		
(*ii*) Deposits of branches outside India		
Total :		

SCHEDULE 4 — BORROWINGS

	As on 31.3.... (Current Year)	As on 31.3.... (Previous Year)
I. Borrowings in India		
(*i*) Reserve Bank of India		
(*ii*) Other banks		
(*iii*) Other institutions and agencies		
II. Borrowings outside India		
Total : (I and II)		

Secured borrowings included in I & II above —Rs.

SCHEDULE 5 — OTHER LIABILITIES AND PROVISIONS

	As on 31.3.... (Current year)	As on 31.3.... (Previous year)
I. Bills payable		
II. Inter-office adjustments (net)		
III. Interest accrued		
IV. Others (including provisions)		
Total :		
(I, II, III and IV)		

SCHEDULE 6 — CASH AND BALANCES WITH RESERVE BANK OF INDIA

	As on 31.3.... (Current year)	As on 31.3.... (Previous year)
I. Cash in hand (including foreign currency notes)		
II. Balances with Reserve Bank of India		
(*i*) in Current Account		
(*ii*) in Other Accounts		
Total :		
(I and II)		

SCHEDULE 7 — BALANCES WITH BANKS & MONEY AT CALL & SHORT NOTICE

	As on 31.3.... (current year)	As on 31.3.... (previous year)
I. In India		
(*i*) Balances with banks		
(*a*) in Current Accounts		
(*b*) in Other Deposit Accounts		
(*ii*) Money at call and short notice		
(*a*) With banks		
(*b*) With other institutions		
Total :		
[(*i*) and (*ii*)]		
II. Outside India		
(*i*) in Current Accounts		
(*ii*) in Other Deposit Accounts		
(*iii*) Money at call and short notice		
Total :		
[(*i*), (*ii*) and (*iii*)]		
Grand Total :		
(I and II)		

SCHEDULE 8 — INVESTMENTS

	As on 31.3.... (Current Year)	As on 31.3.... (Previous Year)
I. Investments in India in		
(*i*) Government securities		
(*ii*) Other approved securities		
(*iii*) Shares		
(*iv*) Debentures and Bonds		

	As on 31.3.... (Current Year)	As on 31.3.... (Previous Year)
(*v*) Subsidiaries and/or joint ventures		
(*iv*) Others (to be specified)		
Total :		
II. Investments outside India in		
(*i*) Government securities (including local authorities)		
(*ii*) Subsidiaries and/or joint ventures abroad		
(*iii*) Other investments (to be specified)		
Total :		
Grand Total : (I & II)		

SCHEDULE 9 — ADVANCES

	As on 31.3.... (Current Year)	As on 31.3.... (Previous Year)
A. (*i*) Bills purchased and discounted		
(*ii*) Cash credits, overdrafts and loans repayable on demand		
(*iii*) Term loans		
Total :		
B. (*i*) Secured by tangible assets		
(*ii*) Covered by Bank/Government guarantees		
(*iii*) Unsecured		
Total :		
C. I. Advances in India		
(*i*) Priority Sectors		
(*ii*) Public Sector		
(*iii*) Banks		
(*iv*) Others		
Total :		
II. Advances outside India		
(*i*) Due from banks		
(*ii*) Due from others		
(*a*) Bills purchased and discounted		
(*b*) Syndicated loans		
(*c*) Others		
Total :		
Grand Total : (C I and II)		

SCHEDULE 10 - FIXED ASSETS

	As on 31.3.... (Current Year)	As on 31.3.... (Previous Year)
I. Premises		
At cost as on 31st March of the preceding year		
Additions during the year		
Deductions during the year		
Depreciation to date		

	As on 31.3.... (Current Year)	As on 31.3.... (Previous Year)
II. Other Fixed Assets (including furniture and fixtures)		
At cost as on 31st March of the preceding year		
Additions during the year		
Deductions during the year		
Depreciation to date		
Total :		
(I and II)		

SCHEDULE 11 — OTHER ASSETS

	As on 31.3.... (Current Year)	As on 31.3.... (Previous Year)
I. Inter-office adjustments (net)		
II. Interest accrued		
III. Tax paid in advance/tax deudcted at source		
IV. Stationery and stamps		
V. Non-banking assets acquired in satisfaction of claims		
VI. Others @		
Total :		

@In case there is any unadjusted balance of loss the same may be shown under this item with appropriate footnote.

SCHEDULE 12 — CONTINGENT LIABILITIES

	Year ended on 31.3... (Current Year)	Year ended on 31.3... (Previous Year)
I. Claims against the bank not acknowledged as debts		
II. Liabilities for party paid investments		
III. Liability on account of outstanding forward exchange contracts		
IV. Guarantees given on behalf of constituents		
(*a*) In India		
(*b*) Outside India		
V. Acceptances, endorsements and other obligations		
VI. Other items for which the bank is contingently liable		
Total :		

Form 'B'
FORM OF PROFIT AND LOSS ACCOUNT
Profit & Loss Account for the year ended 31st March (Year)

(000's ommitted)

	Schedule No.	*Year ended on 31.3... (Current Year)*	*Year ended on 31.3... (Previous Year)*
I. **Income**			
Interest earned	13		
Other income	14		
Total :			
II. **Expenditure**			
Interest expended	15		
Operating expenses	16		
Provisions and contingencies			
Total :			

	Year ended on 31.3... (Current Year)	Year ended on 31.3... (Previous Year)
III. Profit/Loss		
Net profit/Loss (—) for the year		
Profit/Loss (—) brought forward		
Total :		
IV. Appropriations		
Transfer to statutory reserves		
Transfer to other reserves		
Transfer to Government/proposed dividend		
Balance carried over to balance sheet		
Total :		

SCHEDULE 13 — INTEREST EARNED

	Year ended on 31.3.... (Current Year)	Year ended on 31.3.... (Previous Year)
I. Interest/discount on advances/bills		
II. Income on investments		
III. Interest on balances with Reserves Bank of India and other inter-bank funds		
IV. Others		
Total :		

SCHEDULE 14 — OTHER INCOME

	Year ended on 31.3.... (Current Year)	Year ended on 31.3.... (Previous Year)
I. Commission, exchange and brokerage		
II. Profit on sale of investments		
Less : Loss on sale of investments		
III. Profit on revaluation of investments		
Less : Loss on revaluation of investments		
IV. Profit on sale of land, buildings and other assets		
Less : Loss on sale of land, buildings and other assets		
V. Profit on exchange transactions		
Less : Loss on exchange transactions		
VI. Income earned by way of dividends etc. from subsidiaries/companies and/or joint ventures abroad/in India		
VII. Miscellaneous Income		
Total :		

Note : Under items II to V, loss figures may be shown in brackets.

SCHEDULE 15 — INTEREST EXPENDED

	Year ended on 31.3.... (Current Year)	Year ended on 31.3.... (Previous Year)
I. Interest on deposits		
II. Interest on Reserve Bank of India/inter-bank borrowings		
III. Others		
Total :		

SCHEDULE 16 - OPERATING EXPENSES

	Year ended on 31.3... (Current Year)	Year ended on 31.3... (Previous Year)
I. Payments to and provisions for employees		
II. Rent, taxes and lighting		
III. Printing and stationery		
IV. Advertisement and publicity		
V. Depreciation on bank's property		
VI. Directors' fees, allowances and expenses		
VII. Auditors' fees, allowances and expenses (including branch auditors)		
VIII. Law Charges		
IX Postages, Telegrams, Telephones, etc.		
X. Repairs and maintenance		
XI. Insurance		
XII. Other expenditure		
Total :		

It may be noted that formats of Balance Sheet and Profit and Loss Account cover all items likely to appear in the statements. In case a bank does not have any particular item to report, it may be omitted from the formats. Figures should be rounded off to the nearest thousand rupees. Unless otherwise indicated, the banks in these statements will include banking companies, nationalised banks, State Bank of India, associate banks and all other institutions including co-operatives carrying on the business of banking whether or not incorporated or operating in India.

Guidelines of Reserve Bank of India :

The following is a note containing guidelines of the Reserve Bank of India for compilation of financial statements as per the revised formats :-

D. Note containing guidelines of RBI for compilation of Financial Statements
Balance Sheet

Item	Schedule	Coverage		Notes and instructions for compilation
Capital	1	**Nationlised Banks** Capital (Fully Owned by Central Government)		The capital owned by Central Government as on the date of the Balance Sheet including contribution from Government, if any, for participating in World Bank Projects should be shown.
		Banking companies incorporated outside India	(*i*)	The amount brought in by banks by way of start-up capital as prescribed by RBI should be shown under this head.
			(*ii*)	The amount of deposit kept with RBI under sub-section 2 of section 11 of the Banking Regulation Act, 1949 should also be shown.
		Other Banks (Indian) Authorised Capital (....Shares of Rs..... each) Issued Capital (.... Shares of Rs..... each) Subscribed Capital (....Shares of Rs. ....each) Called-up Capital (....Shares of Rs...., each		Authorised, Issued, Subscribed, Called-up Capital should be given separately. Calls-in--arrears will be deducted from Called up Capital while the paid-up value of the forfeited shares should be added thus arriving at the paid-up capital. Where necessary, items which can be combined should be shown under one head, for instance 'Issued and Subscribed Capital'.

		Less : Calls Unpaid *Add* : Forfeited Shares	**Notes - General** The changes in the above items, if any, during the year, say, fresh contribution made by Government, fresh issue of capital, capitalisation of reserves, etc. may be explained in the notes.
Reserves and Surplus	2	**(I) Statutory Reserves**	Reserves created in terms of section 17 or any other section of Banking Regulation Act must be separately disclosed.
		(II) Capital Reserves	The expression 'capital reserves' shall not include any amount regarded as free for contribution through the profit and loss account. Surplus on revaluation should be treated as Capital Reserve. Surplus on translation of the final instalment of foreign branches (which includes fixed assets also) is not a revaluation reserve.
		(III) Securities Premium	Premium on issue of share capital may be shown separately under this head.
		(IV) Revenue and other Reserves	The expression 'Revenue Reserve,' called any reserve other than capital reserve, will include all reserves other than those separately classified. The expression Reserve shall not include any amount retained by way of providing renewals or diminution in value of assets or retained by way of providing fund for known liability.
		(V) Balance of Profit	Includes balance of profit after appropriations. In case of loss the balance may be shown as deduction. **Notes - General** Movement in various categories of Reserves should be shown as indicated in the schedule.
Deposits	3	**A. (I) Demand Deposits**	Includes all bank deposits repayable on demand.
		(*i*) from banks (*ii*) from others	Includes all demand deposits of the non-bank sectors. Credit balances in overdrafts, cash credit accounts, deposits payable at call, overdue deposits, inoperative current accounts, matured time deposits and cash certificates, certificates of deposits, etc. are to be included under this category.
		(II) Savings Bank Deposits	Includes all savings bank deposits (including inoperative savings bank accounts)
		(III) Term Deposits	
		(*i*) from banks	Includes all types of bank deposits repayable after a specified term.
		(*ii*) from others	Includes all types of deposits of the non-bank sectors repayable after a specified term. Fixed deposits, cumulative and recurring deposits, cash certificates, certificates of deposits, annuity deposits, deposits mobilised under various schemes, ordinary staff deposits, foreign currency non-resident deposits accounts, etc. are to be included under this category.

		B. (*i*) Deposits of branches in India (*ii*) Deposits of branches outside India	The total of these two items will agree with the total deposits.
			Notes - General *a*) Interest payable on deposits which is accrued but not due should not be included but shown under other liabilities. *b*) Matured time deposits and cash certificates, etc. should be treated as demand deposits. *c*) Deposits under special schemes should be included under term deposits if they are not payable on demand. When such deposits have matured for payments they should be shown under demand deposits. *d*) Deposits from banks will include deposits from the banking system in India, co-operative banks, foreign banks which may or may not have a presence in India.
Borrowings	4	I) Borrowings in India *i*) Reserve Bank of India	Includes borrowings/refinance obtained from Reserve Bank of India.
		ii) Other banks	Includes borrowings/refinance obtained from commercial banks (including co-operative banks).
		iii) Other institutions and agencies	Includes borrowings/refinance obtained from Industrial Development Bank of India, Export-Import Bank of India, National Bank for Agriculture and Rural Development and other institutions, agencies (including liability against participation certificates, if any).
		II) Borrowings outside India Secured borrowings included above.	Includes borrowing of Indian branches abroad as well as borrowings of foreign branches. This item will be shown separately. Includes secured borrowings/refinance in India and outside India.
			Notes - General (*i*) The total of I & II will agree with the total borrowings shown in the balance sheet. (*ii*) Inter-office transactions should not be shown as borrowings. (*iii*) Funds raised by foreign branches by way of certificates of deposits, notes, bonds, etc. should be classified depending upon documentation, as 'deposits', 'borrowings', etc. (*iv*) Refinance obtained by banks from Reserve Bank of India and various institutions are being brought under the head 'Borrowings'. Hence, advances will be shown at the gross amount on the assets side.
Other liabilities and provisions	5	I. Bills payable	Includes drafts, telegraphic transfers, traveller cheques, mail transfers payable, pay slips, bankers cheques and other miscellaneous items.
		II. Inter-office adjustments (net)	The inter-office adjustments balance, if in credit, should be shown under this head. Only net

			position of inter-office accounts, inland as well as foreign, should be shown here.
		III. Interest accrued	Includes interest accrued but not due on deposits and borrowings.
		IV Others (including Provisions)	Includes the net provision for income tax and other taxes like interest tax (less advance payment, tax deducted at source etc.), surplus in aggregate in provisions for bad debts account, surplus in aggregate in provisions for depreciation in securities, contingency funds which are not disclosed as a reserve but are actually in the nature of reserves, proposed dividend/transfer to Government, other liabilities which are not disclosed under any of the major heads such as unclaimed dividend, provisions and fund kept for specific purposes, unexpired discount, outstanding charges like rent, conveyance etc. Certain types of deposits like staff security deposits, margin deposits, etc. where the repayment is not free, should also be included under this head. **Notes - General** (*i*) For arriving at the net balance of inter-office adjustments all connected inter-office accounts should be aggregated and the net balance only will be shown, representing mostly items in transit and unadjusted items. (*ii*) The interest accruing on all deposits, whether the payment is due or not, should be treated as a liability. (*iii*) It is proposed to show only pure deposits under the head 'deposits' and hence all surplus provisions for bad and doubtful debts, contingency funds, secret reserves, etc. which are not netted off against the relative assets, should be brought under the head 'Others (including provisions)'
Cash and Balances with the Reserve Bank of India	6	I. Cash in hand (including foreign currency notes) II. Balances with Reserve Bank of India (*i*) in Current Account (*ii*) in Other Accounts	Includes cash in hand including foreign currency notes and also foreign branches in case of banks having such branches.
Balances with banks and money at call and short notice	7	**I. In India** (*i*) Balances with banks (*a*) in current accounts (*b*) in other deposit accounts	Includes all balances with banks in India (including co-operative banks). Balances in current accounts and deposit accounts should be shown separately.
		(*ii*) Money at call and short notice (*a*) with banks (*b*) with other institutions	Includes deposits repayable within 15 days or less than 15 days notice lent in the inter-bank call money market.
		II. Outside India (*i*) Current accounts (*ii*) Deposit accounts	Includes balances held by foreign branches and balances held by Indian branches of the banks outside India. Balances held with foreign

			branches by other branches of the bank should not be shown under this head but should be included in inter-branch accounts. The amount held in 'current accounts' and 'deposit accounts' should be shown separately.
		(*iii*) Money at call and short notice	Includes deposits usually classified in foreign countries as money at call and short notice.
Investments	8	**I. Investments in India**	
		i) Government securities	Includes Central and State Government securities and Government treasury bills. These securities should be shown at the book value. However, the difference between the book value and market value should be given in the notes to the balance sheet.
		(*ii*) Other approved securities	Securities other than Government securities, which according to the Banking Regulation Act, 1949 are treated as approved securities, should be included here.
		(*iii*) Shares	Investments in shares of companies and corporations not included in item (*ii*) should be included here.
		(*iv*) Debentures and Bonds	Investments in debentures and bonds of companies and Corporations not included in item (*ii*) should be included here
		(*v*) Investment in subsidiaries/joint ventures	Investments in subsidiaries / joint ventures (including RRBs) should be included here.
		(*vi*) Others	Includes residual investments, if any, like gold. commercial paper and other instruments in the nature of shares/debenture/bonds.
		II. Investments outside India	
		(*i*) Government securities (including local authorities)	All foreign Government securities including securities issued by local authorities may be classified under this head.
		(*ii*) Subsidiaries and/or joint ventures abroad	All investments made in the share capital of subsidiaries floated outside India and/or joint ventures abroad should be classified under this head.
		(*iii*) Others	All other investments outside India may be shown under this head.
Advances	9	A. (*i*) Bills purchased and discounted	In classification under section 'A' all outstanding — in India as well as outside — less provisions made, will be classified under three heads as indicated and both secured and unsecured advances will be included under these heads.
		(*ii*) Cash credits, overdrafts and loans repayable on demand	
		(*iii*) Term loans	Including overdue instalments.
		B. (*i*) Secured by tangible assets	All advances or part of advances which are secured by tangible assets may be shown here. The item will include advances in India and outside India.
		(*ii*) Covered by Bank/ Government Guarantee	Advances in India and outside India to the extent they are covered by guarantees of Indian and foreign governments and Indian and foreign banks and DICGC & ECGC are to be included.

	(*iii*) Unsecured	All advances not classified under (i) and (ii) will be included here. Total of 'A' should tally with the total of 'B'.
	C. I. Advances in India (*i*) Priority sectors (*ii*) Public sector (*iii*) Banks (*iv*) Others **C. II. Advances outside India** (*i*) Due from banks (*ii*) Due from others (*a*) Bills purchased and discounted (*b*) Syndicate loans (*c*) Others	Advances should be broadly classified into 'Advances in India' and 'Advances outside India'. Advances in India will be further classified on the sectoral basis as indicated. Advances to sectors which for the time being are classified as priority sectors according to the instructions of the Reserve Bank are to be classified under the head 'Priority sectors'. Such advances should be excluded from item (*ii*) i.e. advances to public sector. Advances to Central and State governments and other undertakings including Government companies and corporations which are, according to the status, to be treated as public sector companies are to be included in the category "Public Sector". All advances to the banking sector including co-operative bank will come under the head 'Banks'. All the remaining advances will be included under the head 'Others' and typically this category will include non-priority advances to the private, joint and co-operative sectors. **Notes - General** (*i*) The gross amount of advances including refinance and rediscounts but excluding provisions made to the satisfaction of auditors should be shown as advances. (*ii*) Term loans will be loans not repayable on demand. (*iii*) Consortium advances would be shown net of share from other participating banks/institutions.
Fixed Assets	10. I. Premises (*i*) At cost as on 31st March of the preceding year (*ii*) Additions during the year (*iii*) Deductions during the year (*iv*) Depreciation to date	Premises wholly or partly owned by the banking Company for the purpose of business including residential premises should be shown against 'Premises'. In the case of premises and other year fixed assets, the previous balance, additions thereto and deductions therefrom during the year as also the total depreciation written off should be shown. Where sums have been written off on reduction of capital or revaluation of assets. Every balance sheet after the first balance sheet subsequent to the reduction or revaluation should show the revised figures for a period of five years with the date and amount of the revision made.
	II. Other Fixed Assets (including furniture and fixtures) (*i*) At cost on 31st March of the preceding year	Motor vehicles and other fixed assets other than premises but including furniture should be shown under this head.

		(ii) Additions during the year	
		(iii) Depreciation to date	
Other Assets	11	I. Inter-office adjustments (net)	The inter-office adjustments balance, if in debit, should be shown under this head. Only net position of inter-office accounts, inland as well as foreign, should be shown here. For arriving at the net balance of inter-office adjustment accounts, all connected inter-office accounts should be aggregated and the net balance, if in debit, only should be shown representing mostly items in transit and unadjusted items.
		II. Interest accrued	Interest accrued but not due on investments and advances and interest due but not collected on investments will be the main components of this item. As banks normally debit the borrowers' accounts with interest due on the balance sheet date, usually there may not be any amount of interest due on advances. Only such interest as can be realised in the ordinary course should be shown under this head.
		III. Tax paid in advance/ tax deducted at source	The amount of tax deducted at source on securities, advance tax paid etc. to the extent that these items are not set off against relative tax provisions should be shown against this item.
		IV. Stationery and stamps	Only exceptional items of expenditure on stationery like bulk purchase of security paper, loose leaf or other ledgers, etc. which are shown as quasi-asset to be written off over a period of time should be shown here. The value should be on a realistic basis and cost escalation should not be taken into account, as these items are for internal use.
		V. Non-banking assets acquired in satisfaction of claims	Immovable properties/tangible assets acquired in satisfaction of claims are to be shown under this head.
		VI. Others	This will included items like claims which have not been meet, for instance, clearing items, debit items representing addition to assets or reduction in liabilities which have not been adjusted for technical reasons, want of particulars, etc., advances given to staff by a bank as an employer and not as a banker, etc. Items which are in the nature of expenses which are pending adjustments should be provided for and the provision netted against this item so that only realisable value is shown under this head. Accrued income other than interest may also be included here.
Contingent Liabilities	12	I. Claims against the bank not acknowledged as debts.	
		II. Liability for partly	Liabilities on partly paid shares, debentures,

		paid investments	etc. will be included under this head. -
		III. Liability on account of outstanding forward exchange contract	Outstanding forward exchange contracts may be included here.
		IV. Guarantees given on behalf of constituents (*i*) In India (*ii*) Outside India	Guarantees given for constituents in India and outside India may be shown separately.
		V. Acceptances, endorsements and other obligations.	This item will include letters of credit and bills accepted by the bank on behalf of customers.
		VI. Other items for which the Bank is contingently liable	Arrears of cumulative dividends, bills rediscounted under underwriting contracts, estimated amounts of contracts remaining to be executed on capital account and not provided for, etc. are to be included here.
Bills for Collection			Bills and other items in the course of collection and not adjusted will be shown against this item in the summary version only. No separate schedule is proposed.
		Profit and Loss Account	
Interest earned	13	I. Interest/discount on advances/bills	Includes interest and discount on all types of loans and advances like cash credit, demand loans, overdraft, export loans, term loans, domestic and foreign bills purchased and discounted (including those rediscounted), overdue interest and also interest subsidy, if any, relating to such advances/ bills.
		II. Income on investment	Includes all income derived from the investment portfolio by way of interest and dividend.
		III. Interest on balances with Reserve Bank of India and other inter-bank funds	Includes interest on balances with Reserve Bank and other banks, call loans, money market placements, etc.
		IV. Others	Includes any other interest/discount income not included in above heads.
Other Income	14	I. Commission, exchange and brokerage	Includes all remuneration on services such as commission on collections, commission/ exchange on remittances and transfers, commission on letters of credit, letting out of lockers and guarantees, commission on Government business, commission on other permitted agency business including consultancy and other services, brokerage, etc. on securities. If does not include foreign exchange income.
		II. Profit on sale of investments *Less :* Loss on sale of investments etc. III. Profit on revaluation of investments *Less :* Loss on revalu-	Includes profit/loss on sale of securities, furniture, land and building, motor vehicle, gold, silver. Only the net position should be shown. If the net position is a loss, the amount should be shown as a deduction. The net profit/ loss on revaluation of assets may also be shown under this item.

		ation of investments	
		IV. Profit on sale of land, buildings and other assets *Less :* Loss on sale of land, buildings and other assets.	
		V. Profit on exchange transactions *Less :* Loss *Less :* Loss on exchange transactions	Includes profit/loss on dealing in foreign exchange, all income earned by way of foreign exchange, commission and charges on foreign exchange transactions excluding interest which will be shown under interest. Only the net position should be shown. If the net position is a loss, it is to be shown as a deduction.
		VI. Income earned by way of dividends etc from subsidiaries, companies joint ventures abroad/in India	
		VII. Miscellaneous income	Includes recoveries from constituents for the godown rents, income from bank's properties, security charges, insurance etc. and any other miscellaneous income. In case any item under this head exceeds one percentage of the total income, particulars may be given in the notes.
Interest	15	I. Interest on deposits	Includes interest paid on all types of deposits including deposits from banks and other institutions.
		II. Interest on Reserve Bank of India/inter-bank borrowings	Includes discount/interest on all borrowings and refinance from Reserve Bank of India and other banks.
		III. Others	Includes discount/interest on all borrowings/ refinance from financial institutions. All other payments like interest on participation certificates, penal interest paid, etc. may also be included here.
Operating expenses	16	I. Payments to and Provisions for employees	Includes staff salaries/wages, allowances, bonus, other staff benefits like providend fund, pension, gratuity, liveries to staff, leave fare concessions, staff welfare, medical allowance to staff etc.
		II. Rent, taxes and lighting	Includes rent paid by the banks on building and other municipal and other taxes paid (excluding income tax and interest tax), electricity and other similar charges and levies. House rent allowance and other similar payments to staff should appear under the head 'Payments to and provisions for employees'.
		III. Printing and Stationery	Includes books and forms and stationery used by the bank and other printing charges which are not incurred by way of publicity expenditure.
		IV. Advertisement and publicity	Includes expenditure incurred by the bank for advertisement and publicity purposes including printing charges of publicity matter.
		V. Depreciation on Bank's property	Includes depreciation on bank's own property, motor cars and other vehicles, furniture, electric fittings, vaults, lifts, leasehold properties non-banking assets, etc.

VI. Directiors' fees, allowances and expenses	Includes sitting fees and all other items of expenditure incurred on behalf of directors. The daily allowances, hotel charges, conveyance charges, etc. which though in the nature of reimbursement of expenses incurred may be included under this head. Similar expenses of local Committee members may also be included under this head.
VII. Auditors' fees and expenses (including branch auditors' fees and expenses)	Includes fees paid to the statutory auditors and branch auditors for professional services rendered and all expenses for performing their duties, even though they may be in the nature of reimbursement of expenses. If external auditors have been appointed by banks themselves for internal inspections and audits and other services, the expenses incurred in that context including fees may not be included under this head but shown under 'other expenditure'.
VIII. Law charges	All legal expenses and reimbursement of expenses incurred in connection with legal services are to be included here.
IX. Postage, telegrams telephones, etc.	Includes all postal charges like stamps, telegram, telephones, teleprinter, etc.
X. Repairs and maintenance	Included repairs to banks' property, their maintenance charges etc.
XI. Insurance	Includes insurance charges on banks's property, insurance premia paid to Deposit Insurance and Credit Guarantee Corporation, etc. to the extent they are not recovered from the concerned parties.
XII. Other expenditure	All expenses other than those not included in any of the other head like, license fees, donations, subscriptions to papers, periodicals, entertainment expenses, travel expenses, etc. may be included under this head. In case any particular item under this head exceeds one percentage of the total income, particulars may be given in the notes.
Provisions and contingencies	Includes all provisions made for bad and doubtful debts, provisions for taxation, provisions for diminution in the value of investments, transfers to contingencies and other similar items.

Notes on Accounts and Discolure of Accounting Policies :

As per a Circular dated 28.2.91 of the Reserve Bank of India, the banks are to disclose the accounting policies regarding key areas of operation along with notes on accounts in their financial statements. The Reserve Bank of India also issued a specimen form in which a bank may disclose the accounting policies; the bank make the necessary modification to the specimen to suit its individual needs. A bank may give Notes on Accounts as Schedule-17 and state Principal Accounting Policies followed by it as Schedule-18 attatched to its financial statements.

Notes on Accounts vary from case to case. The following is an example with imaginary facts and figures :-

Schedule 17 — Notes on Accounts for 2009-2010

1. Figures of the previous year have been re-grouped, wherever necessary.
2. Under inter-branch reconciliation, initial matching of entries upto 31.03.2010 has been done. Through various effective steps taken by the Bank including decentralisation of reconciliation work to locate, reconcile and adjust the same, the Bank has achieved substantial reduction in the clearance of outstanding entries. However, there are certain old and current items pending to be cleared under inter-branch transactions.
3. In respect of unaudited branches, wherever information in regard to classification of advances was inadequate, the same has been reclassified to the extent possible on the basis of information available at the Head Office.
4. The excess of book value over market value of investments in Indian Government securities as on 31.03.10 amounts to Rs. 1,205 lakhs.
5. Premises include properties, book value of which is Rs. 87 lakhs, for which registration formalities are in progress.

As regards Accounting Policies, the following is the specimen form circulated by the Reserve Bank of India indicating broadly the areas where the accounting policies followed by the bank should be disclosed :-

SPECIMEN FORM OF ACCOUNTING POLICIES

Schedule 18— Principal Accounting Policies

(1) General

The accompanying financial statements have been prepared on the historical cost basis and conform to the statutory provisions and practices prevailing in the country.

(2) Transactions involving foreign exchange

(*a*) Monetary assets and liabilities have been translated at the exchange rate prevailing at the close of the year. Non-monetary assets have been carried in the books at the historical cost.

(*b*) Income and expenditure items in respect of the Indian branches have been translated at the exchange rates ruling on the date of the transaction and in respect of overseas branches at the exchange rates prevailing at the close of the year.

(*c*) Profit or loss on pending forward contracts has been accounted for.

(3) Investments

(*a*) Investments in Government and other approved securities in India are valued at the lower of cost or market value.

(*b*) Investment in subsidiary companies and in some companies (*i.e.* companies in which at least 25% of the share capital) have been accounted for on the historical cost basis.

(*c*) All other investments are valued at the lower of cost or market value.

(4) Advances

(*a*) Provisions for doubtful advances have been made to the satisfaction of the auditors :-

(*i*) in respect of the identified advances, based on a periodical review of advances and after taking into account the portion of advance guaranteed by the Deposit Insurance and Credit Guarantee Corporation and similar statutory bodies.

(*ii*) in respect of general advances as a percentage of total advances taking into account guidelines issued by the Government of India and the Reserve Bank of India.

(*b*) Provisions in respect of doubtful advances have been deducted from advances to the extent necessary and the excess has been includes under "Other liabilities and provisions".

(*c*) Provisions have been made on a gross basis. Tax relief which will be available when the advance is written off will be accounted for in the year of write off.

(5) Fixed Assets

(*a*) Premises and other fixed assets have been accounted for at their historical cost. Premises which have been revalued are accounted for at the values determined on the basis of such revaluation made by professional valuers. Profit arising on revalutions has been credited to Capital Reserve.

(*b*) Depreciation has been provided for on the straight line/diminishing balance method.

(*c*) In respect of revalued assets, depreciation is provided for on the revalued figure and an amount equal to the additional depreciation consequent on revaluation is transferred annually from the Capital Reserve to the General Reserve/Profit and Loss Account.

(6) Staff Benefits

Provisions for gratuity/pension benefits to staff has been made on an accrual/cash basis. Separate funds for gratuity/pension have been created.

(7) Net Profit

(*a*) the net profit disclosed in the profit and loss account is after :
  (*i*) provisions for taxes on income in accordance with statutory requirements,
  (*ii*) provision for doubtful advances,
  (*iii*) adjustments to the value of "current investments'' in Government and other approved securities in India valued at lower of cost or market value,
  (*iv*) transfers to contingency funds,
  (*v*) other usual or necessary provisions.

(*b*) Contingency funds have been grouped in the Balance Sheet under the head "Other Liabilities and Provisions".

Capital Adequacy Norms :

In July, 1988 the Committee on Banking Regulations and Supervisory Practices (known as Basle Committee) adopted minimum capital adequacy standards based on risk assets ratio system for both balance sheet as well as off-balance sheet business. The objectives of the Committee were (*i*) to stop reckless lending by banks thereby strengthening the soundness and stability of the banking system and (*ii*) to put banks from different countries on a more even competitive footing. The Narasimham Committee on Financial System also recommended to adopt the system in a phased manner. Accordingly, the Reserve Bank of India introduced a risk asset ratio system. The BIS standard, as this system is called, seeks to measure capital adequancy as the ratio of capital funds to risk weighted assets.

The Basle Committee talks of Tier-I capital and Tier-II capital. Tier-I capital, also known as core capital, provides the permanent and readily available cover to the bank against unexpected losses. Tier-II capital contains elements that are less permanent in nature and less readily available. The Reserve Bank of India has established norms to identify Tier-I capital and Tier-II capital for Indian banks and foreign banks.

In case of Indian banks, Tier-I capital means, (*i*) paid up capital, (*ii*) statutory reserves and (*iii*) other free reserves, if any. Capital reserves representing surplus arising out of sale proceeds of assets will also be reckoned for this purpose. Equity investments in subsidiaries, intangible assets and losses in the current period and those brought forward from previous periods will be deducted from Tier-I capital.

Tier-II capital consists of (*i*) undisclosed reserves and cumulative perpetual preference assets, (*ii*) revaluation reserves, (*iii*) general provisions and loss reserves, (*iv*) hybrid debt capital instruments and (*v*) subordinated debts, (*vi*) from 1996-97, excess depreciation on investments written back.

Undisclosed reserves and cumulative perpetual preference shares : Undisclosed reserves, to be included here, must represent accumulations of post-tax profits, must not be encumbered by any known liability and should not be routinely used for absorbing normal or operating losses. Cumulative perpetual preference shares should be fully paid-up and should not contain any clause which permits redemption by the holder.

Revaluation reserves : Revaluation reserves arise from revaluation of assets that are under-valued in bank's books. The extent to which the revaluation reserves can be relied upon as a cushion for unexpected losses depends mainly upon the level of certainty that can be placed on estimates of the market values of the relevant assets. In future there may be a fall in values under difficult market conditions or in case of a forced sale. Therefore, it is prudent to consider revaluation reserves at a discount of 55% effective from 1st April, 1994 while determining their values for inclusion in Tier-II capital. Such reserves will have to be reflected on the face of the balance sheet as revaluation reserve.

General provisions and loss reserves : To be included in Tier-II capital, general provisions and loss reserves must not be attributable to the actual diminution in value or identifiable potential loss in any specific asset. Care must also be taken to see that sufficient provisions have been made to meet all known losses and foreseeable potential losses before considering general provisions and loss reserves as part of Tier-II capital. Moreover, general provisions and loss reserves may be taken only up to a maximum of 1.25% of weighted risk assets.

Hybrid Debt Capital instruments : In this category fall a number of capital instruments which combine certain characteristics of equity and certain characteristics of debt. Where these instruments have close similarity to equity, in particular when they are able to support losses on an ongoing basis without triggering liquidation, they may be included in Tier-II capital.

Subordinated Debt : To be eligible for inclusion in the Tier-II capital, the instruments should be fully paid up, unsecured, subordinated to the claims of other creditors, free of restrictive clauses and should not be redeemable at the initiative of the holders or without the consent of the banks' supervisory authorities. They often carry a fixed maturity and as they approach maturity, they should be subjected to progressive discount. For inclusion in Tier-II capital, instruments with an initial maturity of less than five years or with a remaining maturity of one year should not be included as part of Tier-II capital. Sub-ordinated debt instruments will be limited to 50% of Tier-I capital.

From 1996-97, excess provision for depreciation on Investment written back is also eligible for inclusion in Tier II capital.

The total of Tier II capital cannot exceed 100 per cent of Teir I capital. Banks also need to maintain Tier I capital at five per cent of the open forex position limit approved by the Reserve Bank of India as capital requirement for market risks.

For the foreign banks, elements of Tier-I capital are (*i*) interest-free funds from head office kept in a separate account in Indian books specifically for the purpose of meeting the capital adequacy norms, (*ii*) statutory reserves kept in Indian books, (*iii*) remittable surplus written in Indian books which is not repatriable so long as the bank functions in India, (*iv*) capital reserve representing surplus arising out of sale of assets in India held in a separate account and which is not eligible for repatriation so long as the bank functions in India, (*v*) interest free funds remitted from abroad for the purpose of acquisition of property and held in a separate account in Indian books. The net credit balance, if any, in the inter-office account with Head office/overseas branches will not be recommended as capital funds. However, any debit balance in head office account will have to be set off against the capital.

Elements of Tier-II capital are (*i*) undisclosed reserves and cumulative perpetual preference shares, (*ii*) revaluation reserves (*iii*) general provisions and loss reserves (*iv*) Hybrid debt instruments and (*v*) subordinated debt.

Calculation of Risk Adjusted Assets : Risk adjusted assets mean weighted aggregate of funded and non-funded items as detailed below. Weights have been assigned to assets shown in the balance sheet and credit conversion factors have been assigned to off-balance sheet items. (Off-balance sheet items mean items which are not shown in the balance sheet).

The value of each asset or item is multiplied by relevant weight or credit conversion factor to produce adjusted values of assets and off-balance sheet items. The aggregate is taken into account for calculating Risk Weighted Assets Ratio. The weights assigned to different assets and credit conversion factors assigned to off-balance sheet items are given below :

1. Domestic Operations

A. Funded risk assets	*Percentage weights*
(*i*) Cash, balance with Reserve Bank of India, balance with other banks, money at call and short notice and investment in Government and other trustee securities	0
(*ii*) Claims on commercial banks such as certificates of deposits etc.	0
(*iii*) Other investments	100
(*iv*) Loans and advances including bills purchased and discounted and other credit facilities	0
(*a*) Loans guaranteed by Govt. of India	0
(*b*) Loans guaranteed by State Governments	0
(*c*) Loans granted to public sector undertakings of Government of India.	100
(*d*) Loans granted to public sector undertakings of State Governments	100
(*e*) Others	100
(*v*) Premises, furniture and fixtures	100
(*vi*) Other assets	100

Note : 1. Netting may be done only for advances collateralised by cash margins or deposits and in respect of assets where provisions for depreciation or for bad and doubtful debts have been made.

2. Equity investments in subsidiaries, intangible assets and losses deducted from Tier-I capital should be assigned zero weight.

B. Off-Balance Sheet Items *Instruments*	*Credit conversion factors (per cent)*
(*i*) Direct credit substitutes, *e.g.* general guarantees of indebtedness (including stand-by letters of credit serving as financial guarantee for loans and securities) and acceptances (including endorsements with the character of acceptances)	100
(*ii*) Certain transaction-related contingent items (*e.g.*, performance bonds, bid bonds, warranties and stand-by letters of credit related to particular transactions)	50
(*iii*) Short-term self-liquidating trade-related contigencies (such as documentary credits collateralised by the underlying shipments)	20
(*iv*) Sale and repurchase agreement and asset sales with recourse, where the credit risk remains with the bank	100
(*v*) Forward assets purchases, forward deposits and partly paid shares and securities, which represent commitments with certain drawdown	100
(*vi*) Note issuance facilities and revolving under-writing facilities	50
(*vii*) Other commitments (*e.g.*, formal stand-by facilities and credit lines) with an original maturity of over one year	50

(*viii*) Similar commitments with an original maturity upto one year, or which can be unconditionally cancelled at any time	0
(*ix*) Aggregate outstanding foreign exchange contracts of original maturity	
— less than one year	2
— for each additional year or part thereof	3

Note : 1. Cash margins/deposit shall be deducted before applying the conversion factor.

2. After applying the conversion factors as indicated above, the adjusted off-balance Sheet value shall again be multiplied by the weight attributable to the relevant counterpart as specified in I-A above.

II. Overseas operations (applicable only to Indian banks having branches abroad)

A. Funded risk assets	*Percentage weights*
(*i*) Cash	0
(*ii*) Balances with Monetery Authority	0
(*iii*) Investments in Government securities	0
(*iv*) Balances in current accounts with other banks	20
(*v*) All other claims on banks including but not limited to fund loaned in money markets, deposit placements, investments in CDs/FRNs, etc.,	20
(vi) Investments in non-bank sectors	100
(vii) Loans and advances, bills purchased and discounted and other credit facilities :—	
(*a*) Claims guaranteed by Government of India	0
(*b*) Claims guaranteed by State Governments	0
(*c*) Claims on public sector undertakings of Government of India	100
(*d*) Claims on public sector undertakings of State Governments	100
(*e*) Others	100
(*viii*) All other banking and infrastructural assets	100

Note : Netting may be done only for advances collateralised by cash margins or deposits and in respect of assets where provisions for depreciation or for bad and doubtful debts have been made.

B. Non-funded risk assets	*Credit coversion factors (per cent)*
Instruments	
(*i*) Direct credit substitutes, e.g. general guarantees of indebtedness (including stand-by letters of credit serving as financial guarantees for loans and securities) and acceptances (including endorsements with the character of acceptances)	100
(*ii*) Certain transaction-related contingent items (e.g., performance bonds, bid bonds, warranties and standby letters of credit related to particular transactions)	50
(*iii*) Short-term self-liquidating trade related contingencies (such as documentary credits collateralised by the underlying shipments)	20
(*iv*) Sale and repurchase agreement and assets sales with recourse, where the credit risk remains with the bank	100

(*v*)	Forward assets purchases, forward deposits and partly paid shares and securities, which represent commitments with certain draw-down	100
(*vi*)	Note issuance facilities and revolving underwriting facilities	50
(*vii*)	Other commitments (e.g., formal standby facilities and credit lines) with an original maturity of over one year	50
(*viii*)	Similar commitments with an original maturity upto one year, or which can be unconditionally cancelled at any time	0

Note : 1. Cash margins/deposit shall be deducted before applying the conversion factor.

2. After applying the conversion factor as indicated above, the adjusted off-Balance Sheet value shall again be multiplied by the weight attributable to the relevant counterpart as specified in II-A above.

Risk weighted assets ratio is calculated by applying the following formula :

$$\text{Risk Weighted Assets Ratio} = \frac{\text{Capital Funds}}{\text{Risk Adjusted Assets}} \times 100$$

Banks having branches abroad were required to achieve weighted assets ratio of 8% by 31st March, 1994. Later, the time limit was extended to 31st March, 1996. Other banks were required to achieve capital adequacy norm of 4% by 31st March, 1993 and of 8% by 31st March, 1996. Foreign banks were required to achieve capital adequacy norm of 8% by 31st March, 1993.

Illustration 3:

On 31st March, 2010 Mahalakshmi Commercial Bank has the following capital funds and assets :—

	(Rs. in '000)
Capital Funds :	
Equity Share capital	50,00
Statutory Reserve	61,40
Revaluation Reserve	92
Capital Reserve (arising on sale of fixed assets)	7,91
Assets :	
Cash	1,18,90
Balance with Reserve Bank of India	3,26,78
Balances with other Banks	1,09,35
Money at Call and Short Notice	74,18
Investment in Government Securities	9,10,96
Certificates of Deposits with Commercial Banks	10,75
Other Investments	7,15,18
Loans and Advances :	
(*a*) Loans guaranteed by Government of India	1,52,76
(*b*) Loans granted to public sector undertakings of Government of India	1,78,84
(*c*) Loans granted to public sector undertakings of State Governments	92,86
Premises	1,80,00
Furniture and Fixtures	39,35
Other Assets	52,76
Off-balance Sheet Item :	
Acceptances, Endorsements and Letters of Credit	1,95,51

Calculate Risk Weighted Assets Ratio, giving working notes in detail.

Solution :

$$\text{Risk Weighted Assets Ratio} = \frac{\text{Capital Funds}}{\text{Risk Adjusted Assets}} \times 100$$

$$= \frac{1{,}19{,}72.4}{14{,}54{,}50} \times 100 = 8.23\%$$

Working Notes :

	(*Rs. in '000*)	(*Rs. in '000*)
(*i*) Capital Funds Tier-I :		
Equity Share Capital		50,00
Statutory Reserve		61,40
Capital Reserve on sale of fixed assets		7,91
Capital Funds Tier-II :		
Revaluation Reserve	92	
Less : Discount @ 55%.	50.6	41.4
Total Capital Funds		1,19,72.4

(*ii*) Risk Adjusted Assets :

Funded Risk Assets	*Amount* (*Rs. in '000*)	*Percentage* Weight	*Weighted* Amount (*Rs. in '000*)
Cash	1,18,90	0	—
Balance with RBI	3,26,78	0	—
Balances with other Banks	1,09,35	0	—
Money at call and short notice	74,18	0	—
Investment in Government Securities	9,10,96	0	—
Certificates of Deposits with Commercial Banks	10,75	0	—
Other Investments	7,15,18	100	7,15,18
Loans and Advances :			
(*a*) Guaranteed by Govt. of India	1,52,76	0	—
(*b*) Granted to public sector undertakings of Govt. of India	1,78,84	100	1,78,84
(*c*) Granted to public sector undertakings of State Govts.	92,86	100	92,86
Premises	1,80,00	100	1,80,00
Furniture and Fixtures	39,35	100	39,35
Other Assets	52,76	100	52,76
Off-Balance Sheet Item :		Credit Conversion Factors	
Acceptances, Endorsements and Letters of Credit	1,95,51	100	1,95,51
Total Risk Adjusted Assets			14,54,50

Income From Non-performing Assets :

While closing its books for an accounting year, a bank takes credit for interest accrued on term loans, cash credits, overdrafts, bills purchased and discounted etc. But it must not take such a credit for interest accrued on Non-performing Assets (NPA). The guiding principle, in line with International Accounting Standards, is that the income on NPA should not be recognised on accrual basis and should be treated as income only when actually received. An asset becomes non-performing when it ceases to generate income for bank. The Reserve Bank of India has prescribed the following basis for treating a credit facility as non-performing :-

Term Loans : A term loan facility will be treated as NPA for the year ending 31st March, 1998 and onwards if interest or instalment of principal remains past due for a period of more than 90 days.

Cash Credit and Overdrafts : A cash credit and overdraft account will be treated as NPA if the account remains out of order for a period more than 90 days.

An account is treated as 'out of order' any of the following conditions is fulfilled:–

(a) The outstanding balance remains continuously in excess of the sanctions limit/ during power.

(b) Though the outstanding balance is less than the sanctioned limit / drawing power

(i) there are no credits continuously for more than 90 days as on the date of balance sheet; or

(ii) credits during the aforesaid period are not enough to cover the interest debited during the same period more than 90 days.

(c) Further any amount due to the bank under any credit facility it overdue if it is not paid on the due date fixed by the bank.

Agricultural Advances : With effect from September 30, 2004, Advances granted for agriculture purposes become NPA if interest and / or instalment of principal remains overdue for two crop seasons in case of short duration crops and a loan granted for long duration crops will be treated as NPA, if the instalment of principal or interest thereon remains overdue for one crop season.

Crops having crop season of more than one year i.e. upto the period of harvesting the crops raised will be termed as 'long duration' crops and other crops will be treated as 'short duration' crops.

The above NPA nouns would also be applicable to agricultural term loans.

In respect of other agricultural loans and term loans given to non-agriculturists, identification of NPAs would be done on the basis as per non agricultural advances which is, at present, 90 days delinquency norm.

Exempted Assets : Certain categories of advances have been exempted from being treated as non-performing for the purpose of income determination and / or provisioning, even though they meet the aforesaid criteria. Briefly, they are as follows:–

(*i*) Advances secured against term deposits, National Savings Certificates, Vikas Patras, Kisan Vikas Patras and surrender value of life insurance policies.

(*ii*) Advances guaranteed by Government of India and / or State Governments. But this exemption in only for the purpose of assets classification and provisioning norms and not for the purposes of recognition of income. It means income in respect of the facility will not be recognised until it is actually received.

Also, in the case of state government guarantees, this exemption is available only where the guarantees have not been invoked. The State Government guaranteed accounts which have been invoked upon becoming NPA are to be treated at par with other advances for purpose of asset classification, income recognition and provisioning norms.

Advances Under Rehabilitation Packages : Where additional facilities are granted to a unit under rehabilitation packages approved by the Board for Industrial and Financial Reconstruction (BIFR) or by term-lending institutions or the bank (on its own or under consortium arrangement), provision should continue to be made for the dues in respect of existing credit facilities. As regards the additional facilities, provision need not be made for a period of one year from the date of disbursement in respect of additional facilities sanctioned under rehabilitation packages approved by BIFR/ term - lending institution. Similarly, no provision need be made for a period of one year in respect of additional facilities granted to a sick small-scale industrial unit in accordance with a rehabilitation package / nursing programme drawn up by the bank itself or under a consortium arrangement. After the period of one year, the bank in consultation with its auditors would take a view whether there is need for making provision in respect of the additional facilities sanctioned.

Take-out Finance: In the case of take-out finance, if based on record of recovery, the account is classified by their lending bank as NPA, it should make provision for loan losses as per guidelines. The provision should be reversed when the account is taken over by the taking-over institution. On taking over the account, the taking-over institution should make provisions as per the guidelines.

Advances covered by the guarantees of DICGC / ECGC : In the case of advances guaranteed by Expert Credit Guarantee Corporation (ECGC) or by Deposit Insurance and Credit Guarantee Corporation (DICGC), provision is required to be made only for the balance in excess of the amount guaranteed by these corporations. In case the bank also holds a security in respect of an advance guaranteed by ECGC/DICGC, the realisable value of the security should be deducted from the outstanding balance before the ECGC/DICGC guarantee is off-set.

Classification of Bank Advances.

The banks have to classify their advances into the following four broad groups:–

(*i*) **Standard Assets.** Standard assets are those which do not disclose any problems and which do not carry more than normal risk attached to the business. Such assets are not NPA.

(*ii*) **Sub-standard Assets.** Sub-standard assets are those which have been classified as NPA for a period not exceeding 12 months. In such cases, the current net worth of the borrower / guarantor or the current market value of the security charged is not enough to ensure recovery of the dues to the bank in full. Such assets will have well-defined credit weaknesses that jeopardise the liquidation of the debts and are characterised by the distinct possibility that the bank will sustain some loss, if deficiencies are not corrected.

In the case of the term loans, those where instalments of principal are overdue for period exceeding one year should be treated as sub-standard. An asset where the terms of the loan agreement regarding interest and principal have been renegotiated or rescheduled after commencement of production, should be classified as sub-standard and should remain in such category for at least two years of satisfactory performance under the renegotiated or rescheduled terms.

(*iii*) **Doubtful Debts :** Doubtful debts are those which have remained NPA for a period exceeding 18 months. In the case of term loans, those where instalments of principal have remained overdue for a period exceeding 18 months should be treated as doubtful. As in the case of sub-standard assets, rescheduling does not entitle a bank to upgard the quality of an advance automatically. Collection or liquidation of doubtful debts on the basis of currently known facts is highly questionable and improbable.

(*iv*) **Loss Assets :** Loss assets are those where loss has been identified by the bank or internal or external auditors or the RBI inspection but the amounts have not been written off wholly a partly. Such assets are considered uncollectable and of such little values that their continuance as bank assets in not warranted although there may be some salvage or recovery values.

The above classification is only meant for the purpose of computing amount of provision to be made in respect of advances. As far as the balance sheet presentation is concerned, it is governed by the Third Schedule to Banking Regulation Act, 1949 which requires classification of advances altogether differently.

Provision for Loss : A bank is required to make a provision for loss in respect of different classes of its advances as follows:

(*i*) **Standard Assets :** A general provision of a minimum of 0.4 % of total standard assets should be made.

(*ii*) **Sub-standard Assets:** A general provision of 10% of total outstanding should be made without making any allowance for DICGC/ECGC cover and securities available.

(*iii*) **Doubtful Assets:** (i) Full provision to the extent of the unsecured portion should be made. In doing so, the realisable value of the security available to the bank should be determined on a realistic basis.

DICGC/ECGC cover is also taken into account. In case the advance covered by CGTSI guarantee becomes non-performing, no-provision need be made towards the guaranteed portion but the amount outstanding in excess of the guaranteed portion should be provided for as per the guidelines on provisioning for non-preforming advances.

Additionally, 20%-100% of the secured portion should be provided for, depending upon the period for which the advance has been considered as a doubtful asset, as detailed below:–

Period for which the advance has been considered doubtful	*% of provision required on secured portion*
Upto 1 year	20%
More than 1 year and upto 3 years	30%
More than three years	

(*i*)	Outstanding stock of NPA's as on 31.03.2004	60% w.e.f. 31.03.2005 75% w.e.f. 31.03.2006 100% w.e.f. 31.03.2007
(*ii*)	Advances classified as doubtful for more than 3 years on or after 01.04.2004	100% w.e.f. 31.03.2005

(*iv*) **Loss Assets:** The entire amount should be written off or full provision should be made for the amount outstanding.

Illustration 4. On the following term loan and export loan, the bank has not received interest for more than 3 years.

	Tems Loan	**Export Loan**
Balance Outstanding on 31.03.2009	Rs. 30 lakh	Rs. 40 lakh
DICGC/ ECGC cover	30%	50%
Securities held	Rs. 14 lakh	Rs. 18 lakh
Realiasable value of securities	Rs. 12 lakh	Rs. 16 lakh

Compute the amount of provison to be made for the year ended 31st March, 2009.

Solution :

	Term Loan (Rs. in lakhs)	**Export Loan** (Rs. in lakhs)
Balance outstanding	30.0	40.0
Less : Realisable value of securities	12.0	16.0
	18.0	24.0
Less : DICGC cover @30%	5.4	
ECGC cover @ 50%		12.0
	13.6	12.0
Required provision:		
100% of unsecured portion	13.6	12.0
Add : 100% of secured portion	12.0	16.0
	25.6	28.0

The above mentioned norms and requirements of provision are subject to changes. Student is, therefore, advised to keep himself in touch with the latest developments in this regard.

Illustration 5:

While closing its books of account, a commercial bank has its Advances classified as follows:

	Rs. in lakhs
Standard Assets	16,000
Sub-standard Assets	1,300
Doubtful Assets : upto one year	700
: one to three years	400
: more than three years	200
Loss Assets	500

You are required to calculate the amount of provision to be made by the bank.

Solution :

	Amount Rs. in lakhs	*Percentage reqd. as provision*	*Amount of Provision Rs. in lakhs*
Standard Assets	16,000	0.40	64
Sub-standard Assets	1,300	10	130
Doubtful Assets :			
— upto one year	700	20	140
— one to three years	400	30	120
— more than three years	200	100	200
Loss Assets	500	100	500
			1,154

Now, study the following illustrations on final accounts:—

Illustration 6:

From the following information relating to Adarsh Bank Limited, prepare Profit and Loss Account for the year ended 31st March, 2010 along with the necessary Schedules :-

For the year ended 31.3.09 (Rs. in '000)	*Items*	*For the year ended 31.3.10 (Rs. in '000)*
272,67	Interest/discount on advances/bills	316,28
105,30	Income on investments	118,10
40,64	Interest on balances with Reserve Bank of India	42,43
2814	Commission, exchange and brokerage	29,07
1,23	Profit on sale of investments	1,14
278,39	Interest on deposits	314,04
30,64	Interest on Reserve Bank of India borrowings	33,62
83,97	Payments to and provisions for employees	97,17
8,90	Rent, taxes and lighting	9,55
1,90	Printing and stationery	2,13
34	Advertisement and publicity	87
2,15	Depreciation on Bank's property	2,92
6	Directors' fees, allowances and expenses	7
34	Auditors' fees and expenses	41
17	Law charges	22
2,61	Postages, Telegrams, Telephones, etc.	3,12
72	Repairs and maintenance	91
8,03	Insurance	9,15
9,76	Other expenditure	8,84
10,06	Balance of Profit and Loss Account b/fd	?

The following adjustments are to be made :-

I. Make a Provision for Income Tax (including surcharge) @35%. The rate of taxation for the year ended 31st March, 2009 was also 35. Also make a provision for dividend distribution tax @15%

II. Every year, the bank transfers 20% of profit to Statutory Reserves, and 10% of profit to Revenue Reserve.

III. The Board of Directors propose dividend amounting to Rs. 2,00 thousand for the year ended 31st March, 2010. Last year also, an identical amount of dividend was proposed.

Solution :

Adarsh Bank Limited
Profit and Loss Account for the Year ended 31st March, 2010

	Schedule	*As on 31.3.2010 (Rs. in '000)*	*As on 31.3.2009 (Rs. in '000)*
I. Income			
Interest earned	13	476,81	418,61
Other income	14	30,21	29,37
Total		507,02	447,98
II. Expenditure			
Interest expended	15	347,66	309,03
Operating expenses	16	135,36	118,95
Provisions and contingencies		8,40	7,00
Total		491,42	434,98

	31.3.10	31.3.09
III. Profit		
Net profit for the year	15,60	13,00
Profit brought forward	16,86	10,06
Total	32,46	23,06
IV. Appropriations		
Transfer to Statutory Reserves	3,12	2,60
Transfer to Other Reserves	1,56	1,30
Proposed dividend	2,00	2,00
Provision for divided distribution tax @12%	30	30
Balance carried over to Balance Sheet	25,48	16,86
	32,46	23,06

Schedule 13 —Interest Earned

	Year Ended 31.3.10 *(Rs. in '000)*	*Year Ended* 31.3.09 *(Rs. in '000)*
I. Interest - Discount on advances/bills	316,28	272,67
II. Income on investments	118,10	105,30
III. Interest on balances with Reserve Bank of India	42,43	40,64
Total	476,81	418,61

Schedule 14 —Other Income

I. Commission, exchange and brokerage	29,07	28,14
II. Profit on sale of investments	1,14	1,23
Total	30,21	29,37

Schedule 15— Interest Expended

	Year Ended 31.3.10 *(Rs. in '000)*	*Year Ended* 31.3.09 *(Rs. in '000)*
I. Interest on deposits	314,04	278,39
II. Interest on Reserve Bank of India borrowings	33,62	30,64
Total	347,66	309,03

Schedule 16 — Operating Expenses

I. Payments to and provisions for employees	97,17	83,97
II. Rent, taxes and lighting	9,55	8,90
III. Printing and stationery	2,13	1,90
IV. Advertisement and publicity	87	34
V. Depreciation on Bank's property	2,92	2,15
VI. Directors' fees, allowances and expenses	7	6
VII. Auditors' fees and expenses	41	34
VIII. Law charges	22	17
IX. Postages, Telegrams, Telephones, etc.	3,12	2,61
X. Repairs and maintenance	91	72
XI. Insurance	9,15	8,03
XII. Other expenditure	8,84	9,76
Total	135,36	118,95

Working Notes :

(*i*) Interest earned	476,81	418,61
Add : Other income	30,21	29,37
	507,02	447,98

Less : Interest expended	347,66		309,03	
Operating expenses	135,36	483,02	118,95	427,98
Profit before Tax		24,00		20,00
Income Tax @ 35%		8,40		7,00
Net profit for the year		15.60		13,00
(*ii*) Transfer to Statutory Reserves @ 20%		3,12		2,60
(*iii*) Transfer to Revenue Reserves @ 10%		1,56		1,30

Illustration 7:

The following figures have been obtained from the books of the Rana Bank Ltd. for the year ending 31st March, 2010 :

	Rs. in '000
Interest and discount earned	3,800
Commission and exchange	195
Interest paid	2,000
Salaries and wages	210
Directors' fees	35
Rent and taxes	70
Postage and telegrams	61
Profit on sale of investments	240
Loss on sale of investments	38
Rent received	62
Depreciation	31
Stationery	60
Auditors' fees	8

Additional information :

(*i*) The profit and loss account had a balance of Rs. 10,00,000 on 1st April, 2009.

(*ii*) An advance of Rs. 5,68,000 has become doubtful and it is expected that only 50% of the amount due can be recovered from the security.

(*iii*) The provision for tax be made at 35%.

(*iv*) A dividend @ 10% is proposed. Also provide for dividend tax @15% of the amount proposed to be distributed.

Prepare profit and loss account of the Rana Bank Ltd. for the year ending 31st March, 2003.

Solution :

Schedule 13 — Interest Earned

(*all figures in Rs. '000*)

	Year ending 31.3.2010 Rs.	*Year ending 31.3.2009 Rs.*
Interest and discount earned	3,800	—
Total	3,800	—

Schedule 14 — Other Income

	Rs.	*Year ending 31.3.2010 Rs.*	*Year ending 31.3.2009 Rs.*
Commission and exchange		195	—
Profit on sale of investments	240		
Less : Loss on sale of investents	38		
		2,02	—
Rent		62	—
Total		459	—

Schedule 15 — Interest Expended

	Year ending 31.3.2010 Rs.	Year ending 31.3.2010 Rs.
Interest	2,000	—
Total	2,000	

Schedule 16 — Operating Expenses

	Year ending 31.3.2010 Rs.	Year ending 31.3.2009 Rs.
Payments and provisions for employess	210	—
Rent and taxes	70	—
Stationery	60	—
Direcotrs' fees	35	—
Auditors' fees	8	—
Depreciation	31	—
Postage, Telegrams	61	—
Total	475	—

Rana Bank Ltd.

Profit and Loss Account for the year ended 31st March, 2003

	Schedule Number	Year ending 31.3.2003 Rs. '000	Year ending 31.3.2001 Rs. '000
I. Income :			
Interest Earned	13	3,800	—
Other Income	14	459	—
Total		4,259	—
II. Expenditure :			
Interest Expanded	15	2,000	—
Operating Expenses	16	475	—
Provisions and Contingencies		809	—
Total		3,284	—
III. Profit :			
Net profit for the year		975	—
Profit brought forward		1,000	—
Total		1,975	—
IV. Appropriations :			
Transfer to Statutory Reserve		195	—
Transfer to Other Reserves		NIL	—
Proposed Dividend and Dividend Tax		115	—
Balance carried over to Balance Sheet		16,65	—
Total		1,935	—

Working Notes :

(*i*) *Calculation of amount of income tax :*

	Rs.	Rs.
Income		4,259
Less : Interest expended	2,000	
Operating expenses	475	
Provision for doubtful debts	284	2759
		1,500

Provision for income tax @ 35%	525
(*ii*) *Provisions and contingencies :*	Rs.
Provision for doubtful debts	284
Provisin for income tax	525
	809

(*iii*) *Transfer to Statutory Reserve :*

20% of current year's profit - 20% of Rs. 975 thousand = Rs. 195 thousand.

Illustration 8:

From the following information, prepare a Balance Sheet of International Bank Ltd. as on 31st March 2010, giving the relevant schedules and also specify at least four important Principal Accounting Policies:

	Dr.	*Cr.*
		Rs. in lakhs
Share Capital		198.00
19,80,000 Shares of Rs. 10 each		
Statutory Reserve		231.00
Net Profit before appropriations		150.00
Profit and Loss Account		412.00
Fixed Deposit Account		517.00
Savings Deposit Account		450.00
Current Accounts	28.10	520.12
Bills Payable		0.10
Cash Credits	812.00	
Borrowings from other Banks		110.00
Cash on Hand	160.15	
Cash with RBI	37.88	
Cash with other Banks	155.87	
Money at Call	210.12	
Gold	55.23	
Government Securities	110.17	
Premises	155.70	
Furniture	70.12	
Term Loan	792.88	
	2,588.22	2.588.22

Additional Information:

Bills for collection	18,10,000
Acceptances and endorsements	14,12,000
Claims against the Bank not acknowledged as debt	55,000
Depreciation charges — Premises	1,10,000
— Furnitures	78,000

50% of the Term Loans are secured by Government guarantees. 10% of cash credit is unsecured. Also calculate cash reserves required and statutory liquid reserves required.

Assume that cash reserve required is 3% of demand and time liabilities and liquid reserves required is 30% of demand and time liabilities. [*Adapted C.A.* (*Int.*) *Nov. 1994*]

Balance Sheet of International Bank Ltd.
As on 31st March, 2003

(*Rs. in lacs*)

Capital and Liabilities	*Schedule*	*As on 31.3.2003*	*As on 31.3.2002*
Share Capital	1	1,98.00	
Reserves and Surplus	2	7,93.00	
Deposits	3	14,87.12	
Borrowings	4	1,10.00	
Other liabilities and provisions	5	0.10	
		25,88.22	
Assets			
Cash and balances with RBI	6	2,04.76	
Balances with banks and money at call and short notice	7	3,59.26	
Investments	8	1,65.40	
Advances	9	16,32.98	
Fixed Assets	10	2,25.82	
Other Assets	11		
		25,88.22	
Contingent liabilities	12	14.67	
Bills for collection		18.10	

Schedule 1 — Capital

(*Rs. in lacs*)

Capital and Liabilities	*Schedule*	*As on 31.3.2003*	*As on 31.3.2002*
Authorised Capital			
Issued, Subscribed and Paid up capital			
19,80,000 Shares of Rs. 10 each		1,98.00	

Schedule 2 — Reserves and Surplus

(*i*) Statutory Reserve-Opening Balance	2,31.00	
Additions during the year	30.00	
		2,61.00
(*ii*) Balance in Profit & Loss Account [Working Note (*ii*)]		5,32.00
		7,93.00

Schedule 3 — Deposits

(*i*) Demand Deposits from others	5,20.12
(*ii*) Saving Bank Deposits	4,50.00
(*iii*) Fixed Deposits	5,17.00
	14,87.12

Schedule 4 — Borrowings

Borrowing in India — Other banks	1,10.00

Schedule 5 — Other Liabilities and Provisions

Other liabilities and provisions	0.10

Schedule 6 — Cash and Balances with RBI

(*i*) Cash in hand	1,60.15
(*ii*) Balances with RBI –	
In current account [Working Note (*i*)]	44.61
	2,04.76

Schedule 7 — Balances with Banks & Money at Call and Short Notice

I. In India	
(*i*) Balance with Banks	
(*a*) in Current Accounts [Working Note (*iii*)]	1,49.14
(*ii*) Money at call and short notice	2,10.12
	3,59.26

Schedule 8 — Investments

1. Investments in India in	
(*i*) Government securities	1,10.17
(*ii*) Others – Gold	55.23
	1,65.40

Schedule 9 — Advances

A. (*i*) Cash credits and overdrafts	8.40.10
(*ii*) Term loans	7,92.88
	16,32.98

(Rs. in lacs)

Capital and Liabilities	*Schedule*	*As on 31.3.2003*	*As on 31.3.2002*
B. (*i*) Secured by tangible		11,52.53	
(*ii*) Secured by Bank/Government guarantees		3,96.44	
(*iii*) Unsecured		84.01	
		16.32.98	

Schedule 10 — Fixed Assets

1. Premises	
At cost on 31st March, 1994	156.80
Depreciation to date	1.10
	155.70
2. Other Fixed Assets	
Furniture at cost on 31st March, 1994	70.90
Depreciation to date	0.78
	70.12
Total (1 + 2)	2,25.82

Schedule 11 — Other Assets

Nil

Schedule 12 — Contingent Liabilities

(*i*) Claims against the bank not acknowledged as debts	0.55
(*ii*) Acceptances and endorsements	14.12
	14.67

Working Notes:

(*i*) *Required cash reserve and liquid reserve*:

	Rs. in lakhs
Fixed deposits	517.00
Saving deposits	450.00
Current accounts (credit balances)	520.12
Total demand and time liabilities	1487.12

Cash reserve required = 3% of Rs. 1487.12 lakh = Rs. 44.61 lakh
Liquid reserve required = 30% of Rs. 1487.12 lakh = Rs. 446.14 lakh

(*ii*) *Profit and Loss Account*:

	Rs. in lakhs
Balance of Profit and Loss Account b/fd	412.00
Add: Net profit for the year before appropriations	150.00
	562.00
Less: Transfer to Statutory Reserve, 20% of Rs. 150 lakh	30.00
Balance appearing in balance sheet	532.00

(*iii*) *Cash with other banks*:

	Rs. in lakhs
Liquid assets:	
Cash on hand	160.15
Cash with other banks	155.87
Money at call	210.12
Gold	55.33
Government securities	110.17
	691.54
Liquid reserve required	446.14

Excess liquidity = Rs. (691.54 – 446.14) lakh
= Rs. 245.40 lakhs.

	Rs. in lakhs
Cash reserve required	44.61
Less: Cash with R.B.I.	37.88
Transfer needed to maintain cash reserve	6.73
Cash with other banks	155.87
Less: Transfer to cash with R.B.I.	6.73
Balance appearing in balance sheet	149.14

Principal Accounting Policies

(a) Foreign Exchange Transactions:

(*i*) Monetary assets and liabilities have been translated at the exchange rate prevailing at the close of the year. Non-monetary assets have been carried in the books at the historical cost.

(*ii*) Income and Expenditure in respect of Indian branches have been translated at the exchange rates on the date of transactions and in respect of foreign branches at the exchange rates prevailing at the close of the year.

(*iii*) Profit or Loss on foreign currency position including pending forward exchange contracts have been accounted for at the exchange rates prevailing at the close of the year.

(b) Investments:

Permanent category investments are valued at cost. Valuation of investment in current category depends on the nature of securities. While valuation of government securities held as current investment have been made on yield to maturity basis, the investments in shares of companies are valued on the basis of book value

(c) Advances:

Advances due from sick nationalised units under nursing programmes and in respect of various sticky, suit filed and decreed accounts have been considered good on the basis of —

(*i*) Available estimated value of existing and prospective primary and collateral securities including personal worth of the borrowers and guarantors.

(*ii*) The proposed/on going revival/rehabilitation programmes.

(*iii*) The claim lodged/to be lodged under various credit guarantee schemes.

(*iv*) Pending settlement of claims by Govt.

Provisions to the satisfaction of auditors have been made and deducted from advances. Tax relief available when the advance is written off will be accounted for in the year of write-off.

(d) Fixed Assets:

The premises and other fixed assets except for foreign branches are accounted for at their historical cost. Depreciation has been provided on written down value method at the rates specified in the Income Tax Rules, 1962. Depreciation in respect of assets of foreign branches has been provided as per the local laws.

Illustration 9 :

Lena Dena Bank Limited has a paid-up share capital of Rs. 1 crore. You are required to prepare Profit and Loss Account for the year ended 31st March, 2010 along with the necessary Schedules on the basis of following additional information :-

Items	*For the year ended* 31.3.07 *(Rs. in '000)*
Interest on advances	613,56
Discount on bills	23,11
Income on investments	235,97
Interest on balances with Reserve Bank of India	46,20
Interest on other inter-bank funds	8,71
Commission, exchange and brokerage	51,69
Profit on exchange transactions (net)	8,10
Profit on sale of investments	10,21
Profit on sale of land, building and other assets	32
Interest on Deposits	682,24
Interest on Reserve Bank of India/inter-bank borrowings	19,02
Payments to and provisions for employees	140,28
Rent, taxes and lighting	18,85
Insurance	17,05
Printing and stationery	4,02
Advertisement and publicity	1,86
Depreciation on Bank's property	4,56
Postages, Telegrams, Telephones, etc.	5,32
Repairs and maintenance	1,88
Directors' fees, allowance and expenses	22
Auditors' fees and expenses	73
Law charges	41
Other expenditure	18,34
Balance of Profit and Loss Account b/fd	18,35

The following adjustments have to be made :-

(*a*) Rebate on bills discounted on 31.3.09 and 31.3.10 were Rs. 6,48 thousand and Rs. 7,36 thousand respectively.

(*b*) The abovementioned figure of interest on advances includes Rs. 86 thousand of interest on NPA out of which a sum of Rs. 14 thousand only has been received.

(*c*) Advances of the bank have been classified as follows :

	(Rs. in '000)
Standard Assets	21,74
Sub-standard Assets	3,10
Secured portions of Doubtful Assets :	
— upto one year	90
— one year to three years	60
— more than three years	10
Unsecured portions of Doubtful Assets	54
Loss Assets	9

The necessary provision against the abovementioned advances is to be made.

(*d*) Make a provision for Income Tax (including surcharge) @ 35%.

(*e*) Transfer 20% profit to Statutory Reserve and 10% profit to Revenue Reserve.

(*f*) The Board of Directors proposed a dividend @ 10% of paid-up share capital. Ignore corporation dividend tax.

Solution :

Lena Dena Bank Limited

Profit and Loss Account for the Year ended 31st March, 2010

	Schedule	*As on 31.3.10 (Rs. in '000)*	*As on 31.3.09 (Rs. in '000)*
I. Income			
Interest earned	13	925,95	
Other Income	14	70,32	
Total		996,27	
II. Expenditure			
Interest expended	15	701,26	
Operating expenses	16	213,52	
Provisions and contingencies		29,49	
Total		944,27	
III. Profit			
Net profit for the year		52,00	
Profit brought forward		18,35	
Total		70,35	
IV. Appropriations			
Transfer to Statutory Reserves		10,40	
Transfer to Other Reserves		5,20	
Proposed dividend		10,00	
Balance carried over to Balance Sheet	44,75	18,35	
Total		70,35	

Schedule 13 — Interest Earned

	Year ended 31.3.10 (Rs. in '000)	*Year ended 31.3.09 (Rs. in '000)*
I. Interest/discount on advances/bills	635,07	
II. Income on investments	235,97	
III. Interest on balances with Reserve Bank of India and other inter-bank funds	54,91	
Total	925,95	

Schedule 14 —Other Income

I.	Commission, exchange and brokerage	51,69
II.	Profit on sale of investments	10,21
IV.	Profit on sale of land, building and other assets	32
V.	Profit on exchange transactions (net)	8,10
	Total	70,32

Schedule 15 — Interest Expended

I.	Interest on deposits	682,24
II.	Interest on Reserve Bank of India - inter-bank borrowings	19,02
	Total	701,26

Schedule 16 — Operating Expenses

I.	Payments to and provisions for employees	140,28
II.	Rent, taxes and lighting	18,85
III.	Printing and stationery	4,02
IV.	Advertisement and publicity	1,86
V.	Depreciation on Bank's property	4,56
VI.	Directors' fees, allowances and expenses	22
VII.	Auditors' fees and expenses	73
VIII.	Law charges	41
IX.	Postages, Telegrams, Telephones, etc.	5,32
X.	Repairs and maintenance	1,88
XI.	Insurance	17,05
XII.	Other expenditure	18,34
	Total	213,52

Working Notes :

		(Rs. in '000)
(*i*)	Discount on bills	23,11
	Add : Rebate on bills discounted on 31.3.09	6,48
		29,59
	Less : Rebate on bills discounted on 31.3.10	7,36
		22,23
(*ii*)	Interest on advances	613,56
	Less : Interest on NPA credited but not received (86—14)	72
		612,84
(*iii*)	Calculation of Interest/discount on advances/bills :	
	Interest on advances as per W.N. (*ii*) above	612,84
	Discount on bills as per W.N. (*i*) above	22,23
		635,07

(*iv*) Calculation of provisions against advances :

	Amount (*Rs. in '000*)	*Percentage at which provision is required*	*Amount of provision* (*Rs. in '000*)
Standard Assets	21,74	0.40	9
Sub-standard Assets	3,10	10	31
Secured portions of Doubtful Assets :			
— upto one year	90	20	18
— one year to three years	60	30	18
— more than three years	10	100	10

Unsecured portions of Doubtful Assets	54	100	54
Loss Assets	9	100	9
			1,49
(*v*) Interest earned			925,95
Add : Other income			70,32
			996,27
Less : Interest expended		701,26	
Operating expenses		213,52	
Provision against advances		1,49	916,27
Profit before tax			80,00
Less : Income Tax @ 35%			28,00
Net profit for the year			52,00
(*vi*) Transfer to Statutory Reserves @ 20%			10,40
(*vii*) Transfer to Revenue Reserves @ 10%			528
(*viii*) Proposed dividend @10% of paid-up share capital			10,00
(*ix*) Provisions and contingencies :			
Provisions against advances as per W.N. (*iv*)			1,49
Provisions for Income Tax as per W.N. (*v*)			28,00
			29,49

Illustration 10:

From the following trial balance and the additional information, prepare a balance sheet of Laxmi Bank Ltd. as on 31st March, 2010 giving the relevant schedules :

Debit balances	*Rs. in lakhs*
Cash credits	1,218.15
Cash in hand	240.23
Cash with Reserve Bank of India	67.82
Cash with other banks	132.81
Money at call and short notice	315.18
Gold	82.84
Government securities	365.25
Current accounts	42.00
Premises	133.55
Furniture	95.18
Term loans	1,189.32
	3,882.33

Credit balances	*Rs. in lakhs*
Share capital : 29,70,000 Equity shares of Rs. 10 each, fully paid-up	297.00
Statutory reserves	346.50
Net profit for the year (before appropriations)	225.00
Profit and loss account (opening balance)	618.00
Fixed deposit accounts	775.50
Saving deposit accounts	675.00
Current accounts	780.18
Bills payable	0.15
Borrowings from other banks	165.00
	3,882.33

Additional information :

(i) Bills for collection : Rs. 18,10,000.

(ii) Acceptance and endorsements : Rs. 14,12,000.

(iii) Claims against the bank not acknowledged as debts : Rs. 55,000.

(iv) Depreciation charged on premises : Rs. 1,10,000 and on furniture : Rs. 78,000.

Solution :

Balance sheet of Laxmi Bank Ltd. as on 31st March,2010

	Schedule	As on 31.3.2010 Rs. in lakhs
Capital and liabilities		
Capital	1	297.00
Reserves and Surplus	2	1,189.50
Deposits	3	2,230.68
Borrowings	4	165.00
Other liabilities and provisions	5	0.15
		3,882.33
Assets :		
Cash and balances with Reserve Bank of India	6	308.05
Balances with banks and money at call and short notice	7	447.99
Investments	8	448.09
Advances	9	2,449.47
Fixed Assets	10	228.73
Other Assets	11	Nil
		3,882.33
Contingent liabilities	12	14.67
Bills for collection		18.10

SCHEDULES :

Schedule 1 – Capital

	(Rs. in lakhs)
29,70,000 shares of Rs. 10 each, fully paid-up	297.00

Schedule 2 – Reserves and Surplus

		(Rs. in lakhs)
Statutory Reserves :		
Opening balance	346.50	
Add : 20% of current year's profit	45.00	391.50
Balance in Profit and Loss Account Rs. (618.00 + 225.00-45.00) lakh		798.00
Total		1,189.50

Schedule 3 – Deposits

Demand Deposits	780.18
Savings Bank Deposits	675.00
Term Deposits	775.50
Total	2,230.68

Schedule 4 - Borrowings

Borrowings from other banks	165.00

Schedule 5 – Other Liabilities and Provisions

Bills payable	0.15

Schedule 6 – Cash and Balances with Reserve Bank of India

	(Rs. in lakhs)
Cash in hand	240.23
Balances with Reserve Bank of India	67.82
Total	308.05

Schedule 7 – Balances with Banks & Money at Call and Short Notice

Cash with other banks	132.81
Money at call and short notice	315.18
Total	447.99

Schedule 8 - Investments

Investments in Government Securities	365.25
Gold	82.84
	448.09

Schedule 9 – Advances

Cash credits and overdrafts, Rs. (1,218.15 + 42.00) lakh	1,260.15
Term loans	1,189.32
	2,449.47

Schedule 10 – Fixed Assets

Premises	134.65	
Less : Depreciation	1.10	133.55
Furniture	95.96	
Less : Depreciation	0.78	95.18
		228.73

Schedule 11- Other Assets

(Rs. in lakhs)

Nil

Schedule 12 – Contingent Liabilities

Claims against the bank not acknowledged as debts	0.55
Acceptance and endorsements	14.12
	14.67

Illustration 11:

On the basis of the following balances and the additional information provided thereafter, prepare Balance Sheet of Kuber Bank Limited as on 31st March, 2010 along with the necessary Schedules :

Debit Balances	*Rs. (in '000)*	*Credit Balances*	*Rs. (in '000)*
Cash in hand	18,98	Share Capital :	
Balances with RBI	1,06,42	3 lakh Shares of Rs. 10	30,00
Balances with other Banks	12,81	Statutory Reserves	58,40
Money at Call and Short Notice	3,63	Securities Premium	5,00
Government Securities	1,10,88	Revenue Reserves	97,12
Shares	11,47	Profit & Loss Account	32,18
Gold	8,75	Term Deposits	1,00,76
Bills Purchased and Discounted	80,78	Savings Bank Deposits	85,90
Cash Credits and Overdrafts	2,89,64	Demand Deposits	2,36,42

Premises	19,32	Borrowings from RBI	13,60
Furniture and Fixtures	16,62	Bills Payable	10,01
Inter-office Adjustments (Net)	1,21	Interest Accrued	12,35
Stationery and Stamps	8,96	Provisions	40,46
Non-banking Assets	1,50		
Interest Accrued	23,75		
Tax Paid in Advance	7,48		
	7,22,20		7,22,20

Additional Information :

(*i*) The authorised capital of the bank is Rs. 50,00 thousand divided into 5 lakh shares of Rs. 10 each. Out of this, 3 lakh shares have been issued, subscribed and fully paid-up.

(*ii*) Net profit after tax for the year has been Rs. 25,50 thousand; 20% of which has been transferred to Statutory Reserves.

(*iii*) Advances amounting to Rs. 2,61,52 thousand are secured by tangible assets whereas those amounting to Rs.98,49 thousand are covered by Bank/Govt. guarantees. The remaining advances are unsecured.

(*iv*) On 31st March, 2009 cost of premises in hand was Rs. 36,84 thousand and that of furniture and fixtures was Rs. 23,96 thousand. There has been no addition to or disposal of any of these assets during the year 2009-10.

(*v*) Some of the shares held by the bank as investments are partly paid-up; the total liability for these partly paid shares is Rs. 1,00 thousand.

(*vi*) Bank has given guarantees amounting to Rs. 12,80 thousand on behalf of constituents. Also, there are contingent liabilities amounting to Rs. 23,56 thousand relating to acceptances, and endorsements for the clients.

(*vii*) Bills for collection with the bank on 31st March, 2010 totalled Rs. 9,75 thousand.

Solution :

Balance Sheet of Kuber Bank Limited
as on 31st March, 2010

	Schedule	*As on 31.3.10 (Rs. in '000)*	*As on 31.3.09 (Rs. in '000)*
Capital and Liabilities			
Share Capital	1	30,00	
Reserves and Surplus	2	1,92,70	
Deposits	3	4,23,08	
Borrowings	4	13,60	
Other liabilities and provisions	5	62,82	
Total		7,22,20	
Assets			
Cash and balances with RBI	6	1,25,40	
Balances with banks and money at call and short notice	7	16,44	
Investments	8	1,31,10	
Advances	9	3,70,42	
Fixed Assests	10	35,94	
Other Assets	11	42,90	
Total		7,22,20	
Contingent Liabilities	12	37,36	
Bills for Collection		9,75	

Schedule 1 — Capital

		As on 31.3.10 (Rs. in '000)	As on 31.3.09 (Rs. in '000)
Authorised Capital :			
(5,00,000 Shares of Rs. 10 each)		50,00	50,00
Issued, Subscribed and Called-up Capital :			
(3,00,000 Shares of Rs. 10 each)		30,00	

Schedule 2 — Reserves & Surplus

I. Statutory Reserves :		
Opening Balance	53,30	
Additions during the year	5,10	58,40
III. Securities Premium		5,00
IV. Revenue reserves		97,12
V. Balance in Profit & Loss Account		32,18
Total		1,92,70

Schedule 3 — Deposits

I. Demand Deposits	2,36,42
II. Savings Bank Deposits	85,90
III. Term Deposits	1,00,76
Total	4,23,08

Schedule 4 — Borrowings

I. Borrowings in India	
(i) Reserve Bank of India	13,60

Schedule 5 — Other Liabilities and Provisions

I. Bills payable	10,01
II. Interest accrued	12,35
IV. Others (including provisions)	40,46
Total	62,82

Schedule 6 — Cash and Balances with Reserve Bank of India

I. Cash in hand	18,98
II. Balance with Reserve Bank of India	1,06,42
Total	1,25,40

Schedule 7 — Balances with Banks and Money at Call and Short Notice

In India	
(i) Balances with Banks	12,81
(ii) Money at call and short notice	3,63
Total	16,44

Schedule 8 — Investments

I. Investments in India in	
(i) Government Securities	1,10,88
(iii) Shares	11,47
(vi) Others — Gold	8,75
Total	1,31,10

Schedule 9 - Advances

A.	(i)	Bills purchased and discounted	80,78
	(ii)	Cash Credits and overdrafts	2,89,64
		Total	3,70,42
B.	(i)	Secured by tangible assets	2,61,52
	(ii)	Covered by Bank/Govt. Guarantees	98,49
	(iii)	Unsecured	10,41
		Total	3,70,42

Schedule 10 — Fixed Assets

I.	Premises :		
	At cost as on 31st March, 2009	36,84	
	Depreciation to date	17,52	19,32
II.	Furniture and Fixtures :		
	At cost as on 31st March, 2009	23,96	
	Depreciation to date	7,34	16,62
	Total		35,94

Schedule 11 — Other Assets

I.	Inter-office adjustments (Net)	1,21
II.	Interest accrued	23,75
III.	Tax paid in advance	7,48
IV.	Stationery and stamps	8,96
V.	Non-banking assets acquired in satisfaction of claims	1,50
	Total	42,90

Schedule 12 — Contingent Liabilities

		Schedule	*As on 31.3.10 (Rs. in '000)*	*As on 31.3.09 (Rs. in '000)*
II.	Liability for partly paid shares		1,00	
IV.	Guarantee given on behalf of constituents		12,80	
V.	Acceptances, endorsements and other obligations		23,56	
	Total		37,36	

Illustration 12:

From the following trial balance as on 31st March, 2010, prepare the final accounts of Commercial Bank Ltd.:

Debit Balances	*Rs. (in '000)*	*Credit Balances*	*Rs. (in '000)*
Cash Balance	200	Interest on Advances	800
Balance with other Banks	400	Interest from Investments	125
Cash with RBI	100	Commission, Exchange and Brokerage	200
Investments in Govt. Securities	300	Profit on Sale of Investments	20
Other Approved Securities	100	Other Revenue Receipts	80
Bills Purchased and Discounted	400	Share Capital	2,000
Cash Credits, Overdrafts and Demand Loans	1,420	Statutory Reserve	900
Term Loans	1,285	Profit & Loss Account	650
Premises (Net)	1,220	Fixed Deposits	275
Furniture	250	Savings Deposits	325

Interest Paid	120	Current Accounts	125
Salary	75	Borrowings from other Banks	300
Printing & Stationery	35	Borrowing from RBI	100
Postage & Telegrams	20	Bills Payable	25
Repairs	25	Interest Accured	75
Interest Accrued	50		
	6,000		6,000

Additional Information :

(*i*) Bills for collection as on the abovementioned date totalled Rs. 2,35,000.

(*ii*) Advances made have been classified as under :-

	Cash Credits, Overdrafts, etc. (Rs. in '000)	*Term Loans (Rs. in '000)*	*Bills Purchased and Discounted (Rs. in '000)*
Standard Assets	1,003	985	433
Sub-standard Assets	120	100	—
Doubtful Assets :			
— Upto one year	100	20	—
— One year to three years	120	60	—
— More than three years	50	80	—
Loss Assets	12	22	—
	1,405	1,267	433

No provision has been made against these assets. Doubtful Assets are secured to the extent of 50% of the amounts due. (*iii*) All the activities of the bank are confined to India

(Adapted C.A. Inter. May, 1994)

Solution :

Balance Sheet of Commercial Bank Ltd.
as on 31st March, 2010

Capital and Liabilities	*Schedule*	*As on 31.3.10 (Rs. in '000)*	*As on 31.3.09 (Rs. in '000)*
Capital	1	2,000	
Reserves and Surplus	2	2,115	
Deposits	3	725	
Borrowings	4	400	
Other Liabilities & Provisions	5	100	
Total		5,340	
Assets			
Cash and Balances with Reserve Bank of India	6	300	
Balances with Banks and Money at Call and Short Notice	7	400	
Investments	8	400	
Advances	9	2,720	
Fixed Assets	10	1,470	
Other Assets	11	50	
Total		5,340	
Bills for Collection		235	

Profit and Loss Account for the year ended 31st March, 2007

Capital and Liabilities	*Schedule*	*As on 31.3.10 (Rs. in '000)*	*As on 31.3.09 (Rs. in '000)*
I. **Income**			
Interest Earned	13	925	
Other Income	14	300	
		1,225	
II. **Expenditure**			
Interest Expended	15	120	
Operating Expenses	16	155	
Provisions and Contingencies		385	
		660	
III. **Profit**			
Net Profit for the year		565	
Profit brought forward		650	
		1,215	
IV. **Appropriations**			
Transfer to Statutory Reserves		113	
Balance carried over to Balance Sheet		1,102	
		1,215	

Schedule 1 — Capital

Capital and Liabilities	*Schedule*	*As on 31.3.10 (Rs. in '000)*	*As on 31.3.09 (Rs. in '000)*
For other Banks			
Authorised Capital :			
... Share of Rs... each		?	
Issued Capital :			
... Shares of Rs... each		?	
Subscribed Capital :			
... Shares of Rs... each		?	
Called up Capital :			
... Share of Rs... each		2,000	

Schedule 2 — Reserves and Surplus

I. Statutory Reserves	
Opening Balance	900
Additions during the year	113
	1,013
V. Balance in Profit and Loss Account	1,102
	2,115

Schedule 3 — Deposits

AI. Demand Deposits	125
II. Savings Bank Deposits	325
III. Term Deposits	275
	725

Schedule 4 — Borrowings

I. Borrowing in India	
(*i*) Reserve Bank of India	100
(*ii*) Other Banks	300
	400

Schedule 5 — Other Liabilities and Provisions

Capital and Liabilities	Schedule	As on 31.3.10 (Rs. in '000)	As on 31.3.09 (Rs. in '000)
I. Bills Payable		25	
III. Interest Accrued		75	
		100	

Schedule 6 — Cash and Balances with Reserve Bank of India

I. Cash in hand	200
II. Balance with Reserve Bank of India	100
	300

Schedule 7 — Balance with Bank and Money at Call and Short Notice

In India	
(*i*) Balances with Banks	400

Schedule 8 — Investments

I. Investments in India in	
(*i*) Government Securities	300
(*ii*) Other Approved Securities	100
	400

Schedule 9 — Advances

A. (*i*) Bills Purchased and Discounted	399
(*ii*) Cash Credits, Overdrafts and Loans Repayable on demand	1,203
(*iii*) Term Loans	1,118
	2,720

Schedule 10 — Fixed Assets

I. Premises (Net)	1,220
II. Other Fixed Assets (including Furniture and Fixtures)	250
	1,470

Schedule 11 — Other Assets

II. Interest Accrued	50

Schedule 13— Interest Earned

I. Interest/Discount on Advances/Bills	800
II. Income on Investments	125
	925

Schedule 14 — Other Income

I. Commission Exchange and Brokerage	200
II. Profit on Sale of Investments	20
VII. Miscellaneous Income	80
	300

Schedule 16 — Other Income

I. Interest on Deposits	120

Schedule 15 — Operating Expenses

I. Payments to and Provision for Employees	75

III. Printing & Stationery	35
IX. Postage and Telegrams	20
X. Repairs and Maintenance	25
	155

Working Notes :—

Calculation of Provision against Advances :-

	Cash Credits Overdrafts etc. (Rs. in '000)	*Term Loans (Rs. in '000)*	*Percentage at which provision is required (Rs. in '000)*	*Provision Against :— Cash credits, Overdrafts etc. (Rs. in '000)*	*Term Loans (Rs. in '000)*
Standard Assets	1,003	985	0.40	4	4
Sub-standard Assets	120	100	10	12	10
Secured portions of Doubtful Assets :					
— upto one year	50	10	20	10	2
— one year to three years	60	30	30	18	9
— more than three years	25	40	100	25	40
Unsecured portions of Doubtful Assets :					
— upto one year	50	10	100	50	10
— one year to three years	60	30	100	60	30
— more than three years	25	40	100	25	40
Loss Assets	12	22	100	12	22
	1,405	1,267		216	167

Provison against Bills Purchased and Discounted = 0.40 per cent of standard Assests of Rs. 4000 thousand = Rs. 2 thousand.

Total Provision = Rs. (216 + 167+2) thousand
= Rs. 385 thousand

Note : Total amount of Assets have been arrived at by adding the amounts of (*i*) Cash Credits, Overdrafts etc. (*ii*) Term Loans and (*iii*) Bills Purchased and Discounted. As Doubtful Assets are secured to the extent of 50% of the amounts due, the remaining 50% of the Doubtful Assets have been treated as unsecured.

Illustration 13:

On 31st March, 2010 the following trial balance was extracted from the books of the India Bank Ltd. You are required to prepare the Profit and Loss Account for the year ended 31st March, 2010 and the Balance Sheet as on that date along with the necessary Schedules after taking into consideration the additional information also.

Trial Balance as on 31st March, 2010

Debit Balance :	*(Rs. in '000)*
Cash in hand	21,14
Balance with RBI :	
In current account	7,73,47
In other accounts	9,85
Balance with other banks in current accounts	8,23
Money at call and short notice with banks	25
Premises at cost on 31st March, 2009	3,61
Other Fixed Assets at cost on 31st March, 2009	18,90
Interest accrued.	5,60
Inter-office adjustments (net)	12,74

Tax paid in advance	48,76
Non-banking Assets acquired in satisfaction of claims	5,00
Loss on revaluation of investments	2,15
Interest paid on deposits	2,28,03
Interest on RBI borrowings	4,45
Payments to and provision for employees	1,11,82
Directors' fees and allowances	3,48
Auditors' fees and expenses	16,88
Rent, taxes and lighting.	6,95
Printing and stationery	1,86
Advertisement and publicity	40
Depreciation on bank's property	2,71
Repairs and maintenance	1,16
Insurance	9,35
Law charges	17
Postage, Telegrams, Telephones etc	2,23
Other expenditure	7,15
Investments in Government Securities	9,83,52
Investments in other approved securities	3,78,04
Investments in Shares	12,60
Investments in debentures and bonds	15,17
Bills purchased and discounted	2,18,53
Cash credits and overdrafts	9,97,68
Term loans	7,01,23
Stationery and stamps	1,42
	46,34,53
Credit Balances :	
Paid-up Share Capital : 2,50,000 shares of Rs. 10 each	25,00
Statutory Reserve	75,07
Revenue reserves	55,00
Demand deposits	11,14,30
Savings bank deposits	11,86,05
Term deposits	14,65,20
Interest accrued.	12,56
Interest/discount on advances/bills	3,11,43
Rebate on bills discounted	33,03
Income on investments	1,43,62
Interest on balances with RBI and other inter-bank funds	34,47
Commission, exchange and brokerage	47,52
Profit on sale of investments	1,75
Profit and Loss Account	35,00
Depreciation on premises (to date)	1,09
Depreciation on other fixed assets (to date)	9,70
Borrowings from Reserve Bank of India	29,00
Bills payable	54,74
	46,34,53

Additional Information :

(*i*) The authorised capital of the bank is Rs. 50 lakh divided into 5,00,000 shares of Rs. 10 each; half of it has been issued and subscribed.

(*ii*) Advances amounting to Rs. 16,25,21 thousand are secured by tangible assets, those amounting to Rs. 2,50,12 are covered by bank/Govt. guarantees while the remaining advances are unsecured.

(*iii*) All the advances of the bank are in India. Advances to priority, sectors total Rs. 6,82,21 thousand, to public sectors total Rs. 2,92,76 and to banks total Rs. 27,55 thousand.

(*iv*) There are claims amounting to Rs. 12 thousand against the bank not acknowledged as debts. The bank has given guarantees in India totalling Rs. 1,70,21 thousand on behalf of constituents, in addition, there are acceptances, endorsements and other obligations to the tune of Rs. 2,01,45 thousand.

(*v*) Provision for income-tax including surcharge is to be made @ 35%.

(*vi*) 20% of the profit is to be transferred to statutory reserve.

(*vii*) On 31st March, 2010 the bank held bills amounting Rs. 98,47 thousand for collection on behalf of clients.

Solution :

Balance Sheet of the India Bank Limited as on 31st March, 2010

	Schedule	As on 31.3.10 (Rs. in '000)	As on 31.3.09 (Rs. in '000)
Capital and Liabilities			
Capital	1	25,00	
Reserves and surplus	2	2,56,07	
Deposits	3	37,65,55	
Borrowings	4	29,00	
Other liabilities and provisions	5	1,00,57	
Total		41,76,19	
Assets			
Cash and balances with RBI	6	8,04,46	
Balance with banks and money at call and short notice	7	8,48	
Investments	8	13,89,33	
Advances	9	19,17,44	
Fixed Assets	10	11,72	
Other Assets	11	44,76	
Total		41,76,19	
Contingent liabilities	12	3,71,78	
Bills for collection		98,47	

Profit and Loss Account for the year ended 31st March, 2010

	Schedule	As on 31.3.10 (Rs. in '000)	As on 31.3.09 (Rs. in '000)
I. Income			
Interest earned	13	4,89,52	
Other income	14	47,12	
Total		5,36,64	
II. Expenditure			
Interest expended	15	2,32,48	
Operating expenses	16	1,64,16	
Provisions and contingencies		72,45	
Total		4,69,09	
III. Profit			
Net profit for the year		91,00	
Profit brought forward		35,00	
Total		1,26,00	
IV. Appropriations			
Transfer to Statutory Reserve		18,20	
Balance carried over to Balance Sheet		1,07,80	
Total		1,26,00	

Schedule 1 — Capital

	As on 31.3.10 (Rs. in '000)	As on 31.3.09 (Rs. in '000)
Authorised capital		
(5,00,00 shares of Rs. 10 each)	50,00	
Issued, subscribed, called-up and paid-up capital		
(2,50,00 shares of Rs. 10 each)	25,00	
Total	25,00	

Schedule 2 — Reserves and Surplus

I. Statutory reserve		
Opening balance	75,07	
Addition during the year	18,20	93,27
Revenue reserves		55,00
II. Balance in Profit and Loss Account		1,07,80
Total		2,56,07

Schedule 3— Deposits

A. I. Demand deposits	11,14,30
II. Savings bank deposits	11,86,05
III. Term deposits	14,65,20
Total	37,65,55

Schedule 4— Borrowings

I. Borrowings in India	
(*i*) Reserve Bank of India	29,00
Total	29,00

Schedule 5— Other Liabilities and Provisions

I. Bills payable	54,74
III. Interest accrued	12,56
IV. Others (including provisions)	33,27
Total	1,00,57

Schedule 6—Cash and Balances with Reserve Bank of India

I. Cash in hand	21,14
II. Balances with RBI	
(*i*) In current account	7,73,47
(*ii*) In other accounts	9,85
Total	8,04,46

Schedule 7— Balances with Banks and Money at Call and Short Notice

I. In India	
(*i*) Balances with banks	
(*a*) In current accounts	8,23
(*ii*) Money at call and short notice	
(*a*) With banks	25
Total	8,48

Schedule 8—Investments

I. Investments in India in	
(*i*) Government securities	9,83,52
(*ii*) Other approved securities	3,78,04
(*iii*) Shares	12,60
(*iv*) Debentures and bonds	15,17
TOTAL	13,89,33

Schedule 9 - Advances

			As on 31.3.10 (Rs. in '000)	As on 31.3.09 (Rs. in '000)
A.	(i)	Bills purchased and discounted	2,18,53	
	(ii)	Cash credits and overdrafts	9,97,68	
	(iii)	Term loans	7,01,23	
		Total of A	19,17,44	
B.	(i)	Secured by tangible assets	16,25,21	
	(ii)	Covered by bank/Government guarantees	2,50,12	
	(iii)	Unsecured	42,11	
		Total of B	19,17,44	
C.	(I)	Advances in India		
	(i)	Priority sectors	6,82,21	
	(ii)	Public sectors	2,92,76	
	(iii)	Banks	27,55	
	(iv)	Others	9,14,92	
		Total of C	19,17,44	

Schedule 10 - Fixed Assets

I.	Premises		
	At cost as on 31st March, 2009	3,61	
	Depreciation to date	1,09	2,52
II.	Other fixed assets		
	At cost as on 31st March, 2009	18,90	
	Depreciation to date	9,70	9,20
	Total		11,72

Schedule 11 — Other Assets

I.	Inter-office adjustments (net)	12,74
II.	Interest accrued	25,60
IV.	Stationery and stamps	1,42
V.	Non-banking assets acquired in satisfaction of claims	5,00
	Total	44,76

Schedule 12—Contingent Liabilities

I.	Claims against the bank not acknowledged as debts	12
IV.	Guarantees given on behalf of constituents	
	(a) In India	1,70,21
V.	Acceptances, Endorsements and other obligations	2,01,45
	Total	3,71,78

Schedule 13—Interest Earned

I.	Interest/discount on advances/bills	3,11,43
II.	Income on investments	1,43,62
III.	Interest on balances with RBI and other inter-bank funds	34,47
	Total	4,89,52

Schedule 14—Other Income

I.	Commission, exchange and brokerage	47,52
II.	Profit on sale of investments	1,75
III.	Profit on revaluation of investments	
	Less : Loss on revaluation of investments	2,15 (—)
	Total	47,12

Schedule 15— Interest Expended

	As on 31.3.10 (Rs. in '000)	As on 31.3.09 (Rs. in '000)
I. Interest on deposits	2,28,03	
II. Interest on RBI borrowings	4,45	
Total	2,32,48	

Schedule 16 —Operating Expenses

I. Payments to and provisions for employees	1,11,82
II. Rent, taxes and lighting	6,95
III. Printing and stationery	1,86
IV. Advertisement and publicity	40
V. Depreciation on bank's property	2,71
VI. Directors' fees and allowances	3,48
VII. Auditors' fees and expenses	16,88
VIII. Law charges	17
IX. Postage, Telegrams, Telephones etc.	2,23
X. Repairs and maintenance	1,16
XI. Insurance	9,35
XII. Other expenditure	7,15
Total	1,64,16

Working Notes :

	Rs. in '000	Rs. in '000
(*i*) Interest earned		4,89,52
Add : Other income		47,12
		5,36,64
Less : Interest expended	2,32,48	
Operating expenses	1,64,16	3,96,64
Profit before tax		1,40,00
Less : Provision for income-tax including surcharge @ 35%		49,00
Profit after tax		91,00
Transfer to statutory reserve @ 20%		18,20
(*ii*) Provision for income-tax for the year	49,00	
Less : Tax paid in advance	48,76	
Net provision for income-tax including surcharge		24
Rebate on bills discounted		33,03
Others (including provision) to appear in Schedule 5		33,27

Exercise XXVI

Practical

1. On 31st March, 2010 a bank held the following bills discounted by it earlier :-

Date of bills 2010	*Term of Bills (months)*	*Discounted @ % p.a.*	*Amount to bills Rs.*
(*i*) January 17	4	8.5	7,30,000
(*ii*) February, 7	3	9	14,60,000
(*iii*) March, 9	3	8.75	3,64,000

You are required to calculate the Rebate on Bills Discounted. Also show the necessary journal entry for the rebate. *(Rebate, Rs. 29,270)*

[Hints :

Due date of bills	*No. of days away from 31st March, 2005*	*Rebate*
(*i*) May 20, 2010	50	Rs. 8,500
(*ii*) May 10, 2010	40	Rs. 14,400
(*iii*) June 12, 2010	73	Rs. 6,370]

2. On 1st April, 2008 the opening balance of Rebate on Bills Discounted Account of a bank was Rs. 1,07,500. On 31st March, 2009 the bank finds that its Interest/Discount on Advances/Bills/ Account shows a credit balance of Rs. 2,89,600 and no adjustments have been made in the account as yet. The bank has earned discount by discounting the bills. It is ascertained that the proportionate discount not yet earned on the bills discounted which will mature during the year 2009-10 amounted to Rs. 1,12,750.

Pass adjustment journal entries regarding rebate on bills discounted. Also show the following ledger accounts : -

(*i*) Rebate on Bills Discounted Account, and

(*ii*) Interest/Discount on Advances/Bills Accounts.

3. Following facts have been taken out from the records of Adarsha Bank Ltd., in respect of the year ending March 31, 2010

(*a*) On 1-4-2009 bills for collection were Rs. 7,00,000. During 2009-10 bills received for collection amounted to Rs. 64,50,000 and bills collected were Rs. 47,00,000 and bills dishonored and returned were Rs. 5,50,500. Prepare Bills for collection (Asset) Account and Bills for Collection (Liability) Account.

(*b*) On 1-4-2009, Acceptances, Endorsements, etc., not yet satisfied amounted to Rs. 14,50,000. During the year under question, Acceptances, Endorsements, Guarantee, etc., amounted to Rs. 44,00,000. Bank honoured acceptances to the extent of Rs. 25,00,000 and clients paid off Rs. 10,00,000 against the guaranteed liability. Clients failed to pay Rs. 1,00,000 which the Bank had to pay. Prepare the ''Acceptances, Endorsements and other Obligations Account'' as it would appear in the General Ledger.

(*c*) It is found, from the books, that a loan of Rs. 6,00,000 was advanced on 30-9-2009 @ 18 per cent, p.a. interest payable quarterly, but the loan was outstanding as on 31-3-2010 without any payment recorded in the meantime, either towards principal or towards interest. The security, for the loan, was 10,000 fully paid shares of Rs. 100 each (the market value was Rs. 98, as per the Stock Exchange Information as on 30th September, 2009). But, due to fluctuation the price fell to Rs. 60 per share in January 2010. On 31-3-2010, the price as per Stock Exchange rate was Rs. 82 per share. State how you would classify the loan as Standard Asset, Sub-standard Asset, Doubtful Asset or Loss Asset.

(*d*) The following balances are extracted from the Trial Balance as at 31-3-2010 Interest/ Discount on Advances/Bills (Cr.) Rs. 98,00,000, Rebate for Bills Discounted. (Cr.) Rs. 20,000 and Bills Discounted and Purchased Rs. 4,00,000.

It is ascertained that the proportionate discounts not yet earned for bills to mature in 2010-11 amounts to Rs. 14,000. Prepare ledger accounts. [*Adapted C.A., Final*]

[(*a*) Rs. 18,99,500 (*b*) Rs. 22,50,000 (*c*) Standard Asset
(*d*) Interest/Discount earned Rs. 98,06,000; Unexpired Discount, Rs. 14,000]

4. On the basis of the following information regarding Capital Funds and Assets of a commercial bank as on 31st March, 2010, calculate Risk Weighted Assets Ratio, giving detailed working notes:-

	(*Rs. in '000*)
Capital Funds :	
Equity Share Capital	70,00
Statutory Reserve	95,15
Capital Reserve (on sale of fixed assets)	10,00
Revaluation Reserve	4,00
Assets :	
Cash	1,90,74
Balance with Reserve Bank of India	6,10,17
Balance with other banks	1,13,18
Investments in Government securities	9,78,08
Investments in other approved securities	3,17,45

Investments in shares of joint stock companies in the private sector	50,00
Investments in debentures of joint stock companies in the private sector	3,83,38
Loans and Advances :	
(a) Loans guaranteed by Government of India	1,26,78
(b) Loans granted to public sector undertakings of State Governments	2,19,78
(c) Others	7,17,50
Premises	1,70,28
Furniture and Fixtures	78,24
Other Fixed Assets	1,15,83
Off-balance Sheet Item :	
Acceptances, Endorsements and Letters of Credit	4,63,44

[*8.05%*]

5. While closing its books of accounts on 31st March 2010, a Commercial bank finds that :

(*i*) on a term loan of Rs. one lakh fifty thousand, quarterly interest due on 29th September 2009, 29th December 2009 and 29th March 2010 has not been received.

(*ii*) the outstanding balance of an overdraft account has been continuously in excess of the sanctioned limit of Rs. one lakh since 14th May 2010.

(*iii*) Rs. 75,000, the amount of discounted bill was due on 17th February 2010 but the same has not been received.

Which of the abovementioned credit facilities will be treated as NPA on 31st March, 2010 ? Give reasons in support of your answer. **[*(ii) is N.P.A.*]**

6. On 31st March 2010, Bharat Commercial Bank Ltd. finds its Advances classified as follows:

	Rs. in '000
Standard Assets	74,56,50
Sub-standard Assets	4,64,00
Doubtful Assets : upto one years	1,28,30
one year to three years	78,20
: more than three years	32,90
Loss Assets	51,75

Calculate the amount of provision to be made by the bank against the abovementioned Advances. ***(Rs. 21,002 thousand)***

7. The following are the balances of nominal accounts appearing in the books of Kalyani Bank Limited as on 31st March, 2010 :-

Debit Balances	*(Rs. in '000)*
Interest on deposits	7,61,85
Interest on Reserve Bank of India/inter-bank borrowings	50,47
Payments to and provisions for employees	1,98,03
Rent, taxes and lighting	27,18
Depreciation on bank's property	14,16
Printing and stationery	6,75
Law charges	1,89
Postages, Telegrams, Telephones etc	9,67
Repairs and maintenance	10,49
Insurance	25,90
Auditors' fees and expenses	3,03
Directors' fees, allowances and expenses	1,44
Other expenditure	25,01
Credit Balance :	
Interest on advances	8,37,45
Discount on bills	48,19
Income in investments	2,80,31
Interest on balances with Reserve Bank of India	

and other inter-bank funds	72,33
Commission, exchange and brokerage.	1,03,45
Profit on sale of investments	25,69
Profit on exchange transcations	16,04
Miscellaneous income	1,13

Prepare Profit and Loss Account for the year ended 31st March, 2010 after taking into consideration the following information also :

(*i*) The abovementioned interest on advances includes interests amounting to Rs. 9 thousand on NPA which has not been received.

(*ii*) Rebate on bills discounted on 31st March, 2010 exceeds rebate on bills discounted on 31st March, 2009 by Rs. 21 thousand. The abovementioned amount of discount on the bill is to be adjusted for this excess.

(*iii*) On 31st March, 2010 bank's advances have been classified as below :

	(*Rs. in '000*)
Standard Assets	65,48,21
Secured portion of doubtful Assets :	
— upto one year	4,80
— one year to three years	3,70
— more than three years	1,50
Unsecured portions of Doubtful Assets	2,48
Loss Assets	1,39

You are required to make the necessary provision against advances.

(*v*) Provision is to be made for income-tax including surcharge @ 35%.

(*vi*) Transfer is to be made to Statutory Reserve @ 40% and to Revenue Reserve @ 20%.

(*vii*) The paid-up share capital of the bank is Rs. 1,00,00 thousand. Dividend is proposed @ 25%. There is no corporation dividend tax.

[*Provision against Advances Rs. 35,79 thousand; Net profit after tax, Rs. 1,32,36 thousand*]

8. The authorised capital of the Vishal Commercial Bank Limited is Rs. 3 crores divided into 3 lakh shares of Rs. 100 each. The following ledger balances of the bank as on 31st March, 2010 are given to you. You are required to prepare the bank's balances sheet as on 31st March, 2010 along with the relevant Schedules, taking into consideration the additional information also.

Names of ledger accounts	*Debit Balances (Rs. in '000)*	*Credit Balances (Rs. in '000)*
2 lakh shares of Rs. 100 each		2,00,00
Statutory reserve (on 1.4.09)		1,50,00
Profit and loss account (on 1.4.09)		65,00
Net profit for the year before appropriations		50,00
Demand deposits		18,60,65
Savings bank deposits		28,53,26
Term deposits		65,27,45
Government securities	32,36,65	
Other approved securities	14,48,39	
Debentures	3,10,18	
Borrowings from Reserve Bank of India		2,00
Premises at cost on 31.3.09	38,60	
Depreciation provision on premises till 31.3.10		23,60
Other fixed assets (including furniture and fixtures) at cost on 31.3.09	52,70	
Depreciation provision on other fixed assets till 31.3.10		31,20
Stationery and stamps	25,23	
Balances with Indian banks in current accounts	11,91	
Non-banking assets	10,00	
Cash in hand	85,99	
Balance with Reserve Bank of India in current account	15,20,00	
Interest accrued	2,40,10	80,20

Bills payable	2,85,01	
Money at call and short notice	52,00	
Gold	50,00	
Bills purchased and discounted	7,15,57	
Cash credits, overdrafts and loans repayable on demand	27,71,68	
Term loans	15,59,37	
	1,21,28,37	1,21,28,37

Additional Information :

(*i*) Advanced amounting to Rs. 40,01,83 thousand are secured by tangible assets those totalling Rs. 5,00,00 thousand are covered by bank/Government guarantees whereas the remaining advances are unsecured. Advances to the priority sector aggregate Rs. 15,75,07 thousand, those to public sector total Rs. 4,27,38 thousand whereas advances to the bank amount to Rs. 3,53 thousand.

(*ii*) The bank holds bills for collection amounting to Rs. 5,35,01 thousand.

(*iii*) Contingent Liabilities :

(*a*) Claims against the bank not acknowledged as debts, Rs. 2,50 thousand.

(*b*) Guarantees given on behalf of constituents in India, Rs. 5,68,42 thousand.

(*c*) Acceptances, endorsements and other obligations, Rs. 2,78,56 thousand.

(*d*) Disputed income-tax demand under appeal, Rs. 50,78 thousand.

[*Balance Sheet, Rs. 1,20,73,57 thousand; contingent liabilities, Rs. 9,00,35 thousand*]

9. The following is the trial balance extracted from the books of Bharat Bank. Prepare the Profit and Loss Account for the year ended 31st March, 2010 and Balance Sheet as on that date along with the necessary Schedules after taking into consideration the additional information also.

Trial Balance as on 31st March, 2010

	Rs. in '000
Credit Balances :	
Capital (Fully owned by Central Government)	4,00,00
Statutory Reserves	1,10,50
Revenue and other reserves	6,70
Interest/discount on advances/bills	6,39,10
Income on investments	4,91,26
Interest on balances with Reserve Bank of India and other inter-bank funds	54,84
Commission, exchange and brokerage	1,20,66
Profit on sale of investments	11,83
Profit on exchange transactions	10,16
Demand deposits from banks	10,32
Demand deposits from others	17,47,67
Savings bank deposits	20,25,52
Term deposits from banks	15,84
Term deposits from others	50,27,91
Borrowings from Reserve Bank of India	75,50
Borrowings from other banks	5,30
Borrowings from other institutions and agencies	22
Demand drafts and telegraphic transfers	1,31,89
Interest accrued	1,15,30

Bank	*26.69*
Depreciation on fixed assets to date	5,37
Depreciation on other fixed assets to date	52,30
	1,10,58,19
Debit Balances :	
Cash in hand	1,20,85
Balance in current account with RBI	10,22,50
Money at call and short notice with banks in India	10,13
Interest/discount on deposits	8,26,04
Interest on Reserve Bank of India/inter-bank borrowings	22,55
Investments in India in Government securities	27,76,60
Investments in India in other approved securities	10,40,39
Investments in India in debentures and bonds	2,10,73
Investments in Units of Unit Trust of India	26
Interest accrued	98,05
Tax paid in advance	42,25
Stationery and stamps	36
Premises, at cost as on 31st March, 2009	21,62
Other fixed assets (including furniture and fixtures), at cost as on 31st March, 2009	80,92
Payments to and provisions for employees	2,62,20
Rent, taxes and lighting	23,92
Insurance	25,36
Printing and stationery	8,10
Depreciation on bank's property	7,94
Advertisement and publicity	96
Directors' fees, allowances and expenses	2,11
Remuneration to Managing/Executive Director	2,01
Auditors' fees and expenses	1,32
Law charges	33
Postage, telephones, telegrams etc	4,55
Repairs and Maintenance	3,57
Other expenditure	16,89
Bills purchased and discounted	7,28,45
Cash credits, overdrafts and loans payable on demand.	24,49,41
Term loans	12,42,52
	1,10,58,19

Additional Information :

(*i*) Advances amounting to Rs. 37,42,32 thousand are secured by tangible assets, those totalling Rs. 5,82,64 thousand are covered by bank/Government guarantees while the remaining advances are unsecured.

(*ii*) All the advances are in India. Advances to priority sectors total Rs. 16,62,50 thousand, to public sector total Rs. 3,12,15 thousand and to banks total Rs. 40 thousand,

(*iii*) You are required to make a provision for income-tax including surcharge @ 35%.

(*iv*) 20 % of the profit is to be transfered to statutory reserve. The Directors proposed to pay a dividend @ 15% and transfer the balance in profit and loss account to revenue reserve.

(*v*) On 31st March, 2010 the following were the contingent liabilities of the bank :

(*a*) Guarantees given on behalf of constituents in India, Rs. 3,25,28 thousand,

(*b*) Acceptances, endorsements and other obligations, Rs. 2,98,76 thousand,.

(*vi*) The bills for collection held by the bank on 31st March, 2010 totalled Rs. 1,10,32 thousand.

[*Profit after tax, Rs. 78,00 thousand; Balance Sheet, Rs. 97,50,67 thousand.*]

Essay-type

1. How has banking been defined by the Banking Regulation Act, 1949 ?
2. In addition to the usual banking business, what business may be carried on by a banking company?
3. What do you mean by non-banking assets ? What is the period within which these assets have to be disposed of by a bank ?
4. What are the special points regarding Board of Directors of banks ?
5. What must be the minimum paid up capital and resources of a banking company incorporated outside India :-
   (*i*) if it has a place of business in Mumbai or Kolkata, or
   (*ii*) if the places of business are elsewhere ?
6. What must be the minimum paid up capital and resources of a banking company incorporated in India :—
   (*i*) If the places of business are in more than one state and if any place of business in Mumbai or Kolkata, or
   (*ii*) if the places of business are in more than one state and none of the places of business is in Mumbai or Kolkata, or
   (*iii*) if the places of business are only in one State and none of the places of business is in Mumbai or Kolkata, or
   (*iv*) if the places of business are only in one State and if the places of business are also in Mumbai or Kolkata ?
7. What are the special features of capital structure of a banking company ?
8. What are the restrictions imposed by the Banking Regulation Act, 1949 with regard to creation of a floating charge by a banking company on its property ?
9. How far is it correct to say that a banking company cannot pay dividends unless all its capitalised expenses have been completely written-off ?
10. What is Statutory Reserve created by a banking company ? What is the minimum profit which must be transferred to this reserve every year ?
11. What do you know about cash Reserves which have to be maintained by banking companies ? What are the minimum statutory limits of these reserves ?
12. What are the restrictions imposed on loans and advances granted by banking companies?
13. What are the purposes for which banking companies are allowed to form subsidiary companies ?
14. Enumerate the subsidiary books generally required to be maintained by a bank.
15. Name the chief registers and memorandum of books mostly kept by banks.
16. What is meant by 'rebate on bills discount' ? How is it calculated and treated in the books of account of a bank ?
17. Explain the following :-
   (*i*) Demand draft and Telegraphic Transfer, (*ii*) Letters of Credit.
18. What do you understand by Acceptances, Endorsements and other Obligations ?

19. What is the nature of 'Bills for Collection' ? Where does this item appear in the final accounts of a bank ?
20. Write a detailed note on Capital Adequacy Norms.
21. What do you mean by Non-performing Assets ? How is income accrued in respect of Non-performing Assets dealt with by banks ?
22. Define (*i*) Standard Assets, (*ii*) Sub-standard Assets, (*iii*) Doubtful Assets and (*iv*) Loss Assets. To what extent has provision to be made against them ?

27

ACCOUNTS OF ELECTRICITY COMPANIES
(Including Double Account System)

SYNOPSIS

1.	Legal Provisions	27.1		Contingencies Reserve	27.6
	Depreciation	27.1		Development Reserve	27.6
	Reasonable Return	27.2		General Reserve	27.6
	Clear Profit	27.2	2.	Final Accounts	27.7
	Disposal of Surplus	27.5	3.	Double Account System	27.32
	Tariffs and Dividends Control Reserve	27.6		Replacement of an asset	27.36

1. LEGAL PROVISIONS

Electricity is a public utility industry because ample supplies of electricity at low rates are of vital interest to industry and the general public. The special legislation governing electricity consists of the Indian Electricity Act of 1910 and the Electricity (Supply) Act of 1948. The financial provisions relating to electricity supply are contained in the Sixth Schedule to the 1948 Act. Now, The electricity Act, 2003 as amended in 2003 itself is applicable. The following are the chief provisions relating to accounts.

Depreciation :

Till 1st April, 1979, two methods of depreciation were recognised under para VI of the Sixth Schedule, the Compound Interest and the Straight Line Methods. Under the Compound Interest Method, such an amount as would, together with compound interest at the rate of 4% per annum, amount to 90% of the value of the asset concerned within the life of the asset, had to be set aside as depreciation every year. Under the Straight Line Method, the amount of depreciation is determined by dividing 90% of the cost of the asset by its life as laid down in the Seventh Schedule.

If the Compound Interest Method (really the Sinking Fund Method) was followed, every year interest at the rate of 4% per annum on the opening balance of the Depreciation Reserve had to be transferred from the Profit and Loss Account to the Depreciation Reserve Account. If the full amount could not be credited to this account in any year, the arrears had to be carried forward and charged as an appropriation in the future years, when practicable, after interest on unguaranteed bonds or stocks had been allowed. No dividends could be paid till arrears of depreciation remained.

Following amendment to the Electricity (Supply) Act in 1978, with effect from 1st April 1979, only the Straight Line Method (as stated above) is now allowed. The Central Government has been given the power to prescribe, by notification, the life of various types of assets and the method of depreciation.

No depreciation is to be written off when an asset has been written down to 10 per cent of its original cost. Also, when an asset ceases to be available for use due to obsolescence, inadequacy, superfluity or any other reason, no depreciation is to be written off. A description regarding non-availability for use is to be made in the books of the undertaking. When a fixed asset is discarded,

27

ACCOUNTS OF ELECTRICITY COMPANIES (Including Double Account System)

SYNOPSIS

1.	Legal Provisions	.. 27.1		Contingencies Reserve	.. 27.6
	Depreciation	.. 27.1		Development Reserve	.. 27.6
	Reasonable Return	.. 27.2		General Reserve	.. 27.6
	Clear Profit	.. 27.2	2.	Final Accounts	.. 27.7
	Disposal of Surplus	.. 27.3	3.	Double Account System	.. 27.32
	Tariffs and Dividends Control Reserve	.. 27.6		Replacement of an asset	.. 27.36

1. LEGAL PROVISIONS

Electricity is a public utility industry because ample supplies of electricity at low rates are of vital interest to industry and the general public. The special legislation governing electricity consists of the Indian Electricity Act of 1910 and the Electricity (Supply) Act of 1948. The financial provisions relating to electricity supply are contained in the Sixth Schedule to the 1948 Act. Now, The electricity Act, 2003 as amended in 2003 itself is applicable. The following are the chief provisions relating to accounts.

Depreciation :

Till 1st April, 1979, two methods of depreciation were recognised under para VI of the Sixth Schedule, the Compound Interest and the Straight Line Methods. Under the Compound Interest Method, such an amount as would, together with compound interest at the rate of 4% per annum, amount to 90% of the value of the asset concerned within the life of the asset, had to be set aside as depreciation every year. Under the Straight Line Method, the amount of depreciation is determined by dividing 90% of the cost of the asset by its life as laid down in the Seventh Schedule.

If the Compound Interest Method (really the Sinking Fund Method) was followed, every year interest at the rate of 4% per annum on the opening balance of the Depreciation Reserve had to be transferred from the Profit and Loss Account to the Depreciation Reserve Account. If the full amount could not be credited to this account in any year, the arrears had to be carried forward and charged as an appropriation in the future years, when practicable, after interest on unguaranteed bonds or stocks had been allowed. No dividends could be paid till arrears of depreciation remained.

Following amendment to the Electricity (Supply) Act in 1978, with effect from 1st April 1979 only the Straight Line Method (as stated above) is now allowed. The Central Government has been given the power to prescribe, by notification, the life of various types of assets and the method of depreciation.

No depreciation is to be written off when an asset has been written down to 10 per cent of its original cost. Also, when an asset ceases to be available for use due to obsolescence, inadequacy, superfluity or any other reason, no depreciation is to be written off. A description regarding non-availability for use is to be made in the books of the undertaking. When a fixed asset is discarded, the written down value of the asset is to be carried to a special account which may be called Discarded Assets Account. The account is to be credited with the value realised or expected to be realised by its sale (as scrap or otherwise). Any debit balance remaining in the account is to be charged to Contingencies Reserve. Thus, any profit or loss because of discarding of a fixed asset is to be charged to Contingencies Reserve.

Reasonable Return :

The law seeks to prevent an electricity undertaking from earning too high a profit. For this purpose, "reasonable return" has been defined as consisting of :—

(*a*) an yield at the standard rate, which is the Reserve Bank rate (10% w.e.f. 11th July, 1981) plus two per cent on the capital base as defined below;

(*b*) income derived from investments except investments made against Contingencies Reserve;

(*c*) an amount equal to ½ per cent on loans advanced by the Electricity Board;

(*d*) An amount equal to ½ on the amounts borrowed from organisations or institutions approved by the state government.

(*e*) an amount equal to ½ per cent on Debentures.

(*f*) an amount equal to ½ per cent on the balance of Development Reserve.

(*g*) such other amounts as may be allowed by the control government having regard to the pervading tax structure in the country.

"Capital Base" means :

(*a*) the original cost of fixed assets available for use and necessary for the purpose of the undertaking *less* contribution, if any, made by the consumers for construction of service lines and also amounts written off;

(*b*) the cost of intangible assets;

(*c*) the original cost of works in progress;

(*d*) the amount of investments made compulsorily against Contingencies Reserve together with the amount of such investments from contributions towards depreciation as in the opinion of the central Electricity Authority could not be utilised for the purpose of the business of electricity of the undertaking; and

(*e*) the monthly average of the stores, materials, supplies and cash and bank balances held at the end of each month,

Less :

(*i*) the amounts written off or set aside on account of depreciation of fixed assets and amounts written off in respect of intangible assets in the books of the undertaking;

(*ii*) loans advanced by the Board;

(*iii*) the amount of any loans borrowed from organisations or institutions approved by the state government,

(*iv*) Debentures;

(*v*) security deposits of consumers held in cash;

(*vi*) the amount standing to the credit of the Tariff and Dividends Control Reserve;

(*vii*) the amount set apart for the Development Reserve; and

(*viii*) the amount carried forward in the accounts of the licensee for distribution to consumers.

Clear Profit :

Clear Profit means the difference between the total income and the total expenditure plus specific appropriations. The Act defines the three terms—income, expenditure and appropriations. The provisions are set out below for ready understanding in the form of an account :—

Expenditure	*Rs.*	*Income*	*Rs.*
Cost of generation and purchase of energy		Gross receipts from sale of energy *less* discounts applicable to sale	
Cost of distribution and sale of energy		Rental of meters and other apparatus hired to consumers	
Rent, rates and taxes (excluding taxes on income or profits)		Sale and repair of lamps and apparatus	

	Rs.		*Rs.*
Interest on loans advanced by the Board		Rents, *less* outgoings not otherwise provided for	
Interest on Debentures		Transfer fees	
Interest on security deposits		Interest from investments, fixed and call deposits and bank balances	
Bad debts		Other receipts liable for Indian income-tax and arising from and ancillary or incidental to the business of electricity supply	
Auditors' fees			
Management expenses			
Depreciation			
Other expenses admissible under the Indian Income-tax Act and arising from and ancillary or incidental to the business of electricity supply			
Contribution to provident fund, staff pension, gratuity and apprentice and other training schemes			
Bonus paid to the employees of the undertaking in accordance with the decision of labour tribunal or the State Government			
Balance of profit c/d			
Appropriations		Balance of profit *b/d*	
Previous losses			
All taxes on income and profits			
Instalments in respect of intangible assets and expenses regarding issue of capital			
Contribution to Contingencies Reserve			
Arrears of depreciation			
Development Reserve			
Other appropriations permitted by the State Government			
Balance, being *Clear Profit*			

Disposal of surplus :

Should the clear profit exceed the reasonable return, the surplus has to be disposed of as under—

(*a*) One-third of the surplus not exceeding 5% of the reasonable return will be at the disposal of the undertaking;

(*b*) of the balance, one-half will be transferred to "Tariffs and Dividends Control Reserve"; and

(*c*) the balance will be distributed among consumers by way of reduction of rates or by way of special rebate.

An electricity undertaking must so adjust rates that the amount of clear profit in any year does not exceed the reasonable return by more than 20% of the reasonable return.

Illustration 1:

D Electricity Co. earned a profit of Rs. 26,98,500 after paying Rs. 1,40,000 @ 14% as debenture interest for the year ended March 31, 2010. The following further information is supplied to you :—

	Rs.
Fixed Assets	3,60,00,000
Depreciation written off	1,00,00,000
Loan from Electricity Board	80,00,000
Resere Fund Investments, at par, @ 10%	20,00,000
Contingencies Reserve Investments, at par, @ 10%	15,00,000
Tariff and Dividends Control Reserve	2,00,000
Security deposits of customers	3,00,000
Customers' contribution to assets	1,00,000
Preliminary Expenses	80,000
Monthly average of current assets, including amount due from customers, Rs. 5,00,000	15,20,000
Development Reserve	5,00,000

Show the disposal of profits mentioned above.

Assume bank rate to be 10%

Solution :

Reasonable Return :	Rs.
12% on Capital Base, Rs. 1,85,00,000	22,20,000
½ % on Loan from Electricity Board	40,000
½ % on Development Reserve	2,500
½ % on Debentures	5,000
Income from Reserve Fund investments	2,00,000
	24,67,500
Clear Profit :	26,98,500
Surplus : Rs. 26,98,500 *less* Rs. 24,67,500	2,31,000
Disposal :	
$^1/_3$ for the company being less than 5% of Reasonable Return	77,000
½ of the balance to be credited to Tariffs and Dividends Control Reserve	77,000
½ of the balance to be credited to customers	77,000
Total	2,31,000

The journal entry will be :

		Rs.	Rs.
Profit and Loss Account	Dr.	1,54,000	
To Tariffs and Dividends Control Reserve			77,000
To Benefit to Customers Account			77,000
(Amounts to be credited to the Tariffs and Dividends Control Reserve and to be refunded to consumers because of the excess of the clear profit over reasonable return).			

Capital Base :

	Rs.	Rs.
Fixed Assets *less* Depreciation		2,60,00,000
Preliminary Expenses		80,000
Average Current Assets (other than customers' debts)		10,20,000
Contingencies Reserve Investments		15,00,000
		2,86,00,000
Less :		
Loan from Electricity Board	80,00,000	
Debentures	10,00,000	
Tariffs and Dividends Control Reserve	2,00,000	
Security Deposits	3,00,000	
Customers' Contribution	1,00,000	
Development Reserve	5,00,000	
		1,01,00,000
		1,85,00,000

Illustration 2:

The following balances have been extracted from the books of an electricity company at the end of an accounting year :

	Rs.
Share capital	1,00,00,000
Reserve fund invested in 8% Government securities acquired at par	60,00,000
Contingencies reserve invested in 7% State Loan, at par	12,00,000
Loans from State Electricity Board	25,00,000
12% Debentures	20,00,000
Development reserve	8,00,000
Fixed Assets	2,50,00,000
Depreciation reserve on fixed assets	30,00,000
Consumers' deposits	40,00,000
Amount contributed by consumers towards cost Of fixed assets	2,00,000
Intangible assets	8,00,000
Tariffs and dividend control reserve	10,00,000
Current assets (monthly average)	15,00,000

In the accounting year, the Company earned a profit of Rs. 28,00,000 after tax.

Assuming that the bank rate is 10%, show how you will deal with the profits of the company.

Solution :

Calculation of Capital Base :

	Rs.	Rs.
Original cost of fixed assets	2,50,00,000	
Less : Amount contributed by the customers	2,00,000	2,48,00,000
Add : Cost of intangible assets		8,00,000
Investments against contingency reserve		12,00,000
Monthly average of current assets		15,00,000
Total (*i*)		2,83,00,000
Less : Amount written off on account of depreciation	30,00,000	
Loan from State Electricity Board	25,00,00	
12% Debentures	20,00,000	
Consumers' deposits	40,00,000	
Balance of development reserve	8,00,000	
Balan ce of tariffs and dividend control reserve	10,00,000	
Total (*ii*)		1,33,00,000
Capital Base (*i*) – (*ii*)		1,50,00,000

Calculation of Reasonable Return :

	Rs.
Yield at standard rate i.e. 10%+2% on capital base, 12% of Rs. 1,50,00,000	18,00,000
Add : Income from reserve fund investments, 8% of Rs. 60,00,000	4,80,000
½ % of loans from State Electricity Board, ½ % of Rs. 25,00,000	12,500
½ % of debentures, ½ % of Rs. 20,00,000	10,000
½ % of development reserve, ½ % of Rs. 20,00,000	4,000
Total	23,06,500

Disposal of surplus :

	Rs.
Profit after tax, given	28,00,000
Less : Reasonable return, as calculated above	23,06,500
Surplus	4,93,500
Less : 20% of reasonable return. 20 % of Rs. 23,06,500	4,61,300
Amount to be credited to customers rebate reserve	32,200

Allocation of surplus of Rs. 4,61,300 :

(*i*) 1/3rd of the surplus of the company subject to 5% of reasonable rate of return is at the disposal of the company.

1/3rd of Rs. 4,61,300 = Rs. 1,53,767

5% of Rs. 23,06,500 = Rs. 1,15,325

Being lower of the two, Rs. 1,15,325 is at the disposal of the company.

(*ii*) ½ of the balance is to be credited to Tariff and dividend control reserve

= ½ of Rs. [4,6,300 – 1,15,325] = Rs. 1,72,988

(*iii*) ½ of the balance is to be credited to customers rebate reserve i.e. Rs. 1,72,987

Final Distribution :

	Rs.
(*i*) Refunded to customers, Rs. 32,200 + Rs. 1,72,987	2,05,987
(*ii*) Transfer to tariff dividend control reserve, as ca	1,72,988
(*iii*) At the disposal of the company, Rs. 23,06,500 + Rs. 1,15,325	24,21,825
	28,00,000

Tariffs and Dividends Control Reserve :

This can be utilised whenever the clear profit is less than the reasonable return. The balance in the Reserve must be handed over to the purchaser of the undertaking, if it changes hands.

Contingencies Reserve :

A sum equal to not less than 1/4% and not more than 1/2% of the original cost of fixed assets must be transferred from the revenue account to Contingencies Reserves until it equals 5% of the original cost of fixed assets. The amount of the reserve must be kept invested in trust securities. The reserve can be utilised with the approval of the State Government for the following purposes:—

(*a*) to meet expenses or loss of profits arising out of accidents, strikes or circumstances beyond the control of the management;

(*b*) to meet expenses of replacement or removal of plant or works other than the expenses necessary for normal maintenance or renewal; and

(*c*) to pay compensation payable under law for which no other provision has been made.

Any loss or profit on sale of fixed asset has to be transferred to Contingencies Reserve.

Development Reserve :

An amount equal to income-tax and super tax (calculated at current rates) which would have been paid but for the development rebate allowed by income-tax authorities on installation of new plant and machinery, has to be transferred to the Development Reserve Account.

If, in any accounting year, the clear profit excluding the special appropriation together with the accumulations, if any, in the Tariff and Dividends Control Reserve *less* the amount to be credited to Development Reserve falls short of the reasonable return, the sum to be appropriated to the Development Reserve in respect of such accounting year may be reduced by the amount of the shortfall. Appropriations to the Development Reserve may be made over a period of five years.

Development Reserve can be invested only in the business of electricity supply of the undertaking.

On a transfer of the undertaking, the reserve should be transferred to the purchaser.

General Reserve :

Section 67 lays down that after interest and depreciation have been provided, a contribution to general reserve shall be made at the rate of not exceeding 1/2% of the original cost of the fixed assets until the total of such reserve comes to 8% of the original cost of the assets. This applies only to the Electricity Boards though there is nothing to stop electricity companies from building up reserves.

2. FINAL ACCOUNTS

The final accounts of an electricity company are made every year up to 31st March and submitted to the State Government in the forms prescribed in Annexures IV and V of the Indian Electricity Rules, 1956. These forms are given below. The student should particularly note statements no. III, IV, X and XI. Statements no. III and IV together constitute Revenue Account.

Note :— It should be noted that though the Companies Act permits preparation of the final accounts in the forms prescribed by the Electricity (Supply) Act, electricity companies usually present their final accounts to their shareholders in the form laid down by Schedule VI to the Companies Act. This is because the forms under the Companies Act are much more compact than those under the Electricity Supply Act. Returns to State Governments, however, must be in the forms laid down by the Electricity (Supply) Act.

ANNEXURE IV

Summary of Technical and Financial particulars for the year ended 31st *March,* 20 . . . . .

[*See Rule* 26(3)]

A. TECHNICAL

1. Year of working.
2. Area of supply in square miles.
3. Approximate population in the area of supply.
4. Installed capacity :
   (*a*) Generating plant (excluding retired plant).
      (*i*) Hydraulic — kW
      (*ii*) Steam — kW
      (*iii*) Internal combustion — kW
      Total — kW
   (*b*) Receiving Station.
      Transformers — kWA
5. Normal maximum demand on the system — kW
6. kWh generated :
   (*i*) Hydraulic — kWh
   (*ii*) Steam — kWh
   (*iii*) Internal combustion — kWh
   Total — kWh
7. kWh used for Generating Station Auxiliaries.
8. kWh purchased from other agencies.
9. kWh available for sale (6—7)+8.
10. kWh supplied free (if any) to officers and staff.
11. kWh supplied free (if any) to offices, canteen, etc.
12. kWh sold.
13. kWh unaccounted for [9—(10+11+12)].
   (*a*) (*i*) Coal and/or furnace oil consumed in tonnes.
      (*ii*) Average calorific value per kg. of coal and/or furnace oil consumed.
      (*iii*) Oil consumed in tonnes.
   (*b*) (*i*) Oil consumed in tonnes.
      (*ii*) Average calorific value per kg. of oil consumed.
      (*iii*) Average cost of oil per tonne.
15. Lubricating oil :
   (*a*) Quantity consumed (litres).
   (*b*) Average cost per litre.
16. Consumers : No. connected load kW.
   (*a*) Domestic or residential
   (*b*) Commercial.
   (*c*) Industrial.
      (*i*) Low and medium voltage.
      (*ii*) High and/or extra high voltage.
      Total

17. Segregation of kWh sold—
    (*i*) Domestic or residential :
        *(*a*) Lights and fans.
        (*b*) Heating and small power.
    (*ii*) Commercial :
        *(*a*) Light and Fans
        (*b*) Heating and small power.
    (*iii*) Industrial Power :
        (*a*) Low and Medium Voltage.
        (*b*) High Voltage.
    (*iv*) Public Lighting.
    (*v*) Traction.
    (*vi*) Irrigation.
    (*vii*) Public Water-works and Sewage Pumping.
    (*viii*) Supplies in bulk to Distributing Licensees.

B. FINANCIAL—

1. Share Capital (paid up).
2. Loan Capital (other than loans advanced by the State Electricity Board).
3. Licensee's Capital (1+2)
4. Total Capital Expenditure.
5. Capital Base [*Vide* Paragraph XVII (1) of the Sixth Schedule to the Electricity (Supply) Act, 1948].
6. Reasonable Return [*Vide* Paragraph XVII (9) of the Sixth Schedule to the Electricity (Supply) Act, 1948].
7. Clear Profit [*Vide* Paragraph XVII (2) of the Sixth Schedule to the Electricity (Supply) Act, 1948].
8. Maximum sum permissible for distribution to share - and debentureholders [*vide* Paragraph II (1) of the Sixth Schedule to the Electricity (Supply) Act 1948].
9. Actual sum available for Distribution to share - and debentureholders.
10. Item (9) expressed as a % of item (3).
11. Item (9) expressed as a % of item (4).
12. Item (9) expressed as a % of item (5).
13. Dividend declared for the year :—
    (*a*) On Ordinary Shares.
    (*b*) On Preference Shares.
14. Market Price of Shares.
    (*a*) Ordinary Shares.
    (*b*) Preference Shares.
15. Operating Revenues (*vide* Statement III - Annexure V).
16. Operating Expenses including depreciation (*vide* Statement IV—Annexure V).
17. Depreciation set apart for the year (*vide* Statement V—Annexure V).
18. Revenue per kWh sold (Overall) (Item 15/kWh sold).
19. Revenue per kWh sold :—
    (*i*) Domestic or residential :
        (*a*) Lights* and Fans.
        (*b*) Heating and small power
    (*ii*) Commercial :
        (*a*) Lights* and Fans.
        (*b*) Heating and small power.
    (*iii*) Industrial power :
        (*a*) Low and medium voltage.
        (*b*) High voltage.
    (*iv*) Public Lighting.
    (*v*) Traction.
    (*vi*) Irrigation.
    (*vii*) Public Water-works and Sewage Pumping.
    (*viii*) Supplies in bulk to Distributing Licensees.
20. Cost per kWh sold (overall) Item 16/kWh sold).

---

*Including unmetered supply.

ANNEXURE V

[*See section* 11 *and rule* 26 (3)]

ELECTRIC LICENCE, 20.....

Date of Commencement of Licence :

Name of Undertaking .... *Year of Operation* ....

No. I.—STATEMENT OF SHARE AND LOAN CAPITAL FOR THE YEAR ENDED 31ST MARCH, 20 ......

(*Applicable of Licensees other than Local Authority Licensees*)

Description of Capital	*Balance at the beginning of the year* Rs.	*Receipts during the year* Rs.	*Redeemed during the year* Rs.	*Balance at the end of the year* Rs.	*Remarks*
1	2	3	4	5	6
A—Share Capital :					
Authorised Capital					
.. Equity shares of Rs. each					
.. % Preference shares of Rs. each					
Issued Capital					
.. Equity shares of Rs. each					
.. % Preference shares of Rs. each					
Subscribed Capital					
.. Equity shares of Rs. each					
.. % Preference shares of Rs. each					
Called up Capital					
.. Equity shares of Rs. each					
.. % Preference shares of Rs. each					
ess calls in arrear.					
aid-up capital					
.. Equity shares of Rs. each					
.. % Preference shares of Rs. each					
TOTAL PAID UP CAPITAL					
B—Capital Reserve.					
Share Forfeiture Account.					
Securities Premium Account.					
Other items (to be specified)					
TOTAL CAPITAL RESERVE					
C—Loan Capital.					
Loan from State Electricity Board					
.. % Debenture of Rs........ each					
Other secured loans.					
Unsecured loans and advances.					
TOTAL LOAN CAPITAL					
D—Other Capital.					
Contributions from consumers including local authorities for service lines and public lighting after the commencement of the Electricity (Supply) Act, 1948.					
Special items (to be specified).					
TOTAL OTHER CAPITAL					
TOTAL CAPITAL RAISED AND APPROPRIATED (A + B + C + D).					

Note — Capital invested by proprietor, partnership, co-operative society, company, etc., licensee which is interest-bearing should be shown under 'C - Unsecured loans and advances' and that which are interest-free, should be shown under 'D - Special items (to be specified)'.

ANNEXURE

ELECTRIC LICENCE, 20 ....

DATE OF COMMENCEMENT OF LICENCE ....

Name of Local Authority .... *Year of Operation*..

No. I A (I). STATEMENT OF LOANS RAISED AND REDEEMED FOR THE YEAR ENDED 31ST MARCH, 20 ...

(Applicable to Local Authority Licensees)

Description of loans raised from time to time	*Amount sanctioned* Rs.	*Rate %*	*Period of Payment*		*Amount annual instalment* Rs.	*Amount of loan redeemed up to beginning of the year* Rs.	*Loan redeemed during the year* Rs.	*Total loan redemed up to the end of the year* Rs.	*Balance of loan out-standing at the end of the year* Rs.	*Remarks*
			From	*to*						
1	2	3	4	5	6	7	8	9	10	11
TOTAL LOANS RAISED FOR THE ELECTRIFICATION SCHEME										

No. I. (2) — STATEMENT OF LOAN AND OTHER CAPITAL FOR THE YEAR ENDED 31st MARCH, 20 . . . . . .

Particulars	*Balance at the beginning of the year* *Rs.*	*Received during the year* *Rs.*	*Redeemed during the year* *Rs.*	*Balance at the end of the year* *Rs.*	*Remarks*
1	2	3	4	5	6
A. *Capital Raised*					
Amount of loans outstanding [as per col. 10 of statement I. A (I)].					
Grants and advances made from the general funds of the local authority.					
Grants-in-aid from Government.					
TOTAL CAPITAL					
B. *Capital Reserve*					
Loan redemption account [as per col. 9 of statement I-A (I)].					
Other items (to be specified).					
TOTAL CAPITAL RESERVE					
C. *Other Capital*					
Consumers' contributions for service lines after the commencement of the Electricity (Supply) Act, 1948.					
Special items (to be specified).					
TOTAL OTHER CAPITAL					
TOTAL CAPITAL RAISED AND APPROPRIATED (A + B + C)					

No. II - STATEMENT OF CAPITAL EXPENDITURE FOR THE YEAR ENDED 31st MARCH, 20 . . . . .

Particulars	*Balance at the beginning of the year Rs.*	*Additions during the year Rs.*	*Retirements during the year vide Col. 3 statement II-A Rs.*	*Balance at the and of the year Rs.*	*Remarks*
1	2	3	4	5	6
A. Intangible Assets					
1. Preliminary and Promotional expenses.					
2. Cost of licence.					
3. Other expenses, *e.g.*, expenses incidental to conversion from D.C. to A.C., change of frequency, etc.					
TOTAL INTANGIBLE ASSETS					
B. Hydraulic Power Plant					
1. Land & Rights					
2. Buildings and civil engineering works containing generating plants and equipment.					
3. Hydraulic works forming part of a hydro-electric system including					
(*i*) dams, spillways, weirs, canals, reinforced concrete flumes and syphons,					
(*ii*) reinforced concrete pipe-lines and surge tanks, steel pipe-lines, sluice gates, steel surge tanks, hydraulic control valves and other hydraulic works.					
4. Water wheels, Generators and ancillary equipment including plant foundations.					
5. Switchgear including cable connections.					
6. Miscellaneous power plant equipment.					
7. Other civil works (to be specified).					
TOTAL HYDRAULIC POWER PLANT					
C. Steam Power Plant					
1. Land & Rights					
2. Buildings and civil engineering works containing generating plant.					
3. Boiler plant and equipment including plant foundations.					
4. Engines, Turbines, Generators and ancillary equipment including plant foundations.					
5. Water cooling system comprising cooling towers and circulating water systems.					

(Contd.)

1	2	3	4	5	6
6. Switchgear including cable connections.					
7. Miscellaneous power plant and equipment.					
8. Other civil works (to be specified).					
TOTAL STEAM POWER PLANT					
D. Internal Combustion Power Plant					
1. Land & Rights.					
2. Buildings and civil engineering works containing generating plant and equipment.					
3. Engines, Generators and ancillary equipment including plant foundations.					
4. Water cooling system comprising cooling towers and circulating water systems.					
5. Switchgear including cable connections.					
6. Miscellaneous power plant and equipment.					
7. Other civil works (to be specified).					
TOTAL INTERNAL COMBUSTION POWER PLANT					
E. Transmission Plant (High or Extra High Voltage)					
1. Land & Rights.					
2. Buildings and structures including civil engineering works containing transmission plant and equipment.					
3. Sub-station transformers, transformer kiosks, sub-station equipment and other fixed apparatus including plant foundations :					
(*i*) transformers including foundations having a rating of 100 kilovolt amperes and over.					
(*ii*) Others.					
4. Switchgear including cable connections.					
5. Towers, Poles, Fixtures, Overhead conductors and devices :					
(*i*) lines on steel or reinforced concrete supports operating at nominal voltages higher than 13.2 kilovolts.					
(*ii*) other lines on steel or reinforced concrete supports.					
(*iii*) lines on wood supports.					
6. (*i*) Underground cables and devices including joint boxes and disconnecting boxes.					
(*ii*) Cable duct system.					
TOTAL TRANSMISSION PLANT					

(Contd.)

1	2	3	4	5	6
F. Distribution Plant — High Voltage					
1. Land & Rights.					
2. Buildings and structures including civil engineering works containing distribution plant and equipment.					
3. (*i*) Sub-station transformers, transformer kiosks, sub-station equipment and other fixed apparatus including plant foundations.					
(*ii*) Others.					
4. Switchgear including cable connections.					
5. Towers, Poles, Fixtures, Overhead conductors and devices :					
(*i*) lines on steel or reinforced concrete supports operating at nominal voltages, higher than 13.2 kilovolts.					
(*ii*) other lines on steel or reinforced concrete supports.					
(*iii*) lines on wood supports.					
6. (*i*) Underground cables and devices including joint boxes and disconnecting boxes.					
(*ii*) Cable duct system.					
7. Service lines.					
8. Metering equipment.					
TOTAL DISTRIBUTION PLANT (H.V.)					
G. Distribution Plant — Medium and low voltage					
1. Land and Rights.					
2. Buildings and structures including civil engineering works containing distribution plant and equipment.					
3. Sub-section transformers, transformer kiosks, sub-station equipment and other fixed apparatus including plant foundation :					
(*i*) transformers including foundations having a rating of 100 kilovolt amperes and over.					
(*ii*) Others.					
4. Switchgear including cable connections.					
5. Towers, Poles, Fixtures, Overhead conductors and devices :					
(*i*) lines on steel or reinforced concrete supports.					
(*ii*) lines on wood supports.					
6. (*i*) Underground cables and devices including joint boxes and disconnecting boxes.					
(*ii*) Cable duct system.					

(Contd.)

1	2	3	4	5	6
7. Service lines.					
8. Metering equipment.					
TOTAL DISTRIBUTION (M. & L.V.)					
H. Public Lighting					
1. Street and signal lighting systems.					
I. General equipment (Not allocated to other sub-heads)					
1. Land and Rights.					
2. Buildings and structures.					
3. Office furniture and equipment.					
4. Transportation equipment.					
5. Laboratory and meter testing equipment.					
6. Workshop plant and equipment.					
7. Tools and work equipment.					
8. Communication equipment.					
9. Miscellaneous equipment.					
TOTAL GENERAL EQUIPMENT.					
TOTAL CAPITAL ASSETS IN USE.					

Notes : (1) Capital expenditure on items F 7 and G7 should include contributions made by consumers towards service line charges.

(2) Where it is not possible to give segregation of capital expenditure in respect of certain items and where high, medium or low voltage distribution lines are carried on same supports, the combined figures for such items may be given.

(3) Retirement during the year referred to in Col. 4 in respect of :

(*i*) intangible assets relate to amounts written off during the year.

(*ii*) tangible assets relate to the original cost of assets transferred to the special account, under Paragraph VII of the Sixth Schedule to the Electricity (Supply) Act, 1948.

No. II-A - STATEMENT SHOWING THE WRITTEN-DOWN COST OF FIXED ASSETS RETIRED ON ACCOUNT OF OBSOLESCENCE, INADEQUACY, SUPERFLUITY, ETC.

Particulars of the Assets	Written down cost of assets at the beginning of the year	Written down cost of assets retired during the year vide col. 4 St. II less column 8, Statement V	Written down cost of assets sold during the year	Amount realised during the year	Excess of sale proceeds over written down cost transferred to "Contingencies Reserve" Account vide col. 4 of Statement VI	Annual instalement written-off during the year vide col. 7 Statement VI	Balance of written-down cost at the end of the year
	Rs.	Rs.	Rs.	Rs.	Rs.	Rs.	Rs.
1	2	3	4	5	6	7	8

No. III - STATEMENT OF OPERATING REVENUE FOR THE YEAR ENDED 31st MARCH 20...

Particulars of revenue	*Corresponding amount for the previous year of account* Rs.	*Amount for the year of account* Rs.	*Remarks* Rs.
1	2	3	4
A—NET REVENUE BY SALE OF ELECTRICITY FOR CASH & CREDIT			
1. *Domestic and residential*			
(*a*) Lights and Fans.			
(*b*) Heating and small power.			
2. *Commercial.*			
(*a*) Lights and Fans.			
(*b*) Heating and small power.			
3. *Industrial.*			
(*a*) Low and Medium voltage			
(*b*) High voltage.			
4. Public Lighting.			
5. Public Water-Works and Sewage pumping.			
6. Irrigation.			
7. Traction.			
8. Supplies in bulk to distributing licensees.			
Total Revenue by sale of electricity.			
B—MISCELLANEOUS REVENUE FROM CONSUMERS			
1. *Rent from*			
(*a*) Meters.			
(*b*) Electric motors, fittings, appliances and other apparatus hired to consumers.			
2. Service connection fees.			
3. Public Lighting Maintenance.			
Total Miscellaneous Revenue from consumers.			
C—OTHER REVENUES.			
1. Sale of Stores.			
2. Repair of lamps and apparatus.			
3. Commission for the collection of electricity duty.			
4. Other miscellaneous item (to be specified).			
Total Other Revenue.			
TOTAL OPERATING REVENUES			
Deduct			
Total Operating Expenses are per St. IV			
Net surplus or deficit carried to the Net Revenue and Appropriations Account—St. X.			

NO. IV - STATEMENT OF OPERATING EXPENSES FOR THE YEAR ENDED 31ST MARCH, 20 ....

Particulars of expenses	Corresponding amount for the previous year of account Rs.	Amount for the year of account Rs.	Remarks Rs.
1	2	3	4
A. HYDRAULIC POWER GENERATION.			
(a) Operation.			
1. Water for power.			
2. Lubricants and other consumable stores.			
3. Station supplies and miscellaneous expenses.			
4. Proportion of salaries, allowances, gratuities, etc., of Engineers, Superintendents, Officers, supervisory and other staff.			
5. Wages and gratuities to labour.			
6. Contributions to Provident Fund or Staff Pension.			
Total Operation			
(b) Maintenance.			
1. Salaries for supervisory staff.			
2. Buildings and civil engineering works containing generating plant and equipment.			
3. Hydraulic works forming part of a hydro-electric system, including—			
(i) dams, spillways, weirs, canals, reinforced concrete flumes and syphons.			
(ii) reinforced concrete pipe-lines, and surge tanks, steel pipelines, sluice gates, steel surge tanks, hydraulic control valves and other hydraulic works.			
4. Water wheels, generators and ancillary equipment including plant foundations.			
5. Switchgear including cable connections.			
6. Miscellaneous power plant equipment.			
7. Other civil works (to be specified).			
8. Contributions to Provident Fund or staff pensions.			
Total Maintenance			
(c) Depreciation.			
Depreciation on Hydraulic Power Generating plant and Equipment (from Statement V).			
TOTAL HYDRAULIC POWER GENERATION			
B. STEAM POWER GENERATION			
(a) Operation			
1. Fuel (excluding sale proceeds of steam, ashes, etc.)			

(Contd.)

1	2	3	4
2. Lubricants and other consumable stores.			
3. Water (if purchased separately).			
4. Station supplies and miscellaneous expenses.			
5. Proportion of salaries, allowances, gratuities, etc., of Engineers, Superintendents, Officers, supervisory and other staff.			
6. Wages and gratuities to labour.			
7. Contributions to Provident Fund or staff pension.			
Total Operation			
(*b*) *Maintenance*			
1. Salaries for supervisory staff.			
2. Building and civil engineering works containing generating plant and equipment.			
3. Boiler plant and equipment including plant foundations.			
4. Engines, turbines, generators and ancillary equipment including plant foundations.			
5. Water cooling system comprising cooling towers and circulating water systems.			
6. Switchgear including cable connections.			
7. Miscellaneous power plant and equipment.			
8. Other Civil works (to be specified).			
9. Contribution to Provident Fund or staff pensions.			
Total Maintenance			
(*c*) *Depreciation*			
Depreciation on Steam Power Generating Plant and Equipment (from Statement V)			
TOTAL STEAM POWER GENERATION EXPENSES			
C. INTERNAL COMBUSTION POWER GENERATION			
(*a*) *Operation*			
1. Fuel.			
2. Lubricants and other consumable stores.			
3. Water (if purchased separately).			
4. Station supplies and miscellaneous expenses.			
5. Proportion of salaries, allowances, gratuities, etc. of Engineers, Superintendents, Officers, supervisory and other staff.			
6. Wages and gratuities to labour.			
7. Contributions to Provident Fund or staff pensions.			
Total Operation			
(*b*) *Maintenance*			
1. Salaries for supervisory staff.			

(Contd.)

1	2	3	4
2. Buildings and civil engineering works containing generating plant and equipment.			
3. Engines, generators and ancillary equipment, including plant foundations.			
4. Water cooling system comprising cooling towers and circulating water systems.			
5. Switchgear including cable connections.			
6. Miscellaneous power plant and equipment.			
7. Other civil works (to be specified).			
8. Contributions to Provident Fund or Staff Pension.			
Total Maintenance			
(c) *Depreciation*			
Depreciation on Internal Combustion Power Generating Plant and Equipment (from Statement V).			
TOTAL INTERNAL COMBUSTION POWER GENERATION EXPENSES			
D. POWER PURCHASED ;			
TOTAL PRODUCTION EXPENSES (A + B + C + D)			
E. TRANSMISSION (HIGH OR EXTRA HIGH VOLTAGE)			
(a) *Operation and Maintenance*			
1. Proportion of salaries, allowances, gratuities, etc., of Engineers, Superintendents, Officers, supervisory and other staff.			
2. Wages and gratuities to sub-station labour.			
3. Wages and gratuities to labour on lines.			
4. Buildings and structures including civil engineering works containing transmission plant and equipment.			
5. Sub-station transformer, transformer kiosks, sub-station equipment and other fixed apparatus including plant foundations.			
(i) Trasformers including foundations having a rating of 100 kilovolt-amperes and over.			
(ii) Others.			
6. Switchgear including cable connections.			
7. Towers, Poles, Fixtures, Overhead conductors and devices.			
(i) lines on steel or reinforced concrete supports operating at nominal voltages higher than 13.2 kilovolts.			
(ii) other lines on steel or reinforced concrete supports.			
(iii) lines on wood supports.			
8. (i) Underground cable and devices, joint boxes and disconnecting boxes.			
(ii) Cable duct system.			
9. Contributions to Provident Fund or staff pensions.			
(b) *Depreciation on Transmission Plant & Equipment (from Statement V).*			
Total Transmission Expenses			

(Contd.)

ACCOUNTS OF ELECTRICITY COMPANIES

1	2	3	4
F. DISTRIBUTION (HIGH VOLTAGE)			
(*a*) *Operation and Maintenance*			
1. Proportion of salaries, allowances, gratuities, etc., of Engineers, Superintendents, Officers, supervisory and other staff.			
2. Wages & gratuities to sub-station labour.			
3. Wages & gratuities to labour for mains.			
4. Buildings and structures including civil engineering works containing distribution plant and equipment.			
5. Sub-station transformers, transformer kiosks, sub-station equipment and other fixed apparatus including foundations.			
(*i*) transformers including foundations having a rating of 100 kilovolt amperes and over.			
(*ii*) Others.			
6. Switchgear including cable connections.			
7. Towers, Poles, Fixtures, Overhead conductors and devices :			
(*i*) lines on steel or reinforced concrete supports operating at nominal voltages, higher than 13.2 kilovolts.			
(*ii*) other lines on steel or reinforced concrete supports.			
(*iii*) Lines on wood supports.			
8. (*i*) Underground cables and devices including joint boxes and disconnecting boxes.			
(*ii*) Cable duct system.			
9. Service lines.			
10. Metering Equipment.			
11. Contributions to Provident Fund or Staff Pension.			
(*b*) *Depreciation on Distribution Plant and Equipment (from Statement V).*			
Total Distribution (H.V.) expenses.			
G. DISTRIBUTION (MEDIUM AND LOW VOLTAGE)			
(*a*) *Operation and Maintenance.*			
1. Proportion of salaries, allowances, gratuities, etc., of Engineers, Superintendents, Officers, supervisory & other staff.			
2. Wages & Gratuities to labour.			
3. Buildings & structures including civil engineering works containing transmission plant and equipment.			
4. Sub-station transformers, transformer kiosks, sub-station equipment and other fixed apparatus including plant foundations.			
(*i*) transformers including foundations rating of 100 kilovolt amperes and over.			
(*ii*) others.			
5. Switchgear including cable connections.			
6. Towers, Poles, Fixtures, Overhead conductors and devices :			

(*Contd.*)

ADVANCED ACCOUNTS

1	2	3	4
(*i*) lines on steel or reinforced concrete supports operating at nominal voltages, higher than 13.2 kilovolts.			
(*ii*) lines on steel or reinforced concrete supports.			
(*iii*) lines on wood supports.			
7. (*i*) Underground cables and devices including joint boxes and disconnecting boxes.			
(*ii*) Cable duct system.			
8. Service lines.			
9. Metering Equipment.			
10. Contributions to Provident Fund or Staff Pension.			
(*b*) *Depreciation on Distribution Plant and Equipment (from Statement V)*			
Total Distribution (M. & L. V. Expenses)			
H. PUBLIC LIGHTING			
(*a*) *Operation and Maintenance.*			
1. Operation & Maintenance.			
2. Renewal of lamps.			
(*b*) *Depreciation on P.L. system & equipment (from Statement V).*			
Total Public Lighting Expenses.			
I. CONSUMERS' SERVICING, METER READING, BILLING, CONNECTING, ACCOUNTING, SALES PROMOTING, ETC.			
1. Proportion of salaries, allowances, gratuities etc., of Engineers, Secretary, Accountants, other officers, etc.			
2. Meter reading and inspection.			
3. Billing, Collecting and Accounting.			
4. Exhibitions, Demonstrations and Advertisements.			
5. Merchandising, servicing and contract works.			
6. Miscellaneous expenses.			
7. Contributions to Provident Fund or Staff Pensions.			
8. Depreciation on general assets and equipment, which are not allocated to other sub-heads (from Statement V).			
Total Consumers' Servicing, Meter-reading, etc.			
K. GENERAL ESTABLISHMENT CHARGES			
1. Proportion of salaries, allowances, gratuities, etc., of general officers, executives, etc.			
2. Salaries, wages, gratuities, etc., of general office staff.			
3. Contributions to local authority administration for supervision (applicable to local authority licensee only).			
4. Travelling and other expenses of officers and staff.			

(*Contd.*)

ACCOUNTS OF ELECTRICITY COMPANIES

1	2	3	4
5. Rents and Wayleaves.			
6. Rates and Taxes.			
7. General Office expenses and showroom maintenance and supplies.			
8. Repairs to office buildings, staff quarters, furniture and fixtures, office equipment, etc., and maintenance.			
9. Depreciation on office and general buildings, furniture, etc., not allocated to other sub-heads, from Statement V.			
10. Audit services :			
(*a*) Auditor of company.			
(*b*) Auditor appointed under the provisions of the Act.			
11. Legal services.			
12. Insurance expenses.			
13. Contributions to Provident Fund or Staff Pensions.			
Total General Establishment Charges.			
L. OTHER CHARGES			
1. Interest paid and accrued on :			
(*a*) Loans advanced by State Electricity Board.			
(*b*) Depreciation Fund.			
(*c*) Consumers' security deposits.			
2. Bad Debts written off.			
3. Other items (to be specified).			
Total Other Charges			
M. MANAGEMENT EXPENSES			
1. Directors' fees and expenses and Debentures Trustees fees, if any.			
2. Managing Agents' ordinary remuneration.			
3. Managing Agents' office allowances.			
Total Management expenses.			
TOTAL OPERATING EXPENSES TRANSFERRED TO STATEMENT III.			

Notes : (1) No apportionment of expenses under sub-head 'M' be made to any of the salary items under A-(a)4, B-(a)5, C-(a)5, E(a)1, F-(a)1, G(a)1, J-1 and K-1 which shall include the proportion of salaries and allowances of persons solely employed for the purpose of the undertaking and of the engineering staff employed by the Managing Agents under the provision of sub-para (3) of Para XIII of the Sixth Schedule to the Electricity (Supply) Act 1948.

(2) Managing Agents in this context refer to the Managing Agents appointed under the Companies Act, 1956. (N.B. There can be no managing agents now.)

NO. V — STATEMENT OF PROVISION FOR DEPRECIATION FOR THE YEAR ENDED 31ST MARCH, 20 ....

Description of assets in Groups as per Statement II	Balance of accured depreciation brought forward from last account	Balance of arreas of depreciation brought forward from last account	Additions during the year				Withdrawals during the year vide column 5 statement II A	Balance of accured depreciation carried over to next account	Balance of arrears of depreciation carried over to next account	Remarks
			Interest @ 4% per annum on the balance at the beginning of the year under paragraph VI (I) of the Sixth Schedule to the Electricity (Supply) Act, 1948	Depreciation provided for the year	Arrears of drepciation written off during the year	Total				
	Rs.	Rs.	Rs.	Rs.	Rs.	Rs.	Rs.	Rs.	Rs.	Rs.
1	2	3	4	5	6	7	8	9	10	11
A. Hydraulic Power Plant										
B. Steam Power Plant										
C. Internal Combusion Power Plant										
D. Transmission Plant High or, Extra High Voltage										
E. Distribution Plant-High Voltage										
F. Distribution Plant-Medium and Low Voltage										
G. Public Lighting										
H. General Equipment										
Total										

Notes : (1) Withdrawals from the depreication account are permissible only to the extent of past provisions made in respect of assets withdrawn from use and transferred during the year to the special account under paragraph VII of the Sixth Schedule to the Electricity (Supply) Act, 1948.

(2) A Sum of Rs. .... from the accruals in the depreciation account has been invested in securities in pursuance of the provisions of Paragraph XVII (1) (*d*) of the Sixth Schedule to E (S) Act, 1948.

No. VI — STATEMENT OF CONTINGENCIES RESERVE FOR THE YEAR ENDED 31ST MARCH, 20 .....

Particulars	Balance at the begining of the year	Additions during the year			Withdrawals during the year			Balance at the end of the year	Remarks
		Appropriations during the year	*Additions under paragraph IX of the Sixth Schedule of the Elec. (Supply) Act, 1948 vide Col. 6, statement II-A*	*Total*	*Instalment under sub-para (3) of paragraph VII of the Sixth Schedule to the Elec. (Supply) Act. 1948 vide Col. 7 Statement II-A*	*Expenses and/or compensation under paragraph V of the Sixth Schedule to the Elec. (Supply) Act, 1948*	*Total*		
	Rs.	Rs.	Rs.	Rs.	Rs.	Rs.	Rs.	Rs.	Rs.
1	2	3	4	5	6	7	8	9	10

Note — A sum of Rs. ..... from the balance of the Contingencies Reserve has been invested under the Provisions of paragraph IV (2) of the Sixth Schedule to the Electricity (Supply) Act, 1948.

STATEMENT OF DEVELOPMENT RESERVE ACCOUNT FOR THE YEAR ENDED 31ST MARCH, 20 ....

No. VII — STATEMENT OF TARIFFS AND DIVIDENDS CONTROL RESERVE ACCOUNT FOR THE YEAR ENDED 31ST MARCH, 20 ...

Particulars	*Balance at the beginning of the year* Rs.	*Appropriated during the year* Rs.	*Withdrawn during the year (Part6iculars to the indicated in the Remarks column)* Rs.	*Balance at the end of the year* Rs.	*Remarks* Rs.
1	2	3	4	5	6

No. VIII — STATEMENT OF CONSUMERS' REBATE RESERVE ACCOUNT FOR THE YEAR ENDED 31st MARCH, 20 ...

Particulars	*Balance at the beginning of the year* *Rs.*	*Distributed to consumers during the year under paragraph II(I) of the Sixth Schedule to the E (S) Act, 1948* *Rs.*	*Appropriated during the year* *Rs.*	*Balance at the end of the year* *Rs.*	*Remarks* *Rs.*
1	2	3	4	5	6

No. IX — STATEMENT OF SPECIAL APPROPRIATIONS PERMITED BY STATE GOVERNMENT

Particulars (giving reference to the sanction of the State Govt. permitting the appropriation)	*Balance at the beginning of the year* *Rs.*	*Additions by way of appropriation during the year* *Rs.*	*Transfer by way of reappropriation during the year, details to be given in the remarks column* *Rs.*	*Balance at the end of the year* *Rs.*	*Remarks* *Rs.*
1	2	3	4	5	6

No. X — STATEMENT OF NET REVENUE AND APPROPRIATION ACCOUNT FOR THE YEAR ENDED 31st MARCH, 20 ......

Corresponding figures of previous year *Rs.*	*Particulars*	*Amount* *Rs.*	*Corresponding figures of previous year* *Rs.*	*Particulars*	*Amount* *Rs.*
1	2	3	4	5	6
	1. To Balance of loss brought forward from last account.			1. By Balance of profit brought forward from last account	
	2. To Net Operating deficit as per Statement III.			2. By net operating surplus as per Statement III.	
	3. To Appropriations (applicable to Local Authority Licensee only):—			3. By Interest on securities and investment.	
	(*a*) Interest on loan capital.			4. By Other receipts (non-operating), *e.g.*, rents, (*Less* outgoings not otherwise provided, transfer fee, etc., to be specified).	
	(*b*) Instalment of redemption of loan capital as per col. 8 of St. I-A(I).			5. By Balance of loss carried over.	
	(*c*) General rates.				
	4. To Taxes on income and profits paid.				
	5. To Instalments write-down in respect of intangible assets.				
	6. To Instalment of contribution towards arrears of depreciation, as per Statement V—Column 6.				
	7. To Contribution towards Contingencies Reserve as per Statement VI—Column 3.				
	8. To Appropriation to Tariffs and Dividends Control Reserve, as per Statement VII—Column 3.				
	9. To Appropriation to Consumers Rebate Reserve, as per Statement VIII—Column 4.				
	10. To Other special appropriation permitted by the State Government, as per Statement IX—Column 3.				
	11. To Appropriation towards interest paid and accrued and dividends paid and payable:-				
	(*a*) Interest on debentures.				
	(*b*) Interest on other secured loans.				
	(*c*) Interest on unsecured loans, advances, deposits, bank overdrafts, etc.				
	(*d*) Dividends on preference share capital.				
	(*e*) Dividends on ordinary share capital.				
	To Balance of profit carried over.				

No. XI — GENERAL BALANCE SHEET AS ON 31st MARCH, 20 ....

Corresponding figures of previous year *Rs.*	*Particulars*	*Amount* *Rs.*	*Corresponding figures of previous year* *Rs.*	*Particulars*	*Amount* *Rs.*
1	2	3	4	5	6
	1. Capital raised and appropriated–*vide* Statement I or IA			1. Capital amount expended on Works in Use—Statement II. *Less*—Accumulated provisions for depreciation—Statement V.	
	Reserve and Surplus			*Net Block*	
	2. Non-statutory Reserve			2. Balance of written down cost of obsolete, inadequate, etc., assets—Statement II-A.	
	3. Contingencies Reserve Fund as per Statement VI.			*Current Assets*	
	4. Tariffs & Dividends Control Reserve as per Statement VII.			3. Capital works in progress.	
	5. Consumers' Rebate Reserve as per Statement VIII.		4.	Stores and materials in hand — (*a*) Fuel — Coal and/or oil, etc., at cost. (*b*) General Stores at or below cost.	
	6. Special appropriations (as permitted by the State Govt.) as per Statem,ent IX.			5. Debtors for amounts paid in advance on account of contracts.	
	7. Balance of Net Revenue and Appropriations Account as per Statement X.			6. Sundry debtors for electricity supplied.	
	Current Liabilities and Provisions			7. Other debtors (as per schedule attached).	
	8. Balances due on construction of Plant, Machinery, etc.		8.	Accounts receivable (to be specified). 9. Investments in statutory securities at cost. (*a*) Contingencies Reserve Fund investment (Market value on closing date).	
	9. Creditors on open accounts (as per schedule attached).			(*b*) Depreciation Reserve Fund investment (Market value on closing date). (*c*) Other investments, (Market value on closing date).	
	10. Consumers' security deposits.			10. Special deposits. (*a*) In respect of taxation. (*b*) Others (to be specified).	
	11. Accounts payable (to be specified).			11. Balance at Bank : (*a*) Deposit Account. (*b*) Current account and at Call.	
	12. Temporary accommodations, Bank over-draft and other finances.			12. Cash in hand.	
	13. Other accrued liabilities (to be specified).			*Debit Balances*	
	14. Contingent liabilities and outstanding commitments, if any, to be stated on the faceof this balance sheets.			13. Net Revenue and Appropriations Account: Balance at debit thereof—Statement X.	

Illustration 3:

The following balances were extracted from the books of the Urban Electric Supply Company Ltd., as on 31st March, 2010. Prepare a revenue and appropriation account and balance sheet in the form prescribed under the Electricity Supply Act :—

	Rs.
Power purchased	2,83,397
Distribution Expenses	46,658
Rates and Taxes	15
General Establishment Charges	30,407
Management Expenses	17,730
Sales of Electricity	4,19,434
Meter Rent, Reconnection Fee, etc.	27,546
Depreciation	18,758
Income-tax	18,244
Repairs and Maintenance of Buildings	526
Contribution towards Contingencies Reserve	3,143
Interest paid and accrued	6,089
Plant and Machinery	5,59,968
Public Lighting	81,665
General Equipment	15,367
Capital—paid up	3,55,000
Bill Payable	896
Sundry Creditors—consumers	2,636
Sundry Creditors—others	119
Consumers' Security Deposit	1,87,566
Depreciation Reserve—balance as on 1.4.2009	1,28,785
Contingencies Reserve—balance as on 1.4.2009	6,902
Services advance	7,957
Unpaid wages	18
Income-tax Reserve	18,244
Interest payable	11,905
Stores in hand	48,852
Sundry Debtors for supply of electricity	39,219
Advances to staff	10,045
Cash at Bank	7,334
Cash in hand	1,492

[*Adapted from C.A.* (*Final*)]

Solution :

STATEMENT NO. 1

Statement of Share and Loan Capital for the year ended 31st March. 2010

Description of Capital	*Balance at the beginning of the year Rs.*	*Receipts during the year Rs.*	*Redeemed during the year Rs.*	*Balance at the end of the year Rs.*	*Remarks*
A — Share Capital Authorised Capital Issued Capital Subscribed Capital Called up Capital	?	?	?	?	?
..Shares of Rs...each	3,55,000	..	..	3,55,000	-
Total Paid up Capital	3,55,000			3,55,000	
B — Capital Reserve	—	—	—	—	—
C — Loan Capital	—	—	—	—	—
D — Contributions from consumers including local authorities for service lines, public lighting	—	—	—	—	—
Total Capital Raised	3,55,000			3,55,000	

STATEMENT NO. II

Statement of Capital Expenditure for the year ended 31st March, 2010

Particulars	*Balance at the beginning of the year Rs.*	*Additions during the year Rs.*	*Retirements during the year Rs.*	*Balance at the end of the year Rs.*	*Remarks*
A — Intangible Assets	—	—	—	—	—
B — Hydraulic Power Plant					
C — Steam Power Plant					
D — Internal Combustion Power Plant					
E — Transmission Plant— (High or Extra High Voltage)	5,59,968	—	—	5,59,968	—
F — Distribution Plant— (High Voltage)					
G — Distribution Plant (Medium & Low Voltage)					
H — Public Lighting	81,665	—	—	81,665	—
I — General Equipment	15,367	—	—	15,367	—
Total Capital	6,57,000	—	—	6,57,000	—

STATEMENT NO. III

Statement of Operating Revenue for the year ended 31st March, 2010

Particulars of Revenue	*Corresponding amount for the previous year of account Rs.*	*Amount for the year of account Rs.*	*Remarks*
A—Net Revenue by State of electricity for cash and credit			
1. Domestic and residential			
2. Commercial			
3. Industrial	?	4,19,434	—
4. Public Lighting			
5. Public Water Works & Sewage Pumping			
6. Irrigation			
7. Traction			
8. Supplies in Bulk			
B—Miscellaneous Revenue from consumers—Rentals from meters and Reconnection fees	?	27,546	
C—Other Revenues	?	—	—
Total Operating Revenues	?	4,46,980	—
Deduct Total Operating Expenses as per Statement IV	?	4,03,580	—
Net Surplus carried to Net Revenue and Appropriation Account (Statement No. X)	?	43,400	—

STATEMENT NO. IV

Statement of Operating Expenses for the year ended 31st March, 2010

Particulars of Revenue	*Corresponding amount for the previous year of account* *Rs.*	*Amount for the year of account* *Rs.*	*Remarks*
A—Hydraulic Power Generation	—	—	—
B—Steam Power Generation	—	—	—
C—Internal Combustion Power Generation	—	—	—
D—Power Purchased	?	2,83,397	—
Total Production Expenses (A + B + C + D)	?	2,83,397	—
E—Transmission (High or extra High Voltage)	—	—	—
F—Distribution—High Voltage			
F—Distribution—Medium or Low Voltage	?	46,658	—
Depreciation*	?	18,758*	—
Total Distributions	?	65,416	—
H—Public Lighting	—	—	—
I—Consumers Servicing, etc.	—	—	—
K—General Establishment charges	?	30,407	—
L—Other Charges—			
Interest Paid	—	6,089	—
Repairs & Maintenance of Buildings	—	526	—
Rates and Taxes	—	15	—
Total and other Charges		6,630	
M—Management Expenses	—	17,730	—
Total Operating Expenses	—	—	—
Transferred to Statement III	—	4,03,580	—

STATEMENT NO. X

Net Revenue and Appropriation Account for the year ended 31st March, 2010

Corresponding figures of previous year *Rs.*	*Particulars*	*Amount* *Rs.*	*Corresponding figures of previous year* *Rs.*	*Particulars*	*Amount* *Rs.*
?	To Taxes on Income and Profit	18,244	?	By Balance of profit brought forward from last account	—
?	To Contribution towards Contingencies Reserve	3,143	?	By Net Operating Surplus as per Statement III	43,400
	To Profit being clear profit	22,013			
?		43,400	?		43,400

STATEMENT NO. XI

General Balance Sheet of the Urban Electric Supply Co. Ltd. as on March 31st. 2010

Figures for the previous year *Rs.*	*Liabilities*	*Amount* *Rs.*	*Figures for the previous year* *Rs.*	*Assets*	*Amount* *Rs.*
?	Capital raised and appropriated *vide* Statement No. 1	3,55,000		Capital amount expended on works in use (Statement II) *Rs.* 6,57,000	
	Reserves of Surplus:			*Less*: Accumulated provision for depreciation 1,47,543	5,09,457
	Contingencies Reserve : *Rs.* Balance on 1st April, 2000 6,902 Addition during the year 3,143	10,045		**Current Assets:**	
				Stores in hand	48,852
	Net Revenue Appropriation A/c	22,013		Sundry Debtors for Supply of Electricity	39,219
				Advances to staff	10,045
	Current Liabilities and Provisions:			Cash in hand	1,492
				Cash at Bank	7,334
	Consumers' Security Deposits	1,87,566			
	Interest Payable	11,905			
	Bills payable	896			
	Provisions for taxation	18,244			
	Sundry Creditors—Consumers	2,636			
	Sundry Creditors: Others	119			
	Unpaid Wages	18			
	Service Advance	7,957			
		6,16,399			6,16,399

3. DOUBLE ACCOUNT SYSTEM

Public utility concerns in England were previously required to prepare their accounts under the Double Account System. The Double Account System is merely a way of presentation of final accounts. It should not be confused with the Double Entry System which is the basis of maintaining books of account. Up to the preparation of the trial balance, there is no difference between the Double Account System and the ordinary system. Only when it comes to preparation of the Balance Sheet and the Revenue Account that there is a difference. The chief features of the Double Account System are as follows :—

1. The ordinary balance sheet is split up in two parts. One part contains fixed assets and fixed liabilities. It is called "Receipt and Expenditure on Capital Account." On each side there are three columns for amount—one column to show figures up to the beginning of the year, the second column to show expenditure (assets) or receipts (liabilities) during the year and the third column to show total.

The other part (called General Balance Sheet) contains other assets and liabilities and the balance of the Receipts and Expenditure on Capital Account. In case of electricity companies, however, the total of the expenditure as per Capital Account is shown on the assets side and the total of receipts is shown on the liabilities side.

Receipts and Expenditure on Capital Account
For the year ending 31st March, 20 ......

Dr. *Cr.*

Expenditure	*Expenditure up to end of previous year* Rs.	*Expended during the year* Rs.	*Total Expenditure* Rs.	*Receipts*	*Receipts up to end of* Rs.	*Receipts* Rs.	*Total* Rs.
1. To Preliminary Expenses to specified)				By Equity shares of			
2. To Land including law charges incidental to acquisition				By Preference shares of			
3. To Buildings				By Debenture stock			
4. To Plant				By Mortgages and Bonds			
5. To Mains				By Amounts received in anticipation of calls			
6. To Service connections				By Other receipts (to be specified)			
7. To Transformer, etc.							
8. To Meters and fees for certifying under the Act							
9. To General Stores							
10. To Special items (to be specified)							
Total expenditure							
To Balance of Capital							

General Balance Sheet

Liabilities	*Rs.*	*Assets*	*Rs.*
1. Capital account: amount received as per Account No. II		1. Capital Account: expended for works as per Account No. III.	
2. Sundry Creditors due on construction of plant and machinery, fuel, stores, etc.		2. Stores on hand	
		3. Sundry Debtors	
3. Sundry Creditors on open accounts		4. Preliminary Expenses awaiting adjustment.	
4. Net Revenue Account: Balance at credit thereof		5. Securities as held (cost price)	
5. Reserve Fund Account: Balance at credit thereof		6. Special items (to be specified)	
6. Depreciation Fund Account		7. Cash at bankers	
7. Special items (to be specified)		8. Cash on hand	
Total		Total	

2. A Revenue Account is prepared which is like the ordinary Profit and Loss Account. Also, a Net Revenue Account is prepared which is like the ordinary Profit and Loss Appropriation Account. The exceptions are as follows :—

(*a*) Interest in all cases is debited or credited to Net Revenue Account and not to Revenue Account. In cases of Railways, rent on leased land, etc., is also debited to Net Revenue Account.

(*b*) Depreciation is debited to Revenue Account and credited to Depreciation Reserve. Depreciation Reserve appears on the liability side of the General Balance Sheet.

The forms of the Receipts and Expenditure on Capital Account and the General Balance Sheet are given on page 27.33.

Illustration 4:

Provide for the undermentioned depreciation, and prepare a Receipts and Expenditure on Capital Account, Revenue Account, Net Revenue Account and Balance Sheet from the following Trial Balance. A call of Rs. 20 per share was payable on 30th September, 2009 and arrears are subject to interest @ 15% p.a.

Depreciation to be provided for on : Building @ 5%, Machinery @ 15%, Mains @ 20%, Transformers etc., @ 10%, Meters and Electrical Instrument @ 15%.

THE DYNAMO ELECTRIC LIGHTING CO. LTD.
Trial Balance as at March 31st, 2010

Amount on March 31st, 2009 Rs.		*Rs.*	*Rs.*
	Capital, Nominal, 50,000 Shares of Rs. 100 each		
20,00,000	Subscribed, 25,000 shares of Rs. 100 each	—	25,00,000
15,00,000	14% Debentures	—	15,00,000
6,00,000	Provision for Depreciation	—	6,00,000
—	Calls in arrear	1,00,000	
9,30,000	Freehold Land	9,30,000	
4,00,000	Buildings	5,00,000	
6,00,000	Machinery at station	10,00,000	
5,00,000	Mains	8,00,000	
1,00,000	Transformers etc.	2,00,000	
50,000	Meters	1,50,000	
30,000	Electrical Instruments	40,000	
1,60,000	General Stores (Cables, Mains, Meters etc.)	2,35,000	
25,000	Office Furniture	25,000	
	Coal and Fuel	1,90,000	
	Oil, Waste, Engine-room Stores	75,000	
	Coal, Oil, Waste, etc. in Stock	10,000	
	Wages at Station	3,00,000	
	Repairs and Replacement	50,000	
	Rates and Taxes	30,000	
	Salaries of Secretary, Manager etc.	1,50,000	
	Directors' Fees	1,00,000	
	Stationery, Printing and Advertising	60,000	
	Law and Incidental Expenses	30,000	
	Sale by Meter	—	9,75,000
	Sale by contract	—	5,00,000
	Meter Rents	—	30,000
	Sundry Creditors	—	1,00,000
	Sundry Debtors	5,50,000	
	Cash in hand and at Bank	8,30,000	
	Contingencies Reserve	—	1,50,000
		63,55,000	63,55,000

Soultion:

Receipts and Expenditure on Capital Account for the year ended March 31, 2010

Expenditure	*Expenditure upto March 31, 2000*	*Expenditure during the year*	*Total*	*Receipts upto March 31, 2000*	*Receipts during the year*	*Receipts*	*Total*
	Rs.	*Rs.*	*Rs.*		*Rs.*	*Rs.*	*Rs.*
To Freehold Land	9,30,000	—	9,30,000	By Share Capital	20,00,000	4,00,000*	24,00,000
To Buildings	4,00,000	1,00,000	5,00,000	By 14% Debentures	15,00,000	—	15,00,000
To Machinery at Station	6,00,000	4,00,000	10,00,000				
To Mains	5,00,000	3,00,000	8,00,000				
To Transformers	1,00,000	1,00,000	2,00,000				
To Meters	50,000	1,00,000	1,50,000				
To General Stores	1,60,000	75,000	2,35,000				
To Electrical Instruments	30,000	10,000	40,000				
To Office Furniture	25,000	—	25,000				
Total Expenditure	27,95,000	10,85,000	38,80,000				
To Balance of Capital Account	—	—	20,000				
	27,95,000	10,85,000	39,00,000		35,00,000	4,00,000	39,00,000

*Calls in arrears have been deducted.

Revenue Account for the year ended March 31, 2010

	Rs.			Rs.
A. Generation			By Sale of energy for lighting purposes	9,75,000
To Coal and Fuel	1,90,000		By Sale of energy for power purposes	
To Oil, Waste and Engine-Room Stores	75,000		By Sale of energy by contract	5,00,000
To Wages at Station	3,00,000		By Meter Rent	30,000
To Repairs and Replacement	50,000	6,15,000		
B. Distribution		—		
C. Public Lamps		—		
D. Rent, Rates and Taxes :				
To Rates and Taxes		30,000		
E. Management Expenses :				
To Directors' Fees	1,00,000			
To Secretary's and Manager's Salaries	1,50,000			
To Stationery, Printing and Advertising	60,000			
To Law and Incidental Charges	30,000	3,40,000		
G. Depreciation :**				
Depreciation on :				
Buildings	22,500			
Machinery	1,20,000			
Mains	65,000			
Transformers	30,000			
Meters	15,000			
Electrical Instruments	5,250	2,57,750		
To Balance carried to Net Revenue Account		2,62,250		
		15,05,000		15,05,000

**Depreciation on additions charged for 6 months.

Net Revenue Account

	Rs.		Rs.
To Interest on Debentures, outstanding	2,10,000	By Balance from last account	—
To Contingencies Reserve —transfer*	19,400	By Balance brought from Revenue Account	2,62,250
To Balance c/d	40,350	By Interest due on calls in arrears (on Rs. 1,00,000 @ 15% for 6 months)	7,500
	2,69,750		2,69,750

General Balance Sheet

Liabilities		*Rs.*	*Assets*	*Rs.*
Capital Account : amount received		39,00,000	Capital Account : amount expended for works	38,80,000
Sundry Creditors on open accounts		1,00,000	Stores on hand	10,000
Contingencies Reserve.		1,69,400	Sundry Debtors	5,50,000
Net Revenue Account—Balance		40,350	Interest due on calls in arrears	7,500
Provision for Depreciation:			Cash at bank and in hand	8,30,000
Balance as per last Balance Sheet	6,00,000			
Addition during the year	2,57,750	8,57,750		
Interest on Debentures Outstanding		2,10,000		
		52,77,500		52,77,500

Replacement of an asset :

Ordinarily, the amount standing in books against an asset is written off when the asset is replaced by another. The amount spent on the new asset is capitalised. Under the Double Account System, however, the practice is different. Firstly, the account of the asset which is replaced is not affected at all. An appropriate amount out of the new expenditure is charged to revenue or written off and the balance is capitalised. Secondly, the amount to be written off is the amount which would have been spent *had* the asset been acquired *now*. **Suppose, a railway station built in 1980 at a cost of Rs. 15,00,000 is replaced, in 2010, by a new station costing Rs. 80,00,000. Suppose further that between 1980 and 2010, prices of materials have risen to 700%, that labour rates have trebled and that the proportion of materials and labour in the old station is 4 : 6. The amount to be written off will be arrived at as under :**

			Rs.
Total cost of the old station			15,00,000
Proportion of Materials	15,00,000 × 4/10	or	6,00,000
Proportion of Labour	15,00,000 × 6/10	or	9,00,000
Had the station been built in 2000			
Materials would have cost,	6,00,000 × 700/100		42,00,000
and Labour would have cost	9,00,000 × 3		27,00,000
Total			69,00,000

Out of Rs. 80,00,000 spent in 2010, Rs. 69,00,000 would be written off and Rs. 11,00,000 i.e., 80,00,000—69,00,000 would be capitalised. The total amount capitalised would be Rs. 26,00,000, i.e., Rs. 15,00,000 + Rs. 11,00,000.

The entries to be made are as follows :—

1. Debit Replacement Account with the amount to be written off; Debit Works Account (new) with the amount to be capitalised; and Credit Bank with the amount actually spent.

* It is assumed that the transfer to Contingencies Reserve is @ ½% of the cost of fixed assets; it could be any figure from ¼% or ½%.

2. If any old materials have been used in the new construction :
   Debit Works Account
   Credit Replacement Account.
3. If any old materials have been sold :
   Debit Bank
   Credit Replacement Account.

The logic behind the treatment outlined above is firstly, that additional amount should be capitalised only if there is additional capacity and, secondly, that when an old asset is replaced, the amount lost is the asset's present value rather than its historical cost.

Illustration 5:

The Hindustan Gas Company rebuilt and re-equipped part of their works at a cost of Rs. 5,00,000. The part of the old works thus superseded cost Rs. 3,00,000. The capacity of the new works is double the capacity of the old works. Rs. 20,000 is realised by the sale of old materials, and old materials worth Rs. 10,000 are used in the construction of the new works and included in the total cost of Rs. 5,00,000 mentioned above. The costs of labour and materials are 25% higher than when the old works were built.

Journalise the entries.

Solution :

Journal

			Dr. *Rs.*	*Cr.* *Rs.*
	Replacement Account	Dr.	3,75,000	
	New Works Account	Dr.	1,15,000	
	To Bank			4,90,000
	Being the amount written off (Rs. 3,00,000 + 25%) and the amount capitalised out of the Rs. 4,90,000, spent on reconstruction in cash, *i.e.*, Rs. 5,00,000 — Rs. 10,000.			
	New Works Account	Dr.	10,000	
	To Replacement Account			10,000
	Being the materials used in the new works.			
	Bank	Dr.	20,000	
	To Replacement Account			20,000
	Being the amount realised by the sale of old materials.			
	Revenue Account	Dr.	3,45,000	
	To Replacement Account			3,45,000
	Being the transfer of balance of Replacement Account to Revenue Account.			

Working Notes:

	Rs.
Cost of old works	3,00,000
Add: Increase in cost Rs. $\frac{3,00,000 \times 25}{100}$	75,000
Current cost of old works	3,75,000

Cash cost of new works = Rs. 5,00,000 – Rs. 10,000 = Rs. 4,90,000
Account to be capitalised = Rs. 4,90,000 – Rs. 3,75,000 = Rs. 1,15,000.

Illustration 6:

The Gurgaon Electricity Company Limited decides to replace one of its old plants with a modern one with a larger capacity. The plant when installed in 1975 cost the company Rs. 24 lakhs, the components of materials, labour and overheads being in the ratio of 5:3:2. It is ascertained that the costs of materials and labour have gone up by 40% and 80% respectively. The proportion of overheads to total costs is expected to remain the same as before.

The cost of the new plant as per improved design is Rs. 60 lakhs and in addition, material recovered from the old plant of a value of Rs. 2,40,000 has been used in the construction of the new plant. The old plant was scrapped and sold for Rs. 7,50,000.

The accounts of the company are maintained under Double Account system. Indicate how much would be capitalised and the amount that would be charged to revenue. Show the ledger accounts. [*Adapted C.A.* (*Inter.*)]

Solution:

Dr. **Gurgaon Electricity Company Limited Plant Account** *Cr.*

	Rs.		*Rs.*
To Balance *b/fd*	24,00,000	By Balance *c/d*	49,20,000
To Bank Account (cost of new plant—capitlised)	22,80,000		
To Replacement Account (old parts)	2,40,000		
	49,20,000		49,20,000
To Balance *b/d*	49,20,000		

Dr. **Replacement Account** *Cr.*

	Rs.		*Rs.*
To Bank Account (current cost of replacement)	37,20,000	By Bank Account (sale of scrap)	7,50,000
		By Plant Account (old material used)	2,40,000
		By Revenue Account (transfer)	27,30,000
	37,20,000		37,20,000

Working Notes :

(1) Cost to be incurred for replacement of present plant :

	Cost of Existing Plant Rs.	*Increase %*	*Current Cost Rs.*
Materials	12,00,000	40%	16,80,000
Labour	7,20,000	80%	12,96,000
			29,76,000
Overheads (¼ of above or 1/5 of total)			7,44,000
Current Replacement Cost			37,20,000
Current Replacement cost			37,20,000
Total Cash Cost			60,00,000
Amount capitalised, excluding old materials used			22,80,000

EXERCISE XXVI

Practical

1. Bright Electricity Ltd. earned a profit of Rs. 26,95,000 for the year ended 31st March, 2010 after debenture interest at 14% on Rs. 5,00,000. Calculate the reasonable return after taking into consideration the following facts also :

	Rs.
Fixed assets (original cost)	2,00,00,000
Formation and other expenses	10,00,000
Monthly average of current assetss (net)	50,00,000
Reserve fund (represented by 8% govt. securities)	20,00,000
Contingencies reserve investments	5,00,000
Loan from Electricity Board	30,00,000
Total depreciation on fixed assets, written off to date	40,00,000
Tariffs and dividends control reserve	1,00,000
Security deposits received from customers	4,00,000

Assume the bank rate to be 10%. *[Adapted C.S. (Inter) June, 1999]*

[Capital Base, Rs. 1,85,00,000; Reasonable return, Rs. 23,97,500]

Hints :

Yield @ 12% on capital base	22,20,000
Income from investments other than against contingencies Reserve	1,60,000
1/2 % of Loan from Electricity Board	15,000
1/2 % on Debentures	2,500
	23,97,500

2. The following are the balances as on 31st March, 2010 in the books of the Utopian Railway Company Ltd. Make out the Receipts and Expenditure on Capital Account for the year 2009-2010 and the General Balance Sheet as on 31st March, 2010.

	Rs. '000
Traffic Accounts due from other railways	1,31,900
Expenditure on lines open for traffic	2,88,000
Expenditure on working stock	96,000
Expenditure on motor boats	48,000
Expenditure on docks, harbours and wharves	45,000
Subscription to other companies	30,000
Preference shares paid up as on 31st March, 2010	2,55,000
Equity shares paid up as on 1st April, 2009	2,40,000
Equity shares issued in 2009-2010 and paid up	60,000
Premium on shares as on 1st April, 2009	16,500
Premium on shares received in 2009-2010	6,600
Debentures	99,000
Net Revenue Account, balance at credit	860
Renewals Reserve Account	7,500
Sundry Creditors	3,750
Cash at Bank	4,110
Cash on deposit in bank	13,500
Investments	8,700
Share stock	7,500
Sundry debtors	16,500

(Adapted from C.A., Final)

(Total of Balance Sheet, Rs. 1,82,210 thousand)

3. The following are the balances on 31st March, 2010 in the books of the Guntur Power and Light Co. Limited :—

	Dr. Rs.	Cr. Rs.
Lands on April 1, 2009	60,000	
Lands, expended during the year	2,000	
Machinery on April 1, 2009	2,40,000	

	Dr. Rs.	Cr. Rs.
Machinery, expended during 2009-2010	2,000	
Mains, including cost of laying	80,000	
Mines, expended during 2009-2010	20,400	
Equity Shares		2,19,600
Debentures		80,000
Sundry Creditors		400
Depreciation account		1,00,000
Sundry Debtors for current supplied	16,000	
Other Debtors	200	
Cash	2,000	
Cost for generation of electricity	14,000	
Cost of distribution of electricity	2,000	
Rent, Rates and Taxes	2,000	
Management	4,800	
Depreciation	8,000	
Sale of Current		52,000
Rent of Meters		2,000
Interest on Debentures	4,000	
Interim Dividend	8,000	
Balance of Net Revenue Account, April 1, 2009		11,400
	4,65,400	4,65,400

From the above trial balance, prepare Capital Account, General Balance Sheet, Revenue Account and Net Revenue Account. *(Adapted C.A. Final)*

(Revenue Account Balance, Rs. 23,200; *Total of General Balance Sheet, Rs.* 4,22,600; *Capital Account Total, Rs.* 4,04,400)

4. The Trial Balance of the Lunar Light Co. Ltd. on 31st March, 2010 was as follows :—

Balance on Mar. 31, 2009		Rs.	Rs.
	Authorised Capital :		
	20,000 equity shares of Rs. 500 each		
	Subscribed Paid up Capital :		
56,25,000	15,000 shares of Rs. 500 each, Rs. 400 paid up		60,00,000
	14% First Mortgage Debentures :		
32,00,000	3,200 Debentures of Rs. 1,000 each		32,00,000
36,900	Share Premium Reserve		41,050
8,20,000	Depreciation Fund		8,20,000
	Depreciation Fund Investments	8,20,000	
32,00,000	Freehold Land	33,55,000	
11,50,000	Buildings	12,86,250	
7,76,340	Mains and Meters	8,49,280	
34,82,200	Plant	38,79,000	
32,000	Wages and Vans	47,500	
20,000	Office Furniture	20,000	
	Stock on hand (1st April, 2009) :		
	Coal	3,85,300	
	Other materials	2,160	
	Purchases :		
	Coal	17,13,490	
	Other materials	26,450	
	Repairs and Renewals of Plant	3,68,470	
	Repairs and Maintenance of Mains and Meters	1,89,820	
	Wages	2,79,200	

Contd.

Rs.	*Rs.*	*Rs.*
Salaries	44,550	
Directors' Fees	95,000	
Rates and Taxes	94,600	
Bad Debts	32,100	
Legal Charges	1,300	
Audit Fees	2,450	
General Expenses		
Administrative Expenses	1,06,530	
Sickness and Accident		
Compensation paid to workmen	42,200	
Certificate Fees		200
Sale of electricity—Power		39,88,260
Sale of electricity—lighting, heating, etc.		12,72,500
Dividend Paid	12,44,000	
Interest on Debentures	4,48,000	
Net Revenue Account Balance		4,08,670
Sundry Creditors		1,83,260
Sundry Debtors	4,34,970	
Balance in Current Account at Prosperity Bank Ltd.	1,41,125	
Cash in hand	5,195	
	1,59,13,940	1,59,13,940

Stock on hand on 31st March, 2010 :

Coal	Rs. 3,46,470
Other Materials	Rs. 5,350

Depreciation is to be provided as follows :

15 per cent of value of plant, and 10 per cent of value of buildings on 1st April, 2009.

Prepare Revenue Account, Capital Account, Net Revenue Account and General Balance Sheet under the Double Account System. *(Adapted from C.A., Final)*

(*Profit, Rs.* 15,59,030; *Total of Capital Account, Rs.* 94,37,030 ; *Total of General Balance Sheet, Rs.* 1,11,90,440)

5. A water supply concern had to replace a quarter of the mains and lay an auxiliary main for the remaining length in order to augment supplies of water to a locality. The total cost of the original main was Rs. 8,00,000 ; the auxiliary main cost Rs. 9,00,000 and the new main cost Rs. 3,50,000. It is estimated that cost of laying a main has gone up by 30%. Parts of the old main realised Rs. 15,000. Pass journal entries to record the above. Show your workings.

[C.S. (Inter) June, 1998 Modified]

(Amount to be capitalised, Rs. 90,000)

6. An electricity company laid down a main at a cost of Rs. 5,00,000. Some years later the company laid down an auxiliary main for one-fifth of the length of the old main at a cost of Rs. 1,50,000 and also replaced the rest of the length of the old main at a cost of Rs. 6,00,000, the cost of materials. and labour having gonw up by 15%. Sale of old materials reaslied Rs. 8,000. Old materials valued at Rs. 10,000 were used in renewal and those valued at Rs. 5,000 were used in the construction of the auxiliary main.

You are required to give the journal entries for recording the above transactions. Show how you would apportion the above expenditure between capital and revenue. *[C.S. (Inter) Dec. 1996]*

[Capitalised, Rs. 1,40,000 and Rs. 1,50,000; debits Revenue Account Rs. 4,37,000]

7. An electricity supply compnay rebuilt and re-equipped a power station and the connecting lines during the year ended 31st March, 2010. For the purpose, it purchased materials for Rs. 10,85,000 and used stores costing Rs. 4,90,000 from its existing stock. The cost of labour came to Rr. 5,22,000. The estimated supervisory overheads attributed to this project were Rs. 13,000. the power station was erected during the year ended 31st March, 1980 at a cost of Rs. 5,00,000. The index of costs in the line stood at 385 in the year ended 31st March, 2010, taking the year ended 31st March, 1980 as the base year. Discarded materilas from the old powere station fetched Rs. 12,000.

Show journal entries to record the abovementioned transactions relating to the replacement of the power station. Show all your working notes. [*C.S. (Inter) Dec. 1997, Modified*]

(*Rs. 1,85,000 to be capitalised by debit to Power Station*)

8. A railway station had to be replaced by a new one. The new station cost Rs. 8,00,000, whereas the old one had cost only Rs. 2,00,000, materials forming 3/7ths of the total expenditure and labour accounting for the rest. Prices of materials have doubled and wages rates have gone up by 250% since the old station was built. Materials worth Rs. 38,000 were used in the new station and sale proceeds of the materials were Rs. 11,000. These materials were obtained by pulling down the old station. Pass journal entries and show the total amount capitalised and written off.

(*Amount to be capitalised Rs. 2,28,571*)

9. U Electricity Ltd. earned a profit of Rs. 26,95,000 during the year ended March 31, 2001, after debenture interest at 14% on Rs. 5,00,000. With the help of the figures given below, show the disposal of the profits. Assume the bank rate to be 10%.

	Rs.
Original Cost of Fixed Assets	2,00,00,000
Formation and other expenses	10,00,000
Monthly average of current assets (net)	50,00,000
Reserve Fund (represented by 8% Government Securities)	20,00,000
Contingencies Reserve Investments	5,00,000
Loan from Electricity Board	30,00,000
Total Depreciation written off to date	40,00,000
Tariffs & Dividends Control Reserve	1,00,000
Security Deposits received from customers	4,00,000

(*Rs. 1,98,813 due to customers*)

Essay-type

1. How is an electricity company required to provide depreciation ?
2. What is `reasonable return' for an electricity company ? What is meant by `capital base' in this connection ?
3. For an electricity company, what does `clear profit' mean ?
4. Should the clear profit exceed the reasonable return, how has the surplus to be disposed of by an electricity company ?
5. What do you know about the following reserves created by electricity companies :—
   (*i*) Tariffs and Dividends Control Reserve,
   (*ii*) Contingencies Reserve,
   (*iii*) Development Reserve and
   (*iv*) General Reserve ?
6. What are the special features of the final accounts prepared by electricity companies ?
7. What is meant by Double Account System ? What are its chief features ?
8. Distinguish between Double Entry System and Double Account System.
9. How is replacement of an asset treated under the Double Account System ? Explain with the help of an example, showing the necessary calculations and journal entries.

28

LIQUIDATION

SYNOPSIS

1.	Meaning of liquidation or winding up	..	28.1
	Winding up by National Company Law Tribunal	..	28.1
	Voluntary winding up	..	28.2
	Members' voluntary winding up	..	28.2
	Creditors' voluntary winding up	..	28.2
	Consequences of winding up, generally	..	28.3
	Preferential payments	..	28.3
	Overriding preferential payments	..	28.4
	Liquidator	..	28.5
	Power and duties of liquidator	..	28.5
2	Preparation of statement of affairs	..	28.6
	Deficiency/surplus account	..	28.9
3.	Liquidator's final statement of account	..	28.13
	Receiver for debentureholders	..	28.22
	"B" list of contributories	..	28.28

1. MEANING OF LIQUIDATION OR WINDING UP

A company is a creation of law and it can come to an end only through a process of law. A company ceases to exist when it is dissolved. One of the ways to dissolve a company is to resort to the process of winding up or liquidation. When, therefore, winding up commences, the company is said to be in liquidation. It is not necessary that only an insolvent company should be liquidated. Sometimes, it is necessary to liquidate or wind up even a prosperous and solvent company. The Companies Act, 1956 lays down the procedure by which companies can be wound up. Winding up is roughly of two types: when National Company Law Tribunal orders the company to be wound up (compulsory winding up) and when the members of the company, alone or jointly with creditors, take steps to wind up the company (voluntary winding up).

Winding up by National Company Law Tribunal* :

A winding up by the National Company Law Tribunal, or compulsory winding up, as it is often called, is initiated by an application by way of petition presented to the Tribunal for a winding up order.

Grounds for compulsory winding up. Section 433 provides that a company may be wound up by the Tribunal :—

(*a*) if the company has, by special resolution, resolved to be wound up by the Tribunal;

(*b*) if default is made in delivering the statutory report to the Registrar or in holding the statutory meeting;

(*c*) if the company does not commence its business within a year from its incorporation, or suspends its business for a whole year;

(*d*) if the number of members is reduced, in the case of a public company, below 7, and in the case of a private company, below 2;

(*e*) if the company is unable to pay its debts; and

(*f*) if the Tribunal is of opinion that it is just and equitable that the company should be wound up.

---

* The powers of the Court have been transferred to National Company Law Tribunal by the Companies (Amendment) Act, 2002.

(*g*) if the company has made a default in filing with the Registrar its balance sheet and profit and loss account or annual return for any five consecutive financial years;

(*h*) if the company has acted against the interests of the sovereignty and integrity of India, the security of the State, friendly relations with foreign States, public order, decency or morality.

(*i*) if the Tribunal is of the opinion that the company should be wound up under the circumstances specified in section 424 G (This section deals with winding up of a sick industrial company.)

Provided that the Tribunal should make an order for winding up of a company under clause (*h*) on application made by the Central Government or a State Government.

The power of the Tribunal to wind up a company in all the above cases is discretionary as the word used in sec. 433 is 'may'.

Who may petition. Under sec. 439, the following may petition:— (1) the company; (2) a creditor; (3) a contributory; (4) all or any of the above parties; (5) the Registrar; (6) any person authorised by the Central Government as per section 243, i.e., following upon a report of inspectors appointed to investigate the affairs of the company under section 235; (7) in a case falling under clause (h) of section 433, by the Central Government or a State Government. Section 440 provides that where a company is being wound up voluntarily, a petition for its winding up by the Tribunal may be presented by (a) any person authorised to do so under section 439 or (b) the Official Liquidator. But the Tribunal shall not make a winding up order on a petition presented to it under this section unless it is satisfied that the voluntary winding up cannot be continued with due regard to the interests of the creditors or contributories or both.

Procedure. On hearing the petition, the Tribunal may dismiss it, adjourn it, make an interim order, or make a compulsory order for winding up the company. Where the winding up order is made, the Tribunal will appoint the Official Liquidator satisfying the conditions given in Section 448 of the Companies (Amendment) Act, 2002. The Tribunal will also settle the list of contributories, make calls and settle any question arising out of winding up. The creditors will be asked to prove their claims, where necessary, and the liquidator will realise the assets and distribute the proceeds among the creditors, whereupon the Tribunal may pass an order that the company be dissolved.

Voluntary winding up:

A company may be wound up voluntarily —

(*i*) when the period (if any) fixed for its duration has expired, or an event on the happening of which the company is to be wound up has happened and the company in general meeting has passed an ordinary resolution to wind up; or

(*ii*) if the company passes a special resolution to wind up voluntarily (sec. 484). According to sec. 485, when the resolution has been passed, a notice must be given by the company within 14 days of the passing thereof by advertisement in the Official Gazette, and also in some newspapers circulating in the district where the registered office is situated.

Members' voluntary winding up :

There are two kinds of voluntary winding up, namely, Members' and Creditors'. A company may be wound up as members' voluntary winding up, if a declaration of the company's solvency is made by its directors, or where there are more than 2 directors by the majority of directors, at Board meeting, that they are of opinion that the company has no debts, or that it will be able to pay its debts in full within 3 years from the commencement of winding up.

On the passing of the resolution for winding up, the company must, in general meeting, appoint one or more liquidators and fix his or their remuneration. Remuneration so fixed cannot be increased at all. If in a members' voluntary winding up, the liquidator is of opinion that the company will not be able to pay its debts in full within the period stated in the declaration, or if the period has expired without full payment of debts, he must forthwith call a meeting of the creditors. After such a meeting, it will become a creditors' winding up. According to sec. 496, in the event of the winding up continuing for more than one year, the liquidater must call a general meeting of the company at the end of the first year of the commencement of winding up and of each succeeding year, and must lay before the meeting an account of his acts and dealings and of the conduct of winding up. When the affairs of the company are fully wound up, the liquidator must make up an account and call a final meeting of the company and lay these accounts before the meeting, and, within one week of this meeting, send to the Registrar and the Official Liquidator a copy each of the account and the return to each of them. The Registrar will register the account and the return. The Official Liquidator will scrutinise the books and papers of the company and make a report to the Tribunal that its affairs have not been conducted in a manner prejudicial to the interests of its members or the public interest. Then the company will be deemed to be dissolved from the date of the submission of this report to the Tribunal.

Creditors' voluntary winding up :

Where a declaration of solvency is not made and filed with the Registrar, it is presumed that the company is insolvent. In such a case, the company must call a meeting of its creditors for the day or the day next following the day fixed for company's general meeting for passing the resolution for winding up.

Subject to the rights of the preferential creditors, the assets of a company on its winding up are applied in satisfaction of its liabilities *pari passu*, and any surplus is divided among the members according to their rights and interests in the company (sec. 511).

Consequences of winding up generally :

As to Shareholders. A shareholder is liable to pay the full amount of shares held by him. This liability continues after winding up, but he is then described as a "contributory". By sec. 428, a contributory is every person liable to contribute to the assets of a company in the event of its being wound up, and includes a holder of fully paid-up shares, and also any person alleged to be contributory. Contributories are either present or past, and it is the former who are liable to pay calls, and the latter can be called upon to pay only if the present contributories are unable to pay. The nature of a contributory's liability after winding up is legal and not contractual. He cannot set off his debt against his liability for calls even if there is an express agreement to do so. A person who disposes of partly paid shares can be called upon to contribute if the company is wound up within one year of the sale of the shares and only in respect of debts incurred by the company when he was a shareholder. The above applies to those whose shares are forfeited or surrendered but not to the heirs of those who die.

As to Creditors. A company can never be adjudged insolvent, although it may have become insolvent in the sense that it is unable to pay its debts. Where a solvent company is to be wound up, all claims against the company are admissible, and when they are proved, payment is made. In the case of an insolvent company, the insolvency principles apply. A secured creditor may either—

(*i*) rely on the security and ignore the liquidation; or (*ii*) value his security and prove for the balance of his debt; or (*iii*) give up his security and prove for the whole amount.

Unsecured creditors of an insolvent company are paid in the order —

(*i*) Overriding preferential parforments under section 529–A, (*ii*) preferential payments under sec. 530; and (*iii*) other debts *pari passu.*

Preferential Payments :

Preferential payments are as follows :—

(*a*) all revenues, taxes, cesses and rates due and payable by the company within 12 months preceding the relevant date.

'Relevant date' means —

(*i*) in the case of a compulsory winding up of a company, the date on which a provisional liquidator is appointed, or if he is not appointed, the date of the winding up order. In case the company had commenced to be wound up voluntarily before that date, relevant date means the date of commencement of voluntary winding up.

(*ii*) in the case of a voluntary winding up of a company, the date of the passing of the resolution for the winding up of the company.

(*b*) all wages or salary (including wages for time or piece work and salary earned wholly or in part by way of commission) of any employee due for a period not exceeding four months within the twelve months next before commencement of winding up provided the amount payable to one claimant will not exceed one thousand rupees. [Vide Notification G.S.R. 30(E) dated 17-02-1997, the sum payable to any one claimant in relation to wages and salary shall not exceed Rs. 20,000].

(*c*) all accrued holiday remuneration becoming payable to any employee on account of winding up.

Note. Persons who advance money for the purpose of making preferential payments under (*b*) and (*c*) above will be treated as preferential creditors, provided the money is actually, so used;

(*d*) unless the company is being wound-up voluntarily merely for the purposes of reconstruction or of amalgamation with another company, all contributions payable during the 12 months next before winding up, by the company as the employer of any person, under the Employees' State Insurance Act, 1948 or any other law for the time being in force

(*e*) unless the company is being wound up voluntarily merely for the purposes of reconstruction or of amalgamation with another company or unless it has taken out a workmen's compensation insurance policy, all compensation due under the Workmen's Compensation Act, 1923;

(*f*) all sums due to any employee from a provident fund, a pension fund, a gratuity fund or any other fund for the welfare of the employees, maintained by the company;

(*g*) the expenses of any investigation held under sec. 235 or 237, insofar as they are payable by the company.

Overriding Preferential Payments :

The Companies (Amendment) Act, 1985 has introduced Section 529A according to which certain dues are to be settled in the case of winding up of a company even before the payments to preferential creditors under section 530 are made. Section 529A states that in the event of winding up of a company, workmen's dues and debts due to secured creditors, to the extent such debts rank under Section 529(1)(C), shall be paid in priority to all other debts. The workmen's dues and debts to secured creditors shall be paid in full, unless the assets are insufficient to meet them, in which case they shall abate in equal proportions.

It may be noted here that workmen's dues, in relation to a company, means the aggregate of the following sums due from the company to its workmen :-

(g) all wages or salary including wages payable for time or piece work and salary earned wholly or in part by way of commission of any workman and any compensation payable to any workman under any of the provisions of the Industrial Disputes Act, 1947;

(*ii*) all accrued holiday remuneration becoming payable to any workman on account of winding up ;

(*iii*) unless the company is being wound up voluntarily merely for the purposes of reconstruction or of amalgamation with another company, or unless it has taken out a workmen's compensation insurance policy, all amounts due in respect of any compensation or liability for compensation under Workmen's Compensation Act, 1923 in respect of death or disablement of any workman of the company;

(*iv*) all sums due to any workman from a provident fund, a pension fund, a gratuity fund or any other fund for the welfare of the workmen, maintained by the company.

According to section 529(3)(a) "workmen", in relation to a company, means the employees of the company, being workmen within the meaning of the Industrial Disputes Act, 1947. According to section 2(s) of the Industrial Disputes Act, 1947, "workman" means any person (including an apprentice) employed in any industry to do any manual, unskilled, skilled, technical, operational, clerical or supervisory work for hire or reward, whether the terms of employment be express or implied. It includes any person who has been dismissed, discharged or retrenched in connection with, or as a consequence of an industrial dispute or whose dismissal, or discharge or retrenchment has led to that dispute. But it does not include any such person –

(*i*) who is subject the Air Force Act, 1950, or the Army Act, 1950, or the Navy Act, 1957; or
(*ii*) who is employed in the police service or as an officer or other employee of a prison ; or
(*iii*) who is employed mainly in a managerial or administrative capacity; or
(*iv*) who, being employed in a supervisory capacity, draws wages exceeding one thousand six hundred rupees per mensem or exercises, either by the nature of the duties attached to the office or by reason of the powers vested in him, functions mainly of a managerial nature.

The Companies (Amendment) Act, 1985 has made a distinction between employees and workmen for the purposes of preferential payments. Workmen's dues rank *pari passu* with the secured creditors and are to be paid in priority to the dues payable to an employee.

Persons who claim to be creditors must prove their debts within the time fixed by the Court, or by the voluntary liquidator.

Liquidator :

Compulsory Winding up. The Official Liquidator referred to in clause (c) of sub-section (1) of section 448 of the Act will become the liquidator on a winding up order being passed. He may also be appointed as a provisional liquidator with the same powers.

Powers of Liquidator. As soon as a winding up order is made, or a provisional liquidator is appointed, the liquidator will take into his custody or under his control all the property of the company and its effects and actionable claims (Sec. 456). For the purpose, he can make a request to the Chief Presidency Magistrate or the District Magistrate concerned.

The liquidator may, with the sanction of the Tribunal :—

(*i*) institute or defend any suit, prosecution, or other legal proceeding in the name of the company;
(*ii*) carry on the business of the company for its beneficial winding up;
(*iii*) sell company's property;
(*iv*) raise money on the security of the company's assets; and
(*v*) do all other things necessary for the winding up.

He may, without sanction of the Tribunal :—

(*i*) do all acts, and execute in the name of the company, all deeds, receipts and other documents;
(*ii*) inspect the records and returns of the company on the files of the Registrar without payment of any fee;
(*iii*) prove, rank and claim in the insolvency of any contributor and to receive dividends therefrom;
(*iv*) draw, accept, make, endorse any negotiable instrument in the name of the company;
(*v*) take out, in his official name, letters of administration to any deceased contributory, and do other necessary things to obtain payment; and
(*vi*) appoint an agent.

The liquidator may, with the sanction of the Tribunal or special resolution, according as the winding up is compulsory or voluntary,

(*i*) pay any class of creditors in full;
(*ii*) make compromise or arrangement with creditors; and
(*iii*) compromise with a contributory or debtor.

Duties of Liquidator. Section 460 requires the liquidator to conduct the winding up according to the direction given by the resolution of creditors' or contributories' meeting or by the Committee of Inspection. He must summon meetings of creditors or contributories when requisitioned by the holders of 10% of the amount. His principal duty is to administer the assets and pay the debts and distribute the balance among contributories. He must keep proper books of account, minutes books, and allow inspection thereof, twice in each year present to the Court an account of his receipts and payments in duplicate, and send a copy of the audited accounts to each creditor and contributory. He must keep all the funds of the company in "the Public Account of India" in the Reserve Bank of India: and must not keep any such money in his private account. All papers of the company must indicate that the company is being wound up, e.g., by adding the words "In liquidation" after the name of the company.

Voluntary Liquidator. The voluntary liquidator is appointed by resolution in general meeting of the company and/or of the creditors and his remuneration fixed.

Powers and Duties. A voluntary liquidator is a paid agent of the company and is liable to damages if he neglects his duties as such. He must not make any secret profits and must keep funds of the company in a Scheduled Bank to the credit of a special banking account called "the Liquidation Account of . . . Co. Ltd." or "Private Ltd." or "Company". He must not deposit such money in his personal account, nor must he retain with him more than Rs. 500 for more than 10 days. He will also be liable for misfeasance if he pays any money to a person who has no claim against the company. He may, with the sanctions of members' or creditors' resolution, or of the Committee of Inspection, do what the Official Liquidator can do. Section 512 further empowers him to do without the sanction of the Tribunal everything that the Official Liquidator can do and also exercise some of the powers of the Tribunal, e.g., settle lists of contributories, admit claims, make calls, call general meetings, etc., and perform other functions.

2. PREPARATION OF THE STATEMENT OF AFFAIRS

The officers and directors of a company under liquidation must, according to section 454 read with section 511A, make out and submit, within 21 days of the Tribunal's order (or within such extended time, not exceeding 3 months, as the liquidator or the Tribunal may allow), a statement showing the following:—

(*a*) the assets of the company, stating separately the cash balance in hand and at bank, if any, and the negotiable securities, if any, held by the company;

(*b*) its debts and liabilities;

(*c*) the names, residences and occupations of its creditors, stating separately the amount of secured and unsecured debts and in the case of secured debts, particulars of the securities given, whether by the company or its officers, their value and the dates on which they were given;

(*d*) the debts due to the company and the names, residences and occupations of the persons from whom they are due and the amount likely to be realised on account thereof ;

(*e*) such further or other information as may be prescribed, or as the Official Liquidator may require.

The statement has to be prepared even in case of voluntary winding up.

The statement has to be properly verified by an affidavit. It has to be open for inspection by any person stating himself in writing to be a creditor or contributory of the company, on payment of prescribed fee. The person concerned can also acquire a copy or extract from it. The form in which it has to be made out has been prescribed by the Supreme Court; it is given below:—

Form No. 57
(*See Rule* 127)

In the High Court at..................(*Or*) in the District Court at.......................
Original Jurisdiction.....................In the matter of Companies Act, 1956
In the matter of..........................Ltd.
Company Petition No.......................of 20.....
Statement of Affairs under section 454

Statement of affairs of the above-named company as on the............................day of.....................20...., the date of the winding-up order (or the order appointing Provisional Liquidator or the date directed by the Official Liquidator).

I/we................................of................................do solemnly affirm and say that the statement made overleaf and the several lists hereunto annexed marked 'A' to 'H' are to the best of my/our knowledge and belief, a full, true and complete statement as to the affairs of the above named company, on the ....day of................20.... the date of the winding-up order (or the order appointing Provisional Liquidator or the date directed by the Official Liquidator), and that the said company carries/carried on the following business :

(Here set out nature of company's business)

Signature(s)

Solemnly affirmed......................this...........day of.................20.... , before me.

Commissioner for Oaths

The Commissioner is particularly requested, before swearing the affidavit, to ascertain that the full name, address and description of the deponents are stated, and to initial any crossing-out or other alterations in the printed form. A deficiency in the affidavit in any of the above respects will entail its refusal by the Court, and will necessitate its being re-sworn.

Note. The several lists annexed are not exhibits to the affidavit.

Statement of Affairs and Lists to be Annexed

Statement as to the affairs of......................Ltd., on the..................day of..........20.... being the date of the winding-up order (or order appointing Provisional Liquidator or the date directed by the Official Liquidator, as the case may be) showing assets at estimated realisable values and liabilities expected to rank :—

Assets not specifically pledged (as per list 'A')

	Estimated realisable values Rs.
Balance at Bank	
Cash in Hand	
Marketable Securities	
Bills Receivable	
Trade Debtors	
Loan & Advances	
Unpaid Calls	
Stock in Trade	
Work in Progress	
....	
....	
Freehold Property, Land & Buildings	
Leasehold Property	
Plant & Machinery	
Furniture, Fittings, Utensils, etc.	
Investments other than marketable securities..	
Livestock	
Other property, etc.	
....	
....	

*Assets specifically pledged (as per list 'B')	(a) Estimated realisable values	(b) Due to secured creditors	(c) Deficiency ranking as unsecured	(d) Surplus carried to last column
Freehold property :	Rs.	Rs.	Rs.	Rs.
....				
....				

Rs. Estimated surplus from assets specifically pledged

Estimated total assets available for preferential creditors, debentureholders secured by a floating charge, and unsecured creditors (carried forward) Rs.

Summary of Gross Assets

(d)
Rs.

Gross realisable value of assets specifically pledged

Other Assets .. ..

Gross Assets Rs.

Estimated total assets available for preferential creditors, debentureholders secured by a floating charge, and unsecured creditors (brought forward) ..

Liabilities

(e)
Gross Liabilities (to be deducted from surplus or added to deficiency as the case may be)

Rs.

Secured creditors (as per list 'B') to the extent to which claims are estimated to be covered by assets specifically pledged [item (a) or (b) as above, whichever is less]
(insert in 'Gross Liabilities' column only)

Preferential creditors (as per list 'C') ..

Estimated balance of assets available for Debentureholders secured by a floating charge and unsecured creditors**

Debentureholders secured by a floating charge (as per list 'D') ..

Estimated Surplus/Deficiency as regard Debentureholders

Unsecured Creditors (as per list 'E') :

Estimated unsecured balance of claims of creditors partly secured on specific assets, brought from preceding page (c)

Trade Creditors

Bills Payable

Outstanding Expenses

....

Contingent Liabilities (state nature)

....

*Note. All assets specifically mortgaged, pledged or otherwise given as security should be included under this head. In the case of goods given as security, those in possession of the company and those not in possession should be separately set out.

** The figures must be read subject to the following notes:—

(1) (f) There is no unpaid capital liable to be called up, or

(g) the nominal amount of unpaid capital liable to be called up is Rs..........estimated to produce Rs.........which is/is not charged in favour of Debentureholders [Strike out (f) or (g).]

(2) The estimates are subject to costs of the winding-up and to any surplus or deficiency on trading pending realisation of the assets.

Rs. Estimated Surplus/Deficiency as regards Creditors [being difference between Gross Assets brought from preceding page (d) and Gross Liabilities as per column (e)]
Issued and Called-up Capital :
...............Preference Shares of..................each,
Rs.................called-up (as per list 'F')
......................Equity Shares of.............................each,
Rs....................called-up (as per list 'G')
Estimated Surplus/Deficiency as regards Members
(as per List 'H') *Rs.* ________

Lists A to G containing details of assets and liabilities and supplementary schedules are not given.

List A gives a complete list of assets which are not in the hands of or pledged in favour of secured creditors.

List B gives the list of assets which are specifically pledged with creditors both fully secured and partly secured.

List C is a list of preferential creditors and the amounts due.

List D is a list of debentureholders having a floating charge.

List E contains names of unsecured creditors and the amounts due.

List F gives the names and holdings of preference shareholders.

List G is a list of equity shareholders together with the amount of the shares held.

List H is a statement showing how the surplus or deficiency in the statement of affairs arose as a result of the profits and losses of the company (form given below).

List 'H' — Deficiency or Surplus Account

The period covered by this Account must commence on a date not less than three years before the date of the winding-up order (or the order appointing Provisional Liquidator, or the date directed by the Official Liquidator) or, if the company has not been incorporated for the whole of that period, the date of formation of the company, unless the Official Liquidator otherwise agrees.

Items contributing to Deficiency (or reducing Surplus):—

Rs.

1. Excess (if any) of Capital and Liabilities over Assets on the .... 20 ....as shown by Balance Sheet (copy annexed).
2. Net dividends and bonuses declared during the period from ......20 ...... to the date of the statement.
3. Net trading losses (after charging items shown in note to follow) for the same period.
4. Losses other than trading losses written off or for which provision has been made in the books during the same period (give particulars or annex schedule).
5. Estimated losses now written off or for which provision has been made for the purposes of preparing the statement (give particulars or annex schedule).
6. Other items contributing to Deficiency or reducing Surplus ....

Items reducing Deficiency (or contributing to Surplus):—

7. Excess (if any) of Assets over Capital and Liabilities on the .... 20.......to the date of statement.
9. Profits and income other than trading profits during the same period (give particulars or annex schedule).
10. Other items reducing Deficiency or contributing to Surplus:

Deficiency/Surplus (as shown by the Statement of Affairs). *Rs.* ________

Note as to Net Trading Profits and Losses:	*Rs.*
Particulars are to be inserted here (so far as applicable) of the items mentioned below, which are to be taken into account in arriving at the amount of net trading profits or losses shown in this account:—	
Provisions for depreciation, renewals or diminution in value of fixed assets.	
Charges for Indian income-tax and other Indian taxation on profits.	
Interest on debentures and other fixed loans, payments to directors made by the Company and required by law to be disclosed in the accounts.	
Exceptional or non-recurring expenditure:—	
. . ..	
Less: Exceptional or non-recurring receipts:-	
. . . .	
Balance, being other trading profits or losses.	
Net trading profits or losses as shown in Deficiency or Surplus Account above.	

Signature

Dated ....

Briefly, the scheme of the statement of affairs is as follows:

Put down the "free" assets (assets not specifically pledged) at their realisable values.

Add any surplus expected from securities in the hands of the creditors.

Deduct unsecured creditors together with unsatisfied balance of partly secured creditors.

Deduct Share Capital.

If at any stage the deduction to be made is more than the amount available, deficiency appears: otherwise there is a surplus.

In preparing the statement, the following further points should be noted:—

(*a*) Liability in respect of bills discounted by the company is contingent; any amount expected to be paid in respect of bills discounted should be included in List E. This applies to all contingent liabilities.

(*b*) Bills payable are creditors and should be included in the appropriate lists according to the securities held by the holders of the bills. Generally, Bills Payable are included in unsecured creditors. (List E).

(*c*) Debentures should be assumed to have a floating charge if nothing is mentioned regarding the security held by the debentureholders. (List D).

(*d*) Unclaimed dividends should be included in unsecured creditors.

(*e*) Uncalled capital should not be treated as an asset but calls in arrear should be treated as an asset. (List A).

(*f*) Personal sureties should be ignored.

The student should not be afraid of a surplus appearing in the statement as often prosperous companies are wound up. A company which is being wound up is not necessarily insolvent.

Illustration 1:

The following information was extracted from the books of a limited company on 31st March, 2010 on which date a winding up order was made:

	Rs.
Equity Share Capital—20,000 Shares of Rs. 10 each	2,00,000
14% Preference Share Capital—30,000 Shares of Rs. 10 each	3,00,000
Calls in arrear on Equity Shares (estimated to realise Rs. 2,000)	4,000
14% First Mortgage Debentures secured by a floating charge on the whole of the assets of the company (interest paid to date)	2,00,000
Creditors having a mortgage on the Freehold Land and Buildings	85,000
Creditors having a second charge on Freehold Land and Buildings	90,000

	Rs.
Trade Creditors	2,70,000
Bills Discounted (of these bills for Rs. 15,000 are expected to be dishonored)	40,000
Unclaimed Dividends	6,000
Bills Payable	10,000
Income-tax due	25,000
Salaries and Wages (for five months)	40,000
Bank Overdraft secured by a second charge on the whole of the assets of the company	20,000
Cash in hand	1,200
Debtors (of these Rs. 60,000 are good; Rs. 15,000 are doubtful, estimated to realise Rs. 5,000 and the rest bad)	90,000
Bills of Exchange (considered good)	35,000
Freehold Land and Buildings (estimated to realise Rs. 1,65,000)	1,50,000
Plant and Machinery (estimated to produce Rs. 90,000)	1,20,000
Fixtures and Fittings (estimated to produce Rs. 8,000)	12,000
Stock in trade (estimated to produce 25% less)	80,000
Patents (estimated to produce Rs. 45,000)	70,000

On 31st March, 2004, the company's share capital stood at the same figures as on 31st March, 2010 but in addition, there was a General Reserve of Rs. 65,000. In 2004-05 the company earned a profit of Rs. 1,43,000 but thereafter it suffered trading losses totalling in all Rs. 4,67,000. In 2006-07 a speculation loss of Rs. 91,000 was incurred. Preference dividend was paid for 2004-05 and 2005-06 and on equity shares a dividend of 15% was paid for 2004-05 only.

Excise authorities imposed a penalty of Rs. 1,60,000 for evasion of excise and income tax authorities imposed a penalty of Rs. 60,400 for evasion of tax.

Prepare the Statement of Affairs and the Deficiency Account.

Solution:

The unsecured creditors of the company (List E) are the following:—

	Rs.
Trade Creditors	2,70,000
Liability on Bills Discounted	15,000
Unclaimed Dividends	6,000
Bills Payable	10,000
One month's Salaries and Wages	8,000
Amount uncovered in respect of Partly Secured Creditors	10,000
	3,19,000

Creditors having mortgage on Freehold Land and Buildings are fully secured since the estimated value of the security is Rs. 1,65,000 and the creditors amount to Rs. 85,000, leaving a surplus of Rs. 80,000 which the creditors having a second charge on the asset will get. These creditors, amounting to Rs. 90,000, are partly secured.

The Preferential Creditors (List C) are Rs. 25,000 due for income tax and four months' salaries and wages Rs. 32,000 or Rs. 57,000 in total.

.... Ltd. (In Liquidation)

Statement of Affairs as on March 31, 2010

	Estimated Realisable *values* *Rs.*
Assets not specially pledged-(List A)	
Cash in hand	1,200

	Rs.
Bills of Exchange	35,000
Trade Debtors	65,000
Unpaid Calls	2,000
Stock	60,000
Plant and Machinery	90,000
Fixtures and Fittings	8,000
Patents	45,000

Assets Specifically Pledged (List B):

	Estimated Realisable value Rs.	Due to secured creditors Rs.	Deficiency ranking as unsecured Rs.	Surplus Rs.	
Freehold Land & Buildings	1,65,000	1,75,000	10,000	—	—
Estimated surplus from specifically pledged assets					
Estimated Total Assets available for Preferential Creditors, Debentureholders secured by a floating charge and other creditors, carried forward					3,06,200

Summary of Gross Assets	Rs.
Gross Realisable value of assets specifically pledged	1,65,000
Other Assets	3,06,200
	4,71,200

Estimated Total Assets available for Preferential Creditors, Debentureholders secured by a floating charge and other creditors, brought forward.

Gross Liabilities Rs.	Liabilities		Rs.
			3,06,200
	(to be deducted from surplus or added to deficiency as the case may be)		
1,65,000	Secured creditors (as per list B) to the extent to which claims are estimated to be covered by assets specifically pledged (gross liabilities only)		
57,000	Preferential Creditors (as per list C)		57,000
	Estimated Balance of Assets available for Debentureholders and creditors secured by a floating charge, and unsecured creditors*		2,49,200
2,00,000	Debentureholders secured by a first floating charge (as per list D)		2,00,000
	Estimated Balance of Assets available for Bank Overdraft secured by a floating charge and unsecured creditors (as per list D)		49,200
20,000	Bank Overdraft secured by a second floating charge		20,000
	Estimated surplus as regards Debentureholders and other creditors secured by a floating charge		29,200
	Unsecured Creditors (as per list E)		
	Estimated unsecured balance of claims of creditors partly secured on a specific asset	10,000	
2,90,000	Trade Creditors	2,80,000	
6,000	Unclaimed dividends	6,000	
8,000	Outstanding Expenses	8,000	
15,000	Contingent liability on bill discounted	15,000	3,19,000
7,61,000	Estimated Deficiency as regards creditors (being the difference between Gross Assets and Gross Liabilities)		2,89,800

* The figures must be read subject to the following notes:—

(1) There is no unpaid capital liable to be called up.

(2) The estimates are subject to costs of the winding up and to any surplus or deficiency on trading pending realisation of the assets.

Rs.		*Rs.*	*Rs.*
	Issued and called up capital:		
	30,000 14% Preference shares of Rs. 10 each fully paid (as per list F)	3,00,000	
	20,000 Equity shares of Rs 10 each fully paid *less* calls in arrear (as per list G)	1,98,000	4,98,000
	Estimated Deficiency as regards Members		7,87,800

List H—Deficiency Account

		Rs.	*Rs.*
A.	**Items contributing to Deficiency:—**		
1.	Excess of Capital and Liabilities over Assets on 1st April, 2004 as shown by the Balance Sheet (copy attached)		Nil
2.	Net dividends and bonuses declared during the period from 1st April, 2004 to 31st March, 2010		1,13,400*
3.	Net trading losses after charging depreciation, taxation, interest on debentures, etc.		4,67,000
4.	Losses other than trading losses written off or for which provision has been made in the books during the same period:		
	Speculation Loss	91,000	
	Penalty imposed by Excise Authorities	1,60,000	
	Penalty imposed by Taxation Authorities	60,400	3,11,400
5.	Estimated losses now written off or for which provision has been made for the purpose of preparing the statement:		
	Plant and Machinery	30,000	
	Fixtures and Fittings	4,000	
	Stock in Trade	20,000	
	Patents	25,000	
	Book Debts	25,000	
	Bills Discounted	15,000	1,19,000
6.	Other items contributing to Deficiency		Nil
	Total (A)		10,10,800
B.	**Items reducing Deficiency :—**		
7.	Excess of assets over capital and liabilities on 1st April, 2004 as shown in the Balance Sheet (copy annexed)		65,000
8.	Net trading profits (after charging depreciation, taxation, interest on debentures, etc.) from 1st April, 2004 to 31st March, 2010		1,43,000
9.	Profits and income other than trading profits during the same period		Nil
10.	Other items reducing Deficiency—profit expected on realisation of Freehold Land and Buildings		15,000
	Total (B)		2,23,000
	Deficiency as shown by the Statement of Affairs (A—B)		7,87,800

3. LIQUIDATOR'S FINAL STATEMENT OF ACCOUNT

The liquidator's task is to realise the assets and disburse the amounts among those who have a rightful claim to it; in every case the liquidator has to prepare a statement showing how much he realised and how the amount was distributed. The following is the order in which disbursements will be made by the liquidator:—

(*a*) Secured creditors up to their claim or up to the amount realised by sale of securities held

	Rs.
* 14% on Rs. 3,00,000 for two years	84,000
15% on Rs. 1,96,000, *i.e.*, Rs. 2,00,000 *less* calls in arrear	29,000
	1,13,400

by them, whichever is less. The creditors themselves may sell the securities; they will pay to the liquidator any surplus after meeting their claims. Only the surplus is shown as a receipt; the payment to secured creditors is not shown in the liquidator's final statement of account. The balance left unsatisfied—that is when the claims of the creditors are more than the amount realised by sale of securities—will be added to unsecured creditors. Workmen's dues will rank *parri passu* with the secured creditors. These are called overriding preferntial payments.

(*b*) Legal charges.

(*c*) Remuneration to the liquidator.

(*d*) Costs of winding up.

(*e*) Preferential creditors.

(*f*) Debentureholders or other creditors having a floating charge on the assets of the company. (While preparing the Liquidator's Statement of Account, payment to preferential creditors is shown, however, after the payment to debentureholders having a floating charge.)

(*g*) Unsecured creditors. (This may include liability in respect of dividend or amounts due to shareholders on account of profits. In this case, the amount in respect of dividends, etc., shall be paid only after the outsiders are satisfied.)

(*h*) Preference shareholders.

(*i*) Equity shareholders. Unless the articles contain provisions to the effect that preference shareholders are entitled to participate in the surplus left after meeting the claims of the equity shareholders in full, the whole of the amount left after payment to preference shareholders will go to the equity shareholders.

The various claims have priority in the order mentioned above. Hence, if the amount available is exhausted after paying, say, the preferential creditors, payment cannot be made to unsecured creditors or anybody else coming after the preferential creditors. The form prescribed by the Supreme Court is given later.

While preparing the Liquidator's Statement of Account, it should be remembered that there is no double entry involved. It is only a statement although presented in the form of an account. (It is really a summary of the Cash Book after the start of liquidation).

Some Special Points :

Liquidator's Remuneration. In case of compulsory winding up, the remuneration is fixed by the Court and the amount is payable to the Court since the official liquidator is a salaried employee of the Government. In case of voluntary winding up, the remuneration is fixed by the meeting which appoints the liquidator. The remuneration once fixed cannot be increased.

Usually, the remuneration consists of a commission on assets realised plus a commission on the amount paid to unsecured creditors. Unsecured creditors include preferential creditors unless otherwise stated. The commission on unsecured creditors is on the amount *paid* and hence care should be exercised in calculating the commission. If the commission is 2% on amount paid to unsecured creditors, a payment of Rs. 100 to the unsecured creditors will entail a commission of Rs. 2 to the liquidator, thus absorbing Rs. 102. Hence, if the amount available is *insufficient* to pay the unsecured creditors fully, the commission due to the liquidator will be 2/102 of the amount available; the balance will be paid to the unsecured creditors.

Suppose, the amount realised by sale of assets is Rs. 3,00,000, and the amount due is Rs. 3,40,000 including Rs. 10,000 as preferential creditors. Then, if the liquidator is entitled to a commission of 3% on amounts realised and 2% on amounts distributed among the unsecured creditors, his remuneration will be calculated as follows :—

	Rs.
3% on amount realised by sale of assets, viz., Rs. 3,00,000	9,000
2% on preferential creditors, viz., Rs. 10,000	200
2/102 of the amount remaining viz., 2,80,800 (Rs. 3,00,000 — 9,000 — 200 — 10,000)	5,506
Or 2% on the amount paid to unsecured creditors, viz. Rs. 2,80,800 — 5,506 or Rs. 2,75,294	
	14,706

If the amount available is sufficient to pay all the creditors, the calculation of the remuneration to the liquidator is simple. Suppose, the liquidator is to get 2% on amount distributed among the unsecured creditors whose claims are Rs. 60,000; the amount available, say, is Rs. 80,000. The creditors will be paid Rs. 60,000. The liquidator will get 2% of this figure, viz., Rs. 1,200. The remaining amount (Rs. 80,000 — 60,000 — 1,200) will be paid to the shareholders.

Illustration 2:

The Ultra Optimist Ltd. went into liquidation. Its assets realised Rs. 3,50,000 excluding amount realised by sale of securities held by the secured creditors. The following was the position :—

	Rs.
Share Capital : 50,000 shares of Rs. 10 each	
Secured Creditors (securities realised Rs. 40,000)	35,000
Preferential Creditors	6,000
Unsecured Creditors	1,40,000
Debentures having a floating charge on the assets of the company	2,50,000
Liquidation Expenses	5,000
Liquidator's Remuneration	7,500

Prepare the Liquidator's Final Statement of Account.

Solution :

THE ULTRA OPTMIST LTD.
Liquidator's Final Statement of Account

	Rs.		Rs.
Assets Realised :		Liquidator's Remuneration	7,500
"Other" assets	3,50,000	Liquidation Expenses	5,000
Surplus from Securities	5,000	Debentures having a floating charge	2,50,000
		Preferential Creditors	6,000
		Unsecured Creditors— 61.79% of Rs. 1,40,000*	86,500
	3,55,000		3,55,000

Since the amount is not sufficient to pay the unsecured creditors fully, nothing can be paid to the shareholders.

Illustration 3:

A company went into liquidation on 31st March, 2010 when the following balance sheet was prepared:—

Liabilities	*Rs.*	*Assets*	*Rs.*
Share Capital:		Goodwill	50,000
Subscribed and paid up capital,		Leasehold Property	48,000
19,500 shares of Rs. 10 each	1,95,000	Plant and Machinery	65,500
Sundry Creditors :		Stock	56,800

* $\frac{86,500}{1,40,000} \times 100 = 61.79.$

	Rs.	Rs.		Rs.
Preferential	24,200		Sundry Debtors	64,820
Partly secured	55,310		Cash	2,500
Unsecured	99,790	1,79,300	Profit and Loss Account	98,680
Bank Overdraft (unsecured)		12,000		
		3,86,300		3,86,300

The liquidator realised the assets as follows :—

	Rs.
Leasehold Property which was used in the first instance to pay the partly secured creditors *pro rata*	35,000
Plant and Machinery	51,000
Stock	39,000
Sundry Debtors	58,500
Cash	2,500

The expenses of liquidation amounted to Rs. 1,000 and the liquidator's remuneration was agreed at 2.5% on the amount realised, including cash, and 2% on the amount paid to the unsecured creditors.

You are required to prepare the Liquidator's Final Accounts showing the distribution.

(Adapted from C.A. Final)

Solution:

Liquidator's Final Statement of Account

Receipts	*Estimated value** Rs.	*Value realised* Rs.	*Payments*		Rs.
Assets Realised :			Liquidator's Remuneration**:	Rs.	
Cash	2,500	2,500	2.5% on Rs. 1,86,000	4,650	
Debtors	64,820	58,500	2% on Rs. 24,200	484	
Stock	56,800	39,000	2% on Rs. 1,18,300	2,366	7,500
Plant & Machinery	65,500	51,000	Liquidation Expenses		1,000
			Preferential Creditors		24,200
			Unsecured Creditors (89.55%)		1,18,300
		1,51,000			1,51,000

Note. (i) Goodwill valued at Rs. 50,000 in books is valueless.

(ii) The total amount due to the unsecured creditors is Rs. 1,32,100 calculated as follows:—

	Rs.
Unsatisfied balance of partly secured creditors	20,310
Unsecured creditors	99,790
Bank Overdraft	12,000
	1,32,100

*In absence of estimated value, book figures have been given.

**Commission due to the liquidator will be on the total realisation on the supposition that the securities in the hands of creditors are realised by the liquidator on behalf of the partly secured creditors.

Form No. 156
(See Rule 329)
Companies Act, 1956

* Strike out what does not apply

* Here state whether the winding up is a members' or creditors' voluntary winding-up.

Liquidator's Statement of Account of the Winding-up (Members'/Creditors' Voluntary winding-up)
(Pursuant to Section 497/509)*

1. Name of the company .... Ltd.
2. Nature of proceeding :
3. Date of commencement of the winding-up :
4. Name and address of the Liquidator :

Statement showing how the winding-up has been conducted and the property of the company has been disposed of from .... 20 .... (commencement of winding-up) to .... 20 .... (close of winding-up.)

Receipts	*Estimated Value* *Rs. P*	*Value realised* *Rs. P.*	*Payments*	*Rs. P.*	*Payment* *Rs. P.*
Assets:			Legal Charges		
Cash at Bank ..			Liquidator's remuneration:—		
Cash in hand ..					
Marketable Securities ..			Where applicable —		
Bills Receivable ..			% on Rs. .... realised		
Trade Debtors ..			% on Rs. .... distributed		
Loans and Advances ..			Total		
Stock in Trade ..			(By whom fixed ....)		
Work in Progress ..			Auctioneers' and valuers' charges		
Freehold Property ..			Costs of possession and maintenance of estate		
Leasehold Property ..			Costs of notices in Gazette and news-papers		
Plant and Machinery ..			Incidental outlay (establishment charges and other expenses of liquidation)		
Furniture, Fittings, Utensils, etc. ..			total costs and charges		
Patents, Trade marks, etc. ..					
Investments other than marketable securities ..					

Surplus from Securities ..			(*i*) Debentureholders:		
Unpaid Calls at commencement of winding up ..			Payment of Rs. .... per Rs. .... debenture		
Amounts received from calls on contributories made in the winding-up ..			Payment of Rs. .... per Rs. .... debenture		
Receipts per Trading Account			Payment of Rs. .... per Rs. .... debenture		
Other Property, viz,			(*ii*) Creditors:—		
....			.... * Preferential		
....			.... * Unsecured:—		
Total ...			Dividend (s) ..... P. in the rupee on Rs. (The estimate of the amount expected to rank for dividend was Rs. ......)		
Less			(*iii*) Returns of contributories:—		
Payment to redeem securities ..			.... P. per rupee .... ** share		
Costs of execution ..			.... P. per rupee .... ** share		
Payments per Trading Account ..			.... P. per rupee .... ** share		
			Add balance		

* State the number; Preferential creditors need not be separately shown if all creditors have been paid in full.

** State nominal value and class of share.

(1) The follwoing assets estimated to be of the value of Rs. .... have proved to be unrealisable:—
(Give details of the assets which have proved to be unrealisable).

(2) Amount paid into the Companies Liquidation Account in respect of:—

(*a*) Unclaimated dividends payable to creditors in the winding-up — Rs. ....

(*b*) Other unclaimed distributions in the winding-up — Rs. ....

(*c*) Moneys held by the company in trust in respect of dividends or other sum due before the commencement of the winding up to any person as a member of the company — Rs. ....

(3) Add here any remarks the Liquidator thinks desirable:—

Dated this .... day of 20

(Sd.)
Liquidator.

I declare that the above statement is true and contains a full and accurate account of the winding-up from the commencement to the close of the winding-up.

Dated this .... day of 20

(Sd.)
Liquidator.

Debenture Interest. Debenture interest should be paid to the date of payment if the company is solvent. If the company is insolvent, interest should be paid only up to the date of winding up; the same applies to interest payable to other creditors. A company is solvent if it can pay all its creditors.

Preference Dividend. The position regarding arrears of dividend on preference share capital may be summarised as follows:—

(*i*) The question of arrears does not arise in case of non-cumulative preference shares. But if the shares are not specifically stated as non-cumulative, they should be treated as cumulative.

(*ii*) No dividend is payable for any period falling after the commencement of winding up.

(*iii*) As regards arrears of dividend up to the date of winding-up, the provisions of the Articles of Association will apply. As a rule, a dividend becomes payable only when declared by the shareholders in general meeting. If dividend on preference shares was declared, it is to be paid as a debt and not as an arrear of dividend.

It is settled law that in the case of cumulative preference shares, the arrears of dividend are payable on winding up, subject, of course, to settlement of all claims of outsiders. Thus, if need be and possible, a call should be made on equity shareholders to pay arrears of dividend on cumulative preference shares.

Equity Shareholders are paid last of all, if funds are available. In case the equity shares are partly paid and the amount available is not sufficient to satisfy the claims of preference shareholders in full, the equity shareholders should be called upon to pay a suitable amount.

Example : 1. The amount available after paying all creditors is Rs. 75,000. The company's share capital consists of 10,000 Preference Shares of Rs. 10 each, and 10,000 Equity Shares of Rs. 10 each, Rs. 6 paid. In this case the equity shareholders will have to pay Rs. 2.50 per share so that their contribution (Rs. 2.50 x 10,000) together with the amount already available will enable the preference shareholders to be paid off.

2. But suppose, in the above example, the amount available after paying all creditors is Rs. 20,000, other facts being the same as above. In that case, the equity shareholders will pay Rs. 4 per share because that is the maximum they can be called upon to pay. They will contribute Rs. 40,000 thus making the total amount available to be Rs. 60,000. This will be paid to the preference shareholders.

If the equity shareholders have paid different amounts on their shares, the loss suffered by each equity shareholder should be equal. While distributing cash among them or while calling upon them to pay, care should be taken to see that all equity shareholders suffer equally.

Example : 1. The amount available after paying creditors and preference shareholders is Rs. 80,000. The company's equity share capital consists of 10,000 shares of Rs. 10 each, Rs. 8 paid up and 5,000 shares of Rs. 10 each, Rs. 6 paid up. In this case, first Rs. 2 must be returned on those shares on which Rs. 8 has been paid up. This will make all shares Rs. 6 paid. This will absorb Rs. 20,000; the remaining Rs. 60,000 will be distributed on 15,000 shares, i.e., Rs. 4 per share. The loss suffered by equity shareholders will be Rs. 2 per share.

2. The amount available after paying creditors is Rs. 60,000.

The company's share capital consists of :—

(*a*) 1,000 14% Preference Shares of Rs. 100 each.

(*b*) 4,000 Equity Shares of Rs. 100 each, Rs. 95 paid.

(*c*) 6,000 Equity Shares of Rs. 100 each, Rs. 90 paid.

In this case, the additional amount required for paying the preference shareholders is Rs. 40,000, i.e., 1,00,000 — 60,000. This amount should be raised by first of all calling up Rs. 5 on 6,000 equity shares (which will raise Rs. 30,000 and which will make all equity shares Rs. 95 paid up). The remaining amount of Rs. 10,000 should be raised by calling up a further Re. 1 on all equity shares. Thus holders of 4,000 equity shares will pay Re. 1 per share and those holding 6,000 equity shares will pay Rs. 6 per share.

Illustration 4:

The following information is given to you:—

Balance Sheet of A Ltd. on March 31, 2009

Liabilities	Rs.	*Assets*	Rs.
Share Capital:		Land & Buildings	1,00,000
2,000 14% Preference shares of Rs. 100, fully paid-up	2,00,000	Machinery & Plant	2,50,000
1,000 Equity shares of Rs. 100 each, Rs. 75 paid	75,000	Patents	40,000
3,000 Equity shares of Rs. 100 each, Rs. 60 paid	1,80,000	Stock at cost	55,000
14% Debentures having a floating charge on all assets	1,00,000	Sundry Debtors	1,10,000
Interest Outstanding	14,000	Cash at Bank	75,500
Creditors	1,45,000	Profit & Loss Account	83,500
	7,14,000		7,14,000

The company went into liquidation on the above date.

The preference dividends were in arrear for two years. The arrears are payable automatically on liquidation. Creditors include a loan for Rs. 50,000 on the mortgage of Land and Buildings. The assets were realised as follows :—

	Rs.
Land and Buildings	1,20,000
Machinery and Plant	2,00,000
Patents	30,000
Stock	60,000
Sundry Debtors	80,000

The expenses of liquidation amounted to Rs. 10,900. The liquidator is entitled to a commission of 3 per cent on all assets realised except cash and a commission of 2 per cent on amounts distributed among unsecured creditors. Preferential creditors amount to Rs. 15,000. Assume the payment was made on September 30, 2009.

Prepare the Liquidator's Statement of Account.

Solution :

Liquidator's Statement of Account

Receipts	*Estimated value Rs.*	*Value realised Rs.*	*Payments*	*Rs.*	*Amount paid Rs.*
Assets realised;			Liquidator's remuneration :		
Cash	75,500	75,500	3% on Rs. 4,90,000	14,700	
Debtors	1,10,000	80,000	2% on Rs. 95,000	1,900	16,600
Stock	55,000	60,000	Expenses of liquidation		10,900
Plant and Machinery	2,50,000	2,00,000	Debentures having a floating charge	1,00,000	
Patents	40,00C	30,000			
Surplus from securities		70,000	Interest up to 30th September, 2009	21,000	1,21,000
			Creditors: Preferential		15,000
			Others		80,000
			Preference shareholders		2,00,000
			Arrears of preference dividend		56,000

	Rs.	Rs.			Rs.
			Equity shareholders :		
			Rs. 15 on 1,000 shares	15,000	
			Re. 0.25 on 4,000 shares	1,000	16,000
		5,15,500			5,15,500

Illustration 5:

Miniature Ltd. went into voluntary liquidation on 31st January, 2010. The balances in its books on that day were :—

	Rs.		Rs.
Issued Capital :-			
13,000 14% Preference shares of Rs. 10 each, fully paid up	1,30,000	Furniture at cost	9,360
		Investment at cost	2,21,000
6,500 Equity Shares of Rs. 10 each, Rs. 5 paid up	32,500	Life Insurance Policy received from a debtor	16,900
14% Debentures	26,000	Sundry Debtors	1,04,000
Loan from Bank (guaranteed by Directors)	39,000	Cash at Bank	11,700
		Profit and Loss Account	4,680
Sundry Trade Creditors	1,07,000		
Income Tax	17,550		
Employees' Salaries for 1 month (including Rs. 4,950 for Managing Director)	15,590		
	3,67,640		3,67,640

The Bank called upon the Directors to implement their guarantee. The preference dividend had been paid up to 30th September, 2007. There were no arrears of debenture interest. The amount owing to the Government for income-tax was in respect of assessment years 2008-2009 and 2009-2010 of Rs. 3,250, Rs. 14,300 respectively. The company closes its accounts on 31st March each year.

The Liquidator admitted an amount of Rs. 2,730 for salaries in lieu of notice. The rent was paid up to 31st January, 2010. The premises were held under a lease with annual tenancy. The landlord agreed to waive his right to notice on the Liquidator undertaking to pay him two months' rent, i.e., Rs. 650 and to vacate the premises by 31st March, 2010 which he did.

One of the creditors for Rs. 13,000 was under a contract to deliver certain goods to the Company in March, 2010 and the Company had contracted to supply the same goods to Basic Ltd., who were included in Sundry Debtors at Rs. 6,500. The creditor refused to make delivery but admitted a claim made by the Liquidator for damages at Rs. 1,625. Basic Ltd. made a claim for loss against the Company for Rs. 975 which was admitted by the Liquidator.

Furniture was sold for Rs. 7,800. Investments were found to be valueless. Sums owing by Debtors were all collected and the Insurance Policy was surrendered for Rs. 15,600 after the Liquidator had paid a premium of Rs. 585. A shareholder holding 2,600 equity shares failed to pay the call made by the Liquidator. Legal costs came to Rs. 780 and liquidator's remuneration to Rs. 6,500.

Prepare Liquidator's Final Statement of Account. *(Adapted C.A., Final)*

Solution :

Notes. (*i*) Preferential creditors:

	Rs.
Employees' salaries for one month excluding the remuneration payable to the managing director	10,640
Income tax for 2009-2010 (assuming the assessment for the year was made within 12 months prior to 31st January, 2010	14,300
	24,940

		Rs.
(*ii*)	Unsecured creditors :	
	Loan from bank (Directors for their payment to Bank)	39,000
	Sundry trade creditors	1,07,000
	Income tax for 2008-2009	3,250
	Salary of managing director	4,950
	Amount to be paid to employees in lieu of notice	2,730
		1,56,930
	Less: Amount recoverable from the creditor who did not supply the contracted goods	1,625
		1,55,305
(*iii*)	The expenses of liquidation would consist of :	
	Legal costs	780
	Rent paid up to 31st March, 2010	650
		1,430

(*iv*) It is assumed the debentures have a floating charge on the assets of the company.

(*v*) Basic Ltd. will deduct the sum of Rs. 975 from the amount payable by them.

Liquidator's Final Statement of Account

	Rs.	*Rs.*		*Rs.*
Assets Realised :			Legal Costs	780
Cash at Bank	11,700		Liquidation Remuneration	6,500
Life Policy *less* premium paid	15,015		Liquidation Expenses	650
Sundry Debtors	1,03,025		Debentures having a floating charge	26,000
Furniture	7,800	1,37,540	Preferential Creditors	27,940
Calls on Contributories, Rs. 5 on 3,900 equity shares		19,500	Unsecured Creditors (61.27%)	95,170
		1,57,040		1,57,040

Receiver for Debentureholders :

A receiver is generally appointed by the Court to take possession of certain property for protective purposes or for receiving income and profits from the property and for applying it as directed. Sometimes, a mortgagee is also given the power to appoint a receiver in certain circumstances. The debentureholders may have the power under the Debenture Deed. The Receiver will have the duty of duly accounting for the sums received by him. In case the company is being wound up, the Receiver (if appointed) will have to observe the rule regarding preferential payments and after paying the mortgagee by whom he is appointed (or paying those persons for whose protection he is appointed by the Court) he will have to hand over the surplus to the Liquidator. There will thus be two accounts: (1) the Receiver's Statement of Account and (2) Liquidator's Final Statement of Account. The Receiver is entitled to recover his expenses and remuneration from sums collected by him.

Illustration 6:

The following is the Balance Sheet of Overconfident Ltd. as on 31st March. 2010.

	Rs.		*Rs.*
Share Capital :		Buildings	50,000
10,000 14% Preference Shares of Rs. 10 each, fully paid	1,00,000	Other Sundry Assets	5,29,000
10,000 Equity Shares of Rs. 10 each, fully paid	1,00,000	Preliminary Expenses	10,000
		Profit and Loss Account	33,500

	Rs.	Rs.		Rs.
5,000 Equity Shares of Rs. 10 each, Rs. 8.50 paid		42,500		
14% Debentures		2,50,000		
Loan on Mortgage		30,000		
Bank Overdraft		25,000		
Trade Creditors		55,000		
Due for Income Tax				
- 2008-2009 -	15,000			
2009-2010	5,000	20,000		
		6,22,500		6,22,500

The mortgage was secured on the buildings and the debentures were secured by a floating charge on all the assets of the company. The debentureholders appointed a Receiver. A Liquidator was also appointed, the company being voluntarily wound up. The Receiver was entrusted with the task of realising the Buildings which fetched Rs. 40,000. The Receiver took charge of "Sundry Assets" amounting to Rs. 4,00,000 and sold them for Rs. 3,70,000. The Bank was secured by a personal guarantee of the directors who discharged their obligations in full. The balance of the assets realised Rs. 1,20,000. The costs of the Receiver amounted to Rs. 1,000 and his remuneration to Rs. 1,250. The expenses of liquidation was Rs. 2,000 and the remuneration of the liquidator was Rs. 750. Preference dividend was in arrear for 3 years. According to the Articles, the arrears were payable if there was a surplus on winding up.

Prepare the accounts to be submitted by the Receiver and the Liquidator.

Solution :

Receiver's Receipts and Payments Account

Receipts	*Rs.*	*Rs.*	*Payments*	*Rs.*
Assets Realised			Costs of the Receiver	1,000
..			Remuneration of the Receiver	1,250
..			Preferential Payments	20,000
..		3,70,000	(the assessment is presumed to have been made within 12 months preceding the date of liquidation)	
Surplus Received from Mortgagee				
Proceeds of Buildings	40,000			
Mortgage Paid	30,000	10,000		
			Debentureholders	2,50,000
			Balance transferred to Liquidator	1,07,750
		3,80,000		3,80,000

Liquidator's Final Statement of Account

Receipts	*Rs.*	*Payments*	*Rs.*	*Rs.*
Surplus received from Receiver	1,07,750	Liquidator's Remuneration		750
Sundry Assets realised	1,20,000	Costs of Liquidation		2,000
		Unsecured Creditors		80,000
		Preference Shareholders		1,00,000
		Equity Shareholders:	*Rs.*	
		Rs. 1.50 on 10,000 shares	15,000	
		Rs. 2.00 on 15,000 shares	30,000	45,000
	2,27,750			2,27,750

The equity shareholders suffer a loss of Rs. 6.50 per share.

Since there is insufficient amount to return fully the capital contributed by the equity shareholders, preference shareholders have no claim for arrears of dividend.

Illustration 7:

X-ray Ltd. is a private company, the members' holding being:

	X	*R*	*A*	*Y*	*Total*
Equity shares Rs. 10 each,	—	7,200	5,400	5,400	18,000
14% Preferences Shares (Rs. 10 each)	20,000	5,000	—	—	25,000

The company's balance sheet on 30th September, 2009 was as follows:

Liabilities	*Rs.*	*Assets*	*Rs.*
Share Capital :		Freehold Property	1,20,000
Equity	1,80,000	Leasehold Property	3,00,000
Preference	2,50,000	Plant	1,20,000
Revenue Reserve	3,33,000	Motors	30,000
14% Debentures	2,00,000	Investment—Trade	30,000
Trade Creditors	2,00,000	Quoted	41,000
Liability for Income Tax	50,000	Stock	1,40,000
Directors' Loans : X	50,000	Debtors	1,50,000
R	40,000	Cash at Bank	3,72,000
	13,03,000		13,03,000

Dividends on Preference shares were paid upto 30th September, 2008. Under the Articles, arrears of preference dividend were automatically payable in the event of the company being wound up. Also holders of preference shares are entitled to participate equally with equity shareholders in surplus assets upto Rs. 2 per share.

On 1st October, 2009 it was decided to take the company into liquidation; R, A and Y decided to form a partnership to carry on the business previously carried on by the company. They agreed that the partnership capital should be Rs. 4,50,000 to be provided in the same ratio as that of equity shares held by them. They also agreed that they would bring into the firm, as loan, any cash received by them. X agreed to lend to the firm the amount which he would receive by way of capital on his preference shares.

The liquidator was given power to distribute assets in specie; R, A and Y agreed to take the assets so distributed, bringing them into the firm at the values placed on them by the liquidator.

The liquidation was completed on 31st March, 2010; the liquidator dealt with the assets as follows:

(*i*) Freehold property distributed at a valuation of Rs. 1,80,000.
(*ii*) Leasehold property sold for Rs. 4,15,000.
(*iii*) Plant distributed at Rs. 92,500.
(*iv*) One motor sold for Rs. 7,500; the other distributed at Rs. 25,000.
(*v*) Quoted investments sold for Rs. 81,000.
(*vi*) Trade Investments distributed at Rs. 55,000.
(*vii*) Stock distributed at book values; and
(*viii*) Debtors realised in full subject to bad debts of Rs. 3,500.

The creditors were repaid subject to a discount of Rs. 1,000; other liabilities were paid off on 31st March, 2010.

The liquidator's remuneration was agreed at 1% on the assets converted into cash and, in addition, 2% on the total return of capital to contributories. Liquidation expenses totalled Rs. 2,000.

Prepare the Liquidator's Statement of Account and show the distribution among R, A and Y.

(*Adapted from C.A. Eng., PEI*)

Solution :

Xray Ltd.
Liquidator's Statement of Account

Receipts	*Estimated Value*	*Value Realised Rs.*	*Payments*	*Rs.*	*Payment Rs.*
Cash at Bank		3,72,000	Liquidator's Remuneration		
Quoted Investments		81,000	1% on Rs. 6,50,000	6,500	
Sundry Debtors		1,46,500	2% on Rs. 9,00,000	18,000	24,500
Motor		7,500	Liquidation Expenses		2,000
Leasehold property		4,15,000	Debentures :		
Assets distributed in specie:			Paid up value	2,00,000	
Freehold Property		1,80,000	Interest for 6 months	14,000	2,14,000
Plant		92,500	Creditors :		
Motor		25,000	Preferential	50,000	
Trade Investments		55,000	Others (in full)	2,89,000	3,39,000
Stock		1,40,000	Preference Shareholders :		
			Arrears of Dividend (one year)		35,000
			Rs. 12 per share on 25,000 shares		3,00,000
			Equity Shareholders:		
			Rs. 33.33 per share on 18,000 shares		6,00,000
Total		15,14,500			15,14,500

Statement showing the amount distributed amongst members:

	Total Rs.	*X Rs.*	*R Rs.*	*A Rs.*	*Y Rs.*
Preference Shares @ Rs. 12 per share	3,00,000	2,40,000	60,000	—	—
Equity Shares @ Rs. 12 per share	2,16,000	—	86,400	64,800	64,800
Surplus (in the ratio of 72:54:54 or 4:3:3)	3,84,000	—	1,53,600	1,15,200	1,15,200
Total	9,00,000	2,40,000	3,00,000	1,80,000	1,80,000
Capital in the new firm (Rs. 4,50,000 in the ratio of 4:3:3	4,50,000	—	1,80,000	1,35,000	1,35,000
Balance as Loan	4,50,000	2,40,000	1,20,000	45,000	45,000

Working Notes:

			Rs.
(*i*) Liquidator's Remuneration:			
1% on assets realised in cash Rs. 6,50,000 i.e. Rs. 10,22,000 less Rs. 3,72,000, balance at bank			6,500
2% on amount distributed as capital to contributories:		Rs.	
Total available		15,14,500	
Less Payments : Liquidator's Remuneration	6,500		
Liquidation Expenses	2,000		
Debentures	2,14,000		
Creditors	3,39,000		
Preference Dividend	35,000		
		5,96,500	
		9,18,000	
Liquidator's Remuneration Rs. 9,18,000 × 2/102			18,000
			24,500

		Rs.
(*ii*) Amount available for contributories:		
(Rs. 9,18,000 *less* Liquidator Remuneration)		9,00,000
Distribution: Preference Shareholders Rs. 12 per share		3,00,000
Equity Shareholders Rs. 12 per share		2,16,000
		5,16,000
Surplus for Equity Shareholders		3,84,000
		9,00,000

		Rs.
(*iii*) Cash brought into the new firm:		
Total cash available with liquidator		10,22,000
Cash Payments : Remuneration to Liquidator	24,500	
Expenses	2,000	
Debentures	2,14,000	
Creditors	3,39,000	
Preference Dividend	35,000	6,14,500
Cash distributed among partners and brought into the firm as newly constituted.		4,07,500
Add: Assets distributed in specie		4,92,500
		9,00,000

Illustration 8:

The following is the Balance Sheet of Y Limited as at **31st March, 2009** :

Liabilities	*Rs.*	*Assets*	*Rs.*
Share Capital :		Fixed Assets :	
2,000 Equity Shares of Rs. 100 each,		Land and Buildings	4,00,000
Rs. 75 per share paid up	1,50,000	Plant and Machineries	3,80,000
6,000 Equity Shares of Rs. 100 each,		Current Assets :	
Rs. 60 per share paid up	3,60,000	Stock at cost	1,10,000
2,000 10% Preference Share of		Sundry Debtors	2,20,000
Rs. 100 each, fully paid up	2,00,000	Cash at Bank	60,000
10% Debentures (having a floating		Profit and Loss Account	2,40,000
charge on all assets)	2,00,000		
Interest accrued on Debentures			
(also secured as above)	10,000		
Sundry Creditors	4,90,000		
	14,10,000		14,10,000

On that date, the company went into Voluntary Liquidation. The dividends on preference shares were in arrears for the last two years. Sundry Creditors include a loan of Rs. 90,000 on mortgage of Land and Buildings. The assets realised were as under :

	Rs.
Land and Buildings	3,40,000
Plant and Machineries	3,60,000
Stock	1,20,000
Sundry Debtors	1,60,000

Interest accrued on loan on mortgage of buildings upto the date of payment amounted to Rs. 10,000. The expense of Liquidation amounted to Rs. 4,600. The Liquidator is entitled to a remuneration of 3% on all the assets realised (except cash at bank) and 2% on the amounts distributed among equity shareholders. Preferential creditors included in sundry credittors amount to Rs. 30,000. All payments were made on **30th June, 2009**. Prepare the liquidators' final statement of account.

[*Adapted C.A. (Inter) Nov. 1994*]

Solution :

Liquidator's Statement of Accounts

Receipts	*Estimated Value (Rs)*	*Value Realised (Rs.)*	*Payments*	*(Rs.)*	*Payment (Rs.)*
Assets realised :			Liquidation Expenses		4,600
Cash at Bank	60,000	60,000	Liquidator's Remuneration :		
Sundry Debtors	2,20,000	1,60,000	3% on Rs. 9,80,000 realised	29,400	
Stock	1,10,000	1,20,000	2% on Rs. 50,000 distributed		
Plant and Machinery	3,80,000	3,60,000	among equity shareholders	1,000	30,400
Surplus from Secured			Debentureholders :		
Creditors :			1% Debentures	2,00,000	
Land and Buildings,			Interest accrued on debentures	15,000	2,15,000
Rs. 3,40,000 – Rs. 1,00,000		2,40,000	Creditors :		
			Preferential	30,000	
			Unsecured	3,70,000	4,00,000
			Return to Contributors		
			Preference Shareholders :		
			10% Preference Share Capital	2,00,000	
			Arrears of Dividend	40,000	2,40,000
			Equity Shareholders :		
			Rs. 17.50 per share on 2,000 shares	35,000	
			Rs. 2.50 per share on 6,000 shares	15,000	50,000
		9,40,000			9,40,000

Working Notes :

(*i*) *Interest accrued on debentures :*

	Rs.
Interest accrued upto the date of balance sheet	10,000
Interest accrued for subsequent three months, Rs. 2,00,000 × 3/12 × 10/100	5,000
Total	15,000

(*ii*) *Commission to liquidator on assets realised :*

Land and buildings	3,40,000
Plant and machinery	3,60,000
Stock	1,20,000
Sundry debtors	1,60,000
	9,80,000

Commission @ 3% = Rs. 9,80,000 × 3 / 100 = Rs. 29,400

(*iii*) *Commission to liquidator on amount dsitributed :*

Receipts	9,40,000
Less : Payments, Rs. (4,600 + 29,400 + 2,15,000 + 30,000 + 3,70,000 + 2,40,000)	8,89,000
Amount available before commission	51,000

Commission @ 2% = Rs. 51,000 x 2 / 102 = Rs. 1,000

(*iv*) Total paid up equity share capital = Rs. 5,10,000

Loss to be borne by then = Rs. 5,10,000 - Rs. 50,000 = Rs. 4,60,000

Loss per share = Rs. 4,60,000 / 8,000 = Rs. 57.50

Refund per equity share will paid up value of Rs. 75 = Rs. 75 – Rs. 57.50 = Rs. 17.50

Refund per equity share will paid up value of Rs. 60 = Rs. 60 – Rs. 57.50 = Rs. 2.50

"B" List of contributories:

Those persons who ceased to be shareholders (other than by death) within a year of the date of winding up of the company are liable to pay up the amount unpaid on the shares held by them, if the amount due to various persons, while such former members were shareholders, remains unpaid at the time of winding up. Such former members are not liable to contribute for debts incurred after they ceased to be members. They will not also be liable, if all the creditors can be paid out of the moneys realised from sale of assets or from the shareholders who are members at the time of winding up ("A" List). Also, there will be no liability to pay anything if the present shareholders pay or have paid the amount due on the shares.

Suppose, A held 1,000 shares of Rs. 10 each, Rs. 7.50 paid up. He transferred his shares on 31st October, 2009 to B. The company goes into liquidation on 31st March, 2010. A debt existing on 31st October, 2009 remains unpaid. A can be called upon to pay the debt subject to the maximum limit of Rs. 2,500 because his total liability, when he transferred his shares, was Rs. 2.50 per share. Had A transferred the shares on, say, the 15th March, 2009, there would have been no liability upon him. Also, if B has paid the amount due on the shares, A has no liability. If there are more than one member who ceased to be such within one year of the date of winding up, each would be liable to pay proportionately subject to the maximum due on the shares.

Suppose (1) a company goes into liquidation on 31st October, 2008 leaving a debt of Rs. 2,400 unpaid; (2) it is found that A who held 1,000 shares and B who held 500 shares of Rs. 10 each, Rs. 7 paid up, had transferred the shares on 15th November, 2008; and (3) the debt had been incurred sometime before 15th November, 2008. In this case, A and B will contribute proportionately, that is in the ratio of 2 to 1. A will pay Rs. 1,600 and B will pay Rs. 800.

Illustration 9:

In liquidation which commenced on 1st April, 2010 certain creditors could not receive payment out of the realisation of the assets and out of contribution from "A" list contributories. The following are the details of certain transfers which took place after 1st April, 2009 :—

Shareholders	*Numer of Shares transferred*	*Date of ceasing to be member*	*Creditors remaining unpaid and outstanding on the date of ceasing to be member*
			Rs.
A	1,000	1st May, 2009	6,000
B	1,500	1st July, 2009	7,500
C	300	1st Nov, 2009	8,000
D	200	1st Feb, 2010	9,500

All the shares were of Rs. 10 each, Rs. 6 paid up. Ignoring expenses, remuneration to liquidator etc., show the amount to be realised from the various persons listed above.

Solution :

The amount of Rs. 6,000 outstanding on 1st May, 2009 will have to be contributed by all the four persons in the ratio of number of shares held by them, i.e., in the ratio of 10:15:3:2. Thus *A* will have to contribute Rs. 2,000. *B*, Rs. 3,000; *C*, Rs. 600 and *D*. Rs. 400. Similarly, the further debts incurred between 1st May, 2009 and 1st July, 2009 viz., Rs. 1,500 (for which *A* is not liable) will be contributed by *B,C,* and *D* in the ratio of 15:3:2. *B* will have to contribute Rs. 1,125, *C* will have to contribute Rs. 225 and *D* will have to contribute Rs. 150. The further increase from Rs. 7,500 to Rs. 8,000; viz., Rs. 500 occurring between 1st November will be shared by *C* and *D* who will be liable for Rs. 300 and Rs. 200 respectively. The increase between 1st November and 1st February is solely the responsibility of *D*.

The following statement makes the position clear.

Statement of Liability of *B* List Contributories

Creditors outstanding on date ceasing to be member	*A* 1,000 *share*	*B* 1,500 *shares*	*C* 300 *shares*	*D* 200 *shares*	*Amount to be paid to creditors*
	Rs.	*Rs.*	*Rs.*	*Rs.*	*Rs.*
(1) 6,000	2,000	3,000	600	400	6,000
(2) 1,500	—	1,125	225	150	1,500
(3) 500	—	—	300	200	500
(4) 1,500	—	—	—	1,500	50*
Total (*a*)	2,000	4,125	1,125	2,250	
(*b*) Maximum Liability on shares held4,000	6,000	1,200	800		
(*c*) Amount paid (a) or (b) whichever is lower	2,000	4,125	1,125	800	

Illustration 10:

Pessimist Ltd. has gone into liquidation on 10th May, 2010. The details of members, who have ceased to be members within one year ('B' contributories) are given below. The debts that could not be paid out of realisation of assets and contribution from present members ('A' contributories) are also given with their date-wise break up. Share are of Rs. 10 each Rs. 6 per share paid up.

You are to determine the amount realisable from each person.

Shareholders	*No. of shares transferred*	*Date of transfer*	*Proportionate unpaid debts*
P	1,000	20.4.2009	3,000
Q	1,200	15.5.2009.	5,000
R	1,500	18.9.2009	9,200
S	800	24.12.2009	10,500
T	500	12.3.2010	11,000

[*Adapted C.A. (Inter), Nov. 2000*]

Solution :

P has ceased to be a member more than a year ago from the date of winding up; hence he is not liable as a contributory. The amount of Rs. 5,000 outstanding on 15.5.2009 will have to be contributed by Q, R, S and T in the ratio of number of share held by them i.e. 1200, 1500, 800 and 500 respectively. The additional debts incurred from 15.5.2000 to 18.9.2009 *i.e.* Rs. 4,200 will be contributed by R, S and T in the ratio of 1500, 800 and 500 respectively. The further increase of Rs. 1,300 will be borne by S and T in the ratio of 800 and 500 respectively. Finally, the last increase of Rs. 500 will be the sole responsibility of T, limited to his maximum liability.

The following statement makes the position clear.

* Against D's liability of Rs. 2,250, he can be called upon to pay only Rs. 800; the loss of Rs. 1,450 will have to be suffered by these creditors.

Statement of Liability of B List Contributories

Creditors outstanding on date ceasing to be member	Q 1,200 *shares*	R 1,500 *shares*	S 800 *shares*	T 500 *shares*	Amount to be paid to creditors
	Rs.	*Rs.*	*Rs.*	*Rs.*	*Rs.*
(1) 5,000	1,500	1,875	1,000	625	5,000
(2) 4,200	—	2,250	1,200	750	4,200
(3) 1,300	—	—	800	500	1,300
(4) 500	—	—	—	500	125
Total (*a*)	1,500	4,125	3,000	2,375	10,625
(*b*) Maximum liability on shares held @ Rs. 4 per share	4,800	6,000	3,200	2,000	
(*c*) Amount paid, (*a*) or (*b*) whichever is less	1,500	4,125	3,000	2,000	

Illustration 11:

In a winding up of a company certain creditors remained unpaid. The following persons had transferred their holding sometime before winding up :

Name	*Date of transfer*	*No. of shares transferred*	*Amount due to creditors on the date of transfer*
	2009		*Rs.*
P	January 1	1,000	7,500
Q	February 15	400	12,500
S	March 15	700	18,000
T	March 31	900	21,000
U	April 5	1,000	30,000

The shares were of Rs. 100 each, Rs. 80 being called up and paid up on the date of transfers.

A member, R, who held 200 shares died on 28th February, 2009 when the amount due to creditors was Rs. 15,000. His shares were transmitted to his son X.

Z was the transferee of shares held by T, Z paid Rs. 20 per share as calls in advance immediately on becoming a member.

The liquidation of the company commenced on 1st February, 2010 when the liquidator made a call on the present and the past contributories to pay the amount.

You are asked to quantify the maximum liability of the transferors of shares mentioned in the above table, when the transferees :

(*i*) pay the amount due as 'present' member contributories;

(*ii*) do not pay the amount due as 'present' member contributories.

Also quantify the liability of X to whom shares were transmitted on the demise of his father R.

[*C.A. (Inter), Nov. 1997 Modified*]

Solution :

Statement of liability as contributories of former members

Creditors outstanding on the date of transfer (ceasing to be member)			Q	R/X	S	U	Amount to be paid to creditors
No. of Shares			400	200	700	1,000	
2009		*Rs.*	*Rs.*	*Rs.*	*Rs.*	*Rs.*	*Rs.*
Feb. 15		12,500	2,174	1,087	3,804	5,435	12,500
Feb. 28	15,000 − 12,500	2,500	—	263	921	1,316	2,500

			Q	R/X	S	U	Amount to creditors
March 15	18,000 − 15,000	3,000	—	316	1,105	1,579	3,000
April 5	30,000 − 18,000	12,000	—	2,000	—	10,000	12,000
Total (*a*)		30,000	2,174	3,666	5,830	18,330	30,000
Maximum Liability at Rs. 20 per share on shares held (*b*)			8,000	4,000	14,000	20,000	
Lower of (*a*) and (*b*)			2,174	3,666	5,830	18,330	

Working Notes :

(*i*) The transferors are P, Q, S, T and U. When the transferees pay the amount due as 'present' member contributories, there will not be any liability on the transferors. It is only when the transferees do not pay as 'present' member contributories that the liability would arise in the case of 'past' members as contributories.

(*ii*) X to whom share were transmitted on demise of his father R would be liable as an existing member contributory. He steps into the shoes of his deceased father under section 430. His maximum liability would be at Rs. 20 per share on 200 shares received on transmission i.e. for Rs. 4,000.

(*iii*) P will not be liable to pay any amount as the winding up proceedings commenced after one year from the date of the transfer. T also will not be liable as the transferee Z has paid the balance Rs. 20 per share as call in advance.

(*iv*) Q, R/X, S and U will be liable, as former members, to the maximum extent as indicated, provided the transferees do not pay the calls.

EXERCISE XXVIII

Practical

1. Shri A.B. Govindan is appointed liquidator of a company in voluntary liquidation on 1st July, 2009 and the following balances are extracted from the books on that date :—

	Rs.		*Rs.*
Capital :		Machinery	30,000
8,000 shares of Rs. 10 each	80,000	Leasehold Properties	40,000
Debentures	50,000	Stock-in-trade	1,000
Bank Overdraft	18,000	Book Debts	60,000
Liabilities for Purchases	20,000	Investments	6,000
Provision for Bad Debts	10,000	Calls in arrear	5,000
		Cash in hand	1,000
		Profit and Loss Account	35,000
	1,78,000		1,78,000

Prepare a statement of affairs to be submitted to the meeting of the creditors. The machinery is valued at Rs. 60,000, the Leasehold Properties at Rs. 73,000, investments at Rs. 4,000, Stock in Trade at Rs. 2,000; bad debts are Rs. 2,000, doubtful debts are Rs. 4,000 estimated to realise Rs. 2,000. The Bank Overdrafts is secured by deposit of title deeds of Leasehold Properties. Preferential creditors for taxes and wages are Rs. 1,000. Telephone rent owing is Rs. 80.

(Adapted C.A., Final)

(Gross Assets Rs. 2,01,000; Gross Liabilities Rs. 89,080; Surplus as to Creditors Rs. 1,11,920)

2. The following particulars were extracted from the books of X Ltd. on 1st April, 2010 on which day a winding up order was made :—

	Rs.
Equity Share Capital :	
20,000 shares of Rs. 10 each, Rs. 5 paid up	1,00,000
14% Preference Share Capital:	
20,000 shares of Rs. 10 each, fully paid	2,00,000
14% First Mortgage Debentures, secured by a floating charge upon the whole of the assets of the company, exclusive of the uncalled capital	1,50,000
Fully Secured Creditors (values of securities, Rs. 35,000)	30,000
Partly Secured Creditors (values of securities, Rs. 10,000)	20,000
Preferential creditors for rates, taxes, wages, etc.	6,000
Bills Payable	1,00,000
Unsecured Creditors	70,000
Bank Overdraft	10,000
Bills Receivable in hand	15,000
Bills Discounted (one bill for Rs. 10,000 known to be bad)	40,000
Book Debts—Good	10,000
— Doubtful (estimated to produce 50%)	7,000
— Bad	6,000
Land & Building (estimated to produce Rs. 1,00,000)	1,50,000
Stock in Trade (estimated to produce Rs. 40,000)	50,000
Machinery, Tools, etc. (estimated to produce Rs. 2,000)	5,000
Cash in hand	100

Make out (1) Statement of affairs as regards creditors and contributories, and (2) Deficiency Account, *(Adapted from C.A., Final)*

(Deficiency as regards creditors, contributories, Rs. 1,80,400 and Rs. 4,80,400 respectively)

Hint: Prepare Balance Sheet; excess of liabilities and capital over assets, Rs. 3,79,900.

3. The following information was extracted from the books of a limited company on 31st March, 2010 on which date a winding up order was made—

	Rs.
Equity Share Capital:	
2,00,000 shares of Rs. 10 each	20,00,000
14% Preference Share Capital :	
3,00,000 shares of Rs. 10 each	30,00,000
Calls in arrear (estimated to produce Rs. 20,000)	40,000
14% First Mortgage Debentures secured by a floating charge on the whole of the assets of the company (interest paid to date)	20,00,000
Creditors fully secured (value of securities, Rs. 4,00,000)	3,50,000
Creditors partly secured (value of securities, Rs. 2,00,000)	4,00,000
Preferential creditors for wages, rates and taxes, etc.	75,000
Unsecured Creditors	27,00,000
Bank Overdraft, secured by a second charge on the whole of the assets of the company	2,00,000
Cash in hand	12,000
Books Debts —Good	3,80,000
— Doubtful (estimated to produce Rs. 30,000)	80,000
— Bad	45,000
Stock in Trade (estimated to produce Rs. 6,00,000)	7,20,000
Freehold Land & Buildings (estimated to produce Rs. 18,50,000)	21,00,000
Plant & Machinery (estimated to produce Rs. 6,30,000)	6,00,000
Fixtures & Fittings (estimated to produce Rs. 80,000)	1,20,000

You are required to prepare a statement of affairs of the company.

(Adapted B.Com., Lucknow)

(Deficiency as regards (i) creditors, Rs. 15,23,000 (ii) contributories Rs. 65,03,000)

4. From the following particulars prepare a Statement of Affairs and the Deficiency Account for submission to the Official Liquidator of the Equipments Ltd. which went into liquidation on March 31, 2010:—

	Rs.	Rs.
3,000 Equity Shares of Rs. 100 each, Rs. 80 paid		2,40,000
11% 1,000 Preference Shares of Rs. 100 each, fully paid	1,00,000	
Less: Calls in arrear (expected to produce)	5,000	95,000
10% Debentures having a floating charge on the assets		
(Interest paid up to December 31, 2009)	1,00,000	
Mortgage on Land & Buildings	80,000	
Trade Creditors		2,65,500
Owing for wages		20,000
Secretary's Salary @ Rs. 1,500 p.m. owing		3,000
Managing Director's Salary @ Rs. 6,000 p.m. owing		6,000

Assets :	*Estimated to Produce Rs.*	*Book value Rs.*
Land and Buildings	1,30,000	1,20,000
Plant	1,30,000	2,00,000
Tools	4,000	20,000
Patents	30,000	50,000
Stock	74,000	87,000
Book Debts	60,000	90,000
Investments (in the hands of bank for an overdraft of Rs. 1,90,000)	1,70,000	1,80,000

On 31st March, 2005 the balance sheet of the company showed a general reserve of Rs. 40,000 accompanied by a debit balance of Rs. 25,000 in the Profit and Loss Account. In 2005-06, the company made a profit of Rs. 40,000 and declared a dividend of 10% on equity shares. Besides loss of stock due to fire of Rs. 40,000, the company suffered a total loss of Rs. 1,09,000 during 2006-07, 2007-08 and 2008-2009. For 2009-2010 accounts were not made up.

The cost of winding up is expected to be Rs. 15,000.

[*Deficiency as regards (i) creditors Rs. 64,000 (ii) members, Rs.* 4,04,000]

5. The following particulars relate to a limited company which has gone into voluntary liquidation. You are required to prepare the Liquidator's Final Account, allowing for his remuneration @ 2% on the amount realised, and 2% on the amount distributed among unsecured creditors other than preferential creditors :—

	Rs.
Preferential Creditors	10,000
Unsecured Creditors	32,000
Debentures	10,000

The assets realised the following sums :—

Land and Buildings	20,000
Plant and Machinery	18,650
Fixtures and Fittings	1,000

The liquidation expenses amounted to Rs. 1,000.

(Adapted B.Com., Lucknow)

(Liquidator's Remuneration Rs. 1,143; Amount paid to unsecured creditors, Rs. 17,507)

6. The Sunny Valley Mining Co. Ltd. went into voluntary liquidation on 1st April, 2010, as its mines reached such a state of depletion that it became too costly to excavate further minerals. The

Liquidator, whose remuneration is 3% on realisation of assets and 2% on distribution among shareholders, realised all the assets. The following was the position of the company on 31st March, 2010 :—

	Rs.
Cash on realisation of assets	5,00,000
Expenses of Liquidation	9,000
Unsecured Creditors (including salaries and wages for one month prior to liquidation, Rs. 6,000)	68,000
1,500 14% Preference shares of Rs. 100 each (dividend paid up to 31st March, 2009)	1,50,000
10,000 Equity shares of Rs. 10 each, Rs. 9 per share called and paid up	90,000
General Reserve as on 31st March, 2010	1,20,000
Profit & Loss Account as on 31st March, 2010	20,000

Under the Articles of Association of the company, the Preference shareholders have the right to receive one-third of the surplus remaining after repaying the equity share capital.

(Adapted from C.A., Final)

(Preference shareholders receive Rs. 2,17,333 and equity shareholders receive, Rs. 1,82,667)

7. The following is the Balance Sheet of X Ltd. as on 31st March, 2009 :—

	Rs.		*Rs.*
Authorised & Subscribed Capital :		Land & Buildings	1,90,000
20,000 14% Redeemable Preference shares of Rs. 10 each	2,00,000	Plant & Machinery	1,20,000
10,000 Equity shares of Rs. 10 each, Rs. 9 paid	90,000	Patents	10,000
10,000 Equity shares of Rs. 10 each, Rs. 5 paid	50,000	Investments	40,000
14% Mortgage Debentures (holding a floating charge on all the assets of the company)	1,00,000	Stock	45,000
Interest Outstanding on the Debentures	14,000	Sundry Debtors	90,000
Loan secured by hypothecation of stock	40,000	Cash at Bank	35,000
Trade Creditors	72,000	Profit and Loss Account	65,500
Creditors for salaries and wages	15,000		
Liability for workmen's compensation	2,000		
Owing to Government for Telephone and purchases	2,500		
Owing to Government for taxes	10,000		
	5,95,500		5,95,500

The company went into voluntary liquidation on 1st April, 2009 and a liquidator was appointed with a remuneration of 2 per cent of assets realised with the exception of cash and 2 per cent of the amount distributed among unsecured creditors other than preferential creditors. The dividend of preference shares was not paid for 2008-2009. Stock realised Rs. 30,000 and the other assets excluding cash realised Rs. 4,00,000. All assets were realised and payments made on September 30, 2000. Prepare the Liquidator's Final Statement of Account, assuming the expenses of liquidation were Rs. 5,610. *(Equity shares on which Rs. 5 is paid contribute Rs. 2.67 per share; the other equity shareholders receive Rs. 1.33 per share)*

8. A Ltd. went into voluntary liquidation on September 30, 2009. Its liabilities were as under:—

	Rs.
14% Debentures with a floating charge on the assets except uncalled capital	2,00,000
Interest due on Debentures for one year	28,000

	Rs.
Bank Overdraft (with a lien on Stock)	50,000
Trade Creditors	1,50,000
Loan from a director to pay wages	10,000
Provident Fund of employees	30,000
E.S.I. premium for 6 months to September 30, 2009	1,000

The Capital consisted of :

14% Preference Shares of Rs. 100 each fully paid	1,00,000
Equity Shares of Rs. *100 each, Rs. 90* paid	1,80,000
Equity Shares of Rs. 100 each, Rs. 50 paid	1,00,000

The assets realised as follows :—

	Stock Rs.	*Other Assets* Rs.
October 15, 2009	20,000	1,50,000
November 14, 2009	20,000	1,40,000
December 15, 2009	40,000	1,50,000

The liquidator is entitled to 2% on amounts realised from assets and to 25% on the saving which the equity shareholders would have from their maximum legal liability. The debentureholders waived interest after 30th September, 2009. After reserving Rs. 10,000 for expenses (which ultimately amounted Rs. 8,000 and were paid on December 15, 2009), the liquidator distributed the cash among the various parties according to their rights.

Prepare the Statement of Account which the liquidator would be required to submit.

(Debentureholders get Rs. 95,600 on October 15 and Rs. 1,32,400 on November 14,. *Loss suffered by equity shareholders Rs. 89.48 per share)*

9. The books of A Ltd. at 31st March, 2010 contained the following balances :

	Rs.		Rs.
Share Capital :		Plant & Machinery	60,000
20,000 shares of Rs. 10 each	2,00,000	Stock	40,000
Sundry Creditors	1,50,000	Patent Rights & Trade Marks	1,60,000
		Sundry Debtors	60,000
		Cash	250
		Preliminary Expenses	5,000
		Profit & Loss Account	24,750
	3,50,000		3,50,000

The following scheme of reconstruction was submitted to the shareholders and creditors :—

The company to go into voluntary liquidation and a new company, with *a* nominal capital of Rs. 4,00,000, to be formed to take over all the assets from the liquidator on the following terms :—

(a) Preferential creditors for Rs. 5,000 to be paid in full.

(b) Unsecured creditors to have the option of receiving cash to the extent of 50% in full settlement of their claims or par value in 14% Debentures in the new company.

(c) 20,000 shares of Rs. 10 each, Rs. 5 per share paid up, to be distributed pro rata to shareholders of the old company.

(d) The new company to pay the costs of liquidation.

One-half of the unsecured creditors exercised their option to be paid in cash, and the funds for this and for payment of the liquidation expenses (which amounted to Rs. 3,000) were obtained by calling up the balance of Rs. 5 per share.

Three shareholders holding 1,500 shares dissented, and required their interests to be purchased. The price of Rs. 3 was agreed and was paid to the liquidator by one of the assenting shareholders in return for the transfer of such shares.

Prepare the Liquidator's Account for presentation to the final meeting of members.

(*Adapted from S.A.A Inter*)

(*Cash paid to unsecured creditors Rs. 36,250*)

10. Certain creditors remained unpaid on the liquidation of a company and it was found that certain persons had transferred their shares sometime before the winding up. The following were the details :

Name of Person	*Date of Transfer of shares*	*Number of shares transferred*	*Amount of creditors outstanding on the date of transfer, still unpaid*
			Rs.
A	1st February, 2009	600	10,000
B	1st May, 2009	1,000	15,000
C	15th July, 2009	500	18,000
D	15th November, 2009	400	25,000
E	1st December, 2009	100	26,000

All these shares were of Rs. 100 each, Rs. 80 paid. The company went into liquidation on 1st March, 2010. Prepare a statement of the amount recoverable from any or all of the above persons.

(*A pays nil; B pays Rs. 7,500; C pays Rs. 5,250; D pays Rs. 8,000 and E pays Rs. 2,000*)

Essay-type

1. What is meant by liquidation or winding up of a joint stock company ?
2. Enumerate the grounds on which a company may be wound up by the court.
3. Distinguish between :—
   (*i*) Compulsory winding up and Voluntary winding up.
   (*ii*) Member's voluntary winding up and creditors' voluntary winding up.
4. Enumerate preferential payments in case of winding up of a joint stock company.
5. Distinguish between statement of Affairs and Deficiency/Surplus Account prepared on winding up of a company.
6. What do you understand by liquidator's final statement of account ?
7. Who is Receiver for Debenture holders in winding up of a company ?
8. What is meant by 'B' List of contributories ? What is the liability of contributories included in this list? (*CA. Inter., July, 2001*)

29

COMPUTERISED ACCOUNTING SYSTEM

SYNOPSIS

Meaning	.. 29.1	Enterprise Resource Planning (ERP) Software	.. 29.4
Features	.. 29.1	Outsourcing of Accounting Function	.. 29.4
Codification and Grouping of Accounts	.. 29.1	Choice of an Alternative	.. 29.5
Spread-sheet Software	.. 29.2		
Prepackaged Accounting Software	.. 29.3		
Customised Accounting Software	.. 29.3		

1. Computerised Accounting System

Meaning : When computers are used for performing accounting function and for receiving, storing, operating on and outputting related data, it is called computerised accounting system.

Features : The following are the features of computerised accounting system:–

(*i*) A number of computers are used which are used by the members of the office staff who know how to operate them.

(*ii*) Usually, a number of computer softwares are used. A computer software includes any programme or routine that performs a desired function or set of functions quickly and the documentation required to describe and maintain that programme or routine.

(*iii*) The computer software may be developed by the firm's staff specifically for the business or it may be a software acquired from the market.

Acquired software may consist of a spread-sheet package or may be prepackaged accounting software. Larger organisations may use an Enterprise Resource Planning (ERP) package for developing a customised accounting package.

(*iv*) Work is done with great speed and a very high level of accuracy.

(*v*) Sometimes, the whole function of accounting is outsourced where the firm gets its financial accounting processed by an outside agency which also uses computers to perform the function.

(*vi*) The system poses the problems of controls, security and integrity as information is stored in soft copies inside the computers. There may be unauthorised access to the data.

Codification and Grouping of Accounts

In manual accounting system, account codes are rarely used. In computerised accounting also, there are many accounting softwares available which support non-coded accounting system. But mostly a computerised accounting system uses a well-defined coding system.

Proper codification requires a systematic classification of accounts. The main unit of classification is the major heads which are divided into minor heads. Each of the minor head is further divided into subordinate heads generally known as sub-heads. The sub-heads are further divided into detailed heads. Thus, there may be a four tier arrangement of the classification structure of accounts.

To give you an idea, the following may be a part of codification of accounts in a manufacturing concern:–

Revenues (1000–1499)
1100 Domestic
1200 Export
Expenses (1500–7999)
Manufacturing Expenses (1500–1999)
1500 Raw Materials Consumed
1600 Direct Labour
1601 Wages
1700 Power
1750 Fuel
1800 Carriage Inwards
Selling Expenses (2000–2999)
2000 Advertising
2100 Commission
2200 Discount
Administrative Expenses (3000–3999)
3010 Postage
3011 Telegrams
3013 Telephone
3100 Salary
3205 Repairs to Furniture
3306 Travelling Expenses
3388 Insurance
3389 Rent
3392 Rates
3396 Audit Fee
3397 Depreciation on Furniture

There is always some logic behind the classification. For example, two major heads of a company may be car-manufacture and servicing of cars. Car manufacture may be divided into manufacture of chasis, the door, the front panel etc. The servicing of cars may be divided into servicing under the guarantee period and servicing outside the guarantee period.

The detailed classification of account heads and the order in which the major and minor heads are to appear in account-records must be got approved by the top management and reviewed by the auditor before being introduced in the enterprise.

Spread-sheet Software: Spread sheet package may be used to maintain accounts. In doing so, the user will have to keep a control of the figures also. Special spread sheet controls including physical spread sheet controls like spread sheets locked on a protected shared drive with restricted access and read / write access controls and password protected-cells and formulas with passwords may be used.

Advantages :

The following are its advantages:

1. It is simple to use and easy to understand. Accounts can be easily regulated.
2. Most of the common functions like doing calculations, setting formulas etc. can be easily done.
3. Presentation can be made in various forms including graphical presentations like bar

diagrams, histograms, pie-charts etc.

Disadvantages : The following are the disadvantages:–

1. It can accept data only up to a specified limit.
2. Simultaneous access on a network may not be possible.
3. Double entry is not automatically completed. Also, reports are not automatically generated.

Prepackaged Accounting Software : There are several prepackaged accounting softwares which are available in the market. These softwares are easy to use and relatively inexpensive. The installation of a prepackaged software it very simple. An installation diskette or CD is provided with the software to install the software on a personal computer. A network version of the software is also available which has to be installed in the server and then work can be performed from the various workstations or nodes connected to the server. User manual is also provided to guide the user of software. The vendor to the software normally provides regular updates to take care of the changes of law as well as to provide additional features.

Advantages:

The following are the advantages of prepackaged accounting software;

(*i*) It is easy to install.

(*ii*) It is relatively inexpensive.

(*iii*) It is easy to use.

(*iv*) Backup procedure is simple.

(*v*) It is specially effective for medium sized business houses.

Disadvantages: The following are the disadvantages of prepackaged accounting software:–

(*i*) A standard package may not be able to take care of the complexities of the modern business house. There may be certain peculiarities of the particular business which may not be taken care of by the standard package. Many reports which are required may not be possible.

(*ii*) It may not cover all the functional areas. For example, production process may not be covered.

(*iii*) Customisation may not be possible in most such softwares.

(*iv*) There is lack of security because any person can view data of all concerns with common access password. Customized accounting software does not suffer from this drawback.

(*v*) Usually in the initial years, there are bugs which takes long to be rectified by the vendor.

Consideration while selecting a prepackaged software

To select an appropriate prepackaged software from a number of them available in the market, the following points need to be considered:

(*i*) An attempt should be made to match the requirements of the particular business with the available solutions. The one which fulfils the maximum requirements should be picked up.

(*ii*) Costs of the different packages have also to be taken into account.

(*iii*) It should not be very detailed or cumbersome to use.

(*iv*) Reputation and track record of the vendor will also be considered. A vendor who is prepared to give updates has to be preferred.

Customised Accounting Software

A customised accounting software is one where the software is developed on the basis of requirement specifications provided by the organisation.

First of all, a feasibility study is made, If it is decided to go ahead, requirements of the business unit are noted. Based on these requirements, the system analyst prepares a requirement specification which is handed over to the top management for approval. After the requirement specification has been approved, the designing process is started. After development of the system, it is tested. If it is found satisfying, it is implemented.

Advantages: The following are the advantages of a customised accounting package:

(*i*) All the functional areas are covered as per requirement.

(*ii*) The input screens can be tailor-made to match the input documents for ease of data entry.

(*iii*) The reports can be as per specifications of the organisation.

(*iv*) Bar-code scanners can be used as input devices suitable for the specific needs of an organisation

Disadvantages: The following are the disadvantages that may arise in a customised accounting package:–

(*i*) The system may work in a defective manner if

(*a*) requirement specifications are incomplete or ambiguous.

(*b*) documentation is incomplete, or

(c) control measures are inadequate

(*ii*) Inadequate testing may result in bugs remaining in the software.

(*iii*) Vendor of the software may be unwilling to give support due to other commitments. He may also be not willing to part with the source code or enter into an escrow agreement.

(*vi*) If frequent changes are made to the system and they are not well handled, there may be defective functioning.

Enterprise Resource Planning (ERP) Software

An Enterprise Resource Planning (ERP) Software is an integrated software package that manages the business across the entire organisation. Big organisations often adopt this package.

Advantages: The following are the advantages of an ERP:–

(*i*) An ERP is a generalised package which covers most of the common functions

(*ii*) Most of the desired reports are available. Moreover, these reports are standardised across industry and acceptable to the users.

(*iii*) As it is an integrated package, duplication of data entry is avoided.

(*iv*) Much more information is made available by this package than what is available otherwise.

Disadvantages : The following are the disadvantages of an ERP:–

(*i*) At times, the user may have to modify his business procedure to use ERP effectively.

(*ii*) ERP is often too expensive for the small and medium sized organisations.

(*iii*) There may be implementation hurdles.

(*iv*) It is a complex software.

Choice of an ERP : The following factors determine the choice of an ERP:

(*i*) The ERP that matches most of the requirements of an organisation is preferred. It is evaluated whether all the reports required by the business will be available or not.

(*ii*) The reputation and track record of vendor is considered

(*iii*) Costs of different available ERPs are compared.

Outsourcing of Accounting Function

The accounting function may be outsourced to an outside party for a fee. It is done to save cost and more importantly to take the advantage of expertise of the outside party. Accounting software is used by the outside party which processes the data given to it and which hands over different reports to the client from time to time.

Advantages: The following are the advantages of outsourcing the accounting functions.

(*i*) it is more economical.

(*ii*) It saves time thus enabling the concern to concentrate on the core area of business activity.

(*iii*) It enables the organisation to take the advantage of expert knowledge of the outside party to whom the accounting function is outsourced.

(*iv*) The organisation is not bothered about the people leaving the organisation in accounting department.

Disadvantages: The following are the disadvantages of outsourcing the accounting function:

(*i*) The data related to the organisation is in the hands of an outside party. It may endanger security and confidentiality of the organisation data.

(*ii*) The outside agency may provide inadequate services. The desirable standards may not be met and ultimately the system may prove to be more costly rather than cheaper.

(*iii*) The outside agency may be catering to a large number of clients due to which service may not be timely.

Choice of outsourcing vendor. The following factors are considered while choosing an outsourcing vendor:

(*i*) The extent to which the services offered by the vendor meet the requirements of the concern.

(*ii*) The reputation, background and track-record of the vendor.

(*iii*) The comparative costs proposed by the different vendors.

Choice of an Alternative. To a business concern different alternatives are available. The alternatives include spread-sheet package, pre-packaged accounting software, customised accounting package, ERP package and outsourcing of the accounting function to an outside party. The following points are considered while choosing an alternative:

(*i*) *Scale of operation.* A small or medium sized concern may pick a prepackaged accounting package while a large sized organisation may have to opt for customised software or ERP package.

(*ii*) If the operation to be computerised is complex with several functional areas, a customised software or an ERP package may be the choice.

(*iii*) Customised software is the solution if the organisation has several non-standard requirements.

(*iv*) The capacity of the concern to bear the cost is also considered. The spread sheet and prep-ackaged accounting software are cheaper. The customised software and the ERP package are comparatively costly.

EXERCISE XXIX

Essay Type

1. What is computerised accounting system? Describe its features.
2. Write a note on codification and classification of accounts under computerised accounting system.
3. Briefly describe the advantages and disadvantages of spread-sheet software.
4. What is meant by prepackaged accounting software? What are its advantages and disadvantages?
5. What are the points which you will consider while selecting an appropriate prepackaged software?
6. What is customised accounting software? What are the steps which are taken before it is adopted? Also describe the advantages and disadvantages of customised accounting software.
7. Define Enterprise Resource Planning (ERP) Software. What are its advantages and disadvantages? What are the factors which determine the choice of an ERP?
8. What are the advantages and disadvantages of outsourcing of accounting function? What factors will you consider while choosing an outsourcing vendor?
9. Different alternatives like spread-sheet package, pre-packaged accounting software and ERP package are available to adopt computerised accounting system. What are the points you would consider while choosing an alternative?

30

CRITICISM OF FINANCIAL STATEMENTS

SYNOPSIS

1. Criticism	... 30.1	Presentation	...	30.7
Forms in which accounts are drawn up	... 30.1	Single column or vertical statements	...	30.7
Reliability of information	... 30.5	Method of preparing such statements	...	30.7
2. Critical appreciation	... 30.7	Common measurement statements	...	30.16

1. CRITICISM

An intelligent study of the balance sheet and the profit and loss account of a concern with a view to judging its financial position and earning capacity is known as criticism of accounts. Interpretation is slightly different from criticism; the purpose of interpretation is to explain in simple language, understandable to a layman, the financial standing of a business undertaking but interpretation without proper study or criticism would rather be misleading. Criticism, of course, depends upon the purpose, i.e., whether the purpose is to invest money in the shares of the company or to lend money to it or to purchase the undertaking. Criticism takes broadly the following shapes:—

(*a*) criticism of the form in which the accounts are drawn up;

(*b*) testing the reliability of the information disclosed in the published balance sheet and the profit and loss account; and

(*c*) critical appreciation of the future prospects of the undertaking.

Forms in which accounts are drawn up :

The first involves knowledge of forms prescribed by law, if any, or forms usually adopted by firms in the industry, or those prescribed by custom. Whatever the form, a reader of the balance sheet and the profit and loss account be able to form a clear idea of the various items. For example, "Stores and Spares, Stocks and Work in Progress" does not give as good an idea of the position as separate figures for (*a*) stores and spares, (*b*) stocks of raw materials, (*c*) stocks of finished goods, and (*d*) work in progress, together with the method of valuation. Fixed Assets, Current Assets and Expenses not written off should be separately grouped. On the liability side, clear figures should be available for (*a*) capital; (*b*) reserves and surplus belonging to the shareholders; (*c*) long-term liabilities; and (*d*) current liabilities. The requirements in this respect are illustrated below.

Illustration 1. Criticise the following balance sheet :—

	Rs.			*Rs.*
Share Capital :		**Fixed Assets :**		
Authorised :		Goodwill		3,30,000
12% Redeemable Preference Shares of		Land & Buildings		17,64,000
Rs. 100 each, fully paid	10,00,00	Plant & Machinery		5,91,000
Equity shares of Rs. 100 each,		**Investments** (at cost) : Shares in		
Rs. 90 called up	9,00,000	subsidiary and associated		
Forfeited Shares Account	10,000	companies	Rs. 2,00,100	
Securities Premium Account	40,000	Provident Fund		
Calls in Advance Account	10,000	Investments	19,000	2,19,100
		Loan to X Ltd. (Subsidiary)		80,000

		Rs.		Rs.
Reserve and Surplus :			**Current Assets, Loans and Advances :**	
General Reserve	40,000		Bills Receivable	9,600
Proposed Appropriation	20,000	60,000	Sundry Debtors (including income-tax paid in Advance)	1,58,600
Provident Fund		19,000	Stock	2,89,000
Loans and Advances :			Preliminary Expenses	8,610
Loan from Y Ltd. (Subsidiary)		50,000	Cash in hand (including Rs. 2,500 at a cooperative bank)	5,820
14% Mortgage Debentures	8,40,000			
Add Interest	8,400	8,48,400		
Sundry Liabilities and Provisions :			**Miscellaneous Expenses :**	
Interest on Debentures Outstanding		25,200	Prepaid Expenses	9,300
Accumulated Provision for Depreciation		1,48,030	Calls in Arrear	2,000
Provision for Taxation		57,000		
Profit and Loss Account (details below)		57,000		
Proposed Dividend		1,08,000		
Sundry Creditors		1,34,400		
		34,67,030		34,67,030

Profit and Loss Appropriation Account :

	Rs.	Rs.
Balance from Profit and Loss Account including Rs. 56,000 [being rent of apartments let out to officers fetching 14% (net) of the cost of building]		2,42,000
Less :Proposed transfer to General Reserve	20,000	
Proposed Dividend	1,08,000	
Provision for Taxation	57,000	
Carried forward	57,000	2,42,0000
		—

Solution : Apart from the fact that the name of the company whose balance sheet it is and its date, have not been given, the balance sheet has the following shortcomings :—

(*i*) It has not been drawn up according to the form prescribed in Companies Act, 1956 (Part I of Schedule VI).

(*ii*) Information required to be given has not been provided.

(*iii*) It has not been signed in the manner required by the Act.

(*i*) *Shortcomings as regards form—Liabilities side :*

(*a*) It is necessary that figures for the previous year should be given in a column on the left hand side of each one of the items. The same procedure should be followed on Assets side.

(*b*) Forfeited Shares Account presumably is the profit remaining after reissue of shares (since the number of shares at issue is a round figure). Hence, it should be transferred to Capital Reserve and should be shown under Reserves and Surplus. Securities Premium Account should be similarly shown under Reserves and Surplus.

(*c*) Calls in Advance are usually shown just below share capital.

(*d*) Proposed addition to Reserve should be shown separately.

(*e*) Provident Fund is not a reserve and has to be shown as a Provision under Current Liabilities and Provisions.

(*f*) 'Loans and Advances" is not a term used on the liabilities side. In any case, it must be split into (*a*) Secured Loans and (*b*) Unsecured Loans.

(*g*) Interest accrued should be shown as a current liability and that outstanding should be shown along with Debentures under Secured Loans.

(*h*) Accumulated Provision for Depreciation must be deducted from the fixed asset concerned.

(*i*) Profit and Loss Account balance should be shown under Reserves and Surplus; details of Profit and Loss Appropriation Account are not required.

(*j*) "Sundry Liabilities and Provisions" should be renamed as a Current Liabilities and Provisions and should have two sections, (*A*) Current Liabilities, and (*B*) Provisions.

Assets Side :

(*a*) Arrangement of fixed assets is not proper and these have to be shown at cost less depreciation. Immovable property, cost Rs. 4,00,000 on which rent @ 14% rent is received, should be shown under investments.

(*b*) Loan to X Limited is not an investment and has to be shown under Loans and Advances, together with necessary details to indicate that it is a loan to a subsidiary company.

(*c*) Two separate sections should be given for Current Assets, Loans and Advances. Income tax paid in advance should be shown separately or deducted from the Provision for Taxation.

(*d*) Preliminary Expenses should be shown under Miscellaneous Expenditure (to the extent not yet written off).

(*e*) Prepaid Expenses are to be shown under Loans and Advances.

(*f*) Calls in arrear are to be deducted from Share Capital.

(*ii*) *Shortcomings as regards information—Liabilities Side :*

(*a*) Authorised capital, issued and subscribed capital should be given separately.

(*b*) The date on or after which the preference shares are to be redeemed should be mentioned.

(*c*) Details are required as to calls in arrear due from directors and others, separately.

(*d*) Security in the hands of Debentureholders should be mentioned, together with terms of redemption, etc.

Assets Side :

(*a*) Details are required as to cost of additions and disposal of fixed assets during the year.

(*b*) Market value of investments should be given and these should be split into (*i*) fully paid and partly paid and (*ii*) equity and preference shares.

(*c*) Mode of valuation of stock should be stated.

(*d*) Details regarding Sundry Debtors in respect of -

(*i*) debts outstanding for more than 6 months and others;

(*ii*) security held by the company and whether the debts are considered good; and

(*iii*) debts due from directors and companies and firms in which they are interested.

(*ii*) and (*iii*) are required also for Bills Receivable.

(*e*) The fact that Cooperative Bank is not scheduled should be mentioned.

The balance sheet has been redrawn below in the proper form as far as possible.

Balance Sheet of ....Ltd. as at...............................

Previous year's figures	*Liabilities*	*Rs.*	*Rs.*	*Previous year's figures*	*Assets*	*Rs.*	*Rs.*
	Share Capital:				**Fixed Assets :**		
	Authorised				Goodwill	3,30,000	
	10,000 12% Redeemable Preference Shares of Rs. 100 each	10,00,000			Freehold Land and Buildings (at cost)	13,64,000	
	10,000 Equity Shares of Rs. 100 each	10,00,000	20,00,000		Machinery and Plant 5,91,000 *Less:* Depreciation 1,48,030	4,42,970	21,36,970

	Rs.	Rs.		Rs.	Rs.
Issued & Subscribed :			**Investments** (at cost)		
10,000 12% Redeemable Preference Shares of Rs. 100 each, fully paid (redeemable on or after..)	10,00,000		Shares in Subsidiary and Associated Companies (Market value?) (Details of shares?)	2,00,100	
10,000 Equity Shares of Rs. 100 each, Rs. 90 per share called up	9,00,000		Investment of Provident Fund (Market value?)	19,000	2,19,100
	19,00,000		Immovable Property		4,00,000
Less Calls unpaid	2,000	18,98,000	**Current Assets, Loans and Advances :**		
(*i*) By Directors ?			(A) Current Assets :		
(*ii*) By others ?			Stock in trade (at cost)	2,89,000	
Calls in Advance		10,000	Sundry Debtors :		
Reserves and Surplus :			(a) Debts outstanding for more than 6 months ?		
Capital Reserve	10,000		(b) Other debts 1,01,600		
Share Premium Account	40,000		*Less* Provisions nil	1,01,600	
General Reserve	40,000		Particulars of Sundry Debtors ?		
Profit and Loss Account	57,000		Cash on hand 3,320		
Proposed addition to Reserve	20,000	1,67,000	Bank Balances :		
Secured Loans :			with scheduled Banks	—	
14% Mortgage Debentures (Nature of Security ? Terms of redemption ?)	8,40,000		with others 2,500	5,820	3,96,420
Interest accrued and due	25,200	8,65,200	Particulars of Bank Balance with unscheduled banks ?		
Unsecured Loans :			Balance with Coop. Bank	2,500	
Loan from *Y* Subsidiary Ltd.		50,000	(B) Loans and Advances :		
Current Liabilities and Provisions:			Loan to X Subsidiary Limited		80,000
(A) Current Liabilities :			Bills Receivable		9,600
Sundry Creditors	1,34,400		Income-tax Paid in Advance (assumed)	57,000	
Interest Accrued on Debentures	8,400	1,42,800	Prepaid Expenses	9,300	1,55,900
(B) Provisions :			**Miscellaneous Expenditure** (to the extent not yet written off)—		
Provision for Taxation	57,000				
Proposed Dividends	1,08,000				
Provident Fund	19,000	1,84,000	Preliminary Expenses		8,610
Total		33,17,000	Total		33,17,000

..............Director ....Director ....Director

For presentation to shareholders, the figures should be arranged as follows :—

Summarised Balance Sheet

		Rs.	*Rs.*
Fixed Assets :			
Goodwill			3,30,000
Freehold Land and Buildings less depreciation			13,64,000
Machinery and Plant less depreciation			4,42,970
Total fixed assets			21,36,970
Investments : In Subsidiary and associate companies		2,00,100	
Against Provident Fund		19,000	
Immovable Property		4,00,000	6,19,100
Miscellaneous Expenses not yet written off			8,610
Working Capital :			
Current assets and Loans & Advances :			
Stock		2,89,000	
Book Debts		1,01,600	
Cash in hand and at Bank		5,820	
		Rs.	*Rs.*
Bills Receivable		9,600	
Loans to X Subsidiary Co.		80,000	
Prepaid Expenses		9,300	
Tax Paid in Advance		57,000	
		5,52,320	
Less Current Liabilities	1,42,800		
Provisions	1,84,000	3,26,800	2,25,520
			29,90,200
Less : Secured Loans—Debentures		8,65,200	
Unsecured Loans		50,000	9,15,200
Shareholders' Funds			20,75,000
Represented by :			
Share Capital—			
Preference			10,00,000
Equity			8,98,000
Capital Reserves			50,000
Revenue Reserves, Surplus			1,17,000
Calls in advance			10,000
Total			20,75,000

Reliability of information :

Reliability of figures contained in the balance sheet cannot be established without a careful study of series of balance sheets. The following are only broad rules :

(*i*) If the balance sheet reveals that depreciation has been written off, it is a good sign because it shows that the fixed assets are being maintained. But before final judgment is formed, care should be taken to see that the amount of depreciation written off is adequate having regard to (*a*) the cost, (*b*) the expected life and (c) risk of obsolescence. Obsolete assets should be completely written off. The amount written off in various years as depreciation should be noted. Requirements of section 205 of the Companies Act should be kept in mind.

(*ii*) The method of valuation of investments and stocks (of raw materials, finished goods and work in progress) should be clearly shown in the balance sheet. It will be a sign of confidence if both the market price and cost price are revealed. Violent fluctuations from year to year are rather a bad sign.

(*iii*) Adequate provision against bad debts should be maintained. The figure for book debts should be split into (*a*) debts remaining unpaid for more than 6 months and (*b*) other book debts. Loans made to staff or others should be separately stated. The reason why such loans have to be made should be enquired into.

(*iv*) 'Expenses not written off' should be watched. A good company will write off such expenses in a short time, say three or four years.

(*v*) The security of the long-term liabilities and their due dates for repayment should be clearly stated in the balance sheet. If the date of payment of a particular loan is due to arrive shortly, it should be seen whether adequate cash resources exist to meet the liability. Existence of sinking fund for redemption of liability, supported by investments, shows that the company will not have much difficulty in paying off the liability.

(*vi*) Current and contingent liabilities should be clearly stated. If various items are all added up together, perhaps the company wishes to hide something.

(*vii*) The balance sheet should be judged with reference to profits. The value placed on various assets will be considered reliable only if the company is making good profits. If the company is suffering losses, the real value of an asset, specially a fixed asset, may be much lower than that stated in the balance sheet. This is because the assets are useful to the company as a going concern; if the assets have to be sold, the amount realised may only be a fraction of what is stated in the balance sheet.

The published accounts of a company, viz., the balance sheet and the profit and loss account are of great interest to the shareholders, prospective investors in shares or debentures of the company, creditors of the company and students of economics of the industry concerned. It is rarely, however, that the balance sheet or the profit and loss account will tell a full story except to the informed without being subjected to criticism and analysis, through the use of accounting ratios. (See the next chapter). Before a discussion on them, it would be useful to note the chief points concerning the various parties involved. However, for all the various parties interested in a company, mentioned below two points are common : (*a*) fictitious assets and expenses appearing in the balance sheet should be ignored; and (*b*) everything depends upon the profitability of the company.

(*i*) *Shareholders.* The shareholders come last of all in respect of safety of their funds but they have the most vital interest since their well-being depends on the well-being of the company. From the total assets, all liabilities should be deducted. The 'surplus' in a good company, will well cover the entire share capital. If the surplus is less than the amount of the capital, it means that part of the capital has been lost. Another point of great interest is that the rate of profit (after meeting all expenses, interest, depreciation and taxation) to capital employed should be worked out. A good rate means that the shareholders have not much to fear. As far as equity shareholders are concerned, the preference shareholders' claims should be deducted from the surplus of assets over liabilities, because preference shareholders have priority both as regards return of capital and as regards dividend.

(*ii*) *Preference shareholders* are interested in the safety of their capital and in the degree of certainty with which dividend will be paid. To determine safety all liabilities to outsiders should be deducted from the value of assets and the resultant figure compared with the preference share capital. The former should be two or three times the latter. To ascertain the degree of certainty of dividend, the amount of the preference dividend should be compared with profits remaining after taxes.

(*iii*) *Debentureholders.* The profit of the company (before tax) should be ample to pay the interest comfortably. Also, the value of the mortgaged property (in favour of the debentureholders) should be a good deal more than the claim of the debentureholders. If debentures are secured by a floating charge, the value of all assets minus the preferential creditors should be considered.

(*iv*) *Bank.* The bank is interested, while advancing a loan, in the liquidity of the company. This means that the total current assets should have a comfortable margin over the loan. The bank cannot ignore the existence of current liabilities and, therefore, the bank keeps a watch on the difference between current assets and current liabilities. A long-term loan maturing shortly for payment should be treated as a current liability for this purpose.

(*v*) *Creditors.* Current liabilities have to be paid in a short period which is usually taken as one year; for this purpose the total value of current assets is important. Creditors will not be able to receive payment promptly if the value of current assets is low. Normally, current assets should be twice the current liabilities. "Long term" liabilities due for payment within a year should be treated as part of current liabilities.

(*vi*) *Prospective investors,* specially in the shares of the company, are interested in the safety of their investment and also in the yield on such investment. They will not only try to see whether the company is fully solvent both in the short term and in long term and whether the profits of the company are large enough. Since profits depend upon operating efficiency, prospective investors will try to judge this also. Another point of interest to them will be the prospects of the company using additional funds profitably.

(*vii*) *Labour.* Since workers now-a-days get a bonus based on the profits of the concern, the workers are naturally interested in knowing the real profitability of the concern and their share out of profits. Trade unions now-a-days are as much interested in financial statements as anyone else.

(*viii*) *Government and other public bodies* such as the Reserve Bank of India. Accounts of companies are studied by the Reserve Bank of India and treated statistically on a continuous basis so as to ascertain the trends in profitability and changes in financial structure that may be there. In this case, the reliability of figures is the most important factor.

2. CRITICAL APPRECIATION

Presentation :

Obviously, the first requirement for understanding financial statements is that they should be presented in a readily understandable form. It is conceded generally that the usual two side or "T" form of the balance sheet and the profit and loss account is not very intelligible to the person who is not well versed in accounting. Otherwise, also, it is not amenable to analysis readily. The financial statements, if presented in a vertical or single column form, are better appreciated and understood.

Single Column or Vertical Statement. Though a person having good knowledge of accounting can derive full meaning of the final statements of account as ordinarily prepared (in T form), it is not possible for a layman to grasp the significance of various figures properly on the basis of such statements. It is necessary to redraft them. It is now generally accepted that the statements should be drawn up using layman's language as far as possible and in a form where each figure can be logically drawn from the previous ones. This is possible if statements are drawn up in single column form.

The other advantages of such single column statements are the following : —

(*i*) Figures for many years can be put side by side;

(*ii*) The above makes the progress made by the company, or otherwise, clearly discernible;

(*iii*) The establishment of significant relationships of figures, mutually dependent in cause and effect relationship, or of figures which throw light on the financial position of the firm and its operational efficiency, becomes easy. This is the same as saying that accounting ratios can be easily worked out; and

(*iv*) It is easily possible, in such statements, to separate operating from non-operating items—operating items are those that are connected with the ordinary business of the firm, e.g., capital invested in stock in trade is operating but that in shares of other companies is usually non-operating.

The method of preparing the statement. In case of the balance sheet, the method is as follows:—

*(*i*) Put down the fixed assets showing the cost and the depreciation provided against each asset and total the net figures, to show the amount of the net block at a glance;

*(*ii*) State the figure of the working capital by first detailing current assets and totalling them, then listing current liabilities and totalling them and then extending the difference of the two totals to the outer column;

---

*Some people start with working capital and then add net block.

(*iii*) Total the net block and the working capital; the figure is 'operating capital employed' which is the basis for ascertaining the rate of return or return on investment;

**(*iv*) Add the amount in respect of non-operating assets like investments;

(*v*) Add (*iv*) and (*iii*); the figure is 'Total Equity' or total assets available with the firm; and

(*vi*) Deduct from (*v*) long-term loans. The resultant figure is shareholders' funds or shareholders' equity, i.e., funds belonging to shareholders. The figure should be ruled off.

(*vii*) The details of the figure in (*vi*) should be provided to show the amount of—

(*a*) Preference Share Capital;

(*b*) Equity Share Capital;

(*c*) Reserves not available for dividends or capital reserves; and

(*d*) Revenue reserves or profits available for declaring a dividend.

Note. The amount of expenses or losses not yet written off, such as preliminary expenses, should be deducted from revenue reserves; it is not proper to show them as an asset.

The profit and loss account should be dealt with as follows :

(*a*) Start with Sales;

(*b*) Arrive at the cost of goods sold, i.e., cost of goods produced adjusted for opening and closing stock—the details should be kept out of the main statement and only the net figure should be given;

(*c*) Deduct (*b*) from (*a*) to give the gross profit;

(*d*) Deduct administrative and office expenses and also selling and distributing expenses to give the figure of net operating profit before tax;

(*e*) Put down non-operating income, such as dividend received, and non-operating expenses, such as interest paid, and extend the difference to the outer column; the resulting figure will be net profit before tax; and

(f) Deduct the estimated amount of tax payable out of the current year's profits to give net *profit* after tax and available for distribution.

Note. Since the amount of depreciation depends more or less on the will of the management and is thus rather arbitrary, it should be indicated by way of a note. Of course, it will have been considered when the cost of manufacture of goods is arrived at.

In its annual report to the shareholders, a company may present its abridged balance sheet and abridged profit and loss account along with the necessary notes. Study the following specimen :—

XYZ COMPANY, LIMITED

[Statement containing salient features of the Balance Sheet and Profit and Loss Account, etc. as per Section 219(1)(b)(iv) of the Companies Act, 1956]

Abridged Balance Sheet

as at 31 March, 2010		31 March 2010 *Rs.* Lakhs		31 March 2009 *Rs.* Lakhs
Source of Funds				
Sharesholders' Funds				
Capital :				
Equity	41,49,67		41,49.67	
Reserves and Surplus :				
Premium on Ordinary shares	11,37.67		11,37,67	
Capital Redemption Reserve	40.00		40.00	
Other Capital Reserve	1,00,44		1,00,44	

**Some people write investments immediately after net block; this is not recommended as the figure for operating capital will not then be readily available.

Exports Projects Reserve	9,85.62		10,42.62	
Debenture Redemption Reserve	35,40.00		28,20.00	
General Reserve A	8,06.00		8,06.00	
General Reserve B	79,75.84		47,13.84	
Profit and Loss Account	6,25.56	193,60.80	6,22.45	154,32.69
Loan Funds				
Debentures (secured)	52,22.73		54,04.93	
Public deposits (unsecured)	8,08.42		1.00	
Secured Loans (Other than debentures)	46,21.82		29,82.78	
Unsecured Loans	6,40.52	112,93.49	1,21.69	85,10.40
Total		306,54.29		239,43.09
Application of Funds				
Fixed Assets				
Net block (original cost less depreciation)	83,66.05		78,99.93	
Capital work-in-progress	34,03.61	117,69.66	10,20.86	89,20.79
Investments				
Government Securities	0.91		0.95	
Subsidiary Companies Unquoted	14.00		—	
Others :				
Quoted	4,11.12		3,07.95	
Unquoted	10.06	4,36.09	10.06	3,18.96
Current Assets, Loans and Advances				
Inventories	138,48.18		91,90.46	
Sundry Debtors	65,59.65		49,89.36	
Cash and Bank Balances	3,14.51		2,68.94	
Other Current Assets	83,25.42		66,65.83	
Loans and Advances	35,20.63		14,65.32	
	325,68.39		225,79.91	
Less : Current Liabilities and Provisions				
Liabilities	124,13.91		62,28.87	
Provisions	20,41.85		20,76.07	
	144,55.76		83,04.94	
Net Current Assets		181,12.63		142,74.97
Miscellaneous expenditure (to the extent not written off or adjusted)		3,35.91		4,28.37
Total		306,54.29		239,43.09

Abridged Profit and Loss Account

for the year ended 31 March, 2010

Income		
Sales/Services rendered (Schedule 1)	564,22.85	536,42.58
Dividend	12,66.87	3,39.14
Interest	2,78.91	2,92.07
Other income	4,46.11	5,29.78
Total	584,14.74	548,03.57

Expenditure				
Accretion to stock of finished goods, work-in-progress and process stock				
Opening stock	64,38.55		58,35.15	
Less : closing stock	91,08.22	(26,69.67)	64,38.55	(6,03,40)
Purchase of aluminium including conversion charges		18,85.94		8,17.27
Manufacturing and selling expenses (Schedule 2)		315,84.31		283,84.55
Salaries, wages and other employees benefits		53,98.09		46,03.03
Managerial remuneration		9.13		10.47
Interest		18,08.69		13,32.10
Depreciation		10,09.30		9,83.36
Auditors' remuneration		8,22		7.81
Provision for doubtful debts		(5.87)		(19.39)
Excise duty		116,70.80		106,52.68
Other expenses		71.79		22.22
Total		507,70.73		461,90.70
Profit before tax		76,44.01		86,12.87
Provision before taxation		24,71.00		27,63.00
Profit after tax		51,73.01		58,49.87
Exports Projects Reserve written back		57.00		27.30
Balance brought forward from previous year		6,22.45		2,47.63
Amount available for appropriation		58,52.46		61,24.80
Proposed Dividend :				
Equity shares		11,31.73		11,31.73
Corporate Dividend Tax		113.17		113.17
Transfers to				
Debentures Redemption Reserve		7,20.00		13,50.00
General Reserve B		32,62.00		29,07.45
Balance carried to Balance Sheet		6,25.56		6,22.45

Schedule 1 : Sales by Class of Goods

	2009-2010		2008-2009	
	Tonnes	*Rs. Lakhs*	*Tonnes*	*Rs. Lakhs*
Aluminium				
Ingot and billet	1,285	5,10.05	783	2,71.58
Properzi rod	7,522	27,50.88	7,534	25,07.07
Rolled products	48,082	233,95.11	45,512	209,91.47
Extruded products	7,248	35,33.92	6,690	32,08.68
Foil	5,034	58,31.52	4,640	53,63,23
Powder	216	1,58.72	379	2,32.27
Paste and dried filter cake	322	2,48.56	422	3,06.41
Scrap	121	31.80	125	27.51
	69,830	364,60.56	66,085	329,08.22

Non-Aluminium				
Carbon electrode paste	10,405	10,01.82	11,310	9,21.81
Hydrate and alumina	77,526	64,08.85	94,133	87,36.66
Aluminous laterite	84,378	59.40	74,606	52,43
Vanadium sludge	53	79.68	71	99.25
Pre-baked carbon block	298	1,19.45	4	1.43
China clay	81	0.29	102	0.38
Printed circuit boards (sq. mtrs.)	7,639	6,13.59	3,455	2,05.98
		82,83.08		100,17.94
Conversion				
Ingot	—	—	19	0.78
Properzi rod	—	—	206	8.923
Rolled products	5	6.34	248	41.32
Extruded products	15	2.07	15	5.31
	20	8.41	488	56.34
Works Contracts				
(Developmental activity)		—		7.40
Excise Duty		116,70.80		106,52.68
		564,22.85		536,42.58

Schedule 2 : Manufacturing and selling expenses

		2009-2010 *Rs. Lakhs*		2008-2009 *Rs. lakhs*
Raw materials consumed				
Opening stock	13,09.23		12,60.32	
Add : Purchases	100,00.93		77,37.71	
	113,10.16		89,98.03	
Less : closing stock	27,62.91		13,09.23	
Outward and inter-plant freight		85,47.25		76,88.80
Power and fuel		12,33.34		13,37.44
Consumable stores		157,36.39		144,38.99
Repairs and maintenance-buildings and equipment		3,27.31		2,28.39
Repairs and maintenance-machinery		14,34.43		11,64.35
Rent		1,86.80		1,03.13
Insurance		1,78.40		1,28.41
Rates and taxes		1,96.34		3,54.40
Bad debts		(4.52)		23.07
Sales discounts		2,75.11		1,74.63
Commission		1,93.10		2,55.48
Others		18,17.38		15,49.01
		316,24.53		285,52.53
Less : Transfer to Construction, etc.		40.22		1,67.98
		315,84.31	(a)	283,84.55

(a) Includes selling expenses Rs. 7,76.99 lakhs (2008-2009-Rs. 7,13.30 lakhs).

Extracts from notes to Balance Sheet and Profit and Loss Account as per Section 211 of the Companies Act, 1956.

1. Loans repayable during 2010-2011 :
   (*a*) Secured — Rs. 2,66.94 lakhs
   (*b*) Unsecured — (*i*) Rs. 5,13.90 lakhs
   (*ii*) Rs. 24.68 lakhs is repayable, at the option of the depositors, on expiry of any six month period from the date of deposit.

2. Fixed Assets :
   (*a*) Include leasehold land Rs. 53.74 lakhs (2000-Rs. 53.74 lakhs) of which a lease amounting to Rs. 13.04 lakhs will be converted into sale after expirty of ten years on payment of stamp duty and registration charges.
   (*b*) Include Rs. 0.13 lakh (2000- Rs. 0.13) being cost of shares in Co-operative Housing Societies representing ownership rights in residential flats.
   (*c*) Do not include motor cars and office equipment taken on lease for which lease rental of Rs. 37.78 lakhs has been paid.

4. Inventories :
   Excise duty is payable on clearance under Central Excise Rules. Hence, no provision has been made in these accounts for approximately Rs. 3,44.58 lakhs on stocks of finished goods awaiting clearance. This has no impact on the profits for the year.

5. Sundry Debtors include bills receivable Rs. 3,59.36 lakhs (2009- Rs. 1,75.73 lakhs).

6. Loans and Advances include :
   (*i*) Rs. 20, 39.02 lakhs paid to ABC Limited of which the Company is the promoter. This includes amount adjustable towards Company's contribution to ABC Ltd.'s share capital.
   (*ii*) Rs. 27.74 lakhs paid to PQR Limited of which the Company is one of the co-promoters. This includes amount adjustable towards Company's contribution to PQR Ltd.'s share capital.
   (*iii*) Rs. 0.31 lakh paid to XYZ Exports Limited, which is a subsidiary of the Company.

7. Other Current Assets:
   (*a*) This year the fully paid up short-term investments have been treated as current assets and valued at cost or market price whichever is lower. This change has no significant impact on the profits for the year.
   (*b*) The portfolio investments were awaiting registration in the Company's name as was public sector bond Rs. 5,00.00 lakhs.
   (*c*) Units of the face value Rs. 4,40.00 lakhs have been pledged with a bank as security for a loan disbursed by the bank to ABC Ltd.

8. Provisions - The liability for taxation is net of payments made.

9. Contingent Liabilities :

	31 March 2010 *Rs. Lakhs*	31 March 2009 *Rs. Lakhs*
Bill Discounted	23.69	18.54
Claims not acknowledged as Debts (a) :		
Interest on arrears of contribution to Aluminium Regulation Account considered not payable on the basis of Counsel's opinion	2,11.91	2,11.91
Entry tax on certain materials provisionally assessed but not considered payable and for which appeal is pending	21.05	21.05
Disputed Excise duty fow which appeals are pending	50.43	50.43
Total	3,07.08	3,01.93

(*a*) Excludes Rs. 7,28.50 lakhs under appeal by the excise authorities, considered to be untenable.

10. Estimated amount of contracts remaining to be executed on capital account is Rs. 65,67.16 lakhs (2009— Rs. 50,39.72 lakhs).
11. Interest income includes Rs. 1,96.18 lakhs (2008-2009 — Rs. 2,26.54 lakhs) on tax-free Government securities.
12. Other income includes :
    (*a*) Rs. 87.61 lakhs being claims relating to earlier years settled during the year.
    (*b*) Rs. 38.67 lakhs (2008-2009 - Rs. 95.66 lakhs) being liability written back.
13. Cost off Sales :
    (*a*) No allocation of salary, wages and bonus has been made to repairs, power, etc.
    (*b*) Net of Rs. 59.95 lakhs relating to earlier years.
    (*c*) Depreciation has been provided under straight-line method prescribed in Schedule XVI of the Companies Act, 1956. Assets added up to 31 December 2005 are, however, being depreciated at rates then applicable, Leasehold land and mining leases are amortised over the lives of the respective leases.
14. Auditor's remuneration :

	2009-2010 *Rs. Lakhs*	2008-2009 *Rs. Lakhs*
Statutory Auditors		
Audit fee	3.35	3.35
Tax Audit fee	0.75	0.94
Other services (certificates, etc.)	1.98	1.79
Travelling expenses	0.94	0.72
	7.02	6.80
Cost Auditors		
Audit fee	0.70	0.87
Others including travelling expenses	0.50	0.14
	1.20	1.01

15. Other expenses include debenture issue written off Rs. 22.60 lakhs (2008-2009-Rs. 22.22 lakhs)
16. Managerial Remuneration :
    (*a*) Rs. 3.21 lakhs paid to a former Managing Director for 2006 and Rs. 1,39 lakhs for the period from 1 January, 2007 to 14 June, 2007 in terms of the members' resolution approved at the Annual General Meeting held on 28 April, 2006 await approval of the Central Government.
    (*b*) Appointment of the Managing Director from 1 January, 2010 awaits approval of the members at the forthcoming Annual General Meeting. The amount paid to him for the period from 1 January, 2010 to 31 March, 2010 is Rs. 0.99 lakh.
17. C.I.F. value of imports and expenditure in foreign currencies for commission, interest, net dividend and others amount to Rs. 29,33.89 lakhs (2008-2009-Rs. 16,69.06 lakhs) including Rs. 64.82 lakhs (2008-2009 - Rs. 1,84.20 lakhs) paid in rupees.
18. Earnings in foreign exchange on account of exports (f.o.b. basis) including Rs. 31,27.56 lakhs (2008-2009 - Rs. 60,96.28 lakhs) under rupee contract and canvassing agency income, etc. are Rs. 50,77.12 lakhs (2008-2009 - Rs. 69,48.46 lakhs)
19. Previous year's figures have been recast/rearranged, where necessary.

Illustration 2. The Eastern Malleable Ltd. gives you its balance sheet as at **March 31, 2010 and** the accompanying profit and loss account. Redraft the statements in single column form.

Balance Sheet of Eastern Malleable Ltd. as at 31st March, 2010

	Rs.	Rs.		Rs.	Rs.
Capital :			**Fixed Assets :**		
Authorised, issued & subscribed :			Land & Buildings :		
2,000 Equity Shares of Rs. 100 each, fully paid	2,00,000		Cost to date	5,00,000	
2,000 14% Preference Shares of Rs. 100 each, fully paid	2,00,000	4,00,000	*Less* : Depreciation to date	1,67,500	3,32,500
Reserves			Plant :		
Reserves & Surplus :			Cost to date	3,00,000	
Securities Premium		20,000	*Less* : Depreciation to date	1,20,000	1,80,000
Dividend Equalisation Reserve :					5,12,500
As per last Balance Sheet	20,000		**Investments** (Shares)		2,20,000
Transferred from P&L A/c	15,000	35,000	**Current Assets, Loans & Advances :**		
Profit & Loss Account		82,450	(A) Current Assets :		
Secured Loans	2,00,000		Stock	70,000	
Unsecured Loans	Nil		Debtors	60,000	
			Cash at Bank	50,000	1,80,000
Current Liabilities & Provisions :			**Miscellaneous Expenditure** (not yet adjusted)		14,500
(A) Current Liabilities :					
Creditors		30,385			
(B) Provisions :					
Provision for Taxation	83,165				
Proposed Dividend	69,091	1,94,808			
Total		9,27,000	Total		9,27,000

Profit and Loss Account for the year ended 31st March, 2010

	Rs.		Rs.
To Opening Stock	85,000	By Sales	25,60,000
Materials consumed	12,16,000	Stock	70,000
Wages	6,30,000		
Factory Expenses	3,34,600		
Gross Profit c/d	3,64,400		
	26,30,000		26,30,000
To Establishment	15,000	By Gross Profit b/d	3,64,400
Rent & Taxes	6,000	Dividends	12,300
Audit Fees	2,500	Miscellaneous Receipts	2,300
Selling Expenses	48,000		
Interest	12,000		
Directors' fees	2,000		
Sundry Expenses	6,000		
Managing Directors' remuneration	12,385		

Provision for Depreciation	37,500		
Provision for Taxation	83,165		
Net Profit c/d	1,54,450		
	3,79,000		3,79,000
To Income-tax not provided for last year	6,000	By Balance from last year	25,000
Dividend Equalisation Reserve	15,000	Net Profit b/d	1,54,450
Proposed Dividends : Preference 16,000; Equity 60,000	76,000		
Balance carried forward	82,450		
	1,79,450		1,79,450

Solution :

EASTERN MALLEABLE LTD.
Balance Sheet as at 31st March, 2010

Fixed Assets :	*Cost* Rs.	*Depreciation* Rs.	*Net* Rs.
Land & Buildings	5,00,000	1,67,500	3,32,500
Plant	3,00,000	1,20,000	1,80,000
	8,00,000	2,87,500	5,12,500
Working Capital :			
Current Assets :			
Stock		70,000	
Book Debts		60,000	
Cash at Bank		50,000	
		1,80,000	
Current Liabilities :			
Creditors for goods and expenses	30,385		
Estimated liability for taxes	90,074		
Dividend proposed to be paid			
Preference	16,000		
Equity	53,091	1,89,550	– 9,550
Operating Capital Employed			5,02,950
Investments in shares of other companies			2,20,000
Total Equity (or total resources at the disposal of the company)			7,22,950
Less : Loans (on the security of.....?)			2,00,000
Shareholders' Funds or Equity			5,22,950
Represented by :			
14% Preference Share Capital			2,00,000
Equity Share Capital			2,00,000
Securities Premium			20,000
Profits at the disposal of the company less Miscellaneous Expenditure (not yet charged to revenue)			1,02,950
			5,22,950

Profit and Loss Account for the year ended March 31, 2010

	Rs.	Rs.
Sales affected during the year		25,60,000
Less : Cost of goods sold*		22,33,100
Gross Profit		3,26,900
Less : Administrative Expenses**	43,885	
Selling Expenses	48,000	91,885
Net Operating Profit subject to tax		2,35,015
Non-operating Items :		
Miscellaneous Received	2,300	
Dividends, etc. Received	12,300	
Less : Interest Paid	12,000	2,600
Net Profit		2,37,615
Estimated amount of tax payable out of above		83,165
Profit at the disposal of the company		1,54,450
**Cost of goods sold :*		
Materials used		12,16,000
Wages		6,30,000
Factory Expenses		3,34,600
Depreciation of fixed assets		37,500
Cost of goods produced		22,18,100
Add : Opening Stock on August 1, 1986		85,000
		23,03,100
Less : Closing Stock on July 31, 1987		70,000
Cost of goods sold		22,33,100
**Establishment ;		15,000
Rent & Taxes		6,000
Audit Fees		2,500
Directors' Fees		2,000
Sundry Expenses		6,000
Mg. Director's Remuneration		12,385
		43,885

Common-measurement statements :

Comparison of financial statements of various firms or for various years for the same year yields good results. Even putting the same figures side by side throws up some broad conclusions, but, for strict comparison, the figures should be on a common basis. See, for example, the commonest figures that one comes across in the Profit and Loss Account for the year ending 31st March :

	2009	2010		2009	2010
	Rs.	Rs.		Rs.	Rs.
Opening Stock	2,00,000	2,50,000	Sales	10,00,000	11,80,000
Purchases	5,00,000	6,00,000	Closing Stock	2,50,000	2,36,000
Manufacturing Expenses	1,50,000	2,00,000			
Gross Profit	4,00,000	3,66,000			
	12,50,000	14,16,000		12,50,000	14,16,000

Looking at the figures given above, one is a little mystified as to why with increase in sales, the gross profit should have gone down. The mystery will clear somewhat if, in addition to the absolute figures, percentages are worked out. Also, the figures should be presented in a different way, as shown below :

	2008-2009		2009-2010		
	Rs.	% to Sales	*Rs.*	% to Sales	% Increase over 1999
Purchases	5,00,000	50	6,00,000	51	20.0
Manufacturing Expenses	1,50,000	15	2,00,000	17	33.3
Adjustment for Stock	-50,000*	-5	14,000*	1	112.8
Total	6,00,000	60	8,14,000	69	35.6
Gross Profit	4,00,000	40	3,66,000	31	-8.2
Sales	10,00,000	100	11,80,000	100	18.0

A perusal of the figure will now show that, when costs increase by 35.6%, and sales increase only by 18%, a fall in profits must be expected. In 2008-09, total costs are only 60% of sales, whereas they are 69% of sales in 2009-2010. Thus the simple expedient of working out percentage figures based on sales helps to explain the state of affairs to some extent. Of course, it would have been better to know the different components of opening and closing stocks (raw materials, finished goods, work in progress) because then by adjusting purchases for opening and closing stocks of raw materials, cost of materials used would have been ascertained ; the percentage of cost of materials consumed to sales is always more significant than the percentage of purchases to sales. *Statements, presented as shown above, indicating relationship of various items to turnover are called "Common-measurement Statements;" every item is shown as a percentage of sales and can be readily compared with the corresponding figure in other periods.*

The expedient of working out percentage for figures in the Profit and Loss Account can work well enough but it does not work when it comes to studying the balance sheet. Even for the profit and loss account, percentage figures are rather inadequate—working out the ratios, that is the relationship of one figure with other significant figures, is the proper way of analysing and studying financial statements, both the profit and loss account and the balance sheet. That will be the subject matter of the next chapter. One must study the phenomenon that has largely destroyed the reliability of the financial statements, prepared on historical cost basis, as regards appreciation of the future prospects of the firm concerned. The phenomenon is that of inflation which has gone on for a very long period now.

EXERCISE XXX

Essay-type

1. Compare single column statements with those prepared in the "T" form.
2. The following notes have been appended to the published accounts of a company for the year ended 31st March, 2010.
   (*i*) The company follows the Actual Principle of Accounting but claims for goods lost in transit, are recorded in the books only when settled. During the year under review five claims have been filed against transporters.

*In 2008-2009 stock increases, representing saving in expenses of current year. In 2009-2010 stock is reduced showing that, in addition to current year's expenses, part of last year's saving was used up.

(*ii*) Gratuity is recorded only on payment and is included in salaries and wages. The amount paid during the year totalled Rs. 41,300. [There is no other mention of gratuity in the published accounts.]

Bring out the implications of these two notes and state in what respect they are inadequate.

3. Under Schedule VI, good deal of statistical information is required to be given. What are the uses to which information in respect of opening and closing stocks, materials consumed and turnover can be put.
4. What are the limitations of common measure statements ?
5. While studying published accounts, you come across an item entitled "Net Prior Year Adjustments" on the debit side. How do such adjustments arise ?
6. A company has revalued its fixed assets upwards but has used the revaluation profit to write off underwriting commission and preliminary expenses. Also, it has investments in a company whose accumulated losses exceed its capital but the investments, being trade investments, are carried at cost. Comment on the above.

31

INFLATION ACCOUNTING

SYNOPSIS

Need	.. 31.1	Current Cost Accounting	.. 31.12
Objections	.. 31.3	Evaluation of CCA	.. 31.25
Current Purchasing Power method	.. 31.5	SSAP 16	.. 31.27
		Bills Purchased and Discounted	.. 26.7

Need

Consider the following hypothetical but quite realistic case of a company:

	Rs.
(*i*) Capital employed: Fixed Assets — Cost	50,00,000
Less: Depreciation	20,00,000
	30,00,000
Working Capital	30,00,000
	~~60,00,000~~

(*ii*) Profit after tax @ 35% and depreciation of Rs. 5,00,000 (10% of the original cost of fixed assets) average Rs. 9,00,000.

(*iii*) The replacement cost of the fixed assets at present is Rs. 90 lakh.

One may think that the return on investment is 15%, *i.e.*, $9,00,000 \times 100\sqrt{60,00,000}$. However, let us re-work the figures, taking into account the replacement value of fixed assets:—

	Rs.
Profit as stated	11,70,000
Tax	6,30,000
Add: Depreciation	5,00,000
Add: Profit before depreciation and tax	23,00,000
Less: Depreciation on Rs. 90 lakh @ 10%	9,00,000
	14,00,000
Less: Tax @ 35%	4,90,000
"True" Profit	9,10,000
Capital Employed: Fixed Assets	90,00,000
Less: Depreciation [10% as in (*i*) above]	36,00,000
	54,00,000
Add: Working Capital	36,00,000
	84,00,000

$$\text{Return on investment: } \frac{9,10,000 \times 100}{84,00,000} = 10.83\%$$

This shows that if the effect of inflation is ignored, one will have an unrealistic and exaggerated view of the profit earned or return on investment achieved. Hence, the need for "Inflation Accounting."

To illustrate this point, let us consider the steel plants in India. The plants of various steel companies were established at various points of time. TISCO's plant was erected earlier than even the First World War. The Indian Iron and Steel Company was established in the pre-independence period. The various plants of HSL were established in 1960's. If the performances of these plants are compared through ratio analysis, erroneous and misleading results will be shown because of the following two reasons:—

(*i*) The investment base of all the plants would be different. It is obvious that the plants which were established earlier had a much lower capital cost — the same facilities established by other firms at a later period would have a much higher cost. The investment base of the later companies would be much higher than the investment base of the companies established earlier. Therefore, companies which are established later will show a lower rate of return on investment.

(*ii*) The return showed by the old companies would be unduly high. This is due to the fact that the depreciation charge of such companies would be much lower than warranted by the real present day value of the assets.

A point of great significance, apart from proper measurement and comparability, is that if only historical costs are considered, the amounts collected by way of depreciation charge will be totally inadequate to replace the fixed assets when their life is over. If physical assets are to be maintained, as indeed must be the aim, inflation must be kept fully in view. It is, therefore, important that proper adjustments on account of price level changes are made in the financial statements. A number of studies have been conducted, especially in U.K., to devise a practical method to adjust accounts for price level changes. There are basically two methods by which price level changes can be recognised.

Limitations of historical accounting in a period of inflation. The example given on the previous page shows clearly that when prices have risen substantially, the profit and loss account and the balance sheet drawn up on the basis of historical costs do not permit a proper appraisal of the performance of the concern and its financial position. This is because of the fact that though the sales revenue is in terms of current rupees some of the important charges against revenue are in terms of old rupees. The chief example of this is depreciation; another is the cost of goods sold. Further, the real capital employed is much more than that shown by the balance sheet. Thus, the first limitation is that a meaningful appraisal is not possible if financial statements are drawn up in the traditional manner even though there has been a great increase in prices.

Due to inflation, the matching principle, vital to preparation of proper financial statements, is violated. If sales are entered in the Profit and Loss Account in terms of 2010 rupees, it is but proper that the relevant costs should also be in terms of 2010 rupees. That obviously is not so in the case of depreciation, but will the matching principle be satisfied if the goods sold were purchased say in 2008? To satisfy this principle, it will be necessary to restate the 2008 purchases in terms of 2010 prices. From another angle also, it is important. An important function of the profit and loss account is to show up the factors that have led to the year's profit or loss. This will not be possible unless operating profits are separated from holding gains. The former is the profit earned through the firm's operations of production and sale of goods and the latter from rise in prices (which is a windfall for the firm). Inflation accounting should help in clearly differentiating operating profit from holding gain. In another way, one can say that profit should be computed only in items of physical units and not merely rupees in times of inflation. A buys 100 grams of gold at Rs. 14,400 per ten grams on 1st January, 2009, he sells the entire quantity on 31st December, 2009 at Rs. 14,600 and immediately buys the same quantity again at Rs. 14,600, how much profit has he made? Monetarily Rs. 2,000, but really nothing since he had 100 grams of gold and still has only 100 grams.

The second limitation is regarding faulty decisions that are likely to be made if the costs and profits are not properly ascertained. In the example given earlier the profit shown is Rs. 9 lakh whereas in reality it is only Rs. 7 lakh. If Rs. 9 lakh is distributed, it will only result in a reduction in the capital of the firm. If prices are to be fixed, they are likely to be fixed at an unduly low figure if only historical costs are taken into account. The result will be either very low profits or even losses in real terms. For decision-making purposes, it is essential to consider present day or current costs.

The third, and perhaps the most important is that due to faulty measurement of profit and depreciation charge and decisions based thereon, it is very likely that when the time comes to replace fixed assets, the available funds will not suffice to carry to carry out the replacement. This will force the firm to operate at a very much reduced level of operations. Operational capability is affected by non-replacement of fixed assets of equal efficiency: it is further affected by the fact that due to higher prices larger and larger amounts will be required for working capital. If such large funds are not available, operations will be adversely affected.

Another point, important from the point of view of financial management, is that inflation will require large funds for maintenance of the working capital, both for inventories and book debts, etc. If inventory consists of 10,000 units and if the cost rises from Rs. 40 to Rs. 45, Rs. 50,000 more will be required for maintaining the inventory.

Maintenance of operational capability is the most important objective of inflation accounting. The points made above are all relevant to the maintenance of operational capability of the firm. It must think of its capital in physical terms and arrange to retain sufficient funds in the business to replace fixed assets fully when the time is due and also to maintain the working capital required to carry on the operations of the business at their present level. The method followed for inflation accounting should ensure this as well differentiation of operating profits and holding gains.

Objections. There are still some people who object to inflation accounting. Their grounds mainly are the following:—

(1) Inflation accounting, involving a write-up of assets, violates the cost concept and destroys objectivity. In a way it is true but what is cost — Rupees spent 20 years ago or the cost that would have been incurred today? Prices are generally fixed in terms of current costs of inputs; there is no reason why such costs, if ascertainable, violate the cost principle. Objectively must certainly be maintained as, otherwise, the financial statements will lose their credibility. This is a problem which inflation accounting must satisfactorily solve before it can be accepted. The use of official statistics relating to price should go a long way towards a satisfactory solution.

(2) Profits disclosed by revaluation are capital profits — any distribution among shareholders will certainly dissipate financial strength of the firm. This is valid, but no one proposes that profit on revaluation should be treated as distributable; the profit is capital profit.

(3) Maintenance of capital or operational capability is the duty and function of management. It must adopt suitable financial policies to discharge this duty; there is no need to change accounting principles. It is quite true to say that there must be suitable financial policies but accounting always had the extremely important duty of conveying to the management what the real profit is and how much can be safely distributed among the shareholders. In present times, without inflation accounting, it is impossible to ascertain the correct and real profit.

(4) Inflation accounting may lead to revision of cost of production and hence may lead to increase in prices and a further dose of inflation. There are two fallacies to the argument. It presupposes that prices are generally based on costs; that is not so really since the principle that may operate is "what the traffic will bear". Secondly, for fixing prices firms always take into account current costs and not historical costs as is assumed under the argument. In any case, it is for the society to combat inflation; it cannot do so by refusing to know the facts.

(5) Tax authorities so far have refused to recognise depreciation based on replacement costs and, therefore, even if an inflation-adjusted profit and loss account is prepared. The tax will still be on the basis of profit as per historical profit and loss account. This is quite true

but two points can be made. The survival of the firm is paramount and hence the behaviour of tax officers should not stop the firm from ascertaining the real situation. Secondly, it is quite possible that when an agreed scheme of inflation accounting is adopted, Government agreeing, the tax authorities will also agree to make the necessary changes. In U.K., for example, 100% depreciation allowance is made in the very first year.

Conclusion. It is now generally agreed that there is an imperative need for inflation-adjusted financial statements to be prepared and presented to the shareholders and other interested parties. This is because the phenomenon of inflation is widespread and has continued for a long time now; as a result, financial statements prepared on historical cost basis do not, as a rule, portray the real state of affairs — neither the results of operations nor the financial position. However, "historical cost" financial statements will continue to be presented, only they will be supplemented by financial statements, adjusted for the increase in prices — that is the accepted position both in the U.K. and the U.S.A. In U.K. the position has been formalised by the Institute of Chartered Accountants in England and Wales through SSAP 16 and in U.S.A. the Securities and Exchange Commission has framed regulations to require supplementary inflation-adjusted accounting statements. SEC permits the use of the current purchasing power method called. "Constant Dollar Method" as well as the Current Cost Accounting Method.

In Indian the position is that there is no compulsion as yet for any company to present accounts otherwise than on the basis of historical costs. Some companies have revalued their fixed assets but the purpose in these cases appears to be quite different from that of inflation accounting since even the reported profit remains largely unaffected. A few companies, on their own, have prepared supplementary financial statements on the basis of inflation but the objective seems to have been either to get a prize from the Institute of Chartered Accountants of India (which Institute awards prizes annually for best presented accounts) or to show how the real profits are lower than the reported profits and how tax and bonus to employees were unreasonably high. The exercise undertaken by a company was given up when in one fortunate year prices fell because, then, the reported profits would have been shown to be lower than the real profits. It is not necessary to emphasise the need to present accounts adjusted for inflation but, in all propriety, accounting should be concerned with fall in prices also and hence the proper approach is that of accounting for price level charges and not merely for inflation. It appears, however, that for quite some foreseeable future, it will be inflation which will be bothering us and not a fall in prices.

The Role of Inflation Accounting. The definition of Accounting given by AICPA is : "Accounting is the art of recording, classifying, and summarising in a significant manner and in terms of money, transactions and events which are, in part at least, of a financial character, and interpreting the results thereof". Though Statement 4 issued by the Accounting Principles board of the AICPA talks of the utility of accounting in making economic decisions*, really Financial Accounting has confined itself more or less, to portrayal, in a significant manner, of the profit earned or loss suffered during a period and of the financial position at the end thereof. [Decision-making functions have been left to Management Accounting]. The approach to inflation accounting also has kept this objective mainly in view. In other words, it is considered enough if the reported profit and the balance sheet conform to reality.

This is important but equally important is the question of survival which is bound up intimately with replacement of assets at the end of their life. This means that the firm must have funds to carry out the replacement when due. This is one of the important functions of accounting for depreciation and is quite adequately performed if there is no increase in prices; also if increases in prices are constantly kept in view while providing depreciation, at least partially. The point is that inflation

* The APB says, "Accounting is a service activity. Its function is to provide quantitative information primarily financial in nature, about economic entities that is intended to be useful in making economic decisions — in making reasoned choices among alternative courses of action."

accounting must specifically keep this objective in view; otherwise there is danger that the firm will become sick simply because it does not have adequate funds to acquire new assets when the old assets have yielded all their utility. Some people argue that finding funds for replacement of assets is the function of financial management, may be through a judicious use of profits. Some of them, therefore, even deny any need for inflation accounting. If ascertaining real profit and maintenance of operational capability or capital physically are to be viewed separately, this approach may be quite valid but to do so will be to take a partial view of the state of affair to the detriment of not only the various interested parties but also the firm itself. That the firm should not eat up its capital, that is, it should keep its ability to replace assets by new ones of equal efficiency, when the time comes, is a duty and function of Financial Accounting as well as Financial Management. Perhaps Financial Accounting has a greater responsibility in this regard since it alone can provide the necessary information for the required decisions.

Another question that needs some consideration is : whose viewpoint is to be paramount? — the firm's or the shareholders'? It appears that the shareholders may be interested in maintaining their purchasing power in general. Shareholders as a class have no attachment to any particular industry; they are, therefore, more interested in profits from a general point of view and hence they may not rely on profits reported by a firm using the specific inflation adjustment factors. The firm on the other hand, may be interested in ascertaining profits taking into consideration the price changes that are relevant and specific to its business — the Current Cost Accounting Method, which has now found general acceptance, accepts this view. But in this case also the assumption is that the firm will continue in the same industry as hitherto. Should the management decide to move into another industry as and when funds are released from the present investment, the available funds, even though inflation-adjusted on the basis of CCA, may not be adequate. Suppose prices in general rise by 20% but those pertaining to a particular industry rise by only 10%. How would the share market value the shares of a firm in the industry? Will it take at face value, the profits of the firm as disclosed by the Profit and Loss Account drawn up on taking into account the 10% increase in prices? Or will it discount the reported profit because of a greater fall in the purchasing power in general? Suppose the firm takes care to husband all its profits and depreciation funds in order to be able to move into more promising industry. Will not the firm be interested in knowing what the available funds mean in terms of investment opportunities in real terms?

One may summarise this discussion by stating that inflation accounting should have the following objectives:—

(1) To portray the real profit or loss for the period under consideration as against the profit or loss on the basis of historical costs;

(2) To set out the real financial position, in present day terms rather than the conventional position on historical costs basis and to indicate the real capital employed;

(3) To ensure that sufficient funds will be available to replace the various assets when the replacement becomes due; and

(4) To indicate profits in constant rupees, *i.e.*, having regard to the general movement in prices for the guidance of shareholders as well as of management.

The system of inflation accounting should be such that, with minor modifications, it will yield the necessary information to moderate proper management action. Basically new methods have been recommended to adapt financial statements for inflation accounting.

Current Purchasing Power Method

The Institute of Chartered Accountants in England and Wales recommends that changes in the price level should be reflected in the financial statements through the Current Purchasing Power Method (CPP Method). Under this method any established and approved general price index is used to convert the values of various items in the balance-sheet and the profit and loss account. The main argument is that a change in the price level reflects change in the value of the rupee. This change is denoted by a general price index. In India, we may take a general price index like the Wholesale Price Index of the Reserve Bank of India which would show the changes in the value of the rupee in the past years. Thus, if we want to add up the values of certain assets purchased in 2002, to those of some other assets purchased in 2010, we can do so only after we have converted the rupee values of 2010 in terms of rupees of 2002.

The CPP Method accounts for changes in the value of money. It does not account for changes in the value of the individual assets. Thus, a particular machine may have become cheaper over the last few years, whereas the general price level may have risen; the value of the machine will also be raised in accordance with the general price index. This is because we are not trying to work out the current values of the various assets in the possession of the business. What we are trying to achieve is that the financial statements should be stated in terms of rupees of uniform value.

In 1974, the English Institute of Chartered Accountants recommended that companies should continue to prepare financial statements on historical cost basis but should also prepare supplementary statements showing the various items of the financial statements in terms of the value of the pound as at the end of the period to which they relate. The following extracts from this statement would indicate the basic aspects of the CPP Method:

"1. Inflation, which is the decline in the purchasing power of money as the general price of goods and services rises, affects most aspects of economic life, including investment decisions, wage negotiations, pricing policies, international trade and government taxation policy.

2. It is important that managements and other users of financial accounts should be in a position to appreciate the effects of inflation on the businesses with which they are concerned — for example, the effects on costs, profits distribution policies, dividend cover, the exercise of borrowing powers, returns on funds and future cash needs. The purpose of this statement is the limited one of establishing a standard practice for demonstrating the effect of changes in the purchasing power of money on accounts prepared on the basis of existing conventions. It does not suggest the abandonment of the historical cost convention, but simply that historical costs should be converted from an aggregation of historical pounds of many different purchasing powers into approximate figure of current purchasing power and that this information should be given in a supplement to the basic accounts prepared on the historical cost basis.

* * * * *

11. The method proposed in this statement (the 'current purchasing power' as 'CPP' method) is concerned with removing the distorting effects of changes in the general purchasing power of money on accounts prepared in accordance with established practice. It does not deal with changes in the relative values of non-monetary assets (which occur also in the absence of inflation). It should therefore be distinguished from methods of "replacement cost" and "current value" accounting which deal with a mixture of changes in relative values and changes due to movements in the general price level.

Summary of the principal aspects of the statement of standard accounting practice

12. The main features of the standard are:

(*a*) companies will continue to keep their records and present their basic annual accounts in historical pounds, *i.e.*, in terms of the value of the pound at the time of each transaction or revaluation;

(*b*) in addition, all listed companies should present to their shareholders a supplementary statement in terms of the value of the pound at the end of the period to which the accounts relate;

(*c*) the conversion of the figures in the basic accounts into the figures in the supplementary statement should be by means of a general index of the purchasing power of the pound;

(*d*) The standard requires the directions to provide in a note to the supplementary statement an explanation of the basis on which it has been prepared and it is desirable that directors should comment on the significance of the figures.

13. The form of the supplementary statement is a matter for the directors of the company to decide, provided that they conform to the standard accounting practice. There are a number of ways in which the information required may be shown. An example of a possible presentation is given in Appendix 2 (*not reproduced*). This example includes some ratios as the effect of changes in the purchasing power of the pound on them may be even more significant than on the underlying absolute figures.

Monetary and Non-Monetary Items:

14. In converting the figures in the basic historical cost accounts into those in the supplementary current purchasing power statement a distinction is drawn between :

(*a*) monetary items; and

(*b*) non-monetary items.

15. Monetary items are those whose amounts are fixed by contract or otherwise in terms of numbers of pounds, regardless of changes in general price level. Examples of monetary items are cash, debtors, creditors and loan capital. Holders of monetary assets lose general purchasing power during a period of inflation to the extent that any income from the assets does not adequately compensate for the loss; the converse applies to those having monetary liabilities. A company with a material excess on average over the year of long, and short-term debts (e.g., debentures and creditors) over debtors and cash will show, in its supplementary current purchasing power statement, a gain in purchasing power during the year. This is a real gain to the equity shareholders in purchasing power but it has to be appreciated that there may be circumstances in which it will be accompanied by a dangerously illiquid situation or by excessively high gearing and for this reason any such gain should be shown as a separate figure.

16. It has been argued that the gain on long-term borrowing should not be shown as profit in the supplementary statement because it might not be possible to distribute it without raising additional finance. This argument, however, confuses the measurement of profitability, with the measurement of liquidity. Even in the absence of inflation, the whole of a company's profit may not be distributable without raising additional finance for example because it has been invested in, or earmarked for, investment in non-liquid assets.

17. Moreover, it is inconsistent to exclude such gain when profit has been debited with the cost of borrowing (which must be assumed to reflect anticipation of inflation by the lender during the currency of the loan) and with depreciation on the converted value of fixed assets.

18. Non-monetary items include such assets as stock, plant and buildings. The retention of the historical cost concept requires that holders of non-monetary assets are assumed neither to gain nor to lose purchasing power of the pound (but see paragraphs 21 and 22 below).

19. The owners of a company's equity capital have the residual claim on its net monetary and non-monetary assets. The equity interest is therefore neither a monetary nor a non-monetary item.

The conversion process

20. In converting from basic historical cost accounts to supplementary current purchasing power statements for any particular period

(*a*) monetary items in the balance sheet at the end of the period remain the same;

(*b*) non-monetary items are increased in proportion to the inflation that has occurred since their acquisition or revaluation (and conversely, reduced in times of deflation).

21. In the conversion process, after increasing non-monetary items by the amount of inflation, it is necessary to apply the test of lower of cost (expressed in pounds of current purchasing power) and net realizable value to relevant current assets, *e.g.*, stocks, and further to adjust the figures if necessary. Similarly, after restating fixed assets in terms of pounds of current purchasing power, the

question of the value of the business needs to be reviewed in that context and provision made if necessary. Other matters that will need to be considered include the adequacy of the charge for depreciation on freehold and long leasehold properties and whether it may be necessary to include in the deferred tax account in the supplementary statement, an amount for the corporation tax (in the Republic of Ireland, income tax and corporation profits tax) on any chargeable gain which would arise on sale of the assets at the date of the balance sheet at the amount shown in the supplementary statement.

22. In applying these tests, and during the whole process of conversion, it is important to balance the effort involved against the materiality of the figures concerned. The supplementary current purchasing power statement can be no more than an approximation, and it is pointless to strive for over-elaborate precision.

Index to be used

23. In the United Kingdom there are a number of indices which might be taken as indicators of changes in the general purchasing power of the pound.

24. On the basis of a recommendation from the Central Statistical Office, the use of the following indices is specified for the relevant periods:

for periods up to end-1938, the Ministry of Labour cost of living index;
for periods between end-1938 and end–1961, the consumers expenditure deflator;
for periods from 1962 onwards, the general index of retail prices.

Constant Dollar Accounting. The Securities and Exchange Commission has christened the CPP method as "Constant Dollar Accounting". The SEC now requires inflation-adjusted statements and it permits use of either the Current Cost Accounting Method (discussed below) or the Constant Dollar Accounting. In the latter case, the adjustments to be made are based on movements in the consumer price index for all urban consumers. An important point to be noted is that adjustments may be made either on the basis of "average for the year" or of "end of the year" prices. In the latter case revenue items are adjusted on the assumption that the amounts recorded in the income statement are in terms of prices prevailing in the middle of the year. Further, loss or gain on monetary items, resulting from movements in prices, must also be computed and shown (Under the CPP method as enunicated in U.K. such losses or gains were to be ignored.)

Example 1. A company bought investments at a cost of Rs. 6,00,000 on July 1, 2009 when the price index stood at 300. On 31st March, 2010 the index had moved to 320 and the market value of the investments was Rs. 6,10,000. On CPP basis, what is the loss or profit on the investment?

	Rs.
Answer. The "Cost" on CPP basis on 31st march, 2010, Rs. 6,00,000 × 320/300	6,40,000
Market Value	6,10,000
Loss	30,000

Example 2. Eass Ltd. made a sale of Rs. 67,50,000 during the year ended 31st March, 2010. The price indices were 250 in the beginning of the year, 270 in the middle of year and 300 at the end. Using year-end price adjustment basis, what is the sale under the CPP Method?

Answer. Sale for CPP purposes : Rs. 67,50,000 × 300/270 or Rs. 75,00,000.

Illustration 1.

A firm had Rs. 2,00,000 as cash at bank on April 1, 2009. The consumer price index on that date was 200. During the year ended 31st March, 2010 the receipts and payments were stated below:—

Receipts		*Rs.*	*Index*	*Payments*		*Rs.*	Index
June 1	Sales	1,05,000	210	Sept. 15	Costs	2,15,000	215
January 15	Sales	3,45,000	230	Dec. 1	Plant	2,00,000	225
				Mar. 20	Costs	1,50,000	240

Ascertain the profit or loss on account of price changes; the year end index was 240.

Solution:

Statement showing Profit/Loss on Cash during the year ended 31st March, 2010:—

		Historical Rs.	*Adjustment*	*Constant* Rs.
Opening Balance		2,00,000	240/200	2,40,000
Receipts:	June 1	1,05,000	240/210	1,20,000
	Jan. 15	3,45,000	240/230	3,60,000
		6,50,000		7,20,000
Payments:	Sept. 15	2,15,000	240/215	2,40,000
	Dec. 1	2,00,000	240/225	2,13,333
	Mar. 20	1,50,000	240/240	1,50,000
		5,65,000		6,03,333
Balance		85,000		1,16,667

The balance according to Constant Rupees should have been Rs. 1,16,667 whereas the actual balance is only Rs. 85,000. Therefore, as a result of changes in prices, there has been a loss of Rs. 31,667.

Illustration 2:

PQ Ltd. prepared the following (summarised) final statements of account for the year ended 31st March, 2010:—

Balance Sheet

	Rs.			Rs.
Share Capital	10,00,000	Land & Buildings: Cost		4,00,000
Reserves and Surplus	6,00,000	*Less*: Depreciation		1,50,000
15% Loans	8,00,000			2,50,000
Current Liabilities and Provisions	4,00,000	Plant & Machinery		
		Cost	30,00,000	
		Less: Depreciation	16,00,000	14,00,000
		Stock in Trade		5,10,000
		Sundry Debtors		4,50,000
		Cash in hand and at Bank		1,90,000
	28,00,000			2,80,000

Profit and Loss Account

	Rs.		Rs.
Opening Stock	4,00,000		
Purchases	21,00,000		
Wages and Manufacturing Expenses	9,50,000		
Interest	1,20,000		
Administrative & Selling Expenses	6,30,000		
Depreciation	3,20,000		
Provision for Tax	1,75,000		
Net Profit	2,25,000		
	49,20,000		49,20,000

Additional information:—

1. The balances on account of current liabilities and provisions and book debts on April 1, 2009 were respectively Rs. 3,50,000 and Rs. 4,80,000.
2. The relevant price index moved from 250 on 1st April, 2009 to 280 on 30th September,

2009 and stood 300 at the end of the accounting year. The index was 150 when the company commenced operations.

3. Depreciation is charged at 10% on Plant & Machinery and 5% on Land & Building (on origianl cost).

Draw up the inflation adjusted statements of account using the Current Rupee Method.

Solution:

Inflation Adjusted Profit and Loss Account for the Year ended March 31, 2010

	Rs.			Rs.
Opening Stock (Rs. 4,00,000 × 280/250)	4,48,000	Sales	47,03,570	
Purchases	22,50,000	Miscellaneous Income		21,428
Wages and Manufacturing Expenses	10,17,587	Stock		5,46,428
Interest	1,28,571	Gain on Maonetary Working Capital		47,929
Administrative and Selling Expenses	6,75,000	Loss for the year		14,238
Depreciation (as Calculated)	5,86,666			
Provision for Tax	1,87,500			
	52,93,594			52,93,594

Inflation Adjusted Balance Sheet of P. Ltd. as at March, 31, 2010

Liabilities	Rs.	*Assets*		Rs.
Share Capital	10,00,000	Fixed Assets (as revalued):		
Revaluation Reserve	19,25,666	Land and Buildings	8,00,000	
Other Reserves and Surplus	3,60,762	*Less:* Adjusted		
15% Loans	8,00,000	Depreciation	3,00,000	5,00,000
Current Liabilities and Provisions	4,00,000	Plant and Machinery	60,00,000	
		Less: Adjusted		
		Depreciation	32,00,000	28,00,000
		Stock in Trade		5,46,428
		Sundry Debtors		4,50,000
		Cash in Hand and at Bank		1,90,000
	44,86,428			44,86,428

Working Notes:

(i) Opening Cash Balance

Cash and Bank Account

	Rs.	Rs.		Rs.	Rs.
Sale Proceeds:			Overdraft (Opening— Balancing figure)		3,25,000
Sale	43,90,000		Cash Costs:		
Add: Outstanding on 1.4.2009	43,90,000		Purchases	21,00,000	
	48,70,000		Wages and Manufacturing Expenses	9,50,000	
Less: Outstanding on 31.3.2010	4,50,000	44,20,000	Interest	1,20,000	
Miscellaneous Income		20,000	Administrative and selling Expenses	6,30,000	
			Tax	1,75,000	
				39,75,000	
			Add: Outstanding on 1.4.2010	3,50,000	
				43,25,000	

	Rs.			Rs.
		Less: Outstanding on 31.3.2010	4,00,000	39,25,000
		Closing Balance		1,90,000
	44,40,000			44,40,000

(*ii*) *Profit/Loss on Monetary Working Capital:*

1st April, 2009 Book debts		4,80,000	
Less: Current Liabilities etc.	3,50,000		
Bank Overdraft	3,25,000	6,75,000	
Monetary Working Capital on 1.4.2009		(1,95,000)	
Inflation-Adjusted Monetary Working Capital	(Rs.1,95,000) × 300/250		(2,34,000)
Inflation-Adjusted Receipts (Sales etc.)	Rs. 44,10,000 × 300/280		47,25,000
Inflation-Adjusted Payments	(Rs. 39,75,000) × 300/280		(42,58,929)
Inflation-Adjusted Monetary Working Capital at the end			2,32,071
Actual Monetary Working Capital on 31.3.2010			
Cash Balance	1,90,000		
Book Debts	4,50,000		
	6,40,000		
Less: Current Liabilities	4,00,000		2,40,000
Gain			7,929

(*iii*) *Change in fixed assets:*

	Total Rs.	*Land & Building* Rs.	*Plant & Machinery* Rs.
Cost	34,00,000	4,00,000	30,00,000
Adjustment factor up to 1.4.2009, 250/150			
Value on 1.4.2009, Rs. 34,00,000 × 250/150	56,66,667	6,66,667	50,00,000
Adjustment factor up to 31.3.2010, 300/150			
Value on 31.3.2010, Rs. 34,00,000 × 300/150	68,00,000	8,00,000	60,00,000
Adjusted Book Value as on 31.3.2010 (existing book values × 300/150)	33,00,000	5,00,000	28,00,000

(*iv*) *Depreciation Adjustment*:

Actual amount charged	3,20,000
Adjustment, 3,20,000 × 250/150	5,33,333
Additional Depreciation for 6 months due to increase in value during the year: @ 5% on Rs. 1,33,333	3,333
@ 10% on Rs. 10,00,000	50,000
Total Inflation adjusted depreciation for the year	5,86,666

(*v*) All "Cash" expenses and revenue have been adjusted by the factor: Price index at the end of the accounting year/price index in the middle of the accounting year, *i.e.*, 300/280. This applies to closing stock also but opening stock has been adjusted by 280/250, *i.e.*, price index in the middle of the year divided by that in the beginning.

(*vi*) *Revaluation Reserve*:

	Rs.
Increase in value of fixed assets (*iii*) above)	33,00,000
As per Balance Sheet (historical)	16,50,000
	16,50,000
Increase in: Opening stock	48,000
Purchases	1,50,000

		Rs.
Wages and Manufacturing Expenses		67,857
Interest		8,571
Administrative and Selling Expenses		45,000
Depreciation		2,66,666
Tax Provision		12,500
		22,48,594
Less: Increase in sales	3,13,571	
Miscellaneous Income	1,428	
Gain on Monetary Working Capital	7,929	3,22,928
		19,25,666

(vii) Other Reserves and Surplus:

	Rs.
As per historial Balance Sheet	6,00,000
Less: Profit of Rs. 2,25,000 converted into loss of Rs. 14,238	2,39,238
	3,60,762

Current Cost Accounting

The system of inflation accounting now accepted in U.K. is called the Current Cost Accounting System evolved in the initial stages by the Sandilands Committee. The system has been extensively studied and debated and now it has been finalised by the issue of SSAP 16 (Statement of Standard Accounting Practice) which is reproduced as an appendix to this chapter. This system takes into account price changes relevant to the particular firm or industry rather than the economy as a whole. It seeks to arrive at a profit which can be safely distributed as dividend without impairing the operational capability of the firm. In addition to adjustments for depreciation and cost of sales, it deals with the working capital and also loans raised. The ambit is operation profit and operating capital employed.

Current cost accounting has the following important features:

(*a*) Fixed assets are to be shown in the balance sheet at their value to the business and not at their depreciated original cost.

(*b*) Stocks are to be shown in the balance sheet at their value to the business and not at the lower of their original cost and realisable value.

(*c*) Depreciation for the year is to be calculated on the current value of the relevant fixed assets.

(*d*) The cost of stock consumed during the year is to be calculated on the value to the business of the stock at the date of consumption and not at the date of purchase.

(*e*) The effects of the loss or gain from loans will be computed and set off against interest.

The increased replacement cost of fixed assets and of stocks, the increased requirements for monetary working capital and the under provision of depreciation in the past years may be adjusted through a revaluation reserve.

The fixed assets in the balance sheet should be shown at their 'value to the business', which is defined as the amount which the company would lose if it were deprived of the assets. The value to the business can be defined in one of the following three ways.

(*a*) *Net Replacement Value*: This refers to the money now required to buy a new asset of the same type as the existing one less an amount of depreciation that recognises the fact that the true replacement of the asset would not be a new asset but an asset which has the same remaining useful life as the existing asset. Suppose, a machine whose total life is 10 years can now be procured for Rs. 80,000. Suppose further that the machine is 5 years old. Assuming that the machine has no scrap value, the net replacement cost of the machine would be Rs. 80,000 minus depreciation for 5 years, *i.e.*, Rs. 40,000.

(*b*) *Net Realisable Value*: This is the value which is represented by the net cash proceeds which would be received if the existing asset is sold now.

(*c*) *Economic Value*: This refers to the present value of the net income that will be earned from using the existing asset during the rest of its life. Suppose, the net cash inflow (gross income minus expenditure of the machine in our example) is Rs. 8,000 per annum. This means that in the 5 years of its remaining life it will yield Rs. 40,000 in all. Since the sum (Rs. 40,000) will be accruing over the next 5 years and not immediately, it should be discounted and the present value of the future net cash inflows worked out.

The three values discussed above represent the purchase, sale and the holding value of the asset. According to the exposure draft, the net replacement cost is usually the best indicator of the value to the business of an asset.

The value to the business of the self-occupied land and buildings will normally be the open market value for their existing use plus estimated attributable acquisition costs. The depreciated replacement cost of the buildings and the open market value of land, including the estimated acquisition costs for the existing use, should be taken as their value to the business. Such as valuation should be made by a professionally qualified valuer at intervals of not more than 5 years. In the years between full scale professional valuations, the directors should estimate the value of the land and buildings after consultation with professional valuers and after taking into account market variations and changes in construction costs.

Plant and machinery should be valued at their net current replacement costs. For this purpose, the gross current replacement cost of plant and machinery should be worked out. This is the cost that would have to be incurred to obtain and instal at the date of the valuation, a substantially identical replacement assets in new condition. Since the plant and machinery is not new, the gross replacement cost arrivged at as above should be written down with reference to the number of years that the existing plant and machinery has already served. In other words, depreciation should be charged on the gross current replacement cost on the basis of the expired service potential of the asset in question.

The gross current replacement cost can be known from the following sources:

(*i*) The official price lists or the catalogues of the suppliers;

(*ii*) The estimates made by the company itself based on expert opinion;

(*iii*) Index compiled by the company from its own purchasing experience;

(*iv*) Authorised price indices prepared by external agencies like the Department of Industry or Central Statistical Organisation. These indices are now prepared in the U.K. both with reference to the category of assets and the type of industry.

Investments held by the company, not as current assets, should be valued at their value to business. This implies that the quoted investments should be based on the stock market mid prices and the unquoted investments should be based on the directors' valuation of, on the basis of the current cost, net asset value of the company in which the investments have been made or on the basis of the present value of the likely future income from the unquoted investments.

In case investments are held as current assets, their treatment should be the same as that of stock and work in progress (discussed later).

In case of investments in subsidiaries, the cost of the shares should be adjusted to the movement in reserves or net assets of the subsidiaries after the shares have been acquired.

Stocks and work in progress should be shown in the balance sheet at their value to the business on the balance sheet date. The value to the business of a company's stock is lower of the replacement cost of that stock and its net realisable value. In other words, both the replacement cost of the stock and the net realisable value of the stock should be worked out. The lower of these two amounts would be the value which should be put to the stock in the balance sheet.

Debtors, cash and current liabilities in the current cost balance sheet are shown at their value to the business which is their net realisable value. It is obvious that these amounts would be the same in the historical cost balance sheet and the current cost balance sheet.

The depreciation charge in the current cost profit and loss account should be based on the current value of fixed assets. Thus, the depreciation charge may be based on the average of the opening current value and the closing current value. Further, as the gross value of the asset increases in an inflationary period due to it being at its replacement cost, the accumulated depreciation will not be sufficient. Hence, additional depreciation should be charged to provide for this backlog. However, this additional depreciation should be set off against the surplus arising on the revaluation of the assets. Suppose, a machine is purchased for Rs. 10 lakh on 1st April, 2005. Suppose further that on 1st April, 2009, the current value of the machine is Rs. 20 lakh and on 31st March, 2010, the current value of the machine is Rs. 22 lakh. The depreciation for the year ended 31st March, 2010 will be charged on Rs. 21 lakh. If the life of the machine is 10 years, the depreciation for the year 2009-2010 would be Rs. 2,10,000. Suppose, the accumulated depreciation is Rs. 7 lakh. The total accumulated depreciation now becomes Rs. 9,10,000. This is not enough at the gross replacement cost of the asset on 31st March, 2010. Depreciation on Rs. 22 lakh for five years at 10%, straightline basis, would be Rs. 11 lakh. Hence, a further depreciation charge of Rs. 1,90,000 should be made. The depreciation of Rs. 2,10,000 will be debited to the profit and loss account and the depreciation of Rs. 1,90,000 will be set off against the revaluation surplus.

The figure for sales remains the same in the historical cost account and the current cost accounts. However, the cost of sales is different in the historical cost accounts and the current cost accounts. This is because in historical cost accounts each item of stock sold or consumed is included at FIFO cost. The objective of current cost accounts is to charge against sales revenue, the value to the business of the costs cunsumed at the date they are consumed. The date of consumption of stock is normally the date of sale and to arrive at the current cost of sale it is necessary to substitute the current replacement cost of stock sold at the date of sale in place of the historical cost of stock sold. Since it may not be possible to know the current cost of sale of each individual item of stock, it is suggested that an overall cost of sales adjustment may be made. This adjustment is based on approximation through the averaging method.

It would thus be seen that the current profit and loss account requires two adjustments from the historical profit and loss account – firstly, additional depreciation and, secondly, cost of sales adjustment (including working capital adjustment). The total adjustments are again adjusted for loans taken.

Features

Below we discuss briefly and illustrate main features of CCA and see to what extent it will achieve the objectives set out above. The system concerns operating profits and, naturally, operating capital employed and seeks to make a clear distinction between profits that emerge according to present day terms through operations and profits and those that arise only because of increase in prices, i.e., holding gains. This distinction is of vital importance for judging the efficiency of a firm — the profit and loss account on historical cost basis mixes up the two profits and, hence, makes judgment about operational efficiency very difficult.*

The following are the main features of CCA:

(*i*) Ascertaining the present day values of fixed assets on the basis of either specific price indices for various fixed assets (different types of production equipment being treated as different assets), or if indices are not available, replacement cost or recoverable value* whichever is lower.

---

* In India, because of the quantitative information that has to be published by companies regarding materials consumed and goods produced, it may be possible to work out meaningful input-output ratios.

+ *N.B.* SSAP 16 does not lay down the methods for making various adjustments. The methods given below are therefore only illustrative.

* Recoverable value is the discounted value of benefits expected from the asset in future – it is not the amount expected to be realised on sale of the asset unless the asset is to be disposed of.

Suppose an asset is acquired on 1st April, 2006 at a cost of Rs. 10 lakh with an expected life of 10 years ignoring the scrap value. By 1st April, 2009 the price index for the asset rose by 60% and by 75% by the end of March, 2010. The asset will be valued on historical cost (HC) basis and on CCA basis as shown below:

	April, 1, 2009		*March 31, 2010*	
	HC	*CCA*	*HC*	*CCA*
	Rs.	*Rs.*	*Rs.*	*Rs.*
Cost	10,00,000	16,00,000	10,00,000	17,50,000
Depreciation (3 years and 4 years respectively)	3,00,000	4,80,000	4,00,000	7,00,000
	7,00,000	11,20,000	6,00,000	10,50,000

The *CCA* balance sheet will show the asset on 31st March, 2010 at Rs. 10,50,000. The increase of Rs. 4,50,000, from Rs. 6,00,000 (*HC* basis) to Rs. 10,50,000 (*CCA* basis), will be credited to a (capital) reserve styled as "Current Cost Accounting Reserve". A similar treatment will be accorded to the increase in value of inventories — see (*iii*) below:

(*ii*) Charging the correct or real depreciation to the profit and loss account. In the *HC* accounts, the depreciation, actually charged must have been Rs. 1,00,000.

The proper depreciation, however, is Rs. 1,67,500, *i.e.*,

	Rs.
10% of Rs. 16,00,000, the value in the beginning	1,60,000
10% of half the increase in value during the year, assuming the increase was uniform	7,500
	1,67,500

(*iii*) Arriving at the current cost of materials consumed (at the time of consumption) and other costs incurred that enter into the computation of cost of sales, *i.e.*, making a Cost of Sales Adjustment (*COSA*). Taking a very simple example, suppose on 1st April 2009, a firm had 1,000 tonnes of materials which it had acquired at a cost of Rs. 30 per tonne and that in 2009-2010 it consumed 800 tonnes, making no purchases. The price on April 1, 2009 was Rs. 35, the average price during 2009-2010 was Rs. 40 and that on March 31, 2010, it was Rs. 45. On historical cost basis, the amount debited to the profit and loss account would be Rs. 24,000, *i.e.*, 800 tonnes @ Rs. 30. On *CCA* basis, the amount charged would be Rs. 32,000, *i.e.*, @ 40 per tonne. The HC balance sheet on 31st March, 2010 will show the stock at Rs. 6,000, *i.e.* 200 tonnes @ Rs. 30; the CCA balance sheet will record the value @ Rs. 9,000 *i.e.*, Rs. 45 per tonne — the increase of Rs. 3,000 over the HC basis will be credited to the Current Cost Accounting Reserve.

Information about quantities and the purchase price as also the price prevailing at the time of consumption may not be readily available, at least as far as outsiders are concerned. In such assets, adjustment may be made on the basis of relevant price indices. Suppose the following *HC* information is available for a year:

Opening stock	Rs. 1,00,000	(Price index 200)
Purchase	Rs. 8,00,000	
Closing stock	Rs. 1,41,000	(Price index at the end 240 but 235 when the particular purchase was made).

On *HC* basis, the cost of materials consumed would be Rs. 7,59,000 but on *CCA* basis it will work out to be Rs. 8,58,000, as shown below on the assumptions that the consumption takes place regularly, say a month after the purchase, and that the rise in prices is uniform throughout the year

		Rs.
Opening stock	Rs. $1,00,000 \times \frac{220}{200}$	1,10,000

		Rs.
Purchases	Rs. 8,00,000 + 10% increase*	8,80,000
		9,90,000
Less: Closing Stock	Rs. 1,41,000 × $\frac{220}{235}$	1,32,000
		8,58,000

For the purpose of the *CCA* balance sheet, the closing stock would be written up to Rs. 1,44,000, *i.e.*, Rs. 1,41,000 × 240/235, Rs. 3,000 would be added to the Current Cost Accounting Reserve and Rs. 99,000 *i.e.*, Rs. 8,58,000 *less* Rs. 7,59,000 would be the Cost of Sales Adjustment.

Cost of Sales Adjustment would be necessary also for other items entering the computation of cost of sales, chiefly wages and other operating costs excluding depreciation. Suppose wages and other operating costs amount to Rs. 20,00,000 in a year and it is estimated that the increase, Rs. 1,00,000 should be the COSA in this regard.

(*iv*) Ascertaining the additional requirement of monetary working capital purely because of movement in prices and making an adjustment therefore (MWCA, or Monetary Working Capital Adjustment). It should be noted that the additional requirement due to a change in the scale of operations is to be ignored—only the effect of price changes is to be considered. Monetary working capital normally, means the aggregate of: trade debtors, pre-payments and trade bills receivable less trade creditors, accruals and trade bills payable.*

The Adjustment required in regard to the monetary working capital will be based on the prices of materials in the case of trade creditors and of finished goods in the case of trade debtors. Consider the following:—

	April 1, 2000	*March 31, 2001*
Trade Debtors	Rs. 2,00,000	Rs. 3,60,000
Trade Creditors	Rs. 1,10,000	Rs. 1,84,000
Monetary Working Capital	Rs. 90,000	Rs. 1,76,000

Price in 2000-2001 for materials rose from 200 to 230 and for finished goods from 150 to 180. To ascertain the effect of price changes, first the volume increase should be established; for this purpose both the opening and closing balances should be adjusted on the basis of average movement of prices. Thus:

	April, 1 2000 Rs.		*March 31, 2001* Rs.
Trade Debtors			
Rs. 2,00,000 × $\frac{165}{150}$	2,20,000	Rs. 3,60,000 × $\frac{165}{180}$	3,30,000
Trade Creditors			
Rs. 1,10,000 × $\frac{215}{200}$	1,18,250	Rs. 1,84,000 × $\frac{215}{230}$	1,72,000
Monetary Working Capital	1,01,750		1,58,000

The increase in the monetary working capital because of volume changes is Rs. 56,250, whereas the actual increase is Rs. 86,000. Hence the difference, Rs. 29,750, is the required monetary working capital adjustment.

(*v*) *Gearing Adjustment*: CCA is concerned with ascertaining profits as far as shareholders are concerned. It recognises that a part of the operating capital is obtained by way of loans or other monetary obligations which remain unaffected by changes in prices. Therefore, a part of the adjustments in respect of depreciation for the current year, cost of sales and

*If a firm keeps speculative stocks (or dealing stocks), these will not be subject to COSA but will added to the mometary working capital.

monetary working capital is ascribable to the loan funds or borrowings. In other words, the net total adjustment in respect of the three items mentioned above is to be reduced by the proportion that borrowings bear to (loosely speaking) the total operating capital employed. In the examples given above, the various adjustments are the following:—

		Rs.
Depreciation	(*ii*)	1,67,500
COSA	(*iii*)	99,000
MWCA	(*iv*)	29,750
		2,96,250

These amounts would be charged to the profit and loss account and credited to the Current Cost Accounting Reserve.

It borrowings are 40% of the funds employed (discussed below), Rs. 1,18,500 would be credited to the profit and loss account by debit to the Current Cost Accounting Reserve. In the profit and loss account, the net of the gearing adjustment and the interest to be paid may be shown.

SSAP 16 defines net borrowing as the excess of:

(*a*) The aggregate of all liabilities and provisions fixed on monetary terms (including convertible debentures and deferred tax but excluding proposed dividends) other than those included with monetary working capital and other than those which are, in substance, equity capital over.

(*b*) the aggregate of all current assets other than those subject to a cost of sale adjustment and those included within monetary working capital."

Examples of (*a*) would be debentures, loans, provision for tax, etc, and of (*b*) cash and bank balances and marketable securities.

The equity funds would be all funds belonging to the shareholders on the basis of current cost accounting. The total operating capital would comprise net borrowings and equity funds. If B represents net borrowing and S equity funds, the gearing adjustment would be made on the basis of the ratio $\frac{B}{B+S}$ For greater accuracy, the average of the ratio in the beginning and at the end should be used.

Illustration 3:

Below is given a simplified balance sheet and profit and loss of a company in existence for about 10 years:

Balance Sheet of A Ltd. as at March, 31, 2010

31.3.2009		*Rs. lakhs*	31.3.2009		*Rs. lakhs*
413	Share Capital	413		Fixed Assets:	
—	Reserves	100	1,217	Cost	1,306
1,005	Loans	985	333	Depreciation	569
			884		737
213	Current Liabilities	241	38	Capital Work-in-progress	76
	Provisions	55	922		813
				Inventories:	
			100	Finished Goods	118
			216	Materials & Stores	311
			422	In Process	46
			133	Sundry Debtors	191
			32	Cash and Bank	54
			103	Loans & Advances	261
			83	Profit & Loss Account	
1,631		1,794	1,631		1,794

Balance Sheet of A Ltd. as at March, 31, 2010

31.3.2009		Rs. lakhs	31.3.2009		Rs. lakhs
721	Materials consumed	948	1,741	Sales	2,478
214	Excise Duty	366	124	Other Income	62
320	Expenses — Manufacturing	415			
115	— Others	200			
185	Interest	108			
91	Depreciation*	236			
219	Profit	267			
1,865		2,540	1,865		2,540

*Depreciation charge really comes to Rs. 124 lakhs.

The following facts are established:

(1) The price indices of fixed assets had climbed to 200 in the beginning of 2009-2010 and to 225 by the end of the year with the prices ten years ago being 100; the price increase in 2008-2009 was only 6%. Till the end of 2008-2009 the company had not made any substantial additions to the fixed assets. The company considers the life of the fixed assets to be 20 years and would prefer the straight line basis of depreciation.

(2) Prices of materials rose by 54% and of finished goods by 35% during 2009-2010; rates relating to manufacturing costs increased by 20%.

(3) The value of finished goods stock in the beginning and at the end of the year was respectively Rs. 158 lakhs and Rs. 203 lakhs.

The following assumptions are made:

(*a*) Material stocks are valued on FIFO basis.

(*b*) Loans and advances are against supplies of materials and stores, so also current liabilities. The various adjustments required under CCA are worked out below (to the nearest lakh of rupees):

(*i*) The current cost of fixed assets on the basis of price changes:

		Rs. lakhs
(*a*) March 31, 2008:—		
Present "Cost" 1217 × 200/100		2,434
Less: 9 years' depreciation on straight line basis (life being 20 years)		1,095
		1,339
Add: Work-in-progress 38 plus 3%, *i.e.*, half the increase in prices		39
		1,378
Amount shown in Balance Sheet		922
Credit to Current Cost Accounting Reserve		456
(b) March 31, 2009:		
President cost of assets as on 31.3.2009, 1,217 × 225/100		2,738
Present cost of assets installed during the year (assuming half the increasing price applies, i.e., 82 × 225/212.5		94
		2,832
Less: Depreciation for 10 years on 2,738	1,389	
For ½ year on 94	2	1,371
		1,461
Work-in-progress: 76 plus 6¼, *i.e.*, ½ the increasing prices		81
		1,542
Amount shown in the Balance Sheet		813
Credit to Current Cost Accounting Reserve		729

(*ii*) Depreciation for 2000-2001

	Rs. lakhs
1/20 of 2,434 — the current cost of fixed assets in the beginning	122
1/40 of increasing the values of these assets during 2009-2010 assuming the increase was gradual during the year	8
1/40 of assets installed during the year	2
	132
Depreciation charged in the accounts (236 less 112 which in in the nature of appropriate of profits)	124
Additional depreciation to be charged	8

(*iii*) Increase in value of inventories:

	31.3.2009		31.3.2010
Finished Goods (as given)	158		203
Materials and Stores	216*	$311 \times \frac{154}{127}$	377
Process Stocks	42 *		46 *
	416		626
As per Balance Sheet	358		475
Credit to Current Cost Accounting Reserve	58		151

(*iv*) Cost of Sales Adjustment:

Purchases as per accounts already given:	
Materials consumed	948
Add: Closing Stock of materials and stores	311
	1,259
Less: Opening stock of materials and stores	216
Purchases	1,043
Increase by 27% (half of total in the year)	282
	1,325
Add: Opening stock	216
	1,541
Less: Closing sotck at current value	377
Cost of materials consumed at current cost	1,164
Amount shown in the profit & Loss Account	948
Increased debit required in respect of materials	216
Add: Increase @ 10%, half the increase during the year in manufacturing costs	42
Cost of Sales Adjustment	258

*Since these relate to supplies of materials etc. price changes in materials have been applied

(v) Monetary Working Capital Adjustment:

Changes due to Volume:

		31.3.2009 *Rs. lakhs*		31.3.2010 *Rs. lakhs*
Sundry Debtors	$133 \times \frac{117.5}{100}$	156	$191 \times \frac{117.5}{135}$	166
Advances	$103 \times \frac{127}{100}$	131*	$261 \times \frac{127}{154}$	125*
		287		381
Creditors	$213 \times \frac{127}{100}$	271	$241 \times \frac{127}{154}$	199
Monetary working capital		16		182
Increase due to changes in Volumes (182 – 16)				166
Total increase as per Balance Sheet				188

*Assumed the same as per balance sheet.

	Rs. lakhs	Rs. lakhs
Change due to Prices		22
(vi) Gearing Adjustment:	31.3.2009	31.3.2010
(a) Net Borrowings:		
Loans	1,005	986
Provisions	—	55
	1005	1,040
Less: Cash & Bank Balance	32	54
	973	986
(b) Shareholders' Funds:		
Share Capital	413	413
Reserves	– 83	100
Current Cost Accounting		
Reserve — increase in value of fixed assets	456	729
— inventories	58	151
Other Adjustments: as per (ii), (iv) & (v)	—	288
	844	1,681
(c) Total of (a) and (b)	1,817	2,667
(d) Percentage of (a) to (e)	53.6	37.0
Average of 53.6 and 37.0 = 45.3%		
(e) Gearing Adjustment:		
Additional depreciation charge		8
COSA		258
MWCA		22
Total		288
45.3% of 288		130

The Profit and Loss Adjustments for 2009-2010 may be set out as shown below:

	Rs. lakhs	Rs. lakhs
Operating Profit:		
Profit as given		267
Add: Interest		108
Extra Depreciation		112
		487
C.C.A. Adjustments:		
Depreciation	8	
COSA	258	
MWCA	22	288
		790
Add: Gearing Adjustment: 45.3% of 288	130	
Less: Interest	108	22
Profit as per Current Cost Accounts		221
Less: Appropriation towards Depreciation Reserve		112
		109

The Profit and Loss Account for 2009-2010 itself may be set out as given below:

	Rs. lakhs			Rs. lakhs
Materials Consumed	1,164	Sales		2,478
Excise Duty	366	Other Income		62
Manufacturing Costs	457	Gearing Adjustment	130	
Other Cost	200	*Less*: Interest	108	22
Depreciation	132			
Monetary Working Capital Adjustment	22			
Transfer to Depreciation Reserve	112			
Net Profit	109			
	2,562			2,562

The Current Cost Accounting Reserve on 31.3.2010 will stand at Rs. 1,038 lakh as shown below:

	Rs. lakhs
Increase in the value of: Fixed assets	729
Inventories	151
Adjustment for Depreciation, COSA and MWCA	288
	1,168
Less: Gearing Adjustment	130
	1,038

The Current Cost Accounting Balance Sheet is set out below:

Balance Sheet of A. Ltd. as at March 31, 2010

	Rs. lakhs		Rs. lakhs
Share Capital	413	Fixed assets as valued	2,832
Current Cost Accounting Reserve	1,038	Depreciation till date	1,371
Reserves	58*		1,461
Loans	985	Capital Work-in-progress	81
Current Liabilities	241		1,542
Provisions	55	Inventories:	
		Finished Goods	203
		Materials & Stores	377
		In Process	46
		Sundry Debtors	191
		Cash and Bank Balance	54
		Loans and Advances	261
	2,674		2,674

Some observations: The accounts given above are naturally much too simple compared to the actual situation but, nevertheless, they are based on reality. The following observations on these accounts may be pertinent:—

(*i*) The additional depreciation for the current year is only Rs. 8 lakh; this low figure is because the depreciation actually charged in the accounts is much higher than that warranted on straight line basis with a life of 20 years. Generally, in industrial concerns the adjustment required for depreciation will be heavy.

(*ii*) COSA in the above case is very large. This is because there was a very big increase in the prices of materials — 54%. Normally, the adjustment may not be large. Still the point that emerges is that if prices rise rapidly and if there is big time lag between purchase and consumption, the adjustment in respect of cost of sales will be material. Trading concerns cannot naturally ignore COSA.

(*iii*) The gearing adjustment has reduced the debit to the Profit and Loss Account by Rs. 130 lakhs. Indian companies normally resort to loans in a big way and, hence, for Indian companies this adjustment will be generally substantial. In the case under discussion, interest payment was only Rs. 108 lakhs, showing that due to rise in prices, there was a saving of Rs. 22 lakhs because of the fixed nature of monetary obligations.

Illustration 4:

On 31st March, 2001, when the general price index was say 100, Forward Ltd. purchased fixed assets of Rs. one crore. It had also permanent working capital of Rs. 40 lakh. The entire amount required for purchase and permanent working capital was financed by 10% redeemable preference share capital. Forward Ltd. wants to maintain its physical capital.

*Rs. 100 lakhs less adjustments in the P. & L. A/c. totalling in net to Rs. 158 lakhs.

On 31st March, 2010, the company had reserves of Rs. 1.75 crore. The general price index on this day was 200. The written down value of fixed assets was Rs. 10 lakh and they were sold for Rs. 1.5 crore. The proceeds were utilised for redemption of preference shares.

On the same day (31st March, 2010) the company purchased a new factory for Rs. 10 crore. The ratio of permanent working capital to cost of assets is to be maintained at 0.4 : 1.

The company raised the additional funds required by issue of equity share.

Based on the above information (*a*) Quantify the amount of equity capital raised and (*b*) Show the Balance Sheet as on 1.4.2010.

[*Adapted C.A. (Final) May, 1998*]

Solution:

		(*Rs. in crores*)
(*i*) Preference share capital on 31st March, 2001:		
Fixed assets		1.0
Working capital		0.4
10% Redeemable preference share capital		1.4

To maintain physical capital, the company needs to evaluate the financial capital on 31st March, 2010 which is required to maintain the existing operating capability of the physical assets. On the basis of price index data available, it has been worked out as follows:

$$\text{Rs. } 1.4 \text{ crore } \frac{200}{100} = \text{Rs. } 2.8 \text{ crore}$$

The actual amount has been more than this minimum capital required to be maintained as can be seen below:

		(*Rs in crores*)
(*ii*) Working capital on 31st March 2010; before the given transactions or events:		
Preference share capital		1.40
Add: Reserves		1.75
		3.15
Less: Written down value of fixed assets		0.10
		3.05
(*iii*) Position as on 31st March, 2010, after sale of fixed assets and redemption of preference shares:		
Liabilities:		
Reserves	1.75	—
Add: Profit on sale of fixed assets	1.40	3.15
		3.15
Assets:		
Fixed assets		
Working capital Rs. (3.05 + 1.50 – 1.40) crore		3.15
		3.15
(*iv*) Amount of equity capital raised:		
Amount required for purchase of new factory		10.00
Permanent working capital requirement at 40%		4.00
		14.00
Less: Existing working capital		3.15
		10.85

(b) **Balance Sheet as on 1st April, 2010**

(*Rs. in crores*)

Liabilities	*Rs.*	*Assets*	*Rs.*
Equity Share Capital	10.85	Fixed Assets	10.00
Reserves and surplus	3.15	Working Capital	4.00
	14.00		14.00

Illustration 5:

Zero Limited commenced its business on 1st April, 2009, 2,00,000 equity shares of Rs. 10 each at par and 12.5% debentures of the aggregate value of Rs. 2,00,000 were issued and fully taken up. The proceeds were utilised as under:

	Rs.
Fixtures and Equipments (Estimated life 10 years, no scrap value)	16,00,000
Goods purchased for resale at Rs. 200 per unit	6,00,000

The goods were entirely sold by 31st January, 2010 at a profit of 40% on selling price.

Collections from debtors outstanding on 31st March, 2010 amounted to Rs. 60,000, goods sold were replaced at a cost of Rs. 7,20,000, the number of units purchased being the same as before. A payment of Rs. 40,000 to a supplier was outstanding as on 31st March, 2010.

The replaced goods remained entirely in stock on 31st March, 2010.

Replacement cost as at 31st March, 2010 was considered to be Rs. 280 per unit.

Replacement cost of fixtures and equipments (depreciation on straight line basis) was Rs. 20,00,000 as at 31st March, 2010.

Draft the Profit and Loss Account and the Balance Sheet on replacement cost (entry value) basis and on historical cost basis. [*Adapted C.A. (Final) Nov., 1997*]

Solution:

Profit and Loss Account for the year ended 31st March, 2010

	Historical Cost Basis *Rs.*	*Replacement Cost Basis* *Rs.*
Sales	10,00,000	10,00,000
Less: Cost of Sales	6,00,000	7,20,000
Gross Profit	4,00,000	2,80,000
Less: Depreciation	1,60,000	1,80,000
Profit before interest	2,40,000	1,00,000
Less: Debenture Interest	25,000	25,000
Net Profit	2,15,000	75,000

Balance Sheet of Zero Limited as at 31st March, 2010

	Historical Cost Basis *Rs.*	*Replacement Cost Basis* *Rs.*
Liabilities		
Equity Share Capital	20,00,000	20,00,000
Profit and Loss Account	2,15,000	75,000
Replacement Reserve	—	6,20,000
12.5% Debentures	2,00,000	2,00,000
Creditors	40,000	40,000
	24,55,000	29,35,000

	Rs.	Rs.
Assets		
Fixtures and Equipment	14,40,000	18,00,000
Stock	7,20,000	8,40,000
Debtors	60,000	60,000
Cash and Bank	2,35,000	2,35,000
	24,55,000	29,35,000

Working Notes:

(*i*) Replacement cost of sales on the basis of replacement cost on the date of sale = Rs. 240 × 3,000 = Rs. 7,20,000.

(*ii*) Under replacement cost basis, depreciation, calculated on the average basis = 10% of

$$\frac{\text{Rs.}16{,}00{,}000 + \text{Rs.}20{,}00{,}000}{2} = \text{Rs. } 1{,}80{,}000.$$

(*iii*) Fixtures and equipments at net current replacement cost.

	Rs.
Gross replacement cost	20,00,000
Less: Depreciation, 10% of Rs. 20,00,000	2,00,000
	18,00,000

(*iv*) Replacement Reserve = Realised holding gains + Unrealised holding gains

	Realised holding gains Rs.	*Unrealised holding gain* Rs.
Stocks:		
Sold [replacement cost at the date of sale – historical cost] Rs. (7,20,000 – 6,00,000)	1.20,000	
Unsold [closing stock × (closing rate - rate at the date of purchase)] = 3,000 × Rs. (280 – 240)]		1,20,000
Fixtures and Equipments:		
Depreciation Rs. (1,80,000 – 1,60,000)	20,000	
Net book value at year end, Rs. (18,00,000 – 14,40,000)		3,60,000
	1,40,000	4,80,000

Replacement + Reserve = Rs. 1,40,000 + Rs. 4,80,000 = Rs. 6,20,000.

(*v*) *Cash and Bank*:

Collection from customers, Rs. 10,00,000 – Rs. 60,000		9,40,000
Less: Payments to suppliers, Rs. 7,20,000 – Rs. 40,000	6,80,000	
Debenture interest paid	25,000	7,05,000
Balance on 31st March, 2001		2,35,000

Illustration 6:

The following data relate to Bearing Ltd :

	On 1.4.2009 (Rs. `000)	On 31.3.2010 (Rs. `000)
(a) Net long-term borrowing	25,000	28,000
Creditors	15,000	5,000
Bank overdraft	6,000	10,600

	(Rs. '000)	(Rs. '000)
Taxation	2,000	2,000
Cash	(9,000)	(14,800)
	39,000	30,800
(*b*) Share capital and reserves from current cost balance sheet	74,000	94,000
Proposed dividend	1,160	1,312
	75,160	95,312
(c) Current cost adjustment depreciation		3,400
Fixed assets disposal		3,600
Cost of sales adjustments		3,240
Monetary working capital adjustment		2,240
		12,480

Compute :

(*i*) Gearing adjustment ratio, and

(*ii*) Current cost adjustment after abating gearing adjustment.

Solution :

	On 1.4.2009 (Rs. '000)	On 31.3.2010 (Rs. '000)
Average Net Borrowing	39,000	30,800
Total Shareholders Interest (Average	75,160	95,312
Total	1,14,160	1,26,112

$$\text{Gearing Adjustment Ratio} = \frac{(39{,}000 + 30{,}800)/2}{(1{,}14{,}160 + 1{,}26{,}112)/2} \times 100 = 29.05\ \%$$

Total Current Cost Adjustment	12,480
Less : Gearing (29.05% of 12,480)	3,625
Current Cost Adjustment after abating Gearing Adjustment	8,855

Evaluation of CCA

One may say that as for as measurement of real profits is concerned, CCA does an admirable job; it also partially fulfils the function of compelling the firm to accumulate funds, by way of depreciation, at a level much higher than under the HC system. The following points of criticism against the CCA can still, however, be made:—

(*a*) The system ignores, in reality, the question of backlog depreciation; even if from the very beginning inflation is kept in view, the accumulated depreciation will not be equal to the funds ultimately required for replacement. Properly, the backlong depreciation should be charged against revenue reserves available for dividend — only then will management be restrained from disposing of profits required really for replacement of funds. This question can be solved in quite a few ways, one of which is to credit the Depreciation Provision annually by the interest saved by the firm by employing the funds internally. These is no doubt that attention needs to be paid on a systematic basis to ensure proper replacement

(*b*) Even if the depreciation funds are adequate for replacement, they will be adequate for replacement of similar assets; they may not suffice for moving into another industry. It is surely the duty of management to do constant and serious thinking about its business policies and take stock of its resources, including financial resources, and husband them properly.

(*c*) COSA will be an important figure generally. However, cannot the work be simplified by adopting the base stock method? If this system is adopted and the stocks in excess of base stocks are valued on LEFO basis, cost of sales in respect of materials consumed will be generally the real cost of sales — the difference, if any, will be so small as well make no difference.

(*d*) Similarly, for the sake of simplicity, the monetary working capital adjustment may be arrived at by applying the percentage increase in price of materials to the creditors in the beginning and the increase in price of finished goods to sundry debtors in the beginning and establishing the difference between the two figures thus arrived at. It is not a fine calculation but it will give quite accurate figures of additional monetary working capital required as a result of movement in prices, ignoring volume changes during the year.

(*e*) The system recommends gearing adjustment to be made in respect of current year's depreciation, COSA and MWCA. The reason why it should not apply to revaluation profits is not at all clear. The rationale behind the gearing adjustment is that part of the operating funds is raised by way of borrowings, fixed in monetary terms. This holds goods for all operations and, if gearing adjustment is in order, it should be in order for all profits (or losses) resulting from taking into account price level changes. Further the application of gearing adjustment seeks to imply that the objective of accounting is to ascertain the profit for shareholders and not the firm. This appears to be wrong — the objective should be to ascertain profit of the firm and not for any of the interested parties. The management can certainly arrive at the profits that can be properly distributed among the shareholders even on the basis of the profit for the firm.

There is one point in favour of gearing adjustment. It shows clearly the real annual cost of borrowing since interest paid is adjusted against the gearing adjustment. The gains made by the firm by borrowing in inflationary times are brought out by the adjustment. Still on the whole, gearing adjustment does not appear to be theoretically sound.

Conclusion. Materiality is a recognised principle in accounting; in this regard inflation accounting is not an exception. The implication is that each firm should decide for itself whether any of the adjustments required under CCA can be ignored. Suppose a firm, like an oxygen company, does not use much material; it can probably ignore COSA. Each industry should consider and decide on the extent of applicability of the various adjustments.

Though survival is the prime concern of the management and this should not depend on other considerations, like the attitude of tax authorities, yet many firms will not agree to inflation accounting unless Government and revenue authorities agree to allow depreciation on the basis of present day values. For this purpose, a consensus between industry, the accounting profession and the Government will be essential. The Government has itself a vital interest since it is obviously concerned with prevention of sickness. It is time, therefore, that like the Government in U.K., the Government of India also takes the initiative.

One cannot say that all the recommendations contained in SSAP 16 should apply to India — the system will require simplication before application in this country. But it must ensure proper financial measures to the extent accounting can do that to see that replacement of assets when due is carried out without difficulty. It is expected that the Institute of Chartered Accountants of India will soon make known its recommendations about inflation accounting.

The Stand of the Institute of Chartered Accountants of India. The Institute recommends the adoption of inflation accounting but recognises that much care and caution will have to be taken. It favours the adoption of the Current Cost Accounting Method but would permit not only the CPP Method but also even revaluation of fixed assets and adoption of the LIFO basis as regards inventories. In its "Guidance Note on Accounting for Changing Prices" (published in December 1982), the Institute makes the following recommendations:—

"37. The adoption of a system of accounting for changing prices would require a considerable amount of time, money and specialised skills. Also the various techniques are still in the process of development. However, in view of the importance of the subject, it is recommended that enterprises, particularly the large enterprises, may develop the necessary systems to prepare and present this information.

"38. Out of the various methods of accounting for changing prices discussed above, the Current Cost Accounting method seems to be most appropriate in the context of the economic environment in India. The periodic revaluations of fixed assets and the adoption of LEFO formula for inventory valuation are partial responses to the problem of accounting for changing prices. Current Purchasing Power Accounting, though simple to apply, does not ensure the maintenance of the operating capability of an enterprise. Current Cost Accounting, on the other hand, is a rational and comprehensive system of accounting for changing prices, as it considers the specific effects of changing prices on individual enterprises and thus ensures that profits are reported only after maintaining the operating capability. However, the introduction of a full-fledged system of Current Cost Accounting on a wide scale in India will inevitably take some time. During this transitional phase, periodic revaluations of fixed assets along with adoption of LIFO formula for inventory valuation would reflect the impact of changing prices substantially in the case of manufacturing and trading enterprises.

"39. Adequate data base has presently not been developed in India for accounting for changing prices. Therefore, every enterprise may have to select the price indices depending on its own circumstances. The detailed price published in its monthly bulletin by the Government of India can be adopted in a number of cases. There is no doubt that further steps will have to be taken for the timely publication of statistical information required by various industries for the implementation of accounting for changing prices.

"40. Considering the importance of the information regarding the impact of changing prices it is recommended that while the primary financial statements should continue to be prepared and presented on the historical cost basis, supplementary information reflecting the effects of changing prices may also be provided in the financial statements on a voluntary basis, at least by large enterprises.

"41. Since the presentation of statements adjusted for the impact of changing prices is voluntary, the enterprises may or may not get this information audited. However, the audit of such statements would enhance their credibility.

"42. Apart from its utility in external reporting, accounting for changing prices may also provide useful information for internal management purposes. Accounting information system is designed primarily to provide relevant information to various levels of management with a view to assist in managerial decision-making, control and evaluation. However, in periods of rapid and violent fluctuations in prices, the information provided by historical cost-based accounting system may need to be supplemented by information regarding the impact of changing prices. The areas in which such information may be of prime importance to management include investment decisions and allocation of resources, divisional and overall corporate performance evaluation, pricing policy, dividend policy, etc.

"43. In countries like the United Kingdom, there have been some reforms in the tax structure in the wake of introduction of accounting for changing prices. Though, the tax legislation in India at present does not give recognition to such an accounting system, even then accounting for changing prices would be useful for generating relevant information for internal and external decision-making....".

Appendix : SSAP 16

Part 1 — Explanatory note

1. *Scope*: This Standard applies to most listed companies and other large entities[1] whose

1. Footnotes are at the end of this Appendix.

annual financial statements are intended to give a true and fair view of the financial position and profit or loss. It does not apply to:

(*a*) unlisted entitles unless they would be classified as large companies in the prospective UK/ Irish legislation based on the EEC Fourth Directive on Company Law. (It is intended to adopt the precise definition of large companies used in the legislation when this is enacted and operative in the UK and the Republic of Ireland);

(*b*) Most wholly owned subsidiaries;

(*c*) a number of specific types of entity, on the grounds that the current cost accounting (CCA) system in this Standard may not be wholly appropriate to them. Such entities are encouraged to implement any parts of the Standard that are appropriate to their business, and generally to consider how the impact of price changes can best be reflected in their financial statements.

Introduction

2. In most systems of accounting, profit is determined after making charges against revenue to provide for the maintenance of capital. Since the definition of capital varies according to the accounting concept adopted, the method of determining profit also varies.

3. This Standard provides for current cost information to be included in annual financial statements in addition to historical cost information. The CCA system is based upon a concept of capital which is represented by the net operating assets of a business. These net operating assets (fixed assets, stock and monetary working capital) are the same as those included in historical cost accounts, but in the current cost accounts the fixed assets and stock are normally expressed at current cost. The net operating assets can be said to represent, in accounting terms, the operating capability of the business and usually will have been financed both the shareholders' capital and borrowings.

4. A change in the input prices of goods and services used and financed by the business will affect the amount of funds required to maintain the operating capability of the net operating assets. In contrast to historical cost accounts, current cost accounts are designed to reflect this in the determination of profit and in the balance sheet.

The objective of CCA

5. The basic objective of current cost accounts is to provide more useful information than that available from historical cost accounts alone for the management of the business, the shareholders and others on such matters as:

(*a*) the financial viability of the business;

(*b*) return on investment;

(*c*) pricing policy, cost control and distribution decision; and

(*d*) gearing.

6. In determining current cost profits for an accounting period, the objective is achieved in two stages.

In the first stage, the current cost operating profit is determined. This is surplus arising from the ordinary activities of the business in the period after allowing for the impact of price changes on the funds needed to continue the existing business and maintain its operating capability but without taking into account the way in which it is financed. It is calculated before interest on et borrowing and taxation.

In the second stage the current cost profit attributable to shareholders is determined. In arriving at this profit, account is taken of the way in which the business is financed. To the extent that the net operating assets of the business are financed by borrowing, the full allowance for the impact of price changes on operating capability made in arriving at operating profit may not be required, because the repayment rights of lenders are fixed in monetary amount.

Current cost profit attributable to shareholders therefore reflects the surplus for the period after allowing for the impact of price changes on the funds needed to maintain the shareholders' proportion of the operating capability. It is shown after interest, taxation on gearing adjustment and extraordinary items.

7. In the balance sheet the objective is met by including, where practiable, the assets at their value to the business based on current price levels. This provides a realistic statement of the assets employed in the business and enables a relationship to be established between the current cost profit and the net assets employed.

Current cost operating profit

8. Three main adjustments to trading profit, calculated on the historical cost basis before interest are required to arrive at current cost operating profit. These are called the depreciation, cost of sales and monetary working capital adjustments.

Depreciation adjustment

9. The depreciation adjustment allows for the impact of price changes when determining the charge against revenue for the part of fixed assets consumed in the period. It is the difference between the value to the business of part of fixed assets consumed during the accounting period and the amount of depreciation charged on an historical cost basis. The resulting total depreciation charge thus represents the value to the business of the part of fixed assets consumed in earning the revenue of the period.

Cost of sales adjustment

10. The cost of sales adjustment (COSA) allows for the impact of price changes when determining the charge against revenue for stock consumed in the period. It is the difference between the value to the business of stock consumed and the cost of stock charged on an historical cost basis. The resulting total charge thus represents the value to the business of stock consumed in earning the revenue of the period.

Monetary working capital adjustment

11. Most business have other working capital besides stock involved in their day-to-day operating activities. For example, when sales are made on credit the business has funds tied up in debtors. Conversely, if the suppliers of goods and services allow a period of credit, the amount of funds needed to support working capital is reduced. This monetary working capital is an integral part of the net operating assets of the business. Thus, the Standard provides for an adjustment in respect of monetary working capital[3] when determining current cost operating profit. This adjustment should represent the amount of additional (or reduced) finance needed for monetary working capital as a result of changes in the input prices of goods and services used and financed by the business.

12. In a business which holds stocks, the monetary working capital adjustment (MWCA) complements the COSA and together they allow for the impact of price changes on the total amount of working capital used by the business in its day-to-day operations. For example, the relationship between the MWCA made in respect of trade debtors and trade creditors and the COSA is as follows:

(*a*) when sales are made on credit the business has to finance the changes in its input prices until the sale results in a receipt of cash. The part of the MWCA related to trade debtors, in effect, extends the COSA to allow for this; and

(*b*) conversely, when materials and services are purchased from suppliers who offer trade credit price changes are financed by the supplier during the credit period. To this extent extra funds do not have to be found by the business and this reduces the need for a COSA and in some cases for a MWCA on debtors. The part of the MWCA related to trade creditors reflects this reduction.

A MWCA is equally necessary in a business which does not hold stocks.

13. There can the difficulties in practice in identifying, on an objective basis, those monetary assets and liabilities which are part of the net operating assets of the business. Nevertheless, a practical way of doing this has to be accepted if the operating profit is to be identified. Reasonable accuracy and objectivity may usually be achieved by including only trade debtors and trade creditors within monetary working capital, with an extension in the case of financial institutions. However, fluctuations in the volume of stock, debtors and creditors may lead to contrary fluctuations in cash or overdraft.

It is necessary to include this element of cash or overdraft within monetary working capital if, to do so has a material effect on current cost operating profit. Monetary working capital may also include cash floats required to support the business operations. The treatment adopted should be applied consistently.

14. The Standard allows for the COSA and MWCA to be combined in the current cost profit and loss account.

Purchasing skills

15. The benefit of good buying (and the costs of errors) should be, as which the historical cost system, included in the operating profit at the time the asset is used or sold. As discussed in the Guidance Notes, this normally happens through the inter-relationship of the MWCA with the other adjustments.

The current cost profit attributable to shareholders and the gearing adjustment

16. The net operating assets shown in the balance sheet have usually been financed partly by borrowing and the effect of this is reflected by means of a gearing adjustment in arriving at current cost profit attributable to shareholders. No gearing adjustment arises where a company is wholly financed by shareholders capital. While repayment rights on borrowing are normally fixed in monetary amount, the proportion of net operating assets so financed increases or decreases in value to the business. Thus, when these assets have been realised, either by sale or use in the business, repayment of borrowing could be made so long as the proceeds are not less than the historical cost of those assets.

17. No account has been taken of the existence of borrowing in arriving at current cost operating profit in that the operating adjustments (referred to in para 8) make provision for the impact of price changes on all the net operating assets, howsoever financed. The gearing adjustment therefore abates the operating adjustments in the gearing proportion in deriving the current cost profit attributable to shareholders.

18. The gearing adjustment, subject to interest on borrowing, indicates the benefit or cost to shareholders which is realised in the period, measured by the extent to which a proportion of the net operating assets are financed by borrowing. The current cost profit attributable to shareholders is the surplus after making allowance for the impact of price changes in the shareholders' interest in the net operating assets, having provided for the maintenance of lenders' capital in accordance with their repayments rights.

19. The gearing adjustment included in this standard is necessary to determine the profit defined in para 41. The adjustment is retrospective in that it arises wholly because of the manner in which net operating assets are financed in the period and is not dependent on the ability of the company to refinance any part before it is included in profit. The adjustment is generally practicable and objective and since any credit in the profit and loss account only abates adjustments made when assets are consumed or sold, it conforms with the fundamental accounting concepts set out in SSAP 2, disclosure of Accounting Policies.

20. It is recognised that there are a number of possible methods for calculating a gearing adjustment. For the reasons set out it is believed that the method as defined in the Standard is the most appropriate and, on the grounds of the need for comparability between company accounts, it

has been made definitive. This does not prevent those who wish to show in addition the effect of a different method of calculating a gearing adjustment from doing so by way of a note to the accounts. It would help users it those adopting this course explained their reasons for so doing.

21. There are some types of financing structure, such as those which may be found in certain public bodies, co-operatives and wholly owned subsidiaries, where a gearing adjustment strictly in accordance with the normal formula in this Standard may be inappropriate or give a misleading view of attributable profit. In such cases if an alternative adjustment is considered appropriate to the circumstances it should be made in the profit and loss account and the treatment adopted described in a note. In the interests of achieving consistency in the accounts of nationalised industries these bodies are dealt with specifically in the Standard. The adjustment based on the formula in the Standard should also be disclosed in the note unless this would not be practicable.

Assets surplus to operating requirements and in excess of borrowing

22. Where an entity owns monetary current assets in excess of those needed for working capital such assets are not part of the net operating assets for the purposes of this Standard and any income from them should be dealt with below current cost operating profit. These assets should firstly be set against borrowing when calculating the gearing adjustment. Any excess to these assets over the borrowing is not covered by the current cost framework, being more in the nature of asset held for investment of the kind held by entities excluded from the Standard under para 46(*c*). This situation raises complex issues which have not yet been subject to adequate public debate and no adjustment is therefore required in the Standard. Entities are encouraged to include information on any changes in the value to the business of such excess assets and in their effective purchasing power. This should be given and described in a note to the accounts.

Distributable profit

23. The amounts that can prudently be distributed depend not only on profitability, but also on the availability of funds. This is so with all systems of accounting. When determining distribution policy consideration must be given to factors not reflected in profit, such as capital expenditure plans, changes in the volume of working capital, the effect on funding requirements of changes in production methods and efficiency, liquidity, and new financing arrangements. The current cost profit attributable to shareholders should not be assumed to measure the amount that can prudently be distributed. Although the impact of price changes on the shareholders' interest in the net operating assets has been allowed for, the other factors still need to be considered. Even if the effect of such factors is neutral, a full distribution of the current cost profit attributable to shareholders may make it necessary to arrange additional finance (equal to the gearing adjustment) to avoid an erosion of the operating capability of the business. However, an increase in the value to the business of the assets may provide increased cover for such financing.

The current cost reserve

24. The current cost balance sheet includes a reserve in addition to those included in historical cost accounts. The additional reserve may be referred to as the current cost reserve. The total reserves will include where appropriate:

(*a*) unrealised revaluation surpluses on fixed assets, stock and investments;

(*b*) realised amounts equal to the cumulative net total of the current cost adjustments, that is:

(*i*) the depreciation adjustment (and any adjustments on the disposal of fixed assets),

(*ii*) the two working capital adjustments, and

(*iii*) the gearing adjustment.

25. Changes in the rates used to translate the assets and liabilities of subsidiaries whose accounts are denominated in foreign currencies lead to translation differences arising on consolidation. In most circumstances these differences are, in effect, price changes which do not affect the operating

capability of the group and in these cases they are not included in current cost profits but are directly reflected in reserves.

26. Interpretation of the amounts on current cost reserve can be complex for they depend not only on the impact of price changes on the net operating assets, but also on the first period for which current cost accounts conforming with this Standard are published, the policies adopted in preparing historical cost accounts and other factors. Accordingly, the only specific disclosure requirement is to show movements on the current cost reserve during the period, and these may be combined with equivalent movements on historical cost reserves. However, entities are encouraged to disclose the information set out in the Appendix subject to any modifications they regard as relevant and useful in their circumstances.

Annual financial statements and accounting policies

27. The Standard sets out the current cost information which should be disclosed to provide the user with a clear view of the results for the period and the financial state of the business at the balance sheet date. This consists of a current cost profit and loss account and a current cost balance sheet together with appropriate notes. It is expected that once entities have published their first current cost accounts they will also, where appropriate, disclose current cost information in interim accounts, preliminary statements, prospectuses and other financial statements.

28. The Standard requires entities to publish current cost accounts in addition to historical cost accounts or historical cost information. This enables entities to publish both current cost and full historical cost accounts, and to decide in such circumstances which accounts are to be the main accounts. If they decide that the historical cost accounts are the main accounts (and the great majority of companies will probably so decide) the current cost accounts required by this Standard will be of a supplementary nature. Some entities may, however, wish to publish current cost accounts as their main or only accounts[4] in which case it will be necessary to supplement them with full historical cost accounts or adequate historical cost information. The historical cost disclosure requirements will be clarified when the EEC Fourth Directive is enacted in UK-Irish law. Meanwhile, an entity preparing current cost accounts as its only accounts should provide at least sufficient information to enable the user to ascertain the profit of the period under existing historical cost conventions.

29. Since the CCA system set out in the Standard is an adaptation of the historical cost system, the accounting policies adopted will be generally the same for both. In particular the current cost accounts encompass only those assets which are dealt with in historical cost accounts.

30. Statements of Standard Accounting Practice issued for use with historical cost accounts also apply to current cost accounts excepts set out in SSAP 2 apply, *i.e.*, the 'going concern', 'accrual', 'consistency' and 'prudence' concepts. The 'going concern' concept is particularly appropriate to CCA which relates operating profit to the maintenance of operating capability. The information on accounting policies should cover the current cost accounts. SSAP 10 requires that the annual financial statements should include a statement of source and application of funds. Such a statement should be compatible with the main accounts although entities may present an additional statement compatible with the current cost accounts even if these are not presented as the main accounts. Two examples are given in the Guidance Notes.

Methods appropriate to the preparation of current cost accounts

31. The Standard sets out the basic principles. At this stage the ASC does not believe that it would be right to be prescriptive about the methods which should be adopted when preparing current cost accounts. Guidance Notes have been published which the ASC hopes will be helpful, since they offer practical solutions to some common situations. However, they do not form part of the Standard and accordingly are not mandatory.

Interpretation, uses and limitations

32. Current cost accounts allow for the impact of specific price changes on the net operating

assets, and thus the operating capability, of the business. The same tools of analysis as those applied to historical cost accounts are generally appropriate. The ratios derived from current cost accounts for such items as gearing asset cover, dividend cover and return on capital employed will often differ substantially from those revealed in historical cost accounts but should be more realistic indicators when assessing an entity or making comparisons between entities.

33. As with historical cost accounting, CCA is not a substitute for forecasting when such matters as a change in the size or nature of the business are under consideration. It assists cash flow forecasts, but does not replace them. It does not measure the effect of changes in the general value of money or translate the figure into currency of purchasing power at a specific date. Because of this it is not a system of accounting for general inflation. Further, it does not show changes in the value of the business as a whole or the market value of the equity.

Additional voluntary disclosure

34. It may assist users, particularly initially, if current cost accounts are accompanied by explanations of the operating and attributable profit and assets employed. These explanations could be based on the definitions included in the Standard.

35. Those who wish to give additional information reflecting a gearing adjustment on a basis different from that provided for in the Standard should do so by way of a note (para 20).

36. The Standard does not deal with the maintenance of financial capital in general purchasing power terms. It is recognised that some users may be interested in a statement of the change in the shareholders' net equity interest after allowing for the changes in the general purchasing power of money. A statement may therefore be given to reflect this, on the lines illustrated in the Guidance Notes. This statement may be particularly helpful in situations where there are excess monetary assets (see para 22) or where part of the group has activities exempt under para 46(*c*).

37. As with accounts prepared on the historical cost basis, the CCA figures for profit and capital employed in different years are not comparable unless they are adjusted to a common price basis. It is the intention of the ASC to develop an Exposure Draft as soon as possible indicating how such adjustments should be made, both to comparative figures and 5/10-years statements. Meanwhile, entities are encouraged to give, as additional information, comparative figures adjusted to a common price basis with the period's results and also to adjust any 5/10-year statement similarly.

Part 2 – Definition of terms

Net operating assets

38. The net operating assets comprise the fixed assets (including trade investments), stock and monetary working capital dealt within an historical cost balance sheet.

The operating capability

39. The operating capability of the business is the amount of goods and services which the business is able to supply with its existing resources in the relevant period. These resources are represented in accounting terms by the net operating assets at current cost.

The current cost operating profit

40. The current cost operating profit is the surplus arising from the ordinary activities of the business in the period after allowing for the impact of price changes on the funds needed to continue the existing business and maintain its operating capability[5], whether financed by share capital or borrowing[5]. It is calculated before interest of net borrowings and taxation.

41. The current cost profit attributable to shareholders is the surplus for the period after allowing for the impact of price changes on the funds needed to maintain their proportion of the operating capacity. It is calculated after interest, taxation and extraordinary items.

Value to the business

42. The value to the business is

(*a*) Net current replacement cost; or if a permanent diminution to below net current replacement cost has been recognised,

(*b*) recoverable amount[5].

Recoverable amount

43. The recoverable amount is the greater of the net realisable value of an asset and, where applicable, the amount recoverable from its further use.

Monetary working capital

44. Monetary working capital is the aggregate of:

(*a*) trade debtors, prepayments and trade bills receivable, *plus*

(*b*) stocks not subject to a cost of sales adjustment, *less*

(*c*) trade creditors, accruals and trade bills payable, insofar as they arise from the day-to-day operating activities of the business as distinct from transactions of a capital nature. Bank balances or overdrafts may fluctuate with the volume of stock or the items in (*a*), (*b*) and (*c*) above. That part of bank balances or overdrafts arising from such fluctuations should be included in monetary working capital, together with any cash floats required to support day-to-day operations of the business, if to do so has a material effect on the current cost operating profit.

In the case of banks and other financial businesses this definition is extended to cover other assets and other liabilities insofar as they also arise from the day-to-day operating activities of the business as distinct from transactions of a capital nature.

Net borrowing

45. Net borrowing is the excess of:

(*a*) the aggregate of all liabilities and provisions fixed in monetary terms, (including convertible debentures and deferred tax but excluding proposed dividends) other than those included within monetary working capital and other than those which are, in substance, equity capital.

(*b*) over the aggregate of all current assets other than those subject to a cost of sales adjustment and those included within monetary working capital.

Part 3 — Standard accounting practice

Scope

46. This Accounting Standard applies to all annual financial statements intended to give a true and fair view of the financial position and profit or loss other than those of entities falling within the categories listed below:

(*a*) entities which do not have any class of share or loan capital listed on the Stock Exchange and satisfy at least two of the following three criteria:

(*i*) they have a turnover of less than £ 5,00,000 per annum;

(*ii*) their balance sheet total[6], at the commencement of the relevant accounting period, is less than £ 2,500,000 as shown in the historical cost accounts; and

(*iii*) the average number of their employees in the United Kingdom (UK entities) or in the Republic of Ireland (Republic of Ireland entities) is less than 250;

(*b*) wholly owned subsidiaries of companies or other entities where the parent company is registered in the UK or Republic of Ireland. This exemption does not apply where the parent company is exempted under (*c*) or (*d*) below;

(*c*) (*i*) authorised insurers, (*ii*) property investment and dealing entities, with the exception of such entities as hold the properties of another entity within the group to which the Standard does apply; and (*iii*) investment trust companies, unit trusts and other similar long-term investment entities; and (*d*) entities whose long-term primary financial objective is other than to achieve an operating profit (before interest on borrowing); such entities may include charities, building societies, friendly societies, trade unions and pension funds.

Where an entity exempted under (*c*) or (*d*) above has subsidiaries which are not themselves exempted under these sections and which collectively exceed the limit in (*a*) above, the group accounts should include consolidated current cost information in respect of such subsidiaries.

47. Annual financial statements of entities coming within the scope of the Standard should include, in addition to historical cost accounts or historical cost information, current cost accounts prepared in accordance with this Standard. The current cost accounts should contain a profit and loss account and balance sheet, together with explanatory notes, disclosing the information set out in paras 55-59.

48. This requirement to include current cost accounts in addition to historical cost accounts or historical cost information can be complied with by:

(*a*) presenting historical cost accounts as the main accounts with supplementary current cost accounts which are prominently displayed; or

(*b*) presenting current cost accounts as the main accounts with supplementary historical cost account; or

(*c*) presenting current cost accounts as the only accounts accompanied by adequate historical cost information. The historical cost disclosure requirements will be clarified when the EEC Fourth Directive is enacted in UK/Irish law. Meanwhile, an entity preparing current cost accounts as its only accounts should provide at least sufficient information to enable the user to ascertain the historical cost profit of the period under existing conventions.

The current cost profit and loss account

49. The current cost operating profit[5] is derived by making the following main cost trading profit (before interest on net borrowing[5]) to allow for the impact of price changes on the funds needed to maintain the net operating assets[5]:

(*a*) in relation to fixed assets, a depreciation adjustment being the difference between the proportion of their value to the business[5] consumed in the period and the depreciation calculated on the historical cost basis.

(*b*) in relation to working capital:

(*i*) a cost of sales adjustment being the difference between the value to the business[5] and the historical cost of stock consumed in the period; and

(*ii*) an adjustment based on monetary working capital[5].

50. Where a proportions of the net operating assets is financed by net borrowing[5], a gearing adjustment is required in arriving at the current cost profit attributable to the shareholders[5]. This should be calculated by:

(*a*) expressing net borrowing as a proportion of the net operating assets using average figures for the year from the current cost balance sheets; and

(*b*) multiplying the total of the charges or credits made to allow for the impact of the price changes on the net operating assets of the business by the proportion determined at (*a*).

The adjustment, normally a credit, could be a debit if prices fall.

51. No gearing adjustment should be made in the profit and loss accounts of nationalised industries in view of the special nature of their capital structure. Accordingly, in such cases interest on their net borrowing should be shown after taxation and extraordinary items.

52. This treatment within the current cost profit and loss account of gains and losses on asset disposals, extraordinary and exceptional items, prior year items, income from associates, group consolidation adjustments, minority interest and the translation of foreign currencies, should, where practicable, be consistent with the definitions of profit set out in this Standard. Where this is impracticable the treatment adopted should be disclosed in a note to the current cost account.

The current cost balance sheet

53. Assets and liabilities should be included in the balance sheet, as far as practicable, on the following basis:

(*a*) Land and building, plant and machinery and stock subject to a cost of sales adjustment—at their value to the business.

(*b*) Investments in associated companies either at the applicable proportion of the associated companies net assets stated under this Standard or, where such information is not readily available, at directors' best estimate thereof. Allowance for premium or discount on acquisition should be made as stated under (*e*) below.

(*c*) Other investments (excluding those treated as current assets)—at directors' valuation. Where the investment is listed and the directors' valuation is materially different from mid-market value, the basis of valuation and the reasons for the difference should be stated.

(*d*) Intangible assets (excluding goodwill)—at the best estimate of their value to the business.

(*e*) Goodwill (premium or discount) arising on consolidation—on the basis set out in SSAP 14. Where goodwill is carried at an amount established before the introduction of SSAP 14 it should be reduced to the extent that it represents revaluation surpluses relating to assets held at the date of the acquisition.

(*f*) Current assets, other than those subject to a cost of sales adjustment — on the historical cost basis.

(*g*) All liabilities — on the historical cost basis.

54. Reserve in the current cost balance sheet should include revaluation surpluses or deficits and adjustments made to allow for the impact of price changes in arriving at current cost profit attributable to shareholders. Amounts to reduce assets from net current replacement cost to recoverable amount[5] should be charged to the profit and loss account.

Contents of accounts

Profit and loss account

55. The current cost profit and loss account should show (not necessarily in this order);

(*a*) the current cost operating profit or loss;

(*b*) interest/income relating to the net borrowing on which the gearing adjustment has been based;

(*c*) the gearing adjustment; (*d*) taxation; (*e*) extraordinary items; and

(*f*) current cost profit or loss (after tax) attributable to shareholders.

56. A reconciliation should be provided between the current cost operating profit and the profit or loss before charging interest and taxation calculation on the historical cost basis giving the respective amounts of the following:

(*a*) depreciation adjustment; (*b*) cost of sales adjustment;

(*c*) monetary working capital adjustment and, where material, interest relating to monetary working capital; and

(*d*) other material adjustments made to profits calculated on the historical cost basis when determining current cost operating profit.

The adjustments for cost of sales and monetary working capital may be combined.

Balance sheet

57. The current cost balance sheet (which may be in summarised form when a full historical cost balance sheet is disclosed) should show the assets and liabilities of the entity on the basis required by this Standard. Notes to the balance sheet should disclose the totals of net operating assets and net borrowing and their main elements. The balance sheet should be supported by summaries of the fixed asset accounts and the movements on reserves.

Notes to the accounts

58. The notes attached to the current cost accounts should describe the basis and methods adopted in preparing the accounts particularly in relation to:

(*a*) the value to the business of fixed assets and the depreciation thereon;

(*b*) the value to the business of stock and work-in-progress and the cost of sales adjustment;

(*c*) the monetary working capital adjustment; (*d*) the gearing adjustment;

(*e*) the basis of translating foreign currencies and dealing with translation difference arising;

(*f*) other material adjustment to the historical cost information; and

(*g*) the corresponding amounts.

Earnings per share

59. Listed companies should show the current cost earnings per share based on the current cost profit attributable to equity shareholders before extraordinary items.

Group accounts

60. A company which is the parent of a group and which is required to produce current cost group accounts should produce such group accounts in accordance with the principles set out in this Standard. It need not however produce current cost accounts for itself as a single company where historical cost accounts are the main accounts.

Corresponding amounts

61. In all accounts prepared in accordance with this Standard corresponding amounts for the preceding period should be stated. However unless current cost accounts are the main accounts corresponding amounts need only be included for the first period for which current cost accounts are prepared if they are readily available.

Relationship with other standards

62. Existing Standards issued for use with historical cost accounts apply to current cost accounts except where a conflict exists caused by the conceptual difference between the systems. The four fundamental accounting concepts in SSAP 2 should be observed and information on accounting policies should be given. The source and application of funds statement required to SSAP 10 should be compatible with the main accounts.

Date from which effective

63. The accounting practices set out in this Standard should be adopted as soon as possible. They should be regarded as standard for annual financial statements relating to accounting periods starting on or after 1st January, 1980.

FOOT NOTES

1. In this Standard the term 'entities' includes those companies and other enterprises which normally come within the scope of Statements of Standard Accounting Practice.

The provisions of this Standard of Standard Accounting Practice should be read in conjunction with the explanatory Foreword to Accounting Standards and need not be applied to immaterial items.

In particular, the following extract from the Explanatory Foreword is emphasised to assist those who prepare or use current cost accounts prepared in conformity with this Standard;

Accounting Standards are not intended to be a comprehensive code of rigid rules. It would be impracticable to establish a code sufficiently elaborate for all business situations and circumstances and cater every exceptional or marginal case. Nor could any code of rules provide in advance for innovations in business and financial practice.

Moreover it must be recognised that there may be situations in which for justifiable reasons accounting standards are not strictly applicable because they are impracticable or, exceptionally, having regard to the circumstances, would be inappropriate or give a misleading view.

In such cases modified or alternative treatments most be adopted and, as noted, departure from Standard disclosed and explained. In judging exceptional or border-line cases it will be important to have regard to the spirit of accounting standards as well as to their precise terms; and to bear in mind the overriding requirement to give a true and fair view.

Where Accounting Standards prescribe specific information to be contained in accounts, such disclosure requirements do not override exemptions from disclosure requirements given to and utilised by special classes of companies under Statute.

2. As defined in the definition section of the Standard; 3. As defined in the definition section of the Standard;

4. In the Green Paper 'Company Accounting and Disclosure' (Sept. 1979 Omnd. 7654) the Department of Trade indicates that 'individual companies at present have discretion to adopt full current cost accounts in their main accounts, not merely in additional statements'. Those companies wishing to do so should consider the legal implications for example relation to contractual obligations. In the year of any changeovery, an adequate link with comparative figures should be give.

5. As defined in the definitions section of the Standard.

6. For the purposes of this paragraph, the balance sheet total is defined as the total of the following assets; Fixed asset (net book value) other than Investments, current assets including prepayments and accrued income (before deduction of current liabilities).

APPENDIX

Example of Presentation of Current Cost Accounts

This Appendix does not form part of the Statement of Standard Accounting Practice. The method of presentation used are illustrative of the accounts of a manufacturing company. They are in no way prescriptive and other methods of presention may equally comply with the Standard. The example assumes that historical cost accounts are published as the statutory accounts.

Y Limited and Subsidiaries

Group current cost Profit and Loss Account for the year ended March 31, 1989

1987-88		1988-89
£000		£000
18,000	Turnover	20,000
2,420	Profit before interest and taxation on the historical cost basis	2,900
1,320	*Less*: Current cost operating adjustments (Note 2)	1,510
1,100	Current cost operating profit	1,390

170	Gearing adjustment	(166)
180	Interest payable *Less* receivable	200
10		34
1,090	Current cost profit before taxation	1,356
610	Taxation	730
480	Current cost profit attributable to shareholders	626
400	Dividends	430
80	Retained current cost profit of the year	196
16.0	Current cost earnings per share	20.9p
5.2%	Operating profit return on the average of the new assets	6.0%
	Statement of retained profits/reserves	
80	Retained current cost profit of the year	196
1,850	Movements on current cost reserve (Note 4)	2,054
Nil	Movements on other reserves	Nil
1,930		2,250
14,150	Retained profits/reserves at the beginning of the year	16,080
16,380	Retained profits/reserves at the end of the year	18,330

Where applicable, minority interests and extraordinary items should be presented in a manner consistent with the historical cost account.

Example of Alternative Presentation of Current Cost Profit and Loss Account
Y Limited and Subsidiaries

Group current cost Profit and Loss Account for the year ended March 31, 1989

1987-88		1988-89
£000		£000
18,000	Turnover	20,000
2,420	Profit before interest and taxation on the historical cost basis	2,900
1,320	*Less*: Current cost operating adjustments (Note 2)	1,510
1,100	Current cost operating profit	1,390
180	Interest payable *Less* receivable	200
920		1,190
610	Taxation	730
310	Current cost profit after interest and taxation	460
(170)	Gearing adjustment	(166)
480	Current cost profit attributable to shareholders	626
400	Dividends	430
80	Retained current cost profit of the year	196
16.0	Current cost earnings per share	20.9p
5.2%	Operating profit return on the average of the net operating assets	6.0%
	Statement of retained profits/reserves	
80	Retained current cost profit of the year	196
1,850	Movements on current cost reserve (Note 4)	2,054
Nil	Movements on other reserves	Nil
1,930		2,250
14,150	Retained profits/reserves at the beginning of the year	16,080
16,080	Retained profits/reserves at the end of the year	18,330

Y Limited and Subsidiaries

Summarised Group current cost Balance Sheet as at 31 March, 1989

31.3.1988			31.3.1989	
£000	£000		£000	£000
		Assets employed:		
	18,130	Fixed assets (Note 3)		19,530

		Net current assets:		
3,200		Stock	4,000	
700		Monetary working capital	800	
3,900		Total working capital	4,860	
(400)		Proposed dividends	(430)	
(600)		Other current liabilities (Net)	(570)	
	2,900			3,800
	21,030			23,330
		Financed by:		
		Share capital and reserves:		
3,000		Share capital	3,000	
12,350		Current cost reserve (Note 4)	14,404	
3,730		Other reserves and retained profit	3,926	
	19,080			21,330
	1,950	Loan capital		2,000
	21,030			23,330

Y Limited and Subsidiaries

Notes to the current cost accounts for the year ended 31st March, 1989

1. Explanatory notes:
(see para 58 of Standard and the example in the Guidance Notes)

2. Adjustment made in deriving current cost operating profit:

1979		1989
£000		£000
400	Cost of sales	460
70	Monetary working capital	100
470	Working Capital	560
850	Depreciation	950
1,320	Current cost adjustments	1,510

3. Fixed assets:

	31st March, 1989 Gross	Depreciation	Net	31st March, 1988 Net
	£000	£000	£000	£000
Land and building	8,780	680	3,100	3,070
Plant and machinery	25,780	9,350	16,430	15,060
	29,560	10,030	19,530	18,130

	£000	£000	£000
4. Current cost reserve:			
Balance on 1 April, 1988			12,350
Revaluation surpluses reflecting price changes:			
Land and buildings	200		
Plant and machinery	1,430		
Stock and work-in-progress	490	2,120	
Monetary working capital adjustment		100	
Gearing adjustment		(166)	2,054
			14,404
of which: realised [see (*iii*) below]			2,494
Unrealised			11,910
			14,404

(*i*) Where applicable, surpluses or deficits arising on the following should be shown as a movement on reserves:

(*a*) the revaluation of investments (other than those included in current assets);
(*b*) the restatement of investment in associated companies; and
(*c*) consolidation differences arising on foreign currency translations;

(*ii*) Where relevant, movements should be shown net of minority interests.

(*iii*) The realised element represents the net cumulative total of the current cost adjustments which have been passed through the profit and loss account, including the gearing adjustment.

5. Financing of net operating assets:

The following is the value to the business (normally current replacement cost net of depreciation of fixed assets) of the net operating assets at the balance sheet date, together with the method by which they were financed:

31 March, 1988		31 March, 1989
£000		£000
18130	Fixed assets	19,530
3,900	Working assets	4,800
22,030	Net operating assets	24,330
19,080	Share capital and reserves	21,330
400	Proposed dividends	430
19,480	Total shareholders' interest	21,760
1,950	Loan capital	2,000
600	Other current liabilities	570
2,250	Net borrowing	2,570
22,030	Net operating assets	24,330
	The reconciliation between balance sheet totals and net operating assets as follows:	
21,040	Balance sheet totals	23,330
400	Proposed dividends	430
600	Other current liabilites (net)	570
22,030	Net operating assets	24,330

EXERCISE XXXI

Practical

1. The fixed assets of a company were stated as follows in the balance sheet:

	31.3.2009	31.3.2010
	Rs.	*Rs.*
Land at cost	5,00,000	5,00,000
Building at cost	20,00,000	20,00,000
Plant and Machinery	1,00,00,000	1,25,00,000
	1,25,00,000	1,50,00,000
The depreciation provision was:		
Buildings	2,50,000	3,00,000
Plant and Machinery	50,00,000	62,50,000

The depreciation was provided on straight line basis @ 2½% p.a. on building and 10% p.a. on plant and machinery ignoring scrap value.

The following price indices can be confidently applied to the assets of the company to arrive at present day prices, the base year being 2009-2010.

	31.3.2009	31.3.2010
Land	200	250
Buildings	150	180
Plant and Machinery	200	225

Show the adjustments to be made under the CCA resulting from the information given above.

(*Credit to Current Cost Accounting Reserve on Revaluation Rs. 78,91,1250; Adjustment for Depreciation Rs. 11,88,750*)

2. The following figures have been taken from the published accounts of Exe. Ltd. for the year ended 31st March, 2010.

		Rs.
Materials consumed		25,00,000
Wages and other manufacturing expenses		20,00,000
Inventories (1st April, 2009), at cost;		
Raw materials		2,00,000
Finished goods		5,00,000
	Rs.	Rs.
Inventories (31st March, 2010), at cost:		
Raw materials		3,00,000
Finished goods		4,50,000
The value of the business of the inventories was ascertained at:	1.4.2000	31.3.2001
Raw materials	2,40,000	3,50,000
Finished goods	5,50,000	5,00,000

Price of materials rose during the year steadily by 20% and wages and other manufacturing expenses by 16%. Ascertain the adjustments that would be required in respect of the above under the CCA.

(*Credit to Current Cost Accounting Reserve for change in values Rs. 1,00,000; Cost of Sale Adjustment Rs. 4,85,000*)

3. The balance sheet of Wye Ltd. revealed the following among other things:

	31.3.2009	31.3.2010
Inventories	5,50,000	6,10,000
Book debts	4,50,000	5,50,000
Cash at Bank	60,000	80,000
Advances for supply of materials	1,00,000	1,26,500
Due to suppliers	2,50,000	3,22,000

During 2009-2010 material prices rose by 15% and those of finished goods by 10%. Calculate the Monetary Working Capital Adjustment to be made under the Current Cost Accounting system.

(*Rs. 23,500*)

4. The summarised current cost balance sheet of Zed Ltd. as at 31st March, 2010 is given below:

	31.3.2009 Rs.	31.3.2010 Rs.
Fixed Assets (net)	1,20,00,000	1,40,00,000
Inventories	50,00,000	65,00,000
Book Debts	80,00,000	90,00,000
Prepaid	1,00,000	1,00,000
Cash	5,00,000	7,00,000
	2,56,00,000	3,03,00,000
Share Capital	50,00,000	50,00,000
Revenue Reserves	25,00,000	30,00,000
Current Cost Reserve	50,00,000	60,00,000
Loans	58,00,000	88,00,000
Sundry Creditors	50,00,000	46,00,000
Provision for Taxation	15,50,000	20,00,000
Proposed Dividend	7,50,000	9,00,000
	2,56,00,000	3,03,00,000

What is the gearing ratio under the CCA?

5. Ess Ltd. presents the following summarised historical cost final accounts relating to the year ended 31st March, 2010:

Balance Sheet	31.3.2009 Rs.	31.3.2010 Rs.
Plant and machinery: cost	50,00,000	60,00,000
Depreciation @ 10% on straight line basis according to Sec. of the Companies Act	19,00,000	24,70,000
	31,00,000	35,30,000
Inventories – Raw materials, at cost	2,50,000	4,00,000
– Finished goods, at cost	5,00,000	6,00,000
Book Debts	8,00,000	10,00,000
Cash at Bank	1,00,000	1,70,000
	47,50,000	57,00,000
Share Capital	20,00,000	20,00,000
Reserves	10,00,000	12,50,000
Loans @ 15%	10,00,000	15,00,000
Sundry Creditors for Goods	3,00,000	4,00,000
Provision for Taxation	2,50,000	3,50,000
Proposed Dividend	2,00,000	2,00,000
	47,50,000	57,00,000

Profit and Loss Statement	Rs.	Rs.
Sales (adjusted for finished goods inventory)		50,00,000
Costs : Materials consumed	15,00,000	
Wages	5,00,000	
Other Manufacturing Expenses	5,00,000	
Administration Expenses	3,80,000	
Selling Expenses	6,00,000	
Depreciation	5,70,000	
Interest	2,00,000	42,50,000
Profit before tax		7,50,000
Tax		3,00,000
Profit after tax		4,50,000

The following information is available:—

(1) The company carries on operations in rented premises.

(2) Since it was established, prices of plant and machinery have risen to 150% till 31.3.2009 and to 180% by 31.3.2010.

(3) Prices of raw materials and finished goods rose steadily during 2009-2010 — the former by 20% and the latter by 25%.

(4) The replacement prices of inventories were:

	31.3.2009 Rs.	31.3.2010 Rs.
Raw Materials	2,75,000	4,50,000
Finished Goods	6,00,000	7,50,000

Draw up the statements, to supplement the historical cost statement, as required under CCA.

(Total of C.C.A. Balance Sheet Rs. 81,81,000) (Loss for the year after adjustments; Rs. 80,667)

Essay-type

1. What is meant by inflation accounting?
2. What are the limitations of historical accounting in a period of inflation?
3. What are the objections against inflation accounting?
4. Define operating profit and holding gains. State the need for distinguishing between the two.
5. How can changes in the price level be reflected in the financial statement though the Current Purchasing Power Method?
6. Explain Current Cost Accounting.

32

ACCOUNTING FOR HUMAN RESOURCES OF AN ORGANISATION AND SOCIAL RESPONSIBILITY

SYNOPSIS

Introduction	..	32.1	A Suggested Approach	..	32.4
Cost and Replacement Cost Methods	..	32.1	The Two Sides of the Account	..	32.5
Value Approaches	..	32.2	Value Added Statement	..	32.8

Introduction

Everyone agrees that the only real long lasting asset which an organisation, nay, any society or nation, possesses is the quality and calibre of the people working in it. A firm having incompetent management will soon, run through the physical resources available to it. There have been generals who have got defeated—on the verge of victory just as there have been others who turned almost certain defeat into victory. Fayol, the noted French Management writer, was given charge of an almost bankrupt company but he made it into a very successful concern. It is, however, unfortunate that so far there is no agreed and generally accepted method of putting a value on this vital asset and showing it as part of or along with financial statements. However, work has been done in the western countries to evolve a suitable method. Various methods have been put forward by various authorities which we shall examine.

Methods

Cost and Replacement Cost Methods. Since accountants first undertook the task of putting a value on human resources, it was natural for them to first turn to the historical cost method which has been the traditional method of valuing physical or intangible assets for the purpose of financial statements. In the case of human resources, cost would comprise

(*i*) the amount spent on processes leading upto selection and placement in position;

(*ii*) the cost of formal training imparted to the selected people; and

(*iii*) the cost of informal training, the loss incurred because of the mistakes committed, due to their being new on the job and because of the time taken to reach the normal level of efficiency.

In cost accounting, labour turnover cost has been computed in this manner. To compute a figure which is more uptodate, one can imagine that everyone would leave and then arrive at the cost of replacing all members of the present strength.

Positional replacements costs. This refers to the sacrifice that would have to be incurred if a person presently employed in a specified position were to be replaced today with a substitute capable of providing an equivalent set of services *in that given position.* Position replacement cost typically comprises (*i*) acquisition and learning costs, and (*ii*) separation costs.

Personal replacements costs. This refers to the sacrifice to be incurred to replace a person today with a substitute capable of providing an equivalent set of services *in all the positions that the former might occupy.* The concept of personal replacement cost is akin to the concept of economic value discussed later.

Generally, replacement cost has reference only to the replacement of people in relation to specified positions (positional replacement) rather than with reference to the replacement of persons (personal replacement).

To the extent that the value of anything or person is not more than the amount to be spent. on replacing it or him by something or someone of equal efficiency and effectiveness, one may accept the replacement cost method but only for such categories of staff as can be easily replaced people at the shop floor level and those at middle management levels. Here also, one should note that the real value of human resources flows from the synergistic effect and, to that extent, historical cost or replacement cost cannot be treated as adequate. The method is totally inadequate when it comes to evaluating top management people since identical top management material is difficult to find and team work is vital.

There can be two theoretical objections to both the methods stated above. Firstly it is a recognised fact that people do develop at work and some of them develop so much that they later occupy high positions. Therefore, part of the salary that is paid to them is really development cost; it would be wrong to charge the whole of the salary against revenue. However, to compute the amount that should be treated as development cost is well-nigh impossible. Also, in practice managements will not pay anybody more than the value of his present contribution to the firm. Still, this defect in the cost and replacement cost methods should be noted.

Secondly, all costs on developing men at various levels are soon recovered, or at least are meant to be recovered. Therefore, these are amortised over a short period of life even if they are capitalised for the time being; most firms do not carry forward such costs at all. If the costs are already recovered, how can they be treated as an asset? To count this argument one can say that there are many assets with a firm that are not shown on the balance sheet, such as know-how and goodwill; human resources is the most important such asset. Even if it is not shown on the balance sheet, it can certainly be valued.

Value Approaches

Below we give the more common methods accepted as taking value into account.

Opportunity Cost Method. An interesting method advocated by Hekimian and Jones, called opportunity cost method, is that divisional heads may bid for the services to various people whose services they may require and then include the bid price in the investment base. The method roughly works as shown below. Suppose a division's target ROI is 15%, it has capital base of Rs. 1,00,00,000 but its profit is only Rs. 13,00,000 i.e., Rs. 2,00,000 short of the target. It is felt that if it can acquire the services of a particular executive, its profits can improve by Rs. 90,000 *i.e.*, the profit will be Rs. 15,90,000, Rs. 90,000 more than Rs. 15,00,000. Rs. 90,000 capitalised at 15% comes to Rs. 6,00,000. The division certainly may bid up to Rs. 6,00,000 for the services of the executive. Actually, the maximum bid may even be the capitalised value of Rs. 2,90,000, the extra profit likely to be generated by the executive's availability. The method can work for some of the people but, surely, quite a few people, specially those at the top, will not be available for the auction. It also ignores people that are not scarce.

Adjusted Present Value Method. In his book, "Accounting for Human Assets" Hermanson advocates that earnings for the next five years be estimated and then discounted, the resulting figure being multiplied by an "Efficiency Factor'—the 5 years weighted average of the return on investment of the firm divided by a similar average for the concerned industry [(REO)/RFO)]. The method attempts to bring in the question of effectiveness but the ratio of ROI of the firm to the ROI of the industry, based on past performance, assumes that there were no unusual or extraneous factors—that the performance was entirely due to the efforts of the employees and executives of the firm. If the past returns on investment can be suitably adjusted to remove the effect of all factors beyond the firm's control, the method may approximate to value somewhat.

Economic Valuation Methods. Lev and Schwartz* advocate the estimation of future earnings during the remaining working life of the employees, taking into account the possibility of early death and then arriving at the present value by discounting the estimated earnings at the

* "On the Use of the Economic Concept of Human Capital in Financial Statements". The Accounting Review. January, 1971.

firm's cost of capital. Replacement cost may be either (*a*) positional replacement cost or (*b*) personal replacement cost.

$$V_x = \sum_{t=x}^{T} \frac{I_{(T)}^{x}\ (t)}{(1+r)t - x}$$

where

V_x^* = the human capital value of a person x years old.
$I(t)$ = the person's expected future annual earnings upto retirement.
r = a discount rate specific to the person.
T = retirement age.

The above equation ignores the possibility of death prior to retirement; but that can be easily taken care of by visualising 't' as the age at which the employee may die, if that is before retirement. Mortality tables can help in this regard.

The method ignores the possibility of a person moving from one career to another and the possibility of early exit. The most important defect of the method is that it assumes remuneration of an employee as being equal to his value; further, the synergistic effect is totally ignored.

Flamholtz= seeks to remove the defects pointed out above and value the human resources on the basis of their discounted earnings in the future taking into account changes in their service status and the possibility of early retirement. The two methods stated above would consider each employee individually. As Jaggi and Lau point out, to estimate the career movement and the possibility of early death or retirement for each individual person would be very difficult. Hence the proper approach should be to do the exercise for the entire staff strength, considering various groups of employees. The method commonly in use by those who wish to report the value of their human resources is the one advocated by Jaggi and Lau, that is group by group future earnings are estimated and then discounted, the resultant figures being aggregated.

However, Bharat Heavy Electrical Ltd. uses the Lev and Shwartz model. Stating that the value of human capital embodied in an individual is the present value of his remaining future earnings from employment, the promotion policy and pay scales being assumed as constant, the company reported the following values for its human assets in its published accounts for the year ended March 31, 1988 :—

	Rs. million
Executives	4,744
Supervisors	3,841
Artisans	5,850
Supporting Technical Staff	742
Clerical and Office Supporting Staff	1,106
Unskilled and Semi-Skilled Staff	1,982
	18,265

Objections. One can easily spot the main difficulty with the so called value approaches based on future earnings. Future earnings of employees will be the costs to the firm; how can they be the value to the firm? The assumption, of course, is that the benefits from the services of the employees will be the same as their remuneration. If this is valid, how will the firm survive? The fact is that human beings yield, specially because of their team work, much more than they are paid. Even for individuals as Economic Theory points out, the pay is based on marginal productivity and that naturally leaves a large surplus for the employer. One would think that it is the human resources as a whole, or all employees as a team, that has to be valued ; otherwise the result is likely to be unsatisfactory. Also, the value must be based on the benefit likely to be derived by the firm.

="A Model for Human Resources Valuation: A Stokistic Process with Service Rewards." The Accounting Review, April, 1971. "Towards a Model for Human Resources Valuation", The Accounting Review, April, 1974.

A Suggested Approach. On the quite valid assumption that most human beings are generally equally endowed with intelligence and possess almost the same will to work, it may be supposed that most firms in an industry will be putting in the average performance. If there are 20 firms in an industry, perhaps 12 or 13 will be earning profits at the average level or thereabouts, one or two may do very poorly and only two or three may perform substantially better than the rest. If the human resources of all firms are valued, the figures for the 12 or 13 average firms will cluster round one figure but those for the two or three above average firms will be substantially higher. There is advantage in knowing the values for the above-average firms but there appears to be no advantage for establishing the figure for the average firms.

To put it differently, if a firm claims that it enjoys good human resources, it must prove the claims through actual performance ; if the performance over the years is only average, the claim cannot be accepted as valid. If the performance is better than that of other firms, then to that extent, its human resources are better, or, to that extent, the firm possesses additional human resources. If an attempt is made to value the *additional* human resources, over and above those possessed by firms generally, it may be quite successful. The idea is to measure the extra or special results shown by a firm, not counting extraneous or abnormal factors. In industry, the extra or special results will be in the form of profits or return on investment; therefore, if a firm shows good profit or an ROI in excess of the average and in this computation the effect of abnormal factors or factors beyond one's control is removed, the firm may be said to possess special human resources and a value can be put on these extra or special human resources. This is the goodwill approach, as all accountants will recognise, and valuation of goodwill is something from which no accountant will shrink, even though the result is bound to be subject to many factors where human judgment is necessary.

In valuing human resources, only the permanent factors leading to extra or super profits should be considered but a careful assessment must be made of the various factors in operation; it will certainly be risky to proceed on the basis of profits alone. The following factors must be considered to assess the continued performance of a company in the future :

(*i*) Return on Investment in the light of :
- (*a*) Share of the market and the growth rate of sales;
- (*b*) Value added; and
- (*c*) Replacement programme of assets.

(*ii*) Research and Development :
- (*a*) Development of new products; and
- (*b*) Development of new markets and uses.

(*iii*) Management Capability :
- (*a*) Executive development;
- (*b*) Employee satisfaction and morale;
- (*c*) Customer satisfaction; and
- (*d*) Awareness of changes in the social, technological and economic environment and the ability to meet them.

(*iv*) General:
- (*a*) The problems faced by the firm and the manner in which they were tackled; and
- (*b*) The general image that the firm enjoys among government, bankers, financial institutions, etc.

Many of the factors are capable of precise measurement through use of accounting and statistical techniques though quite a few can be only qualitatively and subjectively judged. It is significant in this regard that people are already talking of management audit. The profession of management consultants is already in existence and, therefore, the valuation process should not be too difficult.

It will be seen that though the goodwill approach is advocated—that the extra performance be established for the firm concerned and that the value of the human resources be either the capitalised value or say 5 years' purchase of this figure—the exercise will be quite analytical to see the future role of the human beings. It will have to be undertaken by a team having at least two members—one of them must be a good forward looking management consultant and the other an accountant. The exercise will not be an easy one and, therefore, it may be undertaken once in three years. The figure arrived at as value of human resources may be reported separately in the published accounts. Rather than the absolute figures, the changes in the figures will be significant, showing whether or not the firm is maintaining its human resources over and above the general run of firms.

The Two Sides of the Account

The Credit Side : Business and industry have contributed immensely to the economic upliftment of the society. The following are the most significant ways in which this has been done:—

(*i*) First and foremost is the great increase in employment. In the developed countries serious unemployment is a thing of the past; even in countries like India, where unemployment certainly remains a serious problem, the situation would have been far worse but for development of industry. Availability of work is of immense psychological and political value; the contribution of business and industry in this regard should be freely recognised.

(*ii*) Another contribution is in the form of development of skills and entrepreneurial ability. There are numerous establishments which are the result of development of talent of the employees resulting from the work and employment. An industrial house thus gives rise to many other small units some of which in turn grow big. This surely enriches the society.

(*iii*) To the extent workers and employees get job satisfaction and are able to build good relations with fellow workers and superiors, work is a source of happiness. One should not imagine that such is a rare or impossible case.

(*iv*) The greatly improved standards of living of the people, as compared to that in the past, is the result of firstly, the development of new products, such as television, man made fibres, etc. and, secondly, of the increase in incomes which enables people to enjoy the new products. In both of these, business makes a significant contribution. It is business which takes various goods to all corners of the country.

(*v*) Business and industry are the instrument of change. It is necessary for a society to adapt itself to the changes that are constantly coming about; industry helps in the process. India, for instance, was made aware of the importance of computers by the IBM.

An example, summarising all of the above, is that of Sir Jamshedji Tata and his Tata Iron and Steel Company, which more than anyone else deserves the credit for creating an atmosphere in the country for development of modern industry. In terms of employment, provision of a vital product and giving an impetus to technological development, TISCO's record has not been beaten.

The Debit Side : On the debit side, the following points may be noted :-

(*i*) Since the profit motive is the dominant motive, business may ignore products and services that the society really needs and, instead, offer those that bring a quick and large profit even if they are injurious.

(*ii*) The products are often not thoroughly tested for safety before they are marketed and the consumers are often misled through strong advertising and sales promotion campaigns.

(*iii*) The prices charged are often out of proportion to costs; thus consumers are in fact robbed through combinations and through a process of hypnotisation resulting from strong sales techniques.

(*iv*) Industry often depletes scarce national resources.

(*v*) There are too many cases of exploitation of labour; in India even of bonded labour.

(*vi*) Generally, the treatment that employees and workers receive leaves them frustrated and unhappy. Often the employees have to give up their conscience since management insists upon results and does not care about the means. An employee must show results which may compel him to resort to means that are not fair.

(*vii*) Through dominance of the economic and political scene, large business has a corrupting influence on all concerned.

The above may perhaps be presented in the form of accounts as indicated below :

Employees' Account

Shortfall of wage below the living wage	Excess of wages above the living wage levels
Strains and stresses because of unethical practices	Development of skills, talent, etc.
Injustice that may be there	Job satisfaction and happiness at work
Balance (Cr.) to the Society's Account	Balance (Dr.) to the Society's Account

Society's Account

Balance (Dr.) from the Employees' Account	Balance (Cr.) from the Employees' Account
Pollution of air or water in excess of permissible limits	Development of entrepreneurial ability Growth of employment
Harm caused by unsafe or harmful products	Development of new useful products
Subsidy afforded by the Society represented by the excess of cost over prices charged for infra-structural facilities like railways, roads, etc.	Net contribution to national income as represented by value added in excess of remunerations of people working in the organisation
Services provided by the society free of cost, e.g., education, medical facilities, etc.	Excess of rates over the cost of social service enjoyed such as for scavenging, etc.
Balance-contribution to the society.	Expenditure on Community Development
	Balance — Society's contribution to the business.

Statement Form: Admittedly, it is difficult to put money value on most of the items mentioned above. Some of the authorities, therefore, believe that until quantification and measurement becomes possible, an account of the social responsibility of the firm and its attempt at the discharge of this responsibility may be given in the form of narrative statements. For example, the Directors may, in their annual report, touch upon the company's attitudes and efforts towards, say, (*i*) increasing employment opportunities, specially among backward classes and backward areas, (*ii*) developing new products and the measures for testing them thoroughly, (*iii*) controlling pollution, (iv) measures for increasing job satisfaction among workers and giving greater satisfaction to the customers, etc.

Prof. Lee Brummet states that there is need for multi-faceted or total performance measurement technique which, *inter alia*, should take note of the following factors:

1. Net income.
2. Human resources contributions.

3. Contribution to the society—i.e., interests outside the enterprise.
4. Environmental contribution.
5. Product or service contribution.

The contribution may of course be plus or minus.

One such statement (of Cement Corporation India Ltd.) is reproduced below :-
Social Income Statement for the years ended March 31, 1986 and March 31, 1987 :—

(Rs. in lakhs)

	1986-87	1985-86
I. SOCIAL BENEFITS AND COSTS TO STAFF		
A. SOCIAL BENEFITS TO STAFF :		
1. Medical and hospital facilities	109.30	100.38
2. Educational facilities	35.40	15.08
3. Canteen facilities	17.40	13.80
4. Recreation, entertainment and cultural activities	10.15	15.35
5. Housing and township facilities	235.65	232.55
6. Water supply, concessional electricity and transport	74.70	68.89
7. Training and career development	13.10	48.19
8. Provident fund, gratuity, bonus, insurance benefits	266.30	220.84
9. Holiday, leave encashment and leave-travel benefits	319.80	288.32
10. Other benefits	21.40	15.17
Total benefits to staff	1103.20	1018.57
B. SOCIAL COSTS OF STAFF :		
1. Lay off and involuntary temination	—	—
2. Extra hours put in by officers voluntarily	34.50	32.08
Total cost to staff	34.50	32.08
Net social income to staff-1 (A-B)	1068.70	986.49
II. SOCIAL BENEFITS AND COSTS TO COMMUNITY		
A. SOCIAL BENEFITS TO COMMUNITY:		
1. Local taxes paid to Panchayat/Municipality	34.35	14.06
2. Environmental improvements	23.70	28.35
3. Generation of job potential	1464.45	1349.56
4. Generation of business	205.40	145.66
Total social benefits to community	1727.90	1537.63
B. SOCIAL COSTS TO COMMUNITY :		
Increase in cost of living in the vicinity on account of the cement plants	350.00	330.00
Net social income to community-II (A-B)	1377.90	1207.63
III. SOCIAL BENEFITS AND COSTS TO GENERAL PUBLIC		
A. SOCIAL BENEFITS TO GENERAL PUBLIC :		
1. Taxes, duties, etc. paid to the State Governments	5625.35	3007.60
2. Taxes, duties, etc. paid to the Central Government	7932.70	7919.60
Total benefits to General Public	13558.05	10927.20
B. SOCIAL COSTS TO GENERAL PUBLIC		
1. State services consumed—electricity service	2794.80	1997.21
2. Central services consumed—telephone, telegrams, postal services and banking	57.10	58.96
Total social costs to general public	2851.90	2056.17
Net social benefits to general public III (A—B)	10706.15	8871.03
NET SOCIAL INCOME TO STAFF, COMMUNITY AND GENERAL PUBLIC (I+II+III)	13152.75	11065 15

The figures and the approach given above are instructive since they attempt to measure the effect on the staff, the community, the general public as also the clients. It appears that figures regarding clients are not really relevant to social responsibility since that is the direct business of the firm. Also, as regards staff most of the items are such against which the firm derives or should derive good benefit in the form of regular attendance, better attitude towards work, etc. However, the amount stated as career advancement represents a real benefit to the staff and. therefore, to the society. The exercise as a whole points the way to measuring the discharge of or accounting for the firm's social responsibility.

Value Added Statement. Kohler defines value added as "That part of the cost of manufactured or semimanufactured product attributable to work performed on constituent raw materials." This is inadequate; the proper term that should have been used is "conversion cost." The definition given by the Bureau of Public Enterprises for value added is more appropriate; it is : "value of production *less* cost of direct materials consumed". In other words, value added means the sale value of the concerned product *minus* the cost of direct materials consumed (though some people also deduct the cost of indirect materials and depreciation). A statement showing value added along with its disposal (wages, expenses, taxes, profit). A statement showing value added along with its disposal (wages, expenses, taxes, profit) is called "Value Added Statement".

The statement shows prominently the monetary contribution made to the society by the concerned organisation, longer the contribution the more efficient the firm. Assuming the concerned product or service is one for the good of the people in general and assuming that the firm is not enjoying or exercising monopolistic powers, the statement indicates efficient use of resources or otherwise—if the value added is large there is efficiency and if it is small the level of efficiency is low. To this extent, from the society's point of view the value added statement is more useful than the usual profit and loss account. Some of the public sector companies have started including the value added statement in their published accounts. One such statement (of Bharat Heavy Electricals Ltd.) is reproduced below.

Value Added Statement

	1987-88	%	1986-87	%	1985-86	%	1984-85	%
Value of Production	24,359.3		20,627.2		18,222.7		15,579.7	
Less : Cost of direct materials and excise duty	15,434.3		12,705.6		11,224.4		9,560.9	
	8,925.0		7,921.6		6,998.3		6,018.8	
Applied in the following ways:								
Salaries, Wages and other benefits to employees	2,868.2	32	2,833.1	36	2,436.0	35	2,116.3	35
Other operating expenses	2,870.9	32	2,369.2	30	1,852.5	26	1,570.8	26
Depreciation	695.2	8	624.5	8	573.0	8	535.2	9
Interest	597.7	7	564.8	7	633.5	9	659.6	11
Income Tax	1,083.6	12	768.0	10	660.1	10	405.9	7
Dividend	244.8	3	244.8	3	244.8	3	195.8	3
Retained Profit	564.6	6	517.2	6	598.4	9	535.2	9
	8,925.0	100	7,921.6	100	6,998.3	100	6,018.8	100

Illustration 1.

One the basis of the following income statement pertaining to Bee Ltd., you are required to prepare

(*i*) Gross Value Added Statement, and

(*ii*) Statement showing reconciliation of Gross Value Added with Profit before Taxation.

Profit and Loss Account of Bee Ltd. for the year ended 31st March, 2009

		Rs. in thousands	Rs. in thousands
Income			
Sales *less* returns			15,27,946
Dividends and interest			130
Miscellaneous income			474
	(A)		15,28,550
Expenditure			
Production and operational expenses :			
Decreases in inventory of finished goods		26,054	
Consumption of raw materials		7,40,821	
Power and lighting		1,20,030	
Wages, salaries and bonus		3,81,760	
Staff welfare expenses		26,240	
Excise duty		14,540	
Other manufacturing expenses		32,565	13,42,010
Administrative expenses:			
Directors' remuneration		7,810	
Other administrative expenses		32,640	40,450
Interest on :			
9% Mortgage debentures		14,400	
Long-term loan from financial institution		10,000	
Bank overdraft		100	24,500
Depreciation on fixed assets			50,590
	(B)		14,57,550
Profit before Taxation		(A) – (B)	71,000
Provision for income-tax @33.99%			24,133
Profit after Taxation			46,867
Balance of account as per last balance sheet			300
			47,167
Transferred to :			
General reserve, 35% of profit after taxation		16,404	
Proposed dividend @26%		26,000	
Corporate dividend tax @16.995%		4,419	46,823
Surplus carried to balance sheet			344
			47,167

[Adapted C.A. (Final) Nov. 2003]

Solution:

Bee Ltd.

Gross Value Added Statement for the year ended 31st March, 2009

	Rs. in thousands	Rs. in thousands
Sales *less* returns		15,27,946

	Rs. in thousands	Rs. in thousands
Less: Cost of bought in materials and serivces (as per working note)	9,34,010	
Administrative expenses	32,640	
Interest on bank overdraft	100	9,66,750
Value added by manufacturing and trading activities		5,61,196
Add: Dividends and interest		130
Miscellaneous income		474
Total value added		5,61,800

Application of value added

	Rs. in thousands	Rs. in thousand	%
To pay employees :			
Wages, salaries and bonus	3,81,760		
Staff welfare expenses	26,240	4,08,000	72.63
To pay directors :			
Directors' remuneration		7,810	1.39
To pay government:			
Income tax	24,133		
Corporate dividened tax	4,419	28,552	5.08
To pay providers of capital :			
Interest on 9% mortagage debentures	14,400		
Interest on long-term loan from financial institution	10,000		
Dividend to shareholders	26,000	50,400	8.97
To provide for maintenance and expansion of the company :			
Deprication on fixed assests	50,590		
Transfer to general reserve	16,404		
Retained profit, Rs. (344 – 300) thousand	44	67,038	11.93
		5,61,800	100

Statement showing reconciliation of Gross Value Added with Profit before Taxation

	Rs. in thousands	Rs. in thousands
Profit before Taxation		71,000
Add back :		
Wages, salaries and bonus	3,81,760	
Staff welfare expenses	26,240	
Directors' remuneration	7,810	
Interest on 9% mortgage debentures	14,400	
Interest on long-term loan from financial institution	10,000	
Depreciation on fixed assets	50,590	4,90,800
Gross Value Added		5,61,800

Working note:

Calculation of cost bought in materials and services:

	Rs. in thousands
Decrease in inventory of finished goods	26,054
Consumption of raw-materials	7,40,821
Power and lighting	1,20,030
Excise duty	14,540
Other manufacturing expenses	32,565
	9,34,010

Illustration 2.

The following is the Profit and Loss Account of Grand Co. Ltd. for the year ended 31st March, 2009. Prepare a Gross Value Added Statement of Grand Ltd. and show also the reconsiliation between Gross Value Added and Profit before Taxation.

Profit and Loss Account for the year ended 31st March, 2009

	Notes	Amount (Rs. in lakhs)	(Rs. in lakhs)
Income :			
Sales (net)			890
Other income			55
			945
Expenditure :			
Production and operational expenses	(*a*)	641	
Administrative expenses (factory)	(*b*)	33	
Interest	(*c*)	29	
Depreciation		17	720
Profit before taxes			225
Provision for taxes			79
Profit after taxes		146	
Balance as per last Balance Sheet			10
			156
Transferred to General Reserve			40
Dividends paid		90	
Corporate dividend tax paid			15
			145
Surplus carried to Balance Sheet			11
			156

Notes :

	(Rs. in lakhs)
(*a*) *Production and operational expenses :*	
Consumption of raw materials	293
Consumption of stores	59

Salaries, wages, gratuities etc. (Admn.)	82
Cess and local taxes	98
Other manufacturing expenses	109
	641

(*b*) Administrative expenses include remuneration to Directors, Rs. 9.00 lakhs and Provision for Doubtfull Debts, Rs. 6.30 lakhs

(*c*) Interest on loan from ICICI Bank for working capital	9
Interest on long-term loan from IFCI for fixed assets	12
Interest on debentures	8
	29

(*d*) The provision for taxes include a transfer of Rs. 3 lakhs to the credit of Deferred Tax Account.

(*e*) Cess and local taxes include excise duty, which is equal to 10% of cost of bought in material.

[Adapted C.A (Final), Nov; 2004]

Solution.

Grand Co. Ltd.

Value Added Statement for the year ended 31st March, 2009

	Amount (Rs. in lakhs)	Amount (Rs. in lakhs)
Sales (net)		890
Less : Cost of bought-in material and services [as per working note (*i*)]	461	
Administrative expenses [as per working note (*ii*)]	24	
Interest on loan for working capital	9	
Excise duty [as per working note (*iii*)]	55	549
		341
Add: Other income		55
Total Value Added		396

Application of Value Added

	(Rs. in lakhs)	(Rs. in lakhs)	%
To Pay employess salaries, wages, gratuities etc.		82	20.71
To Pay Directors Remuneration		9	2.27
To Pay Government :			
Cess and local taxes, [Working note no. (*iv*)]	43		
Income tax [Working note no (*v*)]	76		
Corporate dividend tax	15	134	33.84

To Pay providers of capital :			
Interest on long-term loan from IFCI	12		
Interest on debentures	8		
Dividends paid	90	110	27.78
To Provide for maintenance and expansion:			
Transfer to General Reserve	40		
Transfer to Deferred Tax Account	3		
Depreciation	17		
Retained profits, Rs (11 – 10) lakh	1	61	15.40
		396	100

Statement Showing Reconciliation between Total Value Added and Profit before Taxation

	(Rs. in lakhs)	(Rs. in lakhs)
Profit before Taxation		225
Add back :		
Depreciation	17	
Salaries, wages and gratuities	82	
Directors' remuneration	9	
Cess and local taxes	43	
Interest on debentures	8	
Interest on long-term loan fron IFCI	12	171
Total Value Added		396

Working notes :

		(Rs. in lakhs)
(*i*)	Consumption of raw materials	293
	Consumption of stores	59
	Other manufacturing expenses	109
	Cost of bought in material and services	461
(*ii*)	Administrative expenses (factory) as given	33
	Less: Remuneration to Directors	9
	Amount shown in Value Added Statement	24

(*iii*) *Calculation of excise duty :*

If cost of bought in material and services is x, excise duty is 10% of $\frac{x}{10}$.

Then,

$$x = 461 + 24 + 9 + \frac{x}{10}$$

or $$x = 494 + \frac{x}{10}$$

Multiplying both the sides by 10, we get

$$10x = 4940 + x$$

or $$9x = 4,940$$

or $x = 549$

Excise duty $= 549 - 494 = 55$

(*iv*) Cess and local taxes, as given	98
Less : Excise duty as calculated in working note no. (*iii*) above	55
	43
(*v*) Provision for taxation, as given	79
Less : Deferred Tax Accounts Real provision for taxation	3
	76

Illustration 3.

On the basis of the following Profit and Loss Account of Exe Limited and the supplementary information provided thereafter, prepare Gross Value Added Statement of the company for the year ended 31st March, 2009. Also prepare another statement showing reconciliation of Gross Value Added with Profit before Taxation.

Profit and Loss Account of Exe Limited for the year ended 31st March, 2009

	Amount (Rs. in lakhs)	Amount (Rs. in lakhs)
Income		
Sales		5,010
Other Income		130
		5,140
Expenditure		
Production and Operational Expenses	3,550	
Administrative Expenses	185	
Interest	235	
Depreciation	370	4,340
Profit before Taxation		800
Provison for Taxation		272
Profit after Taxation		528
Credit balance as per last Balance Sheet		12
		540
Appropriations		
Transfer to General Reserve		132
Preference Dividend (Interim), paid		40
Proposed Preference Dividend (Final)		40
Proposed Equity Dividened		250
Corporate Dividend Tax		56
Balance carried to Balance Sheet		22
		540

Supplementary Information

	Amount (Rs. in lakhs)
Production and Operational Expenses consist of	
Raw Materials and Stores Consumed	1,900
Wages, Salaries and Bonus	610

Local Taxes including Cess	220
Other Manufacturing Expenses	820
	3,550

Administrative expenses consist of :

Salaries and Commission to Directors	60
Audit Fee	24
Provision for Bad and Doubtful Debts	20
Other Administrative Expenses	81
	185

Interest is on:

Loan from Bank for working capital	35
Debentures	200
	235

[Adapted C.A. (Final), Nov; 2005]

Solution.

Gross Value Added Statement of Exe. Ltd. for the year ended 31st March, 2009

	(Rs. in lakhs)	(Rs. in lakhs)
Sales		5,010
Less : Cost of raw material, stores and other services consumed [W. N. (*i*)]	2,720	
Administrative expenses [W.N. (*ii*)]	125	
Interest on loan from bank for working capital	35	2,880
Value added by manufacturing and trading activities		2,130
Add : Other income		130
Total Value Added		2260

Application of Value Added

	Rs. (in lakhs)	Rs. (in lakhs)	%
To Pay employees :			
Wages, salaries and bonus		610	26.99
To Pay Directors :			
Salaries and Commission to Directors		60	2.66
To Pay Government :			
Local taxes including Cess	220		
Income tax	272		
Corporate dividend tax	56	548	24.25
To Pay providers of Capital :			
Interest on debentures	200		
Preference dividend	80		
Equity dividend	250	530	23.45
To Provide for the maintenance and expansion of the company :			

Depreciation	370		
Transfer to general reserve	132		
Retained profit, Rs. (22 – 12) lakh	10	512	22.65
		2,260	100

Statement showing reconciliation between Gross Value Added with Profit before Taxation

	(Rs. in lakhs)	(Rs. in lakhs)
Profit before Taxation		800
Add back :		
Wages, salaries and bonus	610	
Salaries and commission to Directors	60	
Local taxes including Cess	220	
Interest on debentures	200	
Depreciation	370	1,460
Gross Value Added		2,260

Working Notes :

	(Rs. in lakhs)
(*i*) Raw materials and stores consumed	1,900
Other manufacturing expenses	820
Cost of raw materials, stores and other services consumed	2,720
(*ii*) Audit fee	24
Provision for bad and doubtful debts	20
Other administrative expenses	81
Administrative expenses	125

EXERCISE XXXII

Essay-type

1. Briefly describe the Cost and Replacement Cost Methods of putting a value on human resources.
2. Explain (*i*) Opportunity Cost Method of evaluating human resource
3. Discuss the various economic valuation methods of evaluating human assets. What are the objections against the value approaches ?
4. In valuing human resources, what approach will you suggest ?

MULTIPLE TYPE QUESTIONS (CHAPTERWISE)

CHAPTER 18

INTRODUCTION–SHARES, DEBENTURES, ETC.

State, with reasons in brief, whether the following statements are true or false:-

(*i*) Schedule VI, part I of the Companies Act gives the form in which the balance sheet of a joint stock company has to be prepared.

(*ii*) Revenue reserves as well as capital reserves can be used to issue fully paid bonus shares.

(*iii*) Usually public deposits accepted from the public by a joint stock company are unsecured loans.

(*iv*) Profit prior to incorporation is a capital profit.

(*v*) Schedule XIV of the Companies Act gives rates of depreciation for various assets.

[**Answers:** All statements are true]

Rewrite the following sentences after filling-up the blank spaces with appropriate word(s)/ figure(s):-

(*i*) The minimum number of directors required in a private company is_______.

(*ii*) A_______ company, by its Articles of Association, restricts its member's right to transfer shares.

(*iii*) The first annual general meeting of a public company must be held within_______months of the incorporation.

(*iv*) The uses of securities premium are mentioned in section_______ of the Companies Act.

(*v*) The effect of surrender of shares is the same as that of_______ of shares.

(*vi*) Convertible debentures are the debentures which can be converted into_______ at the option of the debentureholders.

(*vii*) When an underwriter agrees to buy or subscribe a certain number of shares or debentures irrespective of the result of the issue of the prospectus, it is a case of_______ underwriting.

(*viii*) The shares which are applied for on application forms not bearing the stamp of any underwriter are classified as_______applications.

(*ix*) The memorandum of association of a public company must be signed by at least_______ persons who agree to take at least one share each.

(*x*) _______ companies are the companies which are created by special acts of the legislature, e.g., The State Bank of India, Life Insurance Corporation and State Trading Corporation.

[**Answers:** (*i*) 2; (*ii*) private; (*iii*) 18; (*iv*) 78; (*v*) forfeiture; (*vi*) shares; (*vii*) firm; (*viii*) unmarked; (*ix*) 7; (*x*) Statutory]

Choose the most appropriate answers from the given options in respect of the following:-

(*i*) The minimum number of shareholders in a joint stock company is

(*a*) 2. (*b*) 3.

(*c*) 4. (*d*) 5.

(*ii*) The minimum number of shareholders in a public joint stock company is

(*a*) 3. (*b*) 7.
(*c*) 10. (*d*) 20.

(*iii*) The maximum number of shareholders, excluding present and past employees, in a private limited company is

(*a*) 30. (*b*) 40.
(*c*) 50. (*d*) 60.

(*iv*) The Companies Act has laid down the conditions for issue of shares at a discount in section:-

(*a*) 77. (*b*) 78.
(*c*) 79. (*d*) 80.

(*v*) The conditions which have to be fulfilled for redemption of preference shares have been laid down by the Companies Act in section

(*a*) 78. (*b*) 80.
(*c*) 211. (*d*) 433.

[Answers: (*i*) (*a*); (*ii*) (*b*); (*iii*) (*c*); (*iv*) (*c*) ; (*v*) (*b*)]

CHAPTER 19

FINAL ACCOUNTS

State, with reasons in brief, whether the following statements are true or false:-

(*i*) A public joint stock company can commence business as soon as it receives certificate of incorporation.

(*ii*) The credit balance of securities premium account can be used for issuing to members of the company fully paid bonus shares.

(*iii*) A private joint stock company can be started with as small share capital as Rs. 10,000.

(*iv*) Even a new company can issue shares at a discount.

(*v*) The maximum number of shareholders in the case of private company is 20.

(*vi*) A public company cannot buy-back its equity shares.

(*vii*) There are no restrictions on issue of shares at a premium.

(*viii*) If a public company adopts Table A as its Articles of Association, it may charge interest on calls in arrear @ 5% per annum.

(*ix*) The maximum underwriting commission that can be paid to underwriters by a company with regard to a public issue of shares is 5% of the issue price of shares underwritten.

(*x*) The applications for shares on application forms bearing the stamp of an underwriter are classified as marked applications.

[Answers: (*ii*), (*vii*), (*viii*) and (*x*) are true. Other statements are false.]

Rewrite the following sentences after filling-up the blank spaces with appropriate word(s)/ figure(s):-

(*i*) Profit remaining after reissue of forfeited shares is transferred to________ reserve and________ available for distribution by way of dividend.

(*ii*) In the balance sheet of a joint stock company, patents, trade marks and designs are shown under the heading________.

(*iii*) Preliminary expenses have to be treated as________–incorporation expenses while allocating expenses between pre-incorporation and post-incorporation periods.

(*iv*) Schedule________ part II of the Companies Act deals with remuneration payable by joint stock companies to their managerial personnel.

(*v*) The total remuneration payable to the manager of a joint stock company cannot exceed________ per cent of the net profits, except with the approval of the Central Government.

[**Answers:** (*i*) capital, is not; (*ii*) fixed assets; (*iii*) post; (*iv*) XIII; (*v*) five.]

Choose the most appropriate answers from the given options in respect of the following:-

(*i*) In the final accounts of a joint stock company, the item 'Dividend Paid' appears on the
(*a*) debit side of Trading Account.
(*b*) debit side of Profit and Loss Account.
(*c*) debit side of Profit and Loss Appropriation Account.
(*d*) liabilities side of Balance Sheet.

(*ii*) Conditions to be fulfilled for the appointment of a manager or whole-time director or a manager without the approval of the Central Government have been prescribed by the Indian Companies Act in its
(*a*) schedule VI, part I. (*b*) schedule XIII, part I.
(*c*) schedule XIII, part II. (*d*) schedule XIV.

(*iii*) 'Contingencies and events occurring after the balance sheet date' is the topic of
(*a*) Accounting Standard 2. (*b*) Accounting Standard 3.
(*c*) Accounting Standard 4. (*d*) Accounting Standard 5.

(*iv*) While allocating various expenses between pre-incorporation period and post-incorporation period, the amount of salaries will be allocated in the ratio of
(*a*) time. (*b*) sales.
(*c*) wholly pre-incorporation expense. (*d*) wholly post-incorporation expense.

(*v*) According to a Government rule, where the dividend proposed by a public joint stock company exceeds 12.5 per cent but does not exceed 15 per cent of the paid– up capital, the company will have to transfer to the reserves an amount which shall not be less than:–
(*a*) 2.5 per cent of the current profits. (*b*) 5 per cent of the current profits.
(*c*) 7.5 per cent of the current profits. (*d*) 10 per cent of the current profits.

[**Answers:** (*i*) (*c*); (*ii*) (*b*); (*iii*) (*c*); (*iv*) (*a*) ; (*v*) (*b*)]

CHAPTER 20

VALUATION OF INTANGIBLE ASSETS, GOODWILL AND SHARES; REORGANISATION AND RECONSTRUCTION OF SHARE CAPITAL

State, with reasons in brief, whether the following statements are true or false :

(*i*) Intangible assets normally do not have an active market.

(*ii*) An intangible asset should be derecognised on disposal or when no future economic benefits are expected from its use and subsequent disposal.

(*iii*) There may be a need of evaluating the goodwill of a joint stock company when its business is being sold to another joint stock company.

(*iv*) One of the methods of valuation of goodwill of a joint stock company is called Annuity Method.

(*v*) A joint stock company cannot increase its authorised share capital.

[Answers: (*i*) to; (*iv*) are true; (*v*) is false.]

Rewrite the following sentences after filling up the blank spaces with appropriate word (s)/ figure (s):-

(*i*) Accounting Standard (AS) ...., issued by the Institute of Chartered Accountants of India deals with Intangible Assets.

(*ii*) The cost of an intangible asset less residual ...., if any, is allocated over the useful life of the asset as an expense.

(*iii*) There is a rebuttable assumption that the useful life of an intangible asset will not exceed .... years from the date when the asset is available for use.

(*iv*) In .... reconstruction, the company which is being reconstructed is not wound up.

(*v*) When a joint stock company has lost a part of its share capital due to heavy losses suffered by it and the company prepares a scheme of reconstruction, goodwill account appearing in the books must be .... completely.

(*vi*) A joint stock company may sub-divide its 1 lakh fully paid equity shares of Rs. 100 each into ....lakh fully paid equity shares of Rs. 100 each.

[Answer: (*i*) 26; (*ii*) value; (*iii*) ten; (*iv*) internal; (*v*) written off; (*vi*) 10.]

Choose the most appropriate answers from the given options in respect of the following:

(*i*) With regard to intangible assets, the amortisation period and the amortisation method should be reviewed at least at :–

(*a*) each financial year-end. (*b*) the end of every 2 years

(*c*) the end of every 3 years (*d*) the end of every 5 years.

(*ii*) Loss arising from the retirement or disposal of an intangible asset will appear in the final accounts of the concern on the debit side of :

(*a*) Manufacturing Account (*b*) Trading Account

(*c*) Profit and Loss Account. (*d*) Profit and Loss (Appropriation) Account.

(*iii*) When internal reconstruction falses place in a joint stock company, the following special account is opened :–

(*a*) Revaluation Account (*b*) Reconstruction Account

(*c*) Realisation Account (*d*) None of the above accounts.

(*vi*) If a credit balance is left in Reconstruction Account after a scheme of internal reconstruction has been implemented, it is transferred to:–

(*a*) Capital Reserve (*b*) General Reserve

(*c*) Profit and Loss Account (*d*) Profit and Loss Appropriation Account.

(*v*) In internal reconstruction, the following account need not necessarily be written off:–

(*a*) Debit balance of Profit and Loss Account. (*b*) Preliminary Expenses Account

(*c*) Cost of Issue of Shares Account. (*d*) Patents and Trade Marks Account.

[Ans. (*i*) (*a*); (*ii*) (*c*); (*iii*) (*b*); (*iv*) (*a*); (*v*) (*d*).]

CHAPTER 21

AMALGAMATION AND EXTERNAL RECONSTRUCTION

State, with reasons in brief, whether the following statements are true or false:-

(*i*) The subject matter of Accounting Standard 14 is Amalgamation.

(*ii*) In an amalgamation, the transferee company means the company which is amalgamated into another company.

(*iii*) The pooling of interests method is applicable to an amalgamation in the nature of merger.

(*iv*) In an amalgamation in the nature of merger, the transferee company records in its books even the reserves of the transferor company.

(*v*) In external reconstruction, no new company may be formed.

[**Answers:** (*i*), (*iii*) and (*iv*) are true; (*ii*) and (*v*) are false.]

Rewrite the following sentences after filling-up the blank spaces with appropriate word(s)/ figure(s):-

(*i*) Amalgamation may be in the nature of (a)_______ or (b) purchase.

(*ii*) Depending upon the type of amalgamation, there are two methods of accounting, namely (a) the _______ of interests method and (b) the purchase method.

(*iii*) Intrinsic _______ method is one of the methods of calculating consideration in an amalgamation.

(*iv*) In_______ reconstruction, one joint stock company is wound up and its business is taken over by another joint stock company.

(*v*) In an amalgamation, there are two parties called the_______ company and the transferee company.

[**Answers:** (*i*) merger; (*ii*) pooling; (*iii*) worth; (*iv*) external; (*v*) transferor]

Choose the most appropriate answers from the given options in respect of the following:-

(*i*) In case of an amalgamation, the expenses of winding up of the transferor company are necessarily borne

(*a*) according to the agreement between the transferor company and the transferee company.

(*b*) exclusively by the transferor company.

(*c*) solely by the transferee company.

(*d*) by the transferor company and the transferee company equally.

(*ii*) In amalgamation, in the books of the transferor company, the following special account is opened:-

(*a*) Reconstruction Account (*b*) Realisation Account

(*c*) Revaluation Account (*d*) Reorganisation Account

(*iii*) On the date of amalgamation, the books of the transferor company had the following balances:

Fully paid Equity Share Capital	Rs. 20 lakh
Fully paid 9% Preference Share Capital	Rs. 10 lakh
Fully paid 7% Debentures	Rs. 7 lakh

In the amalgamation agreement, the transferee company agreed: to allot fully paid equity shares for Rs. 40 lakh to satisfy equity shareholders;

to allot fully paid 10% preference share for Rs. 10 lakh and pay Rs. 1 lakh in cash to satisfy preference shareholders; and to convert debentures of the transferor company into its own fully paid 8% debentures for Rs. 7 lakh.

The amount of consideration was:

(*a*) Rs. 40 lakh (*b*) Rs. 50 lakh

(*c*) Rs. 51 lakh (*d*) Rs. 58 lakh

[**Answers:** (*i*) (*a*); (*ii*) (*b*); (*iii*) (*c*).]

CHAPTER 22

HOLDING COMPANIES

State, with reasons in brief, whether the following statements are true or false:-

(*i*) A subsidiary is an enterprise that is controlled by another enterprise, known as parent

(*ii*) A holiday company receives dividend from its subsidiary out of the post-acquisition profits. The holding company will credit the dividend to Shares in Subsidiary Account.

(*iii*) Minority interest in a subsidiary does not include the paid up value of the preference shares of the holding company held by the outsiders.

[**Answers:** (*i*) is true, (*ii*) and (*iii*) are false]

Rewrite the following sentences after filling-up the blank spaces with appropriate word(s)/ figure(s):-

(*i*) A subsidiary sold to the holding company goods costing Rs. 20,000 for Rs. 25,000. On the date of consolidation of balance sheets, one-fourth of the goods were still there in the godowns of the holding company as unsold. In the balance sheet, unrealised profit will be shown at Rs._____

(*ii*) On the date of consolidation of balance sheets, the balance sheet of the subsidiary showed bills payable at Rs. 50,000. Half of these acceptances were in favour of its holding company which held all these acceptances in hand. In the consolidated balance sheet, mutual owings will be shown at Rs. ______ .

(*iii*) A holding company receives dividends from its subsidiary out of pre-acquisition profits. The holding company will credit the dividend received to _______ in Subsidiary Company Account.

[**Answers:** (*i*) Rs. 1,250; (*ii*) Rs. 25,000; (*iii*) Shares]

Choose the most appropriate answers from the given options in respect of the following:-

(*i*) A holding company purchased 70% of the equity shares of its subsidiary at a cost of Rs. 65 lakh. On the date of consolidation of balance sheets, the books of account of the subsidiary reveal the following:-

Fully paid equity share capital	Rs. 50 lakh
Capital reserves	Rs. 10 lakh
Revenue reserves	Rs. 30 lakh

The cost of control is

(*a*) Rs. 30 lakh. (*b*) Rs. 23 lakh.

(*c*) Rs. 9 lakh. (*d*) Rs. 2 lakh.

(*ii*) The minority shareholders of a subsidiary hold 20% shares of the company. On the date of consolidation of balance sheets, the books of account of the subsidiary reveal the following:-

Fully paid equity share capital	Rs. 75 lakh

Capital reserves Rs. 15 lakh
Revenue reserves Rs. 30 lakh

The minority interest will be shown at:

(*a*) Rs. 15 lakh. (*b*) Rs. 18 lakh.
(*c*) Rs. 21 lakh. (*d*) Rs. 24 lakh.

(*iii*) Consolidated Financial Statements are dealt with in:

(*a*) Accounting Standard 2. (*b*) Accounting Standard 3.
(*c*) Accounting Standard 14. (*d*) Accounting Standard 21.

[**Answers:** (*i*) (*b*); (*ii*) (*d*); (*iii*) (*d*).]

CHAPTER 23

CASH AND FUNDS FLOW STATEMENTS, CASH BUDGETS AND WORKING CAPITAL

State, with reasons in brief, whether the following statements are true or false:-

(*i*) In cash flow statement, payment made to buy office furniture will appear under flows from operating activities.

(*ii*) In connection with cash flow statements, cash comprises cash on hand and demand deposits with banks.

(*iii*) Funds flow statement is another name of cash flow statement.

(*iv*) Terms of credit to customers have no effect on the working capital requirements of a business concern.

(*v*) In a cash budget, estimated receipts and payments of cash over a specified period are shown.

(*vi*) Net working capital is the excess of current assets over current liabilities.

(*vii*) SEBI requires every listed company to prepare cash flow statement.

[**Answers:** (*ii*), (*v*), (*vi*) and (*vii*) are true. (*i*), (*iii*) and (*iv*) are false.]

Rewrite the following sentences after filling-up the blank spaces with appropriate word(s)/ figure(s):-

(*i*) Cash collected by issue of shares will appear in a cash flow statement under the heading of cash flows from _______ activities.

(*ii*) In cash flow statement, excess of cash inflows over cash outflows from all the activities taken together is shown as net _______ in cash and cash equivalents.

(*iii*) The direct method and the indirect method of the preparation of cash flow statement differ only in the method of calculation of _______ from operating activities.

(*iv*) Along with _______ flow statement, statement showing changes in working capital has also to be presented.

(*v*) There are two methods of preparation of cash flow statement namely the direct method and the _______ method.

(*vi*) In the beginning and at the end of an accounting year, Machinery Account showed balances of Rs. 5,00,000 and Rs. 7,35,000 respectively. Depreciation on machinery for the year was Rs. 65,000. There was no sale of machinery during the year. The cash outflow due to purchase of machinery during the year was Rs. _______.

(*vii*) On 31st March, 2008 current assets and current liabilities of a firm totalled Rs. 5,00,000 and

Rs. 2,40,000 respectively. The net working capital on that date was Rs. _______.

[**Answers:** (*i*) financing; (*ii*) increase; (*iii*) flows; (iv) funds; (*v*) indirect; (*vi*) 3,00,000; (*vii*) Rs. 2,60,000]

Choose the most appropriate answer from the given options in respect of the following:-

(*i*) Profit and loss account for an accounting year shows a net profit of Rs. 2,00,000. The profit has been arrived at after taking into account the following items also:-

Depreciation on Fixed Assets	Rs. 60,000
Cost of Issue of Debentures, written off	Rs. 10,000
Profit on Sale of Investments	Rs. 5,000

Funds from trading operations for the year are :

(*a*) Rs. 2,75,000 (*b*) Rs. 2,70,000
(*c*) Rs. 2,65,000 (*d*) Rs. 1,35,000

(*ii*) It is estimated that in a particular month, cash sales and cash collections from debtors will total Rs. 1,60,000 and Rs. 2,40,000 respectively. The following are the estimated cash payments for different expenses:-

Wages	1,00,000
Materials	1,25,000
Other Variable Expenses	75,000
Fixed Expenses	60,000.

Cash Budget for the month will show :

(*a*) requirement of Rs. 40,000. (*b*) surplus of Rs. 40,000.
(*c*) surplus of Rs. 1,00,000. (*d*) requirement of Rs. 30,000.

(*iii*) Profit and loss account for an accounting year showed expenditure on account of salaries to employees at Rs. 12,70,000. Salaries outstanding in the beginning and at the end of the year totalled Rs. 1,00,000 and Rs. 1,10,000. In the cash flow statement, cash paid to employees will appear at:

(*a*) Rs. 12,50,000. (*b*) Rs. 12,60,000.
(*c*) Rs. 12,70,000. (*d*) Rs. 12,80,000.

(*iv*) In an accounting year, credit purchases, purchases returns and discount received from trade creditors totalled Rs. 10,70,000 Rs. 70,000 and Rs. 20,000 respectively. Opening and closing trade creditors were Rs. 1,00,000 and Rs. 1,10,000. Cash paid to suppliers during the year stands at:

(*a*) Rs. 9,70,000. (*b*) Rs.9,90,000.
(*c*) Rs. 10,00,000. (*d*) Rs. 11,00,000.

[**Answers:** (*i*) (*c*); (*ii*) (*b*); (*iii*) (*b*); (*iv*) (*a*).]

CHAPTER 24

ACCOUNTING RATIOS

State, with reasons in brief, whether the following statements are true or false:-

(*i*) Trading on equity is resorted to in order to increase the rate of earning on equity.

(*ii*) Current ratio shows relationship between current assets and fixed assets.

(*iii*) The ideal ratio of current assets to current liabilities is 5.

(*iv*) Debt-equity ratio shows the relationship between long-term loans and total funds.

(*v*) Accounting ratios facilitate the comparison of efficiency of one firm with that of another firm.

[**Answers:** (*i*), (*iv*) and (*v*) are true. (*ii*) and (*iii*) are false]

Rewrite the following sentences after filling-up the blank spaces with appropriate word(s)/ figure(s):-

(*i*) Liquidity ratio or quick ratio is also called_______ test ratio.

(*ii*) 'Earning per share' is the topic of accounting standard _______.

(*iii*) Proprietary ratio is the ratio of funds belonging to_______ to the total assets of the company.

(*iv*) Average daily credit sales is calculated by dividing total net credit sales for the year by_______.

(*v*) Ideally, working capital ratio should be about_______.

[**Answers:** (*i*) acid; (*ii*) 20; (*iii*) shareholders; (iv) 365; (*v*) 2]

Choose the most appropriate answer from the given options in respect of the following:-

(*i*) Debtors ratio is.

(*a*) not an accounting ratio.
(*b*) a profitability ratio.
(*c*) a turnover ratio.
(*d*) a ratio to judge financial position.

(*ii*) Margin =

(*a*) $\frac{\text{Net profit}}{\text{Net sales}} \times 100$
(*b*) $\frac{\text{Gross profit}}{\text{Net sales}} \times 100$

(*c*) $\frac{\text{Gross profit}}{\text{Cost of production}} \times 100$
(*d*) $\frac{\text{Net profit}}{\text{Cost of production}} \times 100$

[**Answers:** (*i*) (*c*) and (*ii*) (*a*)]

CHAPTER 25

INSURANCE COMPANIES

State, with reasons in brief, whether the following statements are true or false:-

(*i*) Life insurance is also called life assurance.

(*ii*) Policy is the document containing terms of contract of insurance between insurer and the insured.

(*iii*) In connection with life insurance policy, reversionary bonus is the policyholder's share in the profits of the insurance company which is payable only on the maturity of the policy.

(*iv*) Endowment policy is a life insurance policy which matures only on the death of the insured.

(*v*) Paid-up value of a life policy is the amount which the policyholder can get immediately in cash from the insurance company if he stops paying future premiums.

[**Answers:** (*i*), (*ii*) and (*iii*) are true. (*iv*) and (*v*) are false]

Rewrite the following sentences after filling-up the blank spaces with appropriate word(s)/ figure(s):-

(*i*) In a contract of insurance, there are two parties namely the insurer and the_______.

(*ii*) _______ insurance covers the risks of loss of or damage to goods, ship and freights due to perils of sea-transport.

(*iii*) First year's premium is the premium paid by the policyholder in the first year of the life policy. Premiums paid in later years are known as_______ premiums.

(*iv*) _______ is an annual payment guaranteed by the insurance company as long as the insured lives in consideration of a lump sum paid by the insured in the beginning of the contract.

[**Answers:** (*i*) insured; (*ii*) Marine; (*iii*) renewal; (*iv*) Annuity.]

Choose the most appropriate answers from the given options in respect of the following:-

(*i*) Every year, the accounting year of every insurance company is to end on

(*a*) 31st March. (*b*) 30th June.
(*c*) 30th September. (*d*) 31st December.

(*ii*) For every insurance company carrying on exclusively the business as a reinsurer, the minimum paid up equity capital is

(*a*) Rs. 100 crore. (*b*) Rs. 200 crore.
(*c*) Rs. 300 crore. (*d*) Rs. 500 crore.

(*iii*) In an endowment life insurance policy, the insurance company is required to pay the policy amount

(*a*) only on the death of the insured.
(*b*) only on the expiry of the fixed period of time.
(*c*) on the death of the insured or the expiry of the fixed period, whichever is earlier.
(*d*) on the death of the insured or the expiry of the fixed period, whichever is later.

(*iv*) While preparing the final accounts of an insurance company carrying on general insurance business, the minimum reserve for unexpired risks that has to be kept in respect of marine business is

(*a*) 25% (*b*) 50%
(*c*) 75% (*d*) 100%

of the premium, net of reinsurances, received or receivable.

(*v*) For an accounting year, the following are the particulars regarding commission expenses incurred by an insurance company

Commission expense on direct business	... Rs. 250 lakh
Commission on reinsurance accepted	... Rs. 65 lakh
Commission on reinsurance ceded	... Rs. 45 lakh

The net commission appearing in schedule 2 of company's revenue account will be:–

(*a*) Rs. 250 lakh (*b*) Rs. 315 lakh
(*c*) Rs. 270 lakh (*d*) Rs. 230 lakh

[**Answers:** (*i*) (*a*); (*ii*) (*b*); (*iii*) (*c*); (*iv*) (*d*); (*v*) (*c*).]

CHAPTER 26

BANK

State, with reasons in brief, whether the following statements are true or false:-

(*i*) In the final accounts of a banking company, Rebate on Bills Discounted is not shown as a separate item in the Balance Sheet or any of its Schedules.

(*ii*) The Reserve Bank of India has no authority of supervision of banks.

(*iii*) The total amount of the bills receivable lying with the bank for collection at the end of the year is shown separately at the foot of the Balance Sheet of the bank.

[**Answers:** (*i*) and (*iii*) are true. (*ii*) is false]

Rewrite the following sentences after filling-up the blank spaces with appropriate word(s)/ figure(s):-

(*i*) A banking company cannot create a floating charge on the undertaking or any property of the company or any part thereof except upon a certificate from the_______Bank of India.

(*ii*) In a bank, a term-loan facility is treated as non-performing asset if interest or instalment of principal remains past due for a period of_______ quarters.

(*iii*) In the books of a bank, provision has to be made @_______ % on the outstanding balances of Loss Assets.

[**Answers:** (*i*) Reserve; (*ii*) two; (*iii*) 100]

Choose the most appropriate answers from the given options in respect of the following:-

(*i*) Non-banking assets must be disposed of by a banking company within

(*a*) six months. (*b*) one year.
(*c*) three years. (*d*) seven years.

(*ii*) A banking company carrying on business in India must see to it that its subscribed capital is not less than

(*a*) 30% of its authorised capital. (*b*) 40% of its authorised capital.
(*c*) 50% of its authorised capital. (*d*) 60% of its authorised capital.

(*iii*) Section 17 of the Banking Regulation Act, 1949 lays down that every banking company must transfer a specified minimum per cent of the profits prior to declaration of dividend to its Reserve Fund. The specified minimum percentage is

(*a*) 6. (*b*) 10.
(*c*) 15. (*d*) 20.

[**Answers:** (*i*) (*d*); (*ii*) (*c*); (*iii*) (*d*).]

CHAPTER 27

ACCOUNTS OF ELECTRICITY COMPANIES

State, with reasons in brief, whether the following statements are true or false:-

(*i*) Double Account System and Double Entry System mean the same thing.

(*ii*) An electricity company is allowed to adopt only the Sinking Fund Method of depreciation.

(*iii*) Like any other business enterprise, an electricity company is free to earn profits at any rate.

[**Answers:** All statements are false]

Rewrite the following sentences after filling-up the blank spaces with appropriate word(s)/ figure(s):-

(*i*) Under double account system, the balance sheet is prepared in two parts; one part is called________Account and the other part is called General Balance Sheet.

(*ii*) With reference to an electricity company, clear profit means the excess of the total________ over the total expenditure and certain specific appropriations.

(*iii*) In an electricity company, when an old plant is replaced with a modern one, the current cost of the old plant is debited to________Account.

[**Answers:** (*i*) Receipts and Expenditure on Capital; (*ii*) income; (*iii*) Replacement]

Choose the most appropriate answers from the given options in respect of the following:-

(*i*) In an electricity company, fixed assets may be depreciated by

(*a*) annuity method only.

(*b*) sinking fund method only.

(*c*) straight line method only.

(*d*) either sinking fund method or straight line method.

(*ii*) In an electricity company, the per centage of the cost of the fixed assets that is taken to be divided by life of the asset as laid down in the seventh schedule to determine the amount of depreciation is:–

(*a*) 85. (*b*) 90.

(*c*) 95. (*d*) 98.

(*iii*) In an electricity company, any profit or loss because of discarding of a fixed asset is to be charged to:–

(*a*) Contingencies Reserve. (*b*) Emergency Reserve.

(*c*) Renewal Reserve. (*d*) Development Reserve.

[**Answers:** (*i*) (*c*); (*ii*) (*b*); (*iii*) (*a*).]

CHAPTER 28

LIQUIDATION

State, with reasons in brief, whether the following statements are true or false:-

(*i*) In case of voluntary winding up of a joint stock company, the liquidator's remuneration, once fixed, cannot be increased.

(*ii*) Like an individual, a joint stock company can also be adjudged insolvent.

(*iii*) In liquidation of a joint stock company, debenture interest has to be paid to the date of payment in all cases.

[**Answers:** (*i*) is time; (*ii*) and; (*iii*) are false.]

Rewrite the following sentence after filling-up the blank spaces with appropriate word(s)/ figure(s):-

(*i*) When a joint stock company is wound up due to a winding up order by the National Company Law Tribunal, it is called_______winding up.

(*ii*) According to section 529 A of the Companies Act, certain dues, called overriding preferential payments, have to be settled in case of winding up of a company even before the payment to_______ creditors under section 530 are made.

(*iii*) There are two kinds of voluntary winding up, namely, Members' and_______.

[**Answers:** (*i*) compulsory; (*ii*) preferential; (*iii*) Creditors']

Choose the most appropriate answers from the given options in respect of the following:-

(*i*) In liquidation of a joint stock company, debentureholders having a floating charge are included in List

(*a*) A. (*b*) B.
(*c*) C. (*d*) D.

(*ii*) Deficiency or Surplus Account prepared by the liquidator in case of liquidation of a joint stock company is also called

(*a*) List E. (*b*) List F.
(*c*) List G. (*d*) List H.

(*iii*) The liquidator of a joint stock company is entitled to a commission of 3% on all assets realised except cash and a commission of 2% on amount distributed among unsecured creditors. He sold all the assets for Rs. 10,00,000. The amount finally available for distribution among unsecured creditors and for payment of liquidator's remuneration was Rs. 3,06,000. The total remuneration received by the liquidator was:–

(*a*) Rs. 30,000. (*b*) Rs. 33,000.
(*c*) Rs. 36,000. (*d*) Rs. 39,000.

[**Answers:** (*i*) (*d*); (*ii*) (*d*); (*iii*) (*c*).]

CHAPTER 29

MECHANISED ACCOUNTING

State, with reasons in brief, whether the following statements are true or false:-

(*i*) Accounting machines decrease job satisfaction among staff members.

(*ii*) Accounting machines should be installed only if there is sufficiently large volume of work to justify their installation.

(*iii*) In big concerns, it has become essential that every office clerk knows how to operate a computer.

[**Answers:** (*ii*) and (*iii*) are true (*i*) is false]

Rewrite the following sentences after filling-up the blank spaces with appropriate word(s)/ figure(s):-

(*i*) With reference to a computer, the full form of C.P.U. is_______.

(*ii*) Ledger posting machines are a combination of the_______ and comptometer so that the necessary details can be typed.

(*iii*) FORTRAN is the oldest compiler_______.

[**Answers:** (*i*) Central Processing Unit; (*ii*) typewriter; (*iii*) language]

CHAPTER 30

CRITICISM OF FINANCIAL STATEMENTS

State, with reasons in brief, whether the following statements are true or false:-

(*i*) Critical appreciation of the future prospects of the undertaking on the basis of the study of its final accounts is not a part of criticism of accounts.

(*ii*) Common-measurement statements are used in criticism of accounts.

[**Answers:** (*i*) is false; (*ii*) is true]

Rewrite the following sentences after filling-up the blank spaces with appropriate word(s)/ figure(s):-

(*i*) An intelligent study of the balance sheet and the profit and loss account of a concern with a view to judging its financial position and earning capacity is known as_______of accounts.

(*ii*) In criticism of accounts, it is also seen whether the final accounts have been prepared in the_______ forms (if any) or not.

[**Answers:** (*i*) criticism; (*ii*) prescribed.]

CHAPTER 31

INFLATION ACCOUNTING

State, with reasons in brief, whether the following statements are true or false:-

(*i*) When current purchasing power method of accounting is used, historical cost method of accounting has no role to play.

(*ii*) The conclusions drawn on the basis of study of final accounts prepared on the basis of historical cost method of accounting may become misleading due to inflation.

[**Answers:** (*i*) is false; (*ii*) is true]

Rewrite the following sentences after filling-up the blank spaces with appropriate word(s)/ figure(s):-

(*i*) During the course of an accounting year, when the price index stood at 270, a company purchased investments at a cost of Rs. 5,40,000. At the end of the year, the price index had moved to 300 and the market value of investments was Rs. 6,20,000. On CPP basis, the profit on investments is Rs._______.